BRIT SOLO SONG

A guide for singers, teachers, librarians and the music trade of songs currently available

Michael Pilkington

Foreword by
Benjamin Luxon, CBE

Thames / Elkin

First edition published 1997 as *English Solo Song*
Second edition (revised) 1998

Third edition, with additions and corrections, published 2003
by Thames/Elkin Publications,
a division of William Elkin Music Services
Station Road Industrial Estate
Salhouse, Norwich, Norfolk NR13 6NS
Email: sales@elkinmusic.co.uk

Text copyright © Michael Pilkington 2003
Presentation copyright © Thames Publishing 2003

Type management by John Saunders
Printed and bound in Great Britain by Thanet Press Ltd
Union Crescent, Margate, Kent CT9 1NU

Contents

Foreword by Benjamin Luxon, CBE	v
Introduction	vi
Publishers	vii
Anthologies	xi
Songs with piano, by composer	1
Appendix 1: Settings of foreign texts	176
Appendix 2: Other accompaniments	184
Index of titles	216
Index of poets	289
Index of translators	306

Foreword *by Benjamin Luxon,* CBE

THE ENGLISH SONG-WRITING of the 20th century is, without doubt, one of this country's major musical achievements and legacies. The way was paved by the amazingly prolific and fertile outpourings of the Victorian composers of popular songs, ballads and music-hall material. The nation was singing; in the home, town and village halls, concert-halls, churches and chapels. Reputations and fortunes were being made by successful song-writers, lyricists and music publishers.

It is not surprising then that the serious composers of the 20th century turned to the song as an essential means of artistic expression. As in every great tradition of song-writing (e.g. the German Lied and French Chanson), composers looked not only to great poets and literary figures of the past but to the poetry of their contemporaries. Thus, in the most natural way, music and literature converged to create a unique artistic and sociological comment on the taste, fashion and attitudes of an era.

After World War II, and particularly since the 1970s, the interest in our song tradition has fallen away. This is not altogether surprising. With the incredible developments in sound recording, television and the pop-music industry, the populace in general has gradually and inexorably shifted from an active to a passive role as regards their music.

The market-place has become obsessed with being cost-effective, and printed music, recordings, even performances, do not survive for long if they do not generate a healthy market. In the world of vocal music, opera, with its combination of theatre and music, has become the darling of the vocal arts, and interest in song, particularly in live performance, has greatly diminished. All of this is nobody's fault, but the inevitable result of the commercialisation that has swept through all aspects of our modern life-style.

Unlike myself, who was brought up, so to speak, and trained in this song repertoire, many young singers today have, through no fault of their own, lost touch with so much of their native song repertoire. In the light of all these developments this volume incorporates the three requirements of success: it comes at the right time; in the right place; and it is compiled and published by the right people.

Michael Pilkington and Thames Publishing have produced a treasure house of practical information which will, without doubt, open the door to a largely neglected and forgotten tradition of song-writing. Would that it had existed some ten years or so ago, when I made a series of archival recordings with Chandos on some of the major English song-writers. At that time the problems of tracking down material that was no longer published became a small nightmare, and in retrospect I realise that I missed out on many marvellous songs.

However, this problem, with the aid of this volume, no longer exists for the enthusiast of English song, be he or she amateur or professional, young or old, teacher or performer. Using a very simple and easily decipherable system the song output of every serious British composer is laid out for us.

One heartening observation to do with the English song repertoire is the increasing number of anthologies and compilations being published. Wherever applicable, Michael Pilkington has also noted where songs appear in collections and volumes.

In short, I have been amazed at the amount of information available in this concise and clearly documented publication. Apart from having the music in front of you, I cannot conceive of a better method of conveying information about individual songs and the means of acquiring them.

My heartfelt congratulations go to Michael Pilkington for his research and industry in producing this mammoth volume, and to John Bishop of Thames Publishing for putting on to the market such an invaluable book of reference and inspiration.

Canterbury, 1997

Introduction

BRITISH SOLO SONG is a new edition of English Solo Song, first published in 1997 and reissued in 1998. The original book was commissioned by John Bishop who also wrote the first two paragraphs of the introduction. These still apply and are given below.

'This repertoire guide is not concerned with value-judgments. It has one simple aim: to spread knowledge in a convenient form about the availability of English solo song – what can be bought over the counter or as an authorised photocopy. This information has not, it is thought, previously been collected in one place, and we hope singers, teachers, music librarians, retail shops, and others interested will be encouraged to explore as well as find answers to their queries quickly and accurately.

'There has been a determined effort to make the book as comprehensive and up-to-date as possible – not always easy in today's publishing world. The aim is to revise and reissue it at regular intervals; computer technology helps to make this easier than it would have been in the past. Readers are invited to write to the publisher with corrections or additions that would make a future edition more complete.'

The guide lists virtually all recital songs by British composers currently in print or available from publishers' archives. This new edition also attempts to list songs available from self-publishing composers. Material that is available only from the British, Welsh or Scottish Music Information Centres is not listed in detail, but BMIC, WMIC or SMIC is given after the composer's name. Songs such as Victorian and Edwardian ballads are only given if they are included in recent anthologies or have been reissued within the last few years. Settings of foreign texts are given in Appendix 1; and accompaniments other than piano alone, up to six players, as well as unaccompanied songs, are listed in Appendix 2. Note that lute songs are placed in the main catalogue.

Entries in the main catalogues are laid out as below. Note that this is an imaginary entry designed to show all possibilities. In a number of cases it has not been possible to supply all these details, but it was decided to include whatever is known, rather than omit available material:

Doe, John. 1800–1850. *See also* App. 1, 2. B&H.
Collections: *Summer Amusements*, B&H/Classical; *Songs of Sorrow,* [John Champion], [high, low], B&H (James Jones).
    Happy Days, *Harry Parks*, C [c'-d''](f), B&H/Classical Amusements, B&H.
    Holidays, *Sappho* tr. *Edward Jones,* Am [bb-f''], B&H Amusements/Classical, B&H *Heritage 1,* Schirmer *2nd Mezzo*; *Gm*, B&H.
    Seascape, [medium], Novello.

Explanations – line 1: Further songs by John Doe can be found in Appendix 1: Settings of foreign texts, and Appendix 2: Other accompaniments; and more songs are available from the archives of Boosey & Hawkes.

    Collections: The songs in 'Summer Amusements' can be sung separately, and are listed below. They are published by Boosey & Hawkes and by Classical Music Reprints. 'Songs of Sorrow' may be a true cycle, or perhaps details of the individual songs were not available. The words of these songs are by John Champion; they are published in high and low keys, and have been edited by James Jones.

    Songs: 'Happy Days' has words by Harry Parks, it is in C, with range from middle C to the D nine notes above, and is more suited to female voices; it comes in the volume 'Summer Amusements' and was also published as a single copy.

    'Holidays' has words by Sappho, translated by Edward Jones; it is in A minor with range from B flat below middle C to F at the top of the stave; it is in the volume 'Summer Amusements', also in the B&H anthology 'Heritage 1' and the Schirmer anthology '2nd

Mezzo'; Boosey & Hawkes also published it separately in the key of G minor, this is given in italics as it is known that A minor was the original key.

'Seascape' is listed in the Novello catalogue as a song for medium voice, but no further details are available.

Arrangements: If the composer has written any arrangements these are listed separately at the end of the entry.

In previous editions, songs shown between round brackets were those that could be obtained from the publisher's archives, or on special order. With so many publishers now using photocopying to provide copies as required, this no longer seemed appropriate. On the other hand, a number of publishers have taken over firms which had extensive British song collections, but are unable to confirm that copies of the songs in these older collections still exist. Songs given in brackets in this volume are songs which it is reasonable to suppose are available from the publisher concerned, although no confirmation of the fact has been possible.

In this edition songs in Welsh have not been included unless English singing translations are available. English songs by Welsh composers are represented as fully as possible. It is hoped that a Welsh edition of this book might be a future possibility.

In the Index of Titles an attempt has been made to provide cross-references between different titles which are in fact settings of the same poem. There is also a new Index of Poets which should prove useful in constructing recital programmes.

I must record my thanks to the publishers here represented, all of whom have been helpful in providing catalogues and other information. In addition to thanks recorded in previous editions, I have received much detailed information from a number of self-publishers, more help, as always, from Dr Rhian Davies, and the use of the library of the Royal Academy of Music. Use has also been made of a number of web-sites, although the information provided there varies considerably. Special thanks must also go to Philip G. Hayward of Wellington, New Zealand, who provided much useful information and valuable critical comments on the previous edition.

This book was the brain-child of the late John Bishop (Thames Publishing), who provided support and assistance throughout the project ever since he suggested I take on the task of researching the immense amount of material available. This revised and enlarged edition is dedicated to his memory. Having studied this repertoire for some fifty years it is a pleasure to be able to provide the means for others to enjoy exploring this treasure house of English music.

Michael Pilkington.
Old Coulsdon, 2002

Publishers

A & C Black = A & C Black Publishers Ltd. Music Department, 37 Soho Square, London W1D 3QZ. tel: 020 7758 0200; Fax 020 0222/0333; e-mail: enquiries@acblack.com.

Animus = Animus Music Publishing. 4 Rawlinson Street, Dalton in Furness, Cumbria LA15 8AL. Tel: 01229 467432; e-mail: selfmusic@aol.com.

Alfred = Alfred Publishing Co (UK) Ltd. Burnt Mill, Elizabeth Way, Harlow, Essex CM20 2HX. Tel: 01279 828960; Fax 01279 828961; e-mail: music@alfredpublishing.demon.co.uk.

Andresier = Andresier Editions. 63 Marlborough Mansions, Cannon Hill, West Hampstead, London NW6 1JS. Tel. & Fax: 020 7794 9108; Fax: 01296 428609; e-mail: 101464.2670@ compuserve.com.

AR Music = AR Music. 39 Park Crescent, Elstree, Herts WD6 3PT. Tel: 0208 953 4805.

Ascherberg = *see* IMP

Ashdown = Edwin Ashdown *see* Music Sales.

Augener = *see* S&B.

viii Publishers

Aureus = Aureus Publishing. 24 Mafeking Road, Cardiff, CF23 5DQ. Tel. & Fax: 029 2045 5200; e-mail: meuryn.hughes@aureus.co.uk.

Banks = Banks Music Publications. The Old Forge, Sand Hutton, York YO41 1LB. Tel: 01904 468472; Fax: 01904 468679; e-mail: banksramsey@cwcom.net.

Bardic = Bardic Edition. 6 Fairfax Crescent, Aylesbury, Bucks HP20 2ES. Tel. & Fax: 01296 428609; e-mail: info@bardic-music.com .

Bayley & Ferguson = Bayley & Ferguson. 65 Berkeley Street, Glasgow G3 7DZ. Tel: 0141 221 9444.

Bedford = David Bedford, 12 Oakwood Road, Henleaze, Bristol, BS9 4NR. Tel. & Fax: 0117 962 4202; e-mail: dvbmus@AOL.com.

Belwin = *see* Concord.

Bèrben = Bèrben Edizioni (Ancona) *see* Fentone.

B&H = Boosey & Hawkes Music Publishers Ltd. 295 Regent Street, London W1B 2JH. Tel: 020 7580 2060; Fax: 020 7291 7109/7637 3490 (promotion)/7291 7199 (sales); e-mail: marketing.uk@ boosey.com. Major publishers of English song, with a large archive collection, from which photocopies can be supplied. There is reasonably complete information on the songs in the archive, which can be visited by arrangement.

BMIC = British Music Information Centre. 10 Stratford Place, London W1C 1BA. Tel: 020 7499 8567; Fax: 020 7499 4795; e-mail: info@bmic.co.uk. A large collection of 20th-century English music, printed, privately published and manuscript. All the material is available for study, and some of it may be photocopied.

BMP = The OUP archive collection, held by Banks Music, see above for address.

Boston = Boston Music Co. *see* Music Sales.

Bosworth = *see* Music Sales.

Braydeston = *see* William Elkin.

Breitkopf = Breitkopf & Härtel. Broome Cottage, The Street, Suffield, Norwich NR11 7EQ. Tel: 01263 768732; Fax: 01263 768733; e-mail: sales@breitkopf.com. Photocopies of archive material can be supplied from Germany.

Brett = Brett. 4 The Causeway, Boxford, Sudbury, Suffolk CO10 5JR. Tel: 01787 211261.

Brunton = Barry Brunton Music Publisher. 52a Broad Street, Ely, Cambs CB7 4AH. Tel: 01353 663252; Fax: 01353 663371. *See also* Impulse.

Caddy = Caddy Publishing, Convent Lodge, Andover Down, Hants SP11 6LR. Tel: 01264 337205; Fax: 01264 350823.

Cambria = Cambria Master Recording and Publishing. Box 374, Lomita, Cal. 90717. Tel: 310831 1322; Fax 310833 7442.

Camden = Camden Music. 19a North Villas, Camden Square, London NW1 9BJ. Tel: 020 7267 8778; Fax: 020 7813 4601; e-mail: info@camdenmusic.com. *see also* Spartan Press.

Campion = Campion Press. Sandon, Buntingford, Herts SG9 0QW. Tel: 01763 247287; Fax: 01763 249984; e-mail: CampionPress@hotmail.com.

Caritas = Caritas Music Publishing. 28 Dalrymple Crescent, Edinburgh EH9 2NX. Tel. & Fax: 0131 667 3633; e-mail: caritas@caritas-music.co.uk.

Cathedral = Cathedral Music. King Charles Cottage, Racton, Chichester, West Sussex PO18 9DT. Tel; 01243 379968; Fax: 01243 379859; e-mail: cathedral_music@compuserve.com.

Chappell = *see* IMP.

Chester = *see* Music Sales.

Chiltern = *see* Cathedral Music.

Classical = Classical Vocal Reprints. 3253 Cambridge Avenue, Riverdale, NY 10463-3618, USA. Tel: 1(800)298-7474; Fax (718)601-1969; e-mail: ClasVocRep@aol.com. Distributor William Elkin.

Clyde = Clyde, R. 6 Whitelands Avenue, Chorleywood, Rickmansworth, Herts WD3 5RD. Tel. & Fax: 01923 283600; e-mail: r.clyde@dial.pipex.com.

Colne = Colne Edition. 11 Christ Church Court, Ireton Road, Colchester, Essex, CO3 3AU. Tel: 01206 562607/513523; e-mail: alan.bullard@ntlworld.com.

Concord = Concord Partnership. 5 Bushey Close, Old Barn Lane, Kenley, Surrey CR8 5AU. Tel 020 8660 4766; Fax: 020 8668 5273; e-mail: concordptnrship@aol.com.

Cramer = Cramer Music. 23 Garrick Street, London WC2E 9RY. Tel: 020 7240 1612; Fax: 020 7240 2639. There is a catalogue of the large archive holding, giving composer and title.

Creativity = Creativity & Music. 26 Morden Court, Morden, Surrey SM4 5HN. Tel. & Fax: 020 8648 1700; e-mail: howat_hiscocks@compuserve.com.

Curiad = Curiad. The Old Library, County Road, Pen-y-Groes, Caernarfon, Gwynedd LL54 6EY. Tel: 01286 882166; Fax: 01286 882692; e-mail: curiad@curiad.co.uk.

Curwen = *see* Music Sales.

Da Capo = Da Capo Music Ltd. 26 Stanway Road, Whitefield, Manchester M45 8EG. Tel: 0161 766 5950; e-mail: colin@dacapomusic.co.uk.

Dalby = Martin Dalby. 23 Muirpark Way, Drymen, Stirlingshire G63 0DX. Tel: 01360660427; Fax: 01360 660397; e-mail: martin.dalby@euphony.net.

Doblinger = *see* Kalmus.
Electrophonic = Electrophonic Music Company. Lancaster Farm, Chipping Lane, Longridge, Preston PR3 2NB. Tel: 01772 783646; Fax: 01772 786026.
Elkin = *see* Music Sales.
Emerson = Emerson Edition Ltd. Windmill Farm, Ampleforth, York YO62 4HF. Tel: 01439 788324; Fax: 01439 788715; e-mail: JuneEmerson@compuserve.com.
EMI = EMI Music Publishing Ltd. 127 Charing Cross Road, London WC2H 0EA. Tel: 020 7434 2131; Fax: 020 7434 3531.
Enigma = Enigma Publications. Turrall House, 2 Turrall Street, Barbourne, Worcester WR3 8AJ. Tel: 01905 611570.
Enoch = *see* Music Sales.
EPSS = English Poetry and Song Society. 76 Lower Oldfield Park, Bath, Somerset BA2 3HP. Tel: 01225 313531; Fax: 01225 464333; e-mail: ricercar@beeb.net.
Faber = Faber Music Ltd. 3 Queen Square, London WC1N 3AU. Tel: 020 7833 7900; Fax: 020 7833 7939; e-mail: information@fabermusic.com. Distribution and Sales: FM Distribution, Burnt Mill, Elizabeth Way, Harlow, Essex CM20 2HX. Tel: 01279 828989; Fax 01279 828990.
Fand = Fand Music Press. The Barony, 16 Sandringham Road, Petersfield, Hants GU32 2AA. Tel. & Fax: 01730 267341; e-mail: sales@fandmusic.com.
Fentone = Fentone Music Ltd. (De Haske Music (UK) Ltd). Fleming Road, Earlstrees, Corby, Northants NN17 4SN. Tel: 01536 260981; Fax: 01536 401075; e-mail: sales@dehaske.co.uk.
Fischer = *see* William Elkin.
Forsyth = Forsyth Brothers Ltd. 126 Deansgate, Manchester M3 2GR. Tel: 0161 834 3281; Fax: 0161 834 0630; e-mail: publishing@forsyths.co.uk.
Fretwork = Fretwork, 16 Teddington Park Road, Teddington, Middlesex, TW11 8ND. Tel: 020 8977 0924; Fax: 020 8404 2414; e-mail: info@fretwork.co.uk.
Goodmusic = Goodmusic. PO Box 100, Tewkesbury, Glos GL20 7YQ. Tel: 01684 773883; Fax: 01684 773884; e-mail: sales@goodmusic-uk.com.
Goodwin & Tabb = *see* Music Sales.
Griffin = Griffin Music. Hill House, 9 Redford Crescent, Edinburgh EH13 0BS. Tel: 0131 441 3035; Fax: 0131 441 5218; e-mail: griffin.music@btinternet.com. *See also* Impulse.
Gwynn = Gwynn Publishing Co. Y Gerlan, Heol y Dwr, Pen-y-groes, Caernafon, Gwynedd LL54 6LR. Tel: 01286 881797; Fax: 01286 882634.
Hardie = The Hardie Press. 17 Harrison Gardens, Edinburgh EH11 1SE. Tel: 0131 313 1383; Fax: 0131 313 1388; e-mail: admin@hardiepress.co.uk.
Impulse = Impulse Edition. 18 Hillfield Park, Muswell Hill, London N10 3QS. Tel: 020 8444 8587; Fax: 020 8245 0358; e-mail: impulse@impulse-music.co.uk.
IMP = International Music Publications Ltd. Griffin House, 161 Hammersmith Road, Hammersmith, London W6 8BS. Tel: 020 8222 9222; Fax: 020 8222 9260.
International = *see* Kalmus.
J.Williams = Joseph Williams *see* S&B.
James Pass = James Pass Music. 71 Smallbrook, Queensway, Birmingham B5 4HX.
Joad = Joad Press. Distributors William Elkin.
Kalmus = Alfred A. Kalmus Ltd/Universal Edition (London) Ltd. 38 Eldon Way, Paddock Wood, Kent TN12 6BE. Tel: 01892 833422; Fax 01892 836038; e-mail: anne.handley@uemusic.co.uk.
Keith Prowse = *see* IMP.
Kronos = Kronos Press. c/o Philip Cannon, Elmdale Cottage, Marsh, Aylesbury, Bucks HP17 8SP. Tel: 01296 613157.
Kunzelmann = *see* Peters.
Lengnick = Alfred Lengnick & Co (division of Complete Music Ltd). 27 Grove Road, Beaconsfield, Bucks HP9 1UR. Tel: 01494 681216; Fax: 01494 670443; e-mail: gbmuswill@aol.com. Distributor William Elkin.
Leonard = Hal Leonard, distributed by Music Sales.
Leslie = Leslie Music Supply (Ontario) *see* Goodmusic.
Lindis = Colin Hand. 9 Manor Close, Sibsey, Boston, Lincs PE22 0SL. Tel: 01205 750135.
Lipkin = Lipkin, Malcolm. Penlan, Crowborough Hill, Crowborough, East Sussex, TN6 2EA. Tel: 01892 652454; e-mail: malcolmlipkin@excite.co.uk.
Longship = Longship Music. Smidskot, Fawells, Keith Hall, Inverurie AB51 0LN. Tel. & Fax: 01651 882174.
Lord = Roger Lord. The Old Meeting House, St James, Shaftesbury, Dorset SP7 8HF. Tel: 01747 854999
Lynwood = Lynwood Music. 2 Church Street, West Hagley, Stourbridge, West Midlands DY9 0NA. Tel. & Fax: 01562 886625; e-mail: downlyn@globalnet.co.uk.
McLelland-Young = Thomas McLelland-Young. 2 Onslow Gardens, Sanderstead, Surrey CR2 9AB. Tel: 020 8651 0072.
Maecenas = Maecenas Music Ltd. *see* Concord Partnership.

x Publishers

MTT = Mansel Thomas Trust. Ty Cerbyd, Station Road, Ponthir, Newport NP18 1GQ. Tel: 01633 421299; e-mail: grace.gilmore-james@solutia.com.
Masters = Masters Music Publications *see* Concord.
Mayhew = Kevin Mayhew Publishers. Buxhall, Stowmarket, Suffolk IP14 3BW. Tel: 01449 737978; Fax: 01449 737834; e-mail: info@kevinmayhewltd.com.
Micropress = Micropress Publishing. Foxglove Bank, 2 Brook Gardens, Gillow Heath, Staffs ST8 6DE. Tel: 01782 379445; e-mail: micropress@supanet.co.uk.
Modus = Modus Music. 21 Canonbury Road, Enfield, Middlesex, EN1 3LW. Tel: 020 8363 2663.
Murdoch = Murdoch *see* Music Sales
Music Exchange = Music Exchange (Manchester) Ltd. Tayborn Publishing, Claverton Road, Wythenshawe, Manchester, M23 9ZA. Tel: 0161 946 1234; Fax: 0161 946 1195; e-mail: mail@ music-exchange.co.uk.
Music Sales = Music Sales Ltd. 8-9 Frith Street, London W1D 3JB. Tel: 020 7434 0066; Fax: 020 7287 6329; e-mail: music@musicsales.co.uk. Distribution: Newmarket Road, Bury St Edmunds, Suffolk IP33 3YB. Tel: 01284 702600; Fax: 01284 768301.
Musography = Musography. 6 Station Road, Catworth, Huntingdon, Cambs, PE28 0PE. Tel: 01832 710227; Fax: 01832 710359; e-mail: chris@musography.freeserve.co.uk.
Novello = *see* Music Sales
Oecumuse = *see* Brunton.
OUP = Oxford University Press Music Department. Great Clarendon Street, Oxford OX2 6DP. Tel: 01865 556767; Fax: 01865 267749; e-mail: music.enquiry@oup.com.
Paterson = *see* Music Sales.
Paxton = *see* Music Sales..
Peters = Peters Edition Ltd. 10-12 Baches Street, London N1 6DN. Tel: 020 7553 4000; Fax: 020 7490 4921; e-mail: info@uk.edition-peters.com.
Presser = *see* Kalmus.
Primavera = Primavera. 11 Langham Place, Highwoods, Colchester, Essex CO4 4GB. Tel: 01206 751522; e-mail: julia.usher@lineone.net.
Queensgate = Queensgate. 120 Downhill Street, Glasgow G12 9ON.
Quilver = Quilver Press. BCM Box 3824, London WC1N 3XX.
Ramsay = Basil Ramsay Publisher of Music Ltd. 604 Rayleigh Road, Eastwood, Leigh-on-Sea, Essex SS9 5HU. Tel: 01702 524305; Fax: 01702 526142; e-mail: basilmusic@freeserve.co.uk.
Redcliffe = Redcliffe Edition. 68 Barrowgate Road, London W4 4QU. Tel. & Fax: 020 8995 1223.
Ricordi = Ricordi & Co (London) Ltd. Bedford House, 69-79 Fulham High Street, London SW6 3JW. Tel: 020 7384 8180/95; Fax: 020 7371 7270/7384 8167; e-mail: Miranda.Jackson@ bmg.co.uk.
Roberton = Roberton Publications. The Windmill, Wendover, Aylesbury, Bucks HP22 6JJ. Tel: 01296 623107; Fax: 01296 696536. Distributor Goodmusic.
Roeginga = Roeginga Edition. 27 Dunedin Road, Rainham, Essex RM13 8HA. Tel: 01708 520774; e-mail: roegingamusic.co.uk.
RTS = RTS Music Partnership. 17 Bradford Road, St Johns, Wakefield, West Yorks WF1 2RF. Tel. & Fax: 01924 370454; e-mail: standford@rtsmusic.demon.co.uk.
Schirmer = *see* Music Sales.
Schott = Schott & Co Ltd. 48 Great Marlborough Street, London W1F 7BB. Tel: 020 7437 1246; Fax 020 7437 0263; e-mail: promotions@schott-music.com. Marketing and Sales Department, Brunswick Road, Ashford, Kent TN23 1EH. Tel: 01233 628987 Fax 01233 610232.
SMIC = Scottish Music Information Centre. 1 Bowmont Gardens, Glasgow G12 9LR. Tel: 0141 334 6393; Fax: 0141 337 1161; e-mail: info@smic.org.uk.
Snell = Snell & Sons. 68 West Cross Lane, West Cross, Swansea SA3 5LU. Tel: 01792 405727; e-mail: snells@welshmusic.demon.uk.
Spartan = Spartan Press Music Publishers Ltd. Strathmashie House, Laggan by Newtonmore, Inverness-shire, PH20 1BH. Tel: 01528 544770; Fax: 01528 544771; e-mail: mail@SpartanPress.co.uk.
Sphemusations = Sphemusations. 12 Northfield Road, Onehouse, Stowmarket, Suffolk, IP14 3HF. Tel: 01449 613388.
S&B = Stainer & Bell Ltd. PO Box 110, Victoria House, 23 Gruneisen Road, Finchley, London N3 1DZ. Tel: 020 8343 3303; Fax: 020 8343 3024; e-mail: post@stainer.co.uk. A large archive collection, fully catalogued, from which photocopies can be supplied. The collection can be visited by arrangement.
Stevenson = The Ronald Stevenson Society. 3 Chamberlain Road, Edinburgh EH10 4DL. Fax: 0131 229 9298; e-mail: rss@medeco.co.uk.
Tann = Hilary Tann. e-mail: tannh@union.edu
Thames = Thames Publishing *see* William Elkin.
UMP = United Music Publishers Ltd (UMP). 42 Rivington Street, London EC2A 3BN. Tel: 020 7729 4700; Fax: 020 7739 6549; e-mail: info@ump.co.uk.
Universal = *see* Kalmus.
Viking = Viking Publications (Whittaker Centenary Fund). The Oast House, Goddards Green, Benenden, Cranbrook, Kent TN17 4AR. Tel: 01580 240377.

Voicebox = see Fretwork.
Weinberger = Josef Weinberger Ltd. 12-14 Mortimer Street, London W1N 7RD. Tel: 020 7580 2827 Fax: 020 7436 9616; e-mail: generalinfo@jwmail.co.uk. Distributor William Elkin.
WMIC = Welsh Music Information Centre. Ty Cerdd, 15 Mount Stuart Square, Cardiff CF10 5DP. Tel: 029 2046 2855; Fax: 029 2046 2733/5700; e-mail: wmic@tycerdd.org.
Westfield = Westfield Music. Malt Shovel Cottage, 76 Old Walkergate, Beverley, East Yorks HU17 9ER. Tel: 01482 860580; e-mail: ahedges@westfieldmusic.karoo.co.uk.
William Elkin = William Elkin Music Services. Station Road Industrial Estate, Salhouse, Norwich, Norfolk NR13 6NS. Tel: 01603 721302; Fax: 01603 721810; e-mail: sales@elkinmusic.demon.co.uk.
Yorke = Yorke Edition, The Bothy, Grove Cottage, Southgate, S/Creake, Norfolk NR21 9PA. Tel: 01328 823 501; Fax : 01328 823 502; e-mail: enquiries@yorkedition.co.uk.

PLEASE NOTE: IF YOU EXPERIENCE ANY DIFFICULTY IN OBTAINING THE MATERIAL FROM THE PUBLISHERS LISTED YOU MAY ORDER IT ALL THROUGH WILLIAM ELKIN MUSIC SERVICES

Anthologies

3 Elegies = Three Elegies, [Timothy Roberts], Voicebox.
Art of Song 2a, 2b = The Art of Song Grades 1-5, volume 2, (high, medium low), Peters.
6 Divine = Six Divine Hymns by Restoration Composers, [Maurice Bevan], Thames.
6 Restoration = Six Restoration Songs for Baritone/Bass and Keyboard, [Maurice Bevan], Thames.
8 Restoration = Eight Restoration Songs for Soprano and Keyboard, [Maurice Bevan], Thames.
12 18th Century = Twelve Eighteenth Century Songs, [arranged Frederick Keel], B&H.
100 Best 1 - 4 = The 100 Best Short Songs, Books 1 - 4, [Gerhardt, Henschel and Harford], Paterson.
Ballad Operas = Songs from the Ballad Operas, [Geoffrey Bush], Novello.
Ballad Album 1 = Boosey Ballad Album [introduction Andrew Lamb], B&H.
Ballad Album 2 = The 2nd Boosey Ballad Album [introduction Andrew Lamb], B&H.
Banquet = Robert Dowland (compiler) A Musical Banquet, [Peter Stroud], S&B.
Baroque = English Songs, Renaissance to Baroque, [Steven Stolen and Richard Walters], (high, low), Hal Leonard.
Cavalier = Cavalier Songs, [Ian Spink], S&B.
Celebrated 1 - 3 = The Chester Books of Celebrated Songs, Books 1 - 3, [Shirley Leah], (high, medium), Chester.
Centuries = Songs Through the Centuries, Fischer.
Century 1 = A Century of English Song, Volume 1, Ten Songs for Soprano and Piano, [John Bishop, Garry Humphreys, Michael Pilkington (Introduction Pilkington)] Thames.
Century 2 = A Century of English Song, Volume 2, Ten Songs for Baritone and Piano, [John Bishop, Garry Humphreys, Michael Pilkington (Introduction Pilkington)] Thames.
Century 3 = A Century of English Song, Volume 3, Ten Songs for Tenor and Piano, [John Bishop, Garry Humphreys, Michael Pilkington (Introduction Pilkington)] Thames.
Century 4 = A Century of English Song, Volume 4, Ten Songs for Mezzo Soprano/Contralto and Piano, [John Bishop, Garry Humphreys, Michael Pilkington (Introduction Pilkington)] Thames.
Century 5 = A Century of English Song, Volume 5, Ten Songs for Soprano and Piano, [John Bishop, Garry Humphreys, Michael Pilkington (Introduction Pilkington)] Thames.
Century 6 = A Century of English Song, Volume 6, Ten Songs for Baritone and Piano, [John Bishop, Garry Humphreys, Michael Pilkington (Introduction Humphreys)] Thames.
Christmas 1, 2 = Christmas Song Album Volumes 1, 2, B&H.
Collection 1, 2 = The Singer's Collection, Books 1, 2: [Alan Ridout], Kevin Mayhew.
Countertenors 1 - 3 = Songs for Countertenors, Volumes 1 - 3, [Frederick Hodgson], Thames.
Dolmetsch 1, 2 = Select English Songs and Dialogues of the 16th and 17th Centuries, Books 1, 2, [Arnold Dolmetsch], Classical/B&H.
Drawing Room = Drawing Room Songs, [Robert Tear], Cramer.
Easy Song = The Boosey & Hawkes 20th Century Easy Song Collection, [Eileen Field], B&H.
Elizabethan = Elizabethan and Jacobean Songs, [arr. for voice and guitar by Mary Criswick], S&B.
(English Recital 1, 2 = The English Recital Song, Volumes 1, 2, [David Patrick], Chappell.)
First Soprano = First Book of Soprano Solos, [Joan Frey Boytin], Schirmer.
First Soprano 2 = First Book of Soprano Solos, Part 2, [Joan Frey Boytin], Schirmer.

xii Anthologies

First Mezzo = First Book of Mezzo-Soprano/Alto Solos, [Joan Frey Boytin], Schirmer.
First Mezzo 2 = First Book of Mezzo-Soprano/Alto Solos, Part 2, [Joan Frey Boytin], Schirmer.
First Tenor = First Book of Tenor Solos, [Joan Frey Boytin], Schirmer.
First Tenor 2 = First Book of Tenor Solos, Part 2, [Joan Frey Boytin], Schirmer.
First Baritone = First Book of Baritone/Bass Solos, [Joan Frey Boytin], Schirmer.
First Baritone 2 = First Book of Baritone/Bass Solos, Part 2, [Joan Frey Boytin], Schirmer.
Folio 1 = The Cramer Song Folio, Volume 1, Cramer.
Four English = Four English Songs of the Early Seventeenth Century, [Peter Warlock], BMP.
Gentlemen's Magazine = Songs from The Gentlemen's Magazine, [Copley & Reitan], Thames.
Georgian 1 = Early Georgian Songs, Book 1, Medium Voice, [Michael Pilkington], S&B.
Georgian 2 = Early Georgian Songs, Book 2, High Voice, [Michael Pilkington], S&B.
Hardy Songbook = A Thomas Hardy Songbook, [Gordon Pullin], Thames.
Harmonia = Five Songs from Harmonia Sacra, [realised by Benjamin Britten], Faber.
Heritage 1 - 4 = A Heritage of 20th Century British Song, Volumes 1 - 4, [Winifred Radford, Lyndon Vanderpump, Michael Pilkington], B&H.
Holy Night = O Holy Night, [Neil Jenkins, (Organ arrangements by Charles MacDonald)], Kevin Mayhew.
Imperial 1 = New Imperial Edition, Soprano Songs, [Sidney Northcote], B&H.
Imperial 2 = New Imperial Edition, Mezzo-Soprano Songs, [Sidney Northcote], B&H.
Imperial 3 = New Imperial Edition, Contralto Songs, [Sidney Northcote], B&H.
Imperial 4 = New Imperial Edition, Tenor Songs, [Sidney Northcote], B&H.
Imperial 5 = New Imperial Edition, Baritone Songs, [Sidney Northcote], B&H.
Imperial 6 = New Imperial Edition, Bass Songs, [Sidney Northcote], B&H.
Love & Affection = Songs of Love and Affection, [Sidney Northcote], B&H.
Lovesongs 1, 2 = Elizabethan Lovesongs, Books 1, 2, [Frederick Keel], (high, low), B&H.
Lute Songs 1, 2 = English Lute Songs, Books 1, 2, [Michael Pilkington], S&B.
McCormack = John McCormack Song Album, B&H.
Mad Songs 1, 2 = Thirteen Mad Songs Books 1, 2, [Timothy Roberts], Voicebox.
Manuscript 1, 2 = Songs from Manuscript Sources: 1, 2, [David Greer], S&B.
MB 33 = English Songs, 1625 - 1660, [Ian Spink], Musica Britannica XXXIII, S&B.
MB 43 = English Songs, 1800 - 1860, [Geoffrey Bush and Nicholas Temperley], Musica Britannica XLIII, S&B.
MB 56 = Songs, 1860 - 1900, [Geoffrey Bush], Musica Britannica LVI, S&B.
Old English = Old English Melodies, [H. Lane Wilson], B&H.
Parlour Songs = Mini Bumper Book of Parlour Songs, IMP.
Printed = Twenty Songs from Printed Sources, [David Greer], S&B.
Recitalist 1 = The Junior Recitalist, Book 1, Soprano, [Noelle Barker], S&B.
Recitalist 2 = The Junior Recitalist, Book 2, Mezzo-Soprano/Contralto, [Noelle Barker], S&B.
Recitalist 3 = The Junior Recitalist, Book 3, Tenor, [Noelle Barker], S&B.
Recitalist 4 = The Junior Recitalist, Book 4, Baritone/Bass, [Noelle Barker], S&B.
Sacred Songs 1 = Sacred Songs for the Soloist, Medium High Voice, [David Patrick], B&H.
Sacred Songs 2 = Sacred Songs for the Soloist, Medium Low Voice, [David Patrick], B&H.
Sarah's Encores = Sarah's Encores, Novello.
Second Soprano = Second Book of Soprano Solos, [Joan Frey Boytin], Schirmer.
Second Mezzo = Second Book of Mezzo-Soprano/Alto Solos, [Joan Frey Boytin], Schirmer.
Second Tenor = Second Book of Tenor Solos, [Joan Frey Boytin], Schirmer
Second Baritone = Second Book of Baritone/Bass Solos, [Joan Frey Boytin], Schirmer
Shakespeare = The Boosey & Hawkes Shakespeare Song Album, [Guy Woolfenden], B&H.
Solo Baritone = Sing Solo Baritone, [John Carol Case], OUP.
Solo Christmas = Sing Solo Christmas, [John Carol Case], (high, low), OUP.
Solo Contralto = Sing Solo Contralto, [Constance Shacklock], OUP.
Solo Sacred = Sing Solo Sacred, [Neil Jenkins], (high, low), OUP.
Solo Soprano = Sing Solo Soprano, [Jean Allister], OUP.
Solo Tenor = Sing Solo Tenor, [Robert Tear], OUP.
Songs from Wales = Songs from Wales, Volume 1, The Guild for the Promotion of Welsh Music.
Songs from Wales = Songs from Wales, Volume 2, The Guild for the Promotion of Welsh Music.
Souvenirs = Among Your Souvenirs, Selected Victorian and Edwardian Ballads, B&H.
Three Spring Songs = Three Spring Songs, Gwynn.
Tuneful Voice = O Tuneful Voice, 25 Classical English Songs, Timothy Roberts. OUP.
Twelve 17th Century = Twelve Seventeenth Century English Songs arranged for voice and guitar by John Williams, S&B.
W&W 1-6 = English Ayres, volumes 1 - 6, Peter Warlock & Philip Wilson, BMP.
World Renowned = World Renowned Songs, Lengnick

Songs with piano, by composer

A

Adams, Stephen. (Michael Maybrick). 1844–1913. *See also* App. 2.
100 more songs, B&H archive.
    Holy City, The, *Fred. E. Weatherly*, C [e′-g′′], B&H *Ballad Album 1*, B&H; A♭, B&H, Classical; B♭, D♭, B&H.
    Nirvana, *Fred. E. Weatherly*, D [f′#-g′′](m), B&H *Ballad Album 1*; C, Cramer *Drawing Room Songs*; (B♭, E♭, B&H).
    Star of Bethlehem, The, *Fred. E. Weatherly*, G [d′-g′′], B&H *Ballad Album 2*; F, Classical; E♭, B&H.
    Thora, *Fred. E. Weatherly*, G [d′-g′′(a′′)](m), B&H *Ballad Album 1*; F, Classical; E♭, B&H.

Adès, Thomas. 1971– *See also* App. 1, 2.
Collection: *Five Eliot Landscapes*, Faber.
    Cape Ann, *T. S. Eliot*, [b♭-d′′′](f), Faber 5 Eliot.
    Life Story, *Tennessee Williams*, [g-a′′](f), Faber.
    New Hampshire, *T. S. Eliot*, [c′-c′′′](f), Faber 5 Eliot.
    Rannoch by Glencoe, *T. S. Eliot*, [d′-c′′′](f), Faber 5 Eliot.
    Usk, *T. S. Eliot*, [d′-d′′′♭](f), Faber 5 Eliot.
    Virginia, *T. S. Eliot*, [b-b′′](f), Faber 5 Eliot.

Aiken, W. A.
    Sigh no more, ladies, *Shakespeare*, F [c′-f′′], S&B; A♭, S&B.
    Shall I compare thee (Sonnet 18), *Shakespeare*, C [c′-f′′], S&B.

Aknai, Jeremy. 1977– BMIC. *See also* App. 2.

Alison, Richard. *fl.*1592–1606.
    O Lord, turn away thy face, *John Markant*, Gm [f′-f′′], S&B (Greer) *Printed*.
    When as we sat in Babylon, *William Whittingham*, B♭ [f′-g′′], S&B (Greer) *Printed*.

Allen, Anthony. 1925–1995.
    I saw in Louisiana, *Walt Whitman*, [b-d′′], EPSS.

Allitsen, Frances. (Mary Frances Bumpus). 1848–1912. *See also* App. 2.
14 more songs, B&H archive; 7 more, Cramer archive.
    Lord is my light and my salvation, The, *Psalm 27*, E♭ [d-a′′♭(b′′♭)], B&H *Ballad Album 2*, Schirmer; D♭, C, B♭, Schirmer.
    (Lute Player, The, *William Watson*, Dm [a-f′′]; Bm, Cm, Ashdown.)

Allport, R. E. H.
    Come away, death, *Shakespeare*, B♭ [f′-a′′♭], BMP.

Alwyn, William. 1905–1985. *See also* App. 2.
Collections: *Invocations*, Lengnick; *Leave-Taking, A*, Lengnick; *Mirages*, Lengnick.
    Aquarium, *William Alwyn*, [e-f′](m), Lengnick *Mirages*.
    Daffodils, *Lord de Tablay*, [e′-b′′(a′′)], Lengnick *Leave-Taking*.
    Drought, *Michael Armstrong*, [e′♭-b′′♭], Lengnick *Invocations*.
    Fortune's Wheel, *Lord de Tablay*, [d′-f′′#], Lengnick *Leave-Taking*.
    Holding the Night, *Michael Armstrong*, [f′-b′′♭], Lengnick *Invocations*.
    Honeysuckle, The, *William Alwyn*, [d#-g′#(f′#)](m), Lengnick *Mirages*.
    Invocation to the Queen of Moonlight, *Michael Armstrong*, [e′-g′′], Lengnick *Invocations*.
    Leave-Taking, A, *Lord de Tablay*, [c′-g′′], Lengnick *Leave-Taking*.
    Metronome, *William Alwyn*, [c-e′](m), Lengnick *Mirages*.
    Ocean Wood, The, *Lord de Tablay*, [d′-b′′(g′′)], Lengnick *Leave-Taking*.
    Our Magic Horse, *Michael Armstrong*, [e′-b′′], Lengnick *Invocations*.
    Paradise, *William Alwyn*, [f-f′#](m), Lengnick *Mirages*.

Pilgrim Cranes, The, *Lord de Tablay*, [c′-g′′], Lengnick Leave-Taking.
Portrait in a Mirror, *William Alwyn*, [d-f′](m), Lengnick Mirages.
Separation, *Michael Armstrong*, [d′-c′′′(b′′b)], Lengnick Invocations.
Slum Song, *Louis MacNeice*, Am [e′-e′′], BMP.
Spring Rain, *Michael Armstrong*, [d′-a′′], Lengnick Invocations.
Study of a Spider, *Lord de Tablay*, [c′-a′′], Lengnick Leave-Taking.
Through the Centuries, *Michael Armstrong*, [e′b-a′′], Lengnick Invocations.
Two Old Kings, The, *Lord de Tablay*, [e′-g′′], Lengnick Leave-Taking.
Undine, *William Alwyn,* [c#-f′#](m), Lengnick Mirages.

Anderson, Avril. 1953–   *See* App. 2.

Anderson, Julian. 1967–   *See* App. 2.

Anderson, William **H**enry. 1882–1955.
Collections: *Four Seasonal Songs,* Leslie; *Omens of Spring,* Leslie.
   April, *Anon,* Eb [d′-e′′b], Leslie Omens.
   Child's Prayer, A, *Constance Barbour,* E [c′#-e′′], Leslie (with 'Old Shepherd's Prayer').
   Evening in Autumn, *Anon,* Eb [c′-e′′b], Leslie Four Seasonal.
   Fairy Cobbler, A, *A. Neil Lyons,* D [d′-e′′], Leslie.
   Hospitality, *Kenneth Macleod,* Cm [c′-e′′b], Roberton; Dm, Roberton.
   Last Year, *Duncan Campbell Scott,* F#m [c′#-c′′#], Roberton.
   Old Shepherd's Prayer, *Helen Shackleton,* Dm [c′#-c′′], Roberton; Fm (with 'A Child's Prayer'), Leslie.
   Omens of Spring, *Anon,* F [f′-e′′b], Leslie Omens.
   See the cherry blossoms swing, *Anon,* D [d′-d′′], Leslie Omens.
   Song for a Baby Sister, *R. H. Grenville,* Eb [d′-e′′b], Leslie (with 'To a baby brother').
   Spring is singing in the garden, *Anon,* G [d′-e′′], Leslie Four Seasonal.
   Summer on the Prairie, *Anon,* G [d′-e′′], Leslie Four Seasonal.
   Sweet Nightingale, *Anon,* D [d′-e′′], Leslie.
   To a Baby Brother, *R. H. Grenville,* D [d′-e′′], Leslie (with 'Song for a Baby Sister').
   To a Girl on her Birthday, *Blanche Pownall Garrett,* F [c′-d′′], Roberton; Ab, Roberton.
   Winter, *Anon,* D [c′#-e′′], Leslie Four Seasonal.
Arrangements: *Two Ukrainian Folksongs,* Em [b-e′′], Roberton.
   Alone, Roberton 2 Ukrainian.
   In the garden flowers are growing, Roberton 2 Ukrainian.

Andrews, Herbert **K**ennedy. 1904–1965.
Collection: *Two Songs,* BMP
   End Piece, An, *F. M. Heuffer,* [c′#-g′′], BMP.
   Glass of Beer, A, *James Stephens,* Dm [b-f′′#](m), BMP.
   Night is freezing fast, The, *A. E. Housman,* Gm [d′-g′′], BMP 2 Songs.
   Rest, *Christina Rossetti,* F#m [c′-f′′#], BMP.
   When cats run home, *Alfred Lord Tennyson,* [c′#-g′′], Thames *Century 3,* BMP 2 Songs.

Anon.
   All Through the Night, *Anon,* [high], Classical, Schirmer *1st Tenor*; G, [medium], Classical.
   Annie Laurie, *Lady John Scott,* Bb [Bb-d′], Schirmer (J. B. Weckerlin) *2nd Baritone.*
   As at noon Dulcina rested, *Anon,* Eb [e′-g′′], S&B (Greer) *Manuscript 2,* (Pilkington) *Lute Songs 1.*
   Ash Grove, The, *Anon,* G [c′-d′′], IMP *Parlour Songs*; Ab, Classical.
   Ay me, can love and beauty so conspire. *Anon,* Gm [e′-e′′b], BMP *W&W 6.*
   Banks of Roses, The, *18th cent. ballad sheet,* F [c′-f′′](m), BMP (Jacob).
   Barbara Allen (It was in and about), *Anon,* [medium], Classical.
   Barbara Ellen (In Scotland I was born), *Anon,* E [baritone], Classical (Cecil Sharp).
   Chloris sighed and sung and wept: *see under* Bales.
   Complaint, The, *Anon,* Em [e′-a′′], Thames (Copley & Reitan) *Gentleman's Magazine.*
   Country Girl's Farewell, The, *18th cent. ballad sheet,* E [d′-e′′](f), BMP (Jacob).
   Danny Boy (Londonderry Air), *Fred. E. Weatherly,* Eb [c′-g′′], B&H *Ballad Album 1,* B&H; C, Schirmer *1st Mezzo II,* B&H; D, B&H.
   David of the White Rock, *Anon,* Em [b-e′′], IMP *Parlour Songs.*
   Death and the Lady, *Anon,* Chester (Michael Holloway) *Celebrated 2.*
   Drink to me only with thine eyes, *Ben Jonson,* Eb [e′b-e′′b], IMP *Parlour Songs;* Db, Fischer *Centuries low.*
   Flow gently, sweet Afton, *Robert Burns,* [medium], Classical.

Gentle Maiden, The, *J. J. Pain,* [c′-f′′], IMP *Parlour Songs.*
Go my flock, go get you hence, *Philip Sidney,* D [d′-d′′](m), S&B (Stroud) *Banquet.*
Go now, my soul, to thy desired rest, *Anon,* Dm [c′-d′′](m), S&B (Greer) *Manuscript 2.*
Go thy ways since thou wilt go, *Anon,* Gm [d′-f′′], S&B (Spink) *MB 33.*
Have I caught my heav'nly jewel? *Philip Sidney,* Bb [f′-g′′](m), S&B (Greer) *Manuscript 1.*
Have you seen but a whyte lillie grow? *Ben Jonson,* F, [e′-f′′], Leonard *Baroque high,*
    B&H/Classical *Dolmetsch 1,* Schirmer (Michael Holloway) *1st Soprano*; G, Paterson (Diack)
    100 Best 1; *D,* Leonard *Baroque low;* Fischer *Centuries low.*
How now, shepherd, what means that? *Anon,* G [e′-e′′](m), S&B (Greer) *Manuscript 2.*
I loathe that I did love, *Thomas Lord Vaux,* C [e′-e′′], BMP *W&W 6.*
I prithee leave, love me no more, *Michael Drayton,* Cm [g′-a′′b](m), S&B (Greer) *Manuscript 2.*
If floods of tears, *Anon,* Cm [g-c′′], S&B (Greer) *Manuscript 1.*
If I freely may discover, *Ben Jonson,* F [c′-c′′](m), S&B (Greer) *Manuscript 2.*
If I seek t'enjoy the fruits, *Anon,* Gm [d′-d′′](m), S&B (Greer) *Manuscript 2.*
If the deep sighs, *Michael Drayton,* Am [f#-g′], S&B (Greer) *Manuscript 1.*
If, when I die, to hell's eternal shade, *William Fowler?* Gm [d′-f′′], S&B (Spink) *MB 33.*
Invitation, The, *Anon,* A [d′#-f′′#](m), Thames (Copley & Reitan) *Gentleman's Magazine.*
Last Rose of Summer, *Thomas Moore,* F, Classical; (E, Cramer).
Like to the damask rose, *Simon Wastell,* [c′-f′′], BMP (Warlock) *Four English.*
Loch Lomond, *Traditional,* F[c′-d′′], IMP *Parlour Songs*; G, Schirmer (Carl Deis) *1st Tenor.*
Londonderry Air, *see* Danny Boy *and* O Mary dear.
Lye still my deare, why dost thou rise? *John Donne?* Am [g′#-f′′], B&H/Classical *Dolmetsch 2.*
Most men do love the Spanish wine, *Anon,* G [G-d′](m), S&B (Greer) *Manuscript 1.*
Music, thou soul of heav'n, *Robert Herrick,* Gm [d′-e′′b], S&B (Greer) *Manuscript 2.*
Must your fair inflaming eye? *Anon,* Gm [g′-g′′](m), S&B (Spink) *MB 33.*
My love is like a red, red, rose, *Robert Burns,* [high], Classical.
My lytell prety one, *Anon,* C [g′-a′′](m), BMP *W & W 4*; *F,* Paterson (Diack) *100 Best 4*; *Bb,*
    B&H/ Classical *Dolmetsch 1.*
My op'ning eyes are purg'd, *Anon,* Cm [c-f′], Thames (Bevan) *6 Restoration.*
My thread is spun, *Anon,* [g′-a′′], BMP (Warlock) *Four English.*
Now ye Springe is come, *Anon,* Em [d′-e′′], B&H/Classical *Dolmetsch 2.*
O can ye sew cushions, *Anon,* F [c′-f′′], Chester (Michael Holloway) *Celebrated 1.*
O dear life, when shall it be? *Philip Sidney,* Gm [d′-d′′](m), S&B (Stroud) *Banquet.*
O death, rock me asleep, *Anne Boleyn?* Am; *Gm* [f′-d′′](f), B&H/Classical *Dolmetsch 2.*
O Lord, whose grace, *Mary Herbert, Countess of Pembroke,* G [c′-e′′], S&B (Greer) *Manuscript 1.*
O Mary dear (Londonderry Air), *John McCormack,* Eb [c′-g′′](m), B&H *McCormack.*
O waly, waly, *Anon,* [medium], Classical (Cecil Sharp).
Oft in the stilly night, *Thomas Moore,* Bb [medium], Classical.
Phillis was a fair maid, *Anon,* E, [d′#-e′′](f), B&H (Keel) *Lovesongs 1b*; G, *Lovesongs 1a,* BMP
    (Warlock) *Four English.*
Poor soul sat sighing, The, *see* Willow Song, The.
Salley in Our Alley, *Henry Carey,* C [e′-f′′](m), Cramer *Drawing Room Songs.*
Shall I weep or shall I sing? *Anon,* Gm [d′-d′′](f), S&B (Greer) *Manuscript 2.*
Sing aloud, harmonious spheres, *William Strode?,* G [d′-e′′], S&B (Spink) *MB 33.*
Skye Boat Song, *Harold Boulton,* Bb, Cramer; E, G, Cramer.
Sleepe, sleepe, *Anon,* F [d′-d′′], B&H (Keel) *Lovesongs 1b*; *A, Lovesongs 1a.*
Sweet muses, nurses of delights, *Anon,* C [c′-c′′], S&B (Greer) *Manuscript 2.*
Sweet, stay awhile, *John Donne?* Gm [f′#-g′′], S&B (Greer) *Manuscript 2,* (Pilkington) *Lute*
    Songs 1.
Tread Juno's steps who list, *Anon,* F [f′-f′′], BMP *W&W 6.*
What if a day, or a month or a year, *Thomas Campion,* Gm [f′#-f′′], BMP *W&W 6.*
When love is kind, *Thomas Moore,* Eb [bb-c′′], Fischer *Centuries low.*
Why dost thou turn away? *Anon,* F [c′-d′′], B&H (Keel) *Lovesongs 1b*; A, *Lovesongs 1a.*
Willow Song, *Anon,* Gm [g′-g′′], BMP *W&W 1*; *Fm* Leonard *Baroque high*; *Dm,* Leonard *Baroque*
    low.
You meaner beauties of the night, *Henry Wotton,* Gm [d′-e′′](m), S&B (Spink) *MB 33.*

ApIvor, Denis. 1916– BMIC; WMIC. *See also* App. 1, 2.

Archer, Malcolm. 1952– See App. 2.

Arne, Michael. *c.*1740–1786.
Collection: included in *Arne Selected Songs,* Cramer (edited and arranged Robert Barclay Wilson).
    Homeward Bound, *Anon,* F [g-d′′] (m), Cramer *Selected.*

4 Arne, Thomas

Lass with the Delicate Air, The, *Anon*, G [d′-g′′], Cramer Selected, Cramer, Schirmer; E, Fischer *Centuries low;* F, BMP (Jacob).

Arne, Thomas Augustine. 1710–1778. *See also* App. 2.
Collections: *Arne Selected Songs,* Cramer (edited and arranged Robert Barclay Wilson); *Twelve Songs for High Voice volumes 1 and 2,* S&B (edited Michael Pilkington); *Twenty Songs,* Classical.
    Bacchus, God of mirth and wine, *Anon*, Db [ab-e′′b], B&H (Northcote) *Imperial 6.*
    (Behold your faithful Ariel fly / Ere you can say, *Shakespeare,* A [e′-a′′](f), Chappell (Young).)
    Beyond Art (Still to be neat), *Ben Jonson,* Ab [e′b-f′′], Schirmer *2nd Tenor.*
    Blow, blow, thou winter wind, *Shakespeare,* Bb; *Ab* [e′b-a′′b], Leonard (Pilkington) *Baroque high,* S&B *12 Songs 1;* Eb Leonard *Baroque low,* Schirmer *1st Baritone II;* F, BMP (Fellowes), Cramer Selected, Paterson (Diack) *100 Best 3.*
    By dimpled brook and fountain trim, *John Milton,* A [e′-a′′], Cramer.
    Come away, death, *Shakespeare,* Em [b(c′)-g′′](m), B&H (Keel) *12 18th Century.*
    Come, calm content, *James Thomson,* Dm [c′-e′′b], Cramer Selected, Thames (Barclay Wilson) *Countertenors 2.*
    Come Mira, idol of the swains, (The Invitation) *Anon*, Eb [c′-f′′], S&B (Ivimey); F, B&H (Keel) *12 18th Century.*
    Complaint, The, *Anon*, G [c′#-g′′](m), B&H (Keel) *12 18th Century.*
    Cymon and Iphigenia, *Anon*, D; *C* [c′-g′′], S&B *12 Songs 1.*
    (Delia (solo cantata), *Anon,* [c′#-g′′(a′′)], Schirmer (Hufstader).)
    Ere you can say: see Behold your faithful Ariel fly.
    Fame's an echo, Gm [d′-g′′], Schirmer *1st Tenor II.*
    Fond Appeal, The, *Anon*, E [b-a′′](f), S&B *12 Songs 2.*
    Go, lovely rose, *Edmund Waller,* G [b-g′′](m), B&H (Keel) *12 18th Century.*
    (Hail, immortal Bacchus, *Isaac Bickerstaffe,* D [A(F#)-e′](m), Elkin (Bevan).)
    (High Queen of State / Honor, riches, *Shakespeare,* G [d′-a′′](f), Chappell (Young).)
    Honor, riches: *see* High Queen of State.
    How engaging, how endearing, *William Congreve,* G; *F* [d′-g′′], Braydestone (Bevan).
    Hymn of Eve, *Thomas Arne,* D [d′-e′′](f), Cramer Selected.
    (If those who live in shepherd's bower, *Thomson & Mallet,* Ab [c′-e′′b], Curwen (Warrack).)
    Invitation, The, *see* Come, Mira.
    Invitation to Ranelagh, *Anon*, G [d′-g′′], S&B (Ivimey).
    Jenny, *Anon*, G [d′-a′′](m), S&B *12 Songs 1.*
    Kind Inconstant, The, *Anon*, G [d′-g′′](m), B&H (Keel) *12 18th Century.*
    Love's a dream of mighty treasure, *Anon*, E [b-c′′](m), Cramer Selected.
    Morning, The (solo cantata), *Anon*, [d′-b′′], Schirmer (Hufstader).
    Now Phoebus sinketh in the west, *John Milton,* G [d′-g′′](m), Cramer Selected.
    O come, O come my dearest, *Pritchard,* G [d′-g′′], S&B *12 Songs 1,* Leonard (Pilkington) *Baroque high,* Schirmer *1st Tenor II; Eb,* Leonard *Baroque low.*
    O how great is the vexation, *Thomas Arne,* Gm; *Fm* [d′-g′′](f), S&B *12 Songs 2.*
    O peace, thou fairest child of heaven, *Thomson & Mallet,* Gm [d′-a′′b], Schirmer (Warrack) *1st Soprano.*
    O ravishing delight, *William Congreve,* [c′#-a′′], Novello (Cummings).
    Plague of Love, The, *see* Tout-ensemble, The.
    Pleasing tales in dear romances, *Thomas Arne,* A [e′-a′′], Novello (Bush) *Ballad Operas,* Novello.
    Polly Willis, G [d′-g′′], Schirmer *2nd Tenor.*
    Preach me not your musty rules, *J. Dalton* after *John Milton,* F [c′-f′′], Fischer *Centuries low.*
    Rule Britannia, *James Thomson,* Bb [e′b-f′′], Cramer Selected.
    See liberty, virtue and honour appearing, *James Thomson,* A [e′-a′′], Banks (Brown).
    Should you ever find her complying, *George Colman,* D [A-d′](m), Novello (Bush) *Ballad Operas.*
    Sleep, gentle cherub, *Isaac Bickerstaffe,* F [e′-a′′](f), S&B *12 Songs 2, Recitalist 1,* Schirmer *2nd Soprano.*
    Soldier tired of war's alarms, The, *Anon*, [soprano], Classical.
    Sycamore Shade, The, *Anon*, D [d′-a′′](f), S&B *12 Songs 2.*
    Thou soft flowing Avon, *David Garrick,* D [c′#-f′′#], Leonard *Baroque high;* Bb, Leonard *Baroque low;* [mezzo], Classical.
    Timely Admonition, The, *Anon*, E [e′-g′′#](f), S&B *12 Songs 2.*
    (To all the sex deceitful, *William Congreve,* Dm [c′#-g′′](m), Elkin (Bevan).)
    Tout-ensemble, The, *Anon*, F [c′-a′′], S&B *12 Songs 1; E,* B&H Michael Head Album 2; Eb, [d′-g′′], B&H (Lane Wilson) *Old English,* (Northcote) *Imperial 5,* Schirmer *2nd Tenor.*
    Under the greenwood tree, *Shakespeare,* F [d′-a′′], S&B *12 Songs 2; Eb,* B&H (Northcote) *Imperial 4,* Chester *Celebrated 1;* Db, Fischer *Centuries low;* C, BMP (Fellowes).
    Warning, A, *Anon*, G [c′-g′′], BMP (Franklin).

Water parted, F, Schirmer *1st Soprano.*
When daisies pied, *Shakespeare,* G [d′-g′′](f), S&B 12 Songs 2, Leonard *Baroque high,* Schirmer *1st Soprano II*; *F,* B&H (Woolfenden) *Shakespeare Album,* (Northcote) *Imperial* 2, Cramer Selected, Paterson (Diack) *100 Best* 2, Peters *Art of Song 2a/b,* S&B (Pilkington); *Eb,* Leonard *Baroque low.*
Where the bee sucks, *Shakespeare,* G [d′-g′′](f), B&H (Northcote) *Imperial 1,* Cramer Selected, Peters *Art of Song 2a,* S&B (Duncan); *F,* B&H (Woolfenden) *Shakespeare Album,* BMP (Wilson), Paterson (Diack) *100 Best* 2, Peters *Art of Song 2b,* Roberton,
Why so pale and wan, fond lover? *John Suckling,* Bm; *Am* [G-d′](m), Braydeston (Bevan), Schirmer *1st Baritone.*
(Ye fauns and ye dryads, *Anon,* B♭ [b♭-f′′], Elkin (Carmichael).)

Arnell, Richard Antony Sayer. 1917– BMIC.
Love lives beyond, *John Clare,* [b♭-e′′b], EPSS.

Arnold, Sir **Malcolm** Henry. 1921–
Collection: *Two John Donne Songs,* Roberton.
Good-morrow, The, *John Donne,* F [d′-g′′], Roberton 2 Donne.
Woman's Constancy, *John Donne,* G [c′#-g′′], Roberton 2 Donne.

Arnold, Samuel. 1740–1802. *See also* App. 2.
Elegy, *Anon,* G, [d′-g′′], OUP (Roberts) *Tuneful Voice.*
Midsummer Wish, The, *John Hawkesworth,* F [f′-g′′], OUP (Roberts) *Tuneful Voice.*

Arundell, Dennis Drew. 1898–1988. *See also* App. 1.
Leave me alone, O love, *Philip Sidney,* [f′-f′′#], BMP.

Aston, Peter George. 1938– *See also* App. 2.
Collection: *Three Shakespeare Songs,* Novello.

Atkins, John. ?–1671.
I can love for an hour when I'm at leisure, *Anon,* C [c′-e′′](m), S&B (Spink) *MB 33.*
This lady ripe and fair and fresh, *William Davenant,* F [e′-f′′], S&B (Spink) *MB 33.*
Wert thou then fairer than thou art, *Walter Montague?* G [f′#-e′′](m), S&B (Spink) *MB 33.*
When the chill Cherocco blows, *Thomas Bonham,* Am [e′-f′′](m), S&B (Spink) *MB 33.*

Atkinson, Geoffrey. *See also* App. 2.
Arrangements: *Where the Heather Grows,* [high, low], Bardic.
Ae fond kiss, and then we sever, *Robert Burns,* [b♭-e′′b] *or* [c′-f′′], Bardic Heather.
Bonnie Mary of Argyle, *Anon,* [c′-e′′b] *or* [e′-g′′], Bardic Heather.
Ca' the yowes to the knowes, *Robert Burns,* [c′-e′′], Bardic Heather.
Duncan Gray, *Robert Burns,* [d′-d′′], Bardic Heather.
John Anderson, my jo, *Robert Burns,* [b-d′′] *or* [d′-f′′], Bardic Heather.
Kate Dalrymple, *William Watt,* [b♭-e′′b] *or* [c′-f′′], Bardic Heather.
Lea-rig, The, *Robert Burns,* [c′-f′′] *or* [d′-g′′], Bardic Heather.
My Heart is Sair for Somebody, *Robert Burns,* [c′-d′′] *or* [e′b-f′′], Bardic Heather.
O my Love is like a red, red rose, *Robert Burns,* [b♭-f′′] *or* [c′-g′′], Bardic Heather.
There was a lad was born in Kyle, *Robert Burns,* [c′-e′′] *or* [d′-f′′#], Bardic Heather.

Atkinson, René. 1920– *See also* App. 1, 2.
Ave Maria, tr. *René Atkinson,* [e′-g′′], OUP *Solo Christmas high*; [c′-e′′b], *Solo Christmas low.*
Hail holy Mary *see* Ave Maria
Arrangements: *Ma Bonny Lad,* Roberton .
Bobby Shaftoe, *Anon,* Roberton Bonny Lad.
Bonny at morn, *Anon,* Roberton Bonny Lad.
Elsie Marley, *Anon,* Roberton Bonny Lad.
Ma bonny lad, *Anon,* Roberton Bonny Lad.
Water of Tyne, The, *Anon,* Roberton Bonny Lad.

Attey, John. *fl.*1622– *d.*1640.
Collection: *The First Booke of Ayres* S&B (edited Edmund Fellowes). Only songs available in anthologies are listed individually here.
On a time the amorous Silvy, *Anon,* G [d′-g′′], First Booke, S&B (Pilkington) *Lute 1,* B&H (Keel) *Lovesongs 1a*; *E, Lovesongs 1b.*

Sweet was the song, *Anon*, Am [e'-a''] First Booke, *Lovesongs 2a*; Fm, B&H (Keel) *Lovesongs 2b*, (Patrick) *Sacred Songs 2*.

Attwood, Thomas. 1765–1838.
Cold Wave my Love Lies Under, The, *Thomas Moore*, Eb [d'-g''], S&B (Bush & Temperley) *MB 43*.
Coronach: He is gone on the mountain, *Walter Scott*, Dm [d'-f''], S&B (Bush & Temperley) *MB 43*.
Go, lovely rose, *Edmund Waller*, F [c'-f''], S&B (Bush & Temperley) *MB 43*, *Recitalist 4*.
In the grove, friend to love, *Thomas Holcroft*, G [d-e'](m), Novello (Bush) *Ballad Operas*.

Austin, Frederic. 1872–1952.
Collections: *All About Me (Poems for a Child)*, [John Drinkwater], B&H; *Three Wessex Songs*, B&H.
Brave Town in Liverpool, *H. Ernest Hunt*, Dm [d'-f''(e''b)], B&H.
Christmas Eve, *John Drinkwater*, C [c'-g''], B&H.
Fiddler, The, *Thomas Hardy*, Em [c'-e''b], B&H 3 Wessex, Thames *Hardy Songbook*.
Orpheus with his lute, *Shakespeare*, Ab [d'-a''b], B&H *Shakespeare Album*.
Though dynasties pass, *Thomas Hardy*, [a-d''], B&H 3 Wessex.
When I set out for Lyonesse, *Thomas Hardy*, F#m [b-d''], B&H 3 Wessex.
Arrangement:
Twelve Days of Christmas, The, *Anon*, G [d'-f''#], Novello; (A, Novello).

B

Bailey, Judith. 1941–
Christmas Night, *Judith Bailey*, [c'-g''], EPSS.

Bain, James Leith Macbeth. c.1860–1925. *See* App. 2.

Bain, Marjorie K.
Arrangement:
O gathering clouds, *Marjorie K. Bain*, Bb [d'-f''], BMP.

Bainbridge, Simon. 1952– *See* App. 2.

Baines, William. 1899–1922.
Fern Song, *John Bannister Tabb*, E [c'#-e''], Banks.
Fountains, *James Elroy Flecker*, E [c'#-g''#], Banks.

Bainton, Edgar Leslie. 1880–1956.
Angel spirits of sleep, *Robert Bridges*, [c'-f''#], BMP.
(Dawn, *Gordon Bottomley*, [d'-f''], B&H.)
Ring out, wild bells, *Alfred Lord Tennyson*, Cm [c'-e''b], BMP; Dm, BMP.
(Sanctuaries, *Gordon Bottomley*, D [e'-g''], B&H.)
(Spring comes, *Gordon Bottomley*, Bb [d'-f''], B&H.)
(Valley-Moonlight, *Gordon Bottomley*, [bb-e''b, B&H.)

Baker, David.
Someone is sending me flowers, *Sheldon Harnick*, C [b-e''], Novello *Sarah's Encores*.

Bales, Alfonso. ? –1635.
Chloris sigh'd, *Anon*, Cm [f'-g''], S&B (Spink) *MB 33*, (Diack Johnstone) *Recitalist 1*; Bm, [d'-f''#] Classical/B&H (Dolmetsch), *Dolmetsch 2*.

Balfe, Michael William. 1808–1870. *See also* App. 1.
10 more songs, Cramer archive, 5 more, B&H.
Arrow and the Song, The, *Longfellow*, G [b-c''], Thames *Countertenors 1*.
Come into the garden, Maude, *Alfred Lord Tennyson*, D [f'#-g''](m), S&B (Bush & Temperley) *MB 43*.
I dreamt that I dwelt in marble halls, *Alfred Bunn*, Eb [e'b-g''](f), Classical.
Sands of Dee, The, *Charles Kingsley*, G [d'-e''], S&B (Bush & Temperley) *MB 43*.
Then you'll remember me, *Alfred Bunn*, Db [g'-a''b](m), Classical; Bb [e'-f''], Banks.
When other lips, *see* Then you'll remember me.

Ball, Derek. *See* App. 2.

Ball, Michael. 1946–
Lindisfarne Fragments, [baritone], Novello.

Bantock, Sir **Granville.** 1868–1946. *See also* App. 2.
Collections: *Five Ghazals of Hafiz,* Breitkopf; *(Five Songs from the Chinese,* Elkin); (*Five Songs from the Chinese Poets, Set 1,* Chester; *Set 2,* Chester; *Set 3,* Elkin; *Set 4,* Murdoch; *Set 5,* Cramer; *Set 6,* J. Williams) N.B. Classical publish one of these sets; *Five Songs of Essex,* Weinberger; *Lyrics from 'Ferishtah's Fancies',* Breitkopf; *Sappho,* Classical/Breitkopf; *Six Jester Songs,* Breitkopf; (*Songs from the Chinese Poets,* Chappell); (*Songs of Arcady,* Curwen); *Songs of Arabia,* Breitkopf; *Songs of China,* Breitkopf; *Songs of Egypt,* Breitkopf; *Songs of India,* Classical/Breitkopf; *Songs of Japan,* Breitkopf; *Songs of Persia,* Classical/Breitkopf; *Songs of the Seraglio,* Classical/B&H; (*Ten Songs from the Chinese,* Goodwin & Tabb); (*Three Celtic Songs,* B&H); *Three Nocturnes,* Cramer; (*Three Sheiling Songs,* Paterson; *Three Songs for Children,* S&B; (*Three Songs from the Greek Anthology,* Weinberger); (*Three Songs of Sister Miriam,* Goodwin and Tabb); (*Two Chinese Songs,* Breitkopf); *(Vale of Arden, The,* Enoch).

Admirals All, *Henry Newbolt,* B♭ [d′-g′′](m), S&B.
Adrift, *Li Po* tr. *L. Cranmer-Byng, Cm* [g′-a′′b], Thames *Century 1,* (Elkin; Cm, Bm, Elkin).
Ala′ya! send the cup around, *Hafiz* tr. *Edwin Arnold,* [baritone], Breitkopf 5 Ghazals.
And There are Tears, *Wang Seng-Ju* tr. *L. Cranmer-Byng,* F#m [c′#-e′′], Cramer 5 Chinese Set 5.
Apple-eating: *see* Bean-stripe, A.
As I ride through the Metijda, *Robert Browning,* Am [c′-e′′](m), B&H.
At the rising of the moon, *Fiona Macleod,* Weinberger.
(Autumn across the frontier, *Po Chü′i,* Murdoch 5 Chinese Set 2).
(Babyland, *Graham Robertson,* A♭ *(d′-e′′b),* Elkin, B♭, Elkin.)
Bean-stripe, A; also, Apple-eating, *Robert Browning,* D [d′#-b′′b(a′′)](m), Breitkopf Ferishtah.
(Bells of Youth, The, *Fiona Macleod,* A [d′#-a′′], Paxton.)
Bird of Arabia, The, *Helen Bantock,* Am [b-e′′], S&B.
Bird of St Bride, The, *Harold Boulton,* [d′-f′′], Cramer.
Blue Men of the Minch, The, *Donald Alexander Mackenzie,* Cm [c′-e′′], B&H
(Bluebell Wood, The, *Alfred Hayes,* F [b-f′′], Enoch Vale of Arden.)
(Boat Song of the Isles, *Harold Boulton,* G [d′-e′′], Elkin; B♭, Elkin.)
Bridal Song, *Helen Bantock,* A♭ [b♭-a′′b], Breitkopf Egypt.
Bridal Song, *Helen Bantock,* F [c′-f′′](f), Classical/Breitkopf Sappho.
Butterfly Song, *Helen Bantock,* Em [d′-f′′#], Breitkopf Japan.
By the Fireside, *Robert Browning,* C [a-e′′], Weinberger; E♭, Weinberger.
By the Ganges, *Helen Bantock,* Fm [c′-b′′b(g′′)](f),Classical India.
By the rivers of Babylon, *Psalm 137,* [c′-g′′], Cramer.
Camel-driver, A, *Robert Browning,* E [b-e′′](m), Breitkopf Ferishtah.
Captain Harry Morgan, *John Marley,* Cm [b-e′′], Weinberger.
Carrowmore, Æ, Dm [d′-f′′], Weinberger.
(Celestial Weaver, The, *T′ung Han-Ching,* tr. *L. Cranmer-Byng,* Am [c′-f′′#], Chester 5 Chinese Set 1.)
Cherries, *Robert Browning,* Em [b-b′′(a′′)](m), Breitkopf Ferishtah.
Chieftain's Battle Song, The, *Helen Bantock,* Gm [e′-f′′#](m), Breitkopf Arabia.
(Confession, *Sister Miriam,* Goodwin & Tabb Sister Miriam.)
Court of Dreams, The, *Sung Chih-Wên* tr. *L. Cranmer-Byng,* F [b♭-g′′], Cramer 5 Chinese Set 5.
(Cradle Song, *Walter Scott,* D [c′#-f′′#](f), Chappell.)
Crippled Faun, The, *Wilfrid Thorley,* [c′-a′′](m), Weinberger.
Dancing, *Alfred Hayes,* Cramer; D [c′#-f′′#], E♭, Cramer 3 Nocturnes.
Dawn, *Raymond Bantock,* A [c′#-e′′], Cramer 3 Nocturnes.
Dead Dryad, The, *Wilfrid Thorley,* [c′-g′′#](m), Weinberger.
Demon of Mazinderán, The, *Helen Bantock,* Gm [c′#-f′′], Classical/Breitkopf Seraglio.
(Desolation, *Kao-Shih* tr. *Cranmer-Byng,* [c′-g′′b], Chester 5 Chinese Set 2.)
(Despair, *Szü-K′ung T′u,* Murdoch 5 Chinese Set 4.)
Dirge, *Helen Bantock,* Bm [b-c′′#], Classical/Breitkopf India.
Doggie, *Alfred Hayes,* C [e′-f′′], S&B 3 for Children.
Down the Hwai, *Po Chü-i* tr. *L. Cranmer Byng,* Cm [c′-g′′], Cramer 5 Chinese Set 5.
(Dream Merchandise, *Graham Robertson,* E♭ [d′-g′′], Elkin; C, F, Elkin.)
(Dream of Spring, A, *Ts′en Ts′an,* tr. *L. Cranmer-Byng,* Am [c′#-e′′], Chester 5 Chinese Set 2.)
(Dreaming at Golden Hill, *Szu-Tung Po,* tr *L. Cranmer-Byng,* Gm [c′-e′′b], J. Williams 5 Chinese Set 6.)
Drinking Song, *Helen Bantock,* Classical/Breitkopf Persia.

(Dryad, The, *Alfred Hayes,* Curwen Arcady.)
Eagle, The, *Robert Browning*, F [d′-g′′#](m), Breitkopf Ferishtah.
Eastern Love Song, An, *Helen Bantock*, C [c′-d′′#], B&H.
Elfin Lover, *Helen Bantock*, A♭ [e′b-g′′], S&B; F, S&B.
(Emperor, The, *Anon* tr. *E. Powys Mathers,* Gm [c′-e′′b], Elkin; Am, Elkin.)
Enchanted Wood, The, *Myrrha Bantock*, Fm [b♭-e′′b], S&B; Am, S&B.
Epilogue: Oh! love – no, love! *Robert Browning*, C [e′-b′′b(a′′)](m), Breitkopf Ferishtah.
Evening Song, *Helen Bantock*, C [a-e′′](f), Classical/Breitkopf Sappho.
(Exile, *Tu Fu* tr *L. Cranmer-Byng,* Am [e′-g′′], J. Williams 5 Chinese Set 6.)
Fairyland, *Alfred Hayes*, F [d′-f′′], S&B 3 for Children.
Faithful Sailor Boy, *L. Cranmer-Byng*, G [d′-e′′], Weinberger 5 Essex.
Fakir's Song, The, *Helen Bantock*, C [c′-g′′], Classical/Breitkopf India.
Family, The, *Robert Browning*, A♭ [c′#-a′′](m), Breitkopf Ferishta.
Fan Song, *Helen Bantock*, D [d′-f′′#], Breitkopf Japan.
(Faun, The, *Alfred Hayes,* A♭ [d′b-a′′b], Curwen Arcady.)
Faun Despondent, The, *Wilfrid Thorley*, [c′-a′′](m), Weinberger.
Feast of Lanterns, A,*Yüan Mei* tr. *L. Cranmer-Byng,* D [f′#-a′′], Thames *Century 3,* Classical; C, B, Classical; (B♭, Novello).
Festal Hymn of Judith, The, *Bowker Andrews*, B♭ [g′-g′′], Weinberger.
Festal Song, *Helen Bantock*, B [f′#-b′′(g′′#)], Breitkopf Egypt.
(Fire Flame, The, *Alfred Hayes,* E♭ [b♭-e′′b], Enoch Vale of Arden.)
Fireside Fancies, *Alfred Hayes,* Cramer.
Flower Song, *Helen Bantock*, Bm [b-f′′#], Breitkopf Japan.
Forsaken, *Helen Bantock*, G [f′#-e′′], Breitkopf China.
Frolic, Æ, E [e′-f′′#], S&B 3 for Children.
(From the Tomb of an Unknown Woman, *Anon,* tr. *L. Cranmer-Byng,* Am [b-f′′], Elkin; Gm, Elkin.)
(Galloping Home, *Yüan Mei* tr *L. Cranmer-Byng,* G [d′-e′′], J. Williams 5 Chinese Set 6.)
(Garden of Bamboos, The, *Annamese* tr. *E. Powys Mathers,* Cm, [f′-g′′](f), Elkin; Am, Gm, Elkin.)
(Garden of Pan, The, *Plato* tr. *Anon,* Weinberger 3 Songs from Greek Anthology.)
(Ghost Road, The, *Tu Fu* tr. *L. Cranmer-Byng,* Am [a(c′)-f′′], Chester 5 Chinese Set 1.)
(Give me the sun, *Sister Miriam,* Goodwin & Tabb Sister Miriam.)
(Give unto the Lord, *Psalm 29*, C [e′-g′′], Paxton; A, Paxton.)
(Golden Nenuphar, The, *Han Yü* tr *L. Cranmer-Byng,* G [b♭-e′′], Elkin; A, Elkin.)
Great is the Lord, *Psalm 48*, C [c′-g′′], Cramer.
Guardian Angel, The, *Robert Browning*, E♭ [d′-a′′b], Weinberger; C, Weinberger.
(Heap Cassia, *Robert Browning,* Gm [c′-f′′], B&H.)
Hedge of Briar, The, *Helen Taylor*, E♭ [c′-e′′b](m), B&H; (D♭, B&H).
Hind in Ambush, The, *Wilfrid Thorley*, [c′-a′′](m), Weinberger.
Home Thoughts, *Robert Browning*, B♭ [a-f′′#], Weinberger; D♭, Weinberger.
Home to Gower, *John Marley*, C [e′-g′′](m), Weinberger.
Hymn of Pan, *Percy Bysshe Shelley*, [c′-a′′](m), Weinberger.
Hymn of the Gebare, *Helen Bantock*, Classical/Breitkopf Persia.
Hymn to Aphrodite, *Helen Bantock*, F [b♭-f′′], Classical/Breitkopf Sappho.
I go to prove my soul, *Robert Browning*, D♭ [d′b-f′′], Weinberger.
I loved thee once, Atthis, long ago, *Helen Bantock*, Cm [B♭-e′′b](f), Classical/Breitkopf Sappho.
(If I were Lord of Tartary, *Walter de la Mare,* Em [a-d′′], Chappell; Gm, Chappell.)
(If that angel of Shiraz, *Hafiz* tr. *J. H. McCarthy,* [baritone], B&H.)
In a dream I spake, *Helen Bantock*, C [b♭-e′′b](f), Classical/Breitkopf Sappho.
(In a myrtle shade, *William Blake,* Novello.)
In a year, *Robert Browning*, Em [b-f′′](f), Weinberger.
In the Desert, *Helen Bantock*, C [e′-g′′](m), Breitkopf Arabia
In the Garden, *Helen Bantock*, Em [c′-a′′], Breitkopf Egypt.
In the Harem, *Helen Bantock*, Classical/Breitkopf Persia.
In the hollows of quiet places, *Fiona Macleod*, C [c′-g′′], Weinberger; D, Weinberger.
(In the Palace, *Anon* tr. *E. Powys Mathers*, F [c′-f′′#], Elkin; E♭, G, Elkin.)
In the Palace, *Helen Bantock*, Am [g′-e′′], Breitkopf China
In the Temple, *Helen Bantock*, E♭ [c′-g′′], Breitkopf Japan.
In the Village, *Helen Bantock*, E♭ [e′b-e′′], Classical/Breitkopf India.
In tyme of olde, *Helen Bantock*, A [c′#-e′′], Breitkopf Jester.
Invocation to the Nile, *Helen Bantock*, E♭ [b♭-e′′b], Breitkopf Egypt, Breitkopf.
(Island of Pines, The, *Po Chü-i,* tr. *L. Cranmer-Byng*, Am [c′#-e′′], Chester 5 Chinese Set 2.)
(Isles of the Sea, *Harold Boulton*, F [c′-f′′], Elkin; G, Elkin.)
Jack Frost, *L. Cranmer-Byng*, B♭ [c′-g′′(e′′b)], Weinberger 5 Essex.

Jester, The, *Helen Bantock*, B♭ [g(c′)-d′′], Breitkopf Jester.
(King of Tang, A, *Wang Po* tr *L. Cranmer-Byng,* B m [b-e′′], J. Williams 5 Chinese Set 6.)
King George the Farmer, *L. Cranmer-Byng*, E♭ [b♭-e′′♭](m), Weinberger 5 Essex.
(Kingfisher's Tower, The, *Wang Ch'ang-Ling,* Murdoch 5 Chinese Set 4)
Lament, *Helen Bantock*, Gm [d′-f′′♭], Breitkopf Arabia.
Lament of Isis, *Helen Bantock*, Cm [b-e′′♭](f), Breitkopf Egypt, Breitkopf; [high], Breitkopf.
Lament of the Bedouin Slave-girl, *Helen Bantock,* D♭ [e′♭-a′′♭], Classical/Breitkopf Seraglio.
(Land of Promise, *Harold Boulton*, C [c-g′′], Elkin; A, Elkin.)
(Last Revel, The, *Ch'ên Tzû-ang* tr. *L. Cranmer-Byng*, D [c′#-e′′], Murdoch 5 Chinese Set 4, Chappell Chinese.)
Life in a love, *Robert Browning*, [c′b-g′′], Weinberger.
(Little Maid, The, *Myrrha Bantock,* Ashdown.)
(Little Papoose Lake, *Porter B. Coolidge,* B&H.)
(Longing, *Fiona Macleod*, Elkin.)
(Lord is my shepherd, The, *Psalm 23*, B♭ [d′b-f′′], Chappell; D♭, Chappell.)
Lord reigneth, The, *Psalm 93,* A♭ [c′-g′′], S&B.
Lost One, The, *Mêng Hao-Jan* tr. *L. Cranmer-Byng*, D♭ [c′-g′′♭], Cramer 5 Chinese Set 5.
Love Song, *Helen Bantock*, Bm [e′♭-f′′#](m), Breitkopf China.
(Love's Secret, *William Blake*, E [e′-g′′](m), Novello.)
Lullaby, A, *Helen Bantock,* G [d′-g′′], Breitkopf China.
(Lullaby, A, *Alexander Stewart*, F [c′-d′′](f), Chappell.)
(Lullabye, *Graham Robertson*, B♭ [e′-d′′], Elkin; D♭, Elkin.)
(March, The, *J. C. Squire,* Am [d′-g′′], Chester.)
Meeting, The, *Helen Bantock*, E♭ [d′-g′′], Breitkopf Arabia.
Melon-seller, The, *Robert Browning*, Gm [c′-g′′#](m), Breitkopf Ferishtah.
Memories with dusk return, *Li Po* tr. *L. Cranmer-Byng*, Cramer 5 Chinese Set 5.
Mihrab Shah, *Robert Browning*, F#m [c′-g′′](m), Breitkopf Ferishtah.
(Mistress Wang, *Helen Bantock*, [d′-g′′], Breitkopf 2 Chinese.)
Molly Green of Maldon Town, *L. Cranmer-Byng*, E♭ [d′-e′′♭], Weinberger 5 Essex.
(Moo-lee flower, The, *Helen Bantock,* [d′-g′′], Breitkopf 2 Chinese.)
Moon has set, The, *Helen Bantock*, Gm [g-f′′](f), Classical/Breitkopf Sappho.
Moon Maiden's Song, The, *Ernest Dowson*, Bm [f′#-g′′#](f), Weinberger.
Morgan le Fay, *Sheila Kaye-Smith*, A♭ [c′#-f′′], Cramer.
Muse of the Golden Throne, *Helen Bantock*, E♭ [c′♭-g′′♭](f), Classical/Breitkopf Sappho.
Musumë's Song, The, *Helen Bantock*, D [a-d′′], Breitkopf Japan.
(My Fairy Lover, *Donald Alexander Mackenzie*, G♭, B&H 3 Celtic, B&H.)
My star, *Robert Browning*, C [e′-g′′], Weinberger; A, Weinberger.
(Naiad, The, *Alfred Hayes,* G [b-g′′], Curwen Arcady.)
Nautch Girl, The, *Helen Bantock*, Cm [c′-g′′], Classical/Breitkopf India.
Never the time and the place, *Robert Browning*, [c′-a′′♭](m), Weinberger.
New moon's silver sickle, The, *Hafiz* tr. *Edwin Arnold*, [baritone], Breitkopf 5 Ghazals.
Night, *Raymond Bantock*, E [b♭-f′′#], Cramer 3 Nocturnes.
Night on the Mountain, *Ch'ang Ch'ien* tr. *L. Cranmer-Byng*, Em [d′-e′′], Cramer 5 Chinese Set 5.
Nightingale's Song, The, *Helen Bantock*, B♭m [d′-g′′](f), Breitkopf Arabia.
(Nightmare Giant, The, *Raymond Bantock,* Ashdown.)
Nocturne, *Raymond Bantock*, F#m [c′-f′′#], Cramer 3 Nocturnes.
Now, *Robert Browning*, A [a-e′′], Weinberger; C, Weinberger.
Odalisque, The, *Helen Bantock,* Fm [e′-f′′], Classical/Breitkopf Seraglio.
Oh! glory of full-mooned fairness, *Hafiz* tr. *Edwin Arnold*, [baritone], Breitkopf 5 Ghazals.
(Old Fisherman of the Mists and Waters, The, *Chang Chi-ho* tr. *L. Cranmer-Byng,* [d′-g′′], Chester 5 Chinese Set 1.)
(On the Banks of Jo-Eh, *Li-Po,* Murdoch 5 Chinese Set 4.)
Out of the depths, *Psalm 130,* [c′-f′′], Cramer.
Ozymandias, *Percy Bysshe Shelley*, [c′-d′′♭], Weinberger.
(Pan's Piping, *Alcaeus of Messina,* Weinberger 3 Songs from Greek Anthology.)
(Parting, The, *Penuel Grant Ross*, G [c′-e′′], Elkin; B♭, Elkin.)
(Pavilion of Abounding Joy, The, *Ou-Yang Hsiu.* tr. *L. Cranmer-Byng*, Am [c′#-e′′], Chester 5 Chinese Set 2.)
(Peach Flower, The, *E. Powys Mathers*, Gm [d′♭-e′′], Elkin; Am, Elkin.)
Pearl, a girl, A, *Robert Browning*, D♭ [e′♭-a′′♭], Weinberger.
Pearl and the Rose, The, *Helen Bantock,* Classical/Breitkopf Persia.
Peer of gods he seems, *Helen Bantock*, G [g-e′′](f), Classical/Breitkopf Sappho.
(Peewee, The, *Donald Alexander Mackenzie*, B♭ [d′-e′′♭], Paterson 3 Sheiling.)
Persian Love song, A, *Helen Bantock,* f′#-g′′], Classical/Breitkopf Seraglio.

Pillar at Sebzavah, A, *Robert Browning*, G [d′-g′′], Breitkopf Ferishtah.
Pippa Passes, *Robert Browning*, E♭ [f′-b′′♭], Weinberger.
Plot-culture, *Robert Browning*, D♭ [c′-b′′♭](m)], Breitkopf Ferishtah.
Praise ye the Lord, *Psalm 150*, A♭ [c′-e′′♭], Cramer; B♭, Cramer.
Prayer to Vishnu, *Helen Bantock*, Gm [b♭-g′′], Classical/Breitkopf India.
(Raindrops, *Myrrha Bantock,* G, Ashdown; B♭, Ashdown.)
(Red Lotus, The, *E. Powys Mathers*, Bm [c′-f′′#], Elkin; Am, Dm, Elkin.)
Reed Player, The, *Fiona Macleod*, Weinberger.
Return, The, *Helen Bantock*, Breitkopf Arabia.
(Return of Spring, *Seu-K'ung T'u*, tr. *L. Cranmer-Byng*, Am [d′-g′′], Chester 5 Chinese Set 1.)
Robin Redbreast, *Alfred Hayes*, A [b-e′′], Cramer; G, Cramer.
Sáki! dye the cup's rim deeper, *Hafiz* tr. *Edwin Arnold*, [baritone], Breitkopf 5 Ghazals.
(Satyr, The, *Alfred Hayes,* [c′-g′′], Curwen Arcady.)
(Seasons, The, *Alfred Hayes*, D [c′#-f′′#], Cramer.
Serenade, *Helen Bantock*, D♭ [a♭-f′′], Breitkopf Jester, Breitkopf; [high], Breitkopf.
Shah Abbas, *Robert Browning*, Cm [e′♭-g′′](m), Breitkopf Ferishtah.
(Sheiling Song, A, *Donald Alexander Mackenzie*, E♭ [e′♭-e′′♭], Paterson 3 Sheiling.)
Silent Strings, *Helen Taylor*, D [d′-e′′], B&H.
Simurgh, The, *Helen Bantock*, Classical/Breitkopf Persia.
Singer in the Woods, The, *Fiona Macleod*, Bm [c′-d′′], Cramer.
Song of the Bells, *Helen Bantock*, Bm [f′#-f′′#], Breitkopf China.
Song of the Genie, *Helen Bantock*, Dm [d′-a′′], Breitkopf.
(Song of the Peach-blossom Fountain, *T'ao Ch'ien* tr. *L. Cranmer-Byng*, A♭ [c′-e′′], Chappell.)
Song of the Sword, *Helen Bantock*, Em [c′-e′′], Breitkopf Japan.
Song to the Seals, *Harold Boulton*, E♭ [g-e′′♭], Thames *Century 4*, Cramer; F, G, Cramer.
(Spirit Song: Life of life, *Percy Bysshe Shelley*, Goodwin & Tabb.)
Spring Song, *Alfred Hayes*, A♭ [e′♭-f′′], Cramer.
Stand face to face, friend, *Helen Bantock*, E [g-g′′](f), Classical/Breitkopf Sappho.
Súfi, hither gaze, *Hafiz* tr. *Edwin Arnold*, [baritone], Breitkopf 5 Ghazals.
Summum bonum, *Robert Browning*, [c′-a′′♭](m), Weinberger.
Sun, The, *Robert Browning*, Fm [d′♭-g′′](m), Breitkopf Ferishta.
There's a wee, wee glen, *Charles Murray*, E♭, Cramer.
(Tomb of Chao-Chün, *Ch'ang Ch'ien,* tr. *L. Cranmer-Byng*, Em [b-e′′], Chester 5 Chinese Set 2.)
Tra-la-la-lie! *Helen Bantock*, C [c′-e′′], Breitkopf Jester.
(Twilight Coast, The, *Donald Alexander Mackenzie*, Paterson 3 Sheiling.)
Two Camels, *Robert Browning*, F# [c′#-a′′(g′′#)](m), Breitkopf Ferishtah.
(Two Roses, The, *Myrrha Bantock*, E♭ [b-e′′♭], Elkin; F, Elkin.)
(Under the Moon, *Li Po*, tr. *L. Cranmer-Byng*, C [c′-e′′], Chester 5 Chinese Set 1.)
Under the Rose, *Helen Bantock*, Dm [a-e′′], Breitkopf Jester.
Unutterable, The, *Helen Bantock*, C [a-c′′], Breitkopf Egypt.
Valley of Silence, The, *Fiona Macleod*, Dm [c′-e′′], Cramer.
(Waking Song, *Harold Boulton*, E [e′-f′′], Elkin.)
Walden Market, *L. Cranmer-Byng*, A♭ [c′-d′′♭](m), Weinberger 5 Essex.
(Wanting is — what? *Robert Browning*, B♭ [g′-f′′], Weinberger.
War Song, *Helen Bantock*, C [d′-g′′](m), Breitkopf China.
Washer of the Ford, The, *Fiona Macleod*, Am [c′-d′′], Cramer.
Wee Folk, The, *Donald Alexander Mackenzie*, E♭ [b♭-e′′♭], B&H.
When you sang to me, *Raymond Bantock*, F [g(b♭)-e′′], Weinberger; D♭, Weinberger.
(White Queen, The, *Alfred Hayes,* B♭ [b♭-c′′#], Enoch Vale of Arden.)
Whither away? *Myrrha Bantock*, Weinberger.
Widow bird sate mourning for her love, A, *Percy Bysshe Shelley*, Bm [e′-f′′#], Weinberger.
(Wild Flower's Song, The, *William Blake*, Novello.)
(Wild Geese, *Ou-Yang Hsiu* tr *L. Cranmer-Byng*, C [c′-d′′], J. Williams 5 Chinese Set 6.)
Wild Welsh Coast, The, *John Marley*, C [d′-g′′], Weinberger.
Will-o′-the-wisp, *Helen Bantock*, D [d′-d′′], Breitkopf Jester.
(Willow Flowers, *Yüan Mei* tr *L. Cranmer-Byng*, E♭ [b♭-g′′], J. Williams 5 Chinese Set 6.)
Wind, The, *Myrrha Bantock*, D♭ [c′-e′′♭], Ashdown.)
(Winter has gone, *May Chorley*, Bm [c′-g′′], B&H.)
Woman's Last Word, A, *Robert Browning*, C [b♭-f′′#](f), Weinberger.
(Wood Music, *Anon,* Weinberger 3 Songs from Greek Anthology.)
(Woven of the sky, *Sister Miriam,* Goodwin & Tabb Sister Miriam.)
Youthful, Charming Chloe, The, *Robert Burns*, E♭ [d′-a′′♭], Cramer.

Yung Yang, *Po Chü-i* tr. *L. Cranmer Byng*, [high], Classical; ([medium], Novello; Cm, Dm, Em, Elkin).
Zál, *Helen Bantock*, Classical/Breitkopf Persia.
Arrangements:
(Easter Hymn, *Helen Bantock*, F [f′-f′′], Chester.)
Lord Rendal, *Anon*, D [c′#-d′′], Cramer.
(Salve Regina (Holy Queen of heaven) [c′-d′′], Chester.)

Barker, Paul. BMIC.

Barley, William. ? –1614.
But this, and then no more, *Arthur Gorges*, C [c′-c′′], S&B (Greer), *Printed*.
How can the tree but waste, *Thomas, Lord Vaux*, Cm [b-b′b], S&B (Greer), *Printed*.
Sweet are the thoughts that savour of content, *Robert Greene*, Dm [d′-f′′], S&B (Greer), *Printed*.
Those eyes that set my fancy on a fire, *Anon*, Dm [a-b′b](m), S&B (Greer) *Printed*.

Barlow, David Frederick. 1927–1975. *See* App. 2.

Barlow, Michael.
Widow bird sat mourning for her love, A, *Percy Bysshe Shelley*, Em [e-a′′](m), Modus.

Barnett, John. 1802–1890.
I arise from dreams of thee, *Percy Bysshe Shelley*, Bb [c′#-g′′], S&B (Bush & Temperley) *MB 43*.
Ossian's Glen, *William Wordsworth*, Ab [c′-f′′], S&B (Bush & Temperley) *MB 43*.

Barratt, Carol. 1945–
Collection: *Six 'Songs' for Singing*, B&H.
Bachelor's Song, The, (I thank you for that!), *Thomas Flatman*, [G-e′](m), B&H 6 Songs.
Farmer's Boy, *John Clare*, Gm [d′-e′′], B&H *Easy Song*.
(Love... a strange disease, Chester.)
Nothing-at-all! *Anon*, Cm [d′b-e′′b], B&H *Easy Song*.
Song (A widow bird sat mourning), *Percy Bysshe Shelley*, [G-d′](m), B&H 6 Songs.
Song (Pious Selinda goes to prayers), *William Congreve*, [d-e′](m), B&H 6 Songs.
Song (Time stands still), *Anon*, [A-d′](m), B&H 6 Songs.
Song Without Words, *no text*, [c-e′b](m), B&H 6 Songs.
Summer Song (Strawberries swimming in the cream), *George Peele*, [c-e′b](m), B&H 6 Songs.

Barrell, Bernard. 1919– BMIC. *See also* App. 2.

Barrell, Joyce. 1917–1989. BMIC. *See also* App. 2.

Barrett, Richard. 1959– BMIC. *See also* App. 2.
Principia, *A. L. Jones* after *Isaac Newton*, [baritone], UMP.

Barry, Gerald. 1952– *See also* App. 2.
Water parted, *Vincent Deane*, [f-g′′], OUP.

Bartlet, John. *fl.*1606–1610.
Collection: *A Booke of Ayres*, S&B (edited Edmund Fellowes). Only songs available in anthologies are listed individually here.
I heard of late, *Anon*, G [d′-g′′], S&B Booke, B&H (Keel) *Lovesongs 2a*; Eb, *Lovesongs 2b*.
If there be anyone, *Anon*, G [d′-d′′], S&B Booke, B&H (Keel) *Lovesongs 2b*; Bb, *Lovesongs 2a*.
O Lord, thy faithfulness, *Anon*, Dm [g′-g′′], S&B Booke, (Pilkington) *Lute Songs 1*.
Pretty duck there was, A, *Anon*, G [g′-a′′], S&B Booke, (Pilkington) *Lute Songs 1*; D, B&H (Keel) *Lovesongs 2b*; F, *Lovesongs 2a*.
What thing is love? *George Peele*, G [d′-e′′], Booke, S&B (Pilkington) *Lute Songs 1*; F, B&H (Keel) *Lovesongs 2b*; A, *Lovesongs 2a*.
When from my love, *Anon*, C [e′-g′′](m), S&B Booke, (Pilkington) *Lute Songs 1*, B&H (Keel) *Lovesongs 2a*; A, *Lovesongs 2b*.
Whither runneth my sweetheart? (arr.) *Anon*, G [d′-g′′], Leonard *Baroque high;* B&H (Keel) *Lovesongs 2a*; E, *Lovesongs 2b*; Eb, Leonard *Baroque low*.
Who doth behold my mistress' face, *Anon*, G [g′-e′′](m), S&B Booke; F, B&H (Keel) *Lovesongs 2b*; F, *Lovesongs 2a*.

Barton, Nicholas. *See* App. 2.

Batchelor, Daniel. *c*.1574– after 1610.
To plead my faith, *Robert Devereux, Earl of Essex*, Cm [f′-f′′](m), S&B (Stroud) *Banquet,* BMP *W&W 6.*

Bauld, Alison. 1944– *See also* App. 2.
Banquo's Buried, *Shakespeare,* [b♭-g′′](f), Novello.
Cry, cock-a-doodle-doo, *Shakespeare,* [a-g′′](f), Novello.
Where should Othello go? [baritone], Novello.

Bax, Sir **Arnold** Edward Trevor. 1883–1953. *See also* App. 1.
Collections: *Album of Seven Songs,* Chester; (*Bard of the Dimbovitza, The,* Chappell); *Celtic Song-Cycle, A,* Classical/(Breitkopf); (*Five Fantasies on Polish Christmas Carols,* Chappell); *Five Irish Songs,* Classical/(Chappell); *Six Songs,* Thames (introduction Lewis Foreman); (*Three Enfantines,* Chester); *Three Irish Songs,* Classical/(Chappell); *Three Songs,* Classical; *Twelve Songs,* Thames (introduction Lewis Foreman).
  Across the Door, *Padraic Colum,* Cm [c′-f′′](f), Classical 5 Irish.
  As I came over the grey, grey hills, *Joseph Campbell,* E♭ [b♭-g′′♭], Classical 5 Irish.
  (Aspiration, *Richard Dehmel* tr. *Clifford Bax,* D♭ [c′-b′′♭], Chappell.)
  At the last, *Fiona Macleod,* Gm [b♭-d′′], Classical Celtic.
  Beg-Innish, *J. M. Synge,* [c′-g′′], Classical 5 Irish.
  (Berceuse, *French* tr. *Edward Agate,* Chester 3 Enfantines.)
  Carrey Clavel, *Thomas Hardy,* Fm [e′♭-g′′](m), Thames 12 Songs.
  Celtic Lullaby, A, *Fiona Macleod,* E♭ [b♭-a′′♭](f), Classical Celtic, Classical, (Chester).
  Christmas Carol, A, *Anon,* F [d′b-a′′], Chester 7 Songs, Chester.
  Closing Doors, *Fiona Macleod,* A [c′#-g′′#], Classical Celtic.
  Cradle Song, *Padraic Colum,* E♭ [d′b-g′′b], Thames *Century 5,* Classical 3 Irish, (Chappell *English Recital 2*).
  Dermott Donn MacMorna, *Padraic Colum,* Dm [a-f′′](f), Thames 6 Songs.
  (Dream Child, *Val Newton,* E♭ [c′-e′′], Chappell *English Recital 1*.)
  Eilidh my Fawn, *Fiona Macleod,* E [b-a′′], Classical Celtic.
  Enchanted Fiddle, The, *Anon,* D [c′-a′′](m), Chester 7 Songs.
  Eternity, *Robert Herrick,* F [d′-a′′], Thames 12 Songs.
  Fairies, The, *William Allingham,* E [b-g′′#], Chester.
  Far in a western brookland, *A. E. Housman,* Dm [d′-f′′], Thames 12 Songs, Classical 3 Songs.
  (Flute, The (Ideala), *Bjørnstjerne Bjørnson* tr. *Edmund Gosse,* Dm [d′-b′′], Murdoch.)
  God is born, *Polish* tr. *Jan Sliwinski,* E♭ [b♭-e′′♭], Chappell Polish Carols.)
  Golden Guendolen, *William Morris,* A [b♭(c′#)-g′′#], Chester.
  (Green grow the rashes O! *Robert Burns,* Gm [e′b-b′′♭], Murdoch, Em, Murdoch.)
  (Gypsy Song, *Rumanian* tr. *Strettell* and *Sylva,* G [d′-g′′], Chappell Dimbovitza.)
  I heard a piper piping, *Joseph Campbell,* [b-e′′], William Elkin, Classical 5 Irish.
  I heard a soldier, *Herbert Trench,* Gm [b♭-f′′#], Thames 12 Songs.
  Ideala *see* Flute, The.
  (In nightly stillness, *Polish* tr. *Jan Sliwinski,* B♭ [f′-e′′♭], Chappell Polish Carols.)
  (In the manger he is lying, *Polish* tr. *Jan Sliwinski,* A♭ [e′b-f′′], Chappell Polish Carols.)
  In the morning, *A. E. Housman,* F [e′-f′′], Thames 12 Songs, *Century 2.*
  (Jean, p'tit Jean, *French* tr. *Edward Agate,* Chester 3 Enfantines.)
  Lullaby, A, *Sheila MacCarthy (Arnold Bax),* E [b-f′′#](f), Thames 6 Songs, Classical 3 Songs.
  (Lullay, dear Jesus, *Polish* tr. *Jan Sliwinski,* E [f′#-e′′], Chappell Polish Carols.)
  Magnificat, (after a picture by D. G. Rossetti), *Luke 1,* G [d′-a′′♭], Chester.
  Market Girl, The, *Thomas Hardy,* F [d′-f′′](m), Thames 12 Songs, *Hardy Songbook.*
  (Merrily to Bethlehem, *Polish* tr. *Jan Sliwinski,* F [e′-f′′], Chappell Polish Carols.)
  Milking Sian, A, *Fiona Macleod,* F [d′-g′′](f), Chester 7 Songs.
  (Misconception, *Rumanian* tr. *Strettell* and *Sylva,* G[b#-f′′#], Chappell Dimbovitza.)
  (My girdle I hung on a tree-top tall, *Rumanian* tr. *Strettell* and *Sylva,* A[f′-a′′], Chappell Dimbovitza.)
  On the Bridge, *Thomas Hardy,* C [c′-f′′](f), Thames 12 Songs.
  (Out and Away, *James Stephens,* [d′-g′′], Murdoch.)
  Parting, Æ, E [d′#-g′′], Thames 12 Songs.
  Pigeons, The, *Padraic Colum,* [b♭-d′′](f), Classical 5 Irish.
  Rann of Exile, *Padraic Colum,* Am [d′-g′′], Thames 12 Songs, Classical 3 Irish.
  Rann of Wandering, *Padraic Colum,* E♭ [b♭-f′′], Thames 12 Songs, Classical 3 Irish.
  Roundel, *Geoffrey Chaucer,* D [c′-f′′#](m), Chester 7 Songs.

Shieling Song, *Fiona Macleod*, F [c′#-a′′](f), Chester 7 Songs.
Song in the Twilight, The, *Freda Bax*, B♭m [b♭-g′′♭], Thames 6 Songs.
(Spinning Song, *Rumanian* tr. *Strettell and Sylva*, G [d′-g′′], Chappell Dimbovitza.)
Spring Rain, *Friedrich Rückert* tr. *Clifford Bax?* G#m [d′#-g′′#], Thames 6 Songs.
Thy dark eyes to mine, *Fiona Macleod*, F#m [c′#-a′′], Classical Celtic.
To Eire, *J. H. Cousins*, F [c′-g′′], Chester 7 Songs.
(Une petite fille, *French* tr. *Edward Agate*, Chester 3 Enfantines.)
Watching the Needleboats, *James Joyce*, Am [e′-g′′], Thames 12 Songs.
(Well of Tears, The, *Rumanian* tr. *Strettell and Sylva*, Bm [c′#-g′′], Chappell Dimbovitza.)
When I was one-and-twenty, *A. E. Housman*, Em [d′-f′′], Thames 12 Songs, Classical 3 Songs.
When we are lost, *Dermot O'Byrne (Arnold Bax)*, A♭ [d′-a′′], Thames 6 Songs.
White Peace, The, *Fiona Macleod*, A♭ [e′b-g′′b], Chester 7 Songs.
Youth, *Clifford Bax*, F [e′b-f′′](m), Thames 6 Songs.
Arrangements:
(I have a house and land in Kent, *Anon*, Chester.)
Jack and Jone, *Thomas Campion*, Chester.
(Maid and the Miller, The, *Anon*, Chester.)
(O dear! what can the matter be, *Anon*, E♭ [d′-e′′b], Chester.)

Bayley, Thomas Haynes.
Long, long ago, *Thomas Haynes Bayley*, F [c′-d′′], Fischer *Centuries low*.

Bayford, Frank. 1941– *See also* App. 2.
Songs for Children's Dreams (cycle), [d′-g′′](f), Modus.

Bayliss, Colin. 1948–
Collections: *Three Hardy Songs*, Da Capo; *Three Settings of Robert Graves*, Da Capo.
B.C.C.I – a satirical song, *Mark Bones*, [baritone], Da Capo.
Carol on a Polish Folk Song, *Mark Bones*, [soprano/tenor], Da Capo.
Cool Web, The, *Robert Graves*, [tenor], Da Capo Graves.
Devil's Advice to Storytellers, *Robert Graves*, [tenor], Da Capo Graves.
Proud Songsters, *Thomas Hardy*, [alto/baritone], Da Capo Hardy.
Snow in the Suburbs, *Thomas Hardy*, [alto/baritone], Da Capo Hardy.
Theme of Death, The, *Robert Graves*, [tenor], Da Capo Graves.
Weathers, *Thomas Hardy*, [alto/baritone], Da Capo Hardy.

Beamish, Sally. 1956– *See also* App. 2.
Ae fond kiss, *Robert Burns*, [soprano], SMIC.
Clara, *Janice Galloway*, [soprano], SMIC.
Darkened Room at Dawn, A, *Simon Hughes*, [voice], SMIC.
Exile (cycle), *Donald Goodbrand Saunders*, [tenor], SMIC.

Beat, Janet. 1937– *See* App. 1, 2.

Bedford, David Vickerman. 1937– *See also* App. 2
Be music, Night, *Kenneth Patchen*, Bedford, (Universal).
Easy Decision, An, *Kenneth Patchen*, [e′-c′′′](f), Universal.
Epitaphs, *Gravestones*, [baritone], Bedford.
Found in a Country Churchyard, *Gravestones*, [soprano], Bedford.
Some Stars above Magnitude 2.9, *Anon*, [d′-c′′′#](f), Universal.

Belben, Philip. *See* App. 2.

Benbow, Edwin.
Heraclitus, *Callimachus* tr. *William Cory*, [a-e′′], BMP.

Benjamin, Arthur. 1893–1960.
Collections: *Three Greek Poems*, B&H 1934; (*Three Impressions*, Curwen).
(Before Dawn, *Walter de la Mare*, F [f′-e′′], Curwen.)
(Calm Sea and Mist, *William Sharp (Fiona Macleod)*, Cm [c′-f′′], Curwen.)
(Diaphenia, *Henry Chettle* or *Henry Constable*, Curwen.)
(Fire of Your Love, *Frank Eyton*, F [c′-g′′(b′′b)], B&H.)
Flower Girl, The, *Dionysius, 2nd century B.C.* tr. *A. C. Benson*, C [e′-g′′], B&H 3 Greek.
Heritage, A, *Arthur Lewis*, A [c′#-f′′#], B&H.

(Hey nonny no, *Anon Christchurch MS, 16th century,* G [d'(a)-f''#(a'')], Curwen.)
Jamaicalypso, *Jamaican folk song,* F [c'-f''], B&H.
Jan, *Anon,* F [c'-d''b(f'')], B&H.
Linstead Market, *Jamaican,* F [e'-f''], B&H.
(Man and Woman, *Peter Anthony Motteux,* D [b-d''], Elkin.)
(Moon, The, *H. Macrae,* Elkin.)
(Mouse, The, *H. Macrae,* Curwen.)
On Deck, *Thrognis, 6th century B.C.* tr. *A. C. Benson,* A [e'-g''], B&H 3 Greek.
(Piper, The, *Seamus O'Sullivan,* F#m [e'-a''(f''#)], Elkin.)
Shepherd's Holiday, *Elinor Wylie,* Gm [c'-f''](f), B&H *Heritage 4.*
Song of the Banana Carriers, *Jamaican folk song,* F [c'-f''], B&H.
(To Phillis, Milking her Flock, *William Drummond,* G [e'-f''#], Elkin; F, Elkin.)
Wind's Work, *Sturge Moore,* C [d'-f''], Thames *Century 1*; Bb, B&H.
Wine Jug, A, *Anon* tr. *A. C. Benson,* Am [e'-a''], B&H 3 Greek.

Benjamin, George. 1960– *See* App. 2.

Bennard, George. 1873–1958. *See* App. 2.

Bennett, Richard Rodney. 1936– *See also* App. 2.
Collections: *Dream-songs,* Novello; *Garland for Marjorie Fleming, A,* Novello; *History of the Thé Dansant, A,* Novello; *Music that Her Echo is,* Universal; *Tenebrae,* Universal.
    Adieu, farewell earth's bliss, *Thomas Nashe,* [A-g'](m), Universal Tenebrae.
    April is in my mistress' face, *Anon,* [e'b-e''], Universal Her Echo.
    Clear or cloudy, *Anon,* [d'-f''], Universal Her Echo.
    Death, be not proud, *John Donne,* [A(c)-f'#](m), Universal Tenebrae.
    Dream-song, *Walter de la Mare,* Gm [c'-e''b], Novello Dream-songs.
    Follow your saint, *Thomas Campion,* [e'-g''], Universal Her Echo.
    Fox-trot, *M. R. Peacocke,* [c'-g''#](f), Novello History.
    Hey nonny no, *Anon,* [Bb-g''](m), Universal Tenebrae.
    In Isas bed, *Marjorie Fleming,* F [d'-g''b](f), Novello Garland.
    Just Friends in Print, [voice], Novello.
    Like to the falling of a star, *Harry King,* [d#-f'#](m), Universal Tenebrae.
    Little Ghost who Died for Love (cycle), The, *Edith Sitwell,* [soprano], Novello.
    Lowest trees have tops, The, *Edward Dyer,* [c'#-a''b], Universal Her Echo.
    Melancholy Lay, A, *Marjorie Fleming,* Gm [bb-f''](f), Novello Garland.
    On Jessy Watson's Elopement, *Marjorie Fleming,* [b-g''#](f), Novello Garland.
    Partridge Pie, [soprano], Novello.
    Sleep wayward thoughts, *Anon,* [d'#-g''], Universal Her Echo.
    Slow Foxtrot, *M. R. Peacocke,* [c'#-g''b](f), Novello History.
    Song of Shadows, The, *Walter de la Mare,* [d'-e''], Novello Dream-songs.
    Song of the Mad Prince, The, *Walter de la Mare,* Fm [c'-e''], Novello Dream-songs.
    Song of the Wanderer, The, *Walter de la Mare,* [c'-f''], Novello Dream-songs.
    Sonnet on a Monkey, *Marjorie Fleming,* G [e'-f''#](f), Novello Garland.
    Sweet Isabell, *Marjorie Fleming,* F [d'-f''](f), Novello Garland.
    Tango, *M. R. Peacocke,* [bb-g''](f), Novello History.
    this is the garden, *E. E. Cummings,* [c'-a''], Novello.
    This Worldes Joie, *Anon,* [c'#-b''b], Novello hire.
    Vocalese, [soprano], Novello hire.
    Written on the Eve of Execution, *Chidiock Tichbourne,* [Ab-g'](m), Universal Tenebrae.

Bennett, Thomas Case Sterndale. 1882–1944. *See also* B&H, Cramer.
Collection: *Four Chinese Love Lyrics,* [Edward Teschemacher], [medium high], Classical.
    Carol singers, The, *Charles Hayes,* G [d'-e''(d'')](m), Cramer *Folio 1.*
    Leanin', *Hugh E. Wright,* G [c'#-e''](m), B&H *Ballad Album 2*; F, IMP *Parlour Songs,* (B&H).
    Seven Whatnots, [medium], Classical.

Bennett, Sir **William Sterndale.** 1816–1875. *See also* App. 1
Collection: *Twelve Songs, Op 23* and *Op 35,* Classical.
    As lonesome through the woods, *Carl Klingemann* tr. *H. F. Johnston,* Gm [d'-e''b], B&H, Classical 12 Songs.
    Castle Gordon, *Robert Burns,* Am [e'-e''], Classical 12 Songs.
    Dawn, gentle flower, *Barry Cornwall,* E [e'-e''], B&H, Classical 12 Songs.
    Forget-me-not, *Letitia Elizabeth Landon,* E [c'#-e''](m), B&H, Classical 12 Songs.

Gentle Zephyr, *Anon*, B♭ [f′-e′′♭](m), S&B (Bush & Temperley) *MB 43,* Classical 12 Songs.
Indian Love, *Barry Cornwall*, Bm [f′#-e′′](f), S&B (Bush & Temperley) *MB 43,* Classical 12 Songs.
May-dew, *Ludwig Uhland*, tr. *H. H. Pierson*, A♭ [e′♭-e′′♭], B&H, Classical 12 Songs.
Musing on the roaring ocean, *Robert Burns*, B♭ [e′-f′′](f), B&H, Classical 12 Songs.
Past, The, *Percy Bysshe Shelley*, E♭ [e′♭-e′′♭], S&B (Bush & Temperley) *MB 43,* Classical 12 Songs.
Sing, maiden, sing, *Barry Cornwall,* D [e′-g′′], Classical 12 Songs.
To Chloe (in sickness), *Robert Burns*, F#m [f′#-e′′], S&B (Bush & Temperley) *MB 43,* Classical 12 Songs.
Winter's gone, *John Clare,* E♭, [d′-f′′](m), B&H, Classical 12 Songs.

Bergmann, Walter George. 1902–1988. *See* App. 2.

Berkeley, Sir **Lennox** Randall Francis. 1903–1989. *See also* App. 1, 2.
Collections: *Another Spring Op. 93*, Chester; *Autumn's Legacy Op. 58*, Chester; *Five Chinese Songs Op. 78*, Chester; *Five Housman Songs Op. 14 No. 3*, Chester; *Five Poems Op. 53*, [W. H. Auden], Chester; *Five Songs Op. 26*, [Walter de la Mare], Chester; *Three Greek Songs Op. 38*, Chester.
   Afraid, *Walter de la Mare*, D♭ [e′♭-g′′], Chester Another Spring.
   All night a wind of music, *Thomas Lovell Beddoes*, [f′-a′′], Chester Autumn's Legacy.
   Another Spring, *Walter de la Mare*, F [b♭-g′′], Chester Another Spring.
   Autumn Wind, The, *Wu-Ti* tr. *Arthur Waley*, [c′#-f′′#], Chester 5 Chinese.
   Beacon Barn, The, *Patrick O'Malley*, F [c′-f′′], Chester.
   Because I liked you better, *A. E. Housman*, D♭ [d′-g′′](m), Chester 5 Housman.
   Bells of Cordoba, *Federico García Lorca* tr. *Stanley Richardson*, [e′♭-g′′], Chester.
   Carry her over the water, *W. H. Auden*, [e′-g′′], Chester 5 Auden.
   (Counting the Beats, *Robert Graves*, Fm [e♭-a′′♭], Thames.)
   Dreaming of a Dead Lady, *Shên-Yo* tr. *Arthur Waley*, [c′-g′′], Chester 5 Chinese.
   Epitaph of Timas, *Sappho* tr. *Anon*, Fm [c′#-e′′♭], Chester 3 Greek.
   Eyes look into the well, *W. H. Auden*, [c′-e′′♭], Chester 5 Auden.
   Half-moon westers low, The, *A. E. Housman*, B [d′#-a′′](m), Chester 5 Housman.
   He would not stay for me, *A. E. Housman*, [d′#-a′′](m), Chester 5 Housman.
   Horseman, The, *Walter de la Mare*, Gm [d′-f′′#], Chester 5 de la Mare.
   How love came in I do not know, *Robert Herrick*, F [e′-f′′], B&H *Heritage 3*.
   Hurrahing in Harvest, *Gerard Manley Hopkins*, [e′♭-a′′], Chester Autumn's Legacy.
   Late Spring, *Yang Knang* tr. *Kotewall & Smith*, [c′-f′′#], Chester 5 Chinese.
   Lauds, *W. H. Auden*, E♭ [d′-f′′#], Chester 5 Auden.
   Lay your sleeping head, my love, *W. H. Auden,* [soprano/tenor], Chester.
   Lesbos, *Lawrence Durrell*, Fm [f′-g′′], Chester Autumn's Legacy.
   Look not in my eyes, *A. E. Housman*, [d′-g′′#](m), Chester 5 Housman.
   Lowlands of Holland, [mezzo/baritone], Chester hire.
   Memory, A, *Louis Labé* tr. *M. D. Calvocoressi*, [c′#-g′′], OUP.
   Mighty thoughts of an Old World, The, *Thomas Lovell Beddoes*, [c′-a′′], Chester Autumn's Legacy.
   Mistletoe, *Walter de la Mare*, F# [c′#-f′′#], Chester 5 de la Mare.
   Night covers up the rigid land, *W. H. Auden*, Cm [c′-g′′♭], Thames *Century 3*.
   O lurcher-loving collier, *W. H. Auden*, B♭ [d′-f′′], Chester 5 Auden.
   People Hide Their Love, *Wu-Ti* tr. *Arthur Waley*, A♭ [d′♭-f′′], Chester 5 Chinese.
   Poetry, *Walter de la Mare*, [c′-f′′#], Chester Another Spring.
   Poor Henry, *Walter de la Mare*, A [c′-g′′#], Chester 5 de la Mare.
   Rich Days, *W. H. Davies*, E♭ [e′♭-g′′♭], Chester Autumn's Legacy.
   Riverside Village, The, *Ssu-K'ung Shu* tr. *Kotewall & Smith*, D♭ [d′♭-f′′], Chester 5 Chinese.
   Silver, *Walter de la Mare*, E♭ [d′-g′′], Chester 5 de la Mare.
   So sweet love seemed, [mezzo/alto/baritone] *Robert Bridges*, Chester.
   Song of the Soldiers, The, *Walter de la Mare*, Dm [c′-a′′♭], Chester 5 de la Mare.
   Sonnet Op. 102, [high], Chester.
   Spring Song, *Antipater* tr. *Anon*, G [c′#-f′′], Chester 3 Greek.
   Street sounds to the soldiers' tread, The, *A. E. Housman*, [d′-a′′♭](m), Chester 5 Housman.
   Thresher, The, *Joachim du Bellay* tr. *M. D. Calvocoressi*, G [d′-g′′], OUP.
   To Aster, *Plato* tr. *Anon*, D♭ [d′♭-f′′♭], Chester 3 Greek.
   Tonight the winds begin to rise, *Alfred Lord Tennyson*, [e′-b′′♭], Chester Autumn's Legacy.
   What's in your mind, my dove, my coney? *W. H. Auden*, [c′-f′′#], Chester 5 Auden.
   When we were idlers with the loitering rills, *Hartley Coleridge*, [e′-a′′#], Chester Autumn's Legacy.

Berkeley, Michael. 1948– *See also* App. 2.
Collection: *Speaking Silence* OUP.
    And is it night? *Anon*, [baritone], OUP Speaking Silence.
    Blow, Northern Wind, *Anon*, [baritone], OUP Speaking Silence.
    Echo, *Christina Rossetti*, [baritone], OUP Speaking Silence.
    Ragged Wood, The, *W. B. Yeats*, [baritone], OUP Speaking Silence.

Bernard, Anthony. 1891–1963.
    (Cherry Tree, The, *C. A. Claye*, A, B&H.)
    (Follow your saint, *Thomas Campion*, G, B&H; E♭, B&H.)
    (When that I was and a little tiny boy, *Shakespeare*, Gm [d′-e′′♭](m), Chester.)

Berners, Lord (Gerald Hugh Tyrwhitt-Wilson). 1883–1950. *See also* App. 1.
Collections: (*The Collected Vocal Music*, Chester); *Three Songs,* Chester.
    (Come on Algernon, *T. E. B. Clarke*, G [b-d′′(b′)], Chester Collected.)
    Dialogue between Tom Filuter and his man, *Anon*, [d′-f′′], Chester, (Chester Collected).
    (Green-eyed Monster, The, *E. L. Duff*, [c′-g′′], Chester Collected.)
    (Lady visitor in the pauper ward, The, *Robert Graves*, [e′b-f′′♯], Chester Collected.)
    (Long time ago, A, *Traditional*, [c′-g′′♯](m), Chester Collected.)
    (Lullaby, *Thomas Dekker*, Fm [d′-f′′], Chester Collected.)
    (Red Roses and Red Noses, *Lord Berners*, B♭ [b-f′′], Chester Collected.)
    (Rio Grande, The, *Traditional*, [d′b-a′′](m), Chester Collected.)
    (Theodore or The Pirate King, *John Masefield*, [c′♯-f′′♯], Chester Collected.)

Bernofsky, Lauren.
Collection: *Five Songs on Poems by Robert Herrick,* Micropress. Note: Micropress publications can be supplied in a wide range of keys.
    Amarillis, *Robert Herrick,* Micropress 5 Robert Herrick.
    Epitaph upon a Child, An, *Robert Herrick,* Micropress 5 Robert Herrick.
    Frozen Heart, The, *Robert Herrick,* Micropress 5 Robert Herrick.
    Nursery Rhyme, *May Sarton,* Micropress.
    Spell, The, *Robert Herrick,* Micropress 5 Robert Herrick.
    Succession of the Foure Sweet Months, The, *Robert Herrick,* Micropress 5 Robert Herrick.

Besley, Maurice. 1888–1945. *See also* B&H.
Collection: *Three Little Fairy Songs,* Classical.
    Blue-bell, Dew-bell, *J. L. Crommelin Brown,* [medium], Classical 3 Little Fairy.
    Canterbury Bells, *J. L. Crommelin Brown,* [medium], Classical 3 Little Fairy.
    Epitaph, An, *Walter de la Mare,* D♭ [c′b(a♭)-e′′♭], William Elkin.
    Fairy Children, The, *J. L. Crommelin Brown,* [medium], Classical 3 Little Fairy.
    Second Minuet, The, *Aubrey Dowdon,* G [d′-d′′], B&H; B♭, B&H.

Bibby, David.
    Bury me again at Wounded Knee, *Anon*, [high baritone], Da Capo.

Biggs, R.
Arrangements:
    Drink to me only with thine eyes, *Ben Jonson*, [e′b-e′′b], BMP.
    Oft in the stilly night, *Thomas Moore*, [e′b-d′′b], BMP.

Bingham, Judith. 1952– *See also* App. 2.
    Alba, *Ezra Pound,* [e′-g′′♯](m), Maecenas.
    Blacker, *Samuel Taylor Coleridge,* [B♭-e′b](m), Maecenas.
    Cocaine Lil *or* Bondage of Opium, A, *Samuel Taylor Coleridge & Anon,* [a-a′′♯](f), Maecenas.
    Shadow Side of Joy Finzi, The, *Joy Finzi and R. D. Blackmore,* [c′-a′′](f), Maecenas.
    (Snowflake, *Anon,* [b-g′′♯](m), Novello.)

Birkett, C. M. 1911–
Collection: *Songs,* Lengnick.
    Apple Tree, The, *C. M. Birkett,* F [c′-f′′], Lengnick Songs.
    Come, my little children, here are songs for you, *R. L. Stevenson,* C [e′b-f′′], Lengnick Songs.
    Dream Pedlary, *Thomas Lovell Beddoes,* C [d′♯-f′′], Lengnick Songs.
    Love Song (To Anthea, who may command him anything), *Robert Herrick,* A [d′-f′′♯], Lengnick
        Songs.

Music when soft voices die, *Percy Bysshe Shelley*, C [e′-f′′], Lengnick Songs.
October: A Haiku Sequence, *Mary Lind*, [c′-f′′#], Lengnick Songs.
On a Fly Drinking out of his Cup, *William Oldys*, F [c′-f′′], Lengnick Songs.
Song (When I am dead, my dearest), *Christina Rossetti*, Fm [f′-g′′], Lengnick Songs.
Suspense, *C. M. Birkett*, F [d′-a′′b], Lengnick Songs.
There is no Season (cycle), *R. L. Stevenson, Walter de la Mare, John Drinkwater*, [c′-g′′], Lengnick Songs.
Tide rises, the tide falls, The, *Longfellow*, Fm [e′-g′′], Lengnick Songs.

Birtwistle, Sir Harrison Paul. 1934– *See* App. 2.

Bishop, Sir Henry Rowley. 1786–1855. *See also* Cramer.
Collection: *Twenty Songs*, Classical.
Ah! can I e'er forget thee, *Charles Dibdin*, F [c′-f′′](m), Classical 20 Songs.
Are you angry, mother? *George Soane*, E [b-e′′](f), Classical 20 Songs.
Be mine, dear maid, *Daniel Terry*, B♭ [f′-g′′](m), Classical 20 Songs.
Bid me discourse, *Shakespeare* (adapted), G [b-a′′)](f), Classical 20 Songs.
Bloom is on the Rye, The, *Edward Fitzball*, B♭ [f′-g′′](m), Classical 20 Songs.
By the simplicity of Venus's doves, *Shakespeare*, E♭, [e′b-g′′], S&B (Bush & Temperley) *MB 43*, Novello (Bush) *Ballad Operas*.
Come live with me, *Marlowe* adapted *Reynolds*, G [c′#-g′′], S&B (Bush & Temperley) *MB 43*.
Come, my love, to me, *Shakespeare*, G [e′-e′′], B&H (Rowley).
Dashing White Sergeant, The, *General Bargoyn*, D [c′#-a′′(g′′)](f), Classical 20 Songs.
Deep in my heart, *Anon*, E♭ [e′b-g′′], B&H (Alec Rowley) *Imperial 2*.
Ev'ry Bullet has its Billet, *Thomas Dibdin*, B♭ [a-d′′](m), Classical 20 Songs.
Home Sweet Home, *John Howard Payne*, E [e′-e′′], Classical 20 Songs, Cramer *Drawing Room Songs*; F, B&H.
Lo! here the gentle lark, *Shakespeare*, F [e′-a′′(c′′′)](f), B&H (Woolfenden) *Shakespeare Album*, *Souvenirs*, Cramer, BMP (Wilson); C, Fischer *Centuries low*.
Love Has Eyes, *Charles Dibdin*, B♭ [f′-g′′(b′′b)], Classical 20 Songs, Schirmer *1st Soprano*.
My Heart and Lute, *Thomas Moore*, E [d′#-f′′#](m), Classical 20 Songs.
My Native Highland Home, *T. Morton*, G [d′-g′′](m), Classical 20 Songs.
My Native Hills, *Geo. Inman*, B♭ [f′-f′′](f), Classical 20 Songs.
Not the soft sighs *see* Deep in my heart.
O firm as oak, *W. Dimond*, E♭ [a♭-e′′b](m), Classical 20 Songs.
Pilgrim of Love, The, *Mrs Amelia Opie*, C [e′-g′′(a′′)], Classical 20 Songs.
Should he upbraid, *Shakespeare* (adapted), G [c′#-g′′](f), Classical 20 Songs, B&H (Northcote) *Imperial 1*, BMP (Wilson).
Soldier's Gratitude, A, *T. Morton*, B♭ [d′-g′′](m), Classical 20 Songs.
Take O take those lips away, *Shakespeare*, E♭ [d′-f′′], S&B (Bush & Temperley) *MB 43, F, Recitalist 3*.
Teach, O Teach me to Forget, *T. H. Bayly*, A [e′-e′′](m), Classical 20 Songs.
Tell me, my heart, *T. Morton*, E♭ [d′-a′′b](f), Classical 20 Songs.
Tis when to sleep, *S. J. Arnold*, E♭ [g-e′′b](m), Classical 20 Songs.
When Green Leaves Come Again, *T. H. Bayly*, F [c′-f′′](f), Classical 20 Songs.

Blackford, Richard. 1954–
From the Song of Songs, *Song of Solomon*, [soprano], Novello.

Blake, David Leonard. 1936– *See also* App. 2.
Beata l'alma (cantata), *Herbert Read*, [a(b♭)-b′′], Novello.
Bones of Chuang Tzu, The (cantata), *Chang Heng* tr. *Arthur Waley*, [A-g′](m), Novello.

Blake, Howard. 1938– *See also* App. 2.
Collections: *Shakespeare Songs*, [medium], Chester; *Three Songs from James Joyce's 'Chamber Music'*, [medium], Chester; *Three Sussex Songs,* [Judith Garrett], [mezzo], Chester.
Coronach, [mezzo], Chester.
Holy Mary, mother mild, [tenor], Chester.
Isabelle, [mezzo], Chester.
It was the time of roses, [voice], Chester.
Land of Counterpane, The, *Robert Louis Stevenson*, [medium] Chester.
Of a rose is all my song, [bass], Chester.
So we'll go no more a-roving, [voice], Chester.
Walking in the air, *Howard Blake*, [c′#-d′′], Faber.

Bliss, Sir **Arthur** Drummond. 1891–1975. *See also* App. 2
Collections: *Angels of the Mind,* Novello; *Ballads of the Four Seasons, The,* Novello; *Nine Songs,* Novello (Preface by George Dannatt); *Seven American Poems,* B&H; *Two American Poems,* B&H; *Two Love Songs,* OUP.
- Autumn, *Li Po* tr. *Shigeyoshi Obata,* [b♭(f)-a′′], Novello 4 Seasons.
- Auvergnat, *Hilaire Belloc,* [e′-g′′#], Novello.
- Being young and green, *Edna St. Vincent Millay,* [b-e′′], B&H 7 American; [e′b-a′′b] B&H Heritage 3, B&H.
- Buckle, The, *Walter de la Mare,* A [b-f′′#], Novello 9 Songs.
- Child's Prayer, A, *Siegfried Sassoon,* [f′-f′′], Novello 9 Songs.
- Fair Annet's song, *Elinor Wylie,* Gm [b-e′′b], B&H 7 American.
- Fair is my love, *Edmund Spenser,* [b♭-f′′](m), OUP 2 Love Songs.
- Fallow Deer at the Lonely House, The, *Thomas Hardy,* E [e′-g′′#], Novello 9 Songs, Thames *Hardy Songbook.*
- Feast, *Edna St. Vincent Millay,* Dm [a-d′′#], B&H 7 American.
- Gone, gone again is summer, *Edna St. Vincent Millay,* E♭ [b♭-e′′b], B&H 7 American, B&H; G, B&H.
- Hare, The, *Walter de la Mare,* [e′-g′′#], Novello 9 Songs.
- Harvest, *Kathleen Raine,* [e′-a′′](f), Novello Angels.
- Humoresque, *Edna St. Vincent Millay,* [e′-g′′#](f), B&H 2 American.
- In Praise of his Daphnis, *John Wotton,* [c′-f′′#], OUP 2 Love Songs.
- In the Beck, *Kathleen Raine,* [d′-g′′](f) Novello Angels.
- Leisure, *W. H. Davies,* G [g′-g′′], Novello 9 Songs.
- Lenten Flowers, *Kathleen Raine,* [d′-f′′](f), Novello Angels.
- Little Elegy, *Elinor Wylie,* D♭ [c′-f′′], B&H 7 American, B&H; E, B&H.
- Lovelocks, *Walter de la Mare,* [d′-f′′#], Novello 9 Songs.
- Nocturne, *Kathleen Raine,* [d′-g′′](f), Novello Angels.
- Rain comes down, *Edna St. Vincent Millay,* C#m [b#-f′′#], B&H 7 American.
- Return from Town, The, *Edna St. Vincent Millay,* G [d′-f′′#](f), Thames *Century 5,* B&H 2 American.
- Rich or Poor, *W. H. Davies,* [e′-f′′], Novello 9 Songs.
- Seed, *Kathleen Raine,* [d′-a′′b](f), Novello Angels.
- Siege, *Edna St. Vincent Millay,* Am [c′-g′′], B&H 7 American.
- Simples, *James Joyce,* E♭ [e′b-f′′#], OUP.
- Spring, *Li Po* tr. *Shigeyoshi Obata,* A♭ [c′-f′′], Novello 4 Seasons.
- Storm, *Kathleen Raine,* [c′#-g′′#](f), Novello Angels.
- Summer, *Li Po* tr. *Shigeyoshi Obata,* [c′#-g′′#], Novello 4 Seasons.
- This Night, *W. H. Davies,* E♭ [c′-g′′], Novello 9 Songs.
- Thunderstorms, *W. H. Davies,* Bm [d′-f′′#], Novello 9 Songs.
- Tramps, The, *Robert Service,* A♭ [e′b-g′′](m), B&H.
- Tune on my pipe *see* In praise of his Daphnis.
- Winter, *Li Po,* tr. *Shigeyoshi Obata,* [d′-a′′], Novello 4 Seasons.
- Worry about Money, *Kathleen Raine,* C [b-a′′b](f), Novello Angels.

Blow, John. 1649–1708. *See also* App. 2.
Collections: *Ten Songs,* S&B (edited Michael Pilkington); *Twelve Songs,* Voicebox (edited Timothy Roberts).
- Boasting fops, *Peter Anthony Motteux,* F [c′-a′′], S&B 10 Songs.
- Clarona, lay aside your lute, *Anon,* Cm [d′-a′′], S&B 10 Songs.
- Fain would I, Chloris, *Anon,* Dm [d′-a′′](m), S&B 10 Songs.
- Fairest work of happy nature, *Anon,* F [f′-a′′], Voicebox 12 Songs.
- Flavia Grown Old, *Anon,* F [c′-a′′], Voicebox 12 Songs.
- Grant me, ye gods, *Abraham Cowley,* Gm [c′-f′′], S&B 10 Songs.
- (Grove, The: Why does Laura shun me? *Anon,* E♭ [b♭-e′′b](m), B&H (Anthony Bernard).)
- Horace to his Lute, *Anon,* C [G-f′](m), Thames (Bevan) *6 Restoration.*
- Lovely Selina, innocent and free, *Anon,* G [b-g′′], Voicebox 12 Songs.
- Lysander I pursue in vain, *Anon,* Gm [c′-a′′](f), Voicebox *Mad Songs 2.*
- No more the dear lovely nymph, *Peter Anthony Motteux,* Am [d′-a′′](m), Voicebox 12 Songs.
- O mighty God, who sit'st on high, *Anon,* Em [b-a′′], Voicebox 12 Songs.
- O turn not those fine eyes away, *Anon,* Dm [d′-a′′], Voicebox 12 Songs.
- Of all the torments, *William Walsh,* Gm [d′-a′′](m), Voicebox 12 Songs; Fm, S&B 10 Songs, *Recitalist 3.*
- Oh! that mine eyes would melt, *Anon,* Gm [d′-a′′], Voicebox 12 Songs, Faber (Britten) *Harmonia.*
- Pastoral Elegy, A, *Thomas Flatman,* Gm [c′-g′′], Voicebox 12 Songs.

Peaceful is he, and most secure, *Thomas Flatman*, Am [c′-f′′], Thames (Bevan) *6 Divine*.
Perfection, The *Thomas D'Urfey*, Dm [d′-a′′], S&B *10 Songs*.
Philander, do not think of arms, *Anon*, D; *C* [e′-a′′](f), S&B *10 Songs*, *Recitalist 1*.
Queen's Epicedium, The, *Mr Herbert*, Cm [g-b′′b], Voicebox *Three Elegies*; Am, Voicebox *Three Elegies*
Sabina has a thousand charms, *Anon*, C [d′-a′′](m), Voicebox *12 Songs*.
Self Banished, The, *Edmund Waller*, G [d′-g′′], S&B *10 Songs*, Schott (Tippett & Bergmann); *F*, Lengnick; *D*, B&H (Northcote) *Imperial 6*, Schott, Paterson (Diack) *100 Best 4*, Elkin.
Tell me no more, *Anon*, A; *G* [c′#-f′′#](m); S&B *10 Songs*, Schott (Tippett & Bergmann), Leonard *Baroque high; Eb*, Leonard *Baroque low*.
What is't to us? *John Howe*, Gm [c′-a′′](m), S&B *10 Songs*.
Why does the morn' in blushes rise? *Anon*, B♭ [f′-g′′](m), Voicebox *12 Songs*.
Why weeps Asteria? *Anon*, Gm [f′-g′′], Voicebox *12 Songs*.

Blyton, Carey. 1932–2002. *See also* App. 1, 2.
Collections: *Lyrics from the East*, Fand; *Mixed Bag* [Enid Blyton], B&H; *Poetry of Dress, The*, IMP; *Prayers from the Ark*, Modus; *Three A. M.*, Modus; *Two Pensive Songs*, Modus.
As the last guest leaves, *David Munro*, F [a-d′′], Modus *3 A. M.*
Blast of Love, The, *Sappho* tr. *Willis Barnstone & William E. McCulloh*, [d′-g′′], Fand Lyrics.
Blue Christmas, *Peter Westmore*, Cm [c′-f′′], Modus.
By Moonlight, *David Munro*, D♭ [b♭-d′′♭], Modus *3 A. M.*
City Sleeps, The, *David Munro*, F# [a#-d′′#], Modus *3 A. M.*
Come, Night, *Donald R. Hills*, E♭ [c′-g′′], Modus Pensive.
Dawn gapes in, The, *David Munro*, [g#-e′′], Modus *3 A. M.*
Dirge for St Patrick's Night, *Elsa Corbluth*, [e′-c′′], Fand.
Evening, the 'Manyoshu' tr. *Leon Zolbrod*, [e′♭-e′′♭], Fand Lyrics.
Flea, The, *Anon*, C [g′-c′′], Modus.
Indigo Blues, *Carey Blyton*, [e′-g′′], Modus.
My love in her attire, *Anon*, [d′-g′′](m), IMP Poetry of Dress.
Night, *Chinese* tr. *T. C. Lai*, [d′-a′′], Fand Lyrics.
Paradise, *Omar Khayyam* tr. *Edward Fitzgerald*, [f′-f′′], Fand Lyrics.
Pianoman, *Carey Blyton*, [c′-d′′], Modus.
Prayer of the Cat, The, *Carmen Bernos de Gasztold* tr. *Godden*, A [c′#-c′′#], Modus Prayers.
Prayer of the Cock, The, *Carmen Bernos de Gasztold* tr. *Godden*, B♭m [d′♭♭-f′′], Modus Prayers.
Prayer of the Goldfish, The, *Carmen Bernos de Gasztold* tr. *Godden*, G [f′#-g′′], Modus Prayers.
Prayer of the Lark, The, *Carmen Bernos de Gasztold* tr. *Godden*, [e′-f′′#], Modus Prayers.
Prayer of the Mouse, The, *Carmen Bernos de Gasztold* tr. *Godden*, F [c′-f′′], Modus Prayers.
Prayer of the Ox, The, *Carmen Bernos de Gasztold* tr. *Godden*, G [d′#-e′′♭], Modus Prayers.
Prayer of the Tortoise, The, *Carmen Bernos de Gasztold* tr. *Godden*, Am [c′-f′′#], Modus Prayers.
Puty-fish, *Central India* tr. *Shushim Shorka*, [f′#-d′′# or d′#-b′], Fand Lyrics.
Robin Redbreast, *Carey Blyton*, [c′-e′′♭], Modus.
Sea-dog's Song, The, *Alan Cunningham*, E♭ [b♭-g′′♭(c′′)](m), Modus.
Sweet disorder in the dress, A, *Robert Herrick*, [d′-g′′](m), IMP Poetry of Dress.
Symphony in Yellow, *Oscar Wilde*, [c′#-g′′], B&H.
Three a. m., *David Munro*, [a-f′′], Modus *3 A. M.*
Two stolen roses, *Carey Blyton*, [d′-f′′], Modus Pensive.
Whenas in silk my Julia goes, *Robert Herrick*, [d′-a′′♭](m), IMP Poetry of Dress.

Boughton, Rutland. 1878–1960.
At Grafton, *John Drinkwater*, F [c′-d′′], B&H.
Evensong, *Thomas Hardy*, Dm [d′-g′′], S&B.
Faery Song, *Fiona Macleod*, E♭ [e′♭-a′′♭], S&B *Recitalist 3*, S&B; D♭, S&B.
Feckenham Men, The, *John Drinkwater*, E♭, [b♭-e′♭], B&H.
Foreboding, *Thomas Hardy*, [e′♭-f′′], S&B; [d′♭-e′′♭], S&B.
In Prison, *William Morris*, B&H.
Lorna's Song, *R. D. Blackmore*, Gm [f′-g′′](f), B&H.
Song of Lyonesse, A, *Thomas Hardy*, Em [d′-g′′](m), S&B; Dm, S&B.

Boulter, Brian. *See* App. 2.

Bowen, Edwin **York**. 1884–1961.
Collection: *Three Royal Lyrics* (with Philip York Bowen), Weinberger.
Cordovan Love Song, *George Leveson Gower*, C [d′-a′′](m), Weinberger; *A*, Weinberger.
England's Ambassador, *Olive Maitland Marsh*, C [c′-f′′], Weinberger *3 Royal*.

England's Monarch, *Olive Maitland Marsh*, G [d'-e''], Weinberger 3 Royal.
England's Rose, *Olive Maitland Marsh*, Em [b-e''], Weinberger 3 Royal.
Fairies' Lullaby, The, *Alexander Field*, B♭ [d'-f''], Weinberger.
If you should frown, *George Leveson Gower*, Gm [f'-a''♭], Weinberger.
In June, *George Leveson Gower*, F [e'-d''], Weinberger; D, E♭, Weinberger.
Love and Death, *George Leveson Gower*, A♭ [d'-f''(a''♭)], Weinberger.
Love Untold, *J. P. Dalton,* A♭ [e'♭-g''], BMP; B♭, BMP.
Love's Reckoning, *George Leveson Gower*, F [e'-a''], Weinberger.
Moonlight Night, A, *Robert Southey*, B♭ [a-e''♭], Weinberger.
Storm Song, *George Leveson Gower*, Bm [b-d''#(f''#)], Weinberger; Dm, Weinberger.
To Myra, *James Thomson*, E♭ [b♭-e''♭](m), Weinberger; G, Weinberger.
Wind's an old woman, The, *Wilfrid Thorley*, Em [b-e''], Weinberger; Dm Weinberger.

Boyce, William. 1711–1779.
Collections: *Five Songs*, S&B (edited Michael Mullinar); *Ten Songs*, S&B (edited Michael Pilkington).
Amour Sans Soucis, *Colley Cibber*, A [e'-f''#](m), S&B 10 Songs.
Balmy sweetness ever flowing, *Edward Moore*, F [d'-g''](m), BMP (Taylor).
Boast not, mistaken swain, *Anon*, G [f'#-g''](f), BMP (Taylor).)
By thy banks, gentle Stour, *Anon*, D♭ [d'-a''♭], OUP (Poston) *Solo Soprano*; B♭, BMP.
Cantata II *see* Tell me, ye brooks.
Declare my pretty maid, *Anon*, D [a-d''](m), S&B 5 Songs.
Fatal Blessing, The, *George Grenville, Lord Lansdowne*, Cm [G-e'♭](m), BMP (Taylor).
For the Lord hath pleasure, [soprano], Schott (Bevan).
Goddess of the dimpling smile, *Anon*, E♭ [d'-f''](f), S&B 10 Songs.
Happy Pair, The, *Anon*, C [b-e''](m), S&B 5 Songs.
How unhappy's the nymph, *Anon*, Gm [f'#-f''], S&B 10 Songs.
Idleness, *Anon*, G [d'-g''], Thames (Copley & Reitan) *Gentleman's Magazine*.
Non-pareil, The, *Anon*, B♭; *G* [d'-g''](m), S&B 10 Songs; E [b-e''], S&B 5 Songs.
Of all the torments, *William Walsh*, D [c'#-d''], S&B 5 Songs.
On a bank beside a willow, *Anon*, Cm [e'♭-g''](f), S&B 10 Songs, (Curwen (Poston)).
Orpheus and Euridice, *Anon*, Dm [d'-a''], S&B 10 Songs.
Pleasures of Spring Gardens, The, *see* Spring Gardens.
Rail no more, ye learned asses, *Anon*, Bm; *Am* [g'-d''](m), BMP (Jacob).
Song of Momus to Mars, The, *John Dryden*, E♭, [b♭-e''♭](m), OUP (Arkwright) *Solo Baritone*, Schirmer *1st Baritone II*.
Spring Gardens, *John Lockman*, D [d'-a''], S&B 10 Songs, S&B (Mullinar); D♭ BMP (Franklin).
Tell me lovely shepherd, *Anon*, D♭ [d'♭-a''♭], OUP (Poston); B♭, BMP (Poston).
Tell me no more, *George Etheridge*, B♭ [d'-a''♭](m), S&B 10 Songs.
Tell me, ye brooks (Cantata II), *Anon*, E♭ [d'-g''](f), S&B 10 Songs.
Though Chloe's out of fashion, *see*: Non-pareil, The.
Venus to soothe my heart, *Anon*, Em [b-c''], S&B 5 Songs.
Well Judging Phyllis, *John Lockman*, Gm [d'-a''], S&B 10 Songs.
What beauties my nymph doth disclose, *Moses Mendez*, A [c'#-f''#](m), BMP (Taylor).
(Whether I grow old or no, *Abraham Cowley*, Cm [F(B♭)-f'](m), Elkin (Bevan).)

Boyle, Ina. *See* App. 2.

Boyle, Rory. 1951– *See also* App. 2.
Collections: *Three Songs on Poems by Dylan Thomas,* [medium], SMIC; *Three Songs on Poems by Louis MacNeice,* [baritone], SMIC.
Bisclaveret, *Judith Kite,* [bass], SMIC.
Songs of Strange Creatures, *Lewis Carroll, Oliver Goldsmith,* [baritone], SMIC.
Arrangements: *Four English Folk Songs,* SMIC.
Lark in the morn, The, *Anon*, [baritone], SMIC 4 Folksongs.
My bonnie, bonnie boy, *Anon*, [baritone], SMIC 4 Folksongs.
My Boy Willie, *Anon*, [baritone], SMIC 4 Folksongs.
Willow Tree, The, *Anon*, [baritone], SMIC 4 Folksongs.

Braham, John. 1774–1856.
Death of Nelson, The, *Anon*, Cm [f'-a''♭], Cramer *Drawing Room Songs*.

Brahe, Mary H. (Mary Hannah Morgan). 1885–1956.
As I went a-roaming, *Helen Taylor,* G [b-e''](f), Schirmer *1st Mezzo II*.

Bless this house, *Helen Taylor*, Eb [d′-a′′b], B&H *Ballad Album 1*, B&H; B*b*, IMP *Parlour Songs*, B&H; C, B&H.

Brand, Margaret. WMIC.

Branson, David. 1909–
Collection: (*Three Elizabethan Poems*, Elkin)
Look not in my eyes, *A. E. Housman*, Ab [d′b-f′′](m), BMP.
(Mortal Glance, The, *Anon*, F [e′-f′′], Elkin 3 Elizabethan.)
(Music, *Anon*, E [e′-g′′#(f′′#)], Elkin 3 Elizabethan.)
Phillida, *Anon*, F [d′-f′′](m), BMP.
Unseen Spring, The, *A. E. Housman*, Eb [e′b-a′′b], BMP.
(Wily Lover, The, *Thomas Campion*, Eb [e′b-f′′](m), Elkin 3 Elizabethan.)

Brewer, Thomas. 1611– *c.*1660-70.
Mistake me not, I am as cold as hot, *Anon*, Gm [d′-f′′], S&B (Spink) *MB 33*.
O that mine eyes could melt into a flood, *Anon*, Cm [g′-g′′], S&B (Spink) *MB 33*.

Brian, Havergal. 1876–1972
Day and Night, *Gerald Cumberland*, [tenor], UMP.
Faery Song, A, *W. B. Yeats*, E [e′b-g′′#], UMP.
Farewell, *William Heber*, [contralto/baritone], UMP.
If I could speak, *Gerald Cumberland*, [tenor], UMP.
Land of Dreams, The, *William Blake*, UMP.
Message, The, *John Donne*, [alto/baritone], UMP.
Piping down the valleys wild, *William Blake*, UMP.
Soliloquy upon an Dead Child (Little Sleeper), *Gerald Cumberland*, [tenor/soprano], UMP.
Sorrow Song, *Samuel Daniel*, [contralto/baritone], UMP.
When I lie ill, *Gerald Cumberland*, [tenor], UMP.
Why dost thou wound and break my heart? *Robert Herrick*, [tenor], UMP.

Bridge, Frank. 1879–1941. *See also* App. 1, 2.
Collections: *Five Early Songs*, Thames (edited with introduction by Paul Hindmarsh); *Four Songs by Frank Bridge* S&B, (introduction by Peter J. Pirie); *Six Songs*, Thames; *Songs,* B&H (introduction by John Bishop).
Adoration, *John Keats*, C [c′-g′′], B&H Songs.
All things that we clasp, *Heinrich Heine* tr. *Emma Lazarus*, Am [e′-g′′], B&H Songs; F*m*, B&H.
Berceuse, *Dorothy Wordsworth*, Em [e′-g′′#](f), Thames 6 Songs.
Blow, blow, thou winter wind, *Shakespeare*, Cm [c′-f′′], B&H Songs, *Shakespeare Album*; D*m*, B&H.
Blow out, you bugles, *Rupert Brooke*, Bb [f′-b′′b](m), B&H Songs.
Come to me in my dreams, *Matthew Arnold*, Eb [d′-f′′], B&H Songs; *Db*, B&H.
Dawn and Evening, *Heinrich Heine* tr. *C. A.*, Gm [d′-f′′#], B&H Songs; F*m*, B&H.
Day after day, *Rabindranath Tagore*, [e′b-e′′](f), S&B 4 Songs.
Dead Violet, A, *Percy Bysshe Shelley*, F#m [e′#-f′′#], Thames 5 Early.
Devon Maid, The, *John Keats*, G [d′-e′′](m), B&H Songs.
Dirge, A: Rough wind that moaneth loud, *Percy Bysshe Shelley*, Fm [c′-f′′], Thames 5 Early.
Dweller in my Deathless Dreams, *Rabindranath Tagore*, [c′-a′′], S&B 4 Songs.
E'en as a lovely flower, *Heinrich Heine* tr. *Kate Kroeker*, G [e′-g′′], B&H Songs, *Imperial 4*; E, Mayhew *Collection 1*, B&H.
Fair daffodils, we weep to see, *Robert Herrick*, A; *G* [d′-e′′], B&H Songs; *F*, B&H.
Go not, happy day, *Alfred Lord Tennyson*, A [c′-f′′#(a′′)](m), B&H Songs, *Heritage 4*, Classical; G, Classical, B&H.
Goldenhair, *James Joyce*, E [e′-g′′], Thames 6 Songs; (C, Chappell *English Recital 2.*)
Into Her Keeping, *H. D. Lowry*, Eb [d′-f′′#], B&H Songs; F, *Db*, B&H.
Isobel, *Digby Goddard-Fenwick*, F#m [c′#-e′′](m), Thames 6 Songs, Classical, (Chappell *English Recital 1*); F*m*, A*m*, Classical, (Chappell).
Journey's End, *Humbert Wolfe*, Gm [d′-e′′], S&B 4 Songs.
Last Invocation, The, *Walt Whitman*, D [e′-f′′#], B&H Songs; *E, C*, B&H.
Love went a-riding, *Mary Coleridge*, Gb [f′-g′′], B&H Songs, *Heritage 3*, Banks, Classical, B&H, (simplified version), B&H; E, Classical, B&H *Love and Affection*, B&H.
Mantle of Blue, *Padraic Colum*, Dm [d′-f′′], B&H Songs; *Cm*, B&H.
My pent-up tears, *Matthew Arnold*, Ebm [d′-e′′], Thames 5 Early.
Night lies on the silent highways, *Heinrich Heine* tr. *Kate Kroeker*, Bm [b-e′′b], Thames 5 Early.

O That It Were So, *Walter Savage Landor*, C [c′-f′′(a′′)], Thames 6 Songs; B♭, D, Classical, (Chappell).
So Early in the Morning, *James Stephens*, E [e′-a′′], B&H Songs.
So Perverse, *Robert Bridges*, F [f′-e′′(f′′)](m), B&H Songs, *Heritage 4*, B&H.
Speak to me, my love, *Rabindranath Tagore*, [d′-g′′](f), S&B 4 Songs.
Strew no more red roses, *Matthew Arnold*, E♭ [e′-f′′#](m), B&H Songs; C#m, B&H.
Tears, idle tears, *Alfred Lord Tennyson*, Am [c′-e′′], Thames 5 Early.
Thy hand in mine, *Mary Coleridge*, G [f′#-g′′], B&H Songs; E♭, B&H.
Tis but a week, *Gerald Gould*, B♭m [f′#-f′′#], B&H Songs; C#m, *Am*, B&H.
Violets blue, The, *Heine*, trans. *James Thomson*, F#m [e′#-g′′], B&H Songs; Em, B&H.
What shall I your true love tell? *Francis Thompson*, E [f′#-f′′#], B&H Songs; *D*, B&H.
When you are old and grey, *W. B. Yeats*, E [d′-g′′], Thames 6 Songs, (Chappell *English Recital 1*).
Where She Lies Asleep, *Mary Coleridge*, D [d′-e′′], B&H Songs.
Arrangement:
Easter Hymn, *early 17th century German*, tr. *Hans Wagemann*, E♭ [e′♭-e′′♭], Thames 6 Songs.

Britten, Edward **Benjamin**. (Lord Britten of Aldeburgh). 1913–1976. *See also* App. 1, 2.
Collections: *Ballads from Paul Bunyan*, Faber; *Beware*, Faber (introduction Rosamund Strode); *Cabaret Songs*, Faber (introduction Donald Mitchell); *Charm of Lullabies, A*, B&H; *Evening, Morning, Night*, B&H 1988; *Fish in the Unruffled Lakes — Six Settings of W. H. Auden*, B&H (introduction Philip Reed); *Four Burns Songs*, Faber (piano version by Colin Matthews of songs from *Birthday Hansel, A*); *Holy Sonnets of John Donne, The*, B&H; *On This Island*, B&H; *Poet's Echo, The*, Faber; *Red Cockatoo and Other Songs, The*, (high, low), Faber; *Six Hölderlin Fragments*, B&H; *Tit for Tat*, Faber; *Who are these Children?* Faber (reissued 1997 with 3 extra songs); *Winter Words*, B&H (reissued 1994 with 2 extra songs).
Afton Water, *Robert Burns*, E [b-g′′#], Faber 4 Burns.
Angel, *Alexander Pushkin* tr. *Peter Pears*, [c′-g′′], Faber Poet's Echo.
Applause of Men, The, *Friedrich Hölderlin* tr. *Mayer & Pears*, F [e′♭-g′′], B&H 6 Hölderlin.
As it is, plenty, *W. H. Auden*, D [d′-g′′], B&H On This Island.
At Day-close in November, *Thomas Hardy*, Dm [d′-a′′♭], B&H Winter Words.
At the Railway Station, Upway, *Thomas Hardy*, [e′-g′′], B&H Winter Words.
At the round earth's imagined corners, *John Donne*, D [d′-a′′], B&H Holy Sonnets.
Auld aik, The, *William Soutar*, E♭ [e′♭-g′′♭](m), Faber Who are these Children?
Autumn, *Walter de la Mare*, Fm [e′♭-e′′♭], Faber Tit for Tat.
Batter my heart, *John Donne*, Cm [c′#-a′′], B&H Holy Sonnets.
Bedtime, *William Soutar*, [d′♭-g′′♭](m), Faber Who are these Children?
Before Life and After, *Thomas Hardy*, D [d′-g′′], B&H Winter Words.
Beware, *German* tr. *Longfellow*, Fm [e′♭-e′′♭], Faber Beware.
Birds, The, *Hilaire Belloc*, E [b-f′′], B&H.
Black Day, *William Soutar*, Am [d′#-g′′](m), Faber Who are these Children?
Calypso, *W. H. Auden*, G [b♭-b′′], Faber Cabaret Songs.
Canticle 1, *see* My beloved is mine.
Charm, A, *Thomas Randolph*, Dm [a#-e′′](f), B&H Charm of Lullabies, *Heritage 3*.
Children, The, *William Soutar*, [b-a′′♭](m), Faber Who are these Children?
Children and Sir Nameless, The, *Thomas Hardy*, C [d′-g′′], B&H Winter Words 1994.
Choirmaster's Burial, The, *Thomas Hardy*, B♭ [g′-g′′](m), B&H Winter Words, *Heritage 4*.
Corpus Christi Carol, *Anon*, [c′-d′′], OUP Solo Baritone.
Cradle Song, A, *William Blake*, E♭ [b♭-e′′], B&H Charm of Lullabies.
Cradle Song, *Louis MacNeice*, B♭m [b♭-a′′(f′′#)], Faber Red Cockatoo; Am, Red Cockatoo.
Dawtie's Devotion, *William Soutar*, [d′-f′′#](m), Faber Who are these Children? 1997.
Death, be not proud, *John Donne*, B [d′#-g′′], B&H Holy Sonnets.
Echo, *Alexander Pushkin* tr. *Peter Pears*, [c′-a′′♭], Faber Poet's Echo.
Epigram, *Alexander Pushkin* tr. *Peter Pears*, [e′-g′′], Faber Poet's Echo.
Epitaph: the Clerk, *Herbert Asquith*, F [c′-f′′], Faber Beware.
Evening, *Ronald Duncan*, B [f′#-e′′♭], B&H Evening, Morning, Night.
Fish in the unruffled lakes, *W. H. Auden*, F# [c′#-a′′#], B&H *Heritage 3*, B&H; revised edition, B&H 6 Auden.
Funeral Blues, *W. H. Auden*, Fm [c′-a′′♭], Faber Cabaret Songs.
Gully, The, *William Soutar*, F, [f′-f′′](m), Faber Who are these Children? 1997.
Highland Balou, The, *Robert Burns*, B [b#-e′′#](f), B&H Charm of Lullabies.
Home, *Friedrich Hölderlin* tr. *Mayer & Pears*, A [e′♭-g′′], B&H 6 Hölderlin.
If it's ever spring again, *Thomas Hardy*, [e′-a′′♭], B&H Winter Words 1994.
If thou wilt ease thy heart, *Thomas Lovell Beddoes*, D [d′-a′′], Faber Red Cockatoo; B♭, Red Cockatoo.

Johnny, *W. H. Auden*, F [f-c'''], Faber Cabaret Songs.
Laddie's Sang, A, *William Soutar*, D [d'-g''](m), Faber Who are these Children?
Larky Lad, The, *William Soutar*, Dm [d'-g''b](m), Faber Who are these Children?
Let the florid music praise, *W. H. Auden*, D [c'#-a''], B&H On This Island.
Lines of Life, *Friedrich Hölderlin* tr. *Mayer & Pears*, Ebm [e'b-g''b], B&H 6 Hölderlin.
Lines Written during a Sleepless Night, *Alexander Pushkin* tr. *Pears*, [c'-a''b], Faber Poet's Echo.
Little Old Table, The, *Thomas Hardy*, Em [e'-g''], B&H Winter Words.
Middle of Life, The, *Friedrich Hölderlin* tr. *Mayer & Pears*, Bb [e'-a''b], B&H 6 Hölderlin.
Midnight on the Great Western, *Thomas Hardy*, Cm [c'-g''], B&H Winter Words.
Morning, *Ronald Duncan*, G [e'-d''], B&H Evening, Morning, Night.
My beloved is mine (Canticle 1), *Francis Quarles*, [high], B&H.
My heart... *Alexander Pushkin* tr. *Peter Pears*, [d'b-f''#], Faber Poet's Echo.
My Hoggie, *Robert Burns*, Cm [c'-a''b], Faber 4 Burns.
Night, *Ronald Duncan*, Bm [c'-f''], B&H Evening, Morning, Night.
Night covers up the rigid land, *W. H. Auden*, Dm [c'-g''], B&H 6 Auden.
Nightingale and the Rose, The, *Alexander Pushkin* tr. *Peter Pears*, [d'#-a''], Faber Poet's Echo.
Nightmare, *William Soutar*, Dm [c'-a''b](m), Faber Who are these Children?
Nocturne, *W. H. Auden*, C#m [c'#-g''#], B&H On This Island, *Heritage 4*, B&H.
Not even summer yet, *Peter Burra*, D [c'#-f''#], Faber Red Cockatoo; C, Red Cockatoo.
Now the leaves are falling fast, *W. H. Auden*, Fm [ab(c')-b''b(a''b], B&H On This Island.
Now thro' night's caressing grip *see* Nocturne.
Nurse's Song, The, *John Philip*, Bb [a-e''](f), B&H Charm of Lullabies.
O might those sighes and teares, *John Donne*, Em [g'-a''], B&H Holy Sonnets.
O that I had ne'er been married, *Robert Burns*, G [d'-g''](m), Faber Beware.
Oh my blacke soule, *John Donne*, Bm [c'-g''], B&H Holy Sonnets.
Oh to vex me, *John Donne*, F#m [c'-g''], B&H Holy Sonnets.
Poison tree, A, *William Blake*, Dm [c'#-f''#], Faber Red Cockatoo; Cm, Red Cockatoo.
Proud Songsters, *Thomas Hardy*, Eb [f'-g''], B&H Winter Words.
Red Cockatoo, The, *Po Chü-i* tr. *Arthur Waley*, [c'#-g''#], Faber Red Cockatoo; [a'#-e''#], Red Cockatoo.
Riddle (the child you were), *William Soutar*, [d'-f''](m), Faber Who are these Children?
Riddle, A, (the earth), *William Soutar*, G [c'-f''#](m), Faber Who are these Children?
Seascape, *W. H. Auden*, C [c'-a''b], B&H On This Island.
Sephestia's Lullaby, *Robert Greene*, Em [a-e''](f), B&H Charm of Lullabies, *Heritage 4*.
Ship of Rio, The, *Walter de la Mare*, [e'b-e''b], OUP.
Silver, *Walter de la Mare*, [b-f''], Faber Tit for Tat.
Since she whom I loved, *John Donne*, Eb [e'-a''b], B&H Holy Sonnets, *Heritage 4*.
Slaughter, *William Soutar*, Cm [c'-a''b](m), Faber Who are these Children?
Socrates and Alcibiades, *Friedrich Hölderlin* tr. *Mayer & Pears*, D [c'#-a''b], B&H 6 Hölderlin.
Song of Enchantment, A, *Walter de la Mare*, Ab [c'-f''], Faber Tit for Tat.
Songs and Proverbs of William Blake (cycle), *William Blake*, [g#-g''b], Faber.
Sun shines down, The, *W. H. Auden*, [bb-g''], B&H 6 Auden.
Supper, *William Soutar*, B [d'#-e''b](m), Faber Who are these Children?
Tell me the Truth about Love, *W. H. Auden*, D [a-a''], Faber Cabaret Songs.
Thou hast made me, *John Donne*, Bbm [e'b-a''b], B&H Holy Sonnets.
Tit for Tat, *Walter de la Mare*, Am [b-e''], Faber Tit for Tat.
To lie flat on the back, *W. H. Auden*, [c'-g''], B&H 6 Auden.
Tradition, *William Soutar*, Dm [d'-e''](m), Faber Who are these Children? 1997.
Underneath the abject willow, *W. H. Auden*, C [a-b''], B&H 6 Auden, B&H.
Vigil, *Walter de la Mare*, Dm [c'-e''], Faber Tit for Tat.
Wagtail and Baby, *Thomas Hardy*, Am [e'-a''], B&H Winter Words, *Heritage 3*.
Wee Willie, *Robert Burns*, G [c'#-g''], Faber 4 Burns.
What if this present? *John Donne*, Gm [d'-b''b], B&H Holy Sonnets.
What's in your mind? *W. H. Auden*, [d'-a''], B&H 6 Auden.
When you're feeling like expressing your affection, *W. H. Auden*, F [c'-f''], Faber Red Cockatoo; E, Red Cockatoo.
Who are these children? *William Soutar*, Em [d'-g''](m), Faber Who are these Children?
Wild with passion, *Thomas Lovell Beddoes*, [d'b-a''b], Faber Red Cockatoo; [bb-f''], Red Cockatoo.
Winter, The, *Robert Burns*, [b#-g''#], Faber 4 Burns.
Youth, *Friedrich Hölderlin* tr. *Mayer & Pears*, G [c'#-a''], B&H 6 Hölderlin.

Arrangements: *Eight Folk Song Arrangements*, Faber (piano version of harp accompaniment by Colin Matthews); *Folksong Arrangements: Volume 1* [high, medium], B&H; *Volume 3*, [high, medium], B&H; *Volume 4, Moore's Irish Melodies*, B&H; *Volume 5*, B&H; *Tom Bowling and Other Song Arrangements*, B&H.

 Ash Grove, The, *Anon*, A♭ [d′ b-f′′], B&H Folksong 1 high; F, Folksong 1 medium.
 At the mid hour of night, *Thomas Moore*, E♭ [e′ b-g′′], B&H Folksong 4.
 Avenging and bright, *Thomas Moore*, Bm [d′-f′′#], B&H Folksong 4.
 Bird Scarer's Song, *Anon*, G [d′-e′′], Faber 8 Folksong.
 Bonnie Earl o' Moray, The, *Anon*, E♭ [g′-g′′], B&H Folksong 1 high; C, Folksong 1 medium.
 Bonny at morn, *Anon*, Em [d′-e′′], Faber 8 Folksong.
 Brisk Young Widow, The, *Anon*, D [d′-f′′#], B&H Folksong 5.
 Ca' the yowes, *Robert Burns*, Bm [d′-f′′#], B&H Folksong 5.
 Come you not from Newcastle? *Anon*, F [d′-g′′](f), B&H Folksong 3 high; D, Folksong 3 medium.
 Crocodile, The, *Lucy Broadwood, J. A. Fuller Maitland*, C [b(c′)-a′′], B&H Tom Bowling.
 David of the White Rock, *Welsh*, tr. *Thomas Oliphant*, Fm [c′-a′′ b], Faber 8 Folksong.
 Deaf Woman's Courtship, The, *Appalachian*, F [f′-c′′], B&H Tom Bowling.
 Dear harp of my country, *Thomas Moore*, F [c′-g′′], B&H Folksong 4.
 Early one morning, *Anon*, G♭ [d′ b-g′′ b], B&H Folksong 5; E♭, B&H *Easy Song*.
 False Knight upon the Road, The, *Anon*, E [b-e′′], Faber 8 Folksong.
 Foggy, Foggy Dew, The, *Anon*, A♭ [e′ b-e′′ b](m), B&H Folksong 3 high; G, Folksong 3 medium.
 Greensleeves, *Traditional*, Gm [d′-f′′], B&H Tom Bowling.
 Holly and the Ivy, The, *Traditional*, A [e′-f′′#], B&H Tom Bowling.
 How sweet the answer, *Thomas Moore*, B [f′#-f′′#], B&H Folksong 4.
 I was lonely and forlorn, *Welsh* tr. *Ossian Ellis*, E♭ [d′-f′′](m), Faber 8 Folksong.
 I wonder as I wonder, *John Jacob Niles*, [f′-g′′], B&H Tom Bowling.
 Last Rose of Summer, The, *Thomas Moore*, E♭ [e′ b-a′′ b], B&H Folksong 4.
 Lemady, *Anon*, B [b-f′′#](m), Faber 8 Folk Song.
 Lincolnshire Poacher, The, *Anon*, C [e′-g′′](m), B&H Folksong 5.
 Little Sir William, *Anon*, F [f′-f′′], B&H Folksong 1 high; D, Folksong 1 medium.
 Lord! I married me a wife, *Anon*, Em [e′-e′′](m), Faber 8 Folksong.
 Miller of Dee, The, *Anon*, Am [e′-e′′], B&H Folksong 3 high; Gm, Folksong 3 medium.
 Minstrel boy to the wars has gone, The, *Thomas Moore*, F# [c′#-f′′#], B&H Folksong 4.
 O can ye sew cushions? *Anon*, A♭ [e′ b-a′′ b], B&H Folksong 1 high; E♭, Folksong 1 medium, *Imperial 3*.
 O the sight entrancing, *Thomas Moore*, C [b-g′′], B&H Folksong 4.
 O waly, waly, *Anon*, A [e′-e′′](f), B&H Folksong 3 high, B&H *Easy Song*; G, Folksong 3 medium.
 Oft in the stilly night, *Thomas Moore*, A♭ [e′ b-d′′ b], B&H Folksong 4.
 Oliver Cromwell, *Anon*, E♭ [e′ b-e′′ b], B&H Folksong 1 high; C, Folksong 1 medium.
 Plough boy, The, *Anon*, B♭ [g′-f′′], B&H Folksong 3 high, B&H; G, Folksong 3 medium.
 Pray goody, *Kate O'Hara*, E [d′#-e′′], B&H Tom Bowling.
 Rich and rare, *Thomas Moore*, D [d′-f′′#], B&H Folksong 4.
 Sail on, sail on, *Thomas Moore*, F [f′-f′′], B&H Folksong 4.
 Salley Gardens, The, *W. B. Yeats*, G♭ [g′ b-a′′ b], B&H Folksong 1 high; D♭, Folksong 1 medium.
 Salley in our Alley, *Henry Carey*, D [d′-g′′](m), B&H Folksong 5.
 She's like the swallow, *Anon*, Dm [d′-f′′](m), Faber 8 Folksong.
 Stream in the Valley, The, *German* tr. *Iris Rogers*, B♭ [d′-g′′], B&H Tom Bowling.
 Sweet Polly Oliver, *Anon*, E [c′#-f′′#], B&H Folksong 3 high; D, Folksong 3 medium.
 There's none to soothe, *Anon*, D♭ [d♭-f′′], B&H Folksong 3 high; B♭, Folksong 3 medium.
 Tom Bowling, *Charles Dibdin*, E♭ [e′ b-g], B&H Tom Bowling.
 Trees they grow so high, The, *Anon*, Am [c′-e′′](f), B&H Folksong 1 high; Gm, Folksong 1 medium.

Brodsky, Nicholas. 1851–1929. *See* App. 2.

Brook, Harry.
Collection: *Two Songs* , BMP.
 By the Small Tree of Thorn, *Molly Kirnan*, E [b-f′′#], BMP 2 Songs.
 Noel, *Molly Kirnan*, F#m [c′#-f′′#], BMP 2 Songs.

Brown, Christopher Roland. 1943– *See* App. 2.
Collection: *Three Elizabethan Songs*, Musography.
 Exequy, The, *Henry King*, [c-e′ b](m), Musography 3 Elizabethan.
 Lullaby, *Richard Rowlands*, [f′-a′′](f), Musography.

My mistress is as fair as fine, *Anon*, [c-d´](m), Musography 3 Elizabethan.
New Year's Carol, A, *Anon*, [c-e´](m), Musography 3 Elizabethan.
Point of Departure, (cycle), *Leonard Clarke*, [c´#-a´´](m), Musography.
Wordsworth Songs, (cycle) *William Wordsworth*, [bb-a´´](f), Musography.

Brown, James. 1923–
Careless Content, *John Byrom*, Ab [e´b-f´´], Banks.
Lass for a Sailor, The, *Thomas Dibdin*, D [d´-e´´](m), Banks.
Nocturne, A, *Wilfred Scawen Blunt*, [c´#-f´´], Banks.
Silent Spring, *V. C. Staples*, [e´-f´´], Banks.
Arrangement:
Portsmouth, *Anon*, Eb, [bb-g´](m), Banks.

Brown, Thomas.
Shepherd! thy demeanour vary, *Anon*, F [e´-c´´´](f), B&H (Lane Wilson) *Old English,* Classical, Schirmer *2nd Soprano*; Db, Fischer (Lane Wilson) *Centuries low.*

Browne, William Charles **Denis.** 1888–1915.
Collections: (*Two Songs*, S&B); *Six Songs*, Thames (Introduction Trevor Hold).
Arabia, *Walter de la Mare*, Gm [f´b-a´´b], Thames 6 Songs.
Diaphenia, *Henry Constable* or *Henry Chettle*, Bb [f´-f´´](m), Thames 6 Songs; Ab, B&H.
Dream-tryst, *Francis Thompson*, Bm [d´-e´´](m), Thames 6 Songs.
Epitaph on Salathiel Pavey, *Ben Jonson*, Em [d´-g´´], Thames *Century 3*; F#m Thames 6 Songs, B&H *Heritage 1.*
Isle of Lost Dreams, The, *William Sharp (Fiona Macleod)*, Gb [f´-f´´], Thames 6 Songs.
Move eastward, happy earth, *Alfred Lord Tennyson*, D [c´#-g´´], S&B 2 Songs.
Snowdrop, The, *Alfred Lord Tennyson*, Am [e´-g´´], S&B 2 Songs.
To Gratiana Dancing and Singing, *Richard Lovelace*, G [d´-g´´], Thames 6 Songs, BMP; *F*, B&H.

Bruce, M. Campbell. 1914–
Migratory birds at Sennen, *Michael Gardiner*, [c´-f´´], Banks.
(Rain, The, *W. H. Davies*, C [c´-e´´], Curwen.)
(Snow, The, *Walter de la Mare*, Am [d´-e´´(f´´)], Curwen.)

Bryan, Robert. 1858–1920.
Abide with me, *Henry Francis Lyte*, [contralto/baritone], Snell.
Adieu, [tenor], Snell.
Annabel Lee, *Edgar Allan Poe*, [contralto], Snell.
Ave Maria, [soprano/tenor], Snell.
Beloved maid, [tenor], Snell.
Come, my love, [tenor], Snell.
How sweet the moonlight sleeps, *Shakespeare*, [tenor], Snell.
I will come to thee, [tenor], Snell.
My dear, [tenor], Snell.
O love that wilt not let me go, *George Matheson*, [contralto/baritone], Snell.
Parting, [soprano/tenor], Snell.
Somebody, [tenor], Snell.
Song of Cambria, A, *Robert Bryan*, [baritone], Snell.
Song of the Cradle, *Ioan Maethlu* tr. *Robert Bryan*, [mezzo/contralto], Snell.
Sweet and low, *Alfred Lord Tennyson*, [contralto/baritone], Snell.

Bryars, Richard **Gavin.** 1943– *See* App. 2.

Bryson, Ernest.
So the year's done with, *Robert Browning*, F#m [e´-e´´], BMP.

Bullard, Alan. 1947– *See also* App. 2.
Collections: *Ten Songs for Voice and Piano,* Colne; *Three Bird Songs,* Colne. N.B. Colne can provide transposed versions.
Come live with me, *Christopher Marlowe*, E [c´#-f´´], Colne 10 Songs.
Dover Beach *see* Sea of Faith, The.
I held love's head, *Robert Herrick*, D [d´-e´´], Colne 10 Songs.
I seek her in the shady grove, *John Clare*, D [d´-d´´], Colne; F, Colne.

Little trotty wagtail, *John Clare,* A [b-e''](m), Colne 3 Bird.
Matin Song, *Thomas Heywood,* G [d'-g''], Colne 10 Songs.
Owl, The, *Alfred Lord Tennyson,* [c'-d''](m), Colne 3 Bird.
Pretty Ring Time *Shakespeare,* F [d'-f'#], Colne 10 Songs.
Sea of Faith, The, *Matthew Arnold,* [d'-a''], Colne.
Solitary Reaper, The, *William Wordsworth,* G [c'#-a''], Colne 10 Songs.
Song of Thanks, *Charles Cotton,* G [bb-d''], Oecamuse.
To Music, *Robert Herrick,* D [d'-e''], Colne 10 Songs.
To Violets, *Robert Herrick,* D [d'-e''], Colne 10 Songs.
When daisies pied, *Shakespeare,* [b-e''b](m), Colne 3 Bird.
When I am dead, my dearest, *Christina Rossetti,* F#m [c#-e''], Colne 10 Songs.
Winter Robin, The, *John Clare,* D [c'#-e''], Colne 10 Songs.
Year's Awakening, The, *Thomas Hardy,* [b-e''], Colne 10 Songs.

Buller, John. 1927– *See* App. 2.

Bullock, Dafydd. WMIC. *See also* App. 1.

Bullock, Sir **Ernest.** 1890–1979.
Close now thine eyes, *Francis Quarles,* D [b-e''b], BMP.
Come away, death, *Shakespeare,* Bbm [high], BMP.
When that I was and a little tiny boy, *Shakespeare,* [high], BMP.

Burgon, Geoffrey. 1941– *See also* App. 2.
Hymn to Venus, *Edith Sitwell,* [a#-g''](f), Chester hire.

Burkinshaw, Sydney. WMIC. *See* App. 1, 2.

Burrell, Diana. 1948– *See also* App. 2.
Tachograph, *Simon Armitage,* [baritone], UMP.

Burrows, Benjamin. 1891–1966. BMIC.
Collection: *Six Songs,* Thames (introduction Alastair Chisholm).
Bride Cometh, The, *Confucius* tr. *Anon,* Gb [d'b-a''b], Thames 6 Songs.
Dusty Miller, The, *Robert Burns,* Cramer.
From far, from eve and morning, *A. E. Housman,* [e'b-f''], EPSS
How long and dreary is the night, *Robert Burns,* Cramer.
Kiss, The, *Charles D'Orleans,* [d'-g''], Thames 6 Songs.
Lake Isle of Innisfree, The, *W. B. Yeats,* [c'-g''#], Thames 6 Songs.
Love was true to me, *J. Boyle O'Reilly* , [c'#-g''], Thames 6 Songs.
Mistress Fell, *Walter de la Mare,* [c'-b''b], Thames *Century 5.*
Queen Djenira, *Walter de la Mare,* [e'-a''], Thames 6 Songs.
Robin Goodfellow, *Anon,* Am [e'-a''], Thames 6 Songs.

Burtch, Mervyn. 1929– BMIC, WMIC. *See also* App. 2.
Collection: *Songs of London Town,* [Eleanor Farjeon] [c'-f''#], Roberton.
Long Barren, *Christina Rossetti* [c'-f''], WMIC.
Ozymandias, *Percy Bysshe Shelley,* [A-c'#](m), WMIC *Songs from Wales 2.*
When Satan fell, *D. H. Lawrence,* [c'-e''], WMIC.

Bury, Winifred.
I know a bank, *Shakespeare,* Eb [bb-e''b], Paterson; G, Paterson.
It was the lovely moon, Paterson.
Moon complaining, The, *Paul Hayse* tr. *Lily Henkel,* Db [e'b-a''b], Paterson; Bb, Paterson.
Sweet nightingale, *Anon,* Paterson.
(There is a lady, *Thomas Ford,* G [e'-g''], Paterson; E, Paterson.)

Busch, William. 1901–1945.
Collections: *Two Songs of William Blake,* BMP 1944; (*Two Songs,* Chester 1944.)
(Centaurs, The, *James Stephens,* Dm [c'-f''], Chester.)
Come, O come, my life's delight, *Thomas Campion,* E [d'#-g''#], BMP.
Echoing Green, The, *William Blake,* E [d'-g''#], BMP 2 Songs.
If thou wilt ease thy heart, *Thomas Lovell Beddoes,* G#m [d'#-e''], Thames *Century 6,* BMP.

(Laughing Song, *William Blake*, F#m [f#(a)-e″], Chester 2 Songs.)
(Memory, hither come, *William Blake*, [g#-b′], Chester 2 Songs.)
Rest, *Æ*, A♭ [c′b-e″b], BMP.
Shepherd, The, *William Blake*, G#m [b(e′)-g″#], BMP 2 Songs.

Bush, Alan. 1900–1996. BMIC.
(Collection: *Four Seafarer's Songs,* S&B 1964.)
    Voices of the Prophets (cycle), *Isaiah 65, John Milton, William Blake, Peter Blackman,* [b-a″](m), S&B.
    (Greenland Fishery, The, *Anon,* A [d′-f″](m), S&B 4 Seafarer's Songs).
    (Jack the Jolly Tar, *Anon,* D [a-f″#](m), S&B 4 Seafarer's Songs).
    (Ratcliffe Highway, *Anon,* Em [d′-g″](m), S&B 4 Seafarer's Songs).
    (Ship in Distress, The, *Anon,* Fm [c′b-f″](m), S&B 4 Seafarer's Songs).

Bush, Geoffrey. 1920–1998. *See also* App. 2.
Collections: *Eight Songs for High Voice,* Novello; *Eight Songs for Medium Voice,* Novello; *Eight Songs for Medium Voice,* S&B; *Five Mediaeval Lyrics,* Novello; *Five Spring Songs,* Novello; (*Four Songs from 'Hesperides',* Novello); *Old Rhymes Reset,* S&B; *Songs of Wonder,* Novello; *Three Elizabethan Songs,* Novello; *Three Songs of Ben Jonson,* Novello; *Two Stevie Smith Songs,* Novello; *Yesterday,* Thames.
    archy at the zoo, (cycle), *don marquis,* [d′-a″], Thames.
    Aubade, *Anon c.1500,* [c′#-a″], S&B Old Rhymes Reset.
    Avondale, *Stevie Smith,* [c′#-a″], Novello 2 Stevie Smith.
    By the Tamar, *Charles Causley,* [d′-g″], Thames Yesterday.
    Carol, *Anon,* [a-f″](m), Novello 8 Medium; [A-f″](m), Novello 5 Mediaeval.
    Colloquy, *Anon,* [A#-f″](m), Novello 5 Mediaeval.
    Confession, *Anon,* [G#-e″](m), Novello 5 Mediaeval.
    Cuisine Provençale, *Virginia Woolf* adapted *Geoffrey Bush,* [c′-g″(a″)], S&B 8 Songs.
    Daniel Brent, *Charles Causley,* C [c′-g″], Thames Yesterday.
    Diaphenia, *Henry Constable* or *Henry Chettle,* [e′b-g″](m), Novello 5 Spring.
    Echo's Lament for Narcissus, *Ben Jonson,* Dm [e′-f″], Novello 8 High, Novello 3 Ben Jonson.
    Encounter, An, *Traditional,* [d′-a″], S&B Old Rhymes Reset.
    End of Love, The, *Kathleen Raine,* [c′-f″], S&B 8 Songs, *Recitalist 2*.
    (Fain would I change that note, *Anon,* G [f′-a″], Elkin.)
    Far-darting Apollo, *Kathleen Raine,* [c′-g″], S&B 8 Songs.
    Fire, fire, *Thomas Campion,* G [d′-g″], Novello 3 Elizabethan.
    Greek Love Songs (cycle), *Melager* tr. *Fitts,* [A-g′](m), Thames 1998.
    Here comes a lusty wooer, *Anon,* Bm [b(c′)-a″], Novello Wonder.
    Impatient Lover, The, *Robert Herrick,* [d′-e″](m), Novello 8 Medium, ([d-e′](m), Hesperides).
    Introspection, *Kathleen Raine,* [b♭-g″], S&B 8 Songs.
    It was a lover and his lass, *Shakespeare,* D [c′-d″], Novello 8 Medium.
    Kiss, The, *Ben Jonson,* [c′-g″], Novello 3 Ben Jonson.
    Lady Jane Grey, *Charles Causley,* Am [d′-a″], Thames Yesterday.
    Lament, *Kathleen Raine,* [c′-g″], S&B 8 Songs.
    Lay a garland on my hearse, *John Fletcher,* Am [e′-g″(a″)], Novello 5 Spring.
    Little Nut Tree, The, *Traditional,* [e′-g″], Novello 8 High, Wonder.
    Love for such a cherry lip, *Thomas Middleton,* F [c′#-f″#](m), S&B 8 Songs, *Recitalist 1*.
    Merciless Beauty, *Geoffrey Chaucer,* [c′#-f″](m), Novello.
    Mirabile Misterium (cycle), *various medieval* adapted *Geoffrey Bush,* [c′-a″] Novello.
    Mistletoe, *Charles Causley,* Em [c′-g″], Thames Yesterday.
    Morwenstow: a dialogue, *Charles Causley,* C [c′-a″b], Thames Yesterday.
    My Cats, *Stevie Smith,* Am [e′-a″], Novello 2 Stevie Smith.
    My true love hath my heart, *Philip Sidney,* [f′-g″](f), Novello 8 High.
    Nonsense Song, *Geoffrey Bush,* [c′-g″], S&B Old Rhymes Reset.
    Now the lusty spring is seen, *John Fletcher,* Am [d′-a″], Novello 8 High, 5 Spring.
    O, the month of May, *Thomas Dekker,* F [c′-f″](m), Novello 8 Medium.
    Old Abram Brown, *Anon,* [e′-a″b], Novello Wonder.
    Polly Lillicote, *Anon,* [c′-a″], Novello Wonder.
    Rebuke, A, *Ben Jonson,* [c-a″](m), Novello 3 Ben Jonson.
    Rutterkin, *Anon,* [g-f″](m), Novello 8 Medium; [G-f″], Novello 5 Mediaeval.
    Severn Sand, *Traditional,* Em [e′-a″], S&B Old Rhymes Reset.
    She hath an eye, *Anon,* F [c′-e″b(f″)](m), Novello 8 Medium.
    Sigh no more, ladies, *Shakespeare,* F [f′-a″], Novello 8 High, 3 Elizabethan.

Sleigh Ride, *Charles Causley,* Am [e′-a′′], Thames *Yesterday.*
Smuggler's Song, *Charles Causley,* Cm [c′-a′′b], Thames *Yesterday.*
Song of Praise, A, *George Herbert,* C [c′-g′′], S&B *8 Songs.*
Songs of the Zodiac (cycle), *David Gascoigne,* [b-a′′], Novello.
Sweet, stay awhile, *John Donne,* Am [e′-g′′], Novello 3 *Elizabethan.*
Test, The, *Traditional,* Bb [c′-g′′], S&B Old Rhymes Reset, *Recitalist 3.*
There is a garden in her face, *Thomas Campion,* Gm [c′-f′′], S&B *8 Songs,* Novello; (Am, Elkin).
To Electra, *Robert Herrick,* [d′b-g′′b](m), Novello 8 Medium, ([db-g′b], *Hesperides*).
Transience, *Charles Causley,* Dm [d′-g′′], Thames *Yesterday.*
(Upon Julia's Clothes, *Robert Herrick,* [G#-e′]m, Novello *Hesperides.*)
(Upon the Loss of his Mistresses, *Robert Herrick,* [e-f′#]m, Novello *Hesperides.*)
Vanity of Human Wishes, The, *Anon,* [D-f′′](m), Novello 5 *Mediaeval.*
Venus and Adonis, *Robert Greene,* [c′-f′′], Novello.
Weep you no more sad fountains, *Anon,* [f′-g′′#(a′′#)], Novello 8 High, 5 *Spring.*
What thing is love, *George Peel,* [d′-a′′], Novello 5 *Spring.*
When daffodils begin to peer, *Shakespeare,* A [f′-a′′](m), Novello 8 *High.*
When May is in his prime, *Richard Edwardes,* D [b-f′′], Novello 8 *Medium.*
Wishes, *Charles Causley,* C [c′-b′′b(a′′b)], Thames *Yesterday.*
Wonder of Wonders, The, *Traditional,* [c′(b)-g′′], Novello 8 High, *Wonder.*

Butler, Martin. 1960– *See* App. 2.

Butt, James. 1929– *See also* App. 2.
Collection: *Five William Blake Songs,* Sphemusations.
Ariel's song, *Shakespeare,* [voice], Sphemusations.
Behoulde a seely tender babe, *Traditional,* Sphemusations
Blessed is the man *see* Psalm 1.
Chimney Sweeper, The, *William Blake,* [c′#-f′′#], Sphemusations 5 *Blake.*
Christmas Carol, A, *Robert Herrick,* [high], B&H.
Cradle Song, *William Blake,* [d′-g′′#], Sphemusations 5 *Blake.*
Fly, The, *William Blake,* [c′-f′′#], Sphemusations 5 *Blake.*
Heap on more wood, the wind is chill, *Walter Scott,* [high], Sphemusations.
Hebridean rainbows, [high], Sphemusations.
I got me flowers, *George Herbert,* [high], Mills.
Laughing Song, *William Blake,* D [d′-g′′#], Sphemusations 5 *Blake.*
Mad Song, *William Blake,* [d′-g′′#], Sphemusations 5 *Blake.*
Psalm 1, Blessed is the man, *Prayer Book,* [medium high], Sphemusations
Sunset, *Walt Whitman,* [medium high], Chappell.
They that have power to hurt and will do none, (Sonnet 94) *Shakespeare,* [high], Sphemusations.
(Up the airy mountain, *William Allingham,* B&H.)
Virtue, *George Herbert,* Em [c′#-f′′#], Thames *Century 4.*
Weathers, *Thomas Hardy,* [soprano], Sphemusations.
When I am dead, *Christina Rossetti,* A [d′-e′′], Thames *Century 6.*
Wild winds weep, The *see* Mad Song.
Arrangements: *Four Canadian Cowboy Songs,* [baritone], Sphemusations.
Bellman's song, *Traditional,* [high], Sphemusations.
Carol of the ship, *Traditional,* Sphemusations.
Joys Seven, *Traditional,* Sphemusations.

Butterfield, J. A.
When you and I were young, Maggie, *George W. Johnson,* G [d′-e′′], IMP *Parlour Songs.*

Butterworth, Arthur Eckersley. 1923– *See* App. 2.

Butterworth, George. 1885–1916. *See also* App. 2.
Collections: *Bredon Hill and Other Songs,* Masters; *Folk Songs from Sussex and Other Songs,* S&B (introduction by Peter J. Pirie); *Love Blows as the Wind Blows,* Masters, Thames (introduction by John Bishop); *Shropshire Lad and Other Songs, A,* S&B (introduction by Peter J. Pirie); *Songs (6) from 'A Shropshire Lad',* Masters.
Bredon Hill, *A. E. Housman,* F [c′-g′′](m), S&B *Shropshire Lad,* Masters *Bredon;* (*G,* S&B).
Fill a glass with golden wine, *W. E. Henley,* [c′#-d′′#], Thames/Masters *Love Blows.*
Haste on, my joys! *Robert Bridges,* Ab [d′-a′′b], Modus.
I fear thy kisses, *Percy Bysshe Shelley,* Fm [bb-e′′](m), S&B *Folk Songs.*
I will make you brooches, *R. L. Stevenson,* D [c′-f′](m), S&B *Folk Songs.*

In the year that's come and gone, *W. E. Henley*, [c'-e''b], Thames/Masters Love Blows.
Is my team ploughing? *A. E. Housman*, B♭ [e'b-e''b](m), S&B Shropshire Lad, Masters Songs; (D♭ S&B).
Lads in their hundreds, The, *A. E. Housman*, F# [c'#-e''](m), S&B Shropshire Lad, Masters Songs; *G*, Mayhew *Collection 1*.
Life in her creaking shoes, *W. E. Henley*, [c'-f''], Thames/Masters Love Blows.
Look not in my eyes, *A. E. Housman*, F [c'-f''](m), S&B Shropshire Lad, Masters Songs.
Loveliest of trees, *A. E. Housman*, E [c'#-e''](m), S&B Shropshire Lad, Masters Songs, Mayhew *Collection 1*.
O fair enough are sky and plain, *A. E. Housman*, Gm [a-e''](m), S&B Shropshire Lad, Masters Bredon Hill.
On the idle hill of summer, *A. E. Housman*, A [c'#-f''](m), S&B Shropshire Lad, Masters Bredon Hill.
On the way to Kew, *W. E. Henley* [c'#-f''], Thames/Masters Love Blows.
Requiescat, *Oscar Wilde*, Fm [c'-f''], S&B Folk Songs; (*Gm*, S&B).
Think no more, lad, *A. E. Housman*, G#m [c'#-f''](m), S&B Shropshire Lad, Masters Songs.
When I was one-and-twenty, *A. E. Housman*, [d'-e''](m), S&B Shropshire Lad, Masters Songs, Mayhew *Collection 2*.
When the lad for longing sighs, *A. E. Housman*, Em [d'-e''](m), S&B Shropshire Lad, Masters Bredon Hill.
With rue my heart is laden, *A. E. Housman*, F#m [c'#-e''], S&B Shropshire Lad, Masters Bredon Hill.
Arrangements: *Folksongs from Sussex*, Masters; *Folk Songs from Sussex and Other Songs*, S&B (introduction by Peter J. Pirie).
Blacksmith courted me, A, *Anon*, C#m [e'-f''#](f), S&B Folk Songs, Masters Folksongs, Mayhew *Collection 2*.
Brisk young sailor courted me, A, *Anon*, E [e'-e''](f), S&B Folk Songs, Masters Folksongs, Mayhew *Collection 1*.
Come my own one, *Anon*, A♭ [c'-f''], S&B Folk Songs, Masters Folksongs; (*F*, S&B).
Cuckoo, The, *Anon*, [d'-d''], S&B Folk Songs, Masters Folksongs.
Lawyer he went out, A, *Anon*, Am [c'-e''], S&B Folk Songs, Masters Folksongs.
Roving in the dew, *Anon*, E♭ [e'b-e''b](m), S&B Folk Songs, Masters Folksongs, Mayhew *Collection 2*.
Seventeen Come Sunday, *Anon*, D [d'-e''](m), S&B Folk Songs, Masters Folksongs.
Sowing the Seeds of Love, *Anon*, F [c'-d''](f), S&B Folk Songs, Masters Folksongs.
Tarry Trousers, *Anon*, Gm [d'-e''], S&B Folk Songs, Masters Folksongs.
True Lover's Farewell, The, *Anon*, Gm [d'-e''b](m), S&B Folk Songs, Masters Folksongs.
Yonder stands a lovely creature, *Anon*, A [c'#-e''](m), S&B Folk Songs, Masters Folksongs.

Butterworth, Neil. 1934– SMIC. *See also* App. 1, 2.
Collections: *Four Miscellaneous Songs*, [low, medium, high], Brunton; *Pussy and Pump*, [Winifred Kingdom-Ward], (10 songs), Chiltern; *Three Shakespeare Songs*, [medium, high], Brunton; *Two Animal Rhymes*, Chiltern; *Two Rhymes*, Chiltern.
Birthday Recitative and Aria, *Anon*, SMIC.
Clown's Song, *Shakespeare*, [medium/high], Brunton 3 Shakespeare.
Dancing in the Sun, *Neil Butterworth*, [high], Brunton.
Dream of a Girl at Sevenoaks, The, *William Brighty Rands*, [high], Chiltern.
Fox Rhyme, The, *Ian Serraillier*, [high], Belwin.
Full fathom five, thy father lies, *Shakespeare*, [medium/high], Brunton 3 Shakespeare.
I saw a jolly hunter, *Charles Causley*, [high], SMIC.
Kettle Rhyme, The, *Ian Serraillier*, [high], Belwin.
Knees, *Spike Milligan*, [high], SMIC.
Letter to the World (cycle), *Emily Dickinson*, [medium], Chiltern.
Make me a willow cabin, *Shakespeare*, [medium/high], Brunton 3 Shakespeare.
Portus, *Neil Butterworth*, [medium], SMIC.
Round about a wood as I walked, *Anon*, [high], SMIC.
She is the violet, *John Skelton*, [high], Brunton.
Three jolly gentlemen, *Walter de la Mare*, [high], Belwin.
When Christ was born of Mary free, *Anon*, [high], Chiltern.
Who shall have my lady fair, *Anon 16th century*, [high], Brunton.

Byrd, William. 1543–1623.
Cradle Song, *Anon*, C; *D* [c'#-c''] Thames (Hodgson) *Countertenors 1*; *G*, OUP (Willcocks) *Solo Christmas high*; E♭, *Solo Christmas low*; *F*, (Fellowes) S&B.

# C

Camidge, John. 1790–1859.
Put thou thy trust in the Lord, *Psalm 37 vv. 3-8,* F [e′-a′′(f′′#)], B&H (Patrick) *Sacred Songs 1.*

Campion, Thomas. 1567–1620. All Campion's songs are obtainable in original keys from S&B. Collections: *Songs from Rosseter's Book of Ayres,* S&B (edited David Scott), [Rosseter]; *The First Book of Ayres,* S&B (edited David Scott); *The Second Book of Ayres,* S&B (edited David Scott); *The Third Book of Ayres,* S&B (edited Thurston Dart); *The Fourth Book of Ayres,* S&B (edited E. H. Fellowes). Note that in the following: Pilkington = *English Lute Songs Book 1,* S&B; Keel 1a, 1b and 2a, 2b = *Elizabethan Lovesongs Books 1 and 2* [high, low], B&H. Only songs available in anthologies are listed individually here.

Author of light, *Campion,* Gm [d′-e′′b], 1st Book, Pilkington.
Beauty is but a painted hell, *Campion,* G 4th Book; *A* [g′-f′′#], Keel 2a; *F,* Keel 2b.
Beauty since you so much desire, *Campion,* G [d′-e′′](m), 4th Book, Pilkington.
Break now, my heart, *Campion,* Gm [c′-e′′b](m), 3rd Book, Keel 2b; *Bm,* Keel 2a.
Come you pretty false-eyed wanton, *Campion,* Gm [f′#-e′′](m), 2nd Book, Pilkington; *Am,* Keel 2a; *Fm,* Keel 2b.
Cypress curtain of the night, The, *Campion,* Gm [g′-f′′], Rosseter, Pilkington.
Every dame affects good fame, *Campion,* F [e′-g′′], 4th Book, Keel 2a; *D,* Keel 2b.
Fair, if you expect admiring, *Campion,* G [d′-e′′] Rosseter, BMP *W & W 3;* *Ab,* Leonard *Baroque high; E,* Leonard *Baroque low.*
Fire, fire, *Campion,* G [e′-e′′], 3rd Book, BMP *W&W 6.*
Follow thy fair sun, *Campion,* Gm [d′-d′′], Rosseter, BMP *W&W 5;* *F#m,* Pilkington.
Follow your saint, *Campion,* Gm [f′-f′′], Rosseter; *Em,* Pilkington.
Her rosy cheeks, *Campion,* G [d′-e′′](m), 2nd Book, BMP *W&W 3, A,* Keel 2a; *F,* Keel 2b.
Here she her sacred bower adorns, *Campion,* G [d′-d′′], 2nd Book, Keel 1b; *Bb,* Keel 1a.
I care not for those ladies, *Campion,* G [d′-e′′](m), Rosseter, BMP *W&W 3.*
I must complain, *Campion,* Gm [g′-f′′], 4th Book, Pilkington.
If Love loves truth, *Campion,* G [d′-d′′](m), 3rd Book, Pilkington.
If thou long'st so much to learn, *Campion,* Cm [c′-e′′b](f), 3rd Book, Pilkington.
It fell on a summer's day, *Campion,* G [f′#-e′′], Rosseter, Pilkington, *Recitalist 4.*
Jack and Joan, *Campion,* G [f′#-e′′], Leonard *Baroque high,* BMP *W&W 3; F,* Leonard *Baroque low.*
Love me or not, *Campion,* Gm [g′-f′′](m), 4th Book, Pilkington, BMP *W&W 1.*
Maids are simple, *Campion,* Gm [d′-d′′](f), 3rd Book, BMP *W&W 5.*
Move now with measured sound, *Campion,* G [d′-e′′], S&B (Greer) *Printed.*
My sweetest Lesbia, *Campion,* G [d′-e′′](m), Rosseter; *F,* Pilkington.
Never love unless you can, *Campion,* Bb [f′-f′′], 3rd Book, Pilkington.
Now hath Flora robb'd her bowers, *Campion,* G [d′-e′′], S&B (Greer) *Printed.*
O dear, that I with thee might live, *Campion,* Gm [d′-d′′], 2nd Book, Keel 2b, *Bm,* Keel 2a.
O never to be moved, *Campion,* Gm [d′-f′′], 3rd Book, BMP *W&W 5.*
O what unhoped for sweet supply, *Campion,* Fm [f′-f′′], 2nd Book, Pilkington.
Oft have I sighed, *Campion,* Dm [d′-d′′](f), 3rd Book, Pilkington, Keel 2b, B&H (Northcote) *Imperial 3,* BMP *W&W 6; Fm,* Keel 2a.
Peaceful western wind, The, *Campion,* G [d′-e′′], 2nd Book, Pilkington; *F,* Keel 2b; *Bb,* Keel 2a.
Secret love or two, A, *Campion,* Gm [d′-e′′b](f), 2nd Book, Pilkington.
Shall I come sweet love to thee? *Campion,* Fm [f′-f′′(m)], 3rd Book, BMP *W&W 3; F#m,* Keel 1a; *Dm,* Keel 1b.
So sweet is thy discourse, *Campion,* Gm [f′#-g′′], 4th Book, B&H (Northcote) *Imperial 1,* BMP *W&W 6.*
There is a garden in her face, *Campion,* G [d′-e′′], 4th Book, Pilkington, Keel 1b, BMP *W&W 4; Ab,* Paterson (Diack) *100 Best 2; Bb,* Keel 1a.
Thrice toss these oaken ashes, *Campion,* Gm [d′-f′′](m), 3rd Book, BMP *W&W 4; Am,* Keel 2a; *Fm,* Keel 2b.
Turn back you wanton flyer, *Campion,* Gm [f′#-f′′], Rosseter, BMP *W&W 5.*
Vain men whose follies, *Campion,* F [f′-f′′](m), 2nd Book, Pilkington.
Veil, love, my eyes, *Campion,* Gm [f′#-e′′b](m), 4th Book, Pilkington.
When to her lute Corinna sings, *Campion,* Gm [d′-f′′], Rosseter, BMP *W&W 6; Em,* Pilkington, Thames *Countertenors 2.*
Where she her sacred bow'r adorns, *Campion,* G [d′-d′′](m), 2nd Book, Keel 1b; *Bb,* Keel 1a.
Woo her and win her, *Campion,* Gm [d′-e′′], S&B (Greer) *Printed.*
Your fair looks inflame my desire, *Campion,* Gm [d′-d′′](m), Rosseter, BMP *W&W 6.*
Your fair looks urge my desire, *Campion,* Gm [d′-d′′](m), 4th Book, Pilkington.

Cannon, Jack **Philip.** 1929– *See also* App. 1, 2.
Collections: *Cinq Chansons de femme,* Kronos; *Three Rivers,* Kronos.
    Angry Wife, The, *Anon* tr. *Jacqueline Laidlaw,* Dm [b♭-g''], Kronos.
    Chabet, The, *Jacqueline Laidlaw,* [c'-g''](m), Kronos.
    Girl in Love, A, tr. *Jacqueline Laidlaw,* Em [d'-g''#], Kronos.
    Girl Whose Love Shines Fair, A, *Anon* tr. *Jacqueline Laidlaw,* Dm [c'-g''], Kronos.
    Granta, The, *Jacqueline Laidlaw,* [b♭-g''](m), Kronos.
    Merry Wife, The, *Olivier Baselin,* tr. *Jacqueline Laidlaw,* A [d'-a''(g'')], Kronos.
    Thames, The, *Jacqueline Laidlaw,* [c'-g''#](m), Kronos.
    Widow, The, *Christine de Pisan,* tr. *Jacqueline Laidlaw,* Fm [b♭-g''], Kronos.

Capel, J. M.
    Love, could I only tell thee, *G. Clifton Bingham,* F [d'(c')-g''(a'')], Cramer *Drawing Room.*

Caradon, Sulyen R. 1942– *See also* App. 2.
    Clouds, *Rupert Brooke,* [a♭-f''], EPSS.
    Lelant, *E. K. Chambers,* [c'-g''], EPSS.

Carcas, Gillian. 1963– BMIC. *See also* App. 2.

Cardew, Cornelius. 1936–1981. BMIC. *See also* App. 2.

Carew, Molly.
    Everywhere I look, *Molly Carew,* F [c'-g''], Schirmer *1st Soprano.*

Carey, Francis **Clive** Saville. 1883–1968.
Collection: *Three Songs of Faery,* B&H 1926.
    (April Children, B&H.)
    Dustman's Song, The, *Algernon Blackwood,* G [d'-e''], B&H 3 Faery.
    Gardener's Song, The, *Algernon Blackwood,* B♭ [f'-d''], B&H 3 Faery.
    (I have loved flowers that fade, *Robert Bridges,* Cm, B&H.)
    In the highlands, *R. L. Stevenson,* D [c'#-d''], BMP.
    Love on my heart from heaven fell, *Robert Bridges,* E♭ [d'-a''♭], B&H *Heritage 2.*
    Melmillo, *Walter de la Mare,* B [d'#-f''#], B&H *Imperial 2.*
    Organ Grinder's Song, The, *Algernon Blackwood,* Gm [d'-d''], B&H 3 Faery.
    (Since thou, O fondest and truest, *Robert Bridges,* B, B&H.)
    (Song of the Sirens, *William Browne,* B♭, B&H.)
    Spring, The, *William Barnes,* E♭ [c'-e''], BMP.
    (Thrice happy she, *Edmund Spenser,* B&H.)
    To a poet a thousand years hence, *James Elroy Flecker,* D [b-f''#], BMP.
    (To violets, *Robert Herrick,* B♭, B&H.)
    (When June is come, *Robert Bridges,* B&H.)
    While the sun was going down, *Mary Coleridge,* E [c'-g''#], B&H.

Carey, Henry. c.1690–1743.
    Friendly Advisor, The *Anon,* Cm [g'-a''♭], Roberton (Cockshott).
    Pastoral, A, (Flocks are sporting), *Anon,* F [c'-a''], B&H (Lane Wilson) *Old English,* Schirmer *2nd Soprano*; G, Paterson (Diack) *100 Best 1*; D, Fischer (Lane Wilson) *Centuries low.*

Carey, Lewis. (Lucinda (Lucy) Johnstone). c.1860–1925.
    Nearer, my God, to Thee, *Sarah Flower Adams,* G [d'-g''(e'')], B&H *Ballad Album 2.*

Carter, Andrew. 1939–
    Pancake Tuesday, *Eleanore Farjeon,* [medium], Banks.

Case, John Carol. 1923–
Arrangements:
    King Herod and the Cock, *Traditional,* B♭m [f'-f''], OUP *Solo Christmas high*; Gm, *Solo Christmas low.*
    Rocking, *Czech traditional,* tr. *Percy Dearmer,* A♭ [e'♭-f''], OUP *Solo Christmas high,* F, *Solo Christmas low.*
    Two Shepherd Boys, The, *German folk-song,* tr. *John Carol Case,* A [e'-f''#], OUP *Solo Christmas high*; F, *Solo Christmas low.*

Casken, John. 1949–
Ia Orana, Gauguin, *John Casken*, [b-b''b](f), Schott.

Cavendish, Michael. *c.*1565–1628.
Collection: *Fourteen Ayres*, S&B 1926 (edited E. H. Fellowes). Only songs available in anthologies are listed individually here.
Cursed be the time, *Anon*, Gm [f#-e''b](m), BMP *W&W 5*.
Down in a valley, *Anon*, F [e'-f''], BMP *W & W 4*.
Heart to rue the pleasure of the eye, The, *Anon*, Gm [d'-e''b], S&B (Pilkington) *Lute Songs 1*, BMP *W&W 1*.
Love is not blind, *Anon*, G [f#-e''], S&B (Pilkington) *Lute Songs 1*, BMP *W&W 1*.
Love, the delight of all well thinking minds, *Fulke Greville*, Gm [d'-d''], BMP *W&W 3*.
Mourn, Marcus, mourn, *Anon*, Dm [d'-f''], BMP *W&W 6*.
Stay, Glycia, stay, *Anon*, G [g'-e''](m), S&B (Pilkington) *Lute Songs 1*.
Sylvia is fair, *Anon*, C [c'-d''](m), BMP *W&W 5*.
Wanton, come hither, *Anon*, Gm [c'-f''](m), S&B (Pilkington) *Lute Songs 1*.

Center, Ronald. 1913–1973.
Collections: *Four Songs in Praise of Spring,* Bardic; *Scottish Songs,* Bardic.
Angel and the Child, The, *Jean Rebone,* Bardic.
Daffodils, that come before the swallow dares, *Shakespeare*, Bardic 4 Songs.
Evensong, *Christian Gibbs,* Bardic.
For Winter's rains and rains are over, *Shakespeare,* Bardic 4 Songs.
If thou art sleeping, maiden, *Santa Teresa of Avila* tr. *Longfellow,* Bardic.
It was a lover and his lass, *Shakespeare,* Bardic 4 Songs.
Serenade, *Longfellow,* Bardic.
Spring Sorrow, *Rupert Brooke,* Bardic.
Sweet o' the year, The, *Shakespeare,* Bardic 4 Songs.
Unchanging, The, *B. R. Gibbs,* Bardic.
Word over all, *Walt Whitman,* Bardic.
Arrangements: *Twentyfour Scottish Songs,* Bardic.
Ca' the yowes, *Robert Burns,* Bardic Scottish.
Corn Riggs, *Robert Burns,* Bardic Scottish.
Deil's awa', The, *Robert Burns,* Bardic Scottish.
Duncan Gray, *Robert Burns,* Bardic Scottish.
Gallant Weaver, The, *Robert Burns,* Bardic Scottish.
I'm owre young to marry yet, *Robert Burns,* Bardic Scottish.
Lassie wi' the lint white locks, *Robert Burns,* Bardic Scottish.
Lass o' Gowrie, The, *Anon,* Bardic Scottish.
Last May a braw wooer, *Robert Burns,* Bardic Scottish.
Loch Lomond, *Robert Burns,* Bardic Scottish.
Man's a man, A, *Robert Burns,* Bardic Scottish.
Mary Morison, *Robert Burns,* Bardic Scottish.
My heart is sair, *Robert Burns,* Bardic Scottish.
My love she's but a lassie yet, *James Hogg? Robert Burns?,* Bardic Scottish.
O' a' the Airt's, *Robert Burns,* Bardic Scottish.
O this is no my ain lassie, *Robert Burns,* Bardic Scottish.
O whistle and I'll come to ye, my lad, *Robert Burns,* Bardic Scottish.
O Willie brewed, *Robert Burns,* Bardic Scottish.
Simmer's a pleasant time, *Robert Burns,* Bardic Scottish.
There was a lad, *Robert Burns,* Bardic Scottish.
There was a lass,*Robert Burns,* Bardic Scottish.
Up wi' the carls o' Dysart, *Robert Burns,* Bardic Scottish.
Willie Wastle, *Robert Burns,* Bardic Scottish.
Ye banks and braes, *Robert Burns,* Bardic Scottish.

Chapple, Brian. 1945–
Collection: *Five Blake Songs*, Chester 1979.
Every night and every morn, *William Blake*, [f'-g''], Chester 5 Blake.
He who mocks the infant's faith, *William Blake*, [d'-a''], Chester 5 Blake.
Joy and woe are woven fine, *William Blake*, [d'b-b''b], Chester 5 Blake.
Light breaks where no sun shines, [soprano], Chester.
Robin redbreast in a cage, A, *William Blake*, [f'-a''], Chester 5 Blake.
To see a world in a grain of sand, *William Blake*, [c'#-g''#], Chester 5 Blake.

Charlesworth, David. *See* App. 2.

Church, John. 1675–1741.
Divine Hymn (O God for ever blest), *Anon*, Fm [c′-a′′b], BMP (Dent).
King of all joys, *Anon*, Gm [d′-g′′], Thames (Bevan) *6 Divine*.
O God for ever blest, *Anon*, Fm [c′-a′′b], Thames (Bevan) *6 Divine*.

Churches, Richard. 1966– BMIC.

Churchyard, Gordon. WMIC.

Clarke, Jeremiah. *c.*1674–1707. *See also* App. 2.
Collection: *Six Songs*, Thames (edited Maurice Bevan).
Alas, here lies the poor Alonso slain, *Thomas Shadwell*, Dm [c′-f′′], Thames 6 Songs.
Bonny grey-ey'd morn, The, *Thomas D'Urfey*, Bb [c′-g′′](f), Thames 6 Songs.
Cease that enchanting song, *Anon*, Cm [d′-a′′b], Thames 6 Songs.
Divine Hymn, A (Blest be those sweet regions), *Anon*, Cm [c′-a′′], Faber (Britten) *Harmonia*.
Evening Hymn, An, *Anon*, Gm [d′-f′′], Thames 6 Songs.
Gentle warmth comes o'er my heart, A, *Anon*, Dm [c′-a′′](m), Thames 6 Songs.
Sleep betray'd the unhappy lover, *Anon*, Am [e′-a′′], Thames 6 Songs.

Clarke, Rebecca. 1886–1979. *See also* App. 2.
Collections: *Song Album*, B&H (introduction by Calum MacDonald); *Songs with Piano*, OUP (edited Christopher Johnson).
Aspidistra, The, *Claude Flight*, G [d′-g′′], Thames *Century 5*, OUP Songs.
Binnorie (A Ballad), *Traditional Scottish*, Em [c′#-g′′], OUP Songs.
Cherry-blossom Wand, The, *Anna Wickham*, Em [c′#-g′′], Thames *Century 1*, OUP Songs.
Cloths of Heaven, The, *W. B. Yeats*, Am [b-f′′], B&H Song Album.
Come, oh come, my life's delight, *Thomas Campion*, Bm [e′-f′′#], OUP Songs.
Cradle Song, *William Blake*, G [e′-g′′](f), OUP Songs, BMP.
Donkey, The, *G. K. Chesterton*, [c′-g′′b], OUP Songs.
Down by the salley gardens, *W. B. Yeats*, Em [d′-e′′], B&H Song Album, *Easy Song*.
Dream, A, *W. B. Yeats*, Gm [d′-g′′], B&H Song Album; Fm, B&H.
Eight o'clock, *A. E. Housman*, [e′b-g′′], B&H Song Album; [d′b-f′′]B&H.
God made a tree, *Katherine Kendall*, [c′-f′′], OUP Songs.
Greeting, *Ella Young*, F [f′-a′′], B&H Song Album; D, B&H.
Infant Joy, *William Blake*, F [c′#-f′′], B&H Song Album; Eb, B&H.
June Twilight, *John Masefield*, F [c′-f′′#], B&H Song Album; Eb, B&H.
Lethe, *Edna St. Vincent Millay*, [b-f′′], OUP Songs.
Psalm of David, when he was in the wilderness of Judah, A, *Psalm 63*, [bb-f′′], OUP Songs.
Seal Man, The, *John Masefield*, [c′-g′′], B&H Song Album.
Shy One, *W. B. Yeats*, F [c′-a′′](m), B&H Song Album; Eb, B&H.
Tiger, tiger, *William Blake*, [c′-f′′], OUP Songs.
Weep you no more, sad fountains, *Anon*, Am [c′-g′′], OUP Songs.

Clarke, Robert Coningsby. 1879–1934. *See also* Chappell.
Collections: *Songs of Summer*, [high], Classical; *Songs of the Malvern Hills*, [high (given below), low], Classical.
Blind Ploughman, The, *Marguerite Radclyffe Hall*, F [f′-g′′](m), Classical; C, Schirmer *1st Baritone*, Classical; D, Classical.
Casend Hill, *Marguerite Radclyffe Hall*, Am [e′-g′′], Classical Malvern high.
From Out the Mist, *H. D. Banning*, D [e′-f′′], Classical Songs of Summer.
I be hopin' you remember, *Marguerite Radclyffe Hall*, F [F′-f′′], Classical Malvern high.
In the City, *Marguerite Radclyffe Hall*, G [d′-g′′], Classical Malvern high.
In the purple glow, dear, *H. D. Banning*, Eb [d′-f′′(g′′)], Classical Songs of Summer.
Ledbury Train, The, *Marguerite Radclyffe Hall*, A [e′-f′′#], Classical Malvern high.
Little Girl from Hanley Way, The, *Marguerite Radclyffe Hall*, F [f′-g′′], Classical Malvern high.
Malvern Hills in Spring, *Marguerite Radclyffe Hall*, G [d′-g′′(f′′#)], Classical Malvern high.
My Girl and I, *Marguerite Radclyffe Hall*, D [e′-g′′], Classical Malvern high.
Once in a garden lovely, *H. D. Banning*, Db [d′b-f′′], Classical Songs of Summer.
When, My Sweet, I Gaze on Thee, *H. D. Banning*, A [e′-f′′#], Classical Songs of Summer.

Clarke-Whitfield, John. 1770–1836.
Here's the vow she falsely swore, *Anon*, D [f′#-a′′](m), S&B (Bush & Temperley) *MB 43*.

One struggle more, and I am free, *Lord Byron*, Fm [c′-f″](m), S&B (Bush & Temperley) *MB 43*.
What voice is this? *Joanna Baillie*, Am [d′#-a″], S&B (Bush & Temperley) *MB 43*.

Clay, Frederick Emes. 1838–1889.
I'll sing thee songs of Araby, *W. G. Wills*, G [d′-g″], IMP *Parlour Songs*; F, Classical.

Clements, John. ? –1986.
Blessed is the man, *Psalm 1*, B♭, Lengnick.
Blue and White, *Mary Coleridge*, G [d′-a″], B&H.
Crossing the Bar, *Alfred Lord Tennyson*, Cramer.
Early one morning, *Anon*, Cramer.
(Elizabeth's Song, *Lascelles Abercrombie*, G [f″#-b″](f), Keith Prowse.)
Gibberish, *Mary Coleridge*, Cramer.
(Herself a Rose, *Christina Rossetti*, C [c′-g″], Chester.)

Clucas, Humphrey. See also App. 2.
Collection: *Reconciling*, (four songs for high voice) Brunton.

Clutsam, George Howard. 1866–1951.
I know of two bright eyes (Myrra), *George Howard Clutsam*, F [d′-d″(f″)], IMP *Parlour Songs*.

Coates, Eric. 1886–1957. See also B&H, Chappell.
Collection: *Four Old English Songs*, [high], Classical/B&H; [medium, low], B&H.
Bird Songs at Eventide, *Royden Barrie*, G [d′-e″(g″)], IMP *Parlour Songs*, William Elkin.
By Mendip Side, *P. J. O'Reilly*, E♭ [e′b(b)-g″], Schirmer *1st Tenor*, (Chappell *English Recital 1*.)
Green Hills of Somerset, The, *Fred E. Weatherly*, E♭ [d′-g″(b″)], Schirmer *2nd Tenor*, (Chappell *English Recital 1*.)
It was a lover and his lass, *Shakespeare*, G [d′-a″], Classical/B&H 4 Old; E♭, F, B&H 4 Old, Schirmer *1st Tenor II*.
Orpheus with his lute, *Shakespeare*, E♭ [d′-g″], B&H *Shakespeare Album*, Schirmer *1st Tenor*; F, Classical/B&H 4 Old; D♭, B&H 4 Old.
(Sigh no more, ladies, *Shakespeare*, G [d′-g″], Chappell *English Recital 2*.)
Stonecracker John, *Fred E. Weatherly*, E♭ [bb-f″(e″b)], B&H *Souvenirs*.
Under the greenwood tree, *Shakespeare*, C [c′-g″], B&H *Shakespeare Album*, 4 Old; D, Classical/B&H 4 Old; B♭, B&H 4 Old.
Who is Sylvia, *Shakespeare*, D [d′-f″], B&H *Shakespeare Album*, 4 Old, Schirmer *1st Tenor II*; E, Classical/B&H 4 Old; C, B&H 4 Old.

Coates, Leon.
Collection: *North-West Passage*, Hardie Press.
Goodnight, *Robert Louis Stevenson*, [c′-g″], Hardie North-West.
In Port, *Robert Louis Stevenson*, [c′#-a″b], Hardie North-West.
Shadow March, *Robert Louis Stevenson*, [d′-g″], Hardie North-West.

Cochrane, Peggy.
Reverie, *L. Rees*, B♭ [high], BMP.

Cockshott, Gerald. 1915–1979.
Arrangements: Collection; *Two Eighteenth Century Songs*, Roberton.
Charming Country Life, A, *Anon*, Am [e′-e″], Roberton 2 18th Cent.
Little Man and the Little Maid, *Anon*, Gm [d-f″], Roberton 2 18th Cent.
Somebody fetch me a flute, *Anon* tr. *Gerald Cockshott*, G [g′-e″], Roberton.
Threshing Song, *Anon* tr. *Gerald Cockshott*, B♭ [f′-g″], BMP.

Coleridge-Taylor, Samuel. 1875–1912.
Collections: *African Romances* Op 17, S&B; (*Five Fairy Ballads*, B&H); *In Memoriam Op 24*, S&B; *Little Songs for Little Folks Op 19/2*, B&H; *Six Sorrow Songs Op 57*, [high, low], S&B; *Songs of Sun and Shade*, [high, low], B&H; *Southern Love Songs Op 12*, S&B; *Three Songs Op 29*, S&B.
African Love Song, An, *P. L. Dunbar*, F [f′-a″b](m), S&B African.
(Alone with Mother, *Kathleen Easmon*, C, [c′-e″], B&H; E♭, B&H.)
Ballad, *P. L. Dunbar*, G [f′#-g″], S&B African.
Big Lady Moon, *Kathleen Easmon*, F [c′-g″], B&H; D♭, E♭, B&H.
Birthday, A, *Christina Rossetti*, B♭ [f′-g″] Cramer; A♭, F, Cramer.
(Candle Lightin' Time, *P. L. Dunbar*, Em, [b-d″], B&H; Gm, B&H.)

(Come in! *Alfred Noyes*, F, B&H; A♭, B&H.)
Corn Song, *P. L. Dunbar*, C [b-e′′], B&H; E♭, B&H.
Dawn, *P L Dunbar*, A♭ [f′-a′′♭], S&B African.
Earth fades! heaven breaks on me, *Robert Browning*, Gm [d′-e′′♭], S&B In Memoriam.
Eleanore, *Eric Mackay*, D [f#′-g′′](m), B&H *Ballad Album 1*; A, C, Classical; (B♭, B&H).
(Eulalie, *Alice Parsons*, G, B&H; A, B&H.)
(Fairy Roses, *Kathleen Easmon*, A♭ [d′-g′′], B&H; F, B&H.)
(Five-and-twenty sailormen, *Greville E. Matheson*, Gm [d′-d′′](m), B&H; Am, B&H.)
Gift Rose, The, *F. Peterson*, D, B&H; B♭, B&H.
How shall I woo thee? *P. L. Dunbar*, G♭ [g′♭-g′′♭](m), S&B African; F, D, S&B.
If thou art sleeping, maiden, *St Teresa of Avila* tr. *Longfellow*, Dm [f′-f′′](m), S&B Southern.
Jessy, *Robert Burns*, C [d′-g′′](m), S&B 3 Songs; B♭, S&B.
(King there lived in Thule, A, *Goethe* tr. *Stephen Phillips & J. Comyns Carr*, Dm, B&H.)
Lament, A, *Christina Rossetti*, B♭ [f′-g′′], Classical.
Life and Death, *Jessie Adelaide Middleton*, A♭ [b-e′′♭], Classical, S&B; B♭, Classical; (D♭, S&B).
(Long years ago, *P. L. Dunbar*, B&H.)
Lovely Little Dream, A, *Sorojini Naidu*, Gm [d′-g′′], Classical, Cramer; Dm, (Fm), Cramer.
Lucy, *William Wordsworth*, E♭ [e′♭-a′′♭], S&B 3 Songs.
Mary, *William Wordsworth*, A [f′#-g′′], S&B 3 Songs.
Minguillo, *Anon* tr. *J. G. Lockhart*, E♭ [e′♭-a′′♭](f), S&B Southern.
My Doll, *Charles Kingsley*, D♭, B&H.
My Love, *St Teresa of Avila*? tr. *Longfellow*, A [e′-g′′#](m), S&B Southern.
Oh, my lonely pillow, *Lord Byron*, Am [e′-a′′](f), S&B Southern.
Oh, roses for the flush of youth, *Christina Rossetti*, E♭m [b♭-e′′♭], S&B Six Sorrow low; Fm, S&B Six Sorrow high.
Oh what comes over the sea, *Christina Rossetti*, Dm [a-e′′], S&B Six Sorrow low; Em, S&B Six Sorrow high.
Onaway, awake, beloved, *Henry W. Longfellow*, G♭ [f′-b′′♭](m), B&H *Ballad Album 2*, Classical.
Over the hills, *P. L. Dunbar*, D [d′-f′′#], S&B African; B. S&B.
Prayer, A, *P. L. Dunbar*, A [d′#-g′′], S&B African.
Question and Answer (Demande et rêponse), *Arthur Stanley*, F [a-e′′], B&H.
Rainbow child, The, *Marguerite Radclyffe Hall*, Em, [b-e′′], B&H Sun & Shade high; Dm, B&H Sun & Shade low.
(Red of the Dawn, *Alfred Noyes*, Bm, B&H.)
She rested by the broken brook, *R. L. Stevenson*, E♭ [b♭-e′′♭], B&H; G, B&H.
She sat and sang alway, *Christina Rossetti*, G [g(♭)-e′′], S&B Six Sorrow low; A, S&B Six Sorrow high.
Shoshone's Adieu, The, *Brice Fennell*, A [b-e′′], B&H; B♭, B&H.
Song of the Nubian girl, *Thomas Moore*, Dm [a-e′′](f), S&B.
Starry night, A, *P. L. Dunbar*, Am [e′-g′′], S&B African.
(Stars, The, *Kathleen Easmon*, Cm [b♭-e′′♭], B&H; Em, B&H.)
Substitution, *Elizabeth Barrett Browning*, B [b-e′′], S&B In Memoriam.
Summer Idyll, A, *Hilda Hammond-Spencer*, F [d′-f′′], Classical.
(Sweet baby butterfly, *Kathleen Easmon*, F [a-c′′#], B&H; A♭, B&H.)
Tears, *Anon*, D♭ [f′-g′′♭], S&B Southern.
This is the island of gardens, *Marguerite Radclyffe Hall*, D♭ [b♭-f′′], B&H Sun & Shade high; C, B&H Sun & Shade low.
Thou art risen, my beloved, *Marguerite Radclyffe Hall*, Fm [c′-f′′], B&H Sun & Shade high; Dm, Sun & Shade low; Gm, B&H.
Thou hast bewitched me, beloved, *Marguerite Radclyffe Hall*, A [e′-f′′], B&H Sun & Shade high; G, B&H Sun & Shade low.
Too late for love, *Christina Rossetti*, Fm [b-e′′♭], S&B Six Sorrow low; Gm, S&B Six Sorrow high.
Unmindful of the roses, *Christina Rossetti*, D [a-d′′], S&B Six Sorrow low; E, S&B Six Sorrow high.
(Until, *Frank Dempster Sherman*, B&H,)
Waiting, *Alfred Noyes*, (scena) Em [d′#-a′′(f′′)], B&H; Dm, B&H.
Weep not, beloved friends, *Chiabrera* tr. *Wordsworth*, E♭ [c′-d′′], S&B In Memoriam.
When I am dead, my dearest, *Christina Rossetti*, F [c′-e′′♭], S&B Six Sorrow low; G, S&B Six Sorrow high.
Willow song, The, *Shakespeare*, Em [b-e′′], Cramer; Fm, Gm, Cramer.
You lay so still in the sunshine, *Marguerite Radclyffe Hall*, C [d′-e′′], B&H Sun & Shade high; B♭, B&H Sun & Shade low.
(Your heart's desire, *Alfred Noyes*, B&H.)
Arrangement:
Three ravens, The, *Anon*, Em [b-d′′], B&H; (Gm, B&H.)

Colling, Aubrey. *See* App. 2.

Collingwood, Lawrance. 1887–1982. BMIC.

Collins, Hal. ? –1929.
    Forget not yet, *Thomas Wyatt,* [d′-g′′], BMP.

Collins, John Henn.
Collection: *Two Songs,* [d′b-d′′], BMP.
    Down by the sally gardens, *W. B. Yeats,* BMP 2 Songs.
    Mirage, *John Henn Collins,* BMP 2 Songs.

Connolly, Justin Riveagh. 1933– BMIC. *See also* App. 1, 2.

Cook, Waddington.
Collection: *Four Songs,* [high], BMP.
    Weep ye not, G [high], BMP.

Cooke, Arnold Atkinson. 1906– BMIC. *See also* App. 2.

Cooper, John. *See* **Coprario, Giovanni.**

Cope, Cecil.
Collection: *Two songs from 'The Wandering Moon',* Roberton.
    Fire, *James Reeves,* Dm [d′-f′′#], Roberton Wandering Moon.
    Shiny, *James Reeves,* C [c′-e′′], Roberton Wandering Moon.

Copley. Ian. 1926–1988
    Twelfth Night, *Hilaire Belloc,* Bm [c′#-d′′#], William Elkin.

Coprario, Giovanni (John Cooper). *c.*1575–1626.
Collections: *Funeral Tears, Songs of Mourning* and *The Masque of Squires,* S&B 1959 (edited Gerald Hendrie and Thurston Dart).
    O sweet flower, *Anon,* C [g′-g′′], Funeral Tears, BMP *W&W 4.*
    So parted you, *Thomas Campion,* G [c′-e′′], Songs of Mourning, BMP *W&W 5.*

Corke, Hilary. 1921– 2001.
    Alba, *Ezra Pound,* F [c′-a′′], Modus.
    Olney Hymns, *John Betjeman,* Eb [d′-g′′], Modus.
    Sweet and low, *Alfred Lord Tennyson,* D [d′-g′′], Modus.

Corkine, William. *fl.*1610–1612.
Collection: *First Book of Ayres,* S&B (edited E. H. Fellowes); *Second Booke of Ayres,* S&B (edited E. H. Fellowes). Only songs available in anthologies are listed individually here.
    Beauty sat bathing, *Anthony Munday,* Am [e′-e′′](m), 1st Book, BMP *W&W 5.*
    Dear, though your mind, *Anon,* C [f′#-a′′], 2nd Booke; *A,* B&H (Keel) *Lovesongs 1a; F, Lovesongs 1b.*
    He that hath no mistress, *Anon,* F [c′-e′′b](m), 1st Book, S&B (Pilkington) *Lute Songs 1.*
    Shall a frown or angry eye, *Anon,* Gm [d′-f′′](m), 1st Book, BMP *W&W 1.*
    Shall a smile or guileful glance? *Anon,* F, [f′-f′′](m), 2nd Booke; *Eb,* B&H (Keel) *Lovesongs 2b; G, Lovesongs 2a.*
    Sweet Cupid, *Anon,* Bb [f′-f′′](m), 1st Book, S&B (Pilkington) *Lute Songs 1;* G, B&H (Keel)
        Lovesongs 1b; B, Lovesongs 1a.
    Sweet, let me go, *Anon,* C [c′-a′′](f), 1st Book, S&B (Pilkington) *Lute Songs 1,* BMP *W&W 3.*

Courteville, Raphael. *fl.*1687– *c*1735.
    Cease Hymen, cease, *Thomas D'Urfey,* D [F#-e′](m), Thames (Bevan) *6 Restoration.*

Cowen, Sir **Frederic** Hymen. 1852–1935. *See also* B&H.
    All for my true love, *Anon,* Em [d′-g′′], S&B MB 56.
    Border Ballad, *Walter Scott,* Bm [d′-f′′(e′′)](m), Classical, B&H.
    My true love hath my heart, *Philip Sidney,* E [e′-g′′#(f′#)](f), S&B MB 56.

Cowie, Edward. 1943– BMIC.

Cox, Bert. *See* App. 2.

Cox, David Vassall. 1916–1997.
    Fine English Days! *Anon 18th cent.*, E♭ [b♭-e′′♭], Thames *Century 4.*

Crawley, Clifford.
    Magic in the air, Leslie.

Crawford, Robert. 1925–
Arrangements:
    Blathrie O'T, The, *Traditional,* [voice], SMIC (Bayley & Ferguson).
    Brisk young lad, *Traditional,* [voice], SMIC (Bayley & Ferguson).
    Gardner wi' his Paidle, *Traditional,* [voice], SMIC (Bayley & Ferguson).
    Johnny Faa, *Traditional,* [voice], SMIC (Bayley & Ferguson).
    Saw ye Johnny Cummin, *Traditional,* [voice], SMIC (Baylcy & Ferguson).
    Waly, waly, *Traditional,* [voice], SMIC (Bayley & Ferguson).

Cresswell, Lyell. 1944– *See also* App. 1, 2.
Collections: *Eight Shaker Songs,* [soprano], SMIC; *Seven Shaker Songs,* [baritone], SMIC; *Six Poems of Amy Lowell,* [soprano], SMIC.
    Snatches from Baptized Generations, *Emily Dickinson,* [tenor], SMIC.

Crocker, David. 1941–
    Merlin's Song, *Alfred Lord Tennyson,* [b♭-d′′], EPSS.

Croft, William. 1678–1727. *See also* App. 2.
    Ah, how sweet, *Thomas D'Urfey,* Gm [d′-a′′], S&B (Pilkington) *Georgian* 2; *Fm,* B&H (Keel) *12 18th Century.*
    How severe is my fate, *Martin,* Cm [d′-a′′♭](m), S&B (Pilkington) *Georgian 2.*
    Hymn on Divine Music, A, *Anon,* Dm [d′-g′′], Faber (Britten) *Harmonia.*
    My heart is ev'ry beauty's prey, *Anon,* A [e′-a′′], Roberton (H. Diack Johnston).
    Song to Celia's Spinet, A, *Richard Steele,* Dm [g-b′♭], Thames (Richard Newton) *Countertenors 2.*

Crosse, Gordon. 1937– *See also* App. 1, 2.
Collection: *The Cool Web ,* OUP hire.
    Allie, *Robert Graves,* [d′-a′′], OUP Cool Web.
    Cool Web, The, *Robert Graves,* [d′-a′′♭], OUP Cool Web.
    Frog Prince, The, *Stevie Smith,* [c′#-a′′], OUP Cool Web.
    New World, The (cycle), *Ted Hughes,* [g-a′′♭], OUP; a version for high voice on hire.
    Vanity, *Robert Graves.* [d′-g′′], OUP Cool Web.
    Voice from the Tomb, The (cycle), *Stevie Smith,* [a♭-f′′#], OUP hire.

Crossley-Holland, Peter Charles. 1916– 2001. *See also* App. 2.
Collections: *Two Songs,* Lengnick; *Songs,* Forsyth.
    Cradle Song, *Padraic Colum,* Bm [d′-g′′], Forsyth Songs.
    Evening is over the land, *Laurence Binyon,* B♭ [g-d′′], Forsyth Songs.
    Into the twilight, *W. B. Yeats,* E [g#-g′′#], Forsyth Songs.
    Land of the west, The, *Samuel Lover,* D♭ [c′-f′′](m), Forsyth Songs.
    Mariner, The, *Winthrop MacWorth Praed,* Dm [d-e′′](m), Forsyth Songs.
    Night Ride, *Ernest Rhys,* Em [B-e′(g′)](m), Forsyth Songs.
    Nightingales, The, *Robert Bridges,* F [c′-a′′], Forsyth Songs.
    Now all is ready for Pentecost, *Henrik Ibsen* tr. *Anon,* E [e′-f′′#](f), Forsyth Songs.
    Piper, The, *Seumas O'Sullivan,* G [d′-g′′], Lengnick 2 Songs, Forsyth Songs.
    Sleep, my boy, *Henrik Ibsen* tr. *Anon,* E [d′-g′′#](f), Forsyth Songs.
    Twilight it is, *John Masefield,* F [c′-g′′(a′′)], Forsyth Songs.
    Wanderer's Night Song, *Goethe* tr. *Percy Pinkerton,* A♭ [a♭-b′♭], Forsyth Songs.
    Weather the Cuckoo Likes, The, *Thomas Hardy,* G [d′-g′′], Lengnick 2 Songs, Forsyth Songs.
    When woods were green, *Longfellow,* G [g-d′′], Forsyth Songs.

Cruft, Adrian. 1921–1987. BMIC. *See also* App. 2.
Collections: *Two Canadian Poems, Op 56,* Joad; *Two Nursery Rhymes, Op 23,* Joad.
    August River 'to Dinah and George Cartmel', [medium], Joad 2 Canadian.
    Cock Robin, *Anon,* [medium], Joad 2 Nursery.

Dead Days 'for Jan and Louis Applebaum', [medium], Joad 2 Canadian.
Fiddle-cum-fee, *Anon,* [medium], Joad 2 Nursery.
Into God's Kingdom (cycle), *Blake, Lydgate, Herrick, Zouche, Baxter, Gascoigne,* [F-e′b](m), Joad.
Mine Own Sweet Jewel, *Anon,* Eb [e′b-f′′], Joad.
Songs of Good Counsel (cycle), *Anon 15th century,* [mezzo], Joad.

Cundell, Edric. 1893–1961.
(Gold o' the world, *Crosbie Garstin,* Eb [f′-g′′](m), Chappell *English Recital 2.*)

D

Dafydd, Einion. *See* App. 2.

Dalby, John **Martin.** 1942– SMIC. *See also* App. 2.
Collections: *Bairnrhymes,* Novello/Impulse; *Eight Songs from the Chinese,* [baritone/counter-tenor], Lengnick/Impulse; *Four Aspects of Faith,* SMIC/Dalby; *Muse of Love,* A, SMIC/Impulse, B&H; *Three Songs from Old Rhymes,* Novello.
Antoinette alone (scena), *Jean Rhys,* [mezzo], Novello.
Cupid and Campaspe, *John Lyly,* [d′-a′′](m), SMIC/Dalby Muse, B&H *Heritage 3.*
Flood, *T'ao Ch'ien* tr. *Arthur Waley,* [a-e′′](m), Lengnick 8 from the Chinese.
Generous Christian, The, *Francis Quarles,* [soprano/tenor], SMIC/ Dalby 4 Aspects.
Herd boy, The, *Lu Yu* tr. *Arthur Waley,* [bb-c′′](m), Lengnick 8 from the Chinese.
I saw a peacock, *Anon,* [soprano/tenor], Novello/Dalby 3 Songs.
Little cart, The, *Ch'ên Tzu-Lung* tr. *Arthur Waley,* [c′b-e′′b](m), Lengnick 8 from the Chinese.
Little lady of Ch'ing-hsi, The, *Anon* tr. *Arthur Waley,* [g-c′′](m), Lengnick 8 from the Chinese.
My song is in sighing, *Richard Rolle of Hampole,* [treble], Novello/Dalby.
New Corn, *T'ao Ch'ien* tr. *Arthur Waley,* [e′-e′′b], Lengnick 8 from the Chinese.
O gentle love, *George Peele,* [d′-g′′], SMIC/Dalby Muse.)
Pedlar of spells, The, *Lu Yu* tr. *Arthur Waley,* [bb-d′′](m), Lengnick 8 from the Chinese.
Plucking the rushes, *Chinese 4th cent.* tr. *Arthur Waley,* [c′-c′′](m), Lengnick 8 from the Chinese.
Soldier's song, A, *Chinese* tr. *Arthur Waley,* [b-d′′](m), Lengnick 8 from the Chinese.
Sweet are the thoughts, *Anon,* (*J. Amners Sacred Hymns),* [soprano/tenor], SMIC/Dalby 4 Aspects.
Take, O take those lips away, *Shakespeare,* [e′b-g′′], SMIC/Dalby Muse.
Tarry Ooo, *Anon,* [soprano/tenor], Novello/Dalby 3 Songs.
There was a king, *Anon,* [soprano/tenor], Novello/Dalby 3 Songs.
Think and be careful, *John Byrom,* [soprano/tenor], SMIC/Dalby 4 Aspects.
Wanderer, (cycle), *Chinese* tr. *Arthur Waley,* {mezzo], SMIC/Ricordi.
What thing is love? *George Peele,* [d′-g′′], SMIC/Dalby Muse.
When to her lute Corinna sings, *Thomas Campion,* [e′-g′′], SMIC/Dalby Muse.
Why dost thou lurk so close? *Francis Quarles,* [soprano/tenor], SMIC/Dalby 4 Aspects.

Dale, Benjamin. 1885–1943. *see also* App. 2.
(Come away, death, *Shakespeare,* Db, Novello; E, Novello.)
(O mistress mine, *Shakespeare,* F [f′-g′′](m), Novello; D, Novello.)

Dale, Mervyn. 1922–1985.
Collection: *Four English Lyrics,* Roberton.
Back and side go bare, *Anon,* F [c′-c′′](m), Roberton 4 English.
Come live with me, *Christopher Marlowe,* F [c′-d′′](m), Roberton 4 English.
Come night and lay thy velvet hand, *George Chapman,* F [c′-b′b], Roberton 4 English.
Fie diddle dee and fie on me, *Joan Lane,* F [c′-e′′], Roberton.
Footprints in the Snow, *Joan Lane,* F [c′-d′′], Roberton.
Snowie the Snowman, *Joan Lane,* F [c′-d′′], Roberton.
Where be ye, my love? *Anon,* C [b-c′′], Roberton 4 English.

Dalway, Ianthe.
Arrangements: *Three Irish Airs,* BMP.
Killiney Strand, *L.A.G. Strong,* BMP 3 Irish.
Love entrapped me, *L.A.G. Strong,* BMP 3 Irish.
Love repaid, *L.A.G. Strong,* BMP 3 Irish.

Danyel, John. 1564– after 1625.
Collection: *Song*s, S&B (edited David Scott). Only songs available in anthologies are listed individually here.
    Coy Daphne fled, *Anon,* D [c′#-e″], BMP *W&W 1.*
    Dost thou withdraw thy grace? *Anon,* Gm [g′-f″], S&B (Pilkington) *Lute Songs 1,* BMP *W&W 5.*
    Eyes, look no more, *Anon,* Am [d′-e″], BMP *W&W 6.*
    Grief, keep within, *Anon,* Dm [c′-f″], BMP *W&W 6.*
    I die whenas I do not see, *Anon,* Am [c′-e″](m), S&B (Pilkington) *Lute Songs 1,* BMP *W&W 1.*
    If I could shut the gate, *Anon,* Am [e′-e″], BMP *W&W 5.*
    Let not Chloris think, *Anon,* Dm [c′-d″], BMP *W&W 5.*
    Like as the lute delights, *Samuel Daniel,* Cm [c′-e″b], S&B (Pilkington) *Lute Songs 1.*
    Stay, cruel, stay, *Anon,* G [d′-e″], BMP *W&W 3.*
    Thou pretty bird, *Anon,* G [d′-f″], BMP *W&W 5.*
    Time, cruel time, *Samuel Daniel,* Cm [e′b-e″b](m), BMP *W&W 4.*
    Why canst thou not? *Anon,* G [e′-f″], S&B (Pilkington) *Lute Songs 1,* BMP *W&W 3.*

Darke, Harold Edwin. 1888–1976.
    I love all beauteous things, *Robert Bridges,* [d′-f″#], BMP.

Darlow, Royston. 1943–
Collection: *Nocturnes for Voice, Op 8,* B&H.
    At the mid hour of night, *Thomas Moore,* Fm [c′-f″], B&H Nocturnes.
    Beauteous Evening, A, *William Wordsworth,* Eb [d′b-e″b], B&H Nocturnes.
    Night Thoughts, *Goethe* tr. *Anon,* Cm [d′-e″b], B&H Nocturnes.
    Nocturne, *Katheen Raine,* G [d′-f″], B&H Nocturnes.
    Now Winter's Nights enlarge, *Thomas Campion,* C [c′-d″], B&H Nocturnes.
    This Night, *Royston Darlow,* Gm [c′-e″b], B&H Nocturnes.

Daubney, Brian. 1929–
    To a Child, *Wilfrid Owen,* [c′#-f″], EPSS.

Davidson, Harold.
Arrangement:
    Harp that once, The, *Thomas Moore,* [c′-e″], BMP.

Davidson, Malcolm. 1891–1949.
    (At the turn of the burn, *Sylvia Townsend Warner,* D, B&H; F, B&H.)
    Bargain, The, *Philip Sidney,* D [d′-f″#], B&H; E, B&H.
    (Beauty, *John Masefield,* D [b-e″], Curwen.)
    Christmas carol, A, *John Masefield,* Am [f′-a″], B&H *Heritage 3*
    Conjuration, *Anon,* G [b′-f″], Cramer; high, Cramer.
    (In Fountain Court, *Arthur Symons,* Cm [d′b-f″#], Curwen.)
    (Lake and a fairy boat, A, *Thomas Hood,* E, B&H.)
    (Rain on the Down, *Arthur Symons,* D, B&H.)
    Sorrow of Mydath, *John Masefield,* D [e′-a″], B&H; (Bb, B&H).
    Stay O sweet, *John Donne?* Cm [d′-f″b], Cramer; high, Cramer.
    (Under the greenwood tree, *Shakespeare,* Curwen.)

Davie, Cedric Thorpe. 1913–1983. SMIC.

Davies, Eiluned. 1913–1999 WMIC. *See also* App. 2.
    For Ann Gregory, *W. B. Yeats,* [c-f″](m), WMIC *Songs from Wales 2.*
    Will you be as hard? *Lady Gregory* tr. *T. H. Parry-Jones,* [c#-e′](m), Gwynn.

Davies, George A. WMIC.

Davies, Janet.
Collection: *Four Christmas Songs,* Lengnick.
    Angel's warning, The, *Janet Davies,* Lengnick
    Festive carol, *Janet Davies,* Lengnick
    Jesus, infant Jesus, *Janet Davies,* Lengnick.
    Star light carol, The, *Janet Davies,* Lengnick.

Davies, Lyn. 1955–
Praise of Summer, Curiad.
Spectres, Curiad.

Davies, Martin Vaughan. *See* App. 2.

Davies, T. Vincent.
My country's hills of gold, [baritone], Snell.

Davies, Sir Henry **Walford.** 1869–1941. *See also* App. 2.
(Hame, *Alan Cunningham*, B♭ [b♭-d''], Chappell; C, D, Chappell.)
I vow to thee, my country, *Cecil Spring-Rice*, Cramer.
(Seal's lullaby, The, *Rudyard Kipling*, [b♭-f''], Novello.)
When childher plays, *T. E. Brown*, A [a-d''], Banks; C, B&H; (D, B&H).
Arrangements:
My loved one's grave, Gwynn.
O blackbird blithe, Gwynn.

Davies, William. 1859–1907.
Starless Crown, *Watkyn Wyn* tr. *Rev. Prof. Rowlands,* [soprano/tenor], Snell.

Dawney, William **Michael.** 1942– WMIC.
The Cattery, (cycle), [medium], Brunton.

Deacon, Helen.
Rabbits, *Anon,* G [d'-g''(e'')], Roberton.

Dean, Roy, arr. Janet Bishop.
Beneath the Bajan Moon, *Roy Dean*, [mezzo/baritone], Da Capo.
Bromley Blues, *Roy Dean*, [alto], Da Capo.
Flying Fish, *Roy Dean*, [contralto], Da Capo.
I can't get fat like father, *Roy Dean*, [mezzo/baritone], Da Capo.
Queen of my heart, *Roy Dean*, [baritone], Da Capo.
Seven Days of Loving, *Roy Dean*, [soprano/tenor], Da Capo.
Spring Weather, *Roy Dean*, [baritone], Da Capo.
Unwanted, The, *C. Day-Lewis,* [soprano/tenor], Da Capo.

Defesch, William. 1687–?1757.
(Colin's Success, *William Boyce*, D [d'-g''](f), Curwen (Poston).)
(Polly of the Plain, *William Boyce*, D [d'-g''], Curwen (Poston).)
(O fie, shepherd, fie, *William Boyce,* D [d'-g''](f), Curwen (Poston).)

Del Riego, Teresa. 1876–1969. *See also* Chappell.
Collection: *Songs of the Ship,* [Harold Simpson], [medium], Classical.
Homing, *Arthur L. Salmon,* C [c'-f''#], Classical; B♭, D, Classical.

Delius, Frederick Theodore Albert. 1862–1934. *See also* App. 1.
Collections: *Four Posthumous Songs,* Universal; *Nineteen Songs,* OUP; *Sixteen Songs,* B&H; *Song Album,* B&H; *Ten Songs,* S&B; *Twenty-two Songs,* S&B.
Autumn, *Ludwig Holstein* tr. *Delius,* E♭ [c'(b♭)-a''], B&H Album, 16 Songs.
Birds' Story, The, *Henrik Ibsen* tr. *Peter Pears,* F [d'(a)-g''#], OUP 19 Songs.
Black Roses, *Ernst Josephson*, tr. *Delius,* B♭ [c'b-f''], OUP 19 Songs.
Cradle Song, *Henrik Ibsen* tr. *Peter Pears,* D♭ [c'-f''], OUP 19 Songs.
Dreamy Nights, *Holger Drachmann* tr. *Delius,* E♭ [c'-g''], S&B 10 Songs, 22 Songs.
Hidden Love, *Bjørnsterne Bjørnson* tr. *Peter Pears,* F [c'-a''], OUP 19 Songs.
Homeward Way, The, *Asmund Olafson Vinje* tr. *Peter Pears,* A♭ [e'b-f''], OUP 19 Songs, BMP.
I hear in the night, *Holger Drachmann* tr. *Jelka Rosen,* D♭ [b-g''b], Universal 4 Posthumous.
I once had a newly cut willow pipe, *Vilhelm Krag* tr. *Lionel Carley,* G♭ [a-g''b], Universal 4 Posthumous.
I-Brasîl, *Fiona Macleod,* [c'-f''], OUP 19 Songs.
In bliss we walked with laughter, *Drachmann* tr. *Addie Funk,* Fm [c'-f''], Universal 4 Posthumous.
In the Garden of the Seraglio, *Jens Peter Jacobsen* tr. *Delius,* E♭ [d'b-g''b], B&H Album, 16 Songs.
Indian Love Song, *Percy Bysshe Shelley,* E♭ [e'b-b''b], OUP 19 Songs.

Irmelin, *Jens Peter Jacobsen* tr. *Delius*, F#m [b-g''], B&H Album, 16 Songs.
It was a lover and his lass, *Shakespeare*, [c'#-a''], B&H Album, 16 Songs; [a-f''], B&H.
Let springtime come, *Jens Peter Jacobsen* tr. *Delius*, A [c'-g''#], OUP 19 Songs.
Longing, *Theodor Kjerulf* tr. *William Grist*, D [c'b(a)-f''#], S&B 10 Songs, 22 Songs.
Love's Philosophy, *Percy Bysshe Shelley*, G [d'#-g''#(a'')], OUP 19 Songs.
Minstrel, The, *Henrik Ibsen* tr. *Peter Pears*, A [b-f''#](m), OUP 19 Songs.
Morning Star, *Paul Verlaine* tr. *John Andrewes*, [d'#-a''], B&H Album.
Nightingale, The, *Johan Welhaven* tr. *William Grist*, Eb [bb-e''b], S&B 22 Songs; G, 10 Songs, S&B.
Nightingale has a lyre of gold, The, *W. E. Henley*, Dm [c'#-g''], OUP 19 Songs, OUP.
Over the Mountains High, *Bjørnsterne Bjørnson* tr. *Anon*, C [c'-e''], S&B 22 Songs.
Page sat in the lofty tower, The, *Jens Peter Jacobsen* tr. *Delius*, Gm [d'-e''b], S&B 10 Songs, 22 Songs.
Silken shoes upon golden lasts, *Jens Peter Jacobsen* tr. *Delius*, F [c'-f''](m), B&H Album, 16 Songs.
Slumber Song, *Bjørnsterne Bjørnson* tr. *William Grist*, G [d'-f''], S&B 10 Songs, 22 Songs.
So white, so soft, so sweet is she, *Ben Jonson*, [b-f''#], B&H Album, 16 Songs, *Songs of Love and Affection*; [g'#-d''#], B&H.
Softly the forest murmurs, *Bjørnstern Bjørnson* tr. *Lionel Carley*, F#m [c'#-f''#], Universal 4 Posthumous.
Spring, the sweet Spring, *Thomas Nashe*, [d'-a''], B&H Album, 16 Songs; [bb-f''], B&H.
Summer Eve, *John Paulsen* tr. *W. Grist*, F# [d'#-f''x], S&B 10 Songs, 22 Songs.
Summer Landscape, *Holger Drachmann* tr. *Delius*, Bb [d'b-f''#], OUP 19 Songs.
Summer Nights, *Holger Drachmann* tr. *Delius*, Ab [c'-g''b], S&B 10 Songs, 22 Songs.
Sunset, *Andreas Munch* tr. *William Grist*, Gb [d'b(bb)-g''b], S&B 10 Songs, 22 Songs.
(Sweet Venevil, *Bjornsterne Bjørnson* tr. *F. S. Copeland*, C [c'-g''(e'')], OUP.)
They are not long, the weeping and the laughter, *Ernest Dowson*, Bb [db-g''], B&H 16 Songs.
Through long long years, *Jens Peter Jacobsen*, tr. *Delius*, Db [bb-f''], S&B 10 Songs, 22 Songs.
To Daffodils, *Robert Herrick*, [c'#-g''#], B&H Album, 16 Songs, *Heritage 2*; ([a#-e''#], B&H).
To the Queen of my Heart, *Percy Bysshe Shelley*, B [d'#-a''#], OUP 19 Songs.
Twilight Fancies, *Bjørnsterne Bjørnson* tr. *F. S. Copeland*, Bm [d'-f''#], OUP 19 Songs; Gm, OUP *Solo Contralto*, (BMP).
Violet, The, *Ludwig Holstein* tr. *Delius*, G [b-g''], B&H Album, 16 Songs.
Wine Roses, *Jens Peter Jacobsen* tr. *Delius*, C#m [c'#-e''], S&B 10 Songs, 22 Songs.
Young Venevil, *Bjørnsterne Bjørnson* tr. *Peter Pears*, C [c'-g''(e'')], OUP 19 Songs.

Demuth, Norman. 1898–1968.
Sleep, *John Fletcher*, Fm [f'-g''], S&B.

Dench, Chris. 1953– *See* App. 2.

Dennis, Brian. 1941–1998. BMIC.
Futility, *Wilfrid Owen*, [d'-g''b], EPSS.

Dent, Edward J. 1876–1957.
Oxen, The, *Thomas Hardy*, E [e'-f''], Thames *Hardy Songbook*.

Diack, J. Michael. 1869–1946. SMIC.
All in the April evening, *Katherine Tynan (Hinkson)*, Fm [d'b-g''], B&H; Dm, Cm, B&H.
(Jack and Jill, *Anon*, [low], Paterson.)
(Little Polly Flinders, *Anon*, F [c'-g''], Paterson; Eb, Paterson.)
Sing a song of sixpence *Anon*, G [d'-a''(g'')] Paterson; (D, Paterson).
Arrangement:
O my love is like a red, red rose, *Robert Burns*, Paterson.

Dibdin, Charles. 1745–1814.
Collection: (*Five Dibdin Airs*, B&H (edited Robert Chignell).)
(Anchorsmiths, The, *Anon*, G [g-e''](m), B&H 5 Dibdin.)
Blow high, blow low, *Charles Dibdin*, Eb [Ab-c'](m), Schirmer *1st Baritone*.
Come, every man now give his toast, *Charles Dibdin*, F [c'-g''](m), Novello (Bush) *Ballad Operas*.
(I locked up all my treasure, *Anon*, Db, [c'-d''b](m) B&H 5 Dibdin.)
(Jolly Young Waterman, The, *Anon*, F [c'-d''], B&H 5 Dibdin.)
Nothing like grog, *Charles Dibdin*, [baritone], Gwynn (Ian Parrott).
(Peggy Perkins, *Anon*, Bb [e'b-g''](m), BMP (Cockshott).)
(Sailor's Journal, The, *Anon*, G [g-e''](m), B&H 5 Dibdin.)
Say, little foolish fluttering thing, S&B (Ivimey).

(Then farewell my trim-built wherry, *Anon*, D♭ [a♭-d″*b*](m), B&H 5 Dibdin.)
Tinker's Song, The *Charles Dibdin*, D♭ [d′*b*-f″(e″*b*)](m), B&H (Lane Wilson) *Old English*.
Tom Bowling, *Charles Dibdin*, E♭ [e′*b*-g″], IMP *Parlour Songs*, B&H (Britten) Tom Bowling and other Song Arrangements.

Dickinson, Peter. 1934– BMIC. *See also* App. 2.
Collections: *Four Auden Songs*, Novello; *Songs in Blue*, Novello; *Three Comic Songs*, Novello.
Carry her over the water, *W. H. Auden*, [e′*b*-g″](f), Novello 4 Auden.
Dylan Thomas cycle, A, *Dylan Thomas*, [baritone], Novello.
E. E. Cummings Song Cycle, An, *E. E. Cummings*, [g#-g″*b*], Novello.
Extravaganzas (cycle), *Gregory Corso*, [a♭-g″], Novello.
Eyes look into the well, *W. H. Auden*, [d′-e″ or f″-g″](f), Novello 4 Auden.
Happy Ending, *W. H. Auden*, [d′-g″], Novello 3 Comic.
Let the florid music praise, *W. H. Auden*, [tenor], Novello.
Look, stranger, *W. H. Auden*, [c′-g″](f), Novello 4 Auden.
My second thoughts, *W. H. Auden*, [e′*b*-g″*b*], Novello 3 Comic.
Over the heather, *W. H. Auden*, [e′*b*-f″#](m), Novello 3 Comic.
Red, Red Rose, A, *Robert Burns*, [mezzo], Novello Songs in Blue.
Schubert in Blue, *Shakespeare*, [mezzo], Novello Songs in Blue.
So we'll go no more a-roving, *Lord Byron*, [mezzo], Novello Songs in Blue.
Stevie's Tunes (cycle), *Stevie Smith*, [b-g″], Novello.
Three songs from 'The Unicorns' (cycle), *John Heath-Stubbs*, [c′#-b″](f), Novello.
What's in your mind? *W. H. Auden*, [d′#-g″#(f′#)](f), Novello 4 Auden.

Dieren, Bernard van. 1887–1936. *See also* App. 1.
Collection: *Seven Songs*, Thames (introduction Alastair Chisholm).
Alone in the Wood, *Heinrich Heine* tr. *Oliver Strachey*, [c′#-f″#], BMP.
Balow, my babe, *Anon*, [c′-f″], (f), BMP.
Come, I will sing you some slow sleepy tune, *P. B. Shelley*, [c′#-e″], BMP.
Dream Pedlary, *Thomas Lovell Beddoes*, [d′*b*-f″], Thames 7 Songs.
Every day the wondrous, *Heine* tr. *Calvocoressi*, [b-f″#], BMP.
Holy Three Magi, The, *Goethe* tr. *Calvocoressi*, [c′-a″*b*], BMP.
Last Days, *Walter Savage Landor*, [d′-e″*b*], Thames 7 Songs.
Levana and Our Ladies of Sorrow, *Thomas de Quincey*, [d′#-f″#](f), BMP.
Love must be gone, *Walter Savage Landor*, [d′-g″], BMP.
Mild is the parting year, *Walter Savage Landor*, [c′#-f″], BMP.
New-blown rose a message brings, A, *Otto Julius Bierbaum* tr. *Calvocoressi*, [b-f″], BMP.
Nightpiece, *James Joyce*, [d′-e″*b*], Bardic.
She I love, *Walter Savage Landor*, [d′-g″](m), BMP.
Song from The Cenci: *see* Come, I will sing you some slow sleepy tune.
Spring, *Thomas Nashe*, [e′-a″], Thames 7 Songs.
Spring Song of the Birds, *King James I of Scotland*, [e′*b*-g″] Thames 7 Songs.
Take O take those lips away, *Shakespeare*, [e′*b*-f″], Thames 7 Songs.
Touch of Love, The, *Walter Savage Landor*, [d′#-f″], BMP.
Weep you no more, sad fountains, *Anon*, [d′*b*-a″*b*], Thames 7 Songs.
Weeping and Kissing, *Sir Edward Sherburne*, [d′#-g″](m), Thames 7 Songs.
What is good King Ringang's daughter's name? *Eduard Mörike* tr. *Calvocoressi*, [b-a″], BMP.
With margeraine gentle, *John Skelton*, [e′-e″#], BMP.

Dillon, James. 1950– *See* App. 2.

Dix, J. Airlie. A further 20 songs in B&H archive.
Trumpeter, The, *J. Francis Barron*, C [e′-g″](m), B&H *Ballad Album 1*, B&H; G, *Souvenirs*, B&H; B♭, Cramer *Drawing Room Songs*; A, F, B&H.

Dodgson, Stephen. 1924– BMIC.

Dorward, David Campbell. 1933– SMIC. *See also* App. 2.
Collection: *Five Clare Songs*, SMIC.

Dowland, John. ?1563–1626. *See also* App. 2.
Collections: *The First Book of Ayres*, S&B (edited Thurston Dart); *The Second Book of Songs*, S&B (edited Thurston Dart)]; *The Third Book of Songs*, S&B (edited Thurston Dart); *Pilgrim's Solace, A*, S&B (edited Thurston Dart); *Fifty Songs Books 1a, 1b and 2a, 2b* [high, low], S&B (edited David Scott). Note

Dowland, John

that in the following: Pilkington = *English Lute Songs Book 2,* S&B; Keel 1a, 1b and 2a, 2b = *Elizabethan Lovesongs Books 1 & 2* [high, low] B&H. Only songs available in anthologies are listed individually here.

Awake sweet love, *Anon,* F [e′-f″](m), 1st Book, 50/1a, Pilkington; *D,* 50/1b.

Away with these self-loving lads, *Fulke Greville,* G [d′-e″](m), 1st Book; *A* Keel 2a; *F,* Keel 2b.

Behold a wonder here, *Anon,* G [g′-e″], 3rd Book, BMP *W&W 3.*

Burst forth, my tears, *Anon,* Gm [d′-d″](m), 1st Book, 50/1b; *Bm,* 50/1a.

By a fountain where I lay, *Anon,* Gm [f′#-f″](m), 3rd Book, 50/2a; *Em,* 50/2b.

Can she excuse my wrongs? *Anon,* Dm [d′-d″](m), 1st Book, 50/1b; *Fm,* 50/1a.

Clear or cloudy, *Anon,* G [d′-e″](m), 2nd Book; *Bb,* 50/2a; *F,* 50/2b, Pilkington.

Come again, sweet love doth now invite, *Anon,* G [d′-e″], 1st Book, Keel 1b, B&H (Sidney Northcote) *Imperial 5,* Schirmer *1st Tenor*; *A,* Keel 1a, Paterson (Diack) *100 Best 2*; *Ab,* 50/1a; *F,* 50/1b, Pilkington.

Come away, come sweet love, *Anon,* Gm [f′#-f″], 1st Book, 50/1a, Pilkington, S&B (H. Diack-Johnstone) *Recitalist 2,* Chester (Shavitz) *Celebrated 2*; *Am,* Keel 2a; *Fm,* Keel 2b; *Em,* 50/1b.

Come heavy sleep, *Anon,* G [d′-e″], 1st Book; *A,* 50/1a; *Eb,* 50/1b.

Daphne was not so chaste, *Anon,* F [e′-f″], 3rd Book, Pilkington, BMP *W&W 6.*

Dear, if you change, *Anon,* Am [d′-e″], 1st Book; *Bm,* 50/1a, Keel 1a, *Gm,* 50/1b, Keel 1b.

Disdain me still, *Anon,* G [d′-e″](m), Pilgrim; *Bb,* 50/2a; *F,* 50/2b.

Far from triumphing court, *Sir Henry Lee,* G [d′-e″], Pilgrim, S&B *Banquet,* BMP *W&W 4*; *A,* 50/2a; *F,* 50/2b, Pilkington.

Farewell, unkind, farewell, *Anon,* G [f′#-e″], 3rd Book; *Bb,* 50/2a, Pilkington; *A,* Keel 2a; *F,* 50/2b, Keel 2b.

Fie on this feigning, *Anon,* F [f′-g″], 3rd Book, Pilkington.

Fine knacks for ladies, *Anon,* F [e′-f″](m), 2nd Book, 50/1a, Pilkington, Classical, Keel 1a; *Eb,* Keel 1b, Paterson (Diack) *100 Best 4*; *D,* 50/1b.

Flow my tears, (Lachrimae), *Anon,* Am [d′-e″], 2nd Book, BMP *W&W 4,* Leonard *Baroque low*; *Cm,* 50/1a, Leonard *Baroque high*; *Bm,* B&H *Dolmetsch 2*; *Gm,* 50/1b, Pilkington.

Flow not so fast ye fountains, *Anon,* Gm [g′-g″], 3rd Book, 50/2a, Pilkington; *F#m,* Keel 2a; *Em,* Keel 1b; *Dm,* 50/2b.

Go, crystal tears, *Anon,* Cm [g′-e″b](m), 1st Book; *Dm* 50/1a; *Bm,* 50/1b.

His golden locks, *Anon,* G [f′#-d″], 1st Book; *Bb,* 50 1a; *F,* 50/1b.

I saw my lady weep, *Anon,* Am [e′-e″], 2nd Book, BMP *W&W 1*; *Cm,* 50/1a; *Gm,* 50/1b, Pilkington.

If my complaints could passions move, *Anon,* Gm [f′#-f″], 1st Book, Pilkington, 50/1a, *Em,* 50/1b.

If that a sinner's sighs, *Anon,* Gm [f′#-g″], Pilgrim, 50/2a; *Dm,* 50/2b.

In darkness let me dwell, *Anon,* Am [c′-e″], Pilgrim, S&B *Banquet,* BMP *W&W 1*; *Cm,* 50/2a; *Gm,* 50/2b, Pilkington.

It was a time when silly bees, *Anon,* Dm [d′-e″b], 3rd Book; *Em,* 50/2a; *Cm,* 50/2b.

Lady, if you so spite me, *Anon,* Gm [g′-f″](m), Pilgrim, S&B *Banquet,* 50/2a, Pilkington, BMP *W&W 1*; *Em,* 50/2b.

Love those beams, *Anon,* Gm [f′#-g″], Pilgrim, 50/2a; *Em,* 50/2b.

Lowest trees have tops, The, *Anon,* Gm [d′-d″], 3rd Book; *Bm,* 50/2a; *F#m,* 50/2b.

Me, me, and none but me, *Anon,* G [g′-e″], 3rd Book; *Bb,* 50/2a; *F,* 50/2b.

Mourn! day is with darkness fled, *Anon,* D [d′-d″], 2nd Book; *F,* 50/1a; *C,* 50/1b.

My heart and tongue were twins, *Anon,* Dm [f′-a″], Pilgrim; *Bm,* 50/2a; *Gm,* 50/2b.

My thoughts are winged with hopes, *Anon,* Cm [g′-g″](m), 1st Book, 50/1a; *Gm,* 50/1b.

Now cease my wandering eyes, *Anon,* F [f′-f″], 2nd Book, 50/1a; *D,* 50/1b.

Now, O now I needs must part, *Anon,* G [e′-e″], 1st Book; *A,* 50/1a, Keel 2a; *F,* 50/1b, Keel 2b, Pilkington, Thames (Hodgson) *Countertenors 3.*

O what hath overwrought? *Anon,* Gm [f′#-f″], 3rd Book, 50/2a; *Em,* 50/2b.

Rest awhile, you cruel cares, *Anon,* G [f′#-d″], 1st Book; *Bb* 50/1a; *F,* 50/1b.

Say love if ever thou didst find, *Anon,* G [f′#-d″], 3rd Book, 50/2b; *Bb,* 50/2a.

Shall I strive with words to move? *Anon,* Em [e′-d″](m), Pilgrim, 50/2b; *Am,* 50/2a.

Shall I sue? *Anon,* Gm [g′-g″], 2nd Book, 50/2a, Pilkington, S&B (H. Diack Johnstone) *Recitalist 3*; *F#m,* Keel 2a; *Dm,* 50/2b, Keel 2b.

Shepherd in a shade, A, *Anon,* G [d′-d″], 2nd Book, 50/1b, Keel 1b; *B,* 50/1a; *Bb,* Keel 1a.

Sleep, wayward thoughts, *Anon,* G [g′-e″], 1st Book; *A,* 50/1a; *Eb,* 50/1b, Pilkington.

Sorrow, stay, *Anon,* Gm [d′-d″], 2nd Book, Keel 2b, BMP *W&W 5*; *Bm,* 50/1a, Keel 2a; *Fm,* 50/1b, Pilkington.

Stay time awhile thy flying, *Anon,* Am [e′-d″], Pilgrim, Keel 2b; *Cm,* Keel 2a.

Sweet stay awhile, *John Donne?* Am [e′-e″], Pilgrim; *Cm,* 50/2a; *Gm,* 50/2b, Pilkington.

Tell me, true love, *Anon,* Gm [d′-d″], Pilgrim, 50/2b; *Bm,* 50/2a.

Time stands still, *Anon,* G [g′-d″](m), 3rd Book, BMP *W&W 3*; *Bb,* 50/2a; *F,* 50/2b, Pilkington.

To ask for all thy love, *Anon,* Gm [e′-g″], Pilgrim, Pilkington.

Toss not my soul, *Anon*, Gm [f'#-f''], 2nd Book, Pilkington.
Unquiet thoughts, *Anon*, Gm [f'-e''*b*](m), 1st Book; *Am*, 50/1a, *Fm*, 50/1b.
Weep you no more, sad fountains, *Anon*, Gm [d'-g''], 3rd Book, 50/2a, Pilkington, Leonard *Baroque high*; F#m, Keel 2a; *Dm*, 50/2b, Leonard *Baroque low*; *Em*, Keel 2b.
Were every thought an eye, *Anon*, Cm [g'-g''], Pilgrim, 50/2a; *Gm*, 50/2b.
What if I never speed? *Anon*, Am [e'-f''], 3rd Book, 50/2, Pilkington, Leonard *Baroque high*; *Bm*, Keel 2a; *Gm*, Keel 2b; *Fm*, 50/2b, Leonard *Baroque low*.
When Phoebus first did Daphne love, *Anon*, G [g'-e''](m), 3rd Book, Pilkington.
Where sin sore wounding, *Anon*, Gm [a'-a''], Pilgrim; *Fm*, 50/2a; *Dm*, 50/2b.
White as lilies was her face, *Anon*, Gm [g'-f''], 2nd Book, 50/1a; *Em*, 50/1b.
Whoever thinks or hopes of love, *Fulke Greville*, Gm [f'-g''], 1st Book, 50/1a; *Fm* B&H (Northcote) *Imperial* 2; Dm, 50/1b.
Wilt thou, unkind, thus reave me? *Anon*, Am [e'-e''], 1st Book; *Bm*, 50/1a; *Fm*, 50/1b.

Downes, Andrew. 1950– *See also* App. 2.
Collections: *Casterbridge Fair, Op 1,* Lynwood; *Old Love's Domain, Op 29,* Lynwood; *Songs from Spoon River, Op 39,* Lynwood.
After the Club Dance, *Thomas Hardy,* [d-e'](m), [d'-e''](f), Lynwood Casterbridge.
After the Fair, *Thomas Hardy,* [d-g'(f')](m), [d'-g''(f')](f), Lynwood Casterbridge.
At Castle Boterel, *Thomas Hardy,* [d'-g''], Lynwood Old Love.
Ballad Singer, The, *Thomas Hardy,* [c*b*-e'*b*](m), [c'*b*-e''*b*](f), Lynwood Casterbridge.
Curtains now are drawn, The, *Thomas Hardy,* [f'-a''], Lynwood Old Love.
Division, The, *Thomas Hardy,* [c'-f''], Lynwood Old Love.
Dora Williams, *Edgar Lee Masters,* [d'-g''*b*](f), Lynwood Spoon River.
Former Beauties, *Thomas Hardy,* [d-f'](m), [d'-f''](f), Lynwood Casterbridge.
Ollie McGee, *Edgar Lee Masters,* [e'*b*-f''](f), Lynwood Spoon River.
Rebecca Wasson, *Edgar Lee Masters,* [e'*b*-f''#](f), Lynwood Spoon River.
Russian Sonia, *Edgar Lee Masters,* [d'-f''](f), Lynwood Spoon River.
Sarah Brown, *Edgar Lee Masters,* [e'-d''#](f), Lynwood Spoon River.
Something tapped, *Thomas Hardy,* [d'-g''], Lynwood Old Love.
Where the Picnic Was, *Thomas Hardy,* [e'*b*-a''*b*], Lynwood Old Love.
Wife Waits, A, *Thomas Hardy,* [c-e'](m), [c'-e''](f), Lynwood Casterbridge.

Doyle, Patrick. *See* App. 1.

Dring, Madeleine. 1923–1977. BMIC.
Collections: *Dedications,* Thames; *Five Betjeman Songs,* Weinberger; *Four Night Songs,* Thames /Cambria; *Love and Time,* Thames; *Seven Shakespeare Songs,* Thames; *Seven Songs,* Thames; *Six Songs,* Thames (introductions to Thames volumes Roger Lord); *Three Shakespeare Songs,* Lengnick; *Two Comedy Numbers,* Micropress; *Two Show Songs,* Micropress; *Two More Show Songs,* Micropress; *Two Songs,* Micropress. Note: Micropress publications can be supplied in a wide range of keys.
Ah, how sweet it is to love, *John Dryden,* [d'-a''](f), Thames Love and Time.
Bay in Anglesey, A, *John Betjeman,* C [b-f''(g'')], Weinberger 5 Betjeman.
Blind Boy, The, *Colley Cibber,* Em [b-e''(g'')], Lord.
Blow, blow thou winter wind, *Shakespeare,* Gm [d'*b*-f''], Thames 7 Shakespeare, Lengnick 3 Shakespeare.
Business Girls, *John Betjeman,* D [d'-f''#], Weinberger 5 Betjeman.
Cherry Blooming, The, *Joseph Ellison,* Gm [b*b*(d')-g''], Thames 6 Songs.
Come away, come sweet love, *Anon,* C [c'#-d''], Thames 7 Songs.
Come away, death, *Shakespeare,* Am [d'-e''], Thames 7 Shakespeare, Lengnick 3 Shakespeare.
Come live with me, *Christopher Marlowe,* [c'-f''(g)], Micropress 2 Songs.
Crabbed age and youth, *Shakespeare,* F [f'-f''](f), Thames 7 Shakespeare.
Cuckoo, The, *Shakespeare,* F [b-g''*b*], Thames 7 Shakespeare.
Devout Lover, A, *Thomas Randolph,* F [a-c''#](m), Thames 7 Songs.
Don't play your sonata tonight, Mr Humphries, *Madeleine Dring,* [a-a''], Micropress.
Echoes, *Thomas Moore,* F#m [e'#-a''], Thames 6 Songs.
Elegy on the Death of a Mad Dog, *Oliver Goldsmith,* Am [d'-e''], Lord.
Enchantment, The, *Thomas Otway,* Gm [c'-g''], Thames 6 Songs.
Encouragements to a Lover, *Sir John Suckling,* E [b-e''], Thames 7 Songs.
Everything detestable is best, *Charlotte Mitchell,* [b-e''], Micropress 2 More Show Songs.
Faithless Lover, The, *Anon,* Dm [c'-g''*b*](m), Thames 7 Songs.
Fly, fly, you happy shepherds, *Sir John Vanbrough,* Bm [b-d''], Lord.
Frosty Night, *Michael Armstrong,* Gm [c'#-g''], Thames 4 Night Songs.
High in the pines, *Sean Rafferty,* [e'-f''#], Micropress 2 Show Songs.

Holding the Night, *Michael Armstrong*, [d′(b♭)-g′′(b′′♭)], Thames 4 Night Songs.
I feed a flame within, *John Dryden*, Gm [e′♭-a′′](f), Thames Love and Time.
I should have trusted you, *D. F. Aitken*, [d′-e′′], Micropress.
It was a lover, *Shakespeare*, E [b-e′′(g′′#)], Thames 7 Shakespeare.
I've brought you away, *Madeleine Dring*, [d′-g′′], Micropress 2 Show Songs.
I've found the Proms, *Madeleine Dring*, [c′-f′′], Micropress Comedy.
Love is a sickness, *Samuel Daniel*, [c′-a′′♭], Thames 6 Songs.
Love Lyric, *Joseph Ellison*, Em [d′-g′′], Lord.
Melisande, The Far-away Princess, *D. F. Aitken*, Gm [f′-f′′](m), Thames 7 Songs.
Model Models, The, *Charlotte Mitchell*, [spoken], Micropress 2 Comedy.
My heart is like a singing bird, *Christina Rossetti*, G [d′-b′′], Lord.
My proper Bess, *John Skelton*, [b♭-d′′](m), Thames 7 Songs.
My true love hath my heart, *Philip Sidney*, A [c′#-a′′](f), Thames 6 Songs.
O lovely nymph, the world's on fire, *Sir John Vanbrough*, G [d′-d′′], Lord.
Parting, The, *Michael Drayton*, C [b(c′)-a′′♭], Thames 6 Songs.
Reconcilement, The, *John Sheffield, Duke of Buckinghamshire*, [c′-a′′](f), Thames Love and Time.
Separation, *Michael Armstrong*, Cm [d′-g′′], Thames 4 Night Songs.
Sister, awake, *Bateson*, [e′♭-b′′♭](f), Thames Love and Time.
Slumber Song, *Joseph Ellison*, E♭ [d′♭-b′′♭], Lord.
Snowman, *Charlotte Mitchell*, [d′-f′′#], Micropress 2 More Show Songs.
Song of a Nightclub Proprietress, *John Betjeman*, Gm [b-e′′♭](f), Weinberger 5 Betjeman.
Take O take those lips away, *Shakespeare*, [g-d′′], Thames 7 Shakespeare.
There's nothing to stop us now, *D. F. Aitken*, [d′-g′′], Micropress.
Through the Centuries, *Michael Armstrong*, E♭ [b♭-g′′#], Thames 4 Night Songs.
To Daffodils, *Robert Herrick*, [f′-f′′], Thames Dedications.
To Music – to becalm a sweetsick youth, *Robert Herrick*, [d′-g′′], Thames Dedications.
To Phyllis – to love and live with him, *Robert Herrick*, A [e′-g′′](m),Thames Dedications.
To the Virgins – to make much of time, *Robert Herrick*, D [c′#-g′′], Thames Dedications.
To the Willow Tree, *Robert Herrick*, G [f′-g′′♭], Thames Dedications.
Undenominational, *John Betjeman*, Gm [d′-g′′], Weinberger 5 Betjeman.
Under the greenwood tree, *Shakespeare*, C [b♭-f′′], Thames 7 Shakespeare, Lengnick 3 Shakespeare.
Upper Lambourne, *John Betjeman*, B♭ [d′-g′′(b′′♭)], Weinberger 5 Betjeman.
Weep you no more, sad fountains, *Anon*, Cm [c′-c′′], Thames 7 Songs.
What a pother of late, *Sir John Vanbrough*, G [d′-e′′(g′′)], Lord.
What I fancy, *Robert Herrick*, [a-d′′], Micropress 2 Songs/EPSS.
When yielding first to Damon's flame, *Sir John Vanbrough*, G [d′-d′′], Lord.

Dubery, David. BMIC.
Birds, The, *Hilaire Belloc*, [a#-c′′#], Banks.

Duff, Arthur K.
Who is Sylvia? *Shakespeare,* [e′♭-g′′], BMP.

Dunhill, Thomas Frederick. 1877–1946.
Collection: (*Four Songs from Vagabondia*, Novello).
April, *Margaret Rose*, F [f′-f′′], Cramer; (A♭, Cramer).
April Rain, *Robert Loveman*, F [b-f′′(a′′)], B&H; (A♭, B&H).
(Child o' mine, *Alfred H. Hyatt*, F, B&H; A♭, B&H.)
Child's Song of Praise, A, *Lizette Woodworth Reese*, F [f′-d′′], Cramer.
Cloths of Heaven, The, *W. B. Yeats*, E♭ [E♭-g′′], S&B/Classical, Schirmer *1st Tenor II*; C, S&B/Classical.
Dandelion, The, *Anon*, G [d′-g′′], S&B; *F*, S&B.
Evening, *Anon*, E♭ [c′-e′′♭], Cramer.
Fiddler of Dooney, The, *W. B. Yeats*, D [d′-g′′], Classical.
Gifts, *James Thomson*, E♭ [b♭-e′′♭(m), Cramer.
Go, pretty birds, *Thomas Heywood*, D [a-d′′], Cramer.
(Happy Man, The, *Harvey Braban*, C [b(g)-e′′](m), Chappell; B♭ [d′-a′′](m), Chappell.)
Haymakers' Roundelay, The, *Anon*, D [c′#-f′′#], S&B.
Holy Babe, The, *William Canton*, E♭ [d′-g′′], Cramer.
(How soft upon the evening air, *Irene Gass*, E [b-c′′#],William Elkin; A, William Elkin, G, Curwen.)
I can hear a cuckoo, *Margaret Rose*, F [f′-g′′], Cramer.
I remember, *Thomas Hood*, D [e′-a′′](m), Cramer.
I think of you, *J. W. Groves,* Cramer.

If ever I marry at all, Cramer.
In the Dawn, *Ida M Stenning*, F#m [d'#-f''#], Cramer.
(Infant Joy, *William Blake*, B&H.)
John Peel, *J. W. Groves*, Cramer.
(Karroo Cradle Song, *Margaret Rose*, F [c'-f''], Paxton.
Little Town of Bethlehem, *Phillips Brooks*, Eb [c'-g''], Cramer; C, Cramer.
Quiet Night, The, *John Irvine*, Cramer.
Ride Straight, *J. W. Groves*, Cramer.
(Sleep sweet babe, *S. T. Coleridge*, B&H.)
Suffolk Owl, The, *Anon*, Ab [e'b-f''], Cramer; Bb, Cramer.
Sweet July, *Margaret Rose*, F [e'-f''], Cramer.
Three fine ships, *Margaret Rose*, D [a-d''(f''#)], Cramer *Folio 1*; C, Cramer.
To dance and sing, *A. P. Herbert*, Cramer.
To the Queen of Heaven, *Anon*, Dm [c'-g''], Thames *Century 3*.
Visit from the Moon, A, *J. Stevens*, Bb [b-f''], Cramer.

Duxbury, Rosemary. BMIC.

Dyson, Sir George. 1883–1964.
Collection: *Three Songs to Julia*, Thames.
Night Piece, *Robert Herrick*, D [c'#-e''](m), Thames Julia.
Poet's Hymn, A, *Robert Herrick*, C [c'-g''(e'')], Cramer.
Sweet, be not proud, *Robert Herrick*, D [d'-e''](m), Thames Julia.
When I behold a forest spread, *Robert Herrick*, D [c'#-e''](m), Thames Julia.
Wife of Bath, The, *Geoffrey Chaucer*, G [d'-b''b](f), Thames.

E

East, Leslie. 1949–
Collection: *Three Betjeman Songs*, S&B.
Harrow-on-the-hill, *John Betjeman*, [c'#-g''], S&B 3 Betjeman.
Metropolitan Railway, The, *John Betjeman* [c'-f''], S&B 3 Betjeman.
Middlesex, *John Betjeman*, Ab [c'-a''b], S&B 3 Betjeman.

Eccles, John. c.1668–1735.
Collection: *Eight Songs*, S&B (edited Michael Pilkington).
Ah, whither shall I fly, *Anon*, Em [d'-g''](f), S&B 8 Songs.
As Cupid roguishly one day, *the Hon. C. B.*, F [c'-g''], B&H (Keel) *12 18th Century*.
Belinda, *Anon*, C [b-f''](m), S&B (Pilkington) *Early Georgian 1*.
Fair Amoret is gone astray, *William Congreve*, C [c'-f''], B&H (Keel) *12 18th Century*.
Find me a lonely cave, *W. Porter*, Gm [bb-f''], S&B (Pilkington) *Early Georgian 1, Recitalist 4*.
Foolish maid, The, *John Crowne*, Am [e'-g''], S&B 8 Songs.
Haste, give me wings, *Anon*, D [d'-g''](f), Voicebox *Mad Songs 2*.
I burn, I burn, *Thomas D'Urfey*, Em [d'#-g''](f), Thames (Bevan) *8 Restoration*, Voicebox *Mad Songs 1*.
I gently touched her hand, *Anon*, Fm [e'b-f''](m), S&B 8 Songs.
If I hear Orinda swear, *Burnaby*, Em [d'-g''], S&B 8 Songs.
Jolly jolly breeze, The, *Anon*, G [b-e''], S&B (Pilkington) *Early Georgian 1*, Schirmer *2nd Mezzo*; Bb, B&H (Keel) *12 18th Century*.
Love's but the frailty of the mind, *William Congreve*, Dm [c'-g''](f), S&B (Pilkington) *Early Georgian 2*.
Must then a faithful lover go? *Peter Anthony Motteux*, Cm [c'-g''](f), Voicebox *Mad Songs 1*.
Nature framed thee, *William Congreve*, Gm [d'-g''](f), S&B 8 Songs.
Nymph and a swain, A, *William Congreve*, D [d'-g''](f), S&B 8 Songs.
Oh! take him gently from the pile, *John Banks*, Dm [d'-g''](f), Voicebox *Mad Songs 1*.
So well Corinna likes the joy, *George Grenville, Lord Lansdowne*, Am [e'-g''], S&B 8 Songs.
Sylvia, how could you, *John Dryden*, Am [d'#-g''], S&B 8 Songs.

Edgar, Alison. 1927–
Fluctuations, *Anne Brontë*, [bb-f''], EPSS.

Edwards, Gabe.
Pair of shoes, A, [any voice], Snell.

Edwards, Henry Oliver. 1902–1979. WMIC.
Fiddler of Pendine, The, *J. T. Jôb* tr. *G. Islwyn Williams* [d′-e′′b], Gwynn.
Winter it is past, The, *Anon*, Gm [d′-e′′b], Gwynn.

Edwards, Paul.
Cloths of Heaven, The, *W. B. Yeats,* D [d′-f′′#](f)], Micropress.

Edwards, Thomas David. 1859–1907
Cymru land of mine, *Rev. T. Gwilym Jones* tr. *T. D. Edwards.* [soprano], Snell.

Elgar, Sir **Edward** William. 1857–1934. *See also* App. 2.
Collections: *Elgar Song Album, An,* Novello (introduction Gerald Northrop Moore); *Four Songs from 'The Fringes of the Fleet',* [high, low], Classical/(Enoch); *Sea Pictures,* B&H; *Thirteen Songs Books 1 & 2,* Thames.
    After, *Philip Bourke Marston,* Fm [c′-d′′b], B&H; Gm, Am, B&H.
    Always and everywhere, *Zygmunt Krasinski* tr. *F. E. Fortey,* Cm [f′-f′′(g′′)](m), B&H.
    Arabian Serenade, *Margery Lawrence,* Gm [f′-g′′](m), B&H.
    Blue-eyes fairy, The, *Algernon Blackwood,* Eb [bb-f′′(e′′b)], Novello Album.
    Chariots of the Lord, The, *John Brownlie,* Db [d′′b-f′′], B&H; Eb, B&H.
    Child Asleep, A, *Elizabeth Barrett Browning,* Eb [d′-e′′b], Novello Album.
    (Come, gentle night, *G. Clifton Bingham,* C [a(b)-e′′(d′′)], B&H; D, Eb, B&H.)
    Dry those fair, those crystal tears, *Henry King,* G [f′#-e′′], Thames 13 Songs 2.
    Fate's Discourtesy, *Rudyard Kipling,* C [e′-e′′] Classical 4 Fringes; Bb, Classical 4 Fringes.
    In Haven, *Caroline Alice Elgar,* C [c′-c′′](f), B&H Sea Pictures, (B&H); Eb, B&H.
    In Moonlight, *Percy Bysshe Shelley,* F [c′(f′)-f′′)], Novello Album; (Eb, G, Novello).
    In the Dawn, *Arthur C. Benson,* C [c′-e′′](m), Thames 13 Songs 2; Eb, E, B&H.
    Is she not passing fair? *Charles D'Orleans,* tr. *Louisa Stuart Costello,* G [f′#-a′′], B&H *Heritage 2, Imperial 4*; F, Thames 13 Songs 2; D, B&H.
    King's Way, The, *Caroline Alice Elgar,* G [d′-e′′(a′′)], B&H; (F, Ab, B&H)
    Land of hope and glory, *Arthur C. Benson,* C [c′-f′′], B&H; Bb, D, Classical/B&H.
    Like to the damask rose, *Simon Wastell,* Bbm [bb(d′b)-g′′], Thames 13 Songs 1, William Elkin, (Chappell *English Recital 2*).
    Lowestoft Boat, The, *Rudyard Kipling,* D [d′-f′′#(g)], Classical 4 Fringes; C, Classical 4 Fringes.
    Modest and fair, *Ben Jonson,* Eb [d′-e′′b], Novello (Percy M. Young) Album.
    My Old Tunes, *Algernon Blackwood,* Bb [d′-e′′b], Novello Album.
    Oh, soft was the song, *Gilbert Parker,* E [b-f′′#], Novello Album.
    Pipes of Pan, The, *Adrian Ross,* Am [c′-e′′(d′′)](m), Thames 13 Songs 2; Bm B&H, (Gm, B&H.)
    Pleading, *Arthur L. Salmon,* G [d′-f′′#], Novello Album, Novello; (F, Ab, Novello.)
    Poet's Life, The, *Ellen Burroughs,* F [d′-a′′(g′′)], Thames 13 Songs 1.
    Queen Mary's Song, *Alfred Lord Tennyson,* Gm [d′-a′′](f), Banks, Thames 13 Songs 1.
    River, The, *Pietro d'Alba (Edward Elgar),* Am [c′(b)-g′′](m), Novello Album.
    Rondel, *Longfellow,* Bb [e′(d′)-a′′(g′′)], Banks, Thames 13 Songs 1.
    Sabbath Morning at Sea, *E. B. Browning,* C [b(c′)-g′′(e′′)](f), B&H Sea Pictures, B&H; Bb, B&H.
    Sea Slumber Song, *Roden Noel,* Em [g(b)-d′′](f), B&H Sea Pictures, (B&H).
    Shepherd's Song, The, *Barry Pain,* F [e′-a′′], Banks, Thames 13 Songs 1, (Chappell *English Recital 1*; Eb, Chappell).
    Song of Autumn, A, *Adam Lindsay Gordon,* F [f′-a′′(f′)], Thames 13 Songs 1.
    Song of Flight, A, *Christina Rossetti,* Ab [d′-e′′b], B&H.
    Song of Liberty, The, *A. P. Herbert,* Eb [bb-e′′b], B&H.
    Speak, music, *Arthur C. Benson,* Bb [e′b-f′′], B&H *Heritage 1*; A, Thames 13 Songs 2; (C, B&H),
    Speak, my heart, *Arthur C. Benson,* C [e′-f′′], B&H.
    Still to be neat, *Ben Jonson,* E [b′-e′′], Novello (Percy M. Young) Album.
    Submarines, *Rudyard Kipling,* Dm [d′-f′′], Classical 4 Fringes; Cm, Classical 4 Fringes.
    Sweepers, The, *Rudyard Kipling,* C [e′-e′′], Classical 4 Fringes; Bb, Classical 4 Fringes.
    Swimmer, The, *Adam Lindsay Gordon,* D [a(b)-a′′(f′)](f), B&H Sea Pictures, (B&H).
    There are seven that pull the thread, *W. B. Yeats,* Em [e′-d′′], Novello Album.
    Through the long days, *John Hay,* C [g′-a′′](m), Thames 13 Songs 1.
    To the Children, *Algernon Blackwood,* Bb [c′-f′′(e′′)], Novello Album.
    Torch, The, *Pietro d'Alba (Edward Elgar),* G [d′-e′′(g′′)], Novello Album, Novello; A, Novello.
    Twilight, *Gilbert Parker,* Bm [e′-d′′], Novello Album.
    War song, A, *C. Flavell Hayward,* Dm [f#(g#)-e′′] Thames *Century 6*, B&H.

Was it some golden star? *Gilbert Parker*, C#m [c'#-e''](m), Novello Album.
Where Corals Lie, *Richard Garnett*, Bm [b(d')-d''](f), B&H Sea Pictures, Classical/B&H, Schirmer *2nd Mezzo*; Dm, Classical (B&H).
Wind at Dawn, The, *Caroline Alice Elgar*, Fm [c'-g''(a'')], Thames 13 Songs 2, B&H.

Elias, Brian. 1948– *See also* App. 1, 2.
Collection: *Two Songs,* [soprano], Chester.
At the edge of time (cycle), *Mervyn Peake*, [c'-b''b](m), Chester hire.

Elliott, Michael. WMIC. *See also* App. 2.

Elliott, Zo.
There's a long, long trail a-winding, *Stoddard King,* Ab [e'b-e''b], IMP *Parlour Songs.*

Ellis, Mark. *See* App. 2.

Elton, Antony. 1935– WMIC. *See also* App. 2.
Music, *Percy Bysshe Shelley,* [c'-f''], EPSS.

Elwyn-Edwards, Dilys. 1918– WMIC. *See also* App. 2.
Collections: *Bro a Mynydd*, WMIC; *In Faery,* Gwynn; *Reflections,* Curiad; *Six Songs for Children*, [d'b-f''], Gwynn; *Songs of the Seasons,* Curiad; *Songs of the Three Birds*, Gwynn.
Autumn, Curiad Seasons.
Berwyn, *Robert Ellis* tr. *John Stoddart,* C [c'-g''(e'')], WMIC Bro a Mynydd.
Beside the wide Menai, Curiad Reflections.
Cloths of Heaven, The, *W. B. Yeats,* D [d'-e''], Roberton.
Curlew, The, [soprano/tenor], Gwynn 3 Birds.
Duckling, The, *I. D. Hooson,* tr. *Wil Ifan,* C, Gwynn 6 for Children.
Eifionydd, *R. Williams Parry* tr. *John Stoddart,* Dm [a-e''], WMIC Bro a Mynydd, *Songs from Wales 2.*
Fairy Hunt, A, *Francis Ledwidge*, C [e'-a''b], Gwynn In Faery.
Find, The, *Francis Ledwidge,* Gm [d'-a''], Gwynn In Faery.
Gold Headed Gitto, *I. D. Hooson,* tr. *Wil Ifan,* D, Gwynn 6 for Children.
Golden Hair, *I. D. Hooson,* tr. *Wil Ifan,* F, Gwynn 6 for Children.
I saw three ships, Curiad.
Isle of Avalon, The, Curiad Reflections
Merry Margaret, *John Skelton,* F [f'-g''], Gwynn.
Morris the Wind, *I. D. Hooson,* tr. *Wil Ifan,* Em, Gwynn 6 for Children.
Noël, Curiad Reflections.
Owls, The, [soprano/tenor], Gwynn 3 Birds.
Pilgrim's Isle, The, Curiad Reflections.
Rabbits, *I. D. Hooson,* tr. *Wil Ifan,* E, Gwynn 6 for Children.
Rowan Tree,The, Gwynn.
Spring, Curiad Seasons.
Summer, Curiad Seasons.
Sweet Suffolk owl, *Thomas Vautor,* [soprano/tenor], Gwynn.
Tell us, Mary, Curiad Reflections.
There's longing in the sea, [soprano/tenor], Gwynn 3 Birds.
Two Fat Geese, The, *I. D. Hooson,* tr. *Wil Ifan,* G, Gwynn 6 for Children.
Wife of Lleu, The, *Francis Ledwidge,* F [d'-g''], Gwynn In Faery.
Winter, Curiad Seasons.

Evans, Christmas E. (Wynalaw).
Casabianca, *Elias Hughes* tr. *Rev. A. E. Jones,* [baritone], Snell.

Evans, D. Pughe. 1866–1897.
(Lead, kindly light, *Cardinal Newman,* F [d'-f''(g'')], Novello.)
Old Minstrel, The, *Myfyr Emlyn* tr. *B. Parry,* [soprano/tenor], Snell; [contralto/baritone], Snell.
Sweet Memories, *Maggie Griffiths,* [soprano/tenor], Snell.
Wreckers of Dunraven, *Watkyn Wyn* tr. *D. J. Snell,* [baritone], Snell.

Evans, David. 1874–1948.
Awake, *Omar Khayyám* tr. *Fitzgerald,* [contralto], Snell.
Maesaleg, *Dafydd ap Gwilym,* tr. *Wil Ifan,* C [c'-d''](m), BMP; F, BMP.

Evans, Elizabeth Myfanwy. WMIC. *See also* App. 2.

Evans, Emlyn.
Oh holy man of sorrows, [contralto/bass], Snell.

Evans, T. Hopkin. 1879–1940.
Aphrodite, *Sappho*, tr. *H Idris Bell*, Eb [c'(b)-a''b(b'')], Gwynn.
Jesus, lover of my soul, *Charles Wesley*, [any voice], Snell.
Through doors ajar, *R. H. Jones* tr. *R. H. Jones & T. Hopkin Evans*, Gm [c'-f''(g'')], Gwynn.

Evans, W. Trevor.
Home, *J. Boncath Evans*, [soprano/tenor; contralto/baritone], Snell.
Long ago, *W. Trevor Evans*, [contralto/baritone], Snell.

F

Farrar, Ernest Bristow. 1885–1918.
Collections: (*Two Pastorals*, Novello); (*Two Songs*, Novello); *Vagabond Songs Op 10*, S&B.
Brittany, *E. V. Lucas*, Eb [bb'-e''b], Thames *Century 4*; G, Novello; (F, Novello).
(Come you, Mary, *Norman Gale*, Novello 2 Pastorals.)
(Diaphenia, *Henry Chettle* or *Henry Constable*, G [b-e''], Novello 2 Songs; Bb, Novello 2 Songs)
(Lover's Appeal, The, *Sir Thomas Wyatt*, Dm [b-d''], Novello 2 Songs; Fm, Novello 2 Songs)
(O mistress mine, *Shakespeare*, Ab [e'b-a''b](m), Novello.)
Roadside fire, The, *Robert Louis Stevenson*, Bb [d'-f''], S&B Vagabond.
Silent noon, *D. G. Rossetti*, [bb-d''], Thames *Century 6*, S&B Vagabond.
Wanderer's song, The, *Arthur Symons*, A [c'-e''](m), S&B Vagabond.
(Who would shepherd pipes forsake, *Norman Gale*, Novello 2 Pastorals.)
Arrangements:
Bonny at morn, *Anon*, [f'-g''], BMP.
Willow tree, The, *Anon*, [d'-e''], BMP.

Ferguson, Howard. 1908–1999
Collections: *Discovery*, B&H; (*Three Mediaeval Carols*, Curwen).
Babylon, *Denton Welch*, Gm [g'-e''], B&H Discovery.
(Cherry-tree Carol, The, *Anon*, Gm [f'-a''b], Curwen 3 Carols.)
Discovery, *Denton Welch*, Ebm [f'-g''], B&H Discovery.
Dreams Melting, *Denton Welch*, Dm [f'#-g''(a'')], B&H Discovery.
(Falcon, The, *Anon*, Fm [e'b-g''], Curwen 3 Carols.)
Freedom of the City, The, *Denton Welch*, Am [e'-f''#], B&H Discovery.
(I saw three ships, *Anon*, Bb [e'-g''], Curwen 3 Carols.)
Jane Allen, *Denton Welch*, Dm [f'#-g''], B&H Discovery.
Love and Reason, *William Golding*, G [b-b''](m), Banks; *C*, Banks.
Lyke-wake Dirge, A, *Anon*, F#m [a-f''#](m), B&H.
Twa Corbies, *Anon*, C# [A#-c'#](m), B&H; E, B&H.
Arrangements: *Five Irish Songs*, B&H 1956.
Apron of Flowers, The, *Anon*, Db [c'-d''b](f), B&H, B&H 5 Irish Songs.
Calen-o, *Anon*, F [c'-c''], B&H 5 Irish Songs.
I'm from over the mountain, *Anon*, Ab [e'b-e''b](m), B&H 5 Irish Songs.
My grandfather died, *Anon*, Db [bb-d''b], B&H 5 Irish Songs.
Swan, The, *Anon*, Bb [bb-e''b](m), B&H 5 Irish Songs.

Ferneyhough, Brian. 1943– *See* App. 2.

Ferrabosco, Alfonso. *c*.1575–1628.
Collection: *Ayres*, S&B (edited E. H. Fellowes). Only songs available in anthologies are listed individually here.
Come, my Celia, *Ben Jonson*, F [c'-e''b](m), Ayres, BMP *W&W 2*.
Drown not with tears, *Anon*, G [d'-f''], Ayres, S&B (Pilkington) *Lute Songs 1*.
Fain I would but O I dare not, *Anon*, G [d'-f''](m), Ayres, S&B (Pilkington) *Lute Songs 1*, BMP *W&W 2*.
I am a lover, but was never loved, *Anon*, G [g'-g''], Ayres, BMP *W&W 2*.

Like hermit poor, *Sir Walter Raleigh?* Gm [d´-e´´b], Ayres, S&B (Pilkington) *Lute Songs 1*, BMP *W&W 2*.
O eyes, O mortal stars, *Anon,* F [f´-g´´], Ayres, BMP *W&W 2*.
Shall I seek to ease my grief? *Anon,* Gm [g´-g´´], Ayres, BMP *W&W 2*.
So, so, leave off this last lamenting kiss, *John Donne,* G [d´-f´´], Ayres, BMP *W&W 2*.
Unconstant love, *Anon,* Cm [g´-g´´], Ayres, S&B (Pilkington) *Lute Songs 1,* BMP *W&W 2*.
Young and simple though I am, *Thomas Campion,* G [g´-g´´](f), Ayres, S&B (Pilkington) *Lute Songs 1*.

Field, Christopher. 1940–
Sleep, little babe, I love thee, *Alfred Noyes,* Fm [c´-f´´], B&H *Easy Song.*

Fielden, T. P. BMIC.

Findlay, Stuart.
Collection: *Five Shakespeare Songs,* B&H 1949.
Current with the gentle murmur glides, The, *Shakespeare,* [c´-e´´], B&H 5 Shakespeare.
How sweet the moonlight, *Shakespeare,* [e´b-e´´b], B&H 5 Shakespeare.
It was a lover and his lass, *Shakespeare,* [d´-e´´b], B&H *Shakespeare Album,* 5 Shakespeare.
Poor soul sat sighing, The, *Shakespeare,* [d´-e´´], B&H *Shakespeare Album,* 5 Shakespeare.
Under the greenwood tree, *Shakespeare,* Eb [d´-e´´], B&H 5 Shakespeare.

Finlay, David. SMIC.
59 (white guardians of the universe of sleep), SMIC.

Finnissy, Michael Peter. 1946–   *See* App. 2.

Finzi, Gerald Raphael. 1901–1956. *see also* App. 2.
Collections: *Before and After Summer,* B&H; *Earth and Air and Rain,* B&H; *I Said to Love,* B&H; *Let us Garlands Bring,* B&H; *Oh Fair to See,* B&H; *Till Earth Outwears,* B&H; *To a Poet,* B&H; *Young Man's Exhortation, A,* B&H.
Amabel, *Thomas Hardy,* Eb [bb-e´´b](m), B&H Before and After.
As I lay in the early sun, *Edward Shanks,* E [c´#-g´´#], B&H Oh Fair to See.
At a Lunar Eclipse, *Thomas Hardy,* Bm [e´-a´´], B&H Till Earth Outwears.
At Middle-field Gate in February, *Thomas Hardy,* G#m [b-e´´](m), B&H I Said to Love.
Before and After Summer, *Thomas Hardy,* Db [ab-f´´(e´´b)](m), B&H Before and After.
Birthnight, The, *Walter de la Mare,* Db [d´b-e´´], B&H To a Poet.
Boy Johnny, *Christina Rossetti,* G [d´-g´´(e´´)], B&H *Easy Song.*
Budmouth Dears, *Thomas Hardy,* F#m [c´#-a´´](m), B&H Young Man.
Channel Firing, *Thomas Hardy,* Cm [g(bb)-f´´](m), B&H Before and After, *Heritage 3.*
Childhood Among the Ferns, *Thomas Hardy,* Eb [bb-f´´](m), B&H Before and After.
Clock of the Years, The, *Thomas Hardy,* Am [f#(a)-f´´#(e)](m), B&H Earth and Air and Rain.
Come away, death, *Shakespeare,* Bm [a#-d´´], B&H Let us Garlands, *Heritage 3.*
Comet at Yell'ham, The, *Thomas Hardy,* [d´-g´´](m), B&H Young Man.
Dance Continued, The, *Thomas Hardy,* Dm [c´(d´)-g´´](m), B&H Young Man.
Ditty, *Thomas Hardy,* G [d´-g´´](m), B&H Young Man.
Epeisodia, *Thomas Hardy,* G [b-e´´](m), B&H Before and After.
Fear no more the heat o' the sun, *Shakespeare,* Bb [bb-e´´b], B&H Let us Garlands, *Heritage 3.*
Ferry me across the water, *Christina Rossetti,* Am [c´-e´´], B&H *Easy Song.*
For life I had never cared greatly, *Thomas Hardy,* D [a-f´´#(d´´)](m), B&H I Said to Love.
Former Beauties, *Thomas Hardy,* Em [d´-a´´](m), B&H Young Man.
Harvest, *Edmund Blunden,* Dm [c´-a´´b], B&H Oh Fair to See.
He Abjures Love, *Thomas Hardy,* Bm [a-e´´](m), B&H Before and After.
Her Temple, *Thomas Hardy,* Eb [d´-a´´b](m), B&H Young Man.
I look into my glass, *Thomas Hardy,* [c´-g´´], B&H Till Earth Outwears.
I need not go, *Thomas Hardy,* E [c´#-e´´], B&H I Said to Love.
I said to Love, *Thomas Hardy,* C [c´-e´´b], B&H I Said to Love.
I say I'll seek her, *Thomas Hardy,* Em [d´-a´´](m), B&H Oh Fair to See.
In a Churchyard, *Thomas Hardy,* [a-d´´](m), B&H Earth and Air and Rain.
In five-score summers, *Thomas Hardy,* Gm [c´#-e´´], B&H I Said to Love.
In the Mind's Eye, *Thomas Hardy,* Gm [d´-f´´](m), B&H Before and After.
In Time of the Breaking of Nations, *Thomas Hardy,* Bbm [Ab-d´b](m), Banks (Ferguson).
In years defaced, *Thomas Hardy,* Dm [c´-a´´], B&H Till Earth Outwears.
Intrada, *Thomas Traherne,* [bb-f´´], B&H To a Poet.

It never looks like summer, *Thomas Hardy,* F [c′-f′′], B&H Till Earth Outwears.
It was a lover and his lass, *Shakespeare,* E [a-e′′], B&H Let us Garlands.
June on Castle Hill, *F. L. Lucas,* Gm [a-e′′b], B&H To a Poet.
Let me enjoy the earth, *Thomas Hardy,* Gb [d′b-a′′b], B&H Till Earth Outwears.
Life laughs onward, *Thomas Hardy,* G [c′-g′′], B&H Till Earth Outwears.
Lily has a smooth stalk, The, *Christina Rossetti,* Fm [c′-f′′], B&H *Easy Song.*
Market-girl, The, *Thomas Hardy,* F [c′-a′′](m), B&H Till Earth Outwears.
O mistress mine, *Shakespeare,* Eb [bb-e′′b](m), B&H Let us Garlands.
Ode, on the Rejection of St Cecilia, *George Barker,* Gm [ab(c′b)-f′′], B&H To a Poet.
Oh fair to see, *Christina Rossetti,* Cm [e′b-g′′], B&H Oh Fair to See.
On parent knees, *Persian* tr. *William Jones,* Em [d′-e′′], B&H To a Poet.
Only the wanderer, *Ivor Gurney,* Fm [e′b-f′′], B&H Oh Fair to See.
Overlooking the River, *Thomas Hardy,* Eb [d′-e′′b](m), B&H Before and After.
Phantom, The, *Thomas Hardy,* Dm [c′-f′′], B&H Earth and Air and Rain.
Proud Songsters, *Thomas Hardy,* Bm [b-d′′], B&H Earth and Air and Rain.
Rollicum-rorum, *Thomas Hardy,* D [a-e′′](m), B&H Earth and Air and Rain, *Heritage 4,* B&H.
Self-unseeing, The, *Thomas Hardy,* Am [g(a)-f′′](m), B&H Before and After.
Shortening Days, *Thomas Hardy,* Dm [d′-a′′](m), B&H Young Man.
Sigh, The, *Thomas Hardy,* G [d′-g′′](m), B&H Young Man, *Heritage 4.*
Since we loved, *Robert Bridges,* G [g′-g′′], B&H Oh Fair to See.
So have I fared, *Thomas Hardy,* F [a-d′′](m), B&H Earth and Air and Rain.
Summer Schemes, *Thomas Hardy,* D [a-e′′](m), B&H Earth and Air and Rain.
To a Poet a Thousand Years Hence, *James Elroy Flecker,* Cm [g(bb)-f′′#], B&H To a Poet, *Heritage 4.*
To Joy, *Edmund Blunden,* Fm [f′b-a′′b], B&H Oh Fair to See.
To Lizbie Browne, *Thomas Hardy,* Eb [bb-e′′b](m), B&H Earth and Air and Rain.
Too Short Time, The, *Thomas Hardy,* [a-f′′](m), B&H Before and After.
Transformations, *Thomas Hardy,* G [d′-a′′](m), B&H Young Man.
Two Lips, *Thomas Hardy,* Fm [c′-f′′](m), B&H I Said to Love.
Waiting Both, *Thomas Hardy,* Eb [c′-f′′], B&H Earth and Air and Rain.
When I set out for Lyonnesse, *Thomas Hardy,* Em [bb-e′′](m), B&H Earth and Air and Rain.
Who is Sylvia? *Shakespeare,* F [a-d′′], B&H Let us Garlands.
Young Man's Exhortation, A, *Thomas Hardy,* Ab [c′(d′)-a′′](m), B&H Young Man.

Fiske, Roger Elwyn. 1910–1987.
Done For, *Walter de la Mare,* Gm [e′#-e′′b], BMP.
Miss Cherry, *Walter de la Mare,* G [c′#-g′′], BMP.
Weathers, *Thomas Hardy,* G [d′-e′′], BMP.

Fleming, Robert.
Collection: *Secrets – Three Songs,* BMP.
Love, like a drop of dew, *W. H. Davies,* Cm [c′-f′′], BMP Secrets.
Oxen, The, *Thomas Hardy,* Fm [c′-f′′], BMP.
Pleasure and Joy, *W. H. Davies,* F [c′#-g′′], BMP Secrets.
See where young love, *W. H. Davies,* Cm [c′-e′′b], BMP Secrets.

Fligg, David. BMIC.

Fogg, Charles William **Eric.** 1903–1939.
Collections: (*Songs of Love and Life* [high, low], Elkin); (*Two Blake Songs,* Elkin.)
Carol of the Little King, C, Bosworth.
(Dawn Song, *W. Donald Suddaby,* Elkin.)
(Devon Maid, The, *John Keats,* Elkin.)
(Dove, The, *John Keats,* Eb [d′-d′′b(e′′b)], Elkin; G, Elkin.)
(Empty House, *Arthur L. Salmon,* Elkin.)
(Free me from the bonds of your sweetness, *Rabindranath Tagore,* [b-e′′], Elkin Love and Life.)
(Hunting song of the Seeonee Pack, *Rudyard Kipling,* Elkin.)
(In the dusky path of a dream, *Rabindranath Tagore,* [ab-d′′], Elkin Love and Life.)
(It was in May, *Rabindranath Tagore,* Eb [b-e′′b], Elkin Love and Life; Db, Elkin.)
(Laughing Song, *William Blake,* A [f′#-g′′(a′′)], Elkin 2 Blake.)
(Lullaby, *Muriel Levy,* G [d′-e′′(g′′)], Elkin.)
(One morning in the flower garden, *Rabindranath Tagore,* E [b-e′′], Elkin Love and Life; G, Elkin.)
(Peace, *Rabindranath Tagore,* F [b-f′′], Elkin Love and Life; Eb, G, Elkin.)
(Spindrift, *James Lansdale Hodson,* Bb [f′-f′′], Elkin.)

(To Morning, *William Blake,* Eb [f´-g´´#(a´´)], Elkin 2 Blake.
(When passion's trance, *Percy Bysshe Shelley,* Elkin.)
(Widow bird, A, *Percy Bysshe Shelley,* D [e´#-e´´], Curwen.)

Ford, Andrew. 1957– BMIC.

Ford, Thomas. *c.*1580–1648.
Collection: *Ten Airs from Musicke of Sundrie Kindes,* S&B 1966 (edited Thurston Dart). Only songs available in anthologies are listed individually here.
    Come Phyllis, come into these bowers, *Anon,* Gm [f´#-f´´](m), 10 Ayres; *Em,* B&H (Keel) *Lovesongs 1b*; *F#m, Lovesongs 1a.*
    Fair, sweet, cruel, *Anon,* Gm [d´-f´´], 10 Ayres, B&H (Keel) *Lovesongs 1a*; *Fm, Lovesongs 1b*; *Em,* S&B (Pilkington) *Lute Songs 1.*
    Not full twelve years, *Henry Morrice,* Dm [d´-a´´], 10 Ayres; *Am,* S&B (Pilkington) *Lute Songs 1.*
    Now I see thy looks were feigned, *Thomas Lodge,* Gm [d´-f´´], 10 Ayres; *Em,* S&B (Pilkington) *Lute Songs 1.*
    Sigh no more, ladies, *Shakespeare,* C [f´-a´´], BMP (Warlock) *Four English Songs.*
    Since first I saw your face, *Anon,* C [c´-c´´], 10 Ayres, S&B (Pilkington) *Lute Songs 1,* Peters *Art of Song 2b,* Leonard *Baroque low*; E, Leonard *Baroque high*; Eb, Paterson (Diack) *100 Best 4,* Peters *Art of Song 2a.*
    Unto the temple of thy beauty, *Anon,* Gm [d´-f´´](m), 10 Ayres, S&B (Pilkington) *Lute Songs 1.*

Foreman, Michael.
Collections: *Three Songs of Mystery,* Micropress; *Two or Three Songs,* Micropress; *Two Songs,* Micropress. Note: Most Micropress publications can be supplied in a wide range of keys.
    Falcon, The, *Anon,* [high], Micropress 3 Mystery.
    I had a boat, *Mary Coleridge (adapted),* [high], Micropress 3 Mystery.
    Memories from Underwater, *Michael Armstrong,* Micropress 2 Songs.
    Queen Nefertiti, *Anon,* [high], Micropress 3 Mystery.
    Summer Lullaby, *Eudora Bumstead,* Micropress 2 or 3 Songs.
    Sunken Garden, The, *Walter de la Mare,* Micropress.
    Two or three, *John Keats,* Micropress 2 or 3 Songs.
    Tyger, tyger, *William Blake,* Micropress 2 or 3 Songs.

Forshaw, David. *See also* App. 2.
    Orcadian Calendars, *George Mackay Brown,* [soprano], Da Capo.

Foss, Hubert James. 1899–1953.
Collection: *Six Songs from Shakespeare* (two are unaccompanied duets), BMP.
    As I walked forth, *William Blake,* Bb [f´-f´´], BMP.
    Castlepatrick, *G. K. Chesterton,* Dm [c´-f´´](m), BMP.
    Clouds, *Rupert Brooke,* Eb [bb-f´´], B&H.
    Fear no more the heat o' the sun, *Shakespeare,* Fm [c´-f´´], BMP 6 Shakespeare.
    Infant Joy, *William Blake,* Bbm [e´b-f´´], BMP.
    New Mistress, The, *A. E. Housman,* F [a-f´´], BMP.
    Nurse's Song, The, *John Philip,* [c´-a´´](f), BMP.
    O mistress mine, *Shakespeare,* F [d´-f´´](m), BMP 6 Shakespeare.
    Riouperoux, *James Elroy Flecker,* [b-e´´], BMP.
    Sergeant's Song, The, *Thomas Hardy,* F#m [c´#(b)-e´´](m), BMP.
    She sauntered by the swinging seas, *W. E. Henley,* Db [f´-g´´b], BMP.
    Unrest, *John Davidson,* [d´-f´´#], BMP.
    When daisies pied, *Shakespeare,* G [d´-g´´], BMP 6 Shakespeare.
    When that I was and a little tiny boy, *Shakespeare,* [c´-f´´], BMP 6 Shakespeare.
Arrangement:
    Trees they do grow high, The, *Anon,* [c-e´´](f), BMP.

Foster, Derek. 1943– *See* App. 2.

Foster, Ivor. 1904–
Collection: *Three Songs* Lengnick.
    Let me enjoy, *Thomas Hardy,* Eb [d´-g´´](m), Lengnick 3 Songs.
    Rose-Ann, *Thomas Hardy,* Cm [e´b-g´´](m), Lengnick 3 Songs.
    (Those evening bells, *Thomas Moore,* G [b-e´´], Ashdown; Bb, Ashdown.)
    Voice of the Thorn, The, *Thomas Hardy,* Dm [f´-f´´], Lengnick 3 Songs.

Foster, Myles B. 1851–1922.
    Under the greenwood tree, *Shakespeare*, E♭ [c′-f″], B&H *Shakespeare Album*.
    (Unity, *Helen Marion Burnside*, E♭, B&H.)

Fouché, Bob.
Collection: *Three American Songs,* Micropress. Note: Micropress publications can be supplied in a wide range of keys.
    My kind of day, Micropress 3 American.
    My own true love, Micropress 3 American.
    Piano Bar, Micropress 3 American.

Foulds, John Herbert. 1880–1939. BMIC. *See also* App. 2
    Dawn, The, (with Nansi Richards [Telynores Maldwyn]), [contralto/baritone], Snell.
    (Allah, *Anon* tr. *Longfellow,* Paxton.)
    (Eastern Lover, An, *Song of Solomon,* Enoch.)
    (Eileen Aroon, *Gerald Griffin,* D [d′-e″], Chappell; E, F, Chappell.)
    (Evoë, *Fiona Macleod,* Paxton.)
    How sweet the name, *John Newton,* [soprano], Snell.
    (Lances of Gold, *Fiona Macleod,* E [c′#-f′′#], Curwen.)
    (Orchill, *Fiona Macleod,* Paxton.)
    (Parting and Meeting, *Martin Cumberland,* [d′-g″(f″#)], Paxton.)
    (Reed Player, The, *Fiona Macleod,* D [a♭-d″], Curwen.)
    (Roses and Rue, *Charles Kingsley,* Paxton.)
    (Shadowy Woodlands, The *Fiona Macleod,* Am [d′-c″], Curwen.)
    (Song of the Blest, Paxton.)
    (Spring Joy, *French* tr. *Longfellow,* Paxton.)

Fowler, Tommy. 1948– *See also* App. 2.
Collection: *Four Songs for Mezzo-soprano and Piano,* [Walter Scott], SMIC.
    Constantly smile, *David Morrison,* [baritone], SMIC.
    Song, *Percy Bysshe Shelley,* [mezzo], SMIC.

Fox, Christopher. 1955– BMIC. *See also* App. 2.

Frankel, Benjamin. 1906–1973.
Collection: *Eight Songs, Op 32,* Novello hire.
    Drop, drop, slow tears, *Phineas Fletcher,* [d′b-g″], Novello 8 Songs.
    Faery Song, *John Keats,* [c′-g″#], Novello 8 Songs.
    Hornpipe, *Cecil Day-Lewis,* [c′-g″#], Novello 8 Songs.
    I had a dove, *John Keats,* [a#-f′′#], Novello 8 Songs.
    Knight of the Grail, The, *Anon,* [e′b-a″b], Novello 8 Songs.
    O solitude, *John Keats,* [c′#-b″b], Novello 8 Songs.
    Retort to a Clarion Call, *John Scott of Amwell,* [e″-b″b], Novello 8 Songs.
    Stay, O sweet, *John Donne,* [c′#-g″], Novello 8 Songs.

Frankel, Ernest.
    Sister awake, *Thomas Bateson,* [f″#-f″#], BMP.

Fraser, George M.
    Bridgebuilders, *John M. Morrison,* E [medium], BMP.

Fraser, Norman. 1904–1986.
Collection: *Six Songs,* B&H.
    Echo's Lament, *Ben Jonson,* A [e′-a″], B&H 6 Songs.
    From the Brazilian, *Cecilia Meireles* tr. *Norman Fraser,* E♭m [b-e″b], B&H 6 Songs.
    From the Chinese, *Chan Fang Shen* tr. *Arthur Waley,* B [b-g″#], B&H 6 Songs.
    From the Greek, *Antipater* tr. *John Addington Symons,* B♭m [d′b-f″], B&H 6 Songs.
    Little Irish Song, *Blanche Beresford,* A♭ [e′b-e″b], B&H 6 Songs.
    Snowdrop in the Wind, The, *Anna de Bary,* [b-e″b], B&H 6 Songs.
    Venice twilight, *Logan Pearsall Smith,* Bm [b♭-f″], BMP.

Fraser, Shena.
    Boating, *James Reeves,* Em [e′-f″], Roberton.
    Grannies to sell, *James Reeves,* C [e′-e″], Roberton.

Fraser-Simson, Harold. 1872–1944.
    Christopher Robin is saying his prayers, *A. A. Milne,* C [c'-e''], Schirmer *1st Mezzo.*

Fricker, Peter Racine. 1920–1990. *See* App. 2.

Fryer, Herbert. 1877–1957. *See also* App. 1.
    Virgin's cradle-hymn, The, *Anon (Latin)* tr. *Arthur Charlton,* F [f'-f''], B&H *Heritage 1.*

Fuller, Stanley.
    Farewell to summer, [high], Brunton.
    Sursum Corda, [high], Brunton.

Fulton, Robert **Norman.** 1910–1980.
Collections: *Three Songs for High Voice,* S&B; *Two Christmas Songs,* BMP; *Two Songs from Twelfth Night; Two Songs of Thomas Lodge,* BMP.
    Cakewalk, The, *Wilfrid Wilson Gibson,* Bbm [eb-e'b](m), BMP.
    Christ keep the hollow land, *William Morris,* [e'-f''], S&B *3 Songs.*
    Come away, death, *Shakespeare,* Eb [d'-e''b](m), BMP *2 Twelfth Night.*
    Lament in spring, A, *Thomas Lodge,* Am [d'-e''], BMP *2 Thomas Lodge.*
    Love in my bosom, *Thomas Lodge,* F#m [c'#-f'#], BMP *2 Thomas Lodge.*
    Make we merry, *Richard Hill,* D [d'-f'#], OUP *Solo Christmas high;* Bb, *Solo Christma*s *low;* BMP *2 Christmas.*
    Never look back, *Will Redgrave,* [d'-a''b], S&B *3 Songs.*
    No room at the inn, *F. N. Robert,* G [d'-e''b], BMP *2 Christmas.*
    O mistress mine, *Shakespeare,* D [c'#-d''](m), BMP *2 Twelfth Night.*
    To the Moon, *Thomas Hardy,* [e'b-f'#], S&B *3 Songs.*
    Willow Song, The, *Shakespeare,* Gm [d'b-f''], BMP.

G

Gange, Kenneth Edward. *See* App.1.

Gardiner, Henry **Balfour.** 1877–1950.
    Stranger's song, The, *Thomas Hardy,* C [c'-e''](m), Thames *Hardy Songbook.*
    (Winter, *Shakespeare,* F [c'-f''], Ascherberg.)

Garton, Graham. *See also* App. 2.
Collection: *Contretemps Songs,* [mezzo], Brunton.
    Face at the window, [medium], Brunton.
    Farewell songs (cycle), [low], Brunton; [medium], Bruton.
    Grief ago, A, (cycle), [soprano], Brunton.
    How sweet is sin, [high], Brunton; [low], Bruton.
    Listen to the lark, [soprano], Brunton.
    No need to tell me (cycle), [high], Brunton.
    Remembrance day, [tenor], Brunton.
    Song of the day, A, (cycle), [soprano or tenor], Brunton.

Gaul, Alfred Robert. 1837–1933.
    Come ye blessed, *St Matthew 25.24,* G [d'-e''], Schirmer *1st Mezzo II.*
    Eye hath not seen, G [b-d''], Schirmer *2nd Mezzo.*
    These are they which came, A [e'-g''#(f'#)], Schirmer *2nd Soprano.*

Geddes, John Maxwell. 1941– SMIC.
Collections: *Ballater-Dunkeld Song Buke, The* SMIC; *Lassies, Love and Life,* SMIC; *Seven Scots Songs,* SMIC.

Geehl, Henry Ernest, 1881–1961. *See also* App. 2.
    For you alone, *P. J. O'Reilly,* Eb [c'-f''(e''b)], IMP *Parlour Songs,* Classical; F, Db, Classical.
    Mountains of Allah, The (cycle), *Edward Teschemacher,* [medium low], Classical.

Gerhard, Roberto. 1896–1970. *See also* App. 1, 2.
Arrangements: *Six Catalan Folksongs*, B&H 1933.
    Dancing in a Sack, *Anon* tr. *J. B. Trend*, [a′b-f′′], B&H 6 Catalan.
    Death and the Maiden, *Anon* tr. *J. B. Trend*, [g′-g′′], B&H 6 Catalan.
    Lark, The, *Anon* tr. *J. B. Trend*, [g′#-f′′#](m), B&H 6 Catalan.
    Old Cotilo, *Anon* tr. *J. B. Trend*, [a′b-g′′b](m), B&H 6 Catalan.
    Ploughboy, The, *Anon* tr. *J. B. Trend*, [a′b-f′′], B&H 6 Catalan.
    Woman-hater, The, *Anon* tr. *J. B. Trend*, [f′-e′′](m), B&H 6 Catalan.

German, Sir Edward. (German Edward Jones). 1862–1936.
Collections: (*Just So Song Book, The*, Novello); *Three Baritone Songs*, Classical/B&H; (*Three Spring Songs*, Cramer).
    All the world awakes today, *Harold Boulton*, F [c′-g′′], Cramer 3 Spring; E♭, Cramer.
    Big Steamers, *Rudyard Kipling*, D [c′#-f′′#(e′′)], Classical, Cramer *Folio 1*; C, Classical/Cramer.
    Bird of Blue, *'Chrystabel'*, Cm [d′-e′′b], B&H.
    (Camel's hump, The, *Rudyard Kipling*, E♭ [c′-e′′b], Novello Just So.)
    Charming Chloe, *Robert Burns*, E♭ [c′-e′′b], Novello.
    Come to the woods, *Samuel Waddington*, E♭ [b♭-f′′], Classical/B&H 3 Baritone.
    Dew upon the lily, *Harold Boulton*, A [e′-f′′#], Cramer 3 Spring; G, A, Cramer.
    Dream o' Day Jill, *Chas. H. Taylor*, F [d′-g′′](f), Braydeston.
    English Rose, The, *Basil Hood*, B♭ [e′-g′′](m), B&H *Ballad Album 1*; G, IMP *Parlour Songs*.
    (First Friend, The, *Rudyard Kipling*, G [d′-e′′], Novello Just So.)
    Glorious Devon! *Harold Boulton*, F [e′-g′′](m), B&H *Ballad Album 1*; C, *Souvenirs*, (D, Classical/B&H 3 Baritone, B&H.
    (I am the most wise Baviaan, *Rudyard Kipling*, D, [b-f′′#], Novello Just So.)
    (I keep six honest serving-men, *Rudyard Kipling*, E♭, [b♭-e′′b], Novello Just So.)
    (Kangaroo and Dingo, *Rudyard Kipling*, A [e′-f′′#(e′′)], Novello Just So.)
    (Merrow Down, *Rudyard Kipling*, E [b-e′′], Novello Just So.)
    My Lady, *Fred. E. Weatherly*, F [b-d′′], Classical/B&H 3 Baritone.
    My song is of the sturdy north, *Harold Boulton*, Dm [d′-f′′], Cramer 3 Spring; Cm, Cramer.
    (Of all the tribe of Tegumai, *Rudyard Kipling*, F [b♭-f′′], Novello Just So.)
    (Riddle, The, *Rudyard Kipling*, Dm [d′-d′′], Novello Just So.)
    Rolling Down to Rio, *Rudyard Kipling*, Am [a-e′′], Classical, (Novello Just So); Gm, Schirmer *1st Baritone II*; [medium], Classical.
    (Sea lullaby, *Harold Boulton*, F [c′-g′′], Chappell *English Recital 2*.)
    (There was never a Queen like Balkis, *Rudyard Kipling*, A [e′-e′′], Novello Just So.)
    (This unhabited island, *Rudyard Kipling*, Gm [d′-d′′], Novello Just So.)
    What 'Dane-geld' means, *Rudyard Kipling*, A Cramer; G, Cramer.
    (When the cabin portholes, *Rudyard Kipling*, Dm [c′-f′′], Novello Just So.)
    Who'll buy my lavender? *Caryl Battersby*, D [d′-f′′#], B&H *Ballad Album 2*, Classical; C, E, Classical/B&H.

Gibbons, Orlando. 1583–1625.
    Silver swan, The, (arr.), *Anon*, E♭ [e′b-f′′], Leonard *Baroque high;* C, Leonard *Baroque low.*

Gibbs, Alan.
Collection: *Five Elizabethan Songs*, Bardic.
    And if I did what then? *George Gascoigne*, [A#-e′](m), Bardic 5 Elizabethan.
    Even such is time, *Walter Raleigh*, [G-e′b](m), Bardic 5 Elizabethan.
    Follow a shadow, *Ben Jonson*, [d-e′](m), Bardic 5 Elizabethan.
    Mark when she smiles, *Edmund Spenser*, [G-e′b](m), Bardic 5 Elizabethan.
    Sir Patrick Spens, *Scottish Ballad*, [G#-f′](m), Bardic.
    With how sad steps, *Philip Sidney*, [B-f′](m), Bardic 5 Elizabethan.

Gibbs, Cecil Armstrong. 1889–1960. *See also* App. 2.
Collections: *Five Children's Songs from 'Peacock Pie'*, B&H; *Joan of Arc Op 102*, B&H; *Old Wine in New Bottles*, B&H; *Song Album 1, Song Album 2*, Novello (introductions by Michael Pilkington); *Songs of the Mad Sea-Captain Op 111*, B&H (introduction by Mollie Petrie); *Three Songs*, Classical; (*Two Old English Lyrics*, Chappell); *Two Songs*, B&H; *Voice in the Dusk, A, Op 91*, B&H.
    Abel Wright, *Bernard Martin*, C [a♭-d′′#](m), B&H Sea-Captain.)
    (Amaryllis, *Anon*, A [e′-f′′#(a′′)](m) Chappell *English Recital 1*; F, 2 Old English).
    Ann's cradle song, *Walter de la Mare*, C#m [d′b-e′′b](f), Novello Album 1.
    Araby, *Walter de la Mare*, F [c′-f′′] (f), Novello Album 1.
    Arrogant Poppies, *Clifford Bax*, Em [g′-g′′](f), Novello Album 2.

As I lay in the early sun, *Edward Shanks*, F [d'-f''](m), B&H.
Ballad of Semmerwater, The, *William Watson*, Gm [gb-e''b] Thames *Century 4*, (Curwen).
Ballad-maker, A, *Padraic Colum*, Cm [c'-e''b](m), B&H; (Ebm, B&H).
Beggar's song, *Walter de la Mare*, Em [b-e''](m), Novello Album 1.
Birch Tree, The, *Georgina Mase*, Am [a'-a''], Novello Album 2.
Birthday, A, *Christina Rossetti*, C [e'-a''](f), BMP.
By a Bier-side, *John Masefield*, C#m [c'#-e''], Novello Album 1.
Candlestick Maker's Song, *Walter de la Mare*, Dm [c'-f''#], Novello Album 2.
(Chains of Love, The, *Clifford Bax*, Bb [bb-e''b](m), Curwen).
Cherry Tree, The, *Margaret Rose*, Bm [b-e''], Novello Album 1, Schirmer *1st Mezzo*.
(Chloris in the Snow, *Anon*, Am [d'-e''b], Chappell 2 Old English; Cm, 2 Old English.)
Covent Garden, *Eileen Carfrae*, C [c'-e''(g')], Roberton; D, E, Roberton.
Crowning, *Mordaunt Currie*, A [c'#-a''](f), B&H Joan of Arc.
Danger, *Mordaunt Currie*, [c'-d''], Novello Album 1.
Defeat, *Mordaunt Currie*, Am [d'-f''](f), B&H Joan of Arc.
Down in yonder meadow, *Anon*, F [c'-f''], B&H 2 Songs.
Dream Song, *Walter de la Mare*, Ab [d'-f''], B&H.
Dusk, *Anon*, F [c'-e''b], B&H *Easy Song*.
Evening in Summer, *John Fletcher*, Db [d'b-f''], BMP.
(Exile, The, *Walter de la Mare*, Am [c'-e''], Chester.)
February, *Mordaunt Currie*, Am [c'-e''], B&H.
Fields are full, The, *Edward Shanks*, Ebm [d'b-g''b], Thames 10 Songs, B&H *Heritage 4*, B&H.
Five Eyes, *Walter de la Mare*, Gm [d'-d''], B&H; *Bbm*, B&H, Classical 3 Songs.
Flooded Stream, The, *Margaret Cropper*, Bm [d'-f''#], Novello Album 2.
For Remembrance, *Edward Shanks*, D [d'-g''], B&H.
Fulfilment, *Mordaunt Currie*, D [d'-a''], Thames 10 Songs.
Galliass, The, *Walter de la Mare*, G [f'#-f''], Novello Album 1.
Gipsies, *H. H. Bashford*, Em [e'-a''], BMP; Em (unison), BMP.
Golden Ray, The, *Bernard Martin*, D [b-d''](m), B&H Sea-Captain.
Gone is my love, *Edith Harrhy*, G [d'-g''], B&H.
Gone were but the winter, *Christina Rossetti*, G [d'-g''], BMP.
Hawthorn Tree, The, *Hilda Maude*, Em [b-g''], B&H; (Gm B&H).
Hidden Treasure, *Bernard Martin*, Gm [g(bb)-d''](m), B&H Sea-Captain.
Hypochondriacus, *Charles Lamb*, [bb-e''], Thames 10 Songs.
If music be the food of love, *Henry Heveningham*, Gb [ab-e''b](m), B&H Old Wine.
Immortality, *Mordaunt Currie*, Am [e'-a''], B&H.
(Impromptu, *Mordaunt Currie*, Fm [c'-e''b](m), Curwen.)
In the faery hills, *John Irvine*, Eb [d'-g''], B&H A Voice.
In the highlands, *R. L. Stevenson*, Eb [e'b-a''b], Novello Album 2.
In the woods in June, *Mordaunt Currie*, A [e'-a''], B&H.
(In Youth is Pleasure, *Robert Wever*, E [b-e''], Elkin; G, Elkin.)
(Jenny Jones, *Doris Rowley*, Bm [a-e''], Curwen.)
John Mouldy, *Walter de la Mare*, Cm [c'-e''b], B&H.
Juliet Anne, *Mordaunt Currie*, D [b-d''], B&H; (A, B&H.)
Lamb and the Dove, The, *Christina Rossetti*, Em [e'-a''b], BMP.
Lament for Robin Hood, *A, Antony Munday*, Fm [medium], BMP.
Lily-bright and shine-a, *Anon*, G [e'-g''], B&H 2 Songs.
Little Green Orchard, The, *Walter de la Mare*, F [e'b-f''], B&H.
Little Salamander, The, *Walter de la Mare*, Gm [g'b-f''], Novello Album 2.
Love is a sickness, *Samuel Daniel*, F [c'-d''], Classical; (F, Bb, Elkin.)
(Love Talker, The, *Ethna Carbery*, [mezzo], B&H.)
Love's Prisoner, *William Blake*, Bb [b-f''], B&H; D, B&H.
Love's Wisdom, *Mordaunt Currie*, Am [e'-a''], B&H; (Dm, Bbm, B&H).
Lullaby, *Walter de la Mare*, Gm [e'-f''], Novello Album 1.
Lyonesse, *Thomas Hardy*, Am [a-f''](m), Thames *Hardy Songbook*, Classical; Cm, B&H.
Mad Prince, The, *Walter de la Mare*, Em [c'-e''](m), Novello Album 1.
(Maritime Invocation, *A. C. Boyd*, Cm [b-f''](m), B&H; (Dm, Ebm, B&H).
Market, The, *James Stephens*, [a-e''](m), Novello Album 1.
Midnight, *Jeffery Lang*, Bbm [c'-f''], B&H.
Mistletoe, *Walter de la Mare*, Fm [e'b-a''b], Novello Album 2.
Moon Magic, *John Irvine*, [e'-g''], B&H A Voice.
Mors Janua Vitae, *Mordaunt Currie*, [c'-b''b](f), B&H Joan of Arc.
Neglected Moon, *Clifford Bax*, Eb [e'b-a''b](f), Novello Album 2.
Nightfall, *Harry Dawson*, C [d'-g''], Novello Album 2.

Nod, *Walter de la Mare*, D [d′-f′′#], B&H *Heritage 3*, Chester *Celebrated 1*.
(O mistress mine, *Shakespeare*, B&H.)
Oh, nightingale upon my tree, *Mordaunt Currie*, B♭ [c′-e′′♭], B&H.
On Duncton Hill, *Gwen Grant*, F#m [f′#-f′′#], Novello Album 2.
Orchard Sings to the Child, The, *Margaret Cropper*, A [e′-f′′#], Novello Album 2.
Oxen, The, *Thomas Hardy*, Fm [d′♭-f′′], Thames 10 Songs.
Padraic the Fidiler, *Padraic Gregory*, [e′-f′′], Novello Album 1.
Philomel, *Richard Barnfield*, Bm [e′♭-g′′], Thames 10 Songs.
Philomela, *Philip Sidney*, E♭ [b♭-e′′♭], B&H.
(Picture me love, *Westlake & Ridley*, B&H.)
Pious Celinda goes to prayers, *William Congreve*, Gm [d′-d′′](m), B&H Old Wine.
(Prayer before Sleep, *L. E. Eeman*, [c′-c′′], Elkin.)
(Proud Maisie, *Walter Scott*, C [d′-e′′], Curwen.)
Rejected Lover, The, *Clifford Bax*, G [d′-g′′](m), Novello Album 2.
Rest in the Lord, *Edmund Beale Sargant*, Gm [b-e′′♭], B&H.
(Resting, *Gwen Grant*, C [d′♭-e′′], Curwen.)
Revelation, *Mordaunt Currie*, D♭ [c′-g′′#](f), B&H Joan of Arc.
Sailing Homeward, *Chan Fang Shen*, tr. *Arthur Waley*, Bm [d′-g′′#], B&H; Gm, B&H.
Scarecrow, The, *Walter de la Mare*, Bm [a-f′′#], Novello Album 1.
Ship of Rio, The, *Walter de la Mare*, E♭ [a♭-e′′♭], B&H *Heritage 3*.
Silver, *Walter de la Mare*, F#m [c′#-f′′#], B&H *Heritage 4*, B&H, Classical 3 Songs; Em, B&H.
(Sledburn Fair, *Anon*, B♭ [c′-e′′♭], B&H.)
Sleeping Beauty, The, *Walter de la Mare*, F [e′♭-f′′], Novello Album 1.
Slow, horses, slow, *Thomas Westwood*, Cm [f′-g′′], Roberton.
Song of Shadows, A, *Walter de la Mare*, E♭ [e′♭-g′′♭], Thames *Century 1*, B&H.
Splendour falls, The, *Alfred Lord Tennyson*, Cm [a♭-e′′], Thames 10 Songs.
Spring, *John Irvine*, B♭ [f′-g′′], B&H A Voice.
(Starlighters, The, *Ann Gibbs*, B&H.)
Summer Night, *Margery Agrell*, C#m [f′-g′′], Novello Album 2.
Summer Palace, The, *Benedict Ellis*, E♭ [e′-a′′♭], B&H.
(Summertime, *Benedict Ellis*, B♭ [d′♭-g′′], B&H.)
(Sussex Ways, *Mordaunt Currie*, E♭ [c′-e′′♭], B&H.)
Sweet sounds, begone, *Walter de la Mare*, B♭m [d′♭-f′′#], B&H.
Take heed, young heart, *Walter de la Mare*, Em [e′-g′′], Novello Album 2.
Tiger Lily, The, *Dorothy Pleydell Bouverie*, C [c′-e′′], Novello Album 1.
Tis wine that inspires, *Anon*, C [g-e′′](m), B&H Old Wine.
Titania, *Mordaunt Currie*, E♭ [b♭-f′′], Thames 10 Songs.
To Anise, *Nathaniel Downes*, D [a-d′′], B&H.
To one who Passed Whistling through the Night, *Margery Agrell*, C [f′-g′′], Novello Album 2, Classical 3 Songs.
Toll the bell, *Bernard Martin*, Dm [a-d′′](m), B&H Sea-Captain.
Tom o' Bedlam, *Anon*, Am [g-e′′♭](m), Thames 10 Songs.
Victory, *Mordaunt Currie*, C#m [e′-g′′#](f), B&H Joan of Arc.
Wanderer, The, *Walter de la Mare*, B♭m [d′♭-f′′], Thames 10 Songs, Novello Album 1.
When Arthur first in Court began, *Anon*, Cm [a-e′′](m), B&H Old Wine.
When I was one-and-twenty, *A. E. Housman*, G [d′-f′′](m), Novello Album 2.
Why do I love? *Ephelia (Joan Philips)*, [c′-a′′♭(g′′♭)], B&H *New Imperial 1*; B&H.
Wind comes softly, The, *John Irvine*, F [e′-f′′#], B&H A Voice.
Witch, The, *Mordaunt Currie*, Em [d′-g′′], Thames 10 Songs.
Arrangements: *Four Songs by Edward Miller*, B&H; *Two Songs*, B&H.
Despairing Shepherd, The, *Air Carr Scroope*, Em [d′-e′′], B&H 4 Miller.
Fyre, fyre, *Anon, Elizabeth Rogers Virginal Booke*, G [d′-e′′], B&H 2 Songs.
Happy Pair, The, *Francis Pilkington*, D [d′-g′′], B&H 4 Miller.
I prithee, send me back my heart, *John Suckling*, G [d′-g′′](m), B&H 4 Miller.
Lye still, my deare, *Anon, Elizabeth Rogers Virginal Booke*, Am [g′#-f′′], B&H 2 Songs.
To Althea, from Prison, *Richard Lovelace*, C [e′-g′′](m), B&H 4 Miller.

Giles, Thomas. *fl*.1607.
Triumph now with joy and mirth, *Thomas Campion*, G [d′-d′′], S&B (Greer) *Printed*.

Gill, Harry. 1897–1987.
Collection: *Three Songs,* BMP.
About my father's farm, *Edward Wright*, [b♭-g′′](f), BMP.
In Memoriam, *H. Percy Dixon*, D [b-e′′], Thames *Century 2*, BMP 3 Songs.

Love Forsaken, *H. Percy Dixon*, B♭m [a-f″], BMP 3 Songs.
Night, The, *Hilaire Belloc*, C [c′-e″♭], BMP.
Obsequy, *H. Percy Dixon*, A [b-e″], BMP 3 Songs.
Saxon Song, A, *Vita Sackville-West*, G [b-e″], BMP.

Gipps, Ruth. 1921–1999. BMIC.

Glennie-Smith, Keith.
From High Savoy to Chelsea Down, (cycle) *Eleanor Farjeon,* [d′-g″], Modus.

Glover, Charles W.
Rose of Tralee, The, *C. Mordaunt Spencer,* B♭ [d′-f″](m), IMP *Parlour Songs*.

Glyn, Gareth. 1951– *See also* App. 2.
Collections: *Life Reborn,* Curiad; *Llanrwst and Other Songs,* Curiad.
Cauldron, The, Curiad Life.
Challenge, Curiad Life.
Futile, Curiad Llanrwst.
Golgotha, Curiad Life.
Herod's Song, Curiad Llanrwst.
Hymn to the Virgin, *Ieuan ap Hywel Swrdwal*, [A#-f″](m) WMIC *Songs from Wales 2*.
Llanrwst, Curiad Llanrwst.
Recalling, Curiad Llanrwst.
Slowly the ticking clock, Curiad Llanrwst.
Snowdrops, Curiad Life.
Songs of the War, Curiad Llanrwst.
Spring, Curiad Life.
Talors, Curiad Llanrwst.

Goard, Henry A.
Gipsy's warning, *Henry A. Goard,* C [c′-e″], IMP *Parlour Songs*.

Godfrey, Graham.
Phillida, *Anon 17th cent.,* Gm [b♭-e″♭(f″)], BMP.

Godfrey, Paul Corfield. WMIC. *See also* App. 2.

Goehr, Peter **Alexander.** 1932– *See also* App. 1, 2.
Collection: *Four Songs from the Japanese,* Schott 1971.
Do torrents spare the fresh bloom flower? *Anon* tr. *Lafcadio Hearn*, [c′-f″], Schott 4 Songs.
I love and I love, *Anon* tr. *Lafcadio Hearn*, [c′-g″♭], Schott 4 Songs.
Things have never changed, *Anon* tr. *Lafcadio Hearn*, [d′-a″#](m), Schott 4 Songs.
Truth is, The, *Anon* tr. *Lafcadio Hearn*, [c′-f″#], Schott 4 Songs.

Gomelskaya, Julia.
Collection: *Waiting,* Micropress. Note: Micropress publications can be supplied in a wide range of keys.
Alone, *Jennie Fontana,* Micropress Waiting.
I know, *Jennie Fontana,* Micropress Waiting.
Waiting, *Jennie Fontana,* Micropress Waiting.
We cut ice, *Jennie Fontana,* Micropress Waiting.
You say, *Jennie Fontana,* Micropress Waiting.

Goodhart, A. M. 1866– ?
Bells of Clermont Town, The, *Hilaire Belloc*, Dm [a-d″], B&H *Heritage 1,* Schirmer *1st Baritone*.

Goossens, Sir Aynsley **Eugene.** 1893–1962. *See also* App. 1.
Collections: *Chamber Music (Six Songs),* Lengnick; *Four Songs,* Chester; *Persian Idylls,* Chester; *Three Songs,* Chester.
All day I hear the noise of waters, *James Joyce*, [d′♭-e″♭], Lengnick Chamber Music.
Appeal, The, *Thomas Wyatt*, [g′-e″], Chester 3 Songs.
Breath of Ney, *Edwin Evans*, [d′#-g″], Chester Persian.
Dear heart, why will you use me so, *James Joyce*, [b-e″], Lengnick Chamber Music.
(Don Juan's Serenade, *Arnold Bennett*, [e♭-d′(g′)](m), Chester.)
Gentle lady, do not sing sad songs, *James Joyce*, [c′#-e″], Lengnick Chamber Music.

Heart of the kalyan, *Edwin Evans,* [d´-a´´b], Chester Persian.
I hear an army, *James Joyce,* [d´-f´´#], Lengnick Chamber Music.
Lotusland, *Cyril Scott,* [f´#-f´´], B&H.
Melancholy, *John Fletcher,* Ebm [d´-e´´], Chester 3 Songs.
Now, O now, *James Joyce,* [c#-f´´#], Lengnick Chamber Music.
O cool is the valley now, *James Joyce,* [f´-e´´b], Lengnick Chamber Music.
Philomel, *Richard Barnfield,* [d´-g´´], Chester 3 Songs.
Seascape *Bettie F. Holmes,* [f´#-g´´], Chester 4 Songs.
Threshold, *Bettie F. Holmes,* [d´-g´´], Chester 4 Songs.
When thou art dead, *Margaret Kennedy,* Dm [f´#-e´´b], Curwen.
Winter-night Idyll, A, *Bettie F. Holmes,* [g´-g´´], Chester 4 Songs.
Woodland Dell, A, *Bettie F. Holmes,* [f´b-g´´], Chester 4 Songs.
Arrangements: *Old Scottish Folksongs,* Chester.
Searching for Lambs, *Anon,* Chester.

Gorb, Adam. 1958– *See* App. 2.

Gow, David. 1924–1993. (BMIC.) *see also* App. 2.
(A West Sussex Drinking Song, *Hilaire Belloc,* Ab [F-e´b](m), B&H.)

Grainger, Ella. (Ella Viola Ström). 1889–1979.
Crying for the Moon, *Ella Grainger,* [bb-e´´b], Bardic.
Farewell to an Atoll, *Ella Grainger,* [e´b-a´´b], Bardic.
Honey Pot Bee, *Ella Grainger,* [c´#-f´´#], Bardic.
Love at First Sight, *Ella Grainger,* [a-e´´], Bardic.
Mermaid, The, *Ella Grainger,* [c´-e´´b], Bardic.
To Echo, *Ella Grainger,* [c´-f´´], Bardic.

Grainger, Percy. 1882–1961. *See also* App. 1, 2.
Afton Water, *Robert Burns,* [c´-e´´], Bardic.
Anchor Song, *Rudyard Kipling,* [c´#-f´´#](m), Bardic.
Dedication, *Rudyard Kipling,* [e´-c´´], Bardic.
Evan Banks, *Robert Burns,* [e´b-g´´], Bardic.
First Chanty, The, *Rudyard Kipling,* [a#-f´´#], Bardic.
Ganges Pilot, *Rudyard Kipling,* [c´-f´´](m), Bardic.
Lukannon, *Rudyard Kipling,* [c´b-g´´], Bardic (realised B P Ould).
Merciful Town, *Rudyard Kipling,* [e´b-e´´b], Bardic.
Northern Ballad, *Rudyard Kipling,* [bb-f´´](m), Bardic.
(Reiver's Neck Verse, *Algernon Charles Swinburne,* [tenor], Schott.)
Ride with an idle whip, *Rudyard Kipling,* [g-f´´#](m), Bardic.
Sailor's Chanty, *Arthur Conan Doyle,* [g´-e´´], Bardic.
Sea-wife, The, *Rudyard Kipling,* [c´#-f´´], Bardic.
Secret of the Sea, The, *Longfellow,* [e´-e´´](m), Bardic.
Soldier, soldier (1st setting), *Rudyard Kipling,* [e´b-c´´](m), Bardic.
Soldier, soldier (2nd setting), *Rudyard Kipling,* [c´#-f´´#], Bardic.
Variations on 'The harmonious blacksmith', *vocalise,* [b-g´´#], Bardic.
Yon wild mossy mountains, *Robert Burns,* [bb-b´b], Bardic.
Young British Soldier, The, *Rudyard Kipling,* [c´#-e´´], Bardic.
Arrangements: *Songs of the North,* Bardic; *Thirteen Folksongs,* Schirmer; *Thirteen Folksongs Volumes 1, 2,* Thames (introduction by Peter Pears, notes by David Tall).
A-hunting we will go, *Henry Fielding,* [bb-e´´b], Bardic.
Bailiff's daughter of Islington, The, *Percy's Reliques,* [d´b-e´´b], Bardic.
Banks of Allen Water, The, *M. G. Lewis,* [d´-f´´], Bardic.
Barbara Allen, *Percy's Reliques,* [f´-f´´], Bardic.
Begone, dull care! *Anon,* [e´-f´´#], Bardic.
Bold William Taylor, *Anon,* [d´-e´´b], Thames Folksongs 2, Schirmer 13 Folksongs.
Bonnie George Campbell, *Scottish Traditional,* [d´-e´´], Bardic North.
Bridegroom Grat, The, *Anon,* [c´-e´´], Bardic.
British Grenadiers, The, *Anon,* [d´-e´´], Bardic.
British Waterside, *Anon,* [e´-e´´], Thames Folksongs 1, Schirmer 13 Folksongs.
Come lassies and lads, *Anon,* [d´b-f´´], Bardic.
Creeping Jane, *Anon,* G [c´#-e´´], Thames Folksongs 2, Schirmer 13 Folksongs, Bardic.
Died for Love, *Anon,* [e´-e´´](f), Thames Folksongs 1, Schirmer 13 Folksongs.
Drink to me only with thine eyes, *Ben Jonson,* [f´-f´´], Bardic.

Drowned, *Rev. A. Stewart*, [d´-d´´], Bardic North.
Early one morning, *Anon,* (1st setting), [c´-f´´], Bardic.
Early one morning, *Anon,* (2nd setting), Fm [c´-c´´´(f´´)], Thames Folksongs 2, Schirmer 13 Folksongs, Bardic.
Fair young Mary, *A. C. Macleod,* [d´-f´´#], Bardic North.
Girl I Left Behind Me, The, *Anon,* [b♭-e´´♭], Bardic.
Hard Hearted Barb'ra (H)ellen, *Anon,* F# [c´#-f´´#](m), Thames Folksongs 2, Schirmer 13 Folksongs, Bardic.
Hunt is up, The, *Anon,* [e´♭-f´´], Bardic.
It was a maid of my country, *Ritsons 'Ancient Songs',* [e´♭-f´´], Bardic.
Jockey to the Fair, *Anon,* [c´-f´´], Bardic.
Jog on, jog on, *Shakespeare,* [e´♭-e´´♭], Bardic.
Land o' the Leal, *Lady Nairne,* [c´-f´´], Bardic.
Lass of Richmond Hill, The, *Leonard McNally,* [c´-f´´], Bardic.
Leather Bottèl, *Anon,* [e´♭-e´´♭], Bardic.
Leezie Lindsay, *Scottish Traditional,* [e´♭-e´´♭], Bardic North.
Little Ole with his umbrella, *Peter Lemche* tr. *Ella & Percy Grainger,* [a-e´´], Bardic.
Lord Maxwell's Goodnight, *Anon,* F [c´-a´´](m), Thames Folksongs 2, Schirmer 13 Folksongs, Bardic.
Mairi Bhan Og *see* Fair young Mary.
My Faithful Fond One, *Anon (Gaelic)* tr. *Blackie,* [d´-e´´], Bardic North.
My lodging is on the cold ground, *Anon,* [e´♭-e´´♭], Bardic.
Near Woodstock Town, *Anon,* [c´-e´´], Bardic.
O glorious, golden era, *Italian* tr. *Percy Grainger,* [f´-e´´♭], Bardic.
O'er the moor, *A. C. Macleod,* [B♭-c´´], Bardic North.
Oh! the oak and the ash, *Anon,* [c´-e´´♭], Bardic.
Ploughboy, The, *Anon,* [c´-f´´], Bardic.
Poor beggar's daughter, A, *Percy's reliques,* [d´-d´´], Bardic.
Power of love, The, *Danish,* tr. *Anon,* [g´#-g´´], Thames Folksongs 2, Schirmer 13 Folksongs, Bardic.
Pretty Maid Milking her Cow, The, *Anon,* [d´-g´´], Thames Folksongs 1, Schirmer 13 Folksongs.
Proud Vesselil, *Anon* tr. *Joan Rockwell,* [c´-a´´], Bardic.
Rag-Time Gal, The, *Ida Emerson,* [f´#-e´´#], Bardic.
Sally in Our Alley, *Henry Carey,* [c´-f´´], Bardic.
Six dukes went a-fishing, *Anon,* [e´-f´´#], Thames Folksongs 1, Schirmer 13 Folksongs.
Skye Boat Song, *Harold Boulton,* [d´-d´´], Bardic North.
Sprig of Thyme, The, *Anon,* A [e´-f´´#](f), Thames Folksongs 1, Schirmer 13 Folksongs.
There was a jolly miller, *Isaac Bickerstaff?* [e´-e´´], Bardic.
This is not my plaid, *W. Haley,* [d´-d´´], Bardic North.
Three Ravens, The, *Anon,* [e´-g´´], Bardic.
Turn ye to me, *Christopher North (John Wilson),* [b-e´´], Bardic North.
Twa Corbies, The, *Anon,* Gm [b♭-g´´](m), Thames Folksongs 1, Schirmer 13 Folksongs.
Vicar of Bray, The, *Edward Ward,* [d´-e´´], Bardic.
Weaving Song, *Scottish Traditional,* [c´-c´´], Bardic North.
Willie's gane to Melville Castle, *Scottish Traditional,* [d´-d´´], Bardic North.
Willow, willow, *Anon,* (1st setting), [e´-e´´], Bardic.
Willow, willow, *Anon,* (2nd setting), Em [e´-e´´], Thames Folksongs 1, Schirmer 13 Folksongs, Schott.
Women are a' gane wud, The, *Scottish Traditional,* [e´-e´´], Bardic North.

Grange, Philip. 1956– *See* App. 2.

Grant, Julian. *See* App. 1.

Graves, John.
Collection: *Four Songs,* Micropress. Note: Micropress publications can be supplied in a wide range of keys.
Cradle Song, *Padraic Colum,* Micropress 4 Songs.
Magnificat, *Mary Coleridge,* Micropress 4 Songs.
Salley Gardens, The, *W. B. Yeats,* Micropress 4 Songs.
Where the Daisies Are, *James Stephens,* Micropress 4 Songs.

Gray, Alan. 1855–1935.
Bredon Hill, *A. E. Housman,* G [low], BMP.

Greaves, Ralph. 1890–1966.
    I arise from dreams of thee, *Percy Bysshe Shelley,* Em [c′#-a″], Thames *Century 5*, BMP.
    I will go look for death, *John Masefield,* [d′-f″], BMP.
    Lady, when your lovely head, *Hilaire Belloc,* [d′-e″], BMP.
    (Maypole is up, The, *Robert Herrick,* [d′-f″], Curwen.)
    Once very long ago, *John Masefield,* [d′-f″], BMP.
    Poplar and the Moon, The, *Siegfried Sassoon,* [d′-g″], BMP.
    Song of the Ronin, *John Masefield,* [c′-g″], BMP.
    When I am dead, my dearest, *Christina Rossetti,* [e′b-e″b], BMP.
    Yellow Wine, *John Masefield,* [e′-a″(b″)], BMP.

Greaves, Terence. 1933– *See* App. 2.

Greaves, Thomas. *fl.*1604.
Collection: *Songes of Sundrie Kindes*, S&B (edited Ian Spink). Only songs available in anthologies are listed individually here.
    Flora, sweet wanton, *Anon,* F [e′-f″](m), Songes, BMP *W&W 1.*
    Inconstant Laura makes me death to crave, *Anon,* Gm [f′#-g″], Songes, BMP *W&W 6.*
    Shaded with olive trees, (Celestina) *Anon,* F [d′-f″], Songes, B&H (Keel) *Lovesongs 1a,* BMP *W&W 3*; E♭, *Lovesongs 1b.*
    What is beauty but a breath? *Anon,* Gm [f′#-f″], Songes, BMP *W&W 5.*
    Ye bubbling springs, *Anon,* Gm [d′-f″], Songes, S&B (Pilkington) *Lute Songs 1.*

Green, David Llewellyn. *See also* App. 1.
Collections: *Cycle of Three Neil Oram Poems, A,* [high], Brunton; *Five Songs of Sorrow and Reconciliation,* (mezzo/baritone), Brunton.
    Reve d'amour, Brunton.

Greene, Maurice. 1696–1755.
Collection: *Seven Sacred Solos,* [high, medium], Bosworth (edited Stanley Roper); [medium], Classical.
    Blessed are they that dwell in thy house, *Psalm 84,* D [d′-f″#], Classical/Bosworth 7 Sacred; E, Bosworth 7 Sacred.
    Eyes of all, The, *Psalms?,* F [e′-f″], BMP (Roper).
    Fair Sally, *Anon,* Cm [c′-f″(g″)], BMP (Fiske).
    Gentiles shall come to thy light, The, *Isaiah 60, v. 3,* F [c′-f″], B&H (Patrick) *Sacred Songs 2.*
    Go, rose, my Chloe's bosom grace, *John Gay,* G [d′-e″], S&B (Pilkington) *Early Georgian 1.*
    I laid me down and slept, Bosworth (Roper).
    I will lay me down in peace, *Psalm 4, v. 9,* E♭ [d′-e″b], Classical/Bosworth 7 Sacred, Bosworth, B&H (Patrick) *Sacred Songs 2*; F, Bosworth 7 Sacred.
    (Like the young god of wine, *Anon,* E♭ [B♭b-e″b](m), Elkin (Taylor).)
    Lord's name is praised, The, *Psalm 113,* D [c′#-e″], Classical/Bosworth 7 Sacred; F, Bosworth 7 Sacred.
    My lips shall speak the praise, *Psalms?,* C [d′-f″], BMP (Roper).
    O give me the comfort, *Psalms?,* Em [c′#(b)-e″], BMP (Roper).
    O praise the Lord, *Psalm 103,* G [d′#-f″#(g)], Classical/Bosworth 7 Sacred, Bosworth; B♭, Bosworth 7 Sacred.
    O that my ways, *Psalm 119,* D♭ [d′b-f″b], Classical/Bosworth 7 Sacred; F, Bosworth 7 Sacred.
    Orpheus with his lute, *Shakespeare,* B♭ [c′-g″], S&B (Pilkington) *Early Georgian 2,* BMP (Goldsborough).
    Praise the Lord, O my soul, *Psalm 103,* E♭ [d′-f″], Classical/Bosworth 7 Sacred.
    Praised be the Lord, *Psalms?,* Cm [c′-f″], BMP (Roper).
    Salvation belongeth unto the Lord, *Psalms?,* B♭ [f′-e″b], BMP (Roper), Schirmer *2nd Baritone.*
    Sun shall be no more thy light, The, *Psalms?,* Cm [d′-f″], Classical/Bosworth 7 Sacred; Dm, Bosworth 7 Sacred, Bosworth, Schirmer *2nd Soprano.*
    Thou openest thine hand, *see* Eyes of all, The.

Gregson, Edward. 1945– BMIC.

Griffiths, Gilmore. WMIC.

Grossner, Sonja.
Collection: *Four Dickinson Songs,* Da Capo .
    Dawn, *Emily Dickinson,* [high], Da Capo.
    I'm nobody, *Emily Dickinson,* [high], Da Capo.

White of the Year, *Emily Dickinson*, [high], Da Capo.
With Flowers, *Emily Dickinson*, [high], Da Capo.

Gurney, Ivor. 1890-1937. *See also* App. 2.
Collections: *First Volume of Ten Songs, A,* BMP; *Twenty Songs Volume 2,* BMP; *Third Volume of Ten Songs, A,* BMP; *Fourth Volume of Ten Songs, A,* BMP; *Fifth Volume of Ten Songs, A,* BMP; *Five Elizabethan Songs,* B&H; *Eleven Songs,* Thames (edited Michael Hurd); *Lights Out,* S&B; *Ludlow and Teme,* S&B (revised edition Michael Pilkington); *Seven Sappho Songs,* Thames (edited and introduced by Richard Carder); *Twenty Favourite Songs,* OUP (selected and introduced by Neil Jenkins); *Western Playland, The,* S&B (revised edition Michael Pilkington).

All night under the moon, *Wilfrid Gibson*, G# [d′#-f′′#], OUP 20 Favourite, BMP First Volume.
Apple Orchard, The, *Bliss Carman*, E♭ [d′#-e′′♭], Thames 7 Sappho, OUP 20 Favourite, BMP Fifth Volume.
Aspens, The, *A. E. Housman*, F [c′-e′′](m), S&B Western Playland.
Black Stichel, *Wilfrid Gibson*, F [d′♭-e′′], OUP 20 Favourite, BMP First Volume.
Blaweary, *Wilfrid Gibson*, F [d′-d′′], BMP Twenty Songs 2.
Boat is chafing, The, *John Davidson*, D♭ [d′♭-e′′], BMP Twenty Songs 2.
Bonnie Earl of Murray, The, *Anon*, Dm [d′-f′′], B&H *New Imperial 5*, Thames 11 Songs.
Bread and Cherries, *Walter de la Mare*, Em [e′-f′′#], OUP 20 Favourite, BMP Twenty Songs 2, Mayhew *Collection 2*.
Bright clouds, *Edward Thomas*, G [d′-f′′], Thames *Century 4* S&B Lights Out.
Brown is my love, *Anon*, D♭ [d′♭-g′′♭](m), OUP 20 Favourite, BMP Fourth Volume.
By a bierside, *John Masefield*, C [a-f′′], BMP Fifth Volume.
Captain Stratton's Fancy, *John Masefield*, G [c′-e′′](m), Thames 11 Songs.
Carol of the Skiddaw Yowes, *Ernest Casson*, Am [d′-e′′], B&H *Heritage 1*.
Cathleen ni Houlihan, *W. B. Yeats*, Am [c′♭-f′′], BMP First Volume.
Cherry trees bend over, The, *Edward Thomas*, E [e′-e′′], BMP Third Volume.
Cloths of Heaven, The, *W. B. Yeats*, E♭ [e′♭-g′′], OUP 20 Favourite, BMP Fifth Volume.
Cock-crow, *Edward Thomas*, B [e′-f′′#], Thames 11 Songs.
Come, O come, my life's delight, *Thomas Campion*, A♭ [b♭-f′′#], Thames 11 Songs.
County Mayo, The, *James Stephens*, Em [c′-f′′](m), Thames 11 Songs.
Cradle Song, A, *W. B. Yeats*, E♭ [e′♭-f′′♭], BMP Fourth Volume.
Desire in Spring, *Francis Ledwidge*, E [b-e′′], OUP 20 Favourite, BMP Fifth Volume; *G*, BMP.
Down by the salley gardens, *W. B. Yeats*, A♭ [d′♭-f′′], OUP 20 Favourite, BMP First Volume, Mayhew *Collection 2*.
Edward, Edward, *Anon*, Dm [c′-f′′], Thames 11 Songs.
Epitaph, An, *Walter de la Mare*, D [d′-e′′], OUP 20 Favourite, BMP Twenty Songs 2; *C, Solo Baritone*.
Epitaph in Old Mode, *John Squire*, D♭ [d′♭-f′′♭], BMP Twenty Songs 2.
Even such is time, *Walter Raleigh*, Em [b-e′′], OUP 20 Favourite, BMP Fourth Volume.
Far Country, The, *A. E. Housman*, F# [c′#-d′′#](m), S&B Western Playland.
Far in a western brookland, *A. E. Housman*, D♭ [d′♭-g′′♭](m), S&B Ludlow and Teme.
Fiddler of Dooney, The, *W. B. Yeats*, E♭ [b♭-f′′](m), BMP Fourth Volume.
Fields are full, The, *Edward Shanks*, E [c′#-e′′], OUP 20 Favourite, BMP Fifth Volume.
Folly of Being Comforted, The, *W. B. Yeats*, C#m [c′#-g′′#(f′′#)](m), BMP Twenty Songs 2.
Golden Friends, *A. E. Housman*, A♭ [e′♭-e′′♭](m), S&B Western Playland.
Goodnight to the meadow, *Robert Graves*, E♭ [c′-e′′♭], BMP Third Volume.
Ha'nacker Mill, *Hilaire Belloc*, F [e′-f′′], BMP First Volume.
Happy Tree, The, *Gerald Gould*, E [c′#-f′′#], BMP Third Volume.
Hawk and Buckle, *John Doyle (Robert Graves)*, Gm [d′-e′′♭], Mayhew *Collection 1*, Twenty Songs 2.
Hesperus, *Bliss Carman*, F# [c′#-f′′](f), Thames 7 Sappho.
I praise the tender flower, *Robert Bridges*, F [c′#-e′′], OUP 20 Favourite, BMP Third Volume.
I shall ever be maiden, *Bliss Carman*, G [d′♭-g′′](f), Thames 7 Sappho, BMP Third Volume.
I will go with my father a-ploughing, *MacCathmhaoil*, Em [d′-e′′], B&H *Heritage 1*.
In Flanders, *F. W. Harvey*, E♭ [c′#-f′′], BMP Fourth Volume.
Is my team ploughing, *A. E. Housman*, Dm [a(b)-e′′](m), S&B Western Playland.
Last Hours, *John Freeman*, Em [b♭-e′′], BMP Twenty Songs 2.
(Latmian Shepherd, The, *Edward Shanks*, E♭ [c′-e′′], BMP First Volume.
Lent Lily, The, *A. E. Housman*, A [e′-a′′](m), S&B Ludlow and Teme.
Lights Out, *Edward Thomas*, D♭ [d′♭-e′′], Thames *Century 2*, S&B Lights Out.
Lonely Night, *Bliss Carman*, B [c′#-e′′], Thames 7 Sappho.
Love shakes my soul, *Bliss Carman*, Bm [b-f′′#](f), Thames 7 Sappho, BMP Fourth Volume.
Loveliest of trees, *A. E. Housman*, D♭ [d′♭-f′′](m), S&B Western Playland.

Ludlow Fair, *A. E. Housman*, Cm [e′b-g′′](m), S&B Ludlow and Teme.
March, *A. E. Housman*, F [c′-f′′](m), S&B Western Playland.
Most holy night, *Hilaire Belloc*, Eb [e′b-e′′], OUP 20 Favourite, BMP Fourth Volume.
Night of Trafalgar, The, *Thomas Hardy*, Dm [d′-f′′](m), BMP Fifth Volume.
Nine of the clock, *John Doyle (Robert Graves)*, G [d′-e′′], Mayhew *Collection 1*, BMP First Volume.
On the Downs, *John Masefield*, Gm [c′-e′′], BMP Fourth Volume.
On the idle hill of summer, *A. E. Housman*, F [e′b-a′′](m), S&B Ludlow and Teme.
On your midnight pallet, *A. E. Housman*, Gm [d′-e′′](m), Thames 11 Songs.
Orpheus, *Shakespeare*, E [d′#-g′′], B&H 5 Elizabethan.
Penny Whistle, The, *Edward Thomas*, Dm [c′#-f′′], S&B Lights Out.
Piper in the streets today, A, *Seumas O'sullivan*, G [e′-f′′], OUP 20 Favourite, BMP Fourth Volume.
Ploughman singing, *John Clare*, B [d′-g′′], BMP Third Volume.
Quiet Mist, The, *Bliss Carman*, F# [e′-g′′#], Thames 7 Sappho.
Reveille, *A. E. Housman*, F [d′-f′′](m), S&B Western Playland.
Scents, *Edward Thomas*, Db [d′b-e′′], S&B Lights Out.
Scribe, The, *Walter de la Mare*, Bm [b♭-e′′], OUP 20 Favourites, Twenty Songs 2.
Severn Meadows, *Ivor Gurney*, D [b-d′′], OUP 20 Favourite, BMP Fifth Volume.
Shepherd's Song, *Ben Jonson*, Db [c′-f′′b], BMP Third Volume.
Ship, The, *John Squire*, Db [d′b-e′′], BMP Third Volume.
Since thou O fondest and truest, *Robert Bridges*, E [d′#-e′′], Thames 11 Songs.
Singer, The, *Edward Shanks*, Bm [d′b-f′′#], OUP 20 Favourite, BMP First Volume.
Sleep, *John Fletcher*, Db [d′b-a′′b], B&H 5 Elizabethan, *New Imperial 4*, (B&H); Bb, B&H Heritage 1, B&H.
Snow, *Edward Thomas*, Fm [e′b-g′′], OUP 20 Favourite, BMP Third Volume.
Soft was the wind, *Bliss Carman*, B [e′-g′′#](f), Thames 7 Sappho.
Song of Ciabhan, *Ethna Carbery*, D [d′-e′′b], BMP Fifth Volume.
Sowing, *Edward Thomas*, (version 1) Cm [c′-e′′], Thames 11 Songs.
Sowing, *Edward Thomas*, (version 2) Cm [c′-e′′], S&B.
Spring, *Thomas Nashe*, E [c′-g′′#], B&H 5 Elizabethan, *Heritage 1*.
Star-talk, *Robert Graves*, D [b′-f′′#], Thames 11 Songs.
Sword, A, *Robin Flower*, Dm [d′-e′′](m), BMP Twenty Songs 2.
Tears, *Anon*, C#m [c′#-e′′], B&H 5 Elizabethan.
(Thou didst delight my eyes, *Robert Bridges*, Db [d′b-e′′b], BMP Third Volume.
Tis time, I think, *A. E. Housman*, F [e′b-g′′b](m), S&B Ludlow and Teme.
To Violets, *Robert Herrick*, G [c′-e′′], OUP 20 Favourite, BMP Fourth Volume.
Trumpet, The, *Edward Thomas*, Ab [d′b-f′′], S&B Lights Out.
Twa Corbies, The, *Anon*, Am [c′-f′′], BMP Fifth Volume.
Twice a week, *A. E. Housman*, Bm [b-f′′](m), S&B Western Playland.
Under the greenwood tree, *Shakespeare*, Am [c′-f′′#], B&H 5 Elizabethan.
Walking Song, *F. W. Harvey*, F [c′-f′′], OUP 20 Favourite, BMP Fifth Volume.
West Sussex Drinking Song, *Hilaire Belloc*, F [c′-f′′](m), Thames 11 Songs.
When death to either shall come, *Robert Bridges*, Db [d′b-e′′b], BMP First Volume.
When I was one-and-twenty, *A. E. Housman*, Am [e′-g′′](m), S&B Ludlow and Teme.
When smoke stood up, *A. E. Housman*, A [d′b-a′′](m), S&B Ludlow and Teme.
Will you come? *Edward Thomas*, F [c′-e′′], S&B Lights Out.
You are my sky, *John Squire*, Db [c′-f′′], BMP First Volume.

Guthrie, John. 1912–1986. SMIC.

Guy, Barry. 1947– See App. 2.

H

Hadley, Patrick Arthur Sheldon. 1899–1973.
Scene from 'The Woodlanders', *Thomas Hardy*, [d-g′′](f), Thames *Hardy Songbook*, BMP.

Hales, Robert. *fl*.1583.
O eyes, leave off your weeping, *Nicholas Breton?* Cm [e′b-e′′b], S&B (Stroud) *Banquet*, BMP W&W 5.

Hall, Richard. 1903–1982. BMIC.

Hamilton, Alasdair.
Collection: *The Plumes of Time,* Roberton.
    Autumnal, *Lewis Spence,* [a-e′′], Roberton Plumes.
    Pieces of Eight, *Lewis Spence,* [a-e′′], Roberton Plumes.
    Plumes of Time, The, *Lewis Spence,* [bb-e′′b], Roberton Plumes.
    Silken Heart, The, *Lewis Spence,* [a-f′′], Roberton Plumes.

Hamilton, Iain Ellis. 1922– 2000.
Collections: *Five Lyrics of Torquato Tasso,* Presser; *Songs of Summer,* Presser.
    Country Glee, *Thomas Dekker,* [d′-a′′], Presser Songs of Summer.
    Dawn, *Anon,* [d′-a′′], Presser Songs of Summer.
    Rose, The, *Thomas Howell,* [e′-f′′#], Presser Songs of Summer.

Hamilton, Janet.
    Bredon Hill, *A. E. Housman,* Dm [c′-e′′], B&H.
    By Wenlock Town, *A. E. Housman,* Ab [e′b-g′′], B&H.
    Cherry Tree, The, *A. E. Housman,* Db [d′b-f′′], B&H.
    Endymion, *Edward Shanks,* A [d′-f′′], B&H.
    Great Child, The, *Edward Shanks,* E [b-f′′#], B&H.
    Music that Love Made, The, *Madeleine Caron Rock,* Db [c′-e′′b], B&H.
    With rue my heart is laden, *A. E. Housman,* F#m [b-c′′#], B&H.

Hand, Colin. 1929– BMIC.
Collections: *Dark Sunset,* [c′-f′′#], Lindis; *Three Songs to Poems by John Fletcher,* [d′-a′′], Brunton.
    Angelus, *Vivian Locke Ellis,* Lindis Sunset.
    Aspatia's Song, *John Fletcher,* Brunton Fletcher.
    Dark Sunset, *Vivian Locke Ellis,* Lindis Sunset.
    God Lyaeus, *John Fletcher,* Brunton Fletcher.
    Hymn to Pan, *John Fletcher,* Brunton Fletcher.
    Tewkesbury Road, *John Masefield,* Eb [c-e′b(f′)]m, Braydestone.
    This Sad Serenity, *Vivian Locke Ellis,* Lindis Sunset.
    Waves, *Vivian Locke Ellis,* Lindis Sunset.

Handel, George Frideric. 1685–1759. *See also* App. 2.
Collection: *Songs and Cantatas,* BMP (edited Donald Burrows).
    Answer to Colin's complaint, An, *Anon,* Em [d′#-e′′](f), BMP Songs.
    Arm, arm ye brave, C [B-e′], Schirmer *2nd Baritone.*
    Art thou troubled, *W. G. Rothery,* Ab [e′b-a′′b], Novello; F, Novello; Eb, Thames *Countertenors 3.*
    Come and trip it, *Charles Jennens,* Cm [e′b-a′′b], Leonard *Baroque high;* Bm, Schirmer *1st Soprano II;* Gm, Leonard *Baroque low.*
    (Come to me, soothing sleep, *Arthur Somervell,* Eb [d′-f′′], Curwen (Somervell).)
    Dear Adonis, beauty's treasure, *John Hughes,* Gm [d′-a′′](f), BMP Songs.
    Forsaken Maid's Complaint, The, *Anon,* A [e′-b′′](f), BMP Songs.
    Forsaken Nymph, The, *Anon,* F [d′-f′′](f), BMP Songs.
    Here amid the shady woods, *Thomas Morell,* F [d′-f′′], Leonard *Baroque high,* Schirmer *1st Soprano II;* D, Leonard *Baroque low.*
    Hymen, haste! thy torch prepare *William Congreve,* Bb [a′-c′′], Thames (Hodgson) *Countertenors 1.*
    I like the am'rous youth, *James Miller,* F [e′-g′′](f), BMP Songs.
    Leave me, loathsome light, *William Congreve,* D, Schirmer *1st Baritone.*
    Let me wander not unseen , *Charles Jennens,* Dm [d′-g′′], Leonard *Baroque high;* Am, Leonard *Baroque low.*
    Like the shadow, A [a-d′′], Schirmer *2nd Baritone.*
    (Lost Love, *Arthur Somervell,* Gm [c′-f′′], Curwen (Somervell).)
    Love's but the frailty of the mind, *William Congreve,* F [e′-g′′](f), BMP Songs.
    More sweet is that name, D [a-d′′], Schirmer *2nd Baritone.*
    O had I Jubal's lyre, A, Schirmer *2nd Soprano.*
    O sleep, why dost thou leave me, *William Congreve,* E, [e′-g′′#], Chester *Celebrated 3;* C, Schirmer *1st Mezzo.*
    Pleasure's gentle zephyrs play, F [bb-e′′], Schirmer *2nd Mezzo.*
    Poor Shepherd, The, *John Gay,* Em [d′-g′′](f), BMP Songs.
    Quite unconcerned, *French,* tr. *Anon,* Dm [d′-f′′](f), BMP Songs.

Silent Worship, *Arthur Somervell*, A [e′-f′′#], Schirmer *1st Tenor*; G, Chester (Somervell) *Celebrated 1*, Roberton, (F, Curwen).
Smiling hours, The, F [bb-d′′], Schirmer *2nd Mezzo*.
(Spring, *Arthur Somervell*, E [d′#-f′′#], Curwen (Somervell); D, Curwen.)
Thou shalt bring them in, E [b-c′′#], Schirmer *2nd Mezzo*.
Total eclipse, Em [d′-g′′], Schirmer *2nd Tenor*.
Transporting joy, *John Hughes*, Cm [d′-g′′](f), BMP Songs.
(Trumpet is calling, The, *Arthur Somervell*, Bb [d′-g′′], Curwen (Somervell).)
Twas when the seas were roaring, *John Gay*, Gm [c′-g′′](f), BMP Songs.
Unhappy Lovers, The, *Anon*, Dm [c′#-g′′](f), BMP Songs.
Weep no more, *John Fletcher*, Bb [bb-c′′], Schirmer *1st Mezzo II*.
Where e'er you walk, *William Congreve*, Bb [f′-g′′], Leonard *Baroque high*, Novello, Schirmer *1st Tenor II*, Schirmer; G, Leonard *Baroque low*, Cramer, S&B, Schirmer; F, Schirmer (Heale).

Handford, George. 1582–1647.
Collections: *Ayres, Books 1 & 2*, S&B (edited Anthony Rooley).
Go weep, sad soul, *Anon*, [e-f′′], BMP W&W 6.

Hardelot, Guy d'. (Mrs W. I. Rhodes, *née* Helen Guyl). 1858–1936. *See also* Chappell.
Because, *Edward Teschemacher*, C [e′-g′′], IMP *Parlour Songs*, Classical; Bb, Ab, Classical.

Harding, Kenneth. *See* App. 2.

Hardy, John. WMIC. *See also* App. 2.
Collection: *Pandemonium*, WMIC.
Maidens came, The, *Anon*, [high], WMIC.

Harries, David. 1933– WMIC. *See also* App. 2.
Last night, *Alun Jones*, tr. John Stoddart, Am [e′-g′′], WMIC *Songs from Wales 1*.

Harrington, Frank. 1963–
Collection: *Where Poppies Blow!* Lynwood.
'1915', *Thomas Hardy*, [G-e′b], Lynwood Poppies.
Base Details, *Siegfried Sassoon*, [c-c′](m), Lynwood Poppies.
Flanders Fields, *John McRae*, [Bb-e′b](m), Lynwood Poppies.
Immortals, The, *Isaac Rosenberg*, [c#-d′](m), Lynwood Poppies.
Trumpet, The, *Edward Thomas*, [c-e′](m), Lynwood Poppies.

Harris, Roger.
Sigh no more, ladies, *Shakespeare*, D [a′-a′′], R.Clyde.

Harris, S. Taylor.
Feast of Christmas, The, *S. T. Harris*, [c′-f′′], BMP.

Harris, William Lewarne. 1929–
Epitaph (Resurrection), *Leigh Henry*, [Bb-f′#](m), Thames *Century 6*.
Piskies, *T. P. Cameron Wilson*, E [B-e′](m), BMP.

Harrison, Annie Fortescue.
In the gloaming, *Meta Orred*, G [d′-e′′], IMP *Parlour Songs*, Classical; F, Classical.

Harrison, Denham.
Give me a ticket to heaven, *Richard Elton*, Eb [d′-e′′b], Cramer *Drawing Room*.

Harrison, Julius Alan Greenway. 1885–1963.
Collections: (*Five English Songs*, Enoch); *Four Narratives from the Ancient Chinese*, B&H; *Four Songs from Twelfth Night*, Lengnick; *Four Songs of Chivalry*, B&H; (*Three Sonnets from Boccaccio*, Enoch).
Ave mors, *Margery Hamilton-Fellowes*, Cm [c′-a′′b], B&H.
Boot, saddle, to horse, *Robert Browning*, G [d′-f′′](m), B&H; A, B&H.
(By a Clear Well, *Boccaccio* tr. D. G. Rossetti, [d′-g′′], Enoch 3 Boccaccio.)
Cavalier to His Lady, A, *William Strode*, F [e′b-g′′](m), B&H; (D, B&H).
Clown's Song, *Shakespeare*, Em [e′-g′′](m), Lengnick 4 Twelfth Night.
Come away death, *Shakespeare*, Fm [f′-a′′b], Lengnick 4 Twelfth Night.
(Escape from Love, The, *Geoffrey Chaucer*, [d′-g′′b], Enoch 5 English.)

Eve of Crecy, The, *William Morris*, E [e´(d´#)-a´´](m), B&H 4 Chivalry.
(Fiammetta Singing, *Boccaccio* tr. *D. G. Rossetti*, [e´b-a´´b](m), Enoch 3 Boccaccio.)
Gilliflower of Gold, The, *William Morris*, A [e´-a´´](m), B&H 4 Chivalry.
Guendolen, *William Morris*, Eb [d´-g´´(b´´b)](m), B&H 4 Chivalry; C, B&H.
(Heliodore, *Meleager* tr. *Andrew Lang*, F#m [e´#-f´´#], Enoch 5 English.)
(I heard a music sweet today, *Thomas MacDonagh*, E [d´#-g´´(f´´#)], Enoch 5 English.)
I know a bank, *Shakespeare*, E [d´#-f´´#(g´´#)], B&H *Shakespeare Album*; D, B&H.
(In Prison, *William Morris*, Cm [c´-f´´], Enoch 5 English.)
Jolly Robin, *Shakespeare*, Ab [e´b-a´´b], Lengnick 4 Twelfth Night.
King Charles, *Robert Browning*, Cm [e´b-g´´](m), B&H; (Am, B&H.)
Last Revel, The, *Ch'en Tzu-ang* tr. *L. Cranmer-Byng*, Gm [c´-f´´], B&H 4 Narratives.
(Last Sight of Fiammetta, The, *Boccaccio* tr. *D. G. Rossetti*, [c´#-a´´](m), Enoch 3 Boccaccio.)
Marching along, *Robert Browning*, Dm [c´#-f´´](m), B&H; Fm, B&H.
Memory Island, *Paul Askew*, F [d´-f´´#](m), B&H; D, B&H.
(Merciless Beauty, *Geoffrey Chaucer*, [d´-f´´], Enoch 5 English.)
O mistress mine, *Shakespeare*, E [e´-f´´#(g´´)](m), Lengnick 4 Twelfth Night.
Philomel, *Shakespeare*, Bb [f´-b´´b(a´´b)], B&H *Heritage 1*; G, B&H.
Recruiting Sergeant, The, *Tu Fu* tr. *L. Cranmer-Byng?* Dm [c´-g´´b(f´´)], B&H 4 Narratives.
Sea Winds, *Paul Askew*, G [c´-e´´], B&H; F, B&H.
Sir Giles' War Song, *William Morris*, Gm [d´-a´´(b´´b)](m), B&H 4 Chivalry.
Soldier, The, *Confucius* tr. *L. Cranmer-Byng?* Fm, [e´b-g´´b(f´´)](m), B&H 4 Narratives.
There was a king of Liang, *Kao-Shih* tr. *Anon*, F#m [c´#-f´´#(d´´)], B&H 4 Narratives.

Harrison, Pamela. 1915–
Collection: *Eight Poems of Walter de la Mare*, BMP.
Blindman's in, *Walter de la Mare*, [d´-e´´], BMP 8 Walter de la Mare.
Dreamland, *Walter de la Mare*, [d´-g´´], BMP 8 Walter de la Mare.
Goldfinch, A, *Walter de la Mare*, [d´-e´´], BMP 8 Walter de la Mare.
Horseman, The, *Walter de la Mare*, [d´-f´´#], BMP 8 Walter de la Mare.
Nicoletta, *Walter de la Mare*, [d´-f´´#], BMP 8 Walter de la Mare.
Where, *Walter de la Mare*, [d´-d´´], BMP 8 Walter de la Mare.
White, *Walter de la Mare*, [c´-g´´], BMP 8 Walter de la Mare.
Why? *Walter de la Mare*, [d´-d´´], BMP 8 Walter de la Mare.

Hart, James. 1647–1718.
Adieu to the pleasures and follies of love, *Thomas Shadwell*, Dm [c´-f´´](f), Thames (Bevan) *8 Restoration*.
Honest shepherd, since you're poor, *Anon*, Am [e´-f´´](f), Thames (Bevan) *8 Restoration*.

Hartley, Walter.
Love Song of the Bride, *Song of Solomon*, [a-b´´](f), Bardic.
Shall I compare thee? *Shakespeare*, [d´-a´´], Bardic.

Harty, Sir Herbert **Hamilton.** 1879–1941.
Collections: *Antrim and Donegal*, B&H; (*Five Irish Poems*, B&H); *Six Songs of Ireland*, B&H; *Three Flower Songs*, B&H.
(Across the Door, *Padraic Colum*, Novello.)
At Easter, *Helen Lanyon*, C#m [c´#-g´´#(e´´)], B&H, (B&H 5 Irish.)
At Sea, *Moira O'Neill*, C [c´-a´´], B&H 6 Songs.
Bonfires, *W. L. Bultitaft*, C [c´-f´´], B&H; Eb, B&H.
By the bivouac's fitful flame, *Walt Whitman*, Eb [a-e´´b], B&H.
Come, O come, my life's delight, *Thomas Campion*, Eb [d´-g´´(a´´b)], B&H.
(Cradle Song, *Padraic Colum*, Novello.)
Denny's daughter, *Moira O'Neill*, Gb [e´b-g´´b(b´´b)](m), B&H, (B&H 5 Irish.)
Dreaming, *Cahir Healy*, Bb [c´-g´´], B&H 6 Songs.
(Drover, A, *Padraic Colum*, Cm [c´-f´´](m), Novello.)
(Fiddler of Dooney, The, *W. B. Yeats*, Bm [f´#-g´´], B&H 5 Irish.)
Flame in the skies of sunset, *Lizzie Twigg*, [c´-e´´], B&H 6 Songs.
Gorse, *L. B. Hay Shaw*, Eb [e´b-g´´](m), B&H 3 Flower.
Grace for Light, *Moira O'Neill*, G [c´-g´´], B&H 6 Songs, B&H.
Herrin's in the bay, *Elizabeth Shane*, D [d´-g´´](f), B&H Antrim.
Hush Song, *Elizabeth Shane*, Am [e´-f´´](f), B&H Antrim.
(Irish Love Song, An, *Katherine Tynan*, Chappell.)
Lane o' the Thrushes, *Cathal O'Byrne* and *Cahir Healy*, E [e´-f´´#], B&H.

Little Son, The, *Moira O'Neill*, B [b-e''](f), B&H Antrim.
Lookin' Back, *Moira O'Neill*, Dm [d'-g''], B&H 6 Songs.
Lullaby, A, *Cathal O'Byrne*, Bbm [e'-g''b], B&H *Imperial* 1, 6 Songs; *Gm, Heritage 1,* Schirmer 2nd Mezzo.
Mayo Love Song, A, *Alice Milligan*, [f'-a''](m), B&H 5 Irish.
Mignonette, *L. B. Hay Shaw*, Eb [bb-g''], B&H 3 Flower.
(Now is the month of maying, *Anon*, G, B&H.)
Ould Lad, The, *Moira O'Neill*, Db [ab-d''b](m), B&H.
Poppies, *L. B. Hay Shaw*, Db [d'b-f''], B&H 3 Flower.
(Rachray Man, The, *Moira O'Neill*, Dm [c'-f''](f), Novello.)
(Rann of Wandering, A, *Padraic Colum*, Bb [d'-f''#], Novello.)
Sailor Man, The, *Moira O'Neill*, Dm [d'-e''](m), B&H 5 Irish, B&H.
Scythe Song, *Riccardo Stephens*, F [c'-e''], B&H *Heritage 2.*
Sea Gypsy, The, *Richard Hovey,* C [e'-f''](m), B&H; Eb, B&H.
Sea Wrack, *Moira O'Neill*, Bb [bb-e''b](f), B&H *Heritage 1, Imperial 3*: C, D, B&H.
Song of Glen Dun, The, *Moira O'Neill*, G [e'b-g''](f), B&H.
Song of the Three Mariners, *Anon,* G [d'-e''(g')](m), B&H *Easy Song.*
(Stranger's Grave, The, *Emily Lawless*, Gm [c'-e''b], Novello.)
(Tell me not, sweet, I am unkind, *Richard Lovelace*, Db, B&H.)
Two Houses, The, *Moira O'Neill*, Am [e'-g''](f), B&H Antrim.
(Wake Feast, The, *Alice Milligan*, Dm [c'#-e''](m), Novello.)
Arrangements: *Three Irish Folksongs,* BMP; *Three Traditional Ulster Airs* (high, low)*,* B&H.
Black Sheela of the Silver Eye, *Seosamh MacCathmhaoil*, Eb [c'-e''b](m) B&H 3 Ulster; Gb, 3 Ulster.
Blue Hills of Antrim, The, *Seosamh MacCathmhaoil*, Bb [bb-d''], B&H 3 Ulster; D, 3 Ulster.
Fairy King's Courtship, The, *P. W. Joyce,*, Eb [e'b-f''], BMP 3 Irish.
Game Played in Erin-go-Bragh, The, *P. W. Joyce*, Cm [c'-e''b](m), BMP 3 Irish.
Lowlands of Holland, The, *P. W. Joyce*, Em [d'-e''](f), BMP 3 Irish.
My Lagan Love, *Seosamh MacCathmhaoil*, C [bb-e''b](m), B&H *Imperial 6, McCormack*; E, 3 Ulster.

Harvey, Frank. 1939–
Dawn, *William Barnes,* [a-f''], EPSS.

Harvey, Jonathan Dean. 1939– *See also* App. 2.
Collection: *Four Songs of Yeats,* (bass-baritone), Novello.
Cantata II (Three Lovescapes), [soprano], Novello.
Correspondences, [mezzo], Novello.
Lullaby for the unsleeping, *John V. Taylor*, [d'-g''](f), Faber.

Harvey, Trevor.
Sailor's Carol, A, *Hilaire Belloc,* [c'-a''], BMP.

Hattey, Philip.
Collections: *Seven Poems of Robert Graves,* B&H; *Three Spirituals,* BMP.
Horizon, *Robert Graves*, E [b-d''], B&H 7 Graves.
Is now the time? *Robert Graves*, [c'-e''b], B&H 7 Graves.
Lift-boy, *Robert Graves*, [b-f''], B&H 7 Graves.
Sharp Ridge, The, *Robert Graves*, Cm [b-e''b], B&H 7 Graves.
She tells her love while half asleep, *Robert Graves*, F#m [c'-e''], B&H 7 Graves.
Two Witches, The, *Robert Graves*, Gm [bb-e''], B&H 7 Graves.
Variables of Green, *Robert Graves*, F [d'-d''b], B&H 7 Graves.

Hatton, John Liptrot. 1808–1886.
Collection: *A Herrick Cycle,* Thames 1997 (selected and edited Richard Graves).
Deluge, The, *Robert Herrick*, Am [e'-e''](m), Thames Cycle.
Enchantress, The, *Robert Herrick*, Am [f'#-e''](f), B&H *New Imperial 3.*
Gather ye rosebuds, *Robert Herrick*, E [e'-e''](m), Thames Cycle.
Hag, The, *Robert Herrick*, F#m [c'#-a''], MB 43; Dm, S&B *Recitalist 2.*
I'm conquered, love, by thee, *J.Duff*, C, Cramer.
In Her Garden, Cramer.
It is early in the morning, Cramer.
Rock of Rubies, The, *Robert Herrick*, E [e'-e''](m), Thames Cycle.
Sands of Dee, The, *Charles Kingsley*, Cramer.

Simon the Cellarer, *W. H. Bellamy,* D [a-e''](m), IMP *Parlour Songs*.
Student's Serenade, *Longfellow,* F, Cramer; A, Cramer.
Teare, The, *Robert Herrick,* C [e'-f''](m), Thames Cycle.
To Anthea, *Robert Herrick,* E [d'#-e''](m), Thames Cycle; [d'#-f''#] S&B *Recitalist 4, MB 43*; Eb, B&H *New Imperial 5*, Paterson *100 Best 3*; F, Cramer, BMP (Wilson).
To Julia, *Robert Herrick,* F#m [c'#-f''#](m), Thames Cycle.
To the Rose, *Robert Herrick,* D [d'-e''](m), Thames Cycle.
To the Willow Tree, *Robert Herrick,* C#m [c'#-e''](m), Thames Cycle.
Uncle Jack, *W. H. Bellamy,* Cramer.
Wanderer, The, *J. Duff,* Cramer.

Hawes, Jack.
Collections: *Two Canzonets,* [medium]; Brunton; *Two English Lyrics,* [medium]; Brunton.
At the last, [medium], Brunton.
Autumn Ritual (cycle), [medium], Brunton.
Dream Fantasy, [medium], Brunton.
Easter Morn, [medium], Brunton.
Lark, The, [medium], Brunton.
Truth, [medium], Brunton.
Wasp, The, [medium], Brunton.
Woodside Rise, The (cycle), [medium], Brunton.

Hawkins of Liverpool.
Ode on the Morning, *Anon,* Em [c'-g''], Thames (Copley & Reitan) *Gentleman's Magazine*.

Hayden, George. ? –1722.
Cypress Grove, A, *Anon,* Bbm [d'b-g''], BMP (Taylor).

Hayes, Morgan. *See also* App. 2.
Collection: *No Glints in it,* S&B.
Creek, *Anne Rouse,* [c'-b''b], S&B Glints.
Glass, *Anne Rouse,* [c'#-f''#], S&B Glints.
Move, *Anne Rouse,* [b-b''], S&B Glints.
My Compass, *Matthew Green,* [e'b-c''], S&B.
Pick-up in Soho, *Anne Rouse,* [b-b''], S&B Glints.

Haynes, Battison.
Arrangement:
Off to Philadelphia, *Anon, revised Stephen Temple,* D [a-f''#(e'')], IMP *Parlour Songs*.

Head, Michael Dewar. 1900–1976. *see also* App. 1, 2.
Collections: *Five Songs,* B&H; *Over the rim of the moon,* [high, low], B&H; *Six Sea Songs,* B&H; *Song Album 1 – Songs of the Countryside, Song Album 2 — Songs of Romance and Delight, Song Album 3 — Songs for Male Voice,* B&H; *Song Album for Mezzo-soprano or Baritone,* [Album Low] B&H; *Song Album for Soprano or Tenor,* [Album High], B&H); *Songs of the Countryside,* B&H; *More Songs of the Countryside,* B&H; *Three Cotswold Songs,* B&H; *Three Songs of Fantasy* [high, medium, low], B&H; *Three Songs of Venice,* B&H.
Acquaint now thyself with Him, *Job 22, Psalms 99, 96, Micah,* adapted *Denice Koch,* Eb [bb-e''b], B&H; G, B&H.
Autumn's Breath, *R. W. Dixon,* B [b-d''], B&H.
Ave Maria, *Latin* tr. *Nancy Bush,* Am [a'-e''], B&H; Cm, B&H.
Back to Hilo, *Cicely Fox Smith,* Em [b'-e''](m), B&H Album Low, 6 Sea.
Be merciful unto me, O God, *Psalm 57,* C [a'-g''(f')], Roberton; Eb, Roberton.
Behold, I send an angel, *Exodus & Isaiah,* adapted *Denice Koch,* G [b-d''], B&H.
Beloved, *Francis Ledwidge,* Bb [bb-f''(g'')], B&H Over the rim, Album Low; C, Over the rim.
Beloved, let us love one another, *John 4,* adapted *Denice Koch,* F [a-f''], B&H.
Bird-song, *Marjorie Rayment,* Fm [c'#-c'''(b'' or f'')](f), B&H.
Blackbird singing, A, *Francis Ledwidge,* E [b-e''], B&H Over the rim, B&H; Ab, Over the rim, B&H.
Blunder, The, *Jan Struther,* Dm [a-f''], B&H 5 Songs, B&H.
Carol of the Field Mice, The, *Kenneth Grahame,* D [d'-e''b(f''#)], B&H *Easy Song*.
Child on the Shore, *Nancy Bush,* D [bb-e''], Roberton.
Claribel, *Alfred Lord Tennyson,* F [c'-f''], B&H; D, B&H.
Come take your lute, *Helen Taylor,* Dm [a-d''(c'')], B&H.

(Comet, The, *Ruth Pitter*, Dm [bb-f″], B&H.
Constancy, *Ruth Pitter*, [a-f″], B&H.
Cotswold Love, *John Drinkwater*, Db [bb-f″(e″b], B&H; D, B&H.
Dear Delight, *Walter de la Mare*, Ab [e′b-a″b], B&H Album 2.
Dog's Life, A, *Cicely Fox Smith*, Dm [a-f″(d″)](m), B&H Album 3, 6 Sea, B&H.
Dove, The, *John Keats*, Gm [f′-g″](f), B&H.
Dreaming Lake, The, *Elizabeth Evelyn Moore*, C [c′-e″], B&H; E, B&H.
Elizabeth's Song, *Lascelles Abercrombie*, G [d′-b″](f), B&H.
Estuary, The, *Ruth Pitter*, Eb [bb-f″], B&H *Heritage 3,* Album Low.
Fairies' Dance, The, *Frank Dempster Sherman*, G [d′-g″], B&H Album 2, 3 Fantasy, Album High; Eb, B&H.
Fairy Tailor, The, *Rose Fyleman*, G [d′-g″(e″)], B&H Album High.
Fallen Veils, *D. G. Rossetti*, [c′-f″], B&H 5 Songs, B&H.
Foxgloves, *Mary Webb*, C [g′-g″], B&H Album 1, B&H; Ab, B&H Album Low, B&H More Countryside, B&H.
Funny Fellow, A, *Frank Dempster Sherman*, Eb [bb-e″b], B&H Album Low; G, 3 Fantasy; F, 3 Fantasy, B&H.
Gaite and Orior, *Alastair Miller*, Fm [e′b-g″], B&H Album High.
Garden Seat, The, *Thomas Hardy*, [b-c″#], B&H Album Low, More Countryside.
Give a man a horse he can ride, *James Thomson*, Eb [bb(c′)-e″b(g″)], B&H.
Gondolier, The, *Nancy Bush*, Bm [b-e″b], B&H 3 Venice.
Green Cornfield, A, *Christina Rossetti*, F [d′-f″], B&H Album 1, *Heritage 3*, B&H; Eb, B&H.
Green Rain, *Mary Webb*, [c′-f″], B&H Album 1, 5 Songs.
Had I a golden pound, *Francis Ledwidge*, C [b-e″(d″)], B&H.
Hail, bounteous May, *John Milton*, Db [e′b-f″(a″b)], B&H.
Happy Wanderer, The, *Helen Taylor*, F [c′(f′)-a″], B&H Album High.
Holiday in Heaven, *Ruth Pitter*, Am [e′-a″], B&H Album 2.
Holy and most blessed Virgin, *St Augustine* tr. *Nancy Bush*, Em [e′-g″#], B&H.
Homecoming of the Sheep, The, *Francis Ledwidge*, C#m [c′#-d″#], B&H.
How sweet the moonlight sleeps, *Shakespeare*, Db [a(bb)-f″(e″)], B&H.
I arise from dreams of thee, *Percy Bysshe Shelley*, G [d′-g″], B&H.
I will lift up mine eyes, *Psalm 121*, C [b-e″], Roberton; F, Roberton.
King of China's Daughter, The, *Edith Sitwell*, Dm [c′-f″](m), B&H 5 Songs, B&H.
Lavender Pond, *Cicely Fox Smith*, Ab [c′b-e″b], B&H *Heritage 3*, 6 Sea.
Lean out of the window, *James Joyce*, Eb [c′-e″b], B&H.
Limehouse Reach, *Cicely Fox Smith*, G [b-e″](m), B&H, Album Low, 6 Sea, B&H.
Little Dreams, The *Eileen M. Reynolds*, Eb [e′b(bb)-g″(f′)], B&H 3 Fantasy; C, Db, B&H.
Little Road to Bethlehem, The, *Margaret Rose*, Ab [eb-a″b], B&H; F, B&H *Souvenirs*, B&H.
Lone Dog, *Irene McCleod*, Cm [c′-e″b](m), B&H Album 3.
Lord's Prayer, The, *Book of Common Prayer,* Eb [bb-e″b], B&H.
Love me not for comely grace, *Anon*, F [c′-g″(a″)](m), B&H Album 2; G, Album High.
Love Rhapsody, A, *Martin MacDermott*, F [f′-a″](m), B&H.
Love's Lament, *Christina Rossetti*, Fm [c′-f″], B&H Album 2.
Ludlow Town, *A. E. Housman*, E [b-e″](m), B&H, Album Low; D, B&H.
Make a joyful noise unto the Lord, *Psalm 100*, E [b-e″(g″#)], Roberton; G, Roberton.
Mamble, *John Drinkwater*, Bb [bb-d″](m), B&H Album 3, Album Low, 3 Cotswold.
Matron Cat's Song, The, *Ruth Pitter*, Am [a-e″](f), B&H Album 3, Album Low, B&H.
Money, O! *W. H. Davies*, Gm [bb(g)-d″](m), B&H *Heritage 4, Imperial 6,* B&H; Bm, B&H.
My sword for the king, *Helen Taylor*, Em [b-g″(f″#)](m), B&H Album 3; Dm, B&H.
Nature's Friend, *W. H. Davies*, Dm [c′-f″#(d″)], B&H Countryside, B&H; Fm, B&H.
Nocturne, *Francis Ledwidge*, Ebm [c′-e″], B&H Over the rim, (B&H); G, Over the rim.
O blessed Virgin, *Latin* tr. *Nancy Bush*, G [d′-g″], B&H.
O let no star compare with thee, *Henry Vaughan*, F [c′-f″], B&H Album 2; A, B&H.
O to be in England, *Robert Browning*, F [d′-a″(g″)], B&H Album 1.
October Valley, *Nancy Bush*, [c′#-e″b], B&H.
Oh, for a March wind, *Winifred Williams*, A [c′#-a″], B&H Album 1.
On a Lady Singing, *Edward Quillinan*, F [d′-a″], B&H Album High.
On the wings of the wind, *Alastair Miller*, Eb [c′-a″(a″b)], B&H Album 1.
Piper, A, *Seumas O'Sullivan*, Dm [c′-e″], B&H Album 3, B&H; Fm, B&H Album 1, B&H.
Primrosy Gown, The, *Edward Lockton*, Ab [g-e″b](m), B&H.
Rain Storm, *Nancy Bush*, F#m [c′#-f″#], B&H 3 Venice.
Robin Redbreast, *W. H. Davies*, Am [c′-e″], B&H Countryside, B&H; Cm, B&H.
Robin's Carol, The, *Patience Strong*, Ab [c′-a″b(f″)], B&H.
Saint Mark's Square, *Nancy Bush*, D [bb-f″#], B&H 3 Venice.

Sea Burthen, A, *Cicely Fox Smith*, Gm [d′-f″], B&H 6 Sea, B&H.
Sea Gypsy, The, *Richard Hovey*, Cm [c′-e″(e″b)](m), B&H Album 3; Bm, Em, B&H.
Ships of Arcady, The, *Francis Ledwidge*, Bb [bb-e″b], B&H Over the rim, B&H; D, Over the rim.
Singer, The, *Bronnie Taylor*, Fm [c′-a″b](f), B&H Album 2, *Imperial 1*, Album High.
Slumber Song of the Madonna, A, *Alfred Noyes*, C [c-e″](f), B&H; Bb, B&H.
Small Christmas Tree, *Mona Gould*, Ab [f′-a″b(f″], B&H.
Star Candles, *Margaret Rose*, Dm [c′-f″], B&H, Album Low.
Summer Idyll, A, *Richard le Gallienne*, F [c′-f″](m), B&H Album 3; Ab, Album High.
Sweet almond blossom, *Samuel Waddington*, G [d′-g″], B&H Album 1.
Sweet chance, that led my steps abroad, *W. H. Davies*, F [c′-f″], B&H Album 1, *Heritage 4*, B&H; D, B&H.
Sweet day, so cool, *George Herbert*, F [e′b-a″b], B&H.
Sweethearts and Wives, *Cicely Fox Smith*, G [d′-e″](m), B&H 6 Sea, B&H.
Temper of a Maid, The, *W. H. Davies*, B [f″#-g″#], B&H Album High, Countryside.
Tewkesbury Road, *John Masefield*, Em [b-f″](m), B&H Album 1, B&H; Dm, B&H.
There's many will love a maid, *Penuel Grant Ross*, D [a-d″(e″)](m), B&H *Love and Affection*; Gb, B&H.
Three Mummers, The, *Helen Taylor*, Ab [e′b-f″], B&H.
Thus spake Jesus, *John 17*, Gm [b-e″], B&H; Bm, B&H.
Twins, The, *H. S. Leigh*, C [c′-e″b](m), B&H Album 2.
Vagabond Song, A, *John Drinkwater*, C#m [g#-e″(m)], B&H 3 Cotswold, B&H.
Viper, The, *Ruth Pitter*, F [c′-e″], B&H Album Low.
Weathers, *Thomas Hardy*, Ab [e′b-a″b], B&H Album High, More Countryside, B&H.
What Christmas Means to Me, *Joan Lane*, F [c′-f″], B&H; Ab, B&H.
When I came forth this morn, *W. H. Davies*, G [d′-e″], B&H Countryside, B&H; Bb, B&H.
When I think upon the maidens, *Philip Ashbrooke*, C [b-e″](m), B&H Album 3, Classical; Eb, Classical; Db, B&H.
When sweet Ann sings, *Margaret Rose*, Eb [bb-e″b(g″)], B&H Album 3; F, B&H Album High.
Why have you stolen my delight? *Francis Brett Young*, Ab [f′-a″b], B&H Album 2, Album High, More Countryside; F, B&H.
Woodpath in Spring,The, *Ruth Pitter*, D [a(b)-f″#(d″)], B&H.
You cannot dream things lovelier, *Humbert Wolfe*, [c′-g″], B&H.
You shall not go a-maying, *Mordaunt Currie*, Eb [e′b-g″], B&H Album 2; C, B&H.

Headington, Christopher John Magenis. 1930–1996. *See also* App. 1.
Collections: *Clouded Starre, A,* Bardic; *Reflections of Summer,* Bardic; *Three Rilke Songs,* Bardic.
August Midnight, An *Thomas Hardy,* [g#-f″], Bardic Reflections.
Easter Hymn, *Henry Vaughan*, [Bb-f″](m), Bardic Clouded.
Love, and Discipline, *Henry Vaughan,* [A#-e′](m), Bardic Clouded.
Morning-Watch, The, *Henry Vaughan,* [A-e′](m), Bardic Clouded.
Out on the lawn I lie abed, *W. H. Auden,* [b-f″], Bardic Reflections.
Peace, *Henry Vaughan,* [c-f″](m), Bardic Clouded.
Pursuit, The, *Henry Vaughan,* [G#-e′](m), Bardic Clouded.
Sheep in the Shade, *William Barnes,* [bb-f″], Bardic Reflections.
Simmer's a pleasant time, *Robert Burns,* [d′-f″], Bardic Reflections.
Space of Summer, *Lady Lindsay,* [bb-f″#], Bardic Reflections.
Towards a Pindaric Ode, Bardic.
Vain Wits and Eyes, *Henry Vaughan,* [A-f″](m), Bardic Clouded.

Hearne, John. 1937– SMIC. *See also* App. 1, 2.
Collections: *Four Songs,* Longship; *Songs for the North,* Longship; *Two Romantic Songs*, Longship.
And then there's sorrow, *Florence Dunlop,* [mezzo], Longship 4 Songs.
End of Season, *William McCorkindale,* [medium], Longship For the North.
Fishmarket, *William McCorkindale,* [medium], Longship For the North.
Flight of the Geese, The, *Charles G. D. Roberts,* [medium], Longship For the North.
Name Unknown, *Florence Dunlop,* [soprano (or tenor)], Longship Romantic.
On Leaving the Summer and Sea, *Florence Dunlop,* [soprano (or tenor)], Longship Romantic.
Pink Roses, *Florence Dunlop* , [mezzo], Longship 4 Songs.
Pre-Spring, *Florence Dunlop,* [mezzo], Longship 4 Songs.
Sailor's Sweetheart, The, *Duncan Campbell Scott,* [medium], Longship For the North.
Starlight, *Florence Dunlop,* [mezzo], Longship 4 Songs.

Hedges, Anthony John. 1931– BMIC.
Collections: *Five Edward Thomas Poems, Op. 130,* [d′#-g′′#](f), Westfield; *Prayers from the Ark, Op. 68,* [d′b-a′′] or [c′b-g′′], Westfield; *Songs of Four Seasons, Op. 128,* [c′-a′′](f), Westfield.
  Autumn, *James Joyce,* [soprano], Westfield 4 Seasons.
  Cock-Crow, *Edward Thomas,* [soprano], Westfield, 5 Edward Thomas.
  Five Songs of Love, Op. 33, (cycle), *The Song of Solomon,* [bb-a′′b](f), Westfield
  If I should ever by chance grow rich, *Edward Thomas,* [soprano], Westfield, 5 Edward Thomas.
  Lights Out, *Edward Thomas,* Westfield, [soprano], 5 Edward Thomas.
  Melancholy, *Edward Thomas,* Westfield, [soprano], 5 Edward Thomas.
  Noah's Prayer, *Carmen Bernos de Gastoldi* tr. Hedges, [high], Westfield Prayers.
  Prayer of the Butterfly, The, *Carmen Bernos de Gastoldi* tr. *Hedges,* [high],Westfield Prayers.
  Prayer of the Cat, The, *Carmen Bernos de Gastoldi* tr. *Hedges,* [high], Westfield Prayers.
  Prayer of the Cock, The, *Carmen Bernos de Gastoldi* tr. *Hedges,* [high], Westfield Prayers.
  Prayer of the Foal, The, *Carmen Bernos de Gastoldi* tr. *Hedges,* [high], Westfield Prayers.
  Prayer of the Goat, The, *Carmen Bernos de Gastoldi* tr. *Hedges,* [high], Westfield Prayers.
  Prayer of the Little Bird, The, *Carmen Bernos de Gastoldi* tr. *Hedges,* [high], Westfield Prayers.
  Prayer of the Little Ducks, The, *Carmen Bernos de Gastoldi* tr. *Hedges,* [high], Westfield Prayers.
  Prayer of the Ox, The, *Carmen Bernos de Gastoldi* tr. *Hedges,* [high], Westfield Prayers.
  Spring, *W. H. Davies,* [soprano], Westfield 4 Seasons.
  Summer, *John Milton,* [soprano], Westfield 4 Seasons.
  Trumpet, The, *Edward Thomas,* [soprano], Westfield, 5 Edward Thomas.
  Ulysses's Farewell, *Alfred Lord Tennyson,* [G-e′](m), Westfield.
  Vocalise, Op. 90, *no text,* [b-a′′b](f), Westfield.
  Winter, *Laurence Binyon,* [soprano], Westfield 4 Seasons.

Helliwell, Piers. 1956– *See* App. 2.

Hely-Hutchinson, Christian **Victor.** 1901–1947.
Collections: (*Alice Songs,* Elkin); *Three Nonsense Songs,* Paterson; *(Three Songs,* Elkin).
  (Adam lay i-bounden, *Anon,* F [c′-c′′], Elkin; A, Elkin.)
  (Bee's Song, The, *Walter de la Mare,* Eb [d′-f′′], Elkin.)
  (Castlepatrick, *G. K. Chesterton,* E [d′-e′′], Elkin.)
  (Cities and thrones and powers, *Rudyard Kipling,* Elkin.)
  (Cuckoo Song, *Rudyard Kipling,* C [e′-g′′], Elkin.)
  Dream Song, *Walter de la Mare,* Bb [e′b-f′′], BMP.
  Duck and the Kangaroo, The, *Edward Lear,* F [c′-f′′], Paterson 3 Nonsense.
  (Father William, *Lewis Carroll,* C [e′b-g′′], Elkin Alice.)
  (Humpty Dumpty, *Lewis Carroll,* Eb [e′b-d′′b], Elkin Alice.)
  Huntsman, The, *Walter de la Mare,* G [d′-g′′], BMP.
  (Jabberwocky, *Lewis Carroll,* C [b-a′′], Elkin Alice.)
  (Jolly Beggar, The, *Traditional,* [c′-e′′b], Elkin.)
  Old mother Hubbard, *Anon,* E [b-e′′], Paterson; (G, Paterson).
  Old Soldier, The, *Walter de la Mare,* Eb [c′-f′′], BMP.
  Owl and the pussy-cat, The, *Edward Lear,* G [d′-f′′], Paterson 3 Nonsense.
  (Queen's Men, The, *Rudyard Kipling,* Eb [c′-e′′b], Elkin.)
  (Rolling English Road, The, *G. K. Chesterton,* D [d′-e′′], Elkin.)
  Silver, *Walter de la Mare,* F [c′-e′′], BMP.
  (Song of Soldiers, The, *Walter de la Mare,* Ab [c′b-e′′b], Novello; Bb, Novello.)
  Table and the Chair, The, *Edward Lear,* Eb [e′b-e′′b], Paterson 3 Nonsense.
  (To the Looking-glass World, *Lewis Carroll,* Eb [bb-e′′b], Elkin Alice.)
  (Trees, *Walter de la Mare,* Fm [e′b-d′′b], Elkin.)
  (Twa Corbies, The, *Anon,* G [d′-e′′], Elkin; A, Elkin.)
  (Tweedledum and Tweedledee, *Lewis Carroll,* F [c′-c′′], Elkin Alice.)
  (Who goes home? *G. K. Chesterton,* Fm [c′-e′′b], Elkin.)

Henry VIII. 1491–1547.
  Pastyme with good companye, *Anon,* Gm [e′-c′′], Thames (Hodgson) *Countertenors 2;* [e′-b′b], Leonard *Baroque low;* Bm [g′#-d′′], Leonard *Baroque high.*
  Whereto shuld I expresse? *Anon,* [d′-b′b], Thames (Hodgson) *Countertenors 2.*

Henry, John. 1859–1914. *See* App. 2.

Henshall, Dalwyn. 1957– WMIC.
  To... *Percy Bysshe Shelley,* Db [e′b-e′′], WMIC *Songs from Wales 2.*

Herbage, Julian Livingstone. 1904–1976.
    (Dream Pedlary, *Thomas Lovell Beddoes,* G [d′-g′′], Paxton.)
    Kirconnel Lee, *Traditional,* D [d′-g′′], BMP; B♭, BMP.

Herbert, Ivy.
    Collection: *Two Songs,* BMP.
    Jenny kissed me, *Leigh Hunt,* A [e′-f′′#], BMP 2 Songs.
    Linnet, The, *Robert Bridges,* F [e′b-f′′#], BMP.
    Widow bird, A, *Percy Bysshe Shelley,* Dm [c′-f′′], BMP 2 Songs.

Herbert, Muriel. 1897– ?
    (Contentment, F [c′-d′′], Elkin; Ab, Elkin.)
    (Faithless Shepherdess, The, *Anon,* F [d′-f′′], Elkin; G, Elkin.)
    (Fountain Court, *Arthur Symons,* E♭ [e′b-e′′b], Elkin; G♭, Elkin.)
    (Lake Isle of Innisfree, The, *W. B. Yeats,* D [d′-e′′], Elkin; E, Elkin.)
    (On a time, *Anon,* Dm [c′#-e′′], Elkin; Em, Elkin.)
    (Violets, E [d′#-e′′], Elkin; G, Elkin.)

Hewitt, Thomas.
    Sanctuary, *Edward Lockton,* G [d′-e′′], IMP *Parlour Songs.*

Higginson, Gary. BMIC.

Higginson, Ian. 1959–
    Everyone Sang, *Siegfried Sassoon,* G [d′-e′′], B&H *Easy Song.*
    Fear no more the heat o' the sun, *Shakespeare,* Em [d′-e′′], B&H *Shakespeare Album.*
    It was a lover and his lass, *Shakespeare,* G [d′-g′′], B&H *Shakespeare Album.*
    O mistress mine, *Shakespeare,* B♭ [d′-g′′](m), B&H *Shakespeare Album.*
    Picture-books in Winter, *R. L. Stevenson,* F [c′-d′′], B&H *Easy Song.*

Hill, Richard. *See* App. 2.

Hilton, John. 1599–1657.
    As Flora slept, *Anon,* C [g#(bb)-e′′], B&H (Keel) *Lovesongs* 1b; E♭, *Lovesongs* 1a.
    Hang golden sleep upon her eyelids fair, *Anon,* Gm [d′-d′′], S&B (Spink) *MB 33, Recitalist 4.*
    Wilt thou forgive the sin where I begun, *John Donne,* Gm [d′-g′′], S&B (Spink) *MB 33, Recitalist 3, Cavalier*; Fm, B&H (Patrick) *Sacred Songs 2.*

Hinchcliffe, Irvin.
    Green Rain, *Mary Webb,* Cm [e′b-f′′], BMP.

Hiscocks, Harry.
    Old Taff River, The, [baritone], Snell.

Hiscocks, Wendy.
Collections: *I look out and see...,* Creativity; *Mother and Child,* Creativity; *Two Poems of Nefra Canning,* Creativity; *Two Shakespeare Songs,* Creativity.
    Benediction, *Rabindranath Tagore,* [c′#-a′′], Creativity Mother and Child.
    Bush Christmas, *David Martin,* [c′#-f′′#], Creativity.
    Champa Flower, The, *Rabindranath Tagore,* [e′#-f′′], Creativity Mother and Child.
    Day of the Singing Birds, The, *Dennis Stoll,* [d′-f′′#], Creativity.
    Dream, The, *David Martin,* [F-c′], Creativity I Look; [baritone] Creativity I Look.
    Elegy, *Anon,* [c′#-a′′], Creativity.
    End, The, *Rabindranath Tagore,* [d′-a′′], Creativity Mother and Child.
    Friendship, *Nefra Canning,* [d′-e′′], Creativity 2 Poems.
    Grace in the Bush, *David Martin,* [E-c′], Creativity I Look; [baritone] Creativity I Look.
    I sit and look out, *Walt Whitman,* [F-c′], Creativity I Look; [baritone] Creativity I Look.
    Last Invocation, The, *Walt Whitman,* [tenor], Creativity.
    Lover's Gift, *Rabindranath Tagore,* [G-d′], Creativity I Look; [baritone] Creativity I Look.
    My Song, *Rabindranath Tagore,* [d′-a′′], Creativity Mother and Child.
    Twenty-ninth Bather, The: *Walt Whitman,* [g#-b′′b], Creativity.
    When icicles hang by the wall, *Shakespeare,* [d′-a′′b], Creativity 2 Shakespeare.
    Where the bee sucks, *Shakespeare,* [d′-g′′], Creativity 2 Shakespeare.
    Winter, *Nefra Canning,* [e′-e′′], Creativity 2 Poems.

Hobbs, Christopher. BMIC.

Hoddinott, Alun. 1929– *See also* App. 2.
Collections: *Ancestor Worship,* OUP; *Five Poems of Gustavo A. Becquer* (tr. Ifan Payne), WMIC; *Landscapes,* BMP; *One must always have love,* WMIC.
    Ancestor Worship, *Emyr Humphreys,* [B-f′#](m), OUP Ancestor.
    Din Lligwy, *Emyr Humphreys,* [d′-g′′#], BMP Landscapes.
    From Father to Son, *Emyr Humphreys,* [c#-f′′](m), OUP Ancestor.
    Hen Gapel, *Emyr Humphreys,* [e′b-a′′], BMP Landscapes.
    Llys Dulas, *Emyr Humphreys,* [e′-a′′b], BMP Landscapes.
    Marro's only son, *Emyr Humphreys,* [Bb-f′#](m), OUP Ancestor.
    Master Plan, *Emyr Humphreys,* [c-f′′#](m), OUP Ancestor.
    Medieval Carol, *Anon* adapted *Jacqueline Froom,* [d′-e′′], BMP.
    Mynydd Bodafon, *Emyr Humphreys,* [f′-g′′b], BMP Landscapes.
    Silver Hound, The, (cycle), *Ursula Vaughan Williams,* [c′-g′′#](m), Lengnick.
    Traeth Bychan, *Emyr Humphreys,* [e′-a′′b], BMP Landscapes.
Arrangements: *Six Welsh Folksongs,* OUP.
    Ap Shenkin, *Anon* tr. Rhiannon Hoddinott, [e′b-g′′], OUP 6 Welsh.
    Fairest Gwen, *Anon* tr. Rhiannon Hoddinott, [f′-g′′](m), OUP 6 Welsh.
    Golden Wheat, The, *Anon* tr. Rhiannon Hoddinott, [f′-g′′](m), OUP 6 Welsh.
    If she were mine, *Anon* tr. Rhiannon Hoddinott, [f′-g′′b](m), OUP 6 Welsh.
    O gentle dove, *Anon* tr. Rhiannon Hoddinott, [e′-g′′](m), OUP 6 Welsh.
    Two hearts remain, *Anon* tr. Rhiannon Hoddinott, [f′-f′′](m), OUP 6 Welsh.

Hodson, Maud. 1977– BMIC. *See also* App. 2.

Hogben, Dorothy.
    Shawl, The, *Lawrence Atkinson,* [c′#-f′′#], BMP.

Holborne, Anthony. ? –1602.
    My heavy sprite, *George Clifford,* Gm [f′#-g′′], S&B (Stroud) *Banquet.*

Holbrooke, Josef. 1878–1958.
Collection: *Six Songs,* Classical.
    In days of old, *W. E. Grogan,* [medium], Classical.
    Killary, *Herbert Trench,* C [b-e′′], Cramer; Eb, Cramer.
    Long ago, *N. Malloch,* Weinberger.
    Marino Faliero (scena), *Lord Byron,* [G(F)-f′#](m), Classical.
    O wavering fires, (scena), [b-a′′b(f′′)], Classical.
    Outsong, An, *T. E. Ellis,* Eb [c′b-a′′b(f′′′b)], Cramer; C, Cramer.
    Where be ye going? *John Keats,* F [c′-d′′(f′′)], Cramer; [high], Cramer.

Hold, Trevor. 1939– BMIC. *See also* App. 2.
Collections: *John Clare Songbook,* A, Thames; *Something Rich and Strange,* Ramsey.
    Angler's Song, The, *William Basse,* [B-e′b](m), Thames *Century 6.*
    Break of Day, *John Clare,* F [e′b-f′′], Thames John Clare.
    Come unto these yellow sands, *Shakespeare,* [e′-g′′], Ramsey Something Rich.
    Country Letter, *John Clare,* C [d′-f′′], Thames John Clare.
    Drinking Song, *John Clare,* Bb [e′b-g′′b](m), Thames John Clare.
    Dying Child, The, *John Clare,* D [d′-e′′b], Thames John Clare.
    Evening, *John Clare,* C [d′-g′′], Thames John Clare.
    Full fathom five, *Shakespeare,* [e′b-f′′], Ramsay Something Rich.
    Lost as Strangers, *John Clare,* Eb [d′-a′′b](m), Thames John Clare.
    Love's Riddle, *John Clare,* G [d′-g′′](m), Thames John Clare.
    Song at night, *Norman Nicholson,* Am [a-e′′], Ramsay, Thames *Century 4*; Cm, Ramsay.
    Sunday Dip, *John Clare,* Ab [e′b-f′′#], Thames John Clare.
    What is Life? *John Clare,* B [c′-g′′b], Thames John Clare.
    Where the bee sucks, *Shakespeare,* [f′-g′′], Ramsay Something Rich.

Holloway, Robin Greville. 1943– *See also* App. 2.
    (Author of Light (cycle), *Quarles, A. W., Campion,* [f(g)-g′′(e′′b)](f), B&H.)
    (Banal Sojourn (cycle), *Wallace Stevens,* [high voice], B&H.)
    (Four Housman Fragments (cycle), *A. E. Housman,* [soprano], B&H.)
    (From High Windows (cycle), *Philip Larkin,* [G-e′](m), B&H.)

(Georgian Songs (cycle), *Blunden, Stephens, Housman, Cornford, Walter de la Mare,* [A-g′](m), B&H.)
(In the Thirtieth Year (cycle), [c′-b′′b](m), B&H.)
(Leaves Cry, The, (cantata), *Wallace Stevens, Christina Rossetti,* [c′-c′′′](f), B&H.)
(Lights Out (cycle), *Edward Thomas,* [F-g′(f′)](m), B&H.)
(Lover's Well, The, (cycle), *Geoffrey Hill,* [baritone], B&H.)
(Medley of Nursery Rhymes and Conundrums, A, (cycle), *Anon,* [mezzo soprano], B&H.)
This is just to say (cycle), *Carlos Williams,* [d′-a′′](m), B&H.
Three Georgian Songs (part of cycle), *Cornford, Walter de la Mare,* [A-e′](m), B&H.
Wherever we may be (cycle), *Robert Graves,* [b(c′)-a′′](f), B&H.

Holst, Gustav Theodore. 1874–1934. *See also* App. 2.
Collections: *Eleven Songs (1896-1903)*, Thames (edited Colin Matthews); *Hymns from the Rig Veda, Op 24*, Chester; *Twelve Humbert Wolfe Songs*, S&B (introduction by Imogen Holst).
(Awake my heart, *Robert Bridges,* B♭ [bb-d′′](m), Enoch; D, Enoch.)
Betelgeuse, *Humbert Wolfe,* [b-f′′], S&B 12 Humbert Wolfe, *Recitalist 2*.
Calm is the morn, *Alfred Lord Tennyson,* E♭ [a#-e′′], Thames 11 Songs.
Cradle Song, *William Blake,* G [d′-f′′#], Thames 11 Songs.
Creation, *Humbert Wolfe,* [bb-f′′], Chester Vedic Hymns.
Dewy Roses, *Alfred H. Hyatt,* A♭ [bb-e′′b], Thames 11 Songs.
Dream-city, The, *Humbert Wolfe,* [d′-g′′b], S&B 12 Humbert Wolfe.
Envoi, *Humbert Wolfe,* [c′-g′′], S&B 12 Humbert Wolfe.
Faith, *Gustav Holst,* F [d′-e′′b], Chester Vedic Hymns.
Floral Bandit, The, *Humbert Wolfe,* [c′#-a′′b], S&B 12 Humbert Wolfe.
Heart Worships, The, *Alice Buckton,* Dm [bb-d′′], S&B, Schirmer *1st Baritone II*; Em, S&B, Classical.
In a Wood, *Thomas Hardy,* [b(g#)-f′′#], Thames *Hardy Songbook*.
In the Street of Lost Time, *Humbert Wolfe,* [e′-g′′], S&B 12 Humbert Wolfe, Mayhew *Collection 2*.
Indra (God of storm & battle), *Gustav Holst,* C [e′-f′′], Chester Vedic Hymns, Mayhew *Collection 2*.
Journey's End, *Humbert Wolfe,* [c′-g′′b], S&B 12 Humbert Wolfe.
Little Music, A, *Humbert Wolfe,* [d′-g′′], S&B 12 Humbert Wolfe.
Lovely kind and kindly loving, *Nicholas Breton,* F [b-f′′], Thames 11 Songs; (G, Chappell *English Recital 2*, B&H; A♭, B&H.)
Margrete's Cradle Song, *Henrik Ibsen* tr. *William Archer,* F [f′-g′′](f), Thames 11 Songs, Bosworth.
Maruts (Stormclouds), *Gustav Holst,* Am [d′b-f′′], Chester Vedic Hymns.
My true love hath my heart, *Philip Sidney,* F [c′-f′′](f), Thames 11 Songs.
Now in these fairylands, *Humbert Wolfe,* [d′-f′′], S&B 12 Humbert Wolfe.
Peace, *Alfred H. Hyatt,* F [c′-f′′], Thames 11 Songs.
Persephone, *Humbert Wolfe,* [d′-g′′b], S&B 12 Humbert Wolfe, *Recitalist 1*.
Rhyme, *Humbert Wolfe,* [d′-g′′], S&B 12 Humbert Wolfe.
Sergeant's Song, The, *Thomas Hardy,* Gm [g-d′′](m), Thames *Hardy Songbook*, William Elkin; Am, William Elkin.
(She who is dear to me, *Walter E. Grogan,* F [f′-g′′](m), Enoch; D, Enoch.)
Slumber Song, *Charles Kingsley,* D [d′-f′′#](f), Thames 11 Songs, Bosworth.
Soft and gently, *Heinrich Heine* tr. *Anon,* C [c′-e′′], Thames 11 Songs, Bosworth.
Song of the Frogs, *Gustav Holst,* Em [b-d′′], Chester Vedic Hymns.
Song of the Woods, *Alfred H. Hyatt,* B♭ [d′-f′′(g′′)], Thames 11 Songs.
Things Lovelier, *Humbert Wolfe,* [d′-g′′], S&B 12 Humbert Wolfe, Mayhew *Collection 1*.
Thought, The, *Humbert Wolfe,* [c′#-f′′#], S&B 12 Humbert Wolfe.
Ushas (Dawn), *Gustav Holst,* B♭ [bb-f′′(d′′)], Chester Vedic Hymns.
Vac (Speech), *Gustav Holst,* E♭ [d′-f′′], Chester Vedic Hymns.
Varuna I (Sky), *Gustav Holst,* C [bb-d′′b], Chester Vedic Hymns.
Varuna II (The Waters), *Gustav Holst,* C [c′-e′′], Chester Vedic Hymns.
Weep you no more, sad fountains, *Anon,* Em [e′-f′′], Thames 11 Songs.
Arrangements: *Folksongs from Hampshire,* Novello.
Masters in this hall, *William Morris,* Dm [c′#-f′′], OUP *Solo Christmas high*; Cm, *Solo Christmas low*.

Holt, Simon. 1958– *See* App. 2.

Hook, James. 1746–1827.
Collection: *Eight Songs for High Voice,* S&B (edited Michael Pilkington).
Awake my fair, *Anon,* G [b′-a′′], S&B (Ivimey).

Cautious Maid, The, *Anon*, A [e′-a′′](f), S&B (Ivimey).
Emigrant, The, *Mrs Amelia Opie*, Eb [eb-g′′], S&B 8 Songs, OUP (Roberts) *Tuneful Voice*.
Hail, lovely rose, *Anon*, C [c′-g′′], S&B (Ivimey).
Lad wha lilts sae sweetly, The, *Charles Dibdin*, Bb [d′-g′′](f), S&B 8 Songs.
Mary of Allendale, *Anon*, Eb [e′b-a′′b](m), B&H (Lane Wilson) *Old English*.
No, no, no, it must not be, *Anon*, A [e′-a′′](m), S&B 8 Songs.
O listen to the voice of love, *Anon*, D [d′-g′′](m), S&B 8 Songs.
On Richmond Hill there lives a lass, Bb [c′-f′′], Schirmer *1st Tenor II*.
Silver Moon, The, *Anon*, G [d′-g′′](f), S&B (Ivimey).
Softly lulling, sweetly thrilling, *Dr Houlton*, Eb [e′b-e′′b](f), Novello (Bush) *Ballad Operas*.
Steadfast Shepherd, The, *George Wither*, C [g′-g′′](m), S&B 8 Songs.
Sweet are the banks, *William Woty*, F [c′-f′′], S&B (Ivimey).
Sweet Little Girl that I Love, The, *Anon*, F [f′-a′′](m), B&H (Lane Wilson) *Old English*.
Take me, take me, some of you, *John Dryden*, Bb [f′-g′′](f), S&B 8 Songs.
Think it not strange, *Anon*, Bb [d′-g′′(b′′)], S&B (Ivimey).
(Trees begin to bud, The, *Anon*, C [f′#-g′′(a′′)], S&B (Ivimey).)
Turtle dove coos round my cot, The, *Anon*, D [d′-f′′](f), S&B 8 Songs.
Warning, The, *Mrs Rowley*, A [e′-a′′], S&B 8 Songs.

Hope, Donald Geoffrey.
Lullay, lullay, thou little tiny child, *Anon*, E [c′#-g′′#], B&H *Heritage 4*.

Hopkins, Antony (Reynolds). 1921–   *See also* App. 1.
(Humble Song to the Birds, A, *Rosencreutz* tr. *Frieda Harries*, [c′-a′′], Chester.)
Melancholy Song, A, *Anon*, D [d′-f′′#](f), Thames *Century 1*, Chester.

Hopkins, Wil.
Watching the Wheat, [soprano/tenor], Snell.

Hopson, Hal.
When love is found, *Brian Wren*, [d′-f′′](f), S&B.

Horder, Mervyn. BMIC.
Collections: *Black Diamonds I & II*, Bardic; *Five Auden Songs*, Bardic; *Five Burns Songs*, Bardic.
Seven Shakespeare Songs, Lengnick; *Shropshire Lad, A*, Lengnick; *Six Betjeman Songs*, Lengnick.
And is it true? *John Betjeman*, [a-g′′], Bardic.
Blow, blow thou winter wind, *Shakespeare*, Bbm [bb-f′′], Lengnick 7 Shakespeare.
Bohemia, *Dorothy Parker*, [Bb-f′′], Bardic Diamonds I.
Bric-à-brac, *Dorothy Parker*, [d′-g′′], Bardic Diamonds II.
Caprice, *John Betjeman*, Db [c′-f′′](m), Lengnick 6 Betjeman.
Carry her over the water, *W. H. Auden*, [d′-a′′], Bardic 5 Auden.
Church's restoration, The, *John Betjeman*, F [b-f′′], Lengnick 6 Betjeman.
Convalescent, *Dorothy Parker*, [b-g′′], Bardic Diamonds II.
Darling Dog, *Anon*, [d′-g′′], Bardic.
Fear no more the heat o' the sun, *Shakespeare*, Eb [bb-f′′], Lengnick 7 Shakespeare.
Goldcups, *A. E. Housman*, G [d′-g′′], Lengnick Shropshire Lad.
How to Get On in Society, *John Betjeman*, C [g-c′′](f), Lengnick 6 Betjeman.
In Westminster Abbey, *John Betjeman*, Eb [c′-e′′b](f), Lengnick 6 Betjeman.
John Anderson, my jo, *Robert Burns*, [d′-g′′], Bardic 5 Burns.
Johnny, *W. H. Auden*, [d′-a′′], Bardic 5 Auden.
Lenten Lily, The, *A. E. Housman*, A [e′-a′′], Lengnick Shropshire Lad.
Loveliest of trees, *A. E. Housman*, G [e′-a′′], Lengnick Shropshire Lad.
Lullaby, *W. H. Auden*, [d′b-a′′b], Bardic 5 Auden.
My Jean, *Robert Burns*, [c′-a′′], Bardic 5 Burns.
My own dear love, *Dorothy Parker*, [c′-f′′], Bardic Diamonds I.
Not to be born, *W. H. Auden*, [e′b-a′′b], Bardic 5 Auden.
O mistress mine, *Shakespeare*, C [b-e′′b](m), Lengnick 7 Shakespeare.
O whistle and I'll come to you, *Robert Burns*, [c′-f′′], Bardic 5 Burns.
Red, Red Rose, A, *Robert Burns*, [d′-b′′], Bardic 5 Burns.
Sigh no more ladies, *Shakespeare*, E [a-f′′#], Lengnick 7 Shakespeare.
Stop all the clocks, *W. H. Auden*, [e′b-a′′b], Bardic 5 Auden.
Subaltern's Love-song, A, *John Betjeman*, G [b-e′′(a′′)](m), Lengnick 6 Betjeman.
Under the greenwood tree, *Shakespeare*, D [c′#-e′′], Lengnick 7 Shakespeare.
Unfortunate Coincidence, *Dorothy Parker*, [c′-f′′], Bardic Diamonds I.

Wail, *Dorothy Parker*, [c′-e″], Bardic Diamonds II.
Westgate-on-Sea, *John Betjeman*, G [b-e″], Lengnick 6 Betjeman.
When daisies pied, *Shakespeare*, G [d′-e″], Lengnick 7 Shakespeare.
When I was one-and-twenty, *A. E. Housman*, A [e′-f″#], Lengnick Shropshire Lad.
White in the moon, *A. E. Housman*, F [c′-g″], Lengnick Shropshire Lad.
Who is Sylvia? *Shakespeare*, B♭ [d′-f″(g″)], Lengnick 7 Shakespeare.
Winter it is past, The, *Robert Burns*, [e′-e″], Bardic 5 Burns.

Horn, Charles Edward. 1786–1849.
Cherry ripe, *Robert Herrick*, B [b-e″], BMP (Wilson); (E♭, Chappell (Lehmann)0.
I know a bank, *Shakespeare*, BMP.
I've been roaming, *Anon*, D [c′-f″#], BMP.

Horne, David. 1970– *See also* App. 2.
Collection: (*Days now Gone*, B&H.)
 (Burned ships, *Henrik Ibsen* tr. *Michael Meyers*, [d′-f″#], B&H 4 Songs.)
 (Gone, *Henrik Ibsen* tr. *Michael Meyers*, [e′-g″#], B&H 4 Songs.)
 (In the picture gallery, *Henrik Ibsen* tr. *Michael Meyers*, [b♭(c′)-g″b], B&H 4 Songs.)
 (Letter, The, *Walt Whitman*, [high voice], B&H.)
 (Rikke Holst, *Henrik Ibsen* tr. *Michael Meyers*, [d′-g″b], B&H 4 Songs.)

Horowitz, Joseph. 1926–
Lady Macbeth (Scena), *Shakespeare*, [d′-f″#](f), Novello.

Horton, John. 1905–
Arrangements:
 Robin's Last Will, The, *Scottish Traditional*, A♭ [c′-c″], Thames *Countertenors 1*.
 Sweet Nightingale, The, *Traditional*, E♭ [b♭-c″], Thames *Countertenors 2*.

Hosier, John. *See* App. 2.

Howard, Michael. 1922–2002.
Collections: *Cantiones Iudithae*, [counter-tenor], Brunton; *Seven Songs*, [counter-tenor], Brunton.
 Painted Rose, The (cycle), [counter-tenor], Brunton 7 Songs.
 Three Middle English Songs, [counter-tenor], Brunton 7 Songs.

Howard, Samuel. 1710–1782.
 Hymen and Fashion, *Anon*, B♭ [c′-g″], Thames (Copley & Reitan) *Gentleman's Magazine*.
 Love in thy youth, *W. Porter*, B [g#-d″#], Paterson (Coleman) *100 Best 4*.
 Nut-brown Maid, The, *Anon*, E [e′-a″](m), Thames (Copley & Reitan) *Gentleman's Magazine*.
 (Soft invader of my soul, *Anon*, B♭ [d′-g″](m), Elkin (Bevan).)

Howe, Albert.
 Sister awake, *Thomas Bateson*, [e′-a″], BMP.

Howells, Herbert Norman. 1892–1983. *See also* App. 2.
Collections: *Five Songs*, Thames (introduced and edited Peter Horton); *Garland for Walter de la Mare, A*, Thames (introduction Christopher Palmer, edited Michael Pilkington); *In Green Ways*, Thames 1992 (introduction Christopher Palmer), BMP; *Peacock Pie*, Roberton; *Songs*, B&H (introduction Christopher Palmer); *Three Rondeaux*, S&B.
 Alas, alack, *Walter de la Mare*, [d′b-f″], Roberton Peacock Pie.
 Andy Battle, *Walter de la Mare*, Bm [c′-f″], Thames Garland.
 Balulalow, *see* O my deir hert.
 Before dawn (1st setting), *Walter de la Mare*, [c′#-f″#], Thames Garland.
 Before dawn (2nd setting), *Walter de la Mare*, [c′#-f″#], Thames Garland.
 By the Grey Stone, *Fiona Macleod*, [a-f″], Thames 5 Songs.
 Come sing and dance, *Anon*, A♭ [d′-a″b], OUP.
 Dunce, The, *Walter de la Mare*, [c′-e″b], Roberton Peacock Pie.
 Flood, *James Joyce*, [e′b-a″b], BMP.
 Full Moon, *Walter de la Mare*, Em [c′-d″#], Roberton Peacock Pie.
 Gavotte, *H Newbolt*, G [d′-g″], OUP *Solo Soprano*, BMP, Thames *Century 1*.
 Girl's Song, *Wilfrid Gibson*, G [d′-e″](f), B&H *Heritage 3, Easy Song, Imperial 2, Songs*.
 Goat Paths, The, *James Stephens*, [c′-a″], Thames/BMP In Green Ways, BMP.
 Goddess of Night, *F. W. Harvey*, E [e′-g″], B&H Songs.

Her Scuttle Hat, *Frank Dempster Sherman*, C [c′-d′′], S&B 3 Rondeaux.
King David, *Walter de la Mare*, [c′#-f′′], Thames A Garland, B&H *Heritage 4,* B&H, B&H
    Songs.
Lady Caroline, The, *Walter de la Mare*, G [d′-a′′b], Thames A Garland.
Little Boy Lost, *William Blake*, Em [d′-e′′], BMP.
Lost Love, *Chinese* tr. *Clifford Bax*, Dm [c′-g′′], B&H Songs.
Madrigal, A, *Austin Dobson*, Eb [e′b-e′′b], B&H *Heritage 4,* Songs.
Mally O! *Anon*, F#m [c′#-c′′#], S&B.
Merry Margaret, *John Skelton*, F [d′-a′′], Thames/BMP In Green Ways, BMP.
Miss T, *Walter de la Mare*, C [c′-d′′b], Roberton Peacock Pie.
Mrs MacQueen, *Walter de la Mare*, G [d′-e′′], Roberton Peacock Pie.
Mugger's Song, The, *Wilfrid Gibson*, D [d′-e′′b](m), B&H Songs.
O, my deir hert, *Luther* tr. *Wedderburn*, [b-e′′], B&H *Imperial 3,* Songs, B&H, Thames
    Countertenors 3.
Old House, The, *Walter de la Mare,* [d′-g′′#], Thames Garland.
Old Meg, *Wilfrid Gibson*, Eb [d′b-e′′b], BMP.
(Old Skinflint, *Wilfrid Gibson*, [d′-f′′], Curwen.)
Old Soldier, The, *Walter de la Mare*, [c′-f′′#], Thames Garland.
Old Stone House, The, *Walter de la Mare*, [b-e′′], Thames Garland.
On the merry first of May, *Burkitt Parker & Claude Aveling*, C [d′-a′′], Thames/BMP In Green
    Ways, BMP.
Queer story, A, *Walter de la Mare*, [bb-a′′], Thames Garland.
Restful Branches, The, *W. A. Byrne*, Db [a-d′′], S&B.
Rondel of Rest, A, *Arthur Symons*, Db [d′b-e′′b], S&B 3 Rondeaux.
Roses, *Charles Camp Tarelli*, D [bb-d′′], S&B 3 Rondeaux.
Some One, *Walter de la Mare*, [c′-e′′], Thames Garland.
Song of the Secret, The, *Walter de la Mare*, [d′b-f′′#], Thames Garland.
St Bride's Song, *Fiona Macleod*, [bb-e′′b], Thames 5 Songs.
There was a maiden, *W. L. Courtney*, Cm [c′-e′′b], B&H Songs.
Three Cherry Trees, The, *Walter de la Mare*, [d′-g′′], Thames Garland.
Tired Tim, *Walter de la Mare*, Cm [c′-e′′b], Roberton Peacock Pie.
Under the greenwood tree, *Shakespeare*, F [e′-b′′], Thames/BMP In Green Ways, BMP.
Valley of Silence, The, *Fiona Macleod*, [b-e′′], Thames 5 Songs.
Wanderers, *Walter de la Mare*, Bbm [b-f′′], Thames Garland.
Wanderer's Night Song, *Goethe* tr. *Howells*, A [e′b-g′′], Thames/BMP In Green Ways, BMP.
When the dew is falling, *Fiona Macleod*, B [b-d′′#], Thames 5 Songs.
When there is Peace, *Fiona Macleod*, B [bb-d′′], Thames 5 Songs.
Widow Bird, The, *Percy Bysshe Shelley*, Em [e′-e′′], B&H Songs.
Arrangements: *Two English Folksongs*, Thames 1996.
    Brisk Young Widow, The, *Anon*, C [c′-e′′], Thames 2 English Folksongs.
    I will give my love an apple, *Anon*, Am [c′-e′′], Thames 2 English Folksongs.

Hoyle, Vernon. *See* App. 2.

Hudes, Eric. 1920– *See also* App. 2.
Collections: *Four Fragments from Hölderlin's Madness,* [b-g′′#], Bardic; *Sappho Fragments,* [b-f′′#],
Bardic; *Shadows of Chrysanthemums,* [c′-f′′#], Bardic.
    And little knowledge but much pleasure, *Friedrich Hölderlin* tr. *David Gascoyne*, Bardic 4
        Fragments.
    And their feet move, *Sappho* tr. *Mary Barnard*, Bardic Sappho Fragments.
    Apex, The, *Dal Strutt*, Bardic.
    Betrothal, A, *E. J. Scovell*, Bardic Shadows.
    Evening Star, The, *Sappho* tr. *Mary Barnard*, Bardic Sappho Fragments.
    Form and Spirit, *Friedrich Hölderlin* tr. *David Gascoyne*, Bardic 4 Fragments.
    Half of Life, The, *Friedrich Hölderlin* tr. *David Gascoyne*, Bardic 4 Fragments.
    I took my lyre, *Sappho* tr. *Mary Barnard*, Bardic Sappho Fragments.
    In the spring twilight, *Sappho* tr. *Mary Barnard*, Bardic Sappho Fragments.
    Now while we dance, *Sappho* tr. *Mary Barnard*, Bardic Sappho Fragments.
    Peace reigned in heaven, *Sappho* tr. *Mary Barnard*, Bardic Sappho Fragments.
    Prayer, *Sappho* tr. *Mary Barnard*, Bardic Sappho Fragments.
    Requiem, *Robert Louis Stevenson*, Bardic.
    Romancero a la muerte de Federico García Lorca, *Leopoldo Urrutia* tr. *Sylvia Townsend Warner*,
        [c′-g′′], Bardic.

Shadows of Chrysanthemums, *E. J. Scovell,* Bardic Shadows.
Sybil, *Friedrich Hölderlin* tr. *David Gascoyne,* Bardic 4 Fragments.
Take, O take those lips away, *Shakespeare,* Bardic.
This way that way, *Sappho* tr. *Mary Barnard,* Bardic Sappho Fragments.
Time for Sleeping, *E. J. Scovell,* Bardic Shadows.
Tonight I've watched the moon, *Sappho* tr. *Mary Barnard,* Bardic Sappho Fragments.
Truly he hath a sweet bed, *Thomas Moult,* [c′-g′′], Bardic.
With his venom, *Sappho* tr. *Mary Barnard,* Bardic Sappho Fragments.
Without warning, *Sappho* tr. *Mary Barnard,* Bardic Sappho Fragments.
Ye spotted snakes, *Shakespeare,* Bardic.
You remind me, *Sappho* tr. *Mary Barnard,* Bardic Sappho Fragments.

Hugh-Jones, Elaine. 1927– BMIC, WMIC. *See also* App. 2.
Collections: *Cornford Cycle, A,* Micropress; *Eight Songs of Walter de la Mare,* Micropress.
Note: Most Micropress publications can be supplied in a wide range of keys.
Back View, A, *Frances Cornford,* [medium], Micropress Cornford Cycle.
Bicker's Cottage, *Frances Cornford,* [medium], Micropress Cornford Cycle.
Dancer, The, *Joseph Campbell,* [d′b-f′′], EPSS.
Echo, *Walter de la Mare,* Micropress 8 Walter de la Mare.
Futility, *Wilfred Owen,* Eb [f′-g′′b], Thames *Century 3.*
Ghosts, *Walter de la Mare,* Micropress 8 Walter de la Mare.
Hare, The, *Walter de la Mare,* Micropress 8 Walter de la Mare.
Madman and the Child, The, *Frances Cornford,* [medium], Micropress Cornford Cycle.
Night Song, *Frances Cornford,* [medium], Micropress Cornford Cycle.
Nightingale near the House, The, *Harold Monro,* [c′-a′′b], Micropress.
Old Woman at the Flower Show, The, *Frances Cornford,* [medium], Micropress Cornford Cycle.
Raven's Tomb, The, *Walter de la Mare,* Micropress 8 Walter de la Mare.
Remember, *Christina Rossetti,* Gm [c′-g′′], Thames *Century 5.*
Ride-by-nights, The, *Walter de la Mare,* Micropress 8 Walter de la Mare.
Road to Coursegoules, The, *Frances Cornford,* [medium], Micropress Cornford Cycle.
Silver, *Walter de la Mare,* Micropress 8 Walter de la Mare.
Solitude, *Walter de la Mare,* Micropress 8 Walter de la Mare.
Starlight Night, The, *Gerard Manly Hopkins,* [d′-g′], Micropress.
To a Young Cat in the Orchard, *Frances Cornford,* [medium], Micropress Cornford Cycle.
Watch, The, *Frances Cornford,* [medium], Micropress Cornford Cycle.
Winter, *Walter de la Mare,* Micropress 8 Walter de la Mare.

Hughes, Arwel. 1909–1988.
Birds of Rhiannon, *Gwenallt,* tr. *John Stoddart,* [d′-f′′], WMIC *Songs from Wales 1.*
Good Friday, *Rhiannon Bowen Thomas* tr. *H. Idris Bell,* Am [e′-a′′], Gwynn.
Passing, The, [tenor], Aureus.
Romany, *Crwys* tr. *G. Crwys Williams,* G [d′-a′′], Gwynn.
Song from 'Song of Deliverance', [soprano], Aureus.
Wander-thirst, [e′-a′′](m) Aureus.

Hughes, Brian. 1938– WMIC.
Arrangement:
Fair Lisa, Curiad.

Hughes, Herbert. 1882–1937.
Collections: *Five Songs from 'And So To Bed',* (James Bernard Fagan), B&H; *(Three Satirical Songs,* Enoch); *Two Songs in an Olden Style,* B&H.
Believe me, dear, *J. R. Monsell,* C [d′-b′′](f), B&H.
Boys, those were the days, *J. R. Monsell,* C [b-e′′](m), B&H.
(Carol of Jesus Child, *Enoch.*)
Gaze on me though you gaze in scorn, *Oliver St John Gogarty,* F [f′-a′′], B&H Olden Style.
How mortifying to recall, *J. R. Monsell,* Eb [c′-b′′b](f), B&H.
I cannot change as others do, *John Wilmot, Earl of Rochester,* Ab [eb-a′′b(f′′)](m), B&H.
I fear for every breath she draws, *J. R. Monsell,* Ab [d′b-b′′b](f), B&H.
I meant to tease him, *J. R. Monsell,* C#m [f′#-a′′](f), B&H.
My love is dark, *Oliver St John Gogarty,* D [d′-d′′](m), B&H Olden Style; F, B&H.
My Lydia adores me, I know, *J. R. Monsell,* A [e′-a′′](m), B&H.
O men from the fields, *Padraic Colum,* Bbm [d′b-f′′], B&H *Heritage 2.*

Terrible Robber Men, The, *Padraic Colum,* D [c′#-c′′#], B&H.
Arrangements: *Irish Country Songs Highlights,* B&H (introduction Fiona Richards; *Irish Country Songs Vol 1,* B&H (introduction by Herbert Hughes); (*Songs from Connacht,* B&H); *Three Eighteenth Century Songs,* B&H; *Two Ulster Fragments,* B&H.
Aileen Aroon, *see* How sweet and how pleasing.
Airy Bachelor, The, *Traditional,* C [c′-e′′], B&H.
And ye shall walk in silk attire, *Susanna Blamire,* A [a-f′′#], B&H 2 18th century.
At the mid hour of night, *Thomas Moore,* Gb [g′b-a′′b], B&H.
B for Barney, *Belfast Street Song,* F [c′-d′′](f), B&H Irish Country 1.
Ballynure Ballad, A, *Anon,* Cm [bb-d′′], B&H Highlights, Classical, Irish Country 1; Bbm, Ebm, B&H.
Bard of Armagh, The, *Anon,* Ab [e′b-f′′](m), B&H Highlights, Classical; Bb, Classical, B&H.
Black Ribbon-band, The, *Anon,* G [d′-e′′](m), B&H Highlights.
Boney's on the Sea, *Traditional,* D [a′-d′′], B&H.
Bonny Wee Mare, The, *Anon,* Dm [c′#-e′′](m), B&H Irish Country 1.
Down by the salley gardens, *W. B. Yeats,* Db [d′b-e′′b], B&H Highlights, Irish Country 1, B&H; Eb, B&H *McCormack,* Classical, B&H, Schirmer *1st Tenor II.*
Fanaid Grove, The, *Old Ballad,* Bm [b-d′′], B&H Irish Country 1.
Flower of Finae, The, *Thomas Davis,* A [e′-e′′], B&H; Bb, B&H.
Forlorn Queen, The, *Harold Boulton,* B [d′#-e′′], B&H.
Gartan Mother's Lullaby, The, *Anon,* D [b-e′′](f), Highlights, B&H Irish Country 1.
Good roarin' fire, A, *Anon,* E [e′-e′′](m), B&H Highlights, B&H.
Half a bap, *Traditional,* G [d′-d′′], B&H Ulster Fragments.
Has sorrow thy young days shaded? *Thomas Moore,* E [b-e′′], B&H; F, A, B&H.
How deep in love am I, *Harold Boulton,* Cm [c′-e′′b], B&H; Em, B&H.
How sweet and how pleasing, *Anon,* A [e′-a′′], B&H 3 18th century.
I have a bonnet trimmed with blue, *Anon,* F [f′-d′′](f), B&H Highlights, B&H.
I know my love, *Limerick,* F [c′-f′′], B&H Highlights, Irish Country 1; Eb, B&H.
I know where I'm goin', *Old Song,* Eb [g′-e′′b], Highlights, B&H Irish Country 1; G, B&H.
I saw from the beach, *Thomas Moore,* G [d′-e′′], B&H; A, Bb, B&H.
I will walk with my love, *Anon,* Ab [e′b-f′′](f), B&H Highlights.
I wish I had the shepherd's lamb, *Irish* tr. *P. W. Joyce,* G [c′-e′′](m), B&H Irish Country 1.
Innisfree, *Anon,* Em [d′-e′′], B&H Highlights.
Irish Elegy, An, *Thomas Moore,* F [d′-g′′], B&H Highlights.
Island Spinning Song, An, *Padraic Colum,* B [f′#-f′′#], B&H Irish Country 1.
Johnny, I Hardly Knew Ye, *Anon,* Am [e′-e′′](f), B&H Highlights, B&H.
Kathleen O'More, *George Nugent Reynolds,* Bb [f′-e′′b], B&H.
Kitty my love, will you marry me? *Anon,* Eb [c′-f′′](m), B&H *McCormack,* Classical, B&H.
Lark in the Clear Air, The, *Sir Samuel Ferguson,* A [d′-f′′#], B&H.
Leprehaun, The, *P. W. Joyce,* Am [d′-g′′], B&H Highlights, B&H.
Little Boats, *Harold Boulton,* Dm [d′-d′′], B&H *Easy Song,* B&H; Ebm, B&H.
Little Rose of Gartan, The, *Seosamh MacCathmhaoil,* Ab [e′b-e′′b], B&H Irish Country 1.
Lover's Curse, The, *Anon,* Db [bb-e′′b](f), B&H Irish Country 1; Eb, B&H.
Lowlands of Holland, The, *Traditional,* Dm [c′-e′′], B&H.
Magpie's Nest, The, *Anon,* Bb [a-d′′](m), B&H Highlights.
Minstrel Boy, The, *Thomas Moore,* Eb [bb-e′′b], B&H; F, G, B&H.
Monday, Tuesday, *Anon,* Gb [d′b-c′′], B&H Highlights.
Must I go bound, *Anon,* Cm [c′-c′′](m), B&H Irish Country 1.
My aunt she died a month ago, *Traditional,* Eb [bb-e′′b], B&H Ulster Fragments.
My bonny labouring boy, *Anon,* Eb [e′b-f′′], B&H Highlights.
My child is my treasure, *Thomas O'Kelly* tr. *A. P. Graves,* D [d′-e′′], B&H.
My love, oh, she is my love, *Irish* tr. *Douglas Hyde,* Bb [e′b-f′′](m), B&H Irish Country 1.
Next market day, The, *Tyrone Ballad,* Dm [a-c′′], B&H Highlights, Irish Country 1.
No, not more welcome, *Thomas Moore,* E [e′-e′′], B&H.
Norah O'Neale, *County Derry,* [medium high], Classical.
Oh, breathe not his name, *Thomas Moore,* Eb [c′-e′′b], B&H Highlights.
Old Turf Fire, The, *Anon,* Dm [b-e′′], B&H Highlights, B&H.
Reynardine, *Anon,* A [c′#-f′′](f), B&H Irish Country 1.
Rich and rare, *Thomas Moore,* Db [d′b-f′′], B&H Highlights.
Róisín Dubh, *Thomas Furlong,* Cm [c′-f′′], B&H Highlights.
Saw ye my father? *Traditional,* D [c′#-g′′], B&H 2 18th Century.
She moved thro' the fair, *Padraic Colum,* Db [d′b-e′′b](m), B&H Highlights, Irish Country 1; G, B&H.
Shule Agra, *Anon 18th cent,* Am [c′-e′′](f), B&H Highlights.

Slow by the shadows, *Seosamh MacCathmhaoil*, F [d´-d´´](m), B&H Irish Country 1.
Spanish Lady, The, *Anon,* A [e´-e´´], B&H.
Star of the County Down, The, *Anon*, F#m [c´#-e´´](m), B&H Highlights, B&H; Am, B&H.
Stuttering Lovers, The, *Traditional,* G [d´-e´´], Chappell (William Elkin); A, Classical, (Chappell).
Tigaree Torum Orum, *Anon*, E [d´#-e´´], B&H Highlights.
Verdant Braes of Skreen, The, *Anon*, Bb [f´-f´´], B&H Irish Country 1.
Weaver's Daughter, The, *Anon*, F [e´b-e´´b](f), B&H Irish Country 1.
When he who adores thee, *Thomas Moore,* Bbm [d´b-f´´](m), B&H.
When thro' life unblest we rove, *Thomas Moore,* C [c´-g´´], B&H Irish Country 1, B&H.
You couldn't stop a lover, *Anon*, F [c´-e´´], B&H Irish Country 1.
Young maid stood in her father's garden, A, *Anon*, Ab [e´b-f´´], B&H Highlights.

Hughes, Hugh. 1876–1946.
Shepherd's Song, The, *Richard Crashaw*, Fm [e´-a´´b], Gwynn.

Hughes, John.
My Mother's Picture, [soprano/tenor], Snell.

Hughes, Richard Samuel. 1855–1893.
Sailor Boy's Dream, *B. Parry,*[soprano/tenor], Snell.
Warrior's Return, The, *Anon*, C [any voice], Snell.

Hughes-Jones, Llifon. 1918–1996. WMIC.
Love in Christ, Curiad.
Mill at Trefin, The, *Crwys* tr. *R. Gerallt Jones*, Cm [a-e´´b] WMIC *Songs from Wales 2,* Curiad.

Hugill, Robert. See also App. 2.
Collections: *Angel Food,* Bardic; *Love Remembered,* Bardic; *Songs of Love and Loss,* Bardic.
Chandelier, *Constantine Cavafy* tr. *Noel Leavis & David Streeter,* [d´-f´´], Bardic Love.
Come back, *Constantine Cavafy* tr. *Noel Leavis & David Streeter,* [d´b-f´´], Bardic Love.
Dead Poet, The, *Lord Alfred Douglas,* [a-d´´], Bardic Songs of Love and Loss.
December 1903, *Constantine Cavafy* tr. *Noel Leavis & David Streeter,* [c´-f´´], Bardic Love.
Grey, *Constantine Cavafy* tr. *Noel Leavis & David Streeter,* [c´-f´´], Bardic Love.
Let me stop her, *Constantine Cavafy* tr. *Noel Leavis & David Streeter,* [g´b-g´´], Bardic Love.
Melon, The, *Felice Picano,* [b-d´´], Bardic Angel.
Plum, The, *Felice Picano,* [g-b´], Bardic Angel.
Rose, The, *Felice Picano,* [gb-b´], Bardic Angel.
Soft, for music dies, *M. V. Lively,* [c´#-f´´#], Bardic Songs of Love & Loss.
Their beginning, *Constantine Cavafy* tr. *Noel Leavis & David Streeter,* [c´-f´´#], Bardic Love.
To his Coy Mistress, *Andrew Marvell,* [g-c´´], Bardic.

Hullah, John Pyke. 1812–1884.
Three fishers went sailing, *Charles Kingsley,* C [a-f´´], BMP.

Hume, Tobias. *c.*1569–1645.
Fain would I change that note, *Anon*, G [d´-g´´] S&B (Greer) *Printed,* Leonard *Baroque high,* BMP *W&W 4*; F, B&H (Keel) *Lovesongs 1a*; Eb, *Lovesongs 1b*; D, Leonard *Baroque low.*
Soldier's Song, The, *Anon*, C [g-g´´](m), S&B (Greer) *Printed.*
Tobacco, tobacco, *Anon,* Dm [d´-f´´], S&B (Greer) *Printed,* BMP *W&W 3*; Bbm, B&H (Northcote) *Imperial 6.*
What greater grief, *Anon*, Gm [d´-f´´], S&B (Greer) *Printed.*

Humfrey, Pelham. 1647–1674. See also App. 2.
Hymn to God the Father, A, *John Donne*, Gm [c´#-f´´], Schott (Tippett), Thames (Bevan) *6 Divine Hymns,* OUP (Tear?) *Solo Tenor,* Faber (Britten) *Harmonia*; Fm, Schott (Tippett).
Lord! I have sinned, *Jeremy Taylor,* Fm [e´-a´´b], Faber (Britten) *Harmonia.*
Oh! that I had but a fine man, *Anon*, Gm [d´-d´´](f), Thames (Bevan) *8 Restoration.*
Where the bee sucks, *Shakespeare* adapted *Shadwell,* Am [e´-g´´], Thames (Bevan) *8 Restoration.*

Hurd, Michael John. 1928–
Collection: *Shore Leave,* Novello.
Able Seaman Hodge Remembers Ceylon, *Charles Causley,* C [c´-f´´](m), Novello Shore Leave.
Convoy, *Charles Causley,* Dm [c´-f´´](m), Novello Shore Leave.

Day's Alarm, The, (cycle), *Paul Dehn*, [b-e''](m), Novello.
Elizabethan Sailor's Song, *Charles Causley,* F [c'-f''](m), Novello Shore Leave.
Sailor's Carol, *Charles Causley*, Dm [d'-f''](m), Novello Shore Leave.
Shore Leave, *Charles Causley*, D [d'-e''](m), Novello Shore Leave.

Hurlstone, William Yeates. 1876–1906. *See also* App. 2.
Collection: *Two Miniature Ballads*, Banks.
Blossoms, [medium], Banks.
Darkness, *Olive C. Malvery*, [medium], Banks 2 Miniature.
(Derby Ram, The, *Anon*, Cm [c'-d''], Ashdown.)
(Litany, A, *Phineas Fletcher*, Am, B&H.)
Morning, *Olive Christian Malvery*, [medium], Banks 2 Miniature.
(Wilt thou be my dearie? *Robert Burns*, G [c'-d''](m), Ashdown.)

Hywel, John. 1941– WMIC. *See also* App. 2.
Farewell to Snowdonia, [mezzo/baritone], Gwynn.

I

Inglis, Brian. 1969– BMIC. *See also* App. 2.

Ireland, John. 1879–1962. *See also* App. 2.
Collections: *Complete Works for Voice and Piano volumes 1-5*, S&B (foreword Geoffrey Bush); *Eleven Songs,* S&B (Preface and Notes, John Longmire); *Five XVIth Century Poems*, Braydeston Press; *Land of Lost Content and Other Songs, The,* S&B (Preface and Notes, John Longmire); *Marigold*, B&H; *Mother and Child,* S&B; *Songs of a Wayfarer,* B&H; *Songs Sacred and Profane*, Schott; *Three Arthur Symons Songs*, Chester; *Two Songs and a Melodrama,* S&B; *We'll to the woods no more,* BMP, NB: Two songs and a piano solo, the piano solo omitted in S&B *Complete Works 3*.
  Adoration, The, *Arthur Symons*, Ab m [d'b-f''], S&B Complete 2, Chester 3 Symons; (B m, F#m, Chester).
  Advent, The, *Alice Meynell*, Dm [d'-g''], S&B Complete 1, Schott Sacred.
  All in a Garden Green, *Thomas Howell*, F [d'-e''], S&B Complete 3, Braydeston 5 Poems.
  Aside, An, *Anon*, Bb [bb-e''b], S&B Complete 3, Braydeston 5 Poems.
  Baby, *Christina Rossetti,* D [e'-e''], S&B Complete 2, Mother & Child.
  Bed in Summer, *R. L. Stevenson*, F [c'-d''], S&B Complete 5.
  Bells of San Marie, The, *John Masefield*, Gm [c'-d''], S&B Complete 2, 11 Songs; Cm, Am, S&B.
  Blind, *Eric Thirkell Cooper*, Dm [d'-d''], S&B Complete 5.
  Blind Boy, The, *Christina Rossetti,* Am [e'-e''], S&B Complete 2, Mother & Child.
  Blow out, you bugles, *Rupert Brooke*, Eb [c'-f''], S&B Complete 4.
  Cost, The, *Eric Thirkell Cooper*, Fm [c'-f''], S&B Complete 5.
  Death-parting, *Christina Rossetti,* Em [e'-e''], S&B Complete 2, Mother & Child.
  During Music, *D. G. Rossetti*, Eb [bb-g''b], S&B Complete 2, BMP.
  Earth's Call (A Sylvan Rhapsody), *Harold Monro*, Eb [b-f''#], S&B Complete 4.
  East Riding, The, *Eric Chilman*, Cm [e'b-g''], S&B Complete 1; (Am, Em, Enoch).
  Encounter, The, *A. E. Housman*, C [g'-g''], S&B Complete 1, Lost Content; *A*, S&B.
  English May, *D. G. Rossetti*, Eb [bb-e''b], S&B Complete 4, B&H Wayfarer.
  Epilogue, *A. E. Housman*, Db [f'-a''b], S&B Complete 1, Lost Content; *Bb*, S&B.
  Five Poems by Thomas Hardy, (cycle) [bb-g''b(e'')](m), S&B Complete 3, BMP.
  Friendship in Misfortune, *Anon*, Db [d'b-f''], S&B Complete 5, 11 Songs.
  Garland, The, *Christina Rossetti,* F [d'-f''], S&B Complete 2, Mother & Child.
  Garrison Churchyard, A, *Eric Thirkell Cooper,* Bm [b-d''#], S&B 2 Songs & Melodrama.
  Goal and Wicket, *A. E. Housman*, Em [e'-g''](m), S&B Complete 1, Lost Content; *C#m*, S&B.
  Great Things, *Thomas Hardy*, C [c'-e''(d'')](m), S&B Complete 3, 11 Songs; D, S&B.
  Hawthorn Time, *A. E. Housman*, C [d'-g''], S&B Complete 1; *Bb*, B&H
  Heart's Desire, The, *A. E. Housman*, Db [f'-a''b], S&B Complete 1, B&H *Heritage 4*; B, Bb, B&H.
  Her Song, *Thomas Hardy*, Dm [c'-d''](f), S&B Complete 3; *Dm, F#m*, Cramer; Em, F#m, Cramer.
  Holy Boy, The, *Herbert S. Brown*, Eb [c'-f''(g'')], B&H, Mayhew *Holy Night*; F, B&H *Ballad Album 2,* OUP *Solo Christmas high*; D, *Solo Christmas low*; G, B&H.
  Hope, *Christina Rossetti,* Am [d'-d''], S&B Complete 2, Mother & Child.
  Hope the Hornblower, *Henry Newbolt*, Bb [f'-g''], S&B Complete 5, 11 Songs; C, A, G, B&H.

Hymn for a Child, *Sylvia Townsend Warner*, A [c′#-f′′], S&B Complete 1, Schott Sacred.
I have twelve oxen, *Anon*, F [c′-f′′], S&B Complete 5, B&H *Heritage 3*; G, B&H *New Imperial 1*.
I was not sorrowful, *Arthur Symons*, C [c′-e′′b], S&B Complete 4, B&H Wayfarer.
I will walk the earth, *James Vila Blake*, C [c′-e′′(g′′)], S&B Complete 4, B&H Wayfarer.
If there were dreams to sell, *Thomas Lovell Beddoes*, Eb [c′-f′′], S&B Complete 5; Db, F, B&H.
If we must part, *Ernest Dowson*, G [d′-e′′], S&B Complete 5, Lost Content.
In Boyhood, *A. E. Housman*, [c′#-f′′], S&B Complete 3, BMP We'll to the Woods.
Journey, The, *Ernest Blake*, C [d′-f′′], S&B Complete 5; (D, Bb, Enoch).
Ladslove, *A. E. Housman*, Ab [f′-a′′b], S&B Complete 1, Lost Content; *F*, S&B.
Lent Lily, The, *A. E. Housman*, Em [g′-f′′#], S&B Complete 1, Lost Content; *Dm*, S&B.
Love and Friendship, *Emily Bronte*, [c′-g′′], S&B Complete 5, 11 Songs, *Recitalist 3*.
Love is a sickness full of woes, *Samuel Daniel*, Gb [e′b-g′′], S&B Complete 1, B&H *Heritage 4*;
   F, Eb, B&H.
Memory, *William Blake*, D [b-d′′], S&B Complete 4, B&H Wayfarer, Schirmer *2nd Baritone*.
Merry Month of May, The, *Thomas Dekker*, E [c′#-f′′#], S&B Complete 5; G, D, B&H.
My Fair, *Alice Meynell*, B [e′-g′′], S&B Complete 1, Schott Sacred.
My true love hath my heart, *Philip Sidney*, E [d′#-f′′#(f′′)], S&B Complete 1, 11 Songs, *Recitalist 2*; G, S&B.
Newborn, *Christina Rossetti*, C [d′-f′′], S&B Complete 2, Mother & Child.
One Hope, The, *D. G. Rossetti*, [bb-f′′#], S&B Complete 5, 11 Songs.
Only Child, The, *Christina Rossetti*, C [e′-f′′], S&B Complete 2, Mother & Child.
Penumbra, *D. G. Rossetti*, [a-f′′], S&B Complete 4, B&H Marigold.
Rat, The, *Arthur Symons*, Bm [b-e′′], S&B Complete 2, Chester 3 Symons.
Remember, *Mary Coleridge*, D [e′b-g′′], S&B Complete 1; *C, Bb*, B&H.
Report Song, A, *Nicholas Breton*, Eb [e′b-e′′b], S&B Complete 3, Braydeston 5 Poems.
Rest, *Arthur Symons*, Db [e′b-f′′], S&B Complete 2, Chester 3 Symons.
Sacred Flame, The, *Mary Coleridge*, C [d′b-a′′b], S&B Complete 1; *Bb*, B&H.
Salley Gardens, The, *W. B. Yeats*, Em [e′-e′′], S&B Complete 1, Schott Sacred; *Dm*, Schott.
Santa Chiara (Palm Sunday: Naples), *Arthur Symons*, Gm [c′-e′′b], S&B Complete 2, 11 Songs;
   Am, *Cm*, S&B.
Scapegoat, The, *Sylvia Townsend Warner*, G [e′-f′′], S&B Complete 1, Schott Sacred.
Sea Fever, *John Masefield*, Em [b-d′′](m), S&B Complete 2, 11 Songs, Classical, S&B; Fm, S&B,
   Classical; Gm, Schirmer *1st Tenor II*, S&B; Am, S&B.
Skylark and Nightingale, *Christina Rossetti*, Eb [e′b-e′′b], S&B Complete 2, Mother & Child.
Soldier, The, *Rupert Brooke*, F [d′-f′′], S&B Complete 4; G*b*, Eb, B&H.
Soldier's Return, The, *Sylvia Townsend Warner*, Gm [d′-e′′], S&B Complete 1, Schott Sacred.
Song from o'er the hill, A, *P. J. O'Reilly*, Ab [d′-e′′b], S&B Complete 5.
Spleen, *Ernest Dowson*, [a-d′′], S&B Complete 4, B&H Marigold.
Spring Sorrow, *Rupert Brooke*, F [c′-d′′], S&B Complete 4, B&H *Heritage 3*, B&H; Ab, B&H.
Summer Schemes, *Thomas Hardy*, Ab [c′-f′′], S&B Complete 3; *G*, Cramer *Folio 1*.
Sweet Season, The, *Richard Edwards*, D [d′-e′′], S&B Complete 3, Braydeston 5 Poems.
Thanksgiving, A, *William Cornish*, D [b-e′′], S&B Complete 3, Braydeston 5 Poems.
Trellis, The, *Aldous Huxley*, Ab [c′-g′′], S&B Complete 1, 11 Songs; *F*, S&B.
Tryst (In Fountain Court), *Arthur Symons*, [d′-f′′#], S&B Complete 2, BMP.
Tutto e sciolto, *James Joyce*, [e′-e′′], S&B Complete 5.
Vagabond, The, *John Masefield*, Bb [f′-f′′](m), S&B Complete 2, 11 Songs; Ab, *G, F*, S&B.
Vain Desire, The, *A. E. Housman*, Am [e′-a′′b], S&B Complete 1, Lost Content, F#m, S&B.
Weathers, *Thomas Hardy*, C [c′-d′′], S&B Complete 3; *E, D, C*, Cramer.
We'll to the woods no more, *A. E. Housman*, [c′b-f′′](m), S&B Complete 3, BMP We'll to the Woods.
What art thou thinking of? *Christina Rossetti*, Ab [e′b-g′′b], S&B Complete 2, Lost Content.
When daffodils begin to peer, *Shakespeare*, C [b-e′′(e′′b)](m), S&B Complete 4, B&H
   Shakespeare Album, Wayfarer.
When I am dead, my dearest, *Christina Rossetti*, F [d′-d′′], S&B Complete 2, BMP.
When I am old, *Ernest Dowson*, G [b-e′′], S&B 2 Songs & Melodrama.
When lights go rolling round the sky, *James Vila Blake*, D [d′-f′′#(e′′)], S&B Complete 5, Lost
   Content, (Chappell *English Recital 1*); C, Classical, (Chappell).
Youth's Spring-tribute, *D. G. Rossetti*, Eb [bb-g′′(f′′)], S&B Complete 4, B&H Marigold.
Arrangement:
   Three ravens, The, *Anon*, Fm [c′-e′′b], S&B Complete 5; Gm, B&H.

Irvine, Jessie. 1836–1887. *See* App. 2.

Isherwood, Cherry.
   Sleep, *John Fletcher*, [bb-e′′], BMP.

Ives, Simon. 1600–1662.
    Go bid the swan in silence die, *Anon*, G [e′-g′′], S&B (Spink) *MB 33*.
    Will Chloris cast her sun-bright eyes? *Anon*, Am [g′#-f′′](m), S&B (Spink) *MB 33, Cavalier*.

Ives, Grayston. 1948 -
    Falcon, The, *Anon*, [d′-g′′], Roberton.

J

Jackson, Francis. 1917 -
    Tree at my window, *Robert Frost*, G [d′-a′′], Banks.

Jackson, Robert.
    Slumber Song (Lancashire Lullaby), *Edwin Waugh*, Ab [e′b-c′′], Forsyth.

Jackson, William. 1730–1803.
    Let no mortal sing to me, *Anon*, A [c′#-f′′#], OUP (Roberts) *Tuneful Voice*.

Jacob, Gordon. 1895–1984. *See also* App. 2.
Collection: *Three Songs of Innocence*, BMP 1926.
    Adlestrop, *Edward Thomas*, E [e′-e′′], BMP.
    Cam' ye by? *Anon*, Am [c′-f′′](f), S&B.
    Helen of Kirkconnell, *Anon*, Gm [B-f′](m), S&B.
    Lamb, The, *William Blake*, Em [e′-g′′], BMP 3 Songs.
    Laughing Song, *William Blake*, G [d′-g′′], BMP 3 Songs.
    Love me not for comely grace, *Anon*, C [e′-f′′], S&B.
    Mother, I will have a husband, *Thomas Vautor*, G [d′-e′′](f), Thames *Century 4*.
    Shepherd, The, *William Blake*, F#m [e′-f′′#], BMP 3 Songs.
Arrangements:
    Golden slumbers kiss your eyes, *Anon*, Bb [d′-f′′], BMP.
    Londonderry Air, The, *Anon*, Eb [bb-g′′], BMP.
    Pull away home, *Anon*, F [c′-f′′], BMP.
    Widdecombe Fair, *Anon*, G [d′-d′′], BMP.

Jacobson, Maurice. 1896–1976.
    (Boys, *W. M. Letts*, F#m [e-f′′#], Curwen; Em, Curwen.)
    (Jolly good ale and old, *William Stevenson*, [bb-e′′b], Curwen.)
    (Last Hours, *John Freeman*, D [e′b-f′′#], Curwen.)
    (Lord is my shepherd, The, *Psalm 23*, A [f′#-d′′], Elkin.)
    (Mamble, *John Drinkwater*, [db-f′′#], Curwen.)
    (Queen Mab, *Thomas Hood*, [c′-e′′], Curwen.)
    (Roman Road, The, *Peggy Laing*, Gm [e′-a′′b], Curwen.)
    (Savoury Seal, The, *Edward A. Parry*, Am [e′-c′′#], Curwen.)
    Song of Songs, The, *Song of Solomon*, Bm [a-f′′], Lengnick.
Arrangements:
    (In Praise of Isla, *Anon* tr. *Thomas Pattison*, C [c′-e′′], Curwen.)
    (Jota, *Anon* tr. *Whyte Monk*, D [f′#-g′′#], Curwen.)
    (Song for Christmas, A, *Hermon Ould*, Bm [b-d′′], Curwen.)
    (Swansea Town, *Anon*, D [c′#-e′′](m), Curwen.)
    (Willow Song, *Shakespeare*, Em [e′-e′′], Curwen.)

Jacques, Reginald. 1894–1969.
    Orpheus with his lute, *Shakespeare*, BMP.

Jeffreys, George. *c.*1610–1685. *See also* App. 1.
    Cruel! but once again, *Peter Hausted*, Am [g′-f′′], S&B (Spink) *MB 33*.
    Have pity, grief, I cannot pay, *Peter Hausted*, Gm [d′-f′′], S&B (Spink) *MB 33*.

Jeffreys, John. 1927– *See also* App. 2.
Collections: *Album of Fourteen Songs*, Roberton (preface Colin Sutherland); *Book of Songs*, Roberton; *New Brooms*, Thames; *Second Book of Songs*, Roberton (introduction Alfred David Williams); *Third and Last Book of Songs*, Roberton (preface Kenneth Roberton); *When I was Young* Parts 1, 2, 3, Roberton.

Amaryllis, *Thomas Campion*, G [d´-e´´](m), Roberton 2nd Book.
Ambulance Train, *Wilfrid Gibson*, [c´#-e´´], Roberton Book of Songs.
And would you see my mistress' face? *Campion?* B♭ [f´-e´´♭](m), Roberton Book of Songs.
Appeal, The, *Thomas Wyatt*, B [b-d´´#], Roberton Book of Songs.
As Dew in April, *Anon 15th cent.*, [a´-c´´#], Thames *Countertenors 2*.
Aspatia's Song, *John Fletcher*, Gm [d´-g´´](f), Roberton 14 Songs.
At the cry of the first bird, *Anon tr. Howard Mumford Jones*, [e´b-a´´], Roberton 2nd Book.
Awake thee my Bessy, *J. J. Callanan*, G [d´-g´´](m), Roberton 3rd Book.
Bailey Beareth the Bell Away, The, *Anon*, Am [a´-a´´ or a-a´](f), Roberton 14 Songs.
Be you Blithe and Bonny, *Shakespeare*, E♭ [e´b-g´´♭], Roberton 2nd Book.
Birds, The, *Hilaire Belloc*, E♭m [d´b-e´´♭], Roberton 3rd Book.
Black Stichel, *Wilfrid Gibson*, Bm [d´-f´´#], Roberton 2nd Book.
Brigg Fair, *Anon*, [bb-e´´b(g´´b)](m), Roberton 14 Songs.
Brown is my love, *Anon*, D♭ [d´b-e´´♭](m), Roberton 3rd Book.
Candle Gate, *Wilfrid Gibson*, [d´-d´´], Roberton 2nd Book.
Christ's Nativity, *Anon*, B♭ [f´-f´´], Roberton 2nd Book.
Corncrake, The, *James H. Cousins*, [e´#-e´´], Roberton 14 Songs.
Corpus Christi, *Anon*, Em [e´-g´´], Roberton 3rd Book.
Cruel and bright, *Wilfrid Gibson*, [c´#-e´´](m), Roberton 2nd Book.
Cuckoo, The, *Anon*, G [d´-e´´], Roberton 2nd Book.
Curlew calling, *Wilfrid Gibson*, F#m [f´#-e´´], Roberton Book of Songs.
Dapple Grey, *Anon*, E♭ [d´-e´´♭], Roberton When I was Young 3.
Ding dong bell, *Anon*, E♭ [e´b-e´´♭], Roberton When I was Young 2.
Drop, drop slow tears, *Phineas Fletcher*, Em [g-g´](m), Thames New Brooms.
Drop, drop slow tears, *Phineas Fletcher*, Gm [bb-b´♭], Roberton 14 Songs.
Falcon, The, *Anon*, Em [d´-g´´], Roberton 2nd Book.
Farewell, The, *Robert Burns*, G [d´-e´´](m), Roberton 3rd Book.
Fill me O stars, *Joseph Campbell*, A [d´-e´´], Roberton 3rd Book.
Four and twenty tailors, *Anon*, [d´-f´´], Roberton When I was Young 3.
From Omiecourt, *Ivor Gurney*, F#m [e´-f´´#](m), Roberton Book of Songs.
Full fathom five, *Shakespeare*, Bm [d´-c´´#], Roberton Book of Songs.
Gather ye rosebuds, *Robert Herrick*, A [e´-e´´], Roberton 3rd Book.
Golden slumbers, *Thomas Dekker*, A♭ [e´b-f´´], Roberton 2nd Book.
Gone is my love from the silver stream, *Barry Duane Hill*, Gm [d´-f´´](m), Roberton.
Goosey goosey gander, *Anon*, [d´-e´´], Roberton When I was Young 2.
Hag, The, *Robert Herrick*, Bm [d´-f´´#], Roberton Book of Songs.
Ha'nacker Mill, *Hilaire Belloc*, Am [d´-f´´], Roberton 3rd Book.
High Hills, The, *Ivor Gurney*, [c´#-f´´#], Roberton Book of Songs.
Hill Song, *Barry Duane Hill*, Am [d´-e´´](m), Roberton 2nd Book.
Horror follows horror, *Ivor Gurney*, C#m [f´#-e´´], Roberton Book of Songs.
How many miles to Babylon? *Anon*, Gm [d´-e´´♭](m), Roberton When I was Young 1.
How should I your true love know? *Shakespeare*, [e´-e´´], Roberton 2nd Book.
Humpty Dumpty, *Anon*, Gm [d´-d´´], Roberton When I was Young 3.
I am the gilly of Christ, *Joseph Campbell*, Gm [d´-d´´], Roberton 3rd Book.
I love little kitty, *Anon*, G [d´-e´´], Roberton When I was Young 2.
I was young and foolish, *W. B. Yeats*, E [c´#(d´#)-e´´](m), Roberton Book of Songs.
I will go with my father a-ploughing, *Joseph Campbell*, G [d´-f´´], Roberton; F, Roberton.
I will make you brooches, *R. L. Stevenson*, E [b-e´´](m), Roberton 2nd Book.
If it chance your eye offend you, *A. E. Housman*, Fm [c´-d´´♭], Roberton Book of Songs.
If there were dreams to sell, *Thomas Lovell Beddoes*, [d´-e´´], Roberton 2nd Book.
In a Boat, *Hilaire Belloc*, Gm [f´-f´´], Roberton 3rd Book.
In Marley Wood, *Hugh S. Roberton*, [d´-f´´(g´´)], Roberton 3rd Book.
In pride of May, *Anon*, G [d´-e´´](m), Roberton 2nd Book; E, Roberton 2nd Book.
In Youth is Pleasure, *Robert Wever*, D [d´-d´´](m), Roberton Book of Songs.
It is winter, *Walter de la Mare*, [d´-e´´], Roberton Book of Songs.
It was a lover and his lass, *Shakespeare*, E [e´-e´´], Roberton Book of Songs.
Jack and Jill, *Anon*, E [e´-e´´], Roberton When I was Young 1(m).
Jillian of Berry, *Beaumont & Fletcher?* F [d´-f´´](m), Roberton Book of Songs.
Light Wind, A, *Barry Duane Hill*, [d´-f´´#](m), Roberton 2nd Book.
Little Milkmaid, The, *Thomas Nabbes*, G [d´-g´´]('tenor'), Roberton 2nd Book.
Little Milkmaid, The, *Thomas Nabbes*, G [d´-g´´]('lower voices'), Roberton 2nd Book.
Little pretty nightingale, The, *Anon*, E♭ [e´b-e´´♭](m), Roberton 2nd Book.
Little trotty wagtail, *John Clare*, G [d´-g´´], Roberton 2nd Book.

Lone Bird, The, *Emily Brontë*, [e′-g′′], Roberton 3rd Book.
Long to me thy coming, *Padraic Pearse*, [f′#-e′′], Roberton 14 Songs.
Love me not for comely grace, *Anon*, E [e′-e′′](m), Roberton 3rd Book.
Lovely Playthings, *Ivor Gurney*, [b-d′′](m), Roberton 2nd Book.
Lullaby, *Thomas Dekker*, [f′-e′′b], Roberton 3rd Book.
Lyke-wake Dirge, A, *Anon*, Gm [d′-e′′#], Roberton Book of Songs.
Maid of Kent, *William Wager*, E [g#-a′](m), Thames New Brooms.
Matthew Mark Luke and John, *Anon*, [d′-e′′], Roberton When I was Young 2.
Merry Eye, *Wilfrid Gibson*, Fm [c′(f′)-f′′b], Roberton 3rd Book.
Milkmaid, The, *Thomas Nabbes*, G [d′-e′′], Roberton Book of Songs.
My lady, *Anon*, Eb [e′b-e′′b](m), Roberton 3rd Book.
My little pretty one, *Anon*, E [e′-e′′], Roberton Book of Songs.
My Master hath a garden, *Anon*, B [f′#-f′′#], Roberton 3rd Book.
My mistress frowns, *Anon*, G [d′-f′′](m), Roberton 2nd Book.
My pretty honey one, *Anon*, F [f′-f′′](m), Roberton 2nd Book.
Northumberland, *Wilfrid Gibson*, E [e′-e′′], Roberton 3rd Book, Roberton.
Now is the time of Christemas, *Anon*, G [g-g′](m), Thames New Brooms.
Now wolde, *Anon*, E [b-e′′](m), Roberton 2nd Book.
O good ale, *Anon*, D [d′-d′′](m), Roberton 2nd Book.
O mistress mine, *Shakespeare*, Ab [d′b-f′′](m), Roberton Book of Songs.
O my dere hert, *Martin Luther* tr. *Wedderburn*, Eb [e′b-e′′b], Roberton 2nd Book.
Old mother Hubbard, *Anon*, Fm [e′b-e′′b], Roberton When I was Young 3.
Omens, *James H. Cousins*, [f′#-e′′], Roberton Book of Songs.
Otterburn, *Wilfrid Gibson*, Bm [f′#-f′′#], Roberton Book of Songs.
Passing By, *Anon*, G [f′#-g′′](m), Roberton Book of Songs.
Peter the pumpkin-eater, *Anon*, D [d′-d′′](m), Roberton When I was Young 1.
Pippen Hill, *Anon*, Bb [f′-d′′](m), Roberton When I was Young 1.
Poacher's Dog, The, *Louis Mayerling*, Em [d′-f′′#](m), Roberton.
Quarry, The, *Wilfrid Gibson*, Am [d′-e′′], Roberton 14 Songs.
Queen of Hearts, The, *Anon*, [d′-d′′](m), Roberton When I was Young 1.
Reaper, The, *Barry Duane Hill*, [d′#-d′′#], Roberton 3rd Book.
Reaper, The, *Barry Duane Hill*, Bm [g#-b′](m) Thames New Brooms.
Requiem, *Ivor Gurney*, [d′-e′′], Roberton Book of Songs.
Robin Redbreast, *W. H. Davies*, [f′-g′′], Roberton 2nd Book.
Romance, *R. L. Stevenson*, F [c′-f′′](m), Roberton Book of Songs.
Salley Gardens, The, *W. B. Yeats*, Gb [d′b-g′′b], Roberton 2nd Book.
Salley Gardens, The, *W. B. Yeats*, G [d′-g′′], Roberton 14 Songs.
Salley Gardens, The, *W. B. Yeats*, C [d′-d′′], Roberton 14 Songs.
Sally, *Barry Duane Hill*, A [d′-a′′](m), Roberton 3rd Book.
Seals of Love, *Shakespeare*, Bbm [a′b-e′′b], Roberton 2nd Book.
Season of Ice, *Anon*, [d′-f′′], Roberton 14 Songs.
Severn Meadows, *Ivor Gurney*, [d′-f′′#], Roberton Book of Songs.
She is all so slight, *Richard Aldington*, Eb [bb-e′′b](m), Roberton 2nd Book.
She is ever for the new, *Anon*, G [d′-g′′](m), Roberton 2nd Book.
Sigh no more ladies, *Shakespeare*, G [e′-g′′], Roberton Book of Songs.
Sing no sad songs for me, *Christina Rossetti*, Db [d′b-d′′b], Roberton 14 Songs.
Six Badgers, *Robert Graves*, Ab [d′b-e′′b](m), Roberton 3rd Book.
Sleep, *John Fletcher*, Ab [e′b-a′′b], Roberton Book of Songs.
Snow, *Edward Thomas*, [f′-f′′#], Roberton Book of Songs.
Song of Love, The, *Barry Duane Hill*, [d′-e′′], Roberton 14 Songs.
Songs I had, The, *Ivor Gurney*, Fm [d′-f′′], Roberton Book of Songs.
Stow-on-the-Wold, *Wilfrid Gibson*, Gm [d′-d′′], Roberton Book of Songs.
Sweeney the mad, *Irish* tr. *J. G. O'Keefe*, Gm [d′b-d′′](m), Roberton 3rd Book.
Take O take those lips away, *Shakespeare*, Bb [f′-g′′], Roberton Book of Songs.
That ever I saw, *Anon*, D [d′-e′′](m), Roberton 3rd Book.
There is a lady sweet and kind, *Anon*, E [e′-e′′](m), Roberton Book of Songs.
There was a crooked man, *Anon*, F [d′-f′′], Roberton When I was Young 2.
Thirteen Pence a Day, *A. E. Housman*, [d′-d′′](m), Roberton Book of Songs.
This is the weather, *Thomas Hardy*, [b-e′′], Roberton 2nd Book.
This little pig, *Anon*, E [e′-e′′], Roberton When I was Young 2.
This night, *Padraic Pearse*, tr. *Thomas MacDonagh*, Ebm [e′b-a′′b], Roberton Book of Songs.
Thomas MacDonagh, *Francis Ledwidge*, [c′#-f′′#], Roberton 2nd Book.
Through the streets of Picardy, *Anon*, G [d′-e′′](m), Roberton When I was Young 1.
'Tis time I think, *A. E. Housman*, Cm [e′b-f′′], Roberton Book of Songs.

To bed, to bed, *Anon*, F [c′(f′)-f′′(d′′)], Roberton When I was Young 3.
To make my mistress kind, *Patrick Hannay*, F [e′-f′′](m), Roberton 3rd Book.
Tom the piper's son, *Anon*, E [d′-e′′], Roberton When I was Young 3.
True woman's eye, A, *Anon*, E♭ [e′b-e′′b](m), Roberton 3rd Book.
Under the blossom, *Shakespeare*, E♭ [e′b-f′′], Roberton Book of Songs.
Under the leaves green, *Anon*, C [g-a′](m), Thames New Brooms.
Weep you no more, *Anon*, G [g-g′](m), Thames New Brooms.
Welcome to Spring, *John Lyly*, Bm [a-a′](m) Thames New Brooms.
What evil coil of fate? *Ivor Gurney*, F#m [d′-e′′], Roberton Book of Songs.
What thing is love? *George Peele*, G [d′-d′′](m), Roberton 3rd Book.
When daisies pied, *Shakespeare*, A [c′#(d′)-e′′], Roberton Book of Songs.
When I came at last to Ludlow, *A. E. Housman*, F#m [f′#-e′′#](m), Roberton 3rd Book.
When I was one-and-twenty, *A. E. Housman*, E [b(e′)-e′′](m), Roberton 3rd Book.
When that I was and a little tiny boy, *Shakespeare*, G [d′-g′′(e′′)](m), Roberton Book of Songs.
When that I was and a little tiny boy, *Shakespeare*, C [g-a′](m), Thames New Brooms.
Whenas I wake, *Patrick Hannay*, F [e′-e′′b](m), Roberton 3rd Book.
Whether men do laugh or weep, *Anon*, C [g-g′](m), Thames New Brooms.
Whin, The, *Wilfrid Gibson*, F [d′-g′′](m), Roberton 14 Songs.
White Rose, A, *John Boyle O'Reilly*, C [g-a′](m), Thames New Brooms.
White was the way, *Barry Duane Hill*, F [d′-f′′](m), Roberton 2nd Book.
Who is at my window? *Scottish, before 1600*, Gm [d′-e′′b], Roberton Book of Songs.
Wine, *Henry Carey*, E♭ [b♭-e′′b](m), Roberton 14 Songs.
With rue my heart is laden, *A. E. Housman*, Fm [c′-d′′](m), Roberton 3rd Book.
Yet will I love her, *Anon*, A♭ [f′-f′′](m), Roberton 3rd Book.

Jenkins, David. 1848–1915.
Home for ever, *Dyfed* tr. *M. H. Jones*, [contralto/baritone], Snell.
Lord is my shepherd, The, *Psalm 23*, [soprano/tenor], Snell.
Speak, I pray thee, gentle Jesus, *W. Williams* tr. *R. M. Lewis*, [soprano/tenor], Snell; [contralto/baritone], Snell.

Jenkins, John. 1592–1678.
Cease not, thou heav'nly-voiced glorious creature, *Anon*, Cm [d′-f′′], S&B (Spink) *MB 33*.

Jenkins, Karl.
He wishes for the cloths of heaven, *W. B. Yeats*, [c′#-e′′], B&H.

Jenkins, Trevor.
Gethsemane, *William Lewis* tr. *Llwd*, [soprano/tenor], Snell.

Jenkins, William.
Gipsy Song, [any voice], Snell.
Glory of the Cross, The, [contralto/baritone], Snell.
Speak, I pray thee, gentle Jesus, *W. Williams* tr. *R. M. Lewis*, [soprano/tenor], Snell.

Jepson, David.
Faith, hope and love, [medium], Banks.

Johnson, Robert. *c.*1583–1633.
Collection: *Ayres, Songs and Dialogues,* S&B (edited with introduction Ian Spink). Only songs available in anthologies are listed individually here.
As I walked forth one summer's day, *Anon*, Gm [d′-g′′], Ayres, Leonard *Baroque high*; *Fm,* Classical/ B&H *Dolmetsch 1*; *Dm,* Paterson (Diack), *100 Best 4*, Leonard *Baroque low*.
Dear, do not your fair beauty wrong, *Anon*, F [c′-g′′], Ayres, S&B (Pilkington), *Lute Songs 1*.
Have you seen but the bright lily grow? *Ben Jonson*, F [e′-f′′], Ayres, Classical/B&H *Dolmetsch 1*.

Johnson, Robert Sherlaw. 1932–2000. See App. 2.

Johnstone, Maurice. 1900–1976.
Collection: *Two Songs,* BMP 1944.
At Night, *Alice Meynell*, D [d′-e′′], BMP 2 Songs.
Dover Beach, *Matthew Arnold*, F [b-f′′], Lengnick.
Hush! *James Walker,* [d′-e′′], BMP 2 Songs.
So are you to my thoughts, *Shakespeare*, D♭ [d′b-e′′b], Lengnick.

Jones, Daniel Jenkyn. 1912–1993.
Ballad of the Standard-bearer, The, *Rainer Maria Rilke* tr. *Daniel Jones,* [d′b-b′′b](m), Maecenas.

Jones, Derek. WMIC.

Jones, David **Tawe.**
Dick Fisherman, *A. G. Prys-Jones,* [baritone], Snell.
Roses, *D. Emrys Jones,* Ab [soprano], Snell.

Jones, Elfyn Morris. *See* App. 2.

Jones, Eric. WMIC.

Jones, J. Morian.
Song of the People, [contralto/baritone], Snell.

Jones, Kenneth V. 1924– BMIC.

Jones, M. O.
Ship and the Lighthouse, The, *Seth P. Jones,* [soprano/tenor], Snell.

Jones, Owen.
Happy Breezes, [soprano], Snell.
King of Love, [contralto/baritone], Snell.

Jones, Richard Elfyn. 1944– *See also* App. 2.
Ascension Thursday, *Saunders Lewis,* tr. *Anthony Conran,* [d′-g′′], WMIC *Songs from Wales 1.*

Jones, R. L.
Hail, fellow, hail, *James Clarence Harvey,* [baritone], Snell.

Jones, Richard Roderick. 1947– WMIC.
Oak-tree, The, *William Thomas (Islwyn)* tr. *John Stoddart,* [G(A)-d′](m), WMIC *Songs from Wales 2.*

Jones, Robert. *c.*1570–*c.*1615.
Collections: *First Book of Songs, The,* S&B (edited Thurston Dart); *Second Book of Songs, The,* S&B (edited E H Fellowes); *Muses Gardin for Delights, The,* S&B (edited E H Fellowes); *Musicall Dreame, A,* S&B (edited E H Fellowes); *Ultimum Vale* S&B (edited E H Fellowes). Only songs available in anthologies are listed individually here. Note that in the following: Pilkington = *English Lute Songs Book 2,* S&B; Keel 1a, 1b and 2a, 2b = *Elizabethan Lovesongs Books 1 and 2* [high, low], B&H.
  All my sense thy sweetness gained, *Anon,* Dm [d′-g′′], Ultimum, BMP *W&W 2.*
  As I the silly fish deceive, Anon, G [g′-f′′], Ultimum, BMP *W&W 3.*
  Beauty sat bathing by a spring, *Anthony Munday,* Gm [d′-f′′](m), Ultimum, BMP *W&W 3.*
  Beauty, stand further, *Anon,* G [e′-g′′], 2nd Book, BMP *W&W 5.*
  Did ever man thus love as I? *Anon,* Am [e′-e′′], 2nd Book, BMP *W&W 1.*
  Do not, O do not prize, *Anon,* Gm [d′-d′′], Ultimum, BMP *W&W 4.*
  Dreams and imaginations, *Anon,* Gm [f′#-a′′], 2nd Book, BMP *W&W 3.*
  Fair women like fair jewels are, *Anon,* G [d′-g′′], 2nd Book, BMP W&W 3.
  Fie, what a coil is here, *Anon,* G [d′-g′′](f), 2nd Book, Pilkington, BMP *W&W 3.*
  Go to bed, sweet muse, *Anon,* Gm [d′-f′′], Ultimum, Pilkington, BMP *W&W 1,* Paterson (Diack) *100 Best 2*; *Am,* Keel 1a; *Fm,* Keel 1b.
  I am so far from pitying thee, *Anon,* Gm [d′-g′′], Ultimum, BMP *W&W 2.*
  In Sherwood lived stout Robin Hood, *Anon,* G [d′-g′′], Musical Dreame, Leonard *Baroque high,* BMP *W&W 4*; *Eb,* Leonard *Baroque low.*
  Joy in thy hope, *Anon,* G [g′-f′′], Ultimum, BMP *W&W 2.*
  Love is a pretty frenzy, *Anon,* G [d′-e′′], Muses, BMP *W&W 2.*
  Love's god is a boy, *Anon,* G [g′-g′′], 2nd Book, BMP *W&W 1.*
  My complaining is but feigning, *Anon,* C [d′-g′′], Musical Dreame, BMP *W&W 6.*
  My father fain would have me take, *Anon,* G [g′-g′′](f), Muses, Pilkington, BMP *W&W 2.*
  My love bound me with a kiss, *Anon,* Gm [g′-g′′], 2nd Book, BMP *W&W 3.*
  My love hath her true love betrayed, *Anon,* G [g′-f′′](m), Muses, Pilkington.
  My love is neither young nor old, *Anon,* C [g′-g′′], 2nd Book, BMP *W&W 1.*
  Now what is love? *Anon,* G [d′-d′′], 2nd Book, BMP *W&W 1.*

O how my thoughts do beat me, *Anon,* Gm [e′-g′′], 2nd Book, BMP *W&W 6.*
Once did my thoughts both ebb and flow, *Anon,* G [d′-d′′], Ultimum, BMP *W&W 2.*
Sea has many a thousand sands, The, *Anon,* Dm [d′-g′′], Ultimum, BMP *W&W 2.*
Shall I look to ease my grief, *Anon,* Gm [d′-f′′], Ultimum, BMP *W&W 5.*
Soft, Cupid, soft, *Anon,* G [e′-g′′], Ultimum, BMP *W&W 2.*
Sweet if you like and love me still, *Francis Davison,* Gm [d′-f′′], Ultimum, BMP *W&W 1.*
There was a shepherd, *Dm [d′-g′′],* Ultimum, BMP *W&W 2.*
There was a wily ladde, *Anon,* Gm [f′-g′′], Muses, BMP *W&W 2.*
Walking by a riverside, *Anon,* G [d′-e′′], *Ultimum,* BMP *W&W 2.*
What if I seek for love of thee? *Anon,* Gm [d′-f′′], 1st Book, Pilkington; *Am,* Keel 1a; *F#m,* Keel 1b.
What if I sped? *Anon,* Gm [d′-f′′](m), Ultimum, BMP *W&W 3*; *Am,* Keel 2a; *Fm,* Keel 2b.
Whither runneth my sweetheart? *Anon,* G [g′-g′′], 2nd Book, BMP *W&W 5.*
Who-so is tied must needs be bound, *Anon,* G [f′#-g′′], 2nd Book, BMP *W&W 6.*

Jones, Susan L.
Birthday, A, *Christina Rossetti,* Curiad.
Futility, *Wilfred Owen,* Curiad.
Moderate Sinner, The, Curiad.

Jones, W. Bradwen. 1892–1970. WMIC.
Bard's Paradise, The, *R. Williams Parry* tr. *T. Gwynn Jones,* [soprano/tenor], Snell.
Blow, bugle, blow, *Alfred Lord Tennyson,* F#m [b-f′′#(e′′)], BMP.
Calling, love, for you, *Anon,* E♭ [d′-f′′], Gwynn.
Llanarmon, *Cynan,* Dm [d′-a′′], Gwynn.
My love has a garden, *Eifion Wyn* tr. *Brendan Dunne,* E [c′#-e′′(g′′#)], Gwynn.
Now praise we the famous men, *Ecclesiasticus 44* adapted *Brendan Dunne,* E [c′#-e′′(g′′#)], Gwynn.
Son of the storm, *T. Gwynn Jones* tr. *Arthur L. Salmon,* [baritone], Snell.
Son of the sea, *Eifion Wyn* tr. *Arthur L. Salmon,* [baritone], Snell.

Jordan, John.
Song Cycle, *Christina Rossetti,* [high], Roeginga.

Joseph, Jane. 1894–1929. *See also* App. 2.
Collection: *Mirage* (arr. Alan Gibbs), [c′-g′′#], Bardic.
Echo, *Christina Rossetti,* Bardic Mirage.
Mirage, *Christina Rossetti,* Bardic Mirage.
One foot on sea and one on shore, *Christina Rossetti,* Bardic Mirage.
Song in the Cornfield, *Christina Rossetti,* Bardic Mirage.
Song, *Christina Rossetti,* Bardic Mirage.

Josephs, Wilfred. 1927–1997. *See also* App. 2.
Collection: (*Four Japanese Lyrics,* Novello 1975.)
(If I had known, *Anon,* tr. *Bownas & Thwaite,* [e′-e′′], Novello 4 Japanese.)
(Lullaby, *Anon,* tr. *Bownas & Thwaite,* [b′-a′′](f), Novello 4 Japanese.)
(Silent, but... *Tsuboi Shigeji,* tr. *Bownas & Thwaite,* [f′#-f′′(f)], Novello 4 Japanese.)
(Tourist Japan, *Takenaka Iku,* tr. *Bownas & Thwaite,* [b′-a′′], Novello 4 Japanese.)

Joubert, John. 1927– *See also* App. 2.
Collections: *Five Songs, Op 5,* Novello; *Six Poems of Emily Brontë, Op 63,* Novello; *Turning Wheel, The,* Novello; *Two Invocations,* Novello.
Autumn Jig, *Ruth Dallas,* [d′#-g′′](f), Novello Turning Wheel.
Caged Bird, *Emily Brontë,* [f′#-a′′], Novello 6 Poems.
Fain would I change that note, *Anon,* [c′#-a′′♭](m), Novello 5 Songs.
Harp, *Emily Brontë,* [f′-a′′♭], Novello 6 Poems.
Headlands in Summer, *Ruth Dallas,* [c′-g′′](f), Novello Turning Wheel.
Immortality, *Emily Brontë,* [b-b′′♭], Novello 6 Poems.
Love me not for comely grace, *Anon,* [c′-g′′](m), Novello 5 Songs.
Meditation in Winter, *Ruth Dallas,* [e′♭-a′′♭](f), Novello Turning Wheel.
My love in her attire, *Anon,* [c′-a′′♭](m), Novello.
Narcissus, *Ruth Dallas,* [f′#-g′′#](f), Novello Turning Wheel.
O come, soft rest of cares, *George Chapman,* [c′-b′′♭](m), Novello 5 Songs.
On Offa's Back, (scena), *Stephen Tunnicliffe,* [d′-a′′](m), Maecenas.

Oracle, *Emily Brontë*, [bb-a″], Novello 6 Poems.
Remarkables, Queenstown, The, *Ruth Dallas*, [d′-a″](f), Novello Turning Wheel.
Sea, The, *Ruth Dallas*, [g′-a″](f), Novello Turning Wheel.
Sleep, *Emily Brontë*, [bb-a″], Novello 6 Poems.
Song in Spring, *Ruth Dallas*, [f′-a″](f), Novello Turning Wheel.
Stay, O sweet, and do not rise, *John Donne?* [b#-a″](m), Novello 5 Songs.
Storm, *Emily Brontë*, [bb(a)-a″], Novello 6 Poems.
To Spring, *William Blake*, [f′-b″b](m), Novello 2 Invocations.
To Winter, *William Blake*, [d′#-a″#](m), Novello 2 Invocations.

K

Kahn, Percy B. 1880–1966.
Springtime, *Marshall Roberts*, D [d′-e″], Lengnick.

Kaye, Ernest.
Come away, death, *Shakespeare*, Cm [g-e″b], BMP.

Keel, Frederick. 1871–1954. *See also* App. 2., Chappell, Cramer.
Collections: *Three Salt-Water Ballads*, Classical/B&H; *Four Salt-Water Ballads*, B&H; *Three Old English Lyrics*, B&H; *Four Songs of Childhood*, Classical/B&H.
 (Autolocus' Song, *Shakespeare,* D [a-d″], Enoch; F, Enoch.)
 Bunches of Grapes, *Walter de la Mare,* D [f′-f″#], Classical/B&H 4 Childhood.
 Cape Horn Gospel, *John Masefield,* C [c′-c″](m), B&H 4 Salt-Water.
 Had I a golden pound to spend, *Francis Ledwidge,* Eb [d′-e″b], B&H.
 Hell's Pavement, *John Masefield,* Dm [c′-d″](m), B&H 4 Salt-Water.
 (If she forsake me, *Campion?* F, B&H; A, B&H.)
 John Mouldy, *Walter de la Mare,* D [d′-f″#], Classical/B&H 4 Childhood.
 Lullaby, *Alfred Noyes,* Db [d′b-e″bb], S&B; E, S&B.
 Merry Month of May, The, *Thomas Dekker,* F [e′-a″], B&H.
 Mother Carey, *John Masefield,* Cm [bb-e″b](m), Thames *Century 6,* Classical/B&H 3 Saltwater.
 My true love hath my heart, *Philip Sidney,* Eb [e′b-e″b](f), B&H *Easy Song,* 3 Old English.
 On Eastnor Knoll, *John Masefield,* F [c′-e″], B&H.
 Port of Many Ships, *John Masefield,* Dm [c′-e″b](m), Classical/B&H 3 Saltwater.
 Reverie, *Walter de la Mare,* Am [c′-f″], Classical/B&H 4 Childhood.
 Rose and the Nightingale, The, *Bailey's 'Festus',* F [c′-f″], B&H; G, B&H.
 Sailor's Prayer, A, *John Masefield,* Cm [bb-e″](m), B&H 4 Salt-Water.
 Sigh no more, ladies, *Shakespeare,* F [f′-f″], B&H.
 Sleepy Head, *Walter de la Mare,* C [e′-g″], Classical/B&H 4 Childhood.
 Tell me not, sweet, *Richard Lovelace,* F, B&H.
 There is a garden in her face, *Thomas Campion,* G, B&H; Bb, B&H.
 To Althea, from Prison, *Richard Lovelace,* F [c′-f″], B&H; Ab, B&H.
 Trade Winds, *John Masefield,* Eb [bb-e″b](m), B&H, Classical/B&H 3 Saltwater; F, G, B&H.
 Wanderer's Song, A, *John Masefield,* Am [c′-e″](m), B&H 4 Salt-Water.
Arrangements:
 It was a lover and his lass, *Shakespeare,* (Morley), F [f′-f″], B&H; Eb, B&H.
 Jardin d'amour, *French traditional* tr. *Paul England,* A [e′-f″#], B&H.
 With the pride of the garden, *Thomas Arne,* G, B&H.

Keeley, Robert Ian. *See* App. 2.

Kelly, Bryan. 1934–
Unheard melodies (cycle), [baritone], Brunton.

Kenmuir, Callum.
Collection: *Five Dylan Thomas Poems,* [mezzo], SMIC.

Kennedy, Jimmy.
Let there be peace (The Peace Song), *Jimmy Kennedy,* [d′-e″], Weinberger/William Elkin.

Kennedy-Fraser, Marjory. 1857–1930. SMIC. *See also* App. 1.
 75 more songs in B&H archive.
 Collection: *Four Hebridian Love Lilts,* [high, medium], Classical.
  Eriskay love lilt, An, *Kenneth Macleod,* A [e′-f′′#], B&H *Ballad Album 2*; G, B&H *Souvenirs,* B&H, Classical.
  Land of heart's desire, G [high], Classical.

Kent, James. 1700–1776.
 It is a good thing to give thanks to the Lord, *Psalm 92, vv. 1-3,* D [d′-e′′], B&H (Patrick) *Sacred Songs* 2.
 My song shall be of mercy and judgment, *Psalms 101, vv.1-3, 108, vv. 3-4,* G [d′-f′′#], B&H (Patrick) *Sacred Songs 1.*

Ketèlby, Albert William. 1875–1959.
 Collection: *Four Recital Songs* [baritone], Bosworth.
  Blow, blow, thou winter wind, *Shakespeare,* B♭m [e′b-c′′b], Bosworth; Dm, Bosworth.
  Great Day, The, C, Bosworth; E♭, Bosworth.
  In a Monastery Garden, *A. W. Ketèlby,* E♭, William Elkin.
  In a Persian Market, *A. W. Ketèlby,* C, Bosworth; B♭, Bosworth.
  King Cupid, C, Bosworth.
  Mayfair Cinderella, *A. W. Ketèlby,* C, Bosworth; D, Bosworth.
  My Star of Love, *A. W. Ketèlby,* A, Bosworth.
  Sacred Hour, The, A, Bosworth.
  Sanctuary of the Heart, F, Bosworth; G, A♭, Bosworth.

Kimpton, Geoffrey. 1927–
 O come to my arms, *John Clare,* [b-e′′], EPSS.

King, Reginald. 1919–1991.
 Plantation Mood, *Johnny McClain & Eddie Richman,* [d′-b′′b], Bardic.

King, Robert. *fl.*1676–1728.
 Urge me no more, unhappy swain, *Anon,* B♭ [f′-g′′](f), Thames (Bevan) *8 Restoration.*

Kirkwood, Antoinette. *See also* App. 1, 2.
 Barrel Organ, The, *Michael Ashe,* [b-c′′], Bardic.
 Fly, The, *William Blake,* [d′-a′′], Bardic.
 High Seriousness, *Richard Phibbs,* [d′-g′′], Bardic.
 Morning in Bengal, *Anthony Heyward,* [b-d′′], Bardic.
 Must she go? *James Forsyth,* [G-c′](m), Bardic.
 Oyster Catcher's Song, The, *James Forsyth,* [c′-f′′], Bardic.
 Remembrance, *Eddie McGrory,* [g-c′′], Bardic.
 Remorse, *Michael O'Hagen,* [g-d′′], Bardic.
 Snowflake, *Eddie McGrory,* [d′-d′′], Bardic.
 Song of the Fisherman of Cacru, *James Forsyth,* [c′-e′′], Bardic.
 Tourney, The, *Anthony Heyward,* [b-f′′#], Bardic.
 Visit to the Killing Fields, *Eddie McGrory,* [a-f′′], Bardic.

Kleyn, Howard.
Collections: *Chinese Suite No 2, Op 41,* Lengnick; *Offerings,* Lengnick; *Sheaf of Sonnets, A, Op 36,* Lengnick.
  Country Faith, The, *Norman Gale,* [medium], Lengnick Offerings.
  Hers will I be, *Francesco Petrarca* tr. *Henry Howard, Earl of Surrey,* F [b♭-f′′], Lengnick Sheaf.
  Noonday, *Fan Tseng Hsiang* tr. *Henry Hart,* Am [A-d′′](m), Lengnick Chinese.
  O dearest, *Anon* tr. *T. C. Lai,* adapted Howard Kleyn, D [A-d′](m), Lengnick Chinese.
  Remember me, *Christina Rossetti,* G [d′-g′′], Lengnick Sheaf.
  Supplication, A, *Abraham Cowley,* [medium], Lengnick Offerings.
  Time is flying, *Ronsard* tr. *Andrew Lang,* E [b-e′′], Lengnick Sheaf.
  To a Young Lady, *William Cowper,* [medium], Lengnick Offerings.
  To Lucasta, *Richard Lovelace,* [medium], Lengnick Offerings.
  To One Unnamed, *Li Shang Yin* tr. *Wittner Bynner,* B♭ [d-e′](m), Lengnick Chinese.

Knight, Joseph P.
 Rocked in the cradle of the deep, *Emma Hart Willard,* B♭ [d′-f′′], IMP *Parlour Songs.*

Knight, Tim.
Collection: *Three Songs of the Countryside,* Banks.

Knussen, Oliver. 1952– *See also* App. 2.
Collection: *Whitman Settings,* Faber.
  Dalliance of the Eagles, The, *Walt Whitman,* [c'#-b''](f), Faber Whitman.
  Noiseless patient spider, A, *Walt Whitman,* [b-b''b](f), Faber Whitman.
  Voice of the Rain, The, *Walt Whitman,* [bb-b''b](f), Faber Whitman.
  When I heard the learn'd astronomer, *Walt Whitman,* [c'-b''](f), Faber Whitman.

Koffman, Steven. *See* App. 2.

L

Lambert, Leonard **Constant.** 1905–1951. *See also* App. 2.
Collections: *Four Poems by Li-Po,* BMP; *Three Poems of Li-Po,* Chester.
  Intruder, The, *Li-Po* tr. *Shigeyoshi Obata,* [e'b-f''], Chester 3 Poems.
  Lines, *Li-Po* tr. *Shigeyoshi Obata,* [c'-e''], BMP 4 Li-Po.
  Long-departed Lover, The, *Li-Po* tr. *Shigeyoshi Obata,* [d'b-f''], BMP.
  Nocturne, *Li-Po* tr. *Shigeyoshi Obata,* [d'-e''], BMP 4 Li-Po.
  On the City Street, *Li-Po* tr. *Shigeyoshi Obata,* [e'-g''], Chester 3 Poems.
  Ruin of the Ku-Su Palace, The, *Li-Po* tr. *Shigeyoshi Obata,* [f'b-f''], Chester 3 Poems.
  Summer Day, A, *Li-Po* tr. *Shigeyoshi Obata,* C [c'-f''], BMP 4 Li-Po.
  With a Man of Leisure, *Li-Po* tr. *Shigeyoshi Obata,* [b-f''#], BMP 4 Li-Po.

Lambert, Frank. *See also* Chappell.
  She is far from the land, *Thomas Moore,* Bb [d'-f''], IMP *Parlour Songs.*

Lambert, John. 1926–1995 BMIC.

Lamb, Henry.
  Volunteer Organist, The, *W. B. Glenroy,* Eb [d'-e''b], Cramer *Drawing Room Songs.*

Lampe, John Frederick. 1703–1751.
  By the beer as brown as a berry, *Henry Carey,* Dm [c-d'](m), Novello (Bush) *Ballad Operas.*

Lane, Philip. 1950– *See* App. 2.

Lanier, Nicholas. 1588–1666.
Collection: *Six Songs,* S&B (edited Edward Huws Jones).
  Bring away this sacred tree, *Thomas Campion,* G [d'-f''], S&B (Greer) *Printed.*
  Come, come thou glorious object, *William Killigrew,* Dm [f'-f''], S&B Six Songs.
  Fire! fire! lo here I burn, *Thomas Campion,* G [d'-e''], S&B (Spink) *MB 33.*
  Like hermit poor, *Walter Raleigh,* Gm [d'-d''], S&B (Spink) *MB 33,* Six Songs.
  Love and I of late did part, *Anon,* Gm [d'-e''b](m), S&B (Spink) *MB 33.*
  Mark how the blushful morn, *Thomas Carew,* Dm [d'-f''], S&B Six Songs, (Spink) *MB 33, Cavalier.*
  Neither sighs, nor tears, nor mourning, *Anon,* Dm [c'-d''], S&B (Spink) *MB 33.*
  No more shall meads be deck'd with flowers, *Thomas Carew,* G [b-g''](m), S&B (Spink) *MB 33.*
  Nor com'st thou yet, my slothful love, *Anon,* Dm [c-g''](f), S&B (Spink) *MB 33.*
  Silly heart forbear, *Anon,* F [g'-f''], S&B (Spink) *MB 33.*
  Silly heart forbear, *Anon,* G [g'-g''], S&B (Spink) *MB 33.*
  Stay, silly heart, and do not break, *Anon,* Gm [d'-f''](m), S&B (Spink) *MB 33, Cavalier.*
  Thou art not fair, *Thomas Campion,* G [d'-d''](m), S&B Six Songs.
  Though I am young, *Ben Jonson,* Gm [d'-e''b], S&B Six Songs.
  Weep no more my wearied eyes, *Anon,* F [c'-f''](m), S&B (Spink) *MB 33.*
  Young and simple though I am, *Thomas Campion,* Gm [f'#-e''b](f), S&B Six Songs.

Lawes, Henry. 1596–1662. *See also* App. 2.
Collections: *Ten Ayres,* S&B (edited Thurston Dart); *Six Songs,* Peters (edited Gwilym Beechey).
  About the sweet bag of a bee, *Robert Herrick,* Gm [g'-f''], Classical/B&H *Dolmetsch 1.*

Amidst the mirtles as I walke, *Robert Herrick,* G [e'-e''](m), Classical/B&H *Dolmetsch 1.*
Amintor's Welladay, *Henry Hughes,* Bb [c'-d''], S&B 10 Ayres.
Among Rosebuds, *John Berkenhead,* Gm [e'-e''b], S&B 10 Ayres.
Angler's Song, The, *Isaak Walton,* F [f'-f''](m), Classical/B&H *Dolmetsch 1.*
Ask me why I send you here, *Robert Herrick,* Cm [e'b-a''b], Classical/B&H *Dolmetsch 2.*
Beautiful Mistress, A, *Thomas Carew,* F [e'-f''](m), Peters 6 Songs.
Beauty and love once fell at odds, *Anon,* F [e'-g''], S&B (Spink) *MB 33.*
Bid me but live and I will live, *Robert Herrick,* Cm [g'-f''](m), S&B (Spink) *MB 33, Cavalier,* Classical/ B&H *Dolmetsch 1.*
Break heart in twain, *Anon,* Dm [f'-a''](m), S&B (Spink) *MB 33.*
Come my sweet while ev'ry strain, *William Cartwright,* C [e'-g''], S&B (Spink) *MB 33.*
Complaint against Cupid, A, *William Cartwright,* Em [c'-d''], S&B 10 Ayres.
Cupid as he lay, *Robert Herrick,* Cm [e'b-g''], Peters 6 Songs.
Dissuasion from Presumption, *Henry Harrington,* F [c'-d''], S&B 10 Ayres.
Go thou gentle whisp'ring wind, *Thomas Carew,* Dm [d'-f''](m), S&B (Spink) *MB 33.*
Happy youth, that shalt possess, *Thomas Carew,* C [d'-f''], Peters 6 Songs.
Hard-hearted fair, if thou wilt not consent, *Anon,* Cm [c'-e''b], S&B (Spink) *MB 33.*
Have you e'er seen the morning sun? *Henry Hughes,* C [d'-d''](m), S&B (Spink) *MB 33.*
How happy art thou, *Anon,* D [d'-f''#], Leonard *Baroque high;* Bb, Leonard *Baroque low.*
I am confirm'd a woman can, *John Suckling,* C [c'-e''](m), Classical/B&H *Dolmetsch 1.*
I do confess thou'rt smooth and fair, *Robert Ayton,* F [c'-c''], Paterson (Diack) *100 Best 4.*
I prethee sweet to me be kind, *Anon,* Dm [d'-g''], Classical/B&H *Dolmetsch 2.*
I prithee send me back my heart, *Henry Hughes,* Am [c'-c''], S&B 10 Ayres.
I rise and grieve, *Anon,* Cm [c'-g''], S&B (Spink) *MB 33.*
Lady to a Young Courtier, A, *Henry Hughes,* F [e'-d''](f), S&B 10 Ayres.
Lark, The, *Anon,* F [d'-g''](f), Classical/B&H *Dolmetsch 2.*
No constancy in man, *Henry Lawes,* Dm [d'-d''](f), S&B 10 Ayres.
No, no, fair heretic, it cannot be, *John Suckling,* Dm [e'-f''](m), S&B (Spink) *MB 33, Cavalier.*
O let me groan one word into your ear, *William Herbert,* Gm [d'-f''], S&B (Spink) *MB 33.*
O tell me love! O tell me fate, *Henry Hughes,* Dm [e'-g''](m), S&B (Spink) *MB 33.*
O turn away those cruel eyes, *Thomas Stanley,* Dm [c'#-g''], S&B (Spink) *MB 33.*
Or you, or I, nature did wrong, *Anon,* F [f'-g''], S&B (Spink) *MB 33.*
Out upon it, I have lov'd, *John Suckling,* C [c'-d''](m), S&B (Spink) *MB 33, Cavalier.*
Parting, *Henry Reynolds,* Cm [b-e''b], S&B 10 Ayres.
Persuasions to Enjoy, *Thomas Carew,* [f'#-f''#], Peters 6 Songs.
Primrose, The, *see* Ask me why I send you here.
Read in these roses, *Thomas Carew,* Cm [g'-g''], Peters 6 Songs.
Seest thou those diamonds, *Robert Herrick,* Dm [e'-g''], Peters 6 Songs.
Sleep soft, you cold clay cinders, *Anon,* Gm [d'-f''], S&B (Spink) *MB 33.*
Slide soft you silver floods, *W. Brown,* Gm [d'-f''], S&B (Spink) *MB 33.*
Speak, speak, at last reply, *Anon,* Cm [c'-e''b], S&B (Spink) *MB 33.*
Sufferance, *Aurelian Townshend,* F [d'-d''], S&B 10 Ayres.
Sweet stay awhile, why do you rise, *John Donne?* Gm [d'-g''], S&B (Spink) *MB 33, Cavalier.*
Tis but a frown, I prithee let me die, *Anon,* Dm [d'-f''], S&B (Spink) *MB 33.*
Wert thou yet fairer than thou art, *Walter Montague?* C [g'-g''](m), S&B (Spink) *MB 33.*
When thou, poor excommunicate, *Thomas Carew,* Gm [g'-g''], S&B (Spink) *MB 33.*
Whither are all her false oaths blown, *Robert Herrick,* Gm [d'-a''](m), S&B (Spink) *MB 33.*
(Why should'st thou swear I am forsworn, Paxton.)
Will you know my mistress' face, *Anon,* Eb [e'b-f''](m), S&B (Spink) *MB 33, Cavalier.*
Young Maid's Resolution, A, *Henry Hughes,* Bb [c'-d''](f), S&B 10 Ayres.

Lawes, William. 1602–1645.
Collection: *Six Songs,* Schott (edited with introduction Edward Huws Jones).
Come Adonis, come away, *John Tatham,* C [e'-f''], S&B (Spink) *MB 33.*
Faith, be no longer coy, *Anon,* F [f'-g''](m), S&B (Spink) *MB 33, Cavalier Songs.*
No no, fair heretic, it needs must be, *John Suckling,* G [f'#-f''](m), S&B (Spink) *MB 33.*
O my Clarissa, *Anon,* Bm [d'-f''#](m), Classical/B&H *Dolmetsch 2.*
On the Lilies, *Robert Herrick,* G [e'-e''], Schott 6 Songs.
Persuasions Not to Love, *Robert Herrick,* Gm [f'-g''], Schott 6 Songs.
Pleasures, beauty, youth attend thee, *John Ford,* C [e'-e''], S&B (Spink) *MB 33.*
To Pansies, *Robert Herrick,* Gm [g'-f''], Schott 6 Songs.
To Sycamores, *Robert Herrick,* Cm [e'b-f''], Schott 6 Songs.
To the Dews, *Robert Herrick,* G [d'-f''#], Schott 6 Songs.

To the Virgins, to make much of time (Gather ye rosebuds), *Robert Herrick,* G [g´-e´´], S&B (Spink) *MB 33,* Schott 6 Songs, Classical/B&H *Dolmetsch 1.*
To whom should I complain? *Anon,* Dm [d´-f´´], S&B (Spink) *MB 33.*
Why should great beauty virtuous fame desire? *Sir William Davenant?* Dm [d´-g´´], S&B (Spink) *MB 33.*
Why so pale and wan, fond lover? *John Suckling,* Cm [b-e´´b], S&B (Spink) *MB 33.*

Lawrence, Mark. Note: Micropress publications can be supplied in a wide range of keys.
Cat's Eyes, *Mark Lawrence,* Micropress.
Owls, *Mark Lawrence,* Micropress.
There isn't time, *Mark Lawrence,* Micropress.

Lawrence, Thomas. BMIC.

Lawson, Gordon. 1931– *See also* App. 2.
I love all beauteous things, *Robert Bridges,* Brunton.

Leadbetter, John **Martin.** 1945– BMIC.

Lear, Edward. 1812–1888.
Farewell, A, *Alfred Lord Tennyson,* A [c´#-f´´#], Cramer *Drawing Room Songs.*
Sweet and low, *Alfred Lord Tennyson,* B [d´#-e´´](f), Cramer *Drawing Room Songs.*

LeFanu, Nicola. 1947– *See also* App. 2.
I am Bread (scena), *Kennelly,* [soprano], Novello.
Penny for a Song, A, (cycle), [g-b´´b], Novello.

Le Fleming, Christopher Kaye*.* 1908–1985.
(Egypt's might is tumbled down, *Mary Coleridge,* F#m [c´#-e´´], Chester.)
(Hills of Heaven, The, *Mary Webb,* Eb [bb-e´´], Chester.)
Hymnus, *Sarum Primer,* Gm [d´-f´´], Chester.
If it's ever spring again, *Thomas Hardy,* Ab [e´b-f´´](m), Chester *Celebrated 1,* (Chester.)
(In a sleepless night, *W. H. H.,* Gb [bb-f´´], Chester.)
(O waly, waly, *Anon,* B&H.)
(Once in a while, *Bruce Sevier,* B&H.)
Three Sisters, *Walter de la Mare,* [c´-f´´], Cramer.
(To an Isle in the Water, *W. B. Yeats,* Bbm [d´b-e´´b], Chester.)
Arrangement:
(Sheep shearing, *Anon,* Dm [c´-d´´], Chester.)

Lehmann, Liza Elizabeth (Nina Mary Frederika). 1862–1918. *See also* App. 1., Chappell, Cramer.
Collections: *Album of Nine English Songs,* B&H); *Bird Songs,* [high, medium], Classical/B&H; *Daisy-Chain, The,* [4 solo voices], Classical/B&H; *Fourteen Songs,* Thames (chosen and introduced by Stuart Bedford); *In a Persian Garden,* [4 solo voices], Schirmer; *Life of a Rose, The,* [medium high], Classical; *Nine Favourite Soprano Songs,* B&H; *Well of Sorrows, The,* [contralto], B&H.
Ah, moon of my delight, *Omar Khayyam* tr. *Fitzgerald,* G [c´-a´´](m), Schirmer Persian, Classical, Cramer; *F,* Classical, Cramer.
Ah, not a drop,*Omar Khayyam* tr. *Fitzgerald,* Dm [a-f´´](f), Thames 14 Songs, Schirmer Persian.
Bee, The, *Liza Lehmann,* A [e´-a´´], Classical Life of a Rose; G, Life of a Rose.
Cuckoo, The, *W. B. Rands,* D [d´-b´´(g´´)], Classical.
Dusk in the Valley, *George Meredith,* Cm [c´-f´´](f), Thames 14 Songs.
Evensong, *Constance Morgan,* Db [e´b-a´´b(g´´b)](f), Thames 14 Songs; Bb, Schirmer *1st Mezzo,* (Chappell *English Recital 2.*)
I will make you brooches, *R. L. Stevenson,* C [g-e´´], S&B *MB 56.*
If I built a world for you, *Herbert Fordwych,* F [f´-f´´(a´´)], B&H *Ballad Album 2.*
If no one ever marries me, *Laurence Alma Tadema,* D [d´-a´´(f´#)], Classical; C, Classical.
It was a lover and his lass, *Shakespeare,* Eb [e´b-a´´(a´´b)](f), Thames 14 Songs.
Jim, *Hilaire Belloc,* A [f#(g#)-e´´(d´´)](f), Thames 14 Songs.
June Rapture, *Liza Lehmann,* Bb [e´b-g´´], Classical Life of a Rose; Ab, Life of a Rose.
Lily of a Day, The, *Ben Jonson,* Eb [e´b-b´´b](f), Thames 14 Songs.
Love, if you knew the light, *Robert Browning,* G [a´-e´´](f), Thames 14 Songs.
Lovers in the Lane, *Liza Lehmann,* Eb [e´b-g´´], Classical Life of a Rose; Db, Life of a Rose.
Magdalen at Michael's gate, *Henry Kingsley,* Bm [f´#-b´´(a´´)](f), Thames 14 Songs; (Am, Chappell *English Recital 1.*)

Myself when young, *Omar Khayyam,* tr. *Fitzgerald,* F [f(c´)-e´´](m), Cramer *Folio 1,* Schirmer Persian.
No candle was there and no fire, *Frances Gostling,* C [c´-e´´](f),Thames 14 Songs, Classical; [high], Classical.
Oh, tell me, nightingale, sweet bird, *Friedrich Bodenstedt,* tr. *Anon,* Dm [d´-f´´], S&B *MB 56.*
Owl, The, *Alice Sayers?* D♭ [d´♭-g´´♭], Classical/B&H Bird Songs; E♭, Bird Songs.
Rosa Resurget, *Liza Lehmann,* E [e´-♭´´(a´´♭)], Classical Life of a Rose; D, Life of a Rose.
Roseleaves, *Liza Lehmann,* Em [e´-g´´], Classical Life of a Rose; Dm, Life of a Rose.
Starling, The, *Alice Sayers?* E♭ [b♭-g´´(e´´♭)], Classical/B&H Bird Songs; F, Bird Songs.
Summer Storm, *Liza Lehmann,* Bm [f´#-a´´♭], Classical Life of a Rose; Am, Life of a Rose.
Swing, The, *R. L. Stevenson,* E♭ [e´♭-b´´♭(g)](f), Thames 14 Songs, Classical/B&H Daisy-Chain, Classical.
There are fairies at the bottom of our garden, *Rose Fyleman,* D♭ [c´-a´´♭(e´´♭)], Novello *Sarah's Encores,* Classical; E♭, Classical.
To a Little Red Spider, *L. Ann Cunnington,* F [a(c´#)-f´´#](f), Thames 14 Songs.
Unfolding, *Liza Lehmann,* A [e´-a´´], Classical Life of a Rose; G, Life of a Rose.
When I am dead, my dearest, *Christina Rossetti,* Fm [e´-g´´](f), Thames 14 Songs.
Widow bird sate mourning, A, *Percy Bysshe Shelley,* F#m [c´#-f´´#](f), S&B *MB 56.*
Within a rose love sleeping lay, *Hoffmann von Fallersleben,* tr. *Anon,* D♭ [d´♭-g´´♭(b´´♭)], S&B *MB 56.*
Woodpigeon, The, *Alice Sayers?* G [d´-g´´(e´´)], Classical/B&H Bird Songs; A, Bird Songs.
Wren, The, *Alice Sayers?* G [d´-b´´(a´´)](f), Thames 14 Songs, Classical/B&H Bird Songs; F, Bird Songs.
Yellowhammer, The, *Alice Sayers?* B♭ [d´-f´´#](f), Thames 14 Songs, Classical/B&H Bird Songs; A♭, Bird Songs.

Leighton, Kenneth. 1929–88. *See also* App. 2.
Earth, sweet earth (cantata), *John Ruskin, Gerard Manley Hopkins,* [tenor], Novello.

Lemon, Laura G. 1865–1924.
My Ain Folk, *Wilfrid Mills,* G [d´-g´´] B&H *Ballad Album 1;* E♭, IMP *Parlour Songs*; (F, B&H).

Leveridge, Richard. 1670–1758.
Beggar's Song, The, *Anon,* G [g(a)-d´´](m), B&H (Lane Wilson) *Old English.*
Cure of Care, The, *Anon,* F major [g(a)-e´´](m), S&B (Pilkington) *Georgian 1.*
Oft I'm by the women told, *Anacreon* tr. *Abraham Cowley,* Am [G-d´](m), Thames (Bevan) *6 Restoration;* Cm, B&H (Keel) *12 18th Century.*
When dull care, *Anon,* G [b-e´´(g´´)](m), B&H (Lane Wilson) *Old English.*
(Whilst I'm carousing, *Anon,* Gm [g-e´´♭](m), Keith Prowse; Am, Keith Prowse.)
Who is Sylvia? *Shakespeare,* E♭ [e´♭-g´´], B&H (Keel) *12 18th Century.*

Lewis, Geraint. WMIC.

Lewis, Idris. 1889–1952.
Shepherd of Aberdovey, The, [soprano/tenor], Snell.

Lewis, Jeffrey. WMIC. *See also* App. 2.

Lewis, William Rees. WMIC.

Ley, Henry George. 1887–1962.
Lake Isle of Innisfree, The, *W. B. Yeats,* D [d´-f´´#], BMP.

Liddell, Claire. *c.*1940– SMIC. *See also* App. 2.
Collection: *Five Orkney Scenes,* Roberton.
Beachcomber, *George Mackay Brown,* E♭ [b♭-g´´](f), Roberton 5 Orkney.
Country Girl, *George Mackay Brown,* [d´♭-g´´](f), Roberton 5 Orkney.
Fisherman's Bride, *George Mackay Brown,* [♭-e´´](f), Roberton 5 Orkney.
Old Fisherman with Guitar, *George Mackay Brown,* Em [d´-g´´#](f), Roberton 5 Orkney.
Rhythm of Life, The, (cycle), (female voice), Brunton.
Roads, *George Mackay Brown,* D [d´-f´´#](f), Roberton 5 Orkney.
Arrangements: *The Kindling Fire,* Roberton; *Fine Flowers in the Valley – Five Scots Folk Songs,* Brunton.
Ca' the yowes to the knowes, *Robert Burns,* Em [d´-f´´#], Roberton Kindling Fire.

Comin' thro' the rye, *Robert Burns*, A♭ [e'b-f''](f), Roberton Kindling Fire.
Go fetch to me a pint o' wine, *Robert Burns*, D [d'-g''](m), Roberton Kindling Fire.
I dreamed I lay, *Robert Burns*, F [d'-g''], Roberton Kindling Fire.
I'm o'er young to marry yet, *Robert Burns*, B♭ [b♭-g''](f), Roberton Kindling Fire.
On Cessnock Banks, *Robert Burns*, F [c'-g''], Roberton Kindling Fire.
Rosebud by my early walk, A, *Robert Burns*, E♭ [c'-g''], Roberton Kindling Fire.
Scots wha hae, *Robert Burns*, B♭ [d'-f''](m), Roberton Kindling Fire.
Talk not of love, *Robert Burns*, C [c'-g''], Roberton Kindling Fire.
To a Blackbird, *Robert Burns*, Em [e'-g''], Roberton Kindling Fire.
Wee Willie Gray, *Robert Burns*, F [c'-f''], Roberton Kindling Fire.
Ye banks and braes, *Robert Burns*, A♭ [e'b-f''](f), Roberton Kindling Fire.

Liddle, Samuel. 1867–1951. *See also* App. 2., B&H.
Abide with me, *Henry Francis Lyte*, E♭ [b♭-g''], B&H *Ballad Album 1*; D♭, *World Renowned;* (C, F, B&H).
How lovely are thy dwellings, *Psalm 84* adapted, E♭ [e'b-a''b(g'')], B&H *Ballad Album 2*, Schirmer *1st Soprano II*; (C, D♭, B&H).
Lord is my shepherd, The, *Psalm 23*, F [e'-f''], Schirmer *2nd Tenor.*

Lidgey, C. A. *See also* B&H, Cramer.
Earl Bristol's Farewell, *Anon*, G [d'-f''#], B&H.
See where my love a-maying goes, *Anon 17th cent.*, F [c'-f''](m), B&H *Heritage 2*; G, B&H.
Sunny March, *Norman Gale*, E♭ [b♭-f''](m), B&H *Heritage 1.*

Lindsay, Martin.
Collection: *Two Songs,* (high), BMP.
See where my love a-maying goes, *Anon 17th cent.*, Am [d'-g''], BMP.
Weep you no more, sad fountains, *Anon*, Cm [c'-g''], BMP.

Linley, Thomas Snr. 1733–1795
Collection: *Songs of the Linleys,* S&B (edited Michael Pilkington).
Alas, from the day my poor heart, *Anon*, Cm [c'-g''](f), OUP (Roberts) *Tuneful Voice.*
Lark sings high in the cornfield, The, *Anon*, A [e'-a''], OUP (Roberts) *Tuneful Voice.*
No flower that blows, *George Collier*, A [e'-f''#(g''#)], S&B Songs of the Linleys, Schirmer *1st Soprano II.*
Primroses deck the bank's green side, *Anon*, C [c'-g''], S&B (Ivimey).
Still the lark finds repose, *Mark Lonsdale*, A [e'-f''#], S&B Songs of the Linleys, A♭ [e'b-a''b(b''b)], S&B (Ivimey).
Think not, my love, when secret grief, *Anon*, G [d'-f''#], OUP (Roberts) *Tuneful Voice.*
When a tender maid, *R. B. Sheridan*, Cm [c'-g''], S&B Songs of the Linleys.

Linley, Thomas Jnr. 1756–1778.
Collection: *Songs of the Linleys,* S&B (edited Michael Pilkington).
Awake my lyre, *Anon*, A [e'-g''#](m), S&B Songs of the Linleys.
Flora, *Abraham Portal*, G [d'-a''], S&B Songs of the Linleys.
O mighty judge, *Abraham Portal*, G [d'-g''](f), S&B Songs of the Linleys.
Rill, The, *Anon*, E♭ [d'-g''], S&B Songs of the Linleys.
Though cause for suspicion appears, *R. B. Sheridan*, B♭ [f'-g''](m), Novello (Bush) *Ballad Operas.*
When I was a dyer, *Abraham Portal*, Gm [g'-g''](m), S&B Songs of the Linleys.

Linley, William. 1767–1835.
Orpheus, *Shakespeare*, G [b-e''], BMP (Denis Arundell).
While the foaming billows roll, *Anon*, A♭ [b♭(a♭)-e''♭](m), B&H (Lane Wilson) *Old English.*

Lipkin, Malcolm. 1932– BMIC. *See also* App. 2.
Five Songs for Soprano and Piano (cycle), *Percy Bysshe Shelley*, [c'-b''♭](f), Lipkin.

Lloyd, David John de. 1883–1948. WMIC.
Collection: *Two Songs,* WMIC.
Dainty little maiden, *Alfred Lord Tennyson*, [mezzo/baritone], WMIC 2 Songs.
You are old, father William, *Lewis Carroll*, [mezzo/baritone], WMIC 2 Songs.

Lloyd, John Morgan. 1880–1960.
Dilys, *Rhosyr* tr. *Edgar Jones*, B♭m [d'b-g''♭], Gwynn.

Golden Hour, The, *Crwys* tr. *G. Crwys Williams*, Em [d´#-g´´], Gwynn.
Saint Govan, *A. G. Prys-Jones*, Em [a-e´´b], Gwynn.
Song of the Nightingale, *Alun* tr. *Sarnicol,* [bb-f´´], BMP.

Lloyd, Richard. 1933 -
Ballad of the Judas Tree, The, *Ruth Etchells*, [soprano], Banks.

Lloyd Webber, William. 1914–1982.
Collection: *Songs of William Lloyd Webber, The,* Kevin Mayhew.
Cottage of Dreams, The, *Patience Strong*, Eb [bb-e´´b], Mayhew Songs.
Eutopia, *Francis T. Palgrave*, Bb [f´-g´´], Mayhew Songs.
Forest of Wild Thyme, The, *Alfred Noyes*, D [e´-a´´(f´´#)], Mayhew Songs.
(Half Loaf, The, *Helen Rowe Henze*, Bb [d´-f´´], B&H.)
How do I love thee? *Elizabeth Barrett Browning*, Eb [bb-f´´], Mayhew Songs.
I looked out into the morning, *James Thomson*, D [e´-g´´], Mayhew Songs.
(Love, like a drop of dew, *W. H. Davies*, Ab [e´b-a´´](m), Chappell.)
(O Lord, spread thy wings o'er me, F [c´-f´´], Ashdown.)
Over the Bridge, *James Thomson*, G [d´-g´´], Mayhew Songs.
Pretty Washer-maiden, The, *W. E. Henley*, Eb [e´b-g´´], Mayhew Songs.
Rent for Love, A, *Ivronwy Morgan*, G [e´b-f´´](m), Mayhew Songs.
(Sleep, *John Fletcher*, G [d´-e´´(g´´)], Chappell *English Recital 2.*)
So lovely the rose, *Joseph Murrells*, C [c´-g´´(f)], Mayhew Songs.
To the Wicklow Hills, *R. G. Leigh*, D [d´#-f´´#(d´´)], Mayhew Songs.

Llyn-Owen, M.
Collection: *Two Madonna Songs*, BMP.

Locke, Matthew. *c.*1622–1677. *see also* App. 1.
Collection: *Songs and Dialogues of Matthew Lock*, S&B (edited with introduction and notes Mark Levy).
Despondent Lover's Song, The, *Juan Pérez de Montalván,* tr. *Thomas Stanley*, Am [d´#-g´´], S&B *Songs and Dialogues.*
Lucinda, wink or veil those eyes, *Anon*, C [e´-f´´], S&B *Songs and Dialogues.*
Then from a whirlwind oracle, *Job 58* adapted, [G-e´](m), S&B *Songs and Dialogues.*
To a Lady Singing to Herself by the Thames-side, *William Habington*, [f´-a´´], S&B *Songs and Dialogues.*
Urania to Parthenissa: a dream, *Thomas Flatman*, [e´-g´´], S&B *Songs and Dialogues.*
Wrong not your lovely eyes, *Anon*, Gm [e´-f´´], S&B *Songs and Dialogues.*

Loder, Edward James. 1813–1865.
Dirge: Rough wind that moaneth loud, *P. B. Shelley*, Bm [d´-d´´], S&B (Bush & Temperley) *MB 43.*
Diver, The, *G. Douglas Thompson,* Eb [a-d´´], IMP *Parlour Songs*, B&H.
I heard a brooklet gushing, *Eduard Müller,* tr. *Longfellow*, Ab [e´b-g´´], S&B (Bush & Temperley) *MB 43, Recitalist 3;* Gb, B&H (Northcote) *Imperial 4,* Cramer *Drawing Room Songs,* BMP.
Invocation to the Deep, *Felicia Hemans*, Eb [bb-g´´], S&B (Bush & Temperlay) *MB 43.*
Lamentation, The, *Michael Desmond Ryan*, F#m, [b#-f´´#], S&B (Bush & Temperlay) *MB 43.*
Wake, my love, *George Soane*, Db [f´-b´´b], S&B (Bush & Temperley) *MB 43.*

Lodge, Ernest.
Mantle of Blue, The, *Padraic Colum,* [c´#-d´´], BMP.
Mistletoe, *Walter de la Mare,* [c´-e´´], BMP.

Löhr, Hermann. 1872–1943.
Where my caravan has rested, *Edward Teschemacher,* F [d´-f´´], IMP *Parlour Songs.*

Lord, David Malcolm. 1944–
Wife of Winter, The, (cycle), *Michael Dennis Browne*, [mezzo], Universal.

Lord, Roger.
Collection: *Three Blake Songs,* Micropress. Note: Micropress publications can be supplied in a wide range of keys.
anyone lived in a pretty how town, *E. E. Cummings*, Micropress.
Corn-a-turnin' yellow, *William Barnes,* [c´-f´´], EPSS.
Echoing Green, The, *William Blake*, [d´-g´´], Micropress 3 Blake.

Especially when the October Wind, *Dylan Thomas*, [e′b-g′′], Micropress.
Lamb, The, *William Blake*, [e′b-a′′b], Micropress 3 Blake.
Miranda, *Hilaire Belloc*, [c′-g′′], Micropress.
Piping down the valleys wild, *William Blake*, [e′b-g′′], Micropress 3 Blake.

Luard Selby, Bertram. 1853–1918.
Collections: (*Six Love Songs*, [John Todhunter], Novello); (*Four Rispetti*, [Francesca Alexander], Novello).
(La Marguerite, *William Morris*, D, B&H.)
Widow bird sat mourning, A, *P. B. Shelley*, Gm [d′-d′′], B&H *Heritage 1*.

Lubbock, Mark.
(Love sings in the night, *Christopher Hassall*, Eb [bb-f′′], Schott; G, Schott.)
Whispering Poplar, The, *Christopher Hassall*, G [d′-g′′], Schott.
(Winter Rose, *Christopher Hassall*, Eb [bb-f′′], Schott; G, Schott.)

Luff, Enid. 1935– *See also* App. 2.
Collections: *Five Japanese Songs*, Primavera; *Five Nocturnes*, Primavera.
Counterpoints, [soprano], Primavera.
Sheila na gig, [soprano], Primavera.
Vox ultima crucis, [soprano], Primavera.

Lumsdaine, David. 1931– *See* App. 2.

Lupo, Thomas. 1571–1628.
Shows and nightly revels, *Thomas Campion*, Gm [d′-e′′b], S&B (Greer) *Printed*.
Time, that leads the fatal round, *Thomas Campion*, G [d′-e′′], S&B (Greer) *Printed*.

Lutyens, Agnes Elizabeth. 1906–1983. BMIC. *See also* App. 2.
Collection: (*Nine Stevie Smith Songs*, Universal).
Actress, The, *Stevie Smith*, [c#′-f′′], Universal 9 Stevie Smith.)
(Ceux qui luttant, *Stevie Smith*, [c′-c′′], Universal 9 Stevie Smith.)
(Film Star, The, *Stevie Smith*, [e′-f′′], Universal 9 Stevie Smith.)
(Lady 'Rogue' Singleton, *Stevie Smith*, [a-f′′], Universal 9 Stevie Smith.)
(Pad, pad, *Stevie Smith*, [c′-f′′], Universal 9 Stevie Smith.)
(Progression, *Stevie Smith*, [f′-e′′b], Universal 9 Stevie Smith.)
Refugee Blues, *W. H. Auden*, Bb [bb-f′′], Thames *Century 2*.
(Repentence of Lady T, The, *Stevie Smith*, [c′-c′′], Universal 9 Stevie Smith.)
(Songster, The, *Stevie Smith*, [a-e′′], Universal 9 Stevie Smith.)
(Up and Down, *Stevie Smith*, [g-d′′], Universal 9 Stevie Smith.)

Lyall, Margaret. *See also* App. 2.
Nightshade, *J. W. Turner*, [bb-f′′], Bardic.
O fair, O sweet, *Sir Philip Sidney*, [d′b-e′′], Bardic.
Phillida Flouts Me, *Anon*, [c′-f′′], Bardic.
Rondeau, *Charles d'Orleans*, [bb-f′′], Bardic.
Shall I wasting in despair, *George Wither*, [a-e′′], Bardic.
Twas now the earliest morning, *J. W. Turner*, [d′-g′′], Bardic.
Verses to Music, *J. W. Turner*, [e′-g′′#], Bardic.
Villanelle, *Jean Passerat*, [c′-f′′], Bardic.

M

McCabe, John. 1939– *See also* App. 2.
Collection: *Irish Songbook*, Novello 1994.
In ruin reconciled, *Aubrey de Vere*, [c′#-e′′], Novello Irish.
Lover's Farewell, The, *James Clarence Mangan*, [c′#-e′′], Novello Irish.
Lullaby, *W. B. Yeats*, [bb-g′′b], Novello Irish.
Mother, The, *Padraic Pearse*, [c′#-f′′#](f), Novello Irish.
Nameless Doon, The, *William Larminie*, [d′b-g′′b], Novello Irish.
Question, A, *John M. Synge*, [bb-f′′#], Novello Irish.

Requiem Sequence, *Catholic Rite,* [d′-a″](f), Novello.
White Rose, A, *John Boyle O'Reilly,* [c′-d″], Novello Irish.

McCall, J. P.
Boots, *Rudyard Kipling,* Dm [e′-e″b], Weinberger.

MacCunn, Hamish. 1868–1916. SMIC.
Collections: *Album of Ten Songs,* S&B; *Six Settings of Poems by Robert Bridges,* S&B; *Six Songs,* S&B.
Angel spirits of sleep, *Robert Bridges,* S&B 6 Bridges.
Autumn Song, *Percy Bysshe Shelley,* S&B 10 Songs.
Crown winter with green, *Robert Bridges,* S&B 6 Bridges.
Doubting, *Lady Lindsay,* S&B 6 Songs.
Dreamland, *Lady Lindsay,* S&B 6 Songs.
Fire of heaven whose starry arrow, *Robert Bridges,* S&B 6 Bridges.
Flower Message, A, *Lady Lindsay,* S&B 6 Songs.
Golden Days, *Lady Lindsay,* S&B 6 Songs.
Had I a cave on some wild distant shore, *Robert Burns,* Dm [c′#-f″](m), S&B (Bush) *MB 56.*
Her suffering ended, *James Aldrich,* S&B 10 Songs.
Hesper, *Lady Lindsay,* S&B 6 Songs.
Huntsman's Dirge, The, *Walter Scott,* S&B 10 Songs.
Idle Life, The, *Robert Bridges,* S&B 6 Bridges.
In a Palace Garden, Cramer.
I've found my mountain lyre again, *The Ettrick Shepherd (James Hogg),* S&B.
(Lie there, my lute, *Charles H. Taylor,* Bb [bb-f″], Chappell; Ab, Chappell.)
Love in her sunny eyes, *Abraham Cowley,* S&B 10 Songs.
My bed and pillow are cold, *Robert Bridges,* S&B 6 Bridges.
My Mary dear, farewell, *Professor Blackie,* S&B.
Pedlar's Song, *Robert Bridges,* S&B 6 Bridges.
Princess Helene, Cramer.
Tell her, Oh tell her, *Thomas Moore,* S&B 10 Songs.
There be none of beauty's daughters, *Percy Bysshe Shelley,* S&B 10 Songs.
Thine am I, my faithful fair, *Robert Burns,* Ab [d′-f″](m), S&B (Bush) *MB 56.*
Wishes, *Lady Lindsay,* S&B 6 Songs.
You are free, Cramer.
Young rose I give thee, The, *Thomas Moore,* S&B 10 Songs.
Welcome sweet bird, *Thomas Moore,* S&B 10 Songs.
When the first summer bee, *Thomas Moore,* S&B 10 Songs.
When twilight dews, *Thomas Moore,* S&B 10 Songs.
Wilt thou be my dearie? *Robert Burns,* F [c′-f″](m), S&B (Bush) *MB 56.*

MacDonald, Malcolm Calum. 1948– *See also* App. 1.
Collections: *Breaking the Ice,* Bardic; *From Armageddon in Albyn,* Bardic; *Six Early Songs,* Bardic.
At the Firth of Lorne, *Ian Chrighton Smith,* [c′-e″b], Bardic 6 Early.
Breaking the ice, *Hugh MacDiarmid,* [d′-b″], Bardic Breaking.
Clachàrd, *Aonghas MacNeacail,* [b-a″], Bardic.
Full moonlight, *Auriel Frère,* [bb-b″b], Bardic.
Great Day, The, *W. B. Yeats,* [d′-g″], Bardic 6 Early.
In the golden island, *Hugh MacDiarmid,* [e′b-a″], Bardic.
Last Lauch, The, *Douglas Young,* [c′-a″], Bardic 6 Early.
Luss Village, *Ian Crighton Smith,* [c′-e″b], Bardic 6 early.
Mither's Lament, The, *Sidney Goodsir Smith,* [e′-g″], Bardic From Armageddon.
Paradigm, The, *Sorley Maclean,* [f′-a″], Bardic Breaking.
Simmer Landskip, *Sidney Goodsir Smith,* [f′-b″b], Bardic From Armageddon.
Summer Evening, *Emily Brontë,* [d′-g″], Bardic 6 Early.

McDowell, Cecilia. 1951– BMIC. *See also* App. 2.

Mace, Stephen. ? –1635.
Weep no more, nor sigh nor groan, *Beaumont & Fletcher,* Dm [d′-f″], S&B (Spink) *MB 33.*

McEwen, Sir **John** Blackwood. 1868–1948.
Collection: *Three Songs,* BMP.
Brevity, *Constance Travers,* C [g′-g″] BMP.
Love's but a dance, *Austin Dobson,* Db [d′b-a″], BMP.

Soleils Couchants, *Paul Verlaine* tr. *Ashmore Wingate,* D [d´-f´´#], BMP 3 Songs.
Song of Autumn, *Paul Verlaine* tr. *Ashmore Wingate,* C#m [g#(c´#)-f´´#], BMP 3 Songs.
Wood's Aglow, The, *Paul Verlaine* tr. *Ashmore Wingate,* G♭ [b´b-g´´b], BMP 3 Songs.

Macfarren, Sir **George** Alexander. 1813–1887. *See also* App. 2., Cramer.
Separation, *Arabic,* tr. *Edward William Lane,* Dm [c´#-g´´b], S&B (Bush & Temperley) *MB 43.*

Macgeorge, Alastair. 1931–
Cradle Song, A, *W. B. Yeats,* G♭ [d´b-g´´b](f), Thames *Century 5.*

McGregor, Richard. SMIC. *See also* App. 1.
Collection: *Three Songs of Love,* SMIC.
Prologue, Elegy and Epilogue, [baritone], SMIC.

McGuire, Edward. 1948– *See also* App. 2.
Collections; *City Songs,* [Montgomery, Brecht, Mclean], [baritone], SMIC; *Five Songs,* [Janet Humberger], [mezzo/soprano], SMIC; *Web, The: Five Love Songs,* [Lesley Siddall], [soprano], SMIC.
Scot in China, A, *Edward McGuire,* [voice], SMIC.

Mackenzie, Sir **Alexander** Campbell. 1847–1935. *See also* App. 2. , B&H.
Birthday, A, *Christina Rossetti,* F [d´#-g´´(a´´)], S&B (Bush) *MB 56.*
First Spring Day, The, *Christina Rossetti,* E♭ [c´-g´´], S&B (Bush) *MB 56.*
When I am dead, *Christina Rossetti,* A [e´-f´´#], S&B (Bush) *MB 56.*

Mackie, James. SMIC.
Where our heart of town is, [soprano], SMIC.

McLain, John.
Our father, who art in heaven, *Book of Common Prayer,* [c´-d´´], Bardic.

McLelland-Young, Thomas.
Collections: *Twelve Haiku,* [soprano], McLelland-Young; *Two Poems of W. B. Yeats,* [low], McLelland-Young.
Come to me in my dreams, *Matthew Arnold,* [high], McLelland-Young.
Stanzas from Tintern Abbey (cycle), *William Wordsworth,* [tenor], Brunton.
Sun has set, The, *Emily Brontë,* [soprano], McLelland-Young.

McLeod, John. 1934– *See also* App. 1, 2.
Collections: *Peacocks with a Hundred Eyes,* Griffin; *Three Nocturnes,* Griffin; *Three Poems of Irina Ratushinskaya,* Griffin; *White Flame, The,* Griffin.
Dream of the Birds, The, *J. B. Priestley,* [baritone], Griffin White Flame.
Echo, *Christina Rossetti,* [counter-tenor/mezzo/baritone], Griffin Peacocks.
Farewell, The, *J. B. Priestley,* [baritone], Griffin White Flame.
Here sleeps, *Walter de la Mare,* [tenor/soprano], Griffin 3 Nocturnes.
I will travel through the land, *Irina Ratushinskaya,* tr. *David McDuff,* [soprano], Griffin 3 Poems.
Music when soft voices die, *Percy Bysshe Shelley,* [counter-tenor/mezzo/baritone], Griffin Peacocks.
No, I'm not afraid, *Irina Ratushinskaya,* tr. *David McDuff,* [soprano], Griffin 3 Poems.
Now sleeps the crimson petal, *Alfred Lord Tennyson,* [tenor/soprano], Griffin 3 Nocturnes.
Remember, *Christina Rossetti,* [counter-tenor/mezzo/baritone], Griffin Peacocks.
Rest, *Christina Rossetti,* [tenor/soprano], Griffin 3 Nocturnes.
Song, *Christina Rossetti,* [counter-tenor/mezzo/baritone], Griffin Peacocks.
Treasure, The, *J. B. Priestley,* [baritone], Griffin White Flame.
Where are you, my Prince? *Irina Ratushinskaya,* tr. *David McDuff,* [soprano], Griffin 3 Poems.

MacMahon, Desmond.
Collection: *Six Songs of Happiness,* Chester.

MacMillan, James. 1959– *See also* App. 2.
Ballad, *William Soutar,* Em [b-e´´], B&H.
Children, The, *William Soutar,* D [a-f´´#], B&H.
Scots Song, *William Soutar,* [a´#-f´´], B&H.

MacMurrough, Dermot. 1872–1943.
Macushla, *Josephine V. Rowe,* A♭ [e´b-a´´b(g´´b)](m) B&H *Ballad Album 1;* F, *McCormack.*

MacNutt, Walter. 1910–1996
   O love, be deep, *H. E. Foster*, Db [d′b-e′′b], Roberton.

Maconchy, Dame Elizabeth. 1907–1994. BMIC. *See also* App. 2.
   Collections: *Three Donne Songs*, [tenor], Chester 1966; *Three Songs,* Chester 1982. *See also* BMIC.
      Garland, The, [soprano], Chester.
      (Harp Song of the Dane Women, *Rudyard Kipling*, (f), Chester.)
      Have you seen but a bright lily grow, *Ben Jonson*, Fm [e′b-f′′], BMP.
      (Hymn to God the Father, A, *John Donne*, [c′-a′′], Chester.)
      In memory of W. B. Yeats, [soprano], Chester.
      Meditation for his mistress, A, *Robert Herrick*, Ebm [e′b-g′′b](m), BMP.
      Ophelia's song, *Shakespeare*, [e′b-g′′](f), OUP.
      Sun, Moon and Stars (cycle), *Elizabeth Machonchy*, [bb-b′′b], Chester.
   Arrangement:
      Sho-heen sho-ho, *Anon*, Ab [e′b-e′′b], Lengnick.

McPhee, George.
   My beloved spake, *Song of Solomon 2 vv. 10-13,* [soprano or tenor], Brunton.

MacPherson, Charles. 1870–1927. SMIC.

McQuattie, Shiela.
   From the Percy Reliques, *Anon*, [soprano], Da Capo.
   Hear the Voice of the Bard, *William Blake*, [bass], Da Capo.

Marchant, Robert. 1916–1995.
   Collection: *Four Songs,* Banks.
      Fish in the unruffled lakes, *W. H. Auden*, [high], Banks 4 Songs.
      Hidden Law, The, *W. H. Auden*, [high], Banks 4 Songs.
      Look, stranger, *W. H. Auden*, [high], Banks 4 Songs.
      When Sir Beelzebub, *Edith Sitwell*, [high], Banks 4 Songs.

Mark, Jeffrey.
   Auld Jobby Dixon, *John Richardson*, [Ab-e′b](m), BMP.
   Barley Broth, *Susannah Blamire*, [b-e′′], BMP.
   Lal Dinah Grayson, *Alexander Craig Gibson*, [c′#-e′′], BMP.
   Sally Gray, *Robert Anderson*, [c′#-d′′(f′#)], BMP.
   Where be ye going, *John Keats*, [f′-e′′], BMP.

Marsh, Alfonso. 1627–1681.
   Ah Chloris! would the gods allow, *Anon*, Gm [f′-g′′], S&B (Spink) *MB 33.*

Marsh, Roger. 1949– *See* App. 2.
   Fodder after all, [soprano], Novello.

Marshall, Charles.
   13 more songs in B&H archive.
      I have a garden, *Thomas Moore*, [medium], Banks.
      I hear you calling me, *Harold Harford*, Bb [f′-g′′] B&H *Ballad Album 1*; Eb, *McCormack*; C,
         Cramer *Drawing Room Songs,* Classical; (G, Ab, B&H).

Marshall, Nicholas. *See* App. 2.

Martin, Easthope. 1847–1925.
Collections: *Five Poems by John Masefield,* Classical; *Four Dedications,* [high (given below), medium], Classical; *Four Songs of the Fair,* [high, low (given below)], Classical; *Songs of the Hedgerow,* Classical.
   All For You, *Helen Taylor*, Eb [e′b-a′′b], Classical 4 Dedications.
   An Old Song Resung, *John Masefield*, Ab [c′b-e′′b], Classical 5 Poems.
   Ballad-monger, The, *Helen Taylor*, D [b′-e′′], Classical 4 Songs of the Fair.
   Beauty, *John Masefield*, Gb [d′-g′′b], Classical 5 Poems.
   Cargoes, *John Masefield*, Am [c′-e′′], Classical 5 Poems.
   Carillion, *Helen Taylor*, Eb [e′b-a′′b(g′′)], Classical 4 Dedications.
   Come to the fair, *Helen Taylor*, Bb [f′-f′′], Schirmer *1st Soprano II.*
   Fairings, *Helen Taylor*, A [c′#-e′′], Classical 4 Songs of the Fair.

Harvest Moon, *Helen Taylor,* C [d′-e′′], Classical Songs of the Hedgerow.
Hedgerow Carnival, *Helen Taylor,* Eb [d′-e′′b], Classical Songs of the Hedgerow.
Hedgin' and Ditchin', *Helen Taylor,* Am [c′-e′′(d′′)], Classical Songs of the Hedgerow.
Jock the Fiddler, *Helen Taylor,* G [d′-d′′], Classical 4 Songs of the Fair.
June Twilight, *John Masefield,* A [d′-e′′], Classical 5 Poems.
Langley Fair, *Helen Taylor,* Eb [c′-f′(e′′b)], Classical 4 Songs of the Fair.
Most Wonderful, *Helen Taylor,* Bb [f′-g′′], Classical 4 Dedications.
St Mary's Bells, *John Masefield,* Bbm [e′b-f′′], Classical 5 Poems.
To a Bygone Spring, *Helen Taylor,* F [e′-f′′], Classical 4 Dedications.
When it's blackberry time in September, *Helen Taylor,* Classical Songs of the Hedgerow.
Wild Rose Lane, *Helen Taylor,* Eb [bb-e′′b(c′′)], Classical Songs of the Hedgerow.

Martin, Frank.
Years disarmed, The, (cycle), *Humphrey Clucas,* [medium/high], Brunton.

Martin, Jennifer. 1967– SMIC.
In the bleak midwinter, *Christina Rossetti,* [soprano], SMIC.

Martin, Richard. ?1517–?1618.
Change thy mind since she doth change, *Robert Devereux Earl of Essex,* Gm [g′-g′′](m), S&B (Stroud) *Banquet,* (Pilkington) *Lute Songs 2,* BMP *W&W 3.*

Marzials, Theo.
Twickenham Ferry, *Theo Marzials,* Eb [bb-e′′b], IMP *Parlour Songs.*

Mason, George. *fl.*1610 –1617.
Dido was the Carthage Queen, *Thomas Campion?* C [g′-g′′](m), S&B (Pilkington) *Lute Songs 2.*

Matheson, Iain. 1956– *See also* App. 2.
Collection: *Four Songs,* Proverbs 30 vv. 25-28, [soprano], SMIC; *Three Translations of Silence,* Peritti Saaritsa, Primo Levi, Sylvia Fischerova, [soprano], SMIC.

Mathias, William. 1934– 1992. *See also* App. 2.
Fields of Praise, The (cycle), *Dylan Thomas,* [tenor], OUP.
Vision of Time and Eternity, A, *Henry Vaughan,* [bb-f′′#(g′′#)], BMP.
Arrangements: *Three Welsh melodies,* (high, low), Gwynn.
David of the White Rock, Gwynn 3 Welsh.
Loom, The, Gwynn 3 Welsh.
Miller's Song, The, Gwynn 3 Welsh.

Matthews, Colin. 1946– *See also* App. 1, 2.
Aubade, *Paul Auster,* [high, low], Faber.
Shadows in the water, *Thomas Traherne,* [high], Faber.
Strugnell's Haiku, *Wendy Cope,* [g-e′′], Faber.

Matthews, David. 1943– *See also* App. 2.
Book of Hours, The, [mezzo], Faber.
From Coastal Stations, *Maggie Hemingway,* [medium], Faber.
Golden Kingdom, The (cycle), *Raine, Shelley, Blake,* [high], Faber.

Matthews, E. E.
Collection: *Two Songs by Shelley,* BMP.
If I walk in Autumn's even, *Percy Bysshe Shelley,* [d′-f′′], BMP 2 Shelley.
Music when soft voices die, *Percy Bysshe Shelley,* [d′-g′′], BMP 2 Shelley.

Maude, Caroline.
Magdalen, *Henry Kingsley,* Gm, [b-e′′], B&H *Heritage 2.*

Maw, John Nicholas. 1935– *See also* App. 2.
Three young rats, *Traditional,* G [bb-e′′], B&H *Easy Song.*
Voice of Love, The (cycle), *Peter Porter,* [bb-a′′b], B&H.
Arrangements: *Five American Folksongs,* Faber.
Darlin', *Anon,* G [d′-e′′], Faber 5 Folksongs.
Parting Friends, *Anon,* F#m [e′-f′′#], Faber 5 Folksongs.

Rémon, *Anon (French)*, F [e′-b′′], Faber 5 Folksongs.
This train, *Anon,* B♭ [f′-b′′♭], Faber 5 Folksongs.
Zeb Turney's Gal, *Anon,* [e′-a′′], Faber 5 Folksongs.

Maxim, Piers.
Collection: *Two Songs*, Brunton.

Maxwell, Michael. 1958– *See* App. 2.

Maxwell Davies, Sir **Peter.** 1934– *See also* App. 2.
Yellow Cake Revue, The, *Maxwell Davies,* B&H.

Maynard, John. 1577–after 1615.
Collection: *The Twelve Wonders of the World,* (John Davies), S&B.

Mayo, Kevin. 1964– SMIC.

Merrick, Frank. 1886–1981. BMIC.

Metcalf, John Phillip. 1946– WMIC.

Miles, P. Napier. 1865–1935. *See also* App. 2.
My Master hath a garden, *Anon*, [c′-f′′#], BMP.

Milford, Robin. 1903–1959.
Collection: *Twelve Songs,* Thames (introduction Ian Copley).
Colour, The *Thomas Hardy*, G [e′-g′′], Thames 12 Songs.
Cradle Song, *William Blake*, F [c′-f′′], Thames 12 Songs.
Daybreak, *John Donne*, B♭ [f′-f′′], Thames 12 Songs.
Epitaph, *Walter de la Mare*, [d′-f′′], Thames 12 Songs.
If it's ever spring again, *Thomas Hardy*, G [d′-g′′], Thames 12 Songs.
Laus Deo, [high], Novello; [low], Novello.
Love on my heart, *Robert Bridges*, F# [f′#-f′′#], Thames 12 Songs.
Pink Frock, The, *Thomas Hardy*, Em [e′-d′′](f), Thames 12 Songs.
Pleasure it is, *William Cornish*, G [g′-g′′], Thames 12 Songs.
So sweet love seemed, *Robert Bridges*, B♭ [f′-f′′], Thames 12 Songs, Novello.
This endris night, *Anon 15th cent.*, B♭ [d′-f′′], Thames 12 Songs.
Tolerance, *Thomas Hardy*, [c′-g′′], Thames 12 Songs.
What pleasures have great princes? *Anon*, Dm [d′-f′′], Thames 12 Songs.

Miller, Edward. 1735–1807.
Collection: *Four Songs by Edward Miller,* B&H (Armstrong Gibbs).
Despairing Shepherd, The, *Carr Scroope*, Em [d′-e′′], B&H 4 Miller.
Happy Pair, The, *Francis Pilkington*, D [d′-g′′], B&H 4 Miller.
I prithee, send me back my heart, *John Suckling*, G [d′-g′′](m), B&H 4 Miller.
To Althea, from Prison, *Richard Lovelace*, C [e′-g′′](m), B&H 4 Miller.

Mills, Olga.
Shepherd, The, *William Blake,* [f′-g′′], BMP.
Song of Sorrow, A, *William Blake,* [f′-a′′♭], BMP.

Milner, Anthony Francis Dominic. 1925–2002
Collection: *Our Lady's Hours*, Novello 1959.
Dawn, *Anon*, Em [e′-g′′], Novello Our Lady, Novello.
Dusk, *Hilaire Belloc*, G♭ [d′♭-g′′♭], Novello Our Lady.
Noon, *Gerard Manley Hopkins*, A [b-a′′], Novello Our Lady.

Mitchell, John. *See also* App. 2.
Dirge in Woods, *George Meredith*, F# [c′#-g′′], Modus.
Evolution, *Arthur Shipley,* G [d′-f′′#], Modus.
Field and Lane, *A. E. Housman,* D [d′#-a′′], Modus.
Gentleman Soldier, The, *Traditional,* B♭ [d-f′′](m), Modus.
Sloe was lost in flower, The, *A. E. Housman,* Gm [e′♭-f′′], Modus.

'Tis time, I think, by Wenlock Town, *A. E. Housman,* Em [d´-e´´], Modus.
When green buds hang in the elm like dust, *A. E. Housman,* Fm [d´-e´´], Modus.

Moeran, Ernest John. 1894–1950.
Collections: *Collected Solo Songs 1, 2, 3, 4,* Thames (edited, with introduction and notes, John Talbot); *Four English Lyrics,* B&H; *Four Shakespeare Songs,* Novello [high, medium]; *Ludlow Town,* BMP; *Seven Poems of James Joyce,* BMP; *Six Poems by Seumas O'Sullivan,* S&B; *Twelve Songs,* Thames (introduction Peter Todd); *Two Songs,* Chester.
    Bean Flower, The, *Dorothy L. Sayers,* F#m [g´-a´´](f), Chester 2 Songs, Thames Collected 2.
    Blue-eyed Spring, *Robert Nichols,* G [d´-g´´], Thames Collected 1.
    Bright cap, *James Joyce,* A [d´-e´´], Thames Collected 4, BMP 7 Poems.
    Cherry-ripe, *Thomas Campion,* F [d´-a´´], Thames Collected 1, 12 Songs.
    Come away, death, *Shakespeare,* Am [e´-e´´](m), Thames Collected 4, BMP.
    Constant Lover, The, *William Browne,* G [d´-g´´](m), Thames Collected 1, 12 Songs.
    Cottager, A, *Seumas O'Sullivan,* [d´b-g´´b], Thames Collected 2, S&B 6 Poems.
    Day of Palms, The, *Arthur Symons,* E [c´#-f´´#], Thames Collected 4, Cramer.
    Diaphenia, *Henry Constable* or *Henry Chettle,* A [e´-a´´](m), Thames Collected 1, B&H *Heritage 4.*
    Donneycarney*, James Joyce,* [e´b-e´´b](m), Thames Collected 4, BMP 7 Poems.
    Dream of Death, A, *W. B. Yeats,* [c´-e´´b], Thames Collected 4, 12 Songs.
    Dustman, The (Child's fancy), *Seumas O'Sullivan,* [e´b-f´´], Thames Collected 2, S&B 6 Poems.
    Evening, *Seumas O'Sullivan,* Ab [d´b-g´´b], Thames Collected 2, S&B 6 Poems, 12 Songs.
    Far in a western brookland, (1st setting) *A. E. Housman,* [c´-e´´](m), Thames Collected 3.
    Far in a western brookland, (2nd setting) *A. E. Housman,* [c´-d´´](m), Thames Collected 3.
    Farewell to barn and stack and tree, *A. E. Housman,* [c´-e´´b](m), Thames Collected 3, BMP Ludlow Town.
    Herdsman, The, *Seumas O'Sullivan,* Bm [d´-f´´], Thames Collected 2, S&B 6 Poems.
    If there be any Gods, *Seumas O'Sullivan,* [d´-g´´], Thames Collected 2.
    Impromptu in March, *D. A. E. Wallace,* [f´-g´´]], Chester 2 Songs, Thames Collected 2.
    In Youth is Pleasure, *Robert Wever,* F [f´-g´´](m), Thames Collected 1, 12 Songs.
    Invitation in Autumn, *Seumas O'Sullivan,* G [d´-g´´], Thames Collected 1, Novello.
    Lads in their hundreds, The, *A. E. Housman,* [c´#-e´´](m), Thames Collected 3, BMP Ludlow Town.
    Loveliest of trees, *A. E. Housman,* E [b-e´´], Thames Collected 3, Curwen.
    Lover and his Lass, The, *Shakespeare,* Eb [e´b-f´´], Thames Collected 2, Novello 4 Shakespeare.
    Lullaby, *Seumas O'Sullivan,* Gm [d´b-b´´b], Thames Collected 2, S&B 6 Poems.
    Maltworms, *William Stevenson?* or *Bishop Still,* (with Warlock), F [c´-f´´], Thames Collected 4.
    Mantle of Blue, *Padraic Colum,* E [c´#-d´´#], Thames Collected 2.
    Merry Green Wood, The, *James Joyce,* [e´-e´´], Thames Collected 4, BMP 7 Poems.
    Merry Month of May, The, *Thomas Dekker,* G [d´-g´´](m), Thames Collected 1, BMP.
    Monk's Fancy, The, *H. J. Hope,* Cm [e´b-g´´], Thames Collected 1.
    Now, O now, in this brown land, *James Joyce,* [c´-f´´], Thames Collected 4, BMP 7 Poems.
    Oh fair enough are sky and plain, *A. E. Housman,* Gm [d´b-e´´b](m), Thames Collected 3, Chester *Celebrated 2.*
    Passionate Shepherd, The, *Christopher Marlowe,* A [e´-a´´](m), Thames Collected 1.
    Pleasant Valley, The, *James Joyce,* F [c´-f´´], Thames Collected 4, BMP 7 Poems.
    Poplars, The, *Seumas O'Sullivan,* A [a#-e´´], Thames Collected 2, S&B 6 Poems, 12 Songs.
    Rahoon, *James Joyce,* [c´-e´´], Thames Collected 2, BMP.
    Rain has fallen, *James Joyce,* [c´#-f´´#], Thames Collected 4, BMP 7 Poems.
    Rosaline, *Thomas Lodge,* G [d´-a´´](m), Thames Collected 1.
    Rosefrail, *James Joyce,* C#m [c´#-e´´], Thames Collected 2, S&B, 12 Songs.
    Say, lad, have you things to do, *A. E. Housman,* Eb [d´-e´´b](m), Thames Collected 3, 12 Songs, BMP Ludlow Town.
    Spring goeth all in white, *Robert Bridges,* F [f´-e´´], Thames Collected 4, Curwen.
    Strings in the earth and air, *James Joyce,* Dm [d´-f´´], Thames Collected 4, BMP 7 Poems.
    Sweet o' the Year, The, *Shakespeare,* G [d´-g´´](m), Thames Collected 1, 12 Songs.
    This time of year a twelvemonth past, *A. E. Housman,* Eb [c´-e´´b](m), Thames Collected 3.
    Tilly, *James Joyce,* [c´-g´´b], Thames Collected 2.
    'Tis time, I think, by Wenlock Town, *A. E. Housman,* F [c´-f´´], Thames Collected 3.
    Troll the Bowl, *Thomas Dekker,* Bm [g´-f´´#](m), Thames Collected 4, 12 Songs, BMP.
    Twilight, *John Masefield,* Dm [c´-d´´], Thames Collected 2, 12 Songs.
    Weep you no more, sad fountains, *Anon,* Am [f´#-g´´], Thames Collected 1.
    Westward on the high-hilled plains, *A. E. Housman,* C [bb-d´´], Thames Collected 3.
    When daisies pied, *Shakespeare,* F [c´-g´´], Thames Collected 2, Novello 4 Shakespeare.
    When I came last to Ludlow, *A. E. Housman,* [d´-d´´](m), Thames Collected 3.

When icicles hang by the wall, *Shakespeare*, [d′-g′′], Thames Collected 2, Novello 4 Shakespeare.
When June is come, *Robert Bridges*, D [f′-f′′#(e′′)](m), Thames Collected 4, Curwen.
When smoke stood up from Ludlow, *A. E. Housman*, [c′#-e′′](m) Thames Collected 3, BMP Ludlow Town.
Where the bee sucks, *Shakespeare*, E♭ [c′-f′′], Thames Collected 2, Novello 4 Shakespeare.
Willow Song, *John Fletcher*, Gm [f′-g′′](f), Thames Collected 1, 12 Songs.
Arrangements: *Collected Folksong Arrangements 1*, 2, Thames (edited, with introduction and notes, John Talbot); *(Six Folksongs from Norfolk,* S&B); *(Six Suffolk Folksongs,* Curwen); *Songs from County Kerry,* S&B.
    Blackberry Fold, *Anon*, [c′-d′′], Thames Collected Folksongs 2, (Curwen 6 Suffolk*)*.
    Bold Richard, The, *Anon*, [d′-e′′](m), Thames Collected Folksongs 1, (S&B 6 Norfolk).
    Can't you dance the polka, *Anon*, C [b-c′′], Thames Collected Solo Songs 4.
    Cupid's Garden, *Anon*, [a-e′′](m), Thames Collected Folksongs 2, (Curwen 6 Suffolk).
    Dawning of the Day, The, *Anon*, [c′#-e′′], Thames Collected Folksongs 2, S&B Kerry.
    Down by the Riverside, *Anon*, [d′-e′′], Thames Collected Folksongs 1, (S&B 6 Norfolk).
    Father and Daughter, *Anon*, [f′-e′′], Thames Collected Folksongs 2, (Curwen 6 Suffolk).
    Gaol Song, *Anon*, [g′-d′′](m), Thames Collected Folksongs 1.
    High Germany, *Anon*, [c′-f′′], Thames Collected Folksongs 1.
    Isle of Cloy, The, *Anon*, [d′-e′′], Thames Collected Folksongs 2, (Curwen 6 Suffolk).
    Jolly Carter, The, *Anon*, [b-e′′](m), Thames Collected Folksongs 1.
    Kitty, I am in love with you, *Anon*, [d′-f′′#](m),Thames Collected Folksongs 2, S&B Kerry.
    Little Milkmaid, The, *Anon* [c′-d′′], Thames Collected Folksongs 1.
    Lonely Waters, *Anon*, [c′-d′′](m), Thames Collected Folksongs 1, (S&B 6 Norfolk).
    Lost Lover, The, *Anon*, [d′-f′′](f), Thames Collected Folksongs 2, S&B Kerry.
    Mrs Dyer, the baby farmer, *Anon*, G [d′-d′′], Thames Collected Solo Songs 4.
    Murder of Father Hanratty, The, *Anon*, [e′-f′′],Thames Collected Folksongs 2, S&B Kerry.
    My love passed me by, *Anon*, [c′-e′′](m), Thames Collected Folksongs 2, S&B Kerry.
    Nutting Time, *Anon*, D [c′#-d′′], Thames Collected Folksongs 2, (Curwen 6 Suffolk).
    Oxford Sporting Blade, The, *Anon*, [d′-d′′](m), Thames Collected Folksongs 1, (S&B 6 Norfolk).
    Parson and Clerk, *Anon*, [d′-e′′], Thames Collected Folksongs 1.
    Pressgang, The, *Anon*, [c′-d′′](m), Thames Collected Folksongs 1.
    Roving Dingle Boy, The, *Anon*, [e′-f′′#], Thames Collected Folksongs 2, S&B Kerry.
    Sailor and Young Nancy, The, *Anon*, [c′#-e′′], Thames Collected Folksongs 1, BMP.
    Seaman's Life, A, *Anon*, [d′-e′′],Thames Collected Folksongs 2, (Curwen 6 Suffolk).
    Shooting of his Dear, The, *Anon*, [d′-e′′], Thames Collected Folksongs 1, (S&B 6 Norfolk).
    Tinker's Daughter, The, *Anon*, [c′-e′′](m),Thames Collected Folksongs 2, S&B Kerry.

Moir, Frank L.
    Down the Vale, *Gunby Hadath*, F [e′-f′′], B&H *Souvenirs*.

Molloy, James Lynam. 1837–1909. *See also* B&H, Cramer.
    Kerry Dance, The, *J. L. Molloy*, E♭ [c′-f′′], B&H *McCormack*.
    Love's Old Sweet Song, *G. Clifton Bingham*, G [c′#-e′′(g′′)], B&H *Ballad Album 1, McCormack*; (E♭, F, B&H).

Møller, Paulette.
Collection: *Five Rupert Brooke Songs,* Micropress. Note: Micropress publications can be supplied in a wide range of keys.
    Doubts, *Rupert Brooke,* Micropress 5 Rupert Brooke.
    Hawthorn, The, *Rupert Brooke,* Micropress 5 Rupert Brooke.
    It's not going to happen again, *Rupert Brooke,* Micropress 5 Rupert Brooke.
    There is wisdom in women, *Rupert Brooke,* Micropress 5 Rupert Brooke.
    Way that lovers use, The, *Rupert Brooke,* Micropress 5 Rupert Brooke.

Montague, Stephen. 1943– *See* App. 2.

Montgomery, Robert **Bruce.** 1921–1978.
    (My true love hath a garden, F, Chester.)
    (My true love hath my heart, *Philip Sidney,* Novello.)

Moore, Thomas. 1779–1852.
    Believe me if all those endearing young charms, *Thomas Moore,* D [d′-d′′], IMP *Parlour Songs*.

Morgan, Hilda. WMIC. *See also* App. 2.

Morgan, Howard.
Collection: *Five Lyric Poems,* Forsyth.
    Goblin Revel, *Siegfried Sassoon,* Gm [d´-g´´], Forsyth 5 Lyric.
    Noah, *Siegfried Sassoon,* G [d´-f´´#], Forsyth 5 Lyric.
    October, *Siegfried Sassoon,* [d´-g´´], Forsyth 5 Lyric.
    Old French Poet, An, *Siegfried Sassoon,* D [d´-a´´], Forsyth 5 Lyric.
    Poplar and the Moon, A, *Siegfried Sassoon,* [c´-g´´#], Forsyth 5 Lyric.

Morgan, Islwyn.
    April, [soprano/mezzo/tenor/baritone], Gwynn.

Mordish, Louis. ? –1996.
    My Love I Miss You So, *Louis Mordish,* E*b* [e´*b*-e´´*b*], S&B.

Morley, Thomas. 1557–1602.
Collection: *The First Book of Ayres,* S&B (edited Thurston Dart). Only songs available in anthologies are listed individually here. Note that in the following: Pilkington = *English Lute Songs Book 2,* S&B; Keel 1a, 1b and 2a, 2b = *Elizabethan Lovesongs Books 1 and 2* [high, low], B&H.
    Absence, hear thou my protestation, *John Donne?, Sir John Hoskyns?* G [d´-f´´](m), 1st Book, Pilkington.
    Flora, wilt thou torment me, (arr.) *Anon,* G [d´-g´´], Keel 2a; E, Keel 2b.
    I saw my lady weeping, *Anon,* Am [d´-e´´], 1st Book, Pilkington.
    It was a lover and his lass, *Shakespeare,* G [g´-g´´], 1st Book, B&H (Woolfenden) *Shakespeare Album,* Peters *Art of Song 2a; F,* Pilkington, Paterson (Diack) *100 Best 2,* Peters *Art of Song 2b,* Leonard *Baroque high; D,* Leonard *Baroque low,* Fischer *Centuries low.*
    Love winged my hopes, *Anon,* G [f´-g´´], 1st Book; *F,* B&H/Classical *Dolmetsch 2.*
    O grief, e'en on the bud, *Anon,* F [f´-e´´*b*], Pilkington, S&B (Greer) *Printed.*
    Sweet nymph, come to thy lover, (arr.) *Anon,* G, Keel 1a; E, Keel 1b.
    Thyrsis and Milla, *Anon,* Gm [g´-g´´], 1st Book, S&B (H. Diack Johnston) *Recitalist 1.*
    What if my mistress now? *Anon,* G [e´-g´´](m), 1st Book, B&H/Classical *Dolmetsch 2.*
    When lo, by break of morning, (arr.) *Anon,* F, Keel 1a; D, Keel 1b.
    With my love my life was nestled, *Robert Southwell,* G [g´-g´´], 1st Book; *F,* B&H/Classical *Dolmetsch 2.*

Morris, Andrew. *See also* App. 2.
    Awaking in Heaven, *Thomas Traherne,* [baritone], Da Capo Music.

Morris, Haydn. 1891–1965.
    (Chieftain's Daughter, The, [c´-e´´*b*], Gwynn.)
    Hei ho! [soprano], Snell.

Moss, Katie.
    Floral Dance, The, B*b* [a-e´´*b*(d´´)], Classical; D, [high], Classical.

Moule-Evans, David. 1905–1988.
Collection: *Two Celtic Songs,* S&B.
    I-Brasîl, *Fiona Macleod,* F#m [c´#-g´´#], S&B 2 Celtic.
    When the dew is falling, *Fiona Macleod,* B*b*m [c´-e´´*b*], S&B 2 Celtic.

Moult, Richard. 1968–
Collections: *Clee Songbook Vol. 1,* Quilver; *Companions, The,* Quilver; *Ripley Songs Books 1, 2,* Quilver.
    All Those Lights, *William Ripley,* [b-c´´], Quilver Ripley Songs 2.
    April Gale, *Ivor Gurney,* [c´-f´´], Quilver Companions.
    Boy of Infinities, The, *William Ripley,* [c´#-d´´], Quilver Ripley Songs 1.
    Brave Carpets, *Ivor Gurney,* [e´*b*-g´´], Quilver Companions.
    Clown and the Jackal, The, *William Ripley,* [c´-f´´], Quilver Ripley Songs 1.
    Companions, The, *Ivor Gurney,* [e´*b*-a´´*b*], Quilver Companions.
    Dear Lily, *Steve Dibb,* [b-e´´](m), Quilver Clee Songbook.
    Distant Roar, *William Ripley,* [a-f´´#], Quilver Ripley Songs 2.
    Exile, The, *William Ripley,* [b´*b*-f´´], Quilver Ripley Songs 2.
    French Windows, The, *William Ripley,* [c´-e´´], Quilver Ripley Songs 1.
    Harlech, *William Ripley,* [b-f´´], Quilver Ripley Songs 1.

Iliadian, *Ivor Gurney,* [f′-g′′], Quilver Companions.
Italy, *William Ripley,* [b*b*′-g′′], Quilver Ripley Songs 1.
Lizard, The, *William Ripley,* [c′-f′′], Quilver Ripley Songs 2.
Lovely Playthings, *Ivor Gurney,* [e′*b*-g′′*b*], Quilver Companions.
Love's Emblems, *John Fletcher,* [e′-g′′](f), Quilver Clee Songbook.
Monopoly, *William Ripley,* [e′*b*-g′′], Quilver Ripley Songs 2.
Musings, *William Barnes,* [b-d′′](m), Quilver Clee Songbook.
Now are the hills born new in sparkling light, *Ivor Gurney,* [e′-a′′], Quilver Companions.
Ship, The, *Ivor Gurney,* [c′#-a′′], Quilver Companions.
Space, *William Ripley,* [b-f′′#], Quilver Ripley Songs 2.
Stone, a Flower, a Chinese Vase, A, *William Ripley,* [a-e′′], Quilver Ripley Songs 1.
Visionary, The, *Emily Brontë,* [c-b′′*b*](f), Quilver Clee Songbook.
Wanderer's Night Song, *William Ripley,* [c′#-e′′], Quilver Ripley Songs 1.
Willy, *William Ripley,* [b′-f′′#], Quilver Ripley Songs 2.
Wolfram's Dirge, *Thomas Lovell Beddoes,* [c′#-e′′](m), Quilver Clee Songbook.
Your Deep Blue Eyes, *Jo Woolley,* [e′-f′′#](f), Quilver Clee Songbook.

Mowbray, Robert de.
To Music, *Robert Herrick,* Dm [a-d′′], BMP.

Muldowney, Dominic John. 1952– *See also* App. 1, 2.
Collections: *Songs from 'Out of the East',* [James Fenton], Faber; *Songs from 'The Good Person of Sichuan',* Faber.
In Paris with you, [voice], *James Fenton,* Faber.
Never let me see you suffer, *James Fenton,* Faber.
On Suicide, *Bertolt Brecht* tr. *Michael Hofmann,* [g-g′], Faber Good Person.
Pigs'll fly, *Bertolt Brecht* tr. *Michael Hofmann,* [g-d′′], Faber Good Person.
Song of the Inadequacy of the Gods and the Good, *Bertolt Brecht* tr. *Michael Hofmann,* [b*b*-c′], Faber Good Person.
Song of the Smoke, *Bertolt Brecht* tr. *Michael Hofmann,* [b-c′′], Faber Good Person.
Song of the Waterseller in the Rain, *Bertolt Brecht* tr. *Michael Hofmann,* [b-a′′*b*], Faber Good Person.
Trio of the Vanishing Gods on the Cloud, *Bertolt Brecht* tr. *Hofmann,* [c′*b*-e′′], Faber Good Person.

Mullinar, Michael. 1895–1973.
Collection: *Pippen Hill,* S&B.
(Cotswold love, *John Drinkwater,* Elkin.)
Daisies, The, *James Stephens,* G [d′-g′′], BMP.
Epitaph, An, *Walter de la Mare,* D*b* [b*b*-d′′], BMP.
Farmer went trotting, A, *Anon,* D [d′-f′′], S&B Pippen Hill.
I will go with my father a-ploughing, *Joseph Campbell,* C [d′-a′′], BMP.
Little cock sparrow, A, *Anon,* F [c′-e′′*b*], S&B Pippen Hill.
Over the Water to Charlie, *Anon,* F [c′-d′′], S&B Pippen Hill.
Piper and the Drummer, The, *Anon,* C [c′-e′′](f), S&B Pippen Hill.
Pippen Hill, *Anon,* D [d′-d′′], S&B Pippen Hill.
Pretty Polly Pillicote, *Anon,* F [c′-f′′], S&B Pippen Hill.
Seas are quiet, The, *Edmund Waller,* D*b* [d′*b*-c′′], BMP.
(To Daffodils, *Robert Herrick,* F [c′-e′′], Elkin; A*b*, Elkin.
Wee Willie Winkie, *Anon,* Em [d′-f′′#], S&B Pippen Hill.
(Where Go the Boats? *R. L. Stevenson,* D [d′-e′′], B&H; F, B&H.)

Mumby, A. V.
On silent wings, [mezzo/contralto/baritone], Snell.

Munro, George. ? –1731.
Celia the Fair, *Anon,* G [d′-g′′](m), S&B (Pilkington) *Georgian 2, Recitalist 3.*
Gold a Receipt for Love, *Anon,* D [d′-g′′], S&B (Pilkington) *Georgian 2.*
My lovely Celia, *Anon,* G [d′-g′′](m), B&H (Lane Wilson) *Old English,* Leonard *Baroque high,* Classical, Schirmer *1st Tenor II*; E, Chester *Celebrated 3,* Paterson (Diack) *100 Best 3,* Classical; E*b*, Leonard *Baroque low,* Fischer *Centuries low.*

Murray, Alan.
I'll walk beside you, *Edward Lockton,* E*b* [c′-e′′*b*], IMP *Parlour Songs.*

Murrill, Herbert Henry John. 1909–1952.
Collection: *Five Songs*, Thames (introduction by Carolyn Murrill).
    In Youth is Pleasure, *Robert Wever*, A♭ [e′b-a′′](m), Thames 5 Songs.
    Love is a sickness, *Samuel Daniel*, Am [e′-f′′], Thames 5 Songs.
    Piggësnye, *Anon*, A [f′#-a′′](m), Thames 5 Songs.
    Sleep, *John Fletcher*, F#m [e′#-d′′], Modus.
    Thanksgiving to God, for his house, A, *Robert Herrick*, Cm [c′-a′′], Thames 5 Songs.
    To Music, to becalm his fever, *Robert Herrick*, [e′b-a′′], Thames 5 Songs.

Musgrave, Thea. 1928– *See also* App. 1, 2.
Collections: *Suite O' Bairnsangs, A*, Chester; *Songs for a Winter's Evening*, Novello.
    Bairn's Prayer at Nicht, A, *Maurice Lindsay*, [g′-d′′], Chester Suite.
    Ca' the yowes to the knowes, *Robert Burns*, [c′#-b′′(g′′)](f), Novello Songs.
    Daffins, *Maurice Lindsay*, [f′-f′′#], Chester Suite.
    Gean, The, *Maurice Lindsay*, [f′-g′′], Chester Suite.
    I am my Mammy's ae bairn, *Robert Burns*, [d′-g′′b(g′′)](f), Novello Songs.
    Jamie, come try me, *Robert Burns*, [c′-c′′′(a′′)](f), Novello Songs.
    John Anderson my jo, *Robert Burns*, [e′-a′′](f), Novello Songs.
    Man-in-the-mune, The, *Maurice Lindsay*, [e′b-f′′], Chester Suite.
    O whistle and I'll come to ye my lad, *Robert Burns*, [c′-a′′b](f), Novello Songs.
    Song for Christmas, A, *William Dunbar*? [g-a′′b], Chester.
    Summer's a pleasant time, *Robert Burns*, [e′b-a′′b](f), Novello Songs.
    Willie Wabster, *Maurice Lindsay*, [e′-e′′], Chester Suite.
    Ye banks and braes o' bonnie Doon, *Robert Burns*, [c′-a′′](f), Novello Songs.

N

Nares, James. 1715–1783.
    O Lord my God, I will exalt thee, *Anon*, C [b-d′′], B&H (Patrick) *Sacred Songs 2*.

Nash, Stuart. 1914–
    O were my love yon lilac fair, *Robert Burns*, B♭ [e′b-g′′], B&H.
    Sonnet No 104, *Shakespeare*, E [b(e′)-e′′], B&H *Songs of Love and Affection*.

Naylor, Bernard. 1907–1986.
Collection: *Speaking from the Snow*, Roberton.
    Beauty's end is in sight, *C. Day-Lewis*, [e′bb-a′′], Roberton Speaking.
    Child's carol, A. *Arthur L. Salmon*, A [c′#-f′′], Roberton.
    Dreams of the Sea, *W. H. Davies*, Am [g′-e′′], Roberton.
    Ecstatic, The, *C. Day-Lewis*, Gm [c′-g′′], Roberton; Am, Roberton.
    Fallen Poplar, The, *Mary Webb*, Fm [f′-f′′], Roberton.
    Gentle Sleep, *S. T. Coleridge*, C [c′-b′′b(g′′)], Roberton.
    Now she is like the white tree-rose, *C. Day-Lewis*, [d′-g′′], Roberton Speaking.
    Rest from loving and be living, *C. Day-Lewis*, [c′-a′′], Roberton Speaking.
    Rose Berries, *Mary Webb*, Em [e′-g′′], Roberton.
    Twenty weeks near past, *C. Day-Lewis*, [d′-a′′], Roberton Speaking.

Naylor, John. 1838–1897.
    Come away death, *Shakespeare*, Dm [a-d′′], Roberton (Bernard Naylor); G, Roberton.

Naylor, Peter. *See also* App. 2.
Collections: *Five Bird Songs*, Modus [high, low]; *Love and Life: A Miscellany of Songs*, Brunton; *Movement and Stillness*, Modus.
    Break of Day, *John Donne*, [d′-a′′b], Brunton Love and Life.
    Chough, The, *Rex Warner*, [e′b-g′′](m), Modus Bird high; [bb-f′′](m), Modus Bird low.
    Drink to me only with thine eyes, *Ben Jonson*, Cm [c′-g′′], Modus.
    Eagle, The, *Alfred Lord Tennyson*, [e′b-b′′](m), Modus Bird high; [bb-f′′#](m) Modus Bird low.
    Entreat me not to leave thee, *Book of Ruth*, Em [c′-g′′#], Modus.
    Kingfisher, The, *W. H. Davies*, [c′-g′′#](m), Modus Bird high; [g-e′′b](m), Modus Bird low.
    Lark, The, *Cecil Day-Lewis*, [c′-g′′#](m), Modus Bird high; [bb-f′′#](m) Modus Bird low.
    Linnet, The, *Walter de la Mare*, [e′b-a′′](m), Modus Bird high; [bb-e′′](m), Modus Bird low.
    Lord Jesus Christ, shall I stand still? E♭[d′-e′′] Modus.
    Love is a sickness, *Samuel Daniel*, Gm [e′-g′′], Brunton Love and Life.

My prime of youth is but a frost of cares, *Chidiock Tichborne,* Am [e′-g′′](m)], Brunton; Fm [c′-e′′b](m), Brunton.
O mistress mine, *William Shakespeare,* [f′-a′′](m), Brunton.
She walks in beauty, *Lord Byron,* [d′-a′′](m), Brunton Love and Life; [bb-f](m), Brunton Love and Life.
Spring Scene, *John Gracen Brown,* [c-e′](m), Modus Movement.
Stillness, The, *John Gracen Brown,* [A-d′#](m), Modus Movement.
Storm Wind, The, *John Gracen Brown,* [e-e′b](m), Modus Movement.
Under the wide and starry sky, *Robert Louis Stevenson,* [d′-g′′](m), Brunton Love and Life.
Voice of my Beloved, *Song of Solomon,* [db-a′′], Brunton Love and Life.
Widow bird, A, *Percy Bysshe Shelley,* Em [e′-e′′], Brunton Love and Life.
Wild bird calls, The, *John Gracen Brown,* [eb-e′](m), Modus Movement.

Nelson, Havelock. 1917– 1996.
Collection: *Songs for Joanna,* Roberton.
Black Cat, The, *John o' the North,* [high], Banks.
Dirty Work, *John o' the North,* [medium], Banks.
Ghosts in the Belfry, *John o' the North,* C [d′-e′′], Roberton.
Hermit, The, *Sydney Bell,* D [d′-e′′], Roberton.
I think it will be winter, *Helen Waddell,* C [c′-f′′], Banks.
Little Betty Bland, *John o' the North,* F [d′-f′′], Roberton Joanna.
Love is Cruel, *Thomas MacDonagh,* Gm [d′-g′′b], Banks.
Shivery Sarah, *John o' the North,* Am [e′-f′′], Roberton.
Town Tree, The, *Dorothy Roberts,* F [c′-f′′], B&H.
Windy Story, A, *John o' the North,* Gm [d′-f′′], Roberton Joanna.
Arrangements: *An Irish Folksinger's Album,* Roberton.

Nevens, David. 1945– WMIC. *See also* App. 1, 2
Genesis, *David Cole,* [a#-g′′], WMIC *Songs from Wales 2.*

Neville, David James. *See* App. 2.

Newman, C. BMIC.

Newman, Frank.
Arrangement:
Sweet Polly Oliver, *Traditional,* D [bb-e′′], BMP.

Newson, George. 1932– BMIC. *See also* App. 2.
Collections: *Four Songs,* Lengnick; *More Songs in Exchange,* Lengnick.
Akrotiri, *Michael Longley,* [mezzo/tenor], Lengnick Exchange.
Be Vigilant, *Leonard Smith,* [soprano/tenor], Lengnick 4 Songs.
Cantus Troili, *Geoffrey Chaucer,* [mezzo/tenor], Lengnick Exchange.
Clock of the Years, The, *Thomas Hardy,* [mezzo/tenor], Lengnick Exchange.
Clouds, *Rupert Brooke,* [mezzo/tenor], Lengnick Exchange.
Crossing the Bar, *Alfred Lord Tennyson,* [mezzo/tenor], Lengnick Exchange.
Drunkard and the Pig, The, *Anon,* [mezzo/tenor], Lengnick Exchange.
End of the Owls, The, *Hans Magnus Enzensberger,* [mezzo/tenor], Lengnick Exchange.
Funeral Banquet of Duc Jean Floressas des Esseintes, The, *George Newson (after Huysmans),* [mezzo/tenor], Lengnick Exchange.
Glass of Beer, A, *James Stephens,* [mezzo/tenor], Lengnick Exchange.
Heaven, *Rupert Brooke,* [mezzo/tenor], Lengnick Exchange.
Hour of Magic, The, *W. H. Davies,* [mezzo/tenor], Lengnick Exchange.
I love a small earth, *Leonard Smith,* [soprano/tenor], Lengnick 4 Songs.
I smiled and turned away, *Leonard Smith,* [soprano/tenor], Lengnick 4 Songs.
Inscription on the Tomb of the Painter Henri Rousseau, *Apollinaire,* [mezzo/tenor], Lengnick Exchange.
Nuer Love Song, *Anon,* [mezzo/tenor], Lengnick Exchange.
Ode to a Nightingale (from), *John Keats,* [mezzo/tenor], Lengnick Exchange.
Old Yew, *Alfred Lord Tennyson,* [mezzo/tenor], Lengnick Exchange.
One day I wrote her name upon the strand, *Edmund Spenser,* [mezzo/tenor], Lengnick Exchange.
Richard Jefferies, His Invocation, *George Newson (after Jefferies),* [mezzo/tenor], Lengnick Exchange.
River, The, *Leonard Smith,* [soprano/tenor], Lengnick 4 Songs.

Tall Nettles, *Edward Thomas*, [mezzo/tenor], Lengnick Exchange.
Walking Song, *Marie Scott*, [mezzo/tenor], Lengnick Exchange.

Nicholas, Jeremy.
Funny you should say that, *Jeremy Nicholas*, [voice], Novello.
Place Settings, *Jeremy Nicholas,* D, [d′-d′′(f′′#)], Novello *Sarah's Encores*.
Usherettes Blues, *Jeremy Nicholas*, E♭ [b♭-f′′)], Novello *Sarah's Encores*.

Nicholson, George. 1949– BMIC.

Nieman, Alfred. 1913–1997. BMIC.
Collections: *Three Chinese Songs*, S&B.
How goes the night, *Shih King* tr. *Waddell*, [c′-g′′], S&B 3 Chinese, Thames *Century 3*.
Morning glory, The, *Confucius* tr. *Waddell*, [d′-g′′](f), S&B 3 Chinese.
Sailing Homeward, *Anon* tr. *Waley*, [e′b-f′′#], S&B 3 Chinese.

Noble, Harold. 1903–
Aran Homing Song, *Harold Noble*, D [a-d′′], B&H.
Ballad of Semmerwater, The, *William Watson*, Cm [g#-f′′], Lengnick.
Hebridean Night Song, *Harold Noble*, E [b-e′′], B&H.
Johnny, *Anon*, G [d′-e′′](f), Lengnick.
Naples Bay, *Arthur Symons*, D♭ [b♭-e′′], Lengnick.
Road of Evening, The, *Walter de la Mare*, F [d′-f′′#], Lengnick.
Arrangement:
Maid of Bunclody, The, *Irish Street Ballad,* E♭ [e′♭-f′′], B&H.

Noble, Thomas **Tertius.** 1867–1953.
O sweet content, *Thomas Dekker*, E [e′-f′′#], Banks.

Northcote, Sydney.
While two are one, BMP.
Arrangement:
O dear, what can the matter be, *Anon, 18th cent.,* [d′-f′′], BMP.

Northcott, Bayan Peter. 1940– *See* App. 2.

Norton, Frederic.
Cobbler's Song, *Oscar Asche,* G [b′-d′′](m), IMP *Parlour Songs*.

Novello, Ivor (David Ivor Davies). 1893–1951. *See also* Chappell.
Collections: *From Distant Lands* (Edward Lockton), B&H; *Valley of Rainbows*, *The* (Edward Teschemacher), B&H.
If, *Edward Teschemacher*, Cm [c′-f′′] B&H *Ballad Album 2*.
Little Damozel, The, *Fred. E. Weatherly*, G [d′-a′′], B&H; E♭, F, D, B&H.
Little One, *J. Y. Bailey,* D, B&H.
Megan, *Fred. E. Weatherly*, F, B&H; G, A, B&H.
Valley, The, *Edward Teschemacher,* C [e′-g′′]B&H.

Noyes, Brian Edward. WMIC.

Nyman, Michael. 1944– *See also* App. 1, 2.
Ariel Songs (cycle), *Shakespeare*, [e′b-b′′#](f), Chester.
I am an unusual thing, *W. A. Mozart* tr. *Anon*, [contralto], Chester.
Tich, *Pat Hutchins,* [voice], Chester.

O

O'Brien, Catherine.
Space and Beauty, *Margaret Ormiston,* [f′-f′′], BMP.

O'Connor, Frederick.
Old House, The, *Frederick O'Connor,* F [c′-f′′], Cramer; A♭, Cramer.

Oldham, Arthur William. 1926–
Collections: *Commandment of Love, The,* B&H; *Five Chinese Lyrics,* Novello.
    All vanities forsake, *Richard Rolle,* D [d′-f′′#], B&H Commandment.
    Fishing, *Chinese* tr. *E. D. Edwards,* [c′#-g′′], Thames *Century 3,* Novello 5 Chinese.
    Gentle wind, A, *Fu Hsüan* tr. *Arthur Waley,* F [c′#-a′′], Novello 5 Chinese.
    Herd Boy's Song, The, *Chinese* tr. *E. D. Edwards,* E [d′-g′′], Novello 5 Chinese.
    Ihesu God's Son, *Richard Rolle,* B [f′-a′′b], B&H Commandment.
    Lo, leman sweet, now may thou see, *Richard Rolle,* [d′-f′′#], B&H Commandment.
    My sang is in sighing, *Richard Rolle,* G [d′-g′′], B&H Commandment.
    O Lord right dear, *Richard Rolle,* C [f′-g′′], B&H Commandment.
    Pedlar of Spells, The, *Lu Yu* tr. *Arthur Waley,* A [c′#-a′′], Thames *Century 3,* Novello 5 Chinese.
    Under the Pondweed, *Chinese* tr. *Helen Waddell,* [c′-a′′], Novello 5 Chinese.
    Unkind man give keep til me, *Richard Rolle,* Cm [e′-b′′b], B&H Commandment.

Oliver, Stephen. 1950-1992.
    Running back for more, Novello.

O'Neill, Norman. 1875–1934.
Collections: (*Five Rondels,* Breitkopf); *Songs from the Fairy Play 'Through the Green Door'* (M. Vernon), BMP.
    Birds (cycle), Cramer.
    Blossom Songs, *Japanese* tr. *S. Kimura,* G [d′-g′′#], Cramer.
    Golden Hour of Noon, The, *Ashley Dukes,* Cramer.
    Home of Mine, *Betty Haddon,* F [f′-g′′], Cramer.
    I have a flaunting air, *Ashley Dukes,* G [d′-g′′], Cramer.
    Jewels, *Herbert Asquith,* Cm [d′-f′′](m), B&H.
    (Lilacs are in bloom, The, *George Moore,* E [e′-e′′], Breitkopf 5 Rondels.)
    (Lovely Isle, The, *Anon,* Eb [c′-f′′], Breitkopf 5 Rondels.)
    May Lilies, *E. Rutter Leatham,* Cramer.
    Musette, *Anon* tr. *Rosa Newmarch,* A [e′-a′′], Cramer.
    Norse Lullaby, A, *Eugene Field,* Em [d′(b)-g′′], B&H.
    On a grey day, *E. Temple Thurston,* F [f′-a′′], Cramer; Db, Cramer.
    (Rondeau, *W. E. Henley,* D [b-e′′], Breitkopf 5 Rondels.)
    (Roundel of Rest, A, *Arthur Symons,* C [c′-e′′], Breitkopf 5 Rondels.)
    Song of Lucius, The, *Shakespeare,* [d′-f′′(e′′)], BMP.
    Warrior Lover, The, *William Watson,* Cm [c′-f′′](m), Schott.
    When May walks by, *Betty Haddon,* Eb [e′b-a′′b], Cramer.
    With Strawberries, *W. E. Henley,* F [d′b-f′′], Breitkopf 5 Rondels.)

Openshaw, John.
    Love sends a little gift of roses, *Leslie Leonard Cooke,* Eb [d′-f′′], IMP *Parlour Songs.*

Orchard, W. Arundell.
Collection: *Three Troubadour Songs,* BMP.
    Return of Summer, The, *Anon,* tr. *Jethro Bithell,* [d′-g′′], BMP 3 Troubadour.
    Serenade, *Anon,* tr. *Jethro Bithell,* [e′b-a′′b], BMP 3 Troubadour.
    Winter, *Anon,* tr. *Jethro Bithell,* [e′-b′′b], BMP 3 Troubadour.

Orr, Buxton. 1924–1997. BMIC; SMIC. *See also* App. 2.
Collections: *Eight Songs from the Yuan,* [counter-tenor], SMIC; *Songs of Childhood,* [medium], SMIC.
    Ballad of Mr and Mrs Discobolos, The, *Edward Lear,* [c′-a′′](m), Kunzelmann/SMIC.
    Ten Types of Hospital Visitor, SMIC.

Orr Charles Wilfrid. 1893–1976.
Collections: *Cycle of Songs from 'A Shropshire Lad',* Chester; *Five Songs from A Shropshire Lad,* Roberton; *Four Songs for High Voice,* BMP; *Three Songs from 'A Shropshire Lad',* Chester; *Two Seventeenth Century Poems,* Roberton; *Two Songs from A Shropshire Lad,* Chester.
    Along the field, *A. E. Housman,* Em [b-e′′](m), Chester Cycle.
    Bahnhofstrasse, *James Joyce,* G [e′-g′′], BMP 4 Songs.
    Carpenter's Son, The, *A. E. Housman,* Dm [e′b-a′′](m), Chester.
    Earl of Bristol's Farewell, The, *John Digby,* E [c′#-e′′](m), Roberton Two 17th Century.
    Farewell to barn and stack and tree, *A. E. Housman,* Fm [bb-f′′](m), Chester Cycle.
    Hughley Steeple, *A. E. Housman,* F [bb-f′′](m), Chester Cycle.
    Hymn Before Sleep, *Prudentius,* tr. *Helen Waddell,* G [b-e′′], Roberton.

In valleys green and still, *A. E. Housman*, E♭ [b♭-g″], Roberton.
Into my heart, *A. E. Housman*, F [c′-f″](m), Chester 3 Songs.
Is my team ploughing? *A. E. Housman*, [d′-g″](m), Roberton 5 Songs.
Isle of Portland, The, *A. E. Housman*, E♭ [c′#-e″](m), Chester.
Lads in their hundreds, The, *A. E. Housman*, F [c′-a″](m), Roberton.
Lent Lily, The, *A. E. Housman*, F [c′-f″](m), Chester Cycle.
Loveliest of trees, *A. E. Housman*, Fm [d′b-f″], Chester 2 Songs.
Oh fair enough are sky and plain, *A. E. Housman*, F [c′-e″#](m), Chester Cycle.
Oh see how thick, *A. E. Housman*, E [c′#-g″#](m), Chester 3 Songs.
Oh, when I was in love with you, *A. E. Housman*, Gm [d′-f″](m), Roberton 5 Songs.
On your midnight pallet lying, *A. E. Housman*, Dm [d′-g″](m), Roberton 5 Songs.
Plucking the Rushes, *Chinese* tr. *Arthur Waley*, Bm [b-f″#], Chester.
Requiem, *Anon* tr. *Helen Waddell*, A♭ [e′b-a″b], BMP 4 Songs.
Silent Noon, *D. G. Rossetti*, E [c′#-e″#], Chester.
Since thou, O fondest and truest, *Robert Bridges*, D♭ [d′-b″b], BMP 4 Songs.
Soldier from the wars returning, *A. E. Housman*, D [A-d′](m), Roberton.
This time of year, *A. E. Housman*, G [d′-f″#](m), Roberton 5 Songs.
Time of Roses, The, *Thomas Hood*, B [d′#-g″#], BMP 4 Songs.
Tis time I think by Wenlock Town, *A. E. Housman*, G [e′-f″#-], Chester 2 Songs.
Tryste Noel, *Louise Imogen Guiney*, Cm [c′-g″], Roberton.
Westward on the high-hilled plains, *A. E. Housman*, G [c′#-a″](m), Chester 3 Songs.
When I was one-and-twenty, *A. E. Housman*, Dm [d′-g″](m), Chester.
When I watch the living meet, *A. E. Housman*, Fm [c′b-f″](m), Chester Cycle.
When smoke stood up from Ludlow, *A. E. Housman*, E [b-e″](m), Chester Cycle.
When the lad for longing sighs, *A. E. Housman*, E [d′-g″#], Chester.
Whenas I wake, *Patrick Hannay*, E [e′-e″](m), Roberton Two 17th Century.
While summer on is stealing, *Helen Waddell*, D [d′-e″](m), Roberton.
With rue my heart is laden, *A. E. Housman*, Bm [d′-f″#](m), Roberton 5 Songs.

Orr, Robin. (Robert Kemsley). 1909– BMIC; SMIC. *See also* App. 1, 2.
Collections: *Four Romantic Songs,* [Helen Waddell], [tenor], SMIC; *Kelvin Series of Scots Songs,* SMIC/(Bayley & Ferguson); *Seven Traditional Scots Airs,* SMIC; *Three Chinese Songs,* BMP.
Little cart, The, *Ch'en Tzü-lung,* tr. *Arthur Waley,* [f′-e″b], SMIC, BMP Chinese.
Pastoral, *Ogden Nash,* SMIC.
The Seagull and the Eagull, *Ogden Nash,* SMIC.
Plucking the Rushes, *Chinese, late 6th cent.* tr. *Arthur Waley,* [c′#-d″], SMIC, BMP Chinese.
Tell me now, *Wang Chi,* tr. *Arthur Waley,* [c′#-g″], SMIC, BMP Chinese.

Osborne, Nigel. 1948– *See* App. 2.

Oswald, James. 1711–1769.
Self Banished, The, *Edmund Waller*, Em [e′-g″], Thames (Copley & Reitan) *Gentleman's Magazine*.

Owen, Morfydd. 1891–1918.
Collections: *Early Songs,* BMP; *Four Flower Songs,* WMIC; *Selected Songs,* BMP.
Daisy's Song, *John Keats*, D [d′-f″#], WMIC 4 Flower.
Foredoomed, *Philip Bourke Marston*, [c′#-f″#], WMIC.
God made a lovely garden, *Mabel Spence*, D♭ [d′b-g″#], WMIC 4 Flower.
He prayeth best who loveth best, *S. T. Coleridge*, G♭ [g′b-g″b], BMP Selected.
Impenitent, *Ethel Newman*, B♭ [f′-e″], B&H.
In Cradle Land, *Eos Gwalia*, G [g′-g″], BMP Selected.
Infant Joy, *William Blake*, [e′-f″#], WMIC.
Irish Lullaby, An, *Anon*, G [g′-g″](f), BMP Selected.
Jesus, tender saviour, *Anon*, A♭ [a′b-f″], BMP Selected.
Lamb, The, *William Blake*, [c′-g″], WMIC.
Noon-tide Lullaby, A, *Ethel Newman*, A♭ [g′b-g″b(a″b)], BMP Selected.
Orbits, *Richard le Gallienne*, Gm [e′b-f″], BMP Early.
(Patrick's your boy, *Ethel Newman*, Am [c′-e″(d″)], B&H; Bm, B&H.
Pippa's Song, *Robert Browning*, F [f′-f″#], BMP Early.
Serenade, A, *Anon*, D♭ [f′-a″b], BMP Early.
Shepherd's Love Song, *A. D. Edwards,* A♭ [f′-a″b], B&H.
Slumber Song of the Madonna, A, *Alfred Noyes*, G [c′-a″b], WMIC, Gwynn.
Song of Sorrow, A, *William Blake*, [f′-g″], WMIC.

Speedwell, *Atwyth Eversley*, Em [e´-g´´#], WMIC 4 Flower.
Spring, *William Blake*, F [c´-f´´], WMIC *Songs from Wales 1*, BMP.
To Our Lady of Sorrows, *Wilfred Hinton*, [d´#-g´´#], WMIC.
To Violets, *Robert Herrick*, Fm [f´-f´´], WMIC 4 Flower.
Weeping Babe, The, *Katherine Tynan*, Em [g´-e´´](f), BMP Selected.
When I came at last to Ludlow, *A. E. Housman*, B♭m [f´-g´´♭], BMP Selected.
William, *Eric Hiller*, Fm [f´-f´´](f), BMP Selected.

P

Pain, J. J.
Arrangement:
    Gentle Maiden, The, *J. J. Pain,* F [f´-f´´], IMP *Parlour Songs*.

Paintal, Priti. *See* App. 2.

Painter, Christopher William. *See* App. 1.

Papastávrou, Krinió. *See also* App. 2.
Collection: *Four Greek Canticles,* Bardic; *Seven Songs for a Child*, Bardic; *Three Mesolonghi Songs,* Bardic.
    Adoréd Spring, *Krinió Papastávrou*, [d´-f´´#], Bardic 7 Songs.
    Anemone, *Krinió Papastávrou*, [d´-f´´], Bardic 7 Songs.
    Buzz, buzz, buzz, *Krinió Papastávrou*, [d´-e´´], Bardic 7 Songs.
    By the side of the well, *Alexandra Placotari* tr. *Charles Spinks*, [d´#-b´´], Bardic Mesolonghi.
    Father Time, *Krinió Papastávrou*, [d´-e´´], Bardic 7 Songs.
    Give me a place where I might stand, *Alexandra Placotari* tr. *Charles Spinks,* [c´-a´´], Bardic Mesolonghi.
    Icon from Abroad, *Krinió Papastávrou*, [d´-e´´], Bardic 7 Songs.
    Kyrie, *Anon* tr. *Krinió Papastávrou*, [G-c´](m), Bardic 4 Greek.
    Mother of Mesolonghi, The, *Alexandra Placotari* tr. *Charles Spinks*, [e´♭-b´´♭], Bardic Mesolonghi.
    O Christ, Saviour of the World, *Anon* tr. *Krinió Papastávrou*, [F-e´](m), Bardic 4 Greek.
    Off to School, *Krinió Papastávrou*, [d´-g´´], Bardic 7 Songs.
    Praise God, *Anon* tr. *Krinió Papastávrou*, [E-e´](m), Bardic 4 Greek.
    Three Entities, I glorify, *Anon* tr. *Krinió Papastávrou*, [F#-f´#](m), Bardic 4 Greek.
    Wheel of Life, The, *Krinió Papastávrou*, [e´-g´´], Bardic 7 Songs.

Parke, Dorothy. 1904–1990.
Collection: *By Winding Roads* [John Irvine], Roberton.
    Falling of the Leaves, The, *W. B. Yeats*, F#m [e´♭-f´´#], Roberton.
    House and the Road, The, *Josephine Peabody*, F [c´-f´´], Roberton.
    If, *John Irvine*, Am [e´-e´´♭], Roberton Winding Roads, Roberton (*with* Old man from Kilkenny, *and* Over the hills).
    Kilkeel, *Richard Rowley*, Fm [c´-e´´♭], Roberton.
    (Lord is my refuge, The, *Psalm 91*, B&H.)
    Moon Magic, *John Irvine*, A [c´-e´´], Novello.
    Old Man from Kilkenny, The, *John Irvine*, Dm [d´-d´], Roberton Winding Roads, Roberton (*with* If, *and* Over the hills).
    Over the hills and far away, *John Irvine*, G [d´-d´´], Roberton Winding Roads, Roberton (*with* If, *and* Old man from Kilkenny).
    Road to Ballydare, The, *John Irvine*, Cm [c´-e´´♭], Roberton.
    (Sing heigh-ho, *Charles Kingsley*, [d´-e´´], Elkin.)
    Song in Exile, *John Irvine*, E♭ [b♭-e´´♭], Roberton.
    (Song of Good Courage, A, *Gunby Hadath*, E♭, B&H.)
    St Columba's Poem on Derry, tr. *Dr Sigerson*, E♭ [e´♭-c´´], Cramer.
    (To the Sailors, *John Irvine*, A♭, B&H.)
    Wee Hughie, *Elizabeth Shane*, C [c´-e´´], Roberton; E♭, Roberton.
    Wish, The, *Winifred Letts*, E♭ [e´♭-e´´♭], Roberton.

Parrott, Horace **Ian.** 1916– BMIC; WMIC.
Collections: *Eastern Wisdom*, Brunton; *Two Thoughtful Songs*, Brunton.
    Absence, *John Donne? John Hoskyns?* Am [e´-f´´](m), Welsh Music *Songs from Wales 1*.

Flamingoes, *Jane Wilson*, [c′#-e′′], Brunton.
Fly, The, *William Blake*, [d′#-g′′], Brunton 2 Thoughtful.
I heard a linnet courting, *Robert Bridges*, A [c′#-f′′#(e′′)], Lengnick.
In Phæacia, *James Elroy Flecker*, [c′#-a′′], Lengnick.
Leaves, *Elizabeth Ward*, [b-g′′], Lengnick.
Song of Joy, *W. H. Davies*, [d′-c′′′#(a′′)], Brunton.
Thee, God, I come from, *Gerard Manley Hopkins*, [d′#-a′′(g′′)], Brunton 2 Thoughtful.

Parry, Sir Charles **Hubert** Hastings. 1848–1918. *See also* App. 1.
Collections: (*English Lyrics Sets 1-12*, Novello); *English Lyrics Sets 1, 2*, Masters; *Musica Britannica 49* S&B (edited with introduction Geoffrey Bush); *Seven Songs for High Voice*, S&B (edited Geoffrey Bush); *Three Odes of Anacreon*, S&B; *Twenty English Lyrics Books 1, 2*, Thames (selected and introduced by Michael Pilkington).
And yet I love her till I die, *Anon*, G [c′#-e′′](m), S&B MB 49, (Novello English 6).
Armida's Garden, *Mary Coleridge*, E♭ [d′-g′′], S&B 7 Songs, MB 49, (Novello English 9).
(At the hour the long day ends, *A. P. Graves*, E♭ [d′-e′′♭](m), Novello English 6.)
Away, away, ye men of rules, *Anacreon* tr. *Thomas Moore*, Dm [A-d′](m), S&B 3 Odes.
(Blackbird, The, *A. P. Graves*, G [c′#-e′′], Novello English 11.)
Blow, blow, thou winter wind, *Shakespeare*, Em [e′-g′′#](m), S&B 7 Songs, MB 49, Masters/ (Novello) English 2.
Bright star, *Keats*, A♭ [e′♭-a′′♭](m), Thames *Century 3*, S&B MB 49, (Novello English 4).
(Child and the Twilight, The, *Langdon Elwyn Mitchell*, F [c′-g′′], Novello English 10.)
Concerning Love, *Samuel Daniel*, Cm [c′-e′′♭], B&H.
Contrast, A, *Anon*, Gm [d′-d′′], B&H.
Crabbed age and youth, *Shakespeare?* E♭ [e′♭-g′′♭(a′′♭)](f), Thames 20 Book 2, Novello, (Novello English 5).
Dirge in Woods, *George Meredith*, G [g-e′′′], S&B, MB 49, *Recitalist 2*, (Novello English 8).
Dream Pedlary, *Thomas Lovell Beddoes*, B♭ [c′-g′′♭], S&B 7 Songs, MB 49, (Novello English 12).
Fairy Town, A, (St Andrews), *Mary Coleridge*, G [c′#-g′′], Thames 20 Book 2, (Novello English 9).
(Faithful Lover, The, *A. P. Graves*, D [c′#-e′′](m), Novello English 11.)
Farewell, thou art too dear for my possessing, *Shakespeare*, E♭ [d′-g′′(a′′♭)](m), S&B MB 49.
Fill me, boy, as deep a draught, *Anacreon* tr. *Thomas Moore*, F [A-f′′(e′♭)](m), S&B 3 Odes.
(Follow a shadow, *Ben Jonson*, G [b-d′′](m), Novello English 7.)
From a City Window, *Langdon Elwyn Mitchell*, D [b(c′#)-g′′], Thames *Century 1*, (Novello English 10).
(Girl to Her Glass, A, *Julian Sturgis*, D [e′-g′′](f), Novello English 5.)
Golden hues of life are fled, *Anacreon* tr. *Thomas Moore*, Cm [G-e′♭](m), S&B 3 Odes.
(Gone were but the winter cold, *Alan Cunningham*, Cm [c′-g′′], Novello English 10.)
Good night, *Percy Bysshe Shelley*, B♭ [e′♭-g′′], S&B MB 49, Thames 20 Book 2, Masters/(Novello) English 1.
Grapes, *Julian Sturgis*, F [c′-e′′♭], S&B MB 49, (Novello English 8).
Hymn for Aviators, A, *Mary C. D. Hamilton*, E♭ [d′-e′′♭], B&H; F, G, B&H.
(If I might ride on puissant wing, *Julian Sturgis*, G [c′#-e′′], Novello English 11.)
If thou would'st ease thine heart, *Thomas Lovell Beddoes*, G [c′#-d′′#(e′′)], S&B MB 49, Thames 20 Book 1, (Novello English 3).
Jerusalem, *William Blake*, D [b-e′′], Roberton, Novello, Classical; C (simplified), Roberton.
(Julia, *Robert Herrick*, G [d′-d′′](m), Novello English 7.)
(Laird of Cockpen, The, *Lady Caroline Nairn*, F [g-d′′], Novello.)
Lay a garland on my hearse, *John Fletcher*, Gm [d′-f′′](f), S&B MB 49, (Novello English 5).
Looking Backward, *Julian Sturgis*, A♭ [b-e′′♭], Thames 20 Book 1, (Novello English 8).
(Love and Laughter, *Arthur Gray Butler*, F [d′-g′′♭], Novello English 5.)
Love is a bable, *Anon*, E♭ [c′-e′′♭](m), S&B MB 49, Thames 20 Book 1, Schirmer *2nd Baritone*, (Novello English 6).
(Lover's Garland, A, *A. P. Graves*, G [d′-d′′](m), Novello English 6.)
(Maid of Elsinore, *Harold Boulton*, E♭ [b-e′′♭], Novello.)
Maiden, The, *Mary Coleridge*, A♭ [e′♭-a′′♭], Thames 20 Book 2, (Novello English 9).
Marian, *George Meredith*, F [c′-e′′♭](m), Thames 20 Book 1, (Novello English 8).
Merry Margaret, *John Skelton*, F [c′-f′′(e′′♭)], Banks, B&H.
(Moment of Farewell, A, *Julian Sturgis*, D [f′-a′′(g′′#)], Novello English 10.)
My heart is like a singing bird, *Christina Rossetti*, F [c′-a′′](f), S&B 7 Songs, MB 49, Novello, Schirmer *2nd Soprano*, (Novello English 10).
My true love hath my heart, *Philip Sidney*, F [d′-f′′](f), S&B MB 49, Masters/(Novello) English 1.

Nightfall in Winter, *Langdon Elwyn Mitchell*, Em [c′-e′′(e′′b)], S&B MB 49, Thames 20 Book 1, (Novello English 8).
No longer mourn for me, *Shakespeare*, Fm [e′b(c′)-a′′b], S&B MB 49, Masters/(Novello) English 2.
O mistress mine, *Shakespeare*, F [d′-g′′](m), Masters/(Novello) English 2.
O never say that I was false of heart, *Shakespeare*, Eb [bb-f′′b], S&B MB 49, (Novello English 7).
(O world, O life, O time, *Percy Bysshe Shelley*, F# [c′#-a′′], Novello English 12.)
(Of all the torments, *William Walsh*, G [d′-d′′](m), Novello English 3.)
On a day, alack the day, *Shakespeare*, Gm [c′-e′′b], Banks, B&H.
On a time the amorous Silvy, *Anon*, Eb [bb-e′′b(g′′)], S&B MB 49, (Novello English 7).
(One golden thread, *Julia Chatterton*, D [c′#-f′′#], Novello English 11.)
(One silent night of late, *Robert Herrick*, F [c′-g′′], Novello English 10.)
Poet's Song, The, *Alfred Lord Tennyson*, E [b-e′′], Roberton; *D, F,* Roberton.
Proud Maisie, *Walter Scott*, Eb [d′-f′′], S&B 7 Songs, MB 49, (Novello English 5).
Rosaline, *Thomas Lodge*, Eb [d′-a′′b](m), S&B 7 Songs, MB 49, (Novello English 12).
Sea Dirge, A, *Shakespeare*, Fm [c′-e′′b], B&H.
Shall I compare thee to a summer's day? *Shakespeare*, Eb [e′b-a′′b](m), S&B MB 49, Thames 20 Book 2.
She is my love beyond all thought, *A. P. Graves*, Eb [b-e′′b](m), Thames 20 Book 1, (Novello English 11).
Sleep, *Julian Sturgis*, Db [ab-e′′b], S&B MB 49, (Novello English 7).
(Sound of hidden music, The, *Julia Chatterton*, G [c′#-g′′], Novello English 12.)
(Spirit of the Spring, The, *A. P. Graves*, Ebm [c′b-e′′b](m), Novello English 11.)
Spring Song, A, *Shakespeare*, G [d′-g′′(e′′)], B&H *Heritage 1,* B&H.
Stray Nymph of Dian, A, *Julian Sturgis*, F [e′b-a′′b](f), S&B MB 49, (Novello English 5).
Take O take those lips away, *Shakespeare*, Bb [c′-g′′], S&B MB 49, Thames 20 Book 2, Masters/(Novello) English 2.
(There, *Mary Coleridge*, G [b-g′′′], Novello English 9.)
There be none of beauty's daughters, *Lord Byron*, Bb [f′-a′′](m), S&B MB 49, (Novello English 4).
(Thine eyes still shined for me, *Ralph Waldo Emerson*, D [e′-f′′#](m), Novello English 4.)
Three Aspects, *Mary Coleridge*, Eb [c′-a′′b], Novello English 9.)
Through the Ivory Gate, *Julian Sturgis*, G [b-d′′](m), Thames *Century 2*, (Novello English 3).
To Althea, from Prison, *Richard Lovelace*, Db [bb-e′′b](m), S&B MB 49, Thames 20 Book 1, (Novello English 3).
To Blossoms, *Robert Herrick*, Ab [d′-g′′], S&B MB 49, Thames 20 Book 2, (Novello English 12).
To Lucasta, on Going to the Wars, *Richard Lovelace*, F [c′-e′′](m), S&B MB 49, (Novello English 3).
Under the greenwood tree, *Shakespeare*, G [c′-e′′](m), S&B MB 49, (Novello English 6).
Weep you no more, sad fountains, *Anon*, Gm [d′-g′′], S&B 7 Songs, MB 49, *Recitalist 1;* (Novello English 4).
Welsh Lullaby, A, *Cierog* tr. *E. O. Jones*, F [f′-f′′](f), S&B MB 49, (Novello English 5).
(What part of dread eternity, *C. H. H. Parry?* Em [b-e′′b], Novello English 11.)
When comes my Gwen, *Mynydog* tr. *E. O. Jones*, Eb [d′-e′′b](m), S&B MB 49, Thames 20 Book 1, (Novello English 6).
When icicles hang by the wall, *Shakespeare*, Bb [f′-g′′], Masters/(Novello) English 2.
When in disgrace with fortune and men's eyes, *Shakespeare*, Em [d′#-g′′](m), S&B MB 49.
(When lovers meet again, *Langdon Elwyn Mitchell*, D [e′-g′′], Novello English 4.)
(When the dew is falling, *Julia Chatterton*, Gb [d′b-g′′b], Novello English 12.)
(When the sun's great orb, *H. Warner*, Fm [c′-a′′], Novello English 12.)
When to the sessions of sweet silent thought, *Shakespeare*, D [d′-g′′](m), S&B MB 49, Thames 20 Book 2.
When we two parted, *Lord Byron*, Eb [d′-g′′](m), Thames 20 Book 2, (Novello English 4).
(Whence, *Julian Sturgis*, D [c′#(d′)-e′′b], Novello English 8.)
Where shall the lover rest? *Walter Scott*, Eb [e′b-a′′(g′′)], S&B MB 49, Masters/(Novello) English 1.
(Whether I live, *Mary Coleridge*, Ab [c′-g′′], Novello English 9.)
Why art thou slow? *Philip Massinger*, Fm [b-g′′b](f), S&B MB 49, (Novello English 11).
Why so pale and wan, fond lover? *John Suckling,* G [c′#-e′′](m), S&B MB 49, Thames 20 Book 1, (Novello English 3).
Why so pale and wan, fond lover? *John Suckling,* G [d′-g′′](m), S&B MB 49.
Willow, willow, willow, *Shakespeare*, Em [d′-g′′], S&B MB 49, Thames 20 Book 2, Masters/(Novello) English 1.
(Witches' Wood, The, *Mary Coleridge*, Gm [c′-g′′], Novello English 9.)

Ye little birds that sit and sing, *Thomas Heywood*, A [d'#-d''](m), S&B MB 49, (Novello English 7).
Arrangement:
Noble of air, *Anon* tr. *Paul England*, E♭ [c'-e''♭], B&H.

Parry, Enid. WMIC.

Parry, Joseph. 1841–1903.
Knight, The, [baritone], Snell.
Make new friends but keep the old, G [soprano/tenor], Snell; E♭ [contralto/baritone].
Mother and Child, The, *Morgan Samuel*, [tenor/mezzo/soprano], Snell.
My Blodwen, my darling, [tenor], Snell.
Myfanwy, G [medium], Snell; B♭ [high], Snell.
O ye that love the Lord, [contralto/baritone], Snell.
Our Country's Banner, [tenor/baritone], Snell.
Pleasure-boat on the Niagara, The, [baritone], Snell.
Sailor's Wife, The, *R. Davies,* tr. *H. M. Edwards,* [mezzo/contralto/baritone], Snell.
There will always be Wales, C [contralto/baritone], Snell; E [soprano/tenor], Snell.

Parry, W. H. WMIC.
Collection: *Twelve Traditional Rhymes* [soprano], WMIC, (Elkin).
Bed in Summer, *Robert Louis Stevenson,* [soprano], WMIC.
Billy Boy, *Dorothy King,* [soprano], WMIC, (Curwen).
In the Wood, *Eileen Mathias,* [soprano], WMIC, (A & C Black).
One, two three, *Traditional,* [soprano], WMIC, (Paxton).
Weathers, *Thomas Hardy,* [soprano], WMIC, (James Pass).

Parsons, Robert. *c.*1530–1572.
In youthly years, *Richard Edwards*, Dm [c'-c''](m), S&B (Greer) *Manuscript 1.*

Paterson, Charles.
Rejected Lover, The, [high], Brunton.
Sweet and Twenty, *William Shakespeare*, [high], Brunton.

Patterson, Robert H.
Curtains now are drawn, The, *Thomas Hardy*, E♭ [c'-e''♭](m), Thames *Hardy Songbook.*

Payne, Anthony Edward. 1936–
Adlestrop, *Edward Thomas*, [a-g''], Chester.
Evening Land, [soprano], Chester.

Paynter, John. 1931– *See* App. 2.

Peache, D. A.
Ancient Rune of Hospitality, An, *Anon*, [d'♭-e''♭], BMP.

Peel, Gerald **Graham.** 1877–1937. *See also* B&H, Chappell, Cramer.
Collections: *Country-Lover, The,* Classical; *Songs of a Shropshire Lad,* Classical.
April, *William Watson*, A♭ [a'♭-c'''(b''♭)], Classical Country-Lover.
Early Morning, The, *Hilaire Belloc*, B♭ [e'♭-b''♭], Classical Country-Lover.
(In summertime on Bredon, *A. E. Housman*, E♭ [b♭-e''♭](m), Chappell *English Recital 1*; F, Chappell.)
In the highlands, *R. L. Stevenson*, D♭ [b♭(d'♭)-f''], B&H *Heritage 1.*
Lake Isle of Innisfree, The, *W. B. Yeats,* A [d'#-a''], Classical Country-Lover.
Little Waves of Breffny, The, *Eva Gore-Booth*, B [d'#-g''#], Classical Country-Lover.
Loveliest of trees, *A. E. Housman*, E♭ [b♭-f''], Classical Songs of a Shropshire Lad.
Reveillé, *A. E. Housman*, D [b-f''#], Classical Songs of a Shropshire Lad.
Say lad, have you things to do, *A. E. Housman*, D [b-f''#], Classical Songs of a Shropshire Lad.
Sorrow and Spring, *St John Lucas*, B♭ [f'-g''], B&H *Heritage 2,* A♭, B&H.
Wander-Thirst, *Gerald Gould*, E♭ [d'-b''♭(a'')], Classical Country-Lover.
When the lad for longing sighs, *A. E. Housman*, G [c'-d''], Classical Songs of a Shropshire Lad.
Wind of the Western Sea, *Alfred Lord Tennyson*, D♭ [b♭-f''], Schirmer *1st Mezzo*, (Chappell *English Recital 2*; C, E♭, Chappell.)

Peerson, Martin. c.1527–1651.
    Ah, were she pityful as she is fair, *Anon,* G [d′-d′′], BMP *W&W 4.*
    At her fair hands, *Anon,* Gm [c′-d′′], BMP *W&W 6.*
    Now Robin, laugh and sing, *Anon,* C [c′-c′′], BMP *W&W 4.*
    O precious time, *Anon,* Am [e′-e′′], BMP *W&W 4.*

Pender, Tom.
    Fidele, *William Shakespeare,* Em [e′-a′′b], BMP.
    Shall I compare thee? *William Shakespeare,* F [e′-a′′], BMP.

Penny, Martin.
    Old Gaelic Rune, *Traditional,* [d′-g′′], BMP.
    There was a one, *Dorothy Parker,* D [a-e′′b], BMP.

Perrin, Susan F.
    They evermore do sing, BMP.

Pert, Morris. 1947–
    Four Japanese Verses (cycle), tr. Bownas & Thwaite, [c′-f′′](f), Weinberger.

Peterkin, Norman. 1886–1982. *See also* App. 2.
Collection: *Eight Songs,* Thames (introduction Alastair Chisholm).
    Advice to girls, *Herbert A. Giles,* F#m [c′#(b)-f′′#(e′′)], Thames 8 Songs, BMP.
    All suddenly the wind comes soft, *Rupert Brooke,* F [d′-f′′], BMP.
    Bees' Song, The, *Walter de la Mare,* Em [c′-f′′#], BMP.
    Chestnut blossom, The, *Wilfrid Gibson,* [c′#-e′′], Thames 8 Songs, BMP.
    Dubbuldideery, *Walter de la Mare,* Em [b-f′′], BMP.
    Fiddler, The *I. M. Maunder,* Fm [f′-a′′], BMP.
    Galliass, The, *Walter de la Mare,* Em [c′-e′′], BMP.
    Garden of Bamboos, The, *Annamese,* tr. *E. Powys Mathers,* Db [e′b-f′′](f), Thames 8 Songs, BMP.
    Goneril's Lullaby, *Anon,* C, B&H.
    I heard a piper piping, *Seosamh MacCathmhaoèl,* Gm [g′-f′′], OUP, Thames 8 Songs.
    I love the din of beating drums, *Seosamh MacCathmhaoèl,* [d′-f′′#(e′′)](m), Thames 8 Songs, BMP.
    I wish and I wish, *Joseph Campbell,* E [b-e′′], BMP.
    If I be living in Éirinn, *J. P. McCall,* Am [c′#-f′′#], BMP.
    Little Red Hen, The, *J. P. McCall,* Em [b-e′′], BMP.
    My fidil is singing, *Joseph Campbell,* Db [d′b-f′′], BMP.
    Never more, sailor, *Walter de la Mare,* [b-f′′#], BMP.
    Once and there was a young sailor, *Walter de la Mare,* Em [b-f′′#], BMP.
    Palatine's Daughter, The, *Anon* tr. *J. P. McCall,* C#m [b-e′′], BMP.
    Pierrette in memory, *William Griffith,* F#m [e′-f′′], BMP.
    Rune of the Burden of the Tide, *Fiona Macleod,* Am [b-e′′], BMP.
    She's me forgot, *Walter de la Mare,* Am [b-f′′#], BMP.
    Sleep, white love, *Seosamh MacCathmhaoèl,* D [d′-f′′#], Thames 8 Songs, BMP.
    So we'll go no more a-roving, *Lord Byron,* [d′b-d′′], BMP.
    Song of Asano, *John Masefield,* Bbm [d′b-f′′], Thames 8 Songs, BMP.
    Song of Fionula, The, *Fiona Macleod,* Am [c′-e′′], BMP.
    Song of the Secret, The, *Walter de la Mare,* A [e′(c′#)-f′′#(a′′)], BMP.
    Song of the Water Maiden, *Walter de la Mare,* [e′-f′′#](f), Thames 8 Songs, BMP.
    There is a lady sweet and kind, *Anon,* E [c′-f′′#](m), BMP.
    Tide rises, the tide falls, The, *Longfellow* Cm [c′#-g′′], BMP.
    (Why Thomas Cam was Grumpy, *James Stephens,* B&H.)
Arrangement:
    Little wind came blowing, A, *Marie Peterkin,* F [e′-f′′], BMP.

Peters, James.
    I love a life upon the sea, [baritone], Snell.

Philips, John C. *See* App. 2.

Phillips, Julian. WMIC. *See also* App. 2.

Phillips, Montague Fawcett. 1885–1969. *See also* Chappell.
Collections: *Sea Echoes,* [high (given below), low], Classical; *Songs of Joy, Op 24,* [high (given below), low], Classical.

(Crab Apple, *Nancie B. Marsland*, G [e′-a′′], Chappell *English Recital 2.*)
Every Morning, *Nancie B. Marsland*, D [e′-f′′#], Classical Songs of Joy.
If we sailed away, *Nancie B. Marsland*, F [d′-f′′(a′′)], Classical Sea Echoes.
Little Good People, The, *Nancie B. Marsland*, F [e′-a′′], Classical Songs of Joy.
Love's Spell, *Nora C. Usher*, C [d′-g′′], Classical Songs of Joy.
Nightfall at Sea, *Nancie B. Marsland*, E♭ [d′-a′′♭], Classical Sea Echoes.
(Silent Mill, The, *Beryl Cooper*, F [c′-f′′], Chappell *English Recital 1.*)
Sing, joyous bird, *Nora C. Usher*, C [d′-g′′], Classical Songs of Joy, (Chappell *English Recital 1*).
Song of Rosamund (scena), [soprano], Classical.
Waves, *Nancie B. Marsland*, D [d′-a′′], Classical Sea Echoes.
Wind of the Wheat, *Harold Simpson*, Cm [c′-e′′♭], Schirmer *1st Mezzo II*, (Chappell *English Recital 2.*)

Pickard, John.
Collection: *Borders of Sleep, The,* Bardic.
Gallows, The, *Edward Thomas*, [B♭-f′](m), Bardic Borders.
Lights Out, *Edward Thomas*, [B-f′](m), Bardic Borders.
Mill-Water, The, *Edward Thomas*, [B♭-f′](m), Bardic Borders.
No one cares less than I, *Edward Thomas*, [B-f′](m), Bardic Borders.
Out in the dark, *Edward Thomas*, [A-f′](m), Bardic Borders.
Phoenix, The, *after Cynewulf* tr. *R. K. Gordon*, [b-c′′′](f), Bardic.
Rain, *Edward Thomas*, [B♭-f′](m), Bardic Borders.
Sorrows of True Love, The, *Edward Thomas*, [B-f′#](m), Bardic Borders.
Tall Nettles, *Edward Thomas*, [c#-g′](m), Bardic Borders.
Trumpet, The, *Edward Thomas*, [d-f′](m), Bardic Borders.

Pierce, Dora.
Enchantment, The, *Thomas Otway*, A♭ [c′(a♭)-f′′], BMP.

Pierson, Henry Hugo. 1815–1873.
All my heart's thine own, *Anon*, Am [c′-f′′#], S&B (Bush & Temperley) *MB 43*.
Dirge: Fear no more the heat of the sun, *Shakespeare*, Am [g-d′′], S&B (Bush & Temperley) *MB 43*, *Recitalist 4*.
John Anderson, my jo, *Robert Burns*, F#m [c′#-f′′#](f), S&B (Bush & Temperley) *MB 43*.
Love and Grief, *John Fletcher*, F [f′-a′′](m), S&B (Bush & Temperley) *MB 43*.
Those evening bells, *Thomas Moore*, A♭ [e′♭-a′′♭], S&B (Bush & Temperley) *MB 43*.
White Owl, The, *Alfred Lord Tennyson*, Am [c′(a)-e′′], S&B (Bush & Temperley) *MB 43*, *Recitalist 1*.

Piggott, Harry E. ? –1966.
Long ago I went to Rome, *Celia Furse*, [high], Lengnick; [low], Lengnick.

Pike, Lionel. 1939–
Collections: *Encircled by Sea (Three Manx Pictures)*, Lynwood; *Maxims of St Teresa* [Texts from 'The Wisdom of the Spanish Mystics', Stephen Clissold], Lynwood; *Monkey Music*, Lynwood; *Pilgrim Way, The*, Lynwood.
Advice to those practising contemplative prayer, *St Teresa of Avila*, [c-e′′♭](f), Lynwood Maxims.
Ancient Wisdom, *Robin Flower*, [b-g′′#], Lynwood Monkey.
And Death shall have no dominion, *Dylan Thomas*, [a-f′′#(a′′ shouted)](f), Lynwood Pilgrim.
Beatrice's Vision of Eternity, *Dante Alighieri*, [g#-f′′#](f), Lynwood Pilgrim.
Benediction, *St Teresa of Avila*, [c′-g′′](f), Lynwood Maxims.
Blooming of the Flower, The, *Robin Flower*, [b♭-g′′], Lynwood Monkey.
Call, The, *George Herbert*, [a-f′′](f), Lynwood Pilgrim.
Clock, The, *St Teresa of Avila*, [d′-g′′](f), Lynwood Maxims.
Ellan Vannin, ('The Little Island'), *Rosalie Pike*, [c′-g′′], Lynwood Encircled.
En una noche escura, *St John of the Cross*, tr. *Arthur Symons*, [g-f′′](f), Lynwood Pilgrim.
Exhortation of St Teresa to Her Nuns, An, *St Teresa of Avila*, [d′-a′′](f), Lynwood Maxims.
Forest Ball, The, *Robin Flower*, [b♭-g′′], Lynwood Monkey.
Heaven Haven, *Gerard Manley Hopkins*, [b-c′′#](f), Lynwood Pilgrim.
Interior Life, The, *St Teresa of Avila*, [b-g′′](f), Lynwood Maxims.
Love, *St Teresa of Avila*, [c′-f′′](f), Lynwood Maxims.
Lullaby, *Robin Flower*, [c′#-b′′♭], Lynwood Monkey.
Man, *Robin Flower*, [b-f′′#], Lynwood Monkey.
Maxims of St Teresa, *St Teresa of Avila*, [b-g′′](f), Lynwood Maxims.

Mermaid of Purt-le-Murrey, *Anonymous Folk Tale,*[c′-a′′], Lynwood Encircled.
Monkey Day, The, *Robin Flower,* [b♭-g′′], Lynwood Monkey.
Monkey Sailors, The, *Robin Flower,* [e′-g′′], Lynwood Monkey.
Moon Monkey, The, *Robin Flower,* [a#-f′′#], Lynwood Monkey.
Niarbyl Bay, *Rosalie Pike,* [g#-g′′], Lynwood Encircled.
O Lord, Thou hast searched me out, *Psalm 139 vv. 1-11,* [a-f′′](f), Lynwood Pilgrim.
On St John of the Cross, *St Teresa of Avila,* [b-f′′#](f), Lynwood Maxims.
Paripace and Paripale, *Robin Flower,* [b-a′′], Lynwood Monkey.
Parrot, The, *Robin Flower,* [e′-g′′], Lynwood Monkey.
Partridge and Penance, *St Teresa of Avila,* [d′b-f′′](f), Lynwood Maxims.
Picture of a Lover standing before his earthly judges, *Ramon Lull,* [g#-e′′](f), Lynwood Pilgrim.
Pride, *St Teresa of Avila,* [c′-f′′#](f), Lynwood Maxims.
Rebel, The, *Robin Flower,* [c′-a′′], Lynwood Monkey.
Seeking God, *St Teresa of Avila,* [b♭-f′′#](f), Lynwood Maxims.
To a Gentleman who often escorted her on her journeys, *St Teresa of Avila,* [d′-f′′#](f), Lynwood Maxims.
Walsingham, *16th cent, Philip, Earl of Arundel?* [b-f′′#], Lynwood.
Wood beyond the Wood, The, *Robin Flower,* [b♭-g′′#], Lynwood Monkey.

Pilkington, Francis. c.1570–1638.
Collection: *The First Booke of Songs*, S&B (edited Thurston Dart). Only songs available in anthologies are listed individually here. Note that in the following: Pilkington = *English Lute Songs Book 2,* S&B; Keel 1a, 1b and 2a, 2b = *Elizabethan Lovesongs Books 1 and 2* [high, low], B&H.
Diaphenia, *Henry Constable* or *Henry Chettle,* G [d′-d′′](m), 1st Book, Keel 1b, Leonard *Baroque low*; *B♭,* Keel 1a, Leonard *Baroque high* ; *F*, Pilkington.
Down-a-down, thus Phyllis sang, *Thomas Lodge,* G [d′-d′′], 1st Book, Pilkington, Keel 2b; *B♭,* Keel 2a.
Now let her change, *Thomas Campion,* F [e′-f′′](m), 1st Book, Pilkington.
Rest sweet nymphs, *Anon,* Gm [g′-f′′], 1st Book, Pilkington, B&H (Northcote) *Imperial 4*, Leonard *Baroque high; Em,* Leonard *Baroque low.*
Underneath a cypress shade, *Anon,* F [f′-f′′], 1st Book, Keel 1a; *E♭,* Keel 1b.

Pilkington, James Holme. 1856–1916.
Wynken, Blynken and Nod, *Eugene Field,* E♭ [b′b-e′′b], Thames *Century 4.*

Pilkington, Michael. 1928–
Collection: *Four Epigrams and a Prayer*, Thames.
Evening on the Moselle, *Ausonius* tr. *Helen Waddell,* E♭ [b♭-e′′b], Thames *4 Epigrams.*
Li Fu-Jen, *Wu-ti* tr. *Arthur Waley,* [e′b-e′′], Thames *4 Epigrams.*
Love Song, A, *Greek Anthology* tr. *T. F. Higham,* Gm [c′-f′′], Thames *4 Epigrams.*
Night, *Alcman* tr. *H. T. Wade-Grey,* [a-f′′], Thames *4 Epigrams.*
Spouse to the Beloved, The, *William Baldwin,* Am [a-f′′], Thames *4 Epigrams.*

Pilling, Dorothy. *See also* App. 2.
Collection: *Collected Songs*, Forsyth.
Colours, *Rodney Bennett,* D [e′-f′′#], Forsyth *Collected.*
Nod, *Walter de la Mare,* F#m [c′#-a′′(f′′#)], Forsyth *Collected.*
Silver Point, *John Galsworthy,* Bm [d′-g′′], Forsyth *Collected.*
Splendour falls, The, *Alfred Lord Tennyson,* Bm [b-f′′#], Forsyth *Collected.*
Three jolly gentlemen, *Walter de la Mare,* Am [e′-f′′#], Forsyth *Collected.*
Weathers, *Thomas Hardy,* D [d′-a′′], Forsyth *Collected.*

Pinto, George Frederick. 1785–1806.
Eloisa to Abelard, *Alexander Pope,* Dm [d′-g′′](f), S&B (Bush & Temperley) *MB 43.*
From thee, Eliza, I must go, *Robert Burns,* E♭ [d′b-f′′](m), OUP (Roberts) *Tuneful Voice,* S&B (Bush & Temperley) *MB 43.*
Invocation to Nature, *Anon,* A♭ [d′-f′′], OUP (Roberts) *Tuneful Voice,* S&B (Bush and Temperley) *MB 43, Recitalist 2.*
Shepherd lov'd a nymph so fair, A, *Anon,* G [d′-e′′], OUP (Roberts) *Tuneful Voice.*

Pitfield, Thomas Baron. 1903–1999. *See also* App. 2.
Collection: *Recollections*, [medium], Brunton; *Selected Songs*, Forsyth.
Birds about the morning air, *Thomas Pitfield,* G [d′-g′′(a′′)], Forsyth *Selected.*
By the Dee at Night, *Thomas Pitfield,* E♭ [e′b-e′′b], Forsyth *Selected.*

Child hears Rain at Night, The, *Thomas Pitfield*, Dm [d'-f''], Forsyth Selected.
Christmas Lullaby, *Thomas Pitfield*, G [e'-e''], Forsyth Selected.
Crescent Boat, The, *John Gracen Brown*, Eb [bb-f''], Forsyth Selected.
Cuckoo and Chestnut Time, *Robert Faulds*, G [e'-g''], Forsyth Selected.
Desdemona's Song, *Shakespeare*, Em [c'-g''](f), Brunton.
In an Old Country Church, *Thomas Pitfield*, Db [db-e''], Forsyth Selected.
In the Moonlight, *Anon (French),* tr. *Pitfield*, Cramer.
Lingering Music, (1st setting), *Thomas Pitfield*, Bbm [f'-b''b(g''b)], Forsyth Selected.
Lingering Music, (2nd setting), *Thomas Pitfield*, Am [bb-e''], Forsyth Selected.
Naiad, *Dennis Jones*, G [c'-g''(e'')], Forsyth Selected.
Sands of Dee, The, *Charles Kingsley*, Cm [bb-f''], Forsyth Selected.
September Lovers, *Thomas Pitfield*, B [b-e''], Forsyth Selected.
Shadow March, *R. L. Stevenson*, Dm [c'-f''], Forsyth Selected.
Song of Compassion, *Thomas Pitfield*, [d'-e''(g'')], Forsyth Selected.
Unfulfilled, The, *Pushkin,* tr. *Alice M. Pitfield*, Cm [c'-f''], Forsyth Selected.
Wagon of Life, The, *Pushkin,* tr. *Alice M. Pitfield*, Dm [a-f''], Forsyth Selected.
Willow Song, *Shakespeare*, Bm [d'-f''#], Forsyth Selected.
Winter Evening: Dunham Park, *Thomas Pitfield*, D [bb-a''], Forsyth Selected.
Winter Song, *Katherine Mansfield*, Am [d'-e''], Forsyth Selected.
You frail sad leaves, *Thomas Pitfield*, Em [bb-e''], Forsyth Selected.
Arrangements:
Carrion Crow, The *Anon*, F [f'-f''], Forsyth Selected.
Donkey Riding, *Anon*, E [e'b-e''], Cramer.
Faithful Johnny, *Anon*, F [e'-g''], Forsyth Selected.
So far from my country, *Anon*, Eb [e'b-g''], Forsyth Selected.

Playford, John. 1623–1686.
On a quiet conscience, *Francis Quarles*, Dm [f'-g''], Thames (Bevan) *6 Divine.*

Plumstead, Mary. 1905–1980.
Collection: (*Two Songs,* Chester).
Close thine eyes, *Francis Quarles,* (*Charles I,* in error), Db [bb-d''b], Roberton, Thames *Century 2*; Gb, Roberton.
Down by the salley gardens, *W. B. Yeats*, Cm [a'b-e''b], Roberton.
Grateful Heart, A, *George Herbert*, Db [d'b-f''], Roberton *(with* He was the one*).*
Grey Wind, The, *Vera Wainwright,* Bb [d'b-e''b], Roberton.
Ha'nacker Mill, *Hilaire Belloc*, Cm [bb-e''b], Roberton.
He was the one, *Phyllida Garth*, Em [b-e''], Roberton *(with* Grateful heart, A*).*
Love's Reasons, *William Browne*, Eb [c'-f''], Elkin.
(My true love hath my heart, *Sir Philip Sidney,* E (f), Chester).
(Reed, The, *Geoffrey Johnson,* Bm [b-d''], Chester 2 Songs.)
(Sigh no more, ladies, *Shakespeare*, Bb [bb(f)-e''b], Curwen.)
Song of the Cross, The, *Phyllida Garth*, Em [b-e''], Roberton; Gm, Roberton.
(Song of the Songless, *George Meredith,* Em [d'-d''#], Chester 2 Songs.)
Take O take those lips away, *Shakespeare*, Bm [b-e''], Roberton.
(Tale of the Lamb, The, *Sarah Josepha Hale*, C [g-e''], Chappell.)
Where are you going to, my pretty maid, *Anon*, B&H.
(Wish, A, *Samuel Rogers,* Ab [e'b-e''b], Elkin.)
Arrangements: *Two Songs,* B&H.
Come sweet lass, *Anon*, G [d'-a'']B&H 2 Songs.
Forsaken Lover's Complaint, A, *Robert Johnson*, Am [e'-a''], B&H 2 Songs.

Poole, Geoffrey. 1949– *See also* App. 1, 2.
Bone of Adam (dramatic scena), *Laurence Durrell,* [a-b''b](f), Maecenas.

Pope, Peter.
Collections: *Eleven Songs from 'A Shropshire Lad',* [c'-g''], Micropress; *Five Landscapes,* Micropress; *Five Poems of Alice Meynell,* Micropress; *Five Poems of Frederick Pratt Green,* [d'-e''], Micropress; *Four Poems of Alice Meynell,* Micropress; *Four Poems of Dylan Thomas,* Micropress; *Four Poems of Gerard Manley Hopkins,* Micropress; *Four Poems of Ruth Pitter,* Micropress; *In Valleys Green and Still,* Micropress; *Six Renaissance Songs,* Micropress; *Three Housman Songs,* Micropress; *Three Poems of Walter de la Mare,* Micropress. Note: Most Micropress publications can be supplied in a wide range of keys.
Advent Meditation, *Alice Meynell,* Micropress 5 Alice Meynell.

And will they cast the altars down? *Alice Meynell,* Micropress 4 Alice Meynell.
Bells in tower at evening toll, *A. E. Housman,* Micropress 3 Housman.
Cape Ann, *T. S. Eliot,* Micropress 5 Landscapes.
Chimes, *Alice Meynell,* Micropress 5 Alice Meynell.
Ermine, The, *Ruth Pitter,* Micropress 4 Ruth Pitter.
Far in a western brookland, *A. E. Housman,* [medium], Micropress 11 Shropshire Lad.
Given, not lent, *Alice Meynell,* Micropress 4 Alice Meynell.
Go, lovely rose, *Edmund Waller,* Micropress 6 Renaissance.
Half-moon westers low, The, *A. E. Housman,* Micropress 3 Housman.
Heaven-haven, *Gerard Manley Hopkins,* Micropress 4 Manley Hopkins.
I am the way, *Alice Meynell,* Micropress 4 Alice Meynell.
I walked alone and thinking, *A. E. Housman,* Micropress 3 Housman.
If you came, *Ruth Pitter,* Micropress 4 Ruth Pitter.
In summertime on Bredon, *A. E. Housman,* [medium], Micropress 11 Shropshire Lad.
In valleys green and still, *A. E. Housman,* Micropress In Valleys Green.
Joyous Wanderer, The, *Alice Meynell,* Micropress 5 Alice Meynell.
Lads in their hundreds, The, *A. E. Housman,* [medium], Micropress 11 Shropshire Lad.
Look not in my eyes, *A. E. Housman,* [medium], Micropress 11 Shropshire Lad.
Loveliest of trees, *A. E. Housman,* [medium], Micropress 11 Shropshire Lad.
Lovers' Season, The, *Dylan Thomas,* Micropress 4 Dylan Thomas.
Memory of Liverpool, *Frederick Pratt Green,* [medium], Micropress 5 Pratt Green.
Men walking into the trees, *Dylan Thomas,* Micropress 4 Dylan Thomas.
My Fair, *Alice Meynell,* Micropress 5 Alice Meynell.
New Hampshire, *T. S. Eliot,* Micropress 5 Landscapes.
Next Minute, The, *Frederick Pratt Green,* [medium], Micropress 5 Pratt Green.
Nocturne, *Dylan Thomas,* Micropress 4 Dylan Thomas.
October Redbreast, The, *Alice Meynell,* Micropress 5 Alice Meynell.
Oh see how thick the goldcup flowers, *A. E. Housman,* [medium], Micropress 11 Shropshire Lad.
On Wenlock Edge, *A. E. Housman,* [medium], Micropress 11 Shropshire Lad.
Oystercatchers, *Frederick Pratt Green,* [medium], Micropress 5 Pratt Green.
Pied Beauty, *Gerard Manley Hopkins,* Micropress 4 Manley Hopkins.
Rainy Summer, The, *Alice Meynell,* Micropress 4 Alice Meynell.
Rannock, by Glencoe, *T. S. Eliot,* Micropress 5 Landscapes.
Revelation, *Frederick Pratt Green,* [medium], Micropress 5 Pratt Green.
Slackwater Stillness, *Frederick Pratt Green,* [medium], Micropress 5 Pratt Green.
Song to a Child at Night-time, *Dylan Thomas,* Micropress 4 Dylan Thomas.
Spring, *Gerard Manley Hopkins,* Micropress 4 Manley Hopkins.
Spring and Fall, *Gerard Manley Hopkins,* Micropress 4 Manley Hopkins.
Song of Shadows, The: *Walter de la Mare,* Micropress, 3 Walter de la Mare.
Song of the Mad Prince, *Walter de la Mare,* Micropress, 3 Walter de la Mare.
Spring, the sweet spring, *Thomas Nashe,* Micropress 6 Renaissance.
Summer is icumen in, *Anon,* Micropress.
Tis Spring, come out to ramble, *A. E. Housman,* [medium], Micropress 11 Shropshire Lad.
Tis time I think by Wenlock Town, *A. E. Housman,* [medium], Micropress 11 Shropshire Lad.
To Anthea, *Robert Herrick,* Micropress 6 Renaissance.
To Daffodils, *Robert Herrick,* Micropress 6 Renaissance.
Trees, *Walter de la Mare,* Micropress, 3 Walter de la Mare.
Trophy of arms, A, *Ruth Pitter,* Micropress 4 Ruth Pitter.
Tuft of Violets, The, *Ruth Pitter,* Micropress 4 Ruth Pitter.
Usk, *T. S. Eliot,* Micropress 5 Landscapes.
Virginia, *T. S. Eliot,* Micropress 5 Landscapes.
Weep you no more, sad fountains, *Anon,* Micropress 6 Renaissance.
When green buds hang in the elm, *A. E. Housman,* Micropress In Valleys Green.
When I was one-and-twenty, *A. E. Housman,* [medium], Micropress 11 Shropshire Lad.
With rue my heart is laden, *A. E. Housman,* [medium], Micropress 11 Shropshire Lad.
Young Eternity, *Robert Herrick,* Micropress 6 Renaissance.

Poston, Elizabeth. 1905–1987.
Ardan Mor, *Francis Ledwidge,* [c′-e′′b],B&H.
Aubade, *Sir William Davenant,* Bb [d′-g′′], B&H.
Balulalow, *Luther* tr. *Wedderburn,* B&H.
Be still my sweet sweeting, *John Philip,* G [c′-g′′], B&H.
Bellman's Song, The, *Thomas Ravenscroft,* Db [d′b-e′′b], B&H *Easy Song*; Bb, B&H.
Brown is my love, *Anon,* G [e′-g′′], B&H.

Call for the robin redbreast, *John Webster*, [b-f''], B&H.
Dance to your daddie, *Anon*, B&H.
In Praise of Woman, *Anon*, [d'-e''], B&H.
In Youth is Pleasure, *Robert Wever*, F [c'-f''], B&H.
Lake Isle of Innisfree, The, *W. B. Yeats*, C, [c'-a''b(f')], B&H.
Little Candle to St Anthony, A, *S. J. C. Russell*, F [c'-f'(g'')], B&H.
Maid Quiet, *W. B. Yeats*, F [f'-g''(f'')], B&H.
Queen of Sheba's Song, The, *1 Kings 10*, [c'-f''](f), BMP.
She is all so slight, *Richard Aldington*, E♭ [e'b-e''b](m), B&H.
(Sheepfolds, *Mary Madeleva*, G [d'-d''], Elkin.)
Stockdoves, The, *Andrew Young*, [d'-g''], BMP.
Sweet Suffolk owl, *Thomas Vautor*, A♭ [e'b-a''b], Thames *Century 5*, B&H; F, B&H.
Arrangement:
Bonny at morn, *Anon*, [c'-e''], BMP.

Powell, Marion-Wynn.
Close of Day, [any voice], Snell.

Power, David. WMIC.

Powers, Anthony. 1953– *See also* App. 1.
High Windows (cycle), *Philip Larkin*, [f-f''](Counter-tenor/Mezzo/Contralto), OUP.

Price, Beryl.
Collection: (*Shepherd on a Hill*, Curwen)
(In an arbour green, *Robert Wever*, C [c'-f''](m), Curwen Shepherd.)
(Jig, *John Wotton*, C [c'-g''], Curwen Shepherd.)
(Phillis, *Thomas Lodge*, Am [d'-f''#](m), Curwen Shepherd.)

Price, R. Rhedynog.
Abide with me, *Henry Francis Lyte*, [contralto/baritone], Snell.

Procter, Charles.
Collections: *Five Mystic Songs*, Lengnick; *Four Various Songs*, Lengnick; *Quatre Vocalises*, Brunton; *Three Children's Songs*, Lengnick.
Automne, *no text*, D [e'-g''](f), Brunton Quatre Vocalises.
Childrens' Carol, *Evelyn Forster*, [medium high], Lengnick Childrens
Christ my beloved, *William Baldwin*, Am [g'#-e''], Lengnick 5 Mystic.
Come live with me, *Christopher Marlowe*, [medium high], Lengnick Childrens
Earth's Holiday, The, *Nicholas Breton*, G [d'-a''], Lengnick Various.
Eté, *no text*, Em [b-g''](f), Brunton Quatre Vocalises.
He rode like any king, *Madeleine Chase*, F [c'-f''], Brunton.
Hiver, *no text*, D♭ [e'b-e''b](f), Brunton Quatre Vocalises.
King David, *Walter de la Mare*, Gm [d'-g''], Lengnick Various.
Litany, *Thomas a Kempis*, Am [d'-g''], Lengnick Various.
Little Lamb, *William Blake*, [medium high], Lengnick Childrens
Lord thou art mine, and I am thine, *George Herbert*, A [d'#-f''#], Lengnick 5 Mystic.
Love bade me welcome, *George Herbert*, [c'#-g''], Lengnick 5 Mystic.
Orpheus with his lute, *William Shakespeare*, D [c'#-g''#], Brunton.
Our Lady's, *Richard Verstegen*, D [e'-g''], Lengnick 5 Mystic.
Printemps, *no text*, C [e'-f''#](f), Brunton Quatre Vocalises.
That he whom the sun serves, *Richard Crashaw*, Am [b-a''], Lengnick 5 Mystic.
Vocalise, *No text*, A [c'#-a''], Lengnick Various.

Procter-Gregg, Humphrey. 1895–1980.
(Danube to the Severn, The, *Alfred Lord Tennyson*, A [d'-e''], B&H.)
I know a bank, *Shakespeare*, E♭ [d'-e''b], B&H *Easy Song*.
(In the highlands, *R. L. Stevenson*, G [d'-e''], B&H.)

Purcell, Daniel. *c.*1660–1717.
Cupid, make your virgins tender, *Anon*, Gm [d'-f''](m), S&B (Pilkington) *Georgian 1*.
Let not love on me bestow, *Richard Steele*, A♭ [e'b-e''b], S&B (Pilkington) *Georgian 1*.
Morpheus, thou gentle god, *Abel Boyer*, Gm [d'-g''](f), Voicebox (Roberts) *Mad Songs 1*.

Purcell, Edward Cockram. ? –1932.
  Passing by, *Anon*, F [d′-d″], IMP *Parlour Songs*, Classical; B♭, A♭, A, Classical.

Purcell, Henry. 1659–1695. *see also* App. 1, 2.
Listed here are all songs, whether originally solo songs or songs from stage works, which are currently available in collections of solo songs. Solos occurring in larger works only available in complete scores are not covered, nor are songs available only in Purcell Society complete editions. Note that volumes are referred to under editor's names, publishers only being given in the case of anthologies and single copies.
  Collections: (Britten), *Five Songs,* B&H; *Miscellany of Songs, A,* Faber; *Seven Songs* (7*a,* 7*b*) [high, medium], B&H; *Six Songs* (6*a,* 6*b*) [high, medium], B&H; *Three Divine Hymns,* B&H; *Two Divine Hymns and Alleluia,* B&H; (Cooper), *Fifteen Songs and Airs Sets 1a, 1b,* [high, low], Novello/Masters *and 2a, 2b* [high, low], Novello; (Harley), *Selected Songs,* Cramer; (Kagen), *Four Sacred Songs,* [high, low], International; *Forty Songs volumes 1a, 1b – 4a, 4b* [high, low], International; *Six Songs for Bass* International; (Laurie), *Solo Songs volumes 1-4,* Novello; (Lewis & Fortune) *Six Sacred Songs,* Novello; (Roberts), *30 Songs,* volumes *1a, 1b* and *2a, 2b* [high, low], OUP; (Tippett and Bergmann), *Songs volumes 1-5,* Schott; (Wishart), *Songs* volumes 1-3, S&B. Note that B&H published some single songs edited by Britten, and have now amalgamated *Six* Songs and *Seven* Songs into one volume of *Thirteen Songs.* The Tippett and Bergmann editions all appeared separately.
  Aeolus's Song, *see* John Weldon.
  Ah! Belinda, *Nahum Tate*, Cm [c′-f″](f), Cooper 1a, Kagen 2a; *Bbm*, Cooper 1b, Kagen 2b.
  Ah! cruel nymph! you give despair, *Anon*, Gm [d′-a″](m), Laurie 3.
  Ah! how pleasant 'tis to love, *Anon*, C [g′-g″], Kagen 1a, Laurie 3, Peters *Art of Song 2a*; *A*, Kagen 1b, Peters *Art of Song 2b.*
  Ah! how sweet it is to love, *John Dryden*, Gm [f′#-g″], Roberts 1a, Tippett 2; *Fm*, Wishart 2, S&B (Wishart) *Recitalist 4*; *Em*, Roberts 1b; *Dm*, Tippett 4.
  Alleluia, *see* John Weldon.
  Altisadora's song, *Thomas D'Urfey*, Cm [d′-g″](f), Cooper 1a, Novello (Cooper), Kagen 2a, Tippett 2, Voicebox (Roberts) *Mad Songs 2*; *Bm*, Wishart 2; *Am*, Cooper 1b, Kagen 2b, Tippett 4.
  Amidst the shades and cool refreshing streams, *Anon*, Am [d′-g″], Laurie 1.
  Amintas, to my grief I see, *Anon*, Dm [d′-g″](f), Harley, Laurie 1.
  Amintor, heedless of his flocks, *Anon*, Cm [c′-a″b], Laurie 1.
  Amphitrite's Song, *see* John Weldon.
  Anacreon's Defeat, *Anon*, C [F-e′](m), Kagen 6 for Bass, Laurie 3, Masters (Dent), BMP (Dent).
  Arise, ye subterranean winds, *see* John Weldon.
  Ask me to love no more, *Anthony Hammond*, B♭ [c′-g″](f), Laurie 4.
  Bacchus is a pow'r divine, *Anon*, D [D-d′](m), Laurie 3, 4.
  Beneath a poplar's shadow lay me, *Nathaniel Lee,* Am [e′-a″], Voicebox (Roberts) *Mad Songs 2.*
  Bess of Bedlam, *see* Mad Bess.
  Beware, poor shepherds, *Anon*, Dm [d′-g″](m), Laurie 2.
  Blessed Virgin's Expostulation, The, *Nahum Tate*, Cm [e′b-a″b](f), Britten, Roberts 1a; *Bbm*, Kagen 2a, 4 Sacred high, Tippett 1; *Am*, Roberts 1b; *Gm*, Kagen 2b, 4 Sacred low.
  Bonvica's Song, *Anon*, Cm [d′-a″b](f), Cooper 1a, Harley, Kagen 4a, Roberts 2a; *Bm*, Tippett 2; *Am*, Cooper 1b, Kagen 4b, Roberts 2b; *Gm*, Tippett.
  Cares of lovers, The, *Anthony Motteux*, Gm [d′-g″], Roberts 2a; *Em*, Roberts 2b.
  Cease, anxious world, your fruitless pain, *George Etherege*, Gm [d′-g″](m), Laurie 2.
  Cease, O my sad soul, *Charles Webbe,* Cm [g′-g″](m), Harley, Kagen 3a; *Am*, Kagen 3b.
  Celia's fond, too long I've loved her, *Anthony Motteux*, Dm [d′-g″](m), Laurie 4.
  Come all ye songsters, *Elkanah Settle?* C; *Bb* [f′-g″], Cooper 2a, Kagen 4a; *G*, Cooper 2b, Kagen 4b.
  Corinna is divinely fair, *Anon*, Gm [d′-g″], Harley, Laurie 3.
  Crown the altar, *Nahum Tate*, Gm [d′-d″], Tippett 2; *Bm*, Tippett 5.
  Cupid, the slyest rogue alive, *Anon*, Gm [d′-g″], Laurie 2, Roberts 2a; *Em*, Roberts 2b.
  Dear pretty youth, *Anon*, A [e′-g″](f) Thames (Bevan) *8 Restoration*, Roberts 2a; *G*, Roberts 2b, Wishart 1, S&B (Wishart) *Recitalist 2.*
  Dido's Farewell, *see* Dido's Lament.
  Dido's Lament, *Nahum Tate*, C [c′-g″](f), Cooper 1a, Novello (Cooper), Kagen 2a, Wishart 2; *Am*, Cooper 1b, Kagen 2b.
  Earth trembled, The, *Francis Quarles*, A [c′#-f″#], Harley, Lewis & Fortune.
  Epithalamium, An, *Elkanah Settle?* Gm [d′-g″](f), Cooper 1a, Kagen 1a; *Fm*, Tippett 1; *Em*, Cooper 1b, Kagen 1b; *Dm*, Tippett 4.
  Evening Hymn, An, *William Fuller*, G [d′-g″], Britten 3 Divine, Kagen 4a, 4 Sacred high, Roberts 2a, Tippett 3; *F*, Wishart 3, BMP (Whittaker); *Eb*, Kagen 4b, 4 Sacred low, Roberts 2b, Novello (Harvey Grace); *D*, Tippett 5.
  Fair and serene, *see* John Weldon.

Fairest isle, *John Dryden*, B♭ [f′-a′′(a′′b)], Britten 7a, Roberts 1a; *A♭*, Cooper 1a, Kagen 1a; *G*, Roberts 1b; *F*, Britten 7b, Cooper 1b, Kagen 1b.
Farewell all joys, *Anon*, Gm [d′-f′′](f), Laurie 2.
Fatal hour comes on apace, The, *Anon*, Em [d′#-g′′], Kagen 3a, Laurie 4, Roberts 1a, Tippett 2; *Dm*, Roberts 1b, Wishart 2, S&B (Wishart) *Recitalist 4*; *Cm*, Kagen 3b; *Bm*, Tippett 4.
Fly swift, ye hours, *Anon*, Dm [d′-g′′](m), Laurie 3.
From rosy bowers, *see* Altisadora's song.
From silent shades and the Elysian groves, *see* Mad Bess.
Hail to the myrtle shade, *Nathaniel Lee*, B♭ [a′-g′′], Harley; *A*, Cooper 2a, Curwen (Dunhill); *F*, Cooper 2b; *G*, Curwen (Dunhill).
Halcyon Days, *see* John Weldon.
Hark how all things in one sound rejoice, *Elkanah Settle?* G [d′-f′′](f), Cooper 1a, Kagen 4a, Wishart 2, S&B (Wishart) *Recitalist 1*; *A*, Cooper 1b, Kagen 4b.
Hark the echoing air, *Elkanah Settle?* C [e′-a′′](f), Kagen 3a, Leonard *Baroque high*; *B♭*, Britten 5 Songs, Paterson (Diack) *100 Best 1*, Schirmer (John Reed) *2nd Soprano*; *A♭*, Kagen 3b; *G*, Leonard *Baroque low*.
He himself courts his own ruin, *Anon*, F [c′-f′′](m), Laurie 1.
Hear, ye gods of Britain, *Anon*, Cm [g-e′′♭](m), B&H (Northcote) *Imperial 6*.
Hears not my Phyllis, *see* Knotting Song, The.
Hence with your trifling deity, *Thomas Shadwell*, B♭ [F-e′♭](m), Kagen 6 for Bass.
Here let my life, *Abraham Cowley*, Gm [d′-f′′], Cooper 2a, *Fm*, Cooper 2b.
Here the deities approve, *Christopher Fishburn*, Em [g′-b′′], Harley.
How blest are shepherds, *John Dryden*, G [d′-g′′], Britten 5 Songs.
How I sigh when I think of the charms, *Anon*, Cm [c′-f′′](f), Laurie 1.
How long, great God, *John Norris*, Am [d′-f′′], Lewis & Fortune.
I am come to lock all fast, *see* Mystery's Song.
I attempt from love's sickness, *Robert Howard*, A [d′#-f′′#], Britten 5 Songs, Chester (Holloway) *Celebrated 3*, Cooper 1a, Kagen 4a, Roberts 2a; *A♭*, B&H (Northcote) *Imperial 2*, Leonard *Baroque high*; *G*, Cooper 1b, Roberts 2b, Tippett 1, Wishart 3, Schirmer *1st Tenor*; *F*, Kagen 4b, Leonard *Baroque low*, Paterson (Diack) *100 Best 4*.
I came, I saw, and was undone, *Abraham Cowley*, Am [d′-g′′](m), Laurie 2.
I loved fair Celia, *Bernard Howard*, Dm [e′-a′′](m), Laurie 3.
I love and I must, *Anon*, Cm [f′#-a′′♭](m), Laurie 3; *Dm*, Schirmer *1st Tenor*.
I resolve against cringing, *Anon*, Am [e′-g′′](m), Laurie 1.
I saw that you were grown so high, *Anon*, Dm [d′-f′′], Kagen 1a, Peters *Art of Song 2a*; *Bm*, Kagen 1b, Peters *Art of Song 2b*.
I see she flies me, *John Dryden*, Gm [d′-g′′], Cooper 2a, Roberts 1a; *Em*, Cooper 2b, Roberts 1b.
I take no pleasure in the sun's bright beams, *Chamberlaine?* Am [d′-g′′], Britten 5, Laurie 1.
If grief has any pow'r to kill, *Anon*, Dm [d′-g′′], Laurie 2.
If music be the food of love (Z 379B), *Henry Heveningham*, Am [e′-a′′], Laurie 3, Roberts 1a, *Fm*, Roberts 1b; *Em*, OUP (Shacklock) *Solo Contralto*.
If music be the food of love (Z 379A), *Henry Heveningham*, Gm [d′-g′′], Britten 6a, Kagen 1a, Laurie 3, Roberts 1a, Leonard *Baroque high*; *F#m*, Tippett 1; *Em*, Britten 6b, Roberts 1b; *E♭m*, Kagen 1b; *Dm*, Tippett 4, Leonard *Baroque low*.
If music be the food of love (Z 379C), *Henry Heveningham*, Gm [d′-a′′], Britten 7a, Kagen 1a, Laurie 4, Roberts 1a; *Em*, Britten 7b, Kagen 1b, Roberts 1b.
If thou wilt give me back my love, E♭ [medium], BMP.
If pray'rs and tears, *Anon*, Cm [c′-g′′], Laurie 2.
I'll sail upon the dogstar, *Thomas D'Urfey*, C [d′-a′′](m), Voicebox (Roberts) *Mad Songs 2*; *B♭*, Britten 7a, B&H (Northcote) *Imperial 4*, Kagen 3a, Wishart 3, S&B (Wishart) *Recitalist 3*, Leonard *Baroque high*, Schirmer *2nd Tenor*; *G*, Britten 7b, Kagen 3b, Paterson (Diack) *100 Best 3*, Leonard *Baroque low*, BMP (Jacob).
In Chloris all soft charms agree, *John Howe*, G [d′-g′′](m), Laurie 1.
In the black dismal dungeon of despair, *William Fuller*, Em [c′#-g′′], Britten 2 Divine, Lewis & Fortune.
In vain we dissemble, *Anon*, Dm [d′-g′′](f), Laurie 2.
Job's Curse, *Jeremy Taylor*, Cm [c′-g′′], Britten, Lewis & Fortune.
Kind fortune smiles, *see* John Weldon.
Knotting song, The, *Charles Sedley*, F [f′-g′′](m), Britten Miscellany, B&H (Northcote) *Imperial 4*, Kagen 2a, Laurie 4, Roberts 1a, Peters *Art of Song 2a*, BMP (Arundell); *D*, Roberts 1b, Peters *Art of Song 2b*; *D♭*, Kagen 2b.
Let each gallant heart, *John Turner*, C [c′-g′′](m), Laurie 1; *A*, Schirmer *2nd Baritone*.
Let formal lovers still pursue, *Anon*, Am [e′-g′′](m), Laurie 3.

Purcell, Henry

Let the dreadful engines, *Thomas D'Urfey*, F [c-g′](m), Britten (Faber), Voicebox (Roberts) *Mad Songs 1,* Masters (Dent), BMP (Dent); *Eb*, B&H (Northcote) *Imperial 5*, Tippett 5.
Let the night perish, *see* Job's Curse.
Let us dance, let us sing, G [d′-f′′#], Schirmer *1st Soprano*.
Lord, what is man, *William Fuller*, Gm [d′-a′′], Britten 3 Divine, Kagen 3a, 4 Sacred high, Roberts 2a, Lewis & Fortune; *Em*, Roberts 2b, Wishart 1; *Ebm*, Kagen 3b, 4 Sacred low.
Love arms himself in Celia's eyes, *Matthew Prior*, C [d′-a′′b](m), Laurie 4.
Love is now become a trade, *Anon*, Gm [d′-g′′](m), Harley, Laurie 2.
Love quickly is palled, *Anthony Motteux*, Bb; *A* [e′-g′′#], Cooper 2a, Peters *Art of Song 2a,* Schirmer *1st Tenor II*; *F*, Cooper 2b, Peters *Art of Song 2b*.
Love, thou can'st hear, *Robert Howard*, Cm [d′-a′′](m), Laurie 4.
Lovely Albina's come ashore, *Anon*, C [d′-a′′], Harley, Laurie 4.
Love's pow'r in my heart, *Anon*, C [g′-g′′], Laurie 3.
Mad Bess, *Anon*, C [c′-g′′](f), Britten 6a, Kagen 3a, Laurie 1, Tippett 3, Voicebox (Roberts) *Mad Songs 1*; *Bb*, Britten 6b; *A*, Kagen 3b, Tippett 5.
Man is for the woman made, *Anthony Motteux*, C [e′-g′′], Britten 6a, Cooper 2a, Kagen 2a, Roberts 2a, Tippett 3; *Bb*, Britten 6b; *A*, Cooper 2b, Roberts 2b; *Ab*, Kagen 2b; *G*, Tippett 5.
More love or more disdain I crave, *Charles Webbe*, G [e′-a′′]; *F,* Kagen 2a; *Db*, Kagen 2b; *C*, Paterson (Diack) *100 Best 4*.
Morning Hymn, A, *William Fuller*, Gm [c′-g′′], Britten 2 Divine, Thames (Bevan) *6 Divine*.
Music for a while, *John Dryden*, Cm [g′-a′′b], Britten 7a; *Bbm,* Cooper 2a; *Am*, Kagen 1a, Roberts 2a, Tippett 1; *Gm*, Britten 7b, Cooper 2b, Roberts 2b; *Fm,* Kagen 1b, Tippett 4, Novello.
My dear, my Amphitrite, *see* John Weldon.
My heart, whenever you appear, *Anon*, Dm [d′-g′′](m), Laurie 2.
My op'ning eyes are purged, *see* Anon.
Myrtle Shade, The, *see* Hail to the Myrtle Shade.
Mystery's Song, *Elkanah Settle?* Cm [d′-g′′](f), Cooper 1a, *Am*, Cooper 1b, Schirmer *1st Mezzo II*.
Next winter comes slowly, *Elkanah Settle?* Am [A-e′](m), Kagen 6 for Bass; *Gm,* Schirmer *1st Baritone*.
Not all my torments, *Anon*, Cm [d′-a′′b], Britten 6a, Kagen 4a, Laurie 3, Roberts 2a, Tippett 2; *Am*, Britten 6b, Kagen 4b, Roberts 2b; *Gm*, Tippett 5.
Now that the sun has veiled his light. *see* Evening Hymn, An.
Nymphs and shepherds, come away, *Thomas Shadwell*, G [d′-g′′], Kagen 4a, Roberts 1a, Wishart 3, Leonard *Baroque high,* BMP (Jacob); *F*, Paterson (Diack) *100 Best 2* , Roberts 1b, Schirmer *1st Mezzo II*; *Eb*, B&H (Northcote) *Imperial 2*, Kagen 4b, Leonard *Baroque low*.
O lead me to some peaceful gloom, *see* Bonvica's song.
Oh! fair Cedaria, hide those eyes, *Anon*, C [d′-a′′](m), Laurie 4.
Oh let me weep, *see* The plaint.
Oh solitude, my sweetest choice, *Katherine Philips*, Cm [c′-g′′], Laurie 2, Britten Miscellany, Roberts 1a; *Bbm*, Wishart 3; *Am*, Roberts 1b.
Olinda in the shades unseen, *Anon*, G [d′-a′′], Laurie 4.
On the brow of Richmond Hill, *Thomas D'Urfey*, Bb [f′-a′′b], Britten 7a, Laurie 3, Roberts 2a; *G*, Britten 7b, Roberts 2b.
One charming night, *see* Secresy's Song.
Owl is abroad, The, *see* J. C. Smith.
Pastora's beauties, when unblown, *Anon*, Cm [d′-g′′](m), Laurie 1.
Phillis, I can ne'er forgive it, *Anon*, Gm [e′-g′′](m), Laurie 3.
Phillis, talk no more of passion, *Anon*, Cm [d′-g′′](m), Laurie 2.
Pious Celinda goes to pray'rs, *William Congreve*, Dm [d′-a′′](m), Britten 7a, Laurie 4, Roberts 1a; *Cm*, Wishart 3; *Bm*, Roberts 1b; *Am*, Britten 7b.
Plaint, The, *Elkanah Settle?* Dm [d′-g′′](f), Cooper 1a; *Bm*, Cooper 1b.
Rashly I swore I would disown, *Anon*, Bb [e′-g′′](m), Laurie 1.
Retired from (any) mortal's sight, *Nahum Tate*, Gm [d′-f′′], Cooper 1a, Harley, Roberts 1a; *F#m*, Cooper 1b; *Em*, Roberts 1b.
Sawny is a bonny lad, *Anthony Motteux*, G [d′-g′′](f), Harley, Laurie 4, Roberts 2a; *Eb*, Roberts 2b.
Secresy's Song, Cm [g-a′], *Am*, Cooper 2; *F#m*, Cooper 2.
She loves and she confesses too, *Abraham Cowley*, C [c′-g′′](m), Laurie 1.
She that would gain a faithful lover, *Lady E—M—*, Bb [d′-a′′b](f), Laurie 4, Roberts 2a; *G*, Roberts 2b.
She who my poor heart possesses, *Anon*, Gm [d′-g′′](m), Laurie 1.
Since from my dear Astraea's sight, *The E— of M—*, Dm [d′-f′′], Cooper 2a, Kagen 2a, Wishart 1; *Cm*, Cooper 2b; *Bm*, Kagen 2b, Schirmer *2nd Baritone*.
Since one poor view has drawn my heart, *Anon*, C [c′-g′′](f), Laurie 1.
Sound the trumpet, *Nahum Tate*, C; *Bb* [d-a′′b], Cooper 2*a*, Kagen 3a; *G*, Cooper 2b; *F*, Kagen 3b.

Spite of the god-head, pow'rful love, *Anne Wharton*, Em [d´-g´´](f), Laurie 3.
Strike the viol, *Anon*, Dm [a-b´b]; *Gm* Kagen 3a; *Em*, Kagen 3b.
Sweet, be no longer sad, *Charles Webbe*, Am [g´#-g´´], Kagen 4a; *Fm*, Kagen 4b.
Sweeter than roses, *Richard Norton*, Cm [d´-a´´], Britten 6a, Cooper 1a, Kagen 1a, Roberts 2a; *Bm*, Tippett 1; *Am*, Britten 6b, Cooper 1b, Kagen 1b, Roberts 2b, Wishart 1, S&B (Wishart) *Recitalist 2*; *Gm*, Tippett 4.
Sylvia, now your scorn give over, *Anon*, C [g´-g´´](m), Harley, Kagen 3a, Laurie 3; *G*, Kagen 3b.
Take not a woman's anger ill, *Robert Gould*, B*b* [d´-f´´](m), Britten 5 Songs, Cooper 2a; *Ab*, Cooper 2b.
Tell me, some pitying angel, *see* The blessed Virgin's expostulation.
That I may see, *Psalm 106,* C [a-b´], Thames (Hodgson) *Countertenors 1.*
There's not a swain on the plain, *N. Henley*, Em [b-g´´], Britten 6a, Kagen 4a; *Cm*, Britten 6b, Kagen 4b.
They say you're angry, *Abraham Cowley*, B*b* [d´-g´´](m), Laurie 2.
They tell us that you mighty powers above, *Robert Howard*, or *John Dryden*, Am [e´-g´´](f) Thames (Bevan) *8 Restoration.*
This poet sings the Trojan wars, *see* Anacreon's defeat.
Thou wakeful shepherd, *see* Morning hymn, A.
Thousand sev'ral ways I tried, A, *Anon*, B*b* [d´-g´´], Laurie 1.
Thrice happy lovers, *see* Epithalamium, An.
Through mournful shades, *Richard Duke*, Cm [e´b-g´´], Laurie 1.
Thus to a ripe consenting maid, *William Congreve*, Am [d´-g´´], Cooper 1a, Roberts 2a; *Gm*, Roberts 2b; *F#m*, Cooper 1b.
Thy genius, lo, *Nathaniel Lee*, C [c-f´](m), Thames (Bevan) *6 Restoration.*
Thy hand, Belinda, *see* Dido's lament.
'Tis nature's voice, *Nicholas Brady*, F; *Eb* [e´b-f´´], Cooper 2a, Kagen 3a; *C*, Cooper 2b; *Bb*, Kagen 3b.
Turn then thine eyes *Elkanah Settle?* Am [e´-a´´], Britten 7a; *Em*, Britten 7b; *Dm,* Schirmer *1st Mezzo.*
Twas within a furlong of Edinboro' town, *Thomas D'Urfey*, Gm [d´-g´´], Roberts 2a, Tippett 1; *Em*, Roberts 2b, Tippett 4.
Urge me no more, *Francis Quarles*, Cm [c´-a´´b], Laurie 1.
Vouchsafe, O Lord, (Te Deum in D), Dm [c´-c´´], Thames (Hodgson) *Countertenors 3.*
We sing to him, *Nathaniel Ingelo*, Cm [d´-a´´b], Britten 3 Divine, B&H (Patrick) *Sacred Songs 1*; *Bm*, Kagen 1a, 4 Sacred high; *Gm*, Kagen 1b, 4 Sacred low, Schirmer *2nd Mezzo.*
Welcome, more welcome does he come, *Thomas Flatman*, Em [e´-g´´], Cooper 2a; *Cm,* Cooper 2b.
What a sad fate is mine (Z 428B), *Anon*, Cm [g´-a´´b](m), Laurie 4.
What a sad fate is mine (Z 428A), *Anon*, Am [e´-f´´](m), Laurie 4.
What can we poor females do? *Anon*, Am [e´-g´´](f), Kagen 1a; *Fm*, Kagen 1b.
What shall I do to show how much I love her? *Thomas Betterton?* Dm [f´-a´´], Tippet 2; *Cm*, Kagen 2a, Wishart 1, S&B (Wishart) *Recitalist 3*; *Bm*, Cooper 2a, Schirmer *1st Tenor*; *Am*, Cooper 2b, Kagen 2b; *Gm*, Tippett 5.
When first Amintas sued for a kiss, *Thomas D'Urfey*, A [e´-a´´](f); *G*, Tippett 3; *E*, Tippett 5.
When first my shepherdess and I, *Anon*, Am [d´-g´´](m), Laurie 2.
When her languishing eyes said 'Love', *Anon*, Em [e´-g´´](m), Laurie 1.
When I am laid in earth, *see* Dido's lament.
When I have often heard young maids complaining, *Elkanah Settle?* C [g´-a´´](f), Roberts 1a; *Bb*, Cooper 1a; *G*, Cooper 1b, Roberts 1b, Schirmer *1st Mezzo II.*
When my Aemilia smiles, *Anon*, Bm [f´#-a´´](m), Laurie 4.
When Strephon found his passion vain, *Anon*, G [g´-e´´], Laurie 1.
While Thyrsis, wrapped in downy sleep, *Anon*, F [d´-f´´], Laurie 1.
Whilst Cynthia sung, *Anon*, Dm [d´-g´´], Laurie 2.
Who but a slave, *Anon*, Gm [d´-g´´], Laurie 1.
Who can behold Fiorella's charms, *Anon*, F [d´-g´´], Laurie 4.
With sick and famish'd eyes, *George Herbert*, Gm [c´-g´´], Roberts 1a, Lewis & Fortune, BMP (Boyle); *Em*, Roberts 1b.
Wondrous machine, *Nicholas Brady*, Em, [B-e´](m), Kagen 6 for Bass.
Ye happy swains, whose nymphs are kind, *Anon*, Dm [d´-a´´](m), Laurie 2.
You (Ye) twice ten hundred deities, *Robert Howard*, Gm [G-e´b](m), B&H (Northcote) *Imperial 6*, Kagen 6 for Bass.
Your awful voice I hear, *see* John Weldon.

Purser, **John**. 1932–
Collection: *Six Sea Songs,* SMIC; *Landscapes,* SMIC.

Q

Quilter, Roger. 1877–1953. *See also* App. 1, 2.
Collections: *Four Songs of the Sea, Op 1,* [original *high,* low], Forsyth; *Three Songs of the Sea, Op 1,* [revised *high,* low], Classical; *Four Songs of Mirza Schaffy Op 2,* [*high*], Classical/(Elkin), ([low], Elkin); (*Four Child Songs Op 5* [high, *low*], Chappell); *Three Shakespeare Songs, Op 6* [*high, medium,* low], B&H; *To Julia, Op 8* [high, *low*], Classical/B&H; *Songs of Sorrow, Op 10,* [low], Classical/B&H, [*high*], B&H; *Seven Elizabethan Lyrics, Op 12,* [high], B&H, [*low*], Classical/ B&H; *Four Songs, Op 14* [*high,* low], Classical/B&H; *Three Songs for Baritone or Tenor, Op 18(a),* [low], Classical/(Elkin), ([*high*], Elkin); (*Two September Songs,* Op 18*(b),* [*high,* low], Elkin); *Three Songs of William Blake Op 20* [*high*], Classical/B&H, [low], B&H; (*Three Pastoral Songs Op 22,* [*high,* low], Elkin); *Five Shakespeare Songs, Op 23* [*high,* low], B&H; *Five Jacobean Lyrics Op 28* [high, medium, *low*], B&H; *Four Shakespeare Songs, Op 30* [high, low], B&H; *Twelve Songs,* Thames (Introduction by Trevor Hold).
    Amaryllis at the Fountain, *Anon,* G [d'-a''], B&H; *E,* Thames 12 Songs, Classical/B&H.
    Answer, The, *Laurence Binyon,* Eb, B&H.
    April, *William Watson,* Ab [d'-f''], Classical/B&H Op 14 low; *Bb,* Op 14 high.
    Arab Love Song, *Percy Bysshe Shelley,* Cm [f'-f''], Thames 12 Songs; *Dm, Bm,* B&H.
    At Close of Day, *Laurence Binyon,* Am [c'-f'#], B&H; Cm, B&H.
    Autumn Evening, *Arthur Maquarie,* Gm [c'-e''], Thames 12 Songs, Classical/B&H Op 14 low; *Bbm,* Op 14 high, Schirmer *2nd Tenor.*
    Blossom Time, *Nora Hopper,* G [g'-a''], B&H; *E,* Classical/B&H.
    Blow, blow, thou winter wind, *Shakespeare,* Cm [c'-e''], B&H Op 6 low, *Shakespeare Album,* Schirmer, *1st Baritone*; *Em,* B&H Op 6 high, *Ebm,* Op 6 medium.
    Bracelet, The, *Robert Herrick,* Dm, [e'-a''](m), Classical/B&H Op 8 high; *Bm,* Op 8 low.
    Brown is my love, *Anon,* Bb [f'-g''](m), B&H Op 12 high; *G,* Classical/B&H Op 12 low.
    By a Fountainside, *Ben Jonson,* C#m [c'#-g''#], B&H Op 12 high; *Bbm,* Classical/B&H Op 12 low.
    By the Sea, *Roger Quilter,* Dm [d'-e''], Classical 3 Sea Op 1 low, Forsyth 4 Sea low Op 1; *F,* Classical 3 Sea Op 1 high, Forsyth 4 Sea Op 1 high.
    Cherry ripe, *Robert Herrick,* F [e'-a''](m), Classical/B&H Op 8 high; *D,* Op 8 low.
    (Cherry Valley, *Joseph Campbell,* E [b-e''], Elkin Op 20 low; *G,* Op 20 high.)
    Come away, death, *Shakespeare,* Cm [c'-e''b], B&H Op 6 low; *Em,* Op 6 high; *Ebm,* Op 6 medium.
    Come back, *Roger Quilter?* Classical 2 Songs, Cm, (Elkin).
    Come tender bud, lean close to me, *Friedrich Bodenstedt,* tr. *R. H. Elkin,* G [d'-e''], (Elkin Op 2 low); *Bb,* Classical/(Elkin) Op 2 high.
    Come unto these yellow sands, *Shakespeare,* Eb, B&H.
    Constant Lover, The, *John Suckling,* D [d'-f'#](m), B&H Op 28 medium; *E,* Op 28 high; *C,* Op 28 low.
    Coronal, A, *Ernest Dowson,* Bb [bb-f''], Thames 12 Songs, Classical/B&H Op 10 low; *Db,* B&H Op 10 high.
    (Cradle in Bethlehem, The, *Rodney Bennett,* D [c'#-d''], Curwen.)
    Cuckoo Song, *Alfred Williams,* D [f'-a''], Classical/B&H; *B,* B&H)
    Damask Roses, *Anon,* Eb [f'-a''(g')](m), B&H Op 12 high; *C,* Classical/B&H Op 12 low.
    Daybreak, *William Blake,* Ebm [d'b-e''b], B&H Op 20 low; *F#m,* Classical/B&H Op 20 high.
    Dream Valley, *William Blake,* D [b-d''], B&H, Op 20 low, Schirmer *1st Mezzo II*; *Gb, B&H New Imperial 2,* Classical/B&H Op 20 high; *F,* Thames 12 Songs.
    (Drooping wings, *Edith Sterling-Levis,* Bm [d'-f'#], Chappell *English Recital 2.*)
    Fair House of Joy, *Anon,* Db [f'-a''b], B&H Op 12 high, *Heritage 4,* B&H, Schirmer *2nd Tenor*; *Bb,* Classical/B&H Op 12 low, B&H.
    (Fairy Lullaby, *Roger Quilter,* Ab [e'b-f''], Chappell; B*b,* Chappell.)
    Faithless shepherdess, The, *Anon,* Bbm [f'-a''b], B&H Op 12 high; *Gm,* Classical/B&H Op 12 low.
    Fear no more the heat of the sun, *Shakespeare,* Fm [c'-e''b], B&H Op 23 low; *G#m,* Op 23 high.
    Fill a glass with golden wine, *W. E. Henley,* C [c'-e''], B&H; *E, Eb, Db,* B&H.
    (Foreign Children, *Robert Louis Stevenson,* Em [e'-a''], Chappell Op 5 high; Cm, Chappell Op 5 low.)
    Fuchsia tree, The, *Charles Dalmon?,* Bm [b-f''#], B&H; *C#m, Am,* B&H.
    Glow of summer sun, The, *Friedrich Bodenstedt,* tr. *R. H. Elkin,* Gm [d'-e''b], (Elkin Op 2 low); *Bbm,* Classical/(Elkin) Op 2 high.
    Go, lovely rose, *Edmund Waller,* Gb [f'-g''b](m), (Chappell); *F,* Schirmer, *1st Tenor*; *Eb,* (Chappell *English Recital 1.*)
    Golden sunlight's glory, The, *Friedrich Bodenstedt,* tr. *R. H. Elkin,* F [c'-f''], (Elkin Op 2 low); *Ab,* Classical/(Elkin) Op 2 high.
    (Good Child, A, *Robert Louis Stevenson,* F [d'-a''], Chappell Op 5 high; D, Chappell Op 5 low.)

Hark, hark, the lark, *Shakespeare*, D, B&H.
Hey, ho, the wind and the rain, *Shakespeare*, C [d′-f′′(d′′)](m), B&H Op 23 low; *Eb*, Op 23 high.
How should I your true love know? *Shakespeare*, Bbm [f′-f′′], *Century 1*, B&H Op 30 high; Gm, Thames 12 Songs, B&H Op 30 low.
I arise from dreams of thee, *Percy Bysshe Shelley*, Ebm [g′b-g′′], B&H; *Cm*, B&H.
I dare not ask a kiss, *Robert Herrick*, Db [e′b-e′′b], B&H Op 28 medium; *F,* Op 28 high; *C*, Op 28 low.
I have a friend, *Roger Quilter*, C [c′-d′′], Forsyth 4 Sea Op 1 low; *Eb*, Forsyth 4 Sea Op 1 high.
I sing of a maiden *see* Old carol, An.
(I will go with my father a-ploughing, *Joseph Campbell*, Ab [c′-f′′(e′′b)], Elkin Op 22 low; *Bb*, Op 22 high.)
(I wish and I wish, *Joseph Campbell*, Cm [c′-g′′(e′′b)], Elkin Op 20 low; *Dm*, Op 20 high.)
In Spring, *Ernest Dowson*, E [b-e′′], Thames 12 Songs, Classical/B&H Op 10 low; *G*, Op 10 high.
In the Bud of the Morning-O, *James Stephens*, D [d′-e′′], B&H; *F*, B&H.
(In the highlands, *R. L. Stevenson*, Eb [bb-e′′b], Elkin; *Gb, Elkin*.)
It was a lover and his lass, *Shakespeare*, E [c′#-e′′], B&H Op 23 low; *Ab*, Op 23 high.
Jealous Lover, The, *John Wilmot, Earl of Rochester*, D [d′-f′′#](m), B&H Op 28 medium; *F,* Op 28 high; *C*, Op 28 low.
Jocund Dance, The, *William Blake*, G [d′-e′′], Classical/(Elkin) Op 18(a) low; (*Bb*, Elkin Op 18(a) high).
Julia's Hair, *Robert Herrick*, Fm [e′b-a′′b](m), Classical/B&H Op 8 high; *Dm*, Op 8 low.
June, *Nora Hopper*, E [c′#-e′′], B&H; F, B&H; D, Classical/B&H.
(Lamplighter, The, *Robert Louis Stevenson*, Eb [e′b-b′′b(g)′′], Chappell Op 5 high; C, Chappell Op 5 low.)
Land of Silence, A, *Ernest Dowson*, Db [bb-g′′b(e′′b)], Thames 12 Songs, Classical/B&H Op 10 low; *E*, Op 10 high.
Last Year's Rose, A, *W. E. Henley*, Db [e′b-f′′], Thames 12 Songs, Classical/B&H Op 14 low; *Eb*, Op 14 high.
Love's Philosophy, *Percy Bysshe Shelley*, F [d′-a′′], B&H *Heritage 4*, B&H; *C, D*, B&H.
Magic of thy presence, The,*Friedrich Bodenstedt*, tr. *R. H. Elkin*, Db [c′-f′′], (Elkin Op 2 low; F, Classical/(Elkin) Op 2 high, Schirmer *2nd Soprano*.
Maiden Blush, The, *Robert Herrick*, F [f′-g′′](m), Classical/B&H Op 8 high; *D*, Op 8 low.
Moonlight, *Roger Quilter,* D [c′#-d′′], Classical 3 Sea Op 1 low, Forsyth 4 Sea Op 1low; *F*, Classical 3 Sea Op 1 high, Forsyth 4 Sea Op 1 high.
(Morning song, *Thomas Heywood*, E [f′#-a′′], Chappell; *C,* Chappell *English Recital 2*; *D,* Chappell.*)*
(Music, *Percy Bysshe Shelley*, D [f′#-f′′#], Curwen.)
Music and moonlight, *Percy Bysshe Shelley*, Eb [c′-e′′b], Thames 12 Songs.
Music, when soft voices die, *Percy Bysshe Shelley*, Ab [f′-f′′], Thames 12 Songs; *Bb, Gb*, B&H.
My heart adorned with thee, *Mirza Schaffy (Friedrich Bodenstedt* tr. *Roger Quilter*, [high], Novello.
My life's Delight, *Thomas Campion*, G [g′-a′′], B&H Op 12 high, Schirmer *2nd Tenor*; *E*, Classical/ B&H Op 12 low.
Night piece, The, *Robert Herrick*, C#m [c′#-g′′;](m), Classical/B&H Op 8 high; *Am*, Op 8 low.
Now sleeps the crimson petal, *Alfred Lord Tennyson*, Eb [c′-e′′b], Classical/B&H; *Gb*, B&H *Imperial 4*, Classical/B&H; *F, D*, Classical/B&H.
O mistress mine, *Shakespeare*, Eb [bb-e′′b](m), B&H Op 6 low, *Imperial 5*, *Love and Affection*; *Gb* Op 6 medium; *G*, *Heritage 3,* Op 6 high; *D*, Schirmer *1st Baritone*.
(O, the month of May, *Thomas Dekker,* D [d′-e′′(d′′)], Chappell; *F,* Chappell.)
Old carol, An, *Anon*, D [c′-d′′], Thames *Century 4*; *Gb*, B&H.
(One word is too often profaned, *Percy Bysshe Shelley*, Gb [f′-g′′b], Curwen.)
Orpheus with his lute, *Shakespeare*, C [b-e′′], B&H; *Eb*, B&H.
(Over the land is April, *R. L. Stevenson*, C [d′-e′′], Elkin; *D, Bb*, Elkin.)
Passing Dreams, *Ernest Dowson*, Ebm [bb-f′′], Thames 12 Songs, Classical/B&H Op 10 low; *F#m*, Op 10 high.
Sea-bird, The, *Roger Quilter,* Em [e′-e′′], Forsyth 4 Sea Op 1 low, Classical 3 Sea Op 1 low; *Gm*, Forsyth 4 Sea Op 1 high, Classical 3 Sea Op 1 high.
Secret, A, *Roger Quilter*? Classical, (Elkin).
Sigh no more, ladies, *Shakespeare*, C [c′-d′′], B&H Op 30 low; E*b*, Op 30 high.
Slumber song, *Clifford Mills*, [medium], Classical, (Elkin).
(Song at Parting, A, *Christina Rossetti*, Elkin.)
Song of the Blackbird, *W. E. Henley*, Bb [d′-f′′], B&H *Heritage 3*, Classical/B&H Op 14 low; *C*, Op 14 high, Schirmer *2nd Soprano*.
Song of the Stream, *Alfred Williams*, E [c′#(d′#)-f′′#], B&H; *D*, B&H.
Spring is at the door, *Nora Hopper*, D [a(c′#)-(f′′#(d′′)], Novello, Schirmer *1st Mezzo II*; (*F,* Elkin

Take, O take those lips away, *Shakespeare*, D♭ [e′♭-D′′♭], B&H Op 23 low; *E*, Op 23 high.
Tell me, where is fancy bred, *Shakespeare,* D, B&H.
(There be none of beauty's daughters, *Lord Byron,* E♭ [e′♭-g′′], Chappell; C, B, Chappell.)
(Through the sunny garden, *Mary Coleridge,* E [b-e′′], Novello Op 18(b) low; *G,* Op 18 (b) high)
(Time of Roses, The, *Thomas Hood,* Dm [c′-g′′♭], Chappell; *Em, Cm,* Chappell.)
To Althea from Prison, *Richard Lovelace,* E♭ [d′♭-e′′♭](m), B&H Op 28 medium; *F,* Op 28 high; *D*, Op 28 low.
To Daisies, *Robert Herrick,* D♭ [e′♭-a′′♭](m), Classical/B&H Op 8 high, B&H; *B♭*, Op 8 low, B&H *Heritage 4.*
To wine and beauty, *John Wilmot, Earl of Rochester,* E♭ [b♭(c′)-f′′(e′′♭)], Classical/(Elkin), Op 18(a) low; (*F*, Elkin Op 18(a) high).
Under the greenwood tree, *Shakespeare,* D [d′-d′′], B&H Op 23 low; *F*, Op 23 high.
(Valley and the hill, The, *Mary Coleridge,* Dm [c′-e′′], Novello Op 18 (b) low; *Em,* Op 18(b) high.)
(Walled-in Garden, The, *Arthur Heald,* D, Chappell.)
Weep you no more, *Anon,* Fm [e′♭-g′′], B&H Op 12 high, *Heritage 3,* Schirmer *1st Tenor II*; *Dm,* Classical/B&H Op 12 low, B&H *Easy Song.*
When daffodils begin to peer, *Shakespeare,* A♭ [e′♭-e′′♭](m), B&H *Shakespeare Album*, Op 30 low; C, Op 30 high.
When icicles hang by the wall, *Shakespeare,* C [a′♭-a′′♭(g′′)], B&H *Shakespeare Album*; C, B&H.
Where be you going? *John Keats,* D [c′#-d′′], Classical/(Elkin) Op 18(a) low; (*F*, Elkin Op 18(a) high).
(Where Go the Boats, *Robert Louis Stevenson,* A [e′-g′′#(f′′#)], Chappell Op 5 high; F, Chappell Op 5 low.)
Who is Sylvia? *Shakespeare,* D [f′#-d′′], B&H Op 30 low; F, Op 30 high.
Why so pale and wan? *John Suckling,* C#m [e′-e′′], B&H 5 Op 28 medium; *Dm,* Op 28 high; *Bm,* Op 28 low.
Wild Flower's Song, The, *William Blake,* G [b-d′′], B&H Op 20 low; *B♭*, Classical/B&H Op 20 high.
(Wind from the South, *John Irvine,* F [d′-f′′], Chappell *English Recital 1.*)
Arrangements: *The Arnold Book of Songs,* B&H 1947.
Ash Grove, The, *Rodney Bennett,* A♭ [d′♭-e′′♭], B&H Arnold.
Barbara Allen, *Anon,* D [d′-d′′], B&H Arnold.
Believe me, if all those endearing young charms, *Thomas Moore,* E♭ [e′♭-e′′♭], B&H Arnold.
Ca' the yowes to the knowes, *Robert Burns,* Am [c′-e′′], B&H Arnold.
Charlie is my darling, *Anon,* Cm [c′-e′′♭], B&H Arnold.
Drink to me only, *Ben Jonson,* E♭ [e′♭-e′′♭], B&H Arnold, B&H; *G♭, F,* Classical.
Jolly Miller, The, *Isaac Bickerstaffe,* Gm [d′-d′′], B&H Arnold.
Man Behind the Plough, The, *Anon (French),* tr. *Rodney Bennett,* G [d′-e′′], B&H Arnold.
My Lady Greensleeves, *John Irvine,* Fm [c′-e′′♭](m), B&H Arnold.
My Lady's Garden, *Anon (French),* tr. *Rodney Bennett,* D♭ [d′♭-e′′♭], B&H Arnold.
Oh! 'tis sweet to think, *Thomas Moore,* G [d′-d′′], B&H Arnold.
Over the mountains, *Anon,* G [d′-d′′], B&H Arnold, B&H; *A*, B&H.
Pretty Month of May, *Anon* tr. *Anon,* E♭ [e′♭-e′′♭], B&H Arnold.
Since first I saw your face, *Thomas Ford,* E [e′-e′′](m), B&H Arnold.
Three Poor Mariners, *Anon,* E♭ [b♭-e′′♭](m), B&H Arnold.
Ye banks and braes, *Robert Burns,* G♭ [d′♭-e′′♭], B&H Arnold.

R

Race, Steve. 1921–
Collection: (*My music, my songs,* Novello.)

Rainier, Priaulx. 1903–1986. *See also* App. 2.
Collection: *Three Greek Epigrams,* Schott.
    Bird, A, *Anyte of Tegea* tr. *Richard Aldington,* [d′-e′′♭](f), Schott 3 Greek.
    Dolphin, A, *Anyte of Tegea* tr. *Richard Aldington,* [f′-a′′](f), Schott 3 Greek.
    For a Fountain, *Anyte of Tegea* tr. *Richard Aldington,* F# [d′-g′′#](f), Schott 3 Greek.

Randall, Anthony. *See* App. 2.

Randalls, Jeremy. SMIC.
Collections: *Six Songs,* (William Blake), [mezzo/ tenor], SMIC; *Three Sonnets* (Smith), [soprano], SMIC.
- Astyanax, *Smith,* [soprano], SMIC.
- Lullaby, [soprano], SMIC.
- Song of Iphigenia, *Smith,* [soprano], SMIC.

Rands, Bernard. 1935– *See also* App. 2.
- Ballad 2, *Gilbert Sorrentino,* [c′#-b′′b](f), Universal.

Raphael, Mark. 1900–1988
Collections: *Three Blake Songs,* Roberton; *Three D. H. Lawrence Poems,* Roberton, *Two Thomas Moore Songs,* Roberton.
- At the mid hour of night, *Thomas Moore,* Cm [f′#-g′′b], Roberton 2 Thomas Moore.
- Cherry Robbers, *D. H. Lawrence,* E [g′#-g′′#], Roberton 3 D. H. Lawrence.
- Dog-tired, *D. H. Lawrence,* A [e′-g′′#], Roberton 3 D. H. Lawrence.
- Flapper, *D. H. Lawrence,* G#m [e′-g′′#], Roberton 3 D. H. Lawrence.
- Fly, The, *William Blake,* E [c′#-e′′], Roberton 3 Blake.
- Lamb, The, *William Blake,* F#m [d′-e′′], Roberton 3 Blake.
- (Lay a garland on my hearse, *John Fletcher,* [b-e′′], S&B; [d′-g′′], S&B.)
- (Memory, *William Browne,* [e′#-a′′], S&B.)
- Oh! breathe not his name, *Thomas Moore,* Cm [c′b-e′′b], Roberton.
- Row gently here, *Thomas Moore,* G [d′-f′′#](m), Roberton.
- Shepherd, The, *William Blake,* Fm [d′-f′′], Roberton 3 Blake.
- (Sleep, *John Fletcher,* Bm [a-d′′], Curwen.)
- Weep no more, *John Fletcher,* Dm [c′-f′′], Roberton.
- When through the piazzetta, *Thomas Moore,* G [d′-f′′#], Roberton 2 Thomas Moore.

Rawsthorne, Alan. 1905–1971. *See also* App. 1, 2.
Collections: *Three French Nursery Songs,* B&H; *Two Songs,* BMP.
- Away, delights, *John Fletcher,* [c′#-g′′b], BMP 2 Songs.
- Carol, *W. R. Rodgers,* Bbm [d′b-f′′], BMP.
- Go bye-bye, Peterkin, *Anon (French)* tr. *Alex Cohen,* Bm [f′#-f′′#], B&H 3 French.
- God Lyaeus, *John Fletcher,* [e′-a′′], BMP 2 Songs.
- I'm a darling little baby, *Anon (French),* tr. *Alex Cohen,* C [f′#-f′′], B&H 3 French.
- Oh shepherdess, the rain's here, *Anon (French)* tr. *Alex Cohen,* Em [e′-f′′#], B&H 3 French.
- Two Fish, *Guillaume du Barthas* tr. *Joshua Sylvester,* [d′-a′′b], BMP.
- We three merry maidens, *French* tr. *M D Calvocoressi,* [e′-a′′](f), BMP.

Ray, Lilian.
- Sunshine of your smile, The, *Leonard Cooke,* Eb [c′-e′′b], IMP *Parlour Songs.*

Raynor, John. 1909–1970. *See also* BMIC
Collection: *Eleven Songs,* S&B (introduction by Olwen Picton-Jones).
- Bredon Hill, *A. E. Housman,* G [d′-g′′](m), S&B 11 Songs.
- Californy Song, The, *Hilaire Belloc,* Eb [bb-e′b](m), BMP.
- Come, rock his cradle, *G. R. Woodward,* Gm [f′-d′′], S&B 11 Songs.
- Down by the river, *Anon,* Eb [d′-f′′], S&B 11 Songs.
- Go, songs, *Francis Thompson,* Gb [e′b-a′′b], S&B 11 Songs.
- In Leinster, *Louise Imogen Guiney,* Em [d′-g′′](f), S&B 11 Songs.
- Lelant, *E. K. Chambers,* Bbm [d′b-e′′b], S&B 11 Songs.
- Love is a sickness, *Samuel Daniel,* Fm [f′-f′′], S&B 11 Songs.
- Love me again, *Anon,* Db [d′b-f′′], S&B 11 Songs.
- Loveliest of trees, *A. E. Housman,* E [e′-e′′], S&B 11 Songs.
- Loyal Lover, The, *Anon,* Eb [e′b-g′′](f), BMP.
- My Own Country, *Hilaire Belloc,* A [e′-f′′#], BMP.
- Old Lullaby, An, *Eugene Field,* Eb [e′b-g′′], BMP.
- (Rose, *Hilaire Belloc,* Chappell.)
- Spring, *Thomas Nashe,* B [d′#-b′′(g′′#)], BMP.
- Wakening, The, *Anon,* Gb [d′b-g′′b], S&B 11 Songs.
- West Sussex Drinking Song, *Hilaire Belloc,* D [c′#-f′′#](m), S&B 11 Songs.

Read, Martin M. *See also* App. 2.
- Drawing Details in an Old Church, *Thomas Hardy,* [d′-e′′b], Fand.
- Scenes from Shakespeare, *Shakespeare,* [bb-e′′], Fand.

Redman, Reginald. 1892–1972.
Collections: (*Five Chinese Miniatures*, Elkin); (*Five Settings of Poems from the Chinese*, Curwen); (*Two Short Songs,* Paterson).
    (At the Kuang-Li Pavilion, *Su Tung-P'o* tr. *L. Cranmer-Byng*, [d′b-g′′], Elkin 5 Miniatures.)
    (Clearing at Dawn, *Li Po* tr. *Arthur Waley*, [d′-f′′#], Elkin 5 Miniatures.)
    (Dancing Girl, The, *Li Po* tr. *Shigeyoshi Obata*, [d′b-g′′], Curwen 5 Poems.)
    (Immeasurable Pain, *Li Hou-Chu* tr. *Arthur Waley*, [c′-f′′], Elkin 5 Miniatures.)
    (In the Mountains, *Li Po* tr. *Shigeyoshi Obata*, [c′-f′′#], Curwen 5 Poems.)
    (Last Revel, The, *Ch'én Tzú-ang* tr. *L Cranmer-Bing*, [d′-f′′], Curwen 5 Poems.)
    (Night of Sorrow, The, *Li Po* tr. *Shigeyoshi Obata*, [f′-f′′], Curwen 5 Poems.)
    (Nocturne, *Anon,* E♭ [b♭-e′′], Paterson 2 Short Songs.)
    Nocturne, *Li Po* tr. *Shigeyoshi Obata*, [d′-g′′], Curwen 5 Poems.)
    (Pavilion of Abounding Joy, The, *Ou-Yang Hsui* tr. *L. Cranmer-Byng*, [f′#-a′′], Elkin 5 Miniatures.)
    (Silver, *Walter de la Mare*, Am [e′-g′′], Elkin.)
    (Song of Courtship, A, *Li Po* tr. *Arthur Waley*, [e′-g′′], Elkin 5 Miniatures.)
    (Your Rose, *Herbert J. Brandon*, G♭ [d′b-e′′b], Paterson 2 Short Songs.)

Rees, Delyth.
    Another Day, Curiad.

Rees, Howard. *See* App. 2.

Reizenstein, Franz. 1911–1968. BMIC.
Collection: *Five Sonnets*, Bardic.
    I love thee, *Elizabeth Barrett Browning*, [c′-b′′], Bardic 5 Sonnets.
    I think of thee, *Elizabeth Barrett Browning*, [c′-a′′], Bardic 5 Sonnets.
    Our two souls, *Elizabeth Barrett Browning*, [d′-a′′], Bardic 3 Sonnets.
    Perplexèd music, *Elizabeth Barrett Browning*, [c′#-b′′b], Bardic 5 Sonnets.
    Soul's expression, The, *Elizabeth Barrett Browning*, [d′-b′′b], Bardic 5 Sonnets.

Reynolds, Alfred Charles. 1884–1969.
    Ah! how delightful the morning, *Anon,* A [e′-f′′#], Novello.

Reynolds, Peter. *See* App. 2.

Rhys, Stephen. WMIC. *See also* App. 2.

Rice, Hugh Collins. 1962– *See* App. 2.

Richards, John Eric. WMIC.

Richardson, Alan. 1904–1978.
    Sonnet, *John Keats,* F [c′-f′′], BMP.

Ridley, Mr.
    Hunting Song, A, *C. L. Esq,* D [d′-a′′](m), Thames *Gentleman's Magazine.*

Ridout, Alan. 1934–1996
    When first mine eyes, *Thomas Wyatt,* [c′-b′], Thames *Countertenors 1.*

Roberton, Sir **Hugh S**tevenson. 1874–1952. SMIC. *See also* App. 1.
    All in the April evening, *Katherine Tynan,* E [e′-e′′], Roberton.
    As down by Banna's banks I strayed, *George Ogle,* C [c′-e′′], Roberton.
    As if I didn't know, *P. A. Grand,* E♭ [d′b-e′′b], Roberton.
    Blake's Cradle Song, *William Blake,* A♭ [e′b-g′′], Roberton; F, Roberton.
    Goodmorrow to you, Springtime, *P. A. Grand,* A♭ [e′b-e′′b], Roberton.
    Maureen, *Hugh S. Roberton,* C [c′-d′′], Roberton; E♭, F, Roberton.
    Old Woman, The, *Joseph Campbell,* F [c′-b′b], Roberton; A♭, Roberton.
    Softly fall the shades of evening, *H. W. Godfrey,* B♭ [f′-d′′], Roberton.
Arrangements: *Songs of the Isles,* Roberton.
    Dalmatian Cradle Song, *P. A. Grand,* Dm [c′-d′], Roberton.
    Dance to your daddy, *Anon,* B♭ [c′-f′′], Roberton.
    Fairy Lullaby, *Anon,* A♭ [e′b-e′′b], Roberton.
    Fidgety Bairn, The, *Hugh S. Roberton,* E♭ [e′b-e′′b](f), Roberton Songs of the Isles, Roberton.
    Health and joy be with you, *Professor Blackie,* E♭ [c′-e′′b], Roberton.
    Hebridean Shanty, *Hugh S. Roberton,* E♭ [b♭-e′′b](m), Roberton.

Highland Cradle Song, *Walter Scott*, C [c'-e''](f), Roberton, Songs of the Isles, Roberton.
Island Spinning Song, *Hugh S. Roberton*, F#m [e'-c''#](f), Roberton Songs of the Isles, Roberton.
Joy of my heart, *Hugh S. Roberton*, A [c'#-e''], Roberton, Songs of the Isles, Roberton.
Lewis Bridal Song (Mairi's Wedding), *Hugh S. Roberton*, G [c'-e''], Roberton Songs of the Isles, Roberton.
Mingulay Boat Song, *Hugh S. Roberton*, E [b-e''](m), Roberton Songs of the Isles, Roberton.
None so sweet, *Hugh S. Roberton*, Ab [e'b-e''b](m), Roberton.
Old Harper, The, *Anon*, Bb [bb-d''], Roberton.
Rise and follow, love, *Anon*, G [a-e''], Roberton.
Shuttle and Loom, *Hugh S. Roberton*, A [c'#-e''](f), Roberton, Songs of the Isles, Roberton.
Sing at the wheel, *Hugh S. Roberton*, Fm [c'-f''](m), Roberton, Songs of the Isles, Roberton.
Uist Tramping Song, *Hugh S. Roberton*, (tune John R. Bannerman), G [d'-e''], Roberton, Songs of the Isles, Roberton.
Wee Toun Clerk, The, *Anon*, Bb [d'-e''b], Roberton.
Westering Home, *Hugh S. Roberton*, A [c'#-e''], Roberton, Songs of the Isles, Roberton.
Windjammer, The, *Anon*, F#m [c'#-e''], Roberton.

Roberts, Caradog.
Mystery, The, [mezzo/baritone], Gwynn.

Roberts, J. H.
Don't cry [any voice], Snell.

Roberts, Mervyn William Herbert. 1906–1990. BMIC.
(Christmas Day, *Andrew Young*, G [d'-e''], Novello.)
(Elsewhere, *G. O. Warren*, D [b'-f'#], Novello.)
(Put a rosebud on her lips, *Francis H. King*, F [c'-f''], Novello.)
(Sentry, The, *G. O. Warren*, Db [d'b-f''], Novello.)
(St Govan, *A. G. Prys-Jones*, Fm [c'-f''], Novello.)
Arrangements: *Six Welsh Folksongs*, Gwynn.

Roberts, T. Osborne. 1879–1948.
Black Spring, The *Cynan* tr. *Wil Ifan*, C [c'-e''], Gwynn.
Sea Wrack, *Moira O'Neill*, [mezzo/baritone], Gwynn.
Widow Bird, A, *Percy Bysshe Shelley*, [mezzo], Snell.

Roberts, Trevor. 1940– WMIC. *See also* App. 2.
Stopping by Woods on a Snowy Evening, *Robert Frost*, [c#-d'](m), WMIC *Songs from Wales 2*.
Arrangements: *Five Welsh Folksongs*, [high], Banks.

Robinson, Michael Finlay. WMIC.

Robinson, Thomas. *fl.*1589–1609.
Now Cupid, look about thee, *Anon*, G [d'-g''], S&B (Greer) *Printed*.

Rodgers, Sarah. 1953– *See also* App. 2.
Collection: *Songs of Experience*, Impulse.
Acacia Tree, *Kathleen Raine*, [soprano], Impulse.
Clod and the Pebble, The, *William Blake*, [mezzo], Impulse Experience.
Earth's Answer, *William Blake*, [mezzo], Impulse Experience.
Fly, The, *William Blake*, [mezzo], Impulse Experience.
Hear the voice of the Bard, *William Blake*, [mezzo], Impulse Experience.
Listeners, The, *Walter de la Mare*, [mezzo], Impulse.
Poison Tree, The, *William Blake*, [mezzo], Impulse Experience.
Tyger, tyger, *William Blake*, [mezzo], Impulse Experience.

Roe, Betty. 1930– *See also* App. 2.
Collections: *Compliments of the Season*, Thames; *Nine Songs*, Thames (introduction Betty Roe); *Noble Numbers*, Thames; *Man without Myth*, Thames; *Seven Songs*, Thames (introduction Betty Roe); *These Growing Years*, Thames; *Three Dedications*, Thames (introduction Betty Roe); *Three Eccentrics*, Thames.
After Supper, *John Mole*, [a-e''], Thames Compliments.
As the holly groweth green, *King Henry VIII*, A [a-e''](m), Thames *Century 2*.
Bakery, The, *Anon (Korean)* tr. *Peter Hyun*, [d'-a''](f), Thames 7 Songs.
Beeches, *Diana Carroll*, [d'-f''#], Thames These Growing Years.

Beeny Cliff, *Thomas Hardy,* D [d′-f′′#], Thames 3 Dedications.
Distances, *Edward Storey,* [c′-g′′], Thames 9 Songs.
Gertrude's Prayer, *Rudyard Kipling,* [f′-f′′#](f), Thames 7 Songs.
Harp Song of the Dane Women, *Rudyard Kipling,* [e′-a′′](f), Thames 7 Songs.
His Last Sonnet, *John Keats,* G [c′-e′′], Thames 3 Dedications.
Hot sun, cool fire, *George Peel,* [e′-f′′#], Thames 9 Songs.
In the Fall, *Diana Carroll,* [c′#-g′′], Thames These Growing Years.
Infant Song, *Charles Causley,* [e′b-g′′b](f), Thames 7 Songs.
Legend of Rosemary, *Reginald Arkell,* [c′-g′′](f), Thames 7 Songs.
Lullaby, *Anon (Polish)* tr. *H. E. Kennedy & S. Uminska,* [e′-d′′#], Thames 9 Songs.
Lullaby for a Baby Toad, *Stella Gibbons,* Gm [d′-g′′#], Thames 9 Songs.
Man without Myth, *Ursula Vaughan Williams,* Thames Man without Myth.
Morning and Afternoon, *Leonard Clark,* [c′#-d′′], Thames 9 Songs.
Mr Kartoffel, *James Reeves,* B [a-e′′], Thames 3 Eccentrics.
Mr Tom Narrow, *James Reeves,* E [b-e′′b], Thames 3 Eccentrics.
Music Tree, The, *Peter Thorogood,* B [c′#-g′′#], Thames 3 Dedications.
Musical Chairs, *John Mole,* [a-e′′], Thames Compliments.
My Boy Jack, *Rudyard Kipling,* E [d′-e′′](f), Thames 7 Songs.
My Garden, *T. E. Brown,* D [b-d′′], Thames 9 Songs, *Countertenors 1.*
Nursery Rhyme of Innocence and Experience, *Charles Causley,* E [d′#-e′′], Thames 9 Songs, Thames.
Once upon a time, *Ursula Vaughan Williams,* Thames Man without Myth.
Quarry, The, *Ursula Vaughan Williams,* Thames Man without Myth.
Stop all the clocks, *W. H. Auden,* [a-g′′](f), Thames 7 Songs.
This enders night, *Anon 15th cent.,* [d′-g′′#], Thames 9 Songs.
To God (God gives not onely corne), *Robert Herrick,* [c′-d′′], Thames Noble Numbers.
To God (My God, I'm wounded), *Robert Herrick,* [b-d′′], Thames Noble Numbers, *Countenors 3.*
To His Angrie God, *Robert Herrick,* [b-e′′b], Thames Noble Numbers.
To His Saviour, a Child, *Robert Herrick,* D [a-d′′], Thames Noble Numbers.
To His Sweet Saviour, *Robert Herrick,* [c′-d′′], Thames Noble Numbers.
Triolet, *Diana Carroll,* [d′-a′′(g′′#)], Thames These Growing Years.
Two Gardens, *Walter de la Mare,* D [b-e′′], Thames 9 Songs.
Walk, The, *John Mole,* B♭ [d′-f′′#(e′′)], Thames Compliments.
Zackery Zed, *James Reeves,* [a-e′′], Thames 3 Eccentrics.
Arrangements: *A Garland of Folksongs,* Thames.
All things are quite silent, *Traditional,* [f′-f′′](f), Thames Garland.
Cocky robin, *Traditional,* [c′-e′′], Thames Garland, *Countertenors 3,* William Elkin.
Johnny Has Gone for a Soldier, *Anon,* [e′-f′′](f), Thames Garland.
Lass From the Low Countree, The, *Traditional,* [d′-f′′], Thames Garland, William Elkin.
To People who have Gardens, *Agnes Muir Mackenzie,* [f′-c′′], Thames Garland.
Wee Cooper o' Fife, The, *Anon,* [c′#-e′′], Thames Garland.

Ronald, Sir Landon (Landon Ronald Russell). 1873–1938.
Collections: *Album Leaves,* Classical; *Cycle of Life, A,* [high (given below), medium, low], Classical; *Four Silhouettes,* [high (given below), medium], Classical; *Four Songs of the Hill,* Classical; *Song-Offerings (First Series),* [medium high (given below), low], Classical; *Song-Offerings (Second Series),* [high, low], Classical; *Songs of Springtime,* [low], Classical; *Summertime,* [high, low], Classical; *Twelve Songs,* Thames 1990; *Vignettes,* [medium, low], Classical.
After Love, *Arthur Symons,* E♭ [e′b-a′′b], Classical 4 Silhouettes.
All in a Merry May-Time, *Helen Taylor,* B♭ [a-f′′], Classical Songs of Springtime.
April Love, *Ernest Dowson,* B [a#-d′′#], Classical Songs of Springtime.
Ask me not, dear, *Laurence Binyon,* Classical Vignettes.
At dawn the hill stands silver, *Harold Simpson,* B♭ [b♭-e′′♭], Classical 4 Songs of the Hill.
At Morning, *Temple Thurston,* B [b-d′′#], Classical Songs of Springtime.
At Sunrise, *Howard Fisher,* G [d′-g′′(a′′)], Classical Album Leaves.
Away on the hill there runs a stream, *Harold Simpson,* E [e′-e′′], Classical 4 Songs of the Hill.
Come home, my thoughts, from the hill, *Harold Simpson,* C [b♭-g′′♭(e′′)], Classical 4 Songs of the Hill.
Daybreak, *Edward Teschemacher,* D♭ [f′-a′′♭], Classical Summertime; B♭, Classical Summertime.
Dove, The, *John Keats,* Fm [c′-g′′], Thames 12 Songs.
Down in the forest, *Harold Simpson,* E [e′-a′′], Classical Cycle of Life; E♭, Schirmer *2nd Soprano.*
Drift down, drift down from the skies, *Harold Simpson,* A♭ [d′-a′′♭], Classical Cycle of Life; G, Schirmer *1st Soprano II.*

Early in the day it was whispered, *Rabindranath Tagore*, Classical Song-Offerings 2.
Evening, *Edward Teschemacher*, G♭ [g′♭-a′′♭], Classical Summertime; B♭, Classical Summertime.
Had I the heavens' embroidered cloths, *W. B. Yeats*, E [c′#-f′′#], Thames 12 Songs.
He came and sat by my side, *Rabindranath Tagore*, F#m [c′#-g′′], Classical Song-Offerings 1.
June Rhapsody, *Edward Lockton*, F [c′-f′′], Thames 12 Songs.
Let all the strains of joy, *Rabindranath Tagore*, Classical Song-Offerings 2.
Life of my life, I shall ever try, *Rabindranath Tagore*, Classical Song-Offerings 2.
Light, my light, *Rabindranath Tagore*, G [e′-a′′(b′′)], Classical Song-Offerings 1.
Little winding road, A, *Harold Simpson,* E [b-e′′], Classical 4 Songs of the Hill.
Love I have won you, *Harold Simpson*, A♭ [g′-a′′♭], Thames 12 Songs, Classical Cycle of Life; E♭, Schirmer *2nd Mezzo*.
Love in Dreams, *Arthur Symons,* B [e′-a′′], Classical 4 Silhouettes.
Love's Philosophy, *Percy Bysshe Shelley*, E [c′#-g′′#], Thames 12 Songs.
Moon at the Full, The, *Helen Taylor,* D [d′-e′′], Classical Songs of Springtime.
Morning, *Edward Teschemacher,* F [f′-a′′], Classical Summertime; A, Classical Summertime.
Night *see* Oh lovely night.
None will know, *Dorothy Dickinson,* Fm [c′-g′′], Classical Album Leaves.
O, Falmouth is a fine town, *W. E. Henley,* Classical Vignettes.
Oh lovely night, *Edward Teschemacher*, E♭ [e′♭-g′′(b′′♭)], Classical Summertime, Thames 12 Songs; B♭, Classical Summertime.
Pair Well Matched, A, *John Dryden*, E [e′-b′′(g′′#)](m), Thames 12 Songs.
Pluck this little flower, *Rabindranath Tagore*, F [c′-e′′], Classical Song-Offerings 1.
Prelude, *Harold Simpson,* A♭ [d′-b′′♭(g′′)], Thames 12 Songs, Classical Cycle of Life.
Reason, The, *May Aldington,* A♭ [e′♭-a′′♭], Classical Album Leaves.
Remember, *Christina Rossetti*, Bm [b-e′′], Thames 12 Songs.
Roses red in the garden, *Howard Fisher,* G [d′-f′′#], Classical Album Leaves.
Rushes, The, *Francis Ledwidge,* Classical Vignettes.
Second Thoughts, *Arthur Symons*, G [e′-g′′], Classical 4 Silhouettes; E♭, Mayhew *Collection 2*.
South Winds, The, *Temple Thurston,* B♭ [b♭-d′′], Classical Songs of Springtime.
Strew on her roses, roses, *Matthew Arnold,* Fm [e′♭-a′′♭], Thames 12 Songs.
That I want thee, only thee, *Rabindranath Tagore*, Gm [c′#-g′′], Classical Song-Offerings 1.
To One Beloved, *Julia Cook Watson,* C [d′-a′′], Classical Album Leaves.
Were I the flower, *Edward Teschemacher*, C [c′-e′′], Mayhew *Collection 1*.
When the leaves are fallen, *Herbert Bedford,* Classical Vignettes.
White sea mist, The, *Harold Simpson*, B♭ [d′♭-f′′], Thames 12 Songs.
Winds are calling, The, *Harold Simpson,* Fm [f′-f′′], Classical Cycle of Life.
Yes, I know this is nothing but thy love, *Rabindranath Tagore*, Classical Song-Offerings 2.
You are mine, (Alla Passeretta Bruna), *Arthur Symons,* E [d′-a′′], Classical 4 Silhouettes.
Your waking eyes, *Helen Taylor*, E♭ [e′♭-a′′♭], Thames 12 Songs.

Rooper, Jasper. BMIC.

Rootham, Cyril Bradley. 1875–1938.
Collections: (*Four Dramatic Songs,* Novello); *Siegfried Sassoon Songs*, S&B (introduction by Kenneth Shenton); *Six Songs*, S&B (introduction by Kenneth Shenton).
Beyond the sea, *Thomas Love Peacock*, C [d′-g′′], S&B 6 Songs.
Boy's Song, A, *James Hogg*, [d′-f′′](m), S&B 6 Songs.
Butterflies, *Siegfried Sassoon*, D [f′#-g′′(a′′)], S&B Siegfried Sassoon.
Child's Prayer, A, *Siegfried Sassoon*, D♭ [d′♭-e′′♭], S&B Siegfried Sassoon.
Everyone Sang, *Siegfried Sassoon*, C [f′#-a′′♭], S&B Siegfried Sassoon, Thames *Century 3*.
Helen of Kirkconnell, *Traditional*, F [e′-g′′](m), S&B 6 Songs.
I sorrowed, *Anon*, A [e′♭-e′′], S&B 6 Songs.
Idyll, *Siegfried Sassoon*, Am [e′-f′′#], S&B Siegfried Sassoon.
(Imagination, *Mary Coleridge,* B♭ [e′♭-b′′♭(a′′♭)], Novello 4 Dramatic Songs.)
Morning Glory, *Siegfried Sassoon*, F [d′-e′′♭], S&B Siegfried Sassoon.
Over the hills and far away, *Mary Coleridge,* Em [e′-a′′], Novello 4 Dramatic Songs.
Poplar and the Moon, A, *Siegfried Sassoon*, A [e′-f′′#], S&B Siegfried Sassoon.
South Wind, *Siegfried Sassoon*, D [d′-e′′], S&B Siegfried Sassoon.
(St Andrews, *Mary Coleridge,* Novello 4 Dramatic Songs.)
Spring-time of Life, The, *Thomas Love Peacock*, D [a-d′′], S&B 6 Songs.
Supplication, A, *Thomas Wyatt*, F [d′♭-e′′], S&B 6 Songs.
(Unwelcome, *Mary Coleridge,* Novello 4 Dramatic Songs.)

Rose, John. 1928–
Collections; *Seven Scots Songs,* Bardic; *Two Fly Songs,* Bardic; *Unforgotten Thoughts,* Bardic.
  Auld Rocks, The, *Lilias Scott Chisholm,* [c′-d′′], Bardic 7 Scots.
  Cambridge, *Lilias Scott Chisholm,* [a#-f′′#], Bardic Unforgotten.
  Dream O't, *Lilias Scott Chisholm,* [a#-c′′#], Bardic Unforgotten.
  Fly, The, *William Blake,* [g′-f′′], Bardic 2 Fly.
  Fly, The, *Walter de la Mare,* [c′#-f′′], Bardic 2 Fly.
  Fragment, *Lilias Scott Chisholm,* [c′-f′′], Bardic 7 Scots.
  In the Kirkyaird, *Lilias Scott Chisholm,* [d′-f′′], Bardic 7 Scots.
  Innocence, *Lilias Scott Chisholm,* [f′-f′′], Bardic 7 Scots.
  Johnnie Logie, *Lilias Scott Chisholm,* [d′b-e′′], Bardic 7 Scots.
  Luve, *Lilias Scott Chisholm,* [c′-f′′], Bardic 7 Scots.
  Memories, *Lilias Scott Chisholm,* [c′-e′′], Bardic Unforgotten.
  Requital, *Lilias Scott Chisholm,* [bb-g′′], Bardic Unforgotten.
  Snow in the Year of Mourning, *Lilias Scott Chisholm,* [bb-g′′], Bardic Unforgotten.
  Woman Speaks, A, *Lilias Scott Chisholm,* [c′#-f′′], Bardic 7 Scots.

Ross, Colin.
  Cherry Tree Hung with Snow, *A. E. Housman,* Bbm [f′-b′′b], Curwen.
  Golden Sunset, The, *Longfellow,* [high], Brunton.
  Ode, *Chinese* tr. *Soame Jenkins,* [high], Brunton.

Rosseter, Philip. 1568–1623.
Collection: *A Booke of Ayres,* S&B (edited Thurston Dart). Only songs available in anthologies are listed individually here. Note that in the following: Pilkington = *English Lute Songs Book 1,* S&B; Keel 1a, 1b and 2a, 2b = *Elizabethan Lovesongs Books 1 and 2* [high, low], B&H.
  And would you see my mistress' face, *Thomas Campion?* Gm [g′-f′′](m), Ayres, BMP *W&W 4*.
  Ay me that love, *Thomas Campion?* Gm [f′#-f′′](m), Ayres, BMP *W&W 1*.
  If I hope I pine, *Thomas Campion?* G [f′#-d′′], Ayres, Pilkington, BMP *W&W 5*.
  If I urge my kind desires, *Thomas Campion?* G [f′#-e′′](m), Ayres, Keel 1b; *A*, Keel 1a.
  If she forsake me, *Thomas Campion?* G [d′-e′′](m), Ayres, BMP *W&W 3*; *A*, Keel 1a; *Eb*, Pilkington; *F*, Keel 1b.
  Kind in unkindness, *Thomas Campion?* Gm [f′-d′′](m), Ayres, Pilkington, BMP *W&W 5*.
  Shall I come if I swim? *Thomas Campion?* Dm [d′-d′′](m), Ayres, Pilkington, BMP *W&W 3*.
  Shall then a traitorous kiss, *Thomas Campion?* Gm [f′#-d′′], Ayres, BMP *W&W 5*.
  Sweet, come again, *Thomas Campion?* G [g′-g′′], Ayres, Pilkington.
  Though far from joy, *Thomas Campion?* Gm [f′-f′′], Ayres, Pilkington, BMP *W&W 1*.
  What is a day, *Thomas Campion?* Gm [f′-f′′], Ayres, BMP *W&W 4*.
  What then is love but mourning? *Thomas Campion?* Gm [g′-f′′], Ayres, Pilkington, Chester (Shavitz) *Celebrated 1*, BMP *W&W 1*.
  When Laura smiles, *Thomas Campion?* G [d′-e′′], Ayres, Keel 1b, BMP *W&W 1*; *A*, Keel 1a, Leonard *Baroque high*; *F*, Pilkington, S&B, Leonard *Baroque low*.
  Whether men do laugh or weep, *Thomas Campion?* G [d′-e′′], Ayres, BMP *W&W 4*.

Routh, Francis. 1927– *See also* App. 2.
Collections: *Four Shakespeare Songs, Op 4,* Redcliffe; *Ripeness is all, Op 53,* Redcliffe; *Songs of Farewell, Op 8,* Redcliffe; *Songs of Lawrence Durrell, Op 10,* Redcliffe; *Three Shakespeare Songs, Op 57,* Redcliffe.
  August, *Dachine Rainer,* [tenor], Redcliffe Ripeness.
  Baby's Epitaph, A, *Algernon Charles Swinburne,* [high], Redcliffe Songs of Farewell.
  Birthday Sonnet, *Dachine Rainer,* [tenor], Redcliffe Ripeness.
  Blow, blow, thou winter wind, *Shakespeare,* [high], Redcliffe 4 Shakespeare.
  Comfort to a Youth that had Lost his Love, *Robert Herrick,* [high], Redcliffe Songs of Farewell.
  Death, *Dachine Rainer,* [tenor], Redcliffe Ripeness.
  Death of Iphigenea (scena), Op 40, *Aeschylus* tr. *Gilbert Murray,* [mezzo], Redcliffe.
  Echo, *Lawrence Durrell,* [high], Redcliffe Durrell.
  Encounter, *Dachine Rainer,* [tenor], Redcliffe Ripeness.
  Epithalamium, *Dachine Rainer,* [tenor], Redcliffe Ripeness.
  Farewell, A, *George Gascoigne,* [high], Redcliffe Songs of Farewell.
  Fear no more the heat o' the sun, *Shakespeare,* [medium], Redcliffe 3 Shakespeare.
  Glycine's Song, *Samuel Taylor Coleridge,* [high], Redcliffe Songs of Farewell.
  Here summer ends, *Dachine Rainer,* [tenor], Redcliffe Ripeness.
  How should I your true love know? *Shakespeare,* [high], Redcliffe 4 Shakespeare.
  January Thaw, *Dachine Rainer,* [tenor], Redcliffe Ripeness.

Lesbos, *Lawrence Durrell,* [high], Redcliffe Durrell.
Nemea, *Lawrence Durrell,* [high], Redcliffe Durrell.
Orpheus with his lute, *Shakespeare,* [high], Redcliffe 4 Shakespeare.
Season, *Dachine Rainer,* [tenor], Redcliffe Ripeness.
Sigh no more, ladies, *Shakespeare,* [high], Redcliffe 4 Shakespeare.
Songs of Dachine Rainer (cycle), Op 40, *Dachine Rainer,* [high], Redcliffe.
Songs of Sir Walter Scott (cycle), Op 39, *Sir Walter Scott,* [baritone], Redcliffe.
Sonnet on the Descent from Heaven, *Dachine Rainer,* [tenor], Redcliffe Ripeness.
Spears and Fiddleheads, *Dachine Rainer,* [tenor], Redcliffe Ripeness.
Spring, The, *Kathleen Raine,* [high], Redcliffe Songs of Farewell.
This unimportant morning, *Lawrence Durrell,* [high], Redcliffe Durrell.
Under the greenwood tree, *Shakespeare,* [medium], Redcliffe 3 Shakespeare.
Water Music, *Lawrence Durrell,* [high], Redcliffe Durrell.
When that I was and a little tiny boy, *Shakespeare,* [medium], Redcliffe 3 Shakespeare.
Woman Young and Old, A (cycle), *W. B. Yeats,* [high], Redcliffe.

Rowley, Alec. 1892–1958. *See also* App. 2.
Collections: *Five Songs to Words by John Drinkwater,* B&H; *Pillicock Hill,* BMP; *Three Mystical Songs,* B&H.
Birds, The, *Hilaire Belloc,* Em [c′-e′′], B&H; Gm, B&H.
Birthday, The, *Traditional,* Am [e′-a′′], B&H 3 Mystical.
Blue Water, *Edward Shenton,* F [c′-d′′], B&H.
Cotswold Love, *John Drinkwater,* D [d′-e′′], B&H Drinkwater.
(Counting Sheep, *Doris Rowley,* F, Elkin.)
Derbyshire Song, *John Drinkwater,* D [d′-d′′], B&H Drinkwater.
Fairy Pedlar, The, *Doris Rowley,* E♭ [c′-e′′♭], Cramer; G, Cramer.
Friendly Cow, The, *Robert Louis Stevenson,* G [d′-e′′], Roberton.
From a Railway Carriage, *Robert Louis Stevenson,* B♭ [e′♭-f′′], Roberton.
Heart's Journey, The (cycle), *Siegfried Sassoon,* [d′-a′′], B&H.
How far is it to Bethlehem? *F. Chesterton,* S&B.
Johnny shall have a new bonnet, *Old Rhyme,* E♭ [e′♭-g′′], B&H.
Lorry Driver, The, *Edward Shenton,* [d′-e′′(f′′], Gwynn.
Mad Tom Tatterman, *John Drinkwater,* Gm [c′-e′′♭], B&H Drinkwater.
Molly-O, *Anon,* Dm [f′-f′′], B&H.
My Bower, *George Darley,* F [f′-g′′], B&H.
My love doth love the bees, *Doris Rowley,* F [c′-e′′♭], B&H.
O like a queen, *Sir William Watson,* Gm [b♭-e′′], B&H.
O that I knew where I might find him, *Book of Job,* G [d′-g′′], B&H.
Old Oliver, *John Drinkwater,* Am [d′-f′′], B&H Drinkwater.
On Newlyn Hill, *Crosbie Garstin,* E♭ [c′-e′′♭], B&H.
Paradise Street, *Cicely Fox Smith,* Bm [b-e′′], B&H; Dm, B&H.
Pretty Betty, *Anon,* [d′-d′′], BMP.
Prophecy, The, *Traditional,* Bm [e′-g′′], B&H 3 Mystical.
(Sheep, *W. H. Davies,* Cramer.)
Silkworms, *Rodney Bennett,* D [e′-f′′#(a′′)], B&H.
Song of the Wind, *Edward Shenton,* Dm [d′-f′′], Gwynn.
Supplication, *Doris Rowley,* E♭ [c′-e′′♭], B&H.
(Three jolly shepherds, *Traditional,* D [d′-g′′], B&H 3 Mystical.)
To My Lady, *W. R. Titterton,* D [c′#-e′′], B&H.
Toll-Gate House, The, *John Drinkwater,* Am [c′-e′′], B&H Drinkwater.
When rooks fly homeward, *Joseph Campbell,* E♭, Weinberger, F, G, Weinberger.

Roxburgh, Edwin. 1937–
Collection: *Three Songs,* UMP.
these children, *E. E. Cummings,* [contralto], UMP 3 Songs.
this is the garden, *E. E. Cummings,* [contralto], UMP 3 Songs.
wind has blown the rain away, a, *E. E. Cummings,* [contralto], UMP 3 Songs.

Rubbra, Charles **Edmund.** 1901–1986. *See also* App. 1, 2.
Collections: *Amoretti (2nd Series)* Op 43, S&B; *Four Short Songs,* Lengnick; *Three Psalms, Op 61,* Lengnick; *Two Songs, Op 17,* Lengnick; *Two Songs, Op 22,* Lengnick; *Two Songs for Voice and Harp or Piano,* Lengnick.
Cradle Song, *Padraic Colum,* Am [d′-e′′♭], Lengnick 4 Short Songs.
Duan of Barra, A, *Murdoch Maclean,* C [d′-g′′], Lengnick, BMP.

Fly envious time, *John Milton*, [d´#-g´´], Lengnick.
Fresh Spring, the herald of love's mighty king (Sonnet 70), *Edmund Spenser*, [c´-g´´](m), S&B *Amoretti*.
Hymn to the Virgin, A, *Anon*, Am [d´-g´´], Lengnick 2 for Voice.
In Dark Weather, *Mary Webb*, [b-g´´(b´´)], Lengnick.
Invocation to Spring, *James Thomson*, Dm [f´-g´´], Lengnick 2 Songs Op 17.
It was a lover, *Shakespeare*, [c´-g´´], Lengnick, BMP.
Jesukin, *St Ita*, [e´-f´´#](f), Lengnick 2 for Voice.
Lackyng my love, I go from place to place (Sonnet 78), *Edmund Spenser*, [d´b-f´´#](m), S&B *Amoretti*.
Lord is my shepherd, The, *Psalm 23*, D [a-d´´], Lengnick 3 Psalms.
Lyke as the culver, on the bared bough (Sonnet 89), *Edmund Spenser*, [c´#-a´´b](m), S&B *Amoretti*.
Mark when she smiles with amiable cheare (Sonnet 40), *Edmund Spenser*, [c´-g´´](m), S&B *Amoretti*.
Night, The, *Hilaire Belloc*, [b-e´´], Lengnick.
No swan so fine, *Marianne Moore*, Bb [d´-f´´], Lengnick.
Nocturne, Op 54, *Alcman* tr. *H. T. Wade-Grey*, Gb [c´-f´´], Lengnick.
O Lord, rebuke me not, *Psalm 6*, [f#-e´´], Lengnick 3 Psalms.
Orpheus with his lute, *Shakespeare*, Dm [d´-e´´], Lengnick 4 Short Songs.
Out in the dark, *Edward Thomas*, [g´-a´´b], Thames *Century 1*, Lengnick.
Praise ye the Lord, *Psalm 150*, [bb-f´´], Lengnick 3 Psalms, Thames *Century 4*.
Prayer, A, *Ben Jonson*, Fm [bb-g´´], Lengnick 2 Songs Op 17.
Rosa Mundi, *Rachel Annand Taylor*, [d´-e´´b], Lengnick 4 Short Songs.
Rune of Hospitality, *Kenneth Macleod*, Gm [f´-d´´], Lengnick.
Take O take those lips away, *Shakespeare*, [e´-f´´#], Lengnick 2 Songs Op 22.
What guyle is this, that those her golden tresses? (Sonnet 37), *Edmund Spenser*, [e´-a´´b](m), S&B *Amoretti*.
Why so pale and wan? *John Suckling*, Cm [c´-a´´b], Lengnick 2 Songs Op 22.
Widow bird sate mourning, A, *Percy Bysshe Shelley*, [e´-g´´], Lengnick.

Runswick, Daryl. 1946– *See* App. 2.

Russel, Davidson. *fl.*1735.
Modest Question, The, *John Gay?*, F [c´-f´´](m), S&B (Pilkington) *Georgian 1*.

Russell, Henry. 1812–1900.
Woodman, spare that tree, *P. Morise*, F [c´-d´´], IMP *Parlour Songs*.

Russell, Kennedy. *See also* B&H archive.
Vale (Farewell), *de Burgh d'Arcy*, Bb [f´-g´´(b´´b], Cramer *Drawing Room Songs*.

Rutter, John. 1945– *See also* App. 2.
Shepherd's Pipe Carol, *John Rutter*, F [c´-g´´], OUP *Solo Christmas high*, OUP; Eb, *Solo Christmas low*.

S

Sagar, Nigel. 1926–
Collection: *Seven Love Songs*, Modus.
Cloths of Heaven, The, *W. B. Yeats*, D [a-d´´], Modus Love Songs.
Echoes, *Thomas Moore*, F [a-d´´b], Modus Love Songs.
How do I love thee? *Elizabeth Barrett Browning*, G [b-e´´], Modus Love Songs.
Love's Philosophy, *Percy Bysshe Shelley*, F [c´-d´´], Modus Love Songs.
Now sleeps the crimson petal, *Alfred Lord Tennyson*, D [c´#-d´´#], Modus Love Songs.
Romance, *Robert Louis Stevenson*, D [b-e´´], Modus Love Songs.
Shall I compare thee to a summer's day? *Shakespeare*, F [a-d´´], Modus Love Songs.
So we'll go no more a-roving, *Lord Byron*, B [a#-d´´#], Modus.
Walrus and the Carpenter, The, *Lewis Carroll*, Eb [c-e´´b], Modus.

Salomon, Johann Peter. 1745–1815.
Go, lovely rose, *Edmund Waller*, Eb [c´b-f´´](m), OUP (Roberts) *Tuneful Voice*.
O tuneful voice, *Anne Hunter*, Eb [d´-g´´](f), OUP (Roberts) *Tuneful Voice*.

Say not that minutes swiftly move, *Mary Robinson,* D [d′-f#′′], OUP (Roberts) *Tuneful Voice.*
Why still before these streaming eyes? *Anne Hunter,* Gm [c′#-g′′], OUP (Roberts) *Tuneful Voice.*

Salter, Lionel Paul. 1914–2000
Counsel, *Robert Gould,* [g′-a′′], Lengnick.
High song, The, *Humbert Wolfe,* [high voice], Lengnick.
Shepherdess, The, *Alice Meynell,* Dm [d′-g′′], BMP.

Salter, Timothy. 1942– BMIC.

Salzedo, Leonard Lopès. 1921–2000 BMIC. *See also* App. 1, 2.

Samuel, Harold. 1879–1937.
Call of the Roses, The, *Claude Aveling,* G [d′-a′′(b′′)], B&H.
Daisies, *Edward Teschemacher,* Ab [e′b-e′′], B&H.
Dear little love, *Alfred A. Hyatt,* F [c′-f′′], B&H.
Diaphenia, *Henry Constable* or *Henry Chettle,* D [c′#-f′′#(e′′)](m), B&H *Heritage 1*; C, F, B&H.
Fairy Boat, The, *Annette Horey,* G [d′-g′′], B&H *Heritage 2*; Eb, B&H.
Joggin' along the highway, *Arthur Anderson,* D [d′-e′′](m), IMP *Parlour Songs.*
Nanny, *Thomas Percy,* F [c′-e′′b](m), B&H *Heritage 2.*
New Little Visitor, A, *H. Ernest Hunt,* Eb [a-e′′b], B&H; F, G, B&H.
Oh! my sweeting, *Anon,* Db [d′b-f′′](m), B&H *Heritage 1*, B&H.
Toy band, *Sir Henry Newbolt,* G [b-e′′(g′′)], B&H.
Wrong not, *Sir Walter Raleigh,* G [d′-e′′], B&H.

Samuel, Rhian. WMIC. *See also* App. 2.
Collections: *Ancient Songs,* S&B; *White Amaryllis, The,* S&B.
Before Dawn, *May Sarton,* [c′-g′′#](f), S&B White Amaryllis, S&B.
Celebration, *May Sarton,* [c′#-f′′#], S&B White Amaryllis.
Hare in the Moon, The, *Japanese Folk Tale,* [a-c′′′](f), S&B.
Heledd's Lament, *Early Welsh Lyric,* [c′#-g′′], S&B Ancient Songs.
Lullaby for Dinogat, *Early Welsh Lyric,* [c′#-g′′], S&B Ancient Songs.
Snow Light, The, *May Sarton,* [c′#-f′′#], S&B White Amaryllis.
Young Man's Shirt, The, *Early Welsh Lyric,* [c′#-g′′], S&B Ancient Songs.

Samuels, Cuthbert.
Harp on the willows, [soprano/tenor], Snell.
Lost Happiness, The, [tenor], Snell.
Nightingale, The, [soprano], Snell.
Prometheus, [baritone/bass], Snell.
Sculptor, The, [contralto/baritone], Snell.

Sander, Peter. *See* App. 2.

Sanderson, Wilfrid. 1878–1935. *See also* B&H.
Captain Mac, *P. J. O'Reilly,* D [a(e)-f′′#(e′′)](m) B&H *Ballad Album 2.*
Friend o' Mine, *Fred. E. Weatherly,* C [d′(f′)-g′′] B&H *Ballad Album 1*; Ab, *Souvenirs*; (G, Bb, B&H).
Shipmates o' Mine, *Edward Teschemacher,* G [a-d′′](m) B&H *Ballad Album 1*; (F, A, B&H.).
Until, *Edward Teschemacher,* F [d′(f′)-g′′] B&H *Ballad Album 2.*

Sanger, David.
Collection: *Three Powell Songs,* Banks.
Dancer's end XV, *J. Enoch Powell,* [c′#-e′′], Banks 3 Powell.
Wedding Gift IV, The, *J. Enoch Powell,* [b-e′′], Banks 3 Powell.
Wedding Gift V, The, *J. Enoch Powell,* [a-e′′b], Banks 3 Powell.

Sansom, Chris.
Lovesongs (cycle)*, E. E. Cummings,* [b-b′′], Micropress.

Saxton, Robert. 1953–   *See* App. 2.

Schetky, Johann Georg Christoph. 1737–1824.
Echo, The, *William? Woods,* Bb [f′-a′′], OUP (Roberts) *Tuneful Voice.*

Schofield, Ian.
Collection: *Three Base Diversions,* Caddy Publishing.
    Epitaph, An, *Anon,* [c#-e′*b*], Caddy Base.
    Fill the bowl, Butler, *Anon,* [A-e′(a′)], Caddy Base.
    Phillida and Corydon, *Anon,* [B-d′], Caddy Base.

Scott, Anthony Leonard Winstone. 1911–2000
Collection: *Four Songs from 'The Princess',* B&H.
    As thro' the land at eve we went, *Alfred Lord Tennyson,* [d′-g′′], B&H 4 Songs.
    Lullaby, *Alfred Lord Tennyson,* [e′-d′′](f), B&H.
    O swallow, swallow, flying, flying South, *Alfred Lord Tennyson,* [c′-a′′], B&H 4 Songs.
    Sweet and low, *Alfred Lord Tennyson,* [d′*b*-g′′*b*], B&H 4 Songs.
    Tears, idle tears, *Alfred Lord Tennyson,* [c′-a′′*b*], B&H 4 Songs.

Scott, Cyril Meir. 1879–1970. *See also* App. 2.
Collections: (*Album of Songs (Soprano), Album of Songs (Contralto), Album of Songs (Tenor), Album of Songs (Baritone),* Elkin; *Old Songs in New Guise,* Elkin; *Songs of Old Cathay,* Elkin.)
    (Afterday, *Cyril Scott,* G [d′-d′′], Elkin Baritone; B*b*, C, Elkin.)
    (Alone, *Chinese* tr. *Herbert A. Giles,* [c′(b)-e′′#], Elkin Old Cathay.)
    (And so I made a villanelle, *Ernest Dowson,* B*b* [f′-d′′], Elkin; G, Elkin.)
    (Arietta, *Duffield Bendall,* C [a-e′′], Elkin Baritone; E*b* Elkin Tenor.)
    (Aspiration, *Irene McLeod,* Elkin.)
    (Atwain, *F. Leslie,* low [c′-f′′], Elkin; high, Elkin.)
    Autumn Song, *Rosamund Marriott Watson,* B*b* [b*b*-e′′*b*], Novello; (D, Elkin).
    Autumnal, *Ernest Dowson,* B*b* [b*b*-g′′], B&H.
    (Autumn's Lute, *Rosamund Marriott Watson,* [low], Elkin; [high], Elkin.)
    (Ballad of Fair Helen, The, *Anon,* [d′-f′′](m), Elkin.)
    Ballad Singer, The, *Eric Harben,* D*b* [d′*b*-f′′], B&H.
    (Birthday, A, *Christina Rossetti,* C [b-f′′], Elkin; D, Elkin.)
    Blackbird's Song, *Rosamund Marriott Watson,*D [b-e′′], Novello; (E*b*, F, Elkin).
    (Daffodils, *Ella Erskine,* C [g′-a′′](f), Elkin Soprano; A, B*b*, Elkin.)
    Dairy Song, *Ernest Dowson,* G [d′-e′′], B&H; F, B&H.
    Daphnis and Chloe, *Selwyn Image,* G [d′-g′′], B&H.
    Don't come in sir, please, *Anon,* tr. *Herbert A. Giles,* D [d′-f′′#(e′′)](f), Novello; (E, Elkin Soprano; Elkin.)
    (Drink to me only, Elkin Old in New.)
    (Eastern Lament, An, *Anon* tr. *Herbert A. Giles,* Cm [e′*b*-e′′*b*], Elkin; Em, Elkin.)
    Eileen, *Ellen Mary Rowning,* C [c′-f′′], B&H.
    (Evening, *Ernest Dowson,* C [b-d′′], Elkin Contralto, Elkin; E*b*, Elkin.)
    Evening Hymn, *Latin* tr. *E. Caswall,* D [d′-f′′#], B&H.
    (Evening Melody, *Cyril Scott,* low [b-f′′], Elkin; [high], Elkin.)
    (Exultation, *No text,* Elkin.)
    (For a dream's sake, *Christina Rossetti,* A*b* [a*b*-e′′], Elkin; C, B*b*, Elkin.)
    (From Afar, *Rosamund Marriott Watson,* C [c′-e′′], Elkin; E, Elkin.)
    (Garden of Memory, *Rosamund Mariott Watson,* [d′-g′′], Elkin.)
    (Gift of Silence, A, *Ernest Dowson,* F [c′-f′(e′′)](m), Elkin Contralto, Baritone, Elkin.)
    (Have ye seen him pass by? *Anon* tr. *Geoffrey Whitworth,* Elkin.)
    (Huckster, The, *Edward Thomas,* B*b* [d′-f′′], Elkin; C, Elkin.)
    Immortality, *Bulwer-Lytton,* E*b* [b*b*-e′′*b*], Novello; (F, G, Elkin.)
    (In a Fairy Boat, *Bernard Weller,* C [e′-f′′], Elkin; E*b*, Elkin.)
    (In Absence, *Anon* tr. *Herbert A. Giles,* [c′#-f′′#], Elkin Old Cathay.)
    (In the silver moonbeams, *French* tr. *Cyril Scott,* A [f′#-e′′], Elkin; G, Elkin.)
    (In the Valley, *Rosamund Marriott Watson,* high [e′-a′′], Elkin; [medium], Elkin.)
    (Insouciance, *Anon* tr. *Herbert A. Giles,* low [f′-e′′], Elkin; [high], Elkin.)
    (Invocation, *Margaret Maitland Radford,* D [d′-e′′], Elkin; F, Elkin.)
    (Lady June, *Elizabeth Haddon,* Elkin.)
    Last Word, A, *Ernest Dowson,* B*b* [d′-e′′*b*], B&H.
    (Lilac-time, *Walt Whitman,* C [d′-a′′], Elkin.)
    (Little Bells of Sevilla, The, *Dora Sigerson Shorter,* high [e′*b*-a′′], Elkin; [medium], Elkin.)
    (Little Foreigner, The, *Cyril Scott,* Elkin.)
    (Little song of Picardie, A, *Rosamund Marriott Watson,* E [e′-f′′#], Elkin Soprano; D, Elkin.)
    (Looking Back, *Christina Rossetti,* D*b*, Elkin; E*b*, F, Elkin.)
    Lord Randall, *Anon,* [medium], Novello.
    (Lost Love, A, *Anon* tr. *Herbert Giles,* A*b* [g′-a′′*b*], Elkin Soprano; E*b*, Contralto; F, Elkin.)

(Lovely kind and kindly loving, *Nicholas Breton*, B♭ [f′-g′′], Elkin Tenor; G, Elkin.)
(Love's Aftermath, *Ernest Dowson*, B♭ [c′-e′′], Elkin Contralto, Elkin; D♭, Elkin.)
(Love's Quarrel, *Bulwer-Lytton*, C [g′-a′′], Elkin Tenor; B♭, C, Elkin.)
Lullaby, *Christina Rossetti*, F [d′-g′′#(f′′)](f), Novello, Schirmer *1st Soprano*; D, E♭, Novello.
(March Requiem, A, *Norah Richardson*, Elkin.)
Mary, *Helen Selina, Lady Dufferin*, G [d′-e′′], B&H.
(Meditation, *Ernest Dowson*, B♭, Elkin; C, Elkin.)
(Mermaid's Song, *Tamar Faed*, [d′-f′′], Elkin.)
(Mirage, *Rosamund Marriott Watson*, A♭ [d′-f′′], Elkin Soprano; Elkin.)
(My captain, *Walt Whitman*, F [c′-d′′], Elkin; G, Elkin.)
(My lady sleeps, *Duffield Bendall*, F [e′-a′′], Elkin Tenor; D, Elkin.)
(New Moon, The, *Rosamund Marriott Watson*, G [d′-g′′], Elkin Soprano; E, Elkin.)
Night Song, *Rosamund Marriott Watson*, D♭ [b♭-d′′♭], Novello; (E♭, Elkin.)
(Night Wind, *Teresa Hooley*, Elkin.)
(Nocturne, *Rosamund Marriott Watson*, A♭ [c′-f′′], Elkin; B, Elkin.)
(Old Loves, *Cyril Scott*, G [g′-e′′](m), Elkin; A, Elkin.)
(Old Song Ended, An, *D. G. Rossetti*, F [d′-f′′], Elkin; E♭, Elkin.)
(Oracle, *Cyril Scott*, E♭, [c′-e′′♭], Elkin; F, Elkin.)
(Osme's Song, *George Darley*, D [d′-f′′#], Elkin; F, Elkin.)
(Our Lady of Violets, *Teresa Hooley*, D [d′-f′′#], Elkin; C, Elkin.)
(Pastorale, *No text*, [e′♭-a′′(c′′′)], Elkin.)
(Picnic, A, *Anon* tr. *Herbert A. Giles*, [c′-g′′♭], Elkin Old Cathay.)
(Pierrot and the Moon Maiden, *Ernest Dowson*, D♭ [d′♭-f′′], Elkin; E, Elkin.)
(Pilgrim Cranes, The, *Lord de Tabley*, F [d′♭-e′′], Elkin; G, Elkin.)
(Prayer, A, *Charles Kingsley*, A [c′#-a′], Elkin; C, Elkin.)
Prelude, *Rosamund Mariott Watson*, B♭ [b♭-e′′♭], Novello; (C, D, Elkin.)
(Rain, *Margaret Maitland Radford*, [low], Elkin; [high],Elkin.)
(Reconciliation, *Naomi Carvalho*, B♭, Elkin.)
(Reflection, A, *Anon* tr. *W. R. Paton*, F [e′-g′′], Elkin Tenor; D, Elkin.)
(Requiem, *R. L. Stevenson*, C [c′-e′′], Elkin; E♭, Elkin.)
(Retrospect, *Ernest Dowson*, C [c′-e′′], Elkin; D, Elkin.)
(Rima's Call to the Birds (scena), *W. H. Hudson*, [soprano], Elkin.)
(Roundel of Rest, A, *Arthur Symons*, C [a-e′′], Elkin; E♭, Elkin.)
Sands of Dee, The, *Charles Kingsley*, E♭ [e′♭-g′′], Novello; (C, Elkin.)
(Scotch Lullabye, *Scott*, D [a-d′′], Elkin; F, Elkin.)
(Sea-fret, *Teresa Hooley*, C [d′-d′′#], Elkin; E♭, Elkin.)
(Sea-song of Gafran, *Felicia Hemans*, Elkin.)
(Serenade, A, *Duffield Bendall*, D [d′-f′′#](m), Elkin Baritone; F, Elkin Tenor.)
(She's But a Lassie Yet, *James Hogg?/Robert Burns?*, E♭ [d′-e′′♭], Elkin; F, Elkin.)
(Sleep Song, *William Rands*, Dm [b♭-d′′], Elkin; Fm, Elkin.)
(Song of Arcady, A, *Ernest Dowson*, D, Elkin; F, Elkin.)
(Song of London, A, *Rosamund Marriott Watson*, Em [b♭-e′′(g′′)], Elkin Contralto, Baritone, Elkin.)
(Song of Wine, A, *Anon* tr. *Herbert A. Giles*, [c′-f′′#], Elkin Old Cathay.)
(Sorrow, *Ernest Dowson*, E♭ [b♭-e′′♭], Elkin Contralto, Elkin; F, Elkin.)
(Spring Ditty, A, *Anon* tr. *John Addington Symons*, D [b-f′′#], Elkin; F, Elkin.)
(Spring Song, *Cyril Scott*, high [e′-g′′#], Elkin; [low], Elkin.)
(Summer is a-cumin in, Elkin Old and New.)
(Sundown, *Dorothy Grenside*, D [d′-d′′], Elkin; F, Elkin.)
(Sunshine and Dusk, *Margaret Maitland Radford*, [low], Elkin; [medium], Elkin.)
There comes an end to summer, *Ernest Dowson*, C [d′-g′′], B&H; A♭, B&H.
(Think on me, E♭, Paterson.)
(Think on me, (sacred version), Paterson.)
Time I've lost in wooing, The, *Thomas Moore*, B♭ [c′-d′′], B&H.
(Time o' day, *Olive MacNaghten*, [d′-f′′], Elkin; [e′-g′′], Elkin.)
(Tomorrow, *Christina Rossetti*, [e′-e′′], Elkin.)
Trafalgar, *Thomas Hardy*, C [c′-e′′](m), Thames *Hardy Songbook*, B&H.
(Tranquillity, *No text*, [d′-b′′], Elkin.)
(Trysting Tree, The *Charles Sayle*, C [d′-g′′], Elkin; D, Elkin.)
(Tyrolese Evensong, *Felicia Hemans*, C, Elkin; D, Elkin.)
(Unforseen, The, *Rosamund Marriott Watson*, C [c′-g′′], Novello, (D, B♭, Elkin.)
(Valediction, A, *Ernest Dowson*, G [d′-e′′], Elkin; B♭, Elkin.)
(Valley of Silence, The, *Ernest Dowson*, C [c′-e′′], Elkin; E♭, Elkin.)

Villanelle, *Ernest Dowson*, G [d'-e''], B&H *Heritage 1*, B&H.
(Villanelle of Firelight, *Naomi Carvalho*, B♭ [d'-f''], Elkin; C, Elkin.)
(Villanelle of the Poet's Road, *Ernest Dowson*, C [d'-e''](m), Elkin Baritone, Elkin; E♭, Elkin.)
(Vision, A, *Anon* tr. *Herbert A. Giles*, A [c'#-e''], Elkin.)
(Voices of Vision, *Cyril Scott*, [c'-f''], Elkin.)
(Waiting, *Chinese* tr. *Herbert A. Giles*, [c'-e''], Elkin Old Cathay.)
(Watchman, The, *Jean Hildyard*, B♭, Elkin; C, D, Elkin.)
Waterlilies, *P. J. O'Reilly*, C, Novello; (D♭, E♭, Elkin.)
(Where be ye going, Elkin Old in New.)
(White Knight, The, *Anon* tr. *Rosamund Marriott Watson*, D [d'-d''], Elkin; E, Elkin.)
(Why so pale and wan, *John Suckling*, F [c'-e''], Elkin.)
(Willows, *Cyril Scott*, [c'-f''], Elkin.)
Yvonne of Brittany, *Ernest Dowson*, G [a-e''], B&H; F, B&H.

Scott, Derek B.
Collections: *Five Yeats Songs*, Da Capo; *Four Yeats Songs*, Da Capo; *Shakespeare Sonnets*, Da Capo.
  Against that time (Sonnet 49), *Shakespeare*, [soprano/tenor], Da Capo Shakespeare.
  Ballad of Father Gilligan, The, *W. B. Yeats*, [low], Da Capo 5 Yeats.
  Cap and Bells, The, *W. B. Yeats*, [high], Da Capo 4 Yeats.
  Cradle Song, A, *W. B. Yeats*, [low], Da Capo 5 Yeats.
  Fiddler of Dooney, The, *W. B. Yeats*, [high], Da Capo 4 Yeats.
  He Wishes for the Cloths of Heaven, *W. B. Yeats*, [high], Da Capo 4 Yeats.
  Lake Isle of Innisfree, *W. B. Yeats*, [low], Da Capo 5 Yeats.
  Since I left you (Sonnet 113), *Shakespeare*, [soprano/tenor], Da Capo Shakespeare.
  Song of the Wandering Aengus, The: *W. B. Yeats*, [high], Da Capo 4 Yeats.
  Sorrow of Love, The (original version), *W. B. Yeats*, [low], Da Capo 5 Yeats.
  Weary with toil (Sonnet 27), *Shakespeare*, [soprano *or* tenor], Da Capo Shakespeare.
  Who goes with Fergus? *W. B. Yeats*, [low], Da Capo 5 Yeats.

Scott, Francis George. 1880–1958. SMIC.
Collections: (*Scottish Lyrics Book I – 8 Songs for Female Voice; Book II – 9 Songs for Male Voice; Book III; Book IV–13 Songs for Baritone Voice; Book V – 13 Songs for Medium Voice*, Bayley & Ferguson); (*Seven Songs for Baritone Voice*, Bayley & Ferguson); *Songs*, Roberton, (Preface Neil Mackay); (*Thirty-five Scottish Lyrics and other poems*, Bayley & Ferguson).
  Apprentice Angel, An, *Hugh MacDiarmid*, [c'-e''♭], Roberton Songs.
  Ay waukin, O, *Robert Burns*, [b♭-f''](f), Roberton Songs.
  Country Life, *Hugh MacDiarmid*, [d'-g''], Roberton Songs.
  Crowdieknowe, *Hugh MacDiarmid*, [c'#-e''♭], Roberton Songs.
  Cupid and Venus, *Mark Alexander Boyd*, [e'♭-g''♭], Roberton Songs.
  Deil o' Bogie, The, *German* tr. *Alexander Gray*, [a-d''](m), Roberton Songs.
  Discreet Hint, The, *Robert Burns*, [b♭-d''], Roberton Songs.
  Eemis Stane, The, *Hugh MacDiarmid*, [d'-c''#], Roberton Songs.
  Empty Vessel, *Hugh MacDiarmid*, [b-e''], Roberton Songs.
  First Love, *Hugh MacDiarmid*, [d'-f''](m), Roberton Songs.
  Florine, *Thomas Campbell*, [b♭-e''♭](m), Roberton Songs.
  Kerry Shore – Loch Fyne, The, *George Campbell Hay*, [d'♭-f''](m), Roberton Songs.
  Lourd on my hert, *Hugh MacDiarmid*, [c'-e''], Roberton Songs.
  Love-sick Lass, The, *Hugh MacDiarmid*, [d'♭-e''♭], Roberton Songs.
  Mary Morison, *Robert Burns*, [b-e''](m), Roberton Songs.
  Milkwort and Bog-cotton, *Hugh MacDiarmid*, [c'-d''], Roberton Songs.
  Moonstruck, *Hugh MacDiarmid*, [e'♭-g''#], Roberton Songs.
  My luve is like a red, red rose, *Robert Burns*, [b♭-e''♭](m), Roberton Songs.
  O were my love yon lilac fair, *Robert Burns*, [f'-f''](m), Roberton Songs.
  Of ane Blackamoor, *William Dunbar*, [d'♭-e''♭](m), Roberton Songs.
  Old Fisherman, The, *George Campbell Hay*, [c'-c''](m), Roberton Songs.
  Phillis, *William Drummond*, [d'-e''](m), Roberton Songs.
  Rattlin' Roarin' Willie, *Robert Burns*, [c'-f''], Roberton Songs.
  Reid-E'en, *Hugh MacDiarmid*, [b♭-d''#](m), Roberton Songs.
  Rorate caeli desuper, (Of the Nativity of Christ), *William Dunbar*, [c'-f''], Roberton Songs.
  St Brendan's Graveyard, *Jean Lang*, [f'-f''], Roberton Songs.
  Sang of the Birth of Christ, Ane, *Luther* tr. *Wedderburn*, [d'♭-f''], Roberton Songs.
  Sauchs in the Reuch Heuch Hauch, The, *Hugh MacDiarmid*, [d'-g''], Roberton Songs.
  Scots, wha hae, *Robert Burns*, [b-e''](m), Roberton Songs.

Scroggam, *Robert Burns*, [g-e''](m), Roberton Songs.
Since all thy vows, false maid, *Anon*, [d'b-f''](m), Roberton Songs.
To a Lady, *William Dunbar,* [b-d''](m), Roberton Songs.
To a Loch Fyne Fisherman, *George Campbell Hay*, [bb-d''b], Roberton Songs.
Tryst, The, *William Soutar*, [d'b-g''b](m), Roberton Songs.
Twa Corbies, The, *Anon*, [bb-e''b], Roberton Songs.
Twa Kimmers, The, *William Dunbar*, [c'-e''](m), Roberton Songs.
Watergaw, The *Hugh MacDiarmid*, [c'-e''b], Roberton Songs.
Wee Man, The, *Anon (Auvergnat)* tr. *Willa Muir*, [c'-f''](f), Roberton Songs.
Wee Willie Gray, *Robert Burns*, [c'#-d''], Roberton Songs.
Wha is that at my bower-door? *Robert Burns*, [bb-e''b](f), Roberton Songs.
Wheesht, wheesht, *Hugh MacDiarmid*, [c'-d''](m), Roberton Songs.

Scott, Stuart.
Collection: *Songs of the Night,* [soprano], Da Capo.
Cheshire Verses, *Thomas Pitfield,* [baritone], Da Capo.
Fall, leaves, fall, *Emily Brontë,* [soprano], Da Capo Songs of the Night.
Night Clouds, *Amy Lowell,* [soprano], Da Capo Songs of the Night.

Seaman, Barry. 1946– BMIC.
Gabriel's Greeting, *Anon*, [d'-e''], OUP Solo Christmas high; [bb-c''], Solo Christmas low.

Seamarks, Colin. *See* App. 2.

Searle, Humphrey. 1915–1982. BMIC. *See also* App. 1.
Collections: *Two Songs of A. E. Housman*, S&B; (*Three Songs of Jocelyn Brooke*, Faber.)
Counting the Beats, *Robert Graves*, [c'-b''], Faber.
(Epitaph, *Jocelyn Brooke*, [a#-b''b], Faber 3 Songs.)
March past, *A. E. Housman*, [d'-g''](m), S&B 2 Songs.
(Song for Christmas, *Jocelyn Brooke*, [c'-b''b], Faber 3 Songs.)
Stinging Nettle, The, *A. E. Housman*, [C'#-F''#], S&B 2 Songs.
(White Helleborine, The, *Jocelyn Brooke*, [b-b''b], Faber 3 Songs.)

Seiber, Matyas György. 1905–1960. *See also* App. 2.
Collection: *Four Greek Folksongs*, B&H.
Each time, my love, you say farewell, *Anon*, tr. *Peter Carroll*, [a'b-f''#](f), B&H 4 Greek.
Have pity on me, *Anon*, tr. *Peter Carroll*, G [d'-e''], B&H 4 Greek.
My peace is gone, *Goethe* tr. *Louis MacNeice*, Am [d'-e''](f), S&B.
O my love, how long, *Anon*, tr. *Peter Carroll*, Am [g'-e''], B&H 4 Greek.
O your eyes are dark and beautiful, *Anon*, tr. *Peter Carroll*, Em [e'-d''], B&H 4 Greek.
There was a king in Thule, *Goethe* tr. *Louis MacNeice*, Fm [c'-f''], S&B.
(To Poetry (cycle), *Goethe, Shakespeare, Dunbar*, [d'b-g''], Schott.)

Self, Adrian. *See also* App. 2.
Collection: *Come Back in Dreams,* Animus; *Farewell, Earth's Bliss,* Animus; *From the Song of Songs,* Animus; *Song Album, A,* Brunton; *To Cornwall and Beyond,* Animus;.
Autumn in Cornwall, *Algernon Charles Swinburne*, [e'b-g''], Animus Cornwall.
Balulalow, *Luther* tr. *Wedderburn*, [d'-f''], Brunton Song Album, Brunton.
Batter my heart, *John Donne*, [f'#-g''], Animus Earth's Bliss.
Beauty, *Peter Vincent*, [e'b-g''], Brunton Song Album; [c'-e''], Brunton.
Birthday, A, *Christina Rossetti*, [d'-a''b](f), Animus Dreams.
Drop, drop, slow tears, *Phineas Fletcher,* [d'-g''], Animus Earth's Bliss.
Easter Day, *Henry Vaughan*, [b-a''b], Animus Earth's Bliss.
Echo, *Christina Rossetti*, [b-g''](f), Animus Dreams.
Fox, The, *John Clare*, [bb-f''], Brunton Song Album.
Futility, *Wilfred Owen*, [b-g''], Brunton Song Album.
Herbst: Autumn, *Rainer Maria Rilke* tr. *Margrit Parfitt*, [c'-e''], Brunton Song Album, Brunton.
How many miles to Mylor? *A. L. Rowse*, [c'-f''#], Animus Cornwall.
I am my beloved's, *Song of Solomon*, [d'-f''](f), Animus Song of Songs.
In Falmouth Harbour, *Lionel Johnson*, [c'-g''], Animus Cornwall.
In the time of pestilence, *Thomas Nashe*, [b-a''b], Animus Earth's Bliss.
My beloved spake, *Song of Solomon,* [f'-g''](f), Animus Song of Songs.
Poet's Last Thoughts, A, *John Clare*, [c'-f''], Brunton Song Album.

River Lynher, The, (East Cornwall), *Sir John Carew*, [d′-g′′], Animus Cornwall.
Set me as a seal upon thine heart, *Song of Solomon*, [c′-g′′](f), Animus Song of Songs.
Sleep, *John Fletcher*, [c′-e′′] Brunton Song Album; Brunton.
Song, *Christina Rossetti*, [b-g′′b](f), Animus Dreams.
Spring, *Christina Rossetti*, [c′-g′′](f), Animus Dreams.

Self, Geoffrey. 1930–
At One, *Francis Uren*, [c′-d′′], EPSS.

Senator, Ronald. 1926–
Collection: *Cabaret*, Lengnick.
Ballad, *W. H. Auden*, [bass/baritone], Lengnick Cabaret.
Blues, *W. H. Auden*, [bass/baritone], Lengnick Cabaret.
Poet to His Beloved, A, *W. B. Yeats*, [high], Lengnick.
Popsong, *W. H. Auden*, [bass/baritone], Lengnick Cabaret.
Roman Wall Blues, *W. H. Auden*, [bass/baritone], Lengnick Cabaret.

Serrell, Alys F. ? –1941.
Bullfinches, The, *Thomas Hardy*, E♭ [e′♭-f′′], Thames *Hardy Songbook*.

Shaw, Martin Edward Fallas. 1875–1958.
Collections: *Seven Songs*, S&B (Introduction Michael Pilkington); *Six Songs of War*, B&H; *Two Songs from Shakespeare*, Cramer; *Two Songs of Spring*, B&H.
Accursèd Wood, The, *Harold Boulton*, [c′-e′′♭], Cramer.
Annabel Lee, *Edgar Allan Poe*, F [e′♭-a′′](m), S&B 7 Songs, Cramer; *C*, Cramer.
At Columbine's Grave, *Bliss Carman*, Am [c′-e′′], Cramer.
Bells of Christmas, The, *Eugene Field*, Bm [e′-d′′], Cramer; Am, Dm, Cramer.
Caravan, The, *William Brighty Rands*, F [d′-e′′], Cramer; A, Cramer.
Cargoes, *John Masefield*, D [c′#-e′′], S&B 7 Songs, Cramer.
Carillons, *Dominique Bonnaud* tr. *Anon*, G [d′-f′′], B&H.
Child of the flowing tide, *Geoffrey Dearmer*, A♭ [c′-e′′♭], Schirmer *2nd Baritone*, (Chappell *English Recital 1.*)
Come away, death, *Shakespeare*, Gm [d′-e′′♭], Cramer 2 Songs.
Conjuration, The, *Hung-So-Fan.* tr. *Anon*, B♭ [d′-f′′#](m), Cramer; A♭, Cramer.
Cuckoo, *Anon*, G [d′-d′′], S&B 7 Songs.
Down by the salley gardens, *W. B. Yeats*, [b-e′′], S&B 7 Songs.
(Easter Carol, *Christina Rossetti*, C [c′-e′′], Curwen.)
(England, my England, *W. E. Henley*, C [c′-g′′(e′′♭)], B&H.)
Heffle Cuckoo Fair, *Rudyard Kipling*, A [e′-e′′(a′′)], Schirmer *1st Soprano*, (Curwen.)
Herald, The, *Geoffrey Dearmer*, E♭ [e′♭-b′′♭(a′′♭)], B&H 2 Spring.
I know a bank, *Shakespeare*, F [c′-d′′], Cramer; B♭, Cramer; G, Cramer.
(Land of Heart's Desire, The, *W. B. Yeats*, Am [c′-e′′(g′′)], Curwen.)
Little Waves of Breffny, The, *Eva Gore-Booth*, C [e′-a′′], Cramer.
Melodies You Sing, The, *Clifford Bax*, F [c′#-d′′], Cramer.
Merry Christmas, *Walter Scott*, D [d′-a′′(f′′#)], OUP *Solo Christmas high*; B♭, *Solo Christmas low*.
Merry Wanderer, The, *Shakespeare*, E [e′-a′′♭(a′′)], Cramer.
No, *Thomas Hood*, Em [b-e′′], S&B 7 Songs.
(O, Falmouth is a fine town, *W. E. Henley*, [c′-e′′](m), Curwen.).
Old clothes and fine clothes, *John Pride*, B♭ [b♭-d′′], Cramer; C, Cramer.
(Old Mother Laidinwool, *Rudyard Kipling*, E♭ [c′-e′′], Curwen.)
(Refrain, *Arthur Shearly Cripps*, B♭ [c′-e′′♭], Curwen.)
Rivulet, The, *L. Larcom*, G [d′-f′′], Cramer; A, Cramer.
Ships of Yule, *Eugene Field*, G [d′-e′′], Cramer; F, A, Cramer.
Song of the Palanquin Bearers, *Sarojini Naidu*, E [e′-f′′], S&B 7 Songs, (B♭, Curwen).
Through softly falling rain, *Sybil M. Ruegg*, A [e′-a′′], B&H 2 Spring.
Tides, *John Pride*, C [a′-e′′], Cramer.
To Sea! *Thomas Lovell Beddoes*, G [b♭-f′′], Cramer.
When daisies pied, *Shakespeare*, C [e′-a′′], S&B 7 Songs.
When that I was and a little tiny boy, *Shakespeare*, E♭ [b♭-e′′♭](m), Cramer 2 Songs.
Wood Magic, *John Buchan*, C#m [b-f′′], Cramer; Em, Cramer.
Arrangement:
Banks of Allan Water, The, *M. G. Lewis*, B♭ [d′-f′′], Cramer; A♭, C, Cramer.
Ye banks and braes, *Robert Burns*, A [e′-f′′#](f), Cramer; G, A, Cramer.

Shield, William. 1748–1829. *See also* App. 2.
   Collection: *Four Songs from 'Rosina',* B&H (Leslie Russell).
     Ere bright Rosina met my eyes, *Mrs Frances Brooke,* C [e′-g′′](m), Novello (Bush) *Ballad Operas.*
     Friar of Orders Gray, The, *Anon,* C [G-d′](m), Schirmer *1st Baritone.*
     Hope and Love, *William Pearce,* G [e′-g′′], OUP (Roberts) *Tuneful Voice.*
     Moon returns in saffron drest, The, *Mrs Frances Brooke,* Gm [g′-g′′], B&H Rosina.
     Secret transports, *Mrs Brooke,* D [d′-g′′(a′′)](f), B&H Rosina.
     Tis only no harm to know it, you know, *John O'Keeffe,* B♭ [f′-g′′](f), OUP (Roberts) *Tuneful Voice.*
     When bidden to the wake, *Mrs Frances Brooke,* Cm [b♭-g′′](m), B&H Rosina.
     When William at eve, *Mrs Frances Brooke,* C [e′-c′′′](f), B&H Rosina.
     Wolf, The, *William Shield,* E♭ [f(b♭)-f′′(e′′♭)], IMP *Parlour Songs.*
     Ye balmy breezes gently blow, *John Rannie,* C [d′-g′′](m), OUP (Roberts) *Tuneful Voice.*

Short, Michael. 1937– SMIC. *See also* App. 1, 2.
   Ever, SMIC.

Shur, Laura. SMIC. *See also* App. 2.
   Bird sits high and sings, A (cycle), [soprano], SMIC.
   Love in a life: Life in a love, [voice], SMIC.
   Remember, SMIC.
   Shalom Yerushalayim, SMIC.
Arrangements; *Three Goan Songs,* [mezzo], SMIC.

Siôn, Pwyll ap. 1968–
   My lady, *Rhydwen Williams* tr. *John Stoddart,* [A#-e′](m), WMIC *Songs from Wales 2.*

Slater, Gordon.
   Drinking Song, *John Fletcher,* [d′-f′′], BMP.
   Green Willow, The, *Traditional,* [e′-f′′], BMP.
   In Time of the Breaking of Nations, *Thomas Hardy,* [c′-c′′], BMP.
   Lawn as white as driven snow, *Shakespeare,* [c′-f′′], BMP.
   Minion Wife, A, *Nicholas Udall,* [d′-e′′], BMP.
   Seekers, The, *John Masefield,* [c′-e′′♭], BMP.
   Tewkesbury Road, *John Masefield,* Em [b-f′′#], BMP; Gm, BMP.

Smart, Thomas. *fl.*1783.
   Forsaken Maid, The, *Anon,* F [e′-g′′(a′′)], B&H (Lane Wilson) *Old English.*

Smith, John Christopher. 1712–1795.
   Owl is abroad, The, *Ben Jonson,* G [g-d′′](m), B&H *Imperial 6.*

Smith, Robert. 1922–1998 WMIC.
   Angharad, *Eifion Wyn* tr. *Brinley Rees,* Bm [f′#-g′′], Gwynn.
   Ease me, *John Donne,* [b-d′′], WMIC *Songs from Wales 2.*
   Love, *Eifion Wyn* tr. *John Stoddart,* [A-c′](m), WMIC.

Smith, Theodore. *c.*1740–*c.*1810.
   Content, *Anon,* D [d′-f′′#], OUP (Roberts) *Tuneful Voice.*

Smith Brindle, Reginald. 1917– *See* App. 2.

Smyth, Dame **Ethel** Mary. 1858–1944. *See also* App. 1.
   (Anacreontic Ode, *Leconte de Lisle* tr. *Ethel Smyth,* Fm [c′-g′′](m), Novello.)
   (Chrysilla, *Henri de Regnier* tr. *Alma Strettell,* E♭ [b♭-f′′♭], Novello.)
   (Dance, The, *Henri de Regnier* tr. *Alma Strettell,* Em [b-e′′], Novello.)
   (Odelette, *Henri de Regnier* tr. *Alma Strettell,* Cm [c′-a′′♭], Novello.)

Snell, David. *See also* App. 2.
   Autumn Thoughts, [voice], Modus.
   Lullaby, [voice], Modus.
Arrangements:
   Idle days in Summertime, [voice], Modus.
   Ye Banks and Braes, *Robert Burns,* [voice], Modus.

Sohal, Naresh Kumar. 1939– *See also* App. 2.
   Poems of Tagore No 1, *Rabindranath Tagore,* Novello.

Solomons, David W. 1953– *See also* App. 2.
   Collection: *Songs of Solomons Vol. 2,* Da Capo.
   A OI (To Olympia), *David W. Solomons,* [soprano], Da Capo.
   Christmas Haikus, *A. E. Radcliffe,* [alto], Da Capo Songs.
   Dawn in the Room, *E. M., S. N., D. W. Solomons,* [alto/baritone], Da Capo Songs, Da Capo.
   Greek Wassail, *David W. Solomons,* [alto], Da Capo Songs.
   Haviranosan no Haiku, *Mark Haviland,* [alto], Da Capo Songs.
   Invitation to the Journey, *Charles Baudelaire* tr. *S. N. Solomons,* [alto], Da Capo Songs.
   Lhudhè Sing Tishoo, *David W. Solomons,* [mezzo/alto], Da Capo Songs, Da Capo.
   Lookin', just lookin', *David W. Solomons,* [alto], Da Capo.
   Quiet way you move me, The, *Nevil Frenkiel,* [alto], Da Capo Songs, Da Capo.
   Rose, *Iskan Açikça* tr. *Theo Witty,* [alto], Da Capo Songs.
   Swallows, The, *Gourgen Mahari* tr. *J. R. Russell,* [alto], Da Capo Songs; [tenor], Da Capo.

Someren-Godfery, M. van.
   Collections: (*Five Breton Songs*, B&H); *Four Songs*, S&B; *Six Blake Songs*, S&B; *Three Songs*, S&B.
   (Ad domnulum suam, *Ernest Dowson,* Elkin.)
   Anacreon, *Antipater* tr. *Humbert Wolfe,* Cm [b-e″], S&B.
   (Ballad of Semmerwater, *William Watson,* Gm [c′-e″], Elkin.)
   (Birthright, Elkin.)
   Biton to his Gods, *Humbert Wolfe,* E♭ [b♭-e″](m), S&B.
   Cradle Song, A, *William Blake,* Dm [c′#-e″], S&B 6 Blake.
   Day is no more, The, *Rabindranath Tagore,* E♭ [b-e″], S&B.
   Death, thy servant, *Rabindranath Tagore,* G [c′-f″], S&B.
   Go, teach the swan to swim, *E. N. da C. Andrade,* F [c′-f″], S&B.
   Green Candles, *Humbert Wolfe,* A♭ [e′b-f″(e″)], S&B 4 Songs.
   House on Fire, The, *E. N. da C. Andrade,* Dm [c′#-f″#(f″)], S&B 3 Songs.
   Journey's End, *Humbert Wolfe,* [d(g#)-d″#], S&B 4 Songs.
   Joy is my name, *William Blake,* E♭ [e′b-f″#], S&B 6 Blake.
   (Julienne, *French,* tr. *Ruth Rogers,* G [d′-e″](f), B&H 5 Breton.)
   King of China's Daughter, The, *Edith Sitwell,* E♭ [d′-g″](m), S&B.
   La Belle Dame Sans Merci, *John Keats,* Cm [c′-g″], S&B.
   Lamon to Priapus, *Humbert Wolfe,* F [c′-e″], S&B 4 Songs.
   Little Fête, A, *Li-Tai-Po* tr. *Ian Colvin,* E♭m [c′-e″♭], S&B.
   Love and Peter, *Humbert Wolfe,* C [c′(b)-f″(e″)], S&B 4 Songs.
   Love's Secret, *William Blake,* [c′-e″], S&B 6 Blake.
   (Messenger, The, *French,* tr. *Ruth Rogers,* [c′-f″(e″♭)], B&H 5 Breton.)
   (Nay, nay, *French,* tr. *Ruth Rogers,* Em [d′-e″], B&H 5 Breton.)
   Night Piece, A, *E. N. da C. Andrade,* [d′-e″], S&B 3 Songs.
   Old Nurse's Song, The, *Edith Sitwell,* [b♭-e″♭](f), S&B.
   (Our lady weeps, *French,* tr. *Ruth Rogers,* Fm [c′-f″♭(e″♭)], B&H 5 Breton.)
   Ozymandias, *Percy Bysshe Shelley,* Fm [b♭-e″(f″)], S&B.
   Parting, The, *Ma Huang Tschung* tr. *Ian Colvin,* F [c′-d″], S&B.
   Piping down the valleys, *William Blake,* F [c′-f″(d″)], S&B 6 Blake.
   Poison Apple, A, *William Blake,* A [c′#-e″(g″#)], S&B 6 Blake.
   (Rosebud, The, *French,* tr. *Ruth Rogers,* Fm [c′-d″](f), B&H 5 Breton.)
   Shadow and Smoke, *E. N. da C. Andrade,* Em [c-g″(e″)], S&B 3 Songs.
   Shepherd, The, *William Blake,* D [d′-e″], S&B 6 Blake.
   Tears of St Joseph, The, *Ruth Rogers,* [b-e″], S&B.
   Thou art not fair, *Thomas Campion,* Am [c′#-e″](m), S&B.
   Twa Corbies, The, *Anon,* [c′(a)-e″(f″)], S&B.
   White Dress, The, *Humbert Wolfe,* G [d′-f″#], S&B.

Somers-Cocks, John. 1907– 1994. BMIC.
   Collection: *Four Poems,* Bardic.
   Bells of Magdalen Tower, *John Betjeman,* [e′-g″], Bardic 4 poems.
   Eager Spring, *Gordon Bottomley,* [d′-e″], Bardic.
   Echo, *Christina Rossetti,* [c′-e″], Bardic.
   Eternity, *Joan Boycott,* [f′-g″], Bardic.
   Everyone Sang, *Siegfried Sassoon,* [e′-f″#], Bardic.
   House of Rest, *John Betjeman,* [d′b-g″], Bardic 4 poems.

Love in a Valley, *John Betjeman*, [f′-g′′], Bardic 4 poems.
New Year's Eve, 1913, *Gordon Bottomley*, [c′#-f′′#], Bardic.
Sailing Homeward, *Chan Fang-Shëng* tr. *Arthur Waley*, [e′-g′′], Bardic.
Silence, *Joan Boycott*, [c′#-g′′], Bardic.
Song: When I am dead, my dearest, *Christina Rossetti*, [f′-g′′], Bardic.
Sweet Music, *Edmund Bolton*, [e′-g′′], Bardic.
Youth and Age on Beaulieu River, *John Betjeman*, [f′#-f′′#], Bardic 4 poems.

Somervell, Sir Arthur. 1863–1937.
Collections: *Broken Arc*, A, B&H; *James Lee's Wife*, B&H; *Love in Springtime*, B&H; *Maud*, S&B MB 56, Classical/B&H; *Shropshire Lad*, A, B&H; *Twelve Tennyson Poems*, B&H.
After, *Robert Browning*, Bm [b-e′′], B&H Broken Arc.
Among the Rocks, *Robert Browning*, A♭ [b♭-f′′](f), B&H James Lee.
As through the land (1st setting), *Alfred Lord Tennyson*, D [d′-f′′#](m), B&H.
As through the land (2nd setting), *Alfred Lord Tennyson*, E♭ [b♭-e′′♭](m), B&H 12 Tennyson
Bargain, The, *Philip Sidney*, C [a-e′′], Thames *Century 2*, B&H; E♭, B&H.
Birds in the high hall-garden, *Alfred Lord Tennyson*, E♭ [b♭-d′′♭](m), S&B MB 56, B&H *New Imperial 5*, Classical/B&H Maud, 12 Tennyson.
By the Fireside, *Robert Browning*, Cm [g-g′′(f′′)](f), B&H James Lee.
Come into the garden, Maud, *Alfred Lord Tennyson*, G [g-e′′♭](m), S&B MB 56, B&H *Heritage 1*, Classical/ B&H Maud.
Come to me in my dreams, *Matthew Arnold*, Em [b-e′′], B&H.
Crossing the Bar, *Alfred Lord Tennyson*, E♭ [c′-e′′♭], B&H 12 Tennyson; F, B&H.
Dainty little maiden, *Alfred Lord Tennyson*, F [c′-f′′], B&H Springtime, 12 Tennyson.
Dead, long dead, *Alfred Lord Tennyson*, Gm [a-e′′♭](m), S&B MB 56, Classical/B&H Maud.
Dreamiland, *Ethel Speare*, E♭ [e′b-f′′](m), B&H.
Evening Shadows (Sleep, my baby), *Anon*, D [d′-e′′](f), B&H; E, B&H.
Fain would I change that note, *Anon*, G [d′-g′′], B&H.
Fault was mine, The, *Alfred Lord Tennyson*, E♭m [b♭-d′′♭](m), S&B MB 56, Classical/B&H Maud.
(From 'Easter Day', *Robert Browning*, B♭ [b♭-d′′](m), B&H Broken Arc.
Go not, happy day, *Alfred Lord Tennyson*, F [b♭-e′′♭](m), S&B MB 56, Classical/B&H Maud.
Home they brought her warrior dead, *Alfred Lord Tennyson*, Am [c′(a)-e′′], B&H 12 Tennyson.
I cannot tell what you say, *Charles Kingsley*, A [e′-a′′], B&H Springtime.
I hate the dreadful hollow, *Alfred Lord Tennyson*, Dm [a-e′′](m), S&B MB 56, Classical/B&H Maud.
I have led her home, *Alfred Lord Tennyson*, C [c′-d′′](m), S&B MB 56, Classical/B&H Maud, B&H 12 Tennyson.
In summertime on Bredon, *A. E. Housman*, C [b♭-e′′](m), B&H Shropshire Lad, *Heritage 1*.
In the Doorway, *Robert Browning*, F [d′-f′′](f), B&H James Lee.
In the early dawning, *Ethel Speare*, Em [e′-e′′](f), B&H.
Into my heart an air that kills, *A. E. Housman*, E♭ [b♭-d′′](m), B&H Shropshire Lad.
James Lee's Wife Speaks at the Window, *Robert Browning*, A♭ [a-f′′](f), B&H James Lee.
Kingdom by the Sea, A, *Edgar Allan Poe*, E [e′-g′′](m), Classical, B&H, Schirmer *1st Tenor II*; D, B&H.
Lads in their hundreds, The, *A. E. Housman*, A♭ [d′b-f′′](m), B&H Shropshire Lad, *Heritage 2*.
Love unto love, *Katherine Margeson*, E♭ [b♭-e′′♭], B&H.
Loveliest of trees, *A. E. Housman*, E [b♭-d′′#](m), B&H Shropshire Lad.
Marie at the Window, *Anon*, F [c′-f′′], Thames *Century 6*.
Maud has a garden of roses, *Alfred Lord Tennyson*, B♭ [b♭-d′′](m), S&B MB 56, Classical/B&H Maud, B&H 12 Tennyson.
Meeting at Night, *Robert Browning*, C [d′-e′′](m), B&H Broken Arc.
Mine Own Country, *Katherine Tynan*, G [d′-g′′], B&H; E, F, B&H.
My life has crept so long, *Alfred Lord Tennyson*, B♭m [a-e′′♭](m), S&B MB 56, Classical/B&H Maud.
My Star, *Robert Browning*, E♭ [d′b-e′′♭](m), B&H Broken Arc.
Nay, but you who do not love her, *Robert Browning*, E♭ [e′b-g′′♭](m), B&H Broken Arc.
Night-bird, The, *Charles Kingsley*, G [f′#-g′′], B&H Springtime.
O let the solid ground, *Alfred Lord Tennyson*, C [c′-e′′](m), S&B MB 56, Classical/B&H Maud.
O mistress mine, *Shakespeare*, E♭ [e′b-f′′](m), B&H.
O swallow, swallow, *Alfred Lord Tennyson*, G [d′-f′′(g′′)], B&H 12 Tennyson.
O that 'twere possible, *Alfred Lord Tennyson*, B [c′#-d′′](m), S&B MB 56, Classical/B&H Maud, B&H 12 Tennyson.
O what comes over the sea, *Christina Rossetti*, B [f′#-f′′#], B&H Springtime
On a Summer Morning, *Ethel Speare*, C [c′-g′′(e′′)](f), B&H; B♭, D, B&H.

On the Cliff, *Robert Browning*, B [b-f''](f), B&H James Lee.
On the idle hill of summer, *A. E. Housman*, B [c'#-e''](m), B&H *Shropshire Lad*, *Heritage 1*.
Orpheus with his lute, *Shakespeare*, A♭ [e'♭-e''♭], B&H.
She came to the village church, *Alfred Lord Tennyson*, Dm [a-d''](m), S&B MB 56, Classical/B&H *Maud*, B&H *12 Tennyson*.
Shepherd's Cradle Song, *Anon*, A [e'-f''#], William Elkin, F, E♭, William Elkin.
Silent Voice, The, *Laurence Alma Tadema*, Dm [e'-g''(a'')], B&H.
Spring is here, *E. S.*, C [e'-a''], B&H *Springtime*; *G, B♭*, B&H.
Street sounds to the soldiers' tread, The, *A. E. Housman*, E♭ [b♭-e''♭](m), B&H *Shropshire Lad*.
Such a starved bank of moss, *Robert Browning*, E [f'#-e''](m), B&H *Broken Arc*.
Sweet and low, *Alfred Lord Tennyson*, E♭ [b♭-e''♭], B&H *12 Tennyson*, B&H; *F, D*, B&H.
(Take, O take those lips away, *Shakespeare*, D [d'-d''], Forsyth.)
Tears, idle tears, *Alfred Lord Tennyson*, Dm [d'-e''], B&H *12 Tennyson*; *Fm*, B&H.
There pass the careless people, *A. E. Housman*, Em [b-e''](m), B&H *Shropshire Lad*.
Think no more, lad; laugh, be jolly, *A. E. Housman*, G [g(d')-e''](m), B&H *Shropshire Lad*.
To Lucasta, on Going to the Wars, *Richard Lovelace*, Fm [e'♭-f''](m), B&H.
Underneath the growing grass, *Christina Rossetti*, B♭m [b♭-a''♭], B&H *Springtime*.
Voice by the cedar tree, A, *Alfred Lord Tennyson*, F [a-e''](m), S&B MB 56, Classical/B&H *Maud*.
When I was one-and-twenty, *A. E. Housman*, B [b-d''#](m), B&H *Shropshire Lad*.
When spring returns, *Arthur Somervell*, D♭ [e'♭-a''♭], B&H; *C*, B&H.
White in the moon the long road lies, *A. E. Housman*, Bm [c'#-e''](m), B&H *Shropshire Lad*, *Heritage 2*.
Will you come back home? *Gilbert Parker*, C [c'-e''], B&H.
Worst of it, The, *Robert Browning*, E♭m [b♭-e''♭](m), B&H *Broken Arc*.
Year's at the spring, The, *Robert Browning*, F [c'-f''](m), B&H *Broken Arc*.
Young love lies sleeping, *Christina Rossetti*, B♭ [f'-g''], B&H *Springtime*, *Heritage 2*, B&H; *A♭*, B&H.

Arrangements:
All Through the Night, *Anon*, Cramer.
Gathering Daffodils, *Anon*, A♭, Cramer.
Gentle Maiden, The, *Harold Boulton*, E♭ [b♭-e''♭](m), Cramer; *F*, Cramer.
Oft in the stilly night, *Thomas Moore*, A♭ [e'♭-d''♭], IMP *Parlour Songs*.
Snowy-breasted Pearl, The, *Irish* tr. *Petrie*, E, Cramer.
(Twa Sisters of Binnorie, The, *Anon*, C [g-e''], B&H.)

Sorabji, Kaikhosru Shapurji. 1892–1988. *See* App. 1.

Souster, Timothy Andrew James. 1943–1994. *See* App. 2.

Southam, T. Wallace.
Have you seen but a white lily grow? *Ben Jonson*, E♭ [e'♭-e''♭], BMP.
Lesbos, *Lawrence Durrell*, [g-b'♭], BMP.

Spearing, Robert. WMIC.

Spedding, Frank. 1929–2001 SMIC. *See also* App. 2.
Collection: *Old English Songs*, [tenor], SMIC.
Creditor, The, [baritone], SMIC.
Intimations of Mortality, [baritone], SMIC.

Squire, William Henry. 1871–1963. *See also* B&H, Chappell.
If I might come to you, *Fred. E. Weatherly*, C [g'-g''] B&H *Ballad Album 2*; A♭, B♭, B&H.
In an old-fashioned town, *Ada Leonora Harris*, F [d'-g''] B&H *Ballad Album 2*; D, IMP *Parlour Songs*.
When you come home, dear, *Fred E. Weatherley*, F [c'-f''], IMP *Parlour Songs*.

Stafford, Simeon. *See also* App. 2.
Collection: *Songs from a Rock Opera*, Da Capo.
Another me, *Simeon Stafford*, [soprano], Da Capo Rock Opera.
The Horsemen of Belfast, *Simeon Stafford*, [soprano], Da Capo Rock Opera.
When you're in love, *Simeon Stafford*, [soprano], Da Capo Rock Opera.

Standford, Patric. 1939– *See also* App. 2.
Collections: *Five Valentine Songs*, RTS; *Wayward Thoughts*, RTS.

Happy is the country life, *from Playford*, [c-e''](m), RTS Wayward Thoughts.
In a harbour green, *Robert Wever*, [c#-e′b](m), RTS Wayward Thoughts.
Lady, when I behold the roses, *Anon*, [f-f′](m), RTS Wayward Thoughts.
Lavender's blue, *Anon 17th cent.*, [d′-a''], RTS Valentine.
Over the mountains, *Anon 17th cent.*, [d′-g''], RTS Valentine.
Sleep wayward thoughts, *John Dowland?* [c#-d''](m), RTS Wayward Thoughts.
There is a lady sweet and kind, *Anon 17th cent.*, [f′-g''], RTS Valentine.
This dog may kiss your hand, *Anon 17th cent.*, [d′-a''], RTS Valentine.
Though near the fountain, *Anon 17th cent.*, [d′-a''b], RTS Valentine.
Welcome maids of honour, *Robert Herrick*, [Bb-e′b](m), RTS Wayward Thoughts.

Stanford, Sir Charles Villiers. 1852–1924. *See also* App. 1, 2.
Collections: *Cushendall, Op 118*, S&B; *Fire of Turf, A, Op 139*, S&B; *Five Sonnets from 'The Triumph of Love', Op 82*, B&H; *Irish Idyll, An, Op 77*, [low], Masters/B&H, [high], B&H; *Musica Britannica 52*, S&B (edited with introduction Geoffrey Bush); *Sheaf of Songs from Leinster, A, Op 140*, S&B; *Six Songs from 'The Glens of Antrim' Op 174*, B&H; *Six Songs*, S&B (Introduction Geoffrey Bush); *Songs of Faith Op 97*, B&H; *Songs of the Sea Op 91*, Classical/B&H; *Twelve Songs by Heine*, S&B.
Almansor Dying, *Heinrich Heine*, tr. *Anon*, Ebm [b-g''], S&B 12 Songs.
As the moon's pale likeness quivers, *Heinrich Heine* tr. *Anon*, Eb [d′-f''], S&B 12 Songs.
At Sea, *Moira O'Neill*, Bb [bb-e''b], B&H Songs of Antrim.
Back to Ireland, *Moira O'Neill*, F [c′-e''b], Masters/B&H Irish Idyll; *A*, B&H Irish Idyll.
Battle of Pelusium, The, *Beaumont & Fletcher*, Cm [c′-e''b](m), S&B MB 52.
Blackberry Time, *Winifred Letts*, E [b-d''#], S&B MB 52, Fire of Turf.
Boat Song, *Walter Pollock*, F [e′-f''], B&H; *D*, B&H.
Bold Unbiddable Child, The, *Winifred Letts*, Dm [c′-g''(e''b)], S&B MB 52, 6 Songs, Sheaf; *Cm*, S&B.
Boy from Ballytearim, The, *Moira O'Neill*, Dm [c′-e''b], B&H Songs of Antrim.
Broken Song, A, *Moira O'Neill*, Fm [bb-d''b], Masters/B&H Irish Idyll; *Am*, Thames Century 2, B&H Irish Idyll.
Butterfly's love, The, *Heinrich Heine* tr. *H. W. Hoare*, D [d′-f''#], S&B 12 Songs.
Calico Dress, The, *George H. Jessop*, Ab [e′b-f''(a''b)](f), B&H; *F* B&H.
Carol, A, *Arthur Quiller-Couch*, [medium], Banks.
Chapel on the Hill, The, *Winifred Letts*, Dm [a′-d''], S&B MB 52, 6 Songs, Fire of Turf.
Come away, death, *Shakespeare*, Fm [bb-e''b](m), S&B MB 52.
Come to me when the earth is fair, *Walter Pollock*, G [e′-g''], B&H.
Corrymeela, *Moira O'Neill*, Fm [c′-e''b], Masters/B&H Irish Idyll; *Am*, B&H Irish Idyll.
Corsican Dirge, A, *Anon*, tr. *Alma Strettell*, Dm [c′-g''](f), S&B.
Cowslip Time, *Winifred Letts*, Eb [c′-e''b], S&B MB 52, A Fire of Turf.
Crossing the Bar, *Alfred Lord Tennyson*, Bb [f′-g''], S&B MB 52.
Crow, The, *John Stevenson*, Dm [a-d''], S&B Cushendall.
Cushendall, *John Stevenson*, Bbm [bb-d''], S&B Cushendall.
Cuttin' Rushes, *Moira O'Neill*, F [b-d''], B&H Heritage 2, Masters/B&H Irish Idyll, B&H; *Ab*, B&H Irish Idyll, B&H.
Daddy-long-legs, *John Stevenson*, C [b-d''], S&B Cushendall.
Dainty Davie, *Robert Burns*, F [d′-f''(a'')](f), S&B MB 52.
Denny's daughter, *Moira O'Neill*, Dm [c′-e''], B&H Songs of Antrim.
Devon, O Devon, in Wind and Rain, *Henry Newbolt*, Gm [e′b-e''](m), B&H Songs of the Sea.
Did you ever see the sun? *John Stevenson*, Bb [bb-d''b], S&B Cushendall.
Drake's Drum, *Henry Newbolt*, Dm [c′-e''](m), B&H Songs of the Sea, Heritage 1; *Cm*, B&H.
Drop me a flower, *Alfred Lord Tennyson*, Ab [e′b-g''(a''b)](m), S&B MB 52, Cramer.
Fair, The, *Winifred Letts*, D [d′-d''], S&B MB 52, Fire of Turf.
Fairy Lough, The, *Moira O'Neill*, D [a-e''b], S&B MB 52, B&H Heritage 2, Masters/B&H Irish Idyll, B&H; *F*, B&H Irish Idyll.
Fairy Lures, *Rose Fyleman*, Eb [d′-g''], Cramer.
Faith, *Alfred Lord Tennyson*, Ab [e′b-f''b], B&H Songs of Faith.
Fire of Turf, A, *Winifred Letts*, Da [a-d''](m), S&B MB 52, Fire of Turf.
From the red rose to the apple-blossom, *A. P. Graves*, Ab [c′-f''], S&B MB 52.
God and the Universe, *Alfred Lord Tennyson*, Cm [b-e''(e''b)], B&H Songs of Faith.
Grandeur, *Winifred Letts*, Cm [bb-c''], S&B Sheaf.
Homeward Bound, *Henry Newbolt*, Db [c′-d''], B&H Songs of the Sea.
How does the wind blow, *John Stevenson*, D [a-e''b], S&B Cushendall.
Hymn in Praise of Neptune, A, *Thomas Campion*, C [e′-g''], B&H.
I mind the day, *Moira O'Neill*, Dm [c′-e''b], B&H Songs of Antrim.
I praise the tender flower, *Robert Bridges*, F [f′-g''](m), S&B MB 52.

I seal thy lips with kisses three, *Heinrich Heine,* tr. *Anon,* B [c′#-f′′#], S&B 12 Songs.
I think that we were children (Sonnet 5), *Edmund Holmes,* G [e′b-g′′], B&H Triumph of Love.
Ireland, *John Stevenson,* F [c′-d′′], S&B Cushendall.
Irish Skies, *Winifred Letts,* Cm [bb-d′′], S&B Sheaf.
Jack Tar, *Alfred Lord Tennyson,* Bb [bb-d′′], B&H; C, Eb, B&H.
Japanese Lullaby, A, *Eugene Field,* Db [d′b-f′′b](f), Banks; Bb, Eb, Cramer.
Johneen, *Moira O'Neill,* Db [d′-d′′b], Masters/B&H Irish Idyll; *F,* B&H Irish Idyll, B&H.
Joy, shipmate, joy, *Walt Whitman,* D [c′-d′′], S&B MB 52, B&H Songs of Faith.
La Belle Dame Sans Merci, *John Keats,* Fm [bb-f′′(e′′b)], S&B MB 52, S&B;*Gm,* S&B.
Like as the thrush in winter (Sonnet 48), *Edmund Holmes,* G [d′-g′′], S&B MB 52, B&H Triumph of Love.
Little Peter Morrisey, *Winifred Letts,* Dm [c′-d′′], S&B Leinster.
Lookin' Back, *Moira O'Neill,* C [ab-e′′b], B&H Songs of Antrim.
Luck comes in sleeping, *A Song of Lorraine* tr. *Anon,* Eb [e′b-g′′], S&B MB 52.
Lullaby, A, *Thomas Dekker,* Ab [e′b-f′′](f), S&B MB 52, B&H *Heritage 1.*
Lullaby, *George Leveson Gower,* F [c′-f′′], Cramer.
Lute Song, The, *Alfred Lord Tennyson,* Dm [c′#-d′′](f), S&B.
Merry Month of May, The, *Thomas Dekker,* F [d′-f′′], S&B MB 52, 6 Songs.
Message to Phillis, A, *Thomas Heywood,* Ab [c′-f′′(a′′b)](m), S&B.
Milkmaid's Song, The, *Alfred Lord Tennyson,* F [f′-a′′], S&B.
Monkey's carol, The, *Winifred Letts,* Dm [d′-g′′], Cramer, OUP *Solo Christmas high;* Bm, *Solo Christmas low,* Cramer.
(Mopsa, *Philodemus,* tr. *Thomas Moore,* D [a-d′′](m), Elkin.)
My love is a flower, *Heinrich Heine* tr. *Anon,* Db [c′-f′′], S&B 12 Songs.
Night, *John Stevenson,* F [c′-c′′], S&B Cushendall.
Nonsense Rhymes, *Edward Lear,* set to music by 'Karel Drofnatski', 14 songs for various voices, S&B 1960.
O flames of passion (Sonnet 22), *Edmund Holmes,* Gm [e′b-g′′], S&B MB 52, B&H Triumph of Love.
O mistress mine, *Shakespeare,* F [b-d′′](m), B&H *Shakespeare Album,* S&B MB 52, 6 Songs.
O one deep sacred outlet of my soul (Sonnet 37), *Edmund Holmes,* Cm [d′b-g′′], S&B MB 52, B&H Triumph of Love.
Old Navy, The, *Captain Marryat,* C [bb-e′′](m), B&H; *D,* B&H.
Old Superb, The, *Henry Newbolt,* Bb [bb-e′′b](m), B&H Songs of the Sea, *Heritage 2*; Ab, C, B&H.
On the deep-blue-girdled heaven, *Heinrich Heine* tr. *Anon,* Eb [c′-g′′], S&B 12 Songs.
On thy blue eyes, *Heinrich Heine* tr. *Anon,* G [f′-g′′], S&B 12 Songs.
Out upon it, *John Suckling,* Em [e′-f′′#](m), S&B MB 52.
Outward Bound, *Henry Newbolt,* Ab [e′b-e′′b](m), B&H Songs of the Sea, *Heritage 1.*
Parted, *G. H. Jessop,* Eb [e′b-g′′](m), B&H.
Phoebe, *Thomas Lodge,* Bb [c′-e′′b(f′′)](m), S&B MB 52.
Pibroch, The, *Murdoch Maclean,* Bm [a′-d′′(m)], S&B MB 52, 6 Songs; *C#m,* Classical; (Em, Enoch).
Pilgrimage to Kevlaar, The, (scena), *Heinrich Heine,* tr. *Anon,* Db [c′-a′′b], B&H.
Prince Madoc's Farewell, *Felicia Hemans,* Dm [d′-e′′b](m), B&H.
Prospice, *Robert Browning,* G [c′-f′′](m), S&B MB 52, 6 Songs.
Queen and huntress, *Ben Jonson,* A [c′#-g′′], B&H.
Rain it Raineth Every Day, The, *Shakespeare,* Dm [c′-d′′], S&B MB 52, Thames *Countertenors 3,* B&H *Heritage 2, Shakespeare Album.*
Requiescat, *Matthew Arnold,* Ab [e′b-g′′], B&H.
Rhine Wine, The, *Walter Pollock,* G [f′#-g′′](m), B&H.
Rose of Killarney, The, *Alfred Percival Graves,* F [d′-g′′(a′′)], Cramer; *Eb,* Cramer.
Sad is the spring-time, *Heinrich Heine,* tr. *R. H. Benson,* Em [d′#-f′′#], S&B 12 Songs.
Sailor Man, The, *Moira O'Neill,* Ab [bb-e′′b](m), S&B MB 52, *Recitalist 4,* B&H Songs of Antrim.
Say, O say! saith the music, *Robert Bridges,* F [e′b-f′′](m), S&B MB 52.
Scared, *Winifred Letts,* Cm [bb-e′′b], S&B MB 52, Fire of Turf.
Since thou, O fondest and truest, *Robert Bridges,* D [d′-g′′], S&B MB 52.
Slumber Song, *Heinrich Heine,* tr. *Anon,* D [d′-e′′], S&B 12 Songs.
Soft day, A, *Winifred Letts,* Db [d′b-d′′b], S&B MB 52, Sheaf, S&B, Banks; *F,* S&B.
Song of the Bow, A, *Reginald Heber,* G [d′-g′′],(m), Cramer; *Eb,* Cramer.
Song Written at Sea, *Charles Sackville,* F [c′-f′′](m), B&H; *Ab,* B&H.
Sower's Song, The, *Thomas Carlyle,* Eb [e′b-f′′], Cramer.
Spring, *Heinrich Heine* tr. *R. H. Benson,* Ab [d′-f′′#(a′′b)], S&B 12 Songs.

Spring, *Alfred Lord Tennyson*, E♭ [e′♭-a′′♭](m), S&B MB 52.
Stars above me, golden footed, *Heinrich Heine* tr. *Andrew Lang*, D [c′#-f′′#], S&B MB 52, 12 Songs.
Strong son of God, *Alfred Lord Tennyson*, Dm [a-d′′], B&H Songs of Faith.
Sweeter than the violet, *Meleager,* tr. *Andrew Lang*, E♭ [d′-a′′♭], B&H.
Tears, *Walt Whitman*, Bm [b-e′′(f′′)], S&B MB 52, B&H Songs of Faith.
There be none of beauty's daughters, *Lord Byron*, E♭ [e′♭-f′′](m), S&B MB 52.
Thief of the World, *Winifred Letts*, F [d′-f′′], S&B Leinster.
Thou art my love, *Heinrich Heine* tr. *R. H. Benson*, E♭ [e′♭-g′′], S&B 12 Songs.
To Carnations, *Robert Herrick*, G [d′-g′′], S&B MB 52.
To the Rose, *Robert Herrick*, F [f′-f′′](m), B&H.
To the Skylark, *James Hogg*, G [d′(f′#)-a′′], B&H.
To the Soul, *Walt Whitman*, B♭ [b♭-e′′♭], Thames *Century 6*, S&B MB 52, B&H Songs of Faith.
Tragedy of Life, The (scena), *Heinrich Heine* tr. *Anon*, C [c′-f′′], B&H.
Unknown Sea, The, *Mary Kitson Clark*, F [d′-g′′](f), Cramer.
West Wind, The, *Winifred Letts,* F [c′-e′′♭], S&B MB 52, Fire of Turf.
When in the solemn stillness of the night (Sonnet 63), *Edmund Holmes*, D♭ [d′♭-g′′♭], B&H Triumph of Love.
Why so pale, *John Suckling*, Cm [e′♭-g′′](m), S&B MB 52, *Recitalist 3*.
Winds of Bethlehem, The, *Winifred Letts*, Gm [d′-g′′], Cramer *Folio 1.*
Windy Nights, *R. L. Stevenson*, Dm [d′-f′′], Roberton, S&B MB 52.
Witches Charms, *Ben Jonson*, Fm [c′-f′′], Cramer.
Arrangements: *Irish Melodies of Thomas Moore, Op 60,* Classical; *Irish Songs and Ballads,* Classical; *Songs of Erin,* Classical; *Songs of Old Ireland,* Classical.
Cuckoo, The, *Traditional German*, tr. *Paul England*, F [e′-c′′], B&H *Easy Song.*
Father O'Flynn, B♭ [medium high], Classical.
I'd rock my own sweet childie *see* Irish Lullaby, An.
Irish Lullaby, An, *Anon*, [soprano], Classical.
Molly Branigan, *Traditional,* E♭ [b♭-e♭], Classical.
My love's an arbutus, *A. P. Graves*, A♭ [e′♭-f′′](m), B&H *McCormack,* Classical.
Song of the Banshee, *Geo. H. Jessop,* Fm [e′♭-a′′♭], B&H.

Stanley, Charles **John.** 1712–1786.
(Be pleasant, be airy, *Sir John Hawkins*, G [d′-g′′], Elkin (Bevan).)
Fie, Damon, fie, *a young lady*, Em [d′#-f′′](f), Thames *Gentleman's Magazine*.
Sweet pretty bird, *Mr McClennan*, A♭ [e′♭-a′′♭](f), Braydeston (Bevan).
(Would's thou hope the nymph to gain, *Sir John Hawkins*, G [d′-g′′], Elkin (Bevan).)

Steed, Richard. 1941–
Just War, [tenor], SMIC.
Winter Walk, [tenor], SMIC.

Steel, Charles **Christopher.** 1939–1991. BMIC.
Collection: *Our Joyful'st Feast*, Banks.
So now is come our joyful'st feast, *George Wither*, [high], Banks Feast.
There was a time for shepherds, *Anthea Steel*, [high], Banks Feast.
What sweeter music can we bring? *Robert Herrick*, [high], Banks Feast.

Steele, Douglas. 1910–2000 *See also* App. 2.
Collection: *Selected Songs*, Forsyth.
Autumn Wind, The, *Herman Hesse*, tr. *Ralph Manheim*, C [c-e′′](m), Forsyth Selected.
Between the trees, *A. E. Housman*, F [e′♭-f′′], Forsyth Selected.
Blow, blow thou winter wind, *Shakespeare*, Am [c′-e′′], Forsyth Selected.
Dreams, *Walter de la Mare*, Bm [b♭-d′′], Forsyth Selected.
Faery beam upon you, The, *Ben Jonson*, E♭ [d′-e′′♭], Forsyth Selected.
Farm Child, *R. S. Thomas*, E♭ [d′-f′′], Forsyth Selected.
I heard a linnet courting, *Robert Bridges*, F [c′-f′′], Forsyth Selected.
In the highlands, *R. L. Stevenson*, D [d′-f′′#], Forsyth Selected.
Land of Lost Content, The, *A. E. Housman*, E♭ [c′-e′′♭], Forsyth Selected.
Loveliest of trees, *A. E. Housman*, F [c′-g′′], Forsyth Selected.
O mistress mine (1st setting), *Shakespeare*, E♭ [c′-e′′♭](m), Forsyth Selected.
O mistress mine (2nd setting) *Shakespeare*, F [c′-d′′](m), Forsyth Selected.
Prince of Heaven, The, *Brian Donaldson*, Em [e′-e′′], Forsyth Selected.
Requiem, *R. L. Stevenson*, D [d′-f′′#], Forsyth Selected.

Snow falls, The, *Stephen Bagnall*, Am [c′-d″], Forsyth Selected.
Sweet cyder, *Thomas Hardy*, F [c′-f″], Forsyth Selected.
Thrice toss these oaken ashes in the air, *Thomas Campion*, F [c′-d″], Forsyth Selected.
Under the greenwood tree, *Shakespeare*, Em [d′-e″], Forsyth Selected.
When I was one and twenty, *A. E. Housman*, Dm [d′-f″], Forsyth Selected.

Steptoe, Roger Guy. 1953– *See also* App. 2.
Collections: *Chinese Lyrics Set One*, S&B; *Chinese Lyrics Set Two*, S&B; *Three Sonnets to Delia*, S&B; *Two Songs for Baritone and Piano*, Lengnick.
Aspects (cycle), *Ursula Vaughan Williams*, [c′-a″], S&B.
At the Riverside Village, *Chinese* tr. *Kotewall* and *Smith*, [c′#-d″], S&B Chinese 2.
Beautie sweet love, *Samuel Daniel*, [bb-f″], S&B 3 Sonnets.
Blue iris, *Chinese*, tr. *Helen Waddell*, [e′b-e″b](f), S&B Chinese 1.
Care-charmer sleep, *Samuel Daniel*, [d′-e″], S&B 3 Sonnets.
Crossing the Han river, *Chinese* tr. *Kotewall* and *Smith*, [c′#-c″#], S&B Chinese 2.
Gathering of the Clans, A, *Chinese* tr. *Helen Waddell*, [c′-f″](f), S&B Chinese 1.
Green, green the riverside grass, *Chinese* tr. *Kotewall* and *Smith*, [c′#-e″], S&B Chinese 2.
He Protests his Loyalty, *Chinese* tr. *Helen Waddell*, [f′#-f″#](f), S&B Chinese 1.
Inscribed on a Small Garden Wall, *Chinese* tr. *Kotewall* and *Smith*, [c′-c″#], S&B Chinese 2.
Lament, A, *Percy Bysshe Shelley*, [baritone], Lengnick 2 Songs.
Let others sing of knights and palladines, *Samuel Daniel*, [d′-e″], S&B 3 Sonnets.
Little Music, A, (cycle), *Humbert Wolfe*, [G#-e′](m), Lengnick.
Morning glory, The, *Chinese*, tr. *Helen Waddell*, [c′#-f″#](f), S&B Chinese 1.
Music when soft voices die, *Percy Bysshe Shelley*, [baritone], Lengnick 2 Songs.
Night, *Chinese* tr. *Kotewall* and *Smith*, [c′-e″], S&B Chinese 2.
On Early Morning, *Chinese*, tr. *Helen Waddell*, [c′-g″](f), S&B Chinese 1.
White clouds are in the sky, *Chinese* tr. *Helen Waddell*, [c′-c″#], S&B Chinese 2.

Stevens, Bernard George. 1916–1983.
Collections: *Four John Donne Songs*, S&B (introduction by Bertha Stevens); *Palatine Coast, The*, Lengnick; *Two Songs*, Bardic.
Death, be not proud, *John Donne*, [b-g″#], S&B 4 Donne.
Dream Pedlary, *Thomas Lovell Beddoes*, [d′-g″](m), Bardic 2 Songs.
Go and catch a falling star, *John Donne*, [f′#-a″](m), S&B 4 Donne.
Good-morrow, The, *John Donne*, [c′-a″], S&B 4 Donne.
If we die, *Ethel Rosenberg*, [c′-a″b], Bardic.
Lunar Attraction, *Montague Slater*, [c′-g″], Lengnick Palatine Coast.
May Day Carol, *Montague Slater*, [g′-g″], Lengnick Palatine Coast.
Mother Shipton's Wooing, *Montague Slater*, [d′-g″], Lengnick Palatine Coast.
Song of the Ship, *Thomas Lovell Beddoes*, [d′b-b″b](m), Bardic 2 Songs.
Sweetest love, I do not go, *John Donne*, [e′b-f″#], S&B 4 Donne.
True Dark, The, (cycle), *Randall Swingler*, [A-g″](m), Roberton.

Stevens, James. 1929– BMIC.

Stevenson, Ronald. 1928– *See also* App. 1, 2.
Collections: *Eight Selected Songs*; *Four Songs*; *Selected Songs 1, 2, 3*; *Two Songs* [Poe]; *Two Songs* [Raine]; all Ronald Stevenson Society.
A'e Gowden Lyric, *Hugh MacDiarmid*, [medium-high], Stevenson Selected 1.
Annabel Lee, *Edgar Allen Poe*, [medium], Stevenson 2 Songs (Poe).
At My Father's Grave, *Hugh MacDiarmid*, [baritone], Stevenson Selected 3.
Barren Fig, The, *Hugh MacDiarmid*, [baritone], Stevenson Selected 3.
Bobbin Winder, The, *Hugh MacDiarmid*, [medium-high], Stevenson Selected 2.
Bonnie Broukit Bairn, The, *Hugh MacDiarmid*, [medium-high], Stevenson Selected 1.
Border Boyhood (cycle), *Hugh MacDiarmid*, [tenor], Stevenson.
Bubblyjock, *Hugh MacDiarmid*, [medium-high], Stevenson Selected 1.
Buckie Braes, The, *William Soutar*, [medium], Stevenson 8 Selected.
Child's Garden of Verses, A (cycle), *Robert Louis Stevenson*, [high], Stevenson.
Cophetua, *Hugh MacDiarmid*, [medium-high], Stevenson Selected 1.
Coronach for the End of the World, *Hugh MacDiarmid*, [baritone], Stevenson Selected 3.
Day is Düne, *William Soutar*, [medium], Stevenson 8 Selected.
Droll Wee Man, The, *William Soutar*, [medium], Stevenson 8 Selected.
Eldorado, *Edgar Allen Poe*, [high], Stevenson 2 Songs (Poe).
Fairy Tales, *Hugh MacDiarmid*, [medium-high], Stevenson Selected 1.

Four Vietnamese Miniatures (cycle), *Ho Chi Minh,* [high], Stevenson.
Gaelic Muse, The, *Hugh MacDiarmid,* [medium-high], Stevenson Selected 2.
Hallowe'en Sang, *William Soutar,* [medium], Stevenson 8 Selected.
Hill Sang, *William Soutar,* [medium], Stevenson 8 Selected.
Hills of Home (cycle), *Robert Louis Stevenson,* [baritone], Stevenson.
In the Fall, *Hugh MacDiarmid,* [medium-high], Stevenson Selected 2.
Last Trump, The, *Hugh MacDiarmid,* [baritone], Stevenson Selected 3.
Lines from Buchanan's Epithalamium, *Hugh MacDiarmid,* [baritone], Stevenson Selected 3.
My Love is to the Light of Lights, *Hugh MacDiarmid,* [baritone], Stevenson Selected 3.
Nine Haiku (cycle), *Japanese Poets,* tr. *Keith Boseley,* [high], Stevenson.
O Wha's the Bride? *Hugh MacDiarmid,* [medium-high], Stevenson Selected 2.
Plum Tree, The, *William Soutar,* [medium], Stevenson 8 Selected.
Quiet Comes In, The, *William Soutar,* [medium], Stevenson 8 Selected.
Robber, The, *Hugh MacDiarmid,* [medium-high], Stevenson Selected 2.
Rose of all the World, The, *Hugh MacDiarmid,* [medium-high], Stevenson Selected 1.
Scots Steel and Irish Fire, *Hugh MacDiarmid,* [baritone], Stevenson Selected 3.
Skeleton of the Future, The, *Hugh MacDiarmid,* [baritone], Stevenson Selected 3.
Small Cloud on the Horizon, *Aonghas MacNeacail,* [baritone], Stevenson.
Song of the Nightingale, The, *Hugh MacDiarmid,* [medium-high], Stevenson Selected 2.
Songs from Factories and Fields, (cycle), *Hugh MacDiarmid,* [bass-baritone], Stevenson.
To my Mountain, *Kathleen Raine,* [medium], Stevenson 2 Songs (Raine).
To the Future, *William Soutar,* [medium], Stevenson 8 Selected.
Traighean (Shores), *Sorley MacLean,* [high baritone/tenor], Stevenson.
Triad, *Kathleen Raine,* [medium], Stevenson 2 Songs (Raine).
Trompe l'Oeil, *Hugh MacDiarmid,* [medium-high], Stevenson Selected 1.
Two Songs (diptych), *Rabindranath Tagore,* [soprano], Stevenson.
War, *William Blake,* [baritone], Stevenson.

Stewart, D. M.
Collection: *Four Herrick Songs,* [high, medium (given below), low], B&H
 (Succession of the Four Sweet Months, The, *Robert Herrick,* D [d′-e′′], B&H 4 Herrick Songs.)
 (To Electra, *Robert Herrick,* A♭ [e′♭-f′′], B&H 4 Herrick Songs.)
 (To Violets, *Robert Herrick,* A [f′#-f′′#], B&H 4 Herrick Songs.)
 (Upon a Maid, *Robert Herrick,* B♭m [e′♭-f′′], B&H 4 Herrick Songs.)
 West Wind, The, *John Masefield,* E [b-e′′], S&B; G, S&B.

Still, Robert. 1910–1971.
 Beauty Bathing, *Anthony Munday,* E [b-e′′](m), Lengnick.
 Upon Julia's Clothes, *Robert Herrick,* G [d′-e′′], Lengnick.

Stoker, Richard. 1938– BMIC.
 Aspects 1 in 3 (cycle), *Ralph Waldo Emerson,* [a-f′′#], Peters.
 Music that Brings Sweet Sleep (cycle), *Tennyson, du Maurier, Herrick, Shakespeare,* [c′-g′′], Peters.

Stone, David.
Arrangement:
 When I was young (The foggy dew), *Traditional,* D♭ [c′-e′′♭](m), BMP.

Storace, Stephen. 1762–1796. *See also* App. 2.
Collection: *Seven Songs for High Voice,* S&B (edited Michael Pilkington).
 Be mine, tender passion, *Anon,* E♭ [b♭-b′′♭](f), S&B 7 Songs.
 Captivity, *Joshua Jeans,* E♭ [e′♭-a′′♭](f), OUP (Roberts) *Tuneful Voice.*
 Curfew, The, *Thomas Gray,* Dm [c′#-f′′], S&B 7 Songs, OUP (Roberts) *Tuneful Voice.*
 How mistaken is the lover, *Anon,* G [d′-g′′](f), S&B 7 Songs, (H. Diack Johnston) *Recitalist 1.*
 How sweet the calm of this sequester'd shore, *Anon,* A [e′-f′′#], OUP (Roberts) *Tuneful Voice.*
 My rising spirits thronging, *Anon,* B♭ [f′-a′′](f), S&B 7 Songs.
 No more his fears alarming, *Anon,* A [e′-a′′](f), S&B 7 Songs
 Peaceful slumbering on the ocean, *Anon,* C [c′-g′′](f), S&B 7 Songs.
 Pretty creature, The, *Anon,* F [c′-f′′(d′′)](m), B&H (Lane Wilson) *Old English,* Classical (Lane Wilson), Schirmer (Lane Wilson) *1st Baritone II.*
 Sailor loved a lass, A, *Anon,* E♭ [c′-f′′(e′′♭)], B&H (Lane Wilson) *Old English.*
 Summer heats bestowing, The, *Cobb?* A [e′-a′′](f), S&B 7 Songs, S&B (Ivimey).

Stout, Alastair. 1975– *See* App. 2.

Sullivan, Sir **Arthur** Seymour. 1842–1900. *See also* App. 2., B&H
Collections: *Songs Books 1, 2, 3,* S&B (edited with Prefaces by Alan Borthwick and Robin Wilson); *Window, The* or *Songs of the Wrens, The,* Masters.
    Answer, The, *Alfred Lord Tennyson,* Em [d´-g´´], Masters Window.
    Arabian Love Song, *Percy Bysshe Shelley,* Am [e´-g´´(a´´)](f), S&B Book 2.
    At the Window, *Alfred Lord Tennyson,* E♭ [c´-e´´♭], Masters Window, S&B MB 56.
    Ay de mi, my bird! *George Eliot,* F [c´-f´´], S&B MB 56.
    Chorister, The, *Fred. E. Weatherly,* F [c´-f´´], Cramer *Folio 1.*
    County Guy, *Walter Scott,* Em [b-e´´(f´´#)], S&B Book 3.
    Distant Shore, The, *W. S. Gilbert,* E♭ [b♭-e´´♭], S&B Book 3; (G, Chappell *English Recital 2.*)
    Edward Gray, *Alfred Lord Tennyson,* G [d´-g´´](m), S&B Book 3.
    Free from his fetters, *W. S. Gilbert,* E♭ [f´-g´´], Schirmer *2nd Tenor.*
    Golden Days, *Lionel Lewin,* E♭ [b♭-g´´], Banks.
    Gone! *Alfred Lord Tennyson,* C [e´-f´´], Masters Window.
    I heard the nightingale, *C. H. Townshend,* A♭ [d´(e´♭)-a´´♭], S&B MB 56.
    If doughty deeds, *Graham of Gartmore,* E♭ [b♭-e´´♭](m)), S&B Book 2.
    Let me dream again, *B. C. Stephenson,* D [c´#(b)-f´´#(a)](f), S&B Book 1; C, B&H.
    Letter, The, *Alfred Lord Tennyson,* G [d´-g´´], Masters Window.
    Little Buttercup, *W. S. Gilbert,* C [b-d´´], Schirmer *2nd Mezzo.*
    Lost Chord, The, *Adelaide Ann Proctor,* F [c´-f´], S&B Book 1, IMP *Parlour Songs,* B&H, Classical; G, *Ballad Album 2,* Cramer *Drawing Room Songs, World Renowned,* Classical; E♭, B&H.
    Marriage Morning, *Alfred Lord Tennyson,* E♭ [b♭-g´´], Masters Window.
    Mary Morison, *Robert Burns,* G [d´-e´´](m), S&B Book 3; B♭, B&H.
    No Answer (1), *Alfred Lord Tennyson,* Em [b(d´#)-f´´#], Masters Window.
    No Answer (2), *Alfred Lord Tennyson,* E [d´#-e´´], Masters Window.
    O fair dove! O fond dove, *Jean Ingelow,* D [b-f´´](f), S&B Book 1.
    O mistress mine, *Shakespeare,* G [d´-f´´#(g´´)], S&B MB 56.
    On the Hill, *Alfred Lord Tennyson,* E♭ [d´b-g´´(f´´#)], Masters Window.
    Orpheus with his lute, *Shakespeare,* B♭ [d´-g´´(b´´♭)], S&B Book 1, MB 56, Classical; A, Cramer *Folio 1;* G, Classical, Schirmer *2nd Mezzo.*
    Policeman's Song, The, *W. S. Gilbert,* F [f-v´´], Schirmer *2nd Baritone.*
    Sigh no more, ladies, *Shakespeare,* D [e´-g´´(a´´)](m), S&B Book 3.
    Silver'd is the raven hair, *W. S. Gilbert,* E♭ [b♭-c´´], Schirmer *2nd Mezzo.*
    Sometimes, *Lady Lindsay,* C [d´-g´´], S&B Book 2.
    Spring, *Alfred Lord Tennyson,* E [f´#-g´´#(g´´)], Masters Window.
    Sun whose rays, The, *W. S. Gilbert,* G [d´-g´´], Schirmer *2nd Soprano.*
    Sweethearts, *W. S. Gilbert,* A♭ [c´-g´´], S&B Book 2.
    Tears, idle tears, *Alfred Lord Tennyson,* E♭ [b♭-f´´♭], S&B Book 2.
    What does little birdie say? *Alfred Lord Tennyson,* S&B MB 56.
    When? *Alfred Lord Tennyson,* D [f´#-g´´(a´´)], Masters Window.
    When first my old, old love I knew, *W. S. Gilbert,* D [f´-f´´(a´´)], Schirmer *2nd Tenor.*
    When I was a lad I served a term, *W. S. Gilbert,* B♭ [b♭-d´´], Schirmer *2nd Baritone.*
    Where the bee sucks, *Shakespeare,* B♭ [c´-g´´], S&B Book 1, *Recitalist 1;* (D♭, B&H.)
    Willow Song, The, *Shakespeare,* E [b-e´´(c´´#)], S&B Book 1, *Recitalist 2,* B&H *Shakespeare Album; F,* Schirmer *1st Mezzo II.*
    Winter, *Alfred Lord Tennyson,* Am [d´(a)-f´´#], Masters Window.

Sutherland, Margaret.
Collection: *Five Songs,* BMP.
    For a Child, *John Shaw Neilson,* [e´-f´´#], BMP 5 Songs.
    In the dim counties, *John Shaw Neilson,* [c´-e´´], BMP 5 Songs.
    May, *John Shaw Neilson,* [d´b-f´´], BMP 5 Songs.
    Song be delicate, *John Shaw Neilson,* [c´-f´´], BMP 5 Songs.
    When kisses are as strawberries, *John Shaw Neilson,* [d´-f´´], BMP 5 Songs.

Sutton-Anderson, David. *See* App. 2.

Swain, Freda. 1902–1985. BMIC.
    (Blessing, *Austin Clarke,* F [c´-e´´], Curwen.)
    Experience, *Chinese* tr. *Arthur Waley,* [b-e´´], S&B.
    Green Lad from Donegal, The, *Freda Swain,* Fm [e´b-f´´], S&B.
    Lark on Portsdown Hill, The, *Freda Swain,* [c´-f´´], S&B.
    Winter Field, *A. E. Coppard,* Em [c´-e´´], S&B.

Swann, Donald Ibrahim. 1923–1994. *See also* App. 1.
Collections: *Five Colourisations of Emily Dickinson's Poems,* Lengnick; *Poetic Image, The,* Lengnick (preface Donald Swann); *Seven Poetic Songs,* Thames (Preface Alison Swann Smith and Leon Berger, notes John Jansson); *Six Poetic Songs,* Thames (Preface Alison Swann Smith and Leon Berger, notes John Jansson); *Songs to Poems by William Blake,* Lengnick; *Two Songs by Edna St Vincent Millay,* Lengnick.
    Ah!, sun-flower, *William Blake,* [high], Lengnick Blake.
    And must I then indeed, pain, live with you? *Edna St Vincent Millay,* [high], Lengnick Millay.
    Angel, The, *William Blake,* [high], Lengnick Blake.
    Arcades, *John Milton,* [b-d′′], Thames 7 Poetic.
    Be near me when my light is low, *Alfred Lord Tennyson,* [a-e′′], Lengnick Poetic Image.
    Before Life and After, *Thomas Hardy,* D [a♭-f′′], Lengnick Poetic Image.
    Bitter Resurrection, A, *Christina Rossetti,* E [c′#-g′′#], Lengnick Poetic Image.
    Fly, The, *William Blake,* [high], Lengnick Blake.
    Garden of Love, The, *William Blake,* [high], Lengnick Blake.
    Harlot's House, The, *Oscar Wilde,* [d′-c′′′♭], Lengnick Poetic Image.
    He who binds to himself a joy, *William Blake,* [high], Lengnick Blake.
    He Wishes for the Cloths of Heaven, *W. B. Yeats,* [c′-d′′], Thames 6 Poetic.
    I died for beauty, *Emily Dickinson,* [high], Lengnick Dickinson.
    I felt a funeral in my brain, *Emily Dickinson,* [high], Lengnick Dickinson.
    I had no time to hate, *Emily Dickinson,* [high], Lengnick Dickinson.
    I heard a fly buzz when I died, *Emily Dickinson,* [high], Lengnick Dickinson.
    Invite to Eternity, An, *John Clare,* [b-f′′#], Lengnick Poetic Image.
    It was a lover and his lass, *Shakespeare,* Cm [c′-f′′], Thames 6 Poetic.
    Kingdom of God, The, *Francis Thompson,* [a-f′′#], Thames 6 Poetic.
    Lúthien Tinúviel, *J. R. R. Tolkien,* F [c′-g′′], Thames 7 Poetic.
    Marguerite, *David Marsh,* [b-e′′](m), Thames 6 Poetic.
    Oh yet we trust, *Alfred Lord Tennyson,* [b♭-f′′#], Lengnick Poetic Image.
    Passionate Trencherwoman, The, *David Climie,* [c-g′′](f), Thames 7 Poetic.
    Raider's Dawn, *Alun Lewis,* Dm [a-d′′], Thames 7 Poetic.
    Red, Red Rose, A, *Robert Burns,* E♭ [b♭(c′)-g′′](m), Thames 7 Poetic.
    See, dearest, how the rose, *David Marsh,* C [b-e′′](m), Thames 7 Poetic.
    Sick Rose, The, *William Blake,* [high], Lengnick Blake.
    Stopping by Woods, *Robert Frost,* Em [b-e′′], Thames 6 Poetic.
    There rolls the deep, *Alfred Lord Tennyson,* D♭ [d′b-g′′♭], Lengnick Poetic Image.
    Thou famished grave, *Edna St Vincent Millay,* [high], Lengnick Millay.
    Thoughts of Phena, *Thomas Hardy,* G♭ [d′♭-f′′], Lengnick Poetic Image.
    Tie the strings to my life, O Lord, *Emily Dickinson,* [high], Lengnick Dickinson.
    We'll go no more a-roving, *Lord Byron,* D [c′#-a′′](m), Thames 7 Poetic.
    When I am dead, my dearest, *Christina Rossetti,* D [c′#-f′′#], Lengnick Poetic Image.
    Wish, that of the living whole, The, *Alfred Lord Tennyson,* A♭ [a♭-e′′], Lengnick Poetic Image.
    Word on My Ear, A, *Michael Flanders & Donald Swann,* [d′♭-b′′♭], Novello *Sarah's Encores.*

Swayne, Giles Oliver Cairnes. 1946– *See also* App. 2.
    Goodmorrow, The, *John Donne,* [mezzo], Novello hire.
    Goodnight sweet ladies, *Shakespeare,* [soprano], Novello hire.
    Kiss, The, *John Donne,* [high], Novello hire.

Swinstead, Felix.
Collections: *Four Old English Songs,* BMP; *Sing-Song Cycle,* [Christina Rossetti], [high] BMP.
    Maypole, The, *Anon,* D [c′-e′′], BMP 4 Old English Songs.
    No, no, Nigella, *Anon,* Em [d′-d′′], BMP 4 Old English Songs.
    These dainty daffadillies, *Anon,* G [d′-d′′], BMP 4 Old English Songs.
    What saith my dainty darling, *Anon,* D [e′-e′′], BMP 4 Old English Songs.

Sykes, John. 1909–1962.
Collections: (*Songs of Innocence,* Blake; *Songs of Experience,* Blake; MSS held by BMIC).

Symons, Dom Thomas. 1887– ?
Collection: *Two de la Mare Songs,* BMP.
    First of May, The, E♭ [low], BMP.
    Little Black Boy, *William Blake,* A♭m [d′♭-e′′♭], B&H.
    Quartette, The, *Walter de la Mare,* [d′-f′′#], BMP 2 de la Mare.
    Winter, *Walter de la Mare,* [e′♭-g′′#], BMP 2 de la Mare.

T

Talbot, Joby. 1971–
Collection: *Three Songs from the Underground*, [baritone/mezzo], Chester.
Life Support, [mezzo], Chester.

Tann, Hilary. 1947– *see* App. 2.

Tate, Arthur F.
Somewhere a voice is calling, *Eileen Newton*, D [b-d''], IMP *Parlour* Songs; E♭, F, G, Classical.

Tate, Phyllis Margaret Duncan. 1911–1987. *See also* App. 2.
Collections: *Scenes from Tyneside*, Emerson; *Two Songs*, BMP.
    Cock, The, *Anon*, G [c'#-g''], BMP 2 Songs.
    Cradle Song, *William Blake*, Am [f'-e''](f), BMP.
    Epitaph, *Walter Raleigh*, Am [b-f''], BMP.
    Falcon, The, *Anon*, [c'#-g''], BMP 2 Songs.
    I sing of a maiden, *Anon*, [d'-a''], BMP.
    My love could walk, *W. H. Davies*, C [e'b-a''b], BMP.
    Of all the youths, *Anon*, B♭ [d'-f''](f), Emerson Scenes.
    Quiet Mind, The, *Edward Dyer*, G [a#-f''], BMP.
Arrangements:
    Brother James's Air, [e'-f''], OUP.
    Lark in the Clear Air, The, *Samuel Ferguson*, B♭ [e'b-g''](m), OUP *Solo Baritone*, OUP; A♭, OUP; (F, BMP).
    Long ago in Bethlehem, *C. K. Offer*, G [f'#-g''], OUP *Solo Christmas high* ; E♭, *Solo Christmas low*.
    O, the bonny fisher lad, *Anon*, Gm [b♭-d''], BMP.
    Snowy-breasted Pearl, The, *Anon* tr. *Petrie*, D [d'-f''#], BMP.
    The Water of Tyne, *Anon*, [b-d''], OUP.

Tavener, John Kenneth. 1944– *See also* App. 2.
Collection: *Three Sections from the Four Quartets*, Chester.
    Dove descending breaks the air, The, *T. S. Eliot*, [d'-a''](m), Chester 3 Sections.
    Lady, whose shrine stands on the promontory, *T. S. Eliot*, [e'-f''#](m), Chester 3 Sections.
    Lamentation, Last Prayer and Exaltation, [soprano], Chester.
    Mini Songcycle for Gina, A, *W. B. Yeats*, [d'-a''b], Chester.
    Prayer, for Szymanowski, *Shakespeare,* [bass], Chester.
    Time and the bell have buried the day, *T. S. Eliot*, [d'b-g''b](m), Chester 3 Sections.

Taylor, Colin.
    Afternoon Tea, *Charlotte Mew*, [d'-e''(g'')], BMP.
    Barbara Allen, *Old English*, [f'-f''], BMP.
    Hill, The, *James Stephens*, [c'#-f''], BMP.
    O can ye sew cushions, *Traditional*, [g'-g''], BMP.
    Windmill, The, *from a Sussex Millpost*, [d'-e''], BMP.

Taylor, Cyril V.
Collection: *Three Christmas Songs*, BMP.
    Cradle Song, *Martin Luther*, tr. *Wedderburn*, Fm [e'b-g''], BMP 3 Christmas.
    I sing of a maiden, *Anon*, E [e'-g''#], BMP 3 Christmas.
    Longing (Come to me in my dreams), *Matthew Arnold*, C [a-e''(f'#)], BMP.
    Ode on the Birth of Our Saviour, An, *Robert Herrick*, F [c'-g''], BMP 3 Christmas.
    To Helen, *Edgar Allan Poe*, E♭ [d'-f''], BMP.

Taylor, E. Kendall.
    White in the moon, *A. E. Housman*, [d'-g''], BMP.

Taylor, Matthew. 1964– *See also* App. 2.
Collection: *Three Rupert Brooke Songs,* Maecenas.
    Beauty to Beauty, *Rupert Brooke*, [a-f'#](f), Maecenas Brooke.
    Jolly Company, The, *Rupert Brooke*, [a♭-g''](f), Maecenas Brooke.
    Song, *Rupert Brooke*, [b♭-f''](f), Maecenas Brooke.

Taylor, Timothy. WMIC. *See also* App. 2.

Teed, Roy. 1928–
Collections: *Two Songs*, Chester.
    April Morning, *Bill Adams*, C [c′-e′′], Chester 2 Songs.
    Holy Thursday, *William Blake*, C [c′-g′′(e′′)], Roberton.
    Song for Sunrise, *James Kirkup*, C [e′b-f′′], Chester 2 Songs.
    Three jolly gentlemen, *Walter de la Mare*, Eb [e′b-e′′b], Chester.

Thackray, Rupert.
    Neglectful Edward, *Robert Graves*, Bb [d′-f′′], BMP.

Thiman, Eric. 1900–1975. *See also* App. 2.
Collections: *Thirteen Songs*, S&B (introduction Felix Aprahamian); *Two Sacred Songs*, [low], Novello.
    As Joseph was a-walking, *Anon*, E [c′-e′′], S&B 13 Songs; (G, S&B.)
    (Birds, The, *Hilaire Belloc*, C [d′-f′′], Novello; D, Novello.)
    Carol of the Birds, *K. M. Warburton*, Eb [bb-e′′b], B&H.
    Dainty fine bird, *Anon*, Gm [d′-f′′](m), S&B 13 Songs; Fm, S&B.
    Easter Prayer, An, *Irene Gass*, Am [e′-e′′], Cramer *Folio 1*.
    Evening in Lilac Time, *T. H. Dipnall*, G [d′-d′′], S&B 13 Songs.
    (Flower of Heaven, *Irene Gass*, Eb [bb-e′′b], Elkin; Gb, Elkin.)
    God of love my shepherd is, The, *George Herbert*, Ab [c′-f′′], Novello; F, Novello.
    Happy is the man, Novello 2 Sacred.
    I love all graceful things, *Kathleen Boland*, Ab [e′b-g′′], Schirmer/*1st Soprano*, (Curwen).
    I saw three ships, *Anon*, G [d′-d′′], S&B 13 Songs.
    I wandered lonely as a cloud, *William Wordsworth*, Db [c′-g′′b], S&B 13 Songs, *Recitalist 2*.
    (In the bleak midwinter, *Christina Rossetti*, D, Novello; F, Novello.)
    (Jesus, the very thought of thee, *St Bernard of Clairvaux*, tr. *Caswell*, Bb [bb-d′′], Novello; D, Novello.)
    Madonna and Child, *Gerald Bullett*, F [e′-f′′], S&B 13 Songs, (Chappell; D, Chappell).
    (Maid of Dundee, The, *Sydney Bell*, Cm [c′-e′′b], Curwen.)
    (My bonny lass she smileth, *Anon*, E [c′#-f′′#], Novello.)
    (My Master hath a garden, *Anon*, F [c′-f′′], Novello; G, Novello.)
    Now sleeps the crimson petal, *Alfred Lord Tennyson*, Eb [c′-f′′], S&B 13 Songs, *Recitalist 4*.
    Path to the Moon, The, *Madeline C. Thomas*, Ab [e′b-f′′], B&H *Easy Song*.
    (Piper pipes a merry tune, The, *Anon*, G [d′-g′′], Chappell *English Recital 2*.)
    (Ploughman's Song, The, *Christopher Hassall*, G [e′-f′′], Novello.)
    Rainbow, The, *Christina Rossetti*, E [b-e′′], S&B 13 Songs.
    Shepherd, The, *William Blake*, G [d′-f′′#], S&B 13 Songs.
    (Silver Birch, The, *Edith Nisbet*, C [b-d′′(e′′)], Curwen; F, Curwen.)
    Silver swan, The, *Anon*, Bbm [d′b-f′′], S&B 13 Songs; (Cm, Novello).
    Sleeping, *Anon 17th cent.*, E [b-g′′], S&B 13 Songs; (Db, Augener).
    (Song in Solitude, *Walter Savage Landor*, Ab [e′b-f′′#], Elkin.)
    (Song-thrush, The, *Ann Phillips*, D [d′-g′′], Curwen.)
    Sweet Afton, *Robert Burns*, Db [e′b-a′′b](m), S&B 13 Songs; (Bb, Augener).
    (Wee road from Cushendall, The, *Sydney Bell*, F [c′-f′′], Curwen.)
    Where go the boats? *R. L. Stevenson*, F [c′-d′′], S&B 13 Songs; (Ab, Augener).
    Wilderness, The, Novello 2 Sacred.

Thomas, Arthur Goring. 1850–1892. See App. 1.

Thomas, D. Afan. 1881–1925.
    Land of the Silver Trumpets, E [mezzo/contralto/baritone], Snell.
    Sleep my pearl, *Wil Afan*, [d′-g′′], BMP.

Thomas, David Vaughan. 1873–1934.
Collection: *Seven Songs*, [tenor/soprano], Snell; *Two Songs for Baritone*, Snell.
    Berwyn, [baritone], Snell 2 Songs.
    Enter those enchanted woods, *George Meredith*, D [f′-a′′] WMIC, *Songs from Wales 1*.
    Mountain Stream, The, [baritone], Snell 2 Songs.
    Seagull Fair, The, *Dafydd ap Gwilym* tr. *H. Idris Bell*, Dm [f′-f′′], Gwynn.

Thomas, Elizabeth. WMIC.

Thomas, Elsie.
Snowdonia, [contralto/baritone], Snell.

Thomas, Griffith.
Rock of ages, *A. M. Toplady,* [soprano/tenor], Snell; [contralto/baritone], Snell.

Thomas, Harold Flower.
We'll to the woods no more, *A. E. Housman,* [e′b(b)-e′′#(g′′)], BMP.
Give a man a horse he can ride, *James Thomson,* E [d′-e′′], B&H; G, B&H.

Thomas, J. R.
Eileen Alannah, *E. S. Marble,* F [c′-d′′], Weinberger; G, Ab, Weinberger.

Thomas, Mansel Treharne. 1909–1986.
Collections: *Five Settings of Poems by Idris Davies,* MTT; *Four Prayers from the Gaelic,* Gwynn; *Jack's Songs,* [T. Rowland Hughes, Peter Cobb], [c′-g′′], MTT; *Songs for Grace and Siân,* [I. D. Hooson, Eifion Wyn tr. Iolo Davies], [d′-f′′], Gwynn; *Songs of the Year,* [T. Llew Jones tr. Peter Cobb], [d′-f′′], MTT; *Three Songs for Joanna,* Gwynn; *Three Songs for the Night,* [Alun Lewis], [c′-a′′], MTT, [g-e′′], MTT; *Three Songs to Poems by Roland Mathias,* MTT [high, low]; *Twelve Songs for Children,* Gwynn; *Two Songs of Sleep,* [Alun Lewis], [c′-a′′], MTT, [ab-f′′], MTT.
    Another Picture, *Matthew Arnold,* [c′#-g′′], MTT; [b-f′′], MTT.
    Apple Tree, An, *T. Rowland Hughes* tr. *Peter Cobb,* [e′-g′′], MTT.
    Arianrhod, *Sally Roberts,* [e′b-g′′], MTT; [c′-e′′], MTT.
    Bard, The *see* Poet, The.
    Betty Wyn, *Nellie Williams* tr. *Ben Morgan,* [d′-e′′], MTT.
    Bless to me, God, *Anon* tr. *Alexander Carmichael,* Bb [d′-a′′b], Gwynn 4 Prayers.
    Blessing for a House, *Anon* tr. *Alexander Carmichael,* C [c′-g′′], Gwynn 4 Prayers.
    Blossoms, *R. Silyn Roberts* tr. *Peter Cobb,* [b-g′′], MTT; [a-f′′], MTT.
    Boy's Song, A, *James Hogg,* [d′-e′′](m), Gwynn.
    Broad Sound, *John Stuart Williams,* [d′#-g′′], MTT; [b#-e′′], MTT.
    Carol for a New-born King, *Dorothy Adams-Jeremiah,* [e′b-f′′], MTT.
    Channel Saint, *Roland Mathias,* [d′-g′′#], MTT Mathias; [b-e′′#], MTT Mathias.
    Christmas Star, *T. Llew Jones* tr. *Peter Cobb,* [d′-f′′], Gwynn.
    Come and see the baby, *Margery Morrell,* [c′-e′′], MTT.
    Craswall, *Roland Mathias,* [d′#-g′′], MTT Mathias; [c′-e′′], MTT Mathias.
    Crystal Rill, The, *Eifion Wyn* tr. *Robert Davies,* G [d′-e′′], Gwynn.
    Dawn Trees, *Bryn Jones,* [c′#-f′′], MTT; [c′-e′′], MTT.
    Dulas Carol, The, *Mansel Thomas* and *Peter Cobb,* [d′-d′′], MTT.
    Earth-borne, *Jeremy Hooker,* [c′-g′′](m), MTT; [a-e′′], MTT.
    Eifonydd, *R. Williams Parry* tr. *Peter Cobb,* [d′-a′′b], MTT; [b-f′′], MTT.
    Eze-sur-Mer, *Idris Davies,* [d′-a′′], MTT Davies; [bb-f′′], MTT Davies.
    First Christmas, The, *Peter Cobb,* [d′-g′′], MTT; [b-e′′], MTT.
    Flowering Heather, The, *Wyn Williams* tr. *Peter Cobb,* [c′#-f′′#](m), MTT; [b-e′′], MTT.
    God is, *Roland Mathias,* [f′-g′′#], MTT Mathias; [d′b-e′′], MTT Mathias.
    Goldfish, The, *A. G. Prys-Jones,* [c′-f′′], Gwynn Joanna.
    Grave and the Flower, The, *Robert H. Jones* tr. *Idris Bell,* [d′-g′′], MTT; [b-e′′], MTT.
    Gwynn ap Nudd, *Elfed* tr. *Grace Williams,* [d′-a′′b], Gwynn.
    Henry Morgan's March on Panama, *A. G. Prys-Jones,* [b-f′′](m), MTT.
    Holy Child, The, *Aneirin Talfan Davies,* [d′-f′′], MTT.
    Hymn to God the Father, A, *John Donne,* [c′-e′′](m), MTT.
    I will praise thee, *Dyfed* tr. *Peter Cobb.* [d′-f′′], MTT; [bb-d′′b], MTT.
    In Memoriam (Hywel Davies) (cycle), *Wm Williams (Pantycelyn)* tr. *Peter Cobb* [d′-a′′], MTT.
    Inner Light, The, *Idris Davies,* [e′-g′′], MTT Davies; [c′#-e′′], MTT Davies.
    Jack Frost and Sally Sunshine, *Harri Webb,* [e′b-g′′], MTT; [c′-e′′], MTT.
    Life, *T. Gwynn Jones,* [e′b-a′′b], Gwynn.
    Little Tommy Twinkletoes, *A. G. Prys-Jones,* [d′-f′′#], Gwynn Joanna.
    Love lasts longer, *Idris Davies,* [d′-g′′], MTT Davies; [b-e′′] MTT Davies.
    Lower him gently, *Idris Davies,* [d′-f′′#], MTT Davies; [b-d′′#], MTT Davies.
    Madrigal, *R. S. Thomas,* [e′b-a′′b], MTT; [c′-f′′], MTT.
    Marguerite, *William Morris,* [d′-f′′](m), MTT; [c′-e′′b], MTT.
    Mask of Pity, The, *Bryn Griffiths,* [d′b-a′′b], MTT; [a-f′′b], MTT.
    Maud Gonne, *John Stuart Williams,* [c′-a′′], MTT; [g-e′′], MTT.
    My love is like the flowers of the year, *Hen Benillion* tr. *Peter Cobb,* [e′-g′′](m), MTT; [c′#-e′′], MTT.

One, two, three, *Elfed* tr. *Peter Cobb,* [d′-g′′](m), MTT; [b-e′′], MTT.
Overkill, *John Stuart Williams,* [e′b-a′′], MTT; [c′b-f′′], MTT.
Parable, *Alun Lewis,* [d′#-a′′], MTT; [b#-f′′#], MTT.
Peasants, The, *Alun Lewis,* [e′b-a′′b], MTT; [bb-f′′b], MTT.
Poet, The, *R. Williams Parry* tr. *T. Gwynn Jones,* [e′-f′′], Gwynn.
Raider's Dawn, *Alun Lewis,* [d′b-g′′], MTT; [bb-e′′], MTT.
Remembrance, *Bryn Griffiths,* [c′-a′′b], MTT; [ab-f′′b], MTT.
Rhymney, *Idris Davies,* [d′b-a′′b], MTT Davies; [bb-f′′], MTT Davies.
Rising of Glyndwr, The, *R. S. Thomas,* [e′-a′′b], MTT; [b-e′′b], MTT.
Rob Robin, *A. G. Prys-Jones,* [d′-g′′], Gwynn Joanna.
Salter than salt of the ocean, *Aneirin Talfan Davies* tr. *Peter Cobb,* [d′-e′′](m), MTT.
Sea, The, *Wyn Williams* tr. *Peter Cobb,* [d′b-a′′], MTT; [a-f′′], MTT.
Seagulls, The, *J. Morris-Jones* tr. *Peter Cobb,* [e′-a′′], MTT; [c′-f′′], MTT.
Seagull's Cry, The, *L. Haydn Lewis* tr. *Peter Cobb,* [c′-g′′], MTT; [a-e′′], MTT.
Secret People, The, *A. G. Prys-Jones,* [d′-g′′], WMIC, *Songs from Wales 1*; [c′-f′′], MTT.
Song for July, *Harri Webb,* [e′-a′′b], MTT; [c′#-f′′], MTT.
Song of Little Jesus, The, *Daniel H. Davies,* [c′-f′′], MTT.
Song of the Exile, *A. E. Housman,* [e′b-g′′], MTT; [c′-e′′], MTT.
Sorcery of Olwen, The, *Elfed* tr. *Peter Cobb,* [f′#-g′′](m), MTT; [e′b-e′′], MTT.
Spring Morning, *Enid Parry* tr. *Glyn Jones,* [d′-g′′], MTT; [c′-f′′], MTT.
Sunset and Sea, *Gilbert Ruddock,* [c′-a′′b], MTT; [ab-f′′b], MTT.
Taliesin 1952, *R. S. Thomas,* [e′b-a′′](m), MTT; [b-e′′], MTT.
Thanks to thee, O God, *Anon* tr. *Alexander Carmichael,* G [d′-g′′], Gwynn 4 Prayers.
Thou being of marvels, *Anon* tr. *Alexander Carmichael,* G [c′-g′′], Gwynn 4 Prayers.
Unfading Beauty, The, *Thomas Carew,* [d′-g′′](m), MTT; [b-e′′], MTT.
Water Music, *Alun Lewis,* [d′-a′′], MTT; [bb-f′′], MTT.
When the morn is new, *Elfed* tr. *E. D. Bell,* [d′-g′′], MTT; [b-e′′], MTT.
Wind's Lament, The, *John Morris-Jones* tr. *Peter Cobb,* [d′#-f′′#, MTT; [c′#-e′′], MTT.
Arrangements: *Three Folk-songs for Children,* MTT.
As I wandered one fine morning, *Welsh Traditional,* [d′-d′′](m), MTT.
Caller herrin', *Scottish Borders (Lady Nairne),* [c′-f′′](f), MTT; [bb-e′′b], MTT.
Captain Morgan's March, *Welsh Traditional,* [e′-e′′], MTT.
Crossing the Stile, *Welsh Traditional,* [d′-g′′](m), MTT; [b-e′′], MTT.
David of the White Rock, *Welsh Traditional,* [b-e′′], MTT; [a-d′′], MTT.
Dream, A, *Welsh Traditional,* [b-e′′](m), MTT.
Fair Lisa, *Welsh Traditional,* [f′-f′′](m), MTT; [e′b-e′′b], MTT.
For this early morn, *Eos Iâl* tr. *Illtyd Lewis,* [d′-e′′], MTT.
Going with Tom to Towyn, *Welsh Traditional,* [d′-e′′], MTT.
Gwenllian's Repose, *Welsh Traditional,* [d′-f′′#](f), MTT; [c′-e′′], MTT.
Hob y deri dando, *Welsh Traditional,* [d′-e′′](m), MTT.
Holly and the ivy, The, *English Traditional,* [d′-e′′], MTT.
Lament for the Lark, *Welsh Traditional,* [f′#-d′′], MTT.
Llanberis Pass, *Welsh Traditional,* [e′-e′′], MTT; [d′-d′′], MTT.
Lullaby, *Welsh Traditional,* [c′-f′′], MTT 3 Folksongs.
Maid from Penderyn Parish, The, *Welsh Traditional,* [f′-f′′](m), MTT; [d′-d′′], MTT.
Maid of Sker, The, *Welsh Traditional,* [d′-g′′], MTT; [b-e′′], MTT.
Megan's Daughter, *Welsh Traditional,* [c′-g′′](m), MTT; [bb-f′′], MTT.
Migildi Magildi, *Welsh Traditional,* [g′#-f′′#], MTT; [f′#-e′′], MTT.
Miller's Song, The, *Welsh Traditional,* [d′b-e′′b](m), MTT; [c′-d′′], MTT.
On the Seashore, *Welsh Traditional,* [f′#-f′′#], MTT; [e′-e′′], MTT.
Round the Horn, *Welsh Traditional,* [e′-e′′](m), MTT; [e′b-e′′b], MTT.
Sans Day Carol, The, *Cornish Carol,* [d′-e′′b], MTT.
See my mother coming, *Welsh Traditional,* [e′-e′′], MTT; [d′-d′′], MTT.
Shepherd of the Hafod, The, *Welsh Traditional,* [d′-f′′#](m), MTT; [c′-e′′], MTT.
Song of Good Cheer, A, *Welsh Traditional,* [d′-f′′], MTT; [c′-e′′b], MTT.
Swiftly, swiftly, *Latvian Traditional,* [e′-e′′], MTT.
Village Country School, The, *Welsh Traditional,* [d′-e′′b], MTT 3 Folksongs.
Walking in the salt sea weather, *Welsh Traditional,* [f′-f′′], MTT; [e′b-e′′b], MTT.
War-Song of Glamorgan, *Welsh Traditional,* [c′-f′′], MTT 3 Folksongs.
When I was roaming, *Welsh Traditional,* [e′b-f′′], MTT; [d′b-e′′b], MTT.

Thomas, Muriel. 1898– ?. WMIC.
Buds in Spring, *Rupert Brooke,* Db [d′b-a′′b], B&H.
Faithless as the winds, *Charles Sedley,* [mezzo], Snell.

Let my voice ring out over the earth, *James Thomson*, F [c′#-a′′], Snell.
Music when soft voices die, *Percy Bysshe Shelley*, [soprano/tenor], Snell.
My true love hath my heart, *Philip Sidney*, E [c′#-g′′#](f), B&H.
She walks in beauty, *Percy Bysshe Shelley*, [mezzo/contralto/baritone], Snell.
World of Song, A, [high], Snell; [low], Snell.

Thomas, Ray.
Calling me Home, [contralto/mezzo], Snell.

Thomas, Vincent. 1873–1940.
Collection: *Dream Island,* B&H.
April Days, *Chester Dod*, Fm [e′-f′′], Gwynn *Three Spring Songs*.
Hushed Lagoon, The, *Norman Ingram*, Dm [e′-f′′], B&H *Dream Island*.
In Absence, *Norman Ingram*, E [e′-e′′], B&H *Dream Island*.
Night in the Garden, *Norman Ingram*, Eb [d′-f′′], B&H *Dream Island*.
Return, *Norman Ingram*, Eb [bb-g′′], B&H *Dream Island*; F, B&H.
Reverie, *Norman Ingram*, F [d′-f′′], B&H *Dream Island*.
Song of Dinèdan, *Ernest Rhys*, Gm [d′-g′′], B&H.

Thompson, Lawrie.
There is a land, Curiad.

Thompson, Peter. *See also* App. 2.
Collections: *Three Poems by Helen Clarke*, [bb-d′′], Fand; *Two Robert Southey Poems*, [c′-g′′#], Fand.
Carol, *Elizabeth W. Thompson*, [c′-a′′], Fand.
Echoes, *Walter de la Mare*, [d′-f′′#], Fand.
Green of the Semiquaver, The, *Pat Howell*, [c′-g′′b], Fand.
When I was one-and-twenty, *A. E. Housman*, [c′#-f′′], Fand.

Thwaites, Penelope. 1944– BMIC.
All the days of Christmas, *Phyllis McGinley*, [a-f′′], Bardic.
Forestry, *Michael Thwaites*, [b-f′′], Bardic.
Look at the children, *Penelope Thwaites*, [d′-d′′], Bardic.
Reverie, *Carolyn James*, [c′-d′′], Bardic.

Tippett, Sir **Michael** Kemp. 1905–98. *See also* App. 2.
Collections: *Heart's Assurance, The,* Schott; *Songs for Ariel,* Schott.
Boyhood's End (cantata), *W. H. Hudson*, [c′-b′′b](m), Schott.
Come unto these yellow sands, *Shakespeare*, [d′-e′′b], Schott *Songs for Ariel*.
Compassion, *Alun Lewis*, [c′-b′′(a′′)], Schott *Heart's Assurance*.
Dancer, The, *Alun Lewis*, [d′-a′′], Schott *Heart's Assurance*.
Full fathom five, *Shakespeare*, [c′-d′′], Schott *Songs for Ariel*.
Heart's Assurance, The, *Sidney Keyes*, [c′-a′′b], Schott *Heart's Assurance*.
Remember Your Lovers, *Sidney Keyes*, [d′b-a′′b], Schott *Heart's Assurance*.
Song, *Alun Lewis*, [d′-a′′], Schott *Heart's Assurance*.
Where the bee sucks, *Shakespeare*, [d′-e′′b], Schott *Songs for Ariel*.

Tomlinson, Ernest. 1924– *See also* App. 1
Collection: *Four Shakespeare Songs,* Electrophonic.
Come out, the Spring is roaming, *Ammon Wrigley*, [tenor/soprano], Electrophonic.
Fain would I change that note, *Anon*, [tenor/soprano], Electrophonic.
Fair and true, *Nicholas Breton*, [baritone], Electrophonic.
Follow your saint, *Thomas Campion*, [tenor], Electrophonic.
I know a bank, *Shakespeare*, [soprano/tenor], Electrophonic 4 Shakespeare.
In a May morning early, *Edwin Waugh*, [soprano], Electrophonic.
It was a lover and his lass, *Shakespeare*, [soprano/tenor], Electrophonic 4 Shakespeare.
Lover's Maze, A, *Thomas Campion*? [baritone], Electrophonic.
Love's Philosophy, *Percy Bysshe Shelley*, [tenor/soprano], Electrophonic.
My true love hath my heart, *Philip Sidney*, [soprano], Electrophonic.
O mistress mine, *Shakespeare*, [tenor], Electrophonic 4 Shakespeare.
Orpheus and Euridice, *Samuel Lisle*, [baritone], Electrophonic.
Orpheus with his lute, *Shakespeare*? [soprano/tenor], Electrophonic.
Rivals, The, *James Stephens*, [soprano/tenor], Electrophonic.
Spotted Cow, The, *Anon*, [baritone], Electrophonic.

There be none of beauty's daughters, *Lord Byron*, [tenor], Electrophonic.
There is a lady sweet and kind, *Anon*, [baritone], Electrophonic.
Under the greenwood tree, *Shakespeare*, [soprano/tenor], Electrophonic 4 Shakespeare.

Tommis, Colin. WMIC.

Torphichen, Pamela.
Awakening, The, *Joseph Stansbury*, [e'-e''], Bardic.
Cuckoo by Moonlight, *Sugette Compton*, [d'-g''], Bardic.
Isle, The, *Percy Bysshe Shelley*, [e'b-a''b], Bardic.
Not yet, *Anon*, [d'-f''], Bardic.
Scorpio, *Alfred Marnau*, [b-f'#], Bardic.
Song of Freedom, *Irina Ratushinskaya*, [c'-e''], Bardic.
To Electra, *Robert Herrick*, [e'-a''], Bardic.

Towers, George.
Collection: *Three Songs from Oscar Wilde*, [tenor], Brunton.
Come, sleep, [high], Brunton.

Toye, Francis John. 1883–1964.
(Hans Anderson Song, A, *Frances Cornford*, [d'-g''], Curwen.)
(In Dorset, *Frances Cornford*, [b-e''], Curwen.)
(Inn, The, *Hilaire Belloc*, [c'-e''], Curwen.)
To Daffodils, *Robert Herrick*, Db [c'-e''b], B&H.
(To Musique, to becalm his fever, *Robert Herrick*, [d'-g''(b'')], Curwen.)
(Weathercock on the Moor, The, *Geoffrey Scott*, [c'-g''], Curwen.)

Treharne, Bryceson. 1879–1948.
Collection: *Five Oriental Songs*, B&H.
At the Street Corner, *Monica Savory*, Cm [c'-e''(e''b)], B&H 5 Oriental.
Coy Maiden, The, *Monica Savory*, Eb [e'b-a''b], B&H; C, B&H.
In Sacred Banares, *Monica Savory*, Em [c'-e''], B&H 5 Oriental.
Lady Mine, *Thomas Westwood*, F [b-d''], B&H.
Merchant's Song, A, *Monica Savory*, Am [b-e''], B&H 5 Oriental.
Mixon Bell, The, *B. Parry*, [baritone], Snell.
Mountain Voices, *George Arthur Green*, Bm [e'#-g''], B&H.
Night Rider, The, *Monica Savory*, Bbm [bb-f''], B&H 5 Oriental.
Olwen, [soprano/tenor], Snell.
Shadows, *Sebastian Evans*, Em [b(c'#)-e''], B&H.
Snakecharmer's Song, The, *Monica Savory*, Bb [d'-e''], B&H 5 Oriental.
Thorn, The, *Welsh* tr. *H. Idris Bell*, [g(c')-e''b](m), Gwynn.
Wind, The, *R. Williams Parry* tr. *H. Idris Bell*, [f'-g''(a''b], Gwynn.

Trew, Arthur.
Arrangement:
Brother James's Air, *Psalm 23, Scottish Psalter*, D [c'#-d''], OUP.

Trimble, Joan. 1915–2000.
Green Rain, *Mary Webb*, Db [c'#-f''], B&H.
My grief on the sea, *Douglas Hyde*, Em [b-e''], B&H.

Tucapský, Antonín. 1928– BMIC.

Turnbull, Percy. 1902–1976.
Collections: *Songs, Volumes 1, 2*, Thames (prefaces by Jeremy Dibble and Robin Bowman).
Boy's Song, A, *James Hogg*, F [c'-f''](m), Thames Songs 1.
Cavalier, *John Masefield*, Em [b-e''], Thames Songs 1.
Chloris in the snow, *William Strode*, E [b-e''], Thames Songs 1.
Ejaculation to God, *Robert Herrick*, Cm [d'-e''b], Thames Songs 1.
Guess, guess, *Thomas Moore*, Am [e'-g''](m), Thames Songs 2.
If doughty deeds, *Graham of Gartmore*, E [c'#-f'#](m), Thames Songs 2.
In Fountain Court, *Arthur Symons*, Dm [a-f''], Thames Songs 1.
Moon, The, (1st setting), *R. L. Stevenson*, A [e'-e''], Thames Songs 2.
Moon, The, (2nd setting), *R. L. Stevenson*, A [e'-e''], Thames Songs 2.

My bed is a boat, *R. L. Stevenson*, F [c′-f″], Thames Songs 1.
My Mopsa is little, *Philodemus* tr. *Thomas Moore*, Em [e′-g″](m), Thames Songs 2.
Piping down the valleys wild, *William Blake*, C#m [c′#-e″], Thames Songs 1.
Rainy Day, The, *Longfellow*, Am [g′-a″], Thames Songs 2.
Reminder, The, (1st setting), *Thomas Hardy*, C [g-e″], Thames Songs 1.
Reminder, The, (2nd setting), *Thomas Hardy*, [b♭-f″], Thames Songs 1.
To Blossoms, *Robert Herrick*, F [e′b-f″], Thames Songs 2.
To God, *Robert Herrick*, C#m [g#-e″], Thames Songs 1.
To Julia, *Robert Herrick*, F [e′-a″(f)](m),Thames Songs 2.
When daffodils begin to peer, *Shakespeare*, F#m [c′#-f′#](m), Thames Songs 2.

Turner, John.
Collection: *Christmas Garland, A,* Forsyth.
Balulalow, *Luther* tr. *Wedderburn,* [d′-g″], Forsyth Garland.
Birds, The, *Hilaire Belloc*, [e′-g″], Forsyth Garland.
Cradle, The, *Austrian* tr. *Robert Graves,* [g′-e″], Forsyth Garland.
I sing of a maiden, *Anon, 15th century,* [d′-f″], Forsyth Garland.
Noel, *Hilaire Belloc,* [c′-g″], Forsyth Garland.
World's Desire, The, *G. K. Chesterton,* [e′-g″], Forsyth Garland.

U

Usher, Julia. *See also* App. 2.
Blue Epiphany, *Mary Hadingham,* [soprano], Primavera.
Hand in hand, *Jenni Meredith,* [voice], Primavera.
Price of Experience, The, *William Blake,* [soprano], Primavera.
Ruin, The, *Old English* tr. *M. Alexander,* [baritone], Primavera.

V

Vale, Charles. 1912–1984.
Litany to the Holy Spirit, *Robert Herrick,* Fm [a♭-f″], Banks.

Vaughan Williams, Ralph. 1872–1958. *See also* App. 1, 2.
Collections: *Collected Songs Volumes 1, 2, 3,* OUP; *Five Mystical Songs,* S&B; *Four Last Songs,* BMP; *(House of Life, The,* Ashdown); *Merciless Beauty,* Faber; *On Wenlock Edge,* B&H; *Songs of Travel* [high, low], B&H; *Song Album Volumes 1, 2,* B&H; *Three Poems by Walt Whitman,* BMP; *Two Poems by Seumas O'Sullivan,* BMP.
Antiphon, *George Herbert*, D [e′b-f″(g″)], S&B 5 Mystical.
Bird's Song, The, *Psalm 23*, E♭ [d′b-f″], Collected 3, OUP.
Blackmwore by the Stour, *William Barnes*, E [b-d″], B&H Album 1; G, B&H.
Boy Johnny, *Christina Rossetti,* Em [b-e″], B&H Album 1; F#m, B&H.
Bredon Hill, *A. E. Housman,* [e′b-a″](m), B&H Wenlock Edge.
Bright is the ring of words, *R. L. Stevenson*, C [a♭-d″b](m), B&H Travel; F, B&H Travel; D, B&H Album 2, Schirmer *1st Baritone II.*
Buonaparty, *Thomas Hardy*, Dm [d′-e″](m), B&H Album 2, Thames *Hardy Songbook.*
Call, The, *George Herbert*, E♭ [e′b-f″], S&B 5 Mystical, Schirmer *2nd Tenor.*
Claribel, *Alfred Lord Tennyson,* Fm [c′-f″], B&H Album 1.
Clear midnight, A, *Walt Whitman,* G [e′-f″], OUP Collected 1, BMP 3 Poems.
Clun, *A. E. Housman,* [d′-g″](m), B&H Wenlock Edge.
Cradle song, *S. T. Coleridge,* E♭ [c′-e″b], B&H Album 2, *Easy Song.*
(Death in Love, *D. G. Rossetti,* C [c′-e″], Ashdown House of Life.)
Dream-land, *Christina Rossetti*, D♭ [d′b-f″], B&H Album 1, Schirmer *2nd Tenor.*
Easter, *George Herbert*, E♭ [e′b-f″](m), S&B 5 Mystical.
Four Nights, *Fredegond Shove,* [a♭-e″b], OUP Collected 2.
From far, from eve and morning, *A. E. Housman,* E [g′-e″](m), B&H Wenlock Edge.
Hands, eyes, and heart, *Ursula Vaughan Williams,* E♭ [c′-e″b](f), OUP Collected 1, BMP 4 Last.
(Heart's Haven, *D. G. Rossetti,* E [c′#-e″](m), Ashdown House of Life; D, F, Ashdown.)
How can the tree but wither? *Lord Vaux,* Cm [a-e″b], OUP Collected 2, BMP.

Hugh's Song of the Road, *Harold Child*, Fm [e′b-a′′](m), Faber, (Curwen).
I got me flowers, *George Herbert*, Gb [d′b-e′′b], S&B 5 Mystical.
I have trod the upward and the downward slope, *R. L. Stevenson*, Dm [c′-d′′](m), B&H Travel; *Gm* B&H Travel.
If I were a queen, *Christina Rossetti*, E [b-e′′], B&H Album 2; G, B&H.
In dreams, *R. L. Stevenson*, Cm [d′b-f′′](m), B&H Travel; *Ebm*, B&H Travel.
In the Spring, *William Barnes*, D [c′#-e′′](m), OUP Collected 2.
Infinite shining heavens, The, *R. L. Stevenson*, Dm [c′-e′′](m), B&H Travel; *Fm*, B&H Travel.
Is my team ploughing? *A. E. Housman*, Dm [d′-a′′](m), B&H Wenlock Edge.
Joy, shipmate, joy, *Walt Whitman*, G [e′-f′′], OUP Collected 1, BMP 3 Poems.
Let beauty awake, *R. L. Stevenson*, [e′-e′′](m), B&H Travel; *[g′-g′′]*, B&H Travel.
(Let us now praise famous men, *Ecclesiasticus*, E [e′-g′′#], Curwen.)
Linden Lea, *William Barnes*, G [d′-e′′], B&H Album 1, Classical, Schirmer *1st Tenor II*; F, A, Classical/B&H.
Love bade me welcome, *George Herbert*, Em [d′-f′′], S&B 5 Mystical.
(Love's last gift, *D. G. Rossetti*, F [c′-f′′], Ashdown House of Life.)
(Love's Minstrels, *D. G. Rossetti*, D [a-e′′](m), Ashdown House of Life.)
(Love-sight, *D. G. Rossetti*, A [b-e′′], Ashdown House of Life.)
Menelaus, *Ursula Vaughan Williams*, Cm [c′-e′′], OUP Collected 1.
Motion and Stillness, *Fredegond Shove*, [c′-d′′], OUP Collected 2, BMP 4 Last.
New Ghost, The, *Fredegond Shove*, [d′-f′′], OUP Collected 2, Thames *Century 1*, BMP.
Nocturne, *Walt Whitman*, [b-f′′], OUP Collected 1, BMP 3 Poems.
Oh, when I was in love with you, *A. E. Housman*, [g′-f′′#](m), B&H Wenlock Edge.
On Wenlock Edge, *A. E. Housman*, Gm [d′-g′′](m), B&H Wenlock Edge.
Orpheus with his lute (1st setting), *Shakespeare*, G [d′-g′′], Thames *Century 5*, Classical/(Keith Prowse), Schirmer *2nd Tenor*; F, Classical/(Keith Prowse.)
Orpheus with his lute (2nd setting), *Shakespeare*, G [d′-f′′#], OUP Collected 1.
Oxen, The, *Thomas Hardy*, F#m [e′-f′′#], OUP *Solo Christmas high*, Dm, *Solo Christmas low*.
Pilgrim's Psalm, The, *St Paul & Psalms*, [d′-f′′], OUP Collected 3.
Piper, A, *Seumas O'Sullivan*, [c′-e′′], BMP.
Procris, *Ursula Vaughan Williams*, Em [c′-e′′], OUP Collected 1, BMP 4 Last.
Roadside Fire, The, *R. L. Stevenson*, Db [b-e′′](m), B&H Travel, Album 2; *F*, B&H Travel; *C*, Heritage 1, Schirmer *1st Baritone II*.
See the chariot at hand, *Ben Jonson*, C [c′-f′′#](m), OUP Collected 2.
Silent Noon, *D. G. Rossetti*, Eb [c′-e′′b], Schirmer *1st Mezzo*, Classical, *(*Ashdown House of Life); *Db, F, G*, Classical.
Since I from Love escapëd am so fat, *Geoffrey Chaucer*, [a′-a′′](m), Faber Merciless.
Sky above the roof, The, *Paul Verlaine*, tr. *Mabel Dearmer*, Am [c′-e′′], B&H Album 1, B&H, Thames *Countertenors 3*, Schirmer *1st Mezzo*.
So hath your beauty from your hertë, *Geoffrey Chaucer*, Dm [e′-f′′](m), Faber Merciless.
Song of the Leaves of Life and the Water of Life, The, *Revelations*, [d′-e′′], Collected 3.
Song of the Pilgrims, The, *John Bunyan*, D [d′-e′′], OUP Collected 3.
Song of Vanity Fair, The, *Ursula Vaughan Williams*, Eb [c′-f′′b], OUP Collected 3.
Splendour falls, The, *Alfred Lord Tennyson*, C [e′-f′′], B&H Album 1, B&H; Ab, Bb, B&H.
Take, O take, *Shakespeare*, Em [b-d′′], OUP Collected 1.
Tears, idle tears, *Alfred Lord Tennyson*, Cm [b-f′′], B&H Album 2.
Tired, *Ursula Vaughan Williams*, Db [bb-d′′b], OUP Collected 1, BMP 4 Last.
Twilight People, The, *Seumas O'Sullivan*, [bb-e′′b], OUP Collected 2; [c′-f′′], BMP 2 Poems.
Vagabond, The, *R. L. Stevenson*, Cm [a-e′′b](m), B&H Travel, Album 1, *Heritage 2*, B&H, Schirmer *2nd Baritone*; *Em*, B&H Travel, B&H.
Water Mill, The, *Fredegond Shove*, C [c′-d′′], OUP Collected 2, *Solo Contralto*; Eb, OUP.
Watchful's Song, *Psalms & Isaiah*, [c′#-e′′], OUP Collected 3.
(When I am dead, my dearest, *Christina Rossetti*, Gm [g′-g′′], Keith Prowse; Dm, Keith Prowse.)
When icicles hang by the wall, *Shakespeare*, Fm [e′b-f′′], OUP Collected 1.
Whither Must I Wander? *R. L. Stevenson*, Cm [bb-e′′b](m), B&H Travel, *Heritage 2*, B&H; *Em*, B&H Travel, Schirmer *2nd Tenor*; Dm, B&H.
Winter's willow, The, *William Barnes*, Ab [e′b-g′′](m), B&H Album 1; F, B&H.
Wither's rocking hymn, *George Wither*, Gm [f′-g′′], OUP *Solo Christmas high*, Em, *Solo Christmas low*.
Woodcutter's Song, The, *John Bunyan*, G [d′-e′′], OUP Collected 3, BMP.
Your eyën two will slay me suddenly, *Geoffrey Chaucer*, Gm [c′-a′′](m), Faber Merciless.
Youth and Love, *R. L. Stevenson*, G [c′-e′′](m), B&H Travel, *Heritage 2*; Bb, B&H Travel.
  Arrangements: *Six English Folksongs*, BMP.
    Brewer, The, BMP 6 English.

Greensleeves, *Anon*, Fm [c′-e′′b](m), OUP Collected 1, *Am,* OUP.
King William, BMP 6 English.
Love's Bower, *Anon (French 15th cent.),* tr. *Paul England,* C [c′-d′′], B&H Album 1
One man, two men, BMP 6 English.
Ploughman, The, BMP 6 English.
Réveillez-vous Piccarz, *Anon (French 15th cent.),* tr. *Paul England,* Em [d′-e′′](m), B&H Album 2.
Robin Hood and the Pedlar, BMP 6 English.
Rolling in the dew, BMP 6 English.
She's like the swallow, *Anon*, Dm [d′-f″′](m), OUP *Solo Tenor*.
Spanish Ladies, The, *Traditional,* A [e′-e′′](m), B&H Album 1.

Venables, Ian. *See also* App. 2.
At Malvern, *John Addington Symons,* [db-f″](m), Enigma.
At Midnight, *Edna St Vincent Millay,* [c′-a′′b], Enigma; [Bb-g′b](m), Enigma.
At the court of the poisoned rose, *Marion Angus,* [bb-f″], Mezzo or C-tenor, Enigma.
Easter Song, *Edgar Billingham,* [e′b-b′′b](m), Enigma; [B-f″#], Enigma.
Flying Crooked, *Robert Graves,* [e′b-b′′b(f″)], Enigma.
Fortunate Isles, *John Addington Symons,* [c#-f″](m), Enigma.
Invitation to the Gondola, The, *John Addington Symons,* [d-g′](m), Enigma; [c-f″](m), Enigma.
It rains, *Edward Thomas,* [bb-b′′b](f), Enigma.
Kiss, A, *Thomas Hardy,* [c′-g′′], Enigma.
Love's Voice, *John Addington Symons,* [d-g′](m), Enigma.
Midnight Lamentation, *Harold Monro,* [b-a′′], Enigma; [A-g′](m), Enigma.
Pain, *Ivor Gurney,* [d-a′](m), Enigma.
Passing Stranger, The, *John Addington Symons,* [d-a′](m), Enigma.
Way through, The, *Jennifer Andrews,* [d′-g′′](f), Enigma.

Vignoles, Roger Hutton. 1945–
Arrangements: *The Mermaid and Two Other Water Songs,* Thames.
Flow gently, sweet Afton, *Robert Burns,* Ab [e′b-f″], Thames Mermaid.
Lowlands, *Traditional,* Bb [bb-d′′], Thames Mermaid.
Mermaid, The, *Anon,* G [e′b-e′′(g′′)], Thames Mermaid.

Walker, Ernest. 1870–1949.
Corinna's going a-maying, *Robert Herrick,* Eb [a-e′′b](m), B&H *Heritage 2*; F, B&H.
Sleep song, *Sydney Dobell,* Dm [d′-g′′], BMP.
Summer Rain, *Sydney Dobell,* D [c′-f″′#], BMP.

Walker, Robert Matthew. 1946– *See* App. 2.

Wallace, William Vincent. 1812–1865.
Cradle Song, *Alfred Lord Tennyson,* A [a-c′′#](f), S&B (Bush & Temperley) *MB 43*.

Wallbank, Newell.
Great Time, A, *W. H. Davies,* Bb [d′-g′′], Lengnick.
I gave her cakes and I gave her ale, *Anon,* A [e′-a′′], Lengnick.
It was a lover and his lass, *Shakespeare,* G [d′-g′′], Lengnick.
Rhyme in the Tropics, *Dorothy Una Radcliffe,* Eb [f″-f″′#], Lengnick.

Walsworth, Ivor.
Here where the world is quiet, *Algernon Charles Swinburne,* Bm [b-d′′], BMP.
Sleep on, my love, BMP.

Walters, Gareth. WMIC.

Walters, Leslie. 1902– BMIC, WMIC.
Daffa-down-dilly, *W. Graham Robertson,* D [d′-d′′], Gwynn *Three Spring Songs*.
Love Song, A, *Philip Sidney,* Eb [bb-e′′b], Roberton; G, Roberton.
Plesant Grounde, *Anon,* Eb [c′-g′′], Brunton.
Providence, [high], Brunton; [low], Brunton.

(Singer and the Song, The, *A. J. Redpath*, D [d′-f′′#], Chappell.)
Spring, the travelling man, *Winifred Letts*, F [e′-a′′(g′′)], Cramer.
When I set out for Lyonesse, *Thomas Hardy*, Em [b(d′)-e′′(g′′)](m), Brunton.

Walters, W. Edmund. WMIC.

Walthew, Richard Henry. 1872–1951. *See also* B&H.
Collection: (*Album of Twelve Songs*, B&H).
    Mistress Mine, *Shakespeare*, B♭ [c′-f′′](m), B&H *Heritage 1, 12 Songs,* Schirmer *1st Tenor.*
    Splendour falls, The, *Alfred Lord Tennyson*, E♭ [b♭-e′′♭], B&H *Heritage 2,* Schirmer *1st Baritone.*
    Eldorado, *Edgar Allan Poe*, C [e′-c′′], B&H, Schirmer *1st Baritone II.*

Walton, Sir **William** Turner. 1902–1983. *See also* App. 2.
Collection: *Four Early Songs,* OUP (introduction Alan Cuckston); *Song Album, A,* OUP (introduction, and arrangement of *Anon. in love,* Christopher Palmer); *Song for the Lord Mayor's Table, A,* BMP; *Three Songs,* BMP; *Two Early Songs,* BMP.
    Beatriz's Song, *Louis MacNeice*, Dm [f′-d′′](f), OUP Album.
    Child's Song, *Algernon Charles Swinburne*, Cm [f′-f′′#], OUP 4 Early.
    Contrast, The, *Charles Morris*, C [b♭-g′′](f), OUP Album, BMP Lord Mayor.
    Daphne, *Edith Sitwell*, [c′-a′′](f), OUP Album, BMP 3 Songs.
    Fain would I change that note, *Anon*, [c′#-a′′](m), OUP Album, (Anon. in Love).
    Glide gently, *William Wordsworth*, [a-g′′](f), OUP Album, BMP Lord Mayor.
    Holy Thursday, *William Blake*, [b-g′′](f), OUP Album, BMP Lord Mayor.
    I gave her cakes and I gave her ale, *Anon*, [d′-b′′♭](m), OUP Album, (Anon. in Love).
    Lady, when I behold the roses, *Anon*, [c′-a′′](m), OUP Album, (Anon. in Love).
    Lord Mayor's Table, The, *Thomas Jordan*, A♭ [b♭-a′′♭](f), OUP Album, BMP Lord Mayor.
    Lyke-wake Song, A, *Algernon Charles Swinburne*, Fm [e′♭-f′′], OUP 4 Early.
    My love in her attire, *Anon*, [c′-a′′](m), OUP Album, (Anon. in Love).
    O stay, sweet love, *Anon*, [c′-g′′♭](m), OUP Album, (Anon. in Love).
    Old Sir Faulk, *Edith Sitwell*, [c′#-g′′], OUP Album, BMP 3 Songs.
    Rhyme, *Anon*, [c′-g′′](f), OUP Album, (BMP Lord Mayor).
    Song, *Algernon Charles Swinburne*, [g′♭-g′′], OUP 4 Early.
    Through gilded trellises, *Edith Sitwell*, [c′#-a′′](f), OUP Album, BMP 3 Songs.
    To couple is a custom, *Anon*, [c′-a′′](m), OUP Album, (Anon. in Love).
    Tritons, *William Drummond*, [e′-a′′], OUP Album, BMP 2 Early.
    Under the greenwood tree, *Shakespeare*, Gm [d′-g′′], OUP Album, BMP.
    Wapping Old Stairs, *Anon*, Gm [c′-f′′#](f), OUP Album, (BMP Lord Mayor).
    Winds, The, *A C Swinburne*, Em [e′♭-a′′](f), OUP Album, 4 Early, BMP 2 Early.

Ward, Darman.
    Dear old songs of Wales, The, G [any voice], Snell.

Ward, David. SMIC.
Collections: *Three Poems by J. M. Synge,* [mezzo], SMIC; *Three Sonnets to Orpheus,* [mezzo], SMIC.

Ward-Higgs, W.
    Sussex by the Sea, *W. Ward-Higgs*, C [c′-e′′](m), IMP *Parlour Songs*.

Warlock, Peter (Philip Arnold Heseltine). 1894–1930. *See also* App. 1, 2.
Collections: *Book of Songs, A,* OUP; *Candlelight,* S&B; (*Eight Songs,* Thames); *Lilligay,* Chester/ Masters; *Peterisms, 1st Set,* Chester; *Peterisms Set 2,* Masters/BMP; *Saudades,* Chester/Masters; *Second Book of Songs, A,* OUP; *Song Album,* B&H; *Songs Volumes 1-8,* (introductions by Fred Tomlinson) Thames; *Songs Volumes 1-4,* Masters; *Thirteen Songs for High Voice,* S&B.
    Adam lay ybounden, *Anon*, Cm [c′-f′′], Thames Songs 3.
    After Two Years, *Richard Aldington*, D♭ [d′♭-f′′](m), Thames Songs 8, Masters Songs 4, BMP.
    Along the Stream, *Li Po,* tr. *L. Cranmer Byng*, [e′-f′′#], Thames Songs 1, Masters/Chester Saudades.
    And wilt thou leave me thus? *Thomas Wyatt*, B♭m [c′#-f′′], OUP Book of Songs, Thames Songs 8, Masters Songs 3.
    Arthur O'Bower, *Anon*, G♭ [b′♭♭-g′′♭], Thames Songs 5; A♭, S&B Candlelight.
    As ever I saw, *Anon*, D♭ [d′♭-g′′♭](m), B&H Songs, Thames Songs 2; E♭, Mayhew *Collection 1.*
    Autumn Twilight, *Arthur Symons*, Cm [c′-e′′♭], Thames Songs 4, Masters Songs 4, BMP.
    Away to Twiver, *Anon*, Bm [d′-f′′#], OUP 2nd Book, Thames Songs 6, Masters Songs 3.
    Bachelor, The, *Anon*, F#m [c′#-f′′#](m), S&B 13 Songs, Masters Songs 2; *Em,* Thames Songs 3.

Balulalow, *Martin Luther*, tr. *Wedderburn*, E♭ [e′♭-f″], Thames Songs 2, OUP *Solo Christmas high*; C, *Solo Christmas low*.
Bayly berith the bell away, The, *Anon*, E♭ [g-e″♭], B&H Songs, *Heritage 3*; F, Thames Songs 2; G, B&H.
Bethlehem Down, *Bruce Blunt*, Dm [c′#-e″♭], Thames Songs 8, B&H.
Birds, The, *Hilaire Belloc*, E♭ [d′-e″♭], Thames Songs 6, Mayhew *Collection 1*, S&B 13 Songs.
Bright is the ring of words, *R. L. Stevenson*, A; G♭ [b♭-f″], Thames Songs 2.
Burd Ellen and Young Tamlane, *Anon*, Am [e′-g″#], Masters/Chester Lilligay; Gm, Thames Songs 4.
Captain Stratton's Fancy, *John Masefield*, F [c′-f″](m), S&B 13 Songs, S&B, Thames Songs 3, Mayhew *Singer's Collection 2*; D, Masters Songs 4, S&B; G, S&B.
Carillon, Carilla, *Hilaire Belloc*, G [c′-e″], Thames Songs 8.
Chanson du jour de noël, *Clément Marot*, tr. *David Cox*, A [e′-f″#], Thames Songs 6; (C, B&H).
Chopcherry, *George Peele*, A [e′-e″](m) Chester Peterisms 1, *Celebrated 2*, Thames Songs 4.
Cloths of Heaven, The, *W. B. Yeats*, [c′-g″], Thames Songs 1.
Consider, *Ford Madox Ford*, F [c′-g″], Masters Songs 4, BMP; E♭, Thames Songs 5.
Contented Lover, The, (Celestina) *James Mabbe*, A♭ [e′♭-a″♭], S&B 13 Songs, *Recitalist 3*, Masters Songs 2; F, Thames Songs 8.
Countryman, The, *John Chalkhill*, A♭ [e′♭-a″♭], B&H; F, B&H Songs, Thames Songs 6.
Cradle Song, *John Philip*, [d′-f″](f), OUP Book of Songs, Thames Songs 7.
Cricketers of Hambledon, The, *Bruce Blunt*, E♭ [b♭-f″](m), S&B 13 Songs, Thames Songs 8, Masters Songs 4.
Dedication, *Philip Sidney*, D♭ [d′♭-a″♭](m), B&H; B♭, Thames Songs 2.
Distracted Maid, The, *Anon*, B♭m [d′♭-f″], Thames Songs 4, Masters/Chester Lilligay.
Droll Lover, The, *Anon* 17th cent., F [b-e″♭](m), S&B 13 Songs, Thames Songs 8, Masters Songs 2.
Eloré Lo, *Anon*, F [c′-f″](m), S&B 13 Songs, *Recitalist 4*, Thames Songs 8, Masters Songs 2.
Everlasting Voices, The, *W. B. Yeats*, B♭m [e′♭-a″♭(g″♭)], Thames Songs 1.
Fair and True, *Nicholas Breton*, E♭ [e′♭-e″♭], OUP Book of Songs, Thames Songs 6, Masters Songs 1.
Fairest May, The, *Anon*, C [c′-f″], Thames Songs 8.
Fill the cup, Philip, *Anon*, E♭ [b♭-e″♭](m), Thames Songs 8, (8 Songs).
First Mercy, The, *Bruce Blunt*, [f′-f″], B&H Songs, B&H, Thames Songs 7.
Five Lesser Joys of Mary, *D. L. Kelleher*, D♭ [d′♭-e″♭], Thames Songs 8.
Fox, The, *Bruce Blunt*, Dm [d′-f″#], Thames Songs 8, BMP.
Frostbound Wood, The, *Bruce Blunt*, [d′-e″], Thames Songs 8, Masters Songs 4, BMP.
Good Ale, *Anon*, A♭ [e′♭-a″♭](m), Masters Songs 3, S&B; F, Thames Songs 3.
Ha'nacker Mill, *Hilaire Belloc*, Dm [c′-f″], OUP 2nd Book, Thames Songs 7.
Heraclitus, *Callimachus*, tr. *W. J. Cory*, [c′-f″], Thames Songs 1, Masters/Chester Saudades.
Hey, troly loly lo, *Anon* 16th cent., [c′-f″], S&B 13 Songs, Thames Songs 3, Masters Songs 3.
How many miles to Babylon, *Anon*, Fm [f′-f″], Thames Songs 5, S&B Candlelight.
I asked a thief to steal me a peach, *William Blake*, E♭ [c′-f″](m), Thames Songs 1, (8 Songs).
I had a little pony, *Anon*, Cm [c′-e″], Thames Songs 5, S&B Candlelight.
I have a garden, *Thomas Moore*, Dm [d′-e″], Thames Songs 5, Masters Songs 4.
I held love's head, *Robert Herrick*, Fm [c′-f″], Thames Songs 5, B&H Songs.
I won't be my father's Jack, *Anon*, E♭ [d′-c″], Thames Songs 5, S&B Candlelight.
In an arbour green, *Robert Wever*, G [d′-g″](m), Masters Songs 2, (Paterson); F, Thames Songs 4.
Jennie Gray, *Anon*, Em [d′-e″], Thames Songs 5, (8 Songs).
Jillian of Berry, *Beaumont & Fletcher?* B♭ [d′-f″](m) OUP Book of Songs, Thames Songs 6, Masters Songs 1.
Johnnie wi' the Tye, *Anon*, [d′-g″](f), Masters/Chester Lilligay; [c′-f″], Thames Songs 4;.
Jolly Shepherd, The, *Anon*, G [c′-e″(g″)], Thames Songs 7; A, B&H Songs.
Lake and a fairy boat, A, *Thomas Hood*, [d′-g″♭], Thames Songs 1, (8 Songs).
Late Summer, *Edward Shanks*, E [b-f″#], S&B 13 Songs, Thames Songs 3, Masters Songs 4.
Little Jack Jingle, *Anon*, F [c′-f″], Thames Songs 5, S&B Candlelight.
Little Tommy Tucker, *Anon*, G [d′-e″], Thames Songs 5, S&B Candlelight.
Little trotty wagtail, *John Clare*, Dm [c′-f″], Thames Songs 3, Masters Songs 2.
Love for Love, *Anon*, G [d′-g″](m), B&H, Mayhew *Collection 2*; E, Thames Songs 2, Countertenors 3.
Lover Mourns for the Loss of Love, The, *W. B. Yeats*, [d′-e″♭](m), Thames Songs 1.
Lover's Maze, The, *Thomas Campion?* Fm [e′♭-f″], OUP Book of Songs, Thames Songs 7.
Lullaby, *Thomas Dekker*, Dm [a(b)-d″], B&H Songs, Thames Songs 2; Fm, B&H.
Lusty Juventus, *Robert Wever*, C [d′-a″(g″)](m), OUP 2nd Book, Masters/BMP Peterisms 2; A, Thames Songs 4.

Magpie, The, *Harry Hunter*, E [b-e''], Thames Songs 5.
Maltworms, *Bishop Still* or *William Stevenson*, F [c'-f''](m), OUP 2nd Book, Thames Songs 6.
Milkmaids, *James Smith?*, G [d'-g''], Masters Songs 2; *F*, Thames Songs 4; (*E*, Enoch).
Mr Belloc's Fancy, *John Squire*, G [d'-g''(a'')](m), S&B 13 Songs; *Eb*, Thames Songs 3.
Mockery, *Shakespeare*, [e'-g''], OUP 2nd Book; [*d'-f''*], Thames Songs 7.
Mourn no moe, *John Fletcher*, C [c'-f''], Thames Songs 2; (E*b*, B&H).
Music, when soft voices die, *Percy Bysshe Shelley*, A*b*; *F* [d'-f''], Thames Songs 1, (8 Songs).
My gostly fader, *Charles D'Orleans?* G [e'b-f''#], B&H Songs, Thames Songs 2; (*E*, B&H).
My little sweet darling, *Anon*, G [b-g''](f), B&H *Heritage 3*; *F*, Thames Songs 2; (*E*, B&H).
My Own Country, *Hilaire Belloc*, F [c'-e''], OUP 2nd Book, Thames Songs 7, BMP; A*b*, BMP.
Night, The, *Hilaire Belloc*, Em [d'-e''], OUP 2nd Book, Thames Songs 7.
O my kitten, *Anon*, C [c'-e''], Thames Songs 5; D, S&B Candlelight.
Passing By, *Anon*, G [d'-g''](m), OUP Book of Songs, Thames Songs 7, Masters Songs 1.
Passionate Shepherd, The, *Christopher Marlowe*, G [d'-g''](m), Masters Songs 1; *F,* Thames Songs 8.
Peter Warlock's Fancy, *Anon*, E*b* [b*b*-e''*b*](m), Thames Songs 5; (F, Chappell, Paterson).
Piggesnie, *Anon*, G [d'-g''](m), S&B 13 Songs, Masters Songs 3, Mayhew *Collection 2*; *F*, Thames Songs 3; *E*, S&B.
Play-acting, *Anon*, Dm; *Em* [b-g''](m), Thames Songs 3, (8 Songs).
Prayer to St Anthony of Padua, A, *Arthur Symons*, E*b* [e'*b*-e''*b*], OUP 2nd Book, Masters Songs 4; *Db*, Thames Songs 6.
Pretty Ring-time, *Shakespeare*, E*b* [d'-g''(f'')], OUP Book of Songs, Thames Songs 6.
Queen Anne, *Anon*, C [e'-e''](f), Thames Songs 7.
Rantum-tantum, *Victor Neuburg*, D*b* [d'*b*-f''#], Masters/Chester Lilligay; *C*, Thames Songs 4.
Rest, sweet nymphs, *Anon*, F [f'-f''], OUP Book of Songs, *Solo Tenor*, Thames Songs 3.
Robin and Richard, *Anon*, A [d'#-e''], Thames Songs 5, S&B Candlelight.
Robin Goodfellow, *Anon*, A [e'-f''#], OUP Book of Songs, Thames Songs 6, Masters Songs 1.
Roister Doister, *Nicholas Udall*, F [c'-f''](m), OUP 2nd Book, Masters/BMP Peterisms 2, Thames Songs 4, Mayhew *Collection 1*.
Romance, *R. L. Stevenson*, B*b* [b*b*-f''](m), Thames Songs 2, Masters Songs 3.
Rutterkin, *John Skelton?*, A*b* [e'*b*-a''], Chester Peterisms 1; *F*, Thames Songs 4.
Sad Song, A, *John Fletcher*, Bm [e'#-f''#], Chester Peterisms 1; *Am*, Thames Songs 4.
Shoemaker, The, *Anon*, B*b*m [f'-f''], Thames Songs 4, Masters/Chester Lilligay.
Sick Heart, The, *Arthur Symons*, [c'-g''], OUP 2nd Book, Masters Songs 4; [b*b*-f''], Thames Songs 6.
Sigh no more, ladies, *Shakespeare*, E*b* [e'*b*-f''], OUP Book of Songs, Thames Songs 7.
Singer, The, *Edward Shanks*, G [d'-g''], Masters Songs 4, S&B; *F*, Thames Songs 3.
Sleep, *John Fletcher*, Gm [d'-e''*b*], OUP Book of Songs, *Solo Baritone*, OUP, Thames Songs 3.
Song for Christmas Day, A *see* Chanson du jour de noël.
Spring the sweet spring, *Thomas Nashe*, A*b* [c'-g''*b*], OUP 2nd Book, Masters/BMP Peterisms 2; *G*, Thames Songs 4.
Suky, you shall be my wife, *Anon*, E*b* [e'*b*-f''], Thames Songs 5, S&B Candlelight.
Sweet Content, *Thomas Dekker*, G [d'-g''], B&H Songs, *Heritage 4*; *F*, Thames Songs 2.
Sweet o' the Year, The, *Shakespeare*, F [c'-f''](m), Thames Songs 8, Masters Songs 1.
Sweet-and-twenty, *Shakespeare*, A*b* [e'-f''](m), OUP 2nd Book; *G*, Thames Songs 5, BMP.
Take, O take those lips away (1st setting), *Shakespeare*, [c'-f''], Thames Songs 1, Masters/Chester Saudades.
Take, O take those lips away (2nd setting), *Shakespeare*, Em [b-f''#], Thames Songs 2, B&H; *F#m,* B&H Songs, *Heritage 4*.
There is a lady sweet and kind, *Anon*, B*b* [b*b*-f''](m), B&H Songs, Thames Songs 2; (*Db*, B&H).
There was a man of Thessaly, *Anon*, F#m [b-d''], Thames Songs 5, S&B Candlelight.
There was an old man, *Anon*, B*b*m [f'-f''], Thames Songs 5, S&B Candlelight.
There was an old woman, *Anon*, Fm [c'-f''], Thames Songs 5, S&B Candlelight.
Thou gav'st me leave to kiss, *Robert Herrick*, G [d'-f''], Thames Songs 5, B&H Songs.
To the memory of a great singer, *R. L. Stevenson*, A*b* [d'*b*-g''], S&B 13 Songs, Masters Songs 2; *Gb*, Thames Songs 1.
Tom Tyler, *Anon*, G [d'-f''#(g'')](m), S&B 13 Songs, Thames Songs 8, Masters Songs 2.
Toper's Song, The, *Anon*, Em [b-e''](m), Thames Songs 5.
Twelve Oxen, *Anon*, E [b-e''], OUP Book of Songs, Thames Songs 5, Masters Songs 1.
Tyrley tyrlow, *Anon 16th cent.*, Am [e'-f''], Thames Songs 3.
Walking the woods, *Anon*, F [c'-f''](m), B&H Songs, Thames Songs 7.
Water Lily, The, *Robert Nichols*, [e'-a'']; [d'-g''], Thames Songs 1, (8 Songs).
What cheer? good cheer, *Anon*, E*b* [b*b*-e''*b*], Thames Songs 7.
Whenas the rye reach to the chin, *George Peele*, G [c'-f''#](m), B&H Songs, *Heritage 4*; *F*, Thames Songs 2, B&H.

Where Riches is Everlastingly, *Anon*, Dm [c′-f′′], Thames Songs 7.
Wind from the West, The, *Ella Young*, E♭ [d′-f′′], Thames Songs 1, (8 Songs).
Yarmouth Fair, *Hal Collins*, G [d′-g′′](m), BMP; *F,* Thames Songs 5; *E, D,* OUP.
Youth, *Robert Wever*, F [c′-f′′](m), Thames Songs 8, Masters Songs 1.
Arrangement.
Have you seen but a white lily grow, *Ben Jonson,* F [e′-f′′], Masters Songs 3.
One More River, *Anon (The Weekend Book),* F [c′-d′′], Thames Songs 6.

Warren, Raymond Henry Charles. 1928–
Songs of old age (cycle), *W. B. Yeats,* [a′-g′′], Novello.

Watkins, David. *See* App. 2.

Watkins, Michael Blake. 1948– *See* App. 2.

Watson, Edward.
Twelve Days of Christmas, The, *John Julius Norwich,* [medium], Lengnick.

Watson, Ronald.
Collection: *Two Contrasting Songs*, Brunton [medium/high].

Watt, Howard. WMIC.

Webb, William. *c.*1620–1656.
As life what is so sweet, *Anon*, Cm [c′-e′′♭], S&B (Spink), *Recitalist 2*.
Of thee, kind boy, *John Suckling,* Dm [d′-f′′](m), Classical/B&H *Dolmetsch 1*.
Since 'tis my fate to be thy slave, *Anon*, G [e′-e′′](m), S&B (Spink) *Cavalier,* MB 33.

Weeks, Christopher Richard. *See* App. 2.

Weeks, John. *See* App. 2.

Wegener, Margaret. 1920– *See also* App. 2.
Collection: *Three Rossetti Settings,* Da Capo.
All sounds have been as music, *Wilfrid Owen,* [mezzo/baritone], Da Capo.
Echo, *Christina Rossetti,* [soprano], Da Capo Rossetti.
Faery Song, *Shakespeare,* [d′-f′′], EPSS.
Nod, *Walter de la Mare,* [high], Da Capo.
Remember, *Christina Rossetti,* [soprano], Da Capo Rossetti.
To Sleep, *John Keats,* [high], Da Capo.
When I am dead, my dearest, *Christina Rossetti,* [soprano], Da Capo Rossetti.

Weir, Judith. 1954– *See also* App. 1, 2.
Collections: *Scotch Minstrelsy*, Novello; *Songs from the Exotic,* Chester.
Bessie Bell and Mary Gray, *Anon,* [e′-g′′], Novello Scotch Minstrelsy.
Bonnie James Campbell, *Anon,* [b♯-a′′♭], Novello Scotch Minstrelsy.
Braes of Yarrow, The, *Anon,* [c′♯-e′′], Novello Scotch Minstrelsy.
Gypsy Laddie, The, *Anon,* [c′-g′′], Novello Scotch Minstrelsy.
In the lovely village of Nevesinje, *Anon,* [b-e′′], Chester Exotic.
Lady Isobel and the Elf-knight, *Anon,* [b-a′′♭], Novello Scotch Minstrelsy.
Romance of Count Arnaldos, The, *Anon,* [a-e′′], Chester Exotic.
Sevdalino, my little one, *Anon,* [c′♯-c′′], Chester Exotic.
Song of a Girl Ravished away by the Fairies in South Uist, The, *Anon,* [b-f′′♯], Chester Exotic.

Weldon, John. 1676–1736.
Alleluia (from 'O Lord rebuke me not' *Psalm 6),* Gm [f′-g′′], B&H (Britten) Two Divine Hymns and Alleluia (attributed to Purcell in error).
Amphitrite's Song *see* Halcyon days.
Arise, ye subterranean winds, *Thomas Shadwell,* C [E-d′](m), International (Kagen) 6 Songs for Bass, B&H (Northcote) *New Imperial 6,* Schirmer *2nd Baritone,* (attributed to Purcell in error).
Fair and serene, *Thomas Shadwell,* Cm [G-e′♭](m), Thames (Bevan) *6 Restoration*.
From grave lessons, *Anon,* D [d′-g′′] S&B (Pilkington) *Georgian 2.*
Halcyon days, *Thomas Shadwell,* C [d′-g′′], Novello/Masters (Cooper) 15 Songs 1a; *A,* 15 Songs 1b (attributed to Purcell in error).

He will not suffer thy foot to be moved, *Psalm 121, v. 3,* A [c'#-e''], B&H (Patrick) *Sacred Songs 1.*
Kind fortune smiles, *Thomas Shadwell,* C [c'-f''], Schirmer *2nd Mezzo.*
Lord shall preserve thee from all evil, The, *Psalm 121, v. 7,* A [e'-f''#], B&H (Patrick) *Sacred Songs 1.*
My dear, my Amphitrite, *see* Fair and serene.
Reason, what art thou? *John Lawrance,* Bb [e'b-g''], Voicebox *Mad songs 2.*
Wakeful nightingale, The, *Anon,* Am [e'-g''], B&H (Keel) *12 18th Century*; *Gm,* S&B (Pilkington) *Georgian 1, Recitalist 2.*
Your awful voice, *Thomas Shadwell,* C [e-a']; *Bb,* International (Kagen) *40 Songs 2a,* Novello/Masters (Dent) *15 Songs 2a*; *G,* *40 Songs 2b, 15 Songs 2b* (attributed to Purcell in error).

Wellesz, Egon Joseph. 1885–1974. *See also* App. 1, 2.
Collection: *On Time,* Lengnick.
Ah! fading joy, *John Dryden,* Cm [c-e'](m), Lengnick *On Time.*
On Time, *John Milton,* C [c-e'](m), Lengnick *On Time.*
Poet and the Day, The, *Elizabeth Mackenzie,* Eb [Bb-e'](m), Lengnick *On Time.*

Wesley, Charles. 1757–1834. *See* App. 2.

Wesley, Samuel. 1766–1837.
Collection: *Songs,* (edited and realised Francis Routh), Redcliffe.
Hark! His hands the lyre explore, *Thomas Gray,* [soprano], Redcliffe *Songs.*
Hope away! Enjoyment's come, *Anon,* [soprano], Redcliffe *Songs.*
Might I in thy sight appear, *Charles Wesley,* F [c'-f''], S&B (Bush & Temperley) *MB 43.*
Not heav'n itself, *Horace,* tr. *Dryden,* [soprano], Redcliffe *Songs.*
On Cramer's leaving England: Go, minstrel, go, *Anon,* [soprano], Redcliffe *Songs.*
On Music, *Anon,* [soprano], Redcliffe *Songs.*
Think of me, *Anon,* [soprano], Redcliffe *Songs.*
What shaft of fate's relentless power, *Anon,* Gm [a-a''], S&B (Bush & Temperley) *MB 43.*
Within a cowslip's humble bell, *Anon,* [soprano], Redcliffe *Songs.*

Wesley, Samuel Sebastian. 1810–1876.
By the rivers of Babylon, *Lord Byron,* Em [d'#-f''#], S&B (Bush and Temperley) *MB 43.*
Collect for the Third Sunday in Advent, *Thomas Cranmer,* adapted *W.H.Bellamy,* F [Bb(G)-f''](m), S&B (Bush & Temperley) *MB 43.*
Jesu the very thought of thee, *St Bernard of Clairvaux* tr. *Caswall,* F [f'-g''], Schirmer (James Eason), *1st Tenor.*

Weston, H. Burgess.
Row, burnie, row, *Walter C. Smith,* Eb [bb-e''b](f), B&H *Heritage 2*; (D, F, G, B&H).
(Song of the North, *Walter C. Smith,* D, B&H.)

Westrup, Sir **Jack Allen.** 1904–1975.
Come away, death, *Shakespeare,* [f'#-a''], S&B.
Orpheus with his lute, *Shakespeare,* [f'-a''b], S&B.
Take, O take those lips away, *Shakespeare,* [d'b-a''], S&B.

Wetherell, Eric. 1925–
Collection: *Three Shakespeare Sonnets,* Thames.
How like a winter, *Shakespeare,* Bb [bb-d''], Thames *3 Shakespeare.*
Let me not, *Shakespeare,* F [c'-d''], Thames *3 Shakespeare.*
Shall I compare thee? *Shakespeare,* Dm [bb-e''], Thames *3 Shakespeare.*

White, Alexander.
Collections: *Four Jingles,* Bardic; *Three Hogg Songs,* Bardic.
Auntie's skirts, *Robert Louis Stevenson,* [d'-f''], Bardic *4 Jingles.*
Autumn, *Winifred Busfield,* [c'#-g''], Bardic.
Autumn Fires, *Robert Louis Stevenson,* [bb-e''b], Bardic.
Bed in Summer, *Robert Louis Stevenson,* [d'-g''], Bardic.
Birks of Aberfeldie, The, *Robert Burns,* [d'-g''], Bardic.
Block City, *Robert Louis Stevenson,* [e'-a''], Bardic *4 Jingles.*
Collier's Daughter, The, *Robert Burns,* [c'#-a''], Bardic.
Colour, The, *Thomas Hardy,* [bb-g''], Bardic.

Cow, The, *Robert Louis Stevenson,* [b♭-e′′♭], Bardic.
Deuk's dang o'er my daddie, The, *Robert Burns,* [b♭-a′′♭], Bardic.
Dream, A, *William Blake,* [e′♭-f′′], Bardic.
Dusty Miller, The, *Robert Burns,* [a-f′′], Bardic.
Elibanks and Elibraes, *Robert Burns,* [b♭-a′′♭], Bardic.
Fairy Bread, *Robert Louis Stevenson,* [d′♭-f′′], Bardic.
Fairy Ring, The, *Robert Louis Stevenson,* [b♭-e′′♭], Bardic.
Farewell to the farm, *Robert Louis Stevenson,* [c′-a′′], Bardic.
Flowers, The, *Robert Louis Stevenson,* [f′#-g′′], Bardic.
Foreign Children, *Robert Louis Stevenson,* [g-a′], Bardic.
From a Railway Carriage, *Robert Louis Stevenson,* [a♭-d′′], Bardic.
Galloway Tam, *Robert Burns,* [g′-a′′], Bardic.
Good Boy, A, *Robert Louis Stevenson,* [e′-f′#], Bardic.
Grasshopper green, *Anon,* [g♭-a′′♭], Bardic.
Hayloft, The, *Robert Louis Stevenson,* [d′-d′′], Bardic.
If it's ever spring again, *Thomas Hardy,* [e′-b′′], Bardic.
It was a lover and his lass, *Shakespeare,* [b-d′′], Bardic.
Lady Mary Ann, *Robert Burns,* [b♭-g′′], Bardic.
Lamplighter, The, *Robert Louis Stevenson,* [b-f′#], Bardic.
Land of Nod, The, *Robert Louis Stevenson,* [d′-a′′], Bardic.
Land of Story-books, The, *Robert Louis Stevenson,* [b♭-c′′], Bardic.
Lassie of Yarrow, *James Hogg,* [c′-a′′], Bardic 3 Hogg.
Light foot and tight foot, *Robert Louis Stevenson,* [b♭-c′′], Bardic.
Looking-glass River, *Robert Louis Stevenson,* [b♭-d′′], Bardic.
Lucy Lavender, *Ivy O. Eastwick,* [b-e′′], Bardic.
Magic Whistle, The, *Margaret Rose,* [e′♭-g′′], Bardic.
Marching Song, *Robert Louis Stevenson,* [c′-e′′], Bardic 4 Jingles.
My Kingdom, *Robert Louis Stevenson,* [e′♭-a′′♭], Bardic.
My Shadow, *Robert Louis Stevenson,* [d′-a′′], Bardic.
O, ay my wife she dang me, *Robert Burns,* [c′-a′′], Bardic.
O, guid ale comes, *Robert Burns,* [c′-e′′♭], Bardic.
O saw ye my dear, my Philly? *Robert Burns,* [b♭-c′′], Bardic.
One night as I did wander, *Robert Burns,* [f′-a′′♭], Bardic.
Owl and the Pussycat, The, *Edward Lear,* [d′-a′′], Bardic.
Picture-books in Winter, *Robert Louis Stevenson,* [e′♭-e′′♭], Bardic 4 Jingles.
Sea Fairies, *Eileen Mathias,* [f′#-f′′#], Bardic.
Sea-song from the Shore, A, *James Whitcombe Riley,* [b-d′′#], Bardic.
Singing, *Robert Louis Stevenson,* [d′-e′′], Bardic.
Sir Nickety Nox, *Hugh Chesterman,* [d′-g′′], Bardic.
Skylark, The, *James Hogg,* [d′-f′′#], Bardic 3 Hogg.
Summer's Peace, *Winifred Busfield,* [e′♭-a′′♭], Bardic.
Swing, The, *Robert Louis Stevenson,* [e′-g′′], Bardic.
There's cauld kail in Aberdeen, *Robert Burns,* [d′-g′′], Bardic.
Water Jewels, *Mary F. Butts,* [b-d′′], Bardic.
Waukrife Minnie, A, *Robert Burns,* [d′-e′′], Bardic.
Weary pund o'tow, The, *Robert Burns,* [a-c′′], Bardic.
When the golden day is done, *Robert Louis Stevenson,* [a♭-e′′], Bardic.
Wind, The, *Robert Louis Stevenson,* [a-a′′], Bardic.
Wishing, *William Allingham,* [a♭-c′′], Bardic.
Witch o'Fife, The, *James Hogg,* [e′-a′′], Bardic 3 Hogg.
Arrangements:
Afton Water, *Robert Burns,* [d′-g′′], Bardic.
Bonnie Earl o' Moray, The, *Anon,* [f′#-f′′#], Bardic.
Charlie is my darling, *Lady Nairne,* [d′-f′′], Bardic.
Deil's away wi' th' exciseman, *Robert Burns,* [e′-a′′], Bardic.
Gae bring to me a pint o' wine, *Robert Burns,* [c-f′](m), Bardic.
Johnnie Cope, ?*Adam Skirving,* [B-e′](m), Bardic.
O, rattlin' roarin' Willie, *Robert Burns,* [c′-d′′], Bardic.
O whistle an I'll come to ye my lad, *Robert Burns,* [b-f′′#], Bardic.

White, Maude Valérie. 1855–1937. *See also* App. 1, Chappell.
Collection: *Six Songs,* [high (given below), medium], Classical; *Three Little Songs,* Banks, Classical; *Trois Chansons Taiganes,* B&H; *Two Love Songs,* Banks.

Among the Roses, *Hoffmann von Fallersleben* tr. *Maude Valérie White,* G [f'#-g''], Classical 6 Songs.
Bygone Joys, *N. Minsky* tr. *Paul England,* Fm [c'-e''b], B&H Trois Chansons.
Child's Evening Prayer, *German* tr. *Maude Valérie White,* G [e'-e''], Classical 6 Songs.
Come to the dancing, *N. Minsky* tr. *Paul England,* D [b-f'#], B&H Trois Chansons.
Crabbed age and youth, *Shakespeare?* F [a(g)-d''](f), B&H *Heritage 1,* Schirmer *1st Mezzo.*
Divine Providence, *Sicilian* tr. *Roger Gay,* Ab [c'-f''], Classical 6 Songs.
Earth Will Wake, The, *Emmanuel Giebel* tr. *Adrian Ross,* A [e'-g''#], Classical 6 Songs.
King Charles, *Robert Browning,* [medium], Classical; F [c'-c''], B&H; G, B&H.
Let us forget, *Goethe* tr. *M. Darmesteter,* C [c'-e''], Banks 3 Little Songs.
Memory, A, *Anon,* G [c'-e''], Banks 3 Little Songs.
Old Grey Fox, The, *Conan Doyle,* [medium], Classical.
Ophelia's Song, *Shakespeare,* Em [d'-f''](f), B&H *Heritage 2.*
(So we'll go no more a-roving, *Lord Byron,* C [b-e''], *Chappell* English Recital 1; Db, E, Chappell).
Song of the Flax, *N. Minsky* tr. *Paul England,* Cm [bb-c''], B&H Trois Chansons.
Spring has Come, The, *Maude Valérie White,* Eb [e'b-g''], Classical 6 Songs.
Star, A, *Heinrich Heine* tr. *Adrian Ross,* E [d'#-g''#], Classical 6 Songs.
To God, *Robert Herrick,* C#m [c'#-e''], S&B MB 56.
To Mary, *Percy Bysshe Shelley,* Bb [f'-g''], B&H.
To Music, *Robert Herrick,* Em [g'-g''], S&B MB 56.
When I think on the happy days, *Robert Burns,* Am [e'-f''], Banks 2 Love Songs.
When the swallows homeward fly, *German Volkslied* tr. *Anon,* A [a-e''], Banks 3 Little Songs.
When you return, *Arthur Philip Coxford,* Bb [a-e''b], B&H; C, B&H.
Youth once loved a maiden, A, *Heine,* tr. *M. V. White,* Fm, [b-d''b], S&B MB 56; *A,* Banks 2 Love Songs.

White, Robin le Rougetel. 1908–1979. BMIC.
Where shall we adventure? (cycle), *R. L. Stevenson,* [d'-g''#], Banks.

Whittaker, William Gillies. 1876–1944. SMIC; Viking.
Collection: *Two Lyrics from the Chinese,* BMP.
Ah, let it drift, *Chinese,* tr. *Helen Waddell,* [a-f''#], BMP 2 Chinese.
Bog Love, *Shane Leslie,* [d'-e''], BMP.
Chief Centurians, The, *John Masefield,* [ab-e''], BMP.
Crowder, The, *Wilfrid Gibson,* [bb-e''], BMP.
Empty Purse, The, *Wilfrid Gibson,* [c'-e''], BMP.
Little child mine own *see* Lullay, lullay.
Lullay, lullay, *time of Henry VIII,* Bm [bb-e''], B&H.
Mary is a lady bright *see* Nun gaudet Maria.
My Lord has gone away to serve the king, *Chinese,* tr. *Helen Waddell,* [bb-e''], BMP 2 Chinese.
Nun gaudet Maria, *15th century,* C [b-e''], B&H.
Scatterpenny, *Wilfrid Gibson,* [ab-e''b], BMP.
Song of a lass, O, *Wilfrid Gibson,* [b-e''], BMP.
Spring, *Robert Bridges,* [c'#-e''], BMP.
Stay in town, *Julian Antecessor,* [b-e''], BMP.
Arrangements:
(Blow the wind southerly, *Anon,* G, Elkin.)
Shew's the way to Wallington, *Northumbrian,* [c'-c''], BMP.

Whyte, Ian. 1901–1960. SMIC.
(I love you my dear, *Don Whyte,* F [c'-f''], Curwen.)

Wickens, Dennis. 1926–
Parta Quies, *A. E. Housman,* [bb-d''], EPSS.

Wiegold, Peter. 1949– *See* App. 2.

Wilby, Philip. 1949– *See* App. 1, 2.

Wilkinson, Marc. 1929–
Forget yesterday, *Tom Stoppard,* C [b-d''], Weinberger/Elkin.

Willcocks, Sir **David** Valentine. 1919–
Arrangements:
  Infant King, The, *Sabine Baring-Gould,* F [c′-f′′], OUP *Solo Christmas high,* D, *Solo Christmas low.*
  Sussex Carol, *Anon,* G [d′-e′′], OUP *Solo Christmas high and low.*

Williams, Bryn. WMIC.

Williams, Christmas.
  Gethsemene, [soprano/tenor], Snell.
  Jesu lover of my soul, *Charles Wesley,* [soprano/tenor], Snell.
  Never forgetting thee, [soprano/tenor], Snell.

Williams, D. E.
  Soldier's Song, The, [bass/baritone], Snell.

Williams, Gerrard.
  My sweet sweeting, *Early English,* [d′-g′′], BMP.
  Now wolde I faine some merthes make, *A. Godwhen,* [d′-d′′], BMP.

Williams, Grace Mary. 1906–1977. WMIC. *See also* App. 1, 2.
Collection: *Six Welsh Oxen Songs,* B&H.
  Thou art the One Truth, *Dhan Gopal Mukerji,* [G-f′#](m), WMIC.
  To Death, *Caroline Southey,* Am [c′#-a′′], WMIC *Songs from Wales 1.*
Arrangements:
  Jim Crow, *Anon,* Gwynn.
  Loom, The, *Grace Williams,* Gm [b♭-e′′♭](f), OUP *Solo Soprano,* OUP.
  Watching the Wheat, *Wil Hopkin* tr. *Grace Williams,* E [d′#-f′′#](m), BMP.

Williams, Graham. *See App. 2.*

Williams, Meiron. 1901–1976. WMIC.
  Blossoms by my door, The, *John Evans* tr. *Caerwyn,* Fm [c′-f′′(a′′)], Gwynn.
  Ora pro nobis, [c′-e′′♭] Gwynn.

Williams, Owen.
  Palm Sunday, [any voice], Snell.

Williams, Rhyddid. WMIC. *See also* App. 2.
  O perfect love, *Dorothy F. Gurney,* [soprano/contralto], Snell.

Williams, Roderick. 1965–
  Reading Scheme, *Wendy Cope,* A [d′-a′′#], Thames *Century 5.*
  I asked my lady, *Roger McGough,* [b-e′′], Thames *Century 6.*

Williams, Tydain.
  Hero, The, A [baritone], Snell.

Williams, W. Albert. 1909–1946.
  By the Sea, *Huw Emrys Griffith* tr. *Caerwyn,* Dm [d′-e′′], Gwynn.
  Wind's Lament, The, *John Morris-Jones* tr. *H. Idris Bell,* Dm [b♭-f′′], Gwynn.

Williams, Williams **Matthews.** 1885-1972.
  Bronwen, B♭ [soprano/tenor], Snell.
  John of the Glen, *Lewis Glyn Cothi* tr. *H. Idris Bell,* Cm [c′-f′′], Gwynn.
  Llanfihangel Bachellaeth, *Cynan* tr. *H. Idris Bell,* Fm [c′-e′′♭(f′′)], Gwynn.
  My Land, *Dewi Havesp* tr. *T. Gwynn Jones,* F [c′-f′′], Gwynn.

Williams, William Sydney **Gwynn.** 1896–1978.
Collections: *Three Welsh Lyrics,* Gwynn; (*Two Shakespeare Lyrics,* [d′-f′′], Gwynn).
  Apple Tree, The, *I. D. Hooson* tr. *H. Idris Bell,* Gm [d′-f′′], Gwynn 3 Lyrics, Gwynn.
  Fairies, *T. Gwynn Jones* tr. *Anon,* Fm [e′♭-f′′], Gwynn 3 Lyrics, Gwynn.
  Glyndwr's Dream, *Emyr* tr. *H. Idris Bell,* Gm [d′-e′′♭], Gwynn 3 Lyrics, Gwynn.
  God's Mercy, [mezzo/baritone], Gwynn; [soprano/tenor], Gwynn.

Prayer, A, *John Newton*, Eb [e′b-e′′b], Gwynn *Three Spring Songs*.
Skylark, The, *James Hogg*, Eb [d′-g′′], Gwynn.
(Spring, *Shakespeare,* Gwynn 2 Shakespeare.)
(Winter, *Shakespeare,* Gwynn 2 Shakespeare.)

Williamson, John R. 1929– WMIC.
Collection: *Two Housman Songs,* Da Capo.
    Farms of Home, The, *A. E. Housman,* [baritone], Da Capo 2 Housman/EPSS.
    It nods and curtseys, *A. E. Housman,* [baritone], Da Capo 2 Housman.
    Ploughman, The, *A. E. Housman,* [baritone], Da Capo.
    Recruit, The, *A. E. Housman,* [baritone], Williamson.
    Think no more, lad, *A. E. Housman,* [baritone], Da Capo.
    White in the moon, *A. E. Housman,* [baritone], Da Capo.

Williamson, Malcolm Benjamin Graham Christopher. 1931–2003 *See also* App. 2.
Collections: *From a Child's Garden,* Weinberger; *Six English Lyrics,* Weinberger; *Three Shakespeare Songs,* Weinberger; *Vision of Beasts and Gods, A,* B&H.
    Ballad of Wild Children, The, *George Barker,* [e′-a′′], B&H A Vision.
    Birthday, A, *Christina Rossetti,* G [b-d′′], Weinberger 6 Lyrics.
    Celebration of Divine Love (cycle), *James McAuley,* [d′b-c′′′], Novello.
    Christmas Carol, A, *G. K. Chesterton,* D [c′#-d′′], Weinberger.
    Come away, death, *Shakespeare,* Em [e′-f′′#], Weinberger 3 Shakespeare.
    Crossing the Bar, *Alfred Lord Tennyson,* C [b-d′′], Weinberger 6 Lyrics.
    Dedication, *George Barker,* [f′-f′′#], B&H A Vision.
    Epitaph for Many Young Men, *George Barker,* [d′#-g′′], B&H A Vision.
    Fear no more the heat of the sun, *Shakespeare,* [c′-a′′b], Weinberger 3 Shakespeare.
    Flowers, The, *R. L. Stevenson,* F [f′-f′′#], Weinberger Child's Garden.
    From a Railway Carriage, *R. L. Stevenson,* [e′b-a′′b], Weinberger Child's Garden.
    Full fathom five, *Shakespeare,* (unaccompanied), [db-f′′#], Weinberger 3 Shakespeare.
    Go, lovely rose, *Edmund Waller,* F [c′-c′′](m), Weinberger 6 Lyrics.
    Good Boy, A, *R. L. Stevenson,* F [e′-f′′], Weinberger Child's Garden.
    Happy Thought, *R. L. Stevenson,* Gm [a′-a′′], Weinberger Child's Garden.
    Hasselbacher's Scena, *Sidney Gilliat,* [D-e′](m), Weinberger/Elkin.
    Jenny kiss'd me, *Leigh Hunt,* [c′-d′′], Weinberger 6 Lyrics.
    Lamplighter, The, *R. L. Stevenson,* A [e′-f′′#], Weinberger Child's Garden.
    Looking Forward, *R. L. Stevenson,* Ebm [e′b-a′′b], Weinberger Child's Garden.
    Love Letter, *George Barker,* [e′-a′′b], B&H A Vision.
    Marching Song, *R. L. Stevenson,* [e′b-f′′], Weinberger Child's Garden.
    My bed is a boat, *R. L. Stevenson,* Gb [f′-g′′b], Weinberger Child's Garden.
    On the Death of Manolette, *George Barker,* [d′-a′′], B&H A Vision.
    Rain, *R. L. Stevenson,* D [g′-g′′], Weinberger Child's Garden.
    Sweet and low, *Alfred Lord Tennyson,* Eb [d′b-d′′](f), Weinberger 6 Lyrics.
    Time to rise, *R. L. Stevenson,* [d′-g′′b], Weinberger Child's Garden.
    To a Child, *George Barker,* [f′-g′′], B&H A Vision.
    When I am dead, *Christina Rossetti,* F#m, [a-e′′b], Weinberger 6 Lyrics.
    Where go the boats? *R. L. Stevenson,* A [e′-e′′], Weinberger Child's Garden.
    Whole Duty of Children, *R. L. Stevenson,* Eb [f′-a′′b], Weinberger Child's Garden.
Arrangements: *North Country Songs,* Weinberger 1966.
    Adam Buckham O! *Anon,* [a-b′b], Weinberger North Country.
    Bonny at morn, *Anon,* [bb-c′′], Weinberger North Country.
    Captain Bover, *Anon,* F [c′-e′′b], Weinberger North Country.
    Derwentwater's Farewell, *Anon,* [bb-c′′], Weinberger North Country.

Willink, Simon. 1929–
    Kingfisher, The, *W. H. Davies,* [bb-e′′b], EPSS.

Wills, Arthur. 1926– BMIC. *See also* App. 2.
Collections: *Betjemania,* Fentone; *Dark Lady, The,* Brunton; *Dramatis Personae,* Impulse; *Eternity's Sunrise,* Brunton; *Love's Torment,* Brunton; *When the Spirit Comes,* Brunton.
    Abt Vogler, *Robert Browning,* C [b-f′′]; Impulse Dramatis Personae.
    Buddha-song, *Arthur Wills,* Dm [F-e′](m), Wills.
    Eternity, *William Blake,* [d′#-f′′#](f), Brunton Eternity's Sunrise.
    Hound of Heaven, The, *Francis Thompson,* [g-e′′b], Brunton.
    Hunter Trials, *John Betjeman,* D [d′-f′′#](m), Fentone Betjemania.

Investiture in Wales, *John Betjeman,* C [c´-b´´b](m), Fentone Betjemania.
Lamb, The, *William Blake,* [g´-f´´#](f), Brunton Eternity's Sunrise.
Last Lines, *Emily Brontë,* [g#-a´´](f), Brunton Spirit.
Lenten Thoughts of a High Anglican, *John Betjeman,* Db [d´b-a´´b](m), Fentone Betjemania.
Love is a sickness, *Samuel Daniel,* [d´-f´´], Brunton Love's Torment.
Old Stoic, The, *Emily Brontë,* [a-g´´](f), Brunton Spirit.
Prisoner, The, *Emily Brontë,* [ab-b´´](f), Brunton Spirit.
Rabbi Ben Ezra, *Robert Browning,* C [bb-f´´], Impulse Dramatis Personae.
Rosalind's Madrigal, *Thomas Lodge,* [g-f´´], Brunton Love's Torment.
Sonnet 127, *Shakespeare,* [B-e´#](m), Brunton Dark Lady.
Sonnet 128, *Shakespeare,* [G-e´](m), Brunton Dark Lady.
Sonnet 129, *Shakespeare,* [Ab-f´](m), Brunton Dark Lady.
Sonnet 131, *Shakespeare,* [G-e´b](m), Brunton Dark Lady.
Sonnet 136, *Shakespeare,* [F-e´](m), Brunton Dark Lady.
Sonnet 138, *Shakespeare,* [E-e´](m), Brunton Dark Lady.
Sonnet 146, *Shakespeare,* [G#-e´](m), Brunton Dark Lady.
Sonnet 147, *Shakespeare,* [A-e´](m), Brunton Dark Lady.
Sonnet: An evil spirit, *Michael Drayton,* [g#(b)-e´´b], Brunton Love's Torment.
Spellbound, *Emily Brontë,* [bb-a´´b](f), Brunton Spirit.
Subaltern's Love Song, A, *John Betjeman,* C [c´-c´´](m), Fentone Betjemania.
Tyger, The, *William Blake,* [g´-f´´#](f), Brunton Eternity's Sunrise.
What thing is love, *George Peele,* [a-g´´b], Brunton Love's Torment.

Wilson, H. Lane. 1871–1915.
Collection: *Old English Melodies,* (these songs are unattributed, and they may be original compositions) B&H; *Two Elizabethan Lyrics,* B&H.
Ah! willow, *Anon,* Gm [b-c´´], B&H *Old English,* Schirmer *2nd Baritone.*
Carmeña, D [b-f´#](f), Schirmer *1st Mezzo II.*
Come let's be merry, *Anon,* Bb [b-e´´(f´´)](m), B&H *Old English.*
False Phillis, *Anon,* A [a-d´´(e´´)](m), B&H *Old English;* Schirmer *1st Baritone.*
Happy Lover, The, *Anon,* Eb [bb-e´´b](m), B&H *Old English.*
No sweeter life, *Edward Vere,* C [c´-d´´], B&H 2 Elizabethan.
Ralph's Ramble to London, *Anon,* F [c´-e´´](m), B&H *Old English.*
Sailor's life, The, *Anon,* E [b-e´´](m), B&H *Old English.*
Shall I, wasting in despair, *George Wither,* Eb [bb-e´´b]. B&H 2 Elizabethan.
Slighted Swain, The, *Anon,* C [c´-d´´](m), B&H *Old English,* Schirmer *1st Baritone II.*
Spring morning, A, F [high], Classical.

Wilson, James. 1922– BMIC.

Wilson, John. 1595–1674.
In a season all oppressed, *Anon,* Am [g´#-e´´], S&B (Spink) MB 33, *Cavalier.*
Since love hath in thine and mine eye, *Anon,* Eb [d´-f´´], S&B (Spink) MB 33, *Cavalier.*
Take, O take those lips away, *Shakespeare,* Gm [g´-g´´], S&B (Spink) MB 33, *Cavalier.*
Wherefore peep'st thou, envious day? *John Donne?* G [g´-a´´], S&B (Spink) MB 33, *Cavalier.*

Wilson, Richard. 1941– *See* App. 2.

Wilson, Thomas Brendan. 1927– BMIC; SMIC.
Collection: *Six Scots Songs,* SMIC/Queensgate

Wilson-Dickson, Andrew. *See* App. 2.

Winters, Geoffrey. 1928– BMIC; Brett. *See also* App. 2.

Wishart, Peter Charles Arthur. 1921–1984. BMIC. *See also* App. 1, 2.
Collections: *Twelve Songs* (introduction by Brian Trowell), S&B; *Two Shakespeare Songs,* Banks.
Bedpost, The, *Robert Graves,* G [d´-f´´#], S&B 12 Songs.
Bird of Paradise, *Robert Graves,* [medium], Banks.
Cat Goddesses, *Robert Graves,* [c´#-f´´], S&B 12 Songs.
Fidele, *Shakespeare,* Fm [e´b-f´´], Banks.
Henry and Mary, *Robert Graves,* C [c´-e´´], S&B 12 Songs.
Jackdaw, The, *William Cooper,* Em [c´-e´´], S&B 12 Songs.
Lament, *Anon,* D [b-f´´](f), S&B 12 Songs.

Magpie, The, *James McAuley*, A [a′-f′′#], S&B 12 Songs.
My God, why hast thou forsaken me? *St Augustine*, G [b♭-c′′], S&B 12 Songs.
O mistress mine, *Shakespeare*, [medium], Banks 2 Shakespeare.
Orpheus with his lute, *Shakespeare*, [medium], Banks 2 Shakespeare.
Pessimist, The, *Benjamin King*, D [d′-d′′], S&B 12 Songs.
Spring Sadness, *Anon*, tr. *Helen Waddell*, B [c′#-f′′#], S&B 12 Songs.
Tune for Swans, *James McAuley*, [e′-f′′], S&B 12 Songs.
You are a refuge, *St Augustine*, Cm [c′-c′′], S&B 12 Songs.

Wood, Charles. 1866–1926. *See also* App. 2.
Collections: *Five Songs for High Voice*, B&H; *Ten Songs for Low Voice*, B&H.
    Ask me no more, *Alfred Lord Tennyson*, E♭ [d′-g′′], B&H 5 Songs High, B&H.
    At Sea, *Moira O'Neill*, B♭ [b♭-e′′♭], B&H 10 Songs Low.
    At the mid hour of night, *Thomas Moore*, F [e♭-a′′], B&H 5 Songs High, B&H.
    Birds, *Moira O'Neill*, C [c′-e′′♭], B&H 10 Songs Low.
    Darest thou now, O soul, *Walt Whitman*, D♭ [d′♭-f′′], B&H 10 Songs Low.
    Dead at Clonmacnois, The, *Enoch O'Gillan* tr. *T. W. Rolleston*, E♭ [a♭-f′′♭], B&H 10 Songs Low, B&H.
    Denny's daughter, *Moira O'Neill*, B♭ [a-e′′♭](m), B&H 10 Songs Low.
    Echo, *Christina Rossetti*, D♭ [d′♭-g′′], B&H 5 Songs High, B&H.
    Ethiopia Saluting the Colours, *Walt Whitman*, A [a-d′′], Thames *Century 2*, Classical; A♭, B♭ B&H.
    Fortune and Her Wheel, *Alfred Lord Tennyson*, A [e′-g′′#], B&H 5 Songs High.
    Goldthred's Song, *Walter Scott*, Dm [c′-e′′], B&H 10 Songs Low, B&H.
    Holy Thursday, *William Blake*, Am [d′-f′′], B&H.
    O Captain! my captain, *Walt Whitman*, B♭ [b♭-e′′♭], B&H.
    One morning in May, *Alfred Percival Graves*, E♭ [b♭-e′′♭], B&H.
    Outlaw of Loch Lene, The, *Anon* tr. *J. J. Callanan*, F#m [b-d′′#](m), B&H.
    Potato Song, The, *Alfred Percival Graves*, D [b-d′′], B&H.
    Rover, The, *Walter Scott*, C [b-e′′], B&H 10 Songs Low.
    Sailorman, The, *Moira O'Neill*, Dm [c′-d′′](m), B&H 10 Songs Low.
    Shall I forget? *Christina Rossetti*, B♭ [b♭-e′′♭], B&H 10 Songs Low.
    Song of the Cyclops, *Thomas Dekker*, Cm [c′-e′′♭], B&H 10 Songs Low, B&H.
    Splendour falls, The, *Alfred Lord Tennyson*, E♭ [d′-g′′], B&H 5 Songs High.
Arrangements: (*Irish Folk Songs — Twentyfive Old Irish melodies*, B&H); *Seven Irish Folksongs*, Thames.
    Battle-eve of the Brigade, The, *Thomas Davis*, E♭ [b♭-e′′♭](m), Thames 7 Irish.
    Curly Locks, *J. P. M'Call*, E♭ [b♭-f′′](m), Thames 7 Irish.
    Drinaun dhun, The, *Robert Dwyer Joyce*, B♭ [b♭-d′′](m), Thames 7 Irish.
    His Home and His Own Country, *Emily H. Hickey*, Fm [e′♭-a′′♭](f), Thames 7 Irish.
    Oh, the marriage, *Thomas Davis*, Dm [c′-f′′](f), Thames 7 Irish.
    Oliver's Advice, *William Blacker*, Dm [d′-f′′](m), Thames 7 Irish.
    Sho-ho (or Lullaby), *Alfred Percival Graves*, E♭ [e′♭-f′′](f), Thames 7 Irish.

Wood, Haydn. 1882–1959. *See also* Chappell.
    Brown Bird Singing, A, *Royden Barrie*, G [f′#-g′′(e′′)], IMP *Parlour Songs*.
    Roses of Picardy, *Fred E. Weatherly*, C [e′-f′′(g′′)], IMP *Parlour Songs*, Classical; B♭, D, Classical.
    Love's Garden of Roses, *Ruth Rutherford*, G [d′-e′′(g′′)], IMP *Parlour Songs*.
    (Memories of Yesterday, *Lilian Glanville*, G [d′-g′′], Chappell *English Recital 2*.)

Wood, Hugh Bradshaw. 1932– *See also* App. 2.
Collections: *D. H. Lawrence Songs, Op 14*, Chester; *Horses, The, Op 10*, Chester; *Laurie Lee Songs*, Chester; *Robert Graves Songs Set 1, Op 18*, Chester; *Set 2, Op 22*, Chester; *Set 3, Op 25*, Chester; *Songs, Op 23*, Chester.
    Always, *Robert Graves*, [d′♭-a′′], Chester Graves 1.
    Amor, *Pablo Neruda* tr. *Alastair Reid*, [d′♭-b′′♭], Chester Songs Op 23.
    April Rise, *Laurie Lee*, [high], Chester Laurie Lee.
    Bird of Paradise, *Robert Graves*, [d′♭-b′′♭](m), Chester Graves 3, Chester.
    Blue Coat, The, *Yevgeny Yevtushenko* tr. *Anon*, [c′#-a′′], Chester Op 23.
    Boy in Ice, *Laurie Lee*, [high], Chester Laurie Lee.
    Dog-tired, *D. H. Lawrence*, [c′-b′′♭](m), Chester D. H. Lawrence.
    Door, The, *Robert Graves*, [c′#-g′′](m), Chester Graves 3.
    Easter Green, The, *Laurie Lee*, [high], Chester Laurie Lee.
    Edge of Day, The, *Laurie Lee*, [high], Chester Laurie Lee.

Foreboding, The, *Robert Graves*, [e′b-a′′](m), Chester Graves 1.
Fragment, *Robert Graves*, [d′-a′′b], Chester Graves 2.
Gloire de Dijon, *D. H. Lawrence*, [c′#-b′′b](m), Chester D. H. Lawrence Songs.
Home from Abroad, *Laurie Lee*, [d′b-b′′b], Chester Op 23.
Horses, The, *Ted Hughes*, [a-a′′b], Chester The Horses.
How am I poor tonight? [voice], Chester.
Ice, *Stephen Spender*, [d′-a′′], Chester Songs Op 23.
Green Castle, The, *Robert Graves*, [c′-e′′b](m), Chester Graves 1.
Hazel Grove, The, *Robert Graves*, [d′b-b′′b](m), Chester Graves 3.
Last Poem, A, *Robert Graves*, [c′-b′′b](m), Chester Graves 1.
Lines to Mr Hodgson, *Lord Byron*, [a-c′′](f), Chester.
Ouzo Unclouded, *Robert Graves*, [d′-a′′], Chester Graves 2.
Penines in April, *Ted Hughes*, [a-b′′], Chester The Horses.
Records, *Robert Graves*, [b-b′′b](m), Chester Graves 1.
Rider Victory, The, [high], Chester.
Rose, The, *Robert Graves*, [d′-a′′](m), Chester Graves 1.
Seldom yet now, *Robert Graves*, [c′-a′′b], Chester Graves 2.
September, *Ted Hughes*, [c′#-a′′], Chester The Horses.
Song Cycle to Poems by *Pablo Neruda*, tr. *Christopher Logue*, [high], Chester.
Symptoms of Love, *Robert Graves*, [c′-a′′], Chester Graves 2.
To tell and be told, *Robert Graves*, [c′#-g′′], Chester Graves 3.
Town Owl, *Laurie Lee,* [high], Chester Laurie Lee.
Visitation, The, *Robert Graves*, [c′-a′′b](m), Chester Graves 2.

Woodforde-Finden, Amy. 1860–1919.
Collections: (*Aziza*, [Frederick John Fraser], B&H); *Five Little Japanese Songs,* [Charles Hanson Towne], [low], Classical/B&H; *Four Indian Love Lyrics,* [high (introduction Andrew Lamb), B&H, [high, low], Classical/B&H; *Golden Hours,* [Gilbert Parker] [high, low], B&H; *Lover in Damascus, A,* [Charles Hanson Towne], [medium], B&H; (*Myrtles of Damascus* [Charles Hanson Towne], [high, low], B&H; *On Jhelum River* [Frederick John Fraser], [high], Classical/B&H, [low], B&H); *Stars of the Desert* [Laurence Hope], [high, medium], Classical/(B&H), [low], B&H); *Three Little Mexican Songs,* [Harold Simpson], [medium], Classical/B&H, [high], B&H; *To the Hills,* [Laurence Hope], [medium], Classical/B&H.
(Dream of Egypt, A (cycle), *Charles Hanson Towne*, [high, low], B&H.)
   Kashmiri Song, *Laurence Hope*, D [d′-f′′#], B&H 4 Indian, *Ballad Album 1, World Renowned*; Bb, IMP *Parlour Songs*; C, B&H 4 Indian.
Less than the dust, *Laurence Hope*, Cm [c′-f′′(a′′b)], B&H 4 Indian; A, B&H 4 Indian.
Temple Bells, The, *Laurence Hope*, Em [d′-g′′], B&H 4 Indian; Dm, B&H 4 Indian.
Till I wake, *Laurence Hope*, Dm [d′-f′′], B&H 4 Indian; Cm, B&H 4 Indian.

Woodson, Leonard. *c.*1565–1619.
Marigold of golden hue, The, *Anon*, G [g′-g′′](m), S&B (Greer) *Manuscript 2*.

Woolrich, John. 1954– *See also* App. 1, 2.
Collection: *Three Cautionary Tales,* Faber.
Here is My Country (cycle), *de Quincey, de Nerval, Schumann, Anderson,* [c′#-g′′](f), Faber.
La Cantarina, *Jo Shapcott*, [high soprano] Faber.
North Wind, The, *Traditional*, [b-c′′′(a′′)](f), Faber 3 Cautionary, Faber.
Poor Mr Snail, *Macedonian* tr. *Harvey & Pennington*, [d′-d′′′b(b′′)], Faber 3 Cautionary, Faber.
Submerged Bar, The, *Matthew Sweeney,* [soprano], Faber.
Turkish Mouse, The, *Turkish* tr. *John Woolrich*, [d′-g′′](f), Faber 3 Cautionary.
Unlit Suburbs, The, Faber.

Wordsworth, William Brocklesby. 1908–1988. SMIC. *See also* App. 2.
Come away, death, *Shakespeare*, [medium], Banks.
Constant Lover, The, *John Suckling*, [low], Banks.

Wright, Geoffrey.
Transatlantic Lullaby, *Diana Morgan & Robert MacDermot,* Bb [bb-d′′], Novello *Sarah's Encores*.

Wynne, David. 1900–1983. WMIC. *See also* App. 2.
Go, lovely rose, *Edmund Waller*, [soprano/tenor], Snell.
Irish Lullaby, *Francis A-Fahy*, [bb-f′′](f), Welsh Music.
Sleeping Sea, The, *John Freeman*, [d′b-f′′#], Welsh Music *Songs from Wales 2*.

Young, Anthony. 1685– ? Note: these are three different versions of the same song!
    Phillis, *Michael Diack*, Gm [a-g''](m), Paterson 100 Best 4.
    Phillis has such charming graces, *Anon*, D♭ [e'-g''♭](m), B&H (Lane Wilson) *Old English,* Schirmer *1st Tenor II.*
    Shy Shepherdess, The, Cm [d'-g''](f), S&B (Pilkington) *Georgian 2.*

Young, Derek. 1929– *See* App. 1.

Young, Douglas. 1947–
Collection: (*Four Nature Songs*, Faber.)
    (Cat and the Moon, The, *W. B. Yeats*, [b-a''#], Faber 4 Nature.)
    (Full fathom five, *Shakespeare*, [a'-d''], Faber 4 Nature.)
    (To Blossoms, *Robert Herrick*, [b-e''], Faber 4 Nature.)
    (Wild Swans at Coole, The, *W. B. Yeats*, [b♭-b''(a'')], Faber 4 Nature.)

Young, Peter. 1969– *See* App. 2.

Appendix 1: Settings of foreign texts

Adès, Thomas. 1971–
Collection: *Lover in Winter, The,* [Anon, Latin], [counter-tenor], Faber.

ApIvor, Denis. 1916– WMIC (Spanish)

Arundell, Dennis Drew. 1898–1988.
Arrangements: *Four Old French Songs,* BMP
    Pastourelle, *Anon,* [c′-e′′], BMP Old French.
    Plantons le Romarin, *Anon,* [d′-d′′], BMP Old French.
    Point de Couvent, *Anon,* [e′-e′′], BMP Old French.
    Trois Sereurs, *Anon,* [d′-d′′], BMP Old French.

Atkinson, René. 1920– *See also* App. 2.
    Ave Maria, [e′-g′′], OUP *Solo Christmas high*; [c′-e′′b], *Solo Christmas low*.

Balfe, Michael. 1808–1870.
    Si tu savais, *Sully-Prudhomme,* [medium], Classical.

Bax, Sir **Arnold.** 1883–1953.
Collections: (*Traditional Songs of France,* Chappell); (*Trois Enfantines,* Chester); (*Five Fantasies on Polish Christmas Carols,* Chappell).
    (Berceuse, *Anon,* Chester 3 Enfantines.)
    (Bóg sie rodzi, *Anon,* E♭ [b♭-e′′b], Chappell Polish Carols.)
    (Femmes, battez vos marys, Anon, E [e′-f′′#], Chappell France.)
    Frülingsregen, *Friedrich Ruckert,* G#m [d′#-g′′#], Thames Six Songs.
    (Ideala, *Bjørnstjerne Bjørnson,* Dm [d′-b′′], Murdoch.)
    (Jean, p'tit Jean, *Anon,* Chester 3 Enfantines.)
    (La targo, *Anon,* E [e′-b′], Chappell France.)
    (Languedo d′amours, ma douce fillette, *Anon,* F [d′-f′′], Chappell France.)
    (Lulajze Jesuniu, *Anon,* A♭ [e′b-f′′], Chappell Polish carols.)
    (Me soui mesocu danso, *Anon,* F [f′-f′′], Chappell France.)
    (Przybiezeli di Betlejem, *Anon,* F [e′-f′′], Chappell Polish Carols.)
    (Sarabande, *Anon,* Bm [e′-f′′#], Chappell France.)
    (Une petite fille, *Anon,* Chester 3 Enfantines.)
    (W zlobje Lezy, E *Anon,* [f′#-e′′], Chappell Polish Carols.)
    (Wšró noznej ciszy, *Anon,* B♭ [f′-e′′b], Chappell Polish Carols.)

Beat, Janet. 1937– SMIC.
    Premiers Désirs, [soprano], SMIC.

Bennett, Sir **William Sterndale.** 1816–75.
Collection: *Twelve Songs, Op 23 and 35,* Classical.
    Maienthau, *Ludwig Uhland,* A♭ [e′b-e′′b], Classical 12 Songs.
    Waldeinsamkeit, *Carl Klingemann,* Gm [d′-e′′b], Classical 12 Songs.

Berkeley, Sir **Lennox** Randall Francis. 1903–1989.
Collections: (*Complete French Songs,* Chester); *Three Early Songs,* Chester hire; *Trois Poèmes de Vildrac,* Chester hire.
    Automne, *Guillaume Apollinaire,* [e′b-f′′], Chester hire, (Chester French).
    Ce caillou chaud de soleil, *Charles Vildrac,* F#m [c′#-f′′#], Chester Vildrac, (Chester French).
    Cet enfant de jadis, *Charles Vildrac,* [c′-g′′], Chester Vildrac, (Chester French).
    D'un vanneur de blé aux vents, *Joachim du Bellay,* G [d′-g′′], OUP, (Chester French).
    D'un vanneur de blé aux vents, *Joachim du Bellay,* (early version), [mezzo/tenor] Chester 3 Early.
    Ode du premier jour du Mai, *Jean Passerat,* F [c′#-a′′], Chester (Chester French).
    Pastourelle, *Anon,* [d′-e′′], Chester 3 Early, (Chester French).
    Rondeau, *Charles D'Orleans,* F [A-a′](m), Chester 3 Early, (Chester French).
    Sonnet, *Louise Labé,* [c′#-g′′], Chester, (Chester French).
    Sur quel arbre du ciel, *Charles Vildrac,* Em [d′-d′′], Chester Vildrac, (Chester French).

Tant que mes yeux, *Louise Labé*, [c'#-g''], OUP, (Chester French).
Tombeau (cycle), *Jean Cocteau*, [c'-a''], Chester, (Chester French).

Berners, Lord. 1883–1950.
Collections: (*The Collected Vocal Music*, Chester); *Trois Chansons,* Chester.
(Du bist wie eine Blume, *Heine*, [e'-f''], Chester Collected.)
(Konig Wiswamitra, *Heinrich Heine*, [e'b-f''], Chester Collected.)
La fiancée du timbalier, *G. Jean-Aubry*, [c'-a''b], Chester Trois Chansons, (Chester Collected).
L'étoile filante, *G. Jean-Aubry*, [c'-e''], Chester Trois Chansons, (Chester Collected).
Romance, *G. Jean-Aubry*, [c'-e''], Chester Trois Chansons, (Chester Collected).
(Weihnachtslied, *Heinrich Heine*, [b-d''], Chester Collected.)

Blyton, Carey. 1932–2002
Collection: *Toi et Moi,* Modus.
Doute, *Paul Géraldy,* [a-g''], Modus Toi et Moi.
Dualism, *Paul Géraldy,* [d'-f''#], Modus Toi et Moi.
Habitude, *Paul Géraldy,* [g-e''](m), Modus Toi et Moi.
Mea Culpa, *Paul Géraldy,* [b-e''], Modus Toi et Moi.
Post-scriptum, *Paul Géraldy,* [f(a)-g''#](m), Modus Toi et Moi.

Bridge, Frank. 1889–1941.
Arrangement:
Lasst uns erfreuen heimlich sehr, *Anon early 17th cent.* Eb [e'b-e''b], Thames 6 Songs.

Britten, Benjamin. 1913–1976.
Collections: *Poet's Echo, The,* Faber; *Sechs Hölderlin-Fragmente,* B&H; *Seven Sonnets of Michelangelo,* B&H.
A che più debb' io mai l'intensa voglia (Sonnet 31), *Michelangelo,* Cm [e'-a''](m), B&H 7 Sonnets.
Angel, *Pushkin,* [c'-g''], Faber Poet's Echo.
Die Heimat, *Friedrich Hölderlin,* A [e'b-g''], B&H Hölderlin.
Die Jugend, *Friedrich Hölderlin,* G [c'#-a''], B&H Hölderlin.
Die Linien des Lebens, *Friedrich Hölderlin,* Ebm [e'b-g''b], B&H Hölderlin.
Echo, *Pushkin,* [c'-a''b], Faber Poet's Echo.
Epigram, *Pushkin,* [e'-g''], Faber Poet's Echo.
Hälfte des Lebens, *Friedrich Hölderlin,* Bb [e'-a''b], B&H Hölderlin.
Lines written during a sleepless night, *Pushkin,* [c'-a''b], Faber Poet's Echo.
Menschenbeifall, *Friedrich Hölderlin,* F [e'b-g''], B&H Hölderlin.
My heart... *Pushkin,* [d'b-f''#], Faber Poet's Echo
Nightingale and the rose, The, *Pushkin,* [d'#-a''], Faber Poet's Echo.
Rendete a gli occhi miei, o fonte o fiume (Sonnet 38), *Michelangelo,* [f'-a''b](m), B&H 7 Sonnets.
Sì come nella penna e nell' inchiostro (Sonnet 16), *Michelangelo,* A [c'-a''](m), B&H 7 Sonnets.
Socrates und Alcibiades, *Friedrich Hölderlin,* D [c'#-a''b], B&H Hölderlin.
Spirto ben nato, in cui si specchia e vede (Sonnet 24), *Michelangelo,* [c'-a''](m), B&H 7 Sonnets.
S'un casto amor, s'una pietà superna (Sonnet 32), *Michelangelo,* [f'-f''#](m), B&H 7 Sonnets.
Tu sa' ch' io so, signior mie, che tu sai (Sonnet 55), *Michelangelo,* Bb [d'-a''](m), B&H 7 Sonnets.
Veggio co' bei vostri occhi un dolce lume (Sonnet 30), *Michelangelo,* G [d'-b''](m), B&H 7 Sonnets.
Arrangements: *Eight Folksong Arrangements,* Faber; *Folksongs Volume 2* (high, medium), B&H.
Bugeilio'r Gwenith Gwyn, *Anon,* Faber 8 Folksong arrangements.
Dafydd y Garreg Wen, *Anon,* Faber 8 Folksong arrangements.
Eho! Eho!, *Anon,* Am [a'-g''], B&H Folksongs 2; F#m, Folksongs 2;
Fileuse, *Anon,* G [d'-d''](f), B&H Folksongs 2.
Il est quelqu'un sur terre, *Anon,* Bbm [f'-f''](f), B&H Folksongs 2; Gm, Folksongs 2;
La belle est au jardin d'amour, *Anon,* Bb [f'-d''], B&H Folksongs 2.
La Noël passée, *Anon,* Bbm [f'-g''], B&H Folksongs 2; Gm, Folksongs 2;
Le roi s'en va-t'en chasse, *Anon,* Ab [e'b-e''b], B&H Folksongs 2.
Quand j'étais chez mon père, *Anon,* A [a'-e''](m), B&H Folksongs 2; G, Folksongs 2;
Voici le printemps, *Anon,* Gm [f'#-d''], B&H Folksongs 2.

Bullock, Dafydd. WMIC. (Scots, Spanish).

Burkinshaw, Sydney. WMIC. (French).

Butterworth, Neil.
Pour l'amour de ma douce amye, *Anon 14th century French,* [high], Oecamuse.

Cannon, Jack Philip. 1929–
Collection: *Cinq Chansons de Femme.* Kronos.
 La bien amée, *Anon,* Dm [c′-g″], Kronos Cinq Chansons.
 La bien mariée, *Olivier Basselin,* A [d′-a″(g″)], Kronos Cinq Chansons.
 La mal mariée *Anon* Dm [b♭-g″], Kronos Cinq Chansons.
 L'amoureuse *Anon,* Em [d′-g″#], Kronos Cinq Chansons.
 La veuve, *Christine de Pisan,* Fm [b♭-g″], Kronos Cinq Chansons.

Connolly, Justin Riveagh. 1933–
 Waka (cycle), *Japanese c.1000AD,* [mezzo], Chester.

Cresswell, Lyell. 1944–
Collection: *Three Songs,* SMIC.
 Il Nome, *Marco Bucchieri,* [soprano], SMIC 3 Songs.
 Novembre, *Marco Bucchieri,* [soprano], SMIC 3 Songs.
 Sfiorarci le Mani, *Marco Bucchieri,* [soprano], SMIC 3 Songs.

Crosse, Gordon. 1937–
Collection: *Three Songs to Medieval French Texts,* OUP.
 Aube, *Anon,* [b-e″](f), OUP 3 Songs.
 Motet One, *Anon,* [c′#-f″#](f), OUP 3 Songs.
 Motet Two, *Anon,* [b♭-f″#](f), OUP 3 Songs.

Delius, Frederick Theodore Albert. 1862–1934.
Collections: *Early Versions of Songs to Scandinavian Texts,* B&H; *Nineteen Songs,* OUP; *Sixteen Songs,* B&H; *Song Album,* B&H; *Twenty-two Songs,* S&B.
 Aus deinen Augen fliessen meine Lieder, *Heinrich Heine?* D♭ [e′♭-g″♭], S&B 22 Songs.
 Avant que tu t'en ailles, *Paul Verlaine,* [d′#-a″], B&H 16 Songs.
 Chanson d'Automne, *Paul Verlaine,* [b#-f″], OUP 19 Songs.
 Chanson de Fortunio, *Alfred de Musset,* G [b♭-f″#], S&B 22 Songs.
 Der Einsame, *Friedrich Nietzsche,* [d′-g″], B&H 16 Songs, Song Album.
 Der Fichtenbaum, *Heinrich Heine,* F [e′-f″], S&B 22 Songs.
 Der Wanderer, *Friedrich Nietzsche,* Gm [b-g″], B&H 16 Songs, Song Album.
 Der Wanderer und sein Schatten, *Friedrich Nietzsche,* C#m [c′-e″], B&H 16 Songs, Song Album.
 Det bødes der for, *Jens Peter Jacobsen,* [medium], B&H Early Versions.
 Efterår, *Ludvig Holstein,* [high], B&H Early Versions.
 Ein schöner Stern geht auf in meiner Nacht, *Heinrich Heine,* B [e′#-g″#], S&B 22 Songs.
 Hochgebirgsleben, *Hendrik Ibsen* tr. Passage, Fm [d′♭-c‴(a″♭)], S&B 22 Songs.
 Hör ich das Liedchen klingen, *Heinrich Heine,* A♭ [e′♭♭-a″♭], S&B 22 Songs.
 I Seraillets Have, *Jens Peter Jacobsen,* [high], B&H Early Versions.
 Il pleure dans mon coeur, *Paul Verlaine,* B♭m [c′#-f″#], OUP 19 Songs.
 Irmelin Rose, *Jens peter Jacobsen,* [medium], B&H Early Versions.
 Jeg hevde en nyskåren Seljefløjte, *Vilhelm Krag,* [medium], B&H Early Versions.
 Jeg hører I Natten, *Holger Drachmann,* [medium], B&H Early Versions.
 La lune blanche, *Paul Verlaine,* [c′-f″], OUP 19 Songs.
 Lad Våren komme, *Jens Peter Jacobsen,* [high], B&H Early Versions.
 Le ciel est, par-dessus le toit, *Paul Verlaine,* [d′♭-g″♭], OUP 19 Songs.
 Løft de klingre Glaspokaler, *Jens Peter Jacobsen,* [medium], B&H Early Versions.
 Lyse Nœtter, *Holger Drachmann,* (1st version), [high], B&H Early Versions.
 Lyse Nœtter, *Holger Drachmann,* (2nd version), [medium], B&H Early Versions.
 Mit deinen blauen Augen, *Heinrich Heine,* F [e′♭-a″], S&B 22 Songs.
 Nach neuen Meeren, *Friedrich Nietzsche,* C#m [d′-f″#], B&H 16 Songs, Song Album.
 Noch ein Mal, *Friedrich Nietzsche,* B [B-d′#](m), B&H 16 Songs.
 Nuages, *Jean Richepin,* D♭ [e-g″♭], S&B 22 Songs.
 O schneller mein Ross, *Emanuel Geibel,* D [d′-b″♭(g″)], S&B 22 Songs.
 Pågen højt på Tårnet sad, *Jens Peter Jacobsen,* [high], B&H Early Versions.
 Silkeski over gylden Løst, *Jens Peter Jacobsen,* [medium], B&H Early Versions.
 Skogen gir susende, langsam besked, *Bjørnstjerne Bjørnson,* [medium], B&H Early Versions.
 Sommer I Gurre, *Holger Drachmann,* [medium], B&H Early Versions.
 Svartor Rosor, *Ernst Josephson,* [medium], B&H Early Versions.
 Traum Rosen, *Marie Heinitz,* E♭ [b♭-e″♭], S&B 22 Songs.
 Vi lo jo før så lœnge, *Holger Drachmann,* [medium], B&H Early Versions.
 Viol, *Ludvig Holstein,* [medium], B&H Early Versions.
 Zwei braune Augen, *Hans Christian Andersen,* G [b-c″#], S&B 22 Songs.

Dieren, Bernard van. 1887–1936.
   Chanson, *Nicolas Boileau Despréaux*, [d′b-f′′], BMP.
   Der Asra, *Heinrich Heine*, [b-f′′#], BMP.
   Epiphanias, *Goethe*, [c′-a′′b], BMP.
   Ich wanderte unter den Bäumen, *Heinrich Heine*, [c′#-f′′#], BMP.
   Les Contemplations, *Victor Hugo*, [d′-f′′#], BMP.
   Les Rayons et les Ombres, *Victor Hugo*, c′#-f′′#], BMP.
   Mädchenlied, *Otto Julius Bierbaum*, [b-f′′], BMP.
   Mon bras pressait la taille frêle, *see* Les Contemplations.
   Oh! quand je dors, *see* Les Rayons et les Ombres.
   Rondel, *Charles d'Orleans*, [d′-a′′], BMP.
   Schöne Rohtraut, *E. Mörike*, [b-a′′], BMP.
   Spleen, *Paul Verlaine*, [d′-g′′], BMP.
Arrangement:
   Mon coeur se recommande à vous, *Orlando di Lasso*, [d′-g′′], BMP.

Doyle, Patrick.
   Aoibhneas Thír-na N-Óg, *Traditional*, Dm [a-e′′], Weinberger/Elkin.
   Non nobis, Domine, [d′-g′′], Weinberger/Elkin.

Elias, Brian. 1948–
Collection: *Two Songs*, Chester.
   Chanson d'automne, *Paul Verlaine*, [bb-b′′](f), Chester 2 Songs.
   Le ciel est, par dessus le toit, *Paul Verlaine*, [c′-a′′](f), Chester 2 Songs.

Fryer, Herbert. 1877–1957.
   Dormi, Jesu, *Anon* (Latin), F [f′-f′′], B&H *Heritage 1*.

Gange, Kenneth Edward. WMIC. (French).

Gerhard, Roberto. 1896–1970.
Arrangements: *Six Catalan Folksongs*, B&H, *see* main catalogue; *Cancionero*, B&H.
   Alalá, *Galicia*, C#m [b-g′′], B&H Cancionero.
   Correndes, *Valencia*, E [e′-e′′], B&H Cancionero.
   Farruquiño, *Galicia*, C [g′-g′′], B&H Cancionero.
   La mal maridada, *Catalonia*, [f′#-f′′#], B&H Cancionero.
   La Ximbomba, *Majorca*, D [d′-c′′], B&H Cancionero.
   Laieta, *Catalonia*, E [g′#-f′′#], B&H Cancionero.
   Muera yo..., *Asturia*, B [a′#-f′′#], B&H Cancionero.
   Soledad, *Asturia*, Am [e′-e′′], B&H Cancionero.

Goehr, Peter **Alexander.** 1932–
   Das Gesetz der Quadrille (cycle), *Franz Kafka*, [ab-e′′], Schott.

Goossens, Eugene. 1893–1962.
Collection: *Two Proses Lyriques*, Chester.
   Hier, dans la jardin ensoleillé, *Edwin Evans*, [f′#-a′′], Chester Proses Lyriques.
   Mon chemin c'était assombri, *Edwin Evans*, [e′-f′′#], Chester Proses Lyriques.

Grainger, Percy. 1882–1961.
Arrangement:
   Kjær lighede Styrke, *Anon (Danish)*, [g′#-g′′](f), Thames 13 Folksongs 2, Schirmer 13 Folksongs.

Grant, Julian. BMIC. (Italian).

Green, David Llewellyn.
   Rêve d'amour, Brunton.

Handel, George Frideric. 1685–1757.
Collection: *Songs and Cantatas*, BMP (edited with preface and notes Donald Burrowes).
   Air en langue Allemande, *Anon*, [f′#-g′′#], BMP Songs.
   Air en langue Espagnole, *Anon*, [e′-f′′], BMP Songs.
   Chanson (Quand on suit l'amoureuse), *Anon*, [e′-g′′], BMP Songs.
   Chanson (Sans y pense), *Anon*, [d′-f′′], BMP Songs.

Head, Michael Dewar. 1900–1976.
    Ave Maria, Am [a-e''], B&H; Cm, B&H.
    O gloriosa Domina, G [d'-g''], B&H.
    Sancta et Immaculata Virginitas, *St Augustine*, Em [e'-g''#], B&H.

Headington, Christopher John Magenis. 1930–1996.
Collection: *Three Rilke Songs,* Bardic.
    Die Flamingos, *Rainer Maria Rilke,* [c'-g''], Bardic 3 Rilke.
    Herbst, *Rainer Maria Rilke,* [c'-f''#], Bardic 3 Rilke.
    Lied vom Meer, *Rainer Maria Rilke,* [e'b-g''], Bardic 3 Rilke.

Hearne, John. 1937–
Collection: *Songs for the North,* Longship.
    Einsetumadur einu sinni..., *Icelandic traditional,* [medium], Longship For the North.
    Myndlaus, *Steinn Steinarr,* [medium], Longship For the North.
    Sumarnott, *Jön ür Vör,* [medium], Longship For the North.

Hopkins, Antony. 1921–
Arrangements: *Five French Folk Songs,* Chester.
    Gai lon la, *Quebec-Canada,* Eb [e'-e''b](f), Chester 5 French.
    Hollaïka, *Bretagne,* Gb [g'b-e''b](f), Chester 5 French.
    (La bergère aux champs, *Anon,* A [e'-e''(a'')](f), Chester.)
    (Le Roi Renaud, *Anon,* Dm [a-d''], Chester.)
    Les trois rubans, *Bretagne,* Gb [d'b-d''b](f), Chester 5 French.
    Me suis mise en danse, *Bas Quercy,* E [e'-e''](f), Chester 5 French.
    Quand mon mari se fâchera, *Bretagne,* G [d'-d''](f), Chester 5 French.
    (Recueillement, *Charles Beaudelaire,* [cb(d')-g''], Chester.)

Jeffreys, George. c.1610–1685.
Collection: *Two Devotional Songs,* Novello, (Introduction and Notes Peter Aston).
    O quam suave, *Phillippians 2. vv. 9-10,* Dm [D-d'](m), Novello 2 Devotional.
    Speciosus forma, *Psalm 45. v. 2,* Am [C(B)-d'](m), Novello 2 Devotional.

Jones, Richard Elfyn. WMIC. (French).

Kennedy-Fraser, Marjory. 1857–1930.
    Eriskay Love Lilt, An, *Anon, (Gaelic),* A [e'-f''#], B&H *Ballad Album 2*; G, B&H *Souvenirs,* B&H, Classical.

Kirkwood, Antoinette.
    Der Schiffbrüchige, *Heinrich Heine,* [a-a''], Bardic.
    Krönung, *Heinrich Heine,* [bb-b''b], Bardic.

Lehmann, Liza Elizabeth (Nina Mary Frederika). 1862–1918.
    Die Nachtigall, als ich sie fragte, *Friedrich Bodenstedt,* Dm [d'-f''], S&B (Bush) *MB 56.*
    Im Rosenbusch, *Hoffmann von Fallersleben,* Db [d'b-g''b(b''b)], S&B (Bush) *MB 56.*

Locke, Matthew. c. 1622–1677.
    Bone Jesu verbum patris, *Anon,* [c'-f''#], S&B Songs and Dialogues of Matthew Locke.

MacDonald, Malcolm Calum. 1948–
Collection: *Six Early Songs,* Bardic.
    Ed è sùbito sera, *Salvatore Quasimodo,* [g-g''], Bardic 6 Early.

McGregor, Richard. (SMIC).
    Vita d'un Uomo, [soprano], SMIC.

McLeod, John. 1934–
Collection: *Lieder der Jugend,* Griffin.
    Chansons de la Nuit et du Brouillard [cycle], *Jean Cayrol,* [soprano], Griffin.
    Das irdische Leben, *Das Knaben Wunderhorn,* [tenor], Griffin Lieder.
    Der Tamboursg'sell, *Das Knaben Wunderhorn,* [tenor], Griffin Lieder.
    Selbstgefuhl, *Das Knaben Wunderhorn,* [tenor], Griffin Lieder.
    Wo die schönen Trompeten blasen, *Das Knaben Wunderhorn,* [tenor], Griffin Lieder.

Matthews, Colin. 1946–
    Un Colloque Sentimental (cycle), *Verlaine, Baudelaire, de Nerval,* [a-g''#(f''#)], Faber.

Muldowney, Dominic John. 1952–
  Five Theatre Poems (cycle), *Bertolt Brecht,* [G-f´], Universal.

Musgrave, Thea. 1928-
  Collection: *Two Songs* (Swedish), [baritone], Novello hire.

Nevens, David. WMIC. (Spanish).

Nyman, Michael. 1944–
  Collection: *Six Celan Songs,* Chester.
    Anne de Lucy Songs (cycle), *Fray Luis de León,* [g-b´´](f), Chester .
    Blume, *Paul Celan,* [g-g´´#(e´´)](f), Chester 5 Celan.
    Chanson einer Dame in Schatten, *Paul Celan,* [f-g´´](f), Chester 5 Celan.
    Corona, *Paul Celan,* [f-f´´](f), Chester 5 Celan.
    Es war Erde in ihnen, *Paul Celan,* [g-d´´b](f), Chester 5 Celan.
    Nächlich geschürzt, *Paul Celan,* [eb(f)-d´´](f), Chester 5 Celan.
    Psalm, *Paul Celan,* [f-e´´(e´´b)](f), Chester 5 Celan.

Orr, Robin. 1909– BMIC. (German).
  Liebeslied, *Rainer Maria Rilke,* [mezzo], SMIC.

Painter, Christopher William. WMIC. (French).

Parry, Sir Charles **Hubert** Hastings. 1848–1918.
  Arrangement:
    Von edler Art, *Anon,* Eb[c´-e´´b], B&H.

Poole, Geoffrey. 1949–
  Collection: *Fünf Brecht Lieder,* Maecenas.
    Abgesang, *Berthold Brecht,* [F-f´](m), Maecenas Brecht.
    Alles wandelt sich, *Berthold Brecht,* [Ab-e´b], Maecenas Brecht.
    Der Pfaufenbaum, *Berthold Brecht,* [e-g´](m), Maecenas Brecht.
    Finnland 1940, *Berthold Brecht,* [sprechgesang](m), Maecenas Brecht.
    O Lust des Beginnens, *Berthold Brecht,* [G-e´#(b´)](m), Maecenas Brecht.

Powers, Anthony. 1953– BMIC. (French).
  Souvenirs du Voyage (cycle), *Baudelaire,* [soprano], OUP.

Purcell, Henry. 1659–1695.
  Incassum Lesbia, *see* The Queen's Epicedium.
  Queen's Epicedium, The, *Mr Herbert,* Cm [d´-a´´b], Britten, Kagen 4a, Laurie 4; *Am,*
    Kagen 4b.

Quilter, Roger. 1877–1953.
  Collection: *Four Songs of Mirza Schaffy Op 2* [high], Classical, ([*high,* low] Elkin).
    Die helle Sonne leuchtet, *Friedrich Bodenstedt, Ab* [e´b-a´´b], Classical/Elkin 4 Songs *high*; (F,
      Elkin 4 Songs low).
    Ich fühle deinen Odem, *Friedrich Bodenstedt, F* [e´-a´´b(f´´)], Classical/Elkin 4 Songs *high*; (Db,
      Elkin 4 Songs low).
    Neig' schöne Knospe! Dich zu mir!, *Friedrich Bodenstedt, Bb* [f´-g´´] Classical/Elkin 4 Songs *high*;
      (G, Elkin 4 Songs low).
    Und was die Sonne glüht, *Friedrich Bodenstedt, Bbm* [f´-g´´b], Classical/Elkin 4 Songs *high*; (Gm,
      Elkin 4 Songs low).

Rawsthorne, Alan. 1905–1971.
  Collection: (*Trois Chansons de Nourrice,* B&H.)
    (Fais do-do, Pierrot, *Anon,* Bm [f´#-f´´#], B&H 3 Chansons.)
    (Il pleut, il pleut, bergère, *Anon,* Em [e´-f´´#], B&H 3 Chansons.)
    (Je suis un petit poupon, *Anon,* C [f´#-f´´], B&H 3 Chansons.)
    Nous étions trois filles, *Anon,* [e´-a´´], BMP.

Roberton, Sir **Hugh S**tevenson. 1874–1952,
  Arrangement:
    Null do dh' Uidhist, *Archibald MacDonald,* (tune John R. Bannerman), G [d´-e´´], Roberton.

Rubbra, Edmund. 1901–1986.
  Salve, Regina, *Hermann?* [f-c´´#], Lengnick.

Salzedo, Leonard Lopès. 1921– BMIC. (Spanish).

Searle, Humphrey. 1915–1982. BMIC. (French).

Short, Michael. 1937– SMIC. (French).
Sur la Rivière, [medium], SMIC.
Un soir: Les Horloges, SMIC.

Smyth, Dame **Ethel.** 1858–1944.
Collection: (*Lieder*, Peters).
(Anacreontic Ode, *Leconte de Lisle,* Fm [c′-g′′](m), Novello.)
(Chrysilla, *Henri de Regnier,* E♭ [b♭-f′′♭], Novello.)
(Dance, The, *Henri de Regnier,* Em [b-e′′], Novello.)
(Mittagsruh, *J. von Eichendorff,* Fm [c′-f′′], Peters Lieder.)
(Nachtgedanken, *Paul Heyse,* C#m [c′#-g′′], Peters Lieder.)
(Nachtreiter, *Klaus Groth,* E [c′#-f′′#], Peters Lieder.)
(Odelette, *Henri de Regnier,* Cm [c′-a′′♭], Novello.)
(Schlummerlied, *E. von Wildenbruch,* C [c′-e′′], Peters Lieder.)
(Tanzlied, *Georg Büchner,* Gm [c′#-f′′#], Peters Lieder.)

Sorabji, Kaikhosru Shapurji. 1892–1988. BMIC. (French).
Collection: (*Trois Fêtes Galants,* Curwen).
(À la Promenade, *Paul Verlaine,* [c′-g′′#], Curwen 3 Fêtes.)
(Dans la Grotte, *Paul Verlaine,* [a#-g′′], Curwen 3 Fêtes.)
(L'allée, *Paul Verlaine,* [e′-g′′], Curwen 3 Fêtes.)

Stanford, Sir **Charles Villiers.** 1852–1924.
Collection: *Twelve Songs by Heine,* S&B.
An die blaue Himmelsdecke, *Heinrich Heine,* E♭ [c′-g′′], S&B 12 Songs.
Dass du mich liebst, *Heinrich Heine,* E♭ [e′♭-g′′], S&B 12 Songs.
Der Schmetterling ist in die Rose verliebt, *Heinrich Heine,* D [d′-f′′#], S&B 12 Songs.
Der sterbende Almansor, *Heinrich Heine,* E♭m [b♭-g′′], S&B 12 Songs.
Die Wallfahrt nach Kevlaar, *Heinrich Heine,* D♭ [c′-a′′♭], B&H.
Ernst ist der Frühling, *Heinrich Heine,* Em [d′#-f′′#], S&B 12 Songs.)
Frühling, *Heinrich Heine,* A♭ [d′-f′′#(a′′♭)], S&B 12 Songs.
Ich halte ihr die Augen zu, *Heinrich Heine,* B [c′#-f′′#], S&B 12 Songs.
Ich lieb' eine Blume, *Heinrich Heine,* D♭ [c′-f′′], S&B 12 Songs.
Le bien vient en dormant, *Anon,* E♭ [e′♭-g′′](m), S&B MB 52.
Mit deinen blauen Augen, *Heinrich Heine,* G [f′-g′′], S&B 12 Songs.
Schlummerlied, *Heinrich Heine,* D [d′-e′′], S&B 12 Songs.
Sterne mit den goldnen Füsschen, *Heinrich Heine,* D [c′#-f′′#], S&B MB 52, 12 Songs.
Tragödie, *Heinrich Heine,* Am [c′-f′′], B&H.
Wie des Mondes Abbild zittert, *Heinrich Heine,* E♭ [d′-f′′], S&B 12 Songs.

Stevenson, Ronald. 1928–
Collection: *Four Songs,* Stevenson Society.
Herbst, *Christian Morgenstern,* [medium-high], Stevenson 4 Songs.
Liederbuchlein fur Regina Beate, (cycle), *Christian Morgenstern,* [soprano], Stevenson.
Stör' Nicht, *Christian Morgenstern,* [medium-high], Stevenson 4 Songs.
Wasserfall bei Nacht 1, *Christian Morgenstern,* [medium-high], Stevenson 4 Songs.
Wasserfall bei Nacht 2, *Christian Morgenstern,* [medium-high], Stevenson 4 Songs.

Swann, Donald. 1923–1994.
Je suis le Ténébreux, *Gérard de Nerval,* E [b-e′′](m), Thames 6 Poetic Songs.

Swayne, Giles Oliver Cairns. 1946–
La Rivière, Op 1, [high], Chester hire.

Thomas, Arthur Goring. 1850–1892.
Les papillons, *Théophile Gautier,* B♭ [e′♭-g′′](m), S&B (Bush) *MB 56.*
S'il est un charmant gazon, *Victor Hugo,* E [e′-g′′#], S&B (Bush) *MB 56.*

Tomlinson, Ernest.
Collection: *Three German Lyrics,* Electrophonic.
Die Rosen, *Helmut Friedmann,* [soprano *or* tenor], Electrophonic 3 German Lyrics.

Frühlingslied, *Helmut Friedmann*, [soprano *or* tenor], Electrophonic 3 German Lyrics.
Im Ginster, *Helmut Friedmann*, [soprano *or* tenor], Electrophonic 3 German Lyrics.

Vaughan Williams, Ralph. 1872–1958.
Arrangements: *Two French Folksongs*, BMP.
　　L'amour de moy, *Anon 15th century*, C [c′-d′′], B&H Song Album 1.
　　Reveillez-vous Piccarz, *Anon, 15th century*, Em [d′-e′′](m), B&H Song Album 1.

Warlock, Peter (Philip Arnold Heseltine). 1894–1930.
Arrangements: *French Airs*, BMP.

Weir, Judith. 1954–
　　Spanish Liederbooklet, A (cycle), *Anon*, [e′b-a′′](f), Chester.
　　Stänchen, *Ludwig Rellstab*, [baritone], Chester.

Wellesz, Egon. 1885–1974.
　　Ode an die Musik, *Pindar* tr. *Hölderlin*, [mezzo/baritone], Universal.

White, Maude Valérie. 1855–1937.
Collection: *Six Songs*, Classical.
　　Anfangs wollt' ich fast verzagen, *Heinrich Heine*, Ab [e′-d′′b], S&B (Bush) *MB 56*.
　　Aus meinen Thränen spriessen, *Heinrich Heine*, D [d′-e′′], S&B (Bush) *MB 56*.
　　Des Kindes Abendgebet, *Anon*, G [e′-e′′], Classical 6 Songs.
　　Die Himmelsaugen, *Heinrich Heine*, Bb [d′-d′′], S&B (Bush) *MB 56*.
　　Ein Jüngling liebt ein Mädchen, *Heinrich Heine*, Fm [b-d′′b], S&B (Bush) *MB 56*.
　　Ein Stern, *Heinrich Heine*, E [d′#-g′′#], Classical 6 Songs.
　　Es muss doch Frühling werden, *Emmanuel Giebel*, A [e′-g′′#], Classical 6 Songs.
　　Frühling und Liebe, *Hoffmann von Fallersleben*, G [f′#-g′′], Classical 6 Songs.
　　Im wunderschönen Monat Mai, *Heinrich Heine*, E [b-e′′], S&B (Bush) *MB 56*.
　　Liebe, *Heinrich Heine*, C#m [g#-c′′#], S&B (Bush) *MB 56*.
　　Parle moi, *Alphonse de Lamartine*, Db [d′b-d′′b], S&B (Bush) *MB 56*.
　　Ton nom, *Sully-Prudhomme*, Eb [f′-f′′], S&B (Bush) *MB 56*.

Wilby, Philip. 1949–
Collection: *Ten Songs of Paul Verlaine: Melancholie, Paysage Triste,* Chester.
　　Après trois ans, *Paul Verlaine*, [e′-b-e′′], Chester Melancholie.
　　Chanson d'automne, *Paul Verlaine*, [d′-f′′#], Chester Paysage Triste.
　　Crépuscule du soir mystique, *Paul Verlaine*, [e′b-g′′ or a-e′′], Chester Paysage Triste.
　　L'angoisse, *Paul Verlaine*, [b-e′′(a′′)], Chester Melancholie.
　　Le rossignol, *Paul Verlaine*, [a-f′′#], Chester Paysage Triste.
　　L'heure du berger, *Paul Verlaine*, [e′b-e′′b], Chester Paysage Triste.
　　Mon rêve familier, *Paul Verlaine*, [c′-g′′#], Chester Melancholie.
　　Nevermore, *Paul Verlaine*, [d′#-e′′], Chester Melancholie.
　　Soleils couchants, *Paul Verlaine*, [b-g′′], Chester Paysage Triste.
　　Voie, *Paul Verlaine*, [b-e′′], Chester Melancholie.

Williams, Grace Mary. 1906–1977. WMIC. (French).

Wishart, Peter. 1921–1984.
Collection: *Twelve Songs*, S&B.
　　Quatre petits nègres blancs, *Anon*, E [b-e′′], S&B 12 Songs.

Woolrich, John. 1954–
Collection: *Five Italian Songs*, Faber.

Young, Derek. 1929–
Collection: *Das Buch der Bilder,* Lynwood.
　　Der Knabe, *Rainer Maria Rilke*, [Bb-d′](m), Lynwood Das Buch.
　　Einsamkeit, *Rainer Maria Rilke*, [A-d′](m), Lynwood Das Buch.
　　Herbsttag, *Rainer Maria Rilke*, [Bb-d′(e′)](m), Lynwood Das Buch.
　　Ritter, *Rainer Maria Rilke*, [G#-d′](m), Lynwood Das Buch.

Appendix 2: Other accompaniments

Note: English and foreign texts are included together in this section.

Adams, Stephen. (Michael Maybrick). 1844–1913.
    Holy City, The, *Fred. E. Weatherly*, A♭ [c′-e′′♭], OUP *Solo Sacred* [organ arr. Jenkins].
    Star of Bethlehem, The, *Fred. E. Weatherly*, G [d′-g′′], Mayhew *Holy Night* [organ].

Adès, Thomas. 1971–
    Aubade, *Philip Larkin*, [c#-d′′′](f) Faber hire [unaccompanied].
    Life Story, *Tennessee Williams*, [soprano], Faber hire [2 bass clarinets, double bass].

Aknai, Jeremy. 1977– BMIC [trumpet, tuba].

Allitsen, Frances. (Mary Francis Bumpus). 1848–1912.
    Lord is my light, The, *Psalm 27, vv. 1, 3, 5*, C [b-e′′], OUP *Solo Sacred* [organ arr. Jenkins].

Alwyn, William. 1905–1985.
Collection: *Seascapes*, Forsyth [treble recorder *or* flute, piano].
    Black Gulls, *Michael Armstrong*, [c′-b′′](f), Forsyth Seascapes.
    Dawn at Sea, *Michael Armstrong*, [a′-c′′′](f), Forsyth Seascapes.
    Sea-mist, *Michael Armstrong*, [g′-g′′](f), Forsyth Seascapes.
    Song of the Drowned Man, *Michael Armstrong*, [g′-b′′(a′′)](f), Forsyth Seascapes.

Anderson, Avril. 1953–
Collection: *Five Sephardic Songs*, Andresier [guitar]. (*See also* David Sutton-Anderson).
    Los bilbilcos, *Anon*, [d′-e′′], Andresier Five Sephardic.
    Noches, noches, *Anon*, [e′-e′′], Andresier Five Sephardic.

Anderson, Julian. 1967–
    I'm nobody who are you, *Emily Dickinson*, [tenor/high baritone], Faber hire [violin, piano].
    Seadrift, *Walt Whitman*, [soprano], Faber hire [flute/piccolo, clarinet, piano].

ApIvor, Denis. 1916– WMIC. [string quartet], [piccolo, violin, percussion], [string quintet].
Collection: *Seis Canciones, Op 8*, Bèrben [guitar].
    Canción de jinete, *Federico García Lorca*, [b-a′′♭], Bèrben Canciones.
    La guitarra, *Federico García Lorca*, [e′-g′′], Bèrben Canciones.
    La niña del bello rostro, *Federico García Lorca*, [c′-g′′], Bèrben Canciones.
    Pueblo, *Federico García Lorca*, [f′-g′′], Bèrben Canciones.
    Raíz amarga, *Federico García Lorca*, [c′#-g′′], Bèrben Canciones.
    Virgen con miriñaque, *Federico García Lorca*, [e′-g′′#], Bèrben Canciones.

Archer, Malcolm. 1952–
Arrangement:
    Child in the Manger, *Mary MacDonald* tr. *Lachlan Macbean*, D [d′-e′′], Mayhew *Holy Night* [organ].

Arne, Thomas. 1710–1778, arr. **Henry Lazarus.** 1815–1885.
    When daisies pied, *Shakespeare*, E♭ [b♭-e′′♭](f), Emerson [clarinet, piano].
    Wood Nymph, A, [soprano], Schott [recorder *or* flute, piano; 2 violins, cello, ad lib].

Arnold, Samuel. 1740–1802.
    Elegy, *Anon*, G, [d′-g′′], OUP (Roberts) *Tuneful Voice* [harp].
    Midsummer Wish, The, *John Hawkesworth*, F [f′-g′′], OUP (Roberts) *Tuneful Voice* [harp].

Aston, Peter George. 1938–
Collection: *Five Songs of Crazy Jane*, Novello [unaccompanied].
    Crazy Jane Grown Old Looks at the Dancers, *W. B. Yeats*, [d′#-g′′](f), Novello 5 Songs.
    Crazy Jane Talks with the Bishop, *W. B. Yeats*, [d′-a′′♭](f), Novello 5 Songs.
    I am of Ireland, *W. B. Yeats*, Gm [d′-a′′♭](f), Novello 5 Songs.

Those dancing days are gone, *W. B. Yeats*, [e′-a′′](f), Novello 5 Songs.
Three Things, *W. B. Yeats*, [e′-a′′](f), Novello 5 Songs.

Atkinson, Geoffrey.
Collection: *Where the Heather Grows*, Bardic [treble instrument, piano].
John Anderson, my jo, *Robert Burns*, [b-d′′] or [d′-f′′], Bardic Where the Heather.

Atkinson, René. 1920–
Ave Maria, tr. *René Atkinson*, [e′-g′′], OUP *Solo Christmas high*; [c′-e′′b], *Solo Christmas low* [organ]

Bain, James Leith MacBeth. c.1860–1925.
Brother James' Air, [Psalm 23 in Scottish Psalter 1650], C [b′-f′′], OUP *Solo Sacred* [organ arr. Archer].

Bainbridge, Simon. 1952–
Song from Michelangelo, A, *Michelangelo*, [soprano], UMP [2 clarinets, viola, cello, double bass].

Ball, Derek.
Collection: *Five Settings 'Faerie Queen'*, [soprano], SMIC [bass viol, double bass].

Bantock, Sir **Granville.** 1868–1946.
Praise ye the Lord, *Psalm 150*, A♭ [c′-e′′b], Cramer [organ], B♭, Cramer.

Barlow, David Frederick. 1927–1975. BMIC. [unaccompanied].

Barrell, Bernard. 1919– BMIC. [unaccompanied].
Collections: *Five Shakespeare Songs*, Op 83, {d′-f′′#] Brunton [guitar]; *Three Songs*, Op 50, Brunton [guitar].
Come away, death, *Shakespeare*, [medium], Brunton 5 Shakespeare.
Gather ye rosebuds while ye may, *Robert Herrick*, [d′-f′′], Brunton 3 Songs.
Sigh no more, ladies, *Shakespeare*, [medium], Brunton 5 Shakespeare.
Tell me, where is fancy bred, *Shakespeare*, [medium], Brunton 5 Shakespeare.
When daisies pied, *Shakespeare*, [medium], Brunton 5 Shakespeare.
Whenas in silk my Julia goes, *Robert Herrick*, [e′-g′′], Brunton 3 Songs.
Why so pale and wan, *John Suckling*, [d-f′′], Brunton 3 Songs.
Ye spotted snakes, *Shakespeare*, [medium], Brunton 5 Shakespeare.

Barrell, Joyce. 1917–1989. BMIC. [unaccompanied].

Barrett, Richard. 1959–
Coigitum, *wordless*, [mezzo], UMP [alto flute, oboe d′amore, piano (3 pedals), percussion].
Lieder vom Wasser, *Elisabeth Borchers*, [soprano], UMP [bass clarinet, percussion, double bass].
Sounds, *Samuel Beckett*, [soprano], UMP [2 violins, viola, 2 cellos, tape].

Barry, Gerald. 1952–
Things that gain by being painted, *The Pillow Book of Sei Shonagon*, [singer], OUP hire [speaker, cello, piano].

Barton, Nicholas.
Collection: *Dear Lord (Six Animal Songs to God)*, Andresier [guitar].
Ant, The, *Anon*, [a-e′′], Andresier Dear Lord.
Crocodile, The, *Anon*, [e′-f′′#], Andresier Dear Lord.
Daddy-longlegs, The, *Anon*, [e′b-e′′b], Andresier Dear Lord.
Little Deer, The, *Anon*, [c′#-g′′], Andresier Dear Lord.
Nightingale, The, *Anon*, [d′-g′′], Andresier Dear Lord.
Spider, The, *Anon*, [e′-g′′], Andresier Dear Lord.

Bauld, Alison. 1944–
Egg, [tenor], Novello [flute, cello, percussion].
Humpty Dumpty, [tenor], Novello [flute, guitar].
I loved Miss Watson, [soprano], Novello [piano, trumpet].
Mad Moll, [soprano], Novello [unaccompanied].
One Pearl, [soprano/counter-tenor], Novello [string quartet].
One Pearl II, [soprano], Novello [alto flute, string quartet].

Bayford, Frank. 1941–
　In Terra Pax, *Willam Blake and Traditional,* [e′b-g′′#](f), Modus [clarinet, piano].

Beamish Sally. 1956–
　Collections: *Four Findrinny Songs,* [Donald Goodbrand Sanders], [soprano], SMIC [recorder]; *Three Winter Songs,* [Emily Dickinson], [soprano], SMIC [violin]; *Two Burns Songs,* SMIC [string quartet].
　　Ae fond kiss, *Robert Burns,* [mezzo], SMIC 2 Burns.
　　Buzz, *Emily Dickinson,* [soprano], SMIC [viola].
　　Cramasie Threid (Crimson Thread), *Betty McKellar,* [soprano], SMIC [cello].
　　De'ils awa wi' the Excise man, *Robert Burns,* [mezzo], SMIC 2 Burns.
　　In Dreaming, *Shakespeare,* [tenor], SMIC [2 treble viols, 2 tenor viols, 2 bass viols].
　　Madrigali, *Gesualdo,* [tenor], SMIC [flute/piccolo, oboe, clarinet.bass clarinet, horn, harp, double bass].
　　Magic Moments, *Crawford Little,* [high], SMIC [cello].
　　Mask, *Simon Lewis,* [voice], SMIC [unaccompanied].
　　Oracle Beach, *David Pownall,* [mezzo], SMIC [violin, cello, piano].
　　Sonnet, *Shakespeare,* [soprano], SMIC [flute, oboe d'amore, piano].
　　Tuscan Lullaby, *Anon,* [soprano], SMIC [2 clarinets, viola, cello, double bass].

Beat, Janet. SMIC.
　　Cat's cradle for the Nemuri-Neko, [female voice], SMIC [harp *or* guitar].
　　Landscapes, [tenor], SMIC [oboe].
　　Leaves of my brain, The, [soprano/tenor], SMIC [guitar].
　　Mitylene Mosaics, [soprano], SMIC [3 clarinets].

Bedford, David Vickerman. 1937–
　　Because he liked to be at home, *Kenneth Patchen,* [tenor], Universal [treble recorder (played by singer), harp].
　　Bird of the Mountain, The, *Kenneth Patchen,* [soprano], Bedford [2 clarinets, viola, cello, double bass].
　　Come in here, child, *Kenneth Patchen,* [d′-b′′](f) Bedford [amplified piano], (Universal).
　　Even now, *Ernest Dowson,* [soprano], Universal [2 clarinets, viola, cello, double bass].
　　Found in a Country Churchyard, *Gravestones,* [soprano], Bedford [2 clarinets, viola, cello, double bass].
　　Holy Thursday with Squeakers, *William Blake,* [soprano], Universal [electric piano, viola/organ, soprano saxophone/bassoon, percussion].
　　I thirst for shadows, *Federico García Lorca,* [counter-tenor], Bedford [unaccompanied].
　　Inventress of the Vocal Frame, *John Dryden,* [counter-tenor], Bedford [harpsichord, 2 baroque violins, baroque cello].
　　Juniper Tree, The, *Terry Bagg,* [soprano], Universal [recorder, harpsichord].
　　Maggie's Farewell, *Mrs Thatcher,* [soprano], Bedford [2 clarinets, viola, cello, double bass].
　　Music for Albion Moonlight, *Kenneth Patchen,* [soprano], Universal [flute, clarinet, melodica, piano, violin, cello].
　　O now the drenched land awakes, *Kenneth Patchen,* [baritone], Bedford, [piano duet], (Universal).
　　OCD Band and the Minotaur, The, *Elisabeth Gorla,* [soprano], Universal [flute, clarinet, violin, cello, electric guitar, piano].
　　Tentacles of the dark nebula, The, *Arthur C. Clarke,* [tenor], Universal [3 violins, 2 violas, double bass].
　　Vocoder Sextet, *David Bedford,* [vocalist], Universal [flute, clarinet, violin, cello, EMS recorder].

Belben, Philip.
　Collection: *Songs of Silver,* Da Capo [flute, harp].
　　Inside the pillar of white fire, *Tanith Lee,* [soprano], Da Capo Songs of Silver.
　　Rose by any other name, A, *Tanith Lee,* [soprano], Da Capo Songs of Silver.

Benjamin, George. 1960–
　　Upon Silence, *W. B. Yeats,* [mezzo], Faber [1 treble/bass. 2 tenor, 2 bass viols].

Bennard, George. 1873–1958.
　　Old rugged cross, The, *George Bennard,* B♭ [d′-e′′♭], OUP *Solo Sacred* [organ arr. Archer].

Bennett, Richard Rodney. 1936–
　　Crazy Jane, *W. B. Yeats,* [soprano], Novello [clarinet, cello, piano].
　　Nightpiece, *Charles Baudelaire,* [f′-c′′′#](f), Universal, [tape].
　　Time's Whiter Series, [counter-tenor], Novello hire [lute].
　　(Tom O'Bedlams Song, *Anon,* [c′-a′′♭](m), Novello hire [cello].)

Bergmann, Walter George. 1902–1998.
  Pastorale, [alto], Schott [recorder *or* flute].

Berkeley, Sir **Lennox** Randall Francis. 1902–1989.
  Collections: *Songs of the Half-light*, Chester [guitar]; *Five Herrick Poems Op 89*, Chester [harp].
  All that's past, *Walter de la Mare*, Am [e′-a′′], Chester Half-light.
  Dearest of thousands, *Robert Herrick*, [f′b-g′′b], Chester Herrick.
  Fleeting, The, *Walter de la Mare*, [f′-g′′#], Chester Half-light.
  Full Moon, *Walter de la Mare*, D [d′-g′′], Chester Half-light.
  If nine times you your bridegroom kiss, *Robert Herrick*, [f′-g′′], Chester Herrick.
  Moth, The, *Walter de la Mare*, [e′-a′′], Chester Half-light.
  My God, look on me, *Robert Herrick*, [e′-g′′], Chester Herrick.
  Now is your turne, *Robert Herrick*, [d′-g′′], Chester Herrick.
  Rachel, *Walter de la Mare*, Em [g′-g′′], Chester Half-light.
  These springs were maidens once, *Robert Herrick*, [f′-g′′b], Chester Herrick.
  (Una and the Lion, Op 98, *Edmund Spenser*, [soprano], Chester [recorder, viola da gamba, harpsichord].)

Berkeley, Michael. 1948–
Collection: *Wessex Graves*, OUP [harp]. Medium key version available on hire.
  Ah, are you digging my grave? *Thomas Hardy*, [c′-a′′], OUP Wessex Graves.
  Drummer Hodge, *Thomas Hardy*, [e′-g′′], OUP Wessex Graves.
  Grenadier, The, *A. E. Housman*, [d′-a′′](f), OUP [violin, cello].
  Her Secret, *Thomas Hardy*, [e′b-b′′b], OUP Wessex Graves.
  In the Moonlight, *Thomas Hardy*, [c′#-g′′#], OUP Wessex Graves.
  Rain, *Edward Thomas*, [tenor], OUP hire [violin, cello].
  She at His Funeral, *Thomas Hardy*, [b′-b′′b], OUP Wessex Graves.

Bingham, Judith. 1952–
  Cathedral of Trees, The, *David Lyons*, [bb-b′′b], Maecenas [unaccompanied].
  Ghost of a Candle, The, *Judith Bingham*, [f-e′b](C-Tenor), Maecenas [lute].
  Unheimlich, *Judith Bingham*, [bb-b′′b](f), Maecenas [treble recorder].

Birtwistle, Sir **Harrison** Paul. 1934–
Collection: *Nine Settings of Celan*, (German & English), B&H [2 clarinets, viola, cello, double bass].
  Deowa, [soprano], Universal [clarinet].
  Eye, open, An, (Ein Auge, offen), *Paul Celan* tr. *Paul Hamburger*, [a(b)-c′′′], B&H 9 Celan.
  Four Songs of Autumn (cycle), *Anon*, [soprano], Universal [string quartet].
  Give the Word, *Paul Celan* tr. *Paul Hamburger*, [f′-a′′b], B&H 9 Celan.
  La plage, *Alain Robbe-Grillet*, Universal [3 clarinets, piano, marimba].
  Monody for Corpus Christe, *Anon, Martin Luther* tr. *Wedderburn*, [soprano], Universal [flute, violin, horn].
  Night, (Nacht), *Paul Celan* tr. *Paul Hamburger*, [b-c′′′], B&H 9 Celan.
  Nine Settings of Lorine Niedecker (cycle), *Lorine Neidecker*, [c′-b′′](f), B&H hire [cello].
  Psalm, *Paul Celan* tr. *Paul Hamburger*, [c′-b′′b], B&H 9 Celan.
  Ring a dumb carillon, *Christopher Logue*, [soprano], Universal [clarinet, percussion].
  Tenebrae, *Paul Celan* tr. *Paul Hamburger*, [c′-b′′], B&H 9 Celan.
  Thread Suns, (Fadensonnen), *Paul Celan* tr. *Paul Hamburger*, [c′-b′′], B&H 9 Celan.
  Todtnauberg, *Paul Celan* tr. *Paul Hamburger*, [e′-g′′], B&H 9 Celan.
  White and Light, (Weise und Leicht), *Paul Celan* tr. *Paul Hamburger*, [c′-a′′], B&H 9 Celan.
  With Letter and Clock, (Mit Brief und Uhr), *Paul Celan* tr. *Paul Hamburger*, [e′-b′′], B&H 9 Celan.

Bishop, Sir **Henry.** 1786–1855.
  Lo, here the gentle lark, *Shakespeare*, F [e-a′′(c′′′)], Cramer [flute, piano]. Classical (Deis), [flute, piano].

Blake, David Leonard. 1936–
Collection: *Five Heine Songs,* Novello [oboe *or* clarinet, piano].
  Der Asra, *Heinrich Heine*, [baritone], Novello 5 Heine.
  Heimkehr, *Heinrich Heine*, [baritone], Novello 5 Heine.
  Lumpentum, *Heinrich Heine*, [baritone], Novello 5 Heine.
  Solidität, *Heinrich Heine*, [baritone], Novello 5 Heine.
  Weltlauf, *Heinrich Heine*, [baritone], Novello 5 Heine.

Blake, Howard. 1938–
    Coronach, [mezzo], Chester [string quartet].
    Fear no more the heat of the sun, *Shakespeare,* [Counter-tenor], Chester [organ].
    Shakespeare Songs, [tenor], Chester hire [string quartet].
    Toccata of Galuppi's, A, *Robert Browning,* [baritone], Chester hire [harpsichord].)
    Wedding is great Juno's crown, *Shakespeare,* [soprano], Chester [organ].

Bliss, Sir **Arthur** Drummond. 1891–1975.
Collections: *Two Nursery Rhymes,* Chester [clarinet in A, piano]; *Four Songs for Voice, Violin and Piano,* Novello.
    Christmas Carol, A, *Arthur S. Cripps,* B♭ [e′b-g′′], Novello 4 Songs [violin, piano].
    Dandelion, The, *Frances Cornford,* Em [e′-g′′](f), Chester 2 Nursery [clarinet *or* viola].
    Elegiac Sonnet, *Cecil Day-Lewis,* [tenor],Novello [2 violins, viola, cello, piano].
    Mad Woman of Punnet's Town, The, *L. A. G. Strong,* [d′-a′′], Novello 4 Songs [violin, piano].
    Madam Noy, *E. H. W. Meyerstein,* [soprano], Chester [flute, clarinet, bassoon, harp, viola, double bass].
    Ragwort, The *Frances Cornford,* E [f′#-g′′#](f), Chester 2 Nursery [clarinet *or* viola, piano].
    Rout, *Arthur Bliss,* [soprano], Curwen [piano duet].
    Sea Love, *Charlotte Mew,* [c′-f′#](f), Novello 4 Songs, [violin].
    Vocalise, D [f′#-a′′], Novello 4 Songs [violin].

Blow, John. 1649–1708.
    Oh! that mine eyes would melt, *Anon,* Gm [d′-a′′], Faber (Britten) *Harmonia* [harp].

Blyton, Carey. 1932–2002. BMIC [string quartet].
Collection: *Moresques,* Fentone [flute, harp, piano]; *What then is Love?* Roberton [clarinet in A, piano].
    Blue Christmas, *Peter Westmore,* Cm [c′-f′′], Modus [organ *or* keyboard, optional double bass].
    Love is a sickness full of woes, *Samuel Daniel,* [d′-f′′](f), Roberton What is Love.
    Love-song of the Lady of Granada, *David Munro,* F [c′-a′′b](f), Fentone Moresques.
    Maiden Deceived, The (cycle), *Traditional,* [c′-f′′(c′′′)], Modus [clarinet in B♭, horn, piano].
    Robin Redbreast, *Carey Blyton,* [c′-e′′b], Modus. [organ].
    Simoom, *David Munro,* E♭ [c′-a′′b](f), Fentone Moresques.
    Stay, O sweet, and do not rise, *John Donne,* Dm [e′-e′′](f), Roberton What is Love.
    Symphony in Yellow, *Oscar Wilde,* [c′#-g′′], B&H [harp].
    Tell me where is fancy bred? *Shakespeare,* [d′-g′′](f), Roberton What is Love.
    Western wind, when will thou blow, *Anon,* G [f′-g′′](f), Roberton What is Love.
    Yellow Flower, A, *David Munro,* A [c′#-g′′#](f), Fentone Moresques.
Arrangement:
    Rose and the Nightingale, The, *Rimsky-Korsakov,* Fm [f′-f′′], Fand.

Boulter, Brian.
    Vocalise (no text), [soprano], Da Capo [flute, cello].

Boyle, Ina.
    Thinke then, my soule, [tenor], BMP [string quartet].

Boyle, Rory. 1951–
Collections: *Four Greek Love Songs,* [soprano], SMIC [violin]; *Three Religious Songs,* [George Herbert], [counter-tenor], SMIC [clarinet, horn, bassoon].
    Vigils, *Siegfried Sassoon,* [soprano], SMIC [clarinet, piano].

Bridge, Frank. 1879–1941.
Collection: *Three Songs,* Thames [viola, piano].
    Far, far from each other, *Matthew Arnold,* F#m [d′#-e′′], Thames 3 Songs.
    Music when soft voices die, *Percy Bysshe Shelley,* Cm [c′-e′′], Thames 3 Songs.
    Where is it that our soul doth go? *Heine,* tr. *Kate Kroeker,* Em [e′-e′′], Thames 3 Songs.

Britten, Edward **Benjamin.** Lord Britten of Aldeburgh. 1913–1976.
Collections: *Ballads from Paul Bunyan,* Faber [guitar]; *Cabaret Songs,* Faber [alto saxophone *or* clarinet, trumpet, viola, piano, double bass, drum-kit]; *Songs from the Chinese,* B&H [guitar]; *Evening, Morning, Night,* B&H [harp].
    Autumn Wind, The, *Wu-ti,* tr. *Arthur Waley,* E [e′-f′′#], B&H Chinese.
    Big Chariot, The, *Anon* tr. *Arthur Waley,* F [e′-g′′], B&H Chinese.
    Birthday Hansel, A, (cycle), [c′-b′′b], Faber [harp].

    Canticle III, Still falls the rain, *Edith Sitwell*, [c′-a′′](m), B&H [horn, piano].
    Canticle V, The Death of Saint Narcissus, *T. S. Eliot*, [b-g′′#](m), Faber [harp].
    Dance Song, *Anon* tr. *Arthur Waley*, E [d′-a′′], B&H Chinese.
    Depression, *Po Chü-i* tr. *Arthur Waley*, [e′b-g′′b], B&H Chinese.
    Evening, *Ronald Duncan*, B [f′#-e′′b], B&H Evening.
    Herd-boy, The, *Lu Yu* tr. *Arthur Waley*, Gm [d′-g′′], B&H Chinese.
    Morning, *Ronald Duncan*, G [e′-d′′], B&H Evening.
    Night, *Ronald Duncan*, Bm [c′-f′′], B&H Evening.
    Old Lute, The, *Po Chü-i* tr. *Arthur Waley*, [e′-g′′], B&H Chinese.
    Three Songs from 'The Heart of the Matter' (cycle) *Edith Sitwell*, [d′-g′′](m), B&H [horn, piano].
  Arrangements: *Folksongs Volume 6*, B&H [guitar]; *Eight Folksong Arrangements*, Faber [harp].
    Bird Scarer's Song, *Anon*, B♭ [f′-g′′](m), Faber 8 Folksong.
    Bonny at morn, *Anon*, Gm [f′-g′′], B&H Folksongs 6.
    Bonny at morn, *Anon*, Fm [e′b-f′′], Faber 8 Folksong.
    David of the white rock, *Anon* tr. *Thomas Oliphant*, Fm [c′-a′′b](m), Faber 8 Folksong.
    False Knight upon the Road, The, *Anon*, F [c′-f′′], Faber 8 Folksong.
    I was lonely and forlorn, *Anon* tr. *Ossian Ellis*, F [e′-g′′](m), Faber 8 Folksong.
    I will give my love an apple, *Anon*, Am [c′-e′′](m), B&H Folksongs 6.
    Lemady, *Anon*, [b-f′′#]m, Faber 8 Folksong.
    Lord! I married me a wife, *Anon*, Em [e′-e′′](m), Faber 8 Folksong.
    Master Kilby, *Anon*, A [e′-f′′#], B&H Folksongs 6.
    Sailor-boy, *Anon*, Bm [f′#-f′′#](m), B&H Folksongs 6.
    She's like the swallow, *Anon*, [e′-g′′](m), Faber 8 Folksong.
    Shooting of his Dear, The, *Anon*, F#m [e′-f′′#], B&H Folksongs 6.
    Soldier and the Sailor, The, *Anon*, G [d′-g′′], B&H Folksongs 6.

Brodsky, Nicholas. 1851–1929.
    I'll walk with God, *Paul Francis Webster*, D [a-d′′], OUP *Solo Sacred* [organ arr. Jenkins].

Brown, Christopher Roland. 1943–
  Collection: *All Year Round, Op 46,* Chester [guitar].
    Fine Day, A, *Adrian Bell*, [d′-a′′](m), Chester All Year.
    Nocturnal, *Robert Herrick, John Donne*, [a-d′′](counter-tenor), Musography [violin, cello, double bass, harpsichord].
    Suffolk Harvest Song, *Alice Cochrane*, [d′-a′′](m), Chester All Year.
    Suffolk Mist, *Cloudesley Brereton*, [c′-a′′b](m), Chester All Year.
    Winter: East Anglia, *Edmund Blunden*, [c′-a′′#](m), Chester All Year.

Bryars, Richard **Gavin.** 1943–
    Black River, The, [soprano], Schott [organ].
    Incipit Vita Nova, [alto], Schott [string trio].

Bullard, Alan. 1947–
    Autumn Evening, *James Thomson*, [d′-a′′](f), Colne [clarinet *or* viola, piano].
    Ground-song, *William Barnes*, [d′-a′′](f), Colne [string trio].
    Solitary Reaper, The, *William Wordsworth*, G [c′#-a′′], Colne [violin or treble recorder or oboe].
    When I am dead, my dearest, *Christina Rossetti*, Em [b-d′′], Colne [flute, piano].

Buller, John. 1927–
    (Two Night Pieces from Finnegans Wake (cycle), *James Joyce*, [soprano], OUP [flute, clarinet, cello, piano].)

Burgon, Geoffrey. 1941–
  Collections: (*Three Folksongs*, [high] Chester [guitar]); (*Two Love Songs*, [tenor], Chester [guitar].)
    At the round earth's imagined corners, *John Donne*, [soprano], Chester hire [trumpet, organ].
    Cantata on Medieval Latin Texts, [counter-tenor], Chester hire [flute, oboe, bassoon].
    Dira Vi Amores Terror, [counter-tenor], Chester hire [unaccompanied].
    (Lunar Beauty, [counter-tenor], Chester [lute *or* guitar].)
    Nearing the upper air, [counter-tenor], Chester hire [2 recorders, harpsichord, cello].
    (Night is come, The, [high], Chester [cello].)
    Nunc dimittis, [voice], Chester [organ, optional trumpet].
    Songs of Mary, [mezzo], Chester hire [viola, piano].
    Threnody, [tenor], Chester hire [piano and harpsichord (amplified)].
    Worlde's Bliss, [counter-tenor/contralto], Chester [oboe].

Burkinshaw, Sydney. WMIC. [flute, percussion, piano].

Burrell, Diana. 1948–
Angelus, *wordless,* [high], UMP [cello, double bass, small bells *or* gongs].

Burtch, Mervyn. 1929– WMIC. [flute, piano]; [flute, harp, viola]; [harp]; [flute, violin, viola, cello], [cello, piano], [oboe, piano], [guitar].

Bush, Geoffrey. 1920–1998.
Collection: *Two Stevie Smith Songs,* [high], Novello [oboe, cello, piano].
Holy Innocents Carol, [voice], Novello [piano, percussion].
Mirabile Misterium (cycle), *Various,* [c′-a′′], Novello hire [string quartet, harpsichord].

Butler, Martin. 1960–
Collection: *Three Emily Dickinson Songs,* [soprano], OUP, [clarinet, piano].
Roll it along, [soprano], OUP hire [2 bass clarinets, viola, cello, double bass].

Butt, James. 1929– BMIC. [harp], [organ].
Collection: *For Your Delight,* [high], Sphemusations [flute, piano].
Ariel's Song, *Shakespeare,* [voice], Sphemusations [harp].
I got me flowers, *George Herbert,* [high], Mills [harp].
Psalm 1, *Prayer Book,* [medium high], Sphemusations [organ].
Sunset, [medium high], Chappell [harp].
Virtue, *George Herbert,* Em [c′#-f′′#], Mills [harp].

Butterworth, Arthur Eckersley. 1923–
Night Wind, The, [soprano], Chester [clarinet in A, piano].

Butterworth, George. 1885–1916.
Collection: *Love Blows as the Wind Blows,* Masters [string quartet].
Fill a glass with golden wine, *W. E. Henley,* [c′#-d′′#], Masters Love Blows.
In the year that's come and gone, *W. E. Henley,* [c′-e′′b], Masters Love Blows.
Life in her creaking shoes, *W. E. Henley,* [c′-f′′], Masters Love Blows.
On the way to Kew, *W. E. Henley* [c′#-f′′], Masters Love Blows.

Butterworth, Neil. 1934–
Collections: *Three Shakespeare Songs,* [mezzo], SMIC [guitar]; *Three Pomes,* [voice], SMIC [percussion].

Cannon, Jack **Philip.** 1929–
Collection: *Cinq Chansons de Femme.* Kronos [harp].
La bien amée, (Girl Whose Love Shines Fair), *Anon,* tr. *Laidlaw,* Dm [c′-g′′], Kronos Cinq Chansons.
La bien mariée, (Merry Wife, The), *Olivier Basselin,* tr. *Laidlaw,* A [d′-a′′(g′′)], Kronos Cinq Chansons.
La mal mariée (Angry Wife, The), *Anon* tr. *Laidlaw,* Dm [bb-g′′], Kronos Cinq Chansons.
L'amoureuse (Girl in Love, A), *Anon,* tr. *Laidlaw,* Em [d′-g′′#], Kronos Cinq Chansons.
La veuve (Widow, The), *Christine de Pisan,* tr. *Laidlaw,* Fm [bb-g′′], Kronos Cinq Chansons.

Caradon, Sulyen R. 1942–
Nowhere, *Alan Hodge,* [c′-g′′](f) Da Capo/EPSS [flute, viola, bass clarinet].

Carcas, Gillian. 1963– BMIC. [cello, harpsichord], [flute, viola, cello, harp].

Cardew, Cornelius. 1936–1981. BMIC. [unaccompanied].

Charlesworth, David.
Collection: *Three 'Twelfth Night' Songs,* (Shakespeare), [baritone], Brunton [flute, clarinet].

Clarke, Jeremiah. *c.*1674–1707.
Divine Hymn, A (Blest be those sweet regions), *Anon,* Cm [c′-a′′], Faber (Britten) *Harmonia* [harp].

Clarke, Rebecca. 1886–1979.
Arrangements: *Three Old English Songs,* B&H (Introduction, Calum MacDonald) [violin].
It was a lover and his lass, *Shakespeare (Morley),* Eb [e′b-e′′b], B&H 3 Old English Songs.

Phillis on the new made hay, *Anon*, D [c´#-e´´], B&H 3 Old English Songs.
Tailor and his mouse, The, *Anon*, Gm [d´-d´´], B&H 3 Old English Songs.

Clucas, Humphrey.
Collection: *Two George Herbert Songs*, [high], Brunton [unaccompanied].

Colling, Aubrey.
Collection: *Five Odes,* Da Capo [bassoon, xylophone, piano].
All you Spanish Ladies, *Basil Bunting,* [baritone], Da Capo 5 Odes.
Complaint of the Morpethshire Farmer, *Basil Bunting,* [baritone], Da Capo 5 Odes.
Fearful Symmetry, *Basil Bunting,* [baritone], Da Capo 5 Odes.
Gin the goodwife stint, *Basil Bunting,* [baritone], Da Capo 5 odes.
Stones trip Coquet Burn, *Basil Bunting,* [baritone], Da Capo 5 Odes.

Connolly, Justin Riveagh. 1933-
Poems of Wallace Stevens II Op 14 (cycle), *Wallace Stevens,* [soprano], Chester [clarinet, piano].

Cooke, Arnold Atkinson. 1906–
Collections: *Three Songs of Innocence,* OUP [clarinet in A, piano]; *Nocturnes*, OUP [horn, piano].
Boat Song, *John Davidson,* E♭ [d´-g´´♭](f), OUP Nocturnes.
Echoing Green, The, *William Blake,* Am [d´-a´´](f), OUP 3 Songs.
Moon, The, *Percy Bysshe Shelley*, Am [c´#-g´´](f), OUP Nocturnes.
Owl, The, *Alfred Lord Tennyson*, F [c´-g´´](f), OUP Nocturnes.
Piping down the valleys wild, *William Blake*,A [e´-a´´](f), OUP 3 Songs.
Returning, we hear the larks, *Isaac Rosenberg,* B♭m [c´-g´´](f), OUP Nocturnes.
River Roses, *D. H. Lawrence*, F#m [c´#-f´´](f), OUP Nocturnes.
The Shepherd, *William Blake,*F [f´-f´´](f), OUP 3 Songs.

Cox, Bert.
May the mind, [high], Modus [organ].

Cresswell, Lyell. 1944–
Collection: *Four Sentimental Songs,* [soprano], SMIC [bag of clothes pegs].
Prayer for the Cure of a Strained Back, *Maori* tr. *Arthur S. Thomson,* [soprano], SMIC [unaccompanied].
Words for Music, *C. K. Stead,* [mezzo], SMIC [unaccompanied].

Croft, William. 1678–1727.
Hymn on Divine Music, A, *Anon,* Dm [d´-g´´], Faber (Britten) *Harmonia* [harp].
My heart is every beauty's prey, *Anon,* A [e´-a´´], Roberton [harpsichord *or* piano, cello].

Crosse, Gordon. 1937–
Collection: *Medieval French Songs,* [high], OUP hire [clarinet, piano, percussion].
Corpus Christe Carol, [soprano], OUP hire [clarinet, horn, string quartet].
Verses in Memoriam David Munrow, [counter-tenor], OUP hire [recorder, cello, harpsichord].

Crossley-Holland, Peter. 1916–2001.
Collection: *Songs*, Forsyth.
Plum Blossom Song, *see* Song for a Chinese Play.
Fairy Workers, *Patrick MacGill,* E♭ [c´-g´´], Forsyth Songs [sopranino recorder, piano].
Philosopher Bird, The, *see* Secret, The.
Secret, The, *Kevin Crossley-Holland,* [b♭-g´´], Forsyth Songs [descant recorder, piano].
Song for a Chinese Play, *Lian-Shin Yang,* [e´♭-f´´](f), Forsyth Songs [flute].
This is the fountain of life, *from an ancient liturgy,* Bm [d´-e´´], Forsyth Songs [unaccompanied].
You have put on Christ, *adapted from St Paul,* D [d´-d´´] Forsyth Songs [unaccompanied].

Cruft, Adrian. 1921–1987.
Collection: *Two Songs of Quiet Op 12,* Joad [soprano, violin *or* mezzo, viola].
Heaven and Haven, *Gerard Manley Hopkins,* Joad 2 Songs.
Scallop, *Sir Walter Raleigh,* Joad 2 Songs.

Dafydd, Einion. WMIC. [2 clarinets, piano, double bass].

Dalby, Martin. 1942–
Collections: *A Muse of Love,* for details see main catalogue, SMIC hire [flute, violin, viola, cello, harp];
Three Songs from Ezra Pound, [mezzo], SMIC [flute, clarinet, celeste, viola].
Cantica (cycle), *Tommaso Campanella,* [soprano or tenor], Novello hire [clarinet, viola, piano].

Fiddler, The (cycle), *William Soutar,* [soprano *or* tenor], Novello [violin].
Keeper of the Pass, The (cycle), *Various,* [soprano], Novello hire [Eb clarinet, clarinet/bass clarinet, clarinet/tenor saxophone, piano, percussion].
My song is in sighing, *Richard Rolle of Hampole,* [treble], Novello [organ].

Dale, Benjamin. 1885–1943.
Come away, death, *Shakespeare,* G♭ [d′♭-e′′♭](m), Novello [viola, piano].

Davies, Eiluned. 1913– WMIC. [unaccompanied]

Davies, Martin Vaughan. WMIC. [2 bass clarinets, harp, cello].

Davies, Sir Henry Walford. 1869–1941.
God be in my head, *Sarum Primer (1514),* A [e′-d′′], OUP *Solo Sacred* [organ arr. Jenkins].
Arrangement:
My loved one's grave, Gwynn [harp].

Dench, Chris. 1953–
Shunga, *Kobo Daishi,* [mezzo], UMP [bass flute, oboe d'amore, piano, percussion].

Dickinson, Peter. 1934– BMIC. [harpsichord, cello].
Collection: *Four Poems of Andrew Porter,* [counter-tenor], Novello [harpsichord].
Elegy, [counter-tenor], Novello hire [harpsichord, cello].
Reminiscences, *Lord Byron,* [mezzo], Novello, [saxophone, piano].
Summoned by Mother, *John Betjeman,* [mezzo], Novello [harp].
Surrealist Landscape, *Lord Berners,* [any voice], Novello [piano, tape].

Dillon, James. 1950–
Come live with me, [mezzo], Peters [flute, oboe, percussion, piano].
Evening Rain, Peters [unaccompanied].
Roaring Flame, A, *Anon/Clara d'Anduza,* [g′-b′′♭](f), Peters [double bass].
Time Lag Zero, *The Song of Songs (in Hebrew),* [g#-d′′′](f), Peters [viola].
Who do you love, [voice], Peters [flute, clarinet, violin/viola, cello].

Dorward, David Campbell. 1933– SMIC.
Faustus Scene, A, [baritone], SMIC [violin, cello, piano].
Garden of Love, The, [high], SMIC [horn, piano].
Garland of Flowers and Thistles, [tenor], SMIC [cor anglais, piano].
Horati Carminum, [high], SMIC [guitar].
Meditations, [baritone], SMIC [3 clarinets].

Dowland, John. ?1563–1626.
Collection: *The First Book of Songes or Ayres,* Doblinger (Werner J. Wolff), [guitar].

Downes, Andrew. 1950–
Collections: *Five Holy Songs, Op 11,* Lynwood [3 violins, viola, cello, double bass]; *Lost Love, Op 15,* Lynwood [tenor recorder *or* flute, viola da gamba *or* cello, harpsichord *or* piano].
Dreamland, *Edgar Allen Poe,* [c′#-c′′′#](f), Lynwood. [soprano saxophone, piano]
Hear us, O hear us, Lord, *John Donne,* [c′#-d′′], Lynwood 5 Holy Songs.
I sing the progress of a Deathless Soul, *John Donne,* [e′♭-e′′], Lynwood 5 Holy Songs.
Last Love Word, *Thomas Hardy,* [d′#-f′′](f), Lynwood Lost Love.
Lost Love, *Thomas Hardy,* [f′-f′′#](f), Lynwood Lost Love.
Night in November, *Thomas Hardy,* [c′-f′′](f), Lynwood Lost Love.
Spit in my face, ye Jews, *John Donne,* [b-d′′#], Lynwood 5 Holy Songs.
Virgins, The, *John Donne,* [d′-e′′♭], Lynwood 5 Holy Songs.
Walk, The, *Thomas Hardy,* [f′-g′′(f)], Lynwood Lost Love.
When Senses, which thy Soldiers are, *John Donne,* [e′-c′′#], Lynwood 5 Holy Songs.

Elgar, Sir Edward William. 1857–1934.
Ave verum corpus, *Anon* tr H. N. Oxenham, E [b-c′′#], OUP *Solo Sacred* [organ arr. Jenkins].

Elias, Brian. 1948–
Peroration, [g-c′′′#](f), Chester [unaccompanied].
(Personal Stereo, [soprano], Chester [backing tape].)
Song, *Song of Solomon,* [soprano], Chester hire [hurdy-gurdy].

Elliott, Michael. WMIC. [flute], [harp].

Ellis, Mark.
Collections: *Rosenberg Sketches,* Andresier [guitar]; *Two Songs,* Andresier [guitar].
    Break of Day in the Trenches, *Isaac Rosenberg,* [c′-f′′], Andresier Rosenberg.
    Epilogue, *Isaac Rosenberg,* [d′-e′′b], Andresier Rosenberg.
    Liebeslied, *Rainer Maria Rilke,* [b-d′′], Andresier 2 Songs.
    Marching (as seen from the left file), *Isaac Rosenberg,* [c′-e′′], Andresier Rosenberg.
    On Receiving News of the War, *Isaac Rosenberg,* [b-e′′b], Andresier Rosenberg.
    Schlaflied, *Rainer Maria Rilke,* [b-′′b], Andresier 2 Songs.

Elton, Antony. 1935– WMIC. [various], [cello].

Elwyn-Edwards, Dilys. 1918– WMIC. [clarinet, piano].

Evans, Elizabeth Myfanwy. WMIC. [2 pianos].

Ferneyhough, Brian. 1943–
    Etudes Transcendantales, [soprano], Peters [flute/piccolo/alto flute, oboe/cor anglais, harpsichord, cello].
    On Stellar Magnitudes, [mezzo], Peters [flute/piccolo, clarinet/bass clarinet, piano, violin, cello].

Finnissy, Michael Peter. 1946– BMIC. [unaccompanied].
Collections: *Beuk O'Newcassel Sangs,* OUP [clarinet, piano]; *Three Motets,* [soprano], OUP hire [violin, viola, cello]; *Unknown Ground,* OUP [violin, cello, piano].
    A' the neet ower an' ower, [soprano], OUP Beuk.
    As me an' me marra was gannin' ta wark, [soprano], OUP Beuk.
    Buy broom buzzems, [soprano], OUP Beuk.
    I am nearly blind, [baritone], OUP Unknown.
    I come from London, [baritone], OUP Unknown.
    I don't think of death, [baritone], OUP Unknown.
    I thought to marry a parson, [soprano], OUP Beuk.
    I was afraid, [baritone], OUP Unknown.
    It's O but aw ken weel, [soprano], OUP Beuk.
    Moon's goin' down, *no text,* Universal [unaccompanied].
    Mountainfall, *No text,* [d-a′′](f), Universal [unaccompanied].
    Our lives, [baritone], OUP Unknown.
    Patch of blackened earth, A, [baritone], OUP Unknown.
    There's Quayside fer sailors, [soprano], OUP Beuk.
    Trapped in crystal, [baritone], OUP Unknown.
    Up the Raw, maw bonny, [soprano], OUP Beuk.

Finzi, Gerald Raphael. 1901–1956.
Collection: *By Footpath and Stile,* B&H 1984 [string quartet].
    Christmas Eve, and twelve of the clock, *Thomas Hardy,* [b-e′′](m), B&H Footpath.
    Everybody else, then, going, *Thomas Hardy,* [c′-g′′(e′′b)](m), B&H Footpath.
    I went by footpath and by stile, *Thomas Hardy,* [c′-d′′](m), B&H Footpath.
    These flowers are I, *Thomas Hardy,* [b-f′′(f′′#)](m), B&H Footpath.
    We are budding, master, budding, *Thomas Hardy,* [a(b)-f′′#](m), B&H Footpath.
    Where we made the fire, *Thomas Hardy,* [c′-d′′](m), B&H Footpath.

Forshaw, David.
    Orcadian Calenders, *George Mackay Brown,* [soprano], Da Capo Music [piano, percussion].

Foster, Derek. 1943–
    Songs of Innocence, (cycle), *William Blake,* [c′#-a′′b](f), Modus [clarinet, piano].

Fowler, Tommy. 1948–
Collection: *Four Songs,* [Sir Walter Scott], [mezzo], SMIC [2 violins, viola, cello, double bass].
    Brief Ecstasy, *Ann Ross,* [soprano], SMIC [flute, clarinet, bassoon].
    So much time, *Peter Campbell,* [soprano], SMIC [harp, 2 cellos, double bass]
    Song, *Percy Bysshe Shelley,* [mezzo], SMIC [violin, harp].
    Suicide in the copse, The, *Robert Graves,* [tenor], SMIC [percussion, 2 hand-clappers, piano].

Fox, Christopher. 1955– SMIC. [recorder, lute, dulcimer], [hurdy-gurdy].

Freeman, Roland. 1927–
Rendevous, *A. Seeger*, [f′#-a′′b], EPSS [cello].

Fricker, Peter Racine. 1920–1990.
O mistress mine, *Shakespeare*, [c′-g′′](m), Schott [guitar].

Garton, Graham.
Girl in a butterfly cloak, (lyrical romance), [soprano], Brunton [violin, piano].
How sweet is sin, [high], Brunton [harpsichord]; [low], Brunton [harpsichord].
Li Liang-Ch'en, (meditation and legend), [soprano], Brunton [violin].
Prayer for heretics, A, [high], Brunton [unaccompanied].

Geddes, John Maxwell. 1941– SMIC.
Collection: *Burns Collection, A,* SMIC [flute, violin, guitar].

Geehl, Henry. 1881–1961.
For you alone, F [high], Classical [violin, piano]; Db, Eb, Classical [violin, piano].

Gerhard, Roberto. 1896–1970.
Akond of Swat, The, *Edward Lear*, [a-a′′b](f), OUP hire [percussion].
Seven Haiku (cycle), *J. M. Junoy*, [soprano], B&H hire [flute, oboe, clarinet, bassoon, piano].

Gibbs, Cecil **Armstrong.** 1889–1960.
Collections: *Song Album 2*, Novello 1998.
Oxen, The, *Thomas Hardy*, Fm [d′-f′′], Mayhew *Holy Night* [organ].
Padraic the Fidiler, *Padraic Gregory*, [e′-f′′], Novello Album 2 [violin, piano].

Glyn, Gareth. 1951–
Collection: *Songs of the Marches,* (15th and 17th centuries), [baritone], Llonod [harp].

Godfrey, Paul Corfield. WMIC. [2 flutes, 3 clarinets], [2 trumpets, 3 trombones], [flute, guitar, violin, viola, cello], [flute, bassoon, percussion, guitar], [flute, harp], [viola, piano].

Goehr, Peter **Alexander.** 1932–
Arianna abandonata, [tenor], Schott [guitar].
Mouse metamorphosed into a maid, The, *Marianne Moore,* [bb-c′′′] Schott [unaccompanied].

Gorb, Adam. 1958–
Wedding breakfast: a Tribute to Stravinsky, *Anon*, [a-a′′](f), Lengnick [tambourine, played by singer].

Gow, David. 1924–1993. BMIC. [guitar].)

Grainger, Percy. 1882–1961.
Arrangements:
Bridegroom Grat, The, *Anon,* [c′-e′′], Bardic [2 violas, 3 cellos *or* 2 cellos, double bass].
Foweles in the frith, *Anon*, [f′-b′′b], Bardic [viola].
In Bristol Town, *Anon,* [d′-e′′], Bardic [guitar].
Land o' the Leal, The, *Lady Nairne,* [c′-f′′], Bardic [violin, 2 violas, 2 cellos *or* cello, double bass].
Lord Maxwell's Goodnight, *Anon,* [c′-a′′], Bardic [violin, viola, 2 cellos *or* 2 violins, viola, cello].
Old Woman at the Christening, The, *Anon,* [f′-f′′], Bardic [piano, harmonium].

Grange, Philip. 1956–
As it was, *Edward Thomas,* [soprano], Maecenas [2 clarinets, piano].
Memorials of Sleep, *Lawrence Durrell,* [c′#-a′′](f), Maecenas [2 clarinets, viola, piano].
On this bleak hut, *Edward Thomas,* [c′#-a′′](m), Maecenas [flute, clarinet, cello].
Puzzle of Shadows, A, *Robert Louis Stevenson,* [b-a′′](f), Maecenas [violin, piano].

Greaves, Terence. 1933–
Collections: *A Garden of Weeds*, Thames [clarinet, piano]; *Three Rustic Poems of John Clare*, Emerson [clarinet in A].
Bella donna, *Jacqueline Froom,* [e′-f′′#], Thames Garden.

Buttercup, *Jacqueline Froom*, E♭ [e′b-e′′], Thames Garden.
Little trotty wagtail, *John Clare*, E [c′-a′′](f), Emerson 3 Rustic Poems.
Nettle, *Jacqueline Froom*, Cm [a′b-g′′b(b′′b)], Thames Garden.
November, *John Clare*, [b-g′′](f), Emerson 3 Rustic Poems.
Poppy, *Jacqueline Froom*, Cm [c′-e′′b], Thames Garden.
Quail's nest, *John Clare*, E [c′-f′′#](f), Emerson 3 Rustic Poems.
Thistle, *Jacqueline Froom*, F [e′b-f′′], Thames Garden.

Gurney, Ivor. 1890–1937.
Collections: *Ludlow and Teme*, S&B [string quartet, piano]; *The Western Playland*, S&B [string quartet, piano]. See main catalogue for details.

Guy, Barry. 1947-
Waiata, [tenor (playing some percussion)], Novello [medieval instruments, 1 player].

Handel, George Frideric. 1685–1759.
Blessed are all they that fear the Lord, *Psalm 128, vv. 1,2*, F [c′-f′′], OUP *Solo Sacred* [organ arr. Jenkins].
Come unto Him, *Matthew 11, vv. 28, 29*. F [c′-d′′], OUP *Solo Sacred* [organ arr. Jenkins].
I know that my redeemer liveth, *Job 19, vv. 25, 26; I Corinthians 15, v. 20*, D [d′-f′′#], OUP *Solo Sacred* [organ arr. Jenkins].
Let the bright seraphim, *John Milton*, B♭ [bb-f′′], OUP *Solo Sacred* [organ arr. Jenkins].
Lowly they kneel, *Dorothy F. Gurney*, F [c′-d′′], OUP *Solo Sacred* [(Where'er you walk) organ arr. Jenkins].
Merciful God, *E. S. Palmer*, E♭ [bb-e′′b], OUP *Solo Sacred* [(Largo from Serse) organ arr. Jenkins].

Harding, Kenneth. WMIC. [viola].

Hardy, John. WMIC. [cornetto *or* sackbutt *or* clarinet *or* cor anglais], [2 clarinets, bassoon, viola].

Harries, David. 1933– WMIC. [string quartet, piano].

Harvey, Jonathan Dean. 1939–
Angel Eros, [high], Novello [string quartet].
Cantata III, [soprano], Novello hire [flute, clarinet, piano/organ, violin, cello].
Cantata X (Spirit Music), [soprano], Novello hire [3 clarinets, piano].
In Memoriam, [soprano], Novello hire [flute, clarinet, viola, cello].
Nachtlied, *Goethe , Rudolf Steiner*, [soprano], Faber hire [piano, tape].
(You, [soprano], Faber [clarinet, viola, cello, double bass].)

Hayes, Morgan.
Handbag, *Ruth Fainlight*, [soprano], S&B [B♭ clarinet, bass clarinet, viola, cello, double bass].

Head, Michael. 1900–1976.
Be merciful unto me, O God, *Psalm 57*, C [a-g′′(f′′)], Roberton [organ].
Bird-song, *Marjorie Rayment*, Fm [c′#-c′′′(b′′)(f′′′)], (f), B&H [flute, piano].
Child on the Shore, *Nancy Bush*, D [bb-e′′], Roberton [violin, piano].
(Foxgloves, *Mary Webb*, C [g′-g′′], B&H [string quartet]; A♭, B&H [string quartet].)
(Green Rain, *Mary Webb*, Gm [c′-f′′], B&H [string quartet, harp].)
(I arise from dreams of thee, *Percy Bysshe Shelley*, G [d′-g′′], B&H [cello, piano].)
I will lift up mine eyes, *Psalm 121*, C [b-e′′], Roberton [organ].
Little Road to Bethlehem, The, *Margaret Rose*, A♭ [e′b-a′′b], Mayhew *Holy Night* [organ].
Lord's Prayer, The, *Prayer Book*, D [a-d′′], OUP *Solo Sacred* [organ].
Make a joyful noise unto the Lord, *Psalm 100*, G [d′b′′(g′′)], Roberton [organ].
(O gloriosa Domina, E [b-e′′], B&H [string quartet, piano].)
(Piper, A, *Seumas O'Sullivan*, Dm [c′-e′′], B&H [flute, piano].)
(Sancta et immaculata Virginitas, *St Augustine*, Cm [c′-e′′], B&H [string quartet, piano].)
Singer, The, *Bronnie Taylor*, Fm [c′-a′′b], B&H *Album 2 (Album High)*, [unaccompanied].
World is Mad, The, *Louis MacNeice*, [a-f′′](f), Emerson [clarinet in B♭, piano].

Hearne, John. 1937–
Collection: *Four Songs for High Voice and Harp*, Longship [harp].
Bottom's Dream, *Shakespeare*, [Soprano], Longship [solo trombone, clarinet, violin, cello, piano].

Chestnut Tree, The, *Florence Dunlop,* [high], Longship 4 Songs.
Morning Mist, *Florence Dunlop,* [high], Longship 4 Songs.
Oh could I be..., *Florence Dunlop,* [high], Longship 4 Songs.
Road to Emmaus (Canticle for Easter), *William McCorkindale,* [bass-baritone], Longship [organ, percussion].
Summer, *Florence Dunlop,* [high], Longship 4 Songs.

Helliwell, Piers. 1956–
Fatal Harmony, *Andrew Marvell,* [d′-g′′#], Maecenas [unaccompanied].
Four Delays, *Thomas A. Clark,* [d′-f′′#](f), Maecenas [recorder].
Quem Quæritas, *Anon medieval,* [c′-a′′](f), Maecenas [clarinet, bass-clarinet, viola, cello, double bass].

Henry, John. 1859–1914.
Pluck not the tender flowers, [soprano], Snell [violin, piano].

Hill, Richard.
Collection: *Nocturnes,* [high], SMIC [unaccompanied].

Hiscocks, Wendy.
Collections: *Mother and Child,* Creativity [clarinet, piano]; *Two Bulgarian Songs,* Creativity [viola, piano];
Benediction, *Rabindranath Tagore,* [c′#-a′′](f), Creativity Mother and Child.
Champa Flower, The, *Rabindranath Tagore,* [e′#-f′′#](f), Creativity Mother and Child.
Day of the Singing Birds, The, *Dennis Stoll,* [d′-f′′#], Creativity [flute, piano].
End, The, *Rabindranath Tagore,* [d′-a′′](f), Creativity Mother and Child.
Kladenetsut, *Elisaveta Bagryana,* [a-f′′], Creativity 2 Bulgarian.
Last Invocation, The, *Walt Whitman,* [tenor], Creativity [flute, oboe, viola, cello].
Libretto of the Eight Year Old (cantata), *Wendy Hiscocks,* [soprano/mezzo], Creativity [violin, viola, cello].
Moe sartse, *Elisaveta Bagryana,* [g-e′′b], Creativity 2 Bulgarian.
My Song, *Rabindranath Tagore,* [d′-a′′](f), Creativity Mother and Child.

Hoddinott, Alun. 1929– WMIC.

Hodson, Maud. 1972– BMIC. [brass quintet], [viola].

Hold, Trevor. 1939– BMIC. [guitar].

Holloway, Robin Greville. 1943–
Collection: *Tender only to one Op 12,* B&H hire [unaccompanied]; *The Noon's Repose Op 39,* (Eliot, Stevens, Marvell), B&H hire [harp].
Abominable Lake, The, *Stevie Smith,* [c′-a′′b](f), B&H Tender.
Another Weeping Woman, *Wallace Stevens,* [c′#-a′′](m), B&H Noon's Repose.
Blue Doom of Summer, The, (cantata) Op 35/1, *Ronald Firbank,* [c′#-b′′b], B&H hire [harp].
Conundrums Op 33b, *Anon,* [soprano], B&H hire [wind quintet].
Five Little Songs About Death (cycle) Op 21, *Stevie Smith* [g′-g′′](f) B&H hire [unaccompanied].
Four Housman Fragments Op 7, *A. E. Housman,* [soprano], B&H hire [violin, cello, percussion, piano].
Killing Time (cycle), *Auden, Stevie Smith, Raleigh,* [ab-b′′b](f), B&H hire [unaccompanied].
La figlia che piange, *T. S. Eliot,* [e′b-g′′](m), B&H Noon's Repose.
Love will find out the way, *Anon,* [soprano], B&H hire [2 clarinets, viola, cello, double bass].
Nor we to her of him, *Stevie Smith,* [c′-d′′](f), B&H Tender.
(Nursery Rhymes Op 33, *Anon,* [soprano], B&H [wind quintet].)
Nursery Rhymes Op 33a, *Anon,* [soprano], B&H hire [wind quintet].
On a Drop of Dew, *Andrew Marvell,* [d′-g′′b](m), B&H Noon's Repose.
So to fatness come, *Stevie Smith,* [c′-a′′](f), B&H Tender.
Song of Defiance, *A. E. Housman,* [soprano], B&H hire [piano, string quartet].
Tender only to one, *Stevie Smith,* [e′b-b′′b](f), B&H Tender.
Willow Cycle Op 35/2, *Shakespeare, Raleigh, Anon,* [c′-g′′#(g′′)](m), B&H hire [harp].

Holst, Gustav Theodore. 1874–1934.
Collection: *Four Songs for Voice and Violin,* Chester [violin].
I sing of a maiden, *Anon,* [e′-g′′], Chester 4 Songs.

Jesu sweet, now will I sing, *Anon*, [d'-e''], Chester 4 Songs.
My leman is so true, *Anon*, [d'-e''], Chester 4 Songs.
My soul has nought but fire and ice, *Anon*, [c'-d''], Chester 4 Songs.
Personent hodie, *Piae Cantiones* tr. *Jane Joseph*, Fm [e'b-f''], Mayhew *Holy Night* [organ].

Holt, Simon. 1958–
Clandestiny (cycle), *Emily Dickinson*, [soprano], Chester [organ].
Knot of Time, A, [soprano], Chester [clarinet in A/Eb, viola, cello, double bass].
Six Caprices, *Federico García Lorca*, [counter-tenor *or* mezzo], Chester [unaccompanied].
Song of Crocuses and Lightning, A, *Raymond Carver*, [soprano], Chester [horn, harp, viola, double bass].

Horne, David. 1970–
You, *Emily Dickinson*, [soprano], B&H hire [alto flute/piccolo, piano/claves, cello].

Hosier, John.
Mango Walk, G [medium], BMP [tuned percussion, piano].

Howells, Herbert. 1892–1983.
Balulalow, *Martin Luther* tr. *Wedderburn*, [c'#-f''#], Mayhew *Holy Night* [organ].

Hoyle, Vernon.
Lullay my liking, *Traditional*, Em [c'#-g''#], Banks. [organ].

Hudes, Eric. 1920– BMIC.
Collections: *Sappho Kunopis Kai Mantis (Sappho, Bitch and Philosopher)*, [b-g''#], Bardic [clarinet]; *Shadows of Chrysanthemums*, [c'-f''#], Bardic [flute, clarinet, violin, cello]; *Wakenings*, Bardic [violin, viola, cello].
At my age, *Sappho* tr. *Mary Bernard*, Bardic Sappho Kunopis.
Betrothal, A, *E. J. Scovell*, Bardic Shadows.
Cage, The, *David Gascoyne*, [c'-a''b], Bardic Wakenings.
Divrei Kohelet, *Ecclesiastes*, [c'-f''#], Bardic [cello].
Experience shows us, *Sappho* tr. *Mary Bernard*, Bardic Sappho Kunopis.
If you are squeamish, *Sappho* tr. *Mary Bernard*, Bardic Sappho Kunopis.
I hear that Andromeda, *Sappho* tr. *Mary Bernard*, Bardic Sappho Kunopis.
Morning Dissertation, *David Gascoyne*, [c'-b''b], Bardic Wakenings.
No Solution, *David Gascoyne*, [b-b''], Bardic Wakenings.
Not Winter yet, *Lotte Zurndorfer*, Bardic [oboe, clarinet, violin, viola, cello].
Rich as you are, *Sappho* tr. *Mary Bernard*, Bardic Sappho Kunopis.
Romancero a la muerte de Federico García Lorca, *L. Urrutia* tr. *Sylvia Townsend Warner*, [c'-g''], Bardic [flute, clarinet, viola, guitar].
Sappho when some fool, *Sappho* tr. *Mary Bernard*, Bardic Sappho Kunopis.
Shadows of Chrysanthemums, *E. J. Scovell*, Bardic Shadows.
Strange to say, *Sappho* tr. *Mary Bernard*, Bardic Sappho Kunopis.
Time for Sleeping, *E. J. Scovell*, Bardic Shadows.
Truly he hath a sweet bed, *Thomas Moult*, [c'-g''], Bardic [flute, clarinet, viola, guitar].
We know this much, *Sappho* tr. *Mary Bernard*, Bardic Sappho Kunopis.
Yes it is pretty, *Sappho* tr. *Mary Bernard*, Bardic Sappho Kunopis.

Hugh-Jones, Elaine. 1927– BMIC; WMIC.
Collection: *Seven Songs of Walter de la Mare*, Thames [clarinet, piano].
Echo, *Walter de la Mare*, Fm [bb-f''], Thames 7 Songs.
Ghosts, *Walter de la Mare*, Am [e'-f''], Thames 7 Songs.
Hare, The, *Walter de la Mare*, Fm [c'-g''], Thames 7 Songs.
Ride-by-nights, The, *Walter de la Mare*, C#m [c'#-a''], Thames 7 Songs.
Silver, *Walter de la Mare*, Bbm [e'b-f''], Thames 7 Songs.
Solitude, *Walter de la Mare*, F#m [c'#-f''#], Thames 7 Songs.
Winter, *Walter de la Mare*, Eb [d'b-g''b], Thames 7 Songs.

Hugill, Robert.
Collections: *Four Solo Motets*, Bardic [organ], *Let this Harvest Pass, O Love*, Bardic [guitar], *Songs of Love and Loss*, Bardic.
After the rain, *Carl Cook*, [a-c''#], Bardic Let this Harvest.
Another day without you, *Robert Hugill*, [bb-e''], Bardic Songs of Love [clarinet, piano].

Collect, *Book of Common Prayer,* [c′-f′′], Bardic 4 Solo Motets [organ].
David's Lament for Jonathan, *Peter Abelard* tr. *Helen Waddell,* [b-d′′], Bardic Songs of Love [clarinet].
Faith, hope and charity, *Anon,* [f′-b′′b], Bardic 4 Solo Motets [organ].
For the memories ungranted, *Carl Cook,* [g-c′′#], Bardic Let this Harvest.
Let this harvest pass, *Carl Cook,* [e-d′′], Bardic Let this Harvest.
Let's walk on the beach, *Carl Cook,* [a-c′′#], Bardic Let this Harvest.
Memorare, *M. V. Lively,* [b-g′′], Bardic Songs of Love [clarinet, piano].
Nunc Dimittis, *Book of Job,* [d′-f′′], Bardic 4 Solo Motets [organ].
Of Death, *Carl Cook,* [a-c′′#], Bardic Let this Harvest.
Our world is full of banalities, *Carl Cook,* [a#-c′′#], Bardic Let this Harvest.
Perhaps there is something, *Carl Cook,* [e′-b′′], Bardic Let this Harvest.
Prayer of Humble Access, *Book of Common Prayer,* [e-c′′], Bardic 4 Solo Motets [organ].
Something so simple, *Carl Cook,* [e′-c′′#], Bardic Let this Harvest.
Sweet is the night air, *Carl Cook,* [a-a′], Bardic Let this Harvest.
Try the door, *Carl Cook,* [g-c′′], Bardic Let this Harvest.
We are whatever we are, *Carl Cook,* [bb-b′b], Bardic Let this Harvest.
When all this is over, *Carl Cook,* [d′-d′′], Bardic Let this Harvest.

Humfrey, Pelham. 1647–1674.
Collection: *Complete Solo Devotional Songs* (edited by Peter Dennison), Novello [organ].
Hymn to God the Father, A, *John Donne,* Gm [c′#-f′′], Faber (Britten) *Harmonia*; [harp].
Lord! I have sinned, *Jeremy Taylor,* Fm [e′-a′′b], Faber (Britten) *Harmonia* [harp]; [f#′-b′′b], Novello Devotional.
O the sad day, *Thomas Flatman,* Gm [d′-g′′](m), Novello Devotional.
Sleep downy sleep come close mine eyes, *Anon,* Dm [e′-a′′], Novello Devotional.
Wilt thou forgive that sin (Hymn to God the Father), *John Donne,* Gm [c′-f′′], Novello Devotional.

Hurlstone, William Yeates. 1876–1906.
Cradle song, *Anon,* G [d′-f′′], Mayhew *Holy Night* [organ].

Hywel, John. WMIC. [flute, violin, piano].

Inglis, Brian. 1969– BMIC. [oboe, harp], [unaccompanied].

Ireland, John. 1879–1962.
Lowly, laid in a manger, *Herbert S. Brown,* Fm [c′-g′′], Mayhew *Holy Night* [organ].

Irvine, Jessie. 1836–1887.
Crimond, *Psalm 23, Scottish Psalter 1650,* Eb [bb-c′′], OUP *Solo Sacred* [organ arr. Jenkins].

Jacob, Gordon. 1895–1984.
Collection: *Three Songs,* BMP [clarinet].
Flow my tears, *John Dowland?* Dm [c′#-b′′b(g′′)](f), BMP 3 Songs.
Ho, who comes here? *Thomas Morley?* G [d′-a′′](f), BMP 3 Songs.
Of all the birds that I do know, *Anon,* A [e′-f′′#](f), BMP 3 Songs.

Jeffreys, George. *c.*1610–1685.
Rise, [voice], Novello [organ].

Jeffreys, John. 1927– WMIC. [string quartet], [horn, string quartet].
Collection: *With Words of Love,* Roberton [bassoon].
And would you fain the reason know? *Thomas Campion?,* F [d′-d′′](m), Roberton Words of Love.
My little pretty one, *Anon,* E [e′-e′′](m), Roberton Words of Love.
My mistress frowns, *Anon,* G [d′-f′′](m), Roberton Words of Love.
That ever I saw, *Anon,* D [d′-e′′(d′′)](m), Roberton Words of Love.

Johnson, Robert Sherlaw. 1932–2000.
Hymn to the Seasons (cycle), *David Whitter,* [d′b-b′′](f), OUP [clarinet, piano].
Praises of Heaven and Earth, The, [soprano], BMP [piano, tape].

Jones, Elfyn Morris. WMIC. [flute, guitar].

Jones, Richard Elfyn. WMIC. [2 violins, cello, piano], [organ].

Joseph, Jane. 1894–1929.
Collection: *Mirage,* [c'-g''#], Bardic [string quartet].
  Echo, *Christina Rossetti,* Bardic Mirage.
  Mirage, *Christina Rossetti,* Bardic Mirage.
  One foot on sea, and one on shore, *Christina Rossetti,* Bardic Mirage.
  Song in the Cornfield, *Christina Rossetti,* Bardic Mirage.
  Song, *Christina Rossetti,* Bardic Mirage.

Josephs, Wilfred. 1927–1997
Collection: *Four Japanese Lyrics*, Novello [clarinet, piano]. Note: the clarinet part may be played by oboe, cor anglais, violin, viola or cello, or omitted altogether.
  If I had known, *Anon,* tr. *Bownas & Thwaite,* [e'-e''], Novello 4 Japanese, [piano].
  Lullaby, *Anon,* tr. *Bownas & Thwaite,* [b'-a''](f), Novello 4 Japanese [clarinet, piano].
  Silent, but.... *Tsuboi Shigeji,* tr. *Bownas & Thwaite,* [f'#-f''](f), Novello 4 Japanese [clarinet].
  Tourist Japan, *Takenaka Iku,* tr. *Bownas & Thwaite,* [b'-a''], Novello 4 Japanese [clarinet, piano].

Joubert, John. 1927-
  Crabbed age and youth, *Shakespeare,* [counter-tenor], Novello hire [recorder, harpsichord viola da gamba].
  Hour Hand, The (cycle), *Edward Lowbury,* [soprano], Novello [recorder].
  Landscapes (cycle), *Edward Thomas, Stephen Spender, F. L. Lucas, Walter de la Mare, Thomas Hardy,* [soprano], Novello [violin, cello, piano].
  Roundelay, [soprano], Novello [lute, bass viol].

Keel, Frederick. 1871–1954.
  When the herds were watching, *W. Canton,* F#m [c'#-e''], Mayhew *Holy Night* [organ].

Keeley, Robert Ian. WMIC. [2 clarinets, viola, double bass], [clarinet, piano].

Kirkwood, Antoinette. 1930–
  Must she go? *James Forsyth,* [G-c'], Bardic [2 violins, viola, cello, double bass].

Knussen, Oliver. 1952–
  Four Late Poems and an Epigram of Rainer Maria Rilke (cycle) tr. *Mitchell,* [g(bb)-b''](f), Faber [unaccompanied].
  Hums and Songs of Winnie the Pooh, *A. A. Milne,* [soprano], Faber [flute/piccolo, cor anglais, clarinet/bass clarinet, percussion, cello].
  Rosary Songs, *Georg Trakl,* [soprano], Faber [clarinet, viola, piano].
  Trumpets, *Georg Trakl,* [soprano], Faber [3 clarinets].

Koffman, Steven.
Collection: *Two Song Settings*, Da Capo [woodwind, harp].
  Sleepers, *Christopher Logue,* [mezzo], Da Capo 2 Song Settings.
  Walking, *Christopher Logue,* [mezzo], Da Capo 2 Song Settings.

Lambert, Leonard **Constant.** 1905–1951.
Collection: *Two Songs* , Maecenas [flute, harp].
  Serenade, *Sacheverell Sitwell,* [e'-g''], Maecenas 2 Songs.
  White Nightingale, The, *Sacheverell Sitwell,* [d'b-b''b], Maecenas 2 Songs.

Lane, Philip. 1950– BMIC. [unaccompanied].)

Lawes, Henry. 1596–1662.
Collection: *Hymns to the Holy Trinity,* Allegro (Gwilym Beechey) [organ]).
  To God the Father, *John Crofts,* Gm [d'-f''], Allegro Hymns.
  To God the Holy Ghost, *John Crofts,* Gm [d'-g''], Allegro Hymns.
  To God the Son, *John Crofts,* Gm [c'#-f''], Allegro Hymns.

Lawson, Gordon. 1931–
  Sestette to Fish, *Walter Elliott,* Ab [b-f''], Thames *Century 4* [unaccompanied].

LeFanu, Nicola. 1947–
  But stars remaining, *C. Day Lewis,* [ab-b''b](f), Novello [unaccompanied].
  Il Cantico dei Cantici II, *Song of Songs 2,* [ab-a''](f), Novello [unaccompanied].
  Paysage, *Guillaume Apollinaire,* [baritone], Novello [unaccompanied].

Rondeaux, *French Medieval Love Poems*, [c′-a′′](m), Novello [horn].
Trio 2: Song for Peter (cycle), *Emily Dickinson, Chekhov, Ted Hughes, Sara Teasdale,* Novello hire [clarinet, cello].

Leighton, Kenneth. 1929–1988.
Animal Heaven, [soprano], Novello [recorder, harpsichord, cello].
These are thy wonders, [tenor/soprano], Novello [organ].

Lewis, Jeffrey. WMIC. [cello, harpsichord, piano].

Liddell, Claire. *c.*1940–
Affirmations, [tenor], Brunton [horn, piano].

Liddle, Samuel. 1867–1951.
Abide with me, *Henry Francis Lyte,* C [g-e′′], BMP *Solo Sacred* [organ arr. Jenkins].
Lord is my shepherd, The, *Psalm 23,* D [c′#-d′′], BMP *Solo Sacred* [organ arr. Jenkins].
Whence is that goodly fragrance, *Anon* tr. *Allen Beville Ramsey,* F [f′-f′′], Mayhew *Holy Night* [organ].

Lipkin, Malcolm. 1932–
Four Departures (cycle), *Robert Herrick,* [soprano], Lipkin [violin].

Luff, Enid. 1935–
Collection: *Three Shakespeare Sonnets,* [soprano], Primavera [flute *or* violin, piano].
God our mother, [soprano], Primavera [organ].
Lament for the ashes of language, [soprano], Primavera [clarinet, piano].
Spring bereaved, [baritone], Primavera [guitar].
Weather and Mouth Music, [soprano], Primavera [double bass].

Lumsdaine, David. 1931– BMIC. [recorder].

Lutyens, Elizabeth. 1906–1983. BMIC. [flute, viola, piano *or* accordion], [unaccompanied], [guitar], [lute].

Lyall, Margaret.
Sweet pastorale, *Nicholas Breton,* [bb-f′′], Bardic [flute, piano].

McCabe, John. 1939–
Collection: *Five Folk Songs,* [high], Novello [horn, piano]; *Three Folk Songs,* Novello [clarinet, piano]; *Two Latin Elegies,* [counter-tenor], Novello [treble/tenor recorder, harpsichord, cello]; .
Das Letzte Gerichte, [voice], Novello [guitar, percussion].
Hush-a-ba, Birdie, croon, croon, *Anon,* F#m [e′-f′#], Novello 3 Folk Songs.
John Peel, *Anon,* F [e′-g′′], Novello 3 Folk Songs.
Johnny has gone for a soldier, *Anon,* [e′-e′′], Novello 3 Folk Songs.
Les Soirs Bleus, [soprano], Novello hire [recorder, harpsichord, cello].
Weaving Song, [high], Novello [piano duet].

McDowell, Cecilia. 1951– BMIC. [flute, piano].

Macfarren, Sir George Alexander. 1813–1887.
Collection: (*Three Songs,* B&H [flute, piano].)
(As it fell upon a day, *Shakespeare,* [contralto], B&H 3 Songs.)
(Crabbed age and youth, *Shakespeare,* [contralto], B&H 3 Songs.)
(On a day, alack the day, *Shakespeare,* [contralto], B&H 3 Songs.)
Widow bird, The, *Percy Bysshe Shelley,* Gm [d′-g′′], S&B *MB 43* [clarinet, piano].

McGuire, Edward. 1948–
Collections: *Moonsongs,* [Holub, García Lorca, Lu Hsun], [soprano], SMIC [double bass]; *Five Songs,* [Janet Humberger], [mezzo], SMIC [viola, piano]; *Rhymes my Granny Read,* [W. Montgomery, N. Montgomery, Janet Hamilton], [soprano], SMIC [viola, harp, double bass]; *Songs of New Beginnings,* [Marianne Carey], [mezzo], SMIC [flute, oboe, clarinet, bassoon, horn]; *Web, The: Five Love Songs,* [Lesley Siddall], [soprano], SMIC [flute, viola, guitar, percussion].
Prelude 8, [tenor], SMIC [tape delay].
Sidesteps, *Marianne Carey,* [soprano], SMIC [clarinet, bass-clarinet, viola, cello, double bass].

Mackenzie, Alexander Campbell. 1847–1945.
    Dormi, Jesu, *Anon*, E [e′-e′′], S&B (Bush) *MB 56* [violin *or* cello, piano].

McLeod, John. 1934–
Collections: *Animal Songs,* Griffin [clarinet/bass clarinet, piano]; *Two Carols,* Griffin [viola, piano].
    Angel Gabriel, The, *Traditional,* [mezzo], Griffin 2 Carols.
    Bilbo's Last Song, *J. R. R. Tolkien,* [tenor], Griffin [harpsichord].
    Canto per tre, *Elizabeth Barrett Browning,* [mezzo], Griffin [viola, piano].
    Ding, dong, merrily on high, *Traditional,* [mezzo], Griffin 2 Carols.
    Lamb, The, *William Blake,* [soprano], Griffin Animal.
    Rabbit, The, *Naomi Royde Smith,* [soprano], Griffin Animal.
    Sloth, The, *Theodore Roethke,* [soprano], Griffin Animal.
    Song of the Concubine, *Anon Chinese* tr. *Anon,* [soprano], Griffin [2 clarinets, viola, cello, double bass].

MacIlwham, George. 1926– SMIC. [flute], [flute, piano], [piccolo *or* tin whistle, piano].

MacMillan, James. 1959–
    Scots Song, *William Soutar,* [soprano], B&H hire [2 clarinets, viola, cello, double bass].
    Variations on Johnny Faa', *traditional,* [soprano], B&H hire [flute/piccolo, cello, harp].

Maconchy, Elizabeth. 1907–1994.
Collection: *Three Songs,* Chester [harp].
    Butterflies, [mezzo], Chester [harp].
    Knot there's no untying, The, *Thomas Campbell,* [d′#-g′′#](m), Chester 3 Songs.
    L'Horloge, [soprano], Chester [clarinet, piano].
    So we'll go no more a-roving, *Lord Byron,* [d′-g′′](m), Chester 3 Songs.
    Widow bird sat mourning, A, *Percy Bysshe Shelley,* [c′-g′′#](m), Chester 3 Songs.

Marsh, Roger. 1949–
    Another silly love song, *St Bernard of Clairvaux/Roger Marsh,* [soprano], Novello [clarinet, piano].
    Bhodi Tree, The, [soprano], Novello [trombone].
    Delilah, [soprano], Novello [alto saxophone *or* clarinet in A].
    Dum (cycle), *Various,* [male], Novello hire [percussion].
    Little Snow, A, *Nicanor Parra,* [any solo voice], Maecenas [unaccompanied].
    Lover's Ghost, The, [soprano], Novello hire [2 flutes, 2 clarinets, cello].
    Lover's Ghost, The, [high], Novello hire [harp].
    On and on, [soprano], Novello hire [2 clarinets, bass clarinet].
    PS, [female voice], Novello [double bass, trombone].
    Songs of Devotion (cycle), [soprano], Novello hire [clarinet, guitar].
    Sozu-Baba (music theatre), *Judith Woolf,* [any solo voice], Maecenas [unaccompanied].
    Streim, [soprano], Novello hire [flute, clarinet, trumpet, double bass].
    Words of Love, [baritone], Novello hire [2 oboes, bassoon, harpsichord].
    Wormwood and the Gall, The, [mezzo], Novello hire [flute/alto flute, clarinet, percussion, harp, viola, cello].

Marshall. Nicholas.
Collection: *Seven Folksongs,* Forsyth, [recorder (or other melody instrument) and piano/guitar].
    Brisk Young Widow, The, *Anon,* D [d′-f′′#], Forsyth 7 Folksongs.
    Ca' the yowes, *Robert Burns,* Am [c′-e′′], Forsyth 7 Folksongs.
    Keel Row, The, *Anon,* G [d′-g′′], Forsyth 7 Folksongs.
    Little Red Lark, The, *Alfred Percival Graves,* F [c′-f′′], Forsyth 7 Folksongs.
    Richard of Taunton Dene, *Anon,* A♭ [e′b-f′′], Forsyth 7 Folksongs.
    Soldier, soldier, *Anon,* B♭ [d′-f′′], Forsyth 7 Folksongs.
    Ye banks and braes, *Robert Burns,* G [d′-e′′], Forsyth 7 Folksongs.

Martin, Jennifer. 1967– SMIC. [viola, cello, piano].

Matheson, Iain. 1956–
    Breaking Silence, [soprano], SMIC [clarinet, cello, accordion, percussion, piano].
    Et Tout d'un Coup, *Marcel Proust,* [voice], SMIC [bass clarinet, trumpet, violin, cello, piano].
    Soundbites, *Proverbs 30 v. 15,* [soprano], SMIC [E♭ clarinet/bass clarinet, cello, percussion, musette, piano].

Mathias, William. 1934-1992.
Arrangements: *Three Welsh Melodies,* [high, low], Gwynn [harp].
    David of the White Rock, Gwynn 3 Welsh.
    Loom, The, Gwynn 3 Welsh.
    Miller's Song, The, Gwynn 3 Welsh.

Matthews, Colin. 1946–
    Cantata on the death of Antony, *Dion Cassius*, [soprano], Faber [Eb clarinet, bass clarinet, viola, cello, double bass].
    Five Sonnets: To Orpheus (cycle), *Rainer Maria Rilke*, tr. *J B Leishman*, [a′#(c′#)-a′′b(g′′), (m), Faber [harp].
    Pli de Lin, *Tom Paulin*, (French), [soprano], Faber [2 violins, viola, cello, piano].
    Strugnell's Haiku, *Wendy Cope,* Faber hire [clarinet, bass clarinet, viola/3 tamtams, cello, double bass].

Matthews, David. 1943–
Collection: *Two Housman Songs,* Faber [string quartet].
    Congress of Passions, A, *Sappho*, (Greek), [medium] Faber [oboe, piano].
    Loveliest of trees, *A. E. Housman*, [soprano], Faber [string quartet].
    Marina, *T. S. Eliot*, [baritone], Faber [basset horn, viola, piano].
    Skies are now skies (String Quartet No 7), *D. H. Lawrence, E. E. Cummings, Song of Songs,* [tenor], Faber [string quartet].
    Spell of Sleep, *Kathleen Raine*, [baritone], Faber [clarinet, piano].
    Spell of Sleep, *Kathleen Raine*, [soprano], Faber [2 clarinets, viola, cello, double bass].
    Winter Passions, [voice], Faber hire [5 players].

Maw, John **Nicholas.** 1935–
Collection: *Six Interiors*, B&H [guitar].
    At tea, *Thomas Hardy*, [d′-f′′#], B&H 6 Interiors.
    Head of Orpheus, The, *Robert Kelly*, [soprano], Faberprint [2 clarinets].
    I look into my glass, *Thomas Hardy*, [c′#-f′′], B&H 6 Interiors.
    In tenebris, *Thomas Hardy*, [g-g′′], B&H 6 Interiors.
    Inscriptions for a Peal of Eight Bells, *Thomas Hardy*, [b-a′′b], B&H 6 Interiors.
    Neutral Tones, *Thomas Hardy*, [b-g′′], B&H 6 Interiors.
    Roman Canticle, *Robert Browning*, [mezzo soprano], Faber [flute, viola, harp].
    To Life, *Thomas Hardy*, [d′b-g′′], B&H 6 Interiors.

Maxwell, Michael. 1958–
Arrangement:
    (Water of Tyne, The, *Anon*, Eb [eb-g′′](f), Schott [clarinet, piano].)

Maxwell Davies, Sir **Peter.** 1934– SMIC.
    Anakreontika, [mezzo], Chester [alto flute, cello, harpsichord, percussion].
    Buxtehude 'Also hat Gott die Welt geliebet', [soprano], Chester hire [flute, harpsichord, celeste, violin, cello].
    Dark Angels (cycle), *George Mackay Brown*, [e′b-b′′b](f), B&H [guitar].
    Excuse me, *Charles Dibdin,* [soprano], Chester hire [flute, clarinet, percussion, piano, violin, cello].
    (Fiddlers at the wedding, [soprano], B&H hire [alto flute, mandoline, guitar, percussion].
    (From Stone to Thorn, [mezzo], B&H hire [basset-clarinet, guitar, harpsichord, percussion].)
    Medium, The, (monodrama), *Maxwell Davies*, [d(e)-c′′′](f), B&H [unaccompanied].
    (My Lady Lothian's lilt, [mezzo], B&H [6 players].
    (Tractus, Chester [guitar].)

Miles, P. Napier. 1865-1935.
Collection: *Four Songs*, BMP [oboe].
    Cliff top, The, *Robert Bridges*, [A-e′](m), BMP 4 Songs.
    Poppy, The, *Robert Bridges*, [d′-f′′](m), BMP 4 Songs.
    Thou art alone, fond lover, *Robert Bridges*, [B-f′#](m), BMP 4 Songs.
    When June is come, *Robert Bridges*, [c-f′′](m), BMP 4 Songs.

Mitchell, John.
    Lovely Joan, [medium], Modus [guitar].
    Ship in Distress, The, [soprano], Modus [clarinet, piano].
    West Wind, The, *John Masefield,* Ab [d′b-g′′](f), Modus [clarinet, piano].

Arrangements:
    John Barleycorn *Traditional,* [voice], Modus [guitar].
    Pretty Girl Milking her Cow, *Irish Folk Song,* [medium], Modus [guitar].

Montague, Stephen. 1943–
    Wild nights, *Emily Dickinson,* [soprano], UMP [clarinet, viola, piano].

Morgan, Hilda. WMIC. [3 woodwind *or* organ].

Morris, Andrew.
Collection: *Snowdon Songs,* [from a Celtic Miscellany], [mezzo],Da Capo [clarinets, viola, cello, double bass].
    Bright Field, The, *R. S. Thomas,* [mezzo], Da Capo [clarinets, viola, cello, double bass].
    Flute of Interior Time, *Kabir* [soprano], Da Capo [flute, cello].
    Still Waters, [soprano], Da Capo [flute, clarinet, bassoon, viola, cello].
    Tai Chi on a Rainy Day, *Andrew Morris,* [mezzo], Da Capo [clarinet, viola, cello].

Muldowney, Dominic John. 1952–
Collection: *Songs from 'The Resistable Rise of Arturo Ui',* [Berthold Brecht *tr.* Bolt], [voice], Faber hire [alto saxophone, trumpet, 2 synthesisers, drum-kit].
    On Suicide, *Berthold Brecht,* tr. *Anon,* [soprano], Faber hire [2 clarinets, viola, cello, double bass].
    Out of danger, *James Fenton,* [soprano], Faber hire [2 clarinets, viola, cello, double bass].

Musgrave, Thea. 1928–
Collection: *Five Love Songs,* [soprano], Chester hire [guitar]; *Four Portraits,* [Sir John Davies], [baritone], Chester hire [clarinet, piano].
    A la Esperanza (Hope), [soprano], Chester hire [organ].
    Primavera, *Amalia Elguera,* [a(bb)-c′′′](f), Chester [flute].
    Sir Patrick Spens, *Anon,* [bb-a′′](m), Chester [guitar].

Naylor, Peter. 1933–
    Lord Jesus Christ, shall I stand still? [medium], Modus [guitar].
    My prime of youth is but a frost of cares, *Chidiock Tichborne,* Am [e′-g′′](m)], Brunton [harpsichord]; Fm [c′-e′′b](m), Brunton [harpsichord].

Nevens, David. 1945– WMIC. [oboe], [guitar].

Neville, David James. WMIC. [flute, clarinet, harp, cello].

Newson, George. 1932–
    And when love speaks, *George Newson,* [soprano], Lengnick [clarinet, cor anglais, viola, harp, slide projection].
    Marriage Song, A, *W. H. Auden,* [medium}, Lengnick [any 3 instruments].
    Song for September, A, *George Newson,* [soprano], Lengnick [2 clarinets, violin, viola, double bass].
    Three Interiors, *George Newson,* [soprano], Lengnick [flute, oboe, clarinet, bassoon, horn, double bass].
    Unbroken Circle, The, *George Newson,* [soprano], Lengnick [Eb clarinet/Bb clarinet alto clarinet/ bassett, Bb clarinet/bass clarinet, vibraphone/marimba].

Northcott, Bayan Peter. 1940–
Collections: *Three English Lyrics,* S&B [clarinet, viola, double bass]; *Six Japanese Lyrics,* S&B [clarinet, violin].
    Across the snow, *Mishudo* tr. *Bayan Northcott,* [bb-c′′′](f), S&B 6 Japanese.
    Blaze of sultry noon, *Seiji Tanaka* tr. *Bayan Northcott,* [d′-a′′](f), S&B 6 Japanese.
    Experimenting, *Hokushi* tr. *Bayan Northcott,* [b-b′′](f), S&B 6 Japanese.
    In the Village, *Ryōkan* tr. *Bayan Northcott,* [c′#-b′′](f), S&B 6 Japanese.
    Like a child's kite, *Lady Onitsumi* tr. *Bayan Northcott,* [d′-c′′′](f), S&B 6 Japanese.
    Maidens came, The, *Anon,* [d′-b′′b](f), S&B 3 English.
    Momento, *Hilda Morley,* [c′#-g′′](f), S&B [flute].
    O westron winde, *Anon,* [c′#-f′′#](f), S&B 3 English.
    Pleasure it is, *Cornyshe,* [c′-f′′#](f), S&B 3 English.
    Poet Nightingale, *Anon* tr. *Bayan Northcott,* [c′-b′′](f), S&B 6 Japanese.

Nyman, Michael. 1944–
    Ariel Songs (cycle), *Shakespeare,* [low], Chester [string quartet].

Ballad of Kastriot Renhapi, [soprano], Chester [string quartet].
Grounded, [mezzo], Chester [soprano, alto, tenor saxophones, violin, piano].
Miserere, [soprano], Chester [string quartet].
Mozart on Mortality, *Wolfgang Amadeus Mozart,* tr. *Anon,* [soprano], Chester hire [6 instruments].
Piano sings, The, [soprano *or* contralto], Chester [string quartet].
Polish Love Song, [soprano], Chester hire [6 instruments].
Tomorrow, *No text*, [a*b*-c'''#](f), Chester [organ].

Orr, Buxton. 1924–1997. BMIC.
Canzona, [tenor], SMIC/Gamber [clarinet, string trio].
Knight and the Lady, The, *R. H. Barham,* [any voice], SMIC/Gamber [unaccompanied].
Ten Types of Hospital Visitor, [soprano], SMIC/Gamber [double bass].

Orr, Robin. 1909–
Collection: *Four Romantic Songs,* [Helen Waddell], [tenor], SMIC/Peters [oboe, string quartet].
Journeys and Places, [mezzo], SMIC [string quartet, double bass].

Osborne, Nigel. 1948–
Collection: *Two Spanish Songs*, Universal [unaccompanied].
Como las flores, *Anon*, [soprano], Universal 2 Spanish.
Four loom weaver, *Anon*, [soprano], Universal [tape].
Madeleine de la Ste-Baume, *Latin, Greek, Aramaic*, [soprano], Universal [double bass]
Oyó sus gritos, *Anon*, [a*b*-a''*b*], Universal 2 Spanish.

Paintăl, Priti. BMIC. [clarinet; cello].

Painter, Christopher William. WMIC. [oboe].

Papastávrou, Krinió.
Collections: *Seven Songs for a Child*, Bardic [harp] (For details see main catalogue).
Arrangements: *Six Greek Songs,* Bardic [guitar].
Arcananian Song, *Anon* tr. *Krinió Papastávrou*, [e'-f''#], Bardic 6 Greek.
Chian Girl, The, *Anon* tr. *Krinió Papastávrou*, [g'-e''], Bardic 6 Greek.
Chian Ship, The, *Anon* tr. *Krinió Papastávrou*, [g'-a''], Bardic 6 Greek.
Dance from the Island of Samos, *Anon* tr. *Krinió Papastávrou*, [g'-e''], Bardic 6 Greek.
Macedonian Dance, *Anon* tr. *Krinió Papastávrou*, [g'-d''], Bardic 6 Greek.
Pentozáles, *Anon* tr. *Krinió Papastávrou*, [g'-e''], Bardic 6 Greek.

Paynter, John. 1931–
Shine out, fair sun, *Anon*, [d'*b*-b''*b*], BMP [organ].

Peterkin, Norman. 1886–1982.
Collection: *Three Songs for Voice and Viola*, BMP [viola].
Curse on a Closed Gate, *Joseph Campbell,* [d'-g''], BMP 3 Songs.
Journeyman Weaver, The, *Joseph Campbell,* [c'-f''], BMP 3 Songs.
Piper, A, *Seamus O'Sullivan,* [d'-f''#], BMP 3 Songs.

Philips, John C.
Collection: *Young Jesus Sweit*, Banks [unaccompanied].
O my dear heart, young Jesus sweit, *Martin Luther* tr. *Wedderburn*, [d'-g''], Banks Young Jesus.
There is no rose of such virtue, *Anon*, [c'-a''], Banks Young Jesus.
When Christ was born of Mary free, *Anon*, [c'#-a''], Banks Young Jesus.

Phillips, Julian. WMIC. [viola].

Pilling, Dorothy.
Collection: *Collected Songs*, Forsyth.
Jenny kiss'd me, *Leigh Hunt*, G [d'-g''], Forsyth Collected [descant recorder *or* oboe].

Pitfield, Thomas Baron. 1903–
Collection: *Selected Songs*, Forsyth.
Alone, *Walter de la Mare*, B [f'#-g''#](f), Forsyth Selected [violin].
Desdemona's song, *Shakespeare*, Em [c'-g''], Forsyth Selected [guitar].
Desdemona's Song, Brunton [unaccompanied, *or* harp *or* celtic harp].

Fiddler, The, *Walter de la Mare*, F [f′-a′′](f), Forsyth Selected [violin].
Horseman, The, *Walter de la Mare*, Gm [e′b-b′′b](f), Forsyth Selected [violin].
Song of Compassion, *Thomas Pitfield*, [d′-e′′(g′′)], Forsyth Selected [organ].
Willow, The, *Thomas Pitfield*, Dm [bb-f′′], Forsyth Selected [treble recorder *or* flute *or* clarinet, harpsichord *or* piano].
Winter song, *Katherine Mansfield*, [d′-e′′], Forsyth Selected [sopranino recorder *or* flute *or* oboe, piano].

Poole, Geoffrey. 1949–
Collection: *Calligrammes d'Apollinaire,* [ab-a′′](f), Maecenas [clarinet, piano].

Purcell, Henry. 1659–1695.
Hark the echoing air, *Elkanah Settle*, A [c′#-f′′#], OUP *Solo Sacred* [organ arr. Jenkins].

Quilter, Roger. 1877–1953.
Collection: (*Three Pastoral Songs*, Elkin [violin, cello, piano].)
 (Cherry valley, *Joseph Campbell*, E [b-e′′], Elkin 3 Pastoral.)
 I sing of a maiden (Old Carol, An), *Anon*, G [f′-g′′], Mayhew *Holy Night* [organ].
 (I will go with my father a-ploughing, *Joseph Campbell*, Ab [c′-f′′(e′′b)], Elkin 3 Pastoral.)
 (I wish and I wish, *Joseph Campbell*, Cm [c′-g′′(e′′b)], Elkin 3 Pastoral.)

Rainier, Priaulx. 1903–1986.
Collection: *Cycle for Declamation*, Schott 1954 [unaccompanied]. 'Soprano, Alto or Baritone should transpose to suit the tessitura of the voice.'
 Dance of the Rain, *Eugene Marais* tr. *Uys Krige*, [d′-g′′](m), Schott [guitar].
 In the wombe of the earth, *John Donne*, [f′-g′′], Schott Cycle.
 Nunc, lento sonitu, *John Donne*, [d′-a′′], Schott Cycle.
 Ubunzima, *Zulu poem*, [e′b-b′′b(a′′b)], Schott [guitar].
 Wee cannot bid the fruits, *John Donne*, [e′b-a′′], Schott Cycle.

Randall, Anthony.
Collection: *Three Songs for Soprano, Horn and Piano*, AR Music [horn, piano].
 Autumn, *Thomas Hood*, Am [soprano], AR Music 3 Songs.
 Do not go gentle into that good night, *Dylan Thomas*, [d′-b′′](f), AR Music [horn, piano].
 Lullaby, *Kenneth Reynolds*, G [soprano], AR Music 3 Songs.
 Requiem, *Robert Louis Stevenson*, Dm [soprano], AR Music 3 Songs.

Rands, Bernard. 1935–
 Ballad 3, *Gilbert Sorrentino*, [a-a′′](f), Universal [tape].

Rawsthorne, Alan. 1905–1971.
 Scena Rustica, *John Skelton*, [e′-b′′b](f), BMP [harp].
 Tankas of the Four Seasons, *Charles Riba* tr. *J L Gili*, [tenor], BMP hire [oboe, clarinet, bassoon, violin, cello].

Read, Martin M.
Collection: *Three Songs from 'As You Like It'*, ([Shakespeare], [a-d′′], Fand [flute, clarinet, piano].
 Autumn, *John Keats,* [voice], Fand [cor anglais, viola, cello].
 Full fathom five, *Shakespeare*, [e′-b′′], Fand [oboe *or* clarinet].
 He tells her, *Wendy Cope*, [soprano], Fand [clarinet, viola, cello].

Rees, Howard. WMIC. [flute, oboe, clarinet, bass clarinet], [piano, timpani], [unaccompanied], [flute/picco;o, clarinet, electric organ, violin, cello].

Reynolds, Peter. WMIC. [cello, piano].

Rhys, Stephen. WMIC. [clarinet, side drum], [string quartet].

Rice, Hugh Collins. 1962–
 In the grave, whither thou goest, *Christina Rossetti*, [soprano], Lengnick [clarinet, piano, viola, cello, vibraphone].

Roberts, Trevor. 1940– WMIC. [clarinet, violin], [harp].

Rodgers, Sarah. 1953–
 King of the Golden River, The (cycle), *John Ruskin,* [tenor], Impulse [string quartet].

Roe, Betty. 1930–
Collection: *Cat and Mouse*, Yorke [double bass]; *Four Shakespeare Songs*, Thames [flute, piano]; *Jazz Songs* Yorke [double bass]; *Madam Songs*, Thames [double bass]; *Madam's Three Callers*, Thames [cello]; *Noble Numbers*, Thames [harpsichord], *London Fantasies*, Thames [double bass]; *Verities*, Thames [clarinet].
    Appeal to Cats in the Business of Love, An, *Thomas Flatman*, [d'-a''](f), Yorke Cat and Mouse.
    Carol of the Beasts, *James Reeves*, E♭ [c'-e''♭], Thames [flute, piano].
    Come away, death, *Shakespeare*, [e'-e''], Thames 4 Shakespeare.
    Euphonium Dance, *Jacqueline Froom*, D [a'-f''#](f), Yorke Jazz.
    Firstlings, *Rita Ford*, A♭ [e'♭-g''], Thames [B♭ clarinet, piano].
    Grave by the Sea, *Charles Causley*, [e'-a''♭](f), Thames Verities.
    I am the great sun, *Charles Causley*, [e'-g''](f), Thames Verities.
    Legato Leicester Square, *Jacqueline Froom*, [d'-e''♭], Thames London.
    Madam and her Might-have-been, *Langston Hughes*, [d'#-g''](f), Thames Madam Songs.
    Madam and the Census Man, *Langston Hughes*, Cm [g-e''♭](f), Thames Three Callers.
    Madam and the Fortune Teller, *Langston Hughes*, [c'#-e''](f), Thames Madam Songs.
    Madam and the Minister, *Langston Hughes*, C [g-e''](f), Thames Three Callers.
    Madam and the Minister, *Langston Hughes*, E [b-e''](f) Yorke Jazz.
    Madam and the Wrong Visitor, *Langston Hughes*, Em [b-f''#](f) Thames Three Callers.
    Madam's Calling Cards, *Langston Hughes*, [e'-g'''](f) Thames Madam Songs.
    Mouse, *Clifford Dyment*, [c'-e''](f), Yorke Cat and Mouse.
    Now, *Charles Causley*, [f'#-g''#](f), Thames Verities.
    Nursery Rhyme, *Anon*, [c'-d''](f), Yorke Cat and Mouse.
    Nursery Rhyme, *Anon*, [b-b'](f), Yorke Cat and Mouse.
    Orpheus with his lute, *Shakespeare*, D [d'-d''], Thames 4 Shakespeare.
    Pizzicato Piccadilly, *Jacqueline Froom*, [e'-g''(f'#)], Thames London.
    Sigh no more, *Shakespeare*, G [d'-d''], Thames 4 Shakespeare.
    Silver Hound, The, (cycle), *Ursula Vaughan Williams*, [b-b''♭](m), Thames [horn, piano].
    Thames a tempo, *Jacqueline Froom*, [c'#-e''], Thames London.
    To God (My God, I'm wounded), *Robert Herrick*, [b-d''], Thames Noble Numbers.
    To God (God gives not onely corne), *Robert Herrick*, [c'-d''], Thames Noble Numbers.
    To his Angrie God, *Robert Herrick*, [b-e''♭], Thames Noble Numbers.
    To His Saviour, a Child, *Robert Herrick*, D [a-d''], Thames Noble Numbers.
    To his Sweet Saviour, *Robert Herrick*, [c'-d''], Thames Noble Numbers.
    Two Mice, The, *James Reeves*, [c'-f''](f), Yorke Cat and Mouse.
    Willow Song, The, *Shakespeare*, [d'-d'''], Thames 4 Shakespeare.

Routh, Francis. 1927–
    Circles, Op 18, *Stephen Tunnicliffe*, [soprano], Redcliffe [clarinet, viola, piano].
    Elegy, Op 6, *St John of the Cross* tr. *Campbell*, [soprano], Redcliffe [violin, piano].
    Love's Fool, Op 40a, *Rainer, Yeats, Rainer*, [soprano], Redcliffe [flute, guitar *or* piano].
    Two Cautionary Tales (cycle), *Rhoda Levine*, [counter-tenor], Redcliffe [guitar].
    Vocalise, Op 38, *No text*, [soprano], Redcliffe [clarinet, piano, violin, cello].

Rowley, Alec. 1892–1958.
    O saving victim, [bass], Novello [organ].

Rubbra, Charles Edmund. 1901–1986.
Collections: *Amoretti (2nd Series)*, S&B [string quartet] *see main catalogue for details*; *Ave Maria Gratia Plena*, Lengnick [string quartet]; *Jade Mountain, The,* Lengnick [harp], *Two Songs*, Lengnick [harp]; *Two Sonnets*, Lengnick, [viola, piano].
    Autumn Night Message, An, *Wêi Ying-Wu*, tr. *Wittner Bynner*, [a'-a''♭], Lengnick Jade.
    Cantata Pastorale (cycle), *Plato* tr. *Leaf, St Augustine* tr. *Waddell*, [d'-a''♭], Lengnick [Treble Recorder *or* Flute, Harpsichord *or* Piano, Cello].
    Farewell to a Japanese Buddhist Priest Bound Homeward, *Ch'ien Ch'i*, tr. *Wittner Bynner*, [e'-a''], Lengnick Jade.
    Hymn to the Virgin, A, *Anon*, Am [d'-g''], Lengnick 2 Songs.
    Jesukin, *St Ita*, [e'-f''#], Lengnick 2 Songs.
    Mystery, The, *Ralph Hodgson*, [f'-e''], Lengnick 4 Short [unaccompanied].
    Night Thought on Terrace Tower, A, *Wêi Chuang*, tr. *Witter Bynner*, [e'-b''], Lengnick Jade.
    O excellent Virgin Princess, *François Villon*, tr. *D. G. Rossetti*, [d'-g''], Lengnick Ave.
    O my deir hert, young Jesus sweit, *Martin Luther*, tr. *Wedderburn*, [d'-g''], Lengnick Ave.
    On Hearing Her Play the Harp, *Li Tüan*, tr. *Wittner Bynner*, [g'-g''], Lengnick Jade.
    On the Reed of Our Lord's Passion, *William Alabaster*, [a'-e''], Lengnick 2 Sonnets.
    Rosa mundi, *Rachel Annand Taylor*, Gm [d'-e''♭] Lengnick 4 Short [2 violins].

Salve, Regina, *Hermann?* [f-c''#], Lengnick [harpsichord].
Song of the Southern River, A, *Li Yi*, tr. *Wittner Bynner*, [a'-a''], Lengnick Jade.
Upon the Crucifix, *William Albaster*, D [c'#-e''], Lengnick 2 Sonnets.

Runswick, Daryl. 1946–
Lady Lazarus, *Sylvia Plath*, amplified female voice, Faber [unaccompanied].

Rutter, John. 1945–
Collection: *Shadows*, OUP [guitar].
  Close thine eyes, *Francis Quarles*, E [c'#-d''], OUP Shadows.
  Epicure, The, *Thomas Jordan*, A [a-e''], OUP Shadows.
  Gather ye rosebuds, *Robert Herrick*, E [c'#-e''], OUP Shadows.
  In a goodly night, *Anon*, D [a-d''], OUP Shadows.
  O death, rock me asleep, *Anon* 14th cent. *(Anne Boleyn*?), F#m [c'#-c''#], OUP Shadows.
  Shadows, *Samuel Daniel*, Em [c'-c''], OUP Shadows.
  Sic vita, *Henry King*, Bm [b-d''], OUP Shadows.
  Sonnet, *Samuel Daniel*, G [b-d''], OUP Shadows.

Salzedo, Leonard Lopès. 1921– BMIC. [harp].

Samuel, Rhian. 1944– BMIC.
Collection: *Three Songs*, Andresier [guitar]; *Trois Chansons de Francois Villon*, S&B [flute *or* piccolo].
  Ballade I, *Francois Villon*, [g'-a''], S&B 3 Chansons.
  Ballade II, *Francois Villon*, [d'b-a''b], S&B 3 Chansons.
  Dream Within a Dream, *Edgar Allan Poe*, [e'-g''], Andresier 3 Songs.
  Epistre, *Francois Villon*, [c'#-a''b], S&B 3 Chansons.
  If the owl calls again, *John Haines*, [a-a''], Andresier 3 Songs.
  Hare in the Moon, *Japanese Folk Tale*, [a-c'''](f), S&B [vibraphone, marimba, double bass].
  Night, *Wole Soyinka*, [c'#-g''], Andresier 3 Songs.
  Witch's Manuscript, The, *Carol Rumens*, [soprano], S&B [brass quintet].

Sander, Peter. BMIC. [guitar].

Saxton, Robert. 1953–
  Brise Marine, *Stéphane Mallarmé*, [c'-b''b](f), Chester hire [piano, tape].
  Cantata No 2, [tenor] Chester hire [oboe, piano].
  Prayer Before Sleep, [soprano], Chester [cello, piano].
  Prayer to a Child, [soprano], Chester hire [2 clarinets].
  Where are you going to, my pretty maid, [soprano], Chester hire [flute, clarinet, harp, guitar, violin, cello].

Scott, Cyril Meir. 1879–1970.
  (Idyll, *Cyril Scott*, [d'b-c'''](f), Elkin [flute].)
  Idyllic Fantasy, *Cyril Scott*, [voice], Novello [oboe and cello].

Seamarks, Colin.
  Six Mehitabel Magpies (cycle), *Don Marquis*, [b-b''](f), Yorke [double bass].

Self, Adrian.
Collection: *Song Album, A*; Bruton.
  O sacred head, *P. Gerhard* tr. *H. W. Baker*, [c'-f''], Brunton Album [organ].

Seiber, Matyas György. 1905–1960.
Collections: *Four Hungarian Folksongs*, S&B [violin]; *Drei Morgenstern Lieder*, Universal [clarinet]; *Four French Folk Songs*, Schott [guitar].
  Das Knee, *Morgenstern*, [bb-f''](f), Universal 3 Morgenstern.
  Das Nasobëm, *Morgenstern*, [d'-a''](f), Universl 3 Morgenstern.
  Die Trichter, *Morgenstern*, [bb-a''](f), Universal 3 Morgenstern.
  Farewell, *Anon* tr. *A. L. Lloyd*, [c'-d''], S&B 4 Hungarian.
  J'ai descendu, *Anon*, [e'-e''], Schott 4 French.
  Lament, *Anon* tr. *A. L. Lloyd*, [d'-e''], S&B 4 Hungarian.
  Le Rossignol, *Anon*, [e'-d''], Schott 4 French.
  Marguerite, elle est malade, *Anon*, [e'-e''], Schott 4 French.
  Quarrel, *Anon* tr. *A. L. Lloyd*, [c'-e''], S&B 4 Hungarian.

Réveillez-vous, *Anon*, [a'-e''], Schott 4 French.
Soldier's Song, *Anon* tr. *A. L. Lloyd*, [d'-f''], S&B 4 Hungarian.

Shield, William. 1748–1829.
Hope and Love, *William Pearce*, G [e'-g''], OUP (Roberts) *O Tuneful Voice* [harp].
Tis only no harm to know it, you know, *John O'Keeffe*, B♭ [f'-g''](f), OUP (Roberts) *O Tuneful Voice* [harp].
Ye balmy breezes gently blow, *John Rannie*, C [d'-g''](m), OUP (Roberts) *O Tuneful Voice* [harp].

Short, Michael. 1937– BIMC. [Guitar].
Collection: *Six Mediaeval Lyrics*, Thames [clarinet].
Bird on briar, *Anon*, [f''-g''](f), Thames Lyrics.
Go, heart, *Anon*, [f''-f''](f), Thames Lyrics.
Ivy, chief of trees, *Anon*, [f''-f''], Thames Lyrics.
Now welcome, summer, *Anon*, [e'-g''], Thames Lyrics.
Of ev'ry kind of tree, *Anon*, [e'-e''](f), Thames Lyrics.
There is none so wise a man, *Anon*, [g'-e''], Thames Lyrics.

Shur, Laura. SMIC. [flute, piano], [oboe, piano], [clarinet *or* violin, piano].
Collection: In the Pink, SMIC [oboe *or* flute *or* recorder *or* violin, piano].
At the Cenotaph, *Siegfried Sassoon*, [c'#-e''], SMIC In the Pink.
Attack, *Siegfried Sassoon*, [c'-f''#], SMIC In the Pink.
Everyone Sang, *Siegfried Sassoon*, [c'-f''], SMIC In the Pink.
General, The, *Siegfried Sassoon*, [c'-e''], SMIC In the Pink.
In the Pink, *Siegfried Sassoon*, [c'#-f''#], SMIC In the Pink.
Sounds from the Middle Floor, [soprano], SMIC [flute, piano].
Arrangements:
De'il's Awa' Wi' Th' Exciseman, *Robert Burns*, [voice], SMIC [oboe *or* clarinet *or* flute *or* violin, piano].
Hey, Ca' Thro', *Robert Burns*, [voice], SMIC [oboe *or* clarinet *or* flute *or* violin, piano].
Man's a Man, A, *Robert Burns*, [voice], SMIC [oboe *or* clarinet *or* flute *or* violin, piano].

Smith Brindle, Reginald. 1917–
Collection: *Two Poems of Manley Hopkins*, [low], Schott [guitar].
My own heart, *Gerard Manley Hopkins*, [b♭-e''], Schott 2 Poems.
Windhover, The, *Gerard Manley Hopkins*, [b♭-e''], Schott 2 Poems.

Snell, David.
Collection: *Three Songs to Words of Stevie Smith*, Modus [harp].
Autumn Thoughts, [voice], Modus [harp].
Lullaby, [voice], Modus [harp].
Arrangements:
Idle days in Summertime, [voice], Modus [harp].
Ye Banks and Braes, [voice], Modus [harp].

Sohal, Naresh. 1939–
Kavita II, *John Donne*, [soprano], Novello [flute, piano].

Solomons, David W. 1953–
Collection: *Songs of Solomons Vol. 1*, Da Capo [guitar].
Beetle's Wings, *David Solomons*, [alto], Da Capo [guitar].
Camden Town, *David Solomons*, [alto], Da Capo [guitar].
Christmas Haikus, *A. E. Radcliffe*, [alto], Da Capo Songs.
Dawn in the Room, *E. M., S. N., D. W. Solomons*, [alto *or* baritone], Da Capo Songs, Da Capo.
'Exmass' Carol, An, *David Solomons*, [alto], Da Capo [guitar].
Greek Wassail, *David W. Solomons*, [alto], Da Capo Songs.
Haviranosan no Haiku, *Mark Haviland*, [alto], Da Capo Songs.
Invitation to the journey, *Charles Baudelaire* tr. *S. N. Solomons*, [alto], Da Capo Songs.
Lhudè Sing Tishoo, *Anon*, [mezzo or alto], Da Capo [guitar].
Lookin', just lookin', *David W. Solomons*, [alto], Da Capo.
Quiet way you move me, The, *Nevil Frenkiel*, [alto], Da Capo Songs, Da Capo.
Rose, *Iskan Açikça* tr. *Theo Witty*, [alto], Da Capo Songs.
Sentimental Song, *David Solomons*, [alto], Da Capo [guitar].
Swallows, The, *Gourgen Mahari* tr. *J. R. Russell*, [alto], Da Capo Songs.

Souster, Timothy Andrew James. 1943–1994. BMIC. [Viola].

Spedding, Frank. 1929–2001 SMIC. [guitar].
Collection: *Four Scots Songs,* [tenor], SMIC [guitar].
Man with the axe, The, [tenor], SMIC [guitar].

Stafford, Simeon.
Empire of the Gods, [voice], Da Capo Music [piano, tapes].

Standford, Patric. 1939–
Collections: *Gitanjali (Song Offerings),* RTS [flute, clarinet, horn, harp, violin, cello]; *The Inheritor,* RTS [string quartet].
    Avenues and Circles, *Ursula Vaughan Williams,* [d'-g''], RTS Inheritor.
    City, The, *Ursula Vaughan Williams,* [e'-g''], RTS Inheritor.
    Day is no more, The, *Rabindranath Tagore,* [bb-e''b], RTS Gitanjali.
    I am here to sing you songs, *Rabindranath Tagore,* [d-e''b], RTS Gitanjali.
    Let all the strains of joy, *Rabindranath Tagore,* [b-f''], RTS Gitanjali.
    Lost at Sea, *Ursula Vaughan Williams,* [e'-a''b], RTS Inheritor.
    Mound Burial, The, *Ursula Vaughan Williams,* [e'-g''], RTS Inheritor.
    Museum, The, *Ursula Vaughan Williams,* [e'b-g''], RTS Inheritor.
    Prologue, *Ursula Vaughan Williams,* [c'-f''#], RTS Inheritor.
    Wine Shop, The, *Ursula Vaughan Williams,* [e'-g''], RTS Inheritor.
    You have made me endless, *Rabindranath Tagore,* [bb-f''], RTS Gitanjali.

Stanford, Sir Charles Villiers. 1852–1924.
    Fling out your windows wide, *Arthur Quiller-Couch,* Eb [e'b-f''], Mayhew *Holy Night* [organ].
    Song of Battle, A, *Psalm 124,* Gm [d'-e''], S&B; *Bbm,* S&B [organ].
    Song of Freedom, A, *Psalm 126,* C [e'b-f''], Classical/S&B; *Eb,* S&B [organ].
    Song of Hope, A, *Psalm 130,* Bm [bb-d''], S&B; *Fm,* S&B [organ].
    Song of Peace, A, *Isaiah 9,* A [a'-e''], Classical/S&B; *C,* S&B [organ].
    Song of Trust, A, *Psalm 121,* Db [c'-e''b], S&B; *F,* S&B [organ].
    Song of Wisdom, A, *Ecclesiasticus 24,* C [c'-e''(g'')], S&B; *Eb,* S&B [organ].
    Winds of Bethlehem, The, *Winifred Letts,* Gm [d'-g''], Mayhew *Holy Night* [organ].

Steele, Douglas. 1910–
    Hark shepherds awake, *D. C. Hamley,* G [d'-f''#], Forsyth Selected [treble recorder].

Steptoe, Roger Guy. 1953–
Collection, *Chinese Lyrics Set 1,* S&B, [string quintet] see main catalogue for details.
    From the Spanish Descent, *David Defoe,* Lengnick [violin, cello, piano].
    Arrangements: *Two Folk Song Arrangements for baritone and violin,* S&B [violin].
    Brigg Fair, *Anon,* [E(G)-e'](m), S&B 2 Folk Songs.
    Early one spring, *Anon,* [c-d'](m), S&B 2 Folk Song.

Stevenson, Ronald. 1928–
    Four Vietnamese Miniatures, (cycle), *Ho Chi Minh,* [high], Stevenson [harp].
    Nine Haiku (cycle), *Japanese* tr. *Keith Bosley,* [high], Stevenson [harp].

Storace, Stephen. 1762–1796.
    Captivity, *Joshua Jeans,* Eb [e'b-a''b](f), OUP (Roberts) *Tuneful Voice* [harp].
    Curfew, The, *Thomas Gray,* Dm [c'#-f''], OUP (Roberts) *Tuneful Voice* [harp].
    How sweet the calm of this sequester'd shore, *Anon,* A [e'-f''#], OUP (Roberts) *Tuneful Voice* [harp].

Stout, Alastair. 1975–
Collection: *Songs,* SMIC [violin].
    Evensong: La Chanson des Oiseaux, *Jonathan Lennie,* [mezzo], SMIC Songs.
    In downstairs darkness, *Roger McGough,* [soprano], SMIC [bass clarinet, piano, tam-tam (played by singer)].
    We sat down and wept, *Psalms,* [mezzo], SMIC Songs.

Sullivan, Sir Arthur. 1842–1900.
    God shall wipe away all tears, *Bible,* E [b-e''], OUP *Solo Sacred* [organ arr. Jenkins].
    Lost Chord, The, *Adelaide Procter,* Eb [bb-e''b], OUP *Solo Sacred* [organ arr. Jenkins].
    Refrain thy voice from weeping, *Bible,* Eb [bb-e''b], OUP *Solo Sacred* [organ arr. Jenkins].

Sutton-Anderson, David.
Collection: *Five Sephardic Songs*, Andresier [guitar]. (*see also* Avril Anderson).
    Durme, durme, *Anon,* [f´#-f´´#], Andresier 5 Sephardic.
    Siete hijos tiene hann, *Anon,* [e´-f´´#], Andresier 5 Sephardic.
    Yo m'enamori d'un aire, [e´-e´´b], Andresier 5 Sephardic.

Swayne, Giles Oliver Cairns. 1946–
    Convocation of Wurms, [counter-tenor], Novello hire [organ].
    God-song, *York Mystery Plays,* [mezzo], Novello hire [flute, trombone, cello, piano].

Tann, Hilary. 1947–
    Arachne, *Jordan Smith,* [soprano], Tann, [unaccompanied].
    Girl's Song to Her Mother, A, *Menna Elfyn,* [voice], Tann, [solo instrument].
    Mother and Son, *R. S. Thomas,* [c´-b´´b(g´´)](f), OUP [E♭ clarinet *or* violin, viola, cello].

Tate, Phyllis Margaret Duncan.. 1911–1987.
Collections: *Two Ballads*, BMP [guitar]; *Scenes from Tyneside*, Emerson [clarinet in B♭, piano].
    Ballad of the Red-headed Man, The, *Patricia Beer,* [g-f´´#](f), BMP 2 Ballads.
    Died of Love, *Anon,* [b-g´´](f), Emerson Scenes.
    Elsie Marley, *Anon,* [b♭-f´´](f), Emerson Scenes, [tambourine].
    Gan to the kye wi' me, *Anon,* [d´-g´´](f), Emerson Scenes.
    Lady of Shalott, The, (cantata) *Alfred Lord Tennyson,* [tenor], OUP hire [viola, 2/3 percussion, 2 pianos, celesta].
    Mary, Mary Magdelen, *Charles Causley,* [b♭-f´´#](f), BMP 2 Ballads.
    Of all the youths, *Anon,* B♭ [d´-f´´](f), Emerson Scenes, [unaccompanied].
    Quayside Shaver, The, *Anon,* [b♭-g´´], Emerson Scenes.
    Sandgate Lass's Lament, The, *Anon,* F [b♭-g´´](f), Emerson Scenes.
    Songs of Sundrie Kindes (cycle), *Raleigh, Herrick, Wither, Anon,* [c´-b´´b](m), BMP [lute *or* guitar].
Arrangements: *Trois Chansons Tristes*, BMP [guitar].
    La dernière écuelle, *Anon,* [g´e´´b], BMP Trois Chansons.
    Le vieux blaise, *Anon,* [e´-f´´#], BMP Trois Chansons.
    Les fillettes de mon âge, *Anon,* [f´#-b´´b], BMP Trois Chansons.

Talbot, Joby. 1971–
    Seafarer, The, [mezzo], Chester [percussion trio].

Tavener, John. 1944–
Collections: *Akhmatova Songs* (Russian), [soprano], Chester [cello]; *Six Abbasid Songs*, [tenor], Chester [3 flutes/alto flutes, percussion]; *Three Surrealist Songs*, [e-b´´b](f), Chester hire [tape, piano doubling bongos].
    Child Lived, The, *Mother Thekla,* [soprano], Chester [cello].
    Lament for Constantinople, [baritone], Chester [alto flute].
    Lament for Phaedra, [soprano], Chester [cello].
    Lamentation, Last Prayer and Exaltation, *Gaelic, Latin, Church Slavonic,* [soprano], Chester [handbells].
    Meditation on the Light, *Greek text,* [counter-tenor], Chester [guitar, handbells].)
    Nipson, *Greek text,* [counter-tenor], Chester [2 treble, 2 tenor, bass viols].
    Samaveda, [soprano], Chester [flute, tampura].
    To a Child Dancing in the Wind, [soprano], Chester [alto flute, viola, harp].
    World, The, *Kathleen Raine,* [soprano], Chester [string quartet].

Taylor, Matthew. 1964–
Collection: *Four Pope Epigrams,* Maecenas.
    Of gentle Philips will I ever sing, *Alexander Pope,* [a-b´](m), Maecenas Pope [cello, harpsichord].
    Where Thames translucent waves, *Alexander Pope,* [c´-a´´b](f), Maecenas Pope [cello].

Taylor, Timothy. WMIC. [harp].

Thiman, Eric. 1900–1975.
Collection: *Church Soloist, The: Eight Sacred Songs,* [medium] Novello [organ].

Thomas, Mansel Treherne. 1909–1986.
    Come and see the baby, *Margery Morrell,* [c´-e´´], MTT [organ].

Dulas Carol, The, *Mansel Thomas* and *Peter Cobb,* [d´-d´´], MTT [organ].
Holy Child, The, *Aneirin Talfan Davies,* [d´-f´´], MTT [organ].
Song of Little Jesus, The, *Daniel H. Davies,* [c´-f´´], MTT [organ].
Arrangements:
As I wandered one fine morning, *Welsh Traditional,* [d´-d´´](m), MTT [harp].
David of the White Rock, *Welsh Traditional,* [b-e´´], MTT; [a-d´´], MTT [harp].
For this early morn, *Eos Iâl* tr. *Illtyd Lewis,* [d´-e´´], MTT [harp].
Going with Tom to Towyn, *Welsh Traditional,* [d´-e´´], MTT [harp].
Holly and the ivy, The, *English Traditional,* [d´-e´´], MTT [organ].
Maid from Penderyn Parish, The, *Welsh Traditional,* [f´-f´´](m), MTT; [d´-d´´], MTT [harp].
Megan's Daughter, *Welsh Traditional,* [c´-g´´](m), MTT; [b♭-f´´], MTT [harp].
Round the Horn, *Welsh Traditional,* [e´-e´´](m), MTT; [e´b-e´´b], MTT [harp].
Sans Day Carol, The, *Cornish Carol,* [d´-e´´b], MTT [organ].

Thompson, Peter.
Meditation, *Peter Thompson,* [a-a´´], Fand [flute, harp].

Tippett, Sir **Michael** Kemp. 1905–
Collections: *Songs for Achilles,* Schott [guitar]; *Songs for Ariel,* Schott [harpsichord], see main catalogue for details.
Across the Plain, *Michael Tippett,* [e´-b´´b](m), Schott Achilles.
By the Sea, *Michael Tippett,* [c´#-b´´b](m), Schott Achilles.
In the Tent, *Michael Tippett,* [d´-a´´](m), Schott Achilles.
Arrangement:
Bonny at morn, *Anon,* [voice], Schott [2 recorders].

Usher, Julia.
Blue Epiphany, *Mary Hadingham,* [soprano], Primavera [unaccompanied *or* clarinet].
Causeway, The, *Julia Usher, Charles Dickens,* [soprano], Primavera [trumpet, string trio].
Chess Piece, A, *Julia Usher,* [soprano], Primavera [3 clarinets].
Invocation: Poor naked wretches, *Shakespeare,* [alto], Primavera [recorder, cello, rainstick, piano].
Ordnance Survey, *Julia Usher,* [tenor], Primavera [flute, clarinet, viola, cello].
Out of Deep Waters, *Psalm fragments, Psalm 65,* [baritone], Primavera [cello].
Price of Experience, The, *William Blake,* [soprano], Primavera [vibes, clarinet, flute, cello].
Sacred Physic, *Shakespeare, adapted Julia Usher,* [soprano], Primavera [Harpsichord, cello, oboe, recorders].
Vocalism, *Walt Whitman,* [soprano], Primavera [piano, cello, synthesiser, computer].
When I heard the learned astronomer, *Walt Whitman,* [soprano], Primavera [treble recorder, violin, cello, harpsichord, optional synthesiser (JV 1080)].

Vaughan Williams, Ralph. 1872–1958.
Collections: *Along the Field,* OUP [violin]; *Four Hymns,* B&H [viola, piano]; *On Wenlock Edge,* B&H [string quartet, piano]; *Merciless Beauty,* Faber [string trio]; *Ten Blake Songs,* OUP [oboe]; *Three Vocalises,* OUP [clarinet].
Ah! sun-flower, *William Blake,* Dm [d´-f´´](m), OUP 10 Blake.
Along the field, *A. E. Housman,* [c´-f´´](m), OUP Along the Field
Bredon Hill, *A. E. Housman,* [e´b-a´´](m), B&H Wenlock Edge.
Clun, *A. E. Housman,* [d´-g´´](m), B&H Wenlock Edge.
Come Love, come Lord, *Richard Crashaw,* Gm [g´-g´´](m), B&H 4 Hymns.
Cruelty has a Human Heart, *William Blake,* [c´-g´´], OUP 10 Blake.
Divine Image, The, *William Blake,* Fm [d´b-f´´], OUP 10 Blake, [Unaccompanied].
Eternity, *William Blake,* A♭ [e´b-f´´], OUP 10 Blake.
Evening Hymn, *Robert Bridges,* E [e´-a´´](m), B&H 4 Hymns.
Fancy's Knell, *A. E. Housman,* [b-g´´], OUP Along the Field.
From far, from eve and morning, *A. E. Housman,* [g´-e´´](m), B&H Wenlock Edge.
Good-bye, *A. E. Housman,* [d´-a´´], OUP Along the Field.
Half-moon westers low, The, *A. E. Housman,* [e´-f´´#], OUP Along the Field.
He that is down need fear no fall (The woodcutter's song), *John Bunyan,* F [c´-d´´], OUP *Solo Sacred* [organ arr. Jenkins].
In the morning, *A. E. Housman,* [d´-f´´#], OUP Along the Field.
Infant Joy, *William Blake,* G♭ [e´b-e´´b], OUP 10 Blake.
Is my team ploughing? *A. E. Housman,* [d´-a´´](m), B&H Wenlock Edge.
Lamb, The, *William Blake,* Fm [e´b-f´´](m), OUP 10 Blake.
London, *William Blake,* Dm [d´-f´´](m), OUP 10 Blake, [unaccompanied].

Lord, come away, *Jeremy Taylor*, Dm [d´-b´´b](m), B&H 4 Hymns.
Oh, when I was in love with you, *A. E. Housman*, [g´-f´´#](m), B&H Wenlock Edge.
On Wenlock Edge, *A. E. Housman*, [d´-g´´](m), B&H Wenlock Edge.
Piper, The, *William Blake*, [e´b-f´´#], OUP 10 Blake.
Poison Tree, A, *William Blake*, Dm [d´-f´´](m), OUP 10 Blake.
Prelude, *no text*, [c´-c´´´](f), OUP 3 Vocalises.
Quasi minuetto, *no text*, [c´-c´´´](f), OUP 3 Vocalises.
Scherzo, *no text*, [d´-b´´b](f), OUP 3 Vocalises.
Shepherd, The, *William Blake*, F [d´-g´´], OUP 10 Blake, [unaccompanied].
Sigh that heaves the grasses, The, *A. E. Housman*, [c´-f´´], OUP Along the Field.
Since I from Love escapëd am so fat, *Geoffrey Chaucer*, [a´-a´´](m), Faber Merciless.
So hath your beauty from your hertë, *Geoffrey Chaucer*, Dm [e´-f´´](m), Faber Merciless.
Twilight People, The, *Seumas O'Sullivan*, [bb-e´´b], OUP Collected 2 [unaccompanied]; [c´-f´´], BMP 2 Poems.
We'll to the woods no more, *A. E. Housman*, [d´-g´´], OUP Along the Field.
Who is this fair one? *Isaac Watts*, Fm [e´b-a´´](m), B&H 4 Hymns.
With rue my heart is laden, *A. E. Housman*, [d´-f´´], OUP Along the Field.
Your eyën two will slay me suddenly, *Geoffrey Chaucer*, Gm [c´-a´´](m), Faber Merciless.
Arrangements: *Two English Folk-songs*, OUP [viola and piano].
Lawyer, The, *Anon*, Am [c´-e´´], OUP 2 Folk-songs.
Searching for Lambs, *Anon*, Am [e´-e´´], OUP 2 Folk-songs.

Venables, Ian.
Collection: *Invite, to Eternity,* Enigma [string quartet].
Acton Burnell, *Rennie Parker*, [db-a´b](m), Enigma [viola, piano].
Born upon an angel's breast, *John Clare*, [c-g´](m), Enigma Invite.
Evening Bells, *John Clare*, [f-g´](m), Enigma Invite.
I am, *John Clare*, [eb-a´b](m), Enigma Invite.
Invite, to Eternity, An, *John Clare*, [c-b´b](m), Enigma Invite.

Walker, Robert Matthew. 1946–
Collection: *Six Songs of Mervyn Peake*, Banks [2 clarinets, piano].
Colt, The, *Mervyn Peake*, [high], Banks 6 Songs.
If I could see, no surfaces, *Mervyn Peake*, [high], Banks 6 Songs.
Rather a little pain, *Mervyn Peake*, [high], Banks 6 Songs.
Two Fraternities, The, *Mervyn Peake*, [high], Banks 6 Songs.
Two Seasons, *Mervyn Peake*, [high], Banks 6 Songs.
What is it muffles the ascending moment? *Mervyn Peake*, [high], Banks 6 Songs.

Walton, Sir **William** Turner. 1902–1983.
Collection: *Anon. in love*, Allegro [guitar].
Beatriz's Song, *Louis MacNeice*, Dm [f´-d´´](f), Allegro [guitar *(arr.* Quine).
Fain would I change that note, *Anon*, [c´#-a´´](m), Allegro Anon. in love.
I gave her cakes and I gave her ale, *Anon*, [d´-b´´b](m), Allegro Anon. in love.
Lady, when I behold the roses, *Anon*, [c´-a´´](m), Allegro Anon. in love.
My love in her attire, *Anon*, [c´-a´´](m), Allegro Anon. in love.
O stay, sweet love, *Anon*, [c´-f´´#](m), Allegro Anon. in love.
To couple is a custom, *Anon*, [c´-a´´](m), Allegro Anon. in love.

Warlock, Peter. (Philip Arnold Heseltine). 1894–1930.
Collection: *Songs of Peter Warlock Volume 9*, Thames [string quartet].
Adam lay ybounden, *Anon*, Cm [c´-f´´], Mayhew *Holy Night* [organ].
Balulalow, *Martin Luther* tr. *Wedderburn*, Eb [e´b-f´´], Mayhew *Holy Night* [organ].
Bethlehem Down, *Bruce Blunt*, Dm [c´#-e´´b], Mayhew *Holy Night* [organ].
Carillon, carilla, *Hilaire Belloc*, G [c´-e´´], Thames Songs 8 [organ].
Chopcherry, *George Peele*, A [e´-e´´], Thames Songs.
Curlew, The, (cycle), *W. B. Yeats*, [c´-a´´](m) S&B, Thames, [flute, cor anglais and string quartet].
Fairest May, The, *Anon*, C [c´-f´´], Thames Songs.
First Mercy, The, *Bruce Blunt*, Gm [f´-f´´], Mayhew *Holy Night* [organ].
Mourn no moe, *John Fletcher*, C [c´-f´´], Thames Songs.
My gostly fader, *Charles D'Orleans*, G [e´b-f´´#], Thames Songs.
My lady is a pretty one, *Anon*, [c´-g´´](m), Thames Songs, OUP hire.
My little sweet darling, *Anon*, G [b-g´´], Thames Songs.
Sad Song, A, *John Fletcher*, Cm [f´#-g´´], Thames Songs.

Sleep, *John Fletcher*, [d'-e''b], Thames Songs, (OUP hire).
Take, O take those lips away, *Shakespeare*, Em [b-f''#], Thames Songs.
Where riches is everlastingly, *Anon*, Dm [d'-f''], Mayhew *Holy Night* [organ].

Watkins, David.
Arrangements: *Folk Songs*, S&B [harp].
    Barbara Allen, *Anon*, Db [d'b-d''b], S&B Folk Songs.
    Now is the month of maying (Morley), *Anon*, G [d'-d''] S&B Folk Songs.
    Scarborough Fair, *Anon*, Em [d'-e''](m), S&B Folk Songs.
    Summer is a-coming in, *Anon*, Eb [d'-e''b], S&B Folk Songs.

Watkins, Michael Blake. WMIC. [clarinet, guitar, violin], [guitar], [horn, piano], [lute], [oboe].

Weeks, Christopher Richard. WMIC. [guitar].

Weeks, John. BMIC. [unaccompanied], [clarinet], [viola], [organ].

Wegener, Margaret. 1920–
    Inscription for a Wayside Spring, *Frances Darwin Cornford*, [soprano], Da Capo [oboe, harp].

Wiegold, Peter. 1949–
    Saving the Sun, *Nick Otty*, [c'-a''](m), Universal [tape].
    Sing Lullaby, *Peter Wiegold*, [g-c'''#](f), Universal [double bass].

Weir, Judith. 1954–
    Alps, The, [soprano], Chester [clarinet, viola].
    Broken Branches, *Croatian*, tr. *Anon*, [soprano], Chester [piano, double bass].
    Don't let that horse, *Lawrence Ferlinghetti*, [c'-e''b](f), Chester [horn].
    King Harald's Saga, *Judith Weir*, [f#-b''](f), Novello [unaccompanied].
    Romance of Count Arnaldos, The, [soprano], Chester [2 clarinets, viola, cello, double bass].

Wellesz, Egon Joseph. 1885–1974.
    Leaden Echo and the Golden Echo, The, *Gerard Manley Hopkins*, [high], Schott [violin, clarinet, cello, piano].

Wesley, Charles. 1757–1834.
Collection: *Two Sacred Songs,* OUP (Langley & Webber), [organ].
    Gentle Jesus, meek and mild, OUP 2 Sacred.
    Might I in thy sight appear, OUP 2 Sacred.

Wilby, Philip. 1949–
    Easter Wings, [voice] Chester [2 clarinets, viola, cello, double bass].
    (Winter Portrait in Grey and Gold, [soprano], Chester [clarinet, piano, off-stage melody instrument].)

Williams, Grace Mary. 1906–1977. WMIC. [harp, harpsichord], [flute, harp], [flute, harp, viola].
    Japanese fragments, [soprano], Chester [viola *or* guitar].

Williams, Graham. WMIC. [piano, bass guitar, violin], [3 clarinets], [clarinet, piano], [guitar].

Williams, Rhyddid. WMIC. [organ].
    O perfect love, *Dorothy F. Gurney*, [soprano], Snell [organ].

Williamson, Malcolm Benjamin Graham Christopher. 1931–2003
Collection: *Three Shakespeare Songs*, Weinberger [guitar].
    Come away, death, *Shakespeare*, Em [e'-f''#], Weinberger 3 Shakespeare.
    Fear no more the heat of the sun, *Shakespeare*, [c'-a''b], Weinberger 3 Shakespeare.
    Full fathom five, *Shakespeare*, [db-g''], Weinberger 3 Shakespeare [unaccompanied].
    (Pietà, [soprano], Weinberger, [oboe, bassoon, piano].)

Wills, Arthur. 1926–
Collections: *Eternity's Sunrise,* Brunton [organ]; *Love's Torment*, [a-f''#], Brunton [harpsichord] (1); *Love's Torment*, [f#-e''], Brunton [guitar] (2); *Three Poems by e. e. cummings*, Brunton, [oboe, piano]; *A Woman in Love,* [g-g''](f), Brunton [guitar].

Amo ergo sum, *Kathleen Raine*, [g-g''](f), Brunton Woman.
Eternity, *William Blake*, [d'#-f''#](f), Brunton Eternity.
Evil spirit, An, *Michael Drayton*, [counter-tenor/contralto], Brunton Love's Torment (1).
Evil spirit, An, *Michael Drayton*, [counter-tenor], Brunton Love's Torment (2).
Hound of heaven, The, *Francis Thompson*, [g-e''b], Brunton [organ].
if I have made, my lady, intricate songs, *E. E. Cummings*, [c-a'b](m), Brunton 3 Poems.
it may not always be so; and I say, *E. E. Cummings*, [e-a'b](m), Brunton 3 Poems.
Lamb, The, *William Blake*, [g-f''#](m), Brunton Eternity.
Love is a sickness, *Samuel Daniel*, [counter-tenor/contralto], Brunton Love's Torment (1).
Love is a sickness, *Samuel Daniel*, [counter-tenor/contralto], Brunton Love's Torment (2).
Rosalind's Madrigal, *Thomas Lodge*, [counter-tenor/contralto], Brunton Love's Torment (1).
Rosalind's Madrigal, *Thomas Lodge*, [counter-tenor], Brunton Love's Torment (2).
Sonnet: When our two souls, *Elizabeth Barrett Browning*, [c'-c'''#](f), Spartan [clarinet, piano].
spring! may — , *E. E. Cummings*, [e-a'b](m), Brunton 3 Poems.
Toccata of Galuppi's, A, (scena), *Robert Browning*, [g-f''](counter-tenor)], Brunton [string quartet].
Tyger, The, *William Blake*, [g-f''#](f), Brunton Eternity.
What thing is love, *George Peele*, [counter-tenor/contralto], Brunton Love's Torment (1).
What thing is love, *George Peele*, [counter-tenor], Brunton Love's Torment (2).
Winged Eros, *Kathleen Raine*, [g-g''](f), Brunton Woman.
Woman to Lover, *Kathleen Raine*, [g-f''#](f), Brunton Woman.

Wilson, Richard. 1941–
Ballad of Longwood Glen, The, *Vladimir Nabokov*, [tenor], B&H [harp].

Wilson-Dickson, Andrew. WMIC. [bass clarinet, viola, double bass, piano], [cello, piano], [bass viol], [harpsichord].

Winters, Geoffrey. 1928– BMIC. [guitar; harp].

Wishart, Peter. 1921–1984.
(To the Holy Spirit, [soprano], S&B [flute, viola da gamba, harpsichord].)

Wood, Charles. 1866–1926.
Mater ora filium, *Anon*, E*b* [d'-e''b], Mayhew *Holy Night* [organ].

Wood, Hugh Bradshaw. 1932–
Collection: *Four Songs Op 2*, [contralto], Chester [clarinet, violin, cello].
  Bargain my love, [contralto], Chester 4 Songs.
  Image of love grows, The, [contralto], Chester 4 Songs.
  In the beloved's face, [contralto], Chester 4 Songs.
  Love, do not believe, [contralto], Chester 4 Songs.
  Marina Op 31, *T. S. Eliot*, [soprano], Chester [viola, harp, horn, alto flute].

Woolrich, John. 1954–
Collection: *Four Songs after Hoffmann*, [E. T. A. Hoffmann], [soprano, with percussion], Faber [clarinet, piano]. *Three Cautionary Tales*, Faber hire [soprano saxophone/clarinet, bass clarinet/ clarinet, viola, cello, double bass]; *Three Songs for Alto and Six Viols*, [Fernando Pessoa *tr.* Richard Zenith], Faber.
  Cascades, *Anon*, [soprano], Faber hire [5 players].
  North Wind, The, *Anon*, [b-c'''(a'')](f), Faber hire 3 Cautionary.
  Poor Mr Snail, *Macedonian* tr. *Harvey & Pennington*, [d'-d'''b(b'')], Faber hire 3 Cautionary.
  Turkish Mouse, The, *Turkish* tr. *John Woolrich*, [d'-f''#](f), Faber 3 hire Cautionary.
  Ariadne Laments, *Ottavino Rinuccini*, [soprano, with 2 tuned gongs], Faber [2 violins, viola, cello, double bass].
  Berceuse, *Anon*, [soprano], Faber [alto flute, oboe, clarinet/bass clarinet, viola, cello].
  Harlequinade, *Commedia dell'Arta* tr. *Anon*, [soprano, with percussion], Faber [clarinet/bass clarinet, violin, cello, piano/wood block/whistle].
  Light and Rock, *Anon*, tr. *Andrew Harvey & Anne Pennington*, [soprano], Faber [basset horn in A, piano].
  Malicious Observer, *Elvis Costello*, [soprano], Faber [2 clarinets, viola, cello, double bass]; version for 3 players on hire.
  Serbian Songs, *Serbian folk poem*, tr. *Andrew Harvey and Anne Pennington* [soprano], Faber [clarinet, percussion].
  Songs and broken music, *Elvis Costello*, [soprano], Faber hire [violin, cello, piano].

Wordsworth, William Brocklesby. 1908–1988.
  Solitary reaper, The, *William Wordsworth*, [e'-a''#], Roberton [clarinet, piano].

Wynne, David. 1900–1983. WMIC. [string quartet].

Young, Peter. 1969–
Collection: *Three Songs of Ben*, Banks [clarinet, piano].
  Drink to me only with thine eyes, *Ben Jonson*, [d'-g''], Banks 3 Ben.
  Oh do not wanton with those eyes, *Ben Jonson*, [d'-f''], Banks 3 Ben.
  Still to be neat, still to be dressed, *Ben Jonson*, [e'b-a''b], Banks 3 Ben.

Index of titles

Note: Entries in Appendix 1 (foreign texts) have * after the composer's name; those in Appendix 2 (other accompaniments) have †. If these signs are in brackets, the song title appears in both the Appendix and the main catalogue. No distinction has been made for arrangements. Bold type is used for titles appearing under 'Collections'.

Alternative titles are given in round brackets after the main title; texts by different poets using the same title then give the name of the poet (where known) in square brackets; further titles given in round brackets after the composer or composers give cross references to other known settings of the same words, adding the poet's name in square brackets if necessary.

A

A che più debb'io mai l'intensa voglia: *Britten**
A la Esperanza (Hope): *Musgrave*†
À la Promenade: *Sorabji**
A OI (To Olympia): *Solomons*
A' the neet ower an' ower: *Finnissy*†
Abel Wright: *Gibbs, Armstrong*
Abgesang: *Poole**
Abide with me, fast falls the eventide: *Bryan*; *Liddle*(†); *Price, R.R.*
Able Seaman Hodge remembers Ceylon: *Hurd*
Abominable Lake, The: *Holloway*†
About my father's farm: *Gill*
About the sweet bag of a bee: *Lawes, H.*
Absence, hear thou my protestation: *Morley*; *Parrott*
Abt Vogler: *Wills*
Acacia Tree: *Rodgers*
Accursed Wood, The: *Shaw*
Acquaint now thyself with him: *Head*
Across the Door: *Bax*; *Harty*
Across the plain: *Tippett*†
Across the snow: *Northcott*†
Acton Burnell: *Venables*†
Actress, The: *Lutyens*
Ad domnulum suam: *Someren-Godfery*
Adam Buckham O!: *Williamson, M.*
Adam lay i-bounden, bounden in a bond: *Hely-Hutchinson*; *Warlock*(†)
Adieu: *Bryan*
Adieu, farewell earth's bliss: *Bennett, R.R.*
Adieu to the pleasures and follies of love: *Hart*
Adlestrop: *Jacob*; *Payne*
Admirals All: *Bantock*
Adoration [Keats]: *Bridge*
Adoration, The [Symons]: *Ireland*
Adoréd spring: *Papastávrou*
Adrift: *Bantock*
Advent, The: *Ireland*
Advent Meditation: *Pope*
Advice to Girls: *Peterkin*
Advice to Those Practising Contemplative Prayer: *Pike*
Ae fond kiss: *Atkinson, G*; *Beamish*(†)

A'e Gowden Lyric: *Stevenson*
Aeolus' Song (Your awful voice): *Weldon (Purcell, H)*
Affirmations: *Liddell*†
Afraid: *Berkeley, L.*
African Love Song, An: *Coleridge-Taylor*
African Romances: *Coleridge-Taylor*
After [Bourke]: *Elgar,*
After [Tennyson]: *Somervell*
After Love: *Ronald*
After Supper: *Roe*
After the Club Dance: *Downes*
After the Fair: *Downes*
After the Rain: *Hugill*†
After Two Years: *Warlock* (She is all so slight)
Afterday: *Scott, C.*
Afternoon Tea: *Taylor, C.*
Afton Water: *Britten*; *Grainger, P*; *White, A.* (Flow gently, sweet Afton / Sweet Afton)
Against that time, if ever that time come (Sonnet 49) [Shakespeare]: *Scott, D.B.*
Ah, are you digging my grave?: *Berkeley, M.*†
Ah, Belinda, I am pressed with torment: *Purcell, H.*
Ah! can I e'er forget thee: *Bishop*
Ah, Chloris, would the gods allow: *Marsh, A.*
Ah! cruel nymph, you give despair: *Purcell, H.*
Ah, fading joy how quickly thou art past: *Wellesz*
Ah! how delightful the morning: *Reynolds, A.*
Ah! how pleasant 'tis to love: *Purcell, H.*
Ah, how sweet are the cooling breeze, *Croft*
Ah! how sweet it is to love: *Dring*; *Purcell, H.*
Ah, let it drift: *Whittaker*
Ah, moon of my delight: *Lehmann*
Ah, not a drop: *Lehmann*
Ah, sunflower: *Swann*; *Vaughan Williams*†
Ah, were she pityful as she is fair: *Peerson*
Ah, whither shall I fly: *Eccles*
Ah, willow: *Wilson, H.L.*
A-hunting we will go: *Grainger, F.*
Aileen Aroon (How sweet and how pleasing): *Hughes, Herbert*
Air en Langue Allemande: *Handel**
Air en Langue Espagnole: *Handel**
Airy Bachelor, The: *Hughes, Herbert*
Akhmatova Songs: *Tavener*†
Akond of Swat, The: *Gerhard*†
Akrotiri: *Newson*
Alalá: *Gerhard**
Alas, alack: *Howells*
Alas, from the day my poor heart: *Linley Snr*
Alas, here lies the poor Alonso slain: *Clarke, J.*
Ala'ya! send the cup around: *Bantock*
Alba: *Bingham*; *Corke*
Album Leaves: *Ronald*
Album of Fourteen Songs: *Jeffreys, J.*
Album of Nine English Songs: *Lehmann*
Album of Seven Songs: *Bax*
Album of Songs: *Scott, C.*
Album of Ten Songs: *MacCunn*
Album of Twelve Songs: *Walthew*
Alice Songs: *Hely-Hutchinson*
All About Me (Poems for a Child): *Austin*
All day I hear the noise of waters: *Goossens*

Index of titles 217

All for my true love: *Cowen*
All for You: *Martin, E.*
All in a Garden Green: *Ireland* (Rose, The [Howell])
All in a Merry Maytime: *Ronald*
All in the April evening: *Diack*; *Roberton*
All my heart's thine own, love: *Pierson*
All my sense thy sweetness gained: *Jones, R.*
All night a wind of music: *Berkeley, L.*
All night under the moon: *Gurney*
All sounds have been as music: *Wegener*
All suddenly the wind comes soft: *Peterkin* (Buds in Spring / Spring Sorrow)
All that's past: *Berkeley, L.*†
All the days of Christmas: *Thwaites*
All the world awakes today: *German*
All things are quite silent: *Roe*
All things that we clasp and cherish: *Bridge*
All those lights: *Moult*
All Through the Night: *Anon*; *Somervell*
All vanities forsake: *Oldham*
All Year Round: *Brown, C.*†
All you Spanish Ladies: *Colling*†
Allah: *Foulds*
Alleluia: *Weldon (Purcell, H.)*
Alles wandelt sich: *Poole**
Allie: *Crosse*
Almansor Dying: *Stanford*
Alone [Chinese]: *Scott, C.*
Alone [de la Mare]: *Pitfield*†
Alone [Fontana]: *Gomelskaya*
Alone [Ukranian]: *Anderson, W.H.*
Alone in the Wood: *Dieren*
Alone with Mother: *Coleridge-Taylor*
Along the Field: *Vaughan Williams*†
Along the field as we came by: *Orr, C.W.*; *Vaughan Williams*† (Aspens, The)
Along the Stream: *Warlock*
Alps, The: *Weir*†
Also hat Gott die Welt geliebet: *Maxwell Davies*†
Altisadora's Song (From rosy bowers): *Purcell, H.*
Always: *Wood, Hugh*
Always and everywhere: *Elgar*
Amabel: *Finzi*
Amarillis [Herrick]: *Bernofsky*
Amaryllis [Anon]: *Gibbs, Armstrong*
Amaryllis [Campion]: *Jeffreys, J.* (I care not for those ladies)
Amaryllis at the Fountain [Anon]: *Quilter*
Ambulance Train: *Jeffreys, J.*
Amidst the mirtles as I walk: *Lawes, H.*
Amidst the shades and cool refreshing streams: *Purcell, H.*
Amintas, to my grief I see: *Purcell, H.*
Amintor, heedless of his flocks: *Purcell, H*
Amintor's Welladay: *Lawes, H.*
Amo ergo sum: *Wills*†
Among Rosebuds: *Lawes, H.*
Among the Rocks: *Somervell*
Among the Roses: *White, M.V.*
Amor: *Wood, Hugh*
Amoretti (2nd Series): *Rubbra*(†)
Amour Sans Soucis: *Blow*
Amphitrite's Song (Halcyon days): *Weldon (Purcell, H.)*
An die blaue Himmelsdecke: *Stanford**
An Easy Decision: *Bedford*
Anacreon: *Someren-Godfery*

Anacreon's Defeat (This poet sings the Trojan wars): *Purcell, H.*
Anacreontic Ode: *Smyth*(*)
Anakreontika: *Maxwell Davies*†
Ancestor Worship: *Hoddinott*
Ancestor Worship: *Hoddinott*
Anchor Song: *Grainger, P.*
Anchorsmiths, The: *Dibdin*
Ancient Rune of Hospitality: *Peache*
Ancient Songs: *Samuel, R.*
Ancient Wisdom: *Pike*
And death shall have no dominion: *Pike*
And if I did what then?: *Gibbs, Alan*
And is it night?: *Berkeley, M.*
And is it true?: *Horder*
And little knowledge but much pleasure: *Hudes*
And must I then indeed, pain, live with you?: *Swann*
And so I made a villanelle: *Scott, C.*
And their feet move: *Hudes*
And then there's sorrow: *Hearne*
And There are Tears: *Bantock*
And when love speaks: *Newson*†
And will they cast the altars down: *Pope*
And wilt thou leave me thus?: *Warlock* (Appeal, The / Lover's Appeal, The / Supplication, A [Wyatt])
And would you fain the reason know?: *Jeffreys, J.*†
And would you see my mistress' face? *Jeffreys, J.*; *Rosseter*
And ye shall walk in silk attire: *Blamire, Hughes, Herbert*
And yet I Love Her till I Die: *Parry, C.H.H.* (My Lady / Passing by / There is a lady sweet and kind / Yet will I love her till I die)
Andy Battle: *Howells* (Once and there was a young sailor)
Ane Sang of the Birth of Christ: *Scott, F.G.*. (Balulalow / Cradle Song [Luther] / O my dear heart / O my deir hert)
Anemone: *Papastávrou* (†)
Anfangs wollt' ich fast verzagen: *White, M.V.**
Angel [Pushkin]: *Britten*(*)
Angel, The [Blake]: *Swann*
Angel and the Child, The: *Center*
Angel Eros: *Harvey, J.*†
Angel Food: *Hugill*
Angel Gabriel, The: *McLeod*†
Angel spirits of sleep: *Bainton*; *MacCunn*
Angels of the Mind: *Bliss*
Angel's Warning, The: *Davies, J.*
Angelus [no text]: *Burrell*†
Angelus [Ellis]: *Hand*
Angharad: *Smith, R.*
Angler's Song, The (Basse): *Hold*
Angler's Song, The (Walton): *Lawes, H.*
Angry Wife, The: *Cannon*(†)
Animal Heaven: *Leighton*†
Animal Songs: *McLeod*†
Ann's Cradle Song: *Gibbs, Armstrong*
Annabel Lee: *Bryan*; *Shaw*; *Stevenson* (Kingdom by the Sea, A)
Anne de Lucy Songs (cycle): *Nyman**
Annie Laurie: *Anon*
Anon in Love: *Walton*(†)
Another Day: *Rees, D.*
Another day without you: *Hugill*†
Another me: *Stafford*
Another Picture: *Thomas, Mansel*
Another Silly Love Song: *Marsh*†

218 Index of titles

Another Spring: *Berkeley, L.*
Another Spring: *Berkeley, L.*
Another weeping woman: *Holloway*†
Answer, The [Binyon]: *Quilter*
Answer, The [Tennyson]: *Sullivan*
Answer to Colin's complaint, An: *Handel*
Ant, The: *Barton*†
Antiphon: *Vaughan Williams*
Antoinette Alone (scena): *Dalby*
Antrim and Donegal: *Harty*
anyone lived in a pretty how town: *Lord, R.*
Aoibhneas Thir-na N-Óg: *Doyle**
Ap Shenkin: *Hoddinott*
Apex, The: *Hudes*
Aphrodite: *Evans, T.H.*
Appeal, The: *Goossens*; *Jeffreys, J.* (And wilt thou leave me thus? / Lover's Appeal, The / Supplication, A [Wyatt])
Appeal to Cats in the Business of Love, An: *Roe*†
Applause of Men, The: *Britten*
Apple Orchard, The: *Gurney*
Apple Tree, An [Hughes]: *Thomas, Mansel*
Apple tree, The [Birkett]: *Birkett*
Apple tree, The [Hoosen]: *Williams, W.S.G*
Apple-eating: *Bantock*
Apprentice Angel, An: *Scott, F.G.*
Après trois ans: *Wilby**
April: *Morgan, I.*
April [Anon]: *Anderson, W.H.*
April [Rose]: *Dunhill*
April [Watson]: *Peel; Quilter*
April Children: *Carey, C.*
April Days: *Thomas, V.*
April Gale: *Moult*
April is in my mistress' face: *Bennett, R.R.*
April Love: *Ronald*
April Morning: *Teed*
April Rain: *Dunhill*
April Rise: *Wood, Hugh*
Apron of Flowers, The: *Ferguson*
Aquarium: *Alwyn*
Arab Love Song: *Quilter* (Arabian Lovesong)
Arabia: *Browne*
Arabian Lovesong: *Sullivan* (Arab Love Song)
Arabian Serenade: *Elgar*
Araby: *Gibbs, Armstrong*
Arachne: *Tann*†
Aran Homing Song: *Noble, H.*
Arcades: *Swann*
Arcananian Song: *Papastávrou*†
archy at the zoo (cycle): *Bush, G.*
Ardan Mor: *Poston*
Are you angry, mother? *Bishop*
Ariadne Laments: *Woolrich*†
Arianna Abandonata: *Goehr*†
Arianrhod: *Thomas, Mansel*
Ariel Songs (cycle): *Nyman*(†)
Ariel's Song: *Butt*(†)
Arietta: *Scott, C.*
Arise ye subterranean winds: *Weldon* (*Purcell, H*)
Arm, arm, ye brave: *Handel*
Armida's Garden: *Parry, C.H.H.*
Arnold Book of Songs, The: *Quilter*
Arrogant Poppies: *Gibbs, Armstrong*
Arrow and the Song, The: *Balfe*
Art thou troubled: *Handel*
Arthur O'Bower: *Warlock*
As at noon Dulcina rested: *Anon*

As Cupid roguishly one day: *Eccles*
As Dew in April: *Jeffreys, J.* (I sing of a maiden / Old Carol, An)
As down by Banna's banks I strayed: *Roberton*
As Ever I Saw: *Warlock* (Fairest May, The / That Ever I Saw)
As Flora slept: *Hilton*
As I came over the grey, grey hills: *Bax*
As I lay in the early sun: *Finzi*; *Gibbs, Armstrong*
As I ride through the Metijda: *Bantock*
As I the silly fish deceive: *Jones, R.*
As I walked forth (Blake): *Foss*
As I walked forth one summer's day (Anon): *Johnson, R.*
As I wandered one fine morning: *Thomas, Mansel*(†)
As I went a-roaming: *Brahe*
As if I didn't know: *Roberton*
As it fell upon a day: *Macfarren*† (Philomel [Barnfield])
As it is, plenty: *Britten*
As it was: *Grange*†
As Joseph was a-walking: *Thiman*
As life what is so sweet?: *Webb*
As lonesome through the woods: *Bennett, W.S.*
As me an' me marra was gannin' ta wark: *Finnissy*†
As the holly groweth green: *Roe*
As the last guest leaves: *Blyton*
As the moon's pale likeness quivers: *Stanford*
As through the land at eve we went: *Scott, A.; Somervell*
Ascension Thursday: *Jones, R.E.*
Ash Grove, The: *Anon*; *Britten*; *Quilter*
Aside, An: *Ireland*
Ask me no more: *Wood, C.*
Ask me not, dear: *Ronald*
Ask me to love no more: *Purcell, H.*
Ask me why I send you here: *Lawes, H.* (Primrose, The)
Aspatia's Song: *Hand*; *Jeffreys, J.* (Lay a garland on my hearse / Sad Song, A / Willow Song [Fletcher])
Aspects (cycle): *Steptoe*
Aspects 1 in 3 (cycle): *Stoker*
Aspens, The: *Gurney* (Along the field)
Aspidistra, The: *Clarke, R.*
Aspiration [Dehmell]: *Bax*,
Aspiration [McLeod]: *Scott, C.*
Astyanax: *Randalls*
At a Lunar Eclipse: *Finzi*
At Castle Boterel: *Downes*
At Close of Day: *Quilter*
At Columbine's Grave: *Shaw*
At dawn the hill stands silver: *Ronald*
At Day-close in November: *Britten*
At Easter: *Harty*
At Grafton: *Boughton*
At her fair hands: *Peerson*
At Malvern: *Venables*
At Middlefield Gate in February: *Finzi*
At Midnight: *Venables*
At Morning: *Ronald*
At my age: *Hudes*†
At my Father's Grave: *Stevenson*
At Night: *Johnstone*
At One: *Self, G.*
At Sea: *Harty, Stanford*; *Wood, C.*
At Sunrise: *Ronald*
At Tea: *Maw*†

At the court of the poisoned rose: *Venables*
At the cry of the first bird: *Jeffreys, J.*
At the Edge of Time (cycle): *Elias*
At the Firth of Lorne: *MacDonald*
At the hour the long day ends: *Parry, C.H.H.*
At the Kuang-Li Pavilion: *Redman*
At the last: *Hawes*
At the last [Macleod]: *Bax*
At the mid hour of night: *Britten*; *Darlow*; *Hughes, Herbert*; *Raphael*; *Wood, C.*
At the Railway Station, Upway: *Britten*
At the rising of the moon: *Bantock*
At the riverside village: *Steptoe*
At the round earth's imagined corners, blow: *Britten*; *Burgon*†
At the Street Corner: *Treharne*
At the turn of the burn: *Davidson, M.*
At the Window: *Sullivan*
Atwain: *Scott, C.*
Aubade [Anon]: *Bush, G.*
Aubade [Auster]: *Matthews, C.*
Aubade [Davenant]: *Poston*
Aubade [Larkin]: *Adès*†
Aube: *Crosse**
August: *Routh*
August Midnight, An: *Headington*
August River: *Cruft*
Auld aik's down, The: *Britten*
Auld Jobby Dixon: *Mark*
Auld Rocks, The: *Rose*
Auntie's skirts: *White, A.*
Aus deinen Augen fliessen meine Lieder: *Delius**
Aus meinen Thränen spriessen: *White, M.V.**
Author of Light (cycle): *Holloway*
Author of light, revive my dying sprite: *Campion*
Autolocus' Song: *Keel* (Sweet o' the Year, The / When daffodils begin to peer)
Automne [Apollinaire]: *Berkeley, L.*
Automne [no text]: *Procter*
Autumn: *Elwyn-Edwards*
Autumn [Busfield]: *White, A.*
Autumn [de la Mare]: *Britten*
Autumn [Holstein]: *Delius*
Autumn [Hood]: *Randall*†
Autumn [Joyce]: *Hedges* (Now O now in this brown land)
Autumn [Keats]: *Read*†
Autumn [Li Po]: *Bliss*
Autumn across the frontier: *Bantock*
Autumn Evening [Mcquarie]: *Quilter*
Autumn Evening [Thomson]: *Bullard*†
Autumn Fires: *White, A.*
Autumn in Cornwall: *Self, A.*
Autumn Jig: *Joubert*
Autumn Night Message, An: *Rubbra*†
Autumn Ritual: *Hawes*
Autumn Song [Shelley]: *MacCunn*
Autumn Song [Watson]: *Scott, C.*
Autumn Thoughts: *Snell*(†)
Autumn Twilight: *Warlock*
Autumn Wind, The [Hesse]: *Steele*
Autumn Wind, The [Wu Ti]: *Berkeley, L.*; *Britten*†
Autumn's Breath: *Head*
Autumn's Legacy: *Berkeley, L.*
Autumn's Lute: *Scott, C.*
Autumnal [Dowson]: *Scott, C.*
Autumnal [Spence]: *Hamilton, A.*
Auvergnat: *Bliss*

Avant que tu t'en ailles: *Delius**
Ave Maria Gratia Plena: *Rubbra*(†)
Ave Maria, gratia plena: *Atkinson, R.*(†); *Bryan*; *Head*(*)
Ave mors: *Harrison, J.*
Ave verum corpus: *Elgar*†
Avenging and bright fell the swift sword: *Britten*
Avenues and Circles: *Standford*†
Avondale: *Bush, G.*
Awake: *Evans, D*
Awake my fair: *Hook*
Awake my heart to be loved: *Holst*
Awake my lyre and tell: *Linley Jnr*
Awake sweet love, thou art returned: *Dowland*
Awake thee my Bessy: *Jeffreys, J.*
Awakening, The: *Torphichen*
Awaking in heaven: *Morris, A.*
Away, away ye men of rules: *Parry, C.H.H.*
Away, delights, go seek some other dwelling *Rawsthorne*
Away on the hill there runs a stream: *Ronald*
Away to Twiver: *Warlock*
Away with these self-loving lads: *Dowland*
Ay de mi, my bird: *Sullivan*
Ay me, can love and beauty so conspire: *Anon*
Ay me that love should Nature's work accuse: *Rosseter*
Ay waukin, O: *Scott, F.G.*
Ayres: *Ferrabosco*; *Handford*
Ayres, Songs and Dialogues: *Johnson, R.*
Aziza: *Woodforde-Finden*

B

B for Barney, C for Cross: *Hughes, Herbert*
Baby: *Ireland*
Babyland: *Bantock*
Babylon: *Ferguson*
Baby's Epitaph, A: *Routh*
Bacchus, God of mirth and wine: *Arne, T.*
Bacchus is a pow'r divine: *Purcell, H.*
Bachelor, The: *Warlock*
Bachelor's Song, The: *Barratt*
Back and side go bare: *Dale, M.* (Jolly Good Ale and Old / Maltworms)
Back to Hilo: *Head*
Back to Ireland: *Stanford*
Back View, A: *Hugh-Jones*
Bahnhofstrasse: *Orr, C.W.*
Bailey Beareth the Bell Away, The: *Jeffreys, J.* (Bayly berith the bell away, The / Maidens came, The)
Bailiff's daughter of Islington: *Grainger, P.*
Bairnrhymes: *Dalby*
Bairn's Prayer at Nicht, A: *Musgrave*
Bakery, The: *Roe*
Ballad [Auden]: *Senator*
Ballad [Dunbar]: *Coleridge-Taylor*
Ballad [Soutar]: *MacMillan*
Ballad 2: *Rands*
Ballad 3: *Rands*†
Ballad of Fair Helen, The: *Scott, C.*
Ballad of Father Gilligan: *Scott, D.B.*
Ballad of Kastriot Renhapi: *Nyman*†
Ballad of Longwood Glen, The: *Wilson, R.*†
Ballad of Mr and Mrs Discobolos, The: *Orr, B.*

220 Index of titles

Ballad of Semmerwater, The: *Gibbs, Armstrong*; *Noble, H.*; *Someren-Godfery*
Ballad of the Judas Tree: *Lloyd, R.*
Ballad of the Red-headed Man: *Tate, P.*†
Ballad of the Standard-bearer: *Jones, D.*
Ballad of Wild Children, The: *Williamson, M.*
Ballad Singer, The [Harben]: *Scott, C.*
Ballad Singer, The [Hardy]: *Downes*
Ballad-maker, A: *Gibbs, Armstrong*
Ballad-monger, The: *Martin, E.*
Ballade I: *Samuel, R.*†
Ballade II: *Samuel, R.*†
Ballads from Paul Bunyan: *Britten*(†)
Ballads of the Four Seasons, The: *Bliss*
Ballynure Ballad, A: *Hughes, Herbert*
Balmy sweetness ever flowing: *Boyce*
Balow, my babe: *Dieren*
Balulalow: *Howells*(†); *Poston*; *Self, A.*; *Turner*; *Warlock*(†) (Ane Sang of the Birth of Christ / Cradle Song [Luther] / O my deir hert / O my dear heart)
Banal Sojourn (cycle): *Holloway*
Banks of Allan Water, The: *Grainger, P.*; *Shaw*
Banks of Conway, The: *Lloyd, D.J.de*
Banks of Roses, The: *Anon*
Barbara Allen: *Anon*, *Grainger, P.*; *Quilter*; *Taylor, C.*; *Watkins*†
Barbara Ellen: *Anon*
Bard, The (Poet, The): *Thomas, Mansel*
Bard of Armagh, The: *Hughes, Herbert*
Bard of the Dimbovitza, The: *Bax*
Bard's Paradise: *Jones, W.B.*
Bargain, The: *Davidson, M.*; *Somervell* (Love Song [Sidney] / My true love hath my heart)
Bargain my love: *Wood, Hugh*†
Barley Broth: *Mark*
Barrel Organ, The: *Kirkwood*
Barren Fig, The: *Stevenson*
Base Details: *Harrington*
Batter my heart, three-personed God: *Britten*; *Self, A.*
Battle-eve of the Brigade, The: *Wood, C.*
Battle of Pelusium, The: *Stanford*
Bayly Berith the Bell Away, The: *Warlock* (Bailey beareth the bell away, The / Maidens came, The)
Bay in Anglesey, A: *Dring*
B.C.C.I. – a Satirical Song: *Baylis*
Be merciful unto me, O God (Psalm 57): *Head*(†)
Be mine, dear maid: *Bishop*
Be mine, tender passion: *Storace*
Be music, Night: *Bedford*
Be near me when my light is low: *Swann*
Be pleasant, be airy, and constantly praise: *Stanley*
Be still my sweet sweeting, no longer do cry: *Poston* (Cradle Song [Philip] / Nurse's Song, The)
Be Vigilant: *Newson*
Be you Blithe and Bonny: *Jeffreys, J.* (Sigh no more, ladies)
Beachcomber: *Liddell*
Beacon Barn, The: *Berkeley, L.*
Bean-flower, The: *Moeran*
Bean-stripe & Apple-eating: *Bantock*
Beata l'alma (cantata): *Blake, D.*
Beatrice's Vision of Eternity: *Pike*
Beatriz's Song: *Walton*(†)
Beautie, sweet love, is like the morning dew (Sonnet) [Daniel]: *Steptoe*
Beauteous Evening, A: *Darlow*
Beautiful Mistress, A: *Lawes, H.*

Beauty [Masefield]: *Davidson, M.*; *Martin, E.*
Beauty [Vincent]: *Self, A.*
Beauty and love once fell at odds: *Lawes, H.*
Beauty Bathing: *Still* (Beauty sat bathing)
Beauty is but a painted hell: *Campion*
Beauty sat bathing by a spring: *Corkine*; *Jones, R.* (Beauty Bathing)
Beauty since you so much desire: *Campion*
Beauty stand further: *Jones, R.*
Beauty to Beauty: *Taylor, M.*
Beauty's end is in sight: *Naylor, B.*
Because: *Hardelot*
Because he liked to be at home: *Bedford*†
Because I liked you better: *Berkeley, L.*
Bed in Summer: *Ireland*, *Parry, W.H.*; *White, A.*
Bedpost, The: *Wishart*
Bedtime: *Britten*
Bee, The: *Lehmann*
Beeches: *Roe*
Beeny Cliff: *Roe*
Bees' Song, The: *Hely-Hutchinson*; *Peterkin*
Beetle's Wings: *Solomons*†
Before and After Summer: *Finzi*
Before and After Summer: *Finzi*
Before Dawn [de la Mare]: *Benjamin*; *Howells*
Before Dawn [Sarton]: *Samuel, R.*
Before Life and After: *Britten*; *Swann*
Beggar's Song [de la Mare]: *Gibbs, Armstrong*
Beggar's Song, The [Anon]: *Leveridge*
Beg-Innish: *Bax*
Begone, dull care: *Grainger, P.*
Behold a wonder here: *Dowland*
Behold, I send an angel: *Head*
Behold your faithful Ariel fly: *Arne, T.*
Behoulde a seely tender babe: *Butt*
Being young and green: *Bliss*
Believe me dear: *Hughes, Herbert*
Believe me, if all those endearing young charms: *Moore*; *Quilter*
Belinda: *Eccles*
Bella Donna: *Greaves, Terence*†
Bellman's Song [Traditional]: *Butt*
Bellman's Song, The [Ravenscroft]: *Poston*
Bells in tower at evening toll: *Pope*
Bells of Christmas, The: *Shaw*
Bells of Clermont Town, The: *Goodhart*
Bells of Cordoba: *Berkeley, L.*
Bells of Magdalen Tower: *Somers-Cocks*
Bells of San Marie, The: *Ireland* (St Mary's Bells)
Bells of Youth, The: *Bantock*
Beloved, *Head*
Beloved, let us love one another: *Head*
Beloved maid: *Bryan*
Beneath a poplar's shadow lay me: *Purcell, H.*
Beneath the Bajan moon: *Dean*
Benediction [St Teresa]: *Pike*
Benediction [Tagore]: *Hiscocks, W.*(†)
Berceuse [Agate]: *Bax*(*)
Berceuse [Anon]: *Woolrich*†
Berceuse [Wordsworth, D.]: *Bridge*
Berwyn: *Elwyn-Edwards*; *Thomas, D.V.*
Beside the wide Menai: *Elwyn-Edwards*
Bess of Bedlam (From silent shades / Mad Bess): *Purcell, H.*
Bessie Bell and Mary Gray: *Weir*
Betelgeuse: *Holst*
Bethlehem Down: *Warlock*(†)
Betjemania: *Wills*

Betrothal: *Hudes*(†)
Betty Wynn: *Thomas, Mansel*
Between the trees: *Steele*
Beuk O'Newcassel Sangs: *Finnissey*†
Beware: *Britten*
Beware: *Britten*
Beware, poor shepherds all, beware: *Purcell, H.*
Beyond Art: *Arne, T.* (Still to be neat)
Beyond the sea my heart is gone: *Rootham*
Bhodi Tree, The: *Marsh*†
Bicker's Cottage: *Hugh-Jones*
Bid me but live and I will live: *Lawes, H.* (Love Song [Herrick] / To Anthea)
Bid me discourse: *Bishop*
Big Chariot, The: *Britten*†
Big Lady Moon: *Coleridge-Taylor*
Big Steamers: *German*
Bilbo's Last Song: *McLeod*†
Billy Boy: *Parry, W.H.*
Binnorie (A Ballad): *Clarke, R.* (Two Sisters of Binnorie, The)
Birch Tree, The: *Gibbs, Armstrong*
Bird, A: *Rainier*
Bird of Arabia, The: *Bantock*
Bird of Blue: *German*
Bird of Paradise: *Wishart*; *Wood, Hugh*
Bird of St Bride, The: *Bantock*
Bird of the Mountain: *Bedford*†
Bird on briar: *Short*†
Bird Scarer's Song: *Britten*(†)
Bird sits high and sings, A (cycle): *Shur*
Bird Songs: *Lehmann*
Bird Songs at Eventide: *Coates, E.*
Birds (cycle): *O'Neill*
Birds [O'Neill]: *Wood, C.*
Birds, The [Belloc]: *Britten*; *Dubery*; *Jeffreys, J.*; *Rowley*; *Thiman*; *Turner*; *Warlock*
Birds about the morning air: *Pitfield*
Birds in the high hall-garden: *Somervell*
Birds of Rhiannon, draw anon hither: *Hughes, A.*
Bird's Song, The: *Vaughan Williams* (Lord is my shepherd, The)
Bird's Story, The: *Delius*
Bird-song: *Head*(†)
Birks of Aberfeldy, The: *White, A.*
Birthday, A [Rossetti, C.]: *Coleridge-Taylor*; *Gibbs, Armstrong*; *Jones, S.L.*; *Mackenzie*; *Scott, C.*; *Self, A.*; *Williamson, M.* (My heart is like a singing bird)
Birthday, The [Traditional]: *Rowley*
Birthday Hansel, A (cycle): *Britten*†
Birthday Recitative and Aria: *Butterworth, N.*
Birthday Sonnet: *Routh*
Birthnight, The: *Finzi*
Birthright: *Someren-Godfery*
Bisclaveret: *Boyle, R.*
Biton to his Gods: *Someren-Godfery*
Bitter Resurrection, A: *Swann*
Black Cat, The: *Nelson*
Black Day: *Britten*
Black Diamonds: *Horder*
Black Gulls: *Alwyn*†
Black Ribbon-band, The: *Hughes, Herbert*
Black River, The: *Bryars*†
Black Roses: *Delius*
Black Sheela of the silver eye: *Harty*
Black Spring, The: *Roberts, T.O.*
Black Stichel: *Gurney*; *Jeffreys, J.*

Blackberry Fold: *Moeran*
Blackberry Time: *Stanford*
Blackbird, The: *Parry, C.H.H.*
Blackbird singing, A: *Head*
Blackbird's Song: *Scott, C.*
Blacker: *Bingham*
Blackmwore by the Stour: *Vaughan Williams*
Blacksmith courted me, A: *Butterworth, G.*
Blake's Cradle Song: *Roberton* (Cradle Song [Blake])
Blast of Love, The: *Blyton*
Blathrie O'T, The: *Crawford*
Blaweary: *Gurney*
Blaze of sultry noon: *Northcott*†
Bless this house, O Lord, we pray: *Brahe*
Bless to me, God: *Thomas, Mansel*
Blessed are all they that fear the Lord: *Handel*†
Blessed are they that dwell in thy house: *Greene* (Psalm 84)
Blessed is the man (Psalm 1): *Butt*(†); *Clement*
Blessed Virgin's Expostulation, The (Tell me, some pitying angel): *Purcell, H.*
Blessing: *Swain*
Blessing for a House: *Thomas, Mansel*
Blest be those sweet regions (Divine Hymn, A): *Clarke, J.*(†)
Blind: *Ireland*
Blind Boy, The [Cibber]: *Dring*
Blind Boy, The [Rossetti, C.] *Ireland*
Blind Ploughman, The: *Clarke, R.C.*
Blindman's in: *Harrison, P.*
Block City: *White, A.*
Bloom is on the Rye, The: *Bishop*
Blooming of the flower, The: *Pike*
Blossom Songs: *O'Neill*
Blossom Time: *Quilter*
Blossoms: *Hurlstone*
Blossoms [Roberts]: *Thomas, Mansel*
Blossoms by my door, The: *Williams, M.*
Blow, blow, thou winter wind: *Arne, T.*; *Bridge*; *Dring*; *Horder*; *Ketèlby*; *Parry, C.H.H.*; *Quilter*; *Routh*; *Steele*
Blow, bugle, blow: *Jones, W.B.*
Blow high, blow low: *Dibdin*
Blow, Northern Wind: *Berkeley, M.*
Blow out, you bugles, over the rich dead: *Bridge*; *Ireland*
Blow the wind southerly: *Whittaker*
Blue and White: *Clements*
Blue Coat, The: *Wood, Hugh*
Blue Christmas: *Blyton*(†)
Blue Doom of Summer, The (cantata): *Holloway*†
Blue Epiphany: *Usher*(†)
Blue Hills of Antrim, The: *Harty*
Blue iris sweetest smells: *Steptoe*(†)
Blue Men of the Minch, The: *Bantock*
Blue Water: *Rowley*
Blue-bell, Dew-bell: *Besley*
Bluebell Wood, The: *Bantock*
Blue-eyed Spring: *Moeran*
Blue-eyes Fairy, The: *Elgar*
Blues: *Senator*
Blume: *Nyman**
Blunder, The: *Head*
Boast not, mistaken swain: *Boyce*
Boasting fops who court the fair: *Blow*
Boat is chafing at our long delay, The: *Gurney*
Boat Song [Davidson]: *Cooke*†
Boat Song [Pollock]: *Stanford*

222 Index of titles

Boat Song of the Isles: *Bantock*
Boating: *Fraser, S.*
Bobbin Winder, The: *Stevenson*
Bobby Shaftoe: *Atkinson, R.*
Bog Love: *Whittaker*
Bóg sie rodzi: *Bax**
Bohemia: *Horder*
Bold Richard, The: *Moeran*
Bold Unbiddable Child, The: *Stanford*
Bold William Taylor: *Grainger, P.*
Bone Jesu verbum patris: *Locke**
Bone of Adam (scena): *Poole*
Bones of Chuang Tzu, The (cantata): *Blake, D.*
Boney's on the sea: *Hughes, Herbert*
Bonfires: *Harty*
Bonnie Broukit Bairn, The: *Stevenson*
Bonnie Earl o' Moray: *Britten*; *White, A.*
Bonnie Earl of Murray: *Gurney*
Bonnie George Campbell: *Grainger, P.*
Bonnie James Campbell: *Weir*
Bonnie Mary of Argyle: *Atkinson, G.*
Bonny at Morn: *Atkinson, R.*; *Britten*(†); *Farrar*; *Poston*; *Tippett*†; *Williamson, M.*
Bonny grey-ey'd morn, The: *Clarke, J.*
Bonny Wee Mare, The: *Hughes, Herbert*
Bonvica's Song (O lead me to some peaceful gloom): *Purcell, H.*
Book of Hours, The: *Matthews, D.*
Book of Songs, A: *Jeffreys, J.*; *Warlock*
Booke of Ayres, A: *Bartlet*; *Rosseter*
Boot, saddle, to horse: *Harrison, J.*
Boots: *McCall*
Border Ballad: *Cowen*
Border Boyhood (cycle): *Stevenson*
Borders of Sleep, The: *Pickard*
Born upon an angel's breast: *Venables*†
Bottom's Dream: *Hearne*†
Boy from Ballytearim, The: *Stanford*
Boy in Ice: *Wood, Hugh*
Boy Johnny: *Finzi*; *Vaughan Williams*
Boy of Infinities, The: *Moult*
Boyhood's End (cantata): *Tippett*
Boys: *Jacobson*
Boy's Song, A: *Rootham*; *Thomas, Mansel*; *Turnbull*
Boys, those were the days: *Hughes, Herbert*
Bracelet, The: *Quilter*
Braes of Yarrow, The: *Weir*
Brave Carpets: *Moult*
Brave Town in Liverpool: *Austin*
Bread and Cherries: *Gurney*
Break heart in twain: *Lawes, H.*
Break now, my heart, and die: *Campion*
Break of Day [Clare]: *Hold*
Break of Day [Donne]: *Naylor, P.* (Daybreak / Stay, O sweet, and do not rise)
Break of day in the trenches: *Ellis*†
Breaking Silence: *Matheson*†
Breaking the Ice: *MacDonald*
Breaking the Ice: *MacDonald*
Breath of Ney: *Goossens*
Bredon Hill: *Butterworth, G.*; *Gray*; *Hamilton, J.*; *Raynor*; *Vaughan Williams*(†) (In summertime on Bredon)
Bredon Hill and Other Songs: *Butterworth, G.*
Brevity: *McEwen*
Brewer, The: *Vaughan Williams*
Bric-à-brac: *Horder*
Bridal Song: *Bantock*

Bride cometh, The: *Burrows*
Bridegroom Grat, The: *Grainger, P.*(†)
Bridgebuilders: *Fraser, G.M.*
Brief Ecstasy: *Fowler*†
Brigg Fair, *Jeffreys, J.*; *Steptoe*†
Bright cap and streamers: *Moeran*
Bright clouds of May shade half the pond: *Gurney*
Bright Field, The: *Morris, A.*†
Bright is the ring of words: *Vaughan Williams*, *Warlock* (To the Memory of a Great Singer)
Bright star! would I were steadfast as thou art: *Parry, C.H.H.* (His Last Sonnet)
Bring away this sacred tree: *Lanier*
Brise Marine: *Saxton*†
Brisk young lad: *Crawford*
Brisk young sailor courted me, A: *Butterworth, G.*
Brisk Young Widow, The: *Britten*; *Howells*; *Marshall, N.*†
British Grenadiers, The: *Grainger, P.*
British Waterside: *Grainger, P.*
Brittany: *Farrar*
Bro a Mynydd: *Elwyn-Edwards*
Broad Sound: *Thomas, Mansel*
Broken Arc, A: *Somervell*
Broken Branches: *Weir*†
Broken Song, A: *Stanford*
Bromley Blues: *Dean*
Bronwen: *Williams, W. M.*
Brother James's Air: *Bain*†; *Tate, P.*; *Trew* (Crimond)
Brown Bird Singing, A: *Wood, Haydn*
Brown is my love, but graceful: *Gurney*; *Jeffreys, J.*; *Poston*; *Quilter*
Bubblyjock: *Stevenson*
Buckie Braes, The: *Stevenson*
Buckle, The: *Bliss*
Buddha-song: *Wills*
Budmouth Dears: *Finzi*
Buds in Spring: *Thomas, Muriel* (All suddenly the wind comes soft / Spring Sorrow)
Bugeilio'r Gwenith Gwyn: *Britten**
Bullfinches, The: *Serrell*
Bunches of Grapes: *Keel*
Buonaparty: *Vaughan Williams*
Burd Ellen and Young Tamlane: *Warlock*
Burned Ships: *Horne*
Burst forth, my tears: *Dowland*
Bury me again at Wounded Knee: *Bibby*
Bush Christmas: *Hiscocks, W.*
Business Girls: *Dring*
But stars remaining: *LeFanu*†
But this, and then no more: *Barley*
Buttercup: *Greaves, Terence*†
Butterflies: *Maconchy*†
Butterflies [Sassoon]: *Rootham*
Butterfly Song: *Bantock*
Butterfly's love is the op'ning rose, The: *Stanford*
Buy broom buzzems: *Finnissy*†
Buzz: *Beamish*†
Buzz, buzz, buzz: *Papastávrou*(†)
By a Bier-side: *Gibbs*, *Armstrong*; *Gurney* (Chief Centurians, The)
By a Clear Well: *Harrison, J.*
By a fountain where I lay: *Dowland*
By a Fountainside: *Quilter* (Echo's Lament for Narcissus)
By dimpled brook and fountain trim: *Arne, T.*
By Footpath and Stile: *Finzi*†
By Mendip side: *Coates, E.*

Index of titles

By Moonlight: *Blyton*
By the beer as brown as a berry: *Lampe*
By the bivouac's fitful flame: *Harty*
By the Dee at Night: *Pitfield*
By the Fireside: *Bantock*; *Somervell*
By the Ganges: *Bantock*
By the Grey Stone: *Howells*
By the rivers of Babylon we sat down and wept (Psalm 121): *Bantock*; *Wesley, S.S.*
By the Sea [Griffith]: *Williams, W.A.*
By the Sea [Quilter]: *Quilter*
By the Sea [Tippett]: *Tippett*†
By the side of the well: *Papastávrou*
By the simplicity of Venus' doves: *Bishop*
By the Small Tree of Thorn: *Brook*
By the Tamar: *Bush, G.*
By thy banks, gentle Stour: *Boyce*
By Wenlock Town: *Hamilton, J.* (Hawthorn Time / Tis time I think by Wenlock Town)
By Winding Roads: *Parke*
Bygone Joys: *White, M.V.*

C

Ca' the yowes to the knowes: *Atkinson, G.*; *Britten*; *Center*; *Liddell*; *Marshall, N.*†; *Musgrave*; *Quilter*
Cabaret: *Senator*
Cabaret Songs: *Britten*(†)
Cage, The: *Hudes*†
Caged Bird: *Joubert*
Cakewalk, The: *Fulton*
Calen-o: *Ferguson*
Calico Dress, The: *Stanford*
Californy Song, The: *Raynor*
Call, The: *Pike*; *Vaughan Williams*
Call for the robin redbreast: *Poston*
Call of the Roses, The: *Samuel, H.*
Caller herrin': *Thomas, Mansel*
Calligrammes d'Apollinaire: *Poole*†
Calling, love, for you: *Jones, W.B.*
Calling me home: *Thomas, R.*
Calm is the morn without a sound: *Holst*
Calm Sea and Mist: *Benjamin*
Calypso: *Britten*
Cam' ye by? *Jacob*
Cambridge: *Rose*
Camden Town: *Solomons*†
Camel-driver, A: *Bantock*
Camel's hump is an ugly hump, The: *German*
Can she excuse my wrongs? *Dowland*
Canción de jinete: *Aplvor*†
Cancionero: *Gerhard**
Candle Gate: *Jeffreys, J.*
Candle Lightin' Time: *Coleridge-Taylor*
Candlelight: *Warlock*
Candlestick Maker's Song: *Gibbs, Armstrong*
Can't you dance the polka? *Moeran*
Cantata II (Tell me, ye brooks): *Boyce*
Cantata II (Three Lovescapes): *Harvey, J.*
Cantata III: *Harvey, J.*†
Cantata X (Spirit Music): *Harvey, J.*†
Cantata No. 2: *Saxton*†
Cantata on Medieval Latin Texts: *Burgon*†
Cantata on the Death of Antony: *Matthews, C.*†
Cantata Pastorale (cycle): *Rubbra*†

Canterbury Bells: *Besley*
Cantica (cycle): *Dalby*†
Canticle I: My beloved is mine: *Britten*
Canticle III: Still falls the rain: *Britten*†
Canticle V: The Death of St Narcissus: *Britten*†
Canticle for Easter (Road to Emmaus): *Hearne*†
Cantiones Iudithae: *Howard, M.*
Canto per Tre: *McLeod*†
Cantus Troili: *Newson*
Canzona: *Orr, B.*†
Cap and Bells, The: *Scott, D.B.*
Cape Ann: *Adès, Pope*
Cape Horn Gospel: *Keel*
Caprice: *Horder*
Captain Bover: *Williamson, M.*
Captain Harry Morgan: *Bantock*
Captain Mac: *Sanderson*
Captain Morgan's March: *Thomas, Mansel*
Captain Stratton's Fancy: *Gurney*; *Warlock*
Captivity: *Storace*(†)
Caravan, The: *Shaw*
Carecharmer sleep, son of the sable night (Sonnet) [Daniel]: *Rutter*†; *Steptoe*
Careless Content: *Brown, J.*
Cares of lovers, their alarms, The: *Purcell, H.*
Cargoes: *Martin, E.*; *Shaw*
Carillion: *Martin, E.*
Carillon, Carilla: *Warlock*(†)
Carillons: *Shaw*
Carmeña: *Wilson, H.L.*
Carol [Medieval]: *Bush, G.*
Carol [Rodgers]: *Rawsthorne*
Carol [Thompson]: *Thompson, P.*
Carol, A (Fling out your windows wide) [Quiller-Couch]: *Stanford*
Carol for a Newborn King: *Thomas, Mansel*
Carol of Jesus Child: *Hughes, Herbert*
Carol of the Beasts: *Roe*†
Carol of the Birds: *Thiman*
Carol of the Field Mice, The: *Head*
Carol of the Little King: *Fogg*
Carol of the Ship: *Butt*
Carol of the Skiddaw Yowes: *Gurney*
Carol on a Polish Folk Song: *Bayliss*
Carol Singers, The: *Bennett, T.C.S.*
Carpenter's Son, The: *Orr, C.W.*
Carrey Clavel: *Bax*
Carrion Crow, The: *Pitfield*
Carrowmore: *Bantock*
Carry her over the water: *Berkeley, L.*; *Dickinson*; *Horder*
Casabianca: *Evans, C.E.*
Cascades: *Woolrich*†
Casend Hill: *Clarke, R.C.*
Casterbridge Fair: *Downes*
Castle Gordon: *Bennett, W.S.*
Castlepatrick: *Foss*; *Hely-Hutchinson*
Cat and Mouse: *Roe*†
Cat and the Moon, The: *Young, Douglas*
Cat Goddesses: *Wishart*
Cathedral of Trees, The: *Bingham*†
Cathleen ni Houlihan: *Gurney*
Cat's Cradle for the Nemuri-Neko: *Beat*†
Cats' Eyes: *Lawrence, M.*
Cattery, The (cycle): *Dawney*
Cauldron, The: *Glyn*
Causeway, The: *Usher*†
Cautious Maid, The: *Hook*

224 Index of titles

Cavalier: *Turnbull*
Cavalier to his Lady, A: *Harrison, J.*
Ce caillou chaud de soleil: *Berkeley, L.**
Cease, anxious world, your fruitless pain: *Purcell, H.*
Cease Hymen, cease: *Courteville*
Cease not, thou heav'nly-voiced glorious creature: *Jenkins, J.*
Cease, O my sad soul, cease to mourn: *Purcell, H.*
Cease that enchanting song: *Clarke, J.*
Celebration: *Samuel, R.*
Celebration of Divine Love (cycle): *Williamson, M.*
Celestial Weaver, The: *Bantock*
Celestina (Shaded with olive trees): *Greaves, Thomas*
Celia the Fair (My lovely Celia): *Munro*
Celia's fond, too long I've loved her: *Purcell, H.*
Celtic Lullaby, A: *Bax*
Celtic Song-Cycle, A: *Bax*
Centaurs, The: *Busch*
Cet enfant de jadis: *Berkeley, L.**
Ceux qui Luttent, *Lutyens*
Chabet, The: *Cannon*
Chains of Love, The: *Gibbs, Armstrong*
Challenge, The: *Glyn*
Chamber Music: *Goossens*
Champa Flower, The: *Hiscocks, W.*(†)
Chandelier: *Hugill*
Change thy mind since she doth change: *Martin, R.*
Channel Firing: *Finzi*
Channel Saint: *Thomas, Mansel*
Chanson [Anon]: *Handel**
Chanson [Despréaux]: *Dieren**,
Chanson d'Automne: *Delius**; *Elias**; *Wilby**
Chanson de Fortunio: *Delius**
Chanson du jour de noël: *Warlock*
Chanson einer Dame in Schatten: *Nyman**
Chansons de la Nuit et du Brouillard (cycle): *McLeod**
Chapel on the Hill, The: *Stanford*
Chariots of the Lord, The: *Elgar*
Charlie is my Darling: *Quilter*; *White, A.*
Charm, A: *Britten*
Charm of Lullabies, A: *Britten*
Charming Chloe: *German*
Charming Country Life, A: *Cockshott*
Cherries: *Bantock*
Cherry Blooming, The: *Dring*
Cherry ripe, cherry ripe, ripe, I cry (Herrick): *Horn*; *Quilter*
Cherry Robbers: *Raphael*
Cherry Tree, The [Claye]: *Bernard*
Cherry Tree, The [Housman]: *Hamilton, J.* (Cherry Tree hung with Snow / Loveliest of trees)
Cherry Tree, The [Rose]: *Gibbs, Armstrong*
Cherry Tree Hung with Snow: *Ross* (Cherry Tree, The / Loveliest of trees)
Cherry trees bend over, The: *Gurney*
Cherry Valley: *Quilter*(†)
Cherry-blossom Wand, The: *Clarke, R.*
Cherry-ripe (Campion): *Moeran* (There is a garden in her face)
Cherry-tree Carol, The: *Ferguson*
Cheshire Verses: *Scott, S.*
Chess Piece, A: *Usher*†
Chestnut blossom fell, The: *Peterkin*
Chestnut Tree, The: *Hearne*†
Chian Girl, The: *Papastávrou*†
Chian Ship, The: *Papastávrou*†
Chief Centurians, The: *Whittaker* (By a Bierside)

Chieftain's Battle Song, The: *Bantock*
Chieftain's Daughter, The: *Morris, H*
Child and the Twilight, The: *Parry, C.H.H.*
Child Asleep, A: *Elgar*
Child Hears Rain at Night, The: *Pitfield*
Child in the Manger: *Archer*†
Child Lived, The: *Taverner*†
Child o' Mine: *Dunhill*
Child of the flowing tide: *Shaw*
Child on the Shore: *Head*(†)
Childhood Among the Ferns: *Finzi*
Children, The: *Britten*; *MacMillan*
Children and Sir Nameless, The: *Britten*
Children's Carol: *Procter*
Child's Carol, A: *Naylor, B.*
Child's Evenng Prayer: *White, M.V.*
Child's Garden of Verses (cycle): *Stevenson*
Child's Prayer, A [Barbour]: *Anderson, W.H.*
Child's Prayer, A [Sassoon]: *Bliss*; *Rootham*
Child's Song, A: *Walton*
Child's Song of Praise, A: *Dunhill*
Chimes: *Pope*
Chimney Sweeper, The: *Butt*
Chinese Lyrics: *Steptoe*(†)
Chinese Suite No 2: *Kleyn*
Chloris in the Snow: *Gibbs, Armstrong*; *Turnbull*
Chloris sigh'd and sung and wept: *Bales*
Choirmaster's Burial, The: *Britten*
Chopcherry: *Warlock*(†) (Strawberries Swimming in the Cream / Summer Song / Whenas the rye reach to the chin)
Chorister, The: *Sullivan*
Chough, The: *Naylor, P.*
Christ keep the hollow land: *Fulton*
Christ my beloved: *Procter* (Spouse to the Beloved, The)
Christmas Carol, A [Anon]: *Bax* (There is no rose of such virtue)
Christmas Carol, A [Chesterton]: *Williamson, M.*
Christmas Carol, A [Cripps]: *Bliss*†
Christmas Carol, A [Herrick]: *Butt*
Christmas Carol, A [Masefield]: *Davidson, M.*
Christmas Day: *Roberts, M.*
Christmas Eve (Drinkwater): *Austin*
Christmas eve, and twelve of the clock [Hardy]: *Finzi*† (Oxen, The)
Christmas Garland, A: *Turner*
Christmas Haikus: *Solomons*(†)
Christmas Lullaby: *Pitfield*
Christmas Night: *Bailey*
Christmas Star: *Thomas, Mansel*
Christopher Robin is Saying his Prayers: *Fraser-Simson*
Christ's Nativity: *Jeffreys, J.*
Chrysilla: *Smyth*(*)
Church's restoration, The: *Horder*
Church Soloist, The (Eight Sacred Songs): *Thiman*†
Cinq Chansons de Femme: *Cannon*(*)(†)
Circles: *Routh*†
Cities and thrones and powers: *Hely-Hutchinson*
City, The: *Standford*†
City Sleeps, The: *Blyton*
City Songs: *McGuire*
Clachàrd: *MacDonald*
Clandestiny (cycle): *Holt*†
Clara: *Beamish*
Claribel: *Head*; *Vaughan Williams*

Index of titles

Clarona, lay aside your lute: *Blow*
Clear midnight, A: *Vaughan Williams*
Clear or cloudy, sweet as April showering: *Bennett, R.R.*; *Dowland*
Clearing at Dawn: *Redman*
Clee Songbook: *Moult*
Cliff Top, The: *Miles*†
Clock, The: *Pike*
Clock of the Years, The: *Finzi*; *Newson*
Clod and the Pebble, The: *Rodgers*
Close of Day: *Powell*
Close (now) thine eyes and sleep secure: *Bullock*; *Plumstead*; *Rutter*† (On a Quiet Conscience)
Closing Doors: *Bax*
Cloths of Heaven, The: *Clarke, R.*; *Dunhill*; *Edwards, P.*; *Elwyn-Edwards*; *Gurney*; *Sagar*; *Warlock* (Had I the heaven's embroidered cloths / He Wishes for the Cloths of Heaven)
Clouded Starre, A: *Headington*
Clouds: *Caradon*; *Foss*; *Newson*
Clown and the Jackal, The: *Moult*
Clown's Song: *Butterworth, N.*; *Harrison, J.* (Rain It Raineth Every Day, The / When that I was and a little tiny boy)
Clun: *Vaughan Williams*(†)
Cobbler's Song: *Norton*
Cocaine Lil *or* Bondage of Opium: *Bingham*
Cock, The: *Tate, P.*
Cock Robin: *Cruft*
Cock-crow: *Gurney*; *Hedges*
Cocky Robin: *Roe*
Coigitum: *Barrett*†
Cold wave my love lies under, The: *Attwood*
Colin's Success: *Defesch*
Collect: *Hugill*†
Collect for the Third Sunday in Advent: *Wesley, S.S.*
Collected Folksong Arrangements: *Moeran*
Collected Solo Songs: *Moeran*
Collected Songs: *Pilling*(†); *Vaughan Williams*
Collected Vocal Music, The: *Berners*(*)
Collier's Daughter, The: *White, A.*
Colloquy: *Bush, G.*
Colour, The: *Milford*; *White, A.*
Colours: *Pilling*
Colt, The: *Walker, R.*†
Come Adonis, come away: *Lawes, W.*
Come again, sweet love doth now invite: *Dowland*
Come all ye songsters of the sky: *Purcell, H.*
Come and see the baby: *Thomas, Mansel*(†)
Come and trip it as you go: *Handel*
Come away, come away, death: *Allport*; *Arne, T.*; *Barrell, B.*†; *Bullock*; *Dale, B.*(†); *Dring*; *Finzi*; *Fulton*; *Harrison, J.*; *Kaye*; *Moeran*; *Naylor, J.*; *Quilter*; *Roe*†; *Shaw*; *Stanford*; *Westrup*; *Williamson, M.*(†); *Wordsworth*
Come away, come sweet love: *Dowland*; *Dring*
Come back [Cavafy]: *Hugill*
Come back [Quilter]: *Quilter*
Come Back in Dreams: *Self, A.*
Come, calm content: *Arne, T.*
Come, come thou glorious object of my sight: *Lanier*
Come, every man now give his toast: *Dibdin*
Come, gentle night: *Elgar*
Come heavy sleep, the image of true death: *Dowland*
Come home, my thoughts, from the hill: *Ronald*
Come, I will sing you some slow sleepy tune (Song from 'The Cenci'): *Dieren*
Come in! *Coleridge-Taylor*

Come in here, child: *Bedford*†
Come into the garden, Maud: *Balfe*; *Somervell*
Come lassies and lads: *Grainger, P.*
Come let's be merry, let's be airy: *Wilson, H.L.*
Come live with me and be my love: *Bishop*; *Bullard*; *Dale, M.*; *Dillon*†; *Dring*; *Procter* (Passionate Shepherd, The)
Come Love, come Lord: *Vaughan Williams*†
Come Mira, idol of the swains: *Arne, T.*
Come, my Celia, let us prove: *Ferrabosco*
Come, my little children, here are songs for you: *Birkett*
Come, my love: *Bryan*
Come, my love, to me: *Bishop*
Come my own one, come my fond one: *Butterworth, G.*
Come my sweet while every strain: *Lawes, H.*
Come, Night: *Blyton*
Come night and lay thy velvet hand: *Dale, M.*
Come O come, my life's delight: *Busch*; *Clarke, R.*; *Gurney*; *Harty*
Come on, Algernon: *Berners*
Come out, the Spring is roaming: *Tomlinson*
Come Phyllis, come into these bowers: *Ford, T.*
Come, rock his cradle: *Raynor*
Come Sing and Dance: *Howells*
Come, sleep: *Towers*
Come sweet lass: *Plumstead*
Come take your lute: *Head*
Come tender bud, lean close to me: *Quilter*
Come to me in my dreams, and then: *Bridge*; *McLelland-Young*; *Somervell*; *Taylor, C.V.* (Longing [Arnold])
Come to me, soothing sleep: *Handel*
Come to me when the earth is fair: *Stanford*
Come to the dancing: *White, M.V.*
Come to the Fair: *Martin, E.*
Come to the woods: *German*
Come unto him, all ye that labour: *Handel*†
Come unto these yellow sands: *Hold*, *Quilter*; *Tippett*(†)
Come ye blessed: *Gaul*
Come you, Mary: *Farrar*
Come you not from Newcastle? *Britten*
Come you pretty false-eyed wanton: *Campion*
Comet, The: *Head*
Comet at Yell'ham, The: *Finzi*
Comfort to a Youth that had Lost his Love: *Routh*
Comin' thro' the Rye: *Liddell*
Commandment of Love, The: *Oldham*
Como las flores: *Osborne*†
Companions, The: *Moult*
Companions, The: *Moult*
Compassion: *Tippett*
Complaint, The: *Anon*; *Arne, T.*
Complaint against Cupid, A: *Lawes, H.*
Complaint of the Morpethshire Farmer: *Colling*†
Complete French Songs: *Berkeley, L.**
Complete Solo Devotional Songs: *Humfrey*†
Complete Works for Voice and Piano: *Ireland*
Compliments of the Season: *Roe*
Concerning Love: *Parry, C.H.H.* (Love is a sickness full of woes)
Confession (Anon): *Bush, G.*
Confession (Sister Miriam): *Bantock*
Congress of Passions, A: *Matthews, D.*†
Conjuration: *Davidson, M.*
Conjuration, The: *Shaw*

226 Index of titles

Consider: *Warlock*
Constancy: *Head*
Constant Lover, The [Browne]: *Moeran*
Constant Lover, The [Suckling]:, *Quilter, Wordsworth* (Out upon it, I have lov'd)
Constantly smile: *Fowler*
Content: *Smith, T.*
Contented Lover, The: *Warlock*
Contentment: *Herbert, M.*
Contrast, A [Anon]: *Parry, C.H.H.*
Contrast, The [Morris]: *Walton*
Contretemps Songs: *Garton*
Conundrums: *Holloway*†
Convalescent: *Horder*
Convocation of Wurms: *Swayne*†
Convoy: *Hurd*
Cool Web, The: *Crosse*
Cool Web, The: *Bayliss; Crosse*
Cophetua: *Stevenson*
Cordovan Love Song: *Bowen*
Corinna is divinely fair: *Purcell, H.*
Corinna's Going a-Maying: *Walker, E.*
Corn Riggs: *Center*
Corn Song: *Coleridge-Taylor*
Corn-a-turnin' yellow: *Lord, R.*
Corncrake, The: *Jeffreys, J.*
Cornford Cycle, A: *Hugh-Jones*
Corona: *Nyman**
Coronach: *Blake, H.*(†)
Coronach for the End of the World: *Stevenson*
Coronach: He is gone on the mountain: *Attwood*
Coronal, A: *Quilter*
Corpus Christe: *Jeffreys, J.* (Falcon, The)
Corpus Christe Carol: *Britten; Crosse*† (Falcon, The)
Correndes: *Gerhard**
Correspondences: *Harvey, J.*
Corrymeela: *Stanford*
Corsican Dirge, A: *Stanford*
Cost, The: *Ireland*
Cotswold Love: *Head, Mullinar; Rowley*
Cottage of Dreams, The: *Lloyd Webber*
Cottager, A: *Moeran*
Counsel: *Salter, L.*
Counterpoints: *Luff*
Counting Sheep: *Rowley*
Counting the Beats: *Berkeley, L.; Searle*
Country Faith, The: *Kleyn*
Country Girl: *Liddell*
Country Girl's Farewell, The: *Anon*
Country Glee: *Hamilton, I.*
Country Letter: *Hold*
Country Life: *Scott, F.G.*
Country-Lover, The: *Peel*
Countryman, The: *Warlock*
County Guy: *Sullivan*
County Mayo, The: *Gurney*
Court of Dreams, The: *Bantock*
Covent Garden: *Gibbs, Armstrong*
Cow, The: *White, A.*
Cowslip Time: *Stanford*
Coy Daphne fled from Phoebus' hot pursuit: *Danyel*
Coy Maiden, The: *Treharne*
Crab Apple: *Phillips, M.*
Crabbed age and youth cannot live together: *Dring; Joubert*†; *Macfarren*†; *Parry, C.H.H.; White, M.V.*
Cradle, The: *Turner*
Cradle in Bethlehem, The: *Quilter*

Cradle Song [Anon]: *Hurlstone*†
Cradle Song [Anon]: *Byrd; Warlock* (My little sweet darling)
Cradle Song (A) [Blake]: *Butt; Someren-Godfery; Tate, P.* (Blake's Cradle Song?)
Cradle Song (Sleep, sleep, beauty bright) [Blake]: *Britten; Clarke, R.; Milford* (Blake's Cradle Song?)
Cradle Song (Sweet dreams form a shade) [Blake]: *Holst*
Cradle Song [Coleridge, S.T.]: *Vaughan Williams*
Cradle Song [Colum]: *Bax; Crossley-Holland; Graves; Harty; Rubbra* (Mantle of Blue / O men from the fields)
Cradle Song [Ibsen]: *Delius* (Margrete's Cradle Song)
Cradle Song [Luther]: *Taylor, C.V.* (Ane Sang of the Birth of Christ / Balulalow / O my dear heart / O my deir hert)
Cradle Song [MacNeice]: *Britten*
Cradle Song [Philip]: *Warlock* (Be still, my sweet sweeting / Nurse's Song, The)
Cradle Song [Scott]: *Bantock*
Cradle Song [Tennyson]: *Wallace*
Cradle Song (A), [Yeats]: *Gurney; Macgeorge; Scott, D.B.*
Cramasie Threid: *Beamish*†
Craswall: *Thomas, Mansel*
Crazy Jane: *Bennett, R.R.*†
Crazy Jane Grown Old Looks at the Dancers: *Aston*†
Crazy Jane Talks with the Bishop: *Aston*†
Creation: *Holst*
Creditor, The: *Spedding*
Creek: *Hayes*
Creeping Jane: *Grainger, P.*
Crépuscule du soir mystique: *Wilby**
Crescent Boat, The: *Pitfield*
Cricketers of Hambledon, The: *Warlock*
Crimond: *Irvine*† (Brother James's Air)
Crimson Thread: *Beamish*†
Crippled Faun, The: *Bantock*
Crocodile, The [Anon]: *Barton*†,
Crocodile, The [Broadwood]: *Britten*
Crossing the Bar: *Clements; Newson; Somervell; Stanford; Williamson, M.*
Crossing the Han River: *Steptoe*
Crossing the Stile: *Thomas, Mansel*
Crow, The: *Stanford*
Crowder, The: *Whittaker*
Crowdieknowe: *Scott, F.G.*
Crown the altar, deck the shrine: *Purcell, H.*
Crown winter with green: *MacCunn*
Crowning: *Gibbs, Armstrong*
Cruel and bright as the whin: *Jeffreys, J.*
Cruel, but once again: *Jeffreys, G.*
Cruelty has a human heart: *Vaughan Williams*†
Cry, cock-a-doodle-doo: *Bauld*
Crying for the Moon: *Grainger, E.*
Crystal Rill, The: *Thomas, Mansel*
Cuckoo, The [Rands]: *Lehmann*
Cuckoo, The [Shakespeare]: *Dring* (When daisies pied / Mockery)
Cuckoo and Chestnut Time: *Pitfield*
Cuckoo by Moonlight: *Torphichen*
Cuckoo, cuckoo, pray what do you do?: *Shaw*
Cuckoo is a merry bird, The: *Butterworth, G.*
Cuckoo on a paling sat, The: *Stanford*
Cuckoo Song [Kipling]: *Hely-Hutchinson*
Cuckoo Song [Williams]: *Quilter*

Cuckoo's a bonny bird, The: *Jeffreys, J.*
Cuisine Provençale: *Bush, G.*
Cupid and Campaspe: *Dalby*(†)
Cupid and Venus: *Scott, F.G.*
Cupid as he lay among roses: *Lawes, H.*
Cupid make your virgins tender: *Purcell, D.*
Cupid, the slyest rogue alive: *Purcell, H.*
Cupid's Garden: *Moeran*
Cure of Care, The (When dull care): *Leveridge*
Curfew tolls the knell of parting day, The: *Storace*(†)
Curlew, The: *Elwyn-Edwards*
Curlew, The (cycle) [Yeats]: *Warlock*†
Curlew calling down the slack: *Jeffreys, J.*
Curly locks: *Wood, C.*
Current with the gentle murmur glides, The: *Findlay*
Curse, A: *Bush, G.*
Curse on a Closed Gate, A: *Peterkin*†
Cursed be the time: *Cavendish*
Curtains now are drawn, The: *Downes*; *Patterson*
Cushendall: *Stanford*
Cushendall: *Stanford*
Cuttin' Rushes: *Stanford*
Cycle for Declamation: *Rainier*†
Cycle of Life, A: *Ronald*
Cycle of Love: *Boyd*†
Cycle of Songs from A Shropshire Lad: *Orr, C.W.*
Cycle of Three Neil Oram Poems, A: *Green*
Cymon and Iphigenia: *Arne, T.*
Cymru land of mine: *Edwards, T.D.*
Cypress curtain of the night, The: *Campion*
Cypress grove whose melancholy shade, A: *Hayden*

D

Daddy-long-legs [Stevenson]: *Stanford*
Daddy-long-legs, The [Anon]: *Barton*†
Daffa-down-dilly: *Walters, L.*
Daffins: *Musgrave*
Daffodils [de Tably]: *Alwyn*
Daffodils [Erskine]: *Scott, C.*
Daffodils, that come before the swallow dares: *Center*
Dafydd y Ganreg wen: *Britten**
Dainty Davie: *Stanford*
Dainty fine bird that art encaged there: *Thiman*
Dainty little maiden whither would you wander: *Lloyd, D. J. de*; *Somervell*
Dairy Song: *Scott, C.*
Daisies [Teschermacher]: *Samuel, H.*
Daisies, The [Stephens]: *Mullinar* (In the bud of the morning O / Where the Daisies Are)
Daisy Chain, The: *Lehmann*
Daisy's Song: *Owen*
Dalliance of the Eagles, The: *Knussen*
Dalmatian Cradle Song: *Roberton*
Damask Roses: *Quilter* (Lady, when I behold the roses sprouting)
Dance, The: *Smyth*(*)
Dance Continued, The: *Finzi*
Dance from the Island of Samos: *Papastávrou*†
Dance of the Rain: *Rainier*†
Dance Song: *Britten*†
Dance to your daddy: *Poston*; *Roberton*
Dancer, The [Campbell]: *Hugh-Jones*
Dancer, The [Lewis]: *Tippett*
Dancer's End XV: *Sanger*
Dancing: *Bantock*

Dancing Girl, The: *Redman*
Dancing in a Sack: *Gerhard*
Dancing in the Sun: *Butterworth, N.*
Dandelion, The [Anon]: *Dunhill*
Dandelion, The [Cornford]: *Bliss*†
Danger: *Gibbs, Armstrong*
Daniel Brent: *Bush, G.*
Danny Boy: *Anon* (Londonderry Air / O Mary dear)
Dans la Grotte: *Sorabji**
Danube to the Severn, The: *Procter-Gregg*
Daphne: *Walton*
Daphne was not so chaste as she was changing: *Dowland*
Daphnis and Chloe: *Scott, C.*
Dapple Grey: *Jeffreys, J.* (I had a little pony)
Darest thou now, O soul: *Wood, C.* (To the Soul)
Dark Angels (cycle): *Maxwell Davies*†
Dark Lady, The: *Wills*
Dark Sunset: *Hand*
Dark Sunset: *Hand*
Darkened Room at Dawn, A: *Beamish*
Darkness: *Hurlstone*
Darlin': *Maw*
Darling Dog: *Horder*
Das Buch der Bilder: *Young, Derek**
Das Gesetz der Quadrille (cycle): *Goehr**
Das irdische Leben: *McLeod**
Das Knee: *Seiber*†
Das Letzte Gerichte: *McCabe*†
Das Nasoböm: *Seiber*†
Dashing White Sergeant, The: *Bishop*
Dass du mich liebst: *Stanford**
David of the White Rock: *Anon*; *Britten*(†); *Mathias*(†); *Thomas, Mansel*(†)
David's Lament for Jonathan: *Hugill*†
Dawn [Anon]: *Hamilton, I.*; *Milner*
Dawn [Bantock, R.]: *Bantock*
Dawn [Barnes]: *Harvey, F.*
Dawn [Bottomley]: *Bainton*
Dawn [Dickinson]: *Grossner*
Dawn [Dunbar]: *Coleridge-Taylor*
Dawn, The: *Fould*s
Dawn and Evening: *Bridge*
Dawn at Sea: *Alwyn*†
Dawn gapes in with an ashen face, The: *Blyton*
Dawn, gentle flower, from the morning earth: *Bennett, W.S.*
Dawn in the Room: *Solomons*(†)
Dawn Song: *Fogg*
Dawn Trees: *Thomas, Mansel*
Dawning of the Day, The: *Moeran*
Dawtie's Devotion: *Britten*
Day after day he comes and goes away: *Bridge*
Day and Night: *Brian*
Day is Düne: *Stevenson*
Day is no more, The: *Someren-Godfery*; *Standford*†
Day of Palms, The: *Moeran* (Santa Chiara)
Day of the Singing Birds, The: *Hiscocks, W.*(†)
Daybreak [Blake]: *Quilter*
Daybreak [Donne]: *Milford* (Break of Day / Stay, O sweet, and do not rise)
Daybreak [Teschemacher]: *Ronald*
Day's Alarm, The (cycle): *Hurd*
Days Now Gone: *Horne*
Dead at Clonmacnois, The: *Wood, C.*
Dead Days: *Cruft*
Dead Dryad, The: *Bantock*
Dead, long dead: *Somervell*

Dead Poet, The: *Hugill*
Dead Violet, A: *Bridge*
Deaf Woman's Courtship, The: *Britten*
Dear Adonis, beauty's treasure: *Handel*
Dear Delight: *Head*
Dear, do not your fair beauty wrong: *Johnson, R.*
Dear harp of my country: *Britten*
Dear heart, why will you use me so?: *Goossens*
Dear, if you change I'll never choose again: *Dowland*
Dear Lily: *Moult*
Dear little love: *Samuel, H.*
Dear Lord (Six Animal Songs to God): *Barton*†
Dear old songs of Wales: *Ward, Darman*
Dear pretty youth: *Purcell, H.*
Dear, though your mind stand so averse: *Corkine*
Dearest of thousands: *Berkeley, L.*†
Death: *Routh*
Death and the lady: *Anon*
Death and the Maiden: *Gerhard*
Death, be not proud, though some have called thee: *Bennett, R.R.*; *Britten*; *Stevens, B.*
Death in Love: *Vaughan Williams*
Death of Iphigenea (scena): *Routh*
Death of Nelson, The: *Braham*
Death of St Narcissus, The (Canticle V): *Britten*†
Death, thy servant: *Someren-Godfery*
Death-parting: *Ireland*
December 1903: *Hugill*
Declare my pretty maid: *Boyce*
Dedication [Barker]: *Williamson, M.*
Dedication [Kipling]: *Grainger, P.*
Dedication [Sidney]: *Warlock*
Dedications: *Dring*
Deep in my heart: *Bishop*
Defeat: *Gibbs, Armstrong*
Deil o' Bogey, The: *Scott, F.G.*
Deilen: *Elwyn-Edwards**
De'ils awa wi' the Excise man, The: *Beamish*†; *Center*; *Shur*†; *White, A.*
Delia: *Arne, T.*
Delilah: *Marsh*†
Deluge, The: *Hatton*
Demande et Réponse: *Coleridge-Taylor*
Demon of Mazinderán, The: *Bantock*
Denny's daughter stood a minute: *Harty*; *Stanford*; *Wood, C.*
Deowa: *Birtwistle*†
Depression: *Britten*†
Der Asra: *Blake, D.*†; *Dieren**
Der Einsame: *Delius**
Der Fichtenbaum: *Delius**
Der Knabe: *Young, Derek**
Der Mund spricht zwer gezwungen Nein: *Handel**
Der Pfaufenbaum: *Poole**
Der Schiffbrüchige: *Kirkwood**
Der Schmetterling ist in die Rose verliebt: *Stanford**
Der sterbende Almansor: *Stanford**
Der Tamboursg'sell: *McLeod**
Der Wandrer: *Delius**
Der Wandrer und sein Schatten: *Delius**
Derby Ram, The: *Hurlstone*
Derbyshire Song: *Rowley*
Dermott Donn MacMorna: *Bax*
Derwentwater's Farewell: *Williamson, M.*
Des Kindes Abengebet: *White, M.V.*
Desdemona's Song: *Pitfield*(†) (Poor soul sat sighing, A / Willow, willow / Willow Song, The [Shakespeare])

Desire in Spring: *Gurney*
Desolation: *Bantock*
Despair: *Bantock*
Despairing Shepherd, The: *Gibbs, Armstrong*; *Miller*
Despondent Lover's Song, The: *Locke*
Det bødes der for: *Delius**
Deuk's dang o'er my daddie, The: *White, A.*
Devil's Advice to Storytellers: *Bayliss*
Devon Maid, The: *Bridge, Fogg* (Where be ye (you) going [Keats])
Devon, O Devon, in Wind and Rain: *Stanford*
Devout Lover, A: *Dring*
Dew upon the lily: *German*
Dewy Roses: *Holst*
D. H. Lawrence Songs: *Wood, Hugh*
Dialogue Between Tom Filuter and his Man: *Berners*
Diaphenia, like the daffdowndilly: *Benjamin, A.*; *Browne*; *Bush, G.*; *Moeran*; *Pilkington, F.*; *Samuel, H.*
Dick Fisherman: *Jones, D.T.*
Did ever man thus love as I?: *Jones, R.*
Did you ever see the sun? *Stanford*
Dido was the Carthage Queen: *Mason*
Dido's Farewell: *Purcell, H.* (Dido's Lament / Thy hand, Belinda / When I am laid in earth)
Dido's Lament: *Purcell, H.* (Dido's Farewell / Thy hand, Belinda / When I am laid in earth)
Die Flamingos: *Headington**
Die Heimat: *Britten**
Die Himmelsaugen: *White, M.V.**
Die Jugend: *Britten**
Die Linien des Lebens: *Britten**
Die Nachtigall, als ich sie fragte: *Lehmann**
Die Rosen: *Tomlinson**
Die Trichter: *Seiber*†
Die Wallfahrt nach Kevlaar: *Stanford**
Died for Love: *Grainger, P.*
Died of Love: *Tate, P.*†
Dilys: *Lloyd, J.M.*
Din Lligwy: *Hoddinott*
Ding dong bell, pussy's in the well: *Jeffreys, J.*
Ding, dong, merrily on high: *McLeod*†
Dira Vi Amores Terror: *Burgon*†
Dirge [H. Bantock]: *Bantock*
Dirge: Fear no more the heat of the sun: *Pierson*; *Wishart* (Fidele)
Dirge, A: Rough wind that moaneth loud: *Bridge*; *Loder*
Dirge for St Patrick's Night: *Blyton*
Dirge in Woods: *Mitchell*; *Parry, C.H.H.*
Dirty Work: *Nelson*
Discovery: *Ferguson*
Discovery: *Ferguson*
Discreet Hint, The: *Scott, F.G.*
Disdain me still, that I may ever love: *Dowland*
Dissuasion from Presumption: *Lawes, H.*
Distances: *Roe*
Distant Roar: *Moult*
Distant Shore, The: *Sullivan*
Distracted Maid, The: *Warlock*
Ditty: *Finzi*
Diver, The: *Loder*
Divine Hymn, A (Blest be those sweet regions): *Clarke, J.*(†)
Divine Hymn, A (O God forever blest): *Church*
Divine Image, The: *Vaughan Williams*†
Divine Providence: *White, M.V.*
Division, The: *Downes*

Index of titles 229

Divrei Kohelet: *Hudes*†
Dizente mis Ojes: *Handel**
Do not go gentle into that good night: *Randall*†
Do not, O do not prize: *Jones, R.*
Do torrents spare the fresh bloom flower: *Goehr*
Doggie: *Bantock*
Dog's Life, A: *Head*
Dog-tired: *Raphael*; *Wood, Hugh*
Dolphin, A: *Rainier*
Don Juan's Serenade: *Goossens*
Done For: *Fiske*
Donkey, The: *Clarke, R.*
Donkey Riding: *Pitfield*
Donneycarney: *Moeran*
Don't come in sir, please: *Scott, C.*
Don't cry: *Roberts, J.H.*
Don't let that horse: *Weir*†
Don't play your sonata tonight: *Dring*
Door, The: *Wood, Hugh*
Dora Williams: *Downes*
Dormi, Jesu: *Fryer**; *Mackenzie*† (Virgin's Cradle Hymn, The)
Dost thou withdraw thy grace? *Danyel*
Doubting: *MacCunn*
Doubts: *Møller*
Doute: *Blyton**
Dove, The: *Fogg*; *Head*; *Ronald* (I had a dove)
Dove descending breaks the air, The: *Tavener*
Dover Beach: *Bullard*; *Johnstone* (Sea of Faith, The)
Down by the river: *Raynor*
Down by the Riverside: *Moeran*
Down by the salley gardens: *Clarke, R.*; *Collins, J.H.*; *Gurney*; *Hughes, Herbert*; *Plumstead*; *Shaw* (I was young and foolish / Salley Gardens, The)
Down in a valley: *Cavendish*
Down in the forest something stirred: *Ronald*
Down in yonder meadow: *Gibbs, Armstrong*
Down the Hwai: *Bantock*
Down the Vale: *Moir*
Down-a-down, thus Phyllis sang: *Pilkington, F.*
Drake's Drum: *Stanford*
Dramatis Personae: *Wills*
Drawing Details in an Old Church: *Read*
Dream, A [Blake]: *White, A.*
Dream, A [Welsh traditional]: *Thomas, Mansel*
Dream, The [Martin]: *Hiscocks, W.*
Dream of Death, A (Yeats): *Clarke, R.*; *Moeran*
Dream Child: *Bax*
Dream Fantasy: *Hawes*
Dream Island: *Thomas, V.*
Dream Merchandise: *Bantock*
Dream of a Girl at Sevenoaks: *Butterworth, N.*
Dream of Egypt, A (cycle): *Woodforde-Finden*
Dream of Spring, A: *Bantock*
Dream of the Birds: *McLeod*
Dream O't: *Rose*
Dream Pedlary: *Birkett*; *Dieren*; *Herbage*; *Parry, C.H.H.*; *Stevens, B.* (If there were dreams to sell)
Dream Song: *Bennett, R.R.*; *Gibbs, Armstrong*; *Hely-Hutchinson*
Dream-Songs: *Bennett, R.R.*
Dream Valley: *Quilter* (Memory [Blake] / Memory, hither come)
Dream Within a Dream: *Samuel, R.*†
Dream-city, The: *Holst*
Dreamiland: *Somervell*
Dreaming: *Harty*
Dreaming at Golden Hill: *Bantock*

Dreaming Lake, The: *Head*
Dreaming of a Dead Lady: *Berkeley, L.*
Dreamland [de la Mare]: *Harrison, P.*
Dreamland [Lindsay]: *MacCunn*
Dreamland [Poe]: *Downes*†
Dreamland [Rossetti, C.]: *Vaughan Williams*
Dream-o'-day Jill: *German*
Dreams: *Steele*
Dreams and imaginations: *Jones, R.*
Dreams Melting: *Ferguson*
Dreams of the Sea: *Naylor, B.*
Dream-tryst: *Browne*
Dreamy Nights: *Delius*
Drei Morgenstern Lieder: *Seiber*†
Drift down, drift down from the skies: *Ronald*
Drinaun dhun, The: *Wood, C.*
Drink to me only with thine eyes: *Anon*; *Biggs*; *Grainger, P.*; *Naylor, P.*; *Quilter*; *Young, P.*†; *Scott, C.*
Drinking Song [Bantock, H.]: *Bantock*
Drinking Song [Clare]: *Hold*
Drinking Song [Fletcher]: *Slater*
Droll Lover, The: *Warlock*
Droll Wee Man, The: *Stevenson*
Drooping Wings: *Quilter*
Drop, drop, slow tears: *Frankel, B.*; *Jeffreys, J.*; *Self, A.*
Drop me a flower: *Stanford*
Drought: *Alwyn*
Drover, A: *Harty*
Drown not with tears, my dearest love: *Ferrabosco*
Drowned: *Grainger, P.*
Drummer Hodge: *Berkeley, M.*†
Drunkard and the Pig, The: *Newson*
Dry those fair, those crystal tears: *Elgar*
Dryad, The: *Bantock*
Du bist wie eine Blume: *Berners**
Dualism: *Blyton**
Duan of Barra, A: *Rubbra*
Dubbuldideery: *Peterkin*
Duck and the Kangaroo, The: *Hely-Hutchinson*
Duckling, The: *Elwyn-Edwards*
Dulas Carol, The: *Thomas, Mansel*(†)
Dum (cycle): *Marsh*†
D'un vanneur de blé aux vents: *Berkeley, L.**
Duncan Gray came here to woo: *Atkinson, G.*; *Center*
Dunce, The: *Howells*
During Music: *Ireland*
Durme, durme: *Sutton-Anderson*†
Dusk [Anon]: *Gibbs, Armstrong*
Dusk [Belloc]: *Milner*
Dusk in the Valley: *Lehmann*
Dustman, The: *Moeran*
Dustman's Song, The: *Carey, C.*
Dusty Miller, The: *Burrows*; *White, A.*
Dweller in my Deathless Dreams: *Bridge*
Dying Child, The: *Hold*
Dylan Thomas Cycle, A: *Dickinson*

E

e e cummings song cycle: *Dickinson*
Each time, my love, you say farewell: *Seiber*
Eager Spring: *Somers-Cocks*
Eagle, The [Browning]: *Bantock*
Eagle, The [Tennyson]: *Naylor, P.*

230 Index of titles

Earl Bristol's Farewell: *Lidgey*
Earl of Bristol's Farewell, The: *Orr, C.W.*
Early in the day it was whispered: *Ronald*
Early Morning, The: *Peel*
Early one morning, just as the sun was rising: *Britten; Clements; Grainger, P.*
Early one spring: *Steptoe*†
Early Songs: *Owen*
Earth and Air and Rain: *Finzi*
Earth fades! heaven breaks on me: *Coleridge-Taylor*
Earth, sweet earth: *Leighton*
Earth trembled and heaven's closed eye, The: *Purcell, H.*
Earth Will Wake, The: *White, M.V.*
Earth-borne: *Thomas, Mansel*
Earth's Answer: *Rodgers*
Earth's Call: *Ireland*
Earth's Holiday, The: *Procter*
Ease Me: *Smith, R.* (So, so, leave off this last lamenting kiss)
East Riding, The: *Ireland*
Easter: *Vaughan Williams*
Easter Carol: *Shaw*
Easter Day: *Self, A.*
Easter Green, The: *Wood, Hugh*
Easter Hymn [Bantock, H.]: *Bantock*
Easter Hymn [Vaughan]: *Headington*
Easter Hymn [Wagemann]: *Bridge*
Easter Morn: *Hawes*
Easter Prayer, An: *Thiman*
Easter Song: *Venables*
Easter Wings: *Wilby*†
Eastern Lament, An: *Scott, C.*
Eastern Love Song, An: *Bantock*
Eastern Lover, An: *Foulds*
Eastern Wisdom: *Parrott*
Easy Decision, An: *Bedford*
Echo [de la Mare]: *Hugh-Jones*(†)
Echo [Durrell]: *Routh,*
Echo [Pushkin]: *Britten*(*)
Echo [Rossetti, C.]: *Berkeley, M.; Joseph*(†); *McLeod; Self, A.; Somers-Cocks; Wegener; Wood, C.*
Echo, The: *Schetky*
Echoing Green, The: *Busch; Cooke*†; *Lord, R.*
Echoes [de la Mare]: *Thompson, P.*
Echoes [Moore]: *Dring; Sagar* (How sweet the answer echo makes)
Echo's Lament for Narcissus: *Bush, G.; Fraser, N.* (By a Fountainside)
Ecstatic, The: *Naylor, B.*
Ed è sùbito sera: *MacDonald**
Edge of Day, The: *Wood, Hugh*
Edward, Edward: *Gurney*
Edward Gray: *Sullivan*
Eemis Stane, The: *Scott, F.G.*
E'en as a lovely flower: *Bridge*
Efterår, *Delius**
Egg: *Bauld*
Egypt's might is tumbled down: *Le Fleming*
Eho! eho!: *Britten**
Eifionydd [tr. Cobb]: *Thomas, Mansel*
Eifionydd [tr. Stoddart]: *Elwyn-Edwards*
Eight Folksong Arrangements: *Britten*(†)
Eight O'Clock: *Clarke, R.*
Eight Poems of Walter de la Mare: *Harrison, P.*
Eight Sacred Songs ('The Church Soloist'): *Thiman*
Eight Selected Songs: *Stevenson*
Eight Shaker Songs: *Cresswell*

Eight Songs: *Eccles; Frankel, B.; Peterkin; Warlock*
Eight Songs for High Voice: *Bush, G.; Hook*
Eight Songs for Medium Voice: *Bush, G.*
Eight Songs from the Chinese: *Dalby*
Eight Songs from the Yuan: *Orr, B.*
Eight Songs of Walter de la Mare: *Hugh-Jones*
Eileen: *Scott, C.*
Eileen Alannah: *Thomas, J.R.*
Eileen Aroon: *Foulds*
Eilidh my fawn: *Bax*
Ein Auge, offen: *Birtwistle*†
Ein jüngling liebt ein Mädchen: *White, M.V.**
Ein schöner Stern geht auf in meiner Nacht: *Delius**
Ein Stern: *White, M.V.*
Einsamkeit: *Young, Derek**
Einsetumadur einu sinni: *Hearne**
Ejaculation to God: *Turnbull* (My God! look on me)
Eleänore: *Coleridge-Taylor*
Eldorado: *Stevenson; Walthew*
Elegiac Sonnet: *Bliss*†
Elegy: *Dickinson*†
Elegy [Anon]: *Arnold, S.*(†); *Hiscocks, W.*
Elegy [St John of the Cross]: *Routh*†
Elegy on the Death of a Mad Dog: *Dring*
Eleven Songs: *Gurney; Holst; Ireland; Raynor*
Eleven Songs from 'A Shropshire Lad': *Pope*
Elfin Lover: *Bantock*
Elgar Song Album, An: *Elgar*
Elibanks and Elibraes: *White, A.*
Elizabethan Sailor's Song: *Hurd*
Elizabeth's Song: *Clements; Head*
Ellan Vannin (The Little Island): *Pike*
Eloisa to Abelard: *Pinto*
Eloré Lo: *Warlock*
Elsewhere: *Roberts, M.*
Elsie Marley: *Atkinson, R.; Tate, P.*†
Emigrant, The: *Hook*
Emperor, The: *Bantock*
Empire of the Gods: *Stafford*†
Empty House: *Fogg*
Empty Purse, The: *Whittaker*
Empty Vessel: *Scott, F.G.*
En una noche escura: *Pike*
Enchanted Fiddle, The: *Bax*
Enchanted Wood, The: *Bantock*
Enchantment, The: *Dring; Pierce*
Enchantress, The: *Hatton*
Encircled by Sea (Three Manx Pictures): *Pike*
Encounter [Rainer]: *Routh*
Encounter, An [Anon]: *Bush, G.*
Encounter, The [Housman]: *Ireland* (Street sounds to the soldiers' tread, The)
Encouragements to a Lover: *Dring*
End, The: *Hiscocks, W.*(†)
End of Love, The: *Bush, G.*
End of Season: *Hearne*
End of the Owls, The: *Newson*
End Piece, An: *Andrews*
Endymion: *Hamilton, J.* (Latmian Shepherd, The)
England, my England: *Shaw*
England's Ambassador: *Bowen*
England's Monarch: *Bowen*
England's Rose: *Bowen*
English Lyrics: *Parry, C.H.H.*
English May: *Ireland*
English Rose, The: *German*
Enter these enchanted woods: *Thomas, D.V.*
Entreat me not to leave thee: *Naylor, P.*

Index of titles 231

Envoi: *Holst*
Epeisodia: *Finzi*
Epicure, The: *Rutter*†
Epigram: *Britten*(*)
Epilogue [Housman]: *Ireland*
Epilogue [Rosenberg]: *Ellis*†
Epilogue: Oh! love – no love! [Browning]: *Bantock*
Epiphanias: *Dieren**
Epistre: *Samuel, R.*†
Epitaph, An [Anon]: *Schofield*
Epitaph (An) [de la Mare]: *Besley; Gurney; Milford; Mullinar*
Epitaph [Brooke, J.]: *Searle*
Epitaph [Raleigh]: *Tate, P.*
Epitaph in Old Mode: *Gurney*
Epitaph for Many Young Men: *Williamson, M.*
Epitaph of Timas: *Berkeley, L.*
Epitaph on Salathiel Pavey: *Browne*
Epitaph (Resurrection): *Harris, W.L.*
Epitaph: the Clerk: *Britten*
Epitaph upon a Child, An: *Bernofsky*
Epitaphs: *Bedford*
Epithalamium [Rainer]: *Routh*
Epithalamium, An (Thrice happy lovers) [Settle]: *Purcell, H.*
Ere bright Rosina met my eyes: *Shield*
Ere you can say: *Arne, T.*
Eriskay Love-lilt, An: *Kennedy-Fraser*(*)
Ermine, The: *Pope*
Ernst ist der Frühling: *Stanford**
Es muss doch Frühling werden: *White, M.V.**
Es war Erde in ihnen: *Nyman**
Escape from Love, The: *Harrison, J.* (Since I from Love escapëd am so fat)
Especially when the October Wind: *Lord, R.*
Estuary, The: *Head*
Et tout d'un Coup: *Matheson*†
Eté: *Procter*
Eternity [Blake]: *Vaughan Williams*†, *Wills*(†) (He who binds to himself a joy)
Eternity [Boycott]: *Somers-Cocks*
Eternity [Herrick]: *Bax*
Eternity's Sunrise: *Wills*(†)
Ethiopia Saluting the Colours: *Wood, C.*
Etudes Transcendantales: *Ferneyhough*†
Eulalie: *Coleridge-Taylor*
Euphonium Dance: *Roe*†
Eutopia: *Lloyd Webber*
Evan Banks: *Grainger, P.*
Eve of Crecy: *Harrison, J.*
Even now: *Bedford*†
Even such is time: *Gibbs, Alan; Gurney*
Evening [Anon]: *Dunhill*
Evening [Clare]: *Hold*
Evening [Dowson]: *Scott, C.*
Evening [Duncan]: *Britten*(†)
Evening [Manyoshu]: *Blyton*
Evening [O'Sullivan]: *Moeran*
Evening [Teschemacher]: *Ronald*
Evening Bells: *Venables*†
Evening Hymn [Bridges]: *Vaughan Williams*†
Evening Hymn [Caswall]: *Scott, C.*
Evening Hymn, An [Anon]: *Clarke, J. (*Sleep, downy sleep)
Evening Hymn, An (Now that the sun has veiled his light) [Fuller]: *Purcell, H.*
Evening in Autumn: *Anderson, W.H.*
Evening in Lilac Time: *Thiman*

Evening in Summer: *Gibbs, Armstrong*
Evening is over the land: *Crossley-Holland*
Evening Land: *Payne*
Evening Melody: *Scott, C.*
Evening, Morning, Night: *Britten*(†)
Evening on the Moselle: *Pilkington, M.*
Evening Rain: *Dillon*†
Evening Shadows (Sleep, my baby): *Somervell*
Evening Song: *Bantock*
Evening Star, The: *Hudes*
Evensong [Gibbs]: *Center*
Evensong [Hardy]: *Boughton*
Evensong [Morgan]: *Lehmann*
Evensong: La Chanson des Oiseaux: *Stout*†
Ever: *Short*
Everlasting Voices, The: *Warlock*
Every Bullet has its Billet: *Bishop*
Every dame affects good fame: *Campion*
Every day the wondrous: *Dieren*
Every Morning: *Phillips, M.*
Every night and every morn: *Chapple*
Everybody else, then, going: *Finzi*†
Everyone Sang: *Higginson, I.; Rootham; Somers-Cocks*
Everything detestable is best: *Dring*
Everywhere I look: *Carew*
Evil spirit, your beauty, haunts me still, An (Sonnet) [Drayton]: *Wills*(†)
Evoë: *Foulds*
Evolution: *Mitchell*
Excuse me: *Maxwell Davies*†
Exequy, The: *Brown, C.*
Exhortation of St Teresa to her Nuns: *Pike*
Exile: *Bantock*
Exile (cycle): *Beamish*
Exile, The (de la Mare): *Gibbs, Armstrong*
Exile, The (Ripley): *Moult*
'Exmass' Carol: *Solomons*†
Expense of spirit in a waste of shame, Th' (Sonnet 129) [Shakespeare]: *Wills*
Experience: *Swain*
Experience shows us: *Hudes*†
Experimenting: *Northcott*†
Extravaganzas (cycle): *Dickinson*
Exultation: *Scott, C.*
Eye hath not seen: *Gaul*
Eye, open, An: *Birtwistle*†
Eyes look into the well: *Berkeley, L.; Dickinson*
Eyes, look no more: *Danyel*
Eyes of all, The: *Greene*
Eze-sur-Mer: *Thomas, Mansel*

F

Face at the window: *Garton*
Fadensonnen: *Birtwistle*†
Faery beam upon you, The: *Steele*
Faery Song (Keats): *Frankel, B.*
Faery Song (Macleod): *Boughton*
Faery Song [Shakespeare]: *Wegener*
Faery Song, A [Yeats]: *Brian*
Fain I would but O I dare not: *Ferrabosco*
Fain would I change that note: *Bush, G.; Hume; Joubert; Somervell; Tomlinson; Walton*(†) (Fair House of Joy)
Fain would I, Chloris: *Blow*

Fair, The: *Stanford*
Fair Amoret is gone astray: *Eccles*
Fair and serene, like thee, my queen (My dear, my Amphitrite): *Weldon (Purcell, H.)*
Fair and True: *Warlock*; *Tomlinson* (Lovely kind and kindly loving)
Fair Annet's Song: *Bliss*
Fair daffodils, we weep to see: *Bridge* (To Daffodils)
Fair House of Joy: *Quilter* (Fain would I change that note)
Fair, if you expect admiring: *Campion*
Fair is my love: *Bliss*
Fair Lisa: *Hughes, B.*; *Thomas, Mansel*
Fair Sally loved a bonny seaman: *Greene*
Fair, sweet, cruel, why dost thou fly me?: *Ford, T.*
Fair women like fair jewels are: *Jones, R.*
Fair young Mary: *Grainger, P.*
Fairest Gwen: *Hoddinott*
Fairest isle, all isles excelling: *Purcell, H.*
Fairest May, The: *Warlock*(†) (That ever I saw / As ever I saw)
Fairest work of happy nature: *Blow*
Fairies: *Williams, W.S.G.*
Fairies, The: *Bax*
Fairies' Dance, The: *Head*
Fairies' Lullaby, The: *Bowen*
Fairings: *Martin, E.*
Fairy Boat, The: *Samuel, H.*
Fairy Bread: *White, A.*
Fairy Children, The: *Besley*
Fairy Cobbler, A: *Anderson, W.H.*
Fairy Hunt, A: *Elwyn-Edwards*
Fairy King's Courtship: *Harty*
Fairy Lough, The: *Stanford*
Fairy Lures: *Stanford*
Fairy Lullaby [Anon]: *Roberton*
Fairy Lullaby [Quilter]: *Quilter*
Fairy Pedlar, The: *Rowley*
Fairy Ring, The: *White, A.*
Fairy Roses: *Coleridge-Taylor*
Fairy Tailor, The: *Head*
Fairy Tales: *Stevenson*
Fairy Town, A: *Parry, C.H.H.* (St Andrews)
Fairy Workers: *Crossley-Holland*†
Fairyland: *Bantock*
Fais do-do, Pierrot: *Rawsthorne**
Faith [Holst]: *Holst*
Faith [Tennyson]: *Stanford*
Faith, be no longer coy: *Lawes, W.*
Faith, hope and charity: *Hugill*†
Faith, hope and love: *Jepson*
Faithful Johnny: *Pitfield*
Faithful Lover, The: *Parry, C.H.H.*
Faithful Sailor Boy: *Bantock*
Faithless as the winds: *Thomas, Muriel*
Faithless Lover, The: *Dring*
Faithless Shepherdess, The: *Herbert, M.*; *Quilter*
Fakir's Song, The: *Bantock*
Falcon, The: *Ferguson*; *Foreman*; *Ives, G.*; *Jeffreys, J.*; *Tate, P.* (Corpus Christe)
Fall, leaves, fall: *Scott, S.*
Fallen Poplar, The: *Naylor, B.*
Fallen Veils: *Head*
Falling of the Leaves, The: *Parke*
Fallow Deer at the Lonely House, The: *Bliss*
False knight upon the road, The: *Britten*(†)
False Phillis: *Wilson, H.L.*
Fame's an echo: *Arne, T.*

Family, The: *Bantock*
Fan Song: *Bantock*
Fanaid Grove, The: *Hughes, Herbert*
Fancy's Knell: *Vaughan Williams*†
Far Country, The: *Gurney*(†) (Farms of Home, The / Into my heart an air that kills / Land of Lost Content, The)
Far, far from each other: *Bridge*†
Far from triumphing court and wonted glory: *Dowland*
Far in a western brookland: *Bax*; *Gurney*(†); *Moeran*; *Pope*
Far-darting Apollo: *Bush, G.*
Farewell [d'Arcy]: *Russell, K.*
Farewell [Heber]: *Brian*
Farewell [Hungarian]: *Seiber*†
Farewell, A [Gascoigne]: *Routh*
Farewell, A [Tennyson]: *Lear*
Farewell, The [Burns]: *Jeffreys, J.* (O my love is like a red, red rose / Red Red Rose, A
Farewell, The [Priestley]: *McLeod*
Farewell all joys, when he is gone: *Purcell, H.*
Farewell, Earth's Bliss: *Self, A.*
Farewell Songs (cycle): *Garton*
Farewell, thou art too dear for my possessing (Sonnet 87) [Shakespeare]: *Parry, C.H.H.*
Farewell to a Japanese Buddhist Priest Bound Homeward: *Rubbra*†
Farewell to an Atoll: *Grainger, E.*
Farewell to barn and stack and tree: *Moeran*; *Orr, C.W.*
Farewell to Snowdonia: *Hywel*
Farewell to Summer: *Fuller*
Farewell to the farm: *White, A.*
Farewell, unkind, farewell, to me no more a father: *Dowland*
Farm Child: *Steele*
Farms of Home, The: *Williamson, J.R.* (Far Country, The / Into my heart an air that kills / Land of Lost Content, The)
Farmer went trotting upon his grey mare, A: *Mullinar*
Farmer's Boy: *Barratt*
Farraquiño: *Gerhard**
Fatal Blessing, The: *Boyce*
Fatal Harmony: *Helliwell*†
Fatal hour comes on apace, The: *Purcell, H.*
Fate's Discourtesy: *Elgar*
Father and Daughter: *Moeran*
Father O'Flynn: *Stanford*
Father Time: *Papastávrou*(†)
Father William: *Hely-Hutchinson*
Fault was mine, The: *Somervell*
Faun, The: *Bantock*
Faun Despondent, The: *Bantock*
Faustus Scene, A: *Dorward*†
Fear no more the heat o' the sun: *Blake, H.*†; *Finzi*; *Foss*; *Higginson, I.*; *Horder*; *Pierson*; *Quilter*; *Routh*; *Williamson, M.*(†) (Dirge / Fidele)
Fearful Symmetry: *Colling*†
Feast: *Bliss*
Feast of Christmas, The: *Harris, S.T.*
Feast of Lanterns, A: *Bantock*
February: *Gibbs, Armstrong*
Feckenham Men, The: *Boughton*
Femmes, battez vos marys: *Bax**
Fern Song: *Baines*
Ferry me across the water: *Finzi*
Festal Hymn of Judith, The: *Bantock*

Festal Song: *Bantock*
Festive Carol: *Davies, J.*
Fiammetta Singing: *Harrison, J.*
Fiddle-cum-fee: *Cruft*
Fiddler, The (cycle): *Dalby*†
Fiddler, The [de la Mare]: *Pitfield*†
Fiddler, The [Maunder]: *Peterkin*
Fiddler knows what's brewing, The: *Austin*
Fiddler of Dooney, The: *Dunhill*; *Gurney*; *Harty*; *Scott, D.B.*
Fiddler of Pendine, The: *Edwards, O.*
Fiddlers at the Wedding: *Maxwell Davies*†
Fidele: *Pender*; *Wishart* (Dirge / Fear no more the heat of the sun)
Fidgety Bairn, The: *Roberton*
Fie, Damon, fie: *Stanley*
Fie diddle dee and fie on me: *Dale, M.*
Fie on this feigning: *Dowland*
Fie, what a coil is here: *Jones, R.*
Field and Lane: *Mitchell*
Fields are full of summer still, The: *Gibbs, Armstrong*; *Gurney* (Late Summer)
Fields of Praise, The (cycle): *Mathias*
Fifteen Songs and Airs: *Purcell, H.*
Fifth Volume of Ten Songs, A: *Gurney*
59 (white guardians of the universe of sleep): *Finlay*
Fig Tree in Leaf: *Holloway*
Fileuse: *Britten**
Fill a glass with golden wine: *Butterworth, G.*(†); *Quilter*
Fill me, boy, as deep a draught: *Parry, C.H.H.*
Fill me O stars as with an olden tune: *Jeffreys, J.*
Fill the bowl, Butler: *Schofield*
Fill the cup, Philip, and let us drink a dram: *Warlock*
Film Star, The: *Lutyens*
Find, The: *Elwyn-Edwards*
Find me a lonely cave: *Eccles*
Fine Day, A: *Brown, C.*†
Fine English Days: *Cox*
Fine flowers in the valley: *Liddell*
Fine knacks for ladies, cheap, choice, brave and new: *Dowland*
Finnland 1940: *Poole**
Fire, *Cope*
Fire, fire, fire, fire, lo here I burn in such desire: *Bush, G.*; *Campion*; *Lanier*
Fire Flame, The: *Bantock*
Fire of heaven, whose starry arrow: *MacCunn*
Fire of Turf, A: *Stanford*
Fire of Turf, A: *Stanford*
Fire of your love: *Benjamin, A.*
Fireside Fancies: *Bantock*
First Book of Ayres: *Attey*; *Campion*; *Corkine*; *Dowland*(†); *Morley*
First Book of Songs, The: *Jones, R.*; *Pilkington, F.*
First Chanty, The: *Grainger, P.*
First Christmas, The: *Thomas, Mansel*
First Friend, The: *German*
First Love: *Scott, F.G.*
First Mercy, The: *Warlock*(†)
First of May, The: *Symons*
First Spring Day, The: *Mackenzie*
First Volume of Ten Songs, A: *Gurney*
Firstlings: *Roe*†
Fish in the Unruffled Lakes: *Britten*
Fish in the unruffled lakes: *Britten*; *Marchant*
Fisherman's Bride: *Liddell*
Fishing: *Oldham*
Fishmarket: *Hearne*
Five American Folksongs: *Maw*
Five Auden Songs: *Horder*
Five Betjeman Songs: *Dring*
Five Bird Songs: *Naylor, P.*
Five Blake Songs: *Chapple*
Five Breton Songs: *Someren-Godfery*
Five Burns Songs: *Horder*
Five Children's Songs from 'Peacock Pie': *Gibbs, Armstrong*
Five Chinese Lyrics: *Oldham*
Five Chinese Miniatures: *Redman*
Five Chinese Songs: *Berkeley, L.*; *Karkoff*
Five Clare Songs: *Dorward*
Five Colourisations of Emily Dickinson's Poems: *Swann*
Five Dibdin Airs: *Dibdin*
Five Dylan Thomas Poems: *Kenmuir*
Five Early Songs: *Bridge*
Five Edward Thomas Poems: *Hedges*
Five Eliot Landscapes: *Adès*
Five Elizabethan Songs: *Gibbs, Alan*; *Gurney*
Five English Songs: *Harrison, J.*
Five Eyes: *Gibbs, Armstrong*
Five Fairy Ballads: *Coleridge-Taylor*
Five Fantasies on Polish Christmas Carols: *Bax*(*)
Five Folk Songs: *McCabe*†
Five French Folksongs: *Hopkins, A.**
Five Ghazals of Hafiz: *Bantock*
Five Heine Songs: *Blake, D.*†
Five Herrick Poems: *Berkeley, L.*†
Five Holy Songs: *Downes*†
Five Housman Songs: *Berkeley, L.*
Five Irish Poems: *Harty*
Five Irish Songs: *Bax*; *Ferguson*
Five Italian Songs: *Woolrich**
Five Jacobean Lyrics: *Quilter*
Five Japanese Songs: *Luff*
Five Landscapes: *Pope*
Five Lesser Joys of Mary: *Warlock*
Five Little Japanese Songs: *Woodforde-Finden*
Five Little Songs about Death (cycle): *Holloway*†
Five Love Songs: *Musgrave*†
Five Love Songs (The Web): *McGuire*(†)
Five Lyrics of Torquato Tasso: *Hamilton, I.*
Five Lyric Poems: *Morgan, H.*
Five Mediaeval Lyrics: *Bush, G.*
Five Mystic Songs: *Procter*
Five Mystical Songs: *Vaughan Williams*
Five Nocturnes: *Luff*
Five Odes: *Colling*†
Five Oriental Songs: *Treharne*
Five Orkney Scenes: *Liddell*
Five Poems (Auden): *Berkeley, L.*
Five Poems by John Masefield: *Martin, E.*
Five Poems by Thomas Hardy (cycle): *Ireland*
Five Poems of Alice Meynell: *Pope*
Five Poems of Gustavo A. Becquer: *Hoddinott*
Five Poems of Frederick Pratt Green: *Pope*
Five Rondels: *O'Neill*
Five Rupert Brooke Songs: *Møller*
Five Sephardic Songs: *Anderson, A.*†; *Sutton-Anderson*†
Five Settings 'Faerie Queen': *Ball*†
Five Settings of Poems by Idris Davies: *Thomas, Mansel*
Five Settings of Poems from the Chinese: *Redman*
Five Shakespeare Songs: *Barrell*†; *Findlay*; *Quilter*

234 Index of titles

Five Sixteenth Century Poems: *Ireland*
Five Songs: *Boyce*; *Head*; *Howells*; *Joubert*;
   McGuire(†); *Murrill*; *Purcell, H.*; *Sutherland*
Five Songs (de la Mare): *Berkeley, L.*
Five Songs for High Voice: *Wood, C.*
Five Songs for Soprano and Piano (cycle): *Lipkin*
Five Songs from 'A Shropshire Lad': *Orr, C.W.*
Five Songs from 'And So to Bed': *Hughes, Herbert*
Five Songs from the Chinese: *Bantock*
Five Songs from the Chinese Poets: *Bantock*
Five Songs of Crazy Jane: *Aston*†
Five Songs of Essex: *Bantock*
Five Songs of Love (cycle): *Hedges*
Five Songs of Sorrow and Reconciliation: *Green*
Five Songs on Poems by Robert Herrick: *Bernofsky*
Five Songs to Words by John Drinkwater: *Rowley*
Five Sonnets: *Reizenstein*
Five Sonnets from 'The Triumph of Love':
   Stanford
Five Sonnets: To Orpheus (cycle): *Matthews, C.*†
Five Spring Songs: *Bush, G.*
Five Theatre Poems (cycle): *Muldowney**
Five Valentine Songs: *Standford*
Five Welsh Folksongs: *Roberts, T.*
Five William Blake Songs: *Butt*
Five Yeats Songs: *Scott, D.B.*
Five-and-twenty sailormen: *Coleridge-Taylor*
Flame in the skies of sunset: *Harty*
Flamingoes: *Parrott*
Flanders Fields: *Harrington*
Flapper: *Raphael*
Flavia Grown Old: *Blow*
Flea, The: *Blyton*
Fleeting, The: *Berkeley, L.*†
Flight of the Geese: *Hearne*
Fling out your windows wide (Carol [Quiller-
   Couch]): *Stanford*†
Flocks are sporting (Pastoral, A): *Carey, H.*
Flood [Joyce]: *Howells*
Flood [T'ao Ch'ien]: *Dalby*
Flooded Stream, The: *Gibbs, Armstrong*
Flora: *Linley Jnr*
Flora, sweet wanton: *Greaves, Thomas*
Flora, wilt thou torment me: *Morley*
Floral Bandit, The: *Holst*
Floral Dance, The: *Moss*
Florine: *Scott, F.G.*
Flow gently, sweet Afton: *Vignoles* (Afton Water /
   Sweet Afton)
Flow my tears, fall from your springs (Lachrimae):
   Dowland; *Jacob*†
Flow not so fast, ye fountains: *Dowland*
Flower Girl, The: *Benjamin*
Flower Message, A: *MacCunn*
Flower of Finae, The: *Hughes, Herbert*
Flower of Heaven: *Thiman*
Flower Song: *Bantock*
Flowering Heather: *Thomas, Mansel*
Flowers: *Bush, G.*
Flowers, The: *White, A.*; *Williamson, M.*
Fluctuations: *Edgar*
Flute, The (Ideala): *Bax*
Flute of Interior Time: *Morris, A.*†
Fly, The [Blake]: *Butt*; *Kirkwood*; *Parrott*; *Raphael*;
   Rodgers; *Rose*; *Swann*
Fly, The [de la Mare]: *Rose*
Fly, envious Time, till thou run out thy race: *Rubbra*
Fly, fly you happy shepherds: *Dring*

Fly swift, ye hours, make haste: *Purcell, H.*
Flying Crooked: *Venables*
Flying Fish: *Dean*
Fodder after all: *Marsh*
Foggy, Foggy Dew, The: *Britten*
Folk Songs: *Watkins*†
Folksong Arrangements: *Britten*(*)(†)
Folksongs from Hampshire: *Holst*
Folksongs from Sussex and Other Songs:
   Butterworth, G.
Follow a shadow it still flies you: *Gibbs, Alan*;
   Parry, C.H.H.
Follow thy fair sun, unhappy shadow: *Campion*
Follow your saint, follow with accents sweet: *Bennett,*
   R.R.; *Bernard*; *Campion*; *Tomlinson*
Folly of Being Comforted, The: *Gurney*
Fond Appeal, The: *Arne, T.*
Foolish Maid, The: *Eccles*
Footprints in the Snow: *Dale, M.*
For a Child: *Sutherland*
For a dream's sake: *Scott, C.*
For a Fountain: *Rainier*
For Ann Gregory: *Davies, E.*
For life I had never cared greatly: *Finzi*
For the Lord hath pleasure: *Boyce*
For the memories ungranted: *Hugill*†
For Remembrance: *Gibbs, Armstrong*
For this early morn: *Thomas, Mansel*(†)
For Winter's rains and rains are over: *Center*
For you alone: *Geehl*(†)
For Your Delight: *Butt*†
Foreboding [Hardy]: *Boughton*
Foreboding, The [Graves]: *Wood, Hugh*
Foredoomed: *Owen*
Forest Ball, The: *Pike*
Forest of Wild Thyme, The: *Lloyd Webber*
Forestry: *Thwaites*
Forget not yet: *Collins, H.*
Forget yesterday: *Wilkinson*
Forget-me-not: *Bennett, W.S.*
Foreign Children: *Quilter*; *White, A.*
Forlorn Queen, The: *Hughes, Herbert*
Form and Spirit: *Hudes*
Former Beauties: *Downes*; *Finzi*
Forsaken: *Bantock*
Forsaken Lover's Complaint, A: *Plumstead*
Forsaken Maid, The: *Smart*
Forsaken Maid's Complaint, The: *Handel*
Forsaken Nymph, The: *Handel*
Fortunate Isles: *Venables*
Fortune and her Wheel: *Wood, C.*
Fortune's Wheel: *Alwyn*
Forty Songs: *Purcell, H.*
Found in a Country Churchyard: *Bedford*(†)
Fountain Court: *Herbert, M.* (In Fountain Court /
   Tryst)
Fountains: *Baines*
Four Aspects of Faith: *Dalby*
Four Auden Songs: *Dickinson*
Four Burns Songs: *Britten*
Four Canadian Cowboy Songs: *Butt*
Four Child Songs: *Quilter*
Four Chinese Love Lyrics: *Bennett, T.C.S.*
Four Christmas Songs: *Davies, J.*
Four Dedications: *Martin, E.*
Four Delays: *Helliwell*†
Four Departures (cycle): *Lipkin*†
Four Dickinson Songs: *Grossner*

Index of titles 235

Four Dramatic Songs: *Rootham*
Four Early Songs: *Walton*
Four English Folk Songs: *Boyle, R.*
Four English Lyrics: *Dale, M.*; *Moeran*
Four Epigrams and a Prayer: *Pilkington, M.*
Four Findrinny Songs: *Beamish*†
Four Flower Songs: *Owen*
Four Fragments from Hölderlin's Madness: *Hudes*
Four French Folksongs: *Seiber*†
Four Greek Canticles: *Papastávrou*
Four Greek Folksongs: *Seiber*
Four Greek Love Songs: *Boyle, R.*†
Four Hebridean Love Lilts: *Kennedy-Fraser*
Four Herrick Songs: *Stewart*
Four Housman Fragments (cycle): *Holloway*(†)
Four Hungarian Folksongs: *Seiber*†
Four Hymns: *Vaughan Williams*†
Four Indian Love Lyrics: *Woodforde-Finden*
Four Japanese Lyrics: *Josephs*(†)
Four Japanese Verses (cycle): *Pert*
Four Jingles: *White, A.*
Four John Donne Songs: *Stevens, B.*
Four Last Songs: *Vaughan Williams*
Four Late Poems and an Epigram of Rainer Maria Rilke (cycle): *Knussen*†
Four Loom Weaver: *Osborne*†
Four Miscellaneous Songs: *Butterworth, N.*
Four Narratives from the Ancient Chinese: *Harrison, J.*
Four Nature Songs: *Young, Douglas*
Four Night Songs: *Dring*
Four Nights: *Vaughan Williams*
Four Old English Songs: *Coates, E.*; *Swinstead*
Four Old French Songs: *Arundell**
Four Poems: *Somers-Cocks*
Four Poems by Li-Po: *Lambert, C.*
Four Poems of Alice Meynell: *Pope*
Four Poems of Andrew Porter: *Dickinson*†
Four Poems of Dylan Thomas: *Pope*
Four Poems of Gerard Manley Hopkins: *Pope*
Four Poems of Ruth Pitter: *Pope*
Four Pope Epigrams: *Taylor, M.*†
Four Portraits: *Musgrave*†
Four Posthumous Songs: *Delius*
Four Prayers from the Gaelic: *Thomas, Mansel*
Four Recital Songs: *Ketèlby*
Four Rispetti: *Luard Selby*
Four Romantic Songs: *Orr, R.*†
Four Sacred Songs: *Purcell, H.*
Four Salt-Water Ballads: *Keel*
Four Scots Songs: *Spedding*†
Four Seafarers' Songs: *Bush, A.*
Four Seasonal Songs: *Anderson, W.H.*
Four Sentimental Songs: *Cresswell*†
Four Shakespeare Songs: *Moeran*; *Quilter*; *Roe*†; *Routh*; *Tomlinson*
Four Short Songs: *Rubbra*
Four Silhouettes: *Ronald*
Four Solo Motets: *Hugill*†
Four Songs: *Cook*; *Goossens*; *Graves*; *Fowler*†; *Hearne*; *Marchant*; *Matheson*; *Miles*†; *Newson*; *Quilter*; *Someren-Godfery*; *Stevenson*(*); *Wood, Hugh*†
Four Songs After Hoffman: *Woolrich*†
Four Songs by Frank Bridge: *Bridge*
Four Songs for High Voice: *Orr, C.W.*
Four Songs for High Voice and Harp: *Hearne*†
Four Songs for Mezzo-soprano and Piano: *Fowler*

Four Songs for Voice and Violin: *Holst*†
Four Songs for Voice, Violin and Piano: *Bliss*†
Four Songs from 'Hesperides': *Bush, G.*
Four Songs from 'Rosina': *Shield*
Four Songs from 'The Fringes of the Fleet': *Elgar*
Four Songs from the Japanese: *Goehr*
Four Songs from 'The Princess': *Scott, A.*
Four Songs from 'Twelfth Night': *Harrison, J.*
Four Songs from 'Vagabondia': *Dunhill*
Four Songs in Praise of Spring: *Center*
Four Songs of Autumn (cycle): *Birtwistle*†
Four Songs of Childhood: *Keel*
Four Songs of Chivalry: *Harrison, J.*
Four Songs of Mirza Schaffy: *Quilter*(*)
Four Songs of the Fair: *Martin, E.*
Four Songs of the Hill: *Ronald*
Four Songs of the Sea: *Quilter*
Four Songs of Yeats: *Harvey, J.*
Four Various Songs: *Procter*
Four Vietnamese Miniatures (cycle): *Stevenson*(†)
Four Yeats Songs: *Scott, D.B.*
Four-and-twenty tailors went to kill a snail: *Jeffreys, J.*
Fourteen Ayres: *Cavendish*
Fourteen Songs: *Lehmann*
Fourth Book of Ayres, The: *Campion*
Fourth Volume of Ten Songs, A: *Gurney*
Foweles in the frith: *Grainger, P.*†
Fox, The [Blunt]: *Warlock*
Fox, The [Clare]: *Self, A.*
Fox Rhyme, The: *Butterworth, N.*
Foxgloves: *Head*(†)
Fox-trot: *Bennett, R.R.*
Fragment [Chisholm]: *Rose*
Fragment [Graves]: *Wood, Hugh*
Free from his fetters: *Sullivan*
Free me from the bonds of your sweetness: *Fogg*
Freedom of the City: *Ferguson*
French Airs: *Warlock*
French Windows, The: *Moult*
Fresh Spring, the herald of love's mighty king: *Rubbra*
Friars of Orders Gray, The: *Shield*
Friend o' Mine: *Sanderson*
Friendly Advisor, The: *Carey, H.*
Friendly Cow, The: *Rowley*
Friendship: *Hiscocks, W.*
Friendship in Misfortune: *Ireland*
Frog Prince, The: *Crosse*
Frolic: *Bantock*
From a Child's Garden: *Williamson, M.*
From a City Window: *Parry, C.H.H.*
From a Railway Carriage: *Rowley*; *White, A.*; *Williamson, M.*
From Afar: *Scott, C.*
From Armageddon in Albyn: *MacDonald*
From Coastal Stations: *Matthews, D.*
From Distant Lands: *Novello*
From 'Easter Day': *Somervell*
From far, from eve and morning: *Burrows*; *Vaughan Williams*(†)
From father to son: *Hoddinott*
From grave lessons and restraint: *Weldon*
From High Savoy to Chelsea Down (cycle): *Glennie-Smith*
From High Windows (cycle): *Holloway*
From Omiecourt: *Jeffreys, J.*
From Out the Mist: *Clarke, R.C.*

236 Index of titles

From rosy bowers (Altisadora's Song): *Purcell, H.*
From silent shades and the Elysian groves (Bess of Bedlam / Mad Bess): *Purcell, H.*
From stone to thorn: *Maxwell Davies*†
From the Brazilian: *Fraser, N.*
From the Chinese: *Fraser, N.*
From the Greek: *Fraser, N.*
From the Percy Reliques: *McQuattie*
From the red rose to the apple-blossom: *Stanford*
From the Song of Songs: *Self, A.*
From the Song of Songs: *Blackford*
From the Spanish Descent: *Steptoe*†
From the Tomb of an Unknown Woman: *Bantock*
From thee, Eliza, I must go: *Pinto*
Frostbound Wood, The: *Warlock*
Frosty Night: *Dring*
Frozen Heart, The: *Bernofsky*
Frühling: *Stanford**
Frühling und Liebe: *White, M.V.**
Frühlingslied: *Tomlinson**
Frühlingsregen: *Bax**
Fuchsia Tree, The: *Quilter*
Fulfilment: *Gibbs, Armstrong*
Full fathom five thy father lies: *Butterworth, N.*; *Hold*; *Jeffreys, J.*; *Read*†; *Tippett*(†); *Williamson, M.*(†); *Young, Douglas* (Sea Dirge, A)
Full Moon: *Howells*; *Berkeley, L.*†
Full Moonlight: *MacDonald*
Funeral Banquet of Duc Jean Floressas des Esseintes, The: *Newson*
Funeral Blues: *Britten* (Stop all the clocks)
Funeral Tears: *Coprario*
Fünf Brecht Lieder: *Poole**
Funny Fellow, A: *Head*
Funny you should say that: *Nicholas*
Futile: *Glyn*
Futility: *Dennis*; *Hugh-Jones*; *Jones, S.L.*; *Self, A.*
Fyre, fyre: *Gibbs, Armstrong*

G

Gabriel's Greeting: *Seaman*
Gae bring to me a pint o' wine: *White, A.*
Gaelic Muse, The: *Stevenson*
Gai lon la: *Hopkins, A.**
Gaite and Orior: *Head*
Gallant Weaver, The: *Center*
Galliass, The: *Gibbs, Armstrong*; *Peterkin*
Galloping Home: *Bantock*
Galloway Tam: *White, A.*
Gallows, The: *Pickard*
Game Played in Erin-go-Bragh, The: *Harty*
Gan to the kye wi' me: *Tate, P.*†
Ganges Pilot: *Grainger, P.*
Gaol Song: *Moeran*
Garden of Bamboos, The: *Bantock*; *Peterkin*
Garden of Happiness: *Wood, Haydn*
Garden of Love, The: *Dorward*†
Garden of Love, The [Blake]: *Swann*
Garden of Memory: *Scott, C.*
Garden of Pan, The: *Bantock*
Garden of Weeds, A: *Greaves, Terence*†
Garden Seat, The: *Head*
Gardener's Song, The: *Carey, C.*
Gardner wi' his Paidle: *Crawford*
Garland, The: *Maconchy*

Garland, The [Rossetti, C.]: *Ireland*
Garland for Marjorie Fleming, A: *Bennett, R.R.*
Garland for Walter de la Mare, A: *Howells*
Garland of Flowers and Thistles: *Dorward*†
Garland of Folksongs, A: *Roe*
Garrison Churchyard, A: *Ireland*
Gartan Mother's Lullaby, The: *Hughes, Herbert*
Gather ye rosebuds while ye may: *Barrell, B.*†; *Hatton*; *Jeffreys, J.*; *Rutter*† (To the Virgins – to make much of time)
Gathering Daffodils: *Somervell*
Gathering of the Clans, A: *Steptoe*(†) (How goes the night?)
Gavotte: *Howells*
Gaze on me though you gaze in scorn: *Hughes, Herbert*
Gean, The: *Musgrave*
Generous Christian, The: *Dalby*
Genesis: *Nevens*
Gentiles shall come to thy light, The: *Greene*
Gentle Jesus, meek and mild: *Wesley, C.*†
Gentle lady, do not sing sad songs: *Goossens*
Gentle Maiden, The [Boulton]: *Somervell*
Gentle Maiden, The [Pain]: *Anon*; *Pain*
Gentle Sleep: *Naylor, B.*
Gentle warmth comes o'er my heart, A: *Clarke, J.*
Gentle wind fans the calm night, A: *Oldham*
Gentle Zephyr, as you fly: *Bennett, W.S.*
Gentleman Soldier, The: *Mitchell*
Georgian Songs (cycle): *Holloway*
Gertrude's Prayer: *Roe*
Gethsemane: *Jenkins, T.*; *Williams, C.*
Ghost of a Candle, The: *Bingham*†
Ghost Road, The: *Bantock*
Ghosts: *Hugh-Jones*(†) (Song of Shadows, A)
Ghosts in the Belfry: *Nelson*
Gibberish: *Clements*
Gift of Silence, A: *Scott, C.*
Gift Rose, The: *Coleridge-Taylor*
Gifts: *Dunhill* (Give a man a horse he can ride)
Gillyflower of Gold, The: *Harrison, J.*
Gin the goodwife stint: *Colling*†
Gipsies: *Gibbs, Armstrong*
Gipsy Song: *Jenkins, W.*
Gipsy's Warning: *Goard*
Girl I Left Behind Me, The: *Grainger, P.*
Girl in a Butterfly Cloak: *Garton*†
Girl in Love, A: *Cannon*(†)
Girl to Her Glass, A: *Parry, C.H.H.*
Girl Whose Love Shines Fair, A: *Cannon*(†)
Girl's Song: *Howells*
Girl's Song to her Mother, A: *Tann*†
Gitanjali (Song Offerings): *Standford*†
Give a man a horse he can ride: *Head*; *Thomas, H.F.* (Gifts)
Give me a place where I might stand: *Papastávrou*
Give me a ticket to heaven: *Harrison, D.*
Give me the sun: *Bantock*
Give the Word: *Birtwistle*†
Give unto the Lord (Psalm 29): *Bantock*
Given, not lent: *Pope*
Glass: *Hayes*
Glass of Beer, A: *Andrews*; *Newson*
Glide gently thus for ever: *Walton*
Gloire de Dijon: *Wood, Hugh*
Glorious Devon: *German*
Glory of the Cross, The: *Jenkins, W.*
Glow of summer sun, The: *Quilter*

Glühende Rätsel: *Karkoff**
Glycine's Song: *Routh*
Glyndwr's Dream: *Williams, W.S.G.*
Go and catch a falling star: *Stevens, B.*
Go bid the swan in silence die: *Ives, S.*
Go bye-bye, Peterkin: *Rawsthorne*
Go, crystal tears, like to the morning showers: *Dowland*
Go fetch to me a pint o' wine: *Liddell*
Go, heart: *Short*†
Go, lovely rose: *Arne, T.*; *Attwood*; *Pope*; *Quilter*; *Salomon*; *Williamson, M.*; *Wynne*
Go, minstrel, go (On Cramer's leaving England): *Wesley, S.*
Go my flock, go get you hence: *Anon*
Go not, happy day: *Bridge*; *Somervell*
Go now, my soul, to thy desired rest: *Anon*
Go, pretty birds: *Dunhill*
Go, rose, my Chloe's bosom grace: *Greene*
Go, songs: *Raynor*
Go, teach the swan to swim: *Someren-Godfery*
Go thou gentle whisp'ring wind: *Lawes, H.*
Go thy ways since thou wilt go: *Anon*
Go to bed, sweet muse, take thy rest: *Jones, R.*
Go weep, sad soul: *Handford*
Goal and Wicket: *Ireland* (Twice a week the winter thorough)
Goat Paths, The: *Howells*
Goblin Revel: *Morgan, H.*
God and the Universe: *Stanford*
God be in my head: *Davies, Walford*†
God is: *Thomas, Mansel*
God is born: *Bax*
God Lyaeus, ever young: *Hand*; *Rawsthorne*
God made a lovely garden: *Owen*
God made a tree: *Clarke, R.*
God of love my shepherd is, The: *Thiman*
God our mother: *Luff*†
God shall wipe away all tears: *Sullivan*†
Goddess of Night: *Howells*
Goddess of the dimpling smile: *Boyce*
God's Mercy: *Williams, W.S.G.*
God-song: *Swayne*†
Going with Tom to Towyn: *Thomas, Mansel*(†)
Gold a Receipt for Love: *Munro*
Gold Headed Gitto: *Elwyn-Edwards*
Gold o' the world: *Cundell*
Goldcups: *Horder*
Golden Days (Lewin): *Sullivan*
Golden Days (Lindsay): *MacCunn*
Golden Friends: *Gurney* (With rue my heart is laden)
Golden Guendolen: *Bax* (Guendolen)
Golden Hair: *Elwyn-Edwards*
Golden Hour, The: *Lloyd, J.M.*
Golden Hour of Noon, The: *O'Neill*
Golden Hours: *Woodforde-Finden*
Golden hues of life are fled: *Parry, C.H.H.*
Golden Kingdom, The (cycle): *Matthews, D.*
Golden Nenuphar, The: *Bantock*
Golden Ray, The: *Gibbs, Armstrong*
Golden slumbers kiss your eyes: *Jacob*; *Jeffreys, J.* (Lullaby [Dekker])
Golden sunlight's glory, The: *Quilter*
Golden Sunset, The: *Ross*
Golden Wheat, The: *Hoddinott*
Goldenhair: *Bridge* (Lean out of the window)
Goldfinch, A: *Harrison, P.*
Goldfish, The: *Thomas, Mansel*

Goldthred's song: *Wood, C.*
Golgotha: *Glyn*
Gondolier, The: *Head*
Gone (Ibsen): *Horne*
Gone (Tennyson): *Sullivan*
Gone, gone again is summer: *Bliss*
Gone is my love: *Gibbs, Armstrong*
Gone is my love from the silver stream: *Jeffreys, J.*
Gone were but the winter [Rossetti, C.]: *Gibbs, Armstrong*
Gone were but the winter cold [Cunningham]: *Parry, C.H.H.*
Goneril's Lullaby: *Peterkin*
Good Ale: *Warlock*
Good Boy, A: *White, A.*; *Williamson, M.*
Good Child, A: *Quilter*
Good Friday: *Hughes, A.*
Good morning Life (Spring [Davies]): *Hedges*
Good night, ah no,the hour is ill: *Parry, C.H.H.*
Good roarin' fire, A: *Hughes, Herbert*
Goodbye: *Vaughan Williams*†
Good-morrow, The: *Arnold, M.*; *Stevens, B.*; *Swayne*
Goodmorrow to you, Springtime: *Roberton*
Goodnight: *Coates, L.*
Goodnight sweet ladies: *Swayne*
Goodnight to the meadow: *Gurney*
Goosey goosey gander: *Jeffreys, J.*
Gorse: *Harty*
Grace for Light: *Harty*
Grace in the Bush: *Hiscocks, W.*
Grandeur: *Stanford*
Grant me, ye gods: *Blow*
Granta, The: *Cannon*
Grannies to Sell: *Fraser, S.*
Grapes: *Parry, C.H.H.*
Grasshopper Green: *White, A.*
Grateful Heart, A: *Plumstead*
Grave and the Flower, The: *Thomas, Mansel*
Grave by the Sea: *Roe*†
Great Child, The: *Hamilton, J.*
Great Day, The: *Ketèlby*; *MacDonald*
Great is the Lord (Psalm 48): *Bantock*
Great Things: *Ireland* (Sweet cyder is a great thing)
Great Time: *Wallbank*
Greek Love Songs (cycle): *Bush, G.*
Greek Wassail: *Solomons*(†)
Green Candles: *Someren-Godfery*
Green Castle, The: *Wood, Hugh*
Green Cornfield, A: *Head* (Song in the Cornfield)
Green, green the riverside grass: *Steptoe*
Green grow the rashes O! *Bax*
Green Hills of Somerset, The: *Coates, E.*
Green Lad from Donegal, The: *Swain*
Green of the Semiquaver, The: *Thompson, P.*
Green Rain: *Head*(†); *Hinchcliffe*; *Trimble*
Green Willow, The: *Slater*
Green-eyed Monster, The: *Berners*
Greenland Fishery, The: *Bush, A.*
Greensleeves: *Britten*; *Vaughan Williams* (My Lady Greensleeves)
Greeting: *Clarke, R.*
Grenadier, The: *Berkeley, M.*†
Grey: *Hugill*
Grey Wind, The: *Plumstead*
Grief Ago, A (cycle): *Garton*
Grief, keep within: *Danyel*
Grounded: *Nyman*†
Ground-song: *Bullard*†

Grove, The: Why does Laura shun me: *Blow*
Guardian Angel, The: *Bantock*
Guendolen: *Harrison, J.* (Golden Guendolen)
Guess, guess: *Turnbull*
Gully, The: *Britten*
Gwenllian's Repose: *Thomas, Mansel*
Gwynn ap Nudd: *Thomas, Mansel*
Gypsy Laddie, The: *Weir*
Gypsy Song: *Bax*

H

Habitude: *Blyton**
Had I a cave on some wild distant shore: *MacCunn*
Had I a golden pound to spend: *Head*; *Keel*
Had I the heavens' embroidered cloths: *Ronald* (Cloths of Heaven, The / He Wishes for the Cloths of Heaven)
Hag is astride, the night for to ride, The: *Hatton*; *Jeffreys, J.*
Hail, bounteous May: *Head*
Hail, fellow, hail: *Jones, R.L.*
Hail holy Mary, mother most gracious: *Atkinson, R.*(†)
Hail, immortal Bacchus: *Arne, T.*
Hail, lovely rose, to thee I sing: *Hook*
Hail to the myrtle shade: *Purcell, H.*
Halcyon days, now wars are ending (Amphitrite's Song): *Weldon (Purcell, H.)*
Half a bap: *Hughes, Herbert*
Half Loaf, The: *Lloyd Webber*
Half of Life, The: *Hudes*
Half-moon westers low, my love, The: *Berkeley, L.*; *Pope*; *Vaughan Williams*†
Hälfte des Lebens: *Britten**
Hallowe'en Sang: *Stevenson*
Hame, hame, hame, fain wad I be: *Davies, Walford*
Ha'nacker Mill: *Gurney*; *Jeffreys, J.*; *Plumstead*; *Warlock*
Hand in hand: *Usher*
Handbag: *Hayes*†
Hands, Eyes, and Heart: *Vaughan Williams*
Hang golden sleep upon her eyelids fair: *Hilton*
Hans Anderson Song, A: *Toye*
Happy Breeze: *Jones, O.*
Happy Ending: *Dickinson*
Happy is the country life: *Standford*
Happy is the man: *Thiman*
Happy Lover, The: *Wilson, H.L.*
Happy Man, The: *Dunhill*
Happy Pair, The [Anon]: *Boyce*
Happy Pair, The [Pilkington]: *Gibbs, Armstrong*; *Miller*
Happy Thought: *Williamson, M.*
Happy Tree, The: *Gurney*
Happy Wanderer, The: *Head*
Happy youth, that shalt possess: *Lawes, H.*
Hard Hearted Barb'ra (H)ellen: *Grainger, P.*
Hard-hearted fair, if thou wilt not consent: *Lawes, H.*
Hare, The: *Bliss*; *Hugh-Jones*(†)
Hare in the Moon, The: *Samuel, R.*(†)
Hark, hark, the lark: *Quilter*
Hark! his hands the lyre explore: *Wesley, S.*
Hark how all things in one sound rejoice: *Purcell, H.*
Hark shepherds, awake: *Steele*
Hark the echoing air: *Purcell, H.*(†)
Harlech: *Moult*

Harlequinade: *Woolrich*†
Harlot's House, The: *Swann*
Harp: *Joubert*
Harp on the willows: *Samuels*
Harp Song of the Dane Women: *Maconchy*; *Roe*
Harp that once, The: *Davidson, H.*
Harrow-on-the-Hill: *East*
Harvest [Blunden]: *Finzi*
Harvest [Raine]: *Bliss*
Harvest Moon: *Martin, E.*
Has sorrow thy young days shaded? *Hughes, Herbert*
Hasselbacher's Scena: *Williamson, M.*
Haste, give me wings and let me fly: *Eccles*
Haste on, my joys: *Butterworth, G.*
Have I caught my heav'nly jewel?: *Anon*
Have pity, grief, I cannot pay: *Jeffreys, G.*
Have pity on me: *Seiber*
Have ye seen him pass by? *Scott, C.*
Have you e'er seen the morning sun: *Lawes, H.*
Have you seen but a bright lily grow? *Maconchy*
Have you seen but a white lily grow?: *Southam*; *Warlock* (So white, so soft, so sweet is she)
Have you seen but a whyte lillie grow? *Anon*
Have you seen but the bright lily grow? *Johnson*
Haviranosan no Haiku: *Solomons*(†)
Hawk and Buckle: *Gurney*
Hawthorn, The: *Møller*
Hawthorn Time: *Ireland* (By Wenlock Town / 'Tis time, I think, by Wenlock Town)
Hawthorn Tree, The: *Gibbs, Armstrong*
Hayloft, The: *White, A.*
Haymakers' Roundelay, The: *Dunhill*
Hazel Grove, The: *Wood, Hugh*
He Abjures Love: *Finzi*
He came and sat by my side: *Ronald*
He himself courts his own ruin: *Purcell, H.*
He is gone on the mountain: *Attwood*
He prayeth best who loveth best: *Owen*
He Protests his Loyalty: *Steptoe*(†)
He rode like any king: *Procter*
He tells her: *Read*†
He that hath no mistress: *Corkine*
He that is down need fear no fall (Woodcutter's Song, The): *Vaughan Williams*(†)
He was the one: *Plumstead*
He who binds to himself a joy: *Swann* (Eternity [Blake])
He who mocks the infant's faith: *Chapple*
He will not suffer thy foot to be moved: *Weldon*
He Wishes for the Cloths of Heaven: *Jenkins, K.*; *Scott, D.B.*; *Swann* (Cloths of Heaven, The / Had I the heaven's embroidered cloths)
He would not stay for me: *Berkeley, L.*
Head of Orpheus, The: *Maw*†
Headlands in Summer: *Joubert*
Health and joy be with you: *Roberton*
Heap Cassia: *Bantock*
Heap on more wood: *Butt*
Hear the voice of the bard: *McQuattie*; *Rodgers*
Hear us, O hear us, Lord: *Downes*†
Hear, ye gods of Britain: *Purcell, H.*
Hears not my Phyllis how the birds (Knotting Song, The): *Purcell, H.*
Heart of the kalyan: *Goossens*
Heart to rue the pleasure of the eye, The: *Cavendish*
Heart Worships, The: *Holst*
Heart's Assurance, The: *Tippett*
Heart's Assurance, The: *Tippett*

Heart's Desire, The: *Ireland*
Heart's Haven: *Vaughan Williams*
Heart's Journey, The (cycle): *Rowley*
Heaven: *Newson*
Heaven and Haven [Hopkins, G.M.]: *Cruft*†
Heaven Haven [Hopkins, G.M.]: *Pike*; *Pope*
Hebridean Night Song: *Noble, H.*
Hebridean Rainbows: *Butt*
Hebridean Shanty: *Roberton*
Hedge of Briar, The: *Bantock*
Hedgerow Carnival: *Martin, E.*
Hedgin' and Ditchin': *Martin, E.*
Hei ho! *Morris, H.*
Heffle Cuckoo Fair: *Shaw*
Heimkehr: *Blake, D.*†
Heledd's Lament: *Samuel, R.*
Helen of Kirkconnell: *Jacob*; *Rootham* (Kirconnell Lee)
Heliodore: *Harrison, J.*
Hell's Pavement: *Keel*
Hen Gapel: *Hoddinott*
Hence with your trifling deity: *Purcell, H.*
Henry and Mary: *Wishart*
Henry Morgan's march on Panama: *Thomas, Mansel*
Her rosy cheeks, her ever-smiling eyes: *Campion*
Her Scuttle Hat: *Howells*
Her Secret: *Berkeley, M.*†
Her Song: *Ireland*
Her suffering ended: *MacCunn*
Her Temple: *Finzi*
Heraclitus: *Benbow*; *Warlock*
Herald, The: *Shaw*
Herbst (Morgenstern): *Stevenson**
Herbst (Rilke): *Headington**
Herbst: Autumn (Rilke): *Self, A.*
Herbsttag: *Young, Derek**
Herd Boy, The: *Dalby*; *Britten*†
Herd Boy's Song, The: *Oldham*
Herdsman, The: *Moeran*
Here amid the shady woods: *Handel*
Here comes a lusty wooer: *Bush, G.*
Here is my Country (cycle): *Woolrich*
Here let my life with as much silence slide: *Purcell, H.*
Here she her sacred bower adorns: *Campion*
Here sleeps: *McLeod*
Here summer ends: *Routh*
Here the deities approve: *Purcell, H.*
Here where the world is quiet: *Walsworth*
Here's the vow she falsely swore: *Clarke-Whitfield*
Heritage, A: *Benjamin, A.*
Hermit, The: *Nelson*
Hero, The: *Williams, T.*
Herod's Song: *Glyn*
Herrick Cycle, A: *Hatton*
Herrin's in the Bay: *Harty*
Hers will I be: *Kleyn*
Herself a rose that bore the Rose: *Clements*
Hesper: *MacCunn*
Hesperus, bringing together all: *Gurney*
Hey, Ca' Thro': *Schur*†
Hey, ho, the Wind and the Rain: *Quilter* (Clown's Song, The / Rain it Raineth Every Day, The / When that I was and a little tiny boy)
Hey nonny no: *Benjamin, A.*; *Bennett, R.R.*
Hey, trolly lolly lo, maid, whither go you: *Warlock*
Hidden Law, The: *Marchant*
Hidden Love: *Delius*

Hidden Treasure: *Gibbs, Armstrong*
Hier, dans la jardin ensoleillé: *Goossens**
High Germany: *Moeran*
High hills have a bitterness, The: *Jeffreys, J.*
High in the pines: *Dring*
High Queen of State: *Arne, T.*
High Seriousness: *Kirkwood*
High Song, The: *Salter, L.*
High Windows (cycle): *Powers*
Highland Balou, The: *Britten*
Highland Cradle Song: *Roberton*
Hill Sang [Soutar]: *Stevenson*
Hill Song [Hill]: *Jeffreys, J.*
Hill, The: *Taylor, C.*
Hills of Heaven, The: *Le Fleming*
Hills of Home (cycle): *Stevenson*
Hind in Ambush, The: *Bantock*
His golden locks time hath to silver turned: *Dowland*
His home and his own country: *Wood, C.*
His Last Sonnet: *Roe* (Bright Star! would I were steadfast as thou art)
History of the Thé Dansant, A: *Bennett, R.R.*
Hiver: *Procter*
Ho, who comes here: *Jacob*†
Hob y deri dando: *Thomas, Mansel*
Hochgebirgsleben: *Delius**
Holding the night in the palm of my hand: *Alwyn*; *Dring*
Holiday in Heaven: *Head*
Hollaïka: *Hopkins, A.**
Holly and the Ivy, The: *Britten*; *Thomas, Mansel*(†)
Holy and most blessed Virgin: *Head*
Holy Babe, The: *Dunhill*
Holy Boy, The: *Ireland*
Holy Child, The: *Thomas, Mansel*
Holy City, The: *Adams*(†)
Holy Innocents Carol: *Bush, G.*†
Holy Mary, mother mild: *Blake, H.*
Holy Queen of Heaven: *Bantock*
Holy Sonnets of John Donne, The: *Britten*
Holy Three Magi, The: *Dieren*
Holy Thursday: *Teed*; *Walton*; *Wood, C.*
Holy Thursday with Squeakers: *Bedford*†
Home (Evans): *Evans, W.T.*
Home (Hölderlin): *Britten*
Home for ever: *Jenkins, D.*
Home from Abroad: *Wood, Hugh*
Home of Mine: *O'Neill*
Home, Sweet Home: *Bishop*
Home they brought her warrior dead: *Somervell*
Home Thoughts: *Bantock* (O to be in England)
Home to Gower: *Bantock*
Homecoming of the Sheep, The: *Head*
Homeward Bound (Anon): *Arne, M.*
Homeward Bound (Newbolt): *Stanford*
Homeward Way, The: *Delius*
Homing: *Del Riego*
Honest shepherd, since you're poor: *Hart*
Honeypot Bee: *Grainger, E.*
Honeysuckle, The: *Alwyn*
Honor, riches: *Arne, T.*
Hope: *Ireland*
Hope and Love: *Shield*(†)
Hope away! enjoyment's come: *Wesley, S.*
Hope the Hornblower: *Ireland*
Hör ich das Liedchen klingen: *Delius**
Horace to his Lute: *Blow*
Horati Carminum: *Dorward*†

240 Index of titles

Horizon: *Hattey*
Hornpipe: *Frankel, B.*
Horror follows horror within me: *Jeffreys, J.*
Horseman, The: *Berkeley, L.*; *Harrison, P.*; *Pitfield*†
Horsemen of Belfast, The: *Stafford*
Horses, The: *Wood, Hugh*
Horses, The: *Wood, Hugh*
Hospitality: *Anderson, W.H.*
Hot sun, cool fire, temper'd with sweet air: *Roe*
Hound of Heaven, The: *Wills*(†)
Hour Hand, The (cycle): *Joubert*†
Hour of Magic, The: *Newson*
House and the Road, The: *Parke*
House of Life, The: *Vaughan Williams*
House of Rest: *Somers-Cocks*
House on Fire, The: *Someren-Godfery*
How am I poor tonight? *Wood, Hugh*
How blest are shepherds: *Purcell, H.*
How can the tree but waste: *Barley*
How can the tree but wither? *Vaughan Williams*
How deep in love am I: *Hughes, Herbert*
How do I love thee? *Lloyd Webber*; *Sagar*
How does the wind blow? *Stanford*
How engaging, how endearing: *Arne, T.*
How far is it to Bethlehem? *Rowley*
How goes the night: *Nieman* (Gathering of the Clans, A)
How happy art thou and I: *Lawes, H.*
How I sigh when I think of the charms: *Purcell, H.*
How like a winter hath mine absence been (Sonnet 97) [Shakespeare]: *Wetherell*
How long and dreary is the night: *Burrows*
How long, great God, how long must I: *Purcell, H.*
How love came in I do not know: *Berkeley, L.*
How lovely are thy dwellings: *Liddle*
How many miles to Babylon? *Jeffreys, J.*; *Warlock*
How many miles to Mylor: *Self, A.*
How mistaken is the lover: *Storace*
How mortifying to recall: *Hughes, Herbert*
How now, shepherd, what means that? *Anon*
How oft when thou, my music, music play'st (Sonnet 128) [Shakespeare]: *Wills*
How severe is my fate: *Croft*
How shall I woo thee? *Coleridge-Taylor*
How should I your true love know? *Jeffreys, J.*; *Quilter*; *Routh* (Ophelia's Song)
How soft upon the evening air: *Dunhill*
How sweet and how pleasing: *Hughes, Herbert*
How sweet is sin: *Garton*(†)
How sweet the answer Echo makes: *Britten* (Echoes [Moore])
How sweet the calm of this sequester'd shore: *Storace*(†)
How sweet the moonlight sleeps: *Bryan*; *Findlay*; *Head*
How sweet the name: *Foulds*
How to Get On in Society: *Horder*
How unhappy's the nymph: *Boyce*
How Wonderful: *Martin, E.*
Huckster, The: *Scott, C.*
Hughley Steeple: *Orr, C.W.*
Hugh's Song of the Road: *Vaughan Williams*
Humble Song to the Birds, A: *Hopkins, A.*
Humoresque: *Bliss*
Humpty Dumpty sat on a wall: *Bauld*; *Hely-Hutchinson*; *Jeffreys, J.*
Hums and Songs of Winnie-the-Pooh: *Knussen*†
Hunt is up, The: *Grainger, P.*

Hunter Trials: *Wills*
Hunting Song, A: *Ridley*
Hunting Song of the Seeonee Pack: *Fogg*
Huntsman, The: *Hely-Hutchinson*
Huntsman's Dirge, The: *MacCunn*
Hurrahing in Harvest: *Berkeley, L.*
Hush: *Johnstone*
Hush Song: *Harty*
Hush-a-ba, Birdie, croon, croon: *McCabe*†
Hushed Lagoon, The: *Thomas, V.*
Hymen and Fashion: *Howard, S.*
Hymen, haste! thy torch prepare: *Handel*
Hymn before Sleep: *Orr, C.W.*
Hymn for a Child: *Ireland*
Hymn for Aviators, A: *Parry, C.H.H.*
Hymn in Praise of Neptune, A: *Stanford*
Hymn of Eve: *Arne, T.*
Hymn of Pan: *Bantock*
Hymn of the Gebare: *Bantock*
Hymn on Divine Music, A: *Croft*(†)
Hymn to Aphrodite: *Bantock*
Hymn to God the Father, A: *Humfrey*(†); *Maconchy*; *Thomas, Mansel* (Wilt thou forgive that sin where I begun?)
Hymn to Pan: *Hand*
Hymn to the Seasons (cycle): *Johnson, R.S.*
Hymn to the Virgin (Swrdwal): *Glyn*
Hymn to the Virgin, A (Anon): *Rubbra*(†)
Hymn to Venus: *Burgon*
Hymns from the Rig Veda: *Holst*
Hymns to the Holy Trinity: *Lawes, H.*†
Hymnus: *Le Fleming*
Hypochondriacus: *Gibbs, Armstrong*

I

I am: *Venables*†
I am a lover, yet was never loved: *Ferrabosco*
I am an unusual thing: *Nyman*
I am bread: *LeFanu*
I am come to lock all fast (Mystery's Song): *Purcell, H.*
I am confirmed a woman can: *Lawes, H.*
I am here to sing you songs: *Standford*†
I am my beloved's: *Self, A.*
I am my Mammy's ae bairn: *Musgrave*
I am nearly blind: *Finnissy*†
I am of Ireland: *Aston*†
I am so far from pitying thee: *Jones, R.*
I am the gilly of Christ: *Jeffreys, J.*
I am the great sun: *Roe*†
I am the most wise Baviaan: *German*
I am the way: *Pope*
I arise from dreams of thee: *Barnett*; *Greaves, R.*; *Head*(†); *Quilter* (Indian Love Song)
I asked a thief to steal me a peach: *Warlock*
I asked my lady what she did: *Williams, Roderick*
I attempt from love's sickness to fly: *Purcell, H.*
I be hopin' you remember: *Clarke, R.C.*
I burn, I burn, my brain consumes to ashes: *Eccles*
I came, I saw, and was undone: *Purcell, H.*
I can hear a cuckoo: *Dunhill*
I can love for an hour when I'm at leisure: *Atkins*
I cannot change as others do: *Hughes, Herbert*
I cannot tell what you say, green leaves: *Somervell*
I can't get fat like father: *Dean*

Index of titles 241

I care not for those ladies: *Campion* (Amaryllis [Campion])
I come from London: *Finnissy*†
I dare not ask a kiss: *Quilter* (To Electra)
I die whenas I do not see: *Danyel*
I died for beauty: *Swann*
I do confess thou'rt smooth and fair: *Lawes, H.*
I don't think of death: *Finnissy*†
I dreamed I lay where flowers were springing: *Liddell*
I dreamt that I dwelt in marble halls: *Balfe*
I fear for every breath she draws: *Hughes, Herbert*
I fear thy kisses, gentle maiden: *Butterworth, G.*
I feed a flame within: *Dring*
I felt a funeral in my brain: *Swann*
I gave her cakes and I gave her ale: *Wallbank*; *Walton*(†)
I gently touched her hand: *Eccles*
I go to prove my soul: *Bantock*
I got me flowers: *Butt*(†); *Vaughan Williams*
I had a boat: *Foreman*
I had a dove: *Frankel, B.* (Dove, The)
I had a little pony: *Warlock* (Dapple Grey)
I had no time to hate: *Swann*
I hate the dreadful hollow: *Somervell*
I have a bonnet trimmed with blue: *Hughes, Herbert*
I have a flaunting air: *O'Neill*
I have a friend: *Quilter*
I have a garden of my own: *Marshall*; *Warlock*
I have a house and land in Kent: *Bax*
I have led her home: *Somervell*
I have loved flowers that fade: *Carey, C.*
I have trod the upward and the downward slope: *Vaughan Williams*
I have twelve oxen: *Ireland* (Twelve Oxen)
I hear an army charging upon the land: *Goossens*
I hear in the night: *Delius*
I hear that Andromeda: *Hudes*†
I hear you calling me: *Marshall*
I heard a brooklet gushing: *Loder*
I heard a fly buzz when I died: *Swann*
I heard a linnet courting: *Parrott*; *Steele* (Linnet, The)
I heard a music sweet today: *Harrison, J.*
I heard a piper piping: *Bax*; *Peterkin*
I heard a soldier sing some trifle: *Bax*
I heard of late that Love was fall'n asleep: *Bartlet*
I heard the nightingale: *Sullivan*
I held love's head while it did ache: *Bullard*; *Warlock*
I keep six honest serving-men: *German*
I know: *Gomelskaya*
I know a bank where the wild thyme grows: *Bury*; *Harrison, J.*; *Horn*; *Procter-Gregg*; *Shaw*; *Tomlinson*
I know my love by his way o' walkin': *Hughes, Herbert*
I know of two bright eyes: *Clutsam*
I know that my redeemer liveth: *Handel*†
I know where I'm goin': *Hughes, Herbert*
I laid me down and slept: *Greene*
I like the amorous youth: *Handel*
I loathe that I did love: *Anon*
I locked up all my treasure: *Dibdin*
I look into my glass: *Finzi*; *Maw*†
I look out and see... : *Hiscocks, W.*
I looked out into the morning: *Lloyd Webber*
I love a life upon the sea: *Peters*
I love a small earth: *Newson*
I love all beauteous things: *Darke*; *Lawson*
I love all graceful things: *Thiman*

I love and I love: *Goehr*
I love and I must and yet I would fain: *Purcell, H.*
I love little kitty, her coat is so warm: *Jeffreys, J.*
I love the din of beating drums: *Peterkin*
I love thee: *Reizenstein*
I love you my dear: *Whyte*
I loved fair Celia many years: *Purcell, H.*
I loved Miss Watson: *Bauld*
I loved thee once, Atthis, long ago: *Bantock*
I meant to tease him: *Hughes, Herbert*
I mind the day I'd wish I was a saygull: *Stanford*
I must complain, yet do enjoy my love: *Campion*
I need not go through sleet and snow: *Finzi*
I once had a newly cut willow pipe: *Delius*
I praise the tender flower: *Gurney*; *Stanford*
I prethee sweet to me be kind: *Lawes, H.*
I prithee leave, love me no more: *Anon*
I prithee send me back my heart [Hughes]: *Lawes, H.*
I prithee send me back my heart [Suckling]: *Gibbs*, *Armstrong*; *Miller*
I remember: *Dunhill*
I resolve against cringing and whining: *Purcell, H.*
I rise and grieve: *Lawes, H.*
I said to Love: *Finzi*
I said to Love, it is not now: *Finzi*
I saw a jolly hunter: *Butterworth, N.*
I saw a peacock: *Dalby*
I saw from the beach: *Hughes, Herbert*
I saw in Louisiana: *Allen*
I saw my lady weep: *Dowland*
I saw my lady weeping: *Morley*
I saw rain falling: *Stevenson*
I saw that you were grown so high: *Purcell, H.*
I saw three ships: *Elwyn-Edwards*; *Ferguson*; *Thiman*
I say I'll seek her side: *Finzi*
I seal thy lips with kisses three: *Stanford*
I see she flies me: *Purcell, H.*
I seek her in the shady grove: *Bullard*
I Serraillets Have: *Delius**
I shall be ever maiden: *Gurney*
I should have trusted you: *Dring*
I sing of a maiden: *Holst*†; *Quilter*†; *Tate, P.*; *Taylor, C.V.*; *Turner* (As dew in April / Old Carol, An)
I sing the progress of a deathless soul: *Downes*†
I sit and look out: *Hiscocks, W.*
I smiled and turned away: *Newson*
I sorrowed that the golden day was dead: *Rootham*
I take no pleasure in the sun's bright beams: *Purcell, H.*
I thank you for that! (Bachelor's Song, The): *Barratt*
I think it will be winter when I die: *Nelson*
I think of thee: *Reizenstein*
I think of you: *Dunhill*
I think that we were children long ago: *Stanford*
I thirst for shadows: *Bedford*†
I thought to marry a parson: *Finnissy*†
I took my lyre: *Hudes*
I vow to thee, my country: *Davies, Walford*
I walked alone and thinking: *Pope*
I wandered lonely as a cloud: *Thiman*
I was afraid: *Finnissy*†
I was lonely and forlorn: *Britten*(†)
I was not sorrowful: *Ireland*
I was young and foolish: *Jeffreys, J.* (Down by the salley gardens / Salley Gardens, The)
I went by footpath and by style: *Finzi*†
I will come to thee: *Bryan*
I will give my love an apple: *Britten*†; *Howells*

I will go look for death: *Greaves, R.*
I will go with my father a-ploughing: *Gurney*; *Jeffreys, J*; *Mullinar*; *Quilter*(†)
I will lay me down in peace: *Greene*
I will lift up mine eyes (Psalm 121): *Head*(†)
I will make you brooches: *Butterworth, G.*; *Jeffreys, J.*; *Lehmann* (Roadside Fire, The / Romance [Stevenson])
I will praise thee: *Thomas, Mansel*
I will travel through the land: *McLeod*
I will walk the earth: *Ireland*
I will walk with my love: *Hughes, Herbert*
I wish and I wish: *Peterkin*; *Quilter*(†)
I wish I had the shepherd's lamb: *Hughes, Herbert*
I wonder as I wander: *Britten*
I won't be my father's Jack: *Warlock*
Ia Orana, Gauguin: *Casken*
I-Brasîl: *Delius*; *Moule-Evans*
Ice: *Wood, Hugh*
Ich halte ihr die Augen zu: *Stanford**
Ich lieb' eine Blume: *Stanford**
Ich wanderte unter den Bäumen: *Dieren**
Icon from Abroad: *Papastávrou*(†)
I'd rock my own sweet childie (Irish Lullaby): *Stanford*
Ideala (Flute, The): *Bax*(*)
Idle days in summertime: *Snell*(†)
Idle Life, The: *MacCunn*
Idleness: *Boyce*
Idyll [Sassoon]: *Rootham*
Idyll [Scott]: *Scott, C.*†
Idyllic Fantasy: *Scott, C.*†
If [Irvine]: *Parke*
If [Teschemacher]: *Novello*
If doughty deeds my lady please: *Sullivan*; *Turnbull*
If ever I marry at all: *Dunhill*
If floods of tears: *Anon*
If grief has any pow'r to kill: *Purcell, H.*
If I be living in Éirinn: *Peterkin*
If I built a world for you: *Lehmann*
If I could see, no surfaces: *Walker, R.*†
If I could shut the gate: *Danyel*
If I could speak: *Brian*
If I freely may discover: *Anon*
If I had known that old age would call: *Josephs*(†)
If I have made, my lady, intricate songs: *Wills*†
If I hear Orinda swear: *Eccles*
If I hope I pine: *Rosseter*
If I might come to you: *Squire*
If I might ride on puissant wing: *Parry, C.H.H.*
If I seek t'enjoy the fruits: *Anon*
If I should ever by chance grow rich: *Hedges*
If I urge my kind desires: *Rosseter*
If I walk in Autumn's even: *Matthews, E.E.*
If I were a queen what would I do?: *Vaughan Williams*
If I were Lord of Tartary: *Bantock*
If it chance your eye offend you: *Jeffreys, J.*
If it's ever spring again: *Britten*; *Le Fleming*; *Milford*; *White, A.*
If Love loves truth then women do not love: *Campion*
If music be the food of love: *Gibbs, Armstrong*; *Purcell, H.*
If my complaints could passions move: *Dowland*
If nine times you your bridegroom kiss: *Berkeley, L.*†
If no one ever marries me: *Lehmann*
If pray'rs and tears could passions move: *Purcell, H.*
If she forsake me: *Keel*; *Rosseter*

If she were mine: *Hoddinott*
If that a sinner's sighs: *Dowland*
If that angel of Shiraz: *Bantock*
If the deep sighs of an afflicted breast: *Anon*
If the owl calls again: *Samuel, R.*†
If there be any Gods: *Moeran*
If there be anyone: *Bartlet*
If there were dreams to sell: *Ireland*; *Jeffreys, J.* (Dream Pedlary)
If those who live in shepherd's bower: *Arne, T.*
If thou art sleeping, maiden: *Center*; *ColeridgeTaylor*
If thou long'st so much to learn: *Campion*
If thou wilt ease thy heart: *Britten*; *Busch* (If thou would'st ease thine heart / Wolfram's Dirge)
If thou wilt give me back my love: *Purcell, H.*
If thou would'st ease thine heart: *Parry, C.H.H.* (If thou wilt ease thy heart / Wolfram's Dirge)
If thy soul check thee that I come so near (Sonnet 136) [Shakespeare]: *Wills*
If you came: *Pope*
If we die: *Stevens, B.*
If we must part then let it be like this: *Ireland*
If we sailed away: *Phillips, M.*
If, when I die, to hell's eternal shade: *Anon*
If you are squeamish: *Hudes*†
If you should frown: *Bowen*
Ihesu God's Son: *Oldham*
Il cantico dei cantici II: *LeFanu*†
Il est quelqu'un sur terre: *Britten**
Il Nome: *Creswell**
Il pleure dans mon coeur: *Delius**
Il pleut, il pleut, bergère: *Rawsthorne**
Iliadian: *Moult*
I'll sail upon the dogstar: *Purcell, H.*
I'll sing thee songs of Araby: *Clay*
I'll walk beside you: *Murray*
I'll walk with God: *Brodsky*†
I'm a darling little baby: *Rawsthorne*
I'm conquered, love, by thee: *Hatton*
I'm from over the mountain: *Ferguson*
Im Ginster: *Tomlinson**
I'm nobody who are you?: *Anderson, J.*†; *Grossner*
I'm o'er young to marry yet: *Center*; *Liddell*
Im Rosenbusch: *Lehmann**
Im wunderschönen Monat Mai: *White, M.V.**
Image of love grows, The: *Wood, Hugh*†
Imagination: *Rootham*
Immeasurable pain, my dreaming soul: *Redman*
Immortality [Brontë]: *Joubert*
Immortality [Bulwer-Lytton]: *Scott, C.*
Immortality [Currie]: *Gibbs, Armstrong*
Immortals, The: *Harrington*
Impatient Lover, The: *Bush, G.*
Impenitent: *Owen*
Impromptu: *Gibbs, Armstrong*
Impromptu in March: *Moeran*
In a Boat: *Jeffreys, J.*
In a Churchyard: *Finzi*
In a dream I spake: *Bantock*
In a Fairy Boat: *Scott, C.*
In a goodly night: *Rutter*†
In a harbour green: *Standford* (In an arbour green / In Youth is Pleasure / Lusty Juventus / Youth [Wever])
In a May morning early: *Tomlinson*
In a Monastery Garden: *Ketèlby*
In a myrtle shade: *Bantock*
In a Palace Garden: *MacCunn*

Index of titles 243

In a Persian Garden: *Lehmann*
In a Persian Market: *Ketèlby*
In a season all oppressed: *Wilson, John*
In a sleepless night: *Le Fleming*
In a Wood: *Holst*
In a year: *Bantock*
In Absence [Chinese]: *Scott, C.*
In Absence [Ingram]: *Thomas, V.*
In an arbour green: *Price, B.*; *Warlock* (In a harbour green / In Youth is Pleasure / Lusty Juventus / Youth [Wever])
In an Old Country Church: *Pitfield*
In an old-fashioned town: *Squire*
In bliss we walked with laughter: *Delius*
In Boyhood: *Ireland*
In Bristol Town: *Grainger, P.*†
In Chloris all soft charms agree: *Purcell, H.*
In Cradle Land: *Owen*
In Dark Weather: *Rubbra*
In darkness let me dwell: *Dowland*
In days of old: *Holbrooke*
In Dorset: *Toye*
In downstairs darkness: *Stout*†
In Dreaming: *Beamish*†
In dreams, unhappy, I behold you stand: *Vaughan Williams*
In Faery: *Elwyn-Edwards*
In Falmouth Harbour: *Self, A.*
In five-score summers: *Finzi*
In Flanders: *Gurney*
In Fountain Court: *Davidson, M.*; *Turnbull* (Fountain Court / Tryst)
In Green Ways: *Howells*
In Haven: *Elgar*
In her Garden: *Hatton*
In Isas Bed: *Bennett, R.R.*
In June: *Bowen*
In Leinster: *Raynor*
In Marley Wood: *Jeffreys, J.*
In Memoriam: *Coleridge-Taylor*
In Memoriam: *Harvey, J.*†
In Memoriam [Dixon]: *Gill*
In Memoriam (Hywel Davies) (cycle) [Williams]: *Thomas, Mansel*
In Memory of W.B.Yeats: *Maconchy*
In Moonlight: *Elgar*
In nightly stillness: *Bax*
In Paris with you: *Muldowney*
In Phæcia: *Parrott*
In Port: *Coates, L.*
In Praise of his Daphnis: *Bliss*
In Praise of Isla: *Jacobson*
In Praise of Woman: *Poston*
In pride of May the fields are gay: *Jeffreys, J.*
In Prison: *Boughton*; *Harrison, J.*
In ruin reconciled: *McCabe*
In Sacred Benares: *Treharne*
In Scotland I was born: *Anon*
In Sherwood lived stout Robin Hood: *Jones, R.*
In Spring: *Quilter*
In summertime on Bredon: *Peel*; *Pope*; *Somervell* (Bredon Hill)
In tenebris: *Maw*†
In Terra Pax: *Bayford*†
In the Beck: *Bliss*
In the beloved's face: *Wood, Hugh*†
In the black dismal dungeon of despair: *Purcell, H.*
In the bleak midwinter: *Martin, J.*; *Thiman*

In the bud of the morning-O: *Quilter* (Daisies, The / Where the Daisies Are)
In the City: *Clarke, R.C.*
In the Dawn [Benson]: *Elgar*
In the Dawn [Stenning]: *Dunhill*
In the Desert: *Bantock*
In the dim counties: *Sutherland*
In the Doorway: *Somervell*
In the dusky path of a dream: *Fogg*
In the early dawning: *Somervell*
In the faery hills: *Gibbs, Armstrong*
In the Fall [Carroll]: *Roe,*
In the Fall [MacDiarmid]: *Stevenson*
In the Garden: *Bantock*
In the garden flowers are growing: *Anderson, W.H.*
In the Garden of the Seraglio: *Delius*
In the gloaming: *Harrison, A.F.*
In the golden island: *MacDonald*
In the grave, whither thou goest: *Rice*†
In the grove, friend to love: *Attwood*
In the Harem: *Bantock*
In the highlands, in the country places: *Carey, C.*; *Gibbs, Armstrong*; *Peel*; *Procter-Gregg*; *Quilter*; *Steele*; *Stevenson*
In the hollows of quiet places: *Bantock*
In the Kirkyaird: *Rose*
In the lovely village of Nevesinje: *Weir*
In the manger he is lying: *Bax*
In the Mind's Eye: *Finzi*
In the Moonlight [French]: *Pitfield*
In the Moonlight [Hardy]: *Berkeley, M.*†
In the morning: *Bax*; *Vaughan Williams*†
In the Mountains: *Redman*
In the old age black was not counted fair (Sonnet 127) [Shakespeare]: *Wills*
In the Palace: *Bantock*
In the Picture Gallery: *Horne*
In the Pink (cycle): *Shur*†
In the purple glow, dear: *Clarke, R.C.*
In the silver moonbeams: *Scott, C.*
In the Spring: *Vaughan Williams*
In the spring twilight: *Hudes*
In the Street of Lost Time: *Holst*
In the Temple: *Bantock*
In the Tent: *Tippett*†
In the Thirtieth Year (cycle): *Holloway*
In the Time of Pestilence: *Self, A.*
In the Valley: *Scott, C.*
In the Village [Bantock, H.]: *Bantock*
In the Village [Ryōkan]: *Northcott*†
In the wombe of the earth: *Rainier*†
In the Wood: *Parry, W.H.*
In the Woods in June: *Gibbs, Armstrong*
In the year that's come and gone: *Butterworth, G.*(†)
In Time of the Breaking of Nations: *Finzi*; *Slater*
In tyme of olde: *Bantock*
In vain we dissemble: *Purcell, H.*
In Valleys Green and Still: *Pope*
In valleys green and still: *Orr, C.W.*; *Pope*
In Westminster Abbey: *Horder*
In years defaced and lost: *Finzi*
In Youth is Pleasure: *Gibbs, Armstrong*; *Jeffreys, J.*; *Moeran*; *Murrill*; *Poston* (In a harbour green / In an arbour green / Lusty Juventus / Youth)
In youthly years when first my young desires: *Parsons*
Incassum Lesbia: *Purcell, H.**
Incipit Vita Nova: *Bryars*†

Inconstant Laura makes me death to crave: *Greaves, Thomas*
Indian Love [Cornwall]: *Bennett, W.S.*
Indian Love Song [Shelley]: *Delius* (I arise from dreams of thee)
Indigo Blues: *Blyton*
Indra (God of storm and battle): *Holst*
Infant Joy: *Clarke, R.*; *Dunhill*; *Foss*; *Owen*; *Vaughan Williams*†
Infant King, The: *Willcocks*
Infant Song: *Roe*
Infinite shining heavens rose, The: *Vaughan Williams*
Inheritor, The: *Standford*†
Inn, The: *Toye* (Miranda)
Inner Light, The: *Thomas, Mansel*
Innisfree: *Hughes, Herbert* (Lake Isle of Innisfree, The)
Innocence: *Rose*
Inscribed on a Small Garden Wall: *Steptoe*
Inscription for a Wayside Spring: *Wegener*†
Inscription on the Tomb of the Painter Henri Rousseau: *Newson*
Inscriptions for a Peal of Eight Bells: *Maw*†
Inside the pillar of white fire: *Belben*†
Insouciance: *Scott, C.*
Interior Life, The: *Pike*
Intimations of Mortality: *Spedding*
Into God's Kingdom (cycle): *Cruft*
Into her Keeping: *Bridge*
Into my heart an air that kills: *Orr, C.W.*; *Somervell* (Far Country, The / Farms of Home, The / Land of Lost Content, The)
Into the twilight: *Crossley-Holland*
Intrada: *Finzi*
Introspection: *Bush, G.*
Intruder, The: *Lambert, C.*
Inventress of the Vocal Frame: *Bedford*†
Investiture in Wales: *Wills*
Invitation, The: *Anon*; *Arne, T.*
Invitation in Autumn: *Moeran*
Invitation to Ranelagh: *Arne, T.*
Invitation to the Gondola: *Venables*
Invitation to the Journey: *Solomons*(†)
Invite, to Eternity: *Venables*†
Invite to Eternity (An): *Swann*; *Venables*†
Invocation [Radford]: *Scott, C.*
Invocation (Poor naked wretches) [Shakespeare]: *Usher*†
Invocation to Nature: *Pinto*
Invocation to Spring: *Rubbra*
Invocation to the Deep: *Loder*
Invocation to the Nile: *Bantock*
Invocation to the Queen of Moonlight: *Alwyn*
Invocations: *Alwyn*
Ireland: *Stanford*
Irish Country Songs: *Hughes, Herbert*
Irish Country Songs Highlights: *Hughes, Herbert*
Irish Elegy, An: *Hughes, Herbert*
Irish Folk Songs – 25 Old Irish Melodies: *Wood, C.*
Irish Folksinger's Album, An: *Nelson*
Irish Idyll, An: *Stanford*
Irish Love Song, An: *Harty*
Irish Lullaby (I'd rock my own sweet childie): *Stanford*
Irish Lullaby [A-Fahy]: *Wynne*
Irish Lullaby, An [Anon]: *Owen*
Irish Melodies of Thomas Moore: *Stanford*
Irish Skies: *Stanford*
Irish Songbook: *McCabe*

Irish Songs and Ballads: *Stanford*
Irmelin: *Delius*
Irmelin Rose: *Delius**
Is my team ploughing? *Butterworth, G.*; *Gurney*(†); *Orr, C.W.*; *Vaughan Williams*(†)
Is now the time? *Hattey*
Is she not passing fair? *Elgar*
Isabelle: *Blake, H.*
Island of Pines, The: *Bantock*
Island Spinning Song: (Colum): *Hughes, Herbert*
Island Spinning Song (Roberton): *Roberton*
Isle, The: *Torphichen*
Isle of Avalon, The: *Elwyn-Edwards*
Isle of Cloy, The: *Moeran*
Isle of Lost Dreams, The: *Browne*
Isle of Portland, The: *Orr, C.W.*
Isles of the Sea: *Bantock*
Isobel: *Bridge*
It fell on a summer's day: *Campion*
It is a good thing to give thanks to the Lord: *Kent*
It is early in the morning: *Hatton*
It is Winter: *Jeffreys, J.* (Winter [de la Mare])
it may not always be so: *Wills*†
It never looks like summer here: *Finzi*
It nods and curtseys: *Williamson, J.R.*
It rains: *Venables*
It was a lover and his lass: *Bush, G.*; *Center*; *Clarke, R.*†; *Coates, E.*; *Delius*; *Dring*; *Findlay*; *Finzi*; *Higginson, I.*; *Jeffreys, J.*; *Keel*; *Lehmann*; *Morley*; *Quilter*; *Rubbra*; *Swann*; *Tomlinson*; *Wallbank*; *White, A.* (Lover and his Lass, The / Pretty Ringtime / Spring [Shakespeare] / Spring Song [Shakespeare] / Sweet and Twenty)
It was a maid of my country: *Grainger, P.*
It was a time when silly bees: *Dowland*
It was in and about: *Anon*
It was in May: *Fogg*
It was the lovely moon: *Bury*
It was the time of roses: *Blake, H.*
Italy: *Moult*
It's not going to happen again: *Møller*
It's O but aw ken weel: *Finnissy*†
I've been roaming: *Horn*
I've brought you away: *Dring*
I've found my mountain lyre again: *MacCunn*
I've found the Proms: *Dring*
Ivy, chief of trees: *Short*†

J

Jabberwocky: *Hely-Hutchinson*
Jack and Jill went up the hill: *Diack*; *Jeffreys, J.*
Jack and Joan they think no ill: *Campion*
Jack and Jone: *Bax*
Jack Frost: *Bantock*
Jack Frost and Sally Sunshine: *Thomas, Mansel*
Jack Tar: *Stanford*
Jack the Jolly Tar: *Bush, A.*
Jackdaw, The: *Wishart*
Jack's Songs: *Thomas, Mansel*
Jade Mountain, The: *Rubbra*†
J'ai descendu: *Seiber*†
Jamaicalypso: *Benjamin*
James Lee's Wife: *Somervell*
James Lee's Wife Speaks at the Window: *Somervell*
Jamie, come try me: *Musgrave*

Index of titles 245

Jan: *Benjamin, A.*
Jane Allen: *Ferguson*
January Thaw: *Routh*
Japanese Fragments: *Williams, Graham*†
Japanese Lullaby, A: *Stanford*
Jardin d'amour: *Keel*
Jazz Songs: *Roe*†
Je suis le Ténébreux: *Swann**
Je suis un petit poupon: *Rawsthorne**
Jealous Lover, The: *Quilter*
Jean, p'tit Jean: *Bax*(*)
Jeg havde en nyskåren Seljefløjte: *Delius**
Jeg hører i Natten: *Delius**
Jennie Gray: *Warlock*
Jenny bright as the day: *Arne, T.*
Jenny Jones: *Gibbs, Armstrong*
Jenny kiss'd me when we met: *Herbert, I.*; *Pilling*†; *Williamson, M.*
Jerusalem: *Parry, C.H.H.*
Jessy: *Coleridge-Taylor*
Jester, The: *Bantock*
Jesu sweet, now will I sing: *Holst*†
Jesukin: *Rubbra*(†)
Jesus, infant Jesus: *Davies, J.*
Jesus(s), lover of my soul: *Evans, T.H.*; *Williams, C.*
Jesu, tender saviour: *Owen*
Jesu(s), the very thought of thee: *Thiman, Wesley, S.S.*
Jewels: *O'Neill*
Jig: *Price, B.*
Jillian of Berry: *Jeffreys, J.*; *Warlock*
Jim: *Lehmann*
Jim Crow: *Williams, Grace*
Joan of Arc: *Gibbs, Armstrong*
Job's Curse (Let the night perish): *Purcell, H.*
Jock the Fiddler: *Martin, E.*
Jockey to the Fair: *Grainger, P.*
Jocund Dance, The: *Quilter*
Jog on, jog on: *Grainger, P.*
Jogging along the highway: *Samuel, H.*
John Anderson, my jo: *Atkinson, G.*(†); *Horder*; *Musgrave*; *Pierson*
John Barleycorn: *Mitchell*†
John Clare Songbook: *Hold*
John Mouldy: *Gibbs, Armstrong*; *Keel*
John of the Glen: *Williams, W.M.*
John Peel: *Dunhill, McCabe*†
Johneen: *Stanford*
Johnnie Cope: *White, A.*
Johnnie Logie: *Rose*
Johnny [Anon]: *Noble, H.*
Johnny [Auden]: *Britten*; *Horder*
Johnny Faa: *Crawford*
Johnny has gone for a soldier: *McCabe*†; *Roe*
Johnny, I Hardly Knew Ye: *Hughes, Herbert*
Johnny shall have a new bonnet: *Rowley*
Johnny wi' the Tye: *Warlock*
Jolly Beggar, The: *Hely-Hutchinson*
Jolly Carter, The: *Moeran*
Jolly Company, The: *Taylor, M.*
Jolly Good Ale and Old: *Jacobson* (Back and sides go bare / Maltworms)
Jolly, jolly breeze, The: *Eccles*
Jolly Miller, The: *Quilter* (Miller of Dee / There was a jolly miller)
Jolly Robin: *Harrison, J.*
Jolly Shepherd, The: *Warlock*
Jolly Young Waterman, The: *Dibdin*
Jota: *Jacobson*

Journey, The: *Ireland*
Journeyman Weaver, The: *Peterkin*†
Journeys and Places: *Orr, R.*†
Journey's End: *Bridge*; *Holst*; *Someren-Godfery*
Joy and woe are woven fine: *Chapple*
Joy in thy hope: *Jones, R.*
Joy is my name: *Someren-Godfery*
Joy of my heart: *Roberton*
Joy, shipmate, joy: *Stanford*; *Vaughan Williams*
Joyous Wanderer, The: *Pope*
Joys Seven: *Butt*
Julia: *Parry, C.H.H.* (Rock of Rubies, The)
Julia's Hair: *Quilter*
Juliet Anne: *Gibbs, Armstrong*
Julienne: *Someren-Godfery*
June: *Quilter*
June on Castle Hill: *Finzi*
June Rapture: *Lehmann*
June Rhapsody: *Ronald*
June Twilight: *Clarke, R.*; *Martin, E.*
Juniper Tree, The: *Bedford*†
Just Friends in Print: *Bennett, R.R.*
Just So Song Book, The: *German*
Just War: *Steed*

K

Kangaroo and Dingo: *German*
Karroo Cradle Song: *Dunhill*
Kashmiri Song: *Woodforde-Finden*
Kate Dalrymple: *Atkinson, G.*
Kathleen O'More: *Hughes, Herbert*
Kavita II: *Sohal*†
Keel Row, The: *Marshall, N.*†
Keeper of the Pass, The (cycle): *Dalby*†
Kelvin Series of Scots Songs: *Orr, R.*
Kerry Dance, The: *Molloy*
Kerry Shore – Loch Fyne, The: *Scott, F.G.*
Kettle Rhyme, The: *Butterworth, N.*
Kilkeel: *Parke*
Killary: *Holbrooke*
Killiney Strands: *Dalway*
Killing Time (cycle): *Holloway*†
Kind fortune smiles: *Purcell, H.*
Kind in unkindness, when will you relent: *Rosseter*
Kind Inconstant, The: *Arne, T.*
Kindling Fire, The: *Liddell*
King Charles: *Harrison, J.*; *White, M.V.*
King Cupid: *Ketèlby*
King David was a sorrowful man: *Howells*; *Procter*
King George the Farmer: *Bantock*
King Harald's Saga: *Weir*†
King Herod and the Cock: *Case*
King of all joys and easer of all woes: *Church*
King of China's daughter, The: *Head*; *Someren-Godfery*
King of Love: *Jones, O.*
King of Tang, A: *Bantock*
King of the Golden River, The: *Rodgers*†
King there lived in Thule, A: *Coleridge-Taylor*
King William: *Vaughan Williams*
Kingdom by the Sea, A: *Somervell* (Annabel Lee)
Kingdom of God, The: *Swann*
Kingfisher, The: *Naylor, P.*; *Willink*
Kingfisher's Tower, The: *Bantock*
King's Way, The: *Elgar*

246 Index of titles

Kirconnell Lee: *Herbage* (Helen of Kirconnell)
Kiss, A [Hardy]: *Venables*
Kiss, The [Donne]: *Swayne*
Kiss, The [d'Orleans]: *Burrows* (My gostly fader)
Kiss, The [Jonson]: *Bush, G.*
Kitty, I am in love with you: *Moeran*
Kitty my love, will you marry me? *Hughes, Herbert*
Kjær lighede Styrke: *Grainger, P.**
Kladenetsut: *Hiscocks, W.*†
Knees: *Butterworth, N.*
Knight, The: *Parry, J.*
Knight and the Lady, The: *Orr, B.*†
Knight of the Grail, The: *Frankel, B.*
Knot of Time, A: *Holt*†
Knot There's no Untying, The: *Maconchy*†
Knotting Song, The (Hears not my Phyllis): *Purcell, H.*
Konig Wiswamitra: *Berners**
Krönung: *Kirkwood**
Kyrie: *Papastávrou*

L

La Belle Dame Sans Merci: *Someren-Godfery*; *Stanford*
La belle est au jardin d'amour: *Britten**
La bergère aux champs: *Hopkins, A.**
La bien aimée: *Cannon*(*)(†)
La bien mariée: *Cannon*(*)(†)
La Cantarina: *Woolrich*
La dernière écuelle: *Tate*†
La fiancée du timbalier: *Berners**
La figlia che piange: *Holloway*†
La guitarra: *ApIvor*†
La lune blanche: *Delius**
La mal maridada: *Gerhard**
La mal mariée: *Cannon*(*)(†)
La Marguerite: *Luard-Selby*
La niña del bello rostro: *ApIvor*†
La Noël passée: *Britten**
La plage: *Birtwistle*†
La Rivière: *Swayne**
La targo: *Bax**
La veuve: *Cannon*(*)(†)
La Ximbomba: *Gerhard**
Lachrimae (Flow my tears): *Dowland*
Lackyng my love, I go from place to place: *Rubbra*
Lad Våren komme: *Delius**
Lad wha Lilts sae Sweetly, The: *Hook*
Laddie's Sang, A: *Britten*
Lads in their hundreds, The: *Butterworth, G.*; *Moeran*; *Orr, C.W.*; *Pope*; *Somervell* (Ludlow Fair)
Ladslove: *Ireland* (Look not in my eyes)
Lady Caroline, The: *Howells* (Lovelocks)
Lady if you so spite me: *Dowland*
Lady Isobel and the Elf-knight: *Weir*
Lady Jane Grey: *Bush, G.*
Lady June: *Scott, C.*
Lady Lazarus: *Runswick*†
Lady Macbeth (scena): *Horowitz*
Lady Mary Ann: *White, A.*
Lady mine: *Treharne*
Lady of Shalott: *Tate, P.*†
Lady 'Rogue' Singleton: *Lutyens*
Lady to a Young Courtier, A: *Lawes, H.*

Lady Visitor in the Pauper Ward, The: *Berners*
Lady, when I behold the roses sprouting: *Standford*; *Walton*(†) (Damask Roses)
Lady, when your lovely head: *Greaves, R.*
Lady, whose shrine stands on the promontory: *Tavener*
Laieta: *Gerhard**
Laird of Cockpen, The: *Parry, C.H.H.*
Lake and a fairy boat, A: *Davidson, M.*; *Warlock*
Lake Isle of Innisfree, The: *Burrows*; *Herbert, M.*; *Ley*; *Peel*; *Poston*; *Scott, D.B.* (Innisfree)
Lal Dinah Grayson: *Mark*
L'allée: *Sorabji**
Lamb, The: *Jacob*; *Lord, R.*; *McLeod*†; *Owen*; *Raphael*; *Vaughan Williams*†; *Wills*(†) (Little lamb, who made thee?)
Lamb and the Dove, The: *Gibbs, Armstrong*
Lament [Anon]: *Wishart*
Lament [Bantock, H.]: *Bantock*
Lament [Hungarian]: *Seiber*†
Lament [Raine]: *Bush, G.*
Lament, A [Rossetti]: *Coleridge-Taylor*
Lament, A [Shelley]: *Steptoe*
Lament for a Woman Killed by the Soldiery: *Karkoff*
Lament for Constantinople: *Taverner*†
Lament for Phaedra: *Taverner*†
Lament for Robin Hood: *Gibbs, Armstrong*
Lament for the Ashes of Language: *Lufft*†
Lament for the Lark: *Thomas, Mansel*
Lament in Spring, A: *Fulton*
Lament of Isis: *Bantock*
Lament of the Bedouin Slave-girl: *Bantock*
Lamentation, The: *Loder*
Lamentation, Last Prayer and Exaltation: *Tavener*(†)
Lamon to Priapus: *Someren-Godfery*
L'amour de moy: *Vaughan Williams**
L'amoureuse: *Cannon*(*)(†)
Lamplighter, The: *Quilter*; *White, A.*; *Williamson, M.*
Lancashire Lullaby: *Jackson, R.*
Lances of Gold: *Foulds*
Land of Counterpane, The: *Blake, H.*
Land of Dreams, The: *Brian*
Land of heart's desire: *Kennedy-Fraser*
Land of Heart's Desire, The [Yeats]: *Shaw*
Land of Hope and Glory: *Elgar*
Land of Lost Content and Other Songs: *Ireland*
Land of Lost Content: *Steele* (Far Country, The / Farms of Home, The / Into my heart an air that kills)
Land of Nod, The: *White, A.*
Land of Promise: *Bantock*
Land of silence, A: *Quilter*
Land of Storybooks, The: *White, A.*
Land o' the Leal: *Grainger, P.*(†)
Land of the Silver Trumpets: *Thomas, D.A.*
Land of the West, The: *Crossley-Holland*
Landscapes: *Hoddinott*; *Purser*
Landscapes: *Beat*†
Landscapes (cycle): *Joubert*†
Lane o' the Thrushes: *Harty*
Langley Fair: *Martin, E.*
L'Angoisse: *Wilby**
Languedo d'amours, ma douce fillette: *Bax**
Lark, The: *Hawes*
Lark, The [Anon]: *Lawes, H.*
Lark, The [Catalan]: *Gerhard*
Lark, The [Day-Lewis]: *Naylor, P.*
Lark in the Clear Air, The: *Hughes, Herbert*; *Tate, P.*

Index of titles 247

Lark in the Morn, The: *Boyle, R.*
Lark on Portsdown Hill: *Swain*
Lark sings high in the cornfield, The: *Linley Snr*
Larky lad frae the pantry, The: *Britten*
Lass for a sailor is lively and free, The: *Brown, J.*
Lass from the low countrie, The: *Roe*
Lass o' Gowrie, The: *Center*
Lass of Richmond Hill, The: *Grainger, P.*
Lass with the Delicate Air, The: *Arne, M.*
Lassie of Yarrow, The: *White, A.*
Lassie wi' the lint white locks: *Center*
Lasst uns erfreuen heimlich sehr: *Bridge**
Last Days: *Dieren*
Last Hours: *Gurney*; *Jacobson*
Last Invocation, The: *Bridge*; *Hiscocks, W.*(†)
Last Lauch, The: *MacDonald*
Last Lines: *Wills*
Last Love Word: *Downes*†
Last May a braw Wooer: *Center*
Last Night: *Harries*
Last poem, A: *Wood, Hugh*
Last Revel, The: *Bantock*; *Harrison, J.*; *Redman*
Last Rose of Summer, The: *Anon*; *Britten*
Last Sight of Fiametta, The: *Harrison, J.*
Last Trump, The: *Stevenson*
Last Word, A: *Scott, C.*
Last Year: *Anderson, W.H.*
Last Year's Rose, A: *Quilter*
Late Spring: *Berkeley, L.*
Late Summer: *Warlock* (Fields are full of summer still, The)
Latmian Shepherd, The: *Gurney* (Endymion)
Lauds: *Berkeley, L.*
Laughing Song: *Busch*; *Butt*; *Fogg*; *Jacob*
Laurie Lee Songs: *Wood, Hugh*
Laus Deo: *Milford*
Lavender Pond: *Head*
Lavender's blue: *Standford*
Lawn as white as driven snow: *Slater*
Lawyer, The: *Vaughan Williams*†
Lawyer he went out one day, A: *Butterworth, G.*
Lay a garland on my hearse: *Bush, G.*; *Parry, C.H.H.*; *Raphael* (Aspatia's Song / Sad Song, A / Willow Song [Fletcher])
Lay your sleeping head, my love: *Berkeley, L.*
Le bien vient en dormant: *Stanford**
Le ciel est, par-dessus le toit: *Delius**; *Elias**
Le Roi Renaud: *Hopkins, A.**
Le roi s'en va-t'en chasse: *Britten**
Le rossignol (French): *Seiber*†
Le rossignol (Verlaine): *Wilby**
Le vieux blaise: *Tate*†
Lead, kindly light, amid the encircling gloom: *Evans, D.P.*
Leaden Echo and the Golden Echo, The: *Wellesz*†
Lean out of the window: *Head* (Goldenhair)
Leanin': *Bennett, T.C.S.*
Lea-rig, The: *Atkinson, G.*
Leather Bottèl: *Grainger, P.*
Leave me alone, O love: *Arundell*
Leave me, loathsome light: *Handel*
Leaves: *Parrott*
Leaves Cry, The (cantata): *Holloway*
Leaves of my Brain, The: *Beat*†
Leave-taking, A: *Alwyn*
Leave-taking, A: *Alwyn*
Leaving the Mountains in the Rain from Yellow Dragon Temple: *Karkoff*

Ledbury Train, The: *Clarke, R.C.*
Leezie Lindsay: *Grainger, P.*
Legato Leicester Square: *Roe*†
Legend of Rosemary, The: *Roe*
Leisure: *Bliss*
Lelant: *Caradon*; *Raynor*
Lemady: *Britten*(†)
Lent Lily, The: *Gurney*; *Ireland*; *Orr, C.W.*; *Owen* (Lenten Lily, The / 'Tis Spring, come out to ramble)
Lenten Flowers: *Bliss*
Lenten Lily, The: *Horder* (Lent Lily, The / 'Tis Spring, come out to ramble)
Lenten Thoughts of a High Anglican: *Wills*
Leprehaun, The: *Hughes, Herbert*
Les Contemplations (Mon bras pressait la taille frêle): *Dieren**
Les fillettes de mon âge: *Tate, P.*†
Les papillons: *Thomas, A.G.**
Les Rayons et les Ombres (Oh! quand je dors): *Dieren**
Les Soirs Bleus: *McCabe*†
Les trois rubans: *Hopkins, A.**
Lesbos: *Berkeley, L.*; *Routh*; *Southam*
Less than the dust beneath thy chariot wheel: *Woodforde-Finden*
Let all the strains of joy: *Ronald*; *Standford*†
Let beauty awake in the morn: *Vaughan Williams*
Let each gallant heart: *Purcell, H.*
Let formal lovers still pursue: *Purcell, H.*
Let me dream again: *Sullivan*
Let me enjoy the earth no less: *Finzi*; *Foster, I.*
Let me not to the marriage of true minds admit impediment (Sonnet 116) [Shakespeare]: *Wetherell*
Let me stop her: *Hugill*
Let me wander, not unseen: *Handel*
Let my voice ring out over the earth: *Thomas, Muriel*
Let no mortal sing to me: *Jackson, W.*
Let not Chloris think: *Danyel*
Let not love on me bestow: *Purcell, D.*
Let others sing of knights and palladines (Sonnet) [Daniel]: *Steptoe*
Let springtime come then: *Delius*
Let the bright seraphim: *Handel*†
Let the dreadful engines: *Purcell, H.*
Let the florid music praise: *Britten*; *Dickinson*
Let the night perish (Job's Curse): *Purcell, H.*
Let there be peace: *Kennedy*
Let this Harvest Pass: *Hugill*†
Let this harvest pass: *Hugill*†
Let us dance, let us sing: *Purcell, H.*
Let us forget: *White, M.V.*
Let us Garlands Bring: *Finzi*
Let us now praise famous men: *Vaughan Williams*
Lethe: *Clarke, R.*
L'Etoile filante: *Berners**
Let's walk on the beach: *Hugill*†
Letter, The [Tennyson]: *Sullivan*
Letter, The [Whitman]: *Horne*
Letter to the World (cycle): *Butterworth, N.*
Levana and our Ladies of Sorrow: *Dieren*
Lewis Bridal Song (Mairi's Wedding): *Roberton*
L'heure du berger: *Wilby**
L'Horloge: *Maconchy*†
Lhudhè Sing Tishoo: *Solomons*(†)
Li Fu-Jen: *Pilkington, M.*
Li Liang-Ch'en: *Garton*†

248 Index of titles

Libretto of the Eight Year Old (cantata):
    Hiscocks, W.†
Lie there, my lute: *MacCunn*
Liebe: *White, M.V.**
Liebeslied: *Ellis*†
Lied vom Meer: *Headington**
Lieder: *Smyth**
Lieder der Jugend: *McLeod**
Lieder vom Wasser: *Barrett*†
Liederbuchlein fur Regina Beate (cycle): *Stevenson**
Life: *Thomas, Mansel*
Life and Death: *Coleridge-Taylor*
Life in a love: *Bantock*
Life in her creaking shoes: *Butterworth, G.*(†)
Life Laughs Onward: *Finzi*
Life of a Rose, The: *Lehmann*
Life of my life, I shall ever try: *Ronald*
Life Reborn: *Glyn*
Life Story: *Adès*(†)
Life Support: *Talbot*
Lift-boy: *Hattey*
Light and Rock: *Woolrich*†
Light breaks where no sun shines: *Chapple*
Light foot and tight foot: *White, A.*
Light, my light: *Ronald*
Light wind is sighing over the Severn, A: *Jeffreys, J.*
Lights Out: *Gurney,*
Lights Out: *Gurney*; *Hedges*; *Pickard*
Lights Out (cycle): *Holloway*
Like a child's kite: *Northcott*†
Like as the lute delights: *Danyel*
Like as the thrush in winter: *Stanford*
Like hermit poor in pensive place obscure:
    Ferrabosco; *Lanier*
Like the shadow: *Handel*
Like the young god of wine: *Greene*
Like to the damask rose you see: *Anon*; *Elgar*
Like to the falling of a star: *Bennett, R.R.* (Sic Vita)
Lilacs are in bloom, The: *O'Neill*
Lilac-time: *Scott, C.*
Lilligay: *Warlock*
Lily has a smooth stalk, The: *Finzi*
Lily of a Day, The: *Lehmann*
Lily-bright and shine-a: *Gibbs, Armstrong*
Limehouse Reach: *Head*
Lincolnshire Poacher, The: *Britten*
Linden Lea: *Vaughan Williams*
Lindisfarne Fragments: *Ball, M.*
Lines: *Lambert, C.*
Lines from Buchanan's Epithalamium: *Stevenson*
Lines of Life: *Britten*
Lines to Mr Hodgson: *Wood, Hugh*
Lines Written During a Sleepless Night: *Britten*(*)
Lingering Music: *Pitfield*
Linnet, The (Bridges): *Herbert, I.* (I heard a linnet courting)
Linnet, The (de la Mare): *Naylor, P.*
Linstead Market: *Benjamin, A.*
Listen to the lark: *Garton*
Listeners, The: *Rodgers*
Litany [Thomas à Kempis]: *Procter*
Litany, A [Fletcher]: *Hurlstone*
Litany to the Holy Spirit: *Vale*
Little Bells of Sevilla, The: *Scott, C.*
Little Betty Bland: *Nelson*
Little Black Boy, The: *Symons*
Little boats rock on billows of blue: *Hughes, Herbert*
Little Boy Lost: *Howells*

Little Buttercup: *Sullivan*
Little Candle to St Anthony, A: *Poston*
Little cart jolting and banging, The: *Dalby*; *Orr, R.*
Little child mine own: *Whittaker*
Little cock sparrow, A: *Mullinar*
Little Damozel, The: *Novello*
Little Deer, The: *Barton*†
Little Dreams, The: *Head*
Little Elegy: *Bliss*
Little Fête, A: *Someren-Godfery*
Little Foreigner, The: *Scott, C.*
Little Ghost who Died for Love, The (cycle):
    Bennett, R.R.
Little Girl from Hanley Way, The: *Clarke, R.C.*
Little Good People, The: *Phillips, M.*
Little Green Orchard, The: *Gibbs, Armstrong*
Little Irish Song: *Fraser, N.*
Little Island, The (Ellan Vannin): *Pike*
Little Jack Jingle: *Warlock*
Little Lady of Ch'in-hsi, The: *Dalby*
Little lamb, who made thee?: *Procter* (Lamb, The)
Little Maid, The: *Bantock*
Little Man and the Little Maid: *Cockshott*
Little Milkmaid, The [Anon]: *Moeran*
Little Milkmaid, The [Nabbes]: *Jeffreys, J.*
    (Milkmaid, The)
Little Music, A: *Holst*
Little Music, A (cycle): *Steptoe*
Little Nut Tree, The: *Bush, G.*
Little Old Table, The: *Britten*
Little Ole with his umbrella: *Grainger, P.*
Little One: *Novello*
Little Papoose Lake: *Bantock*
Little Peter Morrisey: *Stanford*
Little Polly Flinders: *Diack*
Little pretty nightingale, The: *Jeffreys, J.*
Little red hen, The: *Peterkin*
Little Red Lark, The: *Marshall, N.*†
Little Road to Bethlehem, The: *Head*(†)
Little Rose of Gartan, The: *Hughes, Herbert*
Little Salamander, The: *Gibbs, Armstrong*
Little Sir William: *Britten*
Little Sleeper (Soliloquy upon a dead child): *Brian*
Little Snow, A: *Marsh*†
Little Son, The: *Harty*
Little Song of Picardie, A: *Scott, C.*
Little Songs for Little Folks: *Coleridge-Taylor*
Little Tommy Tucker sings for his supper: *Warlock*
Little Tommy Twinkletoes: *Thomas, Mansel*
Little Town of Bethlehem: *Dunhill*
Little trotty wagtail, he went in the rain: *Bullard*;
    Greaves, Terence†; *Jeffreys, J.*; *Warlock*
Little Waves of Breffny, The: *Peel*; *Shaw*
Little wind came blowing, A: *Peterkin*
Little winding road, A: *Ronald*
Lizard, The: *Moult*
Llanarmon: *Jones, W.B.*
Llanberis Pass: *Thomas, Mansel*
Llanfihangel Bachellaeth: *Williams, W.M.*
Llanrwst and other Songs: *Glyn*
Llanrwst: *Glyn*
Llys Dulas: *Hoddinott*
Lo! here the gentle lark: *Bishop*(†)
Lo, leman sweet now may thou see: *Oldham*
Loch Lomond: *Anon*; *Center*
Løft de klingre Glaspokaler: *Delius**
London: *Vaughan Williams*†
London Fantasies: *Roe*†

Londonderry Air, The: *Anon*; *Jacob* (Danny Boy / O Mary dear)
Lone Bird, The: *Jeffreys, J.*
Lone Dog: *Head*
Lonely Night: *Gurney*
Lonely Waters: *Moeran*
Long ago [Evans]: *Evans, W.T.*
Long ago [Malloch]: *Holbrooke*
Long ago I went to Rome: *Piggott*
Long ago in Bethlehem the virgin fair: *Tate, P.*
Long barren: *Burtch*
Long, long ago: *Bayley*
Long Time Ago, A: *Berners*
Long to me thy coming: *Jeffreys, J.*
Long years ago: *Coleridge-Taylor*
Long-departed Lover, The: *Lambert, C.*
Longing [Arnold]: *Taylor, C.V.* (Come to me in my dreams)
Longing [Kjerulf]: *Delius*
Longing [Macleod]: *Bantock*
Look at the children: *Thwaites*
Look not in my eyes, for fear: *Berkeley, L.*; *Branson*; *Butterworth, G.*; *Pope* (Ladslove)
Look, stranger: *Dickinson*; *Marchant* (Seascape [Auden])
Lookin' Back [O'Neill]: *Harty*; *Stanford*
Lookin', just lookin': *Solomons*(†)
Looking Back [Rossetti, C.]: *Scott, C.*
Looking Backward: *Parry, C.H.H.*
Looking Forward: *Williamson, M.*
Looking-glass River: *White, A.*
Loom, The: *Mathias*(†); *Williams, Grace*
Lord, come away: *Vaughan Williams*†
Lord, I have sinned: *Humfrey*(†)
Lord! I married me a wife: *Britten*(†)
Lord is my light and my salvation, The: *Allitsen*(†)
Lord is my refuge, The (Psalm 91): *Parke*
Lord is my shepherd, The (Psalm 23): *Bantock*; *Jacobson*; *Jenkins, D.*; *S.Liddle*(†); *Rubbra* (Bird's Song, The)
Lord Jesus Christ, shall I stand still: *Naylor, P.*(†)
Lord Maxwell's Goodnight: *Grainger, P.*(†)
Lord Mayor's Table, The: *Walton*
Lord reigneth, The (Psalm 93): *Bantock*
Lord Randall: *Scott, C.*
Lord Rendal: *Bantock*
Lord shall preserve thee from all evil, The: *Weldon*
Lord thou art mine and I am thine: *Procter*
Lord, what is man, lost man: *Purcell, H.*
Lord's name is praised, The: *Greene*
Lord's Prayer, The: *Head*(†) (Our father, who art in heaven)
Lorna's Song: *Boughton*
Lorry Driver, The: *Rowley*
Los bilbilcos: *Anderson, A.*†
Lost as Strangers: *Hold*
Lost at Sea: *Standford*†
Lost Chord, The: *Sullivan*(†)
Lost Happiness, The: *Samuels*
Lost Love: *Downes*†
Lost Love [Chinese tr. Bax]: *Howells*
Lost Love [Hardy]: *Downes*†
Lost Love [Somervell]: *Handel*
Lost Love, A [Chinese tr. Giles]: *Scott, C.*
Lost Lover, The: *Moeran*
Lost One, The: *Bantock*
Lotusland: *Goossens*
Lourd on my hert as winter lies: *Scott, F.G.*

Love [St Teresa]: *Pike*
Love [Wyn]: *Smith, R.*
Love... a strange disease: *Barratt*
Love and Death: *Bowen*
Love and Discipline: *Headington*
Love and Friendship: *Ireland*
Love and Grief: *Pierson* (Seals of love / Take, O take those lips away)
Love and I of late did part: *Lanier*
Love and Laughter: *Parry, C.H.H.*
Love and Life – A Miscellany of Songs: *Naylor, P.*
Love and Peter: *Someren-Godfery*
Love and Reason: *Ferguson*
Love and Time: *Dring*
Love arms himself in Celia's eyes: *Purcell, H.*
Love at First Sight: *Grainger, E.*
Love bade me welcome: *Procter*; *Vaughan Williams*
Love Blows as the Wind Blows: *Butterworth, G.*(†)
Love, could I only tell thee: *Capel*
Love, do not believe: *Wood, Hugh*†
Love entrapped me: *Dalway*
Love for Love: *Warlock*
Love for such a cherry lip: *Bush, G.*
Love Forsaken: *Gill*
Love Has Eyes: *Bishop*
Love I have won you: *Ronald*
Love, if you knew the light: *Lehmann*
Love in a life: Life in a love: *Shur*
Love in a Valley: *Somers-Cocks*
Love in Christ: *Hughes-Jones*
Love in Dreams: *Ronald*
Love in her sunny eyes: *MacCunn*
Love in my bosom, like a bee: *Fulton*
Love in Springtime: *Somervell*
Love in thy youth: *Howard, S.*
Love is a bable: *Parry, C.H.H.*
Love is a pretty frenzy: *Jones, R.*
Love is a sickness full of woes: *Blyton*†; *Dring*; *Gibbs, Armstrong*; *Ireland*; *Murrill*; *Naylor, P.*; *Raynor*; *Wills*(†) (Concerning Love)
Love is cruel: *Nelson*
Love is not blind but I myself am so: *Cavendish*
Love is now become a trade: *Purcell, H.*
Love lasts longer: *Thomas, Mansel*
Love, like a drop of dew: *Fleming*; *Lloyd Webber*
Love lives beyond: *Arnell*
Love Letter: *Williamson, M.*
Love Lyric: *Dring*
Love me again: *Raynor*
Love me not for comely grace: *Head*; *Jacob*; *Jeffreys, J.*; *Joubert* (True Woman's Eye, A)
Love me or not, love her I must or die: *Campion*
Love must be gone: *Dieren*
Love on my heart from heaven fell: *Carey, C.*; *Milford*
Love quickly is palled: *Purcell, H.*
Love Remembered: *Hugill*
Love Repaid: *Dalway*
Love Rhapsody, A: *Head*
Love sends a little gift of roses: *Openshaw*
Love shakes my soul like a mountain wind: *Gurney*
Love sings in the night: *Lubbock*
Love Song [Bantock, H.]: *Bantock*
Love Song [Herrick] *Birkett* (Bid me but live / To Anthea)
Love Song, A [Latin]: *Pilkington, M.*
Love Song, A [Sidney]: *Walters, L.* (Bargain, The / My true love hath my heart)

Love Song of the Bride: *Hartley*
Love Talker, The: *Gibbs, Armstrong*
Love, the delight of all well-thinking minds: *Cavendish*
Love those beams that breed all day long: *Dowland*
Love, thou can'st hear tho' thou art blind: *Purcell, H.*
Love unto love for ever calls: *Somervell*
Love Untold: *Bowen*
Love was true to me: *Burrows*
Love went a-riding: *Bridge*
Love will find out the way: *Holloway*† (Over the mountains)
Love winged my hopes: *Morley*
Loveliest of trees, the cherry now: *Butterworth, G.*; *Gurney*(†); *Horder*; *Matthews, D.*†; *Moeran*; *Orr, C.W.*; *Peel*; *Pope*; *Raynor*; *Somervell*; *Steele* (Cherry Tree, The / Cherry Tree hung with Snow, The)
Lovelocks: *Bliss* (Lady Caroline, The)
Lovely Albina's come ashore: *Purcell, H.*
Lovely Isle, The: *O'Neill*
Lovely Joan: *Mitchell*†
Lovely kind and kindly loving: *Holst*; *Scott, C.* (Fair and True)
Lovely Little Dream, A: *Coleridge-Taylor*
Lovely Playthings: *Jeffreys, J.*; *Moult*
Lovely Selina, innocent and free: *Blow*
Lover and his Lass, The: *Moeran* (It was a lover and his lass / Pretty Ringtime / Spring Song [Shakespeare] / Sweet and Twenty)
Lover in Damascus, A: *Woodforde-Finden*
Lover in Winter, The: *Adès*
Lover Mourns for the Loss of Love, The: *Warlock*
Lover's Appeal, The: *Farrar* (And wilt thou leave me thus? / Appeal, The / Supplication, A)
Lover's Curse, The: *Hughes, Herbert*
Lover's Farewell, The: *McCabe*
Lover's Garland, A: *Parry, C.H.H.*
Lover's Ghost, The: *Marsh*†
Lover's Gift: *Hiscocks, W.*
Lovers in the Lane: *Lehmann*
Lover's Maze, (A), (The): *Tomlinson*; *Warlock*
Lovers' Season, The: *Pope*
Lover's Well, The (cycle): *Holloway*
Love's a dream of mighty treasure: *Arne, T.*
Love's Aftermath: *Scott, C.*
Love's Bower: *Vaughan Williams*
Love's but a dance: *McEwen*
Love's but the frailty of the mind: *Eccles*; *Handel*
Love's Emblems: *Moult*
Love's Fool: *Routh*†
Love's Garden of Roses: *Wood, Haydn*
Love's god is a boy: *Jones, R.*
Love's Lament: *Head*
Love's Last Gift: *Vaughan Williams*
Love's Minstrels: *Vaughan Williams*
Love's Old Sweet Song: *Molloy*
Love's Philosophy: *Delius*; *Quilter*; *Ronald*; *Sagar*; *Tomlinson*
Love's pow'r in my heart: *Purcell, H.*
Love's Prisoner: *Gibbs, Armstrong*
Love's Quarrel: *Scott, C.*
Love's Reasons: *Plumstead*
Love's Reckoning: *Bowen*
Love's Riddle: *Hold*
Love's Secret: *Bantock*; *Someren-Godfery*
Love's Spells: *Phillips, M.*
Love's Torment: *Wills*(†)

Love's Voice: *Venables*
Love's Wisdom: *Gibbs, Armstrong*
Love-sick Lass, The: *Scott, F.G.*
Love-sight: *Vaughan Williams*
Love-song of the Lady of Granada: *Blyton*†
Lovesongs (cycle): *Sansom*
Lower him gently: *Thomas, Mansel*
Lowest trees have tops, The: *Bennett, R.R.*; *Dowland*
Lowestoft Boat, The: *Elgar*
Lowlands: *Vignoles*
Lowlands of Holland, The: *Berkeley, L.*; *Harty*; *Hughes, Herbert*
Lowly, laid in a manger: *Ireland*†
Lowly they kneel in prayer before thy throne: *Handel*†
Loyal Lover, The: *Raynor*
Lucinda, wink or veil those eyes: *Locke*
Luck comes in sleeping: *Stanford*
Lucy: *Coleridge-Taylor*
Lucy Lavender: *White, A.*
Ludlow and Teme: *Gurney*(†)
Ludlow Fair: *Gurney*(†) (Lads in their hundreds, The)
Ludlow Town: *Moeran*
Ludlow Town: *Head*
Lukannon: *Grainger, P.*
Lulajze Jesuniu: *Bax**
Lullaby: *Randalls*; *Snell*(†)
Lullaby [Auden]: *Horder*
Lullaby [de la Mare]: *Gibbs, Armstrong*
Lullaby, (A), [Dekker]: *Berners*; *Jeffreys, J.*; *Stanford*; *Warlock* (Golden slumbers kiss your eyes)
Lullaby [Flower]: *Pike*
Lullaby [Gower]: *Stanford*
Lullaby (Sho-ho) [Graves]: *Wood, C.*
Lullaby [Japanese]: *Josephs*(†)
Lullaby [Levy]: *Fogg*
Lullaby [Polish]: *Roe*
Lullaby [Noyes]: *Keel*
Lullaby [O'Sullivan]: *Moeran*
Lullaby [Reynolds]: *Randall*†
Lullaby [Rossetti, C.]: *Scott, C.*
Lullaby [Rowlands]: *Brown, C.*
Lullaby [Tennyson]: *Scott, A.*
Lullaby [Welsh]: *Thomas, Mansel*
Lullaby [Yeats]: *McCabe*
Lullaby, A [Bantock, H.]: *Bantock*
Lullaby, A [McCarthy]: *Bax*
Lullaby, A [O'Byrne]: *Harty*
Lullaby, A [Stewart]: *Bantock*
Lullaby for a Baby Toad: *Roe*
Lullaby for Dinogat: *Samuel, R.*
Lullaby for the unsleeping: *Harvey*
Lullabye: *Bantock*
Lullay, dear Jesus: *Bax*
Lullay, lullay: *Whittaker*
Lullay, lullay, thou little tiny child: *Hope*
Lullay my liking: *Hoyle*
Lumpentum: *Blake, D.*†
Lunar Attraction: *Stevens, B.*
Lunar Beauty: *Burgon*†
Luss Village: *MacDonald*
Lusty Juventus: *Warlock* (In a harbour green / In an arbour green / In Youth is Pleasure / Youth)
Lute Player, The: *Allitsen*
Lute Song, The: *Stanford* (Queen Mary's Song)
Lúthien Tinúviel: *Swann*
Luve: *Rose*

Lye still my deare, why dost thou rise? *Anon*; *Gibbs, Armstrong*
Lyke as the culver, on the bared bough: *Rubbra*
Lyke-wake Dirge, A: *Ferguson*; *Jeffreys, J.*
Lyke-wake Song, A: *Walton*
Lyonesse: *Gibbs, Armstrong* (Song of Lyonesse, A / When I set out for Lyonesse)
Lyrics from 'Ferishta's Fancies': *Bantock*
Lyrics from the East: *Blyton*
Lysander I pursue in vain: *Blow*
Lyse Nœtter (På Stranden): *Delius**

M

Ma Bonny Lad: *Atkinson, R.*
Ma Bonny Lad: *Atkinson, R.*
Macedonian Dance: *Papastávrou*†
Macushla: *MacMurrough*
Mad Bess (Bess of Bedlam / From silent shades): *Purcell, H.*
Mad Moll: *Bauld*
Mad Prince, The: *Gibbs, Armstrong*
Mad Song: *Butt*
Mad Tom Tatterman: *Rowley*
Mad Woman of Punnet's Town, The: *Bliss*†
Madam and her Might-have-been: *Roe*†
Madam and the Census Man: *Roe*†
Madam and the Fortune Teller: *Roe*†
Madam and the Minister: *Roe*†
Madam and the Wrong Visitor: *Roe*†
Madam Noy: *Bliss*†
Madam Songs: *Roe*†
Madam's Calling Cards: *Roe*†
Madam's Three Callers: *Roe*†
Mädchenlied: *Dieren**
Madeleine de la Ste-Baume: *Osborne*†
Madonna and Child: *Thiman*
Madman and the Child, The: *Hugh-Jones*
Madrigal [Thomas]: *Thomas, Mansel*
Madrigal, A [Dobson}: *Howells*
Madrigali: *Beamish*
Maesaleg: *Evans, D.*
Magdalen at Michael's gate tirled at the pin: *Lehmann*; *Maude*
Maggie's Farewell: *Bedford*†
Magic in the Air: *Crawley*
Magic Moments: *Beamish*†
Magic of thy presence, The: *Quilter*
Magic Whistle, The: *White, A.*
Magnificat [Coleridge, M]: *Graves*
Magnificat [Luke]: *Bax*
Magpie, The [Hunter]: *Warlock*
Magpie, The [McAuley]: *Wishart*
Magpie's Nest, The: *Hughes, Herbert*
Maid and the Miller, The: *Bax*
Maid from Penderyn Parish, The: *Thomas, Mansel*(†)
Maid of Bunclody, The: *Noble, H.*
Maid of Dundee, The: *Thiman*
Maid of Kent: *Jeffreys, J.*
Maid of Sker, The: *Thomas, Mansel*
Maid Quiet: *Poston*
Maiden, The: *Parry, C.H.H.*
Maiden Blush, The: *Quilter*
Maiden Deceived, The (cycle): *Blyton*†

Maidens came when I was in my mother's bower, The: *Hardy*; *Northcott*† (Bailey beareth the bell away, The; Bayly berith the bell away, The)
Maids are simple: *Campion*
Mairi Bhan Og: *Grainger, P.*
Mairi's Wedding (Lewis Bridal Song): *Roberton*
Make a joyful noise unto the Lord (Psalm 121): *Head*(†)
Make me a willow cabin: *Butterworth, N.*
Make new friends but keep the old: *Parry, J.*
Make we merry both more and less: *Fulton*
Malicious Observer: *Woolrich*†
Mally O: *Howells*
Maltworms: *Moeran*; *Warlock* (Back and side go bare / Jolly Good Ale and Old)
Malvern Hills in Spring: *Clarke, R.C.*
Mamble: *Head, Jacobson*
Man: *Pike*
Man and Woman: *Benjamin* (Man is for the woman made)
Man behind the plough, The: *Quilter*
Man is for the woman made: *Purcell, H.* (Man and Woman)
Man with the Axe, The: *Spedding*†
Man without Myth: *Roe*
Man without Myth: *Roe*
Mango Walk: *Hosier*†
Man-in-the-mune's got cleik-i-the-back, The: *Musgrave*
Man's a Man, A: *Center*; *Shur*†
Mantle of Blue (The): *Bridge*; *Lodge*; *Moeran* (Cradle Song [Colum] / O men from the fields)
March: *Gurney*(†)
March, The: *Bantock*
March Past: *Searle*
March Requiem, A: *Scott, C.*
Marching along: *Harrison, J.*
Marching (as seen from the left file): *Ellis*†
Marching Song: *White, A.*; *Williamson, M.*
Margrete's Cradle Song: *Holst* (Cradle Song [Ibsen])
Marguerite [Marsh]: *Swann*
Marguerite [Morris]: *Thomas, Mansel*
Marguerite, elle est malade: *Seiber*†
Marian: *Parry, C.H.H.*
Marie at the Window: *Somervell*
Marigold: *Ireland*
Marigold of golden hue, The: *Woodson*
Marina: *Matthews, D*†; *Wood, Hugh*†
Mariner, The: *Crossley-Holland*
Marino Faliero (scena): *Holbrooke*
Maritime Invocation: *Gibbs, Armstrong*
Mark how the blushful morn: *Lanier*
Mark when she smiles with amiable cheare: *Gibbs, Alan*; *Rubbra*
Market, The: *Gibbs, Armstrong*
Market Girl, The: *Bax*; *Finzi*
Marriage Morning: *Sullivan*
Marriage Song, A: *Newson*†
Marro's Only Son: *Hoddinott*
Maruts (Stormclouds): *Holst*
Mary [Dufferin]: *Scott, C.*
Mary [Wordsworth]: *Coleridge-Taylor*
Mary is a lady bright: *Whittaker*
Mary, Mary Magdalen: *Tate, P.*†
Mary Morison: *Center*; *Scott, F.G.*; *Sullivan*
Mary of Allendale: *Hook*
Mask: *Beamish*†
Mask of Pity, The: *Thomas, Mansel*

252 Index of titles

Masque of Squires, The: *Coprario*
Master Kilby: *Britten*†
Master Plan: *Hoddinott*
Masters in this hall: *Holst*
Mater ora filium: *Wood, C.*†
Matin Song: *Bullard* (Morning Song)
Matthew, Mark, Luke and John: *Jeffreys, J.*
Matron Cat's Song, The: *Head*
Maud: *Somervell*
Maud Gonne: *Thomas, Mansel*
Maud has a garden of roses: *Somervell*
Maureen: *Roberton*
Maxims of St Teresa: *Pike*
Maxims of St Teresa: *Pike*
May: *Sutherland*
May Day Carol: *Stevens, B.*
May Lilies: *O'Neill*
May the mind: *Cox, B.*†
May-dew: *Bennett, W.S.*
Mayfair Cinderella: *Ketèlby*
Mayo Love Song, A: *Harty*
Maypole, The: *Swinstead*
Maypole is up, The: *Greaves, R.*
Me, me, and none but me: *Dowland*
Me soui mesoco danso: *Bax**
Me suis mise en danse: *Hopkins, A.**
Mea Culpa: *Blyton**
Medieval Carol: *Hoddinott*
Medieval French Songs: *Crosse*†
Meditation [Dowson]: *Scott, C.*
Meditation [Thompson]: *Thompson, P.*†
Meditation for his Mistress, A: *Maconchy*
Meditation in Winter: *Joubert*
Meditation on the Light: *Tavener*†
Meditations: *Dorward*†
Medium, The (monodrama): *Maxwell Davies*†
Medley of Nursery Rhymes and Conundrums, A (cycle): *Holloway*
Meeting, The: *Bantock*
Meeting at Night: *Somervell*
Megan: *Novello*
Megan's Daughter: *Thomas, Mansel*(†)
Melancholie: *Wilby**
Melancholy [Fletcher]: *Goossens*
Melancholy [Thomas]: *Hedges*
Melancholy Lay, A: *Bennett, R.R.*
Melancholy Song, A: *Hopkins, A.*
Melisande, the Far-away Princess: *Dring*
Melmillo: *Carey, C.*
Melodies you sing, The: *Shaw*
Melon, The: *Hugill*
Melon-seller, The: *Bantock*
Memorare: *Hugill*†
Memorials of Sleep: *Grange*†
Memories: *Rose*
Memories from Underwater: *Foreman*
Memories of Yesterday: *Wood, Haydn*
Memories with dusk return: *Bantock*
Memory [Blake]: *Ireland* (Dream Valley)
Memory [Browne]: *Raphael*
Memory, A [Anon]: *White, M.V.*
Memory, A [Labé]: *Berkeley, L.*,
Memory, hither come: *Busch* (Dream Valley / Memory [Blake]
Memory Island: *Harrison, J.*
Memory of Liverpool: *Pope*
Men walking into the trees: *Pope*
Menelaus: *Vaughan Williams*

Menschenbeifall: *Britten**
Merchant's Song, A: *Treharne*
Merciful God, think on the souls: *Handel*†
Merciful Town: *Grainger, P.*
Merciless Beauty: *Vaughan Williams*(†)
Merciless Beauty: *Bush, G.*; *Harrison, J.*
Merlin's Song: *Crocker*
Mermaid, The [Anon]: *Vignoles*
Mermaid, The [Grainger]: *Grainger, E.*
Mermaid and two other Water Songs, The: *Vignoles*
Mermaid of Purt-le-Murrey: *Pike*
Mermaid's Song: *Scott, C.*
Merrily to Bethlehem: *Bax*
Merrow Down: *German*
Merry Christmas: *Shaw*
Merry Eye: *Jeffreys, J.*
Merry Green Wood, The: *Moeran*
Merry Margaret as midsummer flower: *Elwyn-Edwards*; *Howells*; *Parry, C.H.H.*
Merry Month of May, The: *Ireland*; *Keel*; *Moeran*; *Stanford* (O, the month of May)
Merry Wanderer, The: *Shaw*
Merry Wife, The: *Cannon*(†)
Message, The: *Brian*
Message to Phillis, A: *Stanford* (Ye little birds that sit and sing)
Messenger, The: *Someren-Godfery*
Metronome: *Alwyn*
Metropolitan Railway, The: *East*
Middle of Life, The: *Britten*
Middlesex: *East*
Midnight: *Gibbs, Armstrong*
Midnight Lamentation: *Venables*
Midnight on the Great Western: *Britten*
Midsummer Wish, The: *Arnold, S.*(†); *Hurlstone*
Might I in thy sight appear: *Wesley, C.*†; *Wesley, S.*
Mighty thoughts of an old world, The: *Berkeley, L.*
Migildi Magildi: *Thomas, Mansel*
Mignonette: *Harty*
Migratory Birds at Sennen: *Bruce*
Mihrab Shah: *Bantock*
Mild is the parting year: *Dieren*
Milking Sian, A: *Bax*
Milkmaid, The: *Jeffreys, J.* (Little Milkmaid, The)
Milkmaids: *Warlock*
Milkmaid's Song, The: *Stanford*
Milkwort and Bogcotton: *Scott, F.G.*
Mill at Trefin, The: *Hughes-Jones*
Miller of Dee: *Britten* (There was a jolly miller / Jolly Miller, The)
Miller's Song, The: *Matthias*(†); *Thomas, Mansel*
Mill-Water, The: *Pickard*
Mine Own Country: *Somervell*
Mine Own Sweet Jewel: *Cruft*
Minguillo: *Coleridge-Taylor*
Mingulay Boat Song: *Roberton*
Mini Songcycle for Gina, A: *Tavener*
Minion Wife, A: *Slater*
Minstrel, The: *Delius*
Minstrel boy to the war has gone, The: *Britten*; *Hughes, Herbert*
Mirabile Misterium (cycle): *Bush, G.*(†)
Mirage: *Joseph*(†)
Mirage [Collins]: *Collins, J.H.*
Mirage [Rossetti, C.]: *Joseph*(†)
Mirage [Watson]: *Scott, C.*
Mirages: *Alwyn*

Index of titles 253

Miranda: *Lord, R.* (Inn, The)
Miscellany of Songs, A: *Purcell, H.*
Misconception: *Bax*
Miserere: *Nyman*†
Miss Cherry: *Fiske*
Miss T: *Howells*
Mistake me not, I am as cold as hot: *Brewer*
Mr Belloc's Fancy: *Warlock*
Mr Kartoffel: *Roe*
Mr Tom Narrow: *Roe*
Mrs Dyer, the Baby Farmer: *Moeran*
Mrs MacQueen: *Howells*
Mistletoe [Causley]: *Bush, G.*
Mistletoe [de la Mare]: *Berkeley, L.*; *Gibbs, Armstrong*; *Lodge*
Mistress Fell: *Burrows*
Mistress Mine: *Walthew* (O mistress mine / Sweet and Twenty)
Mistress Wang: *Bantock*
Mit Brief und Uhr: *Birtwistle*†
Mit deinen blauen Augen: *Delius**; *Stanford**
Mither's Lament, The: *MacDonald*
Mittagsruh: *Smyth**
Mitylene Mosaics: *Beat*†
Mixed Bag: *Blyton*
Mixon Bell, The: *Treharne*
Mockery: *Warlock* (Cuckoo, The {Shakespeare} / When daisies pied)
Moderate Sinner, The: *Jones, S.L.*
Modest and fair: *Elgar*
Modest Question, The: *Russel*
Model Models: *Dring*
Moe sartse: *Hiscocks, W.*†
Molly Branigan: *Stanford*
Molly Green of Maldon Town: *Bantock*
Molly-O: *Rowley*
Moment of Farewell, A: *Parry, C.H.H.*
Momento: *Northcott*†
Mon bras pressait la taille frêle (Les Contemplations): *Dieren**
Mon chemin c'était assombri: *Goossens**
Mon cœur se recommande à vous: *Dieren**
Mon rêve familier: *Wilby**
Monday, Tuesday: *Hughes, Herbert*
Money, O: *Head*
Monkey Day, The: *Pike*
Monkey Music: *Pike*
Monkey Sailors, The: *Pike*
Monkey's Carol, The: *Stanford*
Monk's Fancy, The: *Moeran*
Monody for Corpus Christe: *Birtwistle*†
Monopoly: *Moult*
Moo-Lee Flower, The: *Bantock*
Moon, The [Macrae]: *Benjamin,*
Moon, The [Shelley]: *Cooke*†
Moon at the Full, The: *Ronald*
Moon Complaining, The: *Bury*
Moon has a face like a clock, The: *Turnbull*
Moon has set, The: *Bantock*
Moon Magic: *Gibbs, Armstrong*; *Parke*
Moon Maiden's Song, The: *Bantock*
Moon Monkey, The: *Pike*
Moon returns in saffron drest, The: *Shield*
Moonlight: *Quilter*
Moonlight Night, A: *Bowen*
Moon's goin' down: *Finnissy*†
Moonsongs: *McGuire*†
Moonstruck: *Scott, F.G.*

Moore's Irish Melodies: *Britten*
Mopsa: *Stanford* (My Mopsa is little)
More love or more disdain I crave: *Purcell, H.*
More Songs in Exchange: *Newson*
More Songs of the Countryside: *Head*
More sweet is that name: *Handel*
Moresques: *Blyton*†
Morgan le Fay: *Bantock*
Morning [Malvery]: *Hurlstone*
Morning [Teschemacher]: *Ronald*
Morning, The: *Arne, T.*
Morning and Afternoon: *Roe*
Morning Dissertation, *Hudes*†
Morning Glory [Sassoon]: *Rootham*
Morning glory climbs above my head, The: *Nieman*; *Steptoe*(†)
Morning Hymn, A (Thou wakeful shepherd): *Purcell, H.*
Morning in Bengal: *Kirkwood*
Morning is only: *Britten*(†)
Morning Mist: *Hearne*†
Morning Song: *Quilter* (Matin Song)
Morning Star: *Delius*
Morning-Watch, The: *Headington*
Morpheus, thou gentle god of soft repose: *Purcell, D.*
Morris the Wind: *Elwyn-Edwards*
Mors Janua Vitae: *Gibbs, Armstrong*
Mortal Glance, The: *Branson* (Why canst thou not as others do)
Morwenstow: a dialogue: *Bush, G.*
Most holy night, that still dost keep: *Gurney* (Night, The)
Most men do love the Spanish wine: *Anon*
Most Wonderful: *Martin, E.*
Motet One: *Crosse**
Motet Two: *Crosse**
Moth, The: *Berkeley, L.*†
Mother, The: *McCabe*
Mother and Child [Rossetti, C.]: *Ireland*
Mother and Child [Tagore]: *Hiscocks, W.*(†)
Mother and Child, The: *Parry, J.*
Mother and Son: *Tann*†
Mother Carey: *Keel*
Mother, I will have a husband: *Jacob*
Mother of Mesolonghi, The: *Papastávrou*
Mother Shipton's Wooing: *Stevens, B.*
Motion and Stillness: *Vaughan Williams*
Mound Burial, The: *Standford*†
Mountain Stream, The: *Thomas, D.V.*
Mountain Voices: *Treharne*
Mountainfall : *Finnissy*†
Mountains of Allah, The (cycle): *Geehl*
Mountebank's Song, The: *Wishart*
Mourn, day is with darkness fled: *Dowland*
Mourn, Marcus, mourn: *Cavendish*
Mourn no moe: *Warlock*(†) (Weep no more, nor sigh nor groan)
Mouse [Dyment]: *Roe*†
Mouse, The [Macrae]: *Benjamin, A.*
Mouse Metamorphosed into a Maid, The: *Goehr*†
Move: *Hayes*
Move eastward, happy earth: *Browne*
Move now with measured sound: *Campion*
Movement and Stillness: *Naylor, P.*
Mozart on Mortality: *Nyman*†
Muera yo: *Gerhard**
Mugger's Song, The: *Howells*
Murder of Father Hanratty, The: *Moeran*

254 Index of titles

Muse of Love, A: *Dalby*(†)
Muse of the golden throne: *Bantock*
Muses Gardin for Delights, The: *Jones, R.*
Musette: *O'Neill*
Museum, The: *Standford*†
Music [Anon]: *Branson*
Music [Shelley]: *Elton*; *Quilter*
Music and Moonlight: *Quilter*
Music for a while shall all your cares beguile: *Purcell, H.*
Music for Albion Moonlight: *Bedford*†
Music that brings sweet sleep (cycle): *Stoker*
Music that Her Echo is: *Bennett, R.R.*
Music that love made, The: *Hamilton, J.*
Music, thou soul (queen) of heaven: *Anon* (To Music)
Music Tree, The: *Roe*
Music, when soft voices die: *Birkett*; *Bridge*†; *McLeod*; *Matthews, E.E.*; *Quilter*; *Steptoe*; *Thomas, Muriel*; *Warlock*
Musical Chairs: *Roe*
Musicall Dreame, A: *Jones, R.*
Musing on the roaring ocean: *Bennett, W.S.*
Musings: *Moult*
Must I go bound and you go free: *Hughes, Herbert*
Must she go? *Kirkwood*(†)
Must then a faithful lover go? *Eccles*
Must your fair inflaming eye? *Anon*
Musumë's Song, The: *Bantock*
My Ain Folk: *Lemon*
My aunt she died a month ago: *Hughes, Herbert*
My bed and pillow are cold: *MacCunn*
My Bed is a Boat: *Turnbull*; *Williamson, M.*
My beloved is mine (Canticle I): *Britten*
My beloved spake: *McPhee*; *Self, A.*
My Blodwen, my darling: *Parry, J.*
My bonnie, bonnie boy: *Boyle, R.*
My bonny labouring boy: *Hughes, Herbert*
My bonny lass she smileth: *Thiman*
My Bower: *Rowley*
My Boy Jack: *Roe*
My Boy Willie: *Boyle, R.*
My Captain: *Scott, C.*
My Cats: *Bush, G.*
My child is my treasure: *Hughes, Herbert*
My Compass: *Hayes*
My complaining is but feigning: *Jones, R.*
My country's hills of gold: *Davies, T.V.*
My dear: *Bryan*
My dear, my Amphitrite (Fair and Serene): *Weldon* (*Purcell, H.*)
My Doll: *Coleridge-Taylor*
My fair, no beauty of thine will last: *Ireland*; *Pope*
My Fairy Lover: *Bantock*
My Faithful Fond One: *Grainger, P.*
My father fain would have me take: *Jones, R.*
My fidil is singing: *Peterkin*
My Garden: *Roe*
My girdle I hung on a tree-top tall: *Bax*
My Girl and I: *Clarke, R.C.*
My God! look on me: *Berkeley, L.*† (Ejaculation to God)
My God, why hast thou forsaken me: *Wishart*
My gostly fader, I me confess: *Warlock*(†) (Kiss, The [d'Orleans])
My grandfather died and I didn't know how: *Ferguson*
My grief on the sea: *Trimble*
My heart adorned with thee: *Quilter*

My Heart and Lute: *Bishop*
My heart and tongue were twins: *Dowland*
My heart, I fancied it was over: *Britten*(*)
My heart is ev'ry beauty's prey: *Croft*(†)
My heart is like a singing bird: *Dring*; *Parry, C.H.H.* (Birthday, A)
My heart is sair for Somebody: *Atkinson, G.*; *Center*
My heart, whenever you appear: *Purcell, H.*
My heavy sprite: *Holborne*
My Hoggie: *Britten*
My Jean: *Horder*
My kind of day: *Fouché*
My Kingdom: *White, A.*
My Lady [Anon]: *Jeffreys, J.* (And yet I love her till I die / Passing By / There is a lady sweet and kind / Yet will I love her till I die)
My lady [Weatherly]: *German*
My Lady [Williams]: *Siôn*
My Lady Greensleeves: *Quilter* (Greensleeves)
My lady is a pretty one: *Warlock*† (My little pretty one / My lytell prety one / My pretty honey one)
My Lady Lothian's Lilt: *Maxwell Davies*†
My Lady Sleeps: *Scott, C.*
My Lady's Garden: *Quilter*
My Lagan Love: *Harty*
My land: *Williams, W.M.*
My leman is so true: *Holst*†
My life has crept so long: *Somervell*
My Life's Delight: *Quilter*
My lips shall speak the praise: *Greene*
My little pretty one: *Jeffreys, J.*(†) (My lady is a pretty one / My lytell prety one / My pretty honey one)
My little sweet darling, my comfort and joy: *Warlock*(†) (Cradle Song (*Byrd*))
My lodging is on the cold ground: *Grainger, P.*
My Lord has gone away to serve the king: *Whittaker*
My Love: *Coleridge-Taylor*
My love bound me with a kiss: *Jones, R.*
My love could walk: *Tate, P.*
My love doth love the bees: *Rowley*
My love has a garden: *Jones, W.B.*
My love hath her true love betrayed: *Jones, R.*
My Love I Miss You So: *Mordish*
My love in her attire doth show her wit: *Blyton*; *Joubert*; *Walton*(†)
My love is a flower but I do not know her: *Stanford*
My love is as a fever, longing still (Sonnet 147) [Shakespeare]: *Wills*
My love is dark: *Hughes, Herbert*
My love (luve) is like a red, red rose: *Anon* (Farewell, A [Burns] / O my love is like a red, red rose / Red, Red Rose, A)
My love is like the flowers of the year: *Thomas, Mansel*
My love is neither young nor old: *Jones, R.*
My love is to the light of lights: *Stevenson*
My love, oh, she is my love: *Hughes, Herbert*
My love passed me by: *Moeran*
My love she's but a lassie yet: *Center*
My loved one's grave: *Davies, Walford*(†)
My lovely Celia, heavenly fair: *Munro* (Celia the Fair)
My love's an arbutus: *Stanford*
My luve (love) is like a red, red rose: *Scott, F.G.* (Farewell, A [Burns] / O my love is like a red, red rose / Red, Red Rose, A)
My Lydia adores me, I know: *Hughes, Herbert*

Index of titles

My lyttell prety one: *Anon* (My lady is a pretty one / My little pretty one / My pretty honey one)
My Mary dear, farewell: *MacCunn*
My Master hath a garden: *Jeffreys, J.*; *Miles*; *Thiman*
My mistress frowns when she should play: *Jeffreys, J.*(†)
My mistress is as fair as fine: *Brown, C.*
My Mopsa is little, my Mopsa is brown: *Turnbull* (Mopsa)
My Mother's Picture: *Hughes, J.*
My Music, my Songs: *Race*
My Name is Tian: *Boyd*†
My Native Highland Home: *Bishop*
My Native Hills: *Bishop*
My old tunes are rather broken: *Elgar*
My op'ning eyes are purg'd: *Anon (Purcell, H.)*
My Own Country: *Raynor*; *Warlock*
My own dear love: *Horder*
My own heart: *Smith Brindle*†
My own true love: *Fouché*
My peace is gone: *Seiber*
My pent-up tears oppress my brain: *Bridge*
My pretty honey one: *Jeffreys, J.* (My lady is a pretty one / My little pretty one / My lytell prety one)
My prime of youth is but a frost of cares: *Naylor, P.*(†) (Written on the Eve of Execution)
My proper Bess: *Dring*
My rising spirits thronging: *Storace*
My sang (song) is in sighing: *Oldham*
My second thoughts: *Dickinson*
My Shadow: *White, A.*
My Song: *Hiscocks, W.*(†)
My song (sang) is in sighing: *Dalby*(†)
My song is of the sturdy north: *German*
My song shall be of mercy and judgment: *Kent*
My soul has nought but fire and ice: *Holst*†
My Star: *Bantock*; *Somervell*
My Star of Love: *Ketèlby*
My sweet sweeting: *Williams, Gerrard* (Oh, my sweeting / Piggesnie)
My sweetest Lesbia, let us live and love: *Campion*
My Sword for the King: *Head*
My thoughts are winged with hopes: *Dowland*
My thread is spun: *Anon*
My true love hath a garden: *Montgomery*
My true love hath my heart and I have his: *Bush, G.*; *Cowen*; *Dring*; *Holst*; *Ireland*; *Keel*; *C.H.H. Parry*; *Plumstead*; *Thomas, Muriel*; *Tomlinson* (Love Song [Sidney] / Bargain, The)
Myfanwy: *Parry, J.*
Myndlaus: *Hearne**
Mynydd Bodafon: *Hoddinott*
Myrtles of Damascus: *Woodforde-Finden*
Myself when young: *Lehmann*
Mystery, The: *Roberts, C.*
Mystery, The [Hodgson]: *Rubbra*†
Mystery's Song (I am come to lock all fast): *Purcell, H.*

N

Nach neuen Meeren: *Delius**
Nächlich geschürzt: *Nyman**
Nacht: *Birtwistle*†
Nachtgedanken: *Smyth**
Nachtlied: *Harvey*†

Nachtreiter: *Smyth**
Naiad: *Pitfield*
Naiad, The: *Bantock*
Name Unknown: *Hearne*
Nameless Doon, The: *McCabe*
Nanny: *Samuel, H.*
Naples Bay: *Noble, H.*
Narcissus: *Joubert*
Nature framed thee sure for loving: *Eccles*
Nature's Friend: *Head*
Nautch Girl, The: *Bantock*
Nay, but you who do not love her: *Somervell*
Nay, nay: *Someren-Godfery*
Near Woodstock Town: *Grainger, P.*
Nearer, my God, to thee: *Carey, L.*
Nearing the upper air: *Burgon*†
Neglected moon, romance and you: *Gibbs, Armstrong*
Neglectful Edward: *Thackray*
Neither sighs, nor tears, nor mourning: *Lanier*
Nemea: *Routh*
Nettle: *Greaves, Terence*†
Neutral Tones: *Maw*†
Never forgetting thee: *Williams, C.*
Never let me see you suffer: *Muldowney*
Never look back: *Fulton*
Never love unless you can: *Campion*
Never more, sailor: *Peterkin*
Never the time and the place: *Bantock*
Nevermore: *Wilby**
New Brooms: *Jeffreys, J.*
New Corn: *Dalby*
New Ghost, The: *Vaughan Williams*
New Hampshire: *Adès*; *Pope*
New Little Visitor, A: *Samuel, H.*
New Mistress, The: *Foss*
New Moon, The: *Scott, C.*
New moon's silver sickle, The: *Bantock*
New World, The (cycle) *Crosse*
New Year's Carol, A: *Brown, C.*
New Year's Eve, 1913: *Somers-Cocks*
New-blown rose a message brings, A: *Dieren*
Newborn: *Ireland*
Next Market Day, The: *Hughes, Herbert*
Next Minute, The: *Pope*
Next winter comes slowly: *Purcell, H.*
Niarbyl Bay: *Pike*
Nicoletta: *Harrison, P.*
Night [Alcman]: *Pilkington, M.* (Nocturne [Alcman])
Night [Bantock, R]: *Bantock*
Night [Celan]: *Birtwistle*†
Night [Chinese tr. Kotewall & Smith]: *Steptoe*
Night [Chinese tr. Lai]: *Blyton*
Night [Soyinka]: *Samuel, R.*†
Night [Stevenson]: *Stanford*
Night (Oh lovely night) [Teschemacher]: *Ronald*
Night, The (Belloc): *Gill*; *Rubbra*; *Warlock* (Most holy night)
Night Clouds: *Scott, S.*
Night covers up the rigid land: *Berkeley, L.*; *Britten*
Night in November: *Downes*†
Night in the Garden: *Thomas, V.*
Night is come, The: *Burgon*†
Night is freezing fast, The: *Andrews*
Night is no more: *Britten*(†)
Night lies on the silent highways: *Bridge*
Night of Sorrow, The: *Redman*
Night of Trafalgar, The: *Gurney* (Trafalgar)
Night on the Mountain: *Bantock*

256 Index of titles

Night Piece, A [Andrade]: *Someren-Godfery*
Night Piece, (The) [Herrick]: *Dyson; Quilter* (To Julia)
Night Ride: *Crossley-Holland*
Night Rider, The: *Treharne*
Night Song [Cornford]: *Hugh-Jones*
Night Song [Watson]: *Scott, C.*
Night Thought on Terrace Tower, A: *Rubbra*†
Night Thoughts: *Darlow*
Night Wind [Hooley]: *Scott, C.*
Night Wind, The: *Butterworth, A.*†
Night-bird, The: *Somervell*
Nightfall: *Gibbs, Armstrong*
Nightfall at Sea: *Phillips, M.*
Nightfall in Winter: *Parry, C.H.H.*
Nightingale, The: *Samuels*
Nightingale, The [Anon]: *Barton*†
Nightingale, The [Kjerulf]: *Delius*
Nightingale and the Rose, The: *Britten*(*)
Nightingale has a lyre of gold, The: *Delius* (Song of the Blackbird)
Nightingale Near the House, The: *Hugh-Jones*
Nightingales, The: *Crossley-Holland*
Nightingale's Song, The: *Bantock*
Nightmare: *Britten*
Nightmare Giant, The: *Bantock*
Nightpiece [Baudelaire]: *Bennett, R.R.*†
Nightpiece [Joyce]: *Dieren*
Nightshade: *Lyall*
Nine Favourite Soprano Songs: *Lehmann*
Nine Haiku (cycle): *Stevenson* (†)
Nine of the clock, oh: *Gurney*
Nine Settings of Celan: *Birtwistle*†
Nine Settings of Lorine Niedecker (cycle): *Birtwistle*†
Nine Songs: *Bliss*; *Roe*
Nine Stevie Smith Songs: *Lutyens*
Nineteen Songs: *Delius*
1915: *Harrington*
Nipson: *Taverner*†
Nirvana: *Adams*
No: *Shaw*
No Answer: *Sullivan*
No candle was there and no fire: *Lehmann*
No constancy in man: *Lawes, H.*
No flower that blows is like this rose: *Linley Snr*
No Glints in it: *Hayes*
No, I'm not afraid: *McLeod*
No longer mourn for me (Sonnet 71) [Shakespeare]: *Parry, C.H.H.*
No more his fears alarming: *Storace*
No more shall meads be decked with flowers: *Lanier*
No more the dear lovely nymph: *Blow*
No need to tell me (cycle): *Garton*
No, no, fair heretic, it cannot be: *Lawes, H.*
No, no, fair heretic, it needs must be: *Lawes, W.*
No, no, Nigella: *Swinstead*
No, no, no, it must not be: *Hook*
No, not more welcome: *Hughes, Herbert*
No one cares less than I: *Pickard*
No room at the inn: *Fulton*
No Solution: *Hudes*†
No Swan so Fine: *Rubbra*
No sweeter life: *Wilson, H.L.*
Noah: *Morgan, H.*
Noah's Prayer: *Hedges*
Noble Numbers: *Roe*(†)
Noble of air: *Parry, C.H.H.*
Noch ein Mal: *Delius**

Noches, noches: *Anderson, A.*†
Nocturnal: *Brown, C.*†
Nocturne [Alcman]: *Rubbra* (Night [Alcman])
Nocturne [Anon]: *Redman*
Nocturne (Now thro' nights caressing grip) [Auden]: *Britten*
Nocturne [Bantock, R.]: *Bantock,*
Nocturne [Ledwidge]: *Head*
Nocturne [Li Po]: *Lambert, C.*; *Redman*
Nocturne [Raine]: *Bliss*; *Darlow*
Nocturne [Thomas, Dylan]: *Pope*
Nocturne [Watson]: *Scott, C.*
Nocturne [Whitman]: *Vaughan Williams*
Nocturne, A [Blunt]: *Brown, J.*
Nocturnes: *Cooke*†; *Hill*†
Nocturnes for Voice: *Darlow*
Nod: *Gibbs, Armstrong*; *Pilling*; *Wegener* (Road of Evening, The)
Noël: *Elwyn-Edwards*
Noel [Belloc]: *Turner*
Noel [Kirwan]: *Brook*
Noiseless patient spider, A: *Knussen*
Non nobis, Domine: *Doyle**
None so sweet: *Roberton*
None will know: *Ronald*
Non-pareil, The: *Boyce*
Nonsense Rhymes: *Stanford*
Nonsense Song: *Bush, G.*
Noon: *Milner*
Noonday: *Kleyn*
Noon's Repose, The: *Holloway*†
Noon-tide Lullaby, A: *Owen*
Nor com'st thou yet, my slothful love: *Lanier*
Nor we to her of him: *Holloway*†
Norah O'Neale: *Hughes, Herbert*
Norse Lullaby, A: *O'Neill*
North Country Songs: *Williamson, M.*
North Wind doth blow, The: *Woolrich*(†)
Northern Ballad: *Grainger, P.*
Northumberland: *Jeffreys, J.*
North-West Passage: *Coates, L.*
Not all my torments: *Purcell, H.*
Not even summer yet: *Britten*
Not full twelve years twice told: *Ford, T.*
Not heav'n itself: *Wesley, S.*
Not the soft sighs: *Bishop*
Not to be born: *Horder*
Not Winter yet: *Hudes*†
Not yet: *Torphichen*
Nothing like grog: *Dibdin*
Nothing-at-all!: *Barratt*
Nous étions trois filles: *Rawsthorne**
November: *Greaves, Terence*†
Novembre: *Creswell**
Now [Browning]: *Bantock*
Now [Causley]: *Roe*†
Now all is ready for Pentecost: *Crossley-Holland*
Now are the hills born new: *Moult*
Now cease my wandering eyes: *Dowland*
Now Cupid, look about thee: *Robinson, T.*
Now hath Flora robbed her bowers: *Campion*
Now I see thy looks were feigned: *Ford, T.*
Now in these fairylands: *Holst*
Now is the month of maying: *Harty*; *Watkins*†
Now is the time for the burning of the leaves (Winter [Binyon]): *Hedges*
Now is the time of Christemas: *Jeffreys, J.*
Now is your turne: *Berkeley, L.*†

Index of titles

Now let her change and spare not: *Pilkington, F.*
Now, O now I needs must part: *Dowland*
Now, O now in this brown land: *Goossens*; *Hedges*; *Moeran* (Autumn [Joyce])
Now Phoebus sinketh in the west: *Arne, T.*
Now praise we the famous men: *Jones, W.B.*
Now, Robin, laugh and sing: *Peerson*
Now she is like the white tree-rose: *Naylor, B.*
Now sleeps the crimson petal: *McLeod*; *Quilter*; *Sagar*; *Thiman*
Now that the sun has veiled his light (Evening Hymn, An [Fuller]): *Purcell, H.*
Now the leaves are falling fast: *Britten*
Now the lusty spring is seen: *Bush, G.*
Now thro' night's caressing grip (Nocturne) [Auden]: *Britten*
Now welcome, summer: *Short*†
Now what is love I pray thee tell? *Jones, R.*
Now while we dance: *Hudes*
Now winter's nights enlarge: *Darlow*
Now wolde I fain some merthes make: *Jeffreys, J.*; *Williams, Gerrard*
Now ye Springe is come: *Anon*
Nowhere: *Caradon*†
Nuages: *Delius**
Nuer Love Song: *Newson*
Null do dh'Uidhist: *Roberton**
Nun gaudet Maria: *Whittaker*
Nunc dimittis [Prayer Book]: *Burgon*†
Nunc dimittis [Book of Job]: *Hugill*†
Nunc, lento sonitu: *Rainier*†
Nursery Rhyme [Anon]: *Roe*†
Nursery Rhyme [Sarton]: *Bernofsky*
Nursery Rhyme of Innocence and Experience: *Roe*
Nursery Rhymes: *Holloway*†
Nurse's Song [Blake]: *Foss*
Nurse's Song, The: *Britten* (Be still my sweet sweeting / Cradle Song [Philip])
Nut-brown Maid, The: *Howard, S.*
Nutting Time: *Moeran*
Nymph and a swain to Apollo once prayed, A: *Eccles*
Nymphs and shepherds come away: *Purcell, H.*

O

O' a' the airts the wind can blow: *Center*
O, see also Oh
O ay, my wife she dang me: *White, A.*
O blackbird blithe: *Davies, Walford*
O blessed Virgin: *Head*
O can ye sew cushions? *Anon*; *Britten*; *Taylor, C.*
O captain, my captain: *Wood, C.*
O Christ, Saviour of the World: *Papastávrou*
O come, O come, my dearest: *Arne, T.*
O come, soft rest of cares: *Joubert*
O come to my arms: *Kimpton*
O cool is the valley now: *Goossens* (Pleasant Valley, The)
O dear life, when shall it be? *Anon*
O dear, that I with thee might live: *Campion*
O dear, what can the matter be: *Bax*; *Northcote*
O dearest: *Kleyn*
O death, rock me asleep: *Anon*; *Rutter*†
O excellent Virgin Princess: *Rubbra*†
O eyes, leave off your weeping: *Hales*
O eyes, O mortal stars: *Ferrabosco*

O fair dove, O fond dove: *Sullivan*
O fair enough are sky and plain: *Butterworth, G.*; *Orr, C.W.*
O fair, O sweet: *Lyall*
O fair to see: *Finzi*
O, Falmouth is a fine town: *Ronald*; *Shaw*
O, firm as oak: *Bishop*
O flames of passion, will you never die: *Stanford*
O gathering clouds: *Bain, M.K.*
O gentle dove: *Hoddinott*
O gentle love: *Dalby*(†)
O give me the comfort: *Greene*
O gloriosa Domina: *Head**(†)
O glorious golden era: *Grainger, P.*
O God for ever blest: *Church* (Divine Hymn, A)
O good ale: *Jeffreys, J.* (Toper's Song, The)
O grief, e'en on the bud: *Morley*
O, guid ale comes: *White, A.*
O had I Jubal's lyre: *Handel*
O how great is the vexation: *Arne, T.*
O how my thoughts do beat me: *Jones, R.*
O lead me to some peaceful gloom (Bonvica's Song): *Purcell, H.*
O let me me groan one word into your ear: *Lawes, H.*
O let no star compare with thee: *Head*
O let the solid ground: *Somervell*
O like a queen: *Rowley*
O listen to the voice of love: *Hook*
O Lord my God, I will exalt thee: *Nares*
O Lord, rebuke me not in thine anger (Psalm 6): *Rubbra*
O Lord right dear: *Oldham*
O Lord, spread thy wings o'er me: *Lloyd Webber*
O Lord, thou hast searched me out (Psalm 139): *Pike*
O Lord, thy faithfulness and praise: *Bartlet*
O Lord, turn away thy face: *Alison*
O Lord, whose grace no limits comprehend: *Anon*
O love, be deep: *MacNutt*
O love that will not let me go: *Bryan*
O lovely nymph, the world's on fire: *Dring*
O lurcher-loving collier, black as night: *Berkeley, L.*
O lust des beginnens: *Poole**
O Mary dear: *Anon* (Danny Boy / Londonderry Air)
O men from the fields: *Hughes, Herbert* (Cradle Song [Colum] / Mantle of Blue)
O might those sighs and tears return again: *Britten*
O mighty God, who sit'st on high: *Blow*
O mighty judge forbear to frown: *Linley Jnr*
O mistress mine, where are you roaming: *Dale, B.*; *Farrar*; *Finzi*; *Foss*; *Fricker*†; *Fulton*; *Gibbs, Armstrong*; *Harrison, J.*; *Higginson, I.*; *Horder*; *Jeffreys, J.*; *Naylor, P.*; *Parry, C.H.H.*; *Quilter*; *Somervell*; *Stanford*; *Steele*; *Sullivan*; *Tomlinson*; *Wishart* (Mistress Mine / Sweet and Twenty)
O my Clarissa, thou cruel fair: *Lawes, W.*
O my dear heart, young Jesus sweet: *Philips*† (Ane Sang of the Birth of Christ / Balulalow / Cradle Song [Luther] / O my deir hert)
O, my deir hert, young Jesus sweet: *Howells*; *Jeffreys, J.*; *Rubbra*† (Ane Sang of the Birth of Christ / Balulalow / Cradle Song [Luther] / O my dear heart)
O my kitten, a kitten: *Warlock*
O my love, how long have we to suffer: *Seiber*
O my love is like a red, red rose: *Atkinson, G.*; *Diack* (Farewell, The [Burns] / My love (luve) is like a red, red rose / Red, Red Rose, A)

258 Index of titles

O never say that I was false of heart (Sonnet 109) [Shakespeare]: *Parry, C.H.H.*
O never to be moved: *Campion*
O now the drenched land awakes: *Bedford*†
O one deep sacred outlet of my soul: *Stanford*
O peace, thou fairest child of heaven: *Arne, T.*
O perfect love: *Williams, Rhyddid*(†)
O praise the Lord ye angels of his: *Greene*
O precious time: *Peerson*
O quam suave: *Jeffreys, G.**
O rattlin' roarin' Willie: *White, A.* (Rattlin' roarin' Willie)
O ravishing delight: *Arne, T.*
O sacred head: *Self, A.*†
O saving victim: *Rowley*†
O saw ye my dear, my Philly? *White, A.*
O schneller mein Ross: *Delius**
O sleep, why dost thou leave me: *Handel*
O solitude: *Frankel, B.*
O stay, sweet love, see here the place: *Walton*(†)
O swallow, swallow, flying, flying south: *Scott, A.; Somervell*
O sweet content: *Noble, T.T.* (Sweet Content)
O sweet fa's the eve: *Moeran*
O sweet flower: *Coprario*
O tell me love! O tell me fate: *Lawes, H.*
O that I had ne'er been married: *Britten*
O that I knew where I might find him: *Rowley*
O That It Were So: *Bridge*
O that mine eyes could melt into a flood: *Brewer*
O that my ways were made so direct: *Greene*
O that 'twere possible: *Somervell*
O, the bonny fisher lad: *Tate, P.*
O, the month of May: *Bush, G.; Quilter* (Merry Month of May, The)
O the sad day: *Humfrey*†
O the sight entrancing: *Britten*
O this is no my ain lassie: *Center*
O to be in England now that April's here: *Head* (Home Thoughts)
O tuneful voice, I still deplore: *Salomon*
O turn away those cruel eyes: *Lawes, H.*
O turn not those fine eyes away: *Blow*
O waly, waly: *Anon; Britten; Le Fleming* (Waly, Waly)
O wavering fires (scena): *Holbrooke*
O were my love yon lilac fair: *Nash; Scott, F.G.*
O westron winde: *Northcott*†
O Wha's the Bride? *Stevenson*
O what comes over the sea: *Somervell*
O what hath overwrought? *Dowland*
O what unhoped for sweet supply: *Campion*
O whistle and I'll come to ye (you) my lad: *Center; Horder; Musgrave; White, A.*
O Willie brewed a peck o' maut: *Center*
O world, O life, O time: *Parry, C.H.H.*
O ye that love the Lord: *Parry, J.*
O your eyes are dark and beautiful: *Seiber*
Oak Tree, The: *Jones, R.R.*
Obsequy: *Gill*
OCD Band and the Minotaur: *Bedford*†
Ocean Wood, The: *Alwyn*
October: *Morgan, H.*
October: a Haiku Sequence: *Birkett*
October Redbreast, The: *Pope*
October Valley: *Head*
Odalisque, The: *Bantock*
Ode: *Ross*

Ode an die Musik: *Wellesz**
Ode du premier jour du Mai: *Berkeley, L.**
Ode on the Birth of Our Saviour, An: *Taylor, C.V.*
Ode on the Morning: *Hawkins*
Ode, on the Rejection of St Cecilia: *Finzi*
Ode to a Nightingale: *Newson*
Odelette: *Smyth*(*)
O'er the moor: *Grainger, P.*
Of a rose is all my song: *Blake, H.*
Of all the birds that I do know: *Jacob*†
Of all the torments, all the cares: *Blow; Boyce; Parry, C.H.H.*
Of all the tribe of Tegumai: *German*
Of all the youths: *Tate, P.*(†)
Of Ane Blackamoor: *Scott, F.G.*
Of Death: *Hugill*†
Of ev'ry kind of tree: *Short*†
Of gentle Philips will I ever sing: *Taylor, M.*†
Of thee, kind boy, I ask no red and white: *Webb*
Off to Philadelphia: *Haynes*
Off to School: *Papastávrou*(†)
Offerings: *Kleyn*
Oft have I sighed: *Campion*
Oft I'm by the women told: *Leveridge* (Whether I grow old or no)
Oft in the stilly night: *Anon; Biggs; Britten; Somervell*
Oh, breathe not his name: *Hughes, Herbert; Raphael*
Oh could I be: *Hearne*†
Oh do not wanton with those eyes: *P.Young*†
Oh! fair Cedaria, hide those eyes: *Purcell, H.*
Oh fair enough are sky and plain: *Moeran; Orr, C.W.*
Oh fair to See: *Finzi*
Oh fair to see: *Finzi*
Oh, fie, shepherd, fie: *Defesch*
Oh, for a March wind from the hills: *Head*
Oh! glory of full-mooned fairness: *Bantock*
Oh had I Jubal's lyre: *Handel*
Oh holy man of sorrows: *Evans, E.*
Oh let me weep (Plaint, The): *Purcell, H.*
Oh! love – no, love! see Epilogue
Oh lovely night, thou sweet and gentle maiden (Night [Teschemacher]): *Ronald*
Oh my blacke soule! now art thou summoned: *Britten*
Oh, my lonely pillow: *Coleridge-Taylor*
Oh, my sweeting, my little pretty sweeting: *Samuel, H.* (My sweet sweeting / Piggesnie)
Oh, nightingale upon my tree: *Gibbs, Armstrong*
Oh, quand je dors (Les Rayons et les Ombres): *Dieren**
Oh, roses for the flush of youth: *Coleridge-Taylor*
Oh see how thick: *Orr, C.W.; Pope*
Oh shepherdess, the rain's here: *Rawsthorne*
Oh, soft was the song in my soul: *Elgar*
Oh solitude, my sweetest choice: *Purcell, H.*
Oh! take him gently from the pile: *Eccles*
Oh, tell me, nightingale, sweet bird: *Lehmann*
Oh, that I had but a fine man: *Humfrey*
Oh! that mine eyes would melt: *Blow*(†)
Oh, the marriage: *Wood, C.*
Oh! the oak and the ash: *Grainger, P.*
Oh, 'tis sweet to think: *Quilter*
Oh to vex me, contraryes meet in one: *Britten*
Oh what comes over the sea: *Coleridge-Taylor*
Oh, when I was in love with you: *Orr, C.W.; Vaughan Williams*(†)
Oh yet we trust: *Swann*
Old Abram Brown: *Bush, G.*

Old Carol, An: *Quilter* (As dew in April / I sing of a maiden)
Old clothes and fine clothes: *Shaw*
Old Cotilo: *Gerhard*
Old English Melodies: *Wilson, H.L.*
Old English Songs: *Spedding*
Old Fisherman, The (Hay): *Scott, F.G.*
Old Fisherman of the mists and the waters, The: *Bantock*
Old Fisherman with Guitar: *Liddell*
Old French Poet, An: *Morgan, H.*
Old Gaelic Rune: *Penny*
Old Grey Fox, The: *White, M.V.*
Old Harper, The: *Roberton*
Old House, The [de la Mare]: *Howells*
Old House, The [O'Connor]: *O'Connor*
Old Loves: *Scott, C.*
Old Love's Domain: *Downes*
Old Lullaby, An: *Raynor*
Old Lute, The: *Britten*†
Old Man from Kilkenny: *Parke*
Old Meg: *Howells*
Old Minstrel, The: *Evans, D.P.*
Old mother Hubbard she went to the cupboard: *Hely-Hutchinson*; *Jeffreys, J.*
Old Mother Laidinwool: *Shaw*
Old Navy, The: *Stanford*
Old Nurse's Song, The: *Someren-Godfery*
Old Oliver: *Rowley*
Old Rhymes Reset: *Bush, G.*
Old Rugged Cross, The: *Bennard*†
Old Scottish Folksongs: *Goossens*
Old Shepherd's Prayer: *Anderson, W.H.*
Old Sir Faulk, tall as a stork: *Walton*
Old Skinflint: *Howells*
Old Soldier, The: *Hely-Hutchinson*; *Howells*
Old Song Ended, An: *Scott, C.*
Old Song Resung, An: *Martin, E.*
Old Songs in New Guise: *Scott, C.*
Old Stoic, The: *Wills*
Old Stone House: *Howells*
Old Superb, The: *Stanford*
Old Taff River, The: *Hiscocks, H.*
Old Turf Fire, The: *Hughes, Herbert*
Old Wine in New Bottles: *Gibbs, Armstrong*
Old Woman, The: *Roberton*
Old Woman at the Christening: *Grainger, P.*†
Old Woman at the Flower Show, The: *Hugh-Jones*
Old Yew: *Newson*
Olinda in the shades unseen: *Purcell, H.*
Olive Tree: *Holloway*
Oliver Cromwell lay buried and dead: *Britten*
Oliver's Advice: *Wood, C.*
Ollie McGee: *Downes*
Olney Hymns: *Corke*
Olwen: *Treharne*
Omens: *Jeffreys, J.*
Omens of Spring: *Anderson, W.H.*
Omens of Spring: *Anderson, W.H.*
On a bank beside a willow: *Boyce*
On a day, alack the day: *Macfarren*†; *Parry, C.H.H.*
On a Drop of Dew: *Holloway*†
On a Fly Drinking Out of His Cup: *Birkett*
On a grey day: *O'Neill*
On a Lady Singing: *Head*
On a Quiet Conscience: *Playford* (Close thine eyes and sleep secure)
On a Summer Morning: *Somervell*

On a time the amorous Silvy: *Attey*; *Herbert, M.*; *Parry, C.H.H.*
On and on: *Marsh*†
On Buying a Horse: *Weir*
On Cessnock Banks a lassie dwells: *Liddell*
On Cramer's Leaving England (Go, minstrel, go): *Wesley, S.*
On Deck: *Benjamin, A.*
On Duncton Hill: *Gibbs, Armstrong*
On Early Morning: *Steptoe*(†)
On Eastnor Knoll: *Keel*
On Hearing Her Play the Harp: *Rubbra*†
On Jessy Watsons Elopement: *Bennett, R.R.*
On Jhelum River: *Woodforde-Finden*
On Leaving the Summer and Sea: *Hearne*
On Music: *Wesley, S.*
On Newlyn Hill: *Rowley*
On Offa's Back (scena): *Joubert*
On parent knees a naked new-born child: *Finzi*
On receiving news of the war: *Ellis*†
On Richmond Hill there lives a lass: *Hook*
On St John of the Cross: *Pike*
On silent wings: *Mumby*
On Stellar Magnitudes: *Ferneyhough*†
On Suicide: *Muldowney*(†)
On the Banks of Jo-Eh: *Bantock*
On the Bridge: *Bax*
On the brow of Richmond Hill: *Purcell, H.*
On the City Street: *Lambert, C.*
On the Cliff: *Somervell*
On the Death of Manolette: *Williamson, M.*
On the deep-blue-girdled heaven: *Stanford*
On the Downs: *Gurney*
On the Hill: *Sullivan*
On the idle hill of summer: *Butterworth, G.*; *Gurney*(†); *Somervell*
On the Lilies: *Lawes, W.*
On the merry first of May: *Howells*
On the Reed of Our Lord's Passion: *Rubbra*†
On the Seashore, *Thomas, Mansel*
On the way to Kew: *Butterworth, G.*(†)
On the wings of the wind: *Head*
On this bleak hut: *Grange*†
On This Island: *Britten*
On thy blue eyes reposing: *Stanford*
On Time: *Wellesz*
On Time: *Wellesz*
On Wenlock Edge: *Vaughan Williams*(†)
On Wenlock Edge the wood's in trouble: *Pope*; *Vaughan Williams*(†)
On your midnight pallet lying: *Gurney*; *Orr, C.W.*
Onaway, awake, beloved: *Coleridge-Taylor*
Once and there was a young sailor: *Peterkin* (Andy Battle)
Once did my thoughts both ebb and flow: *Jones, R.*
Once in a garden lovely: *Clarke, R.C.*
Once in a while: *Le Fleming*
Once upon a time: *Roe*
Once very long ago: *Greaves, R.*
One charming night (Secresy's Song): *Purcell, H.*
One day I wrote her name upon the strand: *Newson*
One Foot on Sea and One on Shore: *Joseph*(†)
One golden thread: *Parry, C.H.H.*
One Hope, The: *Ireland*
One man, two men: *Vaughan Williams*
One More River: *Warlock*
One morning in May: *Wood, C.*
One morning in the flower garden: *Fogg*

One must always have love: *Hoddinott*
One night as I did wander: *White, A.*
One Pearl: *Bauld*
One silent night of late: *Parry, C.H.H.*
One struggle more, and I am free: *Clarke-Whitfield*
One, two, three [Elfed]: *Thomas, Mansel*
One, two, three [Traditional]: *Parry, W.H.*
One word is too often profaned: *Quilter* (To...)
Only Child, The: *Ireland*
Only the wanderer knows England's graces: *Finzi* (Severn Meadows)
Ophelia's Song: *Maconchy*; *White, M.V.* (How should I your true love know?)
Or you, or I, nature did wrong: *Lawes, H.*
Ora pro nobis: *Williams, M.*
Oracle [Brontë]: *Joubert*
Oracle [Scott]: *Scott, C.*
Oracle Beach: *Beamish*†
Orbits: *Owen*
Orcadian Calendars: *Forshaw*(†)
Orchard Sings to the Child, The: *Gibbs, Armstrong*
Orchill: *Foulds*
Ordnance Survey: *Usher*†
Organ Grinder's Song, The: *Carey, C.*
Orpheus and Euridice [Anon]: *Boyce*
Orpheus and Euridice [Lisle]: *Tomlinson*
Orpheus with his lute made trees: *Austin*; *Coates, E.*; *Greene*; *Gurney*; *Jacques*; *Linley, W.*; *Procter*; *Quilter*, *Roe*†; *Routh*; *Rubbra*; *Somervell*; *Sullivan*; *Tomlinson*; *Vaughan Williams*; *Westrup*; *Wishart*
Osme's Song: *Scott, C.*
Ossian's Glen: *Barnett*
Otterburn: *Jeffreys, J.*
Ould Lad, The: *Harty*
Our Country's Banner: *Parry, J.*
Our father, who art in heaven: *McLain* (Lord's Prayer, The)
Our Joyful'st Feast: *Steel*
Our Lady of Violets: *Scott, C.*
Our lady weeps: *Someren-Godfery*
Our Lady's: *Procter*
Our Lady's Hours: *Milner*
Our lives: *Finnissy*†
Our Magic Horse: *Alwyn*
Our two souls: *Reizenstein* (Sonnet [Browning, E.B.])
Our world is full of banalities: *Hugill*†
Out and away: *Bax*
Out in the dark over the snow: *Pickard*; *Rubbra*
Out of Danger: *Muldowney*†
Out of deep waters: *Usher*†
Out of the depths: *Bantock*
Out on the lawn I lie abed: *Headington*
Out upon it, I have lov'd: *Lawes, H.*; *Stanford* (Constant Lover, The [Suckling])
Outlaw of Loch Lene, The: *Wood, C.*
Outsong, An: *Holbrooke*
Outward Bound: *Stanford*
Ouzo Unclouded: *Wood, Hugh*
Over the Bridge: *Lloyd Webber*
Over the Heather: *Dickinson*
Over the Hills [Coleridge, M]: *Rootham*
Over the Hills [Dunbar]: *Coleridge-Taylor*
Over the hills and far away [Irvine]: *Parke*
Over the land is April: *Quilter*
Over the mountains: *Quilter*; *Standford* (Love will find out the way)
Over the mountains high: *Delius*

Over the Rim of the Moon: *Head*
Over the water to Charlie: *Mullinar*
Overkill: *Thomas, Mansel*
Overlooking the River: *Finzi*
Owl, The [Tennyson]: *Bullard*; *Cooke*† (When cats run home / White Owl, The)
Owl, The [Sayers]: *Lehmann*
Owl and the Pussy-cat, The: *Hely-Hutchinson*; *White, A.*
Owl is abroad, The: *Smith, J.C.*; *(Purcell, H.)* (Witches' Charms)
Owls: *Lawrence, M.*
Owls, The: *Elwyn-Edwards*
Oxen, The: *Dent*; *Fleming*; *Gibbs, Armstrong*(†); *Vaughan Williams* (Christmas eve, and twelve of the clock)
Oxford Sporting Blade, The: *Moeran*
Oyó sus gritos: *Osborne*†
Oystercatchers: *Pope*
Oyster Catcher's Song, The: *Kirkwood*
Ozymandias: *Bantock*; *Burtch*; *Someren-Godfery*

P

På Stranden (Lyse Nœtter): *Delius*
Pad, pad: *Lutyens*
Padraic the Fidiler: *Gibbs, Armstrong*(†)
Page sat in the lofty tower, The: *Delius*
Pågen højt på Tårnet sad: *Delius**
Pain: *Venables*
Painted Rose, The (cycle): *Howard, M.*
Pair of Shoes: *Edwards, G.*
Pair Well Matched, A: *Ronald*
Palatine Coast, The: *Stevens, B.*
Palatine's Daughter, The: *Peterkin*
Palm Sunday: *Williams, O.*
Pancake Tuesday: *Carter*
Pandemonium: *Hardy*
Pan's Piping: *Bantock*
Parable: *Thomas, Mansel*
Paradigm, The: *MacDonald*
Paradise [Alwyn]: *Alwyn*
Paradise [Khayyam]: *Blyton*
Paradise Street: *Rowley*
Paripace and Paripale: *Pike*
Parle moi: *White, M.V.**
Parrot, The: *Pike*
Parson and Clerk: *Moeran*
Parta Quies: *Wickens*
Parted: *Stanford*
Parting: *Bryan*
Parting [Æ]: *Bax*
Parting [Reynolds]: *Lawes, H.*
Parting, The [Drayton]: *Dring*
Parting, The [Ross]: *Bantock*
Parting, The [Tschung]: *Someren-Godfery*
Parting and Meeting: *Foulds*
Parting Friends: *Maw*
Partridge and Penance: *Pike*
Partridge Pie: *Bennett, R.R.*
Passing, The: *Hughes, A.*
Passing By: *Jeffreys, J.*; *Purcell, E.C.*; *Warlock* (And yet I love her till I die / My Lady / There is a lady sweet and kind / Yet will I love her till I die)
Passing Dreams: *Quilter* (They are not long, the weeping and the laughter)

Index of titles

Passing Stranger, The: *Venables*
Passionate Shepherd, The: *Moeran*; *Warlock* (Come live with me and be my love)
Passionate Trencherwoman, The: *Swann*
Past, The: *Bennett, W.S.*
Pastoral: *Orr, R.*
Pastoral, A (Flocks are sporting): *Carey, H.*
Pastoral Elegy, A: *Blow*
Pastorale: *Bergmann*†; *Peterkin*; *Scott, C.*
Pastora's beauties, when unblown: *Purcell, H.*
Pastourelle: *Arundell**; *Berkeley, L.**
Pastyme with good companye: *Henry VIII*
Patch of Blackened Earth, A: *Finnissy*†
Path to the Moon: *Thiman*
Patrick's Your Boy: *Owen*
Pavilion of Abounding Joy, The: *Bantock*; *Redman*
Paysage: *LeFanu*†
Paysage Triste: *Wilby**
Peace [Hyatt]: *Holst*
Peace [Tagore]: *Fogg*
Peace [Vaughan]: *Headington*
Peace reigned in heaven: *Hudes*
Peace Song, The: *Kennedy*
Peaceful is he, and most secure: *Blow*
Peaceful slumbering on the ocean: *Storace*
Peaceful western wind, The: *Campion*
Peach Flower, The: *Bantock*
Peacock Pie: *Howells*
Peacocks with a Hundred Eyes: *McLeod*
Pearl, a Girl, A: *Bantock*
Pearl and the Rose, The: *Bantock*
Peasants, The: *Thomas, Mansel*
Pedlar of Spells, The: *Dalby*; *Oldham*
Pedlar's Song: *MacCunn*
Peer of gods he seems: *Bantock*
Peewee, The: *Bantock*
Peggy Perkins: *Dibdin*
Penines in April: *Wood, Hugh*
Penny for a Song, A (cycle): *LeFanu*
Penny Whistle, The: *Gurney*
Pentozáles: *Papastávrou*†
Penumbra: *Ireland*
People hide their love: *Berkeley, L.*
Perfection, The: *Blow*
Perhaps there is something: *Hugill*†
Peroration: *Elias*†
Perplexèd music: *Reizenstein*
Persephone: *Holst*
Persian Idylls: *Goossens*
Persian Love Song, A: *Bantock*
Personal Stereo: *Elias*†
Personent hodie: *Holst*†
Persuasions Not to Love: *Lawes, W.*
Persuasions to Enjoy: *Lawes, H.*
Pessimist, The: *Wishart*
Peter the Pumpkin-eater: *Jeffreys, J.*
Peter Warlock's Fancy: *Warlock*
Peterisms: *Warlock*
Phantom, The: *Finzi*
Philander, do not think of arms: *Blow*
Phillida: *Branson*; *Godfrey, G.*
Phillida and Corydon: *Schofield*
Phillida Flouts Me: *Lyall*
Phillis [Anon]: *Young, A.*
Phillis [Drummond]: *Scott, F.G.*
Phillis [Lodge]: *Price*
Phillis has such charming graces: *Young, A.* (Shy Shepherdess, The)

Phillis, I can ne'er forgive it: *Purcell, H.*
Phillis on the new made hay: *Clarke, R.*†
Phillis, talk no more of passion: *Purcell, H.*
Phillis was a fair maid: *Anon*
Philomel [Barnfield]: *Gibbs, Armstrong*; *Goossens* (As it fell upon a day)
Philomel [Shakespeare]: *Harrison, J.* (Ye spotted snakes)
Philomela [Sidney]: *Gibbs, Armstrong*
Philosopher Bird, The (Secret, The): *Crossley-Holland*†
Phoebe: *Stanford*
Phoenix, The: *Pickard*
Piano Bar: *Fouché*
Piano Sings, The: *Nyman*†
Pianoman: *Blyton*
Pibroch, man, the pibroch, The: *Stanford*
Pick-up in Soho: *Hayes*
Picnic, A: *Scott, C.*
Picture me love: *Gibbs, Armstrong*
Picture of a Lover Standing Before his Earthly Judges: *Pike*
Picture-books in Winter: *Higginson, I.*; *White, A.*
Pieces of Eight: *Hamilton, A.*
Pied Beauty: *Pope*
Pierrette in Memory: *Peterkin*
Pierrot and the Moon Maiden: *Scott, C.*
Pietà: *Williamson, M.*†
Pigeons, The: *Bax*
Piggesnie: *Warlock* (My sweet sweeting / Oh, my sweeting)
Piggësnye: *Murrill* (My sweet sweeting / Oh, my sweeting)
Pigs'll fly: *Muldowney*
Pilgrim cranes are moving to their south, The: *Alwyn*; *Scott, C.*
Pilgrim of Love, The: *Bishop*
Pilgrim Way, The: *Pike*
Pilgrimage to Kevlaar (scena): *Stanford*
Pilgrim's Isle, The: *Elwyn-Edwards*
Pilgrim's Psalm, The: *Vaughan Williams*
Pilgrim's Solace, A: *Dowland*
Pillar at Sebzavah, A: *Bantock*
Pillicock Hill: *Rowley*
Pink Frock, The: *Milford*
Pink Roses: *Hearne*
Pious Selinda goes to prayers: *Gibbs, Armstrong*; *Purcell, H.* (Song [Congreve])
Piper, The (Blake): *Vaughan Williams*† (Piping down the valleys wild)
Piper, (A), (The) (O'Sullivan): *Benjamin, A.*; *Crossley-Holland*; *Head*(†); *Peterkin*; *Vaughan Williams* (Piper in the streets today, A)
Piper and the Drummer, The: *Mullinar*
Piper in the streets today, A: *Gurney* (Piper [O'Sullivan])
Piper pipes a merry tune, The: *Thiman*
Pipes of Pan, The: *Elgar*
Piping down the valleys wild: *Brian*; *Cooke*†; *Lord, R.*; *Someren-Godfery*; *Turnbull* (Piper, The [Blake])
Pippa Passes: *Bantock* (Pippa's Song / Year's at the spring, The)
Pippa's Song: *Owen* (Pippa Passes / Year's at the spring, The)
Pippen Hill: *Mullinar*
Pippen Hill: *Jeffreys, J.*; *Mullinar*
Piskies: *Harris, W.L.*
Pizzicato Piccadilly: *Roe*†

262 Index of titles

Place Settings: *Nicholas*
Plague of Love, The (Tout-ensemble, The): *Arne, T.*
Plaint, The (O let me weep): *Purcell, H.*
Plantation Mood: *King, Reginald*
Plantons le Romarin: *Arundell**
Play-acting: *Warlock*
Pleading: *Elgar*
Pleasant Valley, The: *Moeran* (O cool is the valley now)
Pleasing tales in dear romances: *Arne, T.*
Pleasure and Joy: *Fleming*
Pleasure Boat on the Niagara, The: *Parry, J.*
Pleasure it is to hear iwis the birdes sing: *Milford*; *Northcott*† (Thanksgiving, A)
Pleasures, beauty, youth attend thee: *Lawes, W.*
Pleasure's gentle zephyrs play: *Handel*
Pleasures of Spring Gardens, The (Spring Gardens): *Boyce*
Plesant Grounde: *Walters, L.*
Pli de Lin: *Matthews, C.*†
Plot-culture: *Bantock*
Plough-boy, The [Anon]: *Britten*; *Grainger, P.*
Plough-boy, The [Catalan]: *Gerhard*
Ploughman, The [Anon]: *Vaughan Williams*
Ploughman, The [Housman]: *Williamson, J.R.*
Ploughman Singing: *Gurney*
Ploughman's Song, The: *Thiman*
Pluck not the tender flowers: *Henry*†
Pluck this little flower: *Ronald*
Plucking the Rushes: *Dalby*; *Orr, C.W.*; *Orr, R.*
Plum, The: *Hugill*
Plum Blossom Song (Song for a Chinese Play): *Crossley-Holland*†
Plum Tree, The: *Stevenson*
Plumes of Time, The: *Hamilton, A.*
Plumes of Time, The: *Hamilton, A.*
Poacher's Dog, The: *Jeffreys, J.*
Poems for a Child (All About Me): *Austin*
Poems of Tagore, No 1: *Sohal*
Poems of Wallace Stevens II (cycle): *Connolly*†
Poet, The (Bard, The): *Thomas, Mansel*
Poet and the Day, The: *Wellesz*
Poet Nightingale: *Northcott*†
Poet to His Beloved, A: *Senator*
Poetic Image, The: *Swann*
Poetry: *Berkeley, L.*
Poetry of Dress, The: *Blyton*
Poet's Echo, The: *Britten*(*)
Poet's Hymn, A: *Dyson*
Poet's Last Thoughts, A: *Self, A.*
Poet's Life, The: *Elgar*
Poet's Song, The: *Parry, C.H.H.*
Point de Couvent: *Arundell**
Point of Departure (cycle): *Brown, C.*
Poison Apple, A: *Someren-Godfery* (Poison Tree, A)
Poison Tree, (A), (The): *Britten*; *Rodgers*; *Vaughan Williams*† (Poison Apple, A)
Policeman's Song, The: *Sullivan*
Polish Love Song: *Nyman*†
Polly Lilicote: *Bush, G.*
Polly of the Plain: *Defesch*
Polly Willis: *Arne, T.*
Poor beggar's daughter, A: *Grainger, P.*
Poor Henry: *Berkeley, L.*
Poor Mr Snail: *Woolrich*(†)
Poor naked wretches (Invocation): *Usher*
Poor Shepherd, The: *Handel*
Poor soul sat sighing, The: *Anon*; *Findlay* (Willow Song, The [Shakespeare] / Willow, willow)

Poor soul, the centre of my sinful earth (Sonnet 146) [Shakespeare]: *Wills*
Poppies: *Harty*
Poppy [Froom]: *Greaves, Terence*†
Poppy, The [Bridges]: *Miles*†
Poplar and the Moon, (A), (The): *Greaves, R.*; *Morgan, H.*; *Rootham*
Poplars, The: *Moeran*
Popsong: *Senator*
Port of Many Ships: *Keel*
Portrait in a Mirror: *Alwyn*
Portsmouth: *Brown, J.*
Portus: *Butterworth, N.*
Post-scriptum: *Blyton**
Potato Song, The: *Wood, C.*
Pour l'Amour de ma Douce Amye: *Butterworth, N.**
Power of Love, The: *Grainger, P.*
Praise God: *Papastávrou*
Praise of Summer: *Davies, L.*
Praise the Lord, O my soul: *Greene*
Praise ye the Lord (Psalm 150): *Bantock*(†); *Rubbra*
Praised be the Lord: *Greene*
Praises of Heaven and Earth, The: *Johnson, R.S.*†
Pray Goody: *Britten*
Prayer (Sappho): *Hudes*
Prayer, A (Dunbar): *Coleridge-Taylor*
Prayer, A (Jonson): *Rubbra*
Prayer, A (Kingsley): *Scott, C.*
Prayer, A (Newton): *Williams, W.S.G.*
Prayer before Sleep: *Gibbs, Armstrong*; *Saxton*†
Prayer for Heretics, A: *Garton*†
Prayer, for Szymanowski: *Tavener*
Prayer for the Cure of a Strained Back: *Cresswell*†
Prayer of Humble Access: *Hugill*†
Prayer of the Butterfly, The: *Hedges*
Prayer of the Cat, The: *Blyton*; *Hedges*
Prayer of the Cock, The: *Blyton*; *Hedges*
Prayer of the Foal, The: *Hedges*
Prayer of the Goat, The: *Hedges*
Prayer of the Goldfish, The: *Blyton*
Prayer of the Lark, The: *Blyton*
Prayer of the Little Bird, The: *Hedges*
Prayer of the Little Ducks, The: *Hedges*
Prayer of the Mouse, The: *Blyton*
Prayer of the Ox, The: *Blyton*; *Hedges*
Prayer of the Tortoise, The: *Blyton*
Prayer to a Child: *Saxton*†
Prayer to St Anthony of Padua, A: *Warlock*
Prayer to Vishnu: *Bantock*
Prayers from the Ark: *Blyton*; *Hedges*
Preach me not your musty rules: *Arne, T.*
Prelude (no text): *Vaughan Williams*†
Prelude (Simpson): *Ronald*
Prelude (Watson): *Scott, C.*
Prelude 8: *McGuire*†
Premiers Desirs: *Beat**
Pre-Spring: *Hearne*
Pressgang, The: *Moeran*
Pretty Betty: *Rowley*
Pretty Creature, The: *Storace*
Pretty duck there was, A: *Bartlet*
Pretty Girl Milking Her Cow: *Mitchell*†
Pretty Maid Milking Her Cow, The: *Grainger, P.*
Pretty Polly Pillicote: *Mullinar*
Pretty Ring-time: *Bullard*; *Warlock* (It was a lover and his lass / Lover and his Lass, The / Spring Song [Shakespeare] / Sweet and Twenty)
Pretty Washer-maiden, The: *Lloyd Webber*

Price of Experience, The: *Usher*(†)
Pride: *Pike*
Primavera: *Musgrave*†
Primrose, The (Ask me why I send you here): *Lawes, H.*
Primroses deck the bank's green side: *Linley Snr*
Primrosy Gown, The: *Head*
Prince Madoc's Farewell: *Stanford*
Prince of Heaven, The: *Steele*
Princess Helene: *MacCunn*
Principia: *Barrett*
Printemps: *Procter*
Prisoner, The: *Wills*
Procris is lying at the waterside: *Vaughan Williams*
Progression: *Lutyens*
Prologue: *Standford*†
Prologue, Elegy and Epilogue: *McGregor*
Prometheus: *Samuels*
Prophecy, The: *Rowley*
Prospice: *Stanford*
Proud Maisie is in the wood: *Gibbs, Armstrong*; *Parry, C.H.H.*
Proud Songsters: *Bayliss*; *Britten*; *Finzi*
Proud Vesselil: *Grainger, P.*
Providence: *Walters, L.*
Przbiezeli di Betlejem: *Bax**
PS: *Marsh*†
Psalm (Celan): *Birtwistle*†; *Nyman**
Psalm 1 (Blessed is the man): *Butt*(†); *Clements*
Psalm 6 (O Lord, rebuke me not): *Rubbra*
Psalm 23 (Lord is my shepherd, The): *Bantock*; *Rubbra*
Psalm 29 (Give unto the Lord): *Bantock*
Psalm 48 (Great is the Lord): *Bantock*
Psalm 57 (Be merciful unto me): *Head*
Psalm 63 (Psalm of David, A): *Clarke, R.*
Psalm 93 (Lord reigneth, The): *Bantock*
Psalm 91 (Lord is my refuge, The): *Parke*
Psalm 100 (Make a joyful noise): *Head*
Psalm 121 (I will lift up mine eyes): *Head*
Psalm 121 (Song of Trust, A): *Stanford*
Psalm 124 (Song of Battle, A): *Stanford*
Psalm 126 (Song of Freedom, A): *Stanford*
Psalm 130 (Song of Hope, A): *Stanford*
Psalm 137 (By the rivers of Babylon): *Bantock*
Psalm 139 (O Lord, thou hast searched me out): *Pike*
Psalm 150 (Praise ye the Lord): *Bantock*; *Rubbra*
Psalm of David, when he was in the wilderness of Judah (Psalm 63): *Clarke, R.*
Pueblo: *ApIvor*†
Pull away home: *Jacob*
Pursuit, The: *Headington*
Pussy and Pump: *Butterworth, N.*
Put a rosebud on her lips: *Roberts, M.*
Put thou thy trust in the Lord: *Camidge*
Puty-fish: *Blyton*
Puzzle of Shadows, A: *Grange*†

Q

Quail's Nest: *Greaves, Terence*†
Quand j'étais chez mon père: *Britten**
Quand mon mari se fâchera: *Hopkins, A.**
Quand on suit l'amoureuse: *Handel**
Quarrel: *Seiber*†
Quarry, The [Gibson]: *Jeffreys, J.*
Quarry, The [Williams]: *Roe*
Quartette, The: *Symons*
Quasi Minuetto: *Vaughan Williams*†
Quatre petits nègres blancs: *Wishart**
Quatre Vocalises: *Procter*
Quayside Shaver, The: *Tate, P.*†
Queen and huntress, chaste and fair: *Stanford*
Queen Anne: *Warlock*
Queen Djenira: *Burrows*
Queen Mab: *Jacobson*
Queen Mary's Song: *Elgar* (Lute Song, The)
Queen Nefertiti: *Foreman*
Queen of Hearts she made some tarts, The: *Jeffreys, J.*
Queen of my heart: *Dean*
Queen of Sheba's Song, The: *Poston*
Queen's Epicedium, The: *Purcell, H.**
Queen's Epicedium, The: *Blow*
Queen's Men, The: *Hely-Hutchinson*
Queer Story, A: *Howells*
Quem Queritas: *Helliwell*†
Question, A: *McCabe*
Question and Answer: *Coleridge-Taylor*
Quiet Comes In, The: *Stevenson*
Quiet Mind, The: *Tate, P.*
Quiet Mist, The: *Gurney*
Quiet Night, The: *Dunhill*
Quiet way you move me, The: *Solomons*(†)
Quite unconcerned: *Handel*

R

Rabbi ben Ezra: *Wills*
Rabbit, The: *McLeod*†
Rabbits [Anon]: *Deacon*
Rabbits [Hoosen]: *Elwyn-Edwards*
Rachel: *Berkeley, L.*†
Rachray Man, The: *Harty*
Ragged Wood, The: *Berkeley, M.*
Rag-Time Gal: *Grainger, P.*
Ragwort, The: *Bliss*†
Rahoon: *Moeran*
Raider's Dawn: *Swann*; *Thomas, Mansel*
Rail no more, ye learned asses: *Boyce*
Rain [Radford]: *Scott, C.*
Rain [Stevenson]: *Williamson, M.*
Rain [Thomas]: *Berkeley, M.*†; *Pickard*,
Rain, The [Davies]: *Bruce*
Rain comes down: *Bliss*
Rain has fallen all the day: *Moeran*
Rain It Raineth Every Day, The: *Stanford* (Clown's Song, The / When that I was and a little tiny boy)
Rain on the Down: *Davidson, M.*
Rain Storm: *Head*
Rainbow, The: *Thiman*
Rainbow Child, The: *Coleridge-Taylor*
Raindrops: *Bantock*
Rainy Day, The: *Turnbull*
Rainy Summer, The: *Pope*
Raíz amarga: *ApIvor*†
Ralph's Ramble to London: *Wilson, H.L.*
Rann of Exile: *Bax*
Rann of Wandering, (A): *Bax*; *Harty*
Rannoch by Glencoe: *Adès*; *Pope*
Rantum-tantum: *Warlock*
Rashly I swore I would disown: *Purcell, H.*
Rat, The: *Ireland*

264 Index of titles

Ratcliffe Highway: *Bush, A.*
Rather a little pain: *Walker, R.*†
Rattlin' Roarin' Willie: *Scott, F.G.* (O rattlin' roarin' Willie)
Raven's Tomb, The: *Hugh-Jones*
Read in these roses: *Lawes, H.*
Reading Scheme: *Williams, Roderick*
Reaper, The: *Jeffreys, J.*
Reason, The: *Ronald*
Reason, what art thou? *Weldon*
Rebecca Wasson: *Downes*
Rebel, The: *Pike*
Rebuke, A: *Bush, G.*
Recalling: *Glyn*
Recollections: *Pitfield*
Reconcilement, The: *Dring*
Reconciliation: *Scott, C.*
Reconciling: *Clucas*
Records: *Wood, Hugh*
Recruit, The, *Williamson, J.R.*
Recruiting Sergeant, The: *Harrison, J.*
Recueillement: *Hopkins, A.**
Red Cockatoo and Other Songs, The: *Britten*
Red Cockatoo, The: *Britten*
Red Lotus, The: *Bantock*
Red o' the Dawn: *Coleridge-Taylor*
Red, Red Rose, A: *Dickinson*; *Horder*; *Swann* (Farewell, A [Burns] / My love (luve) is like a red, red rose / O my love is like a red, red rose)
Red Roses and Red Noses: *Berners*
Reed, The: *Plumstead*
Reed Player, The: *Bantock*; *Foulds*
Reflection, A: *Scott, C.*
Reflections: *Elwyn-Edwards*
Reflections of Summer: *Headington*
Refrain: *Shaw*
Refrain thy voice from weeping: *Sullivan*†
Refugee Blues: *Lutyens*
Reid-E'en: *Scott, F.G.*
Reiver's Neck Verse: *Grainger, P.*
Rejected Lover, The: *Paterson*
Rejected Lover, The [Bax]: *Gibbs, Armstrong*
Remarkables, Queenstown, The: *Joubert*
Remember: *Shur*
Remember [Coleridge, M.]: *Ireland*
Remember me when I am gone away: *Hugh-Jones*; *Kleyn*; *McLeod*; *Ronald*; *Shur*; *Wegener*
Remember Your Lovers: *Tippett*
Remembrance [Griffiths]: *Thomas, Mansel*
Remembrance [McGrory]: *Kirkwood*
Remembrance Day: *Garton*
Reminder, The: *Turnbull*
Reminiscences: *Dickinson*†
Rémon: *Maw*
Remorse: *Kirkwood*
Rendete a gli occhi miei, o font o fiume: *Britten**
Rent for Love, A: *Lloyd Webber*
Repentance of Lady T, The: *Lutyens*
Report Song, A: *Ireland*
Requiem [Gurney]: *Jeffreys, J.*
Requiem [Latin]: *Orr, C.W.*
Requiem [Stevenson]: *Hudes*; *Randall*†; *Scott, C.*; *Steele* (Under the wide and starry sky)
Requiem Sequence: *McCabe*
Requiescat [Arnold]: *Stanford* (Strew on her roses, roses)
Requiescat [Wilde]: *Butterworth, G.*
Requital: *Rose*

Rest [Æ]: *Busch*
Rest [Rossetti, C.]: *Andrews*; *McLeod*
Rest [Symons]: *Ireland*
Rest awhile, you cruel cares: *Dowland*
Rest from loving and be living: *Naylor, B.*
Rest in the Lord: *Gibbs, Armstrong*
Rest sweet nymphs, let golden sleep: *Pilkington, F.*; *Warlock*
Restful Branches, The: *Howells*
Resting: *Gibbs, Armstrong*
Retired from (any) mortal(s) sight: *Purcell, H.*
Retort to a Clarion Call: *Frankel, B.*
Retrospect: *Scott, C.*
Return: *Thomas, V.*
Return, The: *Bantock*
Return from Town, The: *Bliss*
Return of Spring: *Bantock*
Return of Summer, The: *Orchard*
Returning, we hear the larks: *Cooke*†
Reve d'amour: *Green*
Revelation [Currie]: *Gibbs, Armstrong*
Revelation [Green]: *Pope*
Reveille: *Gurney*(†); *Peel*
Réveillez-vous : *Seiber*†
Réveillez-vous Piccarz: *Vaughan Williams*(*)
Reverie [de la Mare]: *Keel*
Reverie [Ingram]: *Thomas, V.*
Reverie [James]: *Thwaites*
Reverie [Rees]: *Cochrane*
Reynardine: *Hughes, Herbert*
Rhine Wine, The: *Stanford*
Rhyme [Anon]: *Walton*
Rhyme [Wolfe]: *Holst,*
Rhyme in the Tropics: *Wallbank*
Rhymes my Granny Read: *McGuire*†
Rhymney: *Thomas, Mansel*
Rhythm of life, The (cycle): *Liddell*
Rich and rare were the gems she wore: *Britten*; *Hughes, Herbert*
Rich as you are: *Hudes*†
Rich Days: *Berkeley, L.*
Rich or Poor: *Bliss*
Richard Jefferies, his Invocation: *Newson*
Richard of Taunton Dene: *Marshall, N.*†
Riddle, A (the child you were): *Britten*
Riddle, A (the earth): *Britten*
Riddle, The [Kipling]: *German*
Ride Straight: *Dunhill*
Ride with an idle whip: *Grainger, P.*
Ride-by-nights, The: *Hugh-Jones*(†)
Rider Victory, The: *Wood, Hugh*
Rikke Holst: *Horne*
Rill that from the steep ascent, The: *Linley Jnr*
Rima's Call to the Birds (scena): *Scott, C.*
Ring a Dumb Carillon: *Birtwistle*†
Ring out, wild bells: *Bainton*
Ripeness is All: *Routh*
Ripley Songs: *Moult*
Rio Grande, The: *Berners*
Riouperoux: *Foss*
Rise: *Jeffreys, G.*†
Rise and follow, love: *Roberton*
Rising of Glyndwr, The: *Thomas, Mansel*
Ritter: *Young, Derek**
Rivals, The: *Tomlinson*
River, The [d'Alba]: *Elgar*
River, The [Smith]: *Newson*
River Lynher, The: *Self, A.*

Index of titles 265

River Roses: *Cooke*†
Riverside Village, The: *Berkeley, L.*
Rivulet, The: *Shaw*
Road of Evening, The: *Noble, H.* (Nod)
Road to Ballydare, The: *Parke*
Road to Coursegoules, The: *Hugh-Jones*
Road to Emmaus (Canticle for Easter): *Hearne*†
Roads: *Liddell*
Roadside Fire, The: *Farrar*; *Vaughan Williams* (I will make you brooches / Romance [Stevenson])
Roaring Flame, A: *Dillon*†
Rob Robin: *Thomas, Mansel*
Robber, The: *Stevenson*
Robbers' Den: *Holloway*
Robert Graves Songs: *Wood, Hugh*
Robin and Richard were two pretty men: *Warlock*
Robin Goodfellow: *Burrows*; *Warlock*
Robin Hood and the Pedlar: *Vaughan Williams*
Robin Redbreast [Blyton]: *Blyton*(†)
Robin Redbreast [Davies]: *Head*; *Jeffreys, J.*
Robin Redbreast [Hayes]: *Bantock*
Robin redbreast in a cage, A: *Chapple*
Robin's Carol, The: *Head*
Robin's Last Will, The: *Horton*
Rock of ages: *Thomas, G.*
Rock of Rubies, The: *Hatton* (Julia)
Rocked in the cradle of the deep: *Knight, J.F.*
Rocking: *Case*
Róisín Dubh: *Hughes, Herbert*
Roister Doister: *Warlock*
Roll it along: *Butler*†
Rollicum-rorum: *Finzi* (Sergeant's Song, The)
Rolling Down to Rio: *German*
Rolling English Road, The: *Hely-Hutchinson*
Rolling in the Dew: *Vaughan Williams*
Roman Canticle: *Maw*†
Roman Road, The: *Jacobson*
Roman Wall Blues: *Senator*
Romance [Jean-Aubry]: *Berners**
Romance [Stevenson]: *Jeffreys, J.*; *Sagar*; *Warlock* (I will make you brooches / Roadside Fire, The)
Romance of Count Arnaldos, The: *Weir*(†)
Romancero a la muerte de Federico García Lorca: *Hudes*(†)
Romany: *Hughes, A.*
Rondeau [d'Orleans]: *Berkeley, L.**; *Lyall*
Rondeau [Henley]: *O'Neill*
Rondeaux: *LeFanu*†
Rondel [d'Orleans]: *Dieren**
Rondel [Longfellow]: *Elgar*
Rondel (Roundel) of Rest, A: *Howells*; *O'Neill*
Rorate caeli desuper: *Scott, F.G.*
Rosa Mundi: *Rubbra*(†)
Rosa Resurget: *Lehmann*
Rosalind's Madrigal: *Wills*(†)
Rosaline: *Moeran*; *Parry, C.H.H.*
Rosary Songs: *Knussen*†
Rose [Açikça]: *Solomons*(†)
Rose [Belloc]: *Raynor*
Rose, The [Graves, R.]: *Wood, Hugh*
Rose, The [Howell]: *Hamilton, I.* (All in a garden green)
Rose, The [Picano]: *Hugill*
Rose and the Nightingale, The: *Blyton*†,
Rose and the Nightingale, The [Bailey]: *Keel*
Rose Berries: *Naylor, B.*
Rose by any other name, A: *Belben*†
Rose of All the World, The: *Stevenson*

Rose of Killarney, The: *Stanford*
Rose of Tralee, The: *Glover*
Rose-Ann: *Foster, I.*
Rosebud, The: *Someren-Godfery*
Rose-bud by my early walk, A: *Liddell*
Rosefrail: *Moeran*
Roseleaves: *Lehmann*
Rosenberg Sketches: *Ellis*†
Roses: *Jones, D.T.*
Roses [Tarelli]: *Howells*
Roses and rue: *Foulds*
Roses of Picardy: *Wood, Haydn*
Roses red in the garden: *Ronald*
Rough wind that moaneth loud: *Bridge*; *Loder*
Round about a wood as I walked: *Butterworth, N.*
Round the Horn: *Thomas, Mansel*
Roundel [Chaucer]: *Bax* (Your eyën two will slay me suddenly)
Roundel (Rondel) of Rest, A [Symons]: *Scott, C.*
Roundelay: *Joubert*†
Rout: *Bliss*†
Rover, The: *Wood, C.*
Roving Dingle Boy, The: *Moeran*
Roving in the Dew: *Butterworth, G.*
Row, burnie, row, through the bracken glen: *Weston*
Row gently here: *Raphael*
Rowan Tree, The: *Elwyn-Edwards*
Ruin, The: *Usher*
Ruin of the Ku-Su Palace: *Lambert, C.*
Rule Britannia: *Arne, T.*
Rune of Hospitality: *Rubbra*
Rune of the Burden of the Tide: *Peterkin*
Running back for more: *Oliver*
Rushes, The: *Ronald*
Russian Sonia: *Downes*
Rutterkin is come into our town: *Bush, G.*; *Warlock*

S

Sabbath Morning at Sea: *Elgar*
Sabina has a thousand charms: *Blow*
Sacred Flame, The: *Ireland* (Thy hand in mine)
Sacred Hour, The: *Ketèlby*
Sacred Physic: *Usher*†
Sad is the spring-time: *Stanford*
Sad Song, A: *Warlock*(†) (Aspatia's Song / Lay a garland on my hearse / Willow Song [Fletcher])
Sail on, sail on thou fearless bark: *Britten*
Sailing Homeward: *Gibbs*, *Armstrong*; *Nieman*; *Somers-Cocks*
Sailor and Young Nancy, The: *Moeran*
Sailor Boy's Dream: *Hughes, R.S.*
Sailor loved a lass, A: *Storace*
Sailor Man, The: *Harty*; *Stanford*; *Wood, C.*
Sailor-boy: *Britten*†
Sailor's Carol: *Hurd*
Sailor's Carol, A: *Harvey, T.*
Sailor's Chanty: *Grainger, P.*
Sailor's Journal, The: *Dibdin*
Sailor's Life, The: *Wilson, H.L.*
Sailor's Prayer, A: *Keel*
Sailor's Sweetheart, The: *Hearne*
Sailor's Wife, The: *Parry, J.*
Sáki! dye the cup's rim deeper: *Bantock*

266 Index of titles

Salley Gardens, The: *Britten*; *Graves*; *Ireland*; *Jeffreys, J.* (Down by the salley gardens / I was young and foolish)
Salley in our Alley: *Anon*; *Britten*; *Grainger, P.*
Sally: *Jeffreys, J.*
Sally Gray: *Mark*
Salter than salt of the ocean: *Thomas, Mansel*
Salvation belongeth unto the Lord: *Greene*
Salve Regina (Holy queen of heaven): *Bantock,*
Salve Regina [Hermann]: *Rubbra**
Samaveda: *Taverner*†
Sancta et Immaculata Virginitas: *Head**(†)
Sanctuaries: *Bainton*
Sanctuary: *Hewitt*
Sanctuary of the Heart: *Ketèlby*
Sandgate Lass's Lament, The: *Tate, P.*†
Sands of Dee, The: *Balfe*; *Hatton*; *Pitfield*; *Scott, C.*
Sans Day Carol, The: *Thomas, Mansel*(†)
Sans y penser: *Handel**
Santa Chiara: *Ireland* (Day of Palms, The)
Sappho: *Bantock*
Sappho Fragments: *Hudes*
Sappho Kunopis Kai Mantis (Sappho, Bitch and Philosopher: *Hudes*†
Sappho when some fool: *Hudes*†
Sarabande: *Bax**
Sarah Brown: *Downes*
Satyr, The: *Bantock*
Sauchs in the Reuch Heuch Hauch, The: *Scott, F.G.*
Saudades: *Warlock*
Saving the Sun: *Wiegold*†
Savoury Seal, The: *Jacobson*
Saw ye Johnny Cummin? *Crawford*
Saw ye my father? *Hughes, Herbert*
Sawny is a bonny lad: *Purcell, H.*
Saxon Song, A: *Gill*
Say, lad, have you things to do? *Moeran*; *Peel*
Say, little foolish, fluttering thing: *Dibdin*
Say love if ever thou didst find: *Dowland*
Say not that minutes swiftly move: *Salomon*
Say, O say, saith the music: *Stanford*
Scallop: *Cruft*†
Scapegoat, The: *Ireland*
Scarborough Fair: *Watkins*†
Scarecrow, The: *Gibbs, Armstrong*
Scared: *Stanford*
Scatterpenny: *Whittaker*
Scena Rustica: *Rawsthorne*†
Scene from 'The Woodlanders': *Hadley*
Scenes from Shakespeare: *Read*
Scenes from Tyneside: *Tate, P.*(†)
Scents: *Gurney*
Scherzo: *Vaughan Williams*†
Schlaflied: *Ellis*†
Schlummerlied [Heine]: *Stanford**
Schlummerlied [Wildenbruch]: *Smyth**
Schöne Rohtraut: *Dieren**
Schubert in Blue: *Dickinson*
Scorpio: *Torphichen*
Scot in China, A: *McGuire*
Scotch Lullabye: *Scott, C.*
Scotch Minstrelsy: *Weir*
Scots Song: *MacMillan*(†)
Scots Steel and Irish Fire: *Stevenson*
Scots wha hae wi' Wallace bled: *Liddell*; *Scott, F.G.*
Scottish Lyrics: *Scott, F.G.*
Scottish Songs: *Center*
Scribe, The: *Gurney*

Scroggam: *Scott, F.G.*
Sculpter, The: *Samuels*
Scythe Song: *Harty*
Sea, The [Dallas]: *Joubert*
Sea, The [Williams]: *Thomas, Mansel*
Sea Burthen, A: *Head*
Sea Dirge, A: *Parry, C.H.H.* (Full fathom five)
Sea Echoes: *Phillips, M.*
Sea Fairies: *White, A.*
Sea Fever: *Ireland*
Sea Gypsy, The: *Harty*; *Head*
Sea has many a thousand sands, The: *Jones, R.*
Sea Love: *Bliss*†
Sea Lullaby: *German*
Sea Music: *Dyson*
Sea of Faith, The: *Bullard* (Dover Beach)
Sea Pictures: *Elgar*
Sea Slumber Song: *Elgar*
Sea Winds: *Harrison, J.*
Sea Wrack: *Harty*; *Roberts, T.O.*
Sea-bird, The: *Quilter*
Sea-dog's song, The: *Blyton*
Seadrift: *Anderson, J.*†
Seafarer, The: *Talbot*†
Sea-fret: *Scott, C.*
Seagull and the Eagull: *Orr, R.*
Seagull Fair, The: *Thomas, D.V.*
Seagulls, The: *Thomas, Mansel*
Seagulls' Cry, The: *Thomas, Mansel*
Seal Man, The: *Clarke, R.*
Seal's Lullaby, The: *Davies, Walford*
Seals of Love: *Jeffreys, J.* (Love and Grief / Take, O take those lips away)
Seaman's Life, A: *Moeran*
Sea-mist: *Alwyn*†
Searching for Lambs: *Goossens*; *Vaughan Williams*†
Seas are quiet, The: *Mullinar*
Seascape [Auden]: *Britten* (Look, stranger, on this island now)
Seascape [Holmes]: *Goossens*
Seascapes [Armstrong]: *Alwyn*†
Season: *Routh*
Season of Ice: *Jeffreys, J.*
Sea-song from the Shore: *White, A.*
Sea-song of Gafran: *Scott, C.*
Seasons, The: *Bantock*
Sea-wife, The: *Grainger, P.*
Sechs Hölderlin-Fragmente: *Britten**
Second Book of Ayres, The: *Campion*; *Corkine*
Second Book of Songs, A: *Jeffreys, J.*; *Warlock*
Second Book of Songs, The: *Dowland*; *Jones, R.*
Second Minuet, The: *Besley*
Second Thoughts: *Ronald*
Secresy's Song (One charming night): *Purcell, H.*
Secret, A [Quilter]: *Quilter,*
Secret, The (Philosopher Bird, The) [Crossley-Holland]: *Crossley-Holland*†
Secret love or two I must confess, A: *Campion*
Secret of the Sea: *Grainger, P.*
Secret People, The: *Thomas, Mansel*
Secret transports: *Shield*
Secrets – Three Songs: *Fleming*
See, dearest, how the rose: *Swann*
See liberty, virtue and honour appearing: *Arne, T.*
See my mother coming: *Thomas, Mansel*
See the chariot at hand: *Vaughan Williams*
See the cherry blossoms swing: *Anderson, W.H.*
See where my love a-maying goes: *Lidgey*; *Lindsay*

See where young love: *Fleming*
Seed: *Bliss*
Seekers, The: *Slater*
Seeking God: *Pike*
Seest thou those diamonds: *Lawes, H.*
Seis Canciones: *Aplvor*†
Selbstgefuhl: *McLeod**
Seldom yet now: *Wood, Hugh*
Selected Songs: *Arne, M.*; *Arne, T.*; *Owen*; *Pitfield*(†); *Purcell, H.*; *Steele*; *Stevenson*
Self Banished, The: *Blow*; *Oswald*
Self-unseeing, The: *Finzi*
Sentimental Song: *Solomons*†
Sentry, The: *Roberts, M.*
Separation [Armstrong]: *Alwyn*; *Dring*
Separation hath quickly intervened [Arabic]: *Macfarren*
Sephestia's Lullaby: *Britten*
September: *Wood, Hugh*
September Lovers: *Pitfield*
Serbian Songs: *Woolrich*†
Serenade [Bantock]: *Bantock*
Serenade [Longfellow]: *Center*
Serenade [Sitwell]: *Lambert, C.*†
Serenade [Troubadour]: *Orchard*
Serenade, A [Anon]: *Owen*
Serenade, A [Bendall]: *Scott, C.*
Sergeant's Song, The: *Foss*; *Holst* (Rollicumrorum)
Sestette to Fish: *Lawson*†
Set me as a seal upon thine heart: *Self, A.*
Sevdalino, my little one: *Weir*
Seven American Poems: *Bliss*
Seven Days of Loving: *Dean*
Seven Elizabethan Lyrics: *Quilter*
Seven Folksongs: *Marshall, N.*†
Seven Haiku (cycle): *Gerhard*†
Seven Irish Folksongs: *Wood, C.*
Seven Love Songs: *Sagar*
Seven Poems of Robert Graves: *Hattey*
Seven Poems of James Joyce: *Moeran*
Seven Poetic Songs: *Swann*
Seven Sacred Solos: *Greene*
Seven Sappho Songs: *Gurney*
Seven Scots Songs: *Rose*
Seven Shaker Songs: *Cresswell*
Seven Shakespeare Songs: *Dring*; *Horder*
Seven Songs: *Dieren*; *Dring*; *Howard, M.*; *Purcell, H.*; *Roe*; *Shaw*; *Thomas, D.V.*
Seven Songs for a Child: *Papastavrou*(†)
Seven Songs for Baritone Voice: *Scott, F.G.*
Seven Songs for High Voice: *Parry, C.H.H.*; *Storace*
Seven Songs of Walter de la Mare: *Hugh-Jones*†
Seven Sonnets of Michelangelo: *Britten**
Seven Traditional Scots Airs: *Orr, R.*
Seven Whatnots: *Bennett, T.C.S.*
Seventeen come Sunday: *Butterworth, G.*
Severn Meadows: *Gurney*; *Jeffreys, J.* (Only the wanderer)
Severn Sand: *Bush, G.*
Sfiorarci le Mani: *Creswell**
Shaded with olive trees (Celestina): *Greaves, Thomas*
Shadow and Smoke: *Someren-Godfery*
Shadow March: *Coates, L.*; *Pitfield*
Shadow Side of Joy Finzi, The: *Bingham*
Shadows: *Rutter*†
Shadows [Daniel]: *Rutter*†
Shadows [Evans]: *Treharne*
Shadows in the Water: *Matthews, C.*

Shadows of Chrysanthemums: *Hudes*(†)
Shadows of Chrysanthemums: *Hudes*(†)
Shadowy Woodlands, The: *Foulds*
Shah Abbas: *Bantock*
Shakespeare Songs: *Blake, H.*(†)
Shakespeare Sonnets: *Scott, D.B.*
Shall a frown or angry eye: *Corkine*
Shall a smile or guileful glance? *Corkine*
Shall I come if I swim: *Rosseter*
Shall I come sweet love to thee: *Campion*
Shall I compare thee to a summer's day? (Sonnet 18) [Shakespeare] *Aiken*; *Hartley*; *Parry, C.H.H.*; *Pender*; *Sagar*; *Wetherell*
Shall I forget? *Wood, C.*
Shall I look to ease my grief?: *Jones, R.*
Shall I seek to ease my grief?: *Ferrabosco*
Shall I strive with words to move? *Dowland*
Shall I sue? shall I seek for grace? *Dowland*
Shall I, wasting in despair: *Lyall*; *Wilson, H.L.*
Shall I weep or shall I sing? *Anon*
Shall then a traitorous kiss: *Rosseter*
Shalom Yerushalayim: *Shur*
Sharp Ridge, The: *Hattey*
Shawl, The: *Hogben*
She at his Funeral: *Berkeley, M.*†
She came to the village church: *Somervell*
She hath an eye: *Bush, G.*
She I love: *Dieren*
She is all so slight: *Jeffreys, J.*; *Poston* (After Two Years)
She is ever for the new: *Jeffreys, J.*
She is far from the land: *Lambert, F.*
She is my love beyond all thought: *Parry, C.H.H.*
She is the violet: *Butterworth, N.*
She loves and she confesses too: *Purcell, H.*
She moved thro' the fair: *Hughes, Herbert*
She rested by the broken brook: *Coleridge-Taylor*
She sat and sang alway: *Coleridge-Taylor*
She sauntered by the swinging seas: *Foss*
She tells her love while half asleep: *Hattey*
She that would gain a faithful lover: *Purcell, H.*
She walks in beauty: *Naylor, P.*; *Thomas, Muriel*
She who is dear to me: *Holst*
She who my poor heart possesses: *Purcell, H.*
Sheaf of Songs from Leinster, A: *Stanford*
Sheaf of Sonnets, A: *Kleyn*
Sheep: *Rowley*
Sheep in the Shade: *Headington*
Sheep Shearing: *Le Fleming*
Sheepfolds: *Poston*
Sheila na gig: *Luff*
Sheiling Song [Macleod]: *Bax*
Sheiling Song, A [Mackenzie]: *Bantock*
Shepherd, The: *Busch*; *Cooke*†; *Jacob*; *Mills*; *Raphael*; *Someren-Godfery*; *Thiman*; *Vaughan Williams*†
Shepherd in a shade, A: *Dowland*
Shepherd lov'd a nymph so fair, A: *Pinto*
Shepherd of Aberdovey, The: *Lewis, I.*
Shepherd of the Hafod, The: *Thomas, Mansel*
Shepherd on a Hill: *Price, B.*
Shepherd, thy demeanour vary: *Brown, T.*
Shepherdess, The: *Salter, L.*
Shepherd's Cradle Song: *Somervell*
Shepherd's Holiday: *Benjamin, A.*
Shepherd's Love Song: *Owen*
Shepherd's Pipe Carol: *Rutter*

Index of titles

Shepherd's Song [Jonson]: *Gurney* (Though I am young and cannot tell)
Shepherd's Song, The [Crashaw]: *Hughes, Hugh*
Shepherd's Song, The [Pain]: *Elgar*
She's but a lassie yet: *Scott, C.*
She's like the swallow: *Britten*(†); *Vaughan Williams*
She's me forgot: *Peterkin*
Shew's the way to Wallington: *Whittaker*
Shine out, fair sun: *Paynter*†
Shiny: *Cope*
Ship, The [Gurney]: *Moult*
Ship, The [Squire]: *Gurney*
Ship and the Lighthouse, The: *Jones, M.O.*
Ship in Distress, The: *Bush, A.*; *Mitchell*†
Ship of Rio, The: *Britten*; *Gibbs, Armstrong*
Shipmates o' Mine: *Sanderson*
Ships of Arcady, The: *Head*
Ships of Yule: *Shaw*
Shivery Sarah: *Nelson*
Shoemaker, The: *Warlock*
Sho-heen sho-ho: *Maconchy*
Sho-ho (Lullaby [Graves]): *Wood, C.*
Shooting of his Dear, The: *Moeran*; *Britten*†
Shore Leave: *Hurd*
Shore Leave: *Hurd*
Shores (Traighean): *Stevenson*
Shortening Days: *Finzi*
Shoshone's Adieu, The: *Coleridge-Taylor*
Should he upbraid: *Bishop*
Should you ever find her complying: *Arne, T.*
Shows and nightly revels: *Lupo*
Shropshire Lad, A: *Horder*; *Somervell*
Shropshire Lad and Other Songs, A: *Butterworth, G.*
Shule Agra: *Hughes, Herbert*
Shunga: *Dench*†
Shuttle and Loom: *Roberton*
Shy One: *Clarke, R.*
Shy Shepherdess, The: *Young, A.* (Phillis has such charming graces)
Sì come nella penna e nell' inchiostro: *Britten**
Si tu savais: *Balfe**
Sic vita: *Rutter*† (Like to the falling of a star)
Sick Heart, The: *Warlock*
Sick Rose, The: *Swann*
Sidesteps: *McGuire*†
Siege: *Bliss*
Siegfried Sassoon Songs: *Rootham*
Siete hijos tiene hann: *Sutton-Anderson*†
Sigh, The: *Finzi*
Sigh no more, ladies, sigh no more: *Aiken*; *Barrell, B.*†; *Bush, G.*; *Coates, E.*; *Ford, T.*; *Harris, R.*; *Horder*; *Jeffreys, J.*; *Keel*; *Plumstead*; *Quilter*; *Roe*†; *Routh*; *Sullivan*; *Warlock* (Be you Blithe and Bonny)
Sigh that heaves the grasses, The: *Vaughan Williams*†
S'il est un charmant gazon: *Thomas, A.G.**
Silence: *Somers-Cocks*
Silent, but... : *Josephs*(†)
Silent Mill, The: *Phillips, M.*
Silent Noon: *Farrar*; *Orr, C.W.*; *Vaughan Williams*
Silent Spring: *Brown, J.*
Silent Strings: *Bantock*
Silent Voice, The: *Somervell*
Silent Worship: *Handel*
Silken Heart, The: *Hamilton, A.*
Silken shoes upon golden lasts: *Delius*
Silkesko over gylden Læst: *Delius**

Silkworms: *Rowley*
Silly heart forbear: *Lanier*
Silver: *Berkeley, L.*; *Britten*; *Gibbs, Armstrong*; *Hely-Hutchinson*; *Hugh-Jones*(†); *Redman*
Silver Birch, The: *Thiman*
Silver Hound, The (cycle): *Hoddinott*; *Roe*†
Silver Moon, The: *Hook*
Silver Point: *Pilling*
Silver swan, who living had no note, The: *Gibbons*; *Thiman*
Silver'd is the raven hair: *Sullivan*
Simmer Landskip: *MacDonald*
Simmer's (Summer's) a pleasant time: *Center*; *Headington*
Simon the Cellarer: *Hatton*
Simoom: *Blyton*†
Simples: *Bliss*
Simurgh, The: *Bantock*
Since all thy vows, false maid: *Scott, F.G.*
Since first I saw your face: *Ford, T.*; *Quilter*
Since from my dear Astraea's sight: *Purcell, H.*
Since I from love escapèd am so fat: *Vaughan Williams*(†) (Escape from Love, The)
Since I left you, mine eye is in my mind (Sonnet 113) [Shakespeare]: *Scott, D.B.*
Since love hath in thine and mine eye: *Wilson, John*
Since one poor view has drawn my heart: *Purcell, H.*
Since she whom I lov'd hath pay'd her last debt: *Britten*
Since thou, O fondest and truest: *Carey, C.*; *Gurney*; *Orr, C.W.*; *Stanford*
Since 'tis my fate to be thy slave: *Webb*
Since we loved, the earth shook as we kissed: *Finzi*
Sing a song of sixpence: *Diack*
Sing aloud, harmonious spheres: *Anon*
Sing at the wheel: *Roberton*
Sing heigh-ho: *Parke*
Sing, joyous bird, the summer sun is glowing: *Phillips, M.*
Sing lullaby: *Wiegold*†
Sing, maiden, sing: *Bennett, W.S.*
Sing no sad songs for me: *Jeffreys, J.* (When I am dead, my dearest)
Singer, The [Shanks]: *Gurney*; *Warlock*
Singer, The [Taylor]: *Head*
Singer and the Song, The: *Walters, L.*
Singer in the Woods, The: *Bantock*
Singing: *White, A.*
Sing-Song Cycle: *Swinstead*
Sir Giles' War Song: *Harrison, J.*
Sir Nickety Nox: *White, A.*
Sir Patrick Spens: *Gibbs, Alan*; *Musgrave*†
Sister, awake, close not your eyes: *Dring*; *Frankel, E.*; *Howe*
Six Abbasid Songs: *Taverner*†
Six Badgers: *Jeffreys, J.*
Six Betjeman Songs: *Horder*
Six Blake Songs: *Someren-Godfery*
Six Caprices: *Holt*†
Six Catalan Folksongs: *Gerhard*(*)
Six Celan Songs: *Nyman**
Six dukes went a-fishing: *Grainger, P.*
Six Early Songs: *MacDonald*(*)
Six English Folksongs: *Vaughan Williams*
Six English Lyrics: *Williamson, M.*
Six Folksongs from Norfolk: *Moeran*
Six Greek Songs: *Papastávrou*†
Six Hölderlin Fragments: *Britten*(*)

Six Interiors: *Maw*†
Six Japanese Lyrics: *Northcott*†
Six Jester Songs: *Bantock*
Six Love Songs: *Luard Selby*
Six Mediaeval Lyrics: *Short*†
Six Mehitabel Magpies (cycle): *Seamarks*†
Six Poems by Suemas O'Sullivan: *Moeran*
Six Poems of Amy Lowell: *Cresswell*
Six Poems of Emily Brontë: *Joubert*
Six Poetic Songs: *Swann*
Six Renaissance Songs: *Pope*
Six Sacred Songs: *Purcell, H.*
Six Scots Songs: *Wilson, T.*
Six Sea Songs: *Head*; *Purser*
Six Settings of Poems by Robert Bridges: *MacCunn*
Six Settings of W.H.Auden: *Britten*
Six Songs: *Bax*; *Bridge*; *Browne*; *Burrows*; *Clarke, J.*; *Dring*; *Holbrooke*; *Fraser, N.*; *Lanier*; *Lawes, H.*; *Lawes, W.*; *MacCunn*; *Purcell, H.*; *Randalls*; *Rootham*; *Stanford*; *White, M.V.**
Six Songs for Bass: *Purcell, H.*
Six Songs for Children: *Elwyn-Edwards*
Six 'Songs' for Singing: *Barratt*
Six Songs from the Glens of Antrim: *Stanford*
Six Songs from Shakespeare: *Foss*
Six Songs of Happiness: *MacMahon*
Six Songs of Ireland: *Harty*
Six Songs of Mervyn Peake: *Walker, R.*†
Six Songs of War: *Shaw*
Six Sorrow Songs: *Coleridge-Taylor*
Six Suffolk Folksongs: *Moeran*
Six Welsh Folksongs: *Hoddinott*; *Roberts, M.*
Six Welsh Oxen Songs: *Williams, Grace*
Sixteen Songs: *Delius*
Skeleton of the Future, The: *Stevenson*
Sketches from Baptised Generations: *Cresswell*
Skies are now skies: *Matthews, D.*†
Skogen gir susende, langsam besked: *Delius**
Sky above the roof, The: *Vaughan Williams*
Skye Boat Song: *Anon*; *Grainger, P.*
Skylark, The: *White, A.*; *Williams, W.S.G.* (To the Skylark)
Skylark and Nightingale: *Ireland*
Slackwater Stillness: *Pope*
Slaughter: *Britten*
Sledburn Fair: *Gibbs, Armstrong*
Sleep [Brontë]: *Joubert*
Sleep [Fletcher]: *Demuth*; *Gurney*; *Isherwood*; *Jeffreys, J.*; *Lloyd Webber*; *Murrill*; *Raphael*; *Self, A.*; *Warlock*(†)
Sleep [Sturgis]: *Parry, C.H.H.*
Sleep betrayed the unhappy lover: *Clarke, J.*
Sleep, downy sleep, come close mine eyes: *Humfrey*† (Evening Hymn, An [Anon])
Sleep, gentle cherub: *Arne, T.*
Sleep, little babe, I love thee: *Field*
Sleep, my baby (Evening Shadows): *Somervell*
Sleep, my boy: *Crossley-Holland*
Sleep, my pearl: *Thomas, D.A.*
Sleep on, my love: *Walworth*
Sleep soft, you cold clay cinders: *Lawes, H.*
Sleep Song [Dobell]: *Walker, E.*
Sleep Song [Rands]: *Scott, C.*
Sleep sweet babe: *Dunhill* (Cradle Song [Coleridge, S.T.])
Sleep, wayward thoughts, and rest you with my love: *Bennett, R.R.*; *Dowland*; *Standford*
Sleep, white love, sleep: *Peterkin*

Sleepe, sleepe: *Anon*
Sleeping: *Thiman* (Tears / Weep you no more, sad fountains)
Sleeping Beauty, The: *Gibbs, Armstrong*
Sleeping Sea, The: *Wynne*
Sleepy Head: *Keel*
Sleigh Ride: *Bush, G.*
Slide soft you silver floods: *Lawes, H.*
Slighted Swain, The: *Wilson, H.L.*
Sloe was lost in flower: *Mitchell*
Sloth, The: *McLeod*†
Slow by the shadows of dark Gleann-a-righ: *Hughes, Herbert*
Slow Fox-trot: *Bennett, R.R.*
Slow, horses, slow: *Gibbs, Armstrong*
Slowly the ticking clock: *Glyn*
Slum Song: *Alwyn*
Slumber Song [Bjørnson]: *Delius*
Slumber Song [Ellison]: *Dring*
Slumber Song [Heine]: *Stanford*
Slumber Song [Kingsley]: *Holst*
Slumber Song [Mills]: *Quilter*
Slumber Song [Waugh]: *Jackson, R.*
Slumber Song of the Madonna, A: *Head*; *Owen*
Small Christmas Tree: *Head*
Small Cloud on the Horizon: *Stevenson*
Smiling hours, The: *Handel*
Smuggler's Song: *Bush, G.*
Snake-charmer's Song, The: *Treharne*
Snow [Thomas]: *Gurney*; *Jeffreys, J.*
Snow, The [de la Mare]: *Bruce*
Snow falls, The: *Steele*
Snow in the Suburbs: *Bayliss*
Snow in the Year of Mourning: *Rose*
Snow Light, The: *Samuel, R.*
Snowdon Songs: *Morris, A.*†
Snowdonia: *Thomas, Elsie*
Snowdrop, The: *Browne*
Snowdrop in the Wind, The: *Fraser, N.*
Snowdrops: *Glyn*
Snowflake [Anon]: *Bingham*
Snowflake [McGrory]: *Kirkwood*
Snowie the Snowman: *Dale, M.*
Snowman: *Dring*
Snowy-breasted Pearl, The: *Somervell*; *Tate, P.*
So are you to my thoughts: *Johnston*e
So early in the morning: *Bridge*
So far from my country: *Pitfield*
So hath your beauty from your hertë chased: *Vaughan Williams*(†)
So I have fared: *Finzi*
So lovely the rose: *Lloyd Webber*
So much time: *Fowler*†
So now is come our joyful'st feast: *Steel*
So parted you: *Coprario*
So Perverse: *Bridge*
So, so, leave off this last lamenting kiss: *Ferrabosco* (Ease me)
So sweet is thy discourse: *Campion*
So sweet love seemed that April morn: *Berkeley, L.*; *Milford*
So the year's done with: *Bryson*
So to fatness come: *Holloway*†
So well Corinna likes the joy: *Eccles*
So we'll go no more a-roving: *Blake, H.*; *Dickinson*; *Maconchy*†; *Peterkin*; *Sagar*; *White, M.V.* (We'll go no more a-roving)

So White, so Soft, so Sweet is She: *Delius* (Have you seen but a white lily grow?)
Socrates and Alcibiades: *Britten*
Socrates und Alcibiades: *Britten**
Soft and gently through my soul: *Holst*
Soft, Cupid, soft: *Jones, R.*
Soft day, thank God, A: *Stanford*
Soft, for music dies: *Hugill*
Soft invader of my soul: *Howard, S.*
Soft was the wind in the beech trees: *Gurney*
Softly fall the shades of evening: *Roberton*
Softly lulling, sweetly thrilling: *Hook*
Softly the forest murmurs: *Delius*
Soldier, The [Brooke]: *Ireland*
Soldier, The [Confucius:] *Harrison, J.*
Soldier and the Sailor, The: *Britten*†
Soldier from the wars returning: *Orr, C.W.*
Soldier, soldier: *Grainger, P.*; *Marshall, N.*†
Soldier tired of war's alarms, The: *Arne, T.*
Soldier's Gratitude, A: *Bishop*
Soldier's Return, The: *Ireland*
Soldier's Song [Hungarian]: *Seiber*†
Soldier's Song, A [Chinese]: *Dalby*
Soldier's Song, The: *Williams, D.E.*
Soldier's Song, The [Anon]: *Hume*
Soledad: *Gerhard**
Soleils Couchants: *McEwen*; *Wilby**
Solidität: *Blake, D.*†
Soliloquy upon a Dead Child (Little Sleeper): *Brian*
Solitary Reaper, The: *Bullard*(†); *Wordsworth*†
Solitude: *Hugh-Jones*(†)
Solo Songs: *Purcell, H.*
Some One: *Howells*
Someone is sending me flowers: *Baker*
Some stars above magnitude 2.9: *Bedford*
Somebody: *Bryan*
Somebody fetch me a flute: *Cockshott*
Something Rich and Strange: *Hold*
Something so simple: *Hugill*†
Something tapped: *Downes*
Sometimes when I'm sitting alone: *Sullivan*
Somewhere a voice is calling: *Tate, A.F.*
Sommer i Gurre: *Delius**
Son of the Sea: *Jones, W.B.*
Son of the Storm: *Jones, W.B.*
Song [Anon]: *Barratt* (Time stands still)
Song [Brooke]: *Taylor, M.* (All suddenly the wind comes soft / Buds in Spring / Spring Sorrow)
Song [Lewis]: *Tippett*
Song [Congreve]: *Barratt* (Pius Selinda goes to prayers)
Song [Rossetti, C.]: *Birkett*; *Joseph*(†); *McLeod*; *Self, A.*; *Somers-Cocks* (When I am dead, my dearest)
Song [Shelley]: *Fowler*(†)
Song [Shelley]: *Barratt* (Widow bird, A)
Song [Song of Solomon]: *Elias*†
Song [Swinburne]: *Walton*
Song 1: *Finnissy*†
Song 14: *Finnissy*†
Song 15: *Finnissy*†
Song 16: *Finnissy*†
Song Album: *Clarke, R.*; *Delius*; *Gibbs, Armstrong*(†); *Head*; *Vaughan Williams*; *Warlock*
Song Album, A: *Self, A.*(†), *Walton*
Song Album for Mezzo-soprano or Baritone: *Head*
Song Album for Soprano or Tenor: *Head*
Song at Night: *Hold*
Song at Parting, A: *Quilter*

Song be delicate: *Sutherland*
Song Cycle: *Jordan.*
Song Cycle to Poems by Pablo Neruda: *Wood, Hugh*
Song for a Baby Sister: *Anderson, W.H.*
Song for a Chinese Play (Plum Blossom Song): *Crossley-Holland*†
Song for Christmas [Brooke]: *Searle*
Song for Christmas, A [Dunbar]: *Musgrave*
Song for Christmas, A [Ould]: *Jacobson*
Song for Christmas Day: *Warlock*
Song for July: *Thomas, Mansel*
Song for Peter (Trio 2): *LeFanu*†
Song for September, A: *Newson*†
Song for Sunrise: *Teed*
Song for the Lord Mayor's Table, A: *Walton*
Song from Michelangelo, A: *Bainbridge*†
Song from o'er the hill, A: *Ireland*
Song from 'Song of Deliverance': *Hughes, A.*
Song from 'The Cenci' (Come, I will sing you some slow sleepy tune): *Dieren*
Song in Exile: *Parke*
Song in Solitude: *Thiman*
Song in Spring: *Joubert*
Song in the Cornfield: *Joseph*(†) (Green Cornfield, A)
Song in the Twilight, The: *Bax*
Song of a Girl Ravished away by the Fairies in South Uist: *Weir*
Song of a lass, O: *Whittaker*
Song of a Nightclub Proprietress: *Dring*
Song of Arcady, A: *Scott, C.*
Song of Asano: *Peterkin*
Song of Autumn [Verlaine]: *McEwen*
Song of Autumn, A [Gordon]: *Elgar*
Song of Battle, A [Psalm 124]: *Stanford*†
Song of Cambria, A: *Bryan*
Song of Ciabhan: *Gurney*
Song of Compassion: *Pitfield*(†)
Song of Courtship, A: *Redman*
Song of Crocuses and Lightning: *Holt*†
Song of Defiance: *Holloway*†
Song of Dinèdan: *Thomas, V.*
Song of Enchantment, A: *Britten*
Song of Fionula, The: *Peterkin*
Song of Flight, A: *Elgar*
Song of Freedom [Ratushinskaya]: *Torphichen*
Song of Freedom, A (Psalm 126): *Stanford*†
Song of Glen Dun, The: *Harty*
Song of Good Cheer, A: *Thomas, Mansel*
Song of Good Courage, A: *Parke*
Song of Hope, A (Psalm 130): *Stanford*†
Song of Iphigenia: *Randalls*
Song of Joy: *Parrott*
Song of Liberty, The: *Elgar*
Song of Little Jesus, The: *Thomas, Mansel*(†)
Song of London, A: *Scott, C.*
Song of Love, The: *Jeffreys, J.*
Song of Lucius, The: *O'Neill*
Song of Lyonesse, A: *Boughton* (Lyonesse / When I set out for Lyonesse)
Song of Momus to Mars, The: *Boyce*
Song of Peace, A: *Stanford*†
Song of Praise, A: *Bush, G.*
Song of Rosamund (scena): *Phillips, M.*
Song of Shadows, (A), (The): *Bennett, R.R.*; *Gibbs, Armstrong*, *Pope* (Ghosts)
Song of Soldiers, The: *Hely-Hutchinson*
Song of Songs, The: *Jacobson*
Song of Sorrow, A: *Mills*; *Owen*

Index of titles

Song of Thanks: *Bullard*
Song of the Banana Carriers: *Benjamin, A.*
Song of the Banshee: *Stanford*
Song of the Bells: *Bantock*
Song of the Blackbird: *Quilter* (Nightingale has a lyre of gold, The)
Song of the Blest: *Foulds*
Song of the Bow, A: *Stanford*
Song of the Concubine: *McLeod*†
Song of the Cradle: *Bryan*
Song of the Cross, The: *Plumstead*
Song of the Cyclops: *Wood, C.*
Song of the Day, A (cycle): *Garton*
Song of the Drowned Man: *Alwyn*†
Song of the Exile: *Thomas, Mansel*
Song of the Fisherman of Cacru: *Kirkwood*
Song of the Flax: *White, M.V.*
Song of the Frogs: *Holst*
Song of the Genie: *Bantock*
Song of the Inadequacy of the Gods and the Good: *Muldowney*
Song of the Leaves of Life and the Water of Life, The: *Vaughan Williams*
Song of the Mad Prince, The: *Bennett, R.R.*; *Pope*
Song of the Nightingale [Alun]: *Lloyd, J.M.*
Song of the Nightingale, The [MacDiarmid]: *Stevenson*
Song of the North: *Weston*
Song of the Nubian Girl: *Coleridge-Taylor*
Song of the Palanquin Bearers: *Shaw*
Song of the Peach-blossom Fountain: *Bantock*
Song of the People: *Jones, J.M.*
Song of the Pilgrims, The: *Vaughan Williams*
Song of the Ronin: *Greaves, R.*
Song of the Secret, The: *Howells*; *Peterkin*
Song of the Ship: *Stevens, B.*
Song of the Sirens: *Carey, C.*
Song of the Smoke: *Muldowney*
Song of the Soldiers, The: *Berkeley, L.*
Song of the Songless: *Plumstead*
Song of the Southern River, A: *Rubbra*†
Song of the Stream: *Quilter*
Song of the Sword: *Bantock*
Song of the Three Mariners: *Harty*
Song of the Wanderer, The: *Bennett, R.R.*
Song of the Wandering Aengus: *Scott, D.B.*
Song of the Water Maiden: *Peterkin*
Song of the Waterseller in the Rain: *Muldowney*
Song of the Wind: *Rowley*
Song of the Woods: *Holst*
Song of Trust, A (Psalm 121): *Stanford*†
Song of Vanity Fair, The: *Vaughan Williams*
Song of Wine, A: *Scott, C.*
Song of Wisdom, A: *Stanford*†
Song to a Child at Night-time: *Pope*
Song to Celia's Spinet, A: *Croft*
Song to the Seals: *Bantock*
Song Without Words: *Barratt*
Song Written at Sea: *Stanford*
Song-Offerings: *Ronald*
Songs: *Birkett*; *Bridge*; *Crossland-Holland*(†); *Danyel*; *Howells*; *Purcell, H.*; *Scott, F.G.*; *Stout*†; *Sullivan*; *Turnbull*; *Warlock*; *Wesley, S.*; *Wood, Hugh*
Songs and Broken Music: *Woolrich*†
Songs and Cantatas: *Handel*
Songs and Dialogues of Matthew Locke: *Locke*
Songs and Proverbs of William Blake (cycle): *Britten*

Songs for a Winter's Evening: *Musgrave*
Songs for Achilles: *Tippett*†
Songs for Ariel: *Tippett*(†)
Songs for Children's Dreams (cycle): *Bayford*
Songs for Grace and Siân: *Thomas, Mansel*
Songs for Joanna: *Nelson*
Songs for Male Voice: *Head*
Songs for the North: *Hearne*(*)
Songs from a Rock Opera: *Stafford*
Songs from 'A Shropshire Lad': *Butterworth, G.*
Songs from Connacht: *Hughes, Herbert*
Songs from County Kerry: *Moeran*
Songs from Factories and Fields (cycle): *Stevenson*
Songs from 'Out of the East': *Muldowney*
Songs from Rosseter's Book of Ayres: *Campion*
Songs from Spoon River: *Downes*
Songs from the Chinese: *Britten*†
Songs from the Chinese Poets: *Bantock*
Songs from the Exotic: *Weir*
Songs from the Fairy Play 'Through the Green Door': *O'Neill*
Songs from 'The Good Person of Sichuan': *Muldowney*
Songs from 'The Resistable Rise of Arturo Ui': *Muldowney*†
Songs from 'Twelfth Night': *Harrison, J.*
Songs I had are withered, The: *Jeffreys, J.*
Songs in Blue: *Dickinson*
Songs of a Shropshire Lad: *Peel*
Songs of a Wayfarer: *Ireland*
Songs of Arcady: *Bantock*
Songs of Arabia: *Bantock*
Songs of Childhood: *Orr, B.*
Songs of China: *Bantock*
Songs of Dachine Rainer (cycle): *Routh*
Songs of Devotion (cycle): *Marsh*†
Songs of Egypt: *Bantock*
Songs of Erin: *Stanford*
Songs of Experience: *Rodgers*; *Sykes*
Songs of Faith: *Stanford*
Songs of Farewell: *Routh*
Songs of Four Seasons: *Hedges*
Songs of Good Counsel (cycle): *Cruft*
Songs of India: *Bantock*
Songs of Innocence: *Sykes*
Songs of Innocence (cycle): *Foster, D.*†
Songs of Japan: *Bantock*
Songs of Joy: *Phillips, M.*
Songs of Lawrence Durrell: *Routh*
Songs of London Town: *Burtch*
Songs of Love and Life: *Fogg*
Songs of Love and Loss: *Hugill*(†)
Songs of Mary: *Burgon*†
Songs of Mourning: *Coprario*
Songs of New Beginnings: *McGuire*†
Songs of Old Age (cycle): *Warren*
Songs of Old Cathay: *Scott, C.*
Songs of Old Ireland: *Stanford*
Songs of Persia: *Bantock*
Songs of Peter Warlock: *Warlock*†
Songs of Romance and Delight: *Head*
Songs of Silver: *Belben*†
Songs of Sir Walter Scott (cycle): *Routh*
Songs of Solomons: *Solomons*(†)
Songs of Sorrow: *Quilter*
Songs of Springtime: *Ronald*
Songs of Strange Creatures: *Boyle, R.*
Songs of Summer: *Clarke, R.C.*; *Hamilton, I.*

Songs of Sun and Shade: *Coleridge-Taylor*
Songs of Sundrie Kinds: *Greaves, Thomas*
Songs of Sundrie Kinds (cycle): *Tate, P.*†
Songs of the Countryside: *Head*
Songs of the Half-Light: *Berkeley, L.*†
Songs of the Hedgerow: *Martin, E.*
Songs of the Isles: *Roberton*
Songs of the Linleys: *Linley, T.*
Songs of the Mad Sea-Captain: *Gibbs, Armstrong*
Songs of the Malvern Hills: *Clarke, R.C.*
Songs of the Marches: *Glyn*†
Songs of the Night: *Scott, S.*
Songs of the North: *Grainger, P.*
Songs of the Sea: *Stanford*
Songs of the Seasons: *Elwyn-Edwards*
Songs of the Seraglio: *Bantock*
Songs of the Ship: *del Riego*
Songs of the Three Birds: *Elwyn-Edwards*
Songs of the War: *Glyn*
Songs of the Wrens, The (The Window): *Sullivan*
Songs of the Year: *Thomas, Mansel*
Songs of the Zodiac (cycle): *Bush, G.*
Songs of Travel: *Vaughan Williams*
Songs of William Lloyd Webber, The: *Lloyd Webber*
Songs of Wonder: *Bush, G.*
Songs Sacred and Profane: *Ireland*
Songs to Poems by William Blake: *Swann*
Songs with Piano: *Clarke, R.*
Songster, The: *Lutyens*
Song-thrush, The: *Thiman*
Sonnet (When our two souls) [Browning, E.B.]: *Wills*† (Our Two Souls)
Sonnet (Beautie, sweet love, is like the morning dew) [Daniel]: *Steptoe*
Sonnet (Carecharmer sleep, son of the sable night) [Daniel]: *Rutter*†; *Steptoe*
Sonnet (Let others sing of knights and paladins) [Daniel] *Steptoe*
Sonnet [Drayton] (Evil spirit, your beauty, haunts me still, An): *Wills*(†)
Sonnet [Keats]: *Richardson*
Sonnet [Labé]: *Berkeley, L.*;
Sonnet [Shakespeare]: *Beamish*†
Sonnet 18 (Shall I compare thee to a summer's day? [Shakespeare]: *Aiken*; *Hartley*; *Parry, C.H.H.*; *Pender*; *Sagar*; *Wetherell*
Sonnet 27 (Weary with toil, I haste me to my bed) [Shakespeare]: *Scott, D.B.*
Sonnet 29 (When in disgrace with fortune and men's eyes) [Shakespeare]: *Parry, C.H.H.*
Sonnet 30 (When to the sessions of sweet silent thought) [Shakespeare]: *Parry, C.H.H.*
Sonnet 49 (Against that time, if ever that time come) [Shakespeare]: *Scott, D.B.*
Sonnet 71 (No longer mourn for me when I am dead) [Shakespeare]: *Parry, C.H.H.*
Sonnet 87 (Farewell, thou art too dear for my possessing) [Shakespeare]: *Parry, C.H.H.*
Sonnet 97 (How like a winter hath mine absence been) [Shakespeare]: *Wetherell*
Sonnet 104 (To me, fair friend, you never can be old) [Shakespeare]: *Nash*
Sonnet 109 (O never say that I was false of heart) [Shakespeare]: *Parry, C.H.H.*
Sonnet 113 (Since I left you, mine eye is in my mind) [Shakespeare]: *Scott, D.B.*

Sonnet 116 (Let me not to the marriage of true minds admit impediment) [Shakespeare]: *Wetherell*
Sonnet 127 (In the old age black was not counted fair) [Shakespeare]: *Wills*
Sonnet 128 (How oft when thou, my music, music play'st) [Shakespeare]: *Wills*
Sonnet 129 (Th'expense of spirit in a waste of shame) [Shakespeare]: *Wills*
Sonnet 131 (Thou art as tyrannous, so as thou art) [Shakespeare]: *Wills*
Sonnet 136 (If thy soul check thee that I come so near) [Shakespeare]: *Wills*
Sonnet 138 (When my love swears that she is made of truth) [Shakespeare]: *Wills*
Sonnet 146 (Poor soul, the centre of my sinful earth) [Shakespeare]: *Wills*
Sonnet 147 (My love is as a fever, longing still) [Shakespeare]: *Wills*
Sonnet on a Monkey: *Bennett, R.R.*
Sonnet on the Descent from Heaven: *Routh*
Sonnet Op 102: *Berkeley, L.*
Soontree: *Peterkin*
Sorcery of Olwen, The: *Thomas, Mansel*
Sorrow: *Scott, C.*
Sorrow and Spring: *Peel*
Sorrow of Love, The: *Scott, D.B.*
Sorrow of Mydath: *Davidson, M.*
Sorrow Song: *Brian*
Sorrow, stay: *Dowland*
Sorrows of true love, The: *Pickard*
Soul's expression, The: *Reizenstein*
Sound of hidden music, The: *Parry, C.H.H.*
Sound the trumpet: *Purcell, H.*
Soundbites: *Matheson*†
Sounds: *Barrett*†
Sounds from the Middle Floor: *Shur*†
South Wind: *Rootham*
South Winds, The: *Ronald*
Southern Love Songs: *Coleridge-Taylor*
Souvenirs du Voyage (cycle): *Powers**
Sower's Song, The: *Stanford*
Sowing: *Gurney*
Sowing the seeds of love: *Butterworth, G.*
Sozu-Baba (music theatre): *Marsh*†
Space: *Moult*
Space and Beauty: *O'Brien*
Space of Summer: *Headington*
Spanish Ladies, The: *Vaughan Williams*
Spanish Lady, The: *Hughes, Herbert*
Spanish Liederbooklet, A (cycle): *Weir**
Speak, I pray thee, gentle Jesus: *Jenkins, D.*; *Jenkins, W.*
Speak, music, and bring to me *Elgar*
Speak, my heart: *Elgar*
Speak, speak, at last reply: *Lawes, H.*
Speak to me, my love: *Bridge*
Speaking from the Snow: *Naylor, B.*
Speaking Silence: *Berkeley, M.*
Spears and Fiddleheads: *Routh*
Speciosus forma: *Jeffreys, G.**
Spectres: *Davies, L.*
Speedwell, speedwell, what is your dream: *Owen*
Spell, The: *Bernofsky*
Spell of Sleep: *Matthews, D.*†
Spellbound: *Wills*
Spider, The: *Barton*†
Spindrift: *Fogg*
Spinning Song: *Bax*

Index of titles

Spirit of the Spring, The: *Parry, C.H.H.*
Spirit Song: Life of life: *Bantock*
Spirto ben nato, in cui si specchia e vede: *Britten**
Spit in my face, ye Jews, and pierce my side: *Downes*†
Spite of the god-head, pow'r ful love: *Purcell, H.*
Spleen [Dowson]: *Ireland*
Spleen [Verlaine]: *Dieren**
Splendour falls on castle walls, The: *Gibbs, Armstrong*; *Pilling*; *Vaughan Williams*; *Walthew*; *Wood, C.*
Spotted Cow, The: *Tomlinson*
Spouse to the Beloved, The: *Pilkington, M.* (Christ, my beloved)
Sprig of Thyme, The: *Grainger, P.*
Spring: *Elwyn-Edwards*; *Glyn,*
Spring [Blake]: *Owen*
Spring [Bridges]: *Whittaker*
Spring (Good morning, life) [Davies]: *Hedges*
Spring [Heine]: *Stanford(*)*
Spring [Hopkins]: *Pope*
Spring [Irvine]: *Gibbs, Armstrong,*
Spring [Li Po]: *Bliss*
Spring [Nashe]: *Dieren*; *Gurney*; *Raynor* (Spring, the sweet Spring)
Spring [Rossetti, C.]: *Self, A.*
Spring [Shakespeare]: *Williams, W.S.G.* (It was a lover and his lass / Lover and his Lass, The / Pretty Ringtime / Spring Song [Shakespeare])
Spring [Tennyson]: *Stanford;* *Sullivan*
Spring, The [Barnes]: *Carey, C.*
Spring, The [Raine]: *Routh*
Spring and Fall: *Pope*
Spring bereaved: *Luff†*
Spring comes: *Bainton*
Spring Ditty, A: *Scott, C.*
Spring Gardens (Pleasures of Spring Gardens, The): *Boyce*
Spring goeth all in white: *Moeran*
Spring has Come, The: *White, M.V.*
Spring is at the door: *Quilter*
Spring is coming [Somervell]: *Handel*
Spring is here with bud and blossom: *Somervell*
Spring is singing in the garden: *Anderson, W.H.*
Spring Joy: *Foulds*
spring! may: *Wills†*
Spring Morning [Parry]: *Thomas, Mansel*
Spring Morning, A: *Wilson, H.L.*
Spring Rain [Armstrong]: *Alwyn*
Spring Rain [Ruckert]: *Bax*
Spring Sadness: *Wishart*
Spring Scene: *Naylor, P.*
Spring Song [Antipater]: *Berkeley, L.*
Spring Song [Hayes]: *Bantock*
Spring Song [Scott]: *Scott, C.*
Spring Song, A [Shakespeare]: *Parry, C.H.H.* (It was a lover and his lass / Lover and his Lass, The / Pretty Ringtime / Spring [Shakespeare] / Sweet and Twenty)
Spring Song of the Birds: *Dieren*
Spring Sorrow: *Center*; *Ireland* (All suddenly the wind comes soft / Buds in Spring)
Spring, the sweet Spring: *Delius*; *Pope*; *Warlock* (Spring [Nashe])
Spring, the travelling man: *Walters, L.*
Spring Weather: *Dean*
Springtime: *Kahn*
Spring-time of Life, The: *Rootham*

St Andrews: *Rootham* (Fairy Town, A)
St Brendan's Graveyard: *Scott, F.G.*
St Bride's Song: *Howells*
St Columba's Poem on Derry: *Parke*
St Govan: *Lloyd, J.M.*; *Roberts, M.*
St Mark's Square: *Head*
St Mary's Bells: *Martin, E.* (Bells of San Marie, The)
Stänchen: *Weir**
Stand face to face, friend: *Bantock*
Stanzas from Tintern Abbey (cycle): *McLelland-Young*
Star, A: *White, M.V.*
Star Candles: *Head*
Star Light Carol, The: *Davies, J.*
Star of Bethlehem, The: *Adams*(†)
Star of the County Down, The: *Hughes, Herbert*
Starless Crown: *Davies, William*
Starlight: *Hearne*
Starlight Night, The: *Hugh-Jones*
Starlighters, The: *Gibbs, Armstrong*
Starling, The: *Lehmann*
Starry Night, A: *Coleridge-Taylor*
Stars, The: *Coleridge-Taylor*
Stars above me, golden-footed: *Stanford*
Stars of the Desert: *Woodforde-Finden*
Star-talk: *Gurney*
Stay, cruel, stay: *Danyel*
Stay, Glycia, stay: *Cavendish*
Stay in town: *Whittaker*
Stay, O sweet, and do not rise: *Blyton*†; *Davidson, M.*; *Frankel, B.*; *Joubert* (Daybreak [Donne] / Break of Day)
Stay, silly heart, and do not break: *Lanier*
Stay time awhile thy flying: *Dowland*
Steadfast Shepherd, The: *Hook*
Sterne mit den goldnen Füsschen: *Stanford**
Stevie's Tunes (cycle): *Dickinson*
Still falls the rain (Canticle III): *Britten*†
Still the lark finds repose: *Linley Snr*
Still to be neat, still to be drest: *Elgar*; *P.Young*† (Beyond Art)
Still Waters: *Morris, A.*†
Stillness, The: *Naylor, P.*
Stinging Nettle, The: *Searle*
Stockdoves, The: *Poston*
Stone, a Flower, a Chinese Vase, A: *Moult*
Stonecracker John: *Coates, E.*
Stones trip Coquet Burn: *Colling*†
Stop all the clocks, cut off the telephone: *Roe* (Funeral Blues)
Stopping by Woods on a Snowy Evening: *Roberts, T.*; *Swann*
Stör' nicht: *Stevenson**
Storm [Brontë]: *Joubert*
Storm [Raine]: *Bliss*
Storm Song: *Bowen*
Storm Wind, The: *Naylor, P.*
Stow-on-the-Wold: *Jeffreys, J.*
Strange to say: *Hudes*†
Stranger's Grave, The: *Harty*
Stranger's Song, The: *Gardiner*
Strawberries Swimming in the Cream: *Barratt* (Chopcherry / Summer Song / Whenas the rye reach to the chin)
Stray Nymph of Dian, A: *Parry, C.H.H.*
Stream in the Valley, The: *Britten*
Street sounds to the soldiers' tread, The: *Berkeley, L.*; *Somervell* (Encounter, The [Housman])

274 Index of titles

Striem: *Marsh*†
Strew no more red roses: *Bridge*
Strew on her roses, roses: *Ronald* (Requiescat [Arnold])
Strike the viol, touch the lute: *Purcell, H.*
Strings in the earth and air: *Moeran*
Strong son of God: *Stanford*
Strugnell's Haiku: *Matthews, C.*(†)
Student's Serenade: *Hatton*
Study of a Spider: *Alwyn*
Stuttering Lovers, The: *Hughes, Herbert*
Subaltern's Love-song, A: *Horder*; *Wills*
Submarines: *Elgar*
Submerged Bar, The: *Woolrich*
Substitution: *Coleridge-Taylor*
Succession of the Foure Sweet Months, The: *Bernofsky*; *Stewart*
Such a starved bank of moss: *Somervell*
Sufferance: *Lawes, H.*
Suffolk Harvest Song: *Brown, C.*†
Suffolk Mist: *Brown, C.*†
Suffolk Owl, The: *Dunhill* (Sweet Suffolk Owl)
Súfi, hither gaze: *Bantock*
Suicide in the copse: *Fowler*†
Suite O' Bairnsangs, A: *Musgrave*
Suky, you shall be my wife: *Warlock*
Sumarnott: *Hearne**
Summer: *Elwyn-Edwards*
Summer [Dunlop]: *Hearne*†
Summer [Li Po]: *Bliss*
Summer (Sweet is the breath of morn) [Milton]: *Hedges*
Summer Day, A: *Lambert, C.*
Summer Eve: *Delius*
Summer Evening: *MacDonald*
Summer heats bestowing, The: *Storace*
Summer Idyll, A [Hammond-Spencer]: *Coleridge-Taylor*
Summer Idyll, A [le Gallienne]: *Head*
Summer is a-coming in: *Watkins*†
Summer is a-cumin in: *Scott, C.*
Summer is icumen in: *Pope*
Summer Landscape: *Delius*
Summer Lullaby: *Foreman*
Summer Night: *Gibbs, Armstrong*
Summer Nights: *Delius*
Summer on the Prairie: *Anderson, W.H.*
Summer Palace, The: *Gibbs, Armstrong*
Summer Rain: *Walker, E.*
Summer Schemes: *Finzi*; *Ireland*
Summer Song: *Barratt* (Chopcherry / Strawberries Swimming in the Cream / Whenas the rye reach to the chin)
Summer Storm: *Lehmann*
Summer's (Simmer's) a pleasant time: *Musgrave*
Summer's Peace: *White, A.*
Summertime: *Ronald*
Summertime: *Gibbs, Armstrong*
Summoned by Mother: *Dickinson*†
Summum bonum: *Bantock*
Sun, The: *Bantock*
S'un casto amor, s' una pietà superna: *Britten**
Sun Has Set, The: *McLelland-Young*
Sun, Moon and Stars (cycle): *Maconchy*
Sun shall be no more thy light, The: *Greene*
Sun shines down, The: *Britten*
Sun whose rays are all ablaze, The: *Sullivan*
Sunday Dip: *Hold*

Sundown: *Scott, C.*
Sunken Garden, The: *Foreman*
Sunny March: *Lidgey*
Sunset [Munch]: *Delius*
Sunset [Whitman]: *Butt*(†)
Sunset and Sea: *Thomas, Mansel*
Sunshine and Dusk: *Scott, C.*
Sunshine of your smile, The: *Ray*
Supper: *Britten*
Supplication [Rowley]: *Rowley*
Supplication, A [Cowley]: *Kleyn*
Supplication, A [Wyatt]: *Rootham* (And wilt thou leave me thus? / Appeal, The / Lover's Appeal, The)
Sur la Rivière: *Short**
Sur quel arbre du ciel: *Berkeley, L.**
Surrealist Landscape: *Dickinson*†
Sursum Corda: *Fuller*
Suspense: *Birkett*
Sussex by the Sea: *Ward-Higgs*
Sussex Carol: *Willcocks*
Sussex Ways: *Gibbs, Armstrong*
Svartor Rosor: *Delius**
Swallows, The: *Solomons*(†)
Swan, The: *Ferguson*
Swansea Town: *Jacobson*
Sweeney the Mad: *Jeffreys, J.*
Sweepers, The: *Elgar*
Sweet Afton: *Thiman* (Afton Water / Flow gently, sweet Afton)
Sweet almond blossom: *Head*
Sweet and low: *Bryan*; *Corke*; *Lear*; *Scott, A.*; *Somervell*; *Williamson, M.* (Wind of the Western Sea)
Sweet and Twenty: *Paterson*; *Warlock* (It was a lover and his lass / Lover and his Lass, The / Pretty Ringtime / Spring [Shakespeare] / Spring Song [Shakespeare])
Sweet are the banks: *Hook*
Sweet are the thoughts [Anon]: *Dalby*
Sweet are the thoughts that savour of content [Greene]: *Barley*
Sweet baby butterfly: *Coleridge-Taylor*
Sweet, be no longer sad: *Purcell, H.*
Sweet, be not proud of those two eyes: *Dyson*
Sweet chance, that led my steps abroad: *Head*
Sweet, come again: *Rosseter*
Sweet Content: *Warlock* (O sweet content)
Sweet Cupid, ripen her desire: *Corkine*
Sweet cyder is a great thing: *Steele* (Great Things)
Sweet day, so cool: *Head*
Sweet disorder in the dress, A: *Blyton*
Sweet Echo: *Fiske*
Sweet if you like and love me still: *Jones, R.*
Sweet is the breath of morn (Summer [Milton]): *Hedges*
Sweet is the night air: *Hugill*†
Sweet Isabell: *Bennett, R.R.*
Sweet July, bring me a butterfly: *Dunhill*
Sweet, let me go: *Corkine*
Sweet Little Girl that I Love, The: *Hook*
Sweet Memories: *Evans, D.F.*
Sweet Muses, nurses of delights: *Anon*
Sweet Music: *Somers-Cocks*
Sweet Nightingale: *Anderson, W.H.*; *Bury*
Sweet Nightingale, The: *Horton*
Sweet nymph, come to thy lover: *Morley*

Index of titles 275

Sweet o' the Year, The: *Center*; *Moeran*; *Warlock* (Autolycus' Song / When daffodils begin to peer)
Sweet Pastorale: *Lyall*†
Sweet Polly Oliver: *Britten*; *Newman, F.*
Sweet pretty bird contented rest: *Stanley*
Sweet Season, The: *Ireland* (When May is in his prime)
Sweet sounds, begone: *Gibbs, Armstrong*
Sweet, stay awhile, why will (do) you rise?: *Anon*; *Bush, G.*; *Dowland*; *Lawes, H.*
Sweet Suffolk owl, so trimly dight: *Elwyn-Edwards*; *Poston* (Suffolk Owl, The)
Sweet transports: *Shield*
Sweet Venevil ran with her light young feet (Young Venevil): *Delius*
Sweet was the song the Virgin sung: *Attey*
Sweet-and-twenty: *Paterson*; *Warlock* (Mistress Mine / O mistress mine)
Sweeter than roses: *Purcell, H.*
Sweeter than the violet: *Stanford*
Sweetest love, I do not go: *Stevens, B.*
Sweethearts: *Sullivan*
Sweethearts and Wives: *Head*
Swiftly, swiftly: *Thomas, Mansel*
Swimmer, The: *Elgar*
Swing, The: *Lehmann*; *White, A.*
Sword, A: *Gurney*
Sybil: *Hudes*
Sycamore Shade, The: *Arne, T.*
Sylvia, how could you mistrust: *Eccles*
Sylvia is fair: *Cavendish*
Sylvia, now your scorn give over: *Purcell, H.*
Symphony in Yellow: *Blyton*(†)
Symptoms of Love: *Wood, Hugh*

T

Table and the Chair, The: *Hely-Hutchinson*
Tachograph: *Burrell*
Tai Chi on a Rainy Day: *Morris, A.*†
Tailor and his Mouse, The: *Clarke, R.*†
Take heed, young heart, to Time: *Gibbs, Armstrong*
Take me, take me, some of you: *Hook*
Take not a woman's anger ill: *Purcell, H.*
Take, O take those lips away: *Bishop*; *Dalby*(†); *Dieren*; *Dring*; *Hudes*; *Jeffreys, J.*; *Parry, C.H.H.*; *Plumstead*; *Quilter*; *Rubbra*; *Somervell*; *Vaughan Williams*; *Warlock*(†); *Westrup*; *Wilson, John* (Love and Grief / Seals of Love)
Tale of the Lamb, The: *Plumstead*
Taliesin 1952: *Thomas, Mansel*
Talk not of love, it gives me pain: *Liddell*
Tall Nettles: *Newson*; *Pickard*
Talors: *Glyn*
Tango: *Bennett, R.R.*
Tankas of the Four Seasons: *Rawsthorne*†
Tant que mes yeux: *Berkeley, L.**
Tanzlied: *Smyth**
Tarry Ooo: *Dalby*
Tarry Trousers: *Butterworth, G.*
Tavern: *Mullinar*
Teach, Oh! Teach Me to Forget: *Bishop*
Teare, The [Herrick]: *Hatton*
Tears [Anon]: *Coleridge-Taylor*
Tears [Anon]: *Gurney* (Sleeping / Weep you no more, sad fountains)

Tears [Whitman]: *Stanford*
Tears, idle tears, I know not what they mean: *Bridge*; *Scott, A.*; *Somervell*; *Sullivan*; *Vaughan Williams*
Tears of St Joseph, The: *Someren-Godfery*
Tell her, O tell her: *MacCunn*
Tell me lovely shepherd: *Boyce*
Tell me, my heart: *Bishop*
Tell me no more I am deceived: *Boyce*
Tell me no more you love: *Blow*
Tell me not, sweet, I am unkind: *Harty*; *Keel* (To Lucasta, on Going to the Wars)
Tell me now: *Orr, R.*
Tell me, some pitying angel, quickly say (Blessed Virgin's Expostulation, The): *Purcell, H.*
Tell me the Truth about Love: *Britten*
Tell me, true love: *Dowland*
Tell me, where is fancy bred: *Barrell, B.*†; *Blyton*†; *Quilter*
Tell me, ye brooks (Cantata II): *Boyce*
Tell us, Mary: *Elwyn-Edwards*
Temper of a Maid, The: *Head*
Temple bells are ringing, The: *Woodforde-Finden*
Ten Airs from Musicke of Sundrie Kindes: *Ford, T.*
Ten Ayres: *Lawes, H.*
Ten Blake Songs: *Vaughan Williams*†
Ten Songs: *Blow*; *Boyce*; *Delius*; *Gibbs, Armstrong*
Ten Songs for Low Voice: *Wood, C.*
Ten Songs for Voice and Piano: *Bullard*
Ten Songs from the Chinese: *Bantock*
Ten Types of Hospital Visitor: *Orr, B.*(†)
Ten Songs of Paul Verlaine: *Wilby**
Tender only to one: *Holloway*†
Tender only to one: *Holloway*†
Tenebrae: *Bennett, R.R.*
Tenebrae: *Birtwistle*†
Tentacles of the Dark Nebula: *Bedford*†
Terrible Robber Men, The: *Hughes, Herbert*
Test, The: *Bush, G.*
Tewkesbury Road: *Hand*; *Head*; *Slater*
Thames, The: *Cannon*
Thames a Tempo: *Roe*†
Thanks to thee, O God: *Thomas, Mansel*
Thanksgiving, A: *Ireland* (Pleasure it is to hear iwis the birdes sing)
Thanksgiving to God, for his House, A: *Murrill*
That ever I saw: *Jeffreys, J.*(†) (Fairest May, The / As ever I saw)
That he whom the sun serves: *Procter*
That I may see: *Purcell, H.*
That I want thee, only thee: *Ronald*
Thee, God, I come from: *Parrott*
Their beginning: *Hugill*
Theme of Death, The: *Bayliss*
Then farewell, my trim-built wherry: *Dibdin*
Then from a whirlwind oracle: *Locke*
Then you'll remember me (When other lips): *Balfe*
Theodore or The Pirate King: *Berners*
There are fairies at the bottom of our garden: *Lehmann*
There are seven that pull the thread: *Elgar*
There be none of beauty's daughters: *MacCunn*; *Parry, C.H.H.*; *Quilter*; *Stanford*; *Tomlinson*
There comes an end to summer: *Scott, C.*
There in that other world: *Parry, C.H.H.*
There is a garden in her face: *Bush, G.*; *Campion*; *Keel* (Cherry-ripe)
There is a lady sweet and kind: *Bury*; *Jeffreys, J.*; *Peterkin*; *Standford*; *Tomlinson*; *Warlock* (And

276 Index of titles

yet I love her till I die / My Lady / Passing By / Yet will I love her till I die)
There is a land: *Thompson, L.*
There is no rose of such virtue: *Philips*† (Christmas Carol [Anon])
There is no Season (cycle): *Birkett*
There is none so wise a man: *Short*†
There is wisdom in women: *Møller*
There isn't time: *Lawrence, M.*
There pass the careless people: *Somervell*
There rolls the deep: *Swann*
There was a crooked man: *Jeffreys, J.*
There was a jolly miller: *Grainger, P.* (Jolly Miller, The / Miller of Dee, The)
There was a king: *Dalby*
There was a king in Thule: *Seiber*
There was a king of Liang: *Harrison, J.*
There was a lad was born in Kyle: *Center*; *Atkinson, G.*
There was a lass: *Center*
There was a maiden: *Howells*
There was a man of Thessaly: *Warlock*
There was a one: *Penny*
There was a shepherd: *Jones, R.*
There was a time for shepherds: *Steel*
There was a wily lad: *Jones, R.*
There was an old man in a velvet coat: *Warlock*
There was an old woman went up: *Warlock*
There was never a queen like Balkis: *German*
There will always be Wales: *Parry, J.*
There's a long, long trail a-winding: *Elliott*
There's a wee, wee glen: *Bantock*
There's cauld kail in Aberdeen: *White, A.*
There's longing in the sea: *Elwyn-Edwards*
There's many will love a maid: *Head*
There's none to soothe: *Britten*
There's not a swain on the plain: *Purcell, H.*
There's nothing to stop us now: *Dring*
There's Quayside fer sailors: *Finnissy*†
These are they which came: *Gaul*
These are thy wonders: *Leighton*†
these children: *Roxburgh*
These dainty daffadillies: *Swinstead*
These flowers are I: *Finzi*†
These Growing Years: *Roe*
These springs were maidens once: *Berkeley, L.*†
They are not long, the weeping and the laughter: *Delius* (Passing Dreams)
They evermore do sing: *Perrin*
They say you're angry and rant mightily: *Purcell, H.*
They tell us that you mighty powers above: *Purcell, H.*
They that have power: *Butt*
Thief of the World: *Stanford*
Thine am I, my faithful fair: *MacCunn*
Thine eyes still shined for me: *Parry, C.H.H.*
Things have never changed: *Goehr*
Things Lovelier: *Holst* (You cannot dream things lovelier)
Things that gain by being painted: *Barry*†
Think and be careful: *Dalby*
Think it not strange: *Hook*
Think no more, lad, laugh, be jolly: *Butterworth, G.*; *Somervell*; *Williamson, J.R.*
Think not, my love, when secret grief: *Linley Snr*
Think of me: *Wesley, S.*
Think on me: *Scott, C.*
Thinke then my soule: *Boyle, I.*†

Third and Last Book of Songs: *Jeffreys, J.*
Third Book of Ayres, The: *Campion*
Third Book of Songs, The: *Dowland*
Third Volume of Ten Songs, A: *Gurney*
Thirteen Folksongs: *Grainger, P.*
Thirteen Pence a Day: *Jeffreys, J.*
Thirteen Songs: *Elgar*; *Purcell*; *Thiman*
Thirteen Songs for High Voice: *Warlock*
Thirty Songs: *Purcell, H.*
Thirty-five Scottish Lyrics and Other Poems: *Scott, F.G.*
This dog may kiss your hand: *Standford*
This enders night I saw a sight: *Roe*
This endris night I saw a sight: *Milford*
This is just to say (cycle): *Holloway*
This is not my plaid: *Grainger, P.*
This is the fountain of life: *Crossley-Holland*†
this is the garden: *Bennett, R.R.*; *Roxburgh*
This is the island of gardens: *Coleridge-Taylor*
This is the weather the cuckoo likes: *Jeffreys, J.* (Weather the Cuckoo Likes, The / Weathers)
This lady, ripe and fair and fresh: *Atkins*
This little pig went to market: *Jeffreys, J.*
This Night [Darlow]: *Darlow*
This Night [Pearse]: *Jeffreys, J.*
This night as I sit here alone: *Bliss*
This poet sings the Trojan wars (Anacreon's defeat): *Purcell, H.*
This Sad Serenity: *Hand*
This time of year a twelvemonth past: *Moeran*; *Orr, C.W.*
This train: *Maw*
This unimportant morning: *Routh*
This uninhabited island: *German*
This way that way: *Hudes*
This Worldes Joie: *Bennett, R.R.*
Thistle: *Greaves, Terence*†
Thomas MacDonagh: *Jeffreys, J.*
Thora: *Adams*
Thorn, The: *Treharne*
Those dancing days are gone: *Aston*†
Those evening bells: *Foster, I.*; *Pierson*
Those eyes that set my fancy on a fire: *Barley*
Thou art alone, fond lover: *Miles*†
Thou art as tyrannous, so as thou art (Sonnet 131) [Shakespeare]: *Wills*
Thou art my love, I knew it: *Stanford*
Thou art not fair for all thy red and white: *Lanier*; *Someren-Godfery* (Wily Lover, The)
Thou art risen, my beloved: *Coleridge-Taylor*
Thou art the one truth: *Williams, Grace*
Thou being of marvels: *Thomas, Mansel*
Thou didst delight my eyes: *Gurney*
Thou famished grave: *Swann*
Thou gav'st me leave to kiss: *Warlock*
Thou hast bewitched me, beloved: *Coleridge-Taylor*
Thou hast made me, and shall thy work decay?: *Britten*
Thou openest thine hand: *Greene*
Thou pretty bird, how do I see: *Danyel*
Thou shalt bring them in: *Handel*
Thou soft flowing Avon: *Arne, T.*
Thou wakeful shepherd (Morning Hymn, A): *Purcell, H.*
Though cause for suspicion appears: *Linley Jnr*
Though Chloe's out of fashion: *Boyce*
Though dynasties pass: *Austin*
Though far from joy my sorrows are as far: *Rosseter*

Index of titles

Though I am young and cannot tell: *Lanier* (Shepherd's Song [Jonson])
Though near the fountain: *Standford*
Thought, The: *Holst*
Thoughts of Phena: *Swann*
Thousand sev'ral ways I tried, A: *Purcell, H.*
Thread Suns: *Birtwistle*†
Three AM: *Blyton*
Three a.m. and the rain is falling: *Blyton*
Three American Songs: *Fouché*
Three Arthur Symons Songs: *Ireland*
Three Aspects: *Parry, C.H.H.*
Three Baritone Songs: *German*
Three Base Diversions: *Schofield*
Three Betjeman Songs: *East*
Three Bird Songs: *Bullard*
Three Blake Songs: *Lord*, *Raphael*
Three Cautionary Tales: *Woolrich*(†)
Three Celtic Songs: *Bantock*
Three Cherry Trees, The: *Howells*
Three Children's Songs: *Procter*
Three Chinese Songs: *Nieman*; *Orr, R.*
Three Christmas Songs: *Taylor, C.V.*
Three Comic Songs: *Dickinson*
Three Cotswold Songs: *Head*
Three Dedications: *Roe*
Three D.H. Lawrence Poems: *Raphael*
Three Divine Hymns: *Purcell, H.*
Three Donne Songs: *Maconchy*
Three Early Songs: *Berkeley, L.**
Three Eccentrics: *Roe*
Three Eighteenth Century Songs: *Hughes, Herbert*
Three Elizabethan Poems: *Branson*
Three Elizabethan Songs: *Brown, C.*; *Bush, G.*
Three Emily Dickinson Songs: *Butler*†
Three Enfantines: *Bax*
Three English Lyrics: *Northcott*†
Three Entities, I glorify: *Papastávrou*
Three fine ships go sailing by: *Dunhill*
Three fishers went sailing: *Hullah*
Three Flower Songs: *Harty*
Three Folksongs: *Burgon*†; *McCabe*†
Three Folksongs for Children: *Thomas, Mansel*
Three French Nursery Songs: *Rawsthorne*
Three German Lyrics: *Tomlinson**
Three Georgian Songs (part of cycle): *Holloway*
Three Goan Songs: *Shur*
Three Greek Epigrams: *Rainier*
Three Greek Poems: *Benjamin, A.*
Three Greek Songs: *Berkeley, L.*
Three Hardy Songs: *Bayliss*
Three Housman Songs: *Pope*
Three Impressions: *Benjamin, A.*
Three Interiors: *Newson*†
Three Irish Airs: *Dalway*
Three Irish Folksongs: *Harty*
Three Irish Songs: *Bax*
Three jolly gentlemen: *Butterworth, N.*; *Pilling*; *Teed*
Three Jolly Shepherds: *Rowley*
Three Little Fairy Songs: *Besley*
Three Little Mexican Songs: *Woodforde-Finden*
Three Little Songs: *White, M.V.*
Three Lovescapes (Cantata II): *Harvey, J.*
Three Manx Pictures (Encircled by Sea): *Pike*
Three Mediaeval Carols: *Ferguson*
Three Mesolonghi Songs: *Papastávrou*
Three Middle English Songs: *Howard, M.*
Three Mummers, The: *Head*
Three Motets: *Finnissy*†
Three Mystical Songs: *Rowley*
Three Nocturnes: *Bantock*; *McLeod*
Three Nonsense Songs: *Hely-Hutchinson*
Three Odes of Anacreon: *Parry, C.H.H.*
Three Old English Lyrics: *Keel*
Three Old English Songs: *Clarke, R.*†
Three Pastoral Songs: *Quilter*(†)
Three Poems by E.E. Cummings: *Wills*†
Three Poems by Helen Clarke: *Thompson, P.*
Three Poems by J.M. Synge: *Ward, David*
Three Poems of Irina Ratushiskaya: *McLeod*
Three Poems of Li-Po: *Lambert, C.*
Three Poems of Walt Whitman: *Vaughan Williams*
Three Poems of Walter de la Mare: *Pope*
Three Pomes: *Butterworth, N.*†
Three Poor Mariners: *Quilter*
Three Powell Songs: *Sanger*
Three Psalms: *Rubbra*
Three Ravens, The: *Coleridge-Taylor*; *Grainger, P.*; *Ireland*
Three Religious Songs: *Boyle, R.*†
Three Rilke Songs: *Headington*(*)
Three Rivers: *Cannon*
Three Rondeaux: *Howells*
Three Rossetti Settings: *Wegener*
Three Royal Lyrics: *Bowen*
Three Rupert Brooke Songs: *Taylor, M.*
Three Rustic Poems of John Clare: *Greaves*, *Terence*†
Three Salt-Water Ballads, *Keel*
Three Satirical Songs: *Hughes, Herbert*
Three Sections from the Four Quartets: *Tavener*
Three Settings of Celan (cycle): *Birtwistle*†
Three Settings of Robert Graves: *Bayliss*
Three Shakespeare Songs: *Aston*; *Butterworth, N.*(†); *Dring*; *Quilter*; *Routh*; *Williamson, M.*(†)
Three Shakespeare Sonnets: *Lufft*†; *Wetherell*
Three Sheiling Songs: *Bantock*
Three Sisters: *Le Fleming*
Three Songs: *Barrell, B.*†; *Bax*; *Berners*; *Bridge*†; *Coleridge-Taylor*; *Creswell**; *Foster, I.*; *Gibbs*, *Armstrong*; *Gill*; *Goossens*; *Hely-Hutchinson*; *Jacob*†; *Lawrence*; *McEwen*; *Macfarren*†; *Maconchy*(†); *McEwen*; *Roxburgh*; *Samuel, R.*†; *Someren-Godfery*; *Walton*
Three Songs for Alto and Six Viols: *Woolrich*†
Three Songs for Baritone or Tenor: *Quilter*
Three Songs for Children: *Bantock*
Three Songs for High Voice: *Fulton*
Three Songs for Joanna: *Thomas, Mansel*
Three Songs for Soprano, Horn and Piano: *Randall*†
Three Songs for the Night: *Thomas, Mansel*
Three Songs from a Rock Opera: *Stafford*
Three Songs from 'A Shropshire Lad': *Orr, C.W.*
Three Songs from 'As You Like It': *Read*†
Three Songs from Ezra Pound: *Dalby*†
Three Songs from James Joyce's 'Chamber Music': *Blake, H.*
Three Songs from Old Rhymes: *Dalby*
Three Songs from Oscar Wilde: *Towers*
Three Songs from the Greek Anthology: *Bantock*
Three Songs from 'The Heart of the Matter' (cycle): *Britten*†
Three Songs from the Underground: *Talbot*
Three Songs from 'The Unicorns' (cycle): *Dickinson*
Three Songs of Ben: *Young, P.*†

Three Songs of Ben Jonson: *Bush, G.*
Three Songs of Faery: *Carey, C.*
Three Songs of Fantasy: *Head*
Three Songs of Innocence: *Cooke*†; *Jacob*
Three Songs of Jocelyn Brooke: *Searle*
Three Songs of Love: *McGregor*
Three Songs of Mystery: *Foreman*
Three Songs of Sister Miriam: *Bantock*
Three Songs of the Countryside: *Knight, T.*
Three Songs of the Sea: *Quilter*
Three Songs of Venice: *Head*
Three Songs of Walter de la Mare: *Pope*
Three Songs of William Blake: *Quilter*
Three Songs on Poems by Dylan Thomas: *Boyle, R.*
Three Songs on Poems by Louis MacNiece: *Boyle, R.*
Three Songs to Julia: *Dyson*
Three Songs to Medieval French texts: *Crosse**
Three Songs to Poems by John Fletcher: *Hand*
Three Songs to Poems by Roland Mathias: *Thomas, Mansel*
Three Songs to Words of Stevie Smith: *Snell*†
Three Sonnets: *Randalls*
Three Sonnets from Boccaccio: *Harrison, J.*
Three Sonnets to Delia: *Steptoe*
Three Sonnets to Orpheus: *Ward, David*
Three Spirituals: *Hattey*
Three Spring Songs: *German*
Three Surrealist Songs: *Tavener*†
Three Sussex Songs: *Blake, H.*
Three Things: *Aston*†
Three Traditional Ulster Airs: *Harty*
Three Translations of Silence: *Matheson*
Three Troubadour Songs: *Orchard*
Three 'Twelfth Night' Songs: *Charlesworth*†
Three Vocalises: *Vaughan Williams*†
Three Welsh Lyrics: *Williams, W.S.G.*
Three Welsh Melodies: *Mathias*(†)
Three Wessex Songs: *Austin*
Three Winter Songs: *Beamish*†
Three young rats with black felt hats: *Maw*
Threnody: *Burgon*†
Thresher, The: *Berkeley, L.*
Threshing Song: *Cockshott*
Threshold: *Goossens*
Thrice happy lovers (Epithalamium): *Purcell, H.*
Thrice happy she: *Carey, C.*
Thrice toss these oaken ashes: *Campion*; *Steele*
Through doors ajar: *Evans, T.H.*
Through gilded trellises of the heat: *Walton*
Through long, long years: *Delius*
Through mournful shades: *Purcell, H.*
Through softly falling rain: *Shaw*
Through the centuries I have held your hand: *Alwyn*; *Dring*
Through the Ivory Gate: *Parry, C.H.H.*
Through the long days and years: *Elgar*
Through the streets of Picardy: *Jeffreys, J.*
Through the sunny garden: *Quilter*
Thunderstorms: *Bliss*
Thus spake Jesus: *Head*
Thus to a ripe consenting maid: *Purcell, H.*
Thy dark eyes to mine: *Bax*
Thy genius, lo: *Purcell, H.*
Thy hand, Belinda: *Purcell, H.* (Dido's Farewell / Dido's Lament / When I am laid in earth)
Thy hand in mine: *Bridge* (Sacred Flame, The)
Thyrsis and Milla arm in arm together: *Morley*

Tich: *Nyman*
Tide rises, the tide falls, The: *Birkett*; *Peterkin*
Tides: *Shaw*
Tie the strings to my life, O Lord: *Swann*
Tigaree Torum Orum: *Hughes, Herbert*
Tiger Lily, The: *Gibbs, Armstrong*
Tiger, tiger burning bright: *Clarke, R.* (Tyger, tyger)
Till Earth Outwears: *Finzi*
Till I wake: *Woodforde-Finden*
Tilly: *Moeran*
Time and the bell have buried the day: *Tavener*
Time, cruel time, canst thou subdue that brow: *Danyel*
Time for Sleeping: *Hudes*(†)
Time is flying: *Kleyn*
Time I've lost in wooing, The: *Scott, C.*
Time Lag Zero: *Dillon*†
Time o' day: *Scott, C.*
Time of Roses, The: *Orr, C.W.*; *Quilter*
Time stands still with gazing on her face: *Dowland* (Song [Anon])
Time, that leads the fatal round: *Lupo*
Time to Rise: *Williamson, M.*
Timely Admonition, The: *Arne, T.*
Time's Whiter Series: *Bennett, R.R.*†
Tinker's Daughter, The: *Moeran*
Tinker's Song, The: *Dibdin*
Tired: *Vaughan Williams*
Tired Tim: *Howells*
'Tis but a frown, I prithee let me die: *Lawes, H.*
'Tis but a week since down the glen: *Bridge*
'Tis nature's voice: *Purcell, H.*
'Tis only no harm to know it, you know: *Shield*(†)
'Tis Spring, come out to ramble: *Pope* (Lent Lily, The / Lenten Lily, The)
'Tis time I think by Wenlock Town: *Gurney*; *Jeffreys, J.*; *Mitchell*; *Moeran*; *Orr, C.W.*; *Pope* (By Wenlock Town / Hawthorn Time)
'Tis when to sleep: *Bishop*
'Tis wine that inspires: *Gibbs, Armstrong*
Tit for Tat: *Britten*
Tit for Tat: *Britten*
Titania: *Gibbs, Armstrong*
To... : *Henshall* (One word is too often profaned)
To a Baby Brother: *Anderson, W.H.*
To a Blackbird: *Liddell*
To a Bygone Spring: *Martin, E.*
To a Child [Barker]: *Williamson, M.*
To a Child [Owen]: *Daubney*
To a Child Dancing in the Wind: *Tavener*†
To a Gentleman who often Escorted Her on her Journeys: *Pike*
To a Girl on her Birthday: *Anderson, W.H.*
To a Lady: *Scott, F.G.*
To a Lady Singing to Herself by the Thames-side: *Locke*
To a Little Red Spider: *Lehmann*
To a Loch Fyne Fisherman: *Scott, F.G.*
To a Poet: *Finzi*
To a Poet a Thousand Years Hence: *Carey, C.*; *Finzi*
To a Young Cat in the Orchard: *Hugh-Jones*
To a Young Lady: *Kleyn*
To all the sex deceitful: *Arne, T.*
To Althea, from Prison: *Gibbs, Armstrong*; *Keel*; *Miller*; *Parry, C.H.H.*; *Quilter*
To an Isle in the Water: *Le Fleming*
To Anise: *Gibbs, Armstrong*
To Anthea: *Birkett*; *Hatton*; *Pope* (Bid me but live / Love Song [Herrick])

Index of titles

To ask for all thy love: *Dowland*
To Aster: *Berkeley, L.*
To bed, to bed says sleepy-head: *Jeffreys, J.*
To Blossoms: *Parry, C.H.H.*; *Turnbull*; *Young, Douglas*
To Carnations: *Stanford*
To Chloe, in sickness: *Bennett, W.S.*
To Cornwall and Beyond: *Self, A.*
To couple is a custom: *Walton*(†)
To Daffodils: *Delius*; *Dring*; *Mullinar*; *Pope*; *Toye* (Fair daffodils, we weep to see)
To Daisies: *Quilter*
To dance and sing: *Dunhill*
To Death: *Williams, Grace*
To Echo: *Grainger, E.*
To Eire: *Bax*
To Electra: *Bush, G.*; *Torphichen* (I dare not ask a kiss)
To God: *White, M.V.*
To God (God gives not onely corne): *Roe*(†)
To God (I'll come, I'll creep): *Turnbull*
To God (My God, I'm wounded): *Roe*(†)
To God the Father: *Lawes, H.*†
To God the Holy Ghost: *Lawes, H.*†
To God the Son: *Lawes, H.*†
To Gratiana Dancing and Singing: *Browne*
To Helen: *Taylor, C.V.*
To his Angrie God: *Roe*(†)
To his Coy Mistress: *Hugill*
To his Saviour, a Child: *Roe*(†)
To his Sweet Saviour: *Roe*(†)
To Joy: *Finzi*
To Julia: *Quilter*
To Julia: *Hatton* (Night Piece, The)
To Julia: *Turnbull* (Julia / Rock of Rubies, The)
To lie flat on the back: *Britten*
To Life: *Maw*†
To Lizbie Browne: *Finzi*
To Lucasta, on Going to the Wars: *Kleyn*; *Parry, C.H.H.*; *Somervell* (Tell me not, sweet, I am unkind)
To Make my Mistress Kind: *Jeffreys, J.* (Whenas I wake)
To Mary: *White, M.V.*
To me, fair friend, you never can be old (Sonnet 104) [Shakespeare]: *Nash*
To Morning: *Fogg*
To Music: *Bullard*; *Mowbray*; *White, M.V.* (Music thou queen of heaven)
To Music – to becalm a sweetsick youth: *Dring*
To Music – to becalm his fever: *Murrill*; *Toye*
To My Lady: *Rowley*
To My Mountain: *Stevenson*
To Myra: *Bowen*
To Olympia (A OI): *Solomons*
To One Beloved: *Ronald*
To One Unnamed: *Kleyn*
To One who Passed Whistling Through the Night: *Gibbs, Armstrong*
To Our Lady of Sorrows: *Owen*
To Pansies: *Lawes, W.*
To People who have Gardens: *Roe*
To Phillis, milking her flock: *Benjamin, A.*
To Phyllis – to love and live with him: *Dring*
To plead my faith: *Batchelor*
To Poetry (cycle): *Seiber*
To Sea! *Shaw*
To see a world in a grain of sand: *Chapple*

To Sleep: *Wegener*
To Spring: *Joubert*
To Sycamores: *Lawes, W.*
To tell and be told: *Wood, Hugh*
To the Children: *Elgar*
To the Dance: *Wilson, H.L.*
To the Dews: *Lawes, W.*
To the Future: *Stevenson*
To the Hills: *Woodforde-Finden*
To the Holy Spirit: *Wishart*†
To the Looking-glass World: *Hely-Hutchinson*
To the Memory of a Great Singer: *Warlock* (Bright is the ring of words)
To the Moon: *Fulton*
To the Queen of Heaven: *Dunhill*
To the Queen of my Heart: *Delius*
To the Rose: *Hatton, Stanford*
To the Sailors: *Parke*
To the Skylark: *Stanford* (Skylark, The)
To the Soul: *Stanford* (Darest thou now, O soul)
To the Virgins – to make much of time: *Dring*; *Lawes, W.* (Gather ye rosebuds while ye may)
To the Wicklow Hills: *Lloyd Webber*
To the Willow Tree: *Dring*; *Hatton*
To Violets: *Bullard*; *Carey, C.*; *Gurney*; *Owen*; *Stewart* (Welcome, maids of honour)
To whom should I complain: *Lawes, W.*
To Wine and Beauty: *Quilter*
To Winter: *Joubert*
Tobacco, tobacco: *Hume*
Toccata of Galuppi's, A: *Blake, H.*†; *Wills*†
Todtnauberg: *Birtwistle*†
Toi et Moi: *Blyton**
Tolerance: *Milford*
Toll the bell: *Gibbs, Armstrong*
Toll-gate House, The: *Rowley*
Tom Bowling: *Britten*; *Dibdin*
Tom Bowling and Other Song Arrangements: *Britten*
Tom o' Bedlam: *Gibbs, Armstrong*
Tom o' Bedlam's Song: *Bennett, R.R.*†
Tom the Piper's Son: *Jeffreys, J.*
Tom Tyler: *Warlock*
Tomb of Chao-Chün, The: *Bantock*
Tombeau (cycle): *Berkeley, L.**
Tomorrow (no text): *Nyman*†
Tomorrow (Rossetti, C.): *Scott, C.*
Ton nom: *White, M.V.**
Tonight I've watched the moon: *Hudes*
Tonight the winds begin to rise: *Berkeley, L.*
Too late for love, too late for joy: *Coleridge-Taylor*
Too Short Time, The: *Finzi*
Toper's Song, The: *Warlock* (O good ale)
Torch, The: *Elgar*
Toss not my soul, O love: *Dowland*
Total eclipse: *Handel*
Touch of Love, The: *Dieren*
Tourist Japan: *Josephs*(†)
Tourney, The: *Kirkwood*
Tout-ensemble, The (Plague of Love, The): *Arne, T.*
Towards a Pindaric Ode: *Headington*
Town Owl, The: *Wood, Hugh*
Town Tree, The: *Nelson*
Toy Band: *Samuel, H.*
Tractus: *Maxwell Davies*†
Trade Winds: *Keel*
Tradition: *Britten*
Traditional Songs of France: *Bax**

Traeth Bychan: *Hoddinott*
Trafalgar: *Scott, C.* (Night of Trafalgar, The)
Tragedy of Life, The (scena): *Stanford*
Tragödie (scena): *Stanford**
Traighean (Shores): *Stevenson*
Tra-la-la-lie: *Bantock*
Tramps, The: *Bliss*
Tranquillity: *Scott, C.*
Transatlantic Lullaby: *Wright*
Transformations: *Finzi*
Transience: *Bush, G.*
Transporting joy, tormenting fears: *Handel*
Trapped in crystal: *Finnissy*†
Traum Rosen: *Delius**
Tread Juno's steps who list: *Anon*
Treasure, The: *McLeod*
Tree at my window: *Jackson, F.*
Trees: *Hely-Hutchinson*; *Pope*
Trees they do grow high: *Foss*
Trees they grow so high, The: *Britten*
Trellis, The: *Ireland*
Triad: *Stevenson*
Trio of the Vanishing Gods on the Cloud: *Muldowney*
Trio 2 – Song for Peter (cycle): *LeFanu*†
Triolet: *Roe*
Tritons, which bounding dive: *Walton*
Triumph now with joy and mirth: *Giles*
Trois Chansons: *Berners**
Trois Chansons de François Villon: *Samuel, R.*†
Trois Chansons de Nourrice: *Rawsthorne**
Trois Chansons Taiganes: *White, M.V.*
Trois Chansons Triste: *Tate, P.*†
Trois Enfantines: *Bax*(*)
Trois Fêtes Galants: *Sorabji**
Trois Poèmes de Vildrac: *Berkeley, L.**
Trois Sereurs: *Arundell**
Troll the Bowl: *Moeran*
Trompe l'Oeil: *Stevenson*
Trophy of Arms, A: *Pope*
Trottin' to the fair, me and Moll Malony: *Stanford*
True Dark, The (cycle): *Stevens, B.*
True Lover's Farewell, The: *Butterworth, G.*
True Woman's eye, A: *Jeffreys, J.* (Love me not for comely grace)
Truly he hath a sweet bed: *Hudes*(†)
Trumpet, The: *Gurney*; *Harrington*; *Hedges*; *Pickard*
Trumpet is calling, The: *Handel*
Trumpeter, The: *Dix*
Trumpets: *Knussen*†
Truth: *Hawes*
Truth is, The: *Goehr*
Try the door: *Hugill*†
Tryst, The: *Scott, F.G.*
Tryst (In Fountain Court): *Ireland* (Fountain Court)
Tryste Noel: *Orr, C.W.*
Trysting Tree, The: *Scott, C.*
Tu sa' ch'io so, signior mie, che tu sai: *Britten**
Tuft of Violets, The: *Pope*
Tune for Swans: *Wishart*
Tune on my pipe: *Bliss*
Turkish Mouse, The: *Woolrich*(†)
Turn back you wanton flyer: *Campion*
Turn then thine eyes upon these glories: *Purcell, H.*
Turn ye to me: *Grainger, P.*
Turning Wheel, The: *Joubert*
Turtle Dove Coos Round my Cot, The: *Hook*
Tutto e Sciolto: *Ireland*

Twa Corbies, The: *Ferguson*; *Grainger, P.*; *Gurney*; *Hely-Hutchinson*; *Scott, F.G.*; *Someren-Godfery*
Twa Kimmers, The: *Scott, F.G.*
Twa Sisters of Binnorie, The: *Somervell* (Binnorie)
'Twas now the earliest morning: *Lyall*
'Twas when the seas were roaring: *Handel*
'Twas within a furlong of Edinboro' town: *Purcell, H.*
Tweedledum and Tweedledee: *Hely-Hutchinson*
Twelfth Night: *Copley*
Twelve Days of Christmas, The: *Austin*; *Watson, E.*
Twelve Haiku: *McLelland-Young*
Twelve Humbert Wolfe Songs: *Holst*
Twelve Oxen: *Warlock* (I have twelve oxen)
Twelve Songs: *Arne, T.*; *Bax*; *Bennett, W.S.*; *Blow*; *Milford*; *Moeran*; *Quilter*; *Ronald*; *Wishart*(*)
Twelve Songs by Heine: *Stanford*(*)
Twelve Songs for Children: *Thomas, Mansel*
Twelve Tennyson Poems: *Somervell*
Twelve Traditional Rhymes: *Parry, W.H.*
Twelve Wonders of the World: *Maynard*
Twenty English Lyrics: *Parry, C.H.H.*
Twenty Favourite Songs: *Gurney*
Twenty Songs: *Arne, T.*; *Bishop*
Twenty Songs Volume 2: *Gurney*
Twenty weeks near past: *Naylor, B.*
Twenty-ninth Bather, The: *Hiscocks, W.*
Twenty-two Songs: *Delius*
Twice a week the winter thorough: *Gurney*(†) (Goal and Wicket)
Twickenham Ferry: *Marzials*
Twilight: *Elgar*
Twilight Coast, The: *Bantock*
Twilight Fancies: *Delius*
Twilight it is, and the far woods are dim: *Moeran*; *Crossley-Holland*
Twilight People, The: *Vaughan Williams*(†)
Twins, The: *Head*
Two American Poems: *Bliss*
Two Animal Rhymes: *Butterworth, N.*
Two Ballads: *Tate, P.*†
Two Blake Songs: *Fogg*
Two Bulgarian Songs: *Hiscocks, W.*†
Two Burns Songs: *Beamish*†
Two Camels: *Bantock*
Two Canadian Poems: *Cruft*
Two Canzonets: *Hawes*
Two Carols: *McLeod*†
Two Cautionary Tales (cycle): *Routh*†
Two Celtic Songs: *Moule-Evans*
Two Chinese Songs: *Bantock*
Two Christmas Songs: *Fulton*
Two Comedy Numbers: *Dring*
Two Contrasting Songs: *Watson, R.*
Two de la Mare Songs: *Symons*
Two Devotional Songs: *Jeffreys, G.**
Two Divine Hymns and Alleluia: *Purcell, H.*; *Weldon*
Two Early Songs: *Walton*
Two Eighteenth Century Songs: *Cockshott*
Two Elizabethan Lyrics: *Wilson, H.L.*
Two English Folksongs: *Howells*; *Vaughan Williams*†
Two English Lyrics: *Hawes*
Two fat geese, The: *Elwyn-Edwards*
Two Fish: *Rawsthorne*
Two Fly Songs: *Rose*
Two Folksong Arrangements for Baritone and Violin: *Steptoe*†

Two Fraternities, The: *Walker, R.*†
Two French Folksongs: *Vaughan Williams**
Two gardens see! this of enchanted flowers: *Roe*
Two George Herbert Songs: *Clucas*†
Two hearts remain: *Hoddinott*
Two Houses, The: *Harty*
Two Housman Songs: *Matthews, D.*†; *Williamson, J.R.*
Two Invocations: *Joubert*
Two John Donne Songs: *Arnold, M.*
Two Latin Elegies: *McCabe*†
Two Lips: *Finzi*
Two Love Songs: *Bliss*; *Burgon*†; *White, M.V.*
Two Lyrics from the Chinese: *Whittaker*
Two Madonna Songs: *Llyn-Owen*
Two Mice, The: *Roe*†
Two Miniature Ballads: *Hurlstone*
Two More Show Songs: *Dring*
Two Night Pieces from 'Finnegan's Wake' (cycle): *Buller*†
Two Nursery Rhymes: *Bliss*†; *Cruft*
Two Old English Lyrics: *Gibbs, Armstrong*
Two Old Kings, The: *Alwyn*
Two or Three: *Foreman*
Two or Three Songs: *Foreman*
Two Pastorals: *Farrar*
Two Pensive Songs: *Blyton*
Two Poems by Seamus O'Sullivan: *Vaughan Williams*
Two Poems of Manley Hopkins: *Smith Brindle*†
Two Poems of Nefra Canning: *Hiscocks, W.*
Two Poems of W.B. Yeats: *McLelland-Young*
Two Proses Lyriques: *Goossens**
Two Rhymes: *Butterworth, N.*
Two Robert Southey Poems: *Thompson, P.*
Two Romantic Songs: *Hearne*
Two Roses, The: *Bantock*
Two Sacred Songs: *Thiman*; *Wesley, C.*†
Two Seasons: *Walker, R.*†
Two September Songs: *Quilter*
Two Seventeenth Century Poems: *Orr, C.W.*
Two Shakespeare Lyrics: *Williams, W.S.G.*
Two Shakespeare Songs: *Hiscocks, W.*; *Wishart*
Two Shepherd Boys, The: *Case*
Two Short Songs: *Redman*
Two Show Songs: *Dring*
Two Songs: *Andrews*; *Brook*; *Browne*; *Busch*; *Collins, J.H.*; *Crossley-Holland*; *Dring*; *Elias(*)*; *Ellis*†; *Farrar*; *Foreman*; *Gibbs, Armstrong*; *Herbert, I.*; *Johnstone*; *Lambert, C.*†; *Lindsay*; *Lloyd, D.J. de*; *Maxim*; *Moeran*; *Musgrave**; *Plumstead*; *Quilter*; *Rawsthorne*; *Rubbra(*†*)*; *Stevens, B.*; *Stevenson*; *Tate, P.*; *Teed*
Two Songs and a Melodrama: *Ireland*
Two Songs by Edna St Vincent Millay: *Swann*
Two Songs by Shelley: *Matthews, E.E.*
Two Songs (diptych): *Stevenson*
Two Songs for Baritone: *Thomas, D.V.*
Two Songs for Baritone and Piano: *Steptoe*
Two Songs for Voice and Harp or Piano: *Rubbra*
Two Songs from 'A Shropshire Lad': *Orr, C.W.*
Two Songs from Shakespeare: *Shaw*
Two Songs from 'The Wandering Moon': *Cope*
Two Songs from 'Twelfth Night': *Fulton*
Two Songs in Olden Style: *Hughes, Herbert*
Two Songs of A.E. Housman: *Searle*
Two Songs of Quiet: *Cruft*†
Two Songs of Sleep: *Thomas, Mansel*

Two Songs of Spring: *Shaw*
Two Songs of Thomas Lodge: *Fulton*
Two Songs of William Blake: *Busch*
Two Sonnets: *Rubbra*†
Two Spanish Songs: *Osborne*†
Two Stevie Smith Songs: *Bush, G.*(†)
Two stolen roses in a sun-kissed hand: *Blyton*
Two Thomas Moore Songs: *Raphael*
Two Thoughtful Songs: *Parrott*
Two Ukrainian Folksongs: *Anderson, W.H.*
Two Ulster Fragments: *Hughes, Herbert*
Two Witches, The: *Hattey*
Tyger, The: *Wills*(†) (Tyger, tyger / Tiger, tiger)
Tyger, tyger: *Foreman*; *Rodgers* (Tyger, The / Tiger. tiger)
Tyrley tyrlow: *Warlock*
Tyrolese Evensong: *Scott, C.*

U

Ubunzima: *Rainier*†
Uist Tramping Song: *Roberton*
Ultimum Vale: *Jones, R.*
Ulysses's Farewell: *Hedges*
Un colloque Sentimental (cycle): *Matthews, C.**
Un soir: les Horloges: *Short**
Una and the Lion: *Berkeley, L.*†
Unbroken Circle, The: *Newson*†
Unchanging, The: *Center*
Uncle Jack: *Hatton*
Unconstant love: *Ferrabosco*
Undenominational, but still the church of God: *Dring*
Under the Blossom: *Jeffreys, J.* (Where the bee sucks)
Under the greenwood tree: *Arne, T.*; *Coates, E.*; *Davidson, M.*; *Dring*; *Findlay*; *Foster, M.B.*; *Gurney*; *Horder*; *Howells*; *Parry, C.H.H.*; *Quilter*; *Routh*; *Steele*; *Tomlinson*; *Walton*
Under the leaves green: *Jeffreys, J.*
Under the Moon: *Bantock*
Under the pondweed do the great fish go: *Oldham*
Under the Rose: *Bantock*
Under the wide and starry sky: *Naylor, P.* (Requiem [Stevenson])
Underneath a cypress shade: *Pilkington, F.*
Underneath the abject willow: *Britten*
Underneath the growing grass: *Somervell*
Undine: *Alwyn*
Une petite fille: *Bax*(*)
Unfading Beauty, The: *Thomas, Mansel*
Unfolding: *Lehmann*
Unforgotten: *Moult*
Unforgotten Thoughts: *Rose*
Unforseen, The: *Scott, C.*
Unfortunate Coincidence: *Horder*
Unfulfilled, The: *Pitfield*
Unhappy Lovers, The: *Handel*
Unheard Melodies (cycle): *Kelly*
Unheimlich: *Bingham*†
Unity: *Foster, M.B.*
Unkind man give keep til me: *Oldham*
Unknown Ground: *Finnisey*†
Unknown Sea, The: *Stanford*
Unlit Suburbs, The: *Woolrich*
Unmindful of the roses: *Coleridge-Taylor*
Unquiet thoughts: *Dowland*
Unrest: *Foss*

282 Index of titles

Unseen Spring, The: *Branson*
Until [Sherman]: *Coleridge-Taylor*
Until [Teschemacher]: *Sanderson*
Unto the temple of thy beauty: *Ford, T.*
Unutterable, The: *Bantock*
Unwanted, The: *Dean*
Unwelcome: *Rootham*
Up and Down: *Lutyens*
Up the airy mountain: *Butt*
Up the Raw, maw bonny: *Finnissy*†
Up wi' the carls o' Dysart: *Center*
Upon a Maid: *Stewart*
Upon Julia's Clothes: *Bush, G.*; *Still* (Whenas in silks my Julia goes)
Upon Silence: *Benjamin*†
Upon the Crucifix: *Rubbra*†
Upon the Loss of his Mistresses: *Bush, G.*
Upper Lambourne: *Dring*
Urania to Parthenissa: a Dream: *Locke*
Urge me no more, this airy mirth belongs: *Purcell, H.*
Urge me no more, unhappy swain: *King, Robert*
Ushas (Dawn): *Holst*
Usherettes Blues: *Nicholas*
Usk: *Adès, Pope*

V

Vac (Speech): *Holst*
Vagabond, The [Masefield]: *Ireland*
Vagabond, The [Stevenson]: *Vaughan Williams*
Vagabond Song, A: *Head*
Vagabond Songs: *Farrar*
Vain Desire, The: *Ireland*
Vain men whose follies make a god of love: *Campion*
Vain Wits and Eyes: *Headington*
Vale (Farewell): *Russell, K.*
Vale of Arden, The: *Bantock*
Valediction, A: *Scott, C.*
Valley, The: *Novello*
Valley and the Hill, The: *Quilter*
Valley of Rainbows: *Novello*
Valley of Silence, The [Dowson]: *Scott, C.*
Valley of Silence, The [Macleod]: *Bantock*; *Howells*
Valley-Moonlight: *Bainton*
Vanity: *Crosse*
Vanity of Human Wishes, The: *Bush, G.*
Variables of Green: *Hattey*
Variations on Johnny Faa': *MacMillan*†
Variations on 'The Harmonious Blacksmith': *Grainger, P.*
Varuna I (Sky): *Holst*
Varuna II (Waters, The): *Holst*
Veggio co' bei vostri occhi un dolce lume: *Britten*
Veil, love, my eyes, O hide from me: *Campion*
Venice Twilight: *Fraser, N.*
Venus and Adonis: *Bush, G.*
Venus to soothe my heart: *Boyce*
Verdant Braes of Skeen, The: *Hughes, Herbert*
Verities: *Roe*†
Verses in Memoriam David Munrow: *Crosse*†
Verses to Music: *Lyall*
Vi lo jo før så lœnge: *Delius**
Vicar of Bray, The: *Grainger, P.*
Victory: *Gibbs, Armstrong*
Vigil [de la Mare]: *Britten*
Vigils [Sassoon]: *Boyle, R.*†

Vignettes: *Ronald*
Village Country School, The: *Thomas, Mansel*
Vilanelle [Dowson]: *Scott, C.*
Villanelle [Passerat]: *Lyall*
Villanelle of Firelight: *Scott, C.*
Villanelle of the Poet's Road: *Scott, C.*
Viol: *Delius**
Violet, The: *Delius*
Violets: *Herbert, M.*
Violets blue of the eyes divine, The: *Bridge*
Viper, The: *Head*
Virgen con miriñaque: *ApIvor*†
Virginia: *Adès*; *Pope*
Virgins, The: *Downes*†
Virgin's Cradle Hymn, The: *Fryer* (Dormi, Jesu)
Virtue: *Butt*(†)
Vision, A: *Scott, C.*
Vision of Beasts and Gods, A: *Williamson, M.*
Vision of Time and Eternity: *Mathias*
Visionary, The: *Moult*
Visit from the Moon, A: *Dunhill*
Visit to the Killing Fields: *Kirkwood*
Visitation, The: *Wood, Hugh*
Vita d'un Uomo: *McGregor**
Vocalese: *Bennett, R.R.*
Vocalise: *Bliss*†; *Boulter*†; *Hedges*; *Procter*; *Routh*†
Vocalism: *Usher*†
Vocoder Sextet: *Bedford*†
Voice by the cedar tree, A: *Somervell*
Voice from the Tomb, The (cycle): *Crosse*
Voice in the Dusk, A: *Gibbs, Armstrong*
Voice of Love, The (cycle): *Maw*
Voice of my Beloved: *Naylor, P.*
Voice of the rain, The: *Knussen*
Voice of the Thorn, The: *Foster, I.*
Voices of the Prophets (cycle): *Bush, A.*
Voices of Vision: *Scott, C.*
Voici le Printemps: *Britten**
Voie: *Wilby**
Volunteer Organist, The: *Lamb*
Von edler Art: *Parry, C.H.H.**
Vouchsafe, O Lord: *Purcell, H.*
Vox ultima crucis: *Luff*

W

W zlobje Lezy: *Bax**
Wagon of Life, The: *Pitfield*
Wagtail and Baby: *Britten*
Waiata: *Guy*†
Wail: *Horder*
Waiting: *Gomelskaya*
Waiting [Chinese]: *Scott, C.*
Waiting [Fontana]: *Gomelskaya*
Waiting [Noyes]: *Coleridge-Taylor*
Waiting Both: *Finzi*
Waka: *Connolly**
Wake Feast, The: *Harty*
Wake, my love, all life is stirring: *Loder*
Wakeful nightingale that takes no rest, The: *Weldon*
Wakening, The: *Raynor*
Wakenings: *Hudes*†
Waking Song: *Bantock*
Walden Market: *Bantock*
Walk, The [Hardy]: *Downes*†
Walk, The [Mole]: *Roe*

Index of titles 283

Walking by a riverside: *Jones, R.*
Walking in the air: *Blake, H.*
Walking in the salt sea weather: *Thomas, Mansel*
Walking Song [Harvey]: *Gurney*
Walking Song [Scott]: *Newson*
Walking the woods: *Warlock*
Walled-in Garden, The: *Quilter*
Walrus and the Carpenter, The: *Sagar*
Walsingham: *Pike*
Waly, waly: *Crawford* (O waly, waly)
Wanderer (cycle): *Dalby*
Wanderer, The [de la Mare]: *Gibbs, Armstrong*
Wanderer, The [Duff]: *Hatton*
Wanderers: *Howells*
Wanderer's Night Song [Goethe]: *Crossley-Holland*; *Howells*
Wanderer's Night Song [Ripley]: *Moult*
Wanderer's Song, A [Masefield]: *Keel*
Wanderer's Song, The [Symons]: *Farrar*
Wander-thirst: *Hughes, A.*
Wander-thirst [Gould]: *Peel*
Wanting is – what? *Bantock*
Wanton, come hither: *Cavendish*
Wapping Old Stairs: *Walton*
War: *Stevenson*
War Song [Bantock, H.]: *Bantock*
War Song, A [Hayward]: *Elgar*
War-song of Glamorgan: *Thomas, Mansel*
Warning, A [Anon]: *Arne, T.*
Warning, The [Rowley]: *Hook*
Warrior Lover, The: *O'Neill*
Warrior's Return, The: *Hughes, R.S.*
Was it some golden star? *Elgar*
Washer of the Ford, The: *Bantock*
Wasp, The: *Hawes*
Wasserfall bei Nacht: *Stevenson**
Watch, The: *Hugh-Jones*
Watchful's Song: *Vaughan Williams*
Watching the Needleboats: *Bax*
Watching the Wheat: *Hopkins, W.*; *Williams, Grace*
Watchman, The: *Scott, C.*
Water Jewels: *White, A.*
Water Lily, The: *Warlock*
Water Mill, The: *Vaughan Williams*
Water Music [Durrell]: *Routh*
Water Music [Lewis]: *Thomas, Mansel*
Water of Tyne, The: *Atkinson, R.*; *Tate, P.*; *Maxwell†*
Water parted [Anon]: *Arne, T.*
Water parted [Deane]: *Barry*
Watergaw, The: *Scott, F.G.*
Waterlilies: *Scott, C.*
Waukrife Minnie: *White, A.*
Waves [Ellis]: *Hand*
Waves [Marsland]: *Phillips, M.*
Way that lovers use, The: *Møller*
Way Through, The: *Venables*
Wayward Thoughts: *Standford*
We are budding, master, budding: *Finzi†*
We are whatever we are: *Hugill†*
We cut ice: *Gomelskaya*
We know this much: *Hudes†*
We sat down and wept: *Stout†*
We sing to him whose wisdom form'd the ear: *Purcell, H.*
We three merry maidens: *Rawsthorne*
Weary pund o' tow: *White, A.*
Weary with toil, I haste me to my bed (Sonnet 27) [Shakespeare]: *Scott, D.B.*

Weather and Mouth Music: *Lufft†*
Weather the Cuckoo Likes, The: *Crossley-Holland* (This is the weather the cuckoo likes / Weathers)
Weathercock on the Moor, The: *Toye*
Weathers: *Bayliss*; *Butt*; *Fiske*; *Head*; *Ireland*; *Parry, W.H.*; *Pilling* (This is the weather the cuckoo likes / Weather the Cuckoo Likes, The)
Weaver's Daughter, The: *Hughes, Herbert*
Weaving Song: *Grainger, P.*; *McCabe†*
Web, The (Five Love Songs): *McGuire*(†)
Wedding Breakfast: a Tribute to Stravinsky: *Gorb†*
Wedding Gift IV, The: *Sanger*
Wedding Gift V, The: *Sanger*
Wedding is great Juno's crown: *Blake, H.†*
Wee cannot bid the fruits: *Rainier†*
Wee Cooper of Fife, The: *Roe*
Wee Folk, The: *Bantock*
Wee Hughie: *Parke*
Wee Man, The: *Scott, F.G.*
Wee Road from Cushendall, The: *Thiman*
Wee Toun Clerk, The: *Roberton*
Wee Willie Gray an' his leather wallet: *Britten*; *Liddell*; *Scott, F.G.*
Wee Willie Winkie: *Mullinar*
Weep no more my wearied eyes: *Lanier*
Weep no more, nor sigh nor groan: *Handel*; *Mace*; *Raphael* (Mourn No Moe)
Weep not, beloved friends: *Coleridge-Taylor*
Weep ye not: *Cook*
Weep you no more, sad fountains: *Bush, G.*; *Clarke, R.*; *Dieren*; *Dowland*; *Dring*; *Holst*; *Jeffreys, J.*; *Lindsay*; *Moeran*; *Parry, C.H.H.*; *Pope*; *Quilter* (Sleeping / Tears)
Weeping and Kissing: *Dieren*
Weeping Babe, The: *Owen*
Weinachtslied: *Berners**
Weise und Leicht: *Birtwistle†*
Welcome maids of honour: *Standford* (To Violets)
Welcome, more welcome does he come: *Purcell, H.*
Welcome sweet bird: *MacCunn*
Welcome to Spring: *Jeffreys, J.*
Well Judging Phyllis: *Boyce*
Well of Sorrows, The: *Lehmann*
Well of Tears, The: *Bax*
We'll go no more a-roving: *Swann* (So we'll go no more a-roving)
We'll to the Woods no More: *Ireland*
We'll to the woods no more: *Ireland*; *Thomas, H.F.*; *Vaughan Williams†*
Welsh Lullaby, A: *Parry, C.H.H.*
Weltlauf: *Blake, D.†*
Were every thought an eye: *Dowland*
Were I the flower: *Ronald*
Wert thou then (yet) fairer than thou art: *Atkins*
Wert thou yet (then) fairer than thou art: *Lawes, H.*
Wessex Graves: *Berkeley, M.†*
West Sussex Drinking Song, A: *Gow*; *Gurney*; *Raynor*
West Wind, The [Letts]: *Stanford*
West Wind, The [Masefield]: *Mitchell†*; *Stewart*
Westering home: *Roberton*
Western Playland, The: *Gurney*(†)
Western wind, when will thou blow: *Blyton†*
Westgate-on-Sea: *Horder*
Westward on the high-hilled plains: *Moeran*; *Orr, C.W.*
Wha is that at my bower-door?: *Scott, F.G.*
What a pother of late: *Dring*

Index of titles

What a sad fate is mine: *Purcell, H.*
What art thou thinking of?: *Ireland*
What beauties my nymph doth disclose: *Boyce*
What can we poor females do?: *Purcell, H.*
What cheer? good cheer: *Warlock*
What Christmas means to me: *Head*
What 'Dane-geld' means: *German*
What does little birdie say?: *Sullivan*
What evil coil of fate: *Jeffreys, J.*
What greater grief: *Hume*
What guyle is this, that those her golden tresses?: *Rubbra*
What I fancy, I approve: *Dring*
What if a day, or a month or a year: *Anon*
What if I never speed?: *Dowland*
What if I seek for love of thee?: *Jones, R.*
What if I sped when I least expected?: *Jones, R.*
What if my mistress now?: *Morley*
What if this present were the world's last night?: *Britten*
What is a day, what is a year: *Rosseter*
What is beauty but a breath: *Greaves, Thomas*
What is good King Ringang's daughter's name?: *Dieren*
What is it muffles the ascending moment?: *Walker, R.*†
What is Life?: *Hold*
What is't to us who guides the state?: *Blow*
What part of dread eternity?: *Parry, C.H.H.*
What pleasures have great princes?: *Milford*
What saith my dainty darling: *Swinstead*
What shaft of fate's relentless power?: *Wesley, S.*
What shall I do to show how much I love her?: *Purcell, H.*
What shall I your true love tell?: *Bridge*
What star is this?: *Ridout, G.*
What sweeter music can we bring?: *Steel*
What then is Love: *Blyton*†
What then is love but mourning?: *Rosseter*
What thing is love I pray thee tell: *Bartlet*; *Bush, G.*; *Dalby*(†); *Jeffreys, J.*; *Wills*(†)
What voice is this, thou evening gale?: *Clarke-Whitfield*
What's in your mind, my dove, my coney?: *Berkeley, L.*; *Britten*; *Dickinson*
Wheel of Life, The: *Papastávrou*(†)
Wheesht, wheesht: *Scott, F.G.*
When? *Sullivan*
When a tender maid is first assayed: *Linley Snr*
When all this is over: *Hugill*†
When Arthur first in Court began: *Gibbs, Armstrong*
When as we sat in Babylon: *Alison*
When bidden to the wake: *Shield*
When cats run home and light is come: *Andrews* (White Owl, The / Owl, The [Tennyson])
When childer plays: *Davies, Walford*
When Christ was born of Mary free: *Butterworth, N.*; *Philips*†
When comes my Gwen: *Parry, C.H.H.*
When daffodils begin to peer: *Bush, G.*; *Ireland*; *Quilter*; *Turnbull* (Autolycus' Song / Sweet o' the Year, The)
When daisies pied and violets blue: *Arne, T.*(†); *Barrell, B.*†; *Bullard*; *Foss*; *Horder*; *Jeffreys, J.*; *Moeran*; *Shaw* (Cuckoo, The [Shakespeare] / Mockery)
When death to either shall come: *Gurney*
When dull care (Cure of Care, The): *Leveridge*

When first Amintas sued for a kiss: *Purcell, H.*
When first mine eyes did view and mark: *Ridout, A.*
When first my old, old love I knew: *Sullivan*
When first my shepherdess and I: *Purcell, H.*
When from my love: *Bartlet*
When green buds hang in the elm like dust: *Mitchell*; *Pope*
When Green Leaves Come Again: *Bishop*
When he who adores thee: *Hughes, Herbert*
When her languishing eyes said 'Love': *Purcell, H.*
When I am dead, my dearest: *Birkett*; *Bullard*(†); *Butt*; *Coleridge-Taylor*; *Greaves, R.*; *Ireland*(†); *Lehmann*; *Mackenzie*; *Somers-Cocks*; *Swann*; *Vaughan Williams*; *Wegener*; *Williamson, M.* (Sing no sad songs for me / Song [Rossetti, C.])
When I am laid in earth: *Purcell, H.* (Thy hand, Belinda / Dido's Farewell / Dido's Lament)
When I am old, and sadly steal apart: *Ireland*
When I behold a forest spread: *Dyson*
When I came at last to Ludlow: *Jeffreys, J.*; *Moeran*; *Owen*
When I came forth this morn: *Head*
When I have often heard young maids complaining: *Purcell, H.*
When I heard the learned astronomer: *Knussen*; *Usher*†
When I lie ill: *Brian*
When I set out for Lyoness: *Austin*; *Finzi*; *Walters, L.* (Lyonesse)
When I think on the happy days: *White, M.V.*
When I think upon the maidens: *Head*
When I was a dyer and wrought at my trade: *Linley Jnr*
When I was a lad I served a term: *Sullivan*
When I was one-and-twenty: *Bax*; *Butterworth, G.*; *Gibbs, Armstrong*; *Gurney*(†); *Horder*; *Jeffreys, J.*; *Orr, C.W.*; *Pope*; *Somervell*; *Steele*; *Thompson, P.*
When I was roaming: *Thomas, Mansel*
When I was Young: *Jeffreys, J.*
When I was young: *Stone*
When I watch the living meet: *Orr, C.W.*
When icicles hang by the wall: *Hiscocks, W.*; *Moeran*; *Parry, C.H.H.*; *Quilter*; *Vaughan Williams* (Winter [Shakespeare])
When in disgrace with fortune and men's eyes (Sonnet 29) [Shakespeare]: *Parry, C.H.H.*
When in the solemn stillness of the night: *Stanford*
When it's blackberry time in September: *Martin, E.*
When June is come, then all the day: *Carey, C.*; *Moeran*; *Miles*†
When kisses are strawberries: *Sutherland*
When Laura smiles: *Rosseter*
When lights go rolling round the sky: *Ireland*
When lo, by break of morning: *Morley*
When love is found: *Hopson*
When love is kind: *Anon*
When lovers meet again: *Parry, C.H.H.*
When May is in his prime: *Bush, G.* (Sweet Season, The)
When May walks by: *O'Neill*
When my Aemilia smiles: *Purcell, H.*
When my love swears that she is made of truth (Sonnet 138) [Shakespeare]: *Wills*
When, My Sweet, I Gaze on Thee: *Clarke, R.C.*
When other lips and other hearts (Then you'll remember me): *Balfe*

When our two souls (Sonnet) [Browning, E.B.]: *Wills*†
When passion's trance: *Fogg*
When Phoebus first did Daphne love: *Dowland*
When rooks fly homeward: *Rowley*
When Satan fell: *Burtch*
When senses, which thy Soldiers are: *Downes*†
When Sir Beelzebub: *Marchant*
When smoke stood up from Ludlow: *Gurney*(†); *Moeran*; *Orr, C.W.*
When spring returns: *Somervell*
When Strephon found his passion vain: *Purcell, H.*
When Sweet Ann Sings: *Head*
When that I was and a little tiny boy: *Bernard*; *Bullock*; *Foss*; *Jeffreys, J.*; *Routh*; *Shaw* (Clown's Song, The / Hey, ho, the wind and the rain / Rain It Raineth Every Day, The)
When the cabin portholes are dark and green: *German*
When the chill Cherocco blows: *Atkins*
When the dew is falling [Chatterton]: *Parry, C.H.H.*
When the dew is falling [Macleod]: *Howells*; *Moule-Evans*
When the first summer bee: *MacCunn*
When the golden day is done: *White, A.*
When the herds were watching: *Keel*†
When the lad for longing sighs: *Butterworth, G.*; *Orr, C.W.*; *Peel*
When the leaves are fallen: *Ronald*
When the morn is new: *Thomas, Mansel*
When the Spirit Comes: *Wills*
When the sun's great orb: *Parry, C.H.H.*
When the swallows homeward fly: *White, M.V.*
When there is peace: *Howells*
When thou art dead the birds will stop: *Goossens*
When thou, poor excommunicate: *Lawes, H.*
When thro' life unblest we rove: *Hughes, Herbert*
When through the piazzetta: *Raphael*
When to her lute Corinna sings: *Campion*; *Dalby*(†)
When to the sessions of sweet silent thought: (Sonnet 30) [Shakespeare]: *Parry, C.H.H.*
When twilight dews: *MacCunn*
When we are lost: *Bax*
When we two parted in silence and tears: *Parry, C.H.H.*
When we were idlers with the loitering rills: *Berkeley, L.*
When William at eve: *Shield*
When woods were green: *Crossley-Holland*
When yielding first to Damon's flame: *Dring*
When you and I were young, Maggie: *Butterfield*
When you are old and grey and full of sleep: *Bridge*
When you come home, dear: *Squire*
When you return: *White, M.V.*
When you sang to me: *Bantock*
When you're feeling like expressing your affection: *Britten*
When you're in love: *Stafford*
Whenas I wake I dream oft of my dear: *Jeffreys, J.*; *Orr, C.W.* (To Make my Mistress Kind)
Whenas in silks my Julia goes: *Barrell, B.*†; *Blyton* (Upon Julia's Clothes)
Whenas the rye reach to the chin: *Warlock* (Chopcherry / Strawberries Swimming in the Cream / Summer Song)
Whence: *Parry, C.H.H.*
Whence is that goodly fragrance: *Liddle*†
Where, *Harrison, P.*

Where are you going to, my pretty maid: *Plumstead*; *Saxton*†
Where are you, my prince? *McLeod*
Where be ye (you) going? *Holbrooke*; *Mark*; *Quilter*; *Scott, C.* (Devon Maid, The)
Where be ye, my love? *Dale, M.*
Where be you (ye) going? *Holbrooke*; *Mark*; *Quilter*; *Scott, C.* (Devon Maid, The)
Where Corals Lie: *Elgar*
Where e'er you walk cool gales shall fan the glade: *Handel*
Where go the boats? *Mullinar*; *Quilter*; *Thiman*; *Williamson, M.*
Where is it that our soul doth go? *Bridge*†
Where my caravan has rested: *Löhr*
Where our heart of town is: *Mackie*
Where Poppies Blow: *Harrington*
Where Riches is Everlastingly: *Warlock*(†)
Where shall the lover rest? *Parry, C.H.H.*
Where shall we adventure? (cycle) *White, R.le R.*
Where she her sacred bow'r adorns: *Campion*
Where She Lies Asleep: *Bridge*
Where sin sore wounding: *Dowland*
Where Thames translucent waves: *Taylor, M.*†
Where the bee sucks there suck I: *Arne, T.*; *Hiscocks, W.*; *Hold*; *Humfrey*; *Moeran*; *Sullivan*; *Tippett* (Under the Blossom)
Where the Daisies Are: *Graves* (Daisies, The / In the bud of the morning-O)
Where the Heather Grows: *Atkinson, G.*(†)
Where the Picnic Was: *Downes*
Where we Made the Fire: *Finzi*†
Wherever we may be (cycle): *Holloway*
Wherefore peep'st thou, envious day? *Wilson, John*
Whereto shuld I express? *Henry VIII*
Whether I Grow Old or No: *Boyce* (Oft I'm by the women told)
Whether I live or whether I die: *Parry, C.H.H.*
Whether men do laugh or weep: *Jeffreys, J.*; *Rosseter*
While summer on is stealing: *Orr, C.W.*
While the foaming billows roll: *Linley, W.*
While the sun was going down: *Carey, C.*
While Thyrsis, wrapped in downy sleep: *Purcell, H.*
While two are one: *Northcote*
Whilst Cynthia sung: *Purcell, H.*
Whilst I'm carousing: *Leveridge*
Whin, The: *Jeffreys, J.*
Whispering Poplar, The: *Lubbock*
White: *Harrison, P.*
White Amaryllis, The: *Samuel, R.*
White and Light: *Birtwistle*†
White as lilies was her face: *Dowland*
White clouds are in the sky: *Steptoe*
White Dress, The: *Someren-Godfery*
White Flame, The: *McLeod*
White guardians of the universe of sleep: *Finlay*
White Helleborine, The: *Searle*
White in the moon the long road lies: *Horder*; *Somervell*; *Taylor, E.K.*; *Williamson, J.R.*
White Knight, The: *Scott, C.*
White Nightingale, The: *Lambert, C.*†
White of the Year: *Grossner*
White Owl, The: *Pierson* (When cats run home / Owl, The [Tennyson])
White Peace, The: *Bax*
White Queen, The: *Bantock*
White Rose, A: *Jeffreys, J.*; *McCabe*
White sea mist, The: *Ronald*

White was the way of my lov'd one's brow: *Jeffreys, J.*
Whither are all her false oaths blown: *Lawes, H.*
Whither away? *Bantock*
Whither Must I Wander? *Vaughan Williams*
Whither runneth my sweetheart: *Bartlet*; *Jones, R.*
Whitman Settings: *Knussen*
Who are These Children?: *Britten*
Who are these children?: *Britten*
Who but a slave can well express?: *Purcell, H.*
Who can behold Fiorella's charms?: *Purcell, H.*
Who do you love?: *Dillon*†
Who doth behold my mistress' face: *Bartlet*
Who Goes Home?: *Hely-Hutchinson*
Who goes with Fergus?: *Scott, D.B.*
Who is at my window, who?: *Jeffreys, J.*
Who is Sylvia, what is she?: *Coates, E.*; *Duff*; *Finzi*; *Horder*; *Leveridge*; *Quilter*
Who is this fair one?: *Vaughan Williams*†
Who shall have my lady fair?: *Butterworth, N.*
Who would shepherd pipes forsake: *Farrar*
Whoever thinks or hopes of love: *Dowland*
Whole Duty of Children: *Williamson, M.*
Who'll buy my lavender?: *German*
Who-so is tied must needs be bound: *Jones, R.*
Why?: *Harrison, P.*
Why art thou slow, thou rest of trouble, Death?: *Parry, C.H.H.*
Why canst thou not as others do?: *Danyel* (Mortal Glance, The)
Why do I love?: *Gibbs, Armstrong*
Why does Laura shun me?: (The Grove): *Blow*
Why does the morn' in blushes rise?: *Blow*
Why dost thou lurk so close?: *Dalby*
Why dost thou turn away?: *Anon*
Why dost thou wound and break my heart?: *Brian*
Why have you stolen my delight?: *Head*
Why should great beauty virtuous fame desire?: *Lawes, W.*
Why shouldst thou swear I am forsworn?: *Lawes, H.*
Why so pale and wan, fond lover?: *Arne, T.*; *Barrell, B.*†; *Lawes, W.*; *Parry, C.H.H.*; *Quilter*; *Rubbra*; *Scott, C.*; *Stanford*
Why still before those streaming eyes?: *Salomon*
Why Thomas Cam was Grumpy: *Peterkin*
Why weeps Asteria?: *Blow*
Widdecombe Fair: *Jacob*
Widow, The: *Cannon*(†)
Widow bird sate mourning for her love, (A), (The): *Bantock*; *Barlow, M.*; *Fogg*; *Herbert, I.*; *Howells*; *Lehmann*; *Luard-Selby*; *Macfarren*†; *Maconchy*†; *Naylor, P.*; *Roberts, T.O.*; *Rubbra* (Song [Shelley])
Wie des Mondes Abbild zittert: *Stanford**
Wife of Bath, The: *Dyson*
Wife of Lleu, The: *Elwyn-Edwards*
Wife of Winter (cycle): *Lord, D.*
Wife Waits, A: *Downes*
Wild bird calls, The: *Naylor, P.*
Wild Flower's Song, The: *Bantock*; *Quilter*
Wild Geese: *Bantock*
Wild Nights: *Montague*†
Wild Rose Lane: *Martin, E.*
Wild Swans at Coole, The: *Young, Douglas*
Wild Welsh Coast, The: *Bantock*
Wild winds weep, The (Mad Song): *Butt*
Wild with passion: *Britten*
Will Chloris cast her sun-bright eyes?: *Ives, S.*

Will you be as hard?: *Davies, E.*
Will you come?: *Gurney*
Will you come back home: *Somervell*
Will you know my mistress' face: *Lawes, H.*
William: *Owen*
Willie Wabster: *Musgrave*
Willie Wastle dwells on Tweed: *Center*
Willie's gane to Melville Castle: *Grainger, P.*
Will-o'-the-wisp: *Bantock*
Willow, The: *Pitfield*†
Willow Cycle: *Holloway*†
Willow Flowers: *Bantock*
Willow Song (Fletcher): *Moeran* (Aspatia's Song / Lay a garland on my hearse / Sad Song, A)
Willow Song, (The), (Shakespeare): *Coleridge-Taylor*; *Fulton*; *Jacobson*; *Pitfield*; *Roe*†; *Sullivan* (Desdemona's Song / Poor soul sat sighing, A / Willow, willow)
Willow Tree, The: *Boyle, R.*; *Farrar*
Willow, willow: *Anon*, *Grainger, P.*; *Parry, C.H.H.* (Desdemona's Song / Poor soul sat sighing, A / Willow Song, The [Shakespeare])
Willows: *Scott, C.*
Willy: *Moult*
Wilt thou be my dearie? *Hurlstone*; *MacCunn*
Wilt thou forgive that sin where I begun? *Hilton*; *Humfrey*† (Hymn to God the Father)
Wilt thou, unkind, thus reave me? *Dowland*
Wily Lover, The: *Branson* (Thou art not fair)
Wind, The: *Treharne*
Wind, The [Bantock, M.]: *Bantock*
Wind, The [Stevenson]: *White, A.*
Wind at Dawn, The: *Elgar*
Wind comes softly, The: *Gibbs, Armstrong*
Wind from the South: *Quilter*
Wind from the West, The: *Warlock*
wind has blown the rain away, a: *Roxburgh*
Wind of the Western Sea: *Peel* (Sweet and low)
Wind of the Wheat: *Phillips, M.*
Windhover, The: *Smith Brindle*†
Windjammer, The: *Roberton*
Windmill, The: *Taylor, C.*
Window, The or The Songs of the Wrens: *Sullivan*
Wind, The: *White, A.*
Winds The: *Walton*
Wind's an old woman, The: *Bowen*
Winds are calling, The: *Ronald*
Wind's Lament, The: *Thomas, Mansel*; *Williams, W.A.*
Winds of Bethlehem: *Stanford*(†)
Wind's Work: *Benjamin*
Windy Nights: *Stanford*
Windy Story, A: *Nelson*
Wine: *Jeffreys, J.*
Wine Jug, A: *Benjamin, A.*
Wine Roses: *Delius*
Wine Shop, The: *Standford*†
Winged Eros: *Wills*†
Winter: *Elwyn-Edwards*
Winter [Anon]: *Anderson, W.H.*
Winter (Now is the time for the burning of the leaves) [Binyon]: *Hedges*
Winter [Canning]: *Hiscocks, W.*
Winter [de la Mare]: *Hugh-Jones*(†); *Symons* (It is winter)
Winter [Li Po]: *Bliss*
Winter [Shakespeare]: *Gardiner*, *Williams, W.S.G.* (When icicles hang by the wall)
Winter [Tennyson]: *Sullivan*

Winter [Troubadour]: *Orchard*
Winter: East Anglia: *Brown, C.*†
Winter Evening: Dunham Park: *Pitfield*
Winter Field: *Swain*
Winter has gone: *Bantock*
Winter it is past, The: *Britten*; *Edwards, O.*; *Horder*
Winter Night Idyll, A: *Goossens*
Winter Passions: *Matthews, D.*†
Winter Portrait in Grey and Gold: *Wilby*†
Winter Robin, The: *Bullard*
Winter Rose: *Lubbock*
Winter Song: *Pitfield*(†)
Winter Walk: *Steed*
Winter Words: *Britten*
Winter's gone, the summer breezes: *Bennett, W.S.*
Winter's Willow, The: *Vaughan Williams*
Wish, A [Rogers]: *Plumstead*
Wish, The [Letts]: *Parke*
Wish, that of the living whole: *Swann*
Wishes [Causley]: *Bush, G.*
Wishes [Lindsay]: *MacCunn*
Wishing: *White, A.*
Witch, The: *Gibbs, Armstrong*
Witch o' Fife, The: *White, A.*
Witches' Charms: *Stanford* (Owl is abroad, The)
Witches' Wood, The: *Parry, C.H.H.*
Witch's Manuscript: *Samuel, R.*†
With a Man of Leisure: *Lambert, C.*
With Flowers: *Grossner*
With his venom: *Hudes*
With how sad steps: *Gibbs, Alan*
With Letter and Clock: *Birtwistle*†
With margeraine gentle: *Dieren*
With my love my life was nestled: *Morley*
With rue my heart is laden: *Butterworth, G.*; *Hamilton, J.*; *Jeffreys, J.*; *Orr, C.W.*; *Pope*; *Vaughan Williams*† (Golden Friends)
With sick and famished eyes: *Purcell, H.*
With Strawberries: *O'Neill*
With the pride of the garden: *Keel*
With Words of Love: *Jeffreys, J.*†
Wither's Rocking Hymn: *Vaughan Williams*
Within a cowslip's humble bell: *Wesley, S.*
Within a rose love sleeping lay: *Lehmann*
Without Warning: *Hudes*
Wo die schönen trompeten blasen: *McLeod**
Wolf, The: *Shield*
Wolfram's Dirge: *Moult* (If thou wilt ease thy heart / If thou wouldst ease thine heart)
Woman in Love, A: *Wills*†
Woman Speaks, A: *Rose*
Woman to Lover: *Wills*†
Woman Young and Old (cycle): *Routh*
Woman-hater, The: *Gerhard*
Woman's Constancy: *Arnold, M.*
Woman's Last Word, A: *Bantock*
Women are a' gane wud, The: *Grainger, P.*
Wonder of Wonders, The: *Bush, G.*
Wondrous machine: *Purcell, H.*
Woo her and win her: *Campion*
Wood beyond the wood, The: *Pike*
Wood Magic: *Shaw*
Wood Music: *Bantock*
Wood Nymph, A: *Arne, T.*†
Woodcutter's Song, The (He that is down need fear no fall): *Vaughan Williams*(†)
Woodland Dell, A: *Goossens*
Woodman, spare that tree: *Russell, H.*

Woodpath in Spring, The: *Head*
Woodpigeon, The: *Lehmann*
Wood's Aglow, The: *McEwen*
Woodside Rise, The (cycle): *Hawes*
Word on my ear, A: *Swann*
Word over all: *Center*
Words for Music: *Cresswell*†
Words of Love: *Marsh*†
Wordsworth Songs (cycle): *Brown, C.*
World, The: *Taverner*†
World is Mad, The: *Head*†
World of Song, A: *Thomas, Muriel*
World's Desire, The: *Turner*
Worlde's Bliss: *Burgon*†
Wormwood and the Gall, The: *Marsh*†
Worry about money: *Bliss*
Worst of it, The: *Somervell*
Would'st thou hope the nymph to gain: *Stanley*
Woven of the sky: *Bantock*
Wreckers of Dunraven, The: *Evans, D.F.*
Wren, The: *Lehmann*
Written on the Eve of Execution: *Bennett, R.R.* (My prime of youth is but a frost of cares)
Wrong not, sweet empress of my heart: *Samuel, H.*
Wrong not your lovely eyes: *Locke*
Wśro noznej ciszy: *Bax**
Wynken, Blynken and Nod: *Pilkington, J.H.*

Y

Yarmouth Fair: *Warlock*
Ye balmy breezes gently blow: *Shield*(†)
Ye banks and braes of bonnie Doon: *Center*; *Liddell*; *Marshall, N.*†; *Musgrave*; *Quilter*; *Shaw*; *Snell*(†)
Ye bubbling springs that gentle music makes: *Greaves, Thomas*
Ye fauns and ye dryads: *Arne, T.*
Ye happy swains, whose nymphs are kind: *Purcell, H.*
Ye little birds that sit and sing: *Parry, C.H.H.* (Message to Phillis, A)
Ye spotted snakes: *Barrell, B.*†; *Hudes* (Philomel [Shakespeare])
Ye (You) twice ten hundred deities: *Purcell, H.*
Year's at the spring, The: *Somervell* (Pippa Passes / Pippa's Song)
Year's Awakening, The: *Bullard*
Years Disarmed, The (cycle): *Martin, F.*
Yellow Cake Revue, The: *Maxwell Davies*
Yellow Flower, A: *Blyton*†
Yellow Wine: *Greaves, R.*
Yellowhammer, The: *Lehmann*
Yes, I know this is nothing but thy love: *Ronald*
Yes it is pretty: *Hudes*†
Yesterday: *Bush, G.*
Yet will I love her: *Jeffreys, J.* (And yet I love her till I die / My Lady / Passing By / There is a lady sweet and kind)
Yo m'enamori d'un aire: *Sutton-Anderson*†
Yon wild mossy mountains: *Grainger, P.*
Yonder stands a lovely creature: *Butterworth, G.*
You: *Harvey, J.*†
You [Dickinson]: *Horne*†
You are a refuge for me: *Wishart*
You are free: *MacCunn*
You are mine: *Ronald*
You are my sky: *Gurney*

You are old, Father William: *Lloyd, D.J. de*
You cannot dream things lovelier: *Head* (Things Lovelier)
You couldn't stop a lover: *Hughes, Herbert*
You frail sad leaves: *Pitfield*
You have made me endless: *Standford*†
You have put on Christ: *Crossley-Holland*††
You lay so still in the sunshine: *Coleridge-Taylor*
You meaner beauties of the night: *Anon*
You remind me: *Hudes*
You say: *Gomelskaya*
You shall not go a-maying: *Head*
You (Ye) twice ten hundred deities: *Purcell, H.*
Young and simple though I am: *Ferrabosco*; *Lanier*
Young British Soldier, The: *Grainger, P.*
Young Eternity: *Pope*
Young Jesus Sweit: *Philips*†
Young love lies sleeping: *Somervell*
Young maid stood in her father's garden, A: *Hughes, Herbert*
Young Maid's Resolution, A: *Lawes, H.*
Young Man's Exhortation, A: *Finzi*
Young Man's Exhortation, A: *Finzi*
Young Man's Shirt, The: *Samuel, R.*
Young rose I give thee, The: *MacCunn*
Young Venevil ran with her heart on fire (Sweet Venevil): *Delius*
Your awful voice: *Weldon (Purcell, H.)*
Your deep blue eyes: *Moult*

Your eyën two will slay me suddenly: *Vaughan Williams*(†) (Roundel [Chaucer])
Your fair looks inflame my desire: *Campion*
Your fair looks urge my desire: *Campion*
Your heart's desire: *Coleridge-Taylor*
Your Rose: *Redman*
Your waking eyes: *Ronald*
Youth [Bax]: *Bax*
Youth [Hölderlin]: *Britten*
Youth [Wever]: *Warlock* (In a harbour green / In an arbour green / In Youth is Pleasure / Lusty Juventus)
Youth and Age on Beaulieu River: *Somers-Cocks*
Youth and Love: *Vaughan Williams*
Youth once loved a maiden, A: *White, M.V.*
Youthful, Charming Chloe, The: *Bantock*
Youth's Spring-tribute: *Ireland*
Yung Yang: *Bantock*
Yvonne of Brittany: *Scott, C.*

Z

Zackery Zed was the last man: *Roe*
Zál: *Bantock*
Zeb Turney's Gal: *Maw*
Zwei braune Augen: *Delius**

Index of poets

Note: Entries in Appendix 1 (foreign texts) have * after the composer's name; those in Appendix 2 (other accompaniments) have †. If these signs are in brackets, the song title appears in both the Appendix and the main catalogue. No distinction has been made for arrangements. Bold type is used for titles appearing under 'Collections'.

A

Abelard, Peter (1079-1142): *Hugill*†
Abercrombie, Lascelles (1881-1938): *Clements*; *Head*
Açika, Isan: *Solomons*(†)
Adams, Bill: *Teed*
Adams, Sarah Flower (1805-48): *Carey, L.*
Adams-Jeremiah, Dorothy: *Thomas, Mansel*
Æ (George William Russell) (1867-1935): *Bantock*; *Bax*; *Busch*
Aeschylus (c.525-c.456BC): *Routh*
A-Fahy, Francis: *Wynne*
Afan, Wil: *Thomas, D.A.*
Agrell, Marjorie: *Gibbs, Armstrong*
Aitken, D. F.: *Dring*
Akhmatova, Anna (1889-1966): *Tavener*†
Alabaster, William (1567-1640): *Rubbra*†
Alafon: *Elwyn-Edwards**
Alcaeus of Messina (c.620-c.580BC): *Bantock*
Alcman (fl.620BC): *Pilkington, M*; *Rubbra*
Aldington, May: *Ronald*
Aldington, Richard (1892-1962): *Jeffreys, J.*; *Poston*; *Warlock*
Aldrich, James: *MacCunn*
Alexander, Francesca: *Luard Selby*
Allingham, William (1824-89): *Bax*; *Butt*; *White, A.*
Alma Tadema, Laurence: *Lehmann*; *Somervell*
Alun: *Lloyd, J.M.*
Alwyn, William (1905-85): *Alwyn*
Anacreon (c.570-c.485BC): *Parry, C.H.H.*
Andersen, Hans Christian (1805-75): *Delius**
Anderson: *Woolrich*(†)
Anderson, Arthur: *Samuel, H.*
Anderson, Robert: *Mark*
Andrade, E. N. da C.: *Someren-Godfery*
Andrews, Bowker: *Bantock*
Andrews, Jennifer: *Venables*
Angus, Marion: *Venables*
Antecessor, Julian: *Whittaker*
Antipater (398-319BC): *Berkeley, L.*; *Fraser, N.*; *Someren-Godfery*
Anyte of Tegea: *Rainier*
Apollinaire, Guillaume (1880-1918): *Berkeley, L.**; *LeFanu*†; *Newson*; *Poole*†
Arkell, Reginald: *Roe*
Armitage, Simon (1963-): *Burrell*
Armstrong, Michael (1924-2000): *Alwyn*(†); *Dring*; *Foreman*
Arne, Thomas (1710-78): *Arne, T.*; *Keel*
Arnold, Matthew (1822-88): *Bridge*(†); *Bullard*; *Johnstone*; *McLelland-Young*; *Ronald*; *Somervell*; *Stanford*; *Taylor*; *Thomas, Mansel*
Arnold, S. J.: *Bishop*

Asche, Oscar: *Norton*
Ashbrooke, Philip: *Head*
Ashe, Michael: *Kirkwood*
Askew, Paul: *Harrison, J.*
Asquith, Herbert (1881-1947): *Britten*; *O'Neill*
Atkinson, Lawrence: *Hogben*
Auden, W. H. (1907-73): *Berkeley, L.*; *Britten*(†); *Dickinson*; *Headington*; *Holloway*†; *Horder*; *Lutyens*; *Marchant*; *Newson*†; *Roe*; *Senator*
Augustine, St. (354-430): *Head*(*)(†); *Rubbra*†; *Wishart*
Ausonius (c.309-92): *Pilkington, M.*
Auster, Paul (1947-): *Matthews, C.*
Aveling, Claude (1869-?): *Howells*; *Samuel, H.*
Ayton, Robert (1570-1638): *Lawes, H.*

B

B__, the Hon. C__.: *Eccles*
Bagg, Terry: *Bedford*†
Bagnall, Stephen: *Steele*
Bagrjana, Elisaveta: *Hiscocks, W.*(†)
Bailey, J. Y.: *Keel*; *Novello*
Bailey, Judith: *Bailey*
Baillie, Joanna (1762-1851): *Clarke-Whitfield*
Bain, Marjorie K.: *Bain*
Baldwin, William (?-c.1569): *Pilkington, M.*; *Procter*
Banks, John: *Eccles*
Banning, H. D.: *Clarke, R.C.*
Bantock, Lady Helen (1868-1961): *Bantock*
Bantock, Myrrha: *Bantock*
Bantock, Raymond (1900-?): *Bantock*
Barbour, Constance: *Anderson, W. H.*
Barham, R. H. (1788-1845): *Orr, B.*†
Baring-Gould, Sabine (1834-1924): *Willcocks*
Barker, George (1930-91): *Finzi*; *Williamson, M.*
Barnfield, Richard (1574-1627): *Gibbs, Armstrong*; *Goossens*; *Macfarren*†
Barnes, William (1801-86): *Bullard*†; *Carey, C.*; *Harvey, F.*; *Headington*; *Lord, R.*; *Moult*; *Vaughan Williams*
Barrie, Royden: *E. Coates*; *Haydn Wood*
Barron, J. Francis: *Dix*
Barthas, Guillaume du (1544-90): *Rawsthorne*
Bashford, H. H. (1880-1961): *Gibbs, Armstrong*
Basse, William: *Hold*
Basselin, Olivier: *Cannon*(*)(†)
Bateson, Thomas (c.1570-1630): *Frankel, E.*; *Howe*
Battersby, Caryl: *German*
Baudelaire, Charles (1821-67): *Bennett, R.R.*†; *Hopkins, A.**; *Matthews, C.**; *Powers**; *Solomons*(†)
Bauld, Alison (1944-): *Bauld*†
Bax, Arnold (1883-1953) *see* MacCarthy, Sheila *and* O'Byrne, Dermot
Bax, Clifford (1886-1962): *Bax*; *Gibbs, Armstrong*; *Shaw*
Bax, Freda: *Bax*
Baxter, Richard (1615-91): *Cruft*
Bayley, Thomas Haynes: *Bayley*; *Bishop*
Beaumont, Francis (1584-1616): *Jeffreys, J.*; *Mace*; *Stanford*; *Warlock*

Index of poets

Beckett, Samuel (1906-89): *Barrett*
Becquer, Gustavo A.: *Hoddinott*
Beddoes, Thomas Lovell (1803-49): *Berkeley, L.*;
    Birkett; *Britten*; *Busch*; *Dieren*; *Herbage*; *Ireland*;
    Jeffreys, J.; *Moult*; *Parry, C.H.H.*; *Shaw*;
    Stevens, B.
Bedford, David (1937-): *Bedford*†
Bedford, Herbert: *Ronald*
Beer, Patricia (1924-): *Tate, P.*†
Bell, Adrian: *Brown, C.*†
Bell, Sydney: *Nelson*; *Thiman*
Bellamy, W. H.: *Hatton*; *Wesley, S.S.*
Bellay, Joachim du (1522-60): *Berkeley, L.*(*)
Belloc, Hilaire (1870-1953): *Bliss*; *Britten*; *Copley*;
    Dubery; *Gill*; *Goodhart*; *Gow*; *Greaves, R.*;
    Gurney; *Harvey, T.*; *Jeffreys, J.*; *Lehmann*; *Lord,
    R.*; *Milner*; *Peel*; *Plumstead*; *Raynor*; *Rowley*;
    Rubbra; *Thiman*; *Toye*; *Turner*; *Warlock*(†)
Bendall, Duffield: *Scott, C.*
Benillion, Hen: *Thomas, Mansel*
Bennard, George (1873-1958): *Bennard*†
Bennett, Arnold (1867-1931): *Goossens*
Bennett, Rodney (1890-1948): *Pilling*; *Quilter*; *Rowley*
Benson, Arthur Christopher (1862-1925): *Elgar*
Benson, C. H.: *Elgar*
Beresford, Blanche: *Fraser, N.*
Bergoyn, General: *Bishop*
Berkenhead, Sir John (1617-79): *Lawes, H.*
Bernard of Clairvaux, St (1090-1153): *Marsh*†;
    Thiman; *Wesley, S.S.*
Berners, Lord (1883-1950): *Berners*; *Dickinson*†
Betjeman, Sir John (1906-84): *Corke*; *Dickinson*†;
    Dring; *East*; *Horder*; *Somers-Cocks*; *Wills*
Betterton, Thomas (1635-1710): *Purcell, H.*
Bickerstaffe, Isaac (1713-?1808): *Arne, T.*; *Grainger,
    P.*; *Quilter*
Bierbaum, Otto Julius (1865-1910): *Dieren*(*)
Billingham, Edgar: *Venables*
Bingham, G. Clifton (1859-1913): *Capel*; *Elgar*;
    Molloy
Bingham, Judith (1952-): *Bingham*†
Binyon, Laurence (1869-1943): *Crossley-Holland*;
    Hedges; *Quilter*; *Ronald*
Birkett, C. M. (1911-): *Birkett*
Bjørnson, Bjørnstjerne (1832-1910): *Bax*(*); *Delius*(*)
Blacker, William: *Wood, C.*
Blackie, Professor: *MacCunn*; *Roberton*
Blackman, Peter: *Bush, A.*
Blackmore, Richard D. (1825-1900): *Bingham*;
    Boughton
Blackwood, Algernon (1869-1951): *Carey, C.*; *Elgar*
Blake, Ernest: *Ireland*
Blake, Howard (1938-): *Blake, H.*
Blake, James Vila: *Ireland*
Blake, William (1757-1827): *Bantock*; *Bayford*†;
    Bedford†; *Brian*; *Britten*; *Busch*; *Bush, A.*; *Butt*;
    Chapple; *Clarke, R.*; *Cooke*†; *Cruft*; *Dunhill*; *Fogg*;
    Foreman; *Foss*; *Foster, D.*†; *Gibbs, Armstrong*;
    Holst; *Howells*; *Ireland*; *Jacob*; *Joubert*; *Kirkwood*;
    Lord, R.; *McLeod*†; *McQuattie*; *Matthews, D.*;
    Milford; *Mills*; *Owen*; *Parrott*; *Parry, C.H.H.*;
    Procter; *Quilter*; *Randalls*; *Raphael*; *Roberton*;
    Rodgers; *Rose*; *Someren-Godfery*; *Stevenson*;
    Swann; *Sykes*; *Symons*; *Tate, P.*; *Teed*; *Thiman*;
    Turnbull; *Usher*(†); *Vaughan Williams*†; *Walton*;
    Warlock; *White, A.*; *Wills*(†); *Wood, C.*
Blamire, Susannah: *Hughes, Herbert*; *Mark*
Bliss, Sir Arthur (1891-1975): *Bliss*†

Blunden, Charles Edmund (1896-1974): *Brown, C.*†;
    Finzi; *Holloway*
Blunt, Bruce (1899-1957): *Warlock*(†)
Blunt, Wilfred Scawen (1840-1922): *Brown, J.*
Blyton, Carey (1932-2002): *Blyton*(†)
Blyton, Enid (1897-1968): *Blyton*
Boccaccio, Giovanni (1313-75): *Harrison, J.*
Bodenstedt, Friedrich (1819-92): *Lehmann*(*);
    Quilter(*)
Boland, Kathleen: *Thiman*
Boleyn, Anne (c.1507-36): *Anon*; *Rutter*†
Bolton, Edmund: *Somers-Cocks*
Bones, Mark: *Bayliss*
Bonham, Thomas: *Atkins*
Bonnaud, Dominique: *Shaw*
Borchers, Elizabeth: *Barrett*†
Bottomley, Gordon (1874-1948): *Bainton*; *Somers-Cocks*
Boulton, Sir Harold (1859-1935): *Anon*; *Bantock*;
    German; *Grainger, P.*; *Hughes, Herbert*; *Shaw*;
    Somervell
Bouverie, Dorothy Pleydell: *Gibbs, Armstrong*
Boyce, William (1711-79): *Defesch*
Boycott, Joan: *Somers-Cocks*
Boyd, A. C.: *Gibbs, Armstrong*
Boyd, Mark Alexander (1563-1601): *Scott, F.G.*
Boyer, Abel: *Purcell, D.*
Braban, Harvey: *Dunhill*
Brady, Nicholas (1659-1726): *Purcell, H.*
Brandon, Herbert J.: *Redman*
Brecht, Berthold (1998-1956): *McGuire*;
    Muldowney(*)(†); *Poole**
Brereton, Cloudesley: *Brown, C.*†
Breton, Nicholas (c.1545-c.1626): *Hales*; *Holst*;
    Ireland; *Lyall*†; *Procter*; *Scott, C.*; *Tomlinson*;
    Warlock
Bridges, Robert (1844-1930): *Bainton*; *Berkeley, L.*;
    Bridge; *Butterworth, G.*; *Carey, C.*; *Crossley-Holland*; *Darke*; *Finzi*; *Gurney*; *Herbert, I.*; *Holst*;
    MacCunn; *Miles*†; *Milford*; *Moeran*; *Orr, C.W.*;
    Parrott; *Pope*; *Stanford*; *Steele*; *Vaughan
    Williams*†; *Whittaker*
Broadwood, Lucy (1858-1929): *Britten*
Brontë, Anne (1820-49): *Edgar*
Brontë, Emily (1818-48): *Ireland*; *Jeffreys, J.*; *Joubert*;
    MacDonald; *McLelland-Young*; *Moult*; *Scott, S.*;
    Wills
Brooke, Jocelyn (1908-66): *Searle*
Brooke, Mrs Frances (1724-89): *Shield*
Brooke, Rupert (1887-1915): *Bridge*; *Caradon*; *Center*;
    Foss; *Ireland*; *Møller*; *Newson*; *Peterkin*; *Thomas,
    Muriel*; *Taylor, M.*
Brooks, Phillips (1835-93): *Dunhill*
Brown, George Mackay (1921-1996): *Forshaw*(†);
    Liddell; *Maxwell Davies*†
Brown, Herbert S.: *Ireland*(†)
Brown, John Gracen: *Naylor, P.*; *Pitfield*
Brown, J. L. Crommelin: *Besley*
Brown, Thomas Edward (1830-97): *Walford Davies*;
    Roe
Brown, W.: *Lawes, H.*
Browne, Michael Dennis: *Lord, D.*
Browne, William (1591-1643): *Carey, C.*; *Moeran*;
    Plumstead; *Raphael*
Browning, Elizabeth Barrett (1806-61): *Coleridge-Taylor*; *Elgar*; *Lloyd Webber*; *McLeod*†;
    Reizenstein; *Sagar*; *Wills*†

Browning, Robert (1812-89): *Bantock*; *Blake, H.*†; *Bryson*; *Coleridge-Taylor*; *Harrison, J.*; *Head*; *Lehmann*; *Maw*†; *Owen*; *Somervell*; *Stanford*; *White, M.V.*; *Wills*(†)
Brownlie, John (1857-1925): *Elgar*
Bryan, Robert (1858-1920): *Bryan*
Bucchieri, Marco: *Creswell**
Buchan, John, Baron Tweedsmuir (1875-1940): *Shaw*
Büchner, Georg (1813-37): *Smyth**
Buckinghamshire, Duke of: *see* Sheffield, John
Buckton, Alice: *Holst*
Bullett, Gerald: *Thiman*
Bultitaft, W. L.: *Harty*
Bulwer-Lytton, Edward (1803-73): *Scott, C.*
Bumstead, Eudora: *Foreman*
Bunn, Alfred (c.1797-1860): *Balfe*
Bunting, Basil (1900-85): *Colling*†
Bunyan, John (1828-88): *Vaughan Williams*(†)
Burnaby, Charles (fl.1703): *Eccles*
Burns, Robert (1759-96): *Anon*; *Atkinson, G.*(†); *Bantock*; *Bax*; *Beamish*(†); *Bennett, W.S.*; *Britten*; *Burrows*; *Center*; *Coleridge-Taylor*; *Diack*; *Dickinson*; *German*; *Grainger, P.*; *Headington*; *Horder*; *Hurlstone*; *Jeffreys, J.*; *Liddell*; *MacCunn*; *Marshall, N.*†; *Musgrave*; *Nash*; *Pierson*; *Pinto*; *Quilter*; *Scott, C.*; *Scott, F.G.*; *Shaw*; *Shur*†; *Snell*; *Stanford*; *Sullivan*; *Swann*; *Thiman*; *Vignoles*; *White, A.*; *White, M.V.*
Burnside, Helen Marion: *Foster, M.B.*
Burra, Peter (?1910-1937): *Britten*
Burroughs, Ellen (Sophie Jewett), (1861-1909): *Elgar*
Busfield, Winifred: *White, A.*
Bush, Geoffrey (1920-98): *Bush*
Bush, Nancy: *Head*(†)
Butler, Arthur Gray (1832-1909): *Parry, C.H.H.*
Butterworth, Neil (1934-): *Butterworth, N.*
Butts, Mary F.: *White, A.*
Byrne, W. A.: *Howells*
Byrom, John (1692-1763): *Brown, J.*; *Dalby*
Byron, Lord George (1788-1824): *Clarke-Whitfield*; *Coleridge-Taylor*; *Dickinson*(†); *Holbrooke*; *Maconchy*†; *Naylor, P.*; *Parry, C.H.H.*; *Peterkin*; *Sagar*; *Stanford*; *Swann*; *Tomlinson*; *Wesley, S.S.*; *White, M.V.*; *Wood, Hugh*

C

Callanan, Jeremiah J. (1795-1829): *Jeffreys, J.*
Callimachus (c.310-after 240BC): *Benbow*; *Warlock*
Campanella, Tommaso (1568-1639): *Dalby*†
Campbell, Joseph (1879-1944): *Bax*; *Gurney*; *Harty*; *Hugh-Jones*; *Hughes, Herbert*; *Jeffreys, J.*; *Mullinar*; *Peterkin*†; *Quilter*(†); *Roberton*; *Rowley*
Campbell, Peter: *Fowler*†
Campbell, Thomas (1777-1844): *Maconchy*†; *Scott, F.G.*
Campion, Thomas (1567-1620): *Anon*; *Bax*; *Bennett, R.R.*; *Bernard*; *Branson*; *Busch*; *Bush, G.*; *Campion*; *Clarke, R.*; *Coprario*; *Dalby*(†); *Darlow*; *Ferrabosco*; *Giles*; *Gurney*; *Harty*; *Holloway*; *Jeffreys, J.*(†); *Keel*; *Lanier*; *Lupo*; *Mason*; *Moeran*; *Pilkington, F.*; *Quilter*; *Rosseter*; *Someren-Godfery*; *Stanford*; *Steele*; *Tomlinson*; *Warlock*
Canning, Nefra: *Hiscocks, W.*
Canton, William (1845-1926): *Dunhill*; *Keel*†
Carbery, Ethna (Anna MacManus) (1886-1902): *Gibbs, Armstrong*; *Gurney*

Carew, Sir John: *Self, A.*
Carew, Molly: *Carew*
Carew, Thomas (1595-1639): *Lanier*; *Lawes, H.*; *Thomas, Mansel*
Carey, Henry (c.1681-1743): *Anon*; *Britten*; *Grainger, P.*; *Jeffreys, J.*; *Lampe*
Carey, Marianne: *McGuire*†
Carfrae, Eileen: *Gibbs, Armstrong*
Carlyle, Thomas (1795-1881): *Stanford*
Carman, William Bliss (1861-1929): *Gurney*; *Shaw*
Carroll, Diana: *Roe*
Carroll, Lewis (Charles Lutwidge Dodgson) (1832-98): *Boyle, R.*; *Hely-Hutchinson*; *Lloyd, de*; *Sagar*
Cartwright, William (1611-43): *Lawes, H.*
Carvalho, Naomi: *Scott, C.*
Carver, Raymond (1939-88): *Holt*†
Casken, John (1949-): *Casken*
Cassius, Dion (c.150-c.235): *Matthews, C.*†
Casson, Ernest: *Gurney*
Catholic Rite: *McCabe*
Causley, Charles (1917-): *Bush, G.*; *Butterworth, N.*; *Hurd*; *Roe*(†); *Tate, P.*†
Cavafy, Constantine (1863-1933): *Hugill*
Cayrol, Jean: *McLeod**
Ceirog (John Cierog Hughes) (1832-87): *Parry, C.H.H.*
Celan, Paul (1920-79): *Birtwistle*†; *Nyman*(*)
Chalkhill, John (? -1642): *Warlock*
Chamberlaine: *Purcell, H.*
Chambers, Sir E. K. (1866-1954): *Caradon*; *Raynor*
Chan Fang-Shën (4th century): *Fraser, N.*; *Gibbs, Armstrong*; *Somers-Cocks*
Ch'ang Ch'ien: *Bantock*
Chang Chi-ho (c.750): *Bantock*
Chang Heng: *Blake, D.*
Chapman, George (1560-1634): *Dale, M.*; *Joubert*
Charles I, King of England (1600-49): *Plumstead*
Chase, Madeleine: *Procter*
Chatterton, Julia: *Parry, C.H.H.*
Chaucer, Geoffrey (c.1343-1400): *Bax*; *Bush, G.*; *Dyson*; *Harrison, J.*; *Newson*; *Vaughan Williams*(†)
Chekhov, Anton: *LeFanu*†
Ch'ên Tzû-ang (656-698): *Bantock*; *Harrison, J.*; *Redman*
Ch'ên Tzü-Lung (1607-47): *Dalby*; *Orr, R.*
Chesterman, Hugh: *White, A.*
Chesterton, Frances (? -1938): *Rowley*
Chesterton, G. K. (1874-1936): *Clarke, R.*; *Foss*; *Hely-Hutchinson*; *Turner*; *Williamson, M.*
Chettle, Henry (c.1560-c.1607): *Benjamin, A.*; *Browne*; *Bush, G.*; *Moeran*; *Pilkington, F.*; *Samuel, H.*
Chiabrera, Gabriello (1552-1638): *Coleridge-Taylor*
Ch'ien Ch'i: *Rubbra*†
Child, Harold: *Vaughan Williams*
Chilman, Eric (1893-?): *Ireland*
Chisholm, Lilias Scott: *Rose*
Chorley, May: *Bantock*
Christine de Pisan (c.1363-c.1431): *Cannon*(*)(†)
'Chrystabel': *German*
Cibber, Colley (1671-1757): *Boyce*; *Dring*
Clare, John (1793-1864): *Arnell*; *Barratt*; *Bennett, W.S.*; *Bullard*; *Dorward*; *Greaves, Terence*†; *Gurney*; *Hold*; *Jeffreys, J.*; *Kimpton*; *Self, A.*; *Swann*; *Venables*†; *Warlock*
Clark, Leonard: *Brown, C.*; *Roe*
Clark, Mary Kitson: *Stanford*
Clark, Thomas A.: *Helliwell*†
Clarke, Sir Arthur C. (1917-): *Bedford*†
Clarke, Austin (1896-1974): *Swain*

Clarke, Helen: *Thompson, P.*
Clarke, T. E. B. (1907-1989): *Berners*
Clarinda (Mrs McLehose): *Liddell*
Claye, C. A.: *Bernard*
Clifford, George: *Holborne*
Climie, David (1920-95): *Swann*
Clucas, Humphrey: *F. Martin*
Clutsam, George Howard (1866-1951): *Clutsam*
Cobb: *Storace*
Cobb, Peter: *Thomas, Mansel*(†)
Cochrane, Alice: *Brown, C.*†
Cocteau, Jean (1889-1963): *Berkeley, L.**
Cole, David: *Nevens*
Coleridge, Hartley (1796-1849): *Berkeley, L.*
Coleridge, Mary Elizabeth (1861-1907): *Bridge*; *Carey, C.*; *Clements*; *Foreman*; *Graves*; *Ireland*; *Le Fleming*; *Parry, C.H.H.*; *Quilter*; *Rootham*
Coleridge, Samuel Taylor (1772-1834): *Bingham*; *Naylor, B.*; *Owen*; *Routh*; *Vaughan Williams*
Collier, George: *Linley Snr*
Collins, Hal (?-1929): *Warlock*
Collins, John Henn: *Collins, J.H.*
Colman, George (1732-94): *Arne, T.*
Colum, Padraic (1881-1972): *Bax*; *Bridge*; *Crossley-Holland*; *Gibbs, Armstrong*; *Graves*; *Harty*; *Hughes, Herbert*; *Lodge*; *Moeran*; *Rubbra*
Columba, St: *Parke*
Compton, Sugette: *Torphichen*
Confucius (551-479BC): *Burrows*; *Harrison, J.*; *Nieman*
Congreve, William (1670-1729): *Arne, T.*; *Barratt*; *Eccles*; *Gibbs, Armstrong*; *Handel*; *Purcell, H.*
Constable, Henry (1562-1613): *Benjamin, A.*; *Browne*; *Bush, G.*; *Moeran*; *Pilkington, F.*; *Samuel, H.*
Cook, Carl: *Hugill*†
Cooke, Leslie Leonard: *Openshaw*; *Ray*
Coolidge, Porter B.: *Bantock*
Cooper, Beryl: *Phillips, M.*
Cooper, Eric Thirkell, *Ireland*
Cooper, William (1910-): *Wishart*
Cope, Wendy (1945-): *Matthews, C.*(†); *Read*†; *Williams, Roderick*
Coppard, Alfred Edgar (1878-1957): *Swain*
Corbluth, Elsa: *Blyton*
Corinthians, First Letter to: *Handel*
Cornford, Frances (1886-1960): *Bliss*†; *Holloway*; *Hugh-Jones*; *Toye*; *Wegener*†
Cornish, William (c.1465-1523): *Ireland*; *Milford*; *Northcott*†
Cornwall, Barry (Bryan Waller Procter) (1787-1874): *Bennett, W.S.*
Corso, Gregory (1930-): *Dickinson*
Costello, Elvis (Declan Patrick McManus) (1955-): *Woolrich*†
Cothi, Lewis Glyn: *Williams, W.M.*
Cotton, Charles (1630-87): *Bullard*
Courtney, W. L. (1859-1928): *Howells*
Cousins, James H. (1873-?): *Bax*; *Jeffreys, J.*
Cowley, Abraham (1618-67): *Blow*; *Boyce*; *Kleyn*; *Leveridge*; *MacCunn*; *Purcell, H.*
Cowper, William (1731-1800): *Kleyn*
Coxford, Arthur Philip: *White, M.V.*
Cranmer, Thomas (1489-1556): *Wesley, S.S.*
Cranmer-Byng, Launcelot (1872-1945): *Bantock*
Crashaw, Richard (c.1613-49): *Hughes, Hugh.*; *Procter*; *Vaughan Williams*†
Cripps, Arthur Shearly (1869-?): *Bliss*†; *Shaw*
Crofts, John: *Lawes, H.*†

Cropper, Margaret: *Gibbs, Armstrong*
Crossley-Holland, Kevin: *Crossley-Holland*†
Crowne, John (c.1640-1712): *Eccles*
Crws: *Hughes,, A.*; *Hughes-Jones*; *Lloyd, J.M.*
Cumberland, Gerald: *Brian*
Cumberland, Martin: *Foulds*
Cummings, E. E. (1894-1962): *Bennett, R.R.*, *Dickinson*; *Lord, R.*; *Matthews, D.*†; *Roxburgh*; *Sansom*; *Wills*†
Cunningham, Alan (1784-1842): *Blyton*; *Davies, Walford*; *Parry, C.H.H.*; *Roxburgh*
Cunnington, L. Ann: *Lehmann.*
Currie, Sir Walter Mordaunt (1894-1978): *Gibbs, Armstrong*; *Head*
Cynan: *Jones, W.B.*; *Roberts, T.O.*; *Williams, W.M.*
Cynewulf (late 8th to early 9th cent.): *Pickard*

D

D'Alba, Pietro (Edward Elgar) (1857-1934): *Elgar*
Dallas, Ruth: *Joubert*
Dalmon, Charles: *Quilter*
Dalton, J.: *Arne, T.*
Dalton, J. P.: *Bowen*
D'Anduza, Clara: *Dillon*†
Daniel, Samuel (1562-1619): *Blyton*†; *Brian*; *Danyel*; *Dring*; *Gibbs, Armstrong*; *Ireland*; *Murrill*; *Naylor, P.*; *Parry, C.H.H.*; *Raynor*; *Rutter*†; *Steptoe*; *Wills*(†)
Dante Alighieri (1265-1321): *Pike*
D'Arcy, de Burgh: *Russell, K.*
Darley, George (1795-1846): *Rowley*; *Scott, C.*
Darlow, Royston (1943-): *Darlow*
Davenant, Sir William (1606-68): *Atkins*; *Lawes, W.*; *Poston*
Davidson, John (1857-1909): *Cooke*†; *Foss*; *Gurney*
Davies, Aneirin Talfan: *Thomas, Mansel*(†)
Davies, Daniel H.: *Thomas, Mansel*(†)
Davies, Idris: *Thomas, Mansel*
Davies, Janet: *Davies, J.*
Davies, Sir John (1569-1626): *Maynard*; *Musgrave*†
Davies, R.: *Parry, J.*
Davies, William Henry (1871-1940): *Berkeley, L.*; *Bliss*; *Bruce*; *Fleming*; *Head*; *Hedges*; *Jeffreys, J.*; *Lloyd Webber*; *Naylor, B.*; *Naylor, P.*; *Newson*; *Parrott*; *Rowley*; *Tate, P.*; *Wallbank*; *Willink*
Davis, Thomas (1814-45): *Hughes, Herbert*; *Wood, C.*
Davison, Francis: *Jones, R.*
Dawson, Harry: *Gibbs, Armstrong*
Day-Lewis, Cecil (1904-72): *Dean*; *Bliss*†; *Frankel, B.*; *LeFanu*†; *Naylor, B.*; *Naylor, P.*
de Bary, Anna: *Fraser, N.*
de Gasztoldi, Carmen Bernos: *Blyton*; *Hedges*
de la Mare, Walter (1873-1956): *Bantock*; *Benjamin, G.*; *Bennett, R.R.*; *Berkeley, L.*(†); *Besley*; *Birkett*; *Bliss*; *Britten*; *Browne*; *Bruce*; *Burrows*; *Butterworth,, N.*; *Carey, C.*; *Finzi*; *Fiske*; *Foreman*; *Gibbs, Armstrong*; *Gurney*; *Harrison, P.*; *Head*; *Hely-Hutchinson*; *Holloway*; *Howells*; *Hugh-Jones*(†); *Jeffreys, J.*; *Joubert*†; *Keel*; *Le Fleming*; *Lodge*; *McLeod*; *Milford*; *Mullinar*; *Naylor, P.*; *Noble, H.*; *Peterkin*; *Pilling*; *Pitfield*†; *Pope*; *Procter*; *Redman*; *Rodgers*; *Roe*; *Rose*; *Steele*; *Symons*; *Teed*; *Thompson, P.*; *Wegener*
de Léon, Fray Luis: *Nyman**
de Lisle, Leconte see Leconte de Lisle
de Quincey, Thomas (1785-1859): *Dieren*; *Woolrich*(†)
de Tablay, Lord: *Alwyn*; *Scott, C.*

de Vere, Aubrey Thomas (1814-1902): *McCabe*
Dean, Roy: *Dean*
Deane, Vincent: *Barry*
Dearmer, Geoffrey: *Shaw*
Defoe, David: *Steptoe*†
Dehmel, Richard (1863-1920): *Bax*
Dehn, Paul: *Hurd*
Dekker, Thomas (c.1570-1632): *Berners*; *Bush, G.*; *Hamilton, I.*; *Ireland*; *Jeffreys, J.*; *Keel*; *Moeran*; *Noble, T.T.*; *Stanford*; *Warlock*; *C. Wood*
Despréaux, Nicolas Boileau: *Dieren**
Devereux, Robert, Earl of Essex (1591-1646): *Batchelor*; *Martin, R.*
Diack, Michael (1869-1946): *Young, A.*
Dibb, Steve (1960 -): *Moult*
Dibdin, Charles (1745-1814): *Bishop*; *Britten*; *Dibdin*; *Hook*; *Maxwell Davies*†
Dibdin, Thomas (1776-1847): *Bishop*; *Brown, J.*
Dickens, Charles (1812-70): *Usher*†
Dickinson, Dorothy: *Ronald*
Dickinson, Emily (1830-86): *Anderson*†; *Beamish*†; *Butler*†; *Butterworth, N.*; *Cresswell*; *Grossner*; *Holt*†; *Horne*†; *LeFanu*†; *Montague*†; *Swann*
Digby, George, 2nd Earl of Bristol (1612-77): *Orr, C.W.*
Dimond, W.: *Bishop*
Dionysius (2nd cent. BC): *Benjamin, A.*
Dipnall, T. H.: *Thiman*
Dixon, H. Percy (?1898-1973): *Gill*
Dixon, Richard Watson (1833-1900): *Head*
Dobell, Sydney (1824-74): *Walker, E.*
Dobson, Henry Austin (1840-1921): *Howells*; *McEwen*
Dod, Chester: *Thomas, V.*
Donaldson, Brian: *Steele*
Donne, John (c.1572-1631): *Anon*; *Arnold, M.*; *Bennett, R.R.*; *Blyton*†; *Boyle, I.*†; *Brian*; *Britten*; *Brown, C.*†; *Burgon*†; *Bush, G.*; *Davidson, M.*; *Dowland*; *Downes*†; *Ferrabosco*; *Frankel, B.*; *Hilton*; *Humfrey*(†); *Joubert*; *Lawes, H.*; *Maconchy*; *Milford*; *Morley*; *Naylor, P.*; *Parrott*; *Rainier*†; *Self, A.*; *Sohal*†; *Smith, R.*; *Stevens, B.*; *Swayne*; *Thomas, Mansel*; *Wilson, John*
Douglas, Lord Alfred (1870-1945): *Hugill*
Dowdon, Aubrey: *Besley*
Dowland, John (1563-1626): *Jacob*†; *Standford*
Downes, Nathaniel: *Gibbs, Armstrong*
Dowson, Christopher Ernest (1867-1900): *Bantock*; *Bedford*†; *Delius*; *Ireland*; *Quilter*; *Ronald*; *Scott, C.*; *Someren-Godfery*
Doyle, Sir Arthur Conan (1859-1930): *Grainger, P.*; *White, M.V.*
Doyle, John *see* Robert Graves
Drachmann, Holger (1846-1908): *Delius*(*)
Drayton, Michael (1563-1631): *Anon*; *Dring*; *Wills*(†)
Dring, Madeleine (1923 - 1977): *Dring*
Drinkwater, John (1882-1937): *Austin*; *Birkett*; *Boughton*; *Head*; *Jacobson*; *Rowley*
Drummond (of Hawthornden), William (1585-1649): *Benjamin, A.*; *Scott, F.G.*; *Walton*
Dryden, John (1631-1700): *Bedford*†; *Boyce*; *Dring*; *Eccles*; *Hook*; *Purcell, H.*; *Ronald*; *Wellesz*
du Maurier, George (1834-96): *Stoker*
Duff, E. L.: *Berners*
Duff, J.: *Hatton*
Dufferin, Helen Selina, Lady: *Scott, C.*
Duke, Richard (1658-1711): *Purcell, H.*
Dukes, Ashley (1885-1959): *O'Neill*
Dunbar, Paul Laurence (1872-1906): *Coleridge- Taylor*

Dunbar, William (c.1460-c.1520): *Musgrave*; *Scott, F.G.*; *Seiber*
Duncan, Ronald: *Britten*(†)
Dunlop, Florence: *Hearne*(†)
D'Urfey, Thomas: (1653-1723) *Blow*; *Clarke, J.*; *Courteville*; *Croft*; *Eccles*; *Purcell, H.*
Durrell, Lawrence (1912-90): *Berkeley, L.*; *Grange*†; *Poole*; *Southam*; *Routh*
Dyer, Sir Edward (1543-1607): *Bennett, R.R.*; *Tate, P.*
Dyfed: *Jenkins, D.*; *Thomas, Mansel*
Dyment, Clifford: *Roe*†

E

Easmon, Kathleen: *Coleridge-Taylor*
Eastwick, Ivy O.: *White, A.*
Ecclesiastes: *Hudes*†, *Hugill*
Ecclesiasticus: *Jones, W.B.*; *Stanford*†; *Vaughan Williams*
Edwards, A. D.: *Owen*
Edwards, Richard (?1523-66): *Bush, G.*; *Ireland*; *Parsons*
Eeman, L. E.: *Gibbs, Armstrong*
Eichendorf, Joseph von (1788-1857): *Smyth**
Elfed: *Thomas, Mansel*(*)
Elfyn, Menna: *Tann*†
Elgar, Caroline Alice (?1849-1920): *Elgar*
Elgar, Sir Edward *see* D'Alba, Pietro
Elguera, Amalia: *Musgrave*†
Eliot, George (1819-80): *Sullivan*
Eliot, Thomas Stearns (1888-1965): *Adès*; *Britten*†; *Holloway*†; *Matthews, D.*†; *Pope*; *Tavener*, *Wood, Hugh*†
Elliot, Walter: *Lawson*†
Ellis, Benedict: *Gibbs, Armstrong*
Ellis, Robert: *Elwyn-Edwards*
Ellis, Thomas Evelyn, 8th Baron Howard de Walden (1880-?): *Holbrooke*
Ellis, Vivian Locke: *Hand*
Ellison, Joseph: *Dring*
Elton, Richard: *Harrison, D.*
Emerson, Ida: *Grainger, P.*
Emerson, Ralph Waldo (1803-82): *Parry, C.H.H.*; *Stoker*
Emlyn, Myfyr: *Evans, D.P.*
Emyr: *Williams, W.S.G.*(*)
Enzensberger, Hans Magnus: *Newson*
Ephelia (Joan Philips) (fl. 1679): *Gibbs, Armstrong*
Erskine, Ella: *Scott, C.*
Essex, Earl of *see* Devereux, Robert
Etchells, Ruth: *Lloyd, R.*
Etheridge, Sir George (1635-92): *Boyce*; *Purcell, H.*
Ettrick Shepherd *see* Hogg, James
Evans, Edwin: *Goossens*(*)
Evans, J. Boncath: *Evans, W.T.*
Evans, John: *Williams, M.*
Evans, Sebastian: *Treharne*
Evans, W. T.: *Evans, W.T.*
Eversley, Atwyth: *Owen*
Exodus: *Head*
Eyton, Frank: *Benjamin*

F

Faed, Tamar: *Scott, C.*
Fagan, James Bernard: *Hughes, Herbert*
Fainlight, Ruth: *Hayes*†

294 Index of poets

Fan Tseng Hsiang: *Kleyn*
Fardd, Ieuan: *Wynne*†
Farjeon, Eleanor (1881-1965): *Burtch*; *Carter*; *Glennie-Smith*
Faulds, Robert: *Pitfield*
Fennell, Brice: *Coleridge-Taylor*
Fenton, James (1949-): *Muldowney*(†)
Ferguson, Sir Samuel (1810-86): *Hughes, Herbert*; *Tate, P.*
Ferlinghetti, Lawrence(1919-): *Weir*†
Field, Alexander: *Bowen*
Field, Eugene (1850-95): *O'Neill*; *Pilkington, J.H.*; *Raynor*; *Shaw*; *Stanford*
Fielding, Henry: *Grainger, P.*
Finzi, Joy: *Bingham*
Firbank, Ronald (1886-1926): *Holloway*†
Fishburn, Christopher: *Purcell, H.*
Fisher, Howard: *Bishop*
Fischerova, Sylvia: *Matheson*
Fitzball, Edward (1793-1873): *Bishop*
Flanders, Michael (1922-75): *Swann*
Flatman, Thomas (1637-1688): *Barratt*; *Blow*; *Humfrey*†; *Locke*; *Purcell, H.*; *Roe*†
Flecker, James Elroy (1884-1915): *Baines*; *Carey, C.*; *Finzi*; *Foss*; *Parrott*
Fleming, Marjorie: *Bennett, R.R.*
Fletcher, John (1579-1625): *Bush, G.*; *Demuth*; *Gibbs, Armstrong*; *Goossens*; *Gurney*; *Hand*; *Handel*; *Isherwood*; *Jeffreys, J.*; *Lloyd Webber*; *Mace*; *Moeran*; *Moult*; *Murrill*; *Parry, C.H.H.*; *Pierson*; *Raphael*; *Rawsthorne*; *Self, A.*; *Slater*; *Stanford*; *Warlock*(†)
Fletcher, Phineas (1582-1650): *Frankel, B.*; *Hurlstone*; *Jeffreys, J.*; *Self, A.*
Flight, Claude: *Clarke, R.*
Flower, Robin (1881-1946): *Gurney*; *Pike*
Fontana, Jennie: *Gomelskaya*
Ford, Ford Madox (F. M. Heuffer) (1873-1939): *Warlock*
Ford, John (c.1586-c.1640): *Lawes, W.*
Ford, Rita: *Roe*†
Ford, Thomas (c.1580-1648): *Bury*; *Quilter*
Fordwych, Herbert: *Lehmann*
Forster, Evelyn: *Procter*
Forsyth, James: *Kirkwood*(†)
Foster, H. E.: *MacNutt*
Fouché, Bob: *Fouché*
Fowler, William (1560-1612): *Anon*
Fraser, Frederick John: *Woodforde-Finden*
Freeman, John (1880-1929): *Gurney*; *Jacobson*; *Wynne*
Frenkiel, Nevil: *Solomons*(†)
Frère, Auriel: *MacDonald*
Friedmann, Helmut: *Tomlinson**
Froom, Jacqueline: *Greaves, Terence*†; *Hoddinott*; *Roe*†
Frost, Robert (1874-1963): *Jackson, F.*; *Roberts, T.*; *Swann*
Fu Hsüan (? -278): *Oldham*
Fuller, William (1608-1675): *Purcell, H.*
Fuller Maitland, John Alexander (1856-1936): *Britten*
Furlong, Thomas (1794-1827): *Hughes, Herbert*
Furse, Celia: *Piggott*
Fyleman, Rose (1877-1957): *Head*; *Lehmann*; *Stanford*

G

Gale, Norman (1862-1942): *Farrar*; *Kleyn*; *Lidgey*
Galloway, Janice: *Beamish*

Galsworthy, John (1867-1933): *Pilling*
Gardiner, Michael: *Bruce*
Garnett, Richard (1835-1906): *Elgar*
Garrett, Blanche Pownall: *Anderson, W.H.*
Garrett, Judith: *Blake, H.*
Garrick, David (1717-79): *Arne, T.*
Garstin, Crosbie: *Cundell*; *Rowley*
Garth, Phyllida: *Plumstead*
Gascoigne, George (c.1525-77): *Cruft*; *Gibbs, Alan*; *Routh*
Gascoyne, David (1916-2000): *Bush, G.*; *Hudes*†
Gass, Irene: *Dunhill*; *Thiman*
Gautier, Théophile (1811-72): *Thomas, A.G.**
Gay, John (1685-1732): *Greene*; *Handel*; *Russel*
Geibel, Emanuel (1815-1954): *Delius**; *White, M.V.*
Géraldy, Paul: *Blyton**
Gerhardt, Paul (1607-76): *Self, A.*†
Gesualdo, Don Carlo, Prince of Venosa (c.1560-1613): *Beamish*†
Gibbons, Stella (1902-89): *Roe*
Gibbs, Anne: *Gibbs, Armstrong*
Gibbs, B. R.: *Center*
Gibbs, Christian: *Center*
Gibson, Alexander Craig: *Mark*
Gibson, Wilfrid Wilson (1878-1962): *Fulton*; *Gurney*; *Howells*; *Jeffreys, J.*; *Peterkin*; *Whittaker*
Gilbert, Sir William Schwenk (1836-1911): *Sullivan*
Giles, Herbert A. (1845-1935): *Peterkin*
Gilliat, Sidney: *Williamson, M.*
Glanville, Lilian: *Wood, Haydn*
Glenroy, W. B.: *Lamb*
Goard, Henry A.: *Goard*
Goddard-Fenwick, Digby: *Bridge*
Godfrey, H. W: *Roberton*
Godwhen, A.: *Williams, Gerrard*
Goethe, Johann Wolfgang von (1749-1832): *Coleridge-Taylor*; *Crossley-Holland*; *Darlow*; *Dieren*(*); *Harvey, J.*†; *Howells*; *Seiber*; *White, M.V.*
Gogarty, Oliver St John: *Hughes, Herbert*
Golding, Sir William (1911-93): *Ferguson*
Goldsmith, Oliver (1728-74): *Boyle, R.*; *Dring*
Gordon, Adam Lindsay (1833-70): *Elgar*
Gore-Booth, Eva (1870-1926): *Peel*; *Shaw*
Gorges, Sir Arthur: *Barley*
Gorla, Elizabeth: *Bedford*†
Gostling, Frances: *Lehmann*
Gould, Gerald (1885-1936): *Bridge*; *Gurney*; *Peel*
Gould, Mona: *Head*
Gould, Robert (?-c.1709): *Purcell, H.*; *Salter, L.*
Gower, George Leveson: *Bowen*; *Stanford*
Graham of Gartmore: *Sullivan*; *Turnbull*
Grahame, Kenneth (1859-1932): *Head*
Grainger, Ella: *Grainger, E.*
Grand, P. A: *Roberton*
Grant, Gwen: *Gibbs, Armstrong*
Graves, Alfred Percival (1846-1931): *Marshall, N.*†; *Parry, C.H.H.*; *Stanford*; *Wood, C.*
Graves, Robert (1895-1985): *Bayliss*; *Berkeley, L.*; *Berners*; *Crosse*; *Fowler*†; *Gurney*; *Hattey*; *Holloway*; *Jeffreys, J.*; *Searle*; *Thackray*; *Venables*; *Wishart*; *Wood, Hugh*
Gray, Thomas (1716-71): *Storace*(†); *Wesley, S.*
Green, Frederick Pratt: *Pope*
Green, George Arthur: *Treharne*
Greene, Robert (1558-92): *Barley*; *Britten*; *Bush, G.*
Gregory, Isabella Augusta, Lady (1852-1932): *Davies, E.*
Gregory, Padraic: *Gibbs, Armstrong*(†)

Grenside, Dorothy: *Scott, C.*
Grenville, George, Lord Lansdowne: *Boyce*; *Eccles*
Grenville, R. H.: *Anderson, W.H.*
Greville, Sir Fulke, 1st Baron Brooke (1554-1628): *Cavendish*; *Dowland*
Griffin, Gerald (1803-40): *Foulds*
Griffith, Huw Emrys: *Williams, W.A.*
Griffith, William: *Peterkin*
Griffiths, Bryn: *Thomas, Mansel*
Griffiths, Maggie: *Evans, D.P.*
Grogan, Walter E.: *Holbrooke*; *Holst*
Groth, Klaus (1819-99): *Smyth**
Groves, J. W.: *Dunhill*
Guiney, Louise Imogen (1861-1920): *Orr, C.W.*; *Raynor*
Gurney, Dorothy F. (1858-1932: *Handel*†; *Williams, Rhyddid*(†)
Gurney, Ivor (1890-1937): *Finzi*; *Gurney*; *Jeffreys, J.*; *Moult*; *Venables*
Gwalia, Eos: *Owen*
Gwenallt: *Hughes, A.*
Gwilym, Dafydd ap: *Evans, D.V.*; *Thomas, D.V.*(*); *Wynne*†

H

H__, W. H.: *Le Fleming*
Habington, William (1605-54): *Locke*
Hadath, Gunby (1871-1954): *Moir*; *Parke*
Haddon, Elizabeth (Bettie): *O'Neill*; *Scott, C.*
Hadingham, Mary: *Usher*(†)
Hafiz (c.1326-c.1390): *Bantock*
Haines, John: *Samuel, R.*†
Hale, Sarah Josepha (1788-1879): *Plumstead*
Haley, W.: *Grainger, P.*
Hall, Marguerite Radclyffe (1880-1943): *Clarke, R.C.*; *Coleridge-Taylor*
Hamilton, Janet: *McGuire*†
Hamilton, Mary C. D.: *Parry, C.H.H.*
Hamilton-Fellowes, Margery: *Harrison, J.*
Hamley, D. C.: *Steele*†
Hammond, Anthony (1668-1738): *Purcell, H.*
Hammond-Spencer, Hilda: *Coleridge-Taylor*
Han Yü: *Bantock*
Hannay, Patrick (?-?1629): *Jeffreys, J.*; *Orr, C.W.*
Harben, Eric: *Scott, C.*
Hardy, Thomas (1840-1928): *Austin*; *Bayliss*; *Bax*; *Berkeley, M.*†; *Bliss*; *Boughton*; *Britten*; *Bullard*; *Butt*; *Crossley-Holland*; *Dent*; *Downes*(†); *Finzi*(†); *Fiske*; *Fleming*; *Foss*; *Foster, I.*; *Fulton*; *Gardiner*; *Gibbs, Armstrong*(†); *Gurney*; *Hadley*; *Harrington*; *Head*; *Headington*; *Holst*; *Ireland*; *Jeffreys, J.*; *Joubert*†; *Le Fleming*; *Maw*†; *Milford*; *Newson*; *Parry, W.H.*; *Patterson*; *Pilling*; *Read*; *Roe*; *Scott, C.*; *Serrell*; *Slater*; *Steele*; *Swann*; *Turnbull*; *Vaughan Williams*; *Venables*; *Walters, L.*; *White, A.*
Harford, Harold: *Marshall*
Harnick, Sheldon: *Baker*
Harrhy, Edith: *Gibbs, Armstrong*
Harrington, Henry: *Lawes, H.*
Harris, Ada Leonora: *Squire*
Harvey, Frederick William (1888-1957): *Gurney*; *Howells*
Harvey, James Clarence: *Jones, R.L.*
Hassall, Christopher (1912-63): *Lubbock*; *Thiman*
Hausted, Peter (?-1645): *Jeffreys, G.*
Havesp, Dewi: *Williams, W.M.*(*)
Haviland, Mark: *Solomons*(†)

Hawkins, Sir John (1719-93): *Stanley*
Hawksworth, John: *Arnold, S.*(†)
Hay, George Campbell (1915-1984): *Scott, F.G.*
Hay, John (1838-1905): *Elgar*
Hayes, Alfred (1857-1936): *Bantock*
Hayes, Charles: *Bennett, T.C.S.*
Haley, W.: *Grainger, P.*
Hayward, C. Flavell: *Elgar*
Healy, Cahir: *Harty*
Heath-Stubbs, John (1918-): *Dickinson*
Heber, Bishop Reginald (1783-1826): *Brian*; *Stanford*
Heine, Heinrich (1797-1856): *Berners**; *Blake, D*†; *Bridge*(†); *Delius**: *Dieren*(*); *Holst*; *Kirkwood**; *Stanford*(*); *White, M.V.*(*)
Heinitz, Marie: *Delius**
Hemans, Mrs Felicia (1793-1835): *Loder*; *Scott, C.*; *Stanford*
Hemingway, Maggie: *Matthews, D.*
Henley, N.: *Purcell, H.*
Henley, William Ernest (1849-1903): *Butterworth, G.*(†); *Delius*; *Foss*; *Lloyd Webber*; *O'Neill*; *Quilter*; *Ronald*; *Shaw*
Henry VIII, King of England (1491-1547): *Roe*
Henry, Leigh: *Harris, W.L.*
Henze, Helen Rowe: *Lloyd Webber*
Herbert, Mr: *Purcell, H.**
Herbert, Sir Alan Patrick (1890-1971): *Dunhill*; *Elgar*
Herbert, George (1593-1633): *Boyle*†; *Bush, G.*; *Butt*(†); *Clucas*†; *Head*; *Pike*; *Plumstead*; *Procter*; *Purcell, H.*; *Thiman*; *Vaughan Williams*
Herbert, Mary, Countess of Pembroke (1561-1621) : *Anon*
Herbert, William, Earl of Pembroke (1580-1630): *Lawes, H.*
Hermann: *Rubbra**(†)
Herrick, Robert (1591-1674): *Anon*; *Barrell*, *B*†; *Bax*; *Berkeley, L.*(†); *Bernofsky*; *Birkett*; *Blyton*; *Brian*; *Bridge*; *Brown, C.*†; *Bullard*; *Bush, G.*; *Butt*; *Carey, C.*; *Cruft*; *Delius*; *Mowbray*; *Dring*; *Dyson*; *Greaves, R.*; *Gurney*; *Hatton*; *Horn*; *Jeffreys, J.*; *Lawes, H.*; *Lawes, W.*; *Lipkin*†; *Maconchy*; *Mullinar*; *Murrill*; *Owen*; *Parry, C.H.H.*; *Pope*; *Quilter*; *Roe*(†); *Routh*; *Rutter*†; *Standford*; *Stanford*; *Steel*; *Stewart*; *Still*; *Stoker*; *Tate, P.*†; *Taylor, C.V.*; *Torphichen*; *Toye*; *Turnbull*; *Vale*; *Walker, E.*; *Warlock*; *White, M.V.*; *Young, D.*
Hesse, Herman (1877-1962): *Steele*
Heuffer, F. M. see Ford Madox Ford
Heveningham, Colonel Henry: *Gibbs, Armstrong*; *Purcell, H.*
Heyse, Paul von (1830-1914): *Bury*; *Smyth**
Heyward, Anthony: *Kirkwood*
Heywood, Thomas (c.1574-1641): *Bullard*; *Dunhill*; *Parry, C.H.H.*; *Quilter*; *Stanford*
Hickey, Emily H.: *Wood, C.*
Hildyard, Jean (1895-1919): *Scott, C.*
Hill, Barry Duane: *Jeffreys, J.*
Hill, Geoffrey (1932-): *Holloway*
Hill, Richard: *Fulton*
Hiller, Eric: *Owen*
Hills, Donald R.: *Blyton*
Hinkson, see Tynan, Katherine
Hinton, Wilfred: *Owen*
Hiscocks, Wendy: *Hiscocks, W.*†
Ho Chi Minh: *Stevenson*(†)
Hodge, Alan: *Caradon*†
Hodgson, Ralph (1871-1962): *Rubbra*†
Hodson, James Lansdale: *Fogg*

Hoffmann, E. T. A. (1776-1822): *Woolrich*†
Hoffmann von Fallersleben, August Heinrich (1798-1874): *Lehmann*(*); *White, M.V.*
Hogg, James (1770-1835): *Center*; *MacCunn*; *Rootham*; *Scott, C.*; *Stanford*; *Thomas, Mansel*; *Turnbull*; *White, A.*; *Williams, W.S.G.*
Hokushi: *Northcott*†
Holcroft, Thomas (1745-1809): *Attwood*
Hölderlin, Friedrich (1770-1843): *Britten*(*); *Hudes*
Holmes, Bettie Fleischmann (?-1941): *Goossens*
Holmes, Edmund (1850-1936): *Stanford*
Holst, Gustav (1874-1934): *Holst*
Holstein, Ludwig (1864-1933): *Delius*(*)
Holub, Miroslav (1933-1998): *McGuire*†
Hood, Basil: *German*
Hood, Thomas (1799-1845): *M. Davidson*; *Dunhill*; *Jacobson*; *Orr, C.W.*; *Randall*†; *Shaw*; *Warlock*
Hooker, Jeremy: *Thomas, Mansel*
Hooley, Teresa: *Scott, C.*
Hoosen, I. D.: *Elwyn-Edwards*; *Thomas, Mansel*; *Williams, W.S.G.*(*)
Hope, H. J.: *Moeran*
Hope, Laurence (Adela Florence Cory) (1865 - 1904): *Woodforde-Finden*
Hopkin, Wil: *Williams, Grace*
Hopkins, Gerard Manley (1844-89): *Berkeley, L.*; *Cruft*†; *Hugh-Jones*; *Leighton*; *Milner*; *Parrott*; *Pike*; *Pope*; *Smith Brindle*†; *Wellesz*†
Hopper, Nora: *Quilter*
Horace (65-8BC): *Wesley, S.*
Horey, Annette: *Samuel, H.*
Hoskyns, Sir John: *Morley*; *Parrott*
Houlton, Dr: *Hook*
Housman, Alfred Edward (1859-1936): *Andrews*; *Bax*; *Berkeley, L.*; *Berkeley, M.*†; *Branson*; *Burrows*; *Butterworth, G.*; *Clarke, R.*; *Foss*; *Gibbs, Armstrong*; *Gray*; *Gurney*(†); *Hamilton, J.*; *Head*; *Holloway*(†); *Horder*; *Ireland*; *Jeffreys, J.*; *Matthews, D.*†; *Mitchell*; *Moeran*; *Orr, C.W.*; *Owen*; *Peel*; *Pope*; *Raynor*; *Ross*; *Searle*; *Somervell*; *Steele*; *Taylor, E.K.*; *Thomas, H.F.*; *Thomas, Mansel*; *Thompson, P.*; *Vaughan Williams*(†); *Wickens*; *Williamson, J.R.*
Hovey, Richard (1864-1900): *Harty*; *Head*
Howard, Bernard: *Purcell, H.*
Howard, Sir Robert (1626-1698): *Purcell, H.*
Howe, John: *Blow*, *Purcell, H.*
Howell, Pat: *Thompson, P.*
Howell, Thomas (fl.1568-81): *Hamilton, I.*; *Ireland*
Hudson, William Henry (1841-1922): *Scott, C.*; *Tippett*
Hughes, Elias: *Edwards, C.E.*
Hughes, Henry: *Lawes, H.*
Hughes, John: *Handel*
Hughes, Langston (1902-67): *Roe*†
Hughes, Simon: *Beamish*
Hughes, T. Rowland: *Thomas, Mansel*
Hughes, Ted (1930-98): *Crosse*; *LeFanu*†; *Wood, Hugh*
Hugill, Robert: *Hugill*†
Hugo, Victor (1802-85): *Dieren**; *Thomas, A.G.**
Humphreys, Emyr (1919-): *Hoddinott*
Humberger, Janet: *McGuire*
Hung-So-Fan: *Shaw*
Hunt, H. Ernest: *Austin*; *Samuel, H.*
Hunt, James Henry Leigh (1784-1859), *Herbert, I.*; *Pilling*†; *Williamson, M.*
Hunter, Anne: *Salomon*
Hunter, Harry: *Warlock*
Hutchins, Pat: *Nyman*

Huxley, Aldous (1894-1963): *Ireland*
Huysmans, Joris Karl (1848-1907): *Newson*
Hyatt, Alfred H.: *Dunhill*; *Holst*; *Samuel, H.*
Hyde, Douglas (1860-1949): *Trimble*

I

Iâl, Eos: *Thomas, Mansel*(†)
Ibsen, Henrik (1828-1906): *Crossley-Holland*; *Delius*(*); *Holst*; *Horne*
Image, Selwyn: *Scott, C.*
Ingelo, Nathaniel (c.1650-1692): *Purcell, H.*
Ingelow, Jean (1820-97): *Sullivan*
Ingram, Norman: *Thomas, V.*
Inman, Geo.: *Bishop*
Irvine, John (?-1962): *Dunhill*; *Gibbs, Armstrong*; *Parke*; *Quilter*
Isaiah: *Bush, A.*; *Greene*; *Head*; *Stanford*†; *Vaughan Williams*
Islwyn (William Thomas): *Jones, R.R.*
Ita, St: *Rubbra*(†)

J

Jacobsen, Jens Peter (1847-1885): *Delius*(*)
James I, King of Scotland (1394-1437): *Dieren*
James, Carolyn: *Thwaites*
James, D. Emrys: *Jones, D.T.*
Jean-Aubrey, Georges (1882-1949): *Berners**
Jeans, Joshua: *Storace*(†)
Jefferies, Richard (1848-87): *Newson*
Jennens, Charles (1700-73): *Handel*
Jessop, George Henry (?-1915): *Stanford*
Job, Book of: *Handel*; *Head*; *Hugill*†; *Rowley*
Jôb, J. T.: *Edwards, O.*
John, St: *Head*
John of the Cross, St (1542-91): *Pike*; *Routh*†
Johnson, Geoffrey, *Plumstead*
Johnson, George W.: *Butterfield*
Johnson, Lionel (1867-1902): *Self, A.*
Johnson, Robert: *Plumstead*
Jones, A. L.: *Barrett*
Jones, Alun: *Harries*
Jones, Bryn: *Thomas, Mansel*
Jones, Dennis: *Pitfield*
Jones, Robert H.: *Evans, T.H.*; *Thomas, Mansel*
Jones, Seth P.: *Jones, M.O.*
Jones, Rev. T. Gwilym: *Edwards, T.D.*
Jones, T. Gwynn: *Jones, W.B.*; *Thomas, Mansel*, *Williams, W.S.G.*(*)
Jones, T. Llew: *Thomas, Mansel*
Jones, Sir William (1746-94): *Finzi*
Jonson, Ben (1572-1637): *Anon*; *Biggs*; *Browne*; *Bush, G.*; *Delius*; *Elgar*; *Ferrabosco*; *Fraser, N.*; *Gibbs, Alan*; *Grainger, P.*; *Gurney*; *Johnson, R.*; *Lanier*; *Lehmann*; *Maconchy*; *Naylor, P.*; *Parry, C.H.H.*; *Quilter*; *Rubbra*; *Smith, J.C.*; *Southam*; *Stanford*; *Steele*; *Vaughan Williams*; *Warlock*; *Young, P*†
Jordan, Thomas (c.1612-85): *Rutter*†; *Walton*
Josephson, Ernst (1851-1906): *Delius*(*)
Joyce, James (1882-1941): *Bax*; *Blake, H.*; *Bliss*; *Bridge*; *Bullert*†; *Dieren*; *Goossens*; *Head*; *Hedges*; *Howells*; *Ireland*; *Moeran*; *Orr, C.W.*
Joyce, Patrick Weston (1827-1914): *Harty*; *Hughes, Herbert*
Joyce, Robert Dwyer (1836-83): *Wood, C.*
Junoy, J. M.: *Gerhard*†

K

Kabir: *Morris, A.*†
Kafka, Franz (1883-1924): *Goehr**
Kao-Shih: *Bantock*; *Harrison, J.*
Kaye-Smith, Sheila (1887-1956): *Bantock*
Keats, John (1795-1821): *Bingham*; *Bridge*; *Fogg*; *Foreman*; *Frankel, B.*; *Head*; *Holbrooke*; *Mark*; *Newson*; *Owen*; *Parry, C.H.H.*; *Quilter*; *Read*†; *Richardson*; *Roe*; *Ronald*; *Someren-Godfery*; *Stanford*; *Wegener*
Kellerher, D. L.: *Warlock*
Kelly, Robert: *Maw*†
Kempis, Thomas à (1379-1471): *Procter*
Kendall, Katharine: *Clarke, R.*
Kennedy, Jimmy: *Kennedy*
Kennedy, Margaret (1896-1967): *Goossens*
Kennelly: *LeFanu*
Ketèlby, Albert William (1875-1959): *Ketèlby*
Keyes, Sidney (1922-43): *Tippett*
Khayyám, Omar (c.1050-c.1122): *Blyton*; *Evans, D.*; *Lehmann*
Killigrew, Sir William (?1606-95): *Lanier*
Kim, Don'o: *Boyd*†
King, Benjamin (1857-94): *Wishart*
King, Dorothy: *Parry, W.H.*
King, Francis Henry (1923-): *Roberts, M.*
King, Harry: *Bennett, R.R.*
King, Henry (1592-1669): *Brown, C.*; *Elgar*; *Rutter*†
King, Stoddard: *Elliott, Z.*
Kingdom-Ward, Winifred: *Butterworth, N.*
Kings, First Book of: *Poston*
Kingsley, Charles (1819-75): *Balfe*; *Coleridge-Taylor*; *Foulds*; *Hatton*; *Holst*; *Hullah*; *Parke*; *Pitfield*; *Scott, C.*; *Somervell*
Kingsley, Henry (1830-76): *Lehmann*; *Maude*
Kipling, Rudyard (1865-1936): *Davies, Walford*; *Elgar*; *Fogg*; *German*; *Grainger, P.*; *Hely-Hutchinson*; *McCall*; *Maconchy*; *Roe*; *Shaw*
Kirkup, James (1923-): *Teed*
Kirnan, Molly: *Brook*
Kite, Judith: *Boyle, R.*
Kjerulf, Theodor: *Delius*
Klingemann, Carl: *Bennett, W.S.*
Kobo Daishi: *Dench*†
Koch, Denice: *Head*
Krag, Vilhelm (1846-1908): *Delius*(*)
Krasinski, Zygmunt: *Elgar*

L

L__, C__. Esq: *Ridley*
Labé, Louise (c.1524-66): *Berkeley, L.*(*)
Lady, a young: *Stanley*
Laing, Peggy: *Jacobson*
Lamartine, Alphonse de (1790-1869): *White, M.V.**
Lamb, Charles (1775-1834): *Gibbs, Armstrong*
Landon, Letitia Elizabeth (1802-38): *Bennett, W.S.*
Landor, Walter Savage (1775-1864): *Bridge*; *Dieren*; *Thiman*
Lane, Edward William (1801-76): *MacFarren*
Lane, Joan: *Dale, M.*; *Head*
Lang, Jean: *Scott, F.G.*
Lang, Jeffery: *Gibbs, Armstrong*
Lansdowne, Lord *see* Grenville, George
Lanyon, Helen: *Harty*
Larcom, L.: *Shaw*
Larkin, Philip (1822-85): *Adès*†; *Holloway*; *Powers*

Larminie, William: *McCabe*
Lasso, Orlando di (1532-94): *Dieren**
Lawes, Henry (1596-1662): *Lawes, H.*
Lawless, Emily (1845-1913): *Harty*
Lawrance, John: *Weldon*
Lawrence, David Herbert (1885-1930): *Burtch*; *Cooke*†; *Matthews, D*†; *Raphael*; *Wood, Hugh*
Lawrence, Margery: *Elgar*
Lawrence, Mark: *Lawrence, M*
le Gallienne, Richard (1866-1947): *Head*; *Owen*
Lear, Edward (1812-88): *Gerhard*†; *Hely-Hutchinson*; *Orr, B.*; *Stanford*; *White, A.*
Leatham, E. Rutter: *O'Neill*
Leconte de Lisle (1818-94): *Smyth*(*)
Ledwidge, Francis (1891-1917): *Elwyn-Edwards*; *Gurney*; *Head*; *Jeffreys, J.*; *Keel*; *Poston*; *Ronald*
Lee, Sir Henry (1530-1610): *Dowland*
Lee, Laurie (1914-97): *Wood, Hugh*
Lee, Nathaniel (c.1649-92): *Purcell, H.*
Lee, Tanith: *Belben*†
Lehmann, Liza (1862-1918): *Lehmann*
Leigh, Henry Sambrooke (1837-83): *Head*
Leigh, R. G.: *Lloyd Webber*
Lemche, Peter: *Grainger, P.*
Lennie, Jonathan: *Stout*†
Leslie, F.: *Scott, C.*
Leslie, Sir Shane (1885-1971): *Whittaker*
Letts, Winifred M. (1882-?1950): *Jacobson*; *Parke*; *Stanford*(†); *Walters, L.*
Levi, Primo (1919-87): *Matheson*
Levine, Rhoda: *Routh*†
Levy, Muriel: *Fogg*
Lewin, Lionel: *Sullivan*
Lewis, Alun (1915-44): *Swann*; *Tippett*; *Thomas, Mansel*
Lewis, Arthur: *Benjamin*
Lewis, L. Haydn: *Thomas, Mansel*
Lewis, Matthew Gregory (1775-1818): *Grainger, P.*; *Shaw*
Lewis, Saunders (1893-1958): *Jones, R.E.*
Lewis, Simon: *Beamish*†
Lewis, William: *Jenkins, T.*
Li Hou-Chou: *Redman*
Li Po (Li Tai Po): (c.700-762) *Bantock*; *Bliss*; *Lambert, C.*; *Redman*; *Someren-Godfery*; *Warlock*
Li Shang Yin: *Kleyn*
Li Tüan: *Rubbra*†
Li Yi: *Rubbra*†
Lian-Shin Yang: *Crossley-Holland*†
Lind, Mary: *Birkett*
Lindsay, Lady Anne (1750-1825): *Headington*; *MacCunn*; *Sullivan*
Lindsay, Maurice: *Musgrave*
Lisle, Samuel: *Tomlinson*
Li-Tai-Po *see* Li Po
Little, Crawford: *Beamish*†
Lively, M. V.: *Hugill*(†)
Lockman, John: *Boyce*
Lockton, Edward (Teschemacher, Edward) (c. 1875-1940): *Head*; *Hewitt*; *Murray*; *Novello*; *Ronald*
Lodge, Thomas (c.1558-1625): *Ford, T.*; *Fulton*; *Moeran*; *Parry, C.H.H.*; *Pilkington, F.*; *Price, B.*; *Stanford*; *Wills*(†)
Logue, Christopher (1926-): *Birtwistle*†; *Koffman*†
Longfellow, Henry Wadsworth (1807-82): *Balfe*; *Birkett*; *Center*; *Coleridge-Taylor*; *Crossley-Holland*; *Elgar*; *Grainger, P.*; *Hatton*; *Peterkin*; *Ross*; *Turnbull*

298 Index of poets

Longley, Michael (1939-): *Newson*
Lonsdale, Mark: *Linley Snr*
Lorca, Federico García (1899-1936): *ApIvor*†; *Bedford*†; *Berkeley, L.*; *Holt*†; *McGuire*†
Lovelace, Richard (1618-57/8): *Browne*; *Gibbs, Armstrong*; *Harty*; *Keel*; *Kleyn*; *Miller*; *Parry, C.H.H.*; *Quilter*; *Somervell*
Loveman, Robert: *Dunhill*
Lover, Samuel (1796-1868): *Crossley-Holland*
Lowbury, Edward: *Joubert*†
Lowell, Amy (1874-1925): *Cresswell; Scott, S.*
Lowry, Henry Dawson (1869-1906): *Bridge*
Lu Hsun: *McGuire*†
Lu Yu (1125-1209): *Britten*†; *Dalby*; *Oldham*
Lucas, Edward Verrall (1868-1938): *Farrar*
Lucas, Frank Lawrence (1894-1967): *Finzi*; *Joubert*†
Lucas, St. John: *Peel*
Luke, St: *Bax*
Lull, Ramón (c.1235-1315): *Pike*
Luther, Martin (1483-1546): *Birtwistle*†; *Howells*(†); *Jeffreys, J.*; *Phillips, J.C.*†; *Poston*; *Rubbra*†; *Scott, F.G.*; *Self, A.*; *Taylor, C.V.*; *Turner*; *Warlock*(†)
Lydgate John (c.1370-c.1451): *Cruft*
Lyly, John (c.1554-1606): *Dalby*(†); *Jeffreys, J.*
Lyons, A. Neil: *Anderson, W.H.*
Lyons, David: *Bingham*†
Lyte, Henry Francis (1793-1847): *Bryan*; *Liddle*(†); *Price, R.R.*
Lytton, Lord *see* Bulwer-Lytton, Edward

M

M__, Lady E__: *Purcell, H.*
M__, The E__ of: *Purcell, H.*
Ma Huang Tschung: *Someren-Godfery*
Mabbe, James (1572-1642): *Warlock*
McAuley, James (1917-76): *Williamson, M.*; *Wishart*
McCall, J. P.: *Peterkin*; *Wood, C.*
MacCarthy, Sheila (Arnold Bax): *Bax*
MacCathmhaoil (MacCathmhaoèl), Seosamh : *see* Campbell, Joseph
McClain, Johnny: *King, Reginald*
McClennan, Mr: *Stanley*
McCorkindale, William: *Hearne*(†)
McCormack, John (1884-1945): *Anon*
MacDermot, Robert: *Wright*
MacDermott, Martin (1832-1905): *Head*
MacDiarmid, Hugh (Christopher Murray Grieve) (1892-1978): *MacDonald*; *Scott, F.G.*; *Stevenson*
MacDonagh, Thomas (1878-1916): *J. Harrison*; *Nelson*
MacDonald, Archibald: *Roberton*(*)
MacDonald, Mary: *Archer*†
MacGill, Patrick (1890-1963): *Crossley-Holland*†
McGinley, Phyllis: *Thwaites*
McGough, Roger (1937-): *Stout*†; *Williams, Roderick*
McGrory, Eddie: *Kirkwood*
McGuire, Edward: *McGuire*
Mackay, Eric (1851-98): *Coleridge-Taylor*
McKellar, Betty: *Beamish*†
Mackenzie, Agnes Muir: *Roe*
Mackenzie, Donald Alexander (1873-1936): *Bantock*
Mackenzie, Elizabeth: *Wellesz*
Maclean, Murdoch: *Rubbra*, *Stanford*
Maclean, Sorley (1911-96): *MacDonald*; *McGuire*; *Stevenson*
Macleod, A. C.: *Grainger, P.*

Macleod, Fiona (William Sharp) (1855-1905): *Bantock*; *Bax*; *Benjamin, A.*; *Boughton*; *Browne*; *Delius*; *Foulds*; *Howells*; *Moule-Evans*; *Peterkin*
Macleod, Irene: *Head*; *Scott, C.*
Macleod, Kenneth (1872-1958): *Anderson, W.H.*; *Kennedy-Fraser*; *Rubbra*
MacNaghten, Olive: *Scott, C.*
McNally, Leonard: *Grainger, P.*
MacNeacail, Aonghas: *MacDonald*; *Stevenson*
MacNeice, Louis (1907-63): *Alwyn*; *Boyle, R.*; *Britten*; *Head*†; *Walton*(†)
Maconchy, Elizabeth (1907-1994): *Maconchy*
Macrae, H: *Benjamin, A.*
McRae, John: *Harrington*
Madeleva, Mary: *Poston*
Maethlu, Ioan: *Bryan*
Mahari, Gourgen: *Solomons*(†)
Mallarmé, Stéphane (1842-98): *Saxton*†
Mallet: *Arne, T.*
Malloch, N.: *Holbrooke*
Malvery, Olive Christian (?-1914): *Hurlstone*
Mangan, James Clarence (1803-49): *McCabe*
Mansfield, Katherine (1888-1923): *Pitfield*(†)
Manyoshu, The: *Blyton*
Maquarie, Arthur (1874-?): *Quilter*
Marais, Eugene: *Rainier*†
Marble, E. S.: *Thomas, J.R.*
Margeson, Katherine: *Somervell*
Markant, John: *Alison*
Marley, John: *Bantock*
Marlowe, Christopher (1564-93): *Bishop*; *Bullard*; *Dale, M.*; *Dring*; *Moeran*; *Procter*; *Warlock*
Marnau, Alfred: *Torphichen*
Marot, Clément (c.1497-1544): *Warlock*
Marquis, Don (1878-1937): *Bush*; *Seamarks*†
Marryat, Captain Frederick (1792-1848): *Stanford*
Marsh, David (1923-82): *Swann*
Marsh, Olive Maitland: *Bowen*
Marsh, Roger (1949-): *Marsh*†
Marsland, Nancie: *Phillips, M.*
Marston, Philip Bourke (1850-87): *Elgar*; *Owen*
Marzials, Theo.: *Marzials*
Martin: *Croft*
Martin, Bernard: *Gibbs, Armstrong*
Martin, David: *Hiscocks, W.*
Marvell, Andrew (1621-78): *Helliwell*†; *Holloway*†; *Hugill*
Mase, Georgina: *Gibbs, Armstrong*
Masefield, John (1878-1967): *Berners*; *Clarke, R.*; *Crossley-Holland*; *Davidson, M.*; *Gibbs, Armstrong*; *Greaves, R.*; *Gurney*; *Hand*; *Head*; *Ireland*; *Keel*; *Martin, E.*; *Mitchell*†; *Moeran*; *Peterkin*; *Shaw*; *Slater*; *Stewart*; *Turnbull*; *Warlock*; *Whittaker*
Massinger, Philip (1583-1640): *Parry, C.H.H.*
Masters, Edgar Lee (1869-1950): *Downes*
Mathers, E. Powys: *Bantock*
Matheson, George: *Bryan*
Matheson, Greville E.: *Coleridge-Taylor*
Mathias, Eileen: *Parry, W.H.*; *White, A.*
Mathias, Roland: *Thomas, Mansel*
Matthew, St: *Gaul*; *Handel*
Maude, Hilda: *Gibbs, Armstrong*
Maunder, I. M.: *Peterkin*
Maxwell Davies, Sir Peter (1934-): *Maxwell Davies*(†)
Mayerling, Louis: *Jeffreys, J.*
Meireles, Cecilia: *Fraser, N.*